FOUNDATION OF POLITICAL SCIENCE

FOUNDATION OF POLITICAL SCIENCE

RESEARCH, METHODS, AND SCOPE

Edited by
Donald M. Freeman

THE FREE PRESS

A Division of Macmillan Publishing Co., Inc.

NEW YORK

Collier Macmillan Publishers

LONDON

The Free Press
A Division of Macmillan Publishing Co., Inc.
866 Third Avenue, New York, N.Y. 10022

Collier Macmillan Canada, Ltd.

Library of Congress Catalog Card Number: 76-43130

Printed in the United States of America

printing number

1   2   3   4   5   6   7   8   9   10

Library of Congress Cataloging in Publication Data

Main entry under title:

Foundation of political science.

    Bibliography: p.
    Includes index.
    1. Political science. I. Freeman, Donald M.
JA71.F6   320   76-43130
ISBN 0-02-910670-2

To Harold D. Lasswell

CONTENTS

PREFACE

This book has been designed to serve as a text for courses in the scope and methods of political science and as a reference work for professional political scientists. During the 1960s political scientists used methods texts written for other social sciences, usually for sociology, but in the last decade many undergraduate laboratory manuals and introductions to research, written specifically for political science majors, have appeared in print. Numerous advanced works on approaches and methods have also appeared in recent years, but none fully covers the history, scope, and methods of political science. (See, for example, Kerlinger, 1964; Golembiewski, Welsh, and Crotty, 1969; Haas and Kariel, 1970; Wasby, 1970; Leege and Francis, 1974; Kirkpatrick, 1974; Greenstein and Polsby, 1975; McGaw and Watson, 1976; Smith et al., 1976.)

Since it is highly unlikely that any one scholar has the breadth of training to write a comprehensive treatment of the history, scope, and methods of political science, I organized a collaborative effort. This book is the result. Twenty-four men have worked together for over five years in writing this text—each was essential to the enterprise.

Each part of our book focuses on a distinguishing feature of political science as an academic discipline.

1. A discipline has a *history* (Part 1).
2. A discipline has a *province of special concerns* or a legitimate *scope of interests* that mark the boundaries between it and related disciplines. The scope of a discipline's inquiry can be read in its literature and implied from the activities of its practitioners. Therefore, we surveyed the writings and activities in five traditional fields: comparative politics, American politics and institutions, political theory, the science of administration, and international politics (Part 2).

3. A discipline is set apart, or is distinctive, on account of the *tools* or *techniques* employed by its practitioners (Part 3).
4. A discipline has a fundamental *philosophical orientation* or *foundation* that includes canons of evidence, the logic of discovery, the ends of knowledge, the responsibilities of the scholar, and the whole enterprise of self-analysis or self-criticism. It is distinctive on account of the special language, or *concepts*, employed in its research. Moreover, in the process of analyzing and interpreting data, a discipline employs a particular array of *methods* or *approaches* to research (Part 4).
5. A discipline has a *future* that can be forecast on the basis of its history and current trends. In a concluding chapter (Part 5), I reflect on the contents of the book as a springboard for a discussion of the future of political science.

In essence then, this book constitutes a descriptive definition of the discipline of political science: history, literature, practitioners, tools, techniques, philosophical foundations, concepts, approaches, and methods. This is, of course, a skeleton. In the pages that follow we attempt to fill out the corpus and present it as a very lively animal indeed.

I am obliged to acknowledge my gratitude to the twenty-three scholars who contributed to this work. Special thanks should also go to four political science editors at The Free Press who recognized the merit of this project: Carl Beers, Charles E. Smith, Arthur L. Iamele, and Tita D. Gillespie. I am especially grateful for the commitment of our production supervisor, Claude Conyers. James N. Rosenau and John Wahlke read the manuscript and made helpful suggestions. My secretaries, Kay Trine and Karen Born, showed great patience in typing and retyping endless pages of copy. Finally, a special debt to my wife, Ina Freeman, who supervised the preparation of the manuscript and prepared the lengthy bibliography essential to this book.

NOTES ON CONTRIBUTORS

CARL BECK is a professor of political science and director of the University Center for International Studies at the University of Pittsburgh. After completing his baccalaureate and his master's degree at the University of Pittsburgh, he earned his doctorate at Duke University. His publications have established him as one of the nation's leading authorities in the comparative study of political elites.

EDWIN A. BOCK is a professor of political science and public administration at the Maxwell Graduate School, Syracuse University, and president of the Inter-University Case Program. He attended Dartmouth College and the University of London. Active in comparative administration and national planning studies, he is the author of *Fifty Years of Technical Assistance* and editor of and contributor to numerous case books and collections, including *Essays on the Case Method*.

CHARLES M. BONJEAN attended Drake University and the University of North Carolina. Hogg Professor of Sociology at the University of Texas at Austin, he is widely recognized for the evolution of the *Social Science Quarterly* into a major journal under his editorship. He is coeditor of a number of significant works, including *Political Attitudes and Public Opinion*, *Community Politics*, and *Sociological Measurement*.

WILLIAM BUCHANAN is a professor of political science and chairman of the Department of Political Science at Washington and Lee University. After completing his baccalaureate work at Washington and Lee, he studied for his graduate degrees at Princeton. Professor Buchanan is coauthor of two classics in political science: *The Legislative System* and *How Nations See Each Other*. His *Understanding Political Variables* is one of the most highly regarded undergraduate methods texts.

RALPH C. CHANDLER is an associate professor of political science at Western Michigan University. His education has been eclectic: in addition to his baccalaureate, master's, and doctorate in political science at Stetson, Rutgers, and Columbia, he has degrees from Union and Princeton theological seminaries.

AAGE R. CLAUSEN attended Macalester College and won his master's and doctor's degrees from the University of Michigan. His teaching appointments have been at Göteborg University, the University of Wisconsin, and Ohio State University, where he is currently a professor of political science. He has committed a great deal of his research effort to the study of legislative decision making; the results of his work include several articles and a monograph, *How Congressmen Decide: A Policy Focus*.

JEROME M. CLUBB, who did his undergraduate and graduate work at the University of Washington, is executive director of the Inter-University Consortium for Political and Social Research, a program director in the Center for Political Studies of the Institute for Social Research, and a professor of history at the University of Michigan. He is the author of many articles and is coeditor of *Partisan Change and Stability in American Political History*.

AMITAI ETZIONI earned his baccalaureate and his master's degree from Hebrew University and his doctorate from the University of California at Berkeley. He has since been associated with Columbia University, where he is currently a professor of sociology. He has served as the director of the Center for Policy Research from its inception in 1968. He is the author of *A Comparative Analysis of Complex Organizations*, *The Active Society*, *Political Unification*, *Genetic Fix*, and *Social Problems*.

DONALD M. FREEMAN is a visiting professor of political science at Texas Tech University. After receiving his Ph.D. from the University of North Carolina, he taught at Hollins College, the University of North Carolina at Charlotte, the University of Arizona, and the University of West Florida. His publications include articles on the political behavior of Mexican-Americans and *Political Parties and Political Behavior*, of which he is coeditor.

FRED M. FROHOCK was awarded his baccalaureate and his master's degree by the University of Florida and his doctorate by the University of North Carolina. He is a professor of political science at Syracuse University. In addition to his distinguished articles on political theory, he has written two major monographs: *The Nature of Political Inquiry* and *Normative Political Theory*.

MICHAEL HAAS earned his doctorate at Stanford University. Now a professor of political science at the University of Hawaii, he has held other teaching appointments at San Jose State College, Northwestern University, Purdue University, and the University of California at Riverside. Widely recognized as a leading figure in the field of international politics, Professor Haas has served as a UNITAR consultant on international organizations. Among his major publications are *International Conflict*, *International Systems: Approaches to the Study of Political Science*, and *Basic Documents on Asian Regional Organizations*.

OLE R. HOLSTI, who earned his Ph.D. at Stanford University, is George V. Allen Professor of Political Science at Duke University. He has held other teaching assignments at Stanford University and at the University of British Columbia. His works include *Enemies in Politics; The Analysis of Communi-*

cation Content; Content Analysis for the Social Sciences and Humanities; Crisis, Escalation, War; and *Unity and Disintegration in International Alliances: Comparative Studies.*

ROBERT F. KAUFMAN is a professor of political science at Rutgers University. He did his undergraduate and graduate work at Harvard University. He is the author of *The Politics of Land Reform in Chile, 1950–1970* and of articles on clientelism, dependency, and authoritarianism.

EVRON M. KIRKPATRICK is executive director of the American Political Science Association. He studied for his bachelor's and master's degrees at the University of Illinois and for his doctorate at Yale University. He has taught at Georgetown University, Howard University, and the University of Minnesota. His early publications were on American politics and on Communist propaganda; however, he is now best known for his assessments of movements in political science, notably "Toward a More Responsible Two-Party System" and "The Impact of the Behavioral Approach on Traditional Political Science."

PAUL F. KRESS earned his bachelor's and master's degrees at Wisconsin and his doctorate from the University of California at Berkeley. He is currently a professor of political science at the University of North Carolina at Chapel Hill, and he has held other teaching appointments at the University of Hawaii and at Northwestern University. In addition to several articles on political theory and the philosophy of social science, he is the author of *Social Science and the Idea of Process.*

S. DALE McLEMORE is a professor of sociology at the University of Texas at Austin. His bachelor's and master's degrees are from the University of Texas and his Ph.D. is from Yale University. Among his publications are articles on social research, ethnic relations, and health. He is coauthor of *A Statistical Profile of the Spanish-Surname Population of Texas, Management-Training Effectiveness,* and *Sociological Measurement.*

MAURICE NATANSON is a professor of philosophy at Yale University. He did his graduate work at New York University, the University of Nebraska, and the New School for Social Research. Before going to Yale, Professor Natanson taught at the University of California at Santa Cruz. Among his books are *The Journeying Self, Edmund Husserl,* and *Phenomenology, Role, and Reason.* Among the books he has edited are *Philosphy of the Social Sciences* and *Phenomenology and the Social Sciences.*

JOHN R. RASER is Foundation Professor of Social Sciences and chairman of the School of Social Inquiry at Murdoch University in Perth, Western Australia. He has been a Guggenheim fellow and has held teaching and research appointments at the Claremont Graduate School, the University of Otago in New Zealand, the Mental Health Research Institute, and the Western Behavioral Sciences Institute. His doctorate is from Stanford University. In addition to numerous articles, Professor Raser is the author of *Simulation and Society* and *Cabbages and Kings: Essays on Australian Society.*

JAMES N. ROSENAU, who earned his Ph.D. at Princeton University, is currently a professor of political science and international relations and the director of the School of International Relations at the University of Southern California. He has taught at Rutgers University and Ohio State University. He has written, edited, or coedited numerous works, including *Public Opinion and Foreign Policy, Linkage Politics, International Politics and Foreign Policy, The Scientific Study of Foreign Policy, Citizenship between Elections, The Dramas of Politics,* and *In Search of Global Patterns.*

R. J. SNOW attended the University of Utah and received his Ph.D. degree from Northwestern University. Having previously taught at the University of California at Santa Barbara, he is now an associate professor of political science, director of the Hinckley Institute of Politics, and vice-president for university relations at the University of Utah. He is the author of "The School Superintendent," "The Political Involvement of Students," and "The Politics of Urban Government Reform in France."

DOUGLAS K. STEWART holds a baccalaureate and a master's degree from the University of Utah and a doctorate from the University of Pittsburgh. He is an adjunct research assistant in the Urban Research Center at the University of Pittsburgh and the author of *Social Implications of Social Science Data Archives.*

BERT E. SWANSON is a professor of political science and urban studies at the University of Florida. He did his undergraduate work at George Washington University and his graduate work at the University of Oregon. He has held other teaching appointments at the University of Oregon, Hunter College, and Sarah Lawrence College. He is the author of *The Struggle for Equality* and *The Concern for Community in Urban America* and a coauthor of *Black-Jewish Relations in New York City, The Rulers and the Ruled, Small Town in America,* and *Discovering the Community.*

GORDON TULLOCK did his doctoral work at the University of Chicago. He has taught at the University of South Carolina, the University of Virginia, Rice University, and Virginia Polytechnic Institute and State University, where he is currently University Distinguished Professor. He is editor of the journal *Public Choice.* He is author or coauthor of *The New World of Economics; Private Wants, Public Means; The Logic of the Law; The Calculus of Consent;* and *Toward a Mathematics of Politics.*

LARRY L. WADE is a professor of political science at the University of California at Davis, having held previous academic appointments at the University of North Carolina at Charlotte and Purdue University. His bachelor's, master's, and doctor's degrees were all awarded by the University of Oregon. As author or coauthor, he has published *The Elements of Public Policy, A Primer of Political Analysis, A Theory of Political Exchange, A Logic of Public Policy, Democracy in America: A Public Choice Approach,* and *The Political Economy of Success.*

PART 1
A HISTORY OF THE DISCIPLINE

1. FROM PAST TO PRESENT

Evron Kirkpatrick

The root is man. I don't think it is possible to say anything meaningful about the governance of man without talking about his beliefs, commitments, and values. Man has built nations and empires, created customs and institutions, invented symbols and constitutions, made wars, revolutions, and peace. Politics is the study of why man finds it necessary or desirable to build government, of how and why he decides on public policies. Politics is concerned with the conditions and consequences of human action [Eulau, 1963, p. 3].

WHERE ARE WE NOW?

Since the root is man, since there is almost nothing to which we naturally pay more attention than to our fellow men, since being a man involves living with men and therefore observing them, one might assume that man had long since developed a systematic, comprehensive, sound, and effective knowledge of politics that would enable man to govern himself with reason and decency. To say this is to deny it. Politics, governing, are dangerous activities; they are activities through which man may do much that is good, may confer great benefits upon himself and others but also through which he may, and often does, do great harm. (See Jouvenel, 1963, pp. 29- 40, "On the Nature of Political Science.")

After more than two thousand years of Western civilization, and even considerably longer if one includes the history of Eastern civilizations, man lives more by ideologies than by ideas about politics; more by dogma than by systematic theory; more in ignorance and by trial and error than by knowledge systematically and rationally developed. Why is this so?

3

In part, it is because the science of politics, though it has a long history, is in fact a new discipline, a new science. This should not be surprising. As Jouvenel (1963, pp. 39-40) has pointed out, the science of medicine has had a long history but is fundamentally a new discipline, or is composed of new disciplines. Physiology hardly began before Harvey (b. 1578) and didn't really begin its modern development before Haller (b. 1708). Both politics and medicine, or politics and physiology, have man as their central concern; the health of the body and the health of the body politic are so important to man that it is amazing that the proper functioning of both produced so little interest, so little careful examination of this very functioning. There was, as long ago as the ancient Greeks, a great deal of writing about both the body and the body politic, but it was much more normative than empirical in character. If a science of physiology began only in the eighteenth century, a science of politics began only in the twentieth.[1]

The twentieth century, not only in the more important aspects of method and substance but in quantity of produced data, substantive knowledge, and professional scholars, is the century that political science came of age. There are, perhaps, 17,000 trained political scientists living today. This is substantially more than existed in the whole history of civilization until some very recent year—say, 1930. It is extremely doubtful that by any definition there had been 1,000 political scientists up to and including 1903 when the American Political Science Association was created. If we define political science by the significant writing of which we have record, the number more likely is less than 500. More trained political scientists, as measured by the number of Ph.D.'s given, are turned out today in one year than there were in total in 1900, perhaps even in 1930. Today there are well over one hundred universities giving the Ph.D. degree in political science; in 1900 there were certainly no more than

1. As a science matures, those concerned with it become more interested in its historical development; more interested in its past. This is important because a science, like man, always has elements of its past incapsulated in its present. To have self-knowledge, a man must be aware of his own past, his own history; this also is true of science, and the history of the science of politics is only just beginning. William Anderson (1964) attempted such a history and, before his death, published a first volume dealing with the study and teaching about politics in ancient times. There are, of course, various histories of political philosophy or political theory, but they are not devoted to this problem. Anna Haddow (ed. William Anderson, 1939) is more to the point and deals with the study and teaching about politics in the United States down to 1900. Still more important is the excellent study of the development of political science in the United States by Somit and Tanenhaus (1967). This book should be read by every student seriously interested in or professionally concerned with the discipline. *The International Encyclopedia of the Social Sciences* (ed. David L. Sills, 1968) is an important reference work that should be used extensively by students. It has authoritative articles on most of the topics covered in this volume, and excellent bibliographies follow each article.

a half dozen in the United States and very few elsewhere in the world.

No matter how we measure it quantitatively, the explosive increase in the study and teaching of political science is clear. In 1900, perhaps as late as 1930, it would have been possible for a student during his training as an undergraduate and graduate student in political science to read all the literature in the discipline; today it is hard to read all of the literature in one or two specialized fields. When the *American Political Science Review* began publication in 1906, there were few new books advertised or even reviewed or listed in the early issues; today there are more than a thousand every year. In 1900, even in 1930, it would have taken no more than a few pages to have listed all of the books and articles that had been written on the Congress, state legislatures, even legislatures in general; today it takes a large volume to list them.

Data are being accumulated at an increasingly rapid rate. The Inter-University Consortium for Political and Social Research, the Survey Research Center, the Roper Center at Williams College, the Yale Data Center: archives across the country are collecting, processing, and developing systems for storage and retrieval that make possible easy access to important data that could not even have been collected in 1900, let alone stored in any quickly retrievable fashion. The development of the science of statistics in the twentieth century, the modern computer, the sample survey, content analysis, the speed of travel, easy and rapid communication, are all elements in the complete transformation that has taken place in the study of politics. They not only help account for the great increase in the volume of data, in the amount of research, in the wide range of important publications, but also for the great transformation that has taken place in the character and quality of the work done.

Not only is the explosive increase in data, in research, in publication, and in the number of trained political scientists a phenomenon of the twentieth century, but it is to a striking degree an American phenomenon. If there are 17,000 trained political scientists alive and working today, 14,000 of them are in the United States. Whatever the number of new books and articles produced each year, 95 percent are produced in the United States, even though significant increases are taking place elsewhere in the world.

THE IMPORTANCE OF THE PAST

But quantity is not the most interesting and certainly not the most important part of the story. Further, it is much too easy to

assume that writing produced in Western civilization down to the end
of the nineteenth century was no more valuable in political science
than in physiology or physics. This is not the case. Many, if not all,
of the most important questions about politics were posed by the
Greeks and were elaborated and discussed in the centuries that
followed. Plato, Aristotle, Cicero, St. Augustine, the Church Fathers,
St. Francis, Machiavelli, Hobbes, Locke, Rousseau, Mill, Marx, the
authors of *The Federalist Papers*, all asked and sought to answer
important persisting questions. What forms of government are good?
What forms are bad? What causes forms of government to change?
What accounts for stability? What accounts for revolution? Do people create the institutions of a society or do institutions determine
the nature of people? Is it possible for the people to control their
government? What are the various forms of government, and what
are the differentiating characteristics? How is obedience justified? Is
revolution ever a good thing? What is representation? What is the
best way for a people to be represented? Is freedom good? How can
it be maintained? How are young people socialized into the community? How should they be? What is the relationship of the socialization process to stability, to good government, to change? What is
important: Constitutions or character? Some of these questions are
normative, some empirical; all are important. Anyone who wishes to
sensitize himself to the important questions of politics and to some
of the ways which they can be answered cannot do better than
to read the classics. It is more important for a student of politics to read Aristotle or Hobbes than for a physiologist to read
Harvey. (For an excellent discussion of the multiple values of the
classics, see the group of papers in Pool, 1967; also see the
papers given at the 1972 annual APSA meeting by Mulford Sibley, Mark Blitz, and others.)

To note the value of the classical writing about politics is not to
say that there are no differences between political science in the days
of the Greeks, in the Middle Ages, and in the period of the Renaissance and Reformation from political science as we know it today.
The differences are significant and they are almost all twentieth-
century developments. They are not, it is important to note, differences simply of quantity of data, of scholars, or of scholarly writing;
they are substantive differences that arise from a greater consciousness of self as a political scientist and a concern about what that
means; greater methodological awareness; a greater commitment to
science *qua* science; and a greater recognition of the need to distinguish problems of value (normative theory) from problems of descriptive (empirical) theory. Perhaps the most important substantive
differences arise out of methodological awareness and methodolog-

ical scruples. These in turn arose from the impact of the revolutionary advances in the natural sciences that have been a dominant
feature of modern times.

THE IMPACT OF SCIENCE

The scientific method as we know it did not arrive in its fullest
magnificence until the seventeenth century. Kepler, but even more,
Galileo, possessed it in its completeness. (For an excellent discussion,
see Russell, 1931.) Very little has been added to the fundamentals
since; there have been new techniques, new instruments, improved
technology, a more powerful mathematics, but no fundamental
differences in methodological concepts. It is not easy to keep in
mind that science is a new force in the world. Beginning with Galileo
(1564–1642), it has existed only a little over three hundred years. As
Bertrand Russell points out, during the first half of that period it had
little impact on the thoughts or habits of ordinary men. Only in the
last one hundred and fifty years has it been a major influence in the
lives of almost everyone. In that time, science has introduced more
changes in the life of man and in his habits of thought than had
occurred in the preceding twenty-five hundred years. Science is
knowledge and science is power. It has not only made possible our
voyages to the moon, it has made necessary new forms of human
society. It has changed industry, commerce, and agriculture; it has
profoundly influenced the character of our social and political life; it
has transformed the lives of ordinary men and women. It is no
wonder, therefore, that it should have had a profound influence
upon the development of the discipline of political science.

The profound impact of the sciences of nature upon political
science and the other sciences of man has been the result of two
aspects of the scientific revolution. One is the immense dissatisfaction caused among professionals by a comparison of the great progress of the natural sciences with the very modest progress of political
science and the sciences of man; the second is the adoption by social
scientists (and in fact by the whole society) of the system of
assumptions, values, and beliefs associated with the "scientific" outlook. These assumptions, beliefs, and values have their origin, both in
time and content, in Galileo, and have permeated the whole of
twentieth-century society.

It is not surprising that, under the impact of these forces,
political scientists should have become dissatisfied and should have
sought to make their own work more scientific. In doing so, they

launched an era of methodological preoccupation. Political scientists came to devote much energy to an examination of the subject matter and goals appropriate to a science of politics and to the position of political science in a general social science. In our own time, many political scientists have, with much anxiety, turned to the analysis of their own work and that of their colleagues in an effort to identify and examine the assumptions, procedures, modes of explication and description, and the nature of the findings that characterize the body of scholarship that we know as political science; many have become methodologists.

Perhaps this can be summarized by saying that modern political science has finally arrived at being a science. For this to be meaningful, however, it is necessary to note at the outset the existence of disagreement about the definition of science, and therefore disagreement about precisely what it is that modern political science has arrived at being. (For a discussion of science, see Cohen, 1931; Cohen and Nagel, 1934; Nagel, 1961; Brecht, 1959; Friedrich, 1963; Russell, 1931; Feigl and Brodbeck, 1953; Brodbeck, 1968; Campbell, 1920; Pap, 1962; Natanson, 1963; Braybrooke, 1965; Blume, 1974.) Most political scientists would probably reject the slang usage that equates science with natural science but accept the historical meaning of science as a body of systematic and orderly thinking about a determinate subject matter, and most would agree upon this minimal definition of the profession's goals. But this is a self-conscious age; it has been variously and correctly called an age of analysis and an age of anxiety. Political scientists have not been ready to accept this or some similar definition and proceed about their business. They have not only analyzed the work done in the name of political science but have speculated on the changes in focus, procedure, and goals necessary to advance the discipline. They have not been content to tell their colleagues what they have done, but also have wanted to tell them what to do. They have not been satisfied with telling them what kind and quality of findings have emerged from their research, but have insisted on arguing the merits of particular kinds and orders of findings. To understand the terms and the stakes of this discussion it is necessary to explore a little further the nature of science.

Let us begin with some definitions of science by important men: "Science is knowledge gained by systematic observation, experiment and reasoning" (Pasteur). "Science is knowledge, not of things, but of their relations" (Poincaré). "Science is organized common sense" (Thomas Huxley). "Science is the process which makes knowledge" (Charles Singer). "Science is an attempt to systematize our knowledge of the circumstance in which recognitions occur" (Whitehead). (These definitions are taken from Black, 1952, pp. 401-2.) In his

Idea of History, Collingwood (1946) says that science is finding things out. He says, "Science is a form of thought whereby we ask questions and try to answer them. Science is fastening upon something we do not know and trying to discover it." All of these definitions have much in common with the one given above, namely, science is systematic and orderly thinking about a determinate subject matter. What then is the problem? What is it that men differ about when talking about science? The answer is that they differ about at least two things: (1) some fasten upon one particular method and conclude that only utilization of this method characterizes *true science*; others fasten upon some other method or methods of science, (2) having fastened upon some method, it is concluded that any questions that cannot be answered by this method are meaningless and not within the purview of science. The argument thus becomes one over the appropriate concerns of the discipline. Both these routes to disagreement are based upon a misunderstanding of science and the scientific method. Both involve a failure to divide the problem into appropriate subproblems.

Take a look at what some distinguished people have said about method: Kaplan (1964, p. 27) says in his *Conduct of Inquiry* that he forgoes a definition of the scientific method because "I believe there is no one thing to be defined . . . one could as well speak of 'the method' of baseball," and he quotes, with approval, P. W. Bridgman's remark that "the scientist has no other method than doing his damnedest." James B. Conant says (1953) that the historians and philosophers of science have done a public service in making clear that there is no such thing as *the* scientific method. Cohen and Nagel (1934) say, "The constant and universal feature of science is its general method, which consists in the persistent search for truth, constantly asking: Is it so? To what extent is it so? Why is it so?—that is, What general conditions or considerations determine it to be so? . . . Scientific method is simply the way in which we test impressions, opinions, or surmises by examining the best available evidence for and against them. . . . in essence scientific method is simply the pursuit of truth as determined by logical considerations." Salvemini (1939, pp. 112-13) has said, "The scientist is not one who, wishing to open a door, must once and for all choose from among a bunch of keys the one key which alone is good. Scientific research is a series of successive approaches to the truth, comparable to an exploration in an unknown land. Each explorer checks and adds to the findings of his predecessors, and facilitates for his successors the attainment of the goal they all have in common." The appropriate method is determined by the nature of the subject matter; method or methods cannot be determined a priori. As

Aristotle said of the application of quantitative measurements, you can only expect from any science such exactitude as is apt to the subject matter.

Science, then, is finding out. It is a form of rational thought and dialogue. It is a fastening upon something we do not know and asking and answering questions about it. Science begins with a knowledge of our own ignorance. This is not ignorance in general but ignorance of some specific thing: the cause of cancer, the origin of the U.S. Constitution, why people vote as they do, which form of government is best, how rulers can be kept responsible to those ruled, how the operations of legislatures can be made more responsive to the popular will, how poverty can be eliminated, what can be done to prevent racial discrimination. Science, in the sense we have discussed it, can help us with all of these problems; the methods we use will depend on the subject matter. One science differs from another in that it finds out things of a different kind, deals with different subject matter and contextual conditions, and uses different methods to wring from a reluctant world the answers to the questions it asks.

Fundamentally, the questions asked and the answers sought fall into two quite different categories. One set of questions calls for answers that may be described as empirical theory; the other set calls for answers that may be described as normative theory. Now, all of what has been said about science and about the scientific method applies to both categories of questions, to both orders of findings, to both kinds of theory. We fasten on something we do not know and try to find out. We ask questions and answer them. We do our *intellectual* damnedest. We engage in the *rational* pursuit of truth as determined by logical considerations. But let us look a little more closely at each, for the distinctions between them will furnish a basis for examining the development of political science, for surveying the transition from past to present; even, perhaps, for a glimpse at the future.

EMPIRICAL AND NORMATIVE THEORY

Empirical theory is oriented to the existential world, to the world we touch, taste, feel, hear, and smell. It is related to the out there; it seeks to answer questions about the nature of what is out there. In political science, empirical theory is concerned with the behavior of individuals as they participate in the political processes and institutions of a society. It seeks to provide explanation and understanding of political behavior, political processes, political institutions, and of the interaction of one upon the other. Empirical theory is not only a collection of facts about the political world; it offers interpretation, explanation, prediction. Theory is not anecdote or gossip. It is not who was elected mayor or president, it is not who paid off whom in a city administration, it is not even the extensive case history of a political campaign; for example, it is not Theodore White's several studies on the making of the president. Gossip, anecdote, fact, case history, biography, all have their uses. They provide experience vicariously to those who do not or cannot get it first hand. But this is only a part of what is involved in empirical theory and empirical science. (For a very useful development of these points see Van Dyke, 1960, chaps. 5-10; see also the excellent discussion in Skinner, 1953.)

Science involves not only facts, but theorizing as well. The empirical sciences are systems of theories, and as Karl Popper has said so very well, "Theories are nets cast to catch what we call 'the world'; to rationalize, to explain, and to master it. We endeavor to make the mesh ever finer and finer" (Popper, 1959). We theorize, we attempt explanation, we search for understanding. We use our theories then in the collection of data, the gathering of facts, the classification of facts, the ordering of phenomena, and too, in the testing of our hypotheses. Our empirical theories, to quote Arnold Brecht (Sills, 1968, vol. 12, p. 307), are propositions or sets of propositions

> designed to explain something with reference to data or interrelations not directly observed or otherwise manifest. Mere "description" is no theory. Nor are "proposals" of goals, of policy, or of evaluations. Only the explanations, if any, offered for descriptions or proposals may be theoretical; the description or proposal as such is not. On the other hand, theory does include "prediction" provided that it follows from an explanation.

All of this is to say that knowledge is not to be had by coming face to face with raw data or naked facts, nor, as Darwin said, does knowledge come from gaping at nature with an empty head. T. H. Huxley makes the same point when he says, "Those who refuse to go beyond fact rarely get as far as fact. Almost every great step [in the history of science] has been made by the 'anticipation of nature' that is, by the invention of hypotheses," and Darwin drives the point home, saying, "How odd it is that anyone should not see that all observation must be for or against some view" (quoted in Cohen and Nagel, 1934, p. 197). Empirical theory continually anticipates what it finds; it must always seek to clothe what we do not know with some attributes of the known. Empirical theory then is the interpretation of facts. Facts cover up reality; they hide it. While one is in the midst of "their innumerable swarmings we are in chaos and confusion. . . . Then on our own risk and account, we imagine a reality, or to put it another way, we construct an imaginary reality, a pure invention of our own. . . " (Ortega, 1958, p. 12). We invent theories to understand, to bring order out of confusion, to explain, to predict. (See Popper, 1959, 1962, 1964.) It is then our business to continuously test these theories, to try to falsify them, using whatever tools and techniques are at hand for doing so. The tools, the techniques, the methods, will depend on the nature of the subject we are theorizing about. The more theories we develop that withstand all our efforts to falsify them, the more power we have over our political environment. Such knowledge is power; it provides means to ends.

But empirical theory does not give us ends or goals, it does not give us wisdom. It gives us only knowledge. The power that empirical science and empirical theory may give us is the power to change our environment; if we are wise in our use of this power, we can create a humane and just social and political environment. But empirical theory can never answer questions about the ends and goals of political life—no matter how much it advances. Empirical theory is one of the components needed to build a good social and political order, but it is not the only one; normative theory also is needed.

Normative theory is oriented to the inner world of man, to his hopes, aspirations, dreams, values. Its subject matter is different from that of empirical theory. It seeks to provide the moral imperatives, or at least the moral understanding, that will enable man to live his life in a decent, humane, and civilized community. The subject matter of normative theory is not the actual hopes, aspirations, values of man; empirical science can study these. Normative theory is not concerned with describing what man is, but with examining what he ought to be; it is not concerned with what men and women value, but with what they ought to value; it does not attempt to explain the working of an actual political system, but to illuminate the characteristics of a virtuous polity. It is concerned with the ends government and politics ought to serve; with the obligations of a citizen to himself, his community, his government; with the vision man should have of his relationship to man. These general questions can be made much more concrete; in fact, everyone every day is confronted with concrete examples. Is it ever justifiable to violate a law—for example, to run through a red traffic light? Would it make any difference if you were taking a man to the hospital whose life depended on getting there as soon as possible? Should a man refuse to be drafted into the army? Is he justified in doing so because he considers the war he is being drafted to fight in an immoral one? Is it all right for another man to refuse to pay his taxes because he finds the same war immoral? Innumerable questions can be and are raised by every sensitive and perceptive person. What wrongs in society need righting? Should government undertake to right them? Is it better to live under a democratic government that permits some important wrongs to go unrighted, or is it better to institute an authoritarian regime that will attempt to right all wrong?

Take another example. A law may be objected to on many grounds: because it is too difficult to enforce; because the people of the community do not want its results; because it protects the interest of some special group; because it violates some people's rights; because it costs too much money; because it deals with matters that should not be the subject matter of law, but should be left to individual conscience. Some of these might appear to be matters of fact, answerable by empirical science. But this is misleading; there is no law to which objections in the last analysis do not rest on normative theory. For example, a man might object that a law is bad because it violates the Constitution, but why is a law bad that violates the Constitition? Many answers might be given and then still further questions asked, until the objector is ultimately forced back to an answer in terms of normative theory. Normative questions are vitally important; answers to them affect our lives every day. They most certainly deserve the best application of rational thought.

But it is well to be aware that some philosophers have denied the possibility of normative theory as it relates either to politics or to personal life. There have been and are those who claim that one can never meaningfully assert that you "ought" or "ought not" to have done "that." It is sometimes argued that "ought not" is a meaningless term; or that any meaning assigned to it is simply arbitrary and that statements of obligation are nothing more than statements of preference, and no better than any other meaning that might be assigned; or that no person can ever do anything different than he does do; or that, in any event, we can never know that any act is an "ought not" act. Such views eliminate normative theory as a meaningful subject for rational examination. But having noted these objections, which have much less support today than they did a few decades ago, and which it is not our province to examine in detail, what can be said about the application of rational thought to normative problems?

First, the normal methods of empirical science—hypothesis, deduction, observation, experiment, corroboration—do not serve very well in dealing with normative problems. The difficulty here is the difference between description and prescription; this can be illustrated by the difference between "The legislative act was passed because of the influence of powerful interests" and "The legislative act ought not to have been passed." The methods by which one deals· with the first proposition are quite different from the methods by which one deals with the second. It is fairly easy for people to develop an understanding cf how to deal with the first; less easy to develop an understanding of how to deal with the second.

There are political scientists who argue that normative questions are not a proper concern of political science. Either (a) because they do not believe normative questions are ever meaningful or (b) because, in any case, they are not subject to analysis by the methods appropriate to the empirical world. Other political scientists assert that the most important questions about political life are normative, and that to eliminate them from political science would condemn the discipline to triviality. This discussion has continued for some decades, and its end is not in sight. Normative questions have always been and still are a concern of many who attempt to think systematically about political life.

Normative theory in political science is a branch of ethical theory. It has much in common with both aesthetic and logical theory, neither of which can be tackled with the methods of empirical science. Whenever you ask what are the principles upon which actions may be criticized and revised, you are raising questions of normative theory. The results of such theorizing are not descriptive, as are the results of empirical theorizing; they are critical. A criticism is a judgment made with reference to criteria. The criteria themselves are the subject of rational examination. In criticizing and revising we do seek both to clarify and to justify. The knowledge sought is not the knowledge that conveys power; that is the knowledge of empirical science. The knowledge sought is gained by reflection, not by investigation. The kind of thought involved is that of Plato's *Apology* or Aristotle's *Ethics*.

Before leaving the subject of normative theory, it is important to note that many things often thought to be normative theory are not. Not all normative assertions, not all "ought" and "ought not" statements fall into the category of normative theory. Assertions of personal preference or prejudice are no more normative theory than statements of fact, pieces of gossip, or simple case histories are empirical theory.

Furthermore, many "ought" and "ought not" statements are elliptical statements of empirical propositions. For example, "It is raining, you ought to wear your raincoat" really states an empirical proposition: "If you do not want to get wet, wear your raincoat." It is a proposition of the type "If you wish to accomplish x, do y." Whether or not doing y will enable you to accomplish x is a matter that, in principle, can be tested empirically. "Ought" is here used in an instrumental sense. To be sure, the question of whether x is a thing of value, desirable as well as desired, may lead to a discussion that involves normative theory. To put the matter in political terms, someone might argue as follows: "That law (x) ought to be repealed. Why should it be repealed? It should be repealed because it violates freedom of speech. [This is a matter that can be examined empirically. Some might argue that it does not, in fact, violate free speech.] What difference does it make if it violates freedom of speech? If it violates free speech it will destroy democracy. Who cares? What value has democracy?" Whatever empirical questions may be involved along the way, certainly the last is beginning to move into the field of normative inquiry and normative theory. In fact, "democracy" is almost always, if not always, a normative as well as a descriptive term. Failure to recognize this has caused a great deal of confusion in the literature of political science. (See the excellent discussion of this point in Sartori, 1962, chap. 1. Sartori's book is one of the best discussions of democratic theory and Sartori makes clear the continual interplay of normative and empirical theory.)

Today, as in the past, political scientists undertake both empirical and normative inquiry. Both are important and legitimate modes of rational inquiry about political life.

CATEGORIES OF POLITICAL INQUIRY

Having taken a look at where political science now stands as a discipline, briefly glimpsed the impact of science on its development, noted the importance of the past, especially of the classical writings, and established the important distinction between empirical and normative inquiry, it would be valuable to explore in some detail the history of political science down to modern times, both as a discipline and as a profession. Unhappily, the very sketchy narrative that could be provided in the space at my disposal would be of little value. Therefore, discussion here will be limited to the recent past. (It is important to note that interesting work is now being done and certainly more will be done in exploring the past of political science. See Anderson, 1964, and the many excellent histories of political philosophy: for example, Wolin, 1960; Strauss and Cropsey, 1963, and the literature they cite. Also, every student with an interest in political science should read Somit and Tanenhaus, 1967, for a history of the discipline and the profession since the end of the nineteenth century. For a discussion of American political science down to 1900, see Haddow, 1939. A valuable but technical and difficult book for understanding the background of modern political science is Brecht, 1959, which also has an excellent bibliography.)

To discuss modern developments in political science, it will be valuable to have a shorthand description of the whole discipline within the context of the broad divisions of empirical and normative work already briefly explored. For this purpose it may be useful to classify the work done in political science in five main categories: historical, analytic, descriptive-taxonomic, scientific-theoretical, and prescriptive. This classification oversimplifies a large and complex literature. It risks distortion because it separates analytically types of work often found united between the covers of a single book or in a single article. Still, a brief essay does not provide the opportunity even to describe the multiplicity of factors, problems, approaches, and findings included in the work of political science, much less to explore their subtleties. The proposed categories comprise a roughly accurate descriiption of the kinds of work done by political scientists, past and present. A general understanding of these various types of activity is a prerequisite to understanding the various trends and conflicts within the discipline.

Historical political science is distinguished not by the use of historical data, but by how they are used. Historical political science is genetic. It involves tracing given phenomena through time. It provides accounts about the sequence in which events occurred. The historical approach was dominant in the nineteenth century and the historical school of jurisprudence founded by Eichorn and Savigny had great influence on the study of politics; so did the "evolutionary" theories of Marx, Spencer, and others. Much of the study of politics has always been historical; much historical work goes on today. Many textbooks and many courses in political science devote considerable attention to the historical aspects of their subject. Many contemporary studies of political development are essentially historical. In fact, renewed attention to the historical approach is an important, though not frequently noted, by-product of the emergence of political development as a subject of inquiry.

Political scientists study the history of constitutions, of constitutional law, of particular institutions, policies or activities, such as the presidency, the courts, the political parties, foreign policy, domestic policy, international political interactions, and political campaigning. When it is well done—and much of it is—this historical work follows the methods and achieves the results of all sound historical scholarship. It provides perspective; it widens our experience; it enables us to look at trends through time; it makes us aware of the context in which and processes through which events and actions occur, of how context and process have changed through time, and of the interaction of context, process, and events; it provides data for our generalizing and theorizing. History broadens the basis of fact on which the political scientist can build; it provides him with a wide variety of experience from which he can draw; it provides the long-range perspective that can make political scientists aware of causes of the present that lie outside the present, behind the present; of the ways the past is incapsulated in the present; and it can make him aware of the danger of universalizing a judgment that is true only in the context of a limited time span, or in the context of a given culture. (See the excellent pieces by Beer, 1967; Rowse, 1963; and in Lipset, ed., 1969, "History and Political Science" by Richard Jensen. Jensen's references and notes provide excellent sources for following up his discussion. Richter, 1970, includes essays by Beer, Burnham, Walzer, and others, and provides an excellent discussion of the uses of history in analyzing and developing theory; and Beer, 1966, is an excellent example of the use of history in the analysis of the concepts of representation and party.)

Analytic political science refers to that category of work whose chief aim is the examination of a body of data, a set of concepts, a framework of inquiry, or a policy with the intent to clarify terms, identify component elements, explore logical relations, determine consistency and coherence. Traditionally, political scientists whose work might be described as analytical tended to concentrate on the analysis of such concepts as state, law, sovereignty, authority, rights, justice, toleration, freedom, and the like. Much of the best work in political philosophy falls in this category. Socrates' efforts to clarify the meanings of important terms in current usage in his day, his insistence on exploring logical relations, coherence, and consistency are a prime example, and Socrates has had a long line of distinguished successors. Today one might call attention to T. D. Weldon's *The Vocabulary of Politics*, or to R. G. Collingwood's *The New Leviathan*, or to Bertrand de Jouvenel's *The Pure Theory of Politics*. Also in this category, are excellent analyses of law and constitutions, a field in which American political science has done some of its best work. Finally, one should include the attempts to develop systematic frameworks for inquiry such as David Easton's influential *A Systems Analysis of Political Life*, and Lasswell and Kaplan's important book *Power and Society*.

Descriptive-taxonomic political science is that body of work that makes a systematic effort at gathering and classifying the facts of political life, at describing political institutions, processes, and behavior. A very large part of the work done by political scientists in this century falls into this category. As Charles Hyneman has put it, this literature "describes the organizational structure, the process of decision making and action, the politics of control, the policies and actions, and the human environment of legal government" (Hyneman, 1959, chap. 3). There is no need to mention specific studies or books; every reader of this volume will come across many references to them. Descriptive-taxonomic work is not new. Herodotus classified governments. Aristotle collected constitutions and described governments over two thousand years ago. The range and variety of works of this type defy summary; one cannot do justice to this category of works merely by listing examples. But the textbooks in American and comparative government, in international politics, in political parties, and in local government, are cases in point.

Virtually all single-nation studies fall within the descriptive-taxonomic category. So do most studies of parts of political systems, whether of political parties, the executive, legislatures, regulatory commissions, courts, or voting behavior. These studies map the political world. They inform us about who did what to whom. Their relation to empirical theory is dynamic, reciprocal, and crucial. Generally, the collection of data for descriptive studies is guided by existing hypotheses concerning the relevant phenomena, even though the author does not specifically intend to test the hypotheses. In turn, data presented in the descriptive studies influence the development of new hypotheses, new generalizations, new theory about the nature of the political world. Theory builders are dependent on the work of the describers, even when the describers are indifferent to the needs of theory builders. When the discipline is functioning best, the two work self-consciously in tandem. Work in the development field, among others, has reminded us again of the utility of taxonomy and of its suggestive as well as its descriptive role. Most of the work done in political science falls within the descriptive-taxonomic category. Many of the most creative political scientists have produced this type of literature. Three excellent examples are V. O. Key's *Southern Politics in State and Nation* (1949), Gabriel Almond and Bingham Powell's *Comparative Politics: A Developmental Approach* (1966), and Samuel Huntington's *Political Order in Changing Societies* (1968). Huntington's book is a fine example of a combination of categories. It makes good use of history, of the classic writings, is descriptive-taxonomic, analytical, and theoretical. This is true, of course, of much of the best work in political science.

Scientific political science refers to the work that seeks to develop empirical theory (1) capable of *explaining* a wide range of apparently discrete and disparate political phenomena and (2) capable of being tested and possibly *disproved* by further research. Plato, though rarely thought of in these terms, provides an example of empirical theory. Among other things, *The Republic* sets forth a theory of the relation of constitution to character. To oversimplify, Plato asserts that a society's political institutions depend on the character of the people in the society; and that when character changes, political institutions change. Aristotle, more generally and quite properly thought of as the father of an empirical, scientific, and theoretical political science in the Western world, developed a series of theories concerning political life which he sought to test by observation. Both his *Politics* and his *Constitution of Athens* furnish examples. Both contain many hypotheses about the relations of social and economic factors to political life—hypotheses that postulate causal relations under specified conditions and permit of empirical testing.

While there are many examples, from Plato and Aristotle down to the present, of writers on politics who developed theoretical propositions aimed at explaining political reality, a self-conscious concern with development of empirical theory and exploration of the relevant methodological problems and implications, have been primarily an activity of twentieth-century political science. For all the reasons discussed above, twentieth-century political scientists have been especially involved with the effort to be empirical. In addition, the expansion of the social sciences and the development of new techniques for acquiring and analyzing data have aided in the development of scientific theory. Important here are the development of statistics and of techniques dependent on statistics such as survey research and content analysis, and the development of the modern computer with its capacity to store and retrieve data, perform calculations, and analyze data with great speed. For the past twenty years at least, a very broad segment, perhaps a majority, of political scientists engaged in research and writing have been committed to developing a scientific political science capable of producing theories that will explain the facts of political life. So far we have accumulated a number of middle-range theories concerning the functioning of such discrete aspects of political systems as the consequences of various types of electoral systems in specified contexts, the behavior of voters in specified contexts, the consequences of alternative organizational strategies in specified contexts, and the like.

To understand what scientific theory is and its importance to the discipline, it is important to keep in mind both what it is not and how it relates to other categories of political science. Scientific theory is not talk about scientific theory. Frameworks for analysis are not scientific theory unless they include interlocking testable propositions about the real world. Scientific theory is not theorizing about science. It is theorizing about the real world of politics. It must contain propositions capable of being tested. Further, scientific theory cannot proceed independently of data, independently of looking at the real world to see if there is congruence between it and the theory. For this reason, analysis, data collection, description, and taxonomy are closely related, as has already been noted above. (For further discussion of the scientific enterprise in political science, see Arnold Brecht's excellent but difficult volume, 1959. An account of the development of a scientific political science in the United States is provided in the very readable little volume by Somit and Tanenhaus, 1967. Also, see my essay on the impact of the behavioral on the traditional political science in Ranney, 1962. For an exposition of various problems of a scientific social science, see Brodbeck, 1968. For an excellent discussion of science and the study of politics, see Gregor, 1971, chap. 2. Gregor's book also is valuable for an understanding of the relationship of developments in the philosophy of science to the study of political science, and chapter 9 is a stimulating discussion of normative discourse. For criticisms of the whole effort to develop a scientific political science, see Crick, 1959; Storing, 1962; and Charlesworth, 1962.)

Prescriptive political science includes that part of the literature that is normative. It comprises both books arguing the merits of a particular reform, of a particular governmental system, or of a particular policy or set of policies, as well as books and articles devoted to the development and analysis of normative theory. Prescriptive works may argue for the short ballot, for a more responsible two party system, for a change in the draft law, for increase in foreign aid. They may argue that democracy is the best form of government, that in a pluralistic society the obligation of a citizen does not include the responsibility to obey laws which he disapproves, that violence in support of a good cause is just, that silencing opponents with obnoxious views is justified in terms of a higher good than free speech. In the prescriptive category fall all utopias from Plato's Republic through Harrington's Oceana to Herbert Marcuse's "free society" (see Harrington, 1972; Marcuse, 1969). It includes a wide range of scholarly arguments for reform, such as Woodrow Wilson, *Congressional Government* (1885), Herbert Croly, *The Promise of American Life* (1909), E. E. Schattschneider, *Party Government* (1942), James MacGregor Burns, *The Deadlock of Democracy* (1963), Stephen K. Bailey, *The New Congress* (1966), Charles Beard, *The Open Door at Home! A Trial Philosophy of National Interest* (1934). It should be noted, incidentally, that the latter list includes three former presidents of the American Political

Science Association: Wilson, Beard, and Schattschneider. Another type of book that should be mentioned in this category deals strictly with ethical theory and politics. Examples of such books are Aristotle, *Nicomachean Ethics*, Jeremy Bentham, *The Principles of Morals and Legislation*, John Stuart Mill, *Utilitarianism*, Bertrand Russell, *Human Society in Ethics and Politics* (1955), and E. F. Carritt, *Ethical and Political Thinking* (1947).

The categories or approaches to political science just outlined are to be found in the literature of political science from Plato and Aristotle to the present day. All have made significant contributions to our knowledge about government and politics. (For an excellent discussion of approaches to the study of politics using different categories see Van Dyke, 1960: pt. 35 pp. 113–87; his notes furnish excellent further references. Also, see the useful book edited by Roland Young, 1958.) Needless to say, these categories or approaches are not mutually exclusive. Throughout its history, political science has been eclectic in approach. Many of the books cited above could fall into more than one category. For this reason alone, any attempt to characterize the large body of literature in political science in a single short essay is dangerous, perhaps even foolhardy; furthermore, there are important differences of orientation, emphasis, and quality in work falling within each category. To illustrate by example, the descriptive-taxonomic category includes studies of the formal, constitutional, and legal structure of institutions, but it also includes studies that emphasize function and process as well as studies that depict the interaction of structure, function, and process. Between the time the first chair in political science was established at Columbia University in 1857 and today, significant changes have occurred in descriptive-taxonomic work. Early emphasis was certainly on the formal and juridical structures, but this gave way in time to functionally oriented research coupled with a greater comparative emphasis. The work of A. Lawrence Lowell is an example. The more dynamic character of this work pointed up the importance of nongovernmental groups and informal processes. Arthur Bentley's work is another example. Further, the development of new bodies of quantitative data generated by survey research, the increasing use of roll-call votes, electoral data, and census returns served as the basis for descriptive studies that were quantitative in character. Thus, all studies labeled descriptive-taxonomic are by no means identical either in content or in character. Still, this category, like the others discussed above, has utility in making the discussion of the discipline manageable, in helping organize the discussion of developments through time, and in providing a shorthand vocabulary for varieties of work that are similar in character.

The Behavioral Revolution

By the middle of this century substantial accomplishments had been made by political scientists. They had come to know significantly more about the institutions and processes of government in this country and, to a lesser extent, in other parts of the world, than had ever been known about the loci of power in society and the operations of that power in and on government; about the organization of governments; about the cultural and psychological determinants of political behavior; about electoral and legislative processes; about decision making; about the character and types of political leadership; about the variant relations of ideology to leadership; and so forth. They had learned more than would have been thought possible only forty-seven years earlier (1903) when the American Political Science Association was organized. The increase in published works, and in educational and professional activity, was striking.

The *American Political Science Review* was first published in 1906. Between 1906 and 1910 it contained only 14 advertisements for books; between 1911 and 1920, there were only 25. By the period 1941 to 1950, the number of ads had grown to 230. In comparison, it is interesting to note that between 1961 and 1968, the number had grown to 927. This very rough measure of the quantity of new work believed by publishers to be of interest to political scientists is indicative of the great expansion within the profession. With this expansion came a new self-consciousness on the part of political scientists about their corporate identity, purposes, and organization. Out of the new self-consciousness and self-scrutiny grew what has been called the behavioral revolution. Influenced by developments in the natural sciences, in mathematics and statistics, in the other social sciences, and perhaps even more by such students of science and the scientific method as Morris Cohen (1931), more and more political scientists expressed dissatisfaction with the work done in political science and with the results it produced. They criticized the formalism, the aridity, the legalism of much political science. They protested the lack of recognition by political scientists of what was being done in other disciplines, particularly psychology, sociology, anthropology, and psychiatry; they were unhappy about the bulging inventory of facts that had no relation to theory; they noted the extent to which untenable assumptions and premises influenced and distorted findings; they criticized the failure to make better use of new developments in statistics; they were concerned about the amount of so-called political science that served no function but to bolster the value premises of the author; they pointed to difficulties arising from the lack of comparative data and the lack of comparabil-

ity of data collected. In brief, they accused the profession of digni-
fying sloppy, impressionistic, crudely empirical, and prejudiced research with the name of science. (See my essay in Ranney, 1962, for
my more extensive citation of relevant literature on this subject.)

Dissatisfaction and criticism produced ferment, and ferment produced change. The change was based on the criticisms and on the call
for new units of analysis, new methods, new techniques, and the
development of systematic theory. A good example of this criticism
as it was expressed at mid-century is *The Political System*, by David
Easton (1953). Easton's appeal for the development of theory is an
effective restatement for poltical science of the plea for theory as
against crude empiricism by Morris R. Cohen (1931). In total,
Easton's volume is a most effective criticism of the state of the
discipline at that time. Like many such critical assessments, the
critics and those whose work grew out of the criticism were given a
label, behavioralists, and the approach they represented was designated by the name "political behavior." (For an incisive and lucid
discussion of the behavioral approach, see Eulau, 1963.)

In fact, the word "behavioral" was used to describe a wide
variety of people, propensities, and activities. Published studies and
discussion among political scientists made it abundantly clear that a
number of different, sometimes contradictory, sets of assumptions,
methods, techniques, and data were identified with the political
behavior movement. It included political scientists with a special
interest in or enthusiasm for psychology, for cultural anthropology,
for sociology, for structural functionalism, for systems analysis, for
developing areas, for comparative politics, for voting behavior, for
survey research, for epistemology, and the scientific method. The
only definite requirement was desire for a change in how political
science was conceived and practiced, a change in the direction of
attempting to be more systematic and scientific.

Despite this variety of interests and talents among the carriers of
the behavioral revolution, it is possible to identify the salient characteristics of the "political behavior" movement: (1) Initially, at least,
it rejected institutions as the basic units of analysis and sought to put
in their place the behavior of individuals in political situations. (2) It
emphasized the unity of the social sciences and used the name
"behavioral sciences" to describe this unity. (3) It advocated much
more precision and the use of more precise techniques for observing,
classifying, and measuring data. (4) It strongly urged the use of
quantitative formulations wherever possible and specifically urged far
greater use of the modern science of statistics. (5) It insisted on the
separation of empirical from normative statements and, in many
cases, left the impression or, in fewer cases, asserted that normative

propositions have no place in political science. (6) In the early stages, at least, it tended to deprecate most of the work of the past, including the classical writings. (7) It defined the construction of systematic, empirical theory as the goal of political science. (8) It involved a high sense of professionalism based on the conviction, shared, to be sure, by many traditional scholars, that political science could and should be a scholarly enterprise characterized by skills, commitments, methods, and findings that would distinguish it from the speculations and writings about politics by non-political scientists, distinguish it from gossip, distinguish it from plain reporting.

It needs to be pointed out again that no such list of characteristics as are attributed above to "it" (the political behavior movement) were to be found in any one individual. The term "political behavior" was a sort of umbrella, capacious enough to provide shelter for a heterogeneous group united by dissatisfaction with various aspects of the discipline as they saw it.

The political behavior approach described above has had a long history. Almost all of the behavioral criticisms made at mid-century had been voiced long before. Almost all the types of work advocated by behavioralists had been done by some political scientists decades earlier, except work dependent on new techniques or new machines. Both proponents and opponents of the behavioral tendency have exaggerated the extent to which it broke with the past. Yet this exaggeration lives on in the lore of the profession despite the efforts of numerous commentators to correct it (Somit and Tanenhaus, 1967; Dahl, 1961b; Kirkpatrick in Ranney, 1962). For this reason, it seems worthwhile to cite once more some of the evidence on the life history of the behavioral approach.

Already in the period in which political science was emerging as a separate discipline in the United States, one finds criticisms that appear quite modern, and published work that embodies the essence of the behavioral approach to the study of politics. Woodrow Wilson and James Bryce, both later to become presidents of the American Political Science Association, were already in the late 1800s calling on political scientists to get out of the library and into the field. In an essay written well before the turn of the century, Wilson expressed his dissatisfaction with the dull legalism of much political science and with those who gathered all of their data in libraries. He said, "We are inclined, oftentimes, to take laws and constitutions too seriously, to put implicit faith in their professions without examining their conduct" (Wilson, 1893). He called on persons writing about politics to observe the behavior of those who participated in the operation of government. James Bryce, in his *The American Commonwealth* (1888) said that his purpose was "to paint the institutions and people of America as they are ... to avoid temptations of the deductive method and to present simply the facts of the case" (Bryce, 1926, vol. 1, p. 12). Later, he said in a much quoted passage. "It is facts that are needed. Facts, Facts, Facts" (Bryce, 1921, p. 21). It is important to note (because there has been misunderstanding of this point) that, though both Wilson and Bryce wanted facts, wanted to get out into the field and see how people behave, neither was a crude empiricist without concern for theory, either normative or empirical. Nor were they alone.

As early as the 1890s, J. W. Burgess was concerned about the development of a better comparative literature. (See his *Political Science and Comparative Constititional Law*, 1891; by 1896, A. Lawrence Lowell had written his two-volume *Government and Parties in Continental Europe*, and by 1908, his two-volume *The Government of England.*) While Burgess and Lowell were asking for and producing a better comparative literature, Graham Wallas (1908) was calling attention to the unsatisfactory condition of political science resulting from the persistence of an outdated and mistaken psychology; "nearly all students of politics," he asserted, "analyze institutions and avoid the analysis of man" (1908, vol. 1, p. 14). In the same year (1908), Arthur Bentley urged students of politics to concentrate on the study of human behavior and on functional relations and group processes as the proper focuses of a science of politics. Bentley further argued that "measure conquers chaos" and asserted that "if a statement of social facts which lends itself better to measurement is offered, that characteristic entitles it to attention" (1908, pp. 200–1). It is worth noting also that the sociologist E. A. Ross wrote the first book bearing the title *Social Psychology* in the same year that the books by Wallas and Bentley were published.

In 1910, A. Lawrence Lowell, in his presidential address to the American Political Science Association, expressed dissatisfaction with the discipline. In an address entitled "The Physiology of Politics," he criticized the lack of an adequate nomenclature in the discipline, and made a plea for study to be more dynamic and functional in character. In 1917, Jesse Macy, in his presidential address to the APSA, asserted the need for the more scientific study of politics and argued that the methods of science should be the model for dealing with the problems of politics.

The First World War, however, temporarily shifted attention away from problems of method. The war had a massive impact on American life and American government, an impact that brought the first major shift away from a laissez-faire society toward government control and regulation of business, industry, and agriculture. This in turn produced an unprecedented need for planning and prediction. It was, therefore, only natural that political scientists should fasten upon the natural sciences as a model in the hope that a scientific politics might produce—as the sciences of nature had produced—the kind of knowledge needed to deal more effectively with man's problems.

Charles Merriam, brilliant developer of the political science department at the University of Chicago, became, in the 1920s, the most influential figure calling for a new political science. In 1921, in an article entitled "The Present State of the Study of Politics," he argued that political science was paying inadequate attention to the methods and results of scientific work in social psychology, biology, sociology, ethnology, and statistics (Merriam, 1921). In 1923, as head of a committee of the American Political Science Association, Merriam reported that much more attention should and would be paid to the psychological dimension of political science, and his prediction was borne out in the brilliant and influential work of his most distinguished student, Harold Lasswell. (See Lasswell, 1930, 1935a, 1936, 1948, for examples of Lasswell's contribution to the psychological dimension of the study of politics. For further exploration of the work of Lasswell, whose influence on modern political science has been greater than that of any other figure, see *Politics, Personality and Twentieth Century Political Science: Essays in Honor of Harold D. Lasswell*, edited by Arnold A. Rogow, 1969. The first three chapters of this book are exceedingly interesting discussions of Lasswell by men who have been closely associated with him. The remaining chapters deal with matters to which Lasswell has made significant contributions and, therefore, provide a partial appraisal of his work. Rogow's book also contains the most comprehensive bibliography of Lasswell's published work. It makes clear that he has been the most prodigious worker among modern political scientists; see pp. 407- 43.) In 1925, Merriam, in an important and influential book, *New Aspects of Politics*, set forth and advocated most of the characteristic assumptions, goals, methods, procedures, and emphases of the political behavior movement. In the summers of 1923, 1924, and 1925, Merriam played an influential part in three conferences called to critically examine the methods, procedures, and basic goals of political science. (Reports on these conferences were printed in the *American Political Science Review* for 1924, 1925, and 1926, vol. 18, pp. 119- 66; vol. 19, pp. 104- 62; vol. 20, pp. 124- 70; for a biography of Merriam, see Karl, 1974.)

In this same period, other forces were contributing to push political science in the direction Merriam wished it to go. George Catlin, an English scholar then in the United States, had published in 1927 a significant and influential book entitled *The Science and*

Method of Politics; three years later *A Study of the Principles of Politics* (1930) was published. Catlin urged that power relations were the central concern of political science, and could furnish units of analysis that would forward the scientific development of the study of politics. Lasswell, with great insight into the interaction of power and other basic value categories (from the outset he clearly saw that power itself was value), carried the exploration of power relations even further. (Examples of this work are *World Politic and Personal Insecurity*, 1935; *Politics: Who Gets What, When, How*, 1936; *Power and Personality*, 1948; and *Power and Society*, 1950.) In this same period, a significant push was given to quantitative studies by the publication of Stuart Rice's *Quantitative Methods in Politics* (1928). Rice argued for and demonstrated by example the value of quantification and quantitative techniques. This was consistent with Merriam's report for the APSA committee in 1923 asserting that quantification of data and findings was one of the most important trends in political science.

But the behavioral trend was slowed by forces outside the control of those expressing dissatisfaction and advocating change. As has happened repeatedly in the history of political science, politics intervened to influence the tempo, if not the direction, of development in the discipline. The Great Depression, beginning in 1929; the movement of political scientists in and out of government during the politically exciting days of the New Deal, following Franklin Roosevelt's election in 1932; the Second World War with its disruption of academic life and its even greater utilization of political scientists in government; all imposed a brake on the behavioral movement which had been pushed ahead so vigorously in the 1920s. But, at the same time, these experiences set the stage for renewed behavioral development following the end of the war. Exposure to the actual workings of government and international politics sensitized many political scientists to the inadequacies of the literature of political science. Experience with interdisciplinary research on various practical problems dramatized the benefits to be derived from work going on in other disciplines. Further, the pressure to find answers to practical problems had sped the development, refinement, and application of new techniques and methods.

Equally important for rapid changes in the nature of work being done was the existence of a substantial number of political scientists whose training—largely under Merriam or those trained by Merriam—had prepared them and predisposed them to practice, teach, and preach the behavioral approach to political science. Whatever their view about the role or place of normative propositions and normative theory in the discipline, they had no doubt about the value and importance of the behavioral approach. Among those in positions of influence and leadership in political science after the war who had been trained or influenced by Merriam were Leonard White, Quincy Wright, Harold Gosnell, Harold Lasswell, Roscoe Martin, V. O. Key, Gabriel Almond, Avery Leiserson, Herman Pritchett, Robert Dahl, Herbert Simon, David Truman, David Easton, Ithiel de Sola Pool, and Alfred and Sebastian de Grazia. In measuring Merriam's influence, it is worth noting that not only was he elected president of the American Political Science Association, but two colleagues in the department he headed and five of his students later became its president. The colleagues were Quincy Wright and Leonard White; the students were Gabriel Almond, V. O. Key, Harold Lasswell, Herman Pritchett, and David Truman, all of whom had had a significant impact on the discipline.

At the same time an enormous growth in college enrollment took place; political science departments expanded; an ever increasing number of Ph.D.'s were turned out; money for research became more plentiful; the Social Science Research Council—a product of Merriam's tireless energy and institution-building ability—under the effective direction of E. Pendleton Herring brought both money and leadership; the Ford Foundation came into being with assets ready to be devoted to study and research; the Center for Advanced Study in the Behavioral Sciences was created. The resulting progress of the behavioral emphasis was greater than anyone might have expected in the 1930s and 1940s. (It is impossible to pursue these developments in detail in this summary history, but there are many sources to which those interested may turn. Some sources are Eulau, *Recent Developments in the Behavioral Study of Politics*, 1961; *The Behavioral Persuasion in Politics*, 1963; and *Behavioralism in Political Science*, 1969. See also Eulau, Eldersveld, and Janowitz, *Political Behavior: A Reader in Theory and Research*, 1956; Bailey et al., *Research Frontiers in Politics and Government*, 1955; Somit and Tanenhaus, 1967; the excellent article by David Truman, "The Implications of Political Behavior Research," 1951, and his influential book *The Governmental Process*, 1951; Kirkpatrick, in Ranney, 1962. All these provide further discussion and references to the literature. For a comprehensive and extremely valuable examination of the central problems of political science and for an excellent bibliography and references to the important literature throughout the history of political science, see Friedrich, *Man and His Government: An Empirical Theory of Politics*, 1963. Another review and appraisal of political science is Eulau and March, *Political Science*, 1969, a part of the report prepared by the Behavioral and Social Science Survey Committee appointed jointly by the National Academy of Sciences and the Social Science Research Council.)

The Impact of Behavioralism

The behavioral approach has been the dominant, though never the sole, orientation in political science for over two decades. It has exercised determinative influence on the focus of the discipline. It has had a large impact on the vocabulary of political science, on the criteria of relevance, on the canons of evidence, on the training of graduate students, on the character of work produced, and on the standards of excellence in the discipline.

Starting from the premise that the root of politics is man, that a comprehensive description of governmental structure in action "can be supplied only by systematic observation of actual behavior, not by pure speculation or by the exégesis of texts" (Truman, 1951b, p. 38); starting, that is, from the conviction that the individual in political situations is the proper focus of the discipline, many political scientists undertook research on politically relevant beliefs, values, and personality structures. This interest had substantive consequences for political science; let us consider them briefly. To find out what a man actually wants, fears, hopes, wishes, or knows (not what someone thinks he should believe, hope, fear, want, or know), the surest and most direct way to proceed is to ask him. There is nothing new in this approach, of course. Students of politics have always speculated about the relation of character to constitution. St. Augustine had defined a polity in terms of the value commitments of its inhabitants. Hobbes constructed a theory of politics on a view of human nature, as did Rousseau, John Calvin, the authors of *The Federalist Papers*, and Alexis de Tocqueville. Nor was there anything new about observing men directly or speaking with them to discover their hopes, beliefs, aspirations, or fears. This was, of course, how acute observers of politics had always arrived at views about human nature. What was new was the application to the study of subjectivities of methods and techniques of recent development. Freud's discovery of the method of free association and his development and refinement of in-depth interviewing had put new tools at the disposal of political scientists interested in politically relevant patterns of cognition and valuation. (See Lane, 1962, 1969; Pye, 1962; and, of course, the pioneering work of Lasswell, which is still going forward, 1930, 1948, 1966, 1971.) The development of statistics and its application to the problem of sampling large populations made it possible to collect accurate information about the attitudes of masses by investigating the subjectivities of a limited number. The development and use of the sample survey generated great quantities of new data on the wants, goals, and beliefs of masses and made it possible to test the many hypotheses that abound in the classic writings, in the proposals of reformers, and in the halls of government. Emphasis on the subjective aspects of political life stimulated interest in questionnaire development, sampling techniques, scale construction, attitude measurement, tests of validity and reliability, and a host of other problems that had occupied the attention of psychologists and sociologists for years. The substantive consequences of this emphasis were an increased interest in the relations of politics to personality, in voting behavior, in political culture, and in political socialization. (See, for examples, Greenstein, 1969; Davies, 1963; Lasswell, 1948. Greenstein, 1969, has a valuable bibliographical note by Michael Lerner, pp. 154–84. Anyone wishing to become familiar with the work in this field should first turn to Lerner's bibliographical note.)

Starting from the premise that mathematical and statistical formulations could provide both more precision and new insights into political life and open up new analytic capabilities to the profession, a number of political scientists associated with the behavioral approach developed (in some cases acquired) and utilized skills in statistics and mathematics. Increasingly, a knowledge of statistics came to be regarded as a necessary, rather than only a desirable, tool for political scientists. Examinations in statistics took their place alongside the language examinations as requirements for a Ph.D. degree. At the same time came the development of the modern computer. A number of political scientists became involved in learning computer programming and in otherwise developing skills that would enable them to make use of modern machines and methods. All of this stimulated interest in and concern for a more adequate collection of quantifiable data. New data archives were established. The Yale Data Program, the Roper Center at Williams, the Inter-University Consortium for Political Research, are only a few of the efforts in this direction.

In addition, materials were developed for training undergraduates in political science in the use of modern machines and techniques. (See Flanigan and Repass, 1969, for a manual in the field of electoral behavior. Other manuals are being prepared by members of the University of Minnesota department for use in other fields. See also Oliver Benson's volume *Political Science Laboratory*, 1969; and William Buchanan's *Understanding Political Variables*, 1969, 1974. For a series of handbooks developed under the stimulation of James Robinson, see Backstrom and Hursh, *Survey Research*, 1963; North, Holsti, Zaninovich, and Zinnes, *Content Analysis*, 1963; and others published by Northwestern University Press. For more advanced students, see the valuable and important contribution of Alker, *Mathematics and Politics*, 1965. For a compilation of data, see Russett, Alker, Deutsch, and Lasswell, *World Handbook of Political and Social Indicators*, 1964. For an example of one of the many books on research methods with attention to the quantitative aspects of research, see Simon, 1969. This volume has an excellent bibliography, pp. 483–99.)

Starting from the premise that the proper goal of political science is the development of empirical theory and the corollary conviction that an empirical theory of politics must take account of the full range of the varieties of political experience, many political scientists associated with the behavioral movement turned their attention to comparative politics. The result was a veritable explosion of new literature in the comparative field that tended to emphasize the newer areas of investigation such as political socialization, political culture, leadership, and political development. Also, many scholars developed a new self-consciousness about the comparability of data. A vast literature of books, monographs, and articles has been produced, multiplying by many times our substantive knowledge of the varieties of politics. (See the bibliography in Friedrich, 1963, and articles dealing with the comparative politics field in *The International Encyclopedia of the Social Sciences.*)

Starting from the premise of the unity of the social sciences, political scientists associated with the behavioral movement borrowed concepts, approaches, techniques, and vocabulary from social scientists in other disciplines. Not all these borrowings were necessarily supportive of, or even consistent with, other premises of the behavioral orientation, but in their enthusiasm for interdisciplinary collaboration, some did not seem to notice. Through such borrowings, structural-functionalism and general systems theory entered the discipline. So did such concepts as modal personality, national culture, ideal types, cognitive dissonance, and others too numerous to mention. The borrowed concepts are still being sorted out; it is too early to say which will have proved most useful to the study of politics.

In all fields of political science, studies were produced that showed the impact of the behavioral movement. Certainly these studies made significant and valuable contributions to our knowledge. Behavioral studies were done in fields as diverse as international politics, comparative government, the judicial process, public administration, the study of legislatures and legislation, and local government. Examples abound in the references already given, but in order to be more specific, I shall cite a few examples: the work of Herman Pritchett, Glendon Schubert, Alan Westin, and Jack Peltason on the courts and the judicial process; the massive generation of data and effective analysis of voting behavior at the Survey Research Center; the work on administrative behavior by Herbert Simon, James March, and

Fred Riggs; the study of community power structure by Edward
Banfield, Robert Dahl, and by Robert Agger and his coworkers; the
work of Sidney Verba, Gabriel Almond, and Lucian Pye on comparative political cultures; the studies by James Payne, Robert Ward,
James S. Coleman, and Samuel Huntington on developing nations;
the effective research of Fred Greenstein, Robert Lane, Jack Dennis,
and Herbert McClosky on political socialization and the psychological dimensions of political behavior; the publications of Samuel
Eldersveld, Leon Epstein, Allan Sindler, Duane Lockhard, Dwaine
Marvick, Donald Stokes, Philip Converse, Warren Miller, and Austin
Ranney in the field of parties, elections, and voting behavior; the
work of Vernon Van Dyke, Ernst Haas, James Robinson, James
Rosenau, Morton Kaplan, David Singer, Richard Snyder, and Karl
Deutsch in international politics. To name a few, of course, is unfair
to those who are omitted and to a great many who have made
important contributions to more than one field. References to the
work of many of these and other behavioral scholars will be found
throughout this volume and in the bibliography.

In spite of the substantive contributions that have been made,
too often the behavioral approach to political science has been
criticized for its emphasis on method to the exclusion of all else. To
preclude the possibility that any emphasis on technique and method
in this chapter convey such an impression, the contrary needs to be
made explicit. The technical innovations of survey methods, test
instruments, statistical analysis, content analysis, experiments with
small groups, scaling techniques, mathematical models, game
theory—all these and more—have been associated with the behavioral
approach. But to equate them with the political behavior movement
is to confuse means with ends. Technical innovations did not occur
in a conceptual vacuum: they followed on new conceptions of
political process and political system. They are necessary tools for
generating data and for analyzing aspects of public authority and
political life that had not previously been susceptible to systematic
investigation.

Of course, concern with techniques has preempted the attention
of some, and this is as it should be. If it had preempted the attention
of all behaviorally oriented political scientists, this would have been
unfortunate. Happily, as the results make clear, this was not the case.
Indeed, there have been substantial benefits resulting from the
methodological preoccupation induced by the behavioral orientation.
It has had the salutary effect of making many more political scientists self-conscious about their goals, procedures, and findings. The
interdisciplinary focus has awakened many political scientists to the
existence of alternative approaches, orientations, goals, and methods

open to those concerned with the study of man. It has stimulated wide dissemination of knowledge from other disciplines. Furthermore, the theoretical emphasis has led to a more concerted effort to discover uniformities and regularities, and it may even have aided in bringing about the much needed revival of interest in the political classics (Pool, 1967). All this has resulted in the improvement of substantive studies of political life and public authority.

Because it has significant achievements to its credit, the behavioral approach has long since been incorporated into the mainstream of American political science. An institutional reflection of the speed with which the behavioral approach was assimilated by scholars working in all major fields is found in the programs of the American Political Science Association. In 1956, the association formally recognized the interest of a substantial number of scholars in behavioral studies by including in the program for its annual meeting a series of panel discussions devoted to "political behavior." It did so again in 1957 and 1958. By 1959, however, studies utilizing the behavioral approach were so prevalent in most of the traditional fields of research in politics that the association deliberately abandoned panels so labeled. The results of behavioral research were adequately reported in the traditionally listed fields of political parties, legislation, comparative government, public administration, and so forth.

There were several reasons for the rapid spread of the behavioral orientation in addition to its contributions to increased knowledge in the discipline. Only the more important will be mentioned here. (1) It had deep roots in political science, dating back at least to the turn of the century and involving some of the most distinguished scholars in the profession. (2) It moved political science in the same direction that the other social sciences were moving. (3) It was identified with new tools such as survey research, computer analysis, and mathematical applications that have undoubted importance for any discipline involved in the study of mass aggregates, new tools, and techniques that were becoming an indispensible part of other disciplines and of American life generally. (4) Funds and organizational support were available at a time when they were most needed. (5) Many political scientists of high ability and high productivity were associated with the movement. (6) Many distinguished traditional scholars were receptive to the new ideas and willing to give them an opportunity to develop. (7) Excitement was generated among colleagues and graduate students by early behavioral studies. (8) Finally, the movement produced concepts, methods, tools, goals, and results that were centrally relevant to the tasks of political science as perceived by a great majority of the profession. As a result, the behavioral movement, as well as its products, has enjoyed a great deal of success for over two decades. It has generated excitement and respect for its accomplishments; its members have held a large number of offices in the American Political Science Association; scholarly journals have been filled with articles produced by those associated with it.

It is important, therefore, to be clear first that, despite its prestige, accomplishments, and assimilation into the field of political science, the behavioral approach has never preempted the field of political science and second that influences completely outside it were responsible for some of the changes that took place.

Political science did not develop in a vacuum. It is and always has been influenced by the problems, preoccupations, technological, and social developments of the society in which it exists. The impact of the environment has been reflected in political scholarship from Socrates to the present. The enormous expansion in the study of comparative politics is certainly in part a consequence of increased ease and speed of transportation and communication, of the availability of Fulbright grants and foundation funds that were in turn a reflection of the increased interest of the United States in other parts of the world. Similarly, the study of political development and international politics was greatly stimulated by the end of isolation and the beginning of an era of American involvement in world affairs. The problems of the Cold War no doubt were responsible for stimulating a great expansion of the literature on the Soviet Union and Communism. Finally, a government greatly increased in size made available greatly increased funds for research (in the hope that it would produce knowledge helpful in dealing with pressing problems of American society) and thus made possible research that otherwise probably would not have found support (see Nagi and Corwin, 1972).

NEW TRENDS, NEW CHALLENGES

"If we take the term behaviorism to be simply the ideological flag of a group of men who were once Young Turks in the profession, then clearly with the passage of time and the progression of generations the old heterodoxy has become the new orthodoxy. With that transition of generations the wounds are being healed. Our discipline is enjoying a new coherence, a pleasant sense of unity, a self confident identity that fits its rapid growth and healthy mien. At least until some new generation of rebels comes along, we are enjoying a period in which sterile debate between two camps can be put aside while we explore as serious men the interrelations of various parts of our field" (Pool, ed., 1967, pp. vii- viii). This paragraph, written as part of a foreword to a collection of papers delivered at the plenary sessions of the 1966 annual meeting of the American Political Science Association, is evidence of the extent to which the behavioral movement had been incorporated into the mainstream of American political science. Yet the words "at least until some new generation of rebels comes along" were prophetic. A bare three years later, at the 1969 annual meeting of the American Political Science Association, David Easton opened his presidential address with the words, "A new revolution is under way in American political science. The last revolution—behavioralism—has scarcely been completed before it has been overtaken by the increasing social and political crises of our time. The weight of these crises is being felt within our discipline in the form of a new conflict in the throes of which we now find ourselves. This new and latest challenge is directed against a developing behavioral orthodoxy. This challenge I shall call the post-behavioral revolution" (Easton, 1969, p. 1051).

But as we have already seen, revolutions do not spring full blown from foreheads of scholars at any given moment in time. Dissatisfactions, objections and criticism were expressed at every stage of the behavioral development. By 1969 these criticisms had become more vigorous, more organized, more vituperative. Some of them also contained new anti-intellectual elements radically different from the criticisms of the 1950s and early 1960s.

The criticisms fall into several classes. (1) There were self-criticisms, criticisms of one another that characterized the behavioral movement from the first. These were a product, to a large extent, of the commitment to science shared by most of the leading behavioralists. (2) There were criticisms dealing with the intellectual aspects of the behavioral movement from those not a part of it; often, in fact, vigorously opposed to it. They were leveled both at the methodology and at the substantive product. (3) Finally, and most recently, there have been criticisms that the behavioralists are biased in favor of the status quo, are committed to preserving existing institutions, and seek to "ensure the predominance of conservative scholarship in a conservative society" (Wolfe, 1969). Some of this criticism proceeds on rational and intellectual grounds; some of it has little use for reason and is frankly anti-rational and anti-intellectual. All three of these categories are worthy of at least brief examination to make clear where political science stands in the 1970s.

(1) *Self-criticism*. Behavioralists were—and are—committed to science. Science requires self-criticism. Two aspects of science are specially relevant here. First, scientific development requires free and

full criticism both of method and of substantive results. The scientific attitude requires subjecting all scholarly work to criticism. When scientific work is done, reports of that work are made. Both the scientist and his colleagues are confronted with a challenge to prove the new findings unreliable or invalid. It is rigorous and critical testing and checking by both the scientist and his colleagues that insure the impartiality and objectivity of science. Therefore, science is and must be a public enterprise. Scientific objectivity is, as Popper has made clear, "a product of the social or public character of the scientific method." It is not the product of the scientists' own impartiality. This, incidentally, is true not only of science but of all serious intellectual work. It is basic to the rational approach and to the development of knowledge. (A readable discussion and argument for the public character of science and the related nature of the scientific method is to be found in all Popper's books. The most technical is *Logic of Scientific Discovery*, 1959. The most readable for political scientists, and those that deal directly with political and social problems as well, are *The Poverty of Historicism*, 1964, and *The Open Society and Its Enemies*, 1963. *Conjectures and Refutations: The Growth of Scientific Knowledge*, 1962, is a collection of lectures and papers, some technical, some not. Most interesting for political scientists are chapters 16–20.)

The second aspect of science that has relevance in this discussion is that scientists must and do continuously speak with one another. They seek to speak the same language, a language determined by their scientific experience. Experience here refers to the public character of observations, experiments, and theories. For work to be public, to be replicable, to be testable, it must be published and it must be stated in a form such that it can be understood in detail by colleagues. The requirement that science be public does not, of course, require that it be published in a form that can be understood by the man in the street. It requires only that it be understood by persons who have undergone specialized training and acquired the relevant background knowledge, canons of evidence, technical and methodological skills, and vocabulary.

As a result of their commitment to science, the best behavioralists were not only self-critical; they freely criticized others and freely accepted criticism from others. (In a scholarly work like Eulau, 1969a, there are many examples.) The criticisms, of course, assumed shared goals and shared approaches. They assumed agreement about the proper purposes and the central focus of political science. They therefore dealt mainly with matters of inadequate evidence, improper generalization, improper use of statistics or mathematics, sloppy sampling techniques, unreliability, inadequate validation of scales and measurement instruments, and related matters. Self-criticism of this sort is characteristic of all sciences, of all learned disciplines. It serves as the basis for continuing revision, refinement, and progress.

(2) *Criticism from outside the behavioral ranks.* At every stage of the development of the behavioral movement it met with criticism from outside its ranks; some severe, some moderate; some justified, some not. The most vigorous and persistent critics have not been the "Young Turks," but scholars of established reputation: Leo Straus, David Butler, Herbert Storing, Hans Morgenthau, Christian Bay, Sheldon Wolin, Bernard Crick, Henry Kariel, Robert Horowitz, and Walter Berns. (See Morgenthau, 1946; "Power as a Political Concept" in Young, 1958; Crick, 1959; Butler, 1959; Kariel, 1961; Storing, 1962, which contains essays by a number of scholars, including Straus, Horowitz, and Berns; Bay, 1965, 1970; Wolin, 1969; Kariel, 1970. Also, a useful volume for exploring the criticisms of the behavioral movement is McCoy and Playford, eds., *Apolitical Politics: A Critique of Behavioralism*, 1967.)

The criticisms were wide-ranging and vigorous. Generally, they focused on the following: that the behavioral approach led to a political science that was parochial because it ignored history; shallow because it denied itself the insights of the classics; imitative because it slavishly followed often mistaken notions of what other disciplines had done; pretentious because it relied on an unfamiliar polysyllabic vocabulary; deceptive because its precision was often spurious; sterile because it dealt only with trivial questions that could easily be answered; dull because of its studied neutrality; immoral because it turned aside from normative questions; and unreadable because its statistical and mathematical formulations required knowledge not possessed by most political scientists. Finally, and perhaps most cutting, critics accused the behavioral approach of failing to produce on its promises. Where, asked the critics, was the promised empirical science of politics? Where was the empirical theory of political behavior toward the construction of which so much time, money, and energy had been spent? Critics also attacked the assumption that it was desirable to develop a scientific study of politics; spelled out limitations on the use of quantitative techniques and methods; deplored studies of voting behavior that ignored politics; asserted that political "science" was designed to manipulate and control man. They insisted that the behavioralists made their time and space-bound findings into universal principles of politics, and thereby enshrined the status quo in a permanent place in the political science heavens. They argued that behavioralist pluralism stands in the way of dealing with our pressing problems. They insisted that

democratic theory badly needs restructuring and that behavioral
research pays little attention to the substantive goals that were so
important to some of its early proponents and that are equally
important today.

These critics do not represent any one political or philosophical
viewpoint. Some are conservatives, some liberals, some radicals.
Almost without exception, they have made their criticisms of "scientific" political science in reasoned argument; they have been participants in a rational dialogue. And they have had an impact.

(3) *Some criticisms from leaders of protest movements.* The
criticisms outlined above coincided with the development of behavioralism and continue to the present. To these criticisms, to this
rational dialogue that has influenced the development of the profession by argument and evidence, there was added in the 1960s and
1970s a comprehensive new attack. This attack focused not only on
behavioral political science (though that was a principal target) but
on the entire profession and its most basic norms. It has coincided
with the attack on many of this society's institutions by tactics of
direct action. This attack is borne by a heterogeneous group of
individuals—some young, some old, some middle-aged, some white,
some black, some male, some female—most of whom are associated
with the radical politics of what is often loosely termed the New
Left.

Some charges of these critics repeat those levelled by anti-behav-
ioralists at behavioralists. But even where the criticisms had been
heard before, they were offered in a new key from some New Left
spokesmen.

While no summary will communicate the flavor of these critics,
it can provide a sense of the positions advanced. (For a discussion of
radical politics in sociology, see the articles in the *American Journal
of Sociology*, vol. 87, no. 1, July 1972, particularly the articles of
Becker and Horowitz, Martin, Lipset and Todd, Janowitz and
Rhoads.)

The following are the essential accusations:

1. Virtually the whole of political science has a conservative bias
   that grows out of accepting rather than combatting this
   society, which is, of course, defined as corrupt, materialist,
   imperialist, racist, repressive, and unjust. Because political
   science aims at understanding rather than changing society,
   because it proceeds by description and analysis rather than
   by action, it has accepted an ideology of conservatism.
2. The norms and organization of the political science profession (and of other learned disciplines) force this conservative
   bias on political scientists through its definitions of excellence, standards of evidence, and system of rewards.

3. Behavioral political science is *especially* reprehensible because it fosters an undue concern for method and precision as compared to substance; because it advocates constructing a *science* of politics and maintaining a research posture of detachment; because its language and research procedures result in work that is abstracted from desperate human needs.
4. Political scientists have been inadequately concerned about the normative aspects of their work. They have ignored the pressing problems of the day, *and* have been corrupted by relations with government and foundations.
5. Political scientists have accepted the false gods of reason, objectivity and freedom when
   (a) a rational response to misery is inhuman,
   (b) objectivity is neither possible nor desirable, and
   (c) freedom for noxious ideas should not be permitted.

There are several noteworthy aspects of this indictment that distinguish it from prior disagreements and debates in political science. While the earlier debates turned on questions about intellectual assumptions, methods of inquiry, and the status of findings, these new criticisms are basically political. The earlier disagreements assumed a shared purpose: the study of politics with a view to increasing man's understanding of his political life. (It was also assumed that this understanding could be used by policy makers to achieve the men's goals; see, e.g., Lasswell in Lerner and Lasswell, 1951, and Ranney, 1968.) The new criticisms condemn political science for precisely that purpose—for making understanding rather than action a goal. These criticisms attack political scientists' *political* commitments and actions; the earlier debates turned on questions of scholarly inquiry. Finally, and most important, these new criticisms are more radical than any previous internecine criticisms in political science because they attack the very foundations of the scholarly ethic: reason, objectivity, and freedom. These have been central values of most Western scholars in all disciplines since at least the eighteenth century. They have been believed to be essential to inquiry, to scholarship, to science, to the pursuit of truth—not that they have not come under attack in our times. Nazis, Fascists, Communists, and assorted modern tyrants have denounced reason as enfeebling, objectivity as a sham, and defined truth as whatever served their purposes of the moment. Thus we have had—in our times—various versions of revolutionary truth. We have had Aryan truth, proletarian truth, Fascist truth. But we have *not* had an attack on reason, objectivity, and freedom from *within* the learned professions. The attack and the accompanying activism may—if pushed far enough—threaten the very processes of rational debate that have made possible modern science and the modern university.

As always, those attacking reason, objectivity, and freedom have the highest motives for doing so. One spokesman for the New Left critics remarks, "To plead for reason, detachment, objectivity or patience in the face of abject poverty, political repression or na-palmed women and children is absurd" (Marvin Surkin, *P.S.*, Fall, 1969). Another advocates the establishment of a "social university as the alternative to what we have now. This social university is not primarily concerned with the abstract pursuit of scholarship. . . . It does not recognize the right of its members to do anything they wish in the name of academic freedom . . ." (see Alan Wolfe, 1969). It should be added that Wolfe has not finally decided on whether academic freedom should be abolished generally as well as in his "social university." He does think that academic freedom cannot be *assumed* to be a good, any more than a liberal arts education can be assumed to be desirable. His position, therefore, is less repressive than that of Herbert Marcuse and various other New Leftists who are convinced there should be no freedom of speech (research, etc.) for persons holding views regarded as obnoxious.

The positions characteristic of these critics are found not only in political science but in all departments of the university. As sociol-ogist Robert Nisbet remarked in a recent article, "From radical sociologist to radical political scientist to radical anthropologist, all across the spectrum of the social sciences, the refrain is the same: Social scientists have heretofore sought to understand society. The point, however, is to destroy and then remake society" (Nisbet, 1970). Or in the words of the Australian scholar Hugh Stretton, today's conflict "goes beyond discovering and understanding. It becomes his [the social scientist's] business to win" (quoted in Nisbet, 1970).

Who does not want to win? Who can remain indifferent to poverty and repression? Certainly not most political scientists. The *reason* objectivity is valued and detachment cultivated is *not* because political scientists and other scholars are indifferent to suffering. Does anyone seriously suppose that it is indifference that leads some physicians to abandon the practice of medicine to devote themselves to medical research? Would you rather have a surgeon or your mother remove your appendix? She is doubtless more concerned, less detached. Most medical researchers hate harmful bacteria. But destroying the laboratory in which the bacteria are housed is not likely to eliminate the disease they foster.

Like medicine, political science involves human hopes and human ills. People who are attracted to the study of political science almost always have a strong interest in politics. They are people who *care* about the quality of man's social and political life. Many

American political scientists have been very active in politics. Woodrow Wilson is but one dramatic example. Most, however, have shared with scholars all over the world a commitment to rational inquiry, a belief in the necessity of freedom of inquiry, and a conviction—supported by psychology—that to be successful, inquiry requires a certain degree of objectivity. Above all, it requires the free use of reason. When reason is abandoned force replaces it. As Nisbet said, "What the disciples of social science as action can never seem to understand, is that if action is the magic word, there are always others, less burdened by the trained incapacities of scholarship, who can act more swiftly. And ruthlessly." All of which reminds one of Lincoln's dictum, "If your argument for enslaving your fellow men is based on the darkness of his skin, you better be careful not to come across a man with skin lighter than your own."

While students in the 1960s had no personal memory of it, it would have been well for them to read and reflect on the history of the Nazi movement in Germany. The destruction of freedom in the German university, the development of "Aryan science," the use of force in place of reason, led to the annihilation of much that fostered man's worth and dignity, of many of the finest products of Western civilization.

Political science has changed greatly in its relatively short life as an academic discipline. We have seen that it can accommodate a wide variety of approaches, methods, and orientations. It can thrive on controversy. It cannot survive the loss of reason, objectivity, and freedom.

PART 2

THE SCOPE OF
LEGITIMATE CONCERNS

2. COMPARATIVE POLITICS

Robert R. Kaufman and James N. Rosenau

The field of comparative politics is presently in a state of ferment. Its boundaries are expanding. Its focuses are proliferating. Its research strategies are multiplying. Its storehouse of conceptual equipment is overflowing.

Underlying and enlivening this ferment is a tension between a historic conception of the field in which its boundaries are drawn narrowly and an emerging approach in which they are conceived in extremely broad terms. As will be seen, it seems likely that the broad conception will eventually prevail, but many political scientists still subscribe to the narrower version. To a considerable extent, in fact, the narrow boundaries still serve as a basis for organizing the undergraduate curricula offered by many universities, the training and employment of doctoral candidates, and the meetings and journals of the American Political Science Association and other professional societies to which political scientists belong or subscribe. Stated succinctly, this narrow conception confines the field to the study of politics at the level of single national societies elsewhere than in the United States. To offer a major in comparative politics is to specialize in Europe, Latin America, Asia, or some other region of the world. To attend a panel on comparative politics at a meeting of an American professional society is to expose oneself to analyses of political processes abroad. To read the book reviews grouped under the heading of "comparative government and politics" in the *American Political Science Review* is to be exposed to assessments of foreign institutions.

In contrast to this narrow conception of the field is an emerging one in which it is stressed that "comparative politics" suggests a

Special note: We wish to thank our colleagues, Roy E. Licklider, Neil A. McDonald, Stephen A. Salmore, and Harvey L. Waterman for their helpful advice.

method of research as well as substantive phenomena. Comparison, some argue, is the only genuine method of research in a scientific discipline and therefore all scientifically oriented political scientists are students of comparative politics. To contrast the taxing policies of the American states is to engage in the comparative analysis of political systems. To explore the similarities between the present world of nation-states and the fifteenth-century Italian world of city-states is to undertake comparisons of political systems. To delineate differences between the mayoral and city-council forms of local government is to record a comparative analysis of political systems. To differentiate civil-military relationships in Western societies from those in Eastern societies is to compare political behavior. In short, those who draw the field's boundaries broadly contend that there is no political phenomenon, be it institutional or behavioral, local or international, formal or informal, that falls outside the field of comparative politics.

We welcome the emergence of ferment and the stress upon comparison, and interpret them as necessary to the growth of a genuine science of politics. For this reason it is the broader approach to the field that occupies our attention in the pages that follow. However, we are far from sanguine that the new boundaries, focuses, concepts, and research strategies will necessarily result in continued progress. The broadening of the field has raised as many problems as it has solved, and several of these appear to be especially resistant to solution. The ensuing analysis thus strikes a balance between enthusiasm for recent developments and concern over future ones. First, we elaborate on the nature of the ferment, the broader methodological issues it involves, and the extent to which these issues have penetrated the field as a whole. In the next sections, we turn to an examination of one major attempt to provide guidelines for comparative research—the introduction of structural-functional analysis into the discipline during the 1950s—and to an analysis of its impact on three major substantive areas of research, political culture, political parties, and whole political systems. The concluding section explores the nature and limits of the progress that has been made in these areas and the vexing problems that are posed for future research.

WHY, WHAT, HOW: THE FERMENT IN THE FIELD

The evolution of the field of comparative politics prior to World War II has been incisively outlined by Eckstein (1963). Studies of non-American political phenomena were characterized by configurative national profiles, by minute examinations of the formal-legal structures within individual countries, or by highly abstract discussions of norms and values which bore little relationship to behavior within the empirical world. Few efforts were made to examine the realities of the political processes that lay behind the institutional formalities, and still fewer were made to relate political processes to the larger social milieu in which they occurred. To be sure, a handful of outstanding individuals such as Bryce (1921) and Friedrich (1950), along with a growing number of scholars interested in United States politics, were either fully or partially excepted from this generalization. On the whole, however, this was the way matters stood until the 1940s and 1950s, when the emergence of new, non-European nations, the crises of democratic institutions within Europe itself, and the methodological advances made in the social sciences, induced students of comparative politics to look critically at their own past efforts.

The critiques of that period can be succinctly summarized: comparative politics was essentially noncomparative. Although there were many voices in the chorus of criticism, the battle cry was perhaps sounded most loudly by Macridis (1955). His indictment of the field pointed out that most works which went under the heading of comparative politics were essentially descriptions of one country or parallel descriptions of several countries, selected without significant theoretical criteria. Effort had not been made to extend the scope of analysis beyond the boundaries of Western Europe, to understand the emergence of nondemocratic forms of government, or to examine the factors leading to growth and change within particular political systems. The discipline lacked, argued Macridis, a "systematic frame for comparative analysis." It required a new orientation which would "identify characteristics of political systems in terms of generalized categories that would apply to all or as many systems as possible"; that would "not only identify similarities and differences, but also . . . account for them"; and that would permit the "development of a body of knowledge in the light of which predictions of trends and policy recommendations [could] be made."

By the end of the 1950s, there was widespread agreement in principle with the proposition that comparison was necessary. One compares in order to generalize. A major goal of scientific inquiry is to build theory out of logically related, disprovable hypotheses that encompass an ever wider range of phenomena. Plainly, this goal cannot be accomplished unless one sorts out those phenomena which are in some way similar to each other. To examine only a single case is to preclude the recognition of similarities and thus to thwart the aspiration of science. To be sure, comparison often leads to the identification of dissimilarities which inhibit generalization. Obviously, however, the recognition of dissimilarities is no less crucial than the clustering of similarities. Theories cannot be developed and widened unless the boundaries between the similar phenomena they encompass and the dissimilar ones they exclude are clearly delineated.

To indict the field of comparative politics for its lack of comparison, however, was not to reach consensus on the question of *what* was to be compared and *how* the comparison was to be undertaken. The fact that these questions have been increasingly raised in recent years reflects the broadening scope of the field we noted above. The variety of responses that are given to the questions reflect its state of ferment.

Over a decade ago, the structural-functional approach appeared to offer at least some hope of solving the "what" problem. Concerned with the boundaries that divide political systems from their environments, the approach involved analysts in a search for the social requisites and prerequisites necessary to the maintenance and development of certain types of political activities. In so doing, it alerted them to the possibility that structures which appeared quite dissimilar could, in different societies, perform equivalent (and therefore comparable) functions. In short, the structural-functional approach suggested interrelationships to guide the research process, and it provided analytical categories that could potentially facilitate comparisons between culturally different social orders. But none of this really answered the question of what phenomena might be most fruitfully compared: does one compare entire political systems, different levels or parts of the systems, or individual behavior? Does one compare between systems, or within systems? longitudinally, over time, or in cross-sectional terms? Although the structural-functional approach was, to its great credit, responsible for raising many of these questions, it was not, for reasons that will be discussed in more detail presently, in a position to provide answers.

In many ways, in point of fact, the emergence of the structural-functional approach as the most generally accepted "conceptual framework" within the field of comparative politics helped to induce the tremendous proliferation of perspectives and focuses that now command the attention of political scientists. In an earlier time, at least, the student of "comparative" government could be more or less sure of the subject matter of his discipline: it was a particular set of governmental instititions, legally prescribed, and located within a particular cultural setting. Now, with the emphasis in the structural-functional approach on the interrelationships between the political

system and the environment, and on the complex functional relationships within each political system, the subject matter of comparative
politics mushroomed throughout the entire field of political science
and beyond. As Eckstein has pointed out, "The study of public law,
in which scholars of the past made rich and busy careers, has become
a mere fraction of all the things [the student of comparative politics]
is supposed to study. He must also learn all about informal politics,
relate politics to its setting (ecological, social, economic), and be able
to deal adequately with attitudes and motivations, with culture and
socialization processes" (1963, p. 30). The authors of this essay
concur. Writing with the great advantage over Eckstein of hindsight, we
must confess that we are still unable to delineate the scope
or substance of the field of comparative politics. Indeed, we are hard
pressed to identify any clearly marked out subfields of comparative
politics in which there are general agreements on the units and
properties to be compared.

The question of *how* to compare also spreads out a bewildering
array of alternatives and approaches. On the surface, of course, the
answer to the "how" question appears simple enough: when one
compares, one classifies and describes phenomena by denoting
similar and dissimilar properties. This task, however, is far from easy.
How does one describe data so that their similarities and dissimilarities can be discerned? Is it enough to describe them in detail so
that other analysts can use them for comparative purposes? Or is the
researcher obliged to go beyond description of a single case and
gather data on many cases? And if he does gather data on more than
one case, does he do so by hypothesizing their distribution in
advance or by inspecting the distributions and deriving hypotheses
from them? At whatever point he derives hypotheses, moreover, how
does the analyst who has gathered data on many systems or types of
behavior identify their common and unique features? In short, how
does he know a similarity or dissimilarity when he sees one? It is a
measure of the ferment of the field of comparative politics that it
presently offers a multiplicity of answers to these questions. Many
analysts, especially those who take a narrow approach to the field,
believe it is sufficient to describe and assess a single system or type of
behavior and to leave elucidation of its similarities and contrasts with
other cases to others. Those who subscribe to a broader view of the
field, on the other hand, feel obliged to go beyond description of a
single system or type of behavior. Some do so by collecting data on a
small sample of systems and comparing them qualitatively either in
terms of an explicit model (e.g., Holt and Turner, 1966) or in terms
of what appear to be their similarities and dissimilarities (e.g., Ward
and Rustow, 1964). Others do so by accumulating data on many

systems and subjecting them to quantitative techniques of analysis that trace similarities and dissimilarities in statistical terms. Still others proceed exclusively on the deductive level and offer hypotheses or models rather than data about the behavior of many systems that can be subjected to empirical verification.

In addition to these quantitative and inductive-deductive distinctions, moreover, a variety of methods is used to generate quantitative data. Some analysts employ public records and accumulate aggregate data on the attributes of systems (Russett et al., 1964; Rummel, 1966, 1972). Others generate data on attributes by polling panels of experts (Banks and Textor, 1963). Still others content analyze verbal materials (Stone et al., 1966), conduct interview surveys (Almond and Verba, 1963), and simulate political processes in a laboratory (Scott, Lucas, and Lucas, 1966; Brunner and Brewer, 1971). Nor does methodological variety end with the accumulation of masses of data. The processing of the data can also occur in a multitude of ways, ranging from the use of regression techniques that identify exceptions to central tendencies to the use of factor analytic techniques that identify underlying dimensions of data.

That the question of how to compare thus underlies much of the ferment in the field can be readily demonstrated. One need only examine the bitter exchange between Young (1969) and Russett (1969) to appreciate the depth of the differences that can arise over the choice of research strategies. And the ferment fostered by these differences is stirred further by the fact that answers to the question of how to compare are inextricably linked to those offered to the question of what to compare. Not every research methodology is equally applicable to every substantive problem, with the consequence that analysts also differ over the types of political institutions and behavior that are best probed through quantitative methods and those that lend themselves to the nonquantitative comparison of a few cases. Unfortunately, limitations of time and space prevent us from probing this dimension of the ferment in the field. Indeed, since other essays in this symposium focus on the main research methodologies presently available, we have chosen not to pursue the how-to-compare question any further, preferring instead to focus on the problems posed by the what-to-compare question. The reader should consult these other essays when the interdependence of the what and how questions seems relevant to the substantive problems taken up here.

To what extent is the "ferment" to which we have referred widely distributed among the practitioners of the field? Before going further in our discussion, we feel obliged to put the question into some sort of empirical perspective. Our data consist of a content analysis of the titles of the books reviewed under the heading "Comparative Politics and Government" in the book review section of the *American Political Science Review* between 1949 and 1968. While such data have the obvious limitation that the titles of books do not always accurately reflect their contents, they do serve as a preliminary basis for the analysis of "trends" within the field.

Actually, the assertion that there is ferment in the field does not emerge unscathed from this empirical test. Table 1 divides the books in terms of whether their titles refer to a single actor (party, legislature, bureaucracy, voter, etc.) or to more than one. While there is clearly a noticeable and persistent minority of researchers engaged in enough comparison to justify the inclusion of two or more actors in the titles of their works, the data hardly reflect a growing trend toward comparative analysis. The proportion of titles citing plural actors remains quite constant through time and, indeed, it never exceeds more than a quarter of the books reviewed. Notwithstanding the developments described below, and notwithstanding many of the general critiques levied against the practices of comparative politics during the 1950s, the analysis of single actors would appear from these data to be the dominant tendency of scholars in the field.

T A B L E   1. Singularity or Plurality of the Actors Identified in the Titles of Books Reviewed under the Heading "Comparative Politics and Government" in the *American Political Science Review* from 1949 through 1968

Year	Number of Books Reviewed	Proportion of Books with Titles That Posit a Single Actor
1949-50	39	87
1951	59	76
1952	64	83
1953	78	91
1954	82	90
1955	64	88
1956	65	88
1957	69	97
1958	58	90
1959	85	91
1960	84	89
1961	60	83
1962	56	91
1963	84	88
1964	80	86
1965	84	88
1966	55	93
1967	109	94
1968	111	95

TABLE 2.　Geographic and Time Classification of Titles of Books Reviewed under the Heading "Comparative Government and Politics" in the *American Political Science Review* from 1949 through 1968

Year	Number of Books	Proportion of Books with Titles That Posit an Actor or Actors as Located Only in the				Proportion of Books with Titles That Imply Analysis	
		West[1]	Non-West[2]	Eastern Europe[3]	Other or None	Across Time	At One Time
1949-50	39	44	13	21	22	10	90
1951	59	41	17	24	18	24	76
1952	64	42	31	9	18	23	77
1953	78	36	42	8	14	21	79
1954	82	48	31	11	10	29	71
1955	64	41	25	25	9	27	73
1956	65	43	32	5	20	26	74
1957	69	30	42	14	14	19	81
1958	58	33	33	21	13	21	79
1959	85	45	28	13	11	24	76
1960	84	21	38	17	24	17	83
1961	60	30	40	13	17	28	72
1962	56	31	48	9	12	25	75
1963	84	27	43	12	18	20	80
1964	80	21	41	9	29	14	86
1965	84	27	49	8	16	29	71
1966	55	29	49	11	11	20	80
1967	109	28	41	18	13	21	79
1968	111	27	48	19	6	25	75

[1]includes North America, Western Europe　　[2]includes South America, China　　[3]includes the U.S.S.R.

Another breakdown of the data provides perhaps more clearcut evidence that the field is undergoing change. A picture of expansion in the concern of researchers emerges quite clearly if the titles of the reviewed works are classified in terms of broad geographic focuses (columns 3 through 6 of Table 2). Not only is there a greater balance in the proportion of books that focused, respectively, on Western, non-Western, and Communist actors, but there is also a pronounced trend toward the analysis of non-Western politics. For each of the years from 1960 through 1968 the non-Western category had higher proportions than the Western category, whereas exactly the opposite pattern obtained for every year but two between 1949 and 1959. This reversal of focuses is quite consistent with our conclusion below that the introduction of the structural-functional model into the study of politics in the 1950s provided analysts with a basis for exploring political institutions and processes in the non-Western world.

Some diversity of interests is also apparent when the titles are coded along a time dimension. As can be seen in the seventh and eighth columns of Table 2, which differentiate between those titles that suggest cross-sectional analysis at a moment in time and those that imply analysis across a time span, roughly a quarter of the books reviewed each year contained the implication of a concern with developments through time. Although this proportion indicates that case histories are not the predominant mode of analysis, it is perhaps surprising that more titles were not classified in the time span category. The recent spate of theoretical works devoted to the processes of political development (Apter, 1965, 1971, 1973; Holt and Turner, 1966; Huntington, 1968; Black, 1966; Rustow 1967; Scott, 1973; Tullis, 1973; Inkeles and Smith, 1974; Brunner and Brewer, 1974; etc.) might have been expected to generate greater sensitivity to the dynamics of politics through time than is apparent in the last two columns of Table 2.

In sum, although the field may be far from unified, the ferment appears to be reflected only irregularly in research practices. To be sure, the crude empirical net we have cast almost certainly has not caught many aspects of changing practices, such as a more self-conscious use of comparable categories and questions, or the introduction of replicable data within case work. There may well be a growing methodological sophistication among researchers, not detected by our data, that will make the study of single cases cumulative. Nevertheless, it is also possible that much of the ferment we have discussed above is a qualitative one, stimulated by a relatively few pioneering works that have charted new courses which have yet to be traversed by the vast majority of those in the field.

Much of our ensuing analysis focuses on these pioneering works, but it should be evaluated in light of the central messages of the tables presented above; namely, that the works discussed are qualitatively distinguished but not necessarily quantitatively representative.

THE STRUCTURAL-FUNCTIONAL APPROACH: A "FRAME" OF COMPARATIVE ANALYSIS

Perhaps the theoretical framework that most stimulated the broadening of the politics field was the structural-functional approach, developed earlier in sociology by such men as Parsons (1951) and Levy (1952), and in an anthropology by Radcliffe-Brown (1957). At the bottom of the tremendously complex writings of such scholars lies a relatively simple assumption: that human societies can be viewed in terms of a web of highly interdependent activities and expectations. Within this web, it is analytically possible to distinguish patterns of interactions—structures—and to analyze the effects of these patterns in functional terms; that is, in terms of whether and how they contribute to the emergence or maintenance of other social processes. The approach assumes that the major structures of a society are systematically related: that each can be understood only in terms of its effects on the others and that profound or persistent changes in one structure produce changes in the other basic inter- action patterns.

In the field of comparative politics, structural-functional analysis focused attention on that subset of interrelated structures which perform political functions for the society as a whole. Definitions of "political functions" have, of course, varied from one writer to another, but most usually include three basic components. First, the political function involves the allocation of values (who gets what, when, and how) for a large percentage of the population. Secondly, the structures which engage in this allocation have at their disposal a preponderance, if not a monopoly, of the means of physical compulsion. And finally, the process of allocation and the threat or exercise of compulsion is regarded as legitimate by a sizeable percentage of the population. These components and their relation- ship to one another are not always agreed upon in their entirety by structural-functional theorists and, as we shall see, some aspects of the generally accepted definitions of political functions create diffi- culties for analyzing political processes in those areas of the world undergoing rapid change. Nevertheless, the delineations of the political function in terms of an "authoritative allocation of values"

(Easton, 1953), or as "integration and adaptation . . . by means of the employment, or the threat of employment, of more or less legitimate physical compulsion" (Almond, 1960b), or some other such definition, does suggest a boundary for the "political system," or, more properly speaking, the political subsystem.

For purposes of analysis, the structures operating within the political system, and the functions performed by the system as a whole, have been subdivided still further. Those patterns of inter-action that help to maintain the decision-making structures, or which transmit claims from the larger society into the political system, are termed *input* structures and functions. Those structures and effects that impinge directly on the larger society—i.e., those which actually allocate values, threaten compulsion, etc.—are termed the *output* elements within the system. With this set of sometimes rather heavy conceptual baggage, the student of comparative politics is potentially prepared to sally forth into a variety of societies, seeking out and analyzing the kinds of structures which perform different functions, the factors which produce the emergence of these structures, and the efficiency with which they perform the various functions.

A brief summary of Almond's introduction to *The Politics of Developing Areas* (1960), which was perhaps the most influential effort to apply structural-functional theory to comparative politics, will illustrate how this is so. We have already quoted Almond's definition of the function of the political system. What is perhaps more important in Almond's essay is his effort to subdivide the political system in terms of seven subfunctions. On the input side, these are (1) socialization and recruitment, (2) interest articulation, (3) interest aggregation, and (4) communications. On the output side, Almond distinguishes between (1) rule making, (2) rule application, and (3) rule adjudication. Almond admits that this functional classification is a tentative one, drawn by induction from the rela-tively complex political systems of the West, where "functional differentiation [had] taken place to the greatest extent" (p. 16). Nevertheless, Almond argues, the performance of these or similar functions can be considered universal requisites for the survival of any society which maintains internal and external order; and, equally universally, it can be assumed that in all ordered societies, there are structures which perform these functions. He states that "all political systems, including the simplest ones, have political structures" and that "the same functions are performed in all political systems, even though these functions may be performed with different frequencies, and by different kinds of structures" (p. 11).

On the basis of these universalist assumptions, Almond claimed, it was possible to compare the widest range of political systems, from the by now proverbial Eskimo tribe (which, to our knowledge, has not yet actually been studied) to the most complex of social orders. For with the "universal" functional requisites now clarified, analysts could proceed to identify the structures which performed them, whether or not these were formal-legal institutions, and to compare the various structures in terms of the relative frequency and efficiency in the performance of various functions. Almond suggests a number of dimensions which such a comparison might take into account. Structures could be considered more or less intermittent, more or less specialized in terms of the functions they performed, and the style in which the functions were performed could be expected to involve various mixtures of the Parsonian pattern variables, from a universalistic, specific, achievement oriented, and affectively neutral style, to one which was particularistic, diffuse, ascriptive, and affective. Looking forward to future research, Almond claimed his approach specified the "elements of the polity in such a form as may ultimately make possible statistical and perhaps mathematical formulation."

> In other words, we have specified the elements of two sets, one of functions and one of structures, and we suggested that political systems may be compared in terms of the probabilities of the performance of the specified functions by the specified structures. In addition, we have specified styles of performance of function by structure which makes it possible for us at least to think of a state of knowledge of political systems in which we could make precise comparisons relating the elements of three sets—functions, structures, and styles—in the form of a series of probability statements [p. 59].

Not everyone, it should be noted, has shared Almond's optimism, either about the general structural-functional approach, or about Almond's own particular elucidation of this approach. Running alongside the emergence of structural-functional analysis, for one thing, is a variety of alternative frameworks for analysis, some of which are more or less complementary, and others of which are competitive. Apter and Andrain (1968), for example, have distinguished between structural-functional theories and what they term the normative and behavioral approaches. The former, they note, reaches back to a tradition of analysis begun at least as early as Socrates. Unlike the structural-functional approach, normative theories continue to address themselves explicitly to the question of the direction development politics ought to take and to the morally right choices for political actors. The behavioral approach, on the other hand, is termed by Apter and Andrain as the newest trend in comparative politics. Here, the theoretical focus is on individuals, rather than on structures, and the factors examined concern the determinants of individual choices, rather than the ongoing interaction patterns which place limits on these choices. Actually, neither the normative nor the behavioral approach represents a clear-cut theoretical alternative to structural-functionalism. "Few scholars," observe the authors, "work wholly within one approach." In terms of actual research strategies, however, the different approaches do lead scholars in somewhat different directions, and they demand considerably different techniques of comparison and gathering evidence.

Along with alternative approaches that scholars have developed in preference to structural-functionalism, there have also been some direct and rather serious challenges to the theoretical utility of the structural-functional approach itself. Almond's essay (1960b) was subject to serious criticisms on several grounds. In stressing the importance of specialized structures—parties, legislatures, and autonomous interest groups—which could play "regulatory roles" in the performance of interest articulation and aggregation and rule making, Almond's model appeared to imply that the most effective political system would look significantly like the United States. Although this was clearly a proposition worth investigating empirically, Almond's elaboration of structural-functionalism built this bias into the model itself, making it difficult to evaluate or analyze systems which, like the Soviet Union, are obviously both modern, "effective," and undemocratic. A second problem lay in the static quality of the analytical categories presented in the 1960 essay. Although notions such as functional specificity provide an analytical handle with which to compare and contrast sytems existing at a single point in time, they offer no clues about the way systems might change over time, about the way the effectiveness or nature of a different structure might vary, about the kinds of factors that might give rise to greater (or lesser) functional specificity, or about the kinds of factors that might lead to development or breakdown within the system as a whole.

A final criticism levied against Almond, but perhaps generalizable to the whole of structural-functional analysis, focused on the tendency to define structures in terms of the functions they perform and to leave the definition of "function" itself empty of empirical meaning. As Robert Dowse has persuasively pointed out (1966), this omission in Almond's work tends to render its major propositions tautological, and therefore undisprovable. For example, Almond defines the political system as "that system of interactions . . . [presumably those structures] which perform the functions of integration and adaptation . . ." (1960b, p. 7). To delineate the structures of the political system as those which promote integration and adaptation, however, is to exclude by definition those structures which may be maladaptive or disintegrative for the political system or for the society as a whole. Perhaps even more serious is the fact that neither adaptation nor integration—the two major functions of the political system—are defined in Almond's essay. This clearly makes it operationally impossible to define the "boundaries" of the political system (since these include all activities which contribute to integration and adaptation), to determine when the system "breaks down," or to distinguish between those radical changes which are integrative and adaptive and those which are not.

Further difficulties are created by the way in which Almond elaborated the seven subfunctions said to be characteristic of all political systems. Almond makes no effort to relate these categories to one another or to the larger functions that are supposed to be performed by the political system as a whole. Nothing is lost logically if new functional categories are added or if old ones are recombined, making it impossible in effect to disprove Almond's proposition that the same functions are performed in all political systems. By failing to link the subfunctions logically to the larger ones, finally we are left only with an implied connection between such activities as interest articulation and aggregation and the larger ones of integration and adaptation. This means we do not know how or even whether functionally specialized structures which articulate and aggregate interests actually contribute to the integration and adaptation of the society. Indeed, it is not impossible to imagine cases where structures which are effective in performing subfunctions are in fact dysfunctional for the system as a whole. By failing to define key terms and by not demonstrating a presumed logical connection between them, in short, Almond's essay falls considerably short of what might be considered a viable scientific theory.

In considering these criticisms, it is important to distinguish between Almond's attempt in 1960 to apply the structural-functional approach to the analysis of politics and structural-functionalism in general. Some of the criticisms we have elaborated above—the value biases of Almond's model and the static quality of the analytic categories—are not necessarily generic defects of the approach itself, and a number of more recent analytic schemas (Almond and Powell, 1966; Holt, 1967; Johnson, 1966; Huntington, 1968; Dahl, 1973) have been developed which, in some ways, consider the problem of change and the emergence of nondemocratic political systems, without abandoning structural-functional categories. At the same time it is probably fair to say that the latter criticisms have not yet been resolved satisfactorily. The problems of tautology and teleology (that is, of defining structures in terms of their functions and of assuming that all structures must be functional), of spelling out in operational terms the differences between functional and dysfunctional activities, or of elaborating clearly disprovable propositions about the relations between structures and functions, are pitfalls which continue to plague the structural-functional approach.

Notwithstanding its weaknesses, however, the structural-functional approach *has* proved useful as a *classificatory scheme.* At least it has given researchers useful clues about how to gather and order data. It enables them to avoid regarding the political institutions of separate countries sui generis and, instead, to compare them in terms of the performance and functional consequences of their structures. The attention of researchers can now be directed toward the interconnections between "social" phenomena and the emergence and disappearance of political structures, as well as the functional consequences of political activities for the larger society. Indeed, the present concern of many analysts with the processes of political development and decay—that is, with the dynamics whereby a society's capacity to allocate values and realize goals grows or diminishes over time—was as much a response to the theoretical potential of the structural-functional approach as it was to the changing postwar scene in Africa, Asia, and Latin America. In these respects, the approach represented a vast improvement over the "essentially noncomparative" discipline of comparative politics that Macridis had decried in the mid-1950s.

It is perhaps these properties of the structural-functional ap proach, its utility as a classificatory scheme, and its as yet unfulfilled theoretical promise, that more than anything else account for the extraordinary ferment in the discipline of comparative politics about what to compare. On the one hand, it would appear that, alternative approaches to the contrary notwithstanding, a structural-functional framework of one sort or another has become broadly accepted by political scientists in the field. At least two of the major textbooks in comparative politics (Beer and Ulam, 1958; Macridis and Ward, 1963) explicitly adopt a structural-functional approach as the orienting frame for their discussion. In a series edited by Almond, Pye, and Coleman, analyses of such countries as France, the U.S.S.R., Germany, and Britain have been cast in structural-functional terms (Rose, 1964; Barghoorn, 1966; Edinger, 1968; Ehrmann, 1968) largely for the purpose of teaching at the undergraduate level. The highly influential series of volumes on communications (Pye, 1963), bureaucracy (LaPalombara, 1963), education (Coleman, 1965), parties (LaPalombara and Weiner, 1966), and political culture (Pye and

Verba, 1965), sponsored by the Committee on Comparative Politics
of the Social Science Research Council, also give clear indications of
an indebtedness to structural-functional orientations. In 1963, structural-functionalism was characterized as an approach which was
"new and progressive in a field that is in fact to a large extent
old-fashioned and conservative" (Eckstein, 1963, p. 29). By the end
of the decade, the structural-functional approach was rapidly acquiring a catholicity which, if not *truly* universal, was at least the
"established doctrine" to be attacked or defended.

In part, the structural-functional approach acquired its catholicity by virtue of its theoretically open-ended quality. Precisely
because the approach had not yielded a clearly defined body of
theoretical propositions, it was able to embrace analytically a tremendous diversity of activities and orientations within its framework. Armed with the proposition that one had to go beyond
formal-legal institutions to understand the way functions were performed, and with the notion that political activities were linked to a
variety of nonpolitical patterns, political scientists broadened the
scope of comparative politics to the major continents of the world,
moving to Asia, Latin America, and Africa, as well as to Europe and
North America, and from the halls of government to the streets, the
military barracks, the jungles and mountains, the schools, and even
into the intimacy of family life.

To impose coherence on this rapidly expanding subject matter,
or on the different ways it was treated and compared, is a task well
beyond the scope of this chapter. Thus we have chosen to sample
rather than to classify the literature growing out of the broadening of
the field that occurred in the 1950s and 1960s, to give the reader a
taste rather than a summary of the research that goes under the
heading of comparative politics. For this purpose, the concepts,
problems, and research techniques in three general areas of investigation will be discussed: (1) political culture, (2) political parties, and
(3) entire political systems, although we must emphasize again that
these three areas themselves are only a fraction of the entire subject
matter of the field of comparative politics; and that they crisscross
with each other in a variety of ways.

POLITICAL CULTURE

The notion of political culture is taken by almost all writers who
employ the term to mean the "empirical beliefs, expressive symbols,
and values which define the situation in which political action takes

place" (Verba, 1965, p. 513). Individuals, logically, are the ultimate *empirical* unit of investigation, since cultural orientations relate, in the final analysis, to the subjective beliefs and values held by each person within the social order. It is also widely assumed, however, that within each *society*, there are certain configurations of values that characterize the society as a whole, and it is this configuration which is generally referred to by those who employ the concept. Societies, as well as individuals, can thus be compared along a number of dimensions—the extent of parochialism and of national identity, trust or mistrust for other political actors, allegiance to or alienation from existing governmental structures, the sense of being able to effect governmental actions (civic competence), and ideas about legitimate governmental procedures and governmental output—and the *mixture* of orientations existing within a given society will shape the behavior of its citizens, the nature of its policy outputs, and the stability of the system as a whole.

The major attention of most writers has focused on four broader questions suggested by the concept of political culture: (a) What are the configurations or cultural norms within given societies, and how do they differ from those in other societies? (b) What are the factors which produce these norms: how and through what agencies are norms transmitted from one generation to the next? (c) What is the relationship between the essentially subjective "empirical beliefs, expressive symbols and values" that comprise culture, and objective changes in sociopolitical structures? What, in other words, is the nature of the interaction between "culture" and "socioeconomic and political change"? (d) In what ways do cultural norms condition the actual operation of political structures within a given society?

The first of the questions, although the simplest, is still perhaps furthest from being answered in a systematic manner. The fact that the concept of culture concerns the subjective orientations of individuals suggests a survey research approach as the most reliable and systematic way to identify cultural configurations. This, however, is a difficult and costly process. Devising survey questions that can reliably tap comparable cultural dimensions across many cultures is itself an awesome, although probably not insurmountable, task. More important, survey research requires resources normally beyond the reach of individual scholars, making their efforts dependent on funding from sources outside the university. Cross-cultural surveys involve the additional difficulty of gaining access to a strange milieu, acquiring the permission of foreign governments, and the cooperation of foreign scholars and institutions of higher learning. At the time of this writing, consequently, we have found only a few major studies that use survey techniques across several nations (Almond

and Verba, 1963; Deutsch et al., 1967). Some additional large research projects, including one directed by Inkeles investigating the
effects of factory employment on working class attitudes in India,
Israel, Argentina, Chile, Nigeria, and Pakistan (1969), a projected
Social Science Research Council project covering the "Latin culture
area," and a cross-national analysis of political values in the U.S.,
India, Yugoslavia, and Poland directed by Philip Jacob (1971), will
increase the data base for cross-cultural comparisons in the 1970s.

In the meantime, scholars seeking to describe the culture patterns
in different countries, and particularly the non-Western areas, have
relied primarily on other devices. Many of the individual articles in
one comparative volume (Pye and Verba, 1965) rely heavily on
efforts to infer values from existing or past patterns of behavior—
traditional institutions, authority patterns, etc. The scattered opinion
polls that do exist in the various countries are also used, as are the
field research findings of anthropologists and sociologists, the existing bodies of literature, and statements and actions by political
leaders. The use of such devices is often ingenious, and frequently
leads to valuable insights. Yet the inferences that are sometimes
made can clearly be misleading, even in areas with which the researcher is highly familiar and in which he can draw on a much larger
body of commentary. To give but one example, Almond's earliest
attempt to describe the American political culture (1950) stressed
competitiveness, atomization, and distrust of authority as the dominant culture patterns within American society. These were directly
contradicted by the findings of his *Civic Culture* study of 1963,
which indicated that in American culture there existed a high level of
social trust and a broad, relatively unconditional allegiance to the
political system.

This is not to say, it should be emphasized, that discussions of
political culture must necessarily await the emergence of a broad
data base of cross-cultural survey research. Given the difficulties of
such research, scholars may have little alternative but to rely on the
devices summarized above. Further on, moreover, we shall argue that
perhaps at the micro-political level, more political science field research within single countries should supplement the existing body
of anthropological and sociological literature that already exists, as
well as the larger cross-cultural studies which are projected for the
future. In any event, the problems of gathering reliable data *about*
norms continues to be one of the most difficult and slippery problems involved in the investigation of political cultures.

We now turn to the problems of how cultural norms are formed
and transmitted and how they relate to other, objective patterns of
structural change. Studies of both questions involve the convergence

of at least two distinct earlier traditions of analysis. One involves the study of political socialization, and the other arises out of those studies which have concerned themselves with the history of ideas and the sociological roots of ideological conflicts. Perhaps the two most important major works in the latter tradition are by Louis Hartz, *The Liberal Tradition in America* (1955) and *The Founding of New Societies* (1964). In the first, Hartz argues that the "flight" by carriers of the liberal norms from the old world to the new freed them from the need to confront entrenched feudal institutions with liberal views of authority, community, and freedom. For this reason, Hartz suggests, American political conflicts unfolded within a largely implicit consensus which tended to exclude certain types of policy alternatives from political debate. In his second work, Hartz expands his scope to include other "new" societies (Latin America, French Canada, Australia), in which different cultural fragments (feudalism and socialism) also avoided the need to confront conflicting cultural traditions by fleeing from the old world. In each of these "fragment" societies, Hartz suggests, the early flight from conflict and subsequent cultural isolation produced nonideological political conflicts, conducted largely within the implicitly held norms of the cultural fragment itself.

Taking off from the same macro-level starting point, other scholars (Eckstein, 1958b; Almond and Verba, 1963; Pye, 1962, 1966; Verba, 1965) have focused on those societies of Europe, Asia, and Africa, where there *have* been conflicts between competing systems of values. In these instances, they suggest that the conflict between traditional orientations (parochial, particularistic, and ascriptive) and the elements of modern culture (national, universal, and achievement-oriented) gives rise to a series of crises, the timing and nature of which will shape the evolution of a given political culture. Although different terminology is used to elaborate the nature of the conflicts or to identify the particular crises treated, it is generally agreed that the degree of cultural homogeneity, of agreement on legitimate authority, and of cultural integration will depend on the manner in which these crises are handled. To put it simply, the countries in which crises of legitimacy, participation, and integration are handled sequentially rather than simultaneously, and those in which traditional values and institutions are fused with new ones (rather than supplanted entirely), will enjoy the most stable, homogeneous, and least conflict-ridden political cultures.

A. second body of theoretical literature, that on political socialization, tackles the problem from the opposite direction. Instead of focusing on grand historical crises and events, socialization studies begin at the micro-level, taking the individual and the manner in which he internalizes cultural norms as the primary topics of investigation. Students of the socialization process are concerned in general with the norms that are learned at different stages of the individual's development, with the socializing agencies that transmit these norms (the family, school, peer groups), and with the nature of the learning process. This process may be indirect (as when the individual transfers to politics those norms and values which apply explicitly to nonpolitical realms of social life), or direct (as when expressly political norms are transmitted to the individual through family or schools). Many studies have stressed the importance of early and indirect patterns of socialization. The individual, it is suggested, acquires his basic emotional attachment to the community, and his class, racial, or ethnic loyalties by the age of five or six By the time he is made aware of the larger political issues and gains familiarity with existing political structures, these preformed loyalties and commitments provide an emotional frame through which newly learned facts are ordered and interpreted.

On the surface, this emphasis on the importance of early and indirect training would appear to bring the socialization literature into some conflict with the macro-level tradition described above. Actually, on a theoretical level, the two approaches are complementary. Most students of political socialization emphasize the fact that the learning process is one which occurs throughout the lifetime of an individual, that direct experience with politics as well as indirect learning can be an important part of the learning process, and that secondary agencies (unions, political parties, employment structures) as well as primary groupings can be important agencies of transmission. In moments of profound political crisis and during times of vast socioeconomic transformation (i.e., those situations with which the macro-level approach is concerned), the political values directly or indirectly transmitted through the family and peer groups may become less important than new loyalties or commitments acquired elsewhere in the social system and later in the life of an individual. (See Huntington and Nelson, 1976.)

The problem of reconciling these two traditions occurs less at the level of theory than at the level of research. Most of the socialization studies, until very recently, have been conducted in societies where there is a relatively "close fit" between the values and norms acquired early and indirectly and those acquired later on and more directly in the life of an individual. One principal study of the socialization process (Dawson and Prewitt, 1969) drew its conclusions principally from investigations of American school children (Greenstein, 1965; Hyman, 1959; Hess and Easton, 1960). Considerably less research has been undertaken in societies where there are profound discontinuities, and thus we know little about the manner in which such experience as political revolution, immigration from the countryside into the city, changes in employment, a university education, military service, or party indoctrination may induce value changes. Inkeles and Smith's (1974) cross-cultural study of the effects of factory employment does much to fill this void. Also of considerable value is a growing quantity of descriptive material and replicable survey research fragments undertaken in the developing world, such as Zeitlin's study of the postrevolutionary Cuban working class (1967), or Matheison and Powell's study of Colombian and Venezuelan peasants (1972). But the area is one which continues to cry out for good micro-level case studies and surveys. In the meantime, many of our assumptions about the relations between national political events, socioeconomic transformations, adult socialization, and culture change continues to rest on mixed or highly uncertain empirical foundations.

In view of the existing gaps in our understanding of the content of cultural norms, or of how they are developed, transmitted, and changed, it should not be surprising that there are serious problems involved in determining just how political cultures shape the actual processes and structures within the larger political system Without such underpinnings, the culture concept can become an "analytical wastebasket," to be used for explaining events and behavior that cannot be accounted for in other terms, and it is perhaps for this reason that the area specialist's use of culture as an explanatory device is often justifiably viewed with suspicion by others within the discipline. Systematic attempts to trace the links between the culture and the system, on the other hand, seem few and far between. Even the pioneering study by Almond and Verba (1963) confines itself to a highly speculative and in many ways unsatisfying attempt to relate the "civic" culture that they find existing most purely in Britain and the United States to the requisites of a stable democracy. Their argument boils down to the proposition that the mixture of contradictory norms (parochial, subject, and citizen orientations) which comprise the civic culture is supportive of the contradictory behavior patterns (apathy and involvement, conflict and consensus) of a stable democracy. Since "stable democracy" is not defined very precisely anywhere in the volume, however, and since it is not entirely clear why the only version of democratic stability must be that found in the U.S. or Britain, this aspect of their analysis does not really get us very far.

Nevertheless, it is difficult to deny that the notion of political culture is a potentially useful (and probably unavoidable) theoretical tool for understanding political behavior and that, in spite of the research gaps mentioned above, a number of approaches suggest themselves as ways of solving the problems that attach to the concept. Perhaps the most promising and instructive efforts over the short run have been those which concentrate on studies of elite subcultures. In part this is because survey research techniques do not seem quite so important for ascertaining the content of elite norms and values as they do for those of mass cultures. Reliable inferences about culture may instead be drawn from a nation's literature, from analysis of statements and debates by national leaders, and from direct observation; while the visibility of elites and their location within existing political structures make it possible to identify behavior patterns, to relate these patterns to cultural norms, and to discuss their impact on the larger political system (see Stogdill, 1974). Accordingly, it also becomes possible to employ elite values for such purposes as the classification of systems (Shils, 1960), the analysis of the paths of modernization (Bendix, 1964a; Moore, 1966), and even the delineation of variations in the types and styles of decision making (Brzezinski and Huntington, 1964).

For reasons already discussed, the problems in discerning the effects of mass culture on political behavior are probably greater than those of discussing the effects of elite subcultures. Without survey data to provide an independent measure of "culture," one runs the risk of inferring culture patterns from those very elements of behavior he is trying to explain and thus of casting his analysis in terms of nondisprovable propositions. A variety of inventive proposals for the use of aggregate data, however, may provide at least a partial way around this dilemma. Deutsch (1961), for example, has suggested that data on the rate of urbanization, literacy increase, and the expansion of the communications network can be taken as interrelated indicators of a larger process of social mobilization—the breakdown of old norms and commitments and the "availability" of large segments of the population for the formation of new ones. Content analysis of children's readers was similarly used with interesting effect by McClelland (1961) to analyze the relationship between the level of achievement orientation and economic development. Finally, Eckstein (1969) has proposed that the "performance" of a political system will depend on the congruence between governmental and nongovernmental authority structures, a proposition which has built into it many of the theoretical assumptions about the importance of early and indirect socialization for the development of political culture.

None of these approaches, it should be noted, have as yet paid off in full. Deutsch's work has had a tremendous influence on the comparative politics literature and has generated important efforts to order and analyze aggregate data. Many of these efforts, however, have moved theoretically away from the culture concept toward other explanatory variables, and a discussion of them belongs more properly in our later section on comparing whole systems. McClelland's work taps more directly the culture concept, but it is related to a dependent variable (economic growth) that finesses the more direct concerns of political science. Eckstein's hypothesis, perhaps the most directly concerned with operationalizing propositions about the relationship between mass culture and the political system, is still in the testing stage, although it has been explored in a preliminary way in his earlier study of Norway (1966). Nevertheless, all three approaches are illustrative of the ingenuity that can be employed in linking theoretical concepts to empirical research. The uses of aggregate data, along lines suggested above, put research on the effects of political culture within the reach of scholars who lack the funding for survey research, and they broaden the scope of comparison far beyond what is currently feasible through survey techniques. Approaches such as these are not *substitutes* for survey efforts, since it is only through the polling of individuals that we can be sure about the theoretical inferences that are drawn from the aggregate data. As a *complement* to survey research and to other types of micro-level studies, however, the use of aggregate data for this and other purposes is far from having reached its full potential.

POLITICAL PARTIES

Interest in the study of political parties in the United States and Europe long antedates the emergence of structural-functional theory. In Europe, classic studies of internal party organization were conducted by Michels (1962) and Ostrogorski (1902). Beginning in the 1930s in the United States, explorations of the social determinants of voting behavior were studied by men such as Berelson et al. (1954), Lazarsfeld et al. (1944), and Key (1942), while during the 1950s, a series of studies conducted under the auspices of the Social Science Research Council added greatly to the understanding of the psychological factors involved in the voter's choice (Campbell et al., 1954, 1960). The functions of parties were also explored. They were seen almost unanimously as the most important underpinnings of a democratic order: the organizers of public opinion, the brokers between special interest groups and governmental leaders, and the agents of political choice for the voting public.

The advent of structural-functionalism extended these earlier discussions and made their concerns more explicit. In a wide variety of societies, it was suggested, parties might serve as organizational links between publics and elites, performing among other things the representative functions of interest articulation and aggregation (Almond, 1960b). Furthermore, with the postwar emergence of varying types of party systems and no-party systems in new nations, and the evidence of strain and adaptation within the "totalitarian" one-party systems of the Communist world, it has become apparent that the study of parties need not be confined to democratic orders. LaPalombara and Weiner point out that parties tend to emerge "whenever the notion of political power comes to include the idea that the mass public must participate or be controlled" (1966, p. 3). Beginning in the 1950s, therefore, an extensive monographic literature began to grow about the parties and party systems of almost every major country of Western Europe, about the parties of the Communist world, and about aspects of the party systems in many of the major African, Latin American, and Asian societies. Greater attention than before came to be placed on the temporal qualities of party systems—the fact that they may appear and disappear—and on the variety of functions they might perform in both democratic and nondemocratic societies.

It is perhaps a little surprising, in light of this interest, that literature which makes explicit comparisons between political parties has been slower in coming. One of the reasons, noted by Apter (1963), is the fact that parties' intimate links to the special historical and social circumstances of the countries in which they emerged make them exceedingly difficult to classify and compare. Duverger's now classic effort to categorize parties into cadre, mass, and devotee types (1954), for example, has met with strong criticism on the grounds that the categories are far too narrow to be applied to parties outside the range of continental Europe (Wildavsky, 1959). Even within continental Europe, the nature of parties can change so rapidly that categories which seem appropriate at one point in time appear to have little utility only a short time later. In 1956, for example, Neumann suggested that the "party of integration" (i.e., one which attempted to organize the life of its members, to instill within them the ideological principles of the movement, and to insulate them from outside forces) was the wave of the future. Only ten years later, another distinguished scholar suggested that the trend toward "catchall," nonideological parties principally concerned with nominating and electing officials, was the trend in Western Europe (Kirchheimer, 1966). In any event, during the 1950s so little was known about the party structures and operations outside Britain, the

United States, and to a lesser extent, France and the Soviet Union, that much spade work was deemed necessary before broader level comparisons could be attempted.

By the mid-1960s, however, the beginnings of an explicitly comparative literature did begin to appear on the horizon, with important works by Lipset and Rokkan (1967), Dahl (1966), LaPalombara and Weiner (1966), and Huntington (1968), all appearing within a three year time span. Although continued efforts to elaborate comparative theory and engage in comparative research may lead in unforeseen directions in the future, the current stage of the literature on political parties is such as to call for comment on three general problem areas: the social bases of party support, the problem of origins and change within party systems, and the functions performed by parties within the larger society.

It is probably not surprising that of the three areas of research mentioned above, empirical explorations of the social bases of political parties have advanced the farthest. In most Western European countries and in some parts of Asia and Latin America (India, Chile, Brazil, Argentina, and Mexico, for example), there are fairly reliable electoral records and census data which make ecological studies possible. There has been a growing interest among non-American social scientists, moreover, which has led to the adaptation and proliferation of the survey research techniques developed by American political scientists. Although much of the research has been undertaken in single countries, census records, interview surveys, records of voting participation, and a rough division of parties along a left-right continuum has made possible the accumulation of a rather large body of "findings"—rare in the literature on comparative politics—about who votes and how. (See Palmer, 1975; Mackie and Rose, 1974.)

It is beyond the scope of this chapter to summarize these findings here, but it is possible to denote at least a few of the concerns to which the voting studies have been directed. Participation, for example, has been related cross-nationally to an expansion of communications (Lerner, 1958a), to the absence of cross-pressures (Lipset, 1960), to socioeconomic class and education (Almond and Verba, 1963), and to organizational membership (Nie et al., 1969). Voting support for Marxist parties has been linked to communities which have undergone rapid structural transformations; to isolated communities of workers (miners and fishermen), rather than to factory experience per se (Kornhauser, 1959; Lipset, 1960). *Systems* as well as individuals have also been compared through the use of voting data. Alford (1963), for example, has contrasted the degree of class voting in Britain and Australia with that in Canada and the U.S.

Although considerably fewer cross-national data are available on the social-psychological factors involved in the voters' choice (for example, the relative importance of party identification), some survey efforts (e.g., Converse and Dupeux, 1962; Dennis and McCrone, 1970) have also made a start in this direction.

Survey research has also turned up a few surprises. The proposition that the exposure of rural immigrants to urban life leads to radicalism, for example, which was once widely held by political scientists and sociologists, has been examined critically by Nelson (1969) and Cornelius (1969) and can probably be regarded as disconfirmed. Secondary analyses of the *Civic Culture* data by Nie, Powell, and Prewitt (1969), moreover, have raised serious questions about the proposition that city dwellers tend to participate to a greater extent than those who live in the countryside.

This is not to say that serious gaps and problems do not exist in the exploration of the bases of party support. Understandably, a large empirical gap continues to exist about voting in non-European settings. Recent writings on the subject have tended to downgrade the importance of class or party identification presumed to be important in Europe and the United States, and have stressed instead tribal factors, adherence to charismatic national leaders, or links to local notables. With a few important exceptions (Powell, 1970; Scott, 1969; Weingrod, 1968), however, we know little about the dynamics of party allegiance outside of the developed areas—whether a voter is linked to a political movement through ideology, nationalism, party identification, or personal ties—or about the kinds of demands made upon the party structure. The cross-national voting behavior literature, like the studies of American voting, is also subject to the accusation of being static and theoretically uninformed. While we have some understanding of the factors which underlie support for existing party systems, we have considerably less understanding of how these systems came into being, how they are changing, or the implications of various types of voter-party linkages for the system as a whole.

In spite of these criticisms, however, the importance of this comparative research should not be underestimated. By disconfirming some widely held notions, by exploring the sources of radical voting and the meaning of the vote in Europe, and by developing an array of sophisticated analytical tools, these studies have done much to lay the bases for asking larger theoretical questions. It is to some of these questions—the origins and functions of different party systems—that we now turn.

Three major efforts have recently been made to theorize about the conditions which promote the emergence of various types of parties and party systems. These are LaPalombara and Weiner's *Political Parties and Political Development* (1966), Dahl's *Political Oppositions in Western Democracies* (1966), and Lipset and Rokkan's *Party Systems and Voter Alignments* (1967). In attempting to establish a framework for the study of both Western and non-Western, and competitive and noncompetitive, party systems, LaPalombara and Weiner's book is probably the broadest in scope. Viewing the failures of efforts to establish viable parties in the new African states, they suggest in the first place that a certain level of social modernization is probably necessary for the establishment of genuine parties and, in the second, that the timing of key crises in the process of modernization (legitimacy, integration, and political participation) are both the catalysts and the molders for the emergence of competitive and noncompetitive systems. Dahl, on the other hand, classifies opposition in Western democracies according to such dimensions as their goals (structural and nonstructural), their organizational concentration and distinctiveness, and their strategies; and relates these to five interdependent variables—constitutional and governmental structures, widely shared cultural premises, the existence of distinctive subcultures, the record of grievances against the government, and differences in socioeconomic characteristics. Lipset and Rokkan, finally, view the handling of three major issues associated with the rise of the European nation-states as the determinant factors in voter alignments: the issue of the reformation, the struggle within the new nations over the educational system (the democratic revolution), and the handling of the urban-rural cleavage during the course of the industrial revolution. Each of these works, it should be emphasized, starts from a different position, asks different sets of questions, and comes up with slightly different answers.

Perhaps the more interesting point in this context, however, is the similarity in approach between all three volumes. First, although all three works attach some importance to the nature of constitutional structures in determining variations in parties and party systems, all reject Duverger's earlier emphasis on the importance of electoral machinery in shaping various types of party systems. Second, all of the authors, perhaps taking their cue from earlier studies of variation in the social bases of Marxist voting strength, have argued that examinations of contemporary class or issue configurations are not in themselves sufficient for an understanding of contemporary European party systems. Although there are some interesting differences of emphasis among the authors (Dahl gives much greater weight to contemporary factors than do the others), all the authors attach considerable importance to early patterns of social transformation, giving particular weight to the timing and handling

of certain key issues involved in the overall process of social modernization. Finally, all three works focus on the explanatory importance
of the setting in which the "crisis of participation" occurred within a
given society.

Does this agreement on the types of variables to be examined
presage the development of a more precise theory of political parties? One must be cautious in suggesting such a conclusion, because a
number of difficult problems lie in the way of further theoretical
elaborations. Some of the major variables suggested by the above-
mentioned works, for instance, will probably not yield easily to
operational definitions. How, for example, does one determine when
a "crisis of legitimacy" has begun or ended, or whether the "crisis" is
really of the same nature from one system to another? In other cases,
the categories of analysis are clearly inappropriate for cross-culture
research. Lipset and Rokkan's model, in some ways the most elegant
and precise of the three mentioned, is also the most limited in scope,
since such issues as the Reformation—a critical turning point in the
development of European party systems—have obvious temporal and
cultural limitations. A final problem concerns the data base to be
employed. As Lipset and Rokkan point out, the importance attached
by the three works to a broad time dimension suggests the need for
more, rather than less, ecological voting studies and calls into question the usefulness of much of the current survey and panel studies
now going on in Western Europe. There is thus in the study of parties
the same problem that we find in much of the comparative politics
literature, that of fitting data to theory.

The degree to which these obstacles can be overcome remains to
be seen. However, we are reasonably optimistic that at least some
progress can be made. In the first place, the substantial areas of
agreement among the several mentioned works on the types of
variables to be examined suggest that a useful general framework has
been established within which research can be conducted. Moreover,
the focuses of the several authors appear highly useful. The stress on
such factors as the reciprocal effects of traditional structures and
modernizing influences, on rates of change, and on the initial timing
and conditions under which mass demands for participation occurred, builds the problems of development and change into the research model. And although future research is likely to be complex
and multi-variate, this appears both plausible and necessary from a
theoretical point of view. Perhaps more important, all three works
offer a wealth of middle range propositions that can be explored: the
effects of egalitarian versus hierarchical rural orders on the development of national parties (Lipset and Rokkan, 1967), the handling
of various subcultures by party systems (Dahl, 1966), the relation-

ships between the granting of elite participation and the development of mass parties of integration (LaPalombara and Weiner, 1966). Finally, while there are admittedly difficulties in fitting data to theory, the problem is probably much smaller in this theoretical field than in most others. The data base already established, especially in Western Europe, is impressive (see Rose, 1973); and through the International Committee on Social Sciences Documentation and the building of historical data archives in individual countries, considerable progress has been made during the 1960s to accumulate and coordinate relevant empirical material.

Progress in handling the last mentioned of the theoretical problems concerning parties and party systems—their functional role within the larger political system—may encounter more impediments than that of understanding the preconditions for the emergence of parties. One difficulty is that parties are in an intermediate relationship between polity and society which makes it difficult to disentangle the presumed effects of parties—the management of conflict, the articulation of interests, etc.—from their contribution to the cleavages of each particular society. It is hard, in other words, to avoid tautology in the elaboration of dependent and independent variables. A second difficulty is that both sets of variables, dependent and independent, are difficult to define with precision. Discussions of the functional role of parties (the presumed dependent variable) frequently refer to "conflict management," "moderation," "education," and the like, all of which are elusive concepts when one is confronted with empirical reality. A third question involves the relationship between parties and "output." This requires a much better understanding of the internal organization and processes at the middle and upper levels of party structures, and in this respect there are considerable empirical gaps. As Lipset and Rokkan comment, "We know much less about the internal management and organizational functioning of political parties than we do about their sociocultural base and their external history of participation in decision-making" (1967, p. 51). As was the case in several of the other areas we have discussed, however, these problems need not necessarily remain intractable or unyielding when confronted with imagination and ingenuity. At least three approaches within the literature suggest themselves as useful avenues for exploring and comparing variations in parties' functional roles.

The first of these is suggested by deductive models of politics elaborated by Anthony Downs (1957), William Riker (1962), Mancur Olson (1965), and others. One of the theoretical starting points of Downs's work is that politicians seek to maximize and maintain their power and that, in an electorally based democratic system, the structure of the party system, the modalities of opinion, and the politicians' perceptions of these modalities will shape the policies of party and governmental leaders. From this set of premises, one can deduce a series of hypotheses relating governmental output to various kinds of party structures—competitive versus noncompetitive, multiparty versus two-party, etc.—which at some points can be tested empirically. The deductive approach has the advantage of making simplifying assumptions which may ultimately reduce the difficulties of data collection and expand the range of testable hypotheses. Moreover, recent works by Dye (1966), Dawson and Robinson (1963), and Hofferbert (1966) suggest that the testing of such hypotheses is possible. Using aggregate voting data and records of governmental expenditures, these writers have tested the relationships among the degree of party competition, the level of per capital income, and the expenditures of U.S. state governments. Their findings—that the per capita wealth is more important than the competitiveness of the party system—raise some important questions about Downsian theory and about the role of political parties. The point, however, is that cross-national theory about the relationship between parties and policy may ultimately become possible through the use of deductive theory and aggregate data analysis (see Hayward and Watson, 1975).

Recent work by Huntington (1968) offers a second important approach to the comparative study of parties. Concentrating on system stability, rather than on governmental output, as the major dependent variable, Huntington suggests that the stability of a political system will depend on the relative rates of "political institutionalization" and political participation. Parties are viewed as the principal agents for channeling the impact of newly participant groups, and they thus become critical variables in Huntington's larger theory. Systems in which strong parties develop prior to mass participation, Huntington suggests, are more likely to withstand the destabilizing shocks as the level of participation expands. From this there flow a number of interesting propositions: coups are less frequent when parties are strong; one-party systems are more effective in channeling participation during early stages of the modernization process; one-party systems born in social revolutions are more effective than those produced by nationalist movements, and these in turn are more effective than "those whose struggles were brief and easy" (p. 425); in later stages of modernization, two-party competition becomes more important for sustaining the drive of a society toward mass participation and organization. The foregoing, of course, does not do justice to the theoretical subtlety and complexity of Huntington's work, but it should be enough to indicate its richness in propositions that are potentially testable across a broad range of societies.

A final approach to the comparative study of parties, clearly related to the first two we have mentioned, concerns changes in party functions over time: what is the relative capacity of various types of parties or party systems to take on new tasks as conditions change, or to adjust the loss of old tasks to other structures within the society? These are probably the most interesting questions from a theoretical standpoint, but the most difficult ones to answer without intimate knowledge of particular types of parties and societies. Consequently, there is a relatively small amount of work, either theoretical or empirical, devoted to answering them. Once again, however, Huntington's work (1970) stands out as theoretically promising, although it is still too early to determine the quality of further research based on his propositions. Comparing the adaptability of one-party systems, he suggests that those which have worked to eliminate and/or incorporate dissident groups are more likely to survive than those which are based on the need to exclude significant strata of the population from participation (e.g., the one-party systems in the U.S. South, South Africa, Spain, and Portugal). Kirchheimer's discussion (1966) of the transition of European parties from mass integration to catchall types, with a loss of decision-making functions to the bureaucracy and of socializing functions to other agencies, is another interesting line of approach which, although less developed theoretically than Huntington's discussion, is nonetheless more relevant to the situation in Europe and the United States.

POLITICAL SYSTEMS

Until quite recently, it has been widely assumed that whole political systems, as opposed to individuals or separate structures within the system, were the most difficult units to treat in a comparative manner. The operations of whole systems, after all, are the products of many variables, and the functional impact of the political system on society is extraordinarily multifaceted and complex. Such complexity appears to render the exploration and comparison of the structures and functions of more than a single system as beyond the resources of an individual scholar. Thus it is hardly surprising that even the advent of structural-functional analysis did not lead to a spate of empirical efforts to compare whole political systems. To be sure, several such studies stand out in the literature of the 1960s (especially Brzezinski and Huntington, 1964; Ward and

Rustow, 1964; Eisenstadt, 1963; Bendix, 1964a; Moore, 1966), but these works were exceptions to the central trend. In the main, the field continued to be characterized on the one hand by the elaboration of grand structural-functional theory, usually unsupported by empirical research, and on the other hand by studies of single political systems.

In two respects, however, recent developments within the field of comparative politics have made comparison between whole systems appear a promising area for joining comparative theory and empirical research. One of these developments is the growth in recent years not of grand theory, but of a plethora of middle range propositions about the factors which lead to stable systems, to democratic systems, and to particular types of system outputs (e.g., Huntington, 1968; Eckstein, 1969; Lipset, 1960; Kornhauser, 1959; Moore, 1966; Rosenau, 1966, 1969a). Taken together and in conjunction with a second recent development noted below, these theories and pretheories are varied and provocative enough to seem capable of stimulating empirical comparisons between at least certain kinds of whole political systems in the years ahead.

The second development, in some ways more important and newer than the first, is the extraordinary growth of interest in the collection and/or generation of aggregate data—standardized counts of such variables as literacy, urbanization, gross national product, etc., for all or most of the world's "independent" political systems— and in the use of computerized techniques for processing these data. The pioneer in generalizing and processing aggregate data is Karl Deutsch, who has shown both theoretically and empirically the value of gathering and applying such data (1953, 1961, 1963). In developing the concept of social mobilization, for example, Deutsch demonstrated how it could be measured through the use of existing United Nations sources on urbanization, literacy, and other measures that do not depend on firsthand observations or field research for analysis. Since that time, a number of scholars and organizations, following Deutsch's lead, have made efforts to build data archives consisting of relatively standardized and comparable variables that can be made readily available to researchers. The most important of these within the political science world have been the Yale Data Bank program, data gathered by Banks and Textor (1963), Rummel's Dimensions of Nations project (1966, 1972), the International Population and Urban Research Program at Berkeley, and the longitudinal data archives developed by Banks (1971) and by Flanigan and Fogelman (1970). In addition to these, United Nations agencies have made efforts to standardize, coordinate and advise individual nations in their own data collection efforts (see also Mickiewicz, 1973).

The ultimate objective of this effort is to make possible the testing of complex hypotheses about political events across a broad sample of countries and cultures and to move toward what Almond called (1960b) a "probabilistic" theory of politics with the capacity to gauge the likelihood or degree of a phenomenon, given certain conditions. "As in the input-output analysis of other independent systems," argue the proponents of the technique, "it should be possible to analyze political systems by ascertaining the correlation between different variables of social change and political behavior" (Deutsch, Lasswell, Merritt, and Russett, 1966). By the admission of the most enthusiastic proponents of aggregate data techniques, this goal is still relatively remote. Nevertheless, there has been a growing literature making tentative explorations along comparative lines. In 1960 Lipset reported what is now a classic attempt to explore the correlation between economic development and stable democracy, using a sample of fifty countries. Since that time, efforts have been made to test for a large number of countries a host of propositions about such matters as the relationship between stability and land tenure inequality (Russett, 1964), between political stability and rapid socioeconomic change (Feierabend, 1966), between domestic violence and aggressive international behavior (Tanter, 1966), and between a variety of socioeconomic conditions and military interventions (Putnam, 1967). The list of journal articles treating such matters has increased almost exponentially since 1965.

What are the advantages and limitations of this new approach to the generation and processing of data, and where does it fit into the broader theoretical literature on comparative politics? There has probably been no single development in the discipline that has been subject to more discussion or controversy, and perhaps the most common theme among the critics of aggregate data analysis is that such analyses are atheoretical—that they engage in the tasks of finding *correlations* between variables, rather than *explaining* the presumed causal links between them; and that they "fish" inductively for associated variables, rather than attempt to set forth clearly defined and logically deduced hypotheses (Levy, 1969; Young, 1969). In some instances, these criticisms are probably justified, and to the extent that they are, this could lead to some serious problems. Aggregate data analysis is a *technique*, and as such cannot in itself be a substitute for good theory. By the same token, however, there is nothing inherent in the technique itself that would prevent it from being utilized to enrich and test an enlarging body of political theory. Most of those seeking to develop aggregate data and to explore ways in which it can be used defend their activities on the grounds that further theoretical advance in the field of political science requires the testing of theories against "adequately large and verified bodies of data. Without such enhanced opportunities for testing, the growth of political science may be seriously retarded" (Deutsch et al., 1966, p. 86). We regard this as a plausible contention, and one which renders some of the general criticisms of the early explorations of aggregate data analysis premature and somewhat irrelevant.

Having made this point, however, we also feel that it is important to note some of the constraints under which the developers and users of aggregate data must work at present. One of these constraints is clearly theoretical in nature. Although a host of middle-range propositions about political systems have proliferated, the efforts to build general theory, which can unify and guide research, has made little progress. There is, consequently, virtually no consensus among political scientists about the dependent variables that might be explored (stability? democracy? performance? economic development? equality?), about basic theoretical concepts (just what *is* a political system and what are its boundaries), or even about the appropriate *classification* of political systems. In 1963 Eckstein counted thirteen different ways that systems had been classified since the postwar period. By 1970 there were probably many more. This gap should not, of course, preclude the attempts to proceed toward inductive research which generates new middle-range hypotheses, nor should it preclude the testing of old ones. It does, however, suggest at least the possibility that the absorption with empirical technique may at some point outrace the development of theory and that, if the "dialogue" between theory and data is not to become too one-sided, at least some scholars may have to busy themselves with the attempt to build theory.

Another set of constraints lies in the limitations of aggregate data, both for the building and testing of theoretical propositions. First, in the testing of hypotheses, aggregate data can be used reliably only when the unit of analysis is the whole system or a structure within the system, rather than an individual. Inferences drawn from observed relationships between different aggregate measures of entire populations cannot be reduced to statements about individuals within that population. Although such relationships may suggest propositions about individual behavior, the actual testing of these propositions must be accomplished through survey research or other types of micro-level research in which the individual is the empirical unit of analysis. Secondly, although it may be possible through the use of aggregate units of data to test statistical associations, it is often difficult, as Russett has pointed out, to trace the causal directions underlying such associations. He notes that "the single case study, which loses other types of information, is often uniquely valuable in the identification of cause, at least in the particular case" (1966b, p. 100). Thus, aggregate data analysis may well supplement case work and detailed comparisons between a relatively small number of systems, but it will probably not replace these efforts:

> Each approach leads eventually to the other; the social scientist who discards one does no service either to himself or to his readers. The priorities may of course work either way. Perhaps one observes the individual case, develops a theory, and then tests it against the information from many other cases. Or one may start with a large body of data and then move to the case study to better identify details and causal relationships.

A third set of constraints, one far more subject to control and elimination by researchers themselves, lies in the uneven quality and serious gaps which exist in the data presently accumulated. Measurements of socioeconomic variables are often inaccurate or missing in the non-Western areas of the world. Often these data refer to the attributes of whole political systems, such as the GNP, rather than to intrasystem variation, such as the internal distribution of income. "Political" variables—measures of instability, institutionalization, participation, etc.—are often far cruder and more restricted than other social measures. Precisely because this is a situation which can be directly improved by the generators and users of aggregate data, much of their effort is applied to the task of improving the quality of their archives and filling in gaps. We do not minimize the difficulties in this regard, and we do not deny the present inadequate state of many data banks. Nevertheless, we cannot conclude a discussion of the aggregate data approach without expressing our personal optimism about its promise. The theoretical and operational constraints within which the user of aggregate data must work are considerable, but so are the revolutionary potentialities of this line of investigation. Within the limits outlined above, it enormously expands the number of countries and phenomena which can come under the researchers' reach, enabling him to treat a range of empirical problems that are generally unavailable through various types of micropolitical analysis. Perhaps more important, through the use of the computer, the researcher will be able to deal systematically with a large number of variables, thus coming closer to the goal of comparing whole political systems.

SUMMARY AND CONCLUSIONS

Comparative political research involves, at one stage or another, the description and classification of phenomena and the formulation and testing of hypotheses about the relationships between these phenomena. At the start of the postwar period, many of these tasks lay ahead. It may be useful to review the preceding pages from the perspective of how well we have performed these tasks in the past quarter century.

With respect to the tasks of description and classification, it is clear that some innovative conceptual breakthroughs have occurred and equally plain that these have encouraged more extensive empirical analyses of the phenomena encompassed by the field. As late as the mid-1950s, Almond, Cole, and Macridis (1955) pointed out that students of comparative politics had only rudimentary knowledge of such fundamental areas as the legislative organization and processes of Western European countries, and of nongovernmental structures and processes, and practically none about the countries outside the Western culture area. This, as we have suggested in earlier pages, has changed. The structural-functional approach, whatever its theoretical shortcomings, has provided the necessary rudiments for classification, and based on this, many of the gaps have been filled. We now know a great deal about the structures, functions, and processes of all of the Western European countries and about all of the major non-European nations, and studies of the major social and political processes and institutions in the smaller countries have increased dramatically in the last decade.

Yet even on the relatively elementary level of description and classification, some important gaps and difficulties persist. As we have already seen, no generally accepted classificatory scheme has been established to order the data on political parties or on political systems, although several have been elaborated that have proven useful for particular analytical purposes. Moreover, it is not yet clear that much of the information that has been gathered on the structures and functions of individual countries are subject to comparison in a systematic manner. The field is by no means agreed on just how one identifies and compares the functions performed in different systems by different structures. Although the development and use of aggregate data analysis may be viewed by some as one of the more dazzling or dismaying of the space-age innovations, much of the effort of its developers is designed primarily to solve that simple and rudimentary problem. Efforts to improve data archives, to refine the level and comparability of socioeconomic data, to devise and collect "political" variables, are designed at least initially to facilitate no more than this relatively simple task of classification and description. In spite of the accusations frequently levied against aggregate data users that they are too "high powered," or too "impatient for results," their initial objectives and much of their initial efforts tie them closely to the descriptive and classificatory efforts of area specialists and historians of a more "traditionalist" bent.

Finally, as we noted in our discussion of political culture and the socialization process, descriptive and classificatory probes on the micro-political level are only barely underway. For those who seek to understand such important problems as the way in which political values are transmitted and changed, the manner in which political support is mobilized at the grass-roots level, and the mechanics and processes by which citizens are linked to the state, the new nations of the world and many of the old ones remain virtually uncharted territory.

Perhaps even more disquieting is the scarcity of explicit and integrated hypotheses that have been either formulated or tested. For all its progress and ferment, the field of comparative politics is conspicuously lacking in a growing body of hypotheses, derived either from the newly emerging descriptive materials or the recent strides in theory building that posit correlations between variations in political behavior and the conditions antecedent to it. To be sure, the literature has become richer and more explicit in attempts to account for the presence or absence of political events in a wide variety of circumstances. We have mentioned at least some of these propositions as starting points for future research in the comparison of political cultures, parties, and whole systems. What should also be noted, however, is that most of these propositions are not *hypotheses.* As we understand the nature of hypotheses, they should consist of a number of characteristics. First, the variables in a hypothesis should be defined by setting forth a number of observable properties which permit the grouping of empirical phenomena into separate categories. Second, a hypothesis should set forth rules for determining *variation* in the variables—if these are qualitative variables, for the presence or absence of the attribute being examined; and if they are quantitative measures, these rules should cover changes in the *amount* of the attribute being examined. Finally, a hypothesis should set forth the expected relationships between variables and state the conditions in which these relationships can be considered disproved.

In most of the literature we have discussed, some or all of these characteristics are missing. In discussing the relationships between crises and the origins of political parties, for example, no effort has been made to set forth clearly how the same crisis is to be identified in different societies, when it began or ended, or when different crises occurred sequentially or simultaneously. Or, to take another example, in discussions of the relationship between institutionalization and political stability, each variable shares common properties, and for this reason the postulated relationship is difficult to disprove.

With some important exceptions (Eckstein's hypotheses [1969] about the relationship between the congruence of authority relations and governmental performance, to name one), many of the other propositions in the literature can be found at varying levels of explicitness and at uneven levels of precision.

We wish to emphasize that we are not making this observation critically. None of the authors we have discussed claims he has presented a body of integrated hypotheses. Indeed, doubtless all of them would insist they have done nothing more than make initial explanatory probes into territories that had previously not been treated. As works which point out directions for further research, as literature rich in suggestions for the future formulation of hypotheses, and as careful efforts to make inductions about relationships that can be expanded and explored through further case work and comparative studies, the scholarly works we have examined are groundbreaking efforts which richly deserve the favorable reception they have enjoyed. All we wish to stress—and this is a point with which few would disagree—is that there are few broad, or even middle-range, hypotheses in the comparative politics literature. If the goal is that of accumulating a body of logically related general propositions about political behavior that have been validated through the testing of empirically disprovable hypotheses—a goal to which we personally subscribe—then the progress of the past is miniscule compared to the distance that has yet to be traveled in the future.

Underlying these problems is a still larger gap which yawns before the field of comparative politics as a whole; namely, the problem of focus, of determining what broad areas are relevant to the field of comparative politics, and of how professional effort might best be organized to work toward a presumed collective goal. The discussion of the problems, techniques, and concepts involved in the three general avenues of investigation discussed above covers only a limited fragment of the activities which go under the heading of comparative politics. The pie can in fact be sliced analytically in many other ways: we might have talked more about the differences between micro-politics and macro-politics, about the distinction between inductive and deductive ways of arriving at hypotheses, about various strategies and modes of comparison. Or we might have elaborated many other substantive areas of investigation, since the field of comparative politics, as presently conceived, extends far beyond political culture, parties, and systems to the investigation of legislatures, bureaucracies, private interest groups, courts, militaries, leadership recruitment, decision making, and so on, through a virtually endless list. We have no way of knowing at this point just how, or whether, the individual pieces will someday fit together. Until there are commonly agreed upon theoretical guidelines to channel research efforts, uncertainty about the expenditure of our resources and the nature of our collective and individual priorities is bound to prevail.

This problem has been noted frequently (Apter, 1963; Apter and Andrain, 1968), and a variety of interesting "criteria of relevance" have been put forward (LaPalombara, 1968; Macridis, 1968; Huntington, 1970). At this stage, however, methodological pluralism is probably not only inevitable but desirable. Even our incomplete review of the field should indicate that however promising a number of approaches may appear, none has really paid off in impressive results. We ought to be honest enough to admit this fact, to recognize that individual research efforts may well encounter blind alleys, and to welcome the existence of simultaneous efforts which move in different directions from the one we have chosen. In the long run, the problem of focus, if it is to be solved at all, will be solved through trial and error, rather than through methodological argumentation.

3. AMERICAN INSTITUTIONS AND POLITICAL BEHAVIOR

William Buchanan

The traditional "fields" of American political science are in the process of restructuring, with the once dominant "American government" field breaking down into separate specialities: political socialization, legislative processes, voting behavior, and so forth. Thus the topic of this chapter, American institutions and political behavior, is for convenience, permitting us to look both backward and forward. A few years ago it was accepted that "institution" and "behavior" represented alternative ways of studying government and different things to study; the former focused on structure, the latter on actions of people. Now we are more likely to say with Eulau (1967, p. 36) that the institution is just one of a number of possible theoretical units of analysis; while the behavior of individuals is the empirical unit of analysis.

Of course, no political scientist treats American institutions without at least implicitly considering the British and continental alternatives. Since comparative systems, a variety of theories and techniques of analysis, and American institutions for domestic administration and foreign affairs are treated in other chapters, we need not consider them here. Rather we shall examine such questions as: what does the study of American government include, and how has it come to be structured in this way? What sources of information on American political phenomena have been over- or underexploited? When and how did the "behavioral" approach commence and what effect did it have? What have behavioralists discovered that traditionalists did not? What theories, implicit or explicit, simple or sophisticated, underlie the study of American government? What alternative theories are possible? What might be studied that is now being ignored?

For a starting point, let us take the following pragmatic observation: *the task of the political scientists who treat American institu-*

tions and behavior is to describe the nation's political structure and processes, including their linkages with other social institutions, in a systematic way, maximizing generality and predictability.

In this formulation the term "describe" encompasses both the activities of the empirical theorist, whose model is highly abstract and tentative, though in principle eventually comparable to observed data, and the activities of the data gatherer who works with verbal descriptions of political activity acquired from surveys, the papers generated by governmental agencies, (e.g., court decisions, congressional roll calls and tables of administrative organization), and the effluence of a loquacious governmental elite. It also includes the activities of the teacher, who processes the observations of others into descriptions comprehensible to consumers at several levels. It includes the adviser to people within government and those having to do with the government; his fuction is to describe the system in a fashion that enables them to predict and affect outcomes.

The predictive capacity of these descriptions, particularly those of teachers, is often implicit. One describes "how a bill becomes a law" in the expectation that laws will be made in the same fashion in subsequent sessions of the legislature. The terms "descriptive" and "analytic" have sometimes been used in opposition to one another, but analytic generalizations about American government amount to a rather complex kind of description.

FOCUS

Simple geography is going out of style as the dominant way of classifying political phenomena. Somit and Tanenhaus (1963, p. 54) found 17 percent of American political scientists classified their field as American Government. Another 30 percent listed general politics, public administration, and public law: one suspects they were also predominantly American in their outlook. A more refined breakdown, in which each respondent designated up to six specialized subfields, was used in the American Political Science Association's survey of its membership in 1967, from which it is possible to estimate how much attention is given to American phenomena.

827 International Politics
746 Political Parties and Elections; organization and processes
727 Foreign Policy
575 Administration: organization, processes, behavior
472 Constitutional Law
382 Metropolitan and Urban Government and Politics

342 Legislature: organization, processes, behavior
318 Political Theory and Philosophy (Historical)
311 Political Theory and Philosophy (Normative)
314 State and Local Government and Politics
301 Political Theory and Philosophy (Empirical)
236 Executive: organization, processes, behavior
196 Political Socialization
176 International Organization and Administration
175 Political and Constitutional History
154 National Security Policy
140 International Law
138 Judiciary: organization, processes, behavior
132 Revolutions and Political Violence
129 Political Psychology
125 Methodology
 94 Voting Behavior
 76 Public Opinion
 56 Budget and Fiscal Management
 45 Administrative Law
 44 Personnel Administration
 43 Government Regulation of Business
554 Other

A fourth or a fifth of the respondents are concerned almost exclusively with American phenomena (e.g., constitutional law, metropolitan government). Nearly half are fields now treated predominantly from the American viewpoint, though leavened with foreign perspectives (e.g., parties and elections, foreign policy, administration). The remaining third covers theory and international relations, where American phenomena are no more relevant than any others. One cannot conclude that there is any lessening of attention to American government, although it is generally recognized that the context in which it is viewed is broader than before (Keech and Prothro, 1968). Assuming that about half the 11,000 individual members of the Association are principally concerned with American government and roughly an equal number of nonmembers are teaching in colleges and high schools, we arrive at a figure of the order of 10,000 man-years annually devoted to academic description of government.

Social institutions are changing dramatically as technological developments alter the economy, the capacity of communication networks, the available techniques of violence, and the ability of government to handle and store intelligence. The value systems of those being governed also appear to be altering from a predominant emphasis on food, shelter, and security three decades ago to seeking deference and fulfillment in the 1970s. Faced with changing phenomena, those who describe American government have not sought "laws" of the sort that pertain to more stable physical and biological entities. Rather, they strive for generality at a lower level in the form of relatively stable categories and analogies. Legally defined structures most nearly meet their criteria of visibility and permanence, and the study of American government has long centered about formal enactments. The processes of inductive observation, theoretical conceptualization, data collection, hypothesis testing, synthesis of independent researches, publication, and criticism require time. Therefore, the literature of American governmental institutions and behavior contains at any time a substantial number of statements that once were but no longer are in conformity with the observable data of the "real world," and others which, though accurate today, will turn out to be unsound bases for tomorrow's predictions.

Other limitations under which description proceeds should be recognized. For many years those who did academic research were circumscribed by heavy teaching loads and other constraints (Somit and Tanenhaus, 1967). The dispersion of the phenomena being studied often makes both defining the universe and systematically sampling it nearly impossible.

THE LITERATURE

There is so much offhand talk about "the literature" of American government that we may be justified in trying to describe its compass briefly and critically. Seven categories cover it: textbooks, scholarly journals, monographs, papers, theses and dissertations, current periodicals, and reference works.

(1) The staples of the commercial market for years were *introductory texts* in American government, and many of them are still produced and sold. The theory presented in the course and textbook was already so familiar to the student that he hardly perceived it as theory at all. Its core is federalism and the separation of powers, modified by checks and balances. Each of the branches of government is the subject of a part of the book. There are chapters on the Constitutional Convention and the developing Constitution, parties, elections, public opinion and pressure groups, the federal principle, and urban, state, and local government. Budgeting, regulation, welfare, foreign policy, and economic policy usually are aggregated into a section on programs or functions. Thus, structural theory is implic-

it in the book's table of contents. The student/reader is not often told that this is the theory underlying the book, or that there *is* any theory underlying the book, or that theories provide frames of reference for the study of government, or even that theories exist. The source of the theory of separation of powers in Montesquieu's misconception of British government may be traced, but the notion of checks and balances, or even the distinction, if any, between a "check" and a "balance" is not disclosed, nor is attention called to the origin of this analogy is an era when the dominant science was physical mechanics, and the clock was the most sophisticated mechanism conceivable. James Madison's "Swiss watch concept of government," if mentioned, is not pursued, nor are the other implications of the clockwork model: that the whole is equal to the sum of its parts; that the parts are not modified by one another, nor by their own "history"; and that "each part once placed into its appropriate position, with its appropriate momentum, would remain in place and continue to fulfill its uniquely determined function" (Deutsch, 1963, p. 27). Students remain unaware of the analogy, or even that there is an analogy.

In contrast to textbooks, readers in American government and its subfields contain selections from recent journals, excerpts from important "classics," the more penetrating pieces from periodical literature, and perhaps some documents from governmental sources. These are organized topically, with an introduction and headnotes fitting them into a rather loose theoretical framework. They are an important step in establishing a consensus in the profession as to what articles are important, and they may appear at a crucial stage in delineating a new area as worthy of further treatment in a text.

A somewhat different kind of introductory reader currently in style contains a collection of polemics, usually with some attempt to "balance" the views presented.

What consumers of these descriptions are led to believe and remember about their government has consequences for that government. Hence the description of American government occurs in a political environment of push and tug in which the describer, the thing described, and the reader of the description strive to influence not only its substance but the terms on which it is conducted. Whether a "behavioral" or a "polemical" reader is used, whether the text is "pluralist" (e.g., Dahl, 1967, 1976) or "elitist" (e.g., Dye and Zeigler, 1970, 1977) may have consequences that were never explored when the structural text was standard.

(2) Up to the present, original research in American government has been reported in eight to ten *scholarly journals* published by national or regional political science associations, which also deal

with comparative government and international relations; in several more specialized journals (e.g., public opinion, public administration), and in the journals of allied disciplines such as sociology, history, law, or economics. The communication process remains inefficient, but its inadequacy is being attacked electronically by bibliographers and archivists, and some journals are seeking to clarify their fields of specialization.

(3) *Monographs* in political science are usually devoted to an agency of government or a concept of analysis. Formerly the product of university presses, monographs on political topics are now brought out in paperback by commercial publishers. Shorter monographs and duplicated studies are produced by government agencies, bureaus of governmental research and foundations (e.g., the Citizen's Research Foundation's studies of campaign finance).

(4) *Papers* presented at the American Political Science Association convention for some years have been on sale at the meetings and since 1968 have been abstracted. Other associations are less systematic, but their best papers subsequently appear somewhere as journal articles.

(5) *Theses and dissertations* are only nominally part of the literature except as they are subsequently revised and published. They are available on microfilm or interlibrary loan.

(6) *Current periodicals* contain some of the more penetrating studies of national governmental phenomena. Their style is less pedantic than that of the journals. The freedom their authors have from the need for documenting sources makes them less reliable on details and somewhat harder to check than the scholarly publications. The *New York Times Magazine, Trans-Action* (now called *Society*), *Atlantic, Harpers, Saturday Review, New Republic*, and *Commentary* are often useful.

In a special category is the *Congressional Quarterly*, useful both for keeping up with the output of the federal government on a weekly basis and for full documentation of past political events as far back as the late 1940s.

(7) More important *reference works* include the new *International Encyclopedia of the Social Sciences* (ed. David L. Sills, 1968), Richard Scammon's *America Votes* series, the *Statistical Abstract of the United States*, and the *Book of the States*.

The literature of American government is thoroughly eclectic. The phenomena themselves are dispersed. The purposes of those observing them are diverse, affecting their initial selection of what will be examined and from what viewpoint. Political scientists give some unity and continuity to the subject through a loose and evolving consensus on what is currently "important" or "signifi-

cant." Increasing emphasis on public policy may tighten the consensus, but in the past the literature of American government has,
more than any other, been influenced by the "box office" tastes of
the consumers of research: students, journalists, politicians, and
publishers. Rapid expansion of the quantity of output has produced
a problem of information overload that the discipline has not been
able to cope with. Individual political scientists adopt a variety of
scanning strategies, and a few bibliographical aids have appeared,
among them computerized information retrieval (Janda, 1968).

The American Commonwealth

In the beginning was Bryce.

Before him, no political science, no American government text
worthy of the name, no collection of data. A century of experience
with democracy was enlightened only by *The Federalist Papers*,
Tocqueville's *Democracy in America* (1832), history books, memoirs, and the fine-drawn contentions of legal scholars over state
sovereignty. Contemporary with him is only Woodrow Wilson's
Congressional Government (1885).

Bryce's *The American Commonwealth* (1888) ran to 1700 pages
in two volumes. It contained an able synthesis of constitutional
background, formal structural features, and observed processes of the
federal government in action. It dealt systematically for the first time
with state governments and politics. It treated political parties as
integral parts of the system, with chapters on spoils, rings, bosses,
and corruption. It was the first scholarly effort to come to practical
terms with that mysterious entity, "public opinion," about which so
much had been said so vaguely. Its impact was immediate. Reviews,
including those by Lord Acton and Woodrow Wilson, were overwhelmingly favorable. Seventy-one thousand copies were sold in the
first decade, forty-seven thousand the second, fifty-six thousand the
third, and thirty-one thousand the fourth, indicating a continued
demand for the various revised editions for textbook use (Brooks,
1939).

James, Viscount Bryce, an Oxford professor and member of
Parliament with experience in the Gladstone ministry, had compiled
the material for the volume in a series of visits to the United States
during which he had become acquainted with members of the governing elite, but he had also made a determined and successful effort
to converse with "all sorts and conditions of men," finding occasions
to strike up conversations in railway cars and public gatherings. He
had earlier written a thorough, sound, but not brilliant, Roman

history, and he brought to the task both scholarly and practical experience, as well as a broad familiarity with European governments. The approach was comparative, employing British judicial practice and cabinet government as a standard for appraising judicial review and presidential leadership. His outlook was that of the upper-middle-class establishment with which he was acquainted; he liked Americans, and on balance admired the United States government; but he reflected the views of the circle in which he moved in condemning the looters and the spoilsmen at the lower levels.

Had not the study of American government sprung full-blown from the head of Bryce, had not the acclaim of *The American Commonwealth* been so immediate, enthusiastic and sustained; had it not become at the same time a reformist tract, a classic, and a textbook; the shape of subsequent research and teaching of government in America might have been quite different.

Lord Bryce's approach may fairly be called not merely comparative, but behavioral and empirical as well—criteria which were met by a number of the earlier works in the field (Somit and Tanenhaus, 1967). Half a century before the development of polling, Bryce perceived the importance of systematic interviewing of representatives of the public. Five-sixths of his material, he once estimated, came from personal conversations with citizens and elites. He read newspapers religiously, noted the want ads and the interest rates. He even resorted to such "unobtrusive measures" as smelling dollar bills in Wisconsin to see if they had been handled by the skin traders. He attempted to use the class structure as a framework for analysis, dividing the nation into the wealthy businessmen, professionals (especially lawyers), farmers, small shopkeepers, and manufacturers, and the "ignorant masses." Finding status polarization not far advanced compared to the Continent, he rejected class as an important tool of analysis.

He noted the importance of what would now be called style—as opposed to position—issues, commenting that "there are few issues on which each party traverses the doctrine of the other. Each pummels, not his true enemy, but a stuffed figure set up to represent that enemy" (1888, vol. 2, p. 215). These issue appeals have little effect on the voters, for "the American, like the Englishman, usually votes with his party, right or wrong."

What we would call the "viability of the system" was his object of major concern, and he assessed the "supposed" faults, the "true" faults, and the "strengths" of democratic government. He found little evidence of the faults which political philosophers since Plato had attributed to democracy: weakness in emergencies, instability, internal dissensions, disregard for authority, and majority tyranny, but he found a "want of dignity and elevation" in public affairs, apathy among the *upper* classes, lack of "knowledge, tact and judgment" in legislation and administration, and considerable corruption and mismanagement of public business. He found the system to be stable, the people disposed to obey the laws they had participated in making, adequate limitations on arbitrary authority, no basic class struggle, and a reserve capacity to organize to meet emergencies (chaps. 100, 101, 102).

The approach is entirely inductive: Bryce has an explicit confidence that the "facts of the case" will "speak for themselves." He eschews theoretical speculation: he told an Englishman who asked why there was no chapter on the American theory of the state that "the Americans had no theory of the state, and felt no need of one." He also avoided attempting a historical perspective. He accepted the values of his friends—the "best" people—and their simple-minded belief that better government would result from replacing "bad" machine politicians with "good" public spirited statesman (McCloskey, 1968). His easy use of normative adjectives in the construction of empirical propositions today grates on the behavioral ear. His anecdotal facility, his balanced citation of advantages and disadvantages of political arrangements, his unselfconsciousness of method, his concern with institutions rather than social forces, his compulsion for completeness, and his capacity for I-A-1-a outlining comprise an orientation that characterized American government textbooks for the next half-century.

Once set going on the track of formal-legal-structural description, the study of American institutions ran along smoothly, picking up a good deal of baggage from time to time as new governmental agencies were created, but dropping off very little of its original cargo. For example, detailed descriptions of citizenship provisions were incorporated early in the twentieth century to accommodate the deep interest of immigrants in these rules; but when the wave of immigration diminished, the length of the coverage did not. The moralistic tone of the reformists did diminish, to be replaced with a "balanced" treatment of the pros and cons of every conceivable proposal to change the structure of government (Lowi, 1964b).

By contrast to the smooth-flowing description of institutions, the search for the relationship of these structural entities to the popular will found two generations of scholars of several disciplines wandering in a wilderness, following trails that crisscrossed, separated, converged, and frequently dead-ended, led on by a faint theoretical conflagration that seemed at times a guiding pillar of fire but turned out as often to be a will-o'-the-wisp. The major paths they pursued may be labeled Public Opinion, Elections, and Parties and Groups, terms we choose for their historical relevance rather than their conceptual clarity.

PUBLIC OPINION

The path that opened most broadly was the first to end in a methodological thicket. Walter Lippmann in *Public Opinion* (1922) and *The Phantom Public* (1925) made explicit the consequences of the development of mass media as instruments for informing the public, and assessed gloomily the prospect for sustained, informed, popular control of governmental policy. He advanced the proposition, still popular and intuitively sound but difficult to operationalize, that public opinion sets the bounds and limits within which governmental officials must operate (Wright, 1973). Stuart Rice (1928) perceived the need for empirical study of mass phenomena, and the psychologists of the 1920s and 1930s produced a large body of attitude studies dealing with reactions to propaganda, attitudes toward war, pacifism, prohibition, taxation, and so on. They sought to measure "liberalism" and "conservatism," and to discover the correlates and interrelations of all these attitudes as psychological attributes of individuals. While political scientists remained intuitive, impressionistic, normative, and anecdotal, the psychologists became empirical and statistical, seeking general observations based on replicable measurement of expressed sentiments and behavior in definable (though at first very poorly defined) populations.

The reorientation dates not to an important theoretical advance but to a technical one: the development of public opinion polling by Gallup and others, which made possible empirical statements about the national electorate. They demonstrated that within tolerable limits national samples, when compared with presidential vote percentages, were accurate representations of the entire population. A significant event in 1937 was the founding of the *Public Opinion Quarterly*, an interdisciplinary journal that brought together the findings of psychologists, sociologists, journalists, market researchers, historians, and political scientists.

The statistical rationale eventually had an impact throughout political science, making researchers conscious that not only voters, but government elites, documents, political events, characteristics of of units of government, and the content of significant communications were all susceptible to a mode of analysis that first defined the population to be studied, then systematically or randomly selected a stable number of cases for detailed examination, and finally drew conclusions about the universe from the sample studied.

The immediate effect was an expectation that "public opinion" for the first time could be operationally defined. Transparently, the next step was to show the relationship between polled opinion and governmental action. Cantril (1944, chap. 16) showed how poll responses were shaped by events, including official actions and statements. Cantwell (1946) demonstrated an apparent relationship between public opinion and legislative response in the Supreme Court packing controversy. The mechanisms by which these flows were transmitted proved harder to trace. Direct "linkage" processes such as elections or communications from individuals to government, and linking institutions, notably parties and interest groups, then were examined with more care in an effort to clarify the impact of opinion on policy. The diffuse and undifferentiated entity called public opinion is no longer fashionable as an operational concept, although it remains in use as a title for texts and a name for courses in political science, sociology, psychology, and journalism (see Hennessy, 1975; Erikson and Luttbeg, 1973; Wilcox, 1974; Ippolito et al., 1976; Weissberg, 1976).

ELECTION STUDIES

The second path toward an understanding of the relation of people to their government is through studying the electoral process. It consists of many trails that join and diverge, an almost monumental literature of books and journal articles that cannot be more than sketched here. For example, a bibliography of the articles on American politics and elections published during a five-year period (Garrison, 1968) contained 407 entries. The major book-length works, arranged by chronology, locale, and technique are listed in Table 1.

Someone else might compile a slightly different list, but he would probably substantiate four observations: (1) what we know about voting behavior is largely restricted to presidential elections; (2) the University of Michigan Center for Political Studies supplied the bulk of the data, for their own analysis and reanalysis by others through the facilities of the Inter-University Consortium for Political and Social Research; (3) aggregate data from elections, commercial polls, and local studies have provided sufficient opportunities for replication to turn up any gross distortions in survey findings; (4) the rate of publication has increased almost exponentially.

The first of these studies, by Gosnell and Merriam, demonstrated the effect on turnout of socioeconomic status as indexed by educa-

T A B L E 1. Major Studies of American Elections, 1924-1976*

Pub. Date	Senior Author(s): Short Title	Election Studied	Sample or Technique
1924	Merriam & Gosnell: *Non-Voting*	Mayor, 1923	Chicago, interviews
1927	Gosnell: *Getting Out the Vote*	President, 1924	Chicago, interviews
1937	Gosnell: *Machine Politics: Chicago Model*	President, 1928-36	Chicago, aggregate data
1944	Lazarsfeld: *The People's Choice*	President, 1940	Erie County, Ohio sample, panel
1949	Key: *Southern Politics*	State elections	Southern states, aggregate data
1954	Berelson: *Voting*	President, 1948	Elmira, N.Y., sample, panel
1954	Campbell: *The Voter Decides*	President, 1952	SRC national sample, panel
1956	Key: *American State Politics*	Selected state elections	Aggregate data
1959	Lane: *Political Life*		Synthesis of participation studies
1959	Burdick & Brodbeck: *American Voting Behavior*		A collection of articles
1960	Campbell: *The American Voter*	President, 1952, 1956	SRC national sample, panel
1961	Key: *Public Opinion & American Democracy*		Reanalysis of polls and SRC survey data
1962	McPhee & Glaser: *Public Opinion and Congressional Elections*	Congress, 1950	Regional polls
1962	Eulau: *Class and Party in the Eisenhower Years*	President, 1952, 1956	Reanalysis of SRC data
1964	Boskoff & Zeigler: *Voting Patterns in a Local Election*	Atlanta bond referendum, 1961	Aggregate and survey
1965	Pool: *Candidates, Issues and Strategies*	President, 1960, 1964	National polls, reanalysis
1965	Milbrath: *Political Participation*		Synthesis of participation studies
1966	Key: *The Responsible Electorate*	President, 1936-1960	Reanalysis of national polls

T A B L E 1. (Continued)

Pub. Date	Senior Author(s): Short Title	Election Studied	Sample or Technique
1966	Matthews & Prothro: *Negroes and the New Southern Politics*	President, 1960	Regional sample, aggregate data
1966	Cummings: *Congressmen and the Electorate*	President and Congress, 1920-1964	Aggregate data
1966	Campbell: *Elections and the Political Order*	President, 1952-1964	SRC national samples, panel
1968	Kessel: *The Goldwater Coalition*	President, 1964	Reanalysis of SRC survey data
1968	Flanigan: *Political Behavior of the American Electorate* (3d ed. with Zingale, 1975)		Synthesis of electoral studies
1968	Pomper: *Elections in America*		Synthesis of electoral studies
1970	Burnham: *Critical Elections*	President, 1828-1968; selected states, 1880-1968	Aggregate data
1973-74	Kovenock, Prothro and associates: *Comparative State Election Project: Explaining the Vote*	President, selected states, 1968	National and 13-state interlocked samples
1975	Ladd & Hadley: *Transformations of the American Party System: Political Coalitions from the New Deal to the 1970s*	President and Congress: 1936-1972	Reanalysis of national polls, SRC national surveys
1976	Nie, Verba, & Petrocik: *The Changing American Voter*	President: 1952-1972	SRC and NORC national surveys
1976	Miller & Levitin: *Leadership & Change: The New Politics and the American Electorate*	President: 1948-1974	SRC national surveys

*It has become increasingly difficult to determine which publications should be classified as "voting studies." Several excellent candidates for inclusion in this table are Pomper (1975), Abramson (1975), Trilling (1976), Polsby and Wildavsky (1976), and Niemi and Weisberg (1976).

tion, neighborhood, occupation, and ethnicity, and the cultural restriction on participation in politics by women. They also showed the prevailing indifference and cynicism about politics among low-status citizens. The polls later confirmed these phenomena and also demonstrated the effect of status on party choice as the New Deal measures consolidated the tendency toward Republican voting in the upper and middle classes, and Democratic voting among the working class and relief recipients. That social class was exerting a new influence on politics was dramatically shown in 1936 by the failure of the *Literary Digest* poll, which stratified only geographically, and the simultaneous success of the Gallup and other newspaper predictions, which were based on polls stratified by income.

The panel study, in which the same person is interviewed at different points in the campaign, was introduced by Lazarsfeld et al. (1944) in the Erie County, Ohio, study of the 1940 election, and was reapplied by Berelson et al. (1954) to Elmira, New York, in the 1948 election. It led to a revised theory of voting behavior, the "deterministic" model. Among the findings that supported this theory were that relatively few people changed their opinions during a campaign and that those who did were more likely to have been influenced by primary group pressures than by the issue appeals of the candidates; that few persons attended to communications from the opposing party; that the media output was relayed to primary groups by "opinion leaders" who interpreted it in the light of the concerns felt by members of the group; that occupation, rural or urban residence, religious affiliation, and previous voting habits could be used to predict with substantial accuracy how a person would vote, and that "independent" or shifting voters were not issue-oriented in their outlook.

Lazarsfeld's pithy description (1944, p. 69) of his analysis of those who changed from one party to another in the course of the campaign went:

> These people . . . were the least interested in the election; the least concerned about its outcome; the least attentive to political material in the formal media of communication; the last to settle upon a vote decision; and the most likely to be persuaded, finally, by a personal contact, not an "issue" of the election. . . .
>
> The notion that the people who switch parties during the campaign are mainly the reasoned, thoughtful, conscientious people who were convinced by the issues of the election is just plain wrong. Actually, they were mainly the opposite.

These conclusions were summed up in the succinct phrase "a person thinks, politically, as he is, socially." This deterministic view was a corrective to the overrationalized popular theory of voting which stemmed in part from the failure, unchallenged by political scientists, to make distinctions between normative and empirical statements—in this instance to differentiate between the contention that a voter *should* decide on the basis of issues and should wait to hear out the candidates before doing so, and the empirical evidence that some voters *did* indeed alter their preference during the four years between elections. The popular rationalist theory of the thirties was never very coherent, since the contention of Lippmann and others that "propaganda" in the mass media was very influential, and that voters could be easily manipulated by the "engineers of consent," was accepted along with the "rational voter" theory. The determinist model made the voter as resistant to irrational as to rational appeals.

A related proposition to come out of the Erie County and Elmira studies was the "cross-pressures" hypothesis. This stemmed from the finding that those who are pushed to vote for different parties by primary group or other cultural predispositions will resolve the discomfort by delaying their decisions, and in some instances will fail to vote at all, thus withdrawing from the conflictual situation. The generality of this phenomenon was questioned by findings of Pool et al. (1965) with respect to the 1960 election. It is now seen as a special case of the "cognitive dissonance" principle, according to which people try to bring conflicting perceptions of the world into congruence with one another, and seek to avoid situations in which they cannot do so.

The central core of the analysis of voting behavior for a quarter century was conducted by Angus Campbell and his associates at the University of Michigan (e.g., 1954, 1960, 1966). Their first major contribution was the conceptualization of "party identification": the tendency of citizens, voter and nonvoter alike, to perceive themselves as members of a political party. The notion of party "affiliation" had been implicit in the questions asked by the pollsters from the beginning, but it had not been carefully distinguished from actual "membership," registration, or voting tendencies, nor fully appreciated for its stability and for its utility as a control variable. Through the 1964 election, SRC surveys found 45 to 50 percent of the public identifying themselves as Democrats, 25 to 30 percent as Republicans, about 20 percent as Independents and usually less than 5 percent unwilling to fit into this classification scheme. There was only a trickle of changed identification, usually benefitting the Republicans. The greater loyalty and higher turnout of Republican identifiers helps to remedy the imbalance. Party identification accounted for the vote far better than any other factor.

Therefore, an increase after 1964 in the proportion of Independents to around 30 percent, largely at the expense of the Democrats, became very meaningful. What would have been considered a minor fluctuation in any other attitude series presaged the onset of a critical period of electoral realignment.

As data accumulated on a number of elections, the Michigan research team turned toward explaining the "short-term factors" that accounted for shifts from election to election among independents and weak partisans. Their framework of analysis incorporated the perceived attributes of the two presidential candidates, foreign and domestic issues, the association of the two parties with various groups, and the performance of the parties as "managers of government." The balance between the parties on each of these attributes shifts over time, and makes each election a unique pattern (Flanigan, 1968, p. 112; Stokes, 1966). Yet within the period from 1936 to 1968 these shifts were around an equilibrium point determined by the distribution of partisan identification in the population.

The unwillingness of the mass of voters to resort to ideology as a way of organizing their perceptions of domestic politics remained a source of astonishment to the academic community. The words "liberal" and "conservative" were hazy concepts until well into the 1950s. About the best that the average voter could manage was the recognition that each party favored somewhat different group interests (Campbell et al., 1960; Converse, 1964a). Reanalysis of earlier surveys in the light of recent elections showed that since 1964 there has been a sharpening of partisan differences in attitudes toward even the old familiar issues of welfare liberalism that had been on the SRC schedule since 1956 (Pomper, 1972).

These tendencies for citizens, especially the young ones, to dissociate themselves from the major parties and for partisans to become more consistently opinionated confirmed the nature of the change which other indicators (ticket splitting, regional shifts, convention demonstrations) suggested—that there was a basic reorientation afoot. It was the data from the stable 1950s that provided a benchmark for understanding the change.

The choice those who vote make at the polls is only part of the picture. Who gets to the polls is another part, and is important both as an indication of support for the political system and because differential turnout by one group or party can have a crucial effect on the election outcome.

Turnout was found to be stimulated by the activity of political parties, which are more active in competitive districts. It is reduced by the complexity of the election situation (a confirmation of the cross-pressures effect), with the multiparty presidential contests of 1912, 1924, 1948, and 1968 all having fewer voters participating than the norm for their respective periods and the doubtfulness of the outcome would have led one to expect. There was a steady decline in participation after the turn of the century, which may have been due to lessening competition as each party became dominant in its own area, to the one-sidedness of national elections and to a general weakening of the parties themselves (Burnham, 1965). It might also have been because tighter administration of voting laws reduced the number of both real and fraudulent ballots (Kelley et al., 1967). The findings on participation have been summarized by Milbrath (1965) and Lane (1959). Among them were: persons are more likely to participate if they expose themselves to political stimuli, or are exposed to them through the activity of others; if they are middle-class, urban, male, educated, middle-aged, concerned about the outcome of elections; if they identify with parties, feel efficacious about politics, consider it their duty to participate, are confident of their understanding of government, are sociable and self-confident rather than alienated or cynical; if they perceive the outcome of the election as in doubt and important, and its alternatives as clear; if they have been raised in homes and move in circles where political activity is expected; if they belong to other organizations; and if they have lived in the same community for a long time (see also Verba and Nie, 1974). It is apparent that this complex of social, economic, personality, political-structural and situational factors contains a number of intercorrelations, and that the search for a prime cause requires considerable technical sophistication. It is also apparent that those who are socially and economically advantaged are at the same time politically advantaged. Such findings supported other evidence of elitism that influenced the theories taught even at the level of the introductory American government course, as for example in Dye and Zeigler's textbook (1970, 1977). (See also Parenti, 1974; Dye, 1976.)

Key's last work, *The Responsible Electorate* (1966) advanced "the perverse and unorthodox argument . . . that voters are not fools." Using poll data for the elections from 1936 through 1960, he showed that voters who shifted from one party to another in each election tended strongly to express attitudes on issues and presidential performance which were consonant with their change of preference, and that the larger part of those who join or rejoin the electorate at any election, though not as involved as the party regulars, do express views on issues that can account for their decision to enter the political arena.

For generations it had been known that the presidential party almost always loses seats in Congress in the mid-term election. A plausible explanation, assuming voter rationality and attentiveness, was that whatever actions the administration might take were certain to antagonize a portion of the electorate. The election studies showed, to the contrary, that the congressional victories in presidential years (the coattail effect) are attributable to the turnout of independent and weakly partisan citizens attracted by the personal appeal of the presidential candidates and the furor of the campaign.

Almost absent-mindedly, these marginal participants support their candidate's congressional running mates. In mid-term elections these citizens are likely to stay home, and the underlying partisan distribution of the activists reasserts its effect (Campbell et al., 1966, chap. 3; McPhee and Glaser, 1962).

The most striking example of a hypothesis growing from aggregate analysis being subsequently confirmed by survey findings is the construction of an election typology that takes into account the balance of party identification in the nation at any period, and its interrelation with the transient forces affecting voting in a particular election. The seed of the approach was in Key's "theory of critical elections" (1955) to the effect that occasional stressful events produce a reshuffling of the loyalties of population groups into new party coalitions, resulting in an altered balance between the major parties that then becomes stable for a period of elections (see also Burdick and Brodbeck, 1959, chap. 15; MacRae and Meldrum, 1960; Sellers, 1965). It was shortly recognized that the transition usually requires not one but a series of elections. According to Pomper's version of the typology (1968, pp. 102-4), the election types are *maintaining* elections when the party with the majority of voters mobilizes them to keep control of the White House, as in 1924 and 1940; *deviating* elections when the short-range effects enable the minority of affiliants plus their temporary supporters to win, as in 1912 or 1952. The elections in which a new balance is established—critical elections—are called by the Michigan team *realigning* elections (e.g., 1932), but Pomper divides them into *realigning* and *converting*, the latter occurring when there are substantial changes in the party loyalties of societal groups, but not enough to unseat the majority party (e.g., 1964).

Three categories of voting theories can be distinguished. In the first are the deterministic theories, which would include the Lazarsfeld model of sociological forces and the early Michigan studies employing the "funnel of causality," a variety of Lewin's "field" theory. They account for social determinants in the voter's distant background at the wider, distant end of the funnel narrowing down to political effects immediately before the voting decision at the narrow end (Campbell et al., 1960). This is a "pattern" model (see Golembiewski et al., 1969, pp. 404-6), which does not lead to deductive generalization or predictions, but is useful for organizing a complex set of interrelated variables.

The second set of theories hinges upon some sort of deliberate, conscious reaction on the part of the voter to the actions of the administration and the promises of the parties. Included would be Key's idea of a "responsible" electorate which, incidentally, does not *have* to think in concrete issue terms but may have a "diffuse image" of the parties which includes what they have done in the past and would be likely to do in the future (Stokes, 1968). A more explicitly rational framework is that of Anthony Downs's *Economic Theory of Democracy* (1957), which posits parties consciously selecting positions based on a calculus of voter preferences and an electorate weighing utilities from preferred policies against the cost of information gathering and voting. The work of Downs and Key stimulated a reconsideration of voter rationality and a reexamination of the findings of the 1940s and 1950s that voters were influenced primarily by party identification and social status, and that those who took party affiliation lightly were even less likely to take into consideration the positions of the parties and candidates. Kessel (1972) found some thirty books, articles, and papers, most of them dating from 1968, exploring the proposition that issues have some significant part in determining votes. The Comparative State Election Project study (1973-4) of the 1968 election set out explicitly to examine these theories. The June 1972 *American Political Science Review* carried a series of articles setting forth the findings and methodological problems of the neo-rationalists. The battle over the role of issues or policy in determining the voter's choice continued in the September 1976 issue of the *American Political Science Review* (vol. 70). Approximately one hundred pages were devoted to a report of the Survey Research Center's 1972 election study data and analysis (Miller et al., pp. 753-78), to a critical review of the article (Popkin et al., pp. 779-831), and a spirited rejoinder by the senior authors (Miller and Miller, pp. 832-49).

Recent studies have sought to link the behavior of party elites to the response of the electorate. Kessel (1968) examined the strategies of the 1964 campaign managers from the standpoint of their perceptions of the electorate and the consequences of these strategic decisions when the votes were counted. Pomper (1968, chaps. 7, 8) examined party platforms and found them, contrary to popular belief, to be rather rationally calculated documents, specific on issues where benefits to voting groups were clear, and vague where opinion was uncrystallized, endorsing generally what the majority, or unopposed minorities, favored. He also found that parties in power fulfill platform promises much more often than they fail to do so. Though he did not pursue reactions to administrative action at the national level, he did find in the states that taxing and spending by a governor's administration did not have a clearly discernible effect upon the success of his party at the next election.

In the third category are "systems" theories. It has been remarkable that the most complete and sophisticated body of research on

American political behavior, the voting study, has not explicitly addressed itself to the most popular theoretical model of the 1960s, systems theory. Nor had systems theorists taken account of the voting studies, with one notable exception: Talcott Parsons's article in Burdick and Brodbeck (1959), in which he examined Berelson's *Voting* and found its results entirely consistent with a portion of his own theoretical scheme. However, the later formulation of the Michigan group centered their findings around the concept of a "normal vote"—the standing strength of the two major parties in terms of their loyal identifiers. "Short-term forces" peculiar to each presidential election produce defections from the norm (Campbell et al., 1966, p. 7). The relation of this formulation to general systems theory is seen most clearly in Campbell's description of its application to the 1964 election (Cummings, 1966a), which describes party competition as a homeostatic system which may stabilize at different levels. Fluctuations in turnout and party vote derive from a combination of short-term forces superimposed upon a long-standing balance of identifiers of the two parties. Each of the short-term effects—candidate appeal, policy issues, images of party performance, domestic and international circumstances—varies in its impact from election to election, but the sum of these forces may favor one party or the other, swinging the vote from "normal" balance toward a temporary condition that favors that party. Usually the underlying partisanship will swing the vote back to normal in subsequent elections. Occasionally there will be a redistribution of some groups in the electorate, and a new balance at a different "level" will emerge.

If this is indeed a systems theory of national elections (and Campbell does not call it that), several observations are in order. Balance does not mean that the parties are exactly equal in strength, but are within a region of competition which will permit the minority to occasionally win an election. (Presumably, if the system were to get too far out of balance, the events of the 1820s would repeat themselves and the dominant party would split.) The theory does *not* posit an advantage to the administration through having the initiative in policy, monopoly of national patronage, access to the media, and other advantages of incumbency. In fact, Stokes and Iversen (see Campbell et al., 1966, chap. 10) demonstrate statistically that some unspecified forces have regularly restored equilibrium between the parties. The theory accounts for both the deterministic factors in the basic party balance, and some more or less consciously rational ones among the short-term forces. Most important, it is a predictive model.

The voting studies, helpful as they have been, have been called nonpolitical in the sense that they are concerned with individual behavior and have not explicated the relationships between the inputs from the electorate and the internal conversion processes and outputs of government. Nor have they examined the feedback processes wherein policy decisions and pronouncements impinge upon the electorate and presumably affect the next election. Thus they have focused upon the electoral, not the political, system. Burnham's *Critical Elections* (1970) bridges this gap with historical analysis which both defines and explores the correlates of "critical realignment," a periodic intensive reorganization of major party alignments in a time of socioeconomic stress and ideological polarization which reveals the inadequacies of the existing parties in coping with emergent demands. Groups move from one party to the other, regions suddenly become competitive or one-party, rules of the electoral and legislative process are changed formally or informally, tickets are split, electioneering techniques become obsolete, and institutional structures crumble (see Sundquist, 1973). As the CPS (SRC) election surveys entered the third decade in which consistency of item wording and rigor of sampling had been maintained, it became possible by cohort analysis to chart the fluctuations in behavior of generations of voters and to sort out the effects of chronological age from the common experience of those growing up in a particular time period. (See Abramson, 1975; Nie, Verba, and Petrocik, 1976.)

PARTIES

No human institution is simple, and no institution ordering masses of people is convenient to describe, but the American party system is uncommonly elusive, volatile, and contradictory. David Truman (1951a, p. 273) observed that in the United States the term "party"

> does not have the same meaning at the national, state and local levels; it may not have the same meaning in two states or two localities; finally, in the nation, in a single state, or in a single city the term may not have the same meaning at one point in time as at another, in one campaign year and in the next. It usually means in election campaigns something very different from what it means when applied to the activities in a legislature.

The earliest definition of a political party, by Edmund Burke, was a group of men joined to effect some principle on which they are agreed. Bryce found American parties did not meet this specification; that

> neither party has any clean-cut principles, any distinctive tenets. Both have traditions. Both claim to have tendencies. Both have certainly war cries,

organizations, interests, enlisted in their support. But those interests are in the main the interests of getting or keeping the patronage of the government.

Lacking principle, he concluded, American parties must be bad parties, or no parties at all:

What life is to an organism, principles are to a party. When they which are its soul have vanished, its body ought to dissolve, and the elements that formed it be regrouped in some new organism. . . . But a party does not always thus die. It may hold together long after its moral life is extinct. . . . The American parties now continue to exist, because they have existed [pt. 2, chap. 54].

Thus Bryce advanced a second definition of parties that had in it empirical, moralistic, systemic, and functional elements. Moisei Ostrogorski's *Democracy and the Organization of Political Parties* (1902) accounted for the political machine in terms of the need for organizing citizens who were relatively indifferent about political issues, though strongly motivated by personal interests. He attributed differences between the British and American parties not so much to the constitutional structure as to the social structure, noting the absence of an aristocratic elite with a tradition of governmental service, the opportunities in professional politics for men of low status, the irrelevance of issue principles to local politics and to patronage at the municipal level. He concluded by recommending the abandonment of political parties for transient organizations revolving about single issues. It is not surprising that American political science of that day would focus attention on his pragmatic (though impractical) solution, while his theoretical insights would influence European scholars, including Max Weber and Robert Michels (Lipset, 1968). Continentals, faced with the task of accounting for a variety of national one-, two-, and multiparty states, have shown concern with the theory of parties, and party *systems;* while Americans, who must deal with a national complex containing local examples of all three, have taxed their resources merely to describe a *party.* Thus American analysts have tended until recently to be divided between the comparative scholars interested in theory, and American government scholars interested in process and structure of party organization.

The hortatory tone of both Bryce and Ostrogorski was muted in *Party Organization and Machinery* (1904) by Jesse Macy, one of the first behavioralists, in his detachment and his search for "scientific" generalizations. He saw the need for sustained investigation of "the psychology of the political party," consisting of the "remarkable interaction of the minds of the individual members upon the organic institution, and of the organic institution back upon the mind of the individual," without which the properties of the political party would remain a mystery (p. 126).

Merriam and Gosnell's *The American Party System* (4th ed., 1949), first written by Merriam in 1922, is characteristic of the best of the parties texts of the between-war period. In about equal parts it consisted of a developmental history of the parties, dwelling upon the economic issues upon which they divided; a detailed description of party structure and the laws governing suffrage, primaries, and elections; and observations with respect to bosses, spoils, patronage, and reform. Examination of the "functions" of parties was included, but in the form of conclusions stemming from the examination of the party system, rather than as an analytical framework. These functions were: "(1) selection of official personnel, (2) formulation of public policies, (3) conduct or criticism of government, (4) the party as a nationalizing and educational agency, and (5) intermediation between individual and government" (p. 470).

V. O. Key's *Politics, Parties and Pressure Groups* (5th ed., 1964), whose title indicates its broader scope, came out in 1942. It is squarely in the American style of pure description established by Bryce. Key held theories at arm's length, citing them as very tentative explanations, and did not choose to define his concepts rigorously except at the operational level. He was more concerned with the balance between parties over the long sweep of history than with their "functions and roles" (which terms he treated interchangeably). Key put hitherto impressionistic descriptions into a systematic, statistical context and invented aggregate data measures to test them. His major contribution was a hardheaded evaluation of those trends and tendencies which others believed they had discovered. He exhausted the lexicon in his effort to express in English prose the precise basis for his conclusions as "wisps," "traces," "slivers" and "scintillas" of evidence. He remained "close to his data," eschewed high-level abstractions, and avoided the methodological controversy that engulfed his colleagues. He was not unaware of functionalism—indeed, his dissertation on graft (1936, p. 400) contains an observation on the functional contribution of graft that foreshadowed Merton's famous example of a latent function (1957, pp. 71-82)—but he apparently did not consider it a point worth belaboring.

Ranney and Kendall (1956) treated Anerican parties in the light of democratic theory, and also were responsible for a typology of one-party and competitive states that, with Key's work, laid the groundwork for the subsequent comparative study of American state politics.

Just after World War II there was an outbreak of latter-day reformism in the "responsible party" movement. Schattschneider's *Party Government* (1942a) led to the contention that American parties were not performing the function of translating public wishes into political programs, and eventually the Committee of Political

Parties of the American Political Science Association produced a manifesto, *Toward a More Responsible Two-Party System* (1950) in effect urging the two parties to pull up their socks. "Party responsibility" is a normative theory to the effect that the parties should present to the electorate coherent, contrasting programs so that the voters can choose between them. The winning candidates are then obliged to enact the proffered measures or be held responsible for their misfeasance at the next election. It was felt that the decentralized structure of American parties, and particularly their want of legislative discipline comparable to that enforced in the British Parliament, prevented them from doing so. The most compelling argument against the proposal was empirical: surveys showed that barely half the voters were sufficiently aware of and concerned with party positions on issues to take advantage of those distinctions that were being made. To believe that the parties are capable of altering their behavior by any such act of will, one must perceive them as free agents, not prisoners of their social and political environment. This was the view of the party responsibility school, whose more recent statement is Burns's *Deadlock of Democracy* (1963). (See also Ranney, 1975.)

The work of theory that had the most impact in America was Maurice Duverger's *Political Parties* (1954), which constructed elaborate typologies of the party system. Of these, the distinction between elite (or "cadre") and "mass" parties has been analytically useful, although American parties do not fall neatly into either ideal type. The development of a theory of party organization by a French scholar thus brought together the domestic and comparative study of parties in American political science. Theoretical concern triggered by Duverger inspired two self-consciously theoretical examinations of the American party system. The first was Samuel J. Eldersveld's *Political Parties: A Behavioral Analysis* (1964), an empirical study of workers and leaders of the two parties in the Detroit area, a highly competitive political environment. The researchers interviewed party leaders down to the precinct level, seeking to test their understanding of its structure and goals, its organizational plan and logic, and its ability to perform its social and political functions. Departing from Michels's oligarchical theory, Eldersveld posited an organization that encompasses a series of administrative paradoxes. The party is based on a "mutually exploitative relationship—it is joined by those who would use it; it mobilizes for the sake of power those who would join it" (p. 5). The more voters the party enfolds, the more heterogeneous it becomes and the more its unity is thus threatened by factionalism. Yet it must tolerate and stabilize these conflicting interests because it cannot settle them without losing one faction or another. It is not hierarchically controlled because its leaders are dependent upon volunteers at the bottom level, so it becomes a "stratarchy," with each level conducting its own operation according to a consensual strategy perspective and a "mutual tolerance for ineptness." It relies on ambitious volunteers whose aspirations for power must often be disappointed. It copes with the evaporation of personnel by steady replacement and seeks to motivate its workers with nonpolitical rewards. As an oligarchy it manifests less iron than irony.

Such is the theory. In assessing empirically the performance of this three-legged dog, Eldersveld is torn between observing that it walks badly and marvelling that it walks at all. He finds that the party reaches all strata of society, and that each party recruits a substantial number of "deviant" leaders from the strata dominated by its opponent. Top leaders are under a strain to keep interests satisfied. They deplore their lack of sanctions and rewards, the fissile tendencies of their subordinates, and their own expendability. Even the leaders are caught in conflict between party loyalty and loyalty to their own occupational or ethnic groups. Communication between levels is unsatisfactory, leading to confusion; but some precinct leaders appear to operate efficiently despite their isolation. Republican leaders tend to be conservative, Democratic leaders liberal, but many exceptions are tolerated, producing a wide variation in ideological conformity. A rather large minority of precinct leaders do not understand much about voting behavior, and others fail to acknowledge that the overriding goal of the party is winning elections. A good many of them have left undone those things they ought to have done, particularly canvassing voters. A sample survey of the public showed over half the electorate is not reached by the party, and a good many more citizens profess to be interested in helping the party than are ever asked to do so. However, those who are contacted do, with a few puzzling exceptions, respond to the ministrations of the workers. Contacts with workers help to counter the tendency of the ideologically deviant members of a party to vote against it. Parties do inform the public, particularly its least educated members, leading them to understand better the operation of the political system and to have more confidence in it. In short, in their own bumbling and contentious way, as the theory would predict, parties do perform the manifest functions that keep them afloat and some of the latent functions that contribute to the operation of the political system.

The other significant recent work is Frank J. Sorauf's *Party Politics in America* (1968, 1972, 1976), which wrestles with data, theory, and method. Sorauf views the two parties as "aggregates of mobilizers of influence in the competition for scarce goals and resources" not merely with one another but with other political entities. Individuals, groups, and factions within the parties, interest groups, local elites and ad hoc issue groups outside them struggle for money, skills, work, and other scarce resources. Thus the party itself is not a unit but "a tripartite system of interaction, a great and enigmatic three-headed giant" consisting of (1) the party organization, leaders and activists, (2) the party in office, executives and legislators who have captured its symbols and speak for it, (3) the party in the electorate, "the regular consumers of the party's candidates and appeals." These elements are in tension as well as in coincidence, and Sorauf believes the parties are becoming obsolescent as mobilizing agencies, losing their preeminence to smaller, more specialized, more integrated, less diffuse organizations, which appeal to a sophisticated and particularistic electorate (Sorauf, 1968, pp. 4-12).

Sorauf turned to this structural approach resembling Eldersveld's after a previous effort (1964) to treat parties in functional terms which adapted Merriam's much earlier theory. He is not the first observer of parties to find disconcerting the variety of meanings the term function takes on: vote, activity, requisite, and "unintended consequence" (see Charlesworth, ed., 1967, chaps. 4, 5; Scarrow, 1967).

Burnham's evaluation of the party system flows from his preoccupation with historical cycles, alternating long periods of equilibrium with short, sharp, critical realignments. His thesis is that American political institutions, and particularly the parties, are obsolescent. They cannot adjust to social and economic change incrementally, so the deprivation of regions or classes accumulates. A massive realignment is then necessary to develop a new electoral coalition and policy consensus that will last until the next crisis. At this critical time the voter reverts to his "constitution-making role" (Burnham, 1970, p. 181). The critical election becomes "the chief tension-management device available to so peculiar a political system." Politics as usual between the critical periods is pluralistic, the outcome of group bargaining in which strategically located minorities exercise disproportionate power. But pluralists mislead when they treat equilibrium politics as the whole American political reality.[1]

GROUPS

"Group theory" as an analytical concept has attracted much controversy, but it is here necessary only to examine groups as one of a

1. Space does not permit a treatment of the many parties texts now available. Among the more interesting new additions to this growing list are Gelb and Palley (1975), Henderson (1976), and Feigert and Conway (1976).

number of institutions linking government to the governed. Yet even in this narrow context it is difficult to avoid the question: is "group" an overarching concept, by which *all* politics may be analyzed, or is it the name of one kind of phenomenon which plays a part in the transmission of power to and from governments? Does the term include primary and other small groups; the psychological category of "reference groups"; broad consensual "social movements"; administrative agencies and decision-making groups within government; racial, ethnic, and religious identifications; political parties; and the formal associations identified as "interest" or "pressure" groups? If not all these, then where does one draw the line that will give the concept explanatory power without preempting the space occupied by other concepts? Group theorists argue over whether the breadth and vagueness of the concept is an asset or a liability.

Bryce, preoccupied with parties, was aware of lobbying but strangely oblivious to other group phenomena, and it is from Arthur F. Bentley's *The Process of Government* (1908) that the concept dates. Bentley's place in the annals of political science is a remarkable one. Though this work attracted some attention from sociologists, it was dismissed by political scientists until the 1930s. Yet of all the books written at the turn of the century, his is the most influential today. Bryce no longer needs to be read, for he has been incorporated into the very fibers of the discipline; Bentley must be read because he is still new. He called attention to groups as an essential part of the political process. He developed a theory that all politics may be stated in terms of groups, their interests, and their activities (but for rhetorical purposes, he made the point so stridently that his exaggeration has often derailed analysis). He suggested a quantitative methodology to test the theory long before the data and techniques for doing so were available.

Political science did come to grips with group phenomena, but in quite a different way. The New York insurance scandals of 1913, the efforts to regulate utilities and trusts, and the periodic congressional investigations of the lobby gave evidence that something more than the parties needed to be reformed. The first phase was that of gathering information about these new institutions.

Among the early studies of groups were Rice, *Farmers and Workers in American Politics* (1924); Odegard's study of the Anti-Saloon League (1928); Herring, *Group Representation Before Congress* (1929), which sought to classify the major interest groups and their strategies; Childs, *Labor and Capital in National Politics* (1930); Duffield, *King Legion* (1931); Schattschneider, *Politics, Pressure and the Tariff* (1935); McKean, *Pressures on the Legislature of New Jersey* (1938); and Garceau, *The Political Life of the American*

Medical Association (1941). The institutional histories went back to the origins of the associations, mostly in the period between the Civil War and the Progressive era, and their continuing involvement in government as increasing regulation, higher taxes, and improved government service to business and consumers gave them something to squabble over in the political arena.

The terms "interest," "pressure," and "lobby" all had negative connotations, and the implicit assumption of many of these studies was that a "solution" should be sought to the "problem" of group "power." With his customary mistrust of conventional wisdom, Key (1943) undertook to document the basis of the American Legion's influence, and he discovered that its bonus lobbies from 1922 through 1936 had exhibited a remarkable lack of success in unseating the congressmen who voted against them.

David B. Truman in *The Governmental Process* (1951) pulled together the information from these inductive accounts, and returned to Bentley for theory in a dispassionate and systematic examination of group phenomena. He began with the discussion of groups in general: their social functions, their relations to the individual, their origin, and their organizational structure, including leadership, cohesion, and limitations. Then he turned to their relations to government and party at several points and levels, particularly those relations subsumed under the concept of "access." Truman's study became a classic in the behavioral tradition for its use of empirical theory, and for its adaptation of sociological and psychological insights to political problems. Yet it remained within the framework of political science by its concern with the relevance of these associations to the formal processes of American government.

Earl Latham (1952) called for group analysis as a replacement for "political history," which he defined as covering "the life and hard times of the official functionaries of public government." Groups he perceived as "private governments," not entirely unlike public governments, which seek to make life for their members safe, predictable, and secure by restraining, neutralizing, and conciliating their social environment. Politics is the struggle among these groups, and the legislature "referees the group struggle, ratifies the victories of the successful coalitions and records the terms of the surrenders, compromises and conquests in the form of statutes," though not, of course, without some participation in the struggle by the legislators, who themselves constitute a group. Administrators "carry out the terms of the treaties the legislators have negotiated and ratified."

This antiseptic view of the process generally replaced the evaluative slant that prevailed before Truman, and which even Truman accepted as ultimately appropriate, though premature until more empirical evidence on the functioning of groups was in. Bentley's injunction to measure has been implemented to some extent by the use of systematic interviews with lobbyists (Milbrath, 1963) and legislators (Wahlke et al., 1962). Examples of explicitly theoretical studies in the Bentley-Truman-Latham tradition are Gross (1953), which concentrates on congressional lobbying, and Zeigler (1964), which treats group phenomena in the broader context of the entire political process. Vose (e.g., 1959) interprets litigation undertaken and supported by associations for the advantage of their members in the light of interest group tactics.

When the study of interest groups was coming of age, the significant political conflicts were over economic advantage in the form of governmental subsidies, tariffs, tax relief, organizational autonomy, and freedom from regulation. The indices of group power derived from these studies, e.g., organization, numbers, legislative and administrative access, wealth, and political experience, do not appear completely relevant to more recent struggles over nonmonetary values. Nor does the concept of "interest" explain as much as that of "identification" when one turns to racial, ethnic, and ideological groups and their intransigent approach to competition for deference, rectitude, enlightenment, security, and status. The techniques of demonstrations, sit-ins, and marches pose problems of analysis to which group theory seems adaptable in principle, but not yet in practice.

Something like the old reformist belief appears in Lowi's (1969) rejection of pluralism and behavioralism as reinforcing theories. Pluralism as description is inseparable from pluralism as justification of what he labels "interest groups liberalism." That is, "value-free political science is logically committed to the norm of delegation of power because delegation of power is the self-fulfilling mechanism of prediction in modern political science" (p. 127). If the interest group scholars are really as helplessly captive of their implicit premises as that sentence implies, then the study of groups is back on Square One with Arthur Bentley.

FORMAL INSTITUTIONS

Let us now return to the original domain of political science: the formal government, its structures and processes. Separation of powers and federalism produce a familiar nine-cell table, with the rows labeled Federal, State, and Local, the columns Executive, Legislative, and Judicial. The cell boundaries have governed research, if not for theoretical reasons at least because the institutions to be described are generally found in different buildings in different cities.

The American government text tries to cover the whole territory, but its major emphasis is on the Federal row. The rest of the area was once covered by the state and local government "seed catalog," now happily almost extinct. These *tours de force* presented a summary of structural characteristics (how many justices of the State Supreme Court, in how many states they were elected, in how many appointed, whether the lieutenant governor presided over the Senate, whether railroads and utilities were regulated by the same or different commissions, and so on), plus some observations on political processes in the three or four states and cities familiar to the author, which he hopefully implied were typical of all states and cities. No better example can be found of the profession's compulsion to describe and to cover material in the face of an indescribable profusion of phenomena, an inadequate mechanism for observing and comparing them, the absence of any pressing demand for a text summarizing *all* state practices, and above all a healthy indifference on the part of college students.

Key's *Southern Politics* (1949) severed state from local, and introduced to state government the study of politics and the uses of demography. Regional volumes have since covered the politics of New England (Lockard, 1959), the border and midwestern states (Fenton, 1957, 1966), and the West (Jonas, ed., 1961). Key's (1954) study of state politics utilized *typical* states, but Dawson and Robinson (1963) demonstrated what could be done with data from *every* state when they correlated indices of party competition with state welfare budgets to test the widely accepted proposition that parties compete for votes by welfare spending. The hypothesis was disproved when controls for wealth were made. This correlation technique was further developed in Jacob and Vines (eds.) *Politics in the American States: A Comparative Analysis* (1965, 1971, 1976), which applied rank difference measures to various quantitative and qualitative indices of state performance such as revenues and expenditures, demographic and electoral variables. With these data as points of departure, the contributors examined parties, pressure groups, education, executive power, legislative competition, and other subjects. The statistical approach provided a solution to several problems that have beset those who tried to describe state governments: how to generalize analytically rather than impressionistically, how to describe a profusion of governmental patterns with indices that are more meaningful than simple arrays, ranges, and lists of deviant states. The new method consists in essence of multivariate analysis of a population of politics with $N = 50$. Recent availability of state administrative and fiscal records has enabled researchers to generalize about policy outputs in a fashion hitherto impossible (see Dye, 1966).

This new body of data, being of interval or ratio scale in precision, was subjected to more complex and revealing computation than political scientists were accustomed to: multiple correlation and regression, factor analysis, causal modelling, and cyclical analysis. Because the indices used are derived from data collected for other purposes, largely administrative, and the techniques are borrowed from other disciplines, theory is far behind technique. As Jacob and Lipsky (1968) point out, classification of such measures as input or output variables is primitive. This is to be expected, since classification is an a posteriori decision and will continue to be until researchers can select the variables they need to measure and con the officials into collecting data for them.

Among the challenging (and challenged) findings of this school are that political variables such as legislative apportionment, level of party competition, and even which party controls the government, appear to have less impact than expected upon policy outcomes as measured by the available financial indicators. Of equal or greater impact are the level of economic development of the state, its historical decisions to adopt a particular pattern of services, and regional tendencies (Hofferbert and Sharkansky, 1971). The problem of the audience for descriptions of state government remains, for most consumers are principally interested in the government of only one state and where interested in comparisons look only at its immediate neighbors. The discovery of unexplored regional patterns—for example, the similarity of the four upper middle western states with respect to citizen involvement, acceptance of taxes, local responsibility, and concern with education and dependency—suggests that clustering states may provide an intellectual and pedogogical handle for the problem (Sharkansky, 1970, p. 68).

At the local level, matters are not so simple. Fifty is a manageable number of states, their formal structure is standard, their record-keeping now adequate and comparable. Three thousand counties ranging in population from six hundred to six million, with a like variability in power, performance, and reporting, and 18,000 municipal entities presenting still greater diversity, produce a mass of data that, even if it were readily available, entirely reliable, and approximately comparable, might nevertheless prove indigestible even to a computer.

The community power approach to local government, Key's reintroduction of politics into the study of state government, new data-handling techniques that produce meaningful and sometimes unexpected generalizations about governmental units, recent attention to policy outcomes, and above all the political crises that are wracking the cities (for social scientists still are disposed to study what the society deems important), have given new life and spawned new texts in the once-moribund field of state and local government.

FEDERALISM AND THE THREE BRANCHES

The columns of the chart are the three branches of government, but before turning to each of them, we should note the continuing relevance of the concept of federalism. There is always a place for interpretation of the "new" federalism of each generation, as the balance between nation and states changes with the latest batch of Supreme Court decisions and the latest collection of statutory and administrative mechanisms by which the levels of government influence one another. The changing of the adjectives occurs with regularity: "dual," "cooperative," "creative," "direct," "marble-cake," and now "private" federalism. For the continuing re-evaluation of federal-state relations, no behavioral techniques have supplanted the old-fashioned inductive-descriptive process (e.g., Graves, 1964). A new round of evaluation had begun in 1955 with Anderson's *The Nation and the States: Rivals or Partners?* and MacMahon's *Federalism Mature and Emergent*. The "federalism workshop" at Chicago led to Grodzins's *The American System*, published posthumously (1966), which centered around the notion of "sharing" and the "marble cake" analogy. In this treatment the American system defies the neatness implicit in the formality of dual federalism, having built into it a congeries of informal arrangements for consultation, mutual assistance, professional standards, partisan politics, and fund transfers. Private business and civic organizations participate in the melee, producing a composite of order and chaos, often with "antagonistic cooperation" to achieve common goals. Grodzins's portrait has intuitive appeal, it offers new insights, and it is bolstered by examples, illustrations, and some legal and economic data. But there is no theoretically elegant or systematically predictive way of stating his basic proposition that the federal structure is a hodgepodge. It is a necessary triumph of brute description over clarity and logic.

In the first column of our table, labeled Executive, fall the studies of administration (see chap. 5) and the literature on the governors and the president. Neustadt's *Presidential Power* (1960, 1976), a contemporary classic, differs in theory and method from the earlier classics such as Corwin (1940) largely in its attention to the political rather than the legal-constitutional aspects of the office. Barber's psychological-motivational appraisal, *The Presidential Char-*

acter (1972), will have a great impact on future studies of the chief executive. Studies of the governor and the mayor are usually traditional, and are modeled on the presidential studies (e.g., Ransone, 1956). Schlesinger (1957) uses biographical data in a recruitment study of governors over a period of eighty years. (For other recent treatments of the presidency, see Finer, 1974; Tugwell and Cronin, 1974; Thomas, 1975; Cronin, 1975; Kessel, 1975.)

Attention to Congress traces back to Wilson's *Congressional Government* (1885). It was a forerunner of the realist school because Wilson saw through the formalities to the importance of the committee system, the power relationships it entailed, and the consequences of dispersed congressional power for the political system as a whole. The data were drawn largely from the press, historians, and the *North American Review*. Indeed, Wilson takes it for granted that all the relevant facts about Congress are obvious; the task of the political scientist is to interpret them—in this instance, in the light of the alternative of British government. Nor were the demands of realism so rigorous as to require him to take the train from Baltimore to Washington to observe the body in session.

There was a revival of interest in Congress in the 1950s. Representing the procedural and historical approach are Galloway's studies (1953, 1961). Gross (1953) utilized Bentley's group theory in the analysis of Congress. Behavioral techniques were applied to the upper house by Donald Matthews in *U.S. Senators and Their World* (1960). Matthews interviewed senators and those around them, treated accumulated biographical material statistically, analyzed the ouput of the body, collected the "folkways" and "rules of the game," and appraised their consequences for legislative functioning.

Turner (1951) produced the prototype study of roll-call voting; MacRae (1958) pioneered in systematic Guttmann-scale analysis of issue domains; Froman (1963) dissected partisan, regional, and ideological blocs. Fenno's (1966) study of the House Appropriations Committee was couched in systems terminology. A longitudinal study by Davis et al. (1966) of what agencies ask for and what Congress gives them is at the same time theoretical, pragmatic, and mathematically sophisticated—a combination that is bound to inspire imitation. (See also Fenno, 1973; Wildavsky, 1974; Mayhew, 1974; Brezina and Overmyer, 1974; Ripley, 1967, 1969, 1975.)

An important exception to the earlier observation that voting studies have not usually linked inputs, internal processes, and outputs falls in the area of legislative studies. Miller and Stokes (chap. 16 in Campbell et al., 1966) in a sample of congressional districts surveyed the attitudes of the electorate on several broad policy matters, interviewed the candidates for Congress on their orientations and their perception of their constituency attitudes on these same issues, and finally recorded the congressmen's roll-call votes indicating their formal positions. This research design permitted an examination of the patterns of representation, including such traditional ones as the instructed delegate, the Burkean trustee, the party responsibility, and the virtual representation models. (See also Cnudde and McCrone, 1966, who reanalyzed the same data.) It was found that representation could take several paths and that it differed between issues of civil rights, welfare programs, and foreign policy, with the congressmen having greater leeway to use their own judgment in the latter areas. The research encompassed three critical steps in the flow of policy demands: the orientation of the public, differentiated into minority and majority party; the congressman's perceptions of these orientations, his own viewpoint, and the relation between the two; and his formal action to influence the outcome of a decision. The positive correlations were reassuring: public attitudes *do* have some impact on policy. But the patterns are complex, and even the massive effort involved in this study did not reveal every link in the chain. The legislative processes that take place in committees and party conferences could not be examined, nor could the outcome of the decision in the House of Representatives as it passed through the Senate and the executive processes. Nevertheless, the research reveals that, given large resources, the existing techniques of political research can indeed trace processes crucial to democratic politics.

The American Political Science Association's sponsorship of congressional internships is a demonstration of the scholarly impact of a program that puts young scholars in a position to observe an institution. The monographs that resulted are described by Huitt and Peabody (1969).

At the state level, the pioneer in legislative recruitment and systematic biographical examination was Charles Hyneman (1938, 1940), who sought to discover who legislators were and how this affected what they did. Belle Zeller (1954) under APSA auspices sent questionnaires to qualified observers in every state, and analyzed them to assess the impact of parties and pressure groups. Wahlke and his colleagues interviewed nearly all the members of four state legislatures and produced a work (*The Legislative System*, 1962) that was quantitative, comparative, and explicitly theoretical (see also Rosenthal, 1974). The study of American legislative process in both Congress and the states moved out of the reading-book stage with two texts, Keefe and Ogul (1964, 1968) and Jewell and Patterson (1966, 1972), the latter explicit in its functionalism. It defines the functions of the legislature as "the management of conflict" (by deliberation, decision, adjudication, and catharsis) and the "integration of the polity" (by authorization, legitimation, and representation).

At the local level, legislative bodies are composed of so few members that one may use small-group theory (see Barber, 1966), or may cover a large number of bodies so as to make the municipal council, rather than the individual councilman, the unit of analysis. Census data to describe the community, voting statistics to represent electoral inputs, interviews with councilmen to review either consensual political attitudes or interaction within the group, and municipal budgets and records to gauge policy outputs, all may be combined in this research design. One extensive project has as its source of data eighty-nine California city councils (see Eulau and Eyestone, 1968).

The origins of American political science were in the study of public law, and though this no longer dominates the discipline as it once did, it remains a significant part of the study of American government. The early study of legal philosophy in the German tradition was followed in the 1920s by the case method, with the Cushman case book (1925) in its regular revisions providing the material about which the study of constitutional law revolves. Paradoxically, for a time political scientists were intrigued with doctrine as set forth in the Court's decisions, while some of the justices themselves (e.g., Cardozo, 1921) were insisting that the backgrounds of the justices were an important factor in their decisions. When the Court somersaulted in the late 1930s, the antiseptic doctrinary point of view became untenable. Pritchett (1941) introduced analysis in terms of blocs of like-minded justices, which ultimately led to the school of judicial behavior, represented by the works of John Schmidhauser, David Danelski, Fred Kort, Eloise Snyder, Walter Murphy, Stuart Nagel, Harold Spaeth, Joseph Tanenhaus, Sidney Ulmer, and the prodigious output of Glendon Schubert (1960a, 1960b, 1963, 1964, 1965a, 1965b, 1974). This research, summarized in Jacob (1965) and Pritchett (1968), shows that judges are appointed for reasons of their partisan attachments and policy beliefs, and once on the bench they *tend to* behave as other persons of comparable regional, ideological, denominational, socioeconomic, and professional backgrounds would behave if they were intent upon making their political views prevail—which is not to say that they are uninfluenced by legal precedents. Conclusions as to how justices do behave (which can be only imperfectly known until the norm of judicial reticence further weakness) appear to be influenced by how researchers think they should behave and sometimes, one suspects, by how the researchers think the public should think they behave. Recently it appears that judicial scholars are almost as concerned with the opinions of other judicial scholars as with the opinions of the judges, leading to a spate of methodological polemic that can be sampled in Schubert (1965a) and Becker (1964). In 1961 the *American Political Science Review* gave up its annual summaries of the Supreme Court's decisions started in 1918. The *Supreme Court Review*, edited at the Chicago law school, took their place.

One important strain of writing in American government that does not quite fit into any of the previous categories is political psychology. Lasswell (1930) brought Freudian insights to the examination of political role playing, upsetting some members of the profession by advancing the notion that entirely irrelevant private motives may be displaced onto political objects and causes. Notable examples of this genre are George and George's study of Woodrow Wilson (1956), Smith et al. (1956), Lane (1962), and Edelman (1964). The origins of children's perceptions of politics have recently been investigated in such political socialization studies as Easton and Hess (1962), Sigel (1968), Greenstein (1965), and Weissberg (1974). The internalization of democratic norms in adults was examined by Prothro and Grigg (1960) and McClosky (1964). The problem of disentangling the effects of personality needs, acculturation, and life situation from the reaction to official policies (the political part of political behavior) is a difficult one. Each generation of scholars seeks a fresh start by giving the study a new name. Only 13 percent of those listing political psychology as their field are forty years old or over, compared to 26 percent of those listing voting behavior and 40 percent of those listing public opinion (Eulau, 1969b).

TRENDS

Four obvious developments in the study of American government since Bryce have become apparent:

(1) A widening of scope, from exclusive concern with the state and its formal legal-constitutional arrangements to interest in parties, state and local government, and a vaguely understood entity called public opinion; then to interest groups and mass phenomena, especially voting behavior. As the boundaries of the discipline expanded it was natural that the work of psychologists, sociologists, anthropologists, and economists should become more relevant.

(2) Increasing technical versatility, moving from dependence upon public documents and the impressions of those who happened to witness the actions of prominent figures, onward to systematic mass surveys and elite interviews. With increasing quantification went an understanding of measurement and sampling as well as a self-

consciousness of the relation of the observer to the observed, of the criteria of evidence, and of the tentativeness of one's conclusions.

(3) A decline in didacticism. This was evident first in the separation of normative and factual statements; then in a tendency to present the pros and cons of every proposal to alter institutions, and later in a recognition that merely changing the legal rules does not always have the expected effect, and often sets in motion complex interactions and side-effects. This last viewpoint, perceived by the evangelists in the field as a justification of inaction and support for the status quo, has led to a rejection of behavioralism on their part.

(4) A search for theories that overarch domestic and foreign phenomena, inevitably blurring the earlier distinction between American government and comparative government (see Keech and Prothro, 1968). There is hardly more "theory of American government' today than there was in Bryce's time. But competing, pluralist-versus-elitist approaches to the introductory course may lead to a more ideological stance.

PRESENT CONCERNS

Among the research problems now confronting the discipline are these:

(1) The accumulated findings of the study of voting behavior and the party system still have to be synthesized into a generally acceptable framework. Sorauf, moving from functionalism back to structural analysis, covariation, and "intended, goal-seeking behavior" (1968, p. 424), faces the old problem of inferring causality which the functionalists dodged. He deals with it by examining the party first as a dependent and then as an independent variable. Two other strategies presently offer some prospect of coping with the causality problem. One is path modeling, which depends upon some rather sweeping statistical assumptions. The other is the more familiar reliance upon time sequence, a method that is more promising now that three decades of empirical research results are available for reanalysis. A significant collection of essays resulted from the joint efforts of historians and political scientists to examine the party system concept (Chambers and Burnham 1967).

(2) "Policy ouputs" have been studied by Ranney (1968). Improvement of state and local record handling stimulated the study of outcomes of decentralized policy decisions (Wilson, 1968). We have realized how exclusively the discovery of techniques for understanding mass behavior a generation ago centered our attention on

input processes. The pressure of parents and teachers on school budgets is perceived as political science, but the impact of budgets on children was left to the educationists. How farmers shape farm policy is politics, but what farm policy does to farmers is economics. Or, consider the concerns of *The Coming of Post-Industrial Society* (Bell, 1973), *Energy Politics* (Davis, 1974), *The Politics of Revenue Sharing* (Dommel, 1974), *Presidential Spending Power* (Fisher, 1975), *Political Realities of Urban Planning* (Allensworth, 1975), and *Citizens and the Environment* (Caldwell et al., 1976).

To name a few other things that might have been studied more intensively by political scientists: the effects of *Miranda* and similar decisions on the attitudes of criminals and the incidence of crime and conviction; the consequences of categorical welfare grants upon the orientation of their recipients toward government, employment, and the political system; public responses to taxation increases, decreases, and shifts of incidence; the reaction of the poor to community action programs; and the effect of open-housing laws upon the real estate market.

(3) Study of "conversion" processes within government still uses the techniques of elite interview and documentary analysis, and modern scholars have done little but periodically update the classical studies of the pioneers. Study of "feedback" processes—public response to actions and announcements of officials, and the tendencies to communicate, vote, demonstrate, or confront that these responses generate—need more systematic examination. This may occur after the policy ouput studies have made their contribution.

For its first half century, political science was almost exclusively preoccupied with what went on *within* the box called government. For nearly thirty years it has been primarily concerned with what went *into* that box. If the polity and the discipline that describe it survive that long, perhaps the rest of the century will see more interest manifested in what comes out of it—public policy outputs.

(4) More than any other branch of the discipline, American government has derived its imperative and motive power from the problems that confront the nation. It could hardly be otherwise. These of course have changed: corruption, machines, trusts, tariffs, immigration, naturalization, prohibition, interventionism, depression, unemployment, debt, civil liberties, defense, communism, space, urbanization, poverty, welfare, inflation, conservation, population, ecology, consumerism. Part of the task of American specialists will continue to be description of the institutions and processes through which decisions are made and implemented with respect to each new issue as it arises. Otherwise the contribution of political science would be indistinguishable from history's.

Each new set of issues demands some alteration in technique, and the rising urban violence beginning in Watts in 1965 strained the capacity of a discipline organized to study relatively stable processes. On the whole, the contribution of political scientists along with other behaviorists to the work of the National Advisory Commission on Civil Disorders and the National Commission on the Causes and Prevention of Violence (e.g., Graham and Gurr, 1969) demonstrated adaptability, the capacity to communicate with a large audience and to contribute, if not to the solution, at least to the understanding of a complex and emergent problem

4. POLITICAL THEORY AS HISTORY, PHILOSOPHY, AND SCIENCE

Ralph C. Chandler

The field of political theory is undergoing redefinition. There are those today who doubt that theory ought to be described as a separate field of political science at all. Has theorizing not become a major activity of all fields of the discipline, from organization theory in public administration to process theory in comparative politics? And is not the validity of theoretical propositions in these fields sought in an understanding of empirical phenomena, and by data gathering and operationalizing procedures, which concerned Hobbes and Rousseau not at all? Did not Robert A. Dahl accurately predict in his celebrated "Epitaph" (1961) that the behavioral mood would so permeate the discipline as to become the first victim of its own triumph?

Yet Hobbes and Rousseau are still said to be political theorists. Heinz Eulau wrote that perhaps Dahl was too optimistic, that the social sciences are characterized by "an immanent tension between tradition and innovation, between the ancient and the modern" (1969c). It is a fact that graduate students offering theory as a field of examination are still expected in many schools to be familiar with *Leviathan* and *The Social Contract*, as well as the other classics forming the great tradition of political thought.

Is theory to be understood therefore as an academic field or as an intellectual activity (McDonald and Rosenau, 1968)? Are Deutsch and Rieselbach justified in writing confidently that political theory continues to be "an organized body of human activity" and has "an established structure" (in Haas and Kariel, 1970)? Is everyone who claims to be a theorist therefore a theorist? If so, perhaps no one is. Or, if there are at least two kinds of theorists, empirical ones and nonempirical ones, and various uses of the word theory, do all belong in the same field, or even in the same discipline? Tertullian once exclaimed, "What has Jerusalem to do with Athens?" Might a bewildered graduate student be forgiven for wondering what New Haven, Lasswell, and Almond have to do with Athens, Plato, and Aristotle?

In this chapter I shall attempt to deal with the various and ambiguous meanings of political theory today. This is, of course, a presumptuous undertaking. The reader I have in mind is the graduate student mentioned above, who may be trying to understand the spectrum of thought usually represented in the theory field. The student's spectroscope must be his own eyes as they move along the pages of a hundred books and articles. But which hundred books and articles should he read, and in roughly what order? How do the works selected relate to one another? Can they be classified in some meaningful way?

POLITICAL THEORY AS HISTORY

The reading program could well begin with David Easton's *The Political System* (2d ed., 1971), first published in 1953, just fifty years after the founding of the American Political Science Association. Easton's assessment of, and complaint about, political theory at the time was that it was exclusively interested in philosophical, "normally meaning moral" problems (see especially chap. 18). The study of political theory had been equated with the study of value theory. Further, and much worse, in Easton's opinion, American writers on theory had departed from theory's proper function as a "vehicle whereby articulate and intelligent individuals conveyed their thoughts on the actual direction of affairs and offered for serious consideration some ideas about the desirable course of events" (1953, p. 234).

Their departure was into historicism. The most influential works on theory of the day, those by Dunning (1902–20), McIlwain (1932), and Sabine (1937), were merely repositories of information about the meaning, internal consistency, and historical development of past political values. Political theory, limited therefore as value theory and displayed as something of a museum piece, was not active and constructive in Easton's opinion. Political scientists were not laying bare their moral premises so that the knowable consequences of those premises could be explored and self-consciously compared with the way writers of the past might have viewed standards of right. A student could read Dunning, for example, and not know that Rousseau came much closer to having a conversation with Aristotle about certain common and practical problems than he did to regarding *The Politics* as a historical curiosity. In short, political theory was not being approached as an intellectual *activity* in 1953 (McDonald and Rosenau, 1968).

Times have changed. The impact of the thesis of *The Political System*, not fully explicated here, was so to broaden the meaning of the term "political theory" that a radical transformation of thinking about political thought was accomplished in political science in the 1960s. But Eulau is more right than not in suggesting the reformation was more like a renaissance.

> The history of political science as an independent field of inquiry can be written as a history of successive emancipations from earlier limitations and false starts. Yet, these successive emancipations have been additive rather than cumulative: the old survives with the new, and the old acquires new defenders as the new relies on old apostles. It is impossible to say, therefore, that anything has been disproven as long as conventional tests of proof—the requisites of scientific status in any field of knowledge—are not commonly accepted by political scientists, or, in fact, are rejected by some as altogether irrelevant in political inquiry [Eulau, 1969c, pp. 7-8].

Since a renaissance looks backward as well as forward, and since historicism is still very much in evidence in the theory field, let us take the historicist orientation as seriously as Easton did, though not now with his pessimism (cf. Cobban, 1953; Laslett, 1956; Thorson, 1961), and refer to the three classic examples of the historicist approach.

The first volume of William A. Dunning's three-volume work, *A History of Political Theories*, was published in 1902, the second in 1905, and the third in 1920. The teacher and his *opus magnum* decisively influenced a generation of American political scientists. Charles E. Merriam for example, noted in the preface of his important *American Political Ideas:* "This study is the outgrowth of investigations begun in the Seminar on American political philosophy given by Professor Dunning, in Columbia University, 1896- 97, and the writer wishes to acknowledge his deep sense of obligation for the inspiration given, and for subsequent encouragement in the prosecution of this work" (1920, p. iii). Just five years later, however, Merriam was departing from the "formal" approach of his mentor and calling on the American Political Science Association to pursue "another angle of approach . . . to look at political behavior as one of the essential objects of inquiry" of political scientists (Dahl, 1961b, p. 764). Merriam's presidential address of 1925 is generally considered the opening salvo of the Chicago school, and the Dunning's methodological conservatism did not survive the subsequent barrage.

Dunning's training as a historian shaped his approach. His focus was on the problems and the process of historical change. So far was he from conceiving political theory as any kind of reflection that he

isolated political ideas as the most important causal factors in historical change. History itself he understood as a product of the interplay
of political ideas with social practices and institutions. One derives
political theory *from* history because theory is a summation of
observations about political facts and practices, especially as they are
related to the legal forms of political life. "As discrimination and
selection are inevitable, the present history will prefer those lines of
development in which political ideas appear as legal rather than as
ethical" (1902, p. xxi).

Charles H. McIlwain's *The Growth of Political Thought in the
West* (1932) takes a different view of the relationship between
political ideas and social activity. While Dunning saw political ideas
as a direct influence on the course of events, McIlwain saw them as
an effect of social activity. In his opinion, ideas may condition
subsequent ideas, but they have no necessary impact on action.
Political theory is sets of ideas which themselves have a history. The
history of political theory is largely a history of rationalizations, of
justifications for behavior otherwise determined.

> It is almost a law of the development of political thought that political
> conceptions are the by-product of actual political relations, and oftentimes
> in history these relations have changed materially long before this change
> attracted the notice even of those most affected by it, or became a part of
> their unconscious habits of thought, much less of their political speculation,
> when they had any [1932, p. 391].

If political ideas follow upon practices, and are inconsequential
by themselves, it follows for McIlwain's variation of historicism that
the historical conditions surrounding the emergence of an idea are
the proper research areas for the political theorist. Political theory is
a branch of the sociology of knowledge. The theorist shows the way
in which the social milieu determines political thought. He also
shows the moral side of the theoretical justification for existing
political arrangements. Every governmental system has a moral basis
of political obligation. The theorist making the moral basis explicit
still cannot demonstrate, however, that moral ideas are necessarily
influential in the course of history. McIlwain believed that men must
live by myths, and he had a preferred set of them which formed a
rationale for contemporary democracy. But he consistently maintained that myths seldom have the power to persuade men to act.
German National Socialism in the 1930s might have convinced him
otherwise.

The leading exponent and chief practitioner of the historicist
conception of political theory is George H. Sabine. His *A History of
Political Theory* (1937; 4th ed., 1973) has exercised deeper influence

on political theory in the United States than any other single work. Sabine combines elements from both Dunning and McIlwain. He agrees with Dunning that political thought is an aspect of the political process which interacts with and influences social action. He agrees with McIlwain that an important task of the theorist is the description and analysis of the moral judgments implicit in each system of thought studied. Sabine disagrees with Dunning by insisting that moral judgments are not inferior to factual propositions. And he disagrees with McIlwain by holding that moral judgments need not be viewed as mere rationalizations of activity, but may be influential factors in history.

In two brilliantly argued essays published in 1939, Sabine points out that political theories are operative at two levels: as social philosophy and as ideology. In their ideological aspect, theories are psychological phenomena not subject to empirical verification. They are beliefs. They are "events in people's minds and factors in their conduct" (1939a, p. 10). Events in people's minds can be translated and transformed into events in history. And events in political theory can produce events in politics (1939b, p. 170).

Sabine maintains that a theory does not need to have a measurable impact on human actions to be worth the social scientist's attention. The social scientist must, of course, limit statements about truth and falsity, which are statements made from evidence, to statements referring to factual conditions. But there are moral propositions and statements about values which are "always the reaction of human preferences to some state of social and physical fact" (1937, p. viii), and which are simply not deducible from nor reducible to facts. A major reason the social scientist is interested in moral propositions, understood by Sabine as expressions of emotion not rationally discoverable, is that moral propositions are just as subject to questions of logical consistency as are factual propositions.

A political theory is invariably a statement of preference. It is a value judgment, a moral enterprise, and, taken as a whole, cannot be said to be true. It can be psychologically true. And the theorist ought to be able to isolate the psychological influence of a theory on the actions of men. He can also analyze the factual statements implicit in any theory and set them against the facts as they are known at any given time. Political theory is therefore not devoid of concern for empirical truth. In fact, Sabine feels free to pass judgment on the validity of various causal theories and factual assertions in political thought. It is the duty of the theorist, in his view, to examine the logic of statements embodying value judgments and to comment on their consistency. The full meaning of statements of preference must be exposed.

Sabine considers all of this activity a matter of historical narration. The purpose of studying political theory is to aid our understanding of the development of certain important concepts such as liberalism and democracy. The theorist determines categories for classifying the social and psychological conditions which contributed to the growth, diffusion, or decline of the concepts. He is able to describe a variety of value systems which have emerged in the past, and he has learned how to inquire logically into their meaning and possible consequences. The end served, however, does not go very far beyond a detailed report of the quality of a past theorist's moral speculation. Are there logical incompatibilities in it? Are the assumptions of his moral system made clear? Are the evaluative assumptions of the historian also made clear? Is the description of the social conditions molding the theorist's values reasonably accurate?

At no point in Sabine's *History* is the process of evaluation itself examined. The nature of the process and its problems are ignored as being outside the purview of political theory. Easton rightly asked how a constructive redefinition of political goals is possible if political theory is only a relativistic history of values. Clearly, historicism had put a limitation on theory which it had to throw off if new solutions to recurring problems of thought and practice were to be essayed, and if old speculation about the same problems was to be made more understandable and relevant to modern men.

POLITICAL THEORY AS PHILOSOPHY

We do not come to empiricism yet. Before science there was philosophy.

For about 2300 years there was no distinction made between political theory and political philosophy. The original works constituting the heritage of political hermeneutics through Burke—which the student must read on their own terms—were written by men who were major philosophers as well as prominent political thinkers. Burke is considered the *terminus ad quem* of the tradition in agreement with Deutsch and Rieselbach (in Haas and Kariel, 1970), who point out that after the beginning of the nineteenth century the major preoccupation of political theorists was not with the development of their own theories, but with the explication of the ideas of their predecessors. Among the few proponents of new ideas in the nineteenth century, such as John Stuart Mill, Karl Marx, Vilfredo Pareto, and Max Weber, "none considered himself, or was considered by others, primarily a theorist of politics" (1970, p. 78).

Plato, Aristotle, and Locke wrote about whatever concerned them. When the "field" of political theory was relevant to the discussion at hand, they wrote about political theory. They also wrote about economics, sociology, history, and theology. As Bluhm aptly observed (1965), a modern dean would not know in which department to employ them. There was among these writers a surprising unanimity of opinion about the proper subject matter of political theory. Most of them focused combined normative and realistic considerations on the concept of justice. From the Greek Sophists to Machiavelli and Hobbes, there was also a more exclusively realistic or pragmatic emphasis on the concept of power.

During the long period of what some would describe as its captivity to philosophy, political theory was deemed to have prescriptive and evaluative functions as well as descriptive and explanatory ones. Traditional philosophy, of course, had a deep interest in ethical and normative judgments. So it did not occur to philosophers writing about justice and power to draw the fact-value dichotomy accepted by many political scientists today. Neither did any clear distinctions exist in their work among the burning philosophical, theological, and political issues of the day. When Thomas Aquinas endorsed monarchy, for example, he was in process of addressing himself to the more fundamental problem, for him, of how to provide a just order for a united Christendom in which *regnum* and *sacerdotium* had jurisdictions needing better definition (see Douglass, 1976).

Whatever the conceptual framework philosophers employed in the centuries of the captivity, however, the most impressive evidence of political theory's dependence on philosophy is that theorists were almost always guided by the rules of formal logic and the developments in theories of knowledge which guided philosophy. Yet philosophy itself was in a kind of captivity after Aristotle. John Herman Randall writes entertainingly on the point:

In ignorance of her deeds, it is idle to analyze philosophy's character. It is far wiser to tell the story of her life. She belongs to the oldest profession in the world: she exists to give men pleasure, and to satisfy their imperious needs. When young and blooming, she was a favorite of the rich but cultivated and discriminating Greeks, who kept her in idleness for the sheer delight of her conversation. She had not even to lift a finger; and it was rumored the gods themselves loved her and her alone. But as she grew older, her charms faded, she waxed more austere, and took to giving sound advice on every occasion. And when the Romans burst into her garden, with their American moralism and fear of idleness, they led her off and set her to work as the handmaiden of Morality. She has been a working-girl ever since [1962, p. 4].

Philosophy as the handmaiden of morality and the preoccupation of American students of political theory with history, exegesis, and methodological conservatism was a deadly combination indeed. If the classical tradition were to be resurrected in the United States, many believed the new life had to come in the form of bold and imaginative essays demonstrating the contemporaneity of ancient philosophical discussions. Several works attempt to meet the challenge. A representative sampling of them would include *An Introduction to Political Philosophy* (Murray, 1953); *What Is Political Philosophy?* (Strauss, 1959); *Politics and Vision* (Wolin, 1960); *History of Political Philosophy* (Strauss and Cropsey, 1963); *Man and Society* (Plamenatz, 1963); and *Theories of the Political System* (Bluhm, 1965).

In a little gem of a book, A. R. M. Murray explains why political thinkers tend to divide into scientists on the one hand and philosophers on the other. Murray gives David Hume his due, demonstrating that the only important alternative to Hume's thoroughgoing empiricism in political philosophy is the special type of rationalism known among the initiated as Hegelian Idealism. The dogmatic claims of Plato and other pre-Hegelian rationalists to have discovered moral principles of a priori certainty conceals the basic purpose of philosophy in Murray's view.

> For philosophy consists essentially in directing the process of thinking upon itself with a view to ascertaining what thought consists in, and what it can establish. To lay down moral dogmas about the rights and duties of governments and citizens without first considering how far this is a rational process is the very antithesis of philosophy properly conceived [1953, p. 22].

Perhaps the two most remarkable books on politics published in 1960 were *The American Voter* (Campbell et al.) and *Politics and Vision* (Wolin). Both have to do with integrative identity. *The American Voter* suggests the act of voting to be a choice of personal identity. *Politics and Vision* argues the general theme that political theory has been in disrepair for three hundred years because it could not provide the basis of man's social identity: an agreed-upon set of common involvements, or a consensus drawn from (not imposed upon) the body politic as to the valuable purposes of statecraft.

Sheldon S. Wolin rejects the Platonic answer to the problem of integrative identity because it reduces politics to "the art of imposition" and somehow loses the political dimension in the pursuit of ultimate truth. He admires Christianity for contributing the answer of the community-building properties of belief, but finally appraises Christianity as unable to solve the tension between faith and organi-

zation. In a brilliant analysis of another commonly accepted answer
to the integrative identity problem, liberalism, Wolin describes it as
"a philosophy of sobriety, born in fear, nourished by disenchant-
ment, and prone to believe that the human condition was and was
likely to remain one of pain and anxiety" (1960, pp. 293- 4). Thus
liberalism finds itself in alliance with traditional conservatism and
communism, all three positing social conformity or "socialized
conscience" as the proper standard of behavior. Finally, in Wolin's
interpretation, pluralism is inadequate because it escapes from the
dilemma of modern political philosophy through fragmentation into
group or factional politics.

Standing alongside *Politics and Vision* in the breadth of its
scholarship and the provocativeness of its approach is John Plamenatz's two-volume work, *Man and Society* (1963). Plamenatz sets out
to examine critically the most familiar ideas and assumptions about
society and government inherited from the past. He does so despite
the fact that these ideas and assumptions are "out of fashion"
because "sociologists and political scientists in many places . . . now
believe that they have less to learn from them than from one
another" (1963, p. x). Plamenatz in an unoffensive way reminds
social scientists that for all their efforts to be lucid, precise, and
realistic, they are often more obscure, or looser in their arguments,
or more incoherent, than the makers of the old theories which they
neglect on the ground that they are irrelevant. The modern social
scientist sometimes, though he does not know it, "repeats what has
been said as well, or better, long ago" (1963, p. xii).

Plamenatz recommends, and himself follows, the discipline of
attempting to discover what was really being said in other times: how
Hobbes, for example, used such words as "law," "right," "obligation," and "consent." By seeing how Hobbes used them and what
arguments he constructed, we might learn how better to use the
words, and the concepts, ourselves. Did Hobbes treat *right* as absence
of obligation? The explanations of *Leviathan* may tell the student
that he does. They may also suggest against the relief of Hobbes's
self-assertive and prudent man certain modern distinctions of value.
Plamenatz's perspective and modesty of purpose in *Man and Society*
is reminiscent of Bentham's in *A Fragment on Government* (Mack,
1969). The latter was designed, in Bentham's words, to teach the
student "to place more confidence in his own strength, and less in
the infallibility of great names—to help him to emancipate his judgment from the shackles of authority" (Plamenatz, 1963 p. xii).

On some occasions, what one attempts in scholarship may be
more important than what he accomplishes. In *Theories of the
Political System* (1965), William T. Bluhm has attempted to bridge

the chasm between normative and empirical political theory and point the way toward constructing a grand theoretical design. He fails, as one might expect, but he deserves the serious consideration of students of theory for the imaginative and bold way he links the traditional masters of political philosophy with modern political scientists. His reviewer in the *American Political Science Review* (Riemer, 1965, p. 696) did well to capture Bluhm's heuristic, juxtaposing technique by merely listing his chapter titles: "Naturalistic Political Science: Thucydides and Snyder," "Noumenalist Political Science: Plato and Strauss," "The Aristotelian Bridge: Aristotle, Lipset, and Almond," "The Augustinian Bridge: St. Augustine, Niebuhr, and Morgenthau," "Thomas and Neo-Thomism: St. Thomas and Maritain," "Naturalistic Prudence: Machiavelli and Neustadt," "Mathematics in Naturalistic Political Science: Hobbes, Downs, and Riker," "From Political Science to Ideology: Lockean Theory," "Naturalistic Political Science as Interest-Group Theory: Harrington and Bentley," "The Theory of Democratic Virtue: Rousseau, Friedrich, and Burns," "Conservative Immanentism: Burke and Lippmann," "Marxian Theory: Marx, Engels, and Mills," "Scientific Liberalism: John Stuart Mill and Christian Bay."

Bluhm argues that the "discordant variety" of modern political science can be transcended by a critical, comparative review of classical theories and modern analogues. A synthesis can be constructed in which "political ethics would not swallow up descriptive science, nor would ethical questions be reduced to behavioral ones" (1965, p. 487). The Socratic dialectic of the Platonists can be carried on, but with more elaborate and sophisticated data. Plato can finally sit down with the Sophists. His numbers "would lose their mysticism without losing their moral value" (1965, p. 488).

Bluhm's interpretation of individual "noumenalists" (by which he designates thinkers holding that the good order is known by an intuitive faculty), and of individual "naturalists" (by which he specifies theorists maintaining that reality consists only of empirical phenomena), leaves something to be desired. His dichotomy-drawing method of analysis is questionable as well. But Bluhm has made a solid contribution to thinking about a catholic political theory, the construction of which is perhaps the primary task of the field in the next generation.

Other major attempts to synthesize political philosophy and political description are listed in Deutsch and Rieselbach (in Haas and Kariel, 1970). Among the most influential of these are Carl J. Friedrich's *Man and His Government* (1963), which Deutsch and Rieselbach describe as "the most important work of its kind to appear during the last several decades," and George Catlin's *Syste-*

matic Politics (1962). The latter is the fourth volume of a series begun in 1927 and continued in 1938 and 1939, and which Charles S. Hyneman reviews as both erudite and undisciplined (1963, pp. 956-7). Having a less general purpose, but also constituting efforts to link the tradition of political philosophy to modern science, are Arnold Brecht's *Political Theory* (1959), which champions the cause of positivism, and Leslie Lipson's *The Democratic Civilization* (1964), which combines old and new thinking about the concept of democracy. See also on this subject Cassinelli (1961), Sartori (1962), Thorson (1962), Spitz (1958, 1963), and Pitkin (1965, 1966). Of particular relevance is Christian Bay's *The Structure of Freedom* (1958) and "Politics and Pseudopolitics: A Critical Evaluation of Some Behavioral Literature" (1965, pp. 39-51).

Bay advances certain human goals for politics, largely in psychological terms under Maslow's influence, and relates these goals to classical political theory. He rejects as "pseudopolitics" any theory which does not ask the right question, namely, what is politics *for?* Politics is definitely not for promoting private or interest-group advantage. It is for "activity aimed at improving or protecting conditions for the satisfaction of human needs and demands in a given society or community, according to some universalistic scheme of priorities, implicit or explicit" (1965, p. 40). Eulau chastizes Bay for making politics a definitional game once more and for leaving out of his restrictive definition political activity directed toward evil goals, which surely accounts for some of the most interesting aspects of political phenomena (1969c, p. 13). Eulau suspects that any universalistic scheme for ordering needs and values would be nothing less than a modern version of the closed society. But Bay has sounded a theme which will not easily be put down among younger political scientists. If behavioral political science continues to stake out policy science as one of its domains, the nature of the goals of public policy will be increasingly difficult to set aside as questions better left to the philosophers. Eulau himself once declared the purpose of political inquiry to be man (1963, p. 133). If man is more than a seeker or a victim of power, and if he lives at least a part of his life outside any system, Henry S. Kariel has stated the task of what might be termed neo-normative theory well enough:

I should like to insist only that we resolutely challenge every order of facts and allocation of values said to be "given" or "authoritative" or "official," beginning with those which are most overpowering. . . .

Assuming that institutional boundaries are not settled, we must reject the notion that our intellectual problem is to derive general laws (and, ultimately, causal laws) from the life lived within the boundaries. We must therefore realize that there are limits to systemic analysis, that is, to efforts to index aggregates of behavior within systems and efforts to pyramid generalizations into a body of empirical propositions. We must recognize that such generalizations are not about open-ended systems, about men as agents, or about consciously purposeful action. I am assuming, in other words, that there is something more than immediately describable reality, that there are unacknowledged additional resources, that these might yet be used to satisfy our need to remain alive to undescribed possibilities, and finally that norms might be posited to discover and develop latent potentialities. Insofar as behavioral research confronts what Camus termed the "absurd," normative theorists can dramatize and thereby redeem such absurdities [Haas and Kariel, 1970, pp. 116-18].

An important book which defies categorization but fits generally with contemporary efforts to build intellectual bridges back to political philosophy is James C. Davies's *Human Nature in Politics* (1963). This particular bridge is built largely from the territory occupied by social psychologists. The human nature component of the study of political behavior, so clearly discernible in such writers as Hobbes, Hume, Rousseau Mill, and Marx, has been redefined according to Davies. Social psychologists, notably Abraham H. Maslow (1943, 1954), have led the way. The scientific doubt which prevented positivists from writing about human nature with the kind of authority often springing from innocence has been overcome by the confidence Davies says we can place in a system of basic human needs. These are identified as physical (water, food, sex, etc.), social (love, affection, belongingness, etc.), self-esteem (the need for equality), and self-actualization. Davies's work reflects the extraordinary interest in all primate behavior coming to the fore in the social sciences in the last twenty years. It also adds to theory the plausibility of propositions about whether a political community can develop before the problem of survival has been solved, or whether, for example, demands in economically underdeveloped countries can be manipulated so that widespread loyalties to democratic institutions result.

In connection with the Davies-Maslow discussion, Bay has suggested (1965, p. 49) the production of testable hypotheses for Almond and Coleman's theory of political "input functions" (political socialization and recruitment; interest articulation; interest aggregation; political communication) and "output functions" (rule making, rule application, rule adjudication) (1960, p. vii). What might be the place of each of these functions in satisfying individual personality needs? Can there be research-based knowledge on whether democratic theory or institutions have value for human development? It might be that security, another of Maslow's basic needs which Davies conveniently excludes as not of the "same order" as physical, social, equality, and self-actualization needs, demands conservative forms of political organization. By the standard of organic needs, paternalism, authoritarianism and totalitarianism are as serviceable, in certain environmental conditions, as are liberal institutions. Hobbes, of course, pointed this out first.

One of the major problems in discussing the theory field, to reiterate, is word usage. Murray (1953) and Strauss-Cropsey (1963) use the term "philosophy" in the same way Sabine (1937) and Catlin (1957) use the term "theory." This common interchangeability of terms has led Deutsch and Rieselbach (in Haas and Kariel, 1970) to suggest the following distinction:

> Whenever the emphasis of our inquiry is placed on the understanding of what *is* or exists in politics—on the web of "if . . . then" relations that can be verified regardless of the preferences and values of the observer—we are inclined to speak of *political theory*. By contrast, when our interest is focused on what we think *ought* to be in politics—on the effects of political practices or institutions on the normative aspects, the values and personalities of people *including those of the observer*—then we tend to speak about *political philosophy*. In the first case, we tend to see ourselves in the role of detached observers, and, in effect, in the role of social scientists. In the second case, we tend to see ourselves in the role of political philosophers [1970, p. 74].

Many distinguished political scientists move back and forth between these two roles. Carl J. Friedrich, in *Man and His Government* (1963), for example, focuses on observable and verifiable phenomena in a thoroughgoing empirical study. Four years later he published *An Introduction to Political Theory*, which probes certain perennial issues through the works of the great political philosophers. Herbert Kaufman set out in 1964 to show that the two roles shared common concerns. Andrew Hacker argues that the two roles may indeed have a common concern, i.e., a disinterested search for the principles of the good state and the good society and for knowledge of political and social reality, but that science and philosophy have a common enemy: ideology. Theory in its ideological form is "interestedness." It is a "rationalization for current or future political and social arrangements . . . and a distorted description or explanation of political and social reality" (1961, p. 5). Theory as ideology is illustrated by such statements as those describing Machiavelli as having adopted a "proto-Fascist point of view" (von Martin, in Shklar, 1966, p. 23), or Locke as being a "bourgeois philosopher" whose political thought can best be understood in the light of presuppositions which he, "in common with many others of his class and time," entertained about his own society (Macpherson, in Shklar, 1966, p. 66).

Various writers agree with Hacker's specification of ideology as a specific form of political theory (Smith, 1957; McDonald and Rosenau, 1968). Criticism of ideological thought was a major preoccupation of theorists immediately following World War II. Fascism, Nazism, and communism so clearly challenged their democratic counterparts that political scientists were inclined to spend considerable effort assessing them. The assessment, in general, consciously rejected as "untheoretical" and "unphilosophical" prescriptive systems of thought concerned primarily with moving people to action and getting specified things done. But why people engage in political action did become a continuing matter of concern for theorists (Almond and Verba, 1963).

The extent to which the ideological aspect of political theory may be in decline in recent years is a question of controversy in the literature (LaPalombara, 1966; Lipset, 1966). Judith N. Shklar collected a group of essays, *Political Theory and Ideology*, in which she argues persuasively in the introduction that the major failing of ideological political theory is that "reductionists" make no qualitative distinction between slogans and the considered reflection of both political philosophers and political theorists (1966, p. 18). Slogans can act only as cohesives for mass parties.

Political philosophy is distinguishable from ideology not so much by form, which may be for both a more or less coherent blueprint of the future and a way of achieving it, but primarily in content. Philosophy's general question is about the ethical, logical, metaphysical, aesthetic, espistomological, cosmological, and linguistic *content* of the belief system indicated. Of course, the questioning task of philosophy has itself been overtaken by a "slow and silent revolution" in the last thirty years (White, 1959; Thorson, 1961). The analytical movement is described by one of its proponents as follows:

> The temper and tone of the movement is deflationary and critical; its method linguistic and logical. While some of the sponsors emphasize the importance of reconstructing ordinary language, others insist on the need for describing the behavior of words as ordinarily used. What they all oppose, however, is the pretentious method of those who claim to conduct us to the Truth by way of labyrinthine metaphysical systems, aided by the flimsiest threads [White, in Thorson, 1961, p. 711].

Analyzing only the language and the logic of such statements as "We hold these truths to be self-evident, that all men are created equal, . . ." professional philosophers of the analytical school often assign political philosophy to oblivion. Sometimes they adopt A. J. Ayer's classification system for meaningful statements (1936). Meaningful statements are either (1) subject to verification by sense experience, or (2) tautologies. All other statements are literally senseless. Therefore moral judgments in political philosophy must be considered nonsense (Hare, 1952; Toulmin, 1953; Smith, 1957).

Analytic philosophy becomes analytic *political* philosophy in the hands of T. D. Weldon. His *The Vocabulary of Politics* (1953) is an influential work on the subject. An article, "Political Principles" (in Laslett, 1956), is a brief and concise statement of his position, which is that logically there cannot be self-evident truths or fundamental human rules applicable in all places at all times. No political principle can have "non-contextual validity." Its validity rests on its practical political associations, as when practical reason demands in a com munist state that the means of production should not be privately owned. That the means of production should not be privately owned is beyond question and requires no explanation in the context of a communist state. When explanations are attempted nevertheless, e.g., "because profits involve the exploitation of man by man," the "explanations" constitute a restatement of the principle in question. The "because" in such explanations is therefore misleading. It is practical reason which issues "self-evident" or "intuitively obvious" stop signs. To ask for further reasons in a particular association at a particular point in time is useless. That all men are created equal or that profits involve the exploitation of man by man are not in fact general political principles acceptable to all human beings. Their "truth" is contextual.

Weldon insists that political associations adopt certain propositions as political principles as a matter of conscious or unconscious decision. Any significant change in these propositions or rules constitutes a revolution. Since governing classes think poorly of revolutions, they sanctify what they deem to be the basic or important principles by making inquiries into them or demands for explanations of them illegitimate. Analytic political philosophy asks *why* explanations are thus discouraged. Is the observed fact that political associations have fundamental principles about which no questions may be asked a *logical* must, i.e., part of the meaning of the word "association," or is it just an empirical fact about associations which might be otherwise?

Analytic political philosophy answers its question with emphatic statements about the logical possibility of there being associations in which all the rules are open to question all the time and no propositions have the status of principles. That no such association actually exists is testimony to the *psycho*logical requirements of security and the learned ability of men to live without explanations, which in some cases is called growing up.

Analytic political philosophy's achievement is significant. It has gone far to deprive the abstract ideas of traditional political philosophy of their logical power. For an interesting statement in partial opposition to the analysts, the student should consult Joseph Margolis, "Difficulties in T. D. Weldon's Political Philosophy" (1958, pp. 1113-17). He should see also Flew (1951, 1953), Field (n.d.), Kaplan (1961), McCloskey (1964), Riker and Ordeshook (1973), Wright (1973), Kleinberg (1973), and Dahl and Tufte (1973).

One possible outcome for political philosophy following the analytic and allied attacks is to regard the subject as properly an appendage of political science departments in somewhat the same manner that History of Economic Thought and History of Science courses are handled in many economics and physics departments today.

Earlier the graduate student was advised to become familiar with the principal works of Easton, Dunning, McIlwain, and Sabine. The student or young professor looking for newer texts on the history of political ideas was also advised to consider the essays of Wolin and Plamenatz. To conclude his consideration of political theory as philosophy, the student should read the major writings of one of political philosophy's foremost modern representatives, Leo Strauss.

Strauss and an able group of his students have considered in consternation the challenges of the analytic school in philosophy and the behavioral school in political science, and counterattacked both movements. Consult especially the charges against behavioral political science in Herbert Storing, ed., *Essays on the Scientific Study of Politics* (1962), to which Strauss contributes the epilogue. See also Schaar and Wolin's trenchant review and the replies (1963, p. 125*ff*).

Strauss agrees with the analysts and the behavioralists that political philosophy has fallen on hard times. Everywhere, he says, a distinction is made between a nonphilosophical political science and a nonscientific political philosophy. This distinction "takes away all dignity, all honesty from political philosophy" (1957, p. 347). The rejection of political philosophy as unscientific Strauss lays to present-day positivism in an aberration from Comte's intention to construct a social science modeled on natural science and therefore able to overcome the intellectual anarchy of modern society. Science became instead the one true church. Unlike most churches, however, science does not aim at absolute knowledge of the Why, as theology and metaphysics do, but only at a relative knowledge. Strauss believes that among the practical consequences of positivistic social science is an ethical neutrality on the part of social scientists bordering on nihilism.

The process said to arrive at nihilism is as follows. Social scientists emancipate themselves from moral judgments so that "moral obtuseness is the necessary condition for scientific analysis" (1957, p. 348). The social scientist must, in fact, engage in a constant fight against the preferences he has as a human being and as a citizen, in light of his responsibilities as a scientist to maintain a posture of detachment. Whatever the social scientist's personal preferences or ends might be, attaining adequate knowledge of the means conducive to social ends remains the sole function of his profession. This knowledge itself is a value—the only value—and dedication to it is dedication to truth. But, alas, truth is not a value which it is necessary to choose. One may reject it as well as choose it. The positivistic social scientist *has* chosen it, but it is an ideal he has chosen *in preference to other ideals* (1959). Thus if the positivistic social scientist is to avoid the predicament Socrates led Thrasymachus into in *The Republic*, he must insist that social science cannot pronounce on the question of whether social science itself is good. Neutrality in the conflict between good and evil is nihilism.

It has been said that Strauss and his students counterattacked the analysts and behavioralists. Theirs is not just a defense in the manner of Levinson (1953), Wild (1953a), and Hallowell (1954) defending against Popper's charge that Plato was the intellectual father of modern totalitarianism (1950). Strauss is not content to label himself a Platonist or even a neoclassicist with those (it is presumed) limiting points of view, thus to build fences against the heretics. All political knowledge and action is the ground of his confession. With the philosopher's unique mental equipment, which may be understood as a combination of detachment, passion, and reason, Strauss aspires to subsume empiricism's interest in analyzing political action. The philosopher's task is the inclusive one of discerning the political good served or not served by any action studied.

> The meaning of political philosophy and its meaningful character are as evident today as they have been since the time when political philosophy first made its appearance in Athens. All political action aims at either preservation or change. When desiring to preserve, we wish to prevent a change to the worse; when desiring to change, we wish to bring about something better. All political action is, then, guided by some thought of better or worse. But thought of better or worse implies thought of the good. The awareness of the good which guides all our actions has the character of opinion: it is no longer questioned but, on reflection, it proves to be questionable. The very fact that we can question it directs us toward such a thought of the good as is no longer questionable—toward a thought which is no longer opinion but knowledge. All political action has then in itself a directedness toward knowledge of the good: of the good life, or the good society. For the good society is the complete political good [Strauss, in Eulau, 1969c, pp. 93-4].

Strauss's "classical solution" to the problems of the political world are elaborated in his *Natural Right and History* (1953), a work technically concerned with the problem of the validity of natural right doctrines in view of the historical evidence of their nonrecognition. The "modern solution" he deprecates in the same work begins with the heresy of Machiavelli and ends with that of Nietzsche. It is noteworthy in this connection that both Machiavelli and Nietzsche were writing not about justice and the political good, but about that other major theme of Western political thought which Strauss largely ignores, power.

In all the Strauss corpus there is little evidence that he gives credence to the contention that power, more precisely political activity as power process, may be used by a society's members for a great variety of purposes, and that for the moment of analysis the thought of better or worse may be suspended. To isolate and describe the characteristic patterns of the power process is not necessarily *ever* to pass judgment on the rightness or wrongness of the purposes involved. Many political scientists will not attempt logically to derive values from facts, or facts from values. Yet they finally would rate the purposes and policies of democracy as political goods. This does not make more or less rational, more or less nihilistic, conformist, or philistine, the research judgments made prior to, and arguably independent of, their admission of their human preferences (Almond, 1946; Eulau, 1969c).

POLITICAL THEORY AS SCIENCE

David Easton's call for political theorists to end their field's conservatism, and march alongside other fields in the natural and social sciences in developing new explanatory schemes for their subject matter, has been more than answered in the last twenty years. Scientific modes of investigation and analysis have been introduced into every field of political studies. Theorizing has become a preoccupation of the vanguard of the discipline. Are there organizing concepts which may help the student classify the kinds of theorizing being done *across* the traditional field divisions? Perhaps there are. One organizing concept is that theorizing is done about *individuals*, rather than larger political units. This kind of theorizing may be termed "micropolitics."

Micropolitics

As early as 1944, the Social Science Research Council, under the prodding of E. Pendleton Herring, reached a decision to explore the feasibility of developing a new approach to the study of political behavior. Focused upon the behavior of individuals in political situations, this approach calls for the examination of the political relationships of men—as citizens, administrators, and legislators—by disciplines which can throw light on the problems involved, with the object of formulating and testing hypotheses, concerning uniformities of behavior in different institutional settings [*Annual Report for 1944-45*, quoted in Dahl, 1961b, p. 764].

Easton picked up the SSRC thread as he argued in 1953 that

the research worker wishes to look at participants in the political system as individuals who have the emotions, prejudices, and predispositions of human beings as we know them in our daily lives.... Behavioral research ... has therefore sought to elevate the actual human being to the center of attention. Its premise is that the traditionalists have been reifying institutions, virtually looking at them apart from their component individuals ... [1953, pp. 201-2].

Easton contends in chapter 8 of *The Political System* that the use of physchological terms regarding political problems is by no means a modern innovation. Virtually all speculation in political philosophy rests on a unique set of notions about individuals writ large as "human nature." Plato, Hobbes, Locke, Rousseau, and Bentham made psychological assumptions that played a prominent role in their views about the functioning of the political system. Rousseau, for example, pictured political and social institutions as corrupting or liberating the innocent individual. Bentham proclaimed the greatest happiness of the greatest number as the universal moral standard.

The pioneering scientific work in the area of personality and politics was done almost fifty years ago by Harold Lasswell. His *Psychopathology and Politics* (1930, reissued with an essay "Afterthoughts—Thirty Years Later" in 1960) attempted to show how the neurotic aspects of the personality leave their effects on political life, or perhaps more precisely, how an individual's private affects can be displaced upon public issues. Lasswell did further work adapting political theory to the findings of psychology and psychiatry in *Power and Personality* (1948), *World Politics and Personal Insecurity* (1950), *Politics: Who Gets What, When, How* (1958), and, with Arnold Rogow, in *Power, Corruption and Rectitude* (1963).

Rogow's study of the field of psychiatry in the United States, *The Psychiatrists* (1970), applies various behavioral research techniques to a part of the medical profession. He reported, for example, in an interesting chapter entitled "The Politics of Psychiatry" that "the most orthodox Freudian analyst is apt to take an active interest in politics and in ideological terms to locate himself on the left wing of the Democratic Party" (1970, p. 123). The reader will note the contrast to the ordinary political stance of other members of the medical profession, who vote Republican over 60 percent of the time (1970, p. 123). Rogow speculates in chapter six that much mental illness in the United States is the result of social conditions, a kind of reverse psychological determinism that Abram Kardiner and Ralph Linton had argued for in their *The Individual and His Society* (1939). The political implications of Sigmund Freud's thought are close to the surface in Kardiner and Linton's work, as well as Lasswell's, but are not entirely convincing until Paul Roazen's *Freud: Political and Social Thought* (1968).

Another manifestation of the continuing interest of the profession in individual behavior is the spate of psychologically oriented biographies of political leaders and decisionmakers. Erik H. Erikson's pathfinding *Young Man Luther* (1958) advanced on Lasswell by stressing the need for exploring the public arena of an individual's activity in its own right, not just as a screen for the projection of individual pathology. Individual activity must be explained concurrently on two distinct levels, says Erikson: the personal or psychological, and the social or historical. Only where personal and social need, each serving its own requirements, broadly coincide, does that rare opportunity arise when "an individual is called upon . . . to lift his individual patienthood to the level of a universal one and try to solve for all what he could not solve for himself alone" (1958, p. 67). Operationalizing such concepts as these, psychoanalysts, historians, and social scientists, using the canons of methodology sacred to each, have begun cooperative new studies of the phenomenon of leadership. The student should read carefully the contributions of each genre in *Philosophers and Kings: Studies in Leadership* (Rustow, ed., 1968).

Other notable examples of this type of investigation are Alexander L. George and Juliette L. George, *Woodrow Wilson and Colonel House: A Personality Study* (1956); Arnold A. Rogow, *James Forrestal: A Study of Personality, Politics, and Policy* (1963); Lewis J. Edinger, *Kurt Schumacher: A Study in Personality and Political Behavior* (1965); a collection edited by Edinger, *Political Leadership in Industrialized Societies: Studies in Comparative Analysis* (1967); Fred I. Greenstein, *Children and Politics* (1965); E. Victor Wolfenstein, *The Revolutionary Personality: Lenin, Trotsky, Gandhi* (1967), *Personality and Politics* (1969), studies of Winston Churchill, Malcolm X, and Friedrich Nietzsche; Lucian W. Pye, "Mao Tse-tung's Leadership Style" (1976); and Doris Kearns, "The Benevolent Leader Revisited: Children's Images of Political Leaders in Three Democracies" (1975) and "Lyndon Johnson's Political Personality" (1976).

One of Erikson's important contributions to personality studies is his evidence that personality continues its evolution in successive crises from childhood through adolescence and into maturity. Freud's teachings had left many with the impression that an individual's personality is fully shaped in the first few years of his life, both in its strengths and in its pathology. Erikson's emphasis on "crises" serves to highlight rather the discontinuous, innovative, and creative possibilities in both personal development and in a dynamic process of leadership development (*Childhood and Society*, 1964; *Identity, Youth and Crisis*, 1968a). Erikson (1968b) writes on the nature of psychohistorical evidence for determining a process of leadership development in his "In Search of Gandhi."

Focusing on elements of the Eriksonian identity crisis and using a variety of historical data, James David Barber produced a comprehensive analysis of American presidential styles with the aim of predicting a president's possible actions on the basis of previous responses in psychologically similar circumstances (Barber, 1972). According to Barber, a leader "copes, adapts, leads, and responds not as some shapeless organism in a flood of novelties, but as a man with a memory in a system with a history" (Barber, 1968, pp. 938–9). Memory is the important element in Barber's analysis. It enables a president, for example, to consider his present reaction to a crisis in the light of what worked for him before, perhaps at a time far back in his personal history when he was just emerging as a differentiated and successful human being. The best clue to President Truman's possible actions as president, for example, may not be in his actions as vice president or senator, but in his actions as junior officer in the National Guard in World War I (Barber, 1969, p. 40). In another context, Barber successfully combines political and psychological analysis in his study of Connecticut legislators, *The Lawmakers: Recruitment and Adaptation to Legislative Life* (1965).

The theoretical problems in understanding the leadership process are impressive. A number of approaches have been advanced, including Deutsch's view of leadership as a process of communication or connection (1963, pp. 157–60, 172–76). Dankwart A. Rustow believes the leadership focus to be a productive one in the future of political science.

> In a field like political science, a focus on leadership may help resolve some current methodological dilemmas. The generation that participated in the "successful revolt" waged against the older institutional-legal approach in favor of behaviorism has been engaged ever since in a wide search for a new basic unit of analysis. Some have sought it in a "functional" vocabulary too abstruse to be applied in empirical research, some in the making of

"decisions" that have proved difficult to isolate from the stream of reality, some in an elusive quantitative measure of power, and some in messages of communication so numerous as to defy inventory. The leader as a figure omnipresent in any political process, as the maker of decisions, originator and recipient of messages, performer of functions, wielder of power, and creator or operator of institutions can bring these disparate elements into a single, visible focus. The study of leadership, moreover, can readily be supplemented with an examination of the social and political organization that he founds and transforms, with an analysis of the pyschological appeals and political sanctions, that give leader and organization a hold on their mass following. In short, there may be the elements for a new theoretical view, both comprehensive and dynamic, of the political process as a whole [Rustow, 1968, pp. 688-9].

Political scientists theorize about other individuals than leaders. The study of what the *average* individual does in the act of voting, for example, is one of the oldest examples of empirical research in American political science. A Swede, Herbert Tingsten, showed the way with his study of European elections, *Political Behavior: Studies in Election Statistics* (1937). The survey studies of American voting behavior beginning with *The People's Choice* (1944) have greatly increased the profession's understanding of individual psychology as well as politics in general. The classic of this type, *The American Voter* (1960), theorizes that the act of voting and the choice of a political party are not so much like the choice of a brand of consumer goods, which is largely influenced by expected satisfactions, than like the selection of a preferred role. People vote and act in politics, say Campbell et al., less for what they want to get than for what they want to be.

The fact that a person's self-image and sense of identity may come from his choice of a political or social group constitutes a major stimulus for efforts to construct a new theory of democracy. This is a theory "based upon the opportunity of individuals to choose their small-group affiliations with a considerable degree of freedom, and thus indirectly to choose the future development of their own personality structures and personal identities" (Deutsch and Rieselbach in Haas and Kariel, 1970, p. 83). Hermann Weilenmann, a Swiss, has constructed such a theory in "The Interlocking of Nation and Personality" (1963). A Japanese scholar, Masao Maruyama, adopts the same theoretical approach in his "Patterns of Individuation and the Case of Japan: A Conceptual Scheme" (1965). Maruyama uses a simple scheme with only two variables: the associative or dissociative attitudes of individuals toward one another, and their "centripetal" or "centrifugal" attitudes toward political authority. He uses specific historical, social, and biological evidence from the various stages of the political development of Japan to support the variety of combinations the scheme generates.

The political participation aspect of the investigation of individual behavior, combining, as it must, depth interview methods with statistical data and perceptiveness, is perhaps best represented in the work of Robert E. Lane. His *Political Life* (1959), *Political Ideology* (1962) and *Political Thinking and Consciousness* (1969), have revealing subtitles: "Why and How People Get Involved in Politics," "Why the American Common Man Believes What He Does," and "The Private Life of the Political Mind." Lane originally carried forward the work of Theodor W. Adorno and his associates, who made partial use of questionnaire data in their *The Authoritarian Personality* (1950), and of Smith, Bruner, and White, who combined extended interviews with standarized psychological tests in their *Opinions and Personality* (1956).

Political Ideology (1962) affords an example of Lane's technique, which many political scientists believe represents empirical theorizing at its best. Lane first points out that "ideology" has been defined in a formidable variety of ways by lexicographers, psychologists, and sociologists. He quotes various meanings of the term, such as Webster's "the science of ideas" and Daniel Bell's "the conversion of ideas into social levers" (1960). Lane then lists the ways in which he will use "political ideology": as a body of concepts dealing with such questions as who the rulers will be, how the rulers will be selected, and by what principles they will govern.

Lane postulates that most ideologies will have the qualities of group belief that individuals borrow by identifying or disidentifying with a social group. Further, ideologies will have a body of sacred documents, such as constitutions, bills of rights, declarations, and manifestos. Ideologies will also have heroes, such as founding fathers, sages, originators, and great interpreters. Finally, ideologies imply an empirical theory of cause and effect in the world, and a theory of the nature of man.

Lane is careful to differentiate between the articulated and differentiated political arguments put forward by informed and conscious Marxists or fascists or liberal democrats on the one hand (Ebenstein, *Today's Isms*, 6th ed., 1970), and the loosely structured, unreflective statements of common men. The former variety of ideology he calls "forensic," the latter "latent." The basic question Lane examines is whether the common man does in fact have a set of emotionally charged political beliefs. Does he make some kind of critique of alternative policy proposals on the basis of political beliefs? Does he have a program of reform, however modest? Assuming political beliefs exist, do they embrace certain central values and institutions? Are they rationalizations of interests? Do they serve as moral justifications for daily acts and attitudes?[1]

A political philosopher could write perceptive and logical answers to such questions as these in an exercise of his intellect. Many have done so to the profit of the study of politics. The empirical political theorist seeks data, however. In Lane's case, he conducted extensive interviews with fifteen men of "Eastport," a city of over 100,000 population on the Atlantic seaboard. He found, among other items of particular interest to democratic theorists, that conventional democratic ideals are reflective of personal qualities congenial to those ideals. Each respondent, for example, believed himself to be the master of some portion of his environment, and, with the ego strength which undergirds such a perception, capable of *self* government. Most of the Eastport men had sufficient tolerance of delay, confusion, and ambiguity to suffer along with such meandering democratic institutions as legislatures and executive bureaucracies. They rated "high" on Morris Rosenberg's "faith in people" scale (1956). Lane justifiably claims a quality of realism for his data because it is derived from specific men (Costa, Sullivan, Woodside, etc.) answering specific questions about specific parts of the records of Presidents Roosevelt and Eisenhower.

A well-chosen collection of readings in the "Sociology of American Political Life" is Larson and Wasburn's *Power, Participation and Ideology* (1969). For comparative data on individual political behavior in other cultures, the student is referred to Almond and Verba's *The Civic Culture* (1963), a study of political attitudes in Italy, Mexico, West Germany, and Great Britain, as well as in the United States. The authors used national cross-section samples totaling about 5,000 people, obtaining their data through structured interviews of about an hour each, carried out by respected polling organizations in each country. Follow-up interviews were conducted with individuals who, on the basis of the first interviews, seemed to exemplify certain types of citizens. From the welter of findings there emerged portraits of five quite different political cultures. That of the United States, labeled a "participant civic culture," reinforced Lane's conclusions. The Italian culture was found to be one of political alienation, where low feelings of national pride, distrust of government, and little sense of political obligation obtained. In Mexico there was a combination of alienation and aspiration. In West Germany, Almond and Verba found considerable knowledge of the

1. See Robert E. Lane's review of *The Nature of Human Values* by Milton Rokeach (New York: Free Press, 1973) in the *American Political Science Review* 70 (September 1976): 965–66.

political system, activity in it, and confidence in its fairness. But they also found a lack of involvement in political groups and other informal kinds of political participation. Great Britain's civic culture was marked by similar levels of comprehension to that of the United States and West Germany, but also by a much greater deference to the authority of government. It was classified, then, as a "deferential civic culture."

Other political culture studies, notably those by Hyman (1959), Almond and Coleman (1960), Apter (1963 and 1968), and Dawson (1966), join Almond and Verba in raising basic theoretical questions about the extent to which human nature is uniform in politics and the extent to which politics is shaped by the spirit of the times, of countries, and of peoples. Aristotle and Montesquieu were concerned with the same questions, of course, and might have been somewhat familiar with the basic configuration of memories, attention patterns, and value orientations which are now emerging from empirical investigations.

One of the problems in theorizing about individual behavior anywhere in the world is how particular attitudes and values can best be identified and measured. Helpful works here are Shaw and Wright's *Scales for the Measurement of Attitudes*, a compendium of attitude measures (1967), and Robinson and Shaver's *Measures of Social Psychological Attitudes*, a survey of more than one hundred sources, many of them specifically relevant to political science (1969). Herbert McCloskey's article, "Personality and Attitude Correlates of Foreign Policy Orientation," in Rosenau's *Domestic Sources of Foreign Policy* (1967) is noteworthy, as are earlier efforts by McCloskey (1958), Farris (1960), and Agger, Goldstein, and Pearl (1961). See also Edelman (1971), Lamb, Gilmour, and Gallo (1974), and Renshon (1974).

Macropolitics

If the study of the individual is one focal point for empirical political theory, the other fixed point in the ellipse is the system in which the individual operates. Macropolitics is the view of the political system as a whole, the "aerial view," in Frank J. Sorauf's phrase (1966, p. 39). The nature and composition of the forest is juxtaposed, for organizing and explanatory purposes, with the perspective of the individual tree.

Deutsch is quite right in pointing out that the smallest system in politics is the individual (*Politics and Government*, 1970, p. 126). The drives and complexes operating in the individual's body and personality are studied by medical doctors, psychologists, and psychiatrists, as well as by behavioral political scientists. But analysis of individual drives and complexes cannot fully explain collective decisions. The mechanisms by which individual decisions are aggregated and combined into collective decisions have more and more become the stuff of empirical theorizing. What is the pattern of relationships emerging among individuals interacting? Which elements might be subsystems within a system? Might something be a subsystem in two or more different systems that overlap only in part?

Sociologists were the first to write in terms of social systems. Talcott Parsons, for example, defines a social system in broad terms as having the following characteristics: (1) two or more persons interact with one another; (2) in their actions people take account of how others are likely to act; and (3) sometimes the people in the system act together in pursuit of common goals (Parsons and Shils, 1951, p. 55). Thus, in Parsons's usage, a political or an economic system is a subsystem of a social system. The political function is instrumental. It is that of "facilitating the effective attainment of a collectivity's goals" (Parsons, 1961a). The student should read carefully the collection of seventeen papers by Parsons in *Politics and Social Structure* (1969). William C. Mitchell notes in the forward to this anthology that the papers illustrate the gradual evolution of Parsons's thinking about politics and also point up his persistent concern for practical matters of public policy.

The focus on political *function*, which treats politics as a process or type of activity, is different from a focus on political *structures*, which orients itself toward the various types of institutions dealing with politics on a fulltime basis, and which might be labeled as pertaining to the governmental subsystem of a society. Proponents of the former view among political scientists find political phenomena almost everywhere: in the corporation, the private association, the family, and so forth. Dahl, for example, claims that almost every human association has a political aspect. "In common parlance we speak of the 'government' of a club, a firm, and so on. In fact, we may even describe such a government as dictatorial, democratic, representative, or authoritarian; and we often hear about 'politics' and 'politicking' going on in these associations" (1963, pp. 6–7).

The function-process approach to systems theory is generally concerned with the power ratios present in an association. "Power" is defined in this context as "coercive influence" (Dahl, 1963, p. 50). Aristotle, for example, differentiated the kind of power wielded in a political association, or polis, from that wielded by a master over a slave, a husband over a wife, and parents over children (bk. 1, *The*

Politics, in McKeon, 1941). Weber argued that a political relationship necessarily postulates the power of a ruling authority to exercise its will. An association may be called political "if and in so far as the enforcement of its orders is carried out continually within a given territorial area by the application staff" (1947a, p. 154). Oran R. Young maintains in *Systems of Political Science* that Weber's concern with the governance of territory classifies him in the narrow, i.e., political structures, group of social scientists (1968, pp. 4–5). Lasswell defines political science itself as an empirical discipline engaged in the study of "the shaping and sharing of power" (1950, p. xiv). A political act is one performed "in power perspectives" (1950, p. 240).

The power perspective and the emphasis on the individual as a unit of analysis came together in Lasswell's *Power and Personality* (1948) and in Lasswell and Kaplan's *Power and Society* (1950). Since then, the power concept has been a conspicuous common denominator for theorizing about the system in which scarce resources are allocated unevenly (Bell, 1975; Nagel, 1975). C. Wright Mills saw the American social system as a pyramid with a "power elite" at the apex, the elite constituting a triumvirate from the economic, political, and military sectors of society (1956). Mills's theory of an oligarchy should not have surprised readers of European theorists such as Michels, Mosca, and Pareto. But it did undermine a previous understanding of the American system as a pluralist one. David Riesman was careful to deny the existence of an elite power bloc in the United States. Riesman instead suggested that decisions emanated from the interaction of competing interest groups, some of which have veto power over public policy. Writing in 1961, he observed *The Lonely Crowd* was in agreement with John Kenneth Galbraith's *American Capitalism* in that "there is no single, coherent, self-conscious power elite, but an amorphous set of would-be elites, bidding for and forming coalitions" (1961, p. xxxvi). The work of Mills and Riesman has inspired many interesting essays, some of the best in Domhoff and Ballard, *C. Wright Mills and the Power Elite* (1968), and in Lipset and Lowenthal, *Culture and Social Character: The Work of David Riesman Reviewed* (1961).

In *The Power Structure* (1967), Arnold M. Rose contrasts various theories of political power in the American social system. The work of Mills and Floyd Hunter receives a lengthy critique. Rose refers to their view as the "economic-elite-dominance hypothesis." He interprets the hypothesis to mean that "the economic elite acts in a more-or-less unified fashion to control the political process of the United States" (1967, p. 9). His own view Rose terms the "multi-influence hypothesis," believing society to consist of many elites, "each relatively small numerically and operating in different spheres of life" (1967, p. 4). The bulk of the population is thus classifiable into organized groups and publics.

Rose looks for empirical support of his hypothesis in the writings of Bentley (1908), Herring (1940), Schattschneider (1942a), Truman (1952a), and Key (1959). He follows their lead in concentrating on political processes, but, tipping his hat to his profession, he analyzes the facts of power, "not in a 'narrow' political context, but in the broader context of sociology" (1967, p. 7).

Studies of power in the local community constitute a distinctive species of theorizing about decision making (Debnam, 1975). Hunter's *Community Power Structure* (1953) led the way, with Nelson W. Polsby's *Community Power and Political Theory* (1963) still perhaps the best methodological work on the subject. Like Riesman and Rose, Polsby argues from a pluralist point of view, rejecting the stratification thesis that some group necessarily dominates in a community. "If anything, there seems to be an unspoken notion among pluralist researchers that at bottom nobody dominates in a town, so that their first question to a local informant is not likely to be 'Who runs this community?', but rather 'Does anyone at all run this community?'" (1963, p. 112). The pluralist methodology is based on the study of specific outcomes of a range of issues in order to determine who actually prevails in community decision making. The status of community power research was summarized by John Walton in 1966. He presented and compared the findings of some thirty-three studies, concluding that the next logical step in the investigation of the community decision-making system is comparative studies.

The sociological context of systems theorizing extends further, to theories of organization and role. March and Simon's *Organizations* (1958) and Simon's *Models of Man* (1957), as well as Simon's article "On the Concept of Organization Goal" (1964), constitute important theoretical contributions of political scientists working on the boundaries of several disciplines. The contribution, which seems marginal to some, is the questioning of the assumption that rational actors in government and business have skills and values independent of their social environment. The actors are sometimes thought to maximize these skills and values on the basis of complete information and "an unlimited capacity to think and calculate at no cost in resources or delay" (Deutsch and Rieselbach, 1970, p. 87). Simon, for example, replaces the "optimizing" assumption with a discussion of a "satisficing" decision process in which decision makers, "with limited time and incomplete knowledge, try to substitute relatively better outcomes for less preferable ones, but which often fall short of optimal results" (Deutsch and Rieselbach, 1970, p. 88).

The application of role theory to the study of organizations is thoughtfully investigated by Peter M. Blau in Blau and Scott, *Formal Organizations: A Comparative Approach* (1962). Fred W. Riggs extends the comparative approach to developing countries in *Administration in Developing Countries: The Theory of Prismatic Society* (1964). Wahlke, Eulau, Buchanan, and Ferguson have applied role theory to legislatures in *The Legislative System: Explorations in Legislative Behavior* (1962). Organization theory received perhaps its most interesting treatment in studies of foreign policy decision making. Richard C. Snyder and his associates, for example, utilize both theoretical analysis and actual cases in an attempt to isolate the decision process as the crucial element in organization theory. The student should consult Snyder, Bruck, and Sapin's *Foreign Policy Decision-Making* (1962); Glenn D. Paige's *The Korean Decision* (1968); and Robinson and Majak's "The Theory of Decision-Making," in Charlesworth's *Contemporary Political Analysis* (1967). James N. Rosenau raises several interesting questions in evaluating the decision-making analysis approach in "The Premises and Promises of Decision-Making Analysis," also in Charlesworth (1967a, pp. 189–211). The student should also consider the philosophical analysis of decision making in Braybrooke and Lindblom's *A Strategy of Decision* (1963).

Organization theory and the study of decision processes and cybernetics have in common that they are not limited to any single discipline and that their results can often be expressed in mathematical language. The search for common aspects of organizations, small and large, and in smaller and larger groups, is one way to describe the task of general systems theory. The interdisciplinary use of general systems concepts is adequately surveyed by Young (1964, 1968). Morton A. Kaplan's "Systems Theory" and Herbert J. Spiro's "An Evaluation of Systems Theory" in Charlesworth (1967) is necessary reading for anyone claiming competence in the theory field.

The cutting edge in empirical theory today appears to be how political systems can be represented by mathematical models. Clearly stated primers are Alker, Deutsch, and Stoetzel's *Mathematical Approaches to Politics* (1973) and Herndon and Bernd's *Mathematical Applications in Political Science* (1974). One way of modeling in the recent past was by means of game theory, following von Neumann and Morgenstern's *Theory of Games and Economic Behavior* (3d ed., 1953). Since the mid-1960s the limits of game theory have become better known (Brams, 1975). Its primary application has been in international politics (Schelling, 1960; Boulding, 1962; Rapoport, 1964). The current method is to make consistent use of the concept of probability, rather than determinism, and occasionally to use stochastic processes combining both probabilistic and deterministic elements of analysis. The resource of the electronic high-speed computer is now making it possible to simulate the behavior of very large groups, including whole electorates and international political systems.

The Political Science Panel of the Behavioral and Social Science Survey wrote in 1969:

> As modern computer technology develops, political science is likely to rely increasingly on simulations of political processes as a means to advance knowledge about phenomena that cannot be easily or directly observed in the real world. Simulations, which are basically operating models of real systems controlled by the researcher, may take a variety of forms and have a variety of objectives. . . . The rigor required in constructing completely programmed simulation models aids in unmasking implicit theoretical assumptions and in revealing otherwise unpredicted consequences which may take the form of new theorems [Eulau and March, 1969, pp. 60–1].

The same panel predicted that two trends would dominate political theory in the near future. One is that political thought will receive more and more contextual treatment.[2] Historical documents such as letters, diaries, and biographical materials will be used to describe the conditions and consequences surrounding the emergence, influence, and decline of political philosophies. It was predicted that the psychological roots of the political thought formulations of the classical past will be uncovered. The second trend is for linguistic analysis to be applied increasingly to political problems. This type of theorizing will be concerned with the varied usages of concepts such as "democracy" in all areas of human life and with the relationships among words in a family of words. Its emphasis on linguistic clarification and conceptual rigor should have important consequences for the operational usefulness of political theory in empirical research.

Analytic philosophers say that political theory as an academic field is dead. It has joined God in the mortuary of discarded bodies of knowledge because the language used to describe both theory and conceptualizations of God as commonly understood is no longer relevant to modern men. Are the phenomena therefore dead or uninteresting because the language used to talk about them is inadequate? Is any language adequate? Perhaps an improved language will resurrect certain old and useful ideas yet again. Whether it does or

---

2. The entire special bicentennial issue of the *Journal of Politics* 38 (August 1976) is an example of this. See especially Lewis P. Simpson's "The Symbolism of Literary Alienation in the Revolutionary Age," pp. 79–100. That a professor of English literature (and coeditor of the *Southern Review*) should be contributing to the *Journal of Politics* is evidence of the new contextualism.

not, whether political theory as an academic field survives or not, political theory as an intellectual activity in any of its forms, history, philosophy, or science, will probably remain what it was to the Greeks: "the passionate contemplation of reality." Whether reality consists mostly of a decent respect for the past, a literary search for wisdom and understanding, or a dedication to the gathering and codification of empirical data, most political scientists would agree that elements of all three approaches form some kind of trinity of comprehension. Some might also agree with Heraclitus and Hegel that everything is and is not.

5. THE SCIENCE OF ADMINISTRATION

Larry L. Wade

A SHORT HISTORY

The modern study of public administration in America is normally held to begin with the publication of Woodrow Wilson's article, "The Study of Administration," in an 1887 issue of the *Political Science Quarterly*. For reasons that psychologists might explore, many historians of a science seem to require some fixed historical point from which human concerns with a social process can be dated. There is little to be gained from the imposition of such artificial schemes on history. As Lewis Mumford has shown in *The Myth of the Machine* (1967), the truth, at least the truth of administrative history, is much more complex. Large-scale, consciously organized human activities and the division of labor associated with them probably had their origins in the preliterate rituals of early man, rituals which, in the form of society-wide ceremonials, involved elaborate planning and human positioning. That, and the maintenance of the purity and integrity of the activity, require memory and virtually all of the other processes that we now associate with formal organization. Mumford is persuasive, in fact, in suggesting that these activities probably *preceded* learned speech. Indeed, some *type of formal organization may well have been the first peculiarly human activity*. The elaborate symbolic systems which today are integral to the operation of complex formal organizations were preceded by the symbolic associations of gesture, rhythm, and expression which served to order and integrate the inchoate and seemingly random features of the physical world. Order was the first need of man in society; order was first achieved in incipient ritual; and order is what we mean by contemporary public administration: the order that develops from the patterns and means by which people who count

154

most in society coordinate the activities of others toward politically determined ends. In short, administration and organization are ancient, universal, and uniquely human activities. If man outside of society is either a beast or a god, as Aristotle suggested, it is in good measure because such a man does not participate in the formally organized activities of his society.

We can go further. The "megamachine," to use Mumford's term for early bureaucracy, or the manner in which early historical man was ranked, repressed, motivated, but above all formally coordinated in the interest of social goals, testifies to the administrative genius of the ancient world. Whether we refer to the Step Pyramid at Sakkara, the Great Wall of China, or the Corinth Canal, we must admit first of all to the massive scale of the objectives—massive even by today's engineering and bureaucratic standards—postulated for human achievement, as well as to the astuteness—if not the humaneness— with which they were in fact achieved. The appropriate permutations of human and physical resources necessary to these achievements suggest that the "principles" of administration followed in the ancient world were ones which, if we control for cultural variations, may have expressed the universally intuited imperatives of successful task performance.

The point is this: if administration is taken to mean forethought, deliberation, technical skill, and coordination of others in the execution of a task, the historical evidence suggests that it is as legitimate to speak of man as an administrative animal as it is to speak of him as a political, social, or economic animal. Indeed, if we adopt some anthropologists' definition of man as a tool-making and -using animal, then man is preeminently an administrative animal. His first tool was himself and his primitive symbolic equipment; his second tool was himself and others organized together, with a growing symbolic capability, in the pursuit of some objective. His physical tools— bones, flintrock, ivory—were secondary to all of this. It follows from this that both the Parsonians and the Marxists are wrong in viewing modern technology and its imperatives as the origin of the division of labor and its concomitant, large formal organization, in society (Gouldner, 1955). The symbolic competence of man and his ability to conceive of mighty purposes are at the root of the question. (See also Dunsire, 1973.)

Wilson's 1887 paper is remembered largely because of the contention it seemingly advanced that politics and administration *are* completely separate processes: administration, said Wilson, is involved in politics "only as machinery is part of the manufactured product. . . ." If read as intended, however, as Herbert Simon (1967, pp. 87-8) has recently noted, Wilson was concerned to argue only that politics and administration *ought* to be separated (on the state of public administration, also see Waldo, 1968, 1971; Peabody and Rourke, 1965; Altshuler, 1968; *Public Administration Review*, 1965; Ostrom, 1973). One can now see that even this much weaker request has little to commend it—the prescriptive statement is quite impossible of attainment and even if it were, Wilson would surely not have been willing to accept all of its implications. While one may wish generals to maintain a discrete silence as to the purposes to which their skills are put, it is less clear that public health officials should have nothing to recommend concerning public health policy. With uneven consistency, and certainly not among the more reflective writers in administration, Wilson's view held sway in the less progressive areas of the field for the next fifty years. I shall return to this point later, noting now only that the apogee of Wilson's contention was not reached until some years after its publication.

In his comprehensive treatise, *The Managing of Organizations*, Bertram Gross (1964, pp. 120–48) has singled out five major contributors to the early twentieth-century study of administration. Their work has had an impact on subsequent students of both private and public administration, and it is necessary here to mention briefly their contributions. Their concerns began with what has continued to excite some students of administration: the creation of what might be called "production oriented" models of administration. These strangely nonpolitical, nonsocial models were essentially normative in character, reflecting as they did an uncritical acceptance of the social myths of "economy and efficiency" and the unwillingness to question the meaning of those terms in any context that extended beyond the narrow interests of the managerial class. The economy and efficiency movement, which continues to influence some organizational theorists, served as the point of intellectual departure for succeeding developments in the field. In their view, the job of administration was to do the most work possible with the fewest possible resources. That the central terms of this interest might be ambiguous and their application in some cases self-serving, were rarely raised possibilities.

The early administrative philosophy of the "new industrial civilization," to use Mayo's term (1945), is typified in the work of Frederick Taylor, Henri Fayol, and, to some extent, Luther Gulick and Lyndall Urwick. Gross includes Max Weber in this list, perhaps with some justification. Although they varied greatly in intent, learning, and ultimate influence, they are united, in Gross's view, by their chronological proximity and, more important, their emphasis on bureaucratic efficiency and the neutrality of administrative techniques and, with the exception of Weber, by an apparent disinterest in the political and social undergirdings of organizational forms, activities, and goals. Still, to consider Taylor and Weber in the same breath is to risk serious misunderstanding; of the subtlety and seriousness of their work there is no comparison, and indeed, although he was contemporary with Taylor, Weber's work was not widely read in the United States until after World War II.

The archetypical figure in this movement, which Daniel Bell (1960) has called the "Cult of Efficiency," was Frederick W. Taylor (1929). Implicit in his formulation was a theory of personality which contemporary "Third Force" psychologists and their followers in organizational analysis (Argyris, 1957, 1964; Maslow, 1959, 1962; Dvorin and Simmons, 1972) would be quick to reject. To Taylor, man was naturally indolent, slothful, and amenable to efficient manipulation through the application of the economic whip to occupational discipline. Consider Taylor's statement that "one of the first requirements for a man who is fit to handle pig iron as a regular occupation is that he shall be so stupid and so phlegmatic that he more nearly resembles an ox than any other type." Taylor knew that he was not dealing with a science *for* human beings but rather for those elites that controlled the major, and particularly industrial, institutions of society. If Wilson had been concerned with the analytical separation of politics and administration, Taylor was concerned to make the separation "scientific." In his schema there would be no politics internal to organizational life, nor would external processes of policy formation ever be questioned. Since work could be organized in order to maximize production possibilities, one might, as he said, "as reasonably . . . insist on bargaining about the time and place of the rising and setting sun." Taylor's conception was both mechanical and static, but more than that it was utopian, since it was timeless, "scientific," and, since rewards were adjusted to contributions, "just." Work could be reduced to precisely computed units of time and kinetic energy, a fact which could be used to arrive at rational and efficient allocations of tasks and rewards in an organizational setting. Instances can be found in the work of Taylor's followers; for example, in Gilbreth's "therbligs" and Bedeaux's "B's." It was a utilitarian calculus for privileged interest, and its scientism was consequently false, as Abruzzi (1956) and Gomberg (1955) have shown in more recent days.

With the 1916 publication of Fayol's *General and Industrial Management* (1949), there emerged the first modern effort to establish the "principles" by which an efficient organization should be governed. Among Fayol's fourteen points were such now aged injunctions as the sanctity of unity of command, the commensurability of responsibility and authority, the prerogatives of managerial discipline, and the like. It is at this point, then, that what Simon was later to call the "proverbs of administration" began to enter modern administrative thought. The functions of management, Fayol argued, were to forecast, organize, command, coordinate, and control, a list that was to be refined by Luther Gulick in 1937 into the familiar mnemonic device POSDCORB: planning, organizing, staffing, direcing, coordinating, reporting, budgeting. If these concerns were to appear somewhat naive to a subsequent generation of scholars, Fayol's work did represent a humanistic advance (albeit one still beclouded by a managerial bias) over Taylor's rather primitive Calvinism. Fayol emphasized the importance of internal justice and equity in responsible administration, an emphasis that was later reflected in the so-called human relations approach to management. It was to certain of the problems raised by Fayol that Gulick and Urwick addressed themselves (Gulick and Urwick, 1937; Urwick, 1944). They retained an emphasis on the formal structure of organizations, the neutrality of administration, and the abstract prescriptive principles of "good" management practices.

Succeeding the administrative economy/efficiency period were contributions during the 1930s and 1940s from a group of scholars with very diverse interests and concerns, a diversity that, upon serious examination, leads one to qualify certain widely accepted propositions concerning the development of administrative theory. (It must be understood that the economy/efficiency movement is still very much alive; here it is possible only to discuss general trends.) One such proposition—that a serious scientific concern with administration was a post–World War II development—is actually quite inaccurate, although certainly the magnitude of scientific interest has increased tremendously since 1945. Also requiring qualification are statements to the effect that, until the postwar period, a "simplified model of decision-making and administration has long dominated the literature" (Peabody and Rourke, 1965, p. 805). Both propositions are true of only the less imaginative writers of the prewar period: they in no way reflect the sentiments of the major prewar writers mentioned below. But even more important, what has at times been dismissed as an overly innocent distinction between policy making and administration, stemmed from more than an uncritical view of the actual operation of administration, or from an ideological preoccupation with the fetish of efficiency. Many writers who maintained the distinction were concerned, in a serious and responsible fashion, with the maintenance of a democratic order, and were troubled by the enduring conflict between democracy and bureaucratic power in a mass industrial society (Blau, 1956; Appleby, 1949; Gaus, 1947; Herring, 1940; Hyneman, 1950; Schattschneider, 1942b; Finer, 1941; Friedrich, 1932; Bailey, 1964). How was it possible to keep the political process open and truly public if the hidden decisions of a huge state bureaucracy were accorded legitimacy and often final authority in the policy-making process?

One not entirely pointless answer was to create a new public man, the administrative eunuch, indoctrinated with a narrow, technical, apolitical ideology, a man no more efficacious in the political arena, and perhaps less so, than any other citizen. While this "solution" has not proved altogether practical, few would deny the character of this problem and, indeed, it has been the purpose of many writers on bureaucracy to face it squarely.

Following the relative decline of the economy and efficiency movements in administration, a new group of writers emerged, some of whom continue to dominate certain schools of administrative theory. Among the more important were Mary Parker Follett, Elton Mayo, Fritz Roethlisberger, Chester Barnard, and Herbert Simon. Mary Parker Follett has been an original and still relevant contributor to organizational theory (Metcalf and Urwick, 1942). She was the first modern organizational theorist explicitly interested in power in administration, the social functions of conflict, the processes of conflict resolution, and the psychological analysis of organizational participants. Her outlook was, in the modern sense, thoroughly scientific, although, at the prescriptive level, it was somewhat clouded by remnants of the philosophical idealism that persisted in the pragmatic philosophy to which she subscribed. And contrary to many writers who both preceded and succeeded her, Follett was antiauthoritarian in her perspective (about which more later). Formal discipline and command were, in her view, poor substitutes for reason. Effective organizational performance should and would emerge from an individual's appreciation of the "facts" of the matter, an unalienated understanding of how one's work fit a larger whole and how it constituted an indispensable contribution to a common undertaking.

Follett was clear in her understanding of science as more than a static, classificatory activity. Administration and science ("The greatest need of today is a keen, analytical, objective study of human relations") were dynamic processes, multidirectional and multipurposeful. The formal chartism which, it is said, has been at the root of false administrative analysis, had no part in Follett's work. Kariel (1961, p. 158) has expressed Follett's concerns as well as anyone:

> Behind the facade of the traditional table of organization she made out a complex, informal, and unplanned structure. She questioned the notion of human organizations as rational hierarchies of power. To this view she

opposed her theory of the necessary diffusion of authority, a theory springing from her moral sensibilities as well as from the observations that decisions are never isolated actions but dynamic processes. She cut through rigid organizational forms to their peculiar human constituents whose fundamental needs, irrational reactions, and concealed motives she sought to understand and order. . . . She therefore felt called on to prescribe a new order, one which would rest on objective "laws of association." These laws, when finally known, would constitute both the science of man's behavior and the proper foundation of society.

The parallel between this observation and the interests of Maslow, Fromm, and other contempory psychologists is striking, and testifies to the modernity of Follett's thought. There is no need to cite here Follett's awareness of the importance of experimental inquiry. That the tools of contemporary investigation—survey research, computer simulation, experimental gaming, and the rest—were not developed during her period goes without saying, of course, and to the extent that knowledge is coterminus with the techniques of inquiry, Follett's knowledge of administration was limited compared even to the modest advances of the 1960s.

As I said above, the movements which succeeded the machine models of Taylor and his followers were many. One, the human relations approach, was a movement that focused on the organizational member as a complex human personality which, if sufficiently known, could be molded in the service of an organizational elite's objectives but which, at the same time, might result in objectively improved conditions for the rank and file as well. The ideology of the human relations movement was never stated thus, of course; its ostensible purpose was to remove those frustrations and inhibitions of the worker which prevented his full actualization as an individual. The derivative question—actualization with respect to whose goals?—was rarely raised.

The earliest, and now classic exposition of the human relations approach came with the publication of the Hawthorne plant findings of Elton Mayo and his associates (Roethlisberger and Dickson, 1939). The central proposition of the Mayo group was this: contrary to the prevailing management theory of the late 1920s and early 1930s, alterations in physical settings, working conditions, and monetary incentives bore little relationship to worker productivity. Rather, social satisfactions arising out of one's work—wholesome group and benign leadership relationships—were the important independent determinants of productivity. In spite of numerous studies (Gouldner, 1950; Cartwright and Zander, 1953; Stogdill and Coons, 1957) which undermine the simple elegance of this proposition (in fact, no clear cross-organizational relationship exists, for example, between productivity and leadership styles), the Hawthorne studies have enjoyed extraordinarily wide acceptance among both academics and men of affairs. Alex Carey (1967) has recently argued that a secondary data analysis of the Hawthorne materials points in precisely the opposite direction from that claimed by the Mayo group; i.e., the data suggest that monetary incentives were the *most* important influences on heightened productivity. Beyond this, however, Carey argues that *no* conclusion can actually be made from the studies because of their rather profound failings in research design. Sykes (1965) has taken much the same position.

As much as anyone, Chester Barnard (1938, 1948), a creative and reflective practitioner of the administrative arts, set the tone for much subsequent important theoretical work in administrative science. Barnard called for what has now developed: an approach to the study of organizations that would utilize the techniques and insights of economics, sociology, political science, and psychology in an effort to construct a general theory of administration. Barnard was aware of the systemic character of organizations and of the relevance of the equilibrium concept to an understanding of their processes. An organization he defined as a "system of consciously coordinated personal activities of two or more persons," thus drawing attention to the relational and interactional character of its members. Equilibrium consisted in a balance between contributions and satisfactions, a concept that served to integrate personal and organizational demands into a comprehensive and intricate system of mutually interdependent linkages. This early formulation of an organization conceived as a network of human exchanges is strikingly current in its relevance for contemporary theory.

Barnard was aware as well of the existence and importance of informal organizations and their bearing upon formal structure in both functional and dysfunctional manifestations. Informal systems might inhibit organizational effectiveness by undermining formal authority but, by the same token, might contribute to organizational welfare by improving communications, cohesion, and individual self-esteem. Finally, Barnard was sensitive to organizations as systems of decisions and decision makers, as entities that have a greater capacity for rational analysis and action than individuals. In all of these ideas the reader will detect concerns that were later accepted, extended, and modified, but never completely abandoned, in much contemporary research and theorizing, particularly in the work of Herbert Simon and his associates (Simon, 1957a; Simon, Smithburg, and Thompson, 1957; March and Simon, 1958; Simon, 1960).

Simon's important work began with the publication of his book, *Administrative Behavior* (1947), in which at least three major issues in administrative thought were raised. The first concerned the "principles" of administration as they had developed from, among others, the "wisdom" of Fayol and the "Science" of Gulick. Simon's method was to deal in a rigorously logical manner with traditional propositions such as the separation of line and staff ("the function of staff is to advise, of line to command") which can be shown to be not only empirically false but conceptually naive in its misunderstanding of power and authority. The unity of command exhortation was absurd as a principle of action, given the realities of functional authority, as was the span of control injunction which, instead of reducing communication problems, might actually increase them by expanding the number of formal layers in an organization. Other "principles" were similarly attacked and none has recovered from the onslaught of Simon's logic.

The second major issue addressed in *Administrative Behavior* was the nature of organizational decision making. Decisions extended from two data sources: the empirical realities of an issue and the attitudes, biases, prejudices that people hold with respect to those and other realities. "Facts" and "values," their interpenetration and their control—the manner in which they could be mobilized to affect the behavior of others—comprised the essence of administrative authority and administrative decision making. Thus, the appropriate unit of analysis for organizational inquiry is the decisional "premise," the discrete fact or the private value that guides administrative conduct. An organization is a vast field of such premises which, combined in different fashions (e.g., specialists operating from different factual premises, administrators and rank and file from different value premises), give rise to organizational conflict and, to the extent that premises are shared, cooperation (see Wilensky, 1967 on this point). In the second edition of *Administrative Behavior* (1957), Simon reiterated his support of the decision-making approach and criticized the most popular alternative, role theory, as providing a unit of analysis, the "role," that is too gross for adequate theory-building and research purposes. The role to Simon is a bundle of decisional premises, and to *begin* organizational analysis with the role concept is to forego understanding of the roots of behavior. The third edition of *Administrative Behavior* was published in 1976. Leibenstein (1960) has made efforts to fuse role theory and the decision-making approach.

Simon may well be correct in this view, although it would seem that role theory can provide certain insights and organizing concepts useful in some initial forms of analysis. The role types that have been developed for application to organizational theory are virtually unlimited; some in the literature which provide interesting dimensions for analysis are: task-oriented, technique-oriented, and peo-ple-oriented role types; rule enforcers, rule evaders, and rule blin-kers, regulars, deviants, and isolates; locals and cosmopolitans; upwardly mobiles, indifferents, and ambivalents; rationalists, ideal-ists, and realists; professionals careerists, and missionaries; climb-ers, conservers, mixed-motive officials, advocates, zealots, and statesmen.

Finally, Simon developed the notion of the "satisficing" admin-istrator who, given the "cognitive limits on rationality," lacked the intellectual competence required to maximize in any decision-making situation. This formulation emerged as a response to those schemata (sometimes they are advanced as prescriptions) that describe admin-istrative man as more heroic than he in fact is. To Simon, man is less than an omniscient calculating machine that knows clearly what it wants and how to get it most efficiently. Alternatives are never fully specified, preferences may be ambiguous or, if ranked at all, intransi-tive, and the future is forever uncertain. In such an environment, given the limits to what he can calculate, administrative man does not maximize as does classic "economic man." Opposing the fic-tional rational man of economic theory, Simon posits man as he is, a creature who takes what is satisfactory, not what is "best," who gets along, who accepts what is "adequate."

POLITICO-ADMINISTRATIVE ECONOMY

This conception of human decision making in organizations has provided the focus for much of Simon's later, extremely sophisti-cated work and has stirred debate among decision-making theorists interested in organizations. Within this stormy history there are really two traditions at work—economic, statistical, and game and bargaining theories on the one hand, and a variety of socio-psycho-logical theories on the other. Simon, first alone, and then with March in their classic *Organizations*, was concerned to attack the extension of traditional rational-choice models to administration, models which assume that men maximize their welfare in an unambiguous physical and social setting. Such models may be formulated in a variety of ways, but as frequently advanced they assume the existence of an administrator's "decisional latitude" at the outset of any decisional period; i.e., all options and preferences are specified at the outset of the decisional period, and no inquiry is conducted into their origins. It seems true, as many argue, that no rational-choice, axiomatic model can deal with the question of the origin of perceived alternatives. Only detailed empirical work conducted within a sociopsychological framework is apt to treat the problem effectively.

Rational-choice models also assume the stability of goals, although the alternatives chosen in pursuit of those goals may shift with increases in knowledge or reductions in risks attendant upon those choices. Rational administrative man does not want x and at the same time reject x. Dramatic, quantum-type shifts in goals, by the same token, are explainable by, say, game theory, only in an ex post facto fashion while they may be more clearly deducible from other formulations, e.g., a theory of personality. Finally, theories of individual rationality assume that, as March and Simon put it, there is "a complete utility-ordering (or cardinal function) for all possible sets of consequences." (This is not strictly accurate; somewhat weaker ordinal functions as represented in economics by indifference analysis, and as extended to politics by Curry and Wade, 1968, may be used.)

Braybrooke and Lindblom (1963) have referred to rational-choice models of decision making as "synoptic" or comprehensive constructs which presume a mentally heroic but, for that reason, inaccurate picture of man the decision maker. Lindblom (1965, 1968) has more recently extended their analysis. (Again, it is not logically necessary that all such models be synoptic, although such assumptions are frequently made.) Braybrooke and Lindblom have advanced a notion compatible with satisficing administrative man by the term "disjointed incrementalism," which also purports to describe accurately how administrative decisions get made. Kenneth Boulding has reduced the concept of disjointed incrementalism to two propositions: "Never do anything unless you have to; if you have to do anything, do as little as possible" (Gamson, 1966, pp. 158–9).

Yet, there are good reasons for believing that some formulations of rational-choice decision making are useful in understanding administrative behavior, at least under certain circumstances. For example, it may in some instances be true that all possible alternatives have been specified at a given moment and that no amount of inquiry will expand the available alternatives. For example, the citizen is rarely presented with the question "What form of government shall I choose?" but rather with "For which of two candidates shall I vote?" Whether the decision maker possesses impressive intellectual credentials or not will have little bearing upon the situation. Here, *subjective and objective reality are one.* Practically, his alternatives are limited: he can vote for candidate A or B, abstain, or work, probably "irrationally" in terms of consequences, to expand the range of alternatives. For any given citizen, the latter option is not typically available. Thus, to vote, say for A, would be to "muddle through," yet it might also be the height of rationality. Knowledge has never meant, ipso facto, power. The same is true for administrative man. Thus, the environment may specify the range of available options from which the rational administrator can choose in a relatively unambiguous manner; moreover, the environment itself, from someone's perspective, may itself be regarded as rationally structured, or intendedly organized, precisely so that an administrator can have little effect on it, i.e., can extract no further alternatives from it. A more telling criticism of rational administrative man, however, goes to the question of consequences: how can he rationally choose from among alternatives if he cannot accurately predict the results of his actions? (See also Wamsley and Zald, 1973.)

The problem of unanticipated consequences is a real and troublesome one (March and Simon, 1958, pp. 36–47), but as we improve our knowledge of social systems and of the manifest and latent functions of administrative organizations, the possibility of rational selection of goals, as well as knowledge of their attendant consequences, is increased. Bureaucracies are organized in good part to resolve the problem of a misty future: their routines, programs, information gathering and processing techniques assist in that purpose. Thus, in any given circumstance it largely becomes an empirical question whether or not actual results were anticipated and whether, if unexpected *and* undesirable, they can be reversed or their effects mitigated and subsequent decisions amended accordingly. We should emphasize, too, that not all unanticipated consequences are undesirable, something that more pessimistic observers sometimes fail to note. Of course, to the extent that any decision ramifies through history, its consequences are never fully known, which tends to reduce the question of unanticipated consequences to an obvious truism.

Rational-choice models also typically assume the stability of goals. As for individual goals, there is, of course, some instability, although such instability may be more apparent than real. For example, Maslow's need hierarchy, if correctly stated, would seem to summarize the nature of what might be described as first-order goals, or goals that are enduring and innate; second-order goals (e.g., a preoccupation with professional ethics, job mobility, income) may shift to the extent that such shifts represent more efficient efforts to achieve first-order goals (Argyris, 1957, pp. 49–52). It is true that such shifts are only partly comprehended by rational-choice models. On the other hand, some second-order goals-shifts are comprehensible by such models, as demonstrated by the income and substitution effects in economic theory. In any event, organizational goals are typically social, or more accurately cultural, and not psychological second-order goals or constructs. As a consequence, they are frequently highly, indeed notoriously, stable. Thus, the problem of dramatic goal-shifts, while it may constitute a problem in principle, only infrequently in fact confronts the organizational analyst when organizational and individual goals are integrated. Dramatic alterations in organizational goals are rather deviant cases, at least in any normal research span.

The point is this: bureaucracy, by its very nature, may afford a particularly fruitful area for academic explication through rational-choice models. Not only may organizational goals be relatively unambiguous and reasonably stable, but the relatively self-conscious nature of an organization's role-structure, information-processing system, and authority matrix do tend in the direction of purposeful and rational action (Parsons, 1956). Indeed, the major criticism of bureaucracy—its stifling of individual spontaneity, its enforced discipline, its perverse "efficiency"—stems precisely from this realization. Now, it is true that all of the richness and complexity of organizational life cannot be captured by such formulations; it is also true that any research effort must choose between emphasizing social complexity or social simplicity (Mitchell, 1967b, pp. 19–20). Social scientists have usually preferred to give up nuance for rigor and elaborate and even accurate descriptions for simple, if somewhat less accurate, behavioral propositions.

In 1967 a quite remarkable book by the economist Anthony Downs, *Inside Bureaucracy*, was published. Downs's previous work, *An Economic Theory of Democracy* (1957), is now correctly regarded as a preeminent contribution to political theory. There is reason to believe that *Inside Bureaucracy* will have a similar impact in public administration. The organizing principle of Downs's book is that the style of thinking common in economic analysis can be extended to other social processes and institutions, specifically to organizational analysis. Gordon Tullock's *The Politics of Bureaucracy* (1965) and Niskanen's *Bureaucracy and Representative Government* (1971) provide other examples of this new genre. Downs's work is based upon three quite simple "hypotheses": (1) bureaucrats are rational utility-maximizers; (2) they pursue complex personal goals—power, income, prestige, etc.; and (3) an organization's "social function" influences both its internal and external conduct. These hypotheses, really axioms, are obviously derived from microeconomic theory, but they differ from conventional economic analysis in terms of the environment which Downs postulates for their operations. It is one familiar in orthodox sociological analysis: information is incomplete, both because of its costs and because of, again, the cognitive limits on rationality. The analysis proceeds in four stages. Terms are first defined; hypotheses are derived from the axioms cited above; a rather complete description of the environment is given; and a set of propositions relating to the hypotheses and the environment is advanced.

While Downs's theory does not purport to be general, it does aim to cover most major aspects of bureaucratic behavior, ranging from the processes through which bureaus are established, their internal characteristics (involving both Weberian and non-Weberian components), external relations, and the characteristics of bureaucrats, to organizational communications, organizational dynamics and controls, and bureaucratic ideologies. Within this system, some five role types are employed to explain different behavioral accommodations to bureaucracy. Downs concludes his analytical discussion by posing the questions of social efficiency and individual freedom, the traditional evaluative dimensions of economic analysis.

As a major contribution to the theory of public administration, Downs's book is perhaps the most important volume to appear in years, rivaled only by March and Simon's *Organizations*. Rigorous testing of Downs's formulation remains to be undertaken, but a sense of the fertility of his perspective is given by the 16 "laws" and the 3 central and 162 related hypotheses he articulates, most of which are far from trivial. The nature of the laws that Downs proposes may be illustrated by his "Law of Non-Money Pricing," which holds that "Organizations that cannot charge money for their services must develop non-monetary costs to impose on their clients as a means of rationing their outputs." The "Law of Ever Expanding Control" states that "the quantity and detail of reporting required by monitoring bureaus tends to rise steadily over time, regardless of the amount or nature of the activity being monitored." Many of the derived hypotheses are also stimulating and useful, e.g., "Bureaus are less willing to engage in all-out struggles with each other than are private profit-making firms." And again, "Bureaus that are highly selective in recruiting will do less internal training of recruits than other bureaus performing tasks of the same degree of complexity but exercising less selectivity in recruitment."

Tullock's *The Politics of Bureaucracy* is another (less ambitious) effort to understand (governmental) bureaucracies from an axiomatic and deductive perspective derived from economic theory. Like Downs, Tullock has been concerned with aspects of political theory as well as with organizational analysis. While Tullock's book suffers from certain deficiencies (his analysis is nowhere related to the corpus of administrative literature and his reliance on "understanding" is somewhat retrograde in implication), it nonetheless illustrates further an important approach to the study of public administration. To Tullock, there are two forms of social interaction: exchange, which is voluntary, and coercion, which is not. The organizing principle of his book is that it is useful to understand bureaucracies only in (admittedly simplified) terms of power. Exchange is not to be found in bureaucratic settings. Thus, one should analyze bureaucracies as systems in which "most civil servants, especially at the higher levels, are . . . committed to a career of finding out what their superiors want (frequently not an easy task) and doing it in the hope that these superiors will then reward such behavior with promotions." By building structural variations into the analysis (e.g., cases of the single, group, or multiple "sovereign" or superior) and relating them to his general propositions, Tullock is able to generate an intriguing (if one-dimensional) view of public bureaucracies. Niskanen's proposition that bureaucrats are budget-maximizers leads to an elegant analysis of legislative and agency behavior and contains an explicit statement on the relationship among preferences, rules, outcomes, and reform.

We have now spoken of some three general conceptions of man in organizations and the sorts of behavioral propositions that have been derived from them. March and Simon conceive of these approaches as involving (1) models in which the organizational member has been viewed as a passive receptor of organizational controls; (2) approaches in which the individual has been viewed as endowed with the "attitudes, values, and goals" which give rise to problems of conflict, motivation, and organizational goal-attainment; and (3) perspectives from which the individual has been seen as a "decision-maker and problem-solver" rationally engaged with the organization and its environment. A rough but accurate history of public administration, as well as of administration more generally, shows that academic concerns with administration have developed generally in the order with which the above contentions are given. From the work of Taylor to that of Follett, Simon, Downs, and Niskanen, the movement of administrative theory, with many diverse side currents, has been in this direction. In *Organizations* March and Simon have undertaken an analysis of each of these major models (although for the first model there is little but criticism) and, from that examination, developed hypothetical (and in some instances, well-verified) propositions involving some 206 variables which span nearly the entire range of scientific interest.

March and Simon's basic orientation might be described as a kind of psychological reductionism upon which is constructed a formal organization understood as a complex social system. Man's cognitive, perceptual, and information-processing competencies are the bases from which their analysis proceeds, an analysis built upon an extraordinary range of scientific literature. Administrative man is thus seen as "a choosing, decision-making, problem-solving organism that can do only one or a few things at a time, and that can attend to only a small part of the information recorded in its memory and presented by the environment." One is tempted to say that their masterly overview and extension of a difficult subject is itself evidence that man may be more heroic than their own definition suggests.

Their departure from certain other formulations, e.g., the traditional concept of economic man discussed above, could not be sharper, although it may well be argued that their attack upon such formulations is somewhat misplaced. But the proof of the pudding is in the eating, although my own guess is that the Downsian framework will ultimately prove more productive than March and Simon's. More generously, it may be that the complexity of organizational life as presented by March and Simon will provide a better description than Downs's approach, although the Downs model would seem to have the advantage of greater predictive accuracy and generalizability.

The post-World War II trend in public administration has centered, then, on the development of a systematic and comparative theory of administration, a trend that has involved the parent discipline, political science, with the disciplines of psychology, sociology, and economics in a search for rigorous conceptual schemes, central organizing concepts, testable hypotheses, and more sensitive devices of measurement (Henderson, 1966). The increasingly irrelevant character of the behavioralist-traditionalist struggle that engaged political science in recent years was felt less in public administration than in other areas of the discipline. Unversed as the public administration specialist of the 1930s may have been in social and psychological theory (and often, as in the case of Follett, *was* so versed), he was nonetheless always concerned with the establishment of general propositions of human behavior (although he might, to the dismay of Herbert Simon, refer to those propositions as "principles" and might grant them greater validity than they deserved). Indeed, many thought that some quite important ones had been discovered. The Simon/Waldo debates were peculiar in this sense: Waldo (1952), the antipositivist, defended the traditional explorations of administrative problems; Simon (1952b) attacked them on the presumption that more valid ones could be established. When read now, the debates seem essentially to have turned on whether or not such generalizations were acceptable, the nature of the evidence supporting them, the rigor with which they were posed, and the conditions under which they might or might not hold. If the definition of "science" is

extended beyond a narrow and arbitrary one, it was a debate between scientists, although it was one in which Simon seems clearly to
have had the upper hand. And while Simon's fact/value distinction
stirred some philosophical debate, it was not one that was to persist
in public administration with the same strength as it did in some
other areas of political science.

A second, and corollary, development of the postwar period was
the discovery, or rediscovery, in sociology, of Max Weber's historical
and sociological writings (Henderson and Parsons, 1947; Gerth and
Mills, 1946), an event that sparked a new interest throughout the
social sciences, and not least of all in political science, in the study of
bureaucracy. Indeed, if Weber was correct in his treatment of bureaucracy and authority, the study of administration had to be moved to
a central position in the theoretical structure of political science.

Weber's essential insight did not consist in his analysis of the
transformation of authority systems (from traditional to charismatic
to legal-rational) in history, but rather in his view that the state
bureaucracy was not only the major instrument of policy implementation in modern society but increasingly the channel through which
most public values were operationalized, the avenue through which
political inputs entered the political system and the arena in which
they were converted into public policies. Without slighting in importance the other institutions of political mobilization—interest groups,
political parties, electoral processes—it was the micropolitical state
bureaucracy that more and more linked individual frustrations,
demands, and allegiances to the political order that acted, or failed to
act, upon them, and that finally both expressed and applied public
rules to society. As the firm is the link between household and
macroeconomy, so, in our own time, Weber suggested, is the bureaucracy the important link between citizen and macropolity.

Three things impressed Weber about this development of bureaucracy: its awesome stability, the critical problem of its control, and
its rationality. Of the first we may cite Weber's observation that
"even in case of revolution by force or of occupation by an enemy,
the bureaucratic machinery will normally continue to function just
as it had for the previous government"; and of the second, his remark
that "generally speaking, in the long run the trained permanent
official is more likely to get his way than his nominal superior, the
Cabinet minister, who is not a specialist." On the matter of his third
preoccupation, the matter of bureaucratic rationality, Weber has
frequently been misunderstood. What is rational, he knew, is not
necessarily preferable. Bureaucracy solved certain problems but
posed others. Bureaucracy was rational only in the sense that, relative to alternative means of social organization, it was more precise,

stable, disciplined, and reliable. Greater calculability and scope of operations are the consequences of bureaucracy and would increase to the extent that, as he said, "the purest type" of bureaucratic organization was realized. The pure or ideal type would function as an analytical yardstick or set of hypotheses against which existential organizations could be measured. Its components consisted in: the organization's authority over the official life of the individual member; hierarchy, or ranks of offices; limited spheres of competence for each office; offices staffed through "free contract"; access to bureaucratic postion through technical qualification; fixed salaries; the office as the primary occupation of the bureaucrat; the bureaucratic life as a career; ownership separate from staff; strict organizational discipline; records. These variable sets have become the subjects of much empirical work in organizational analysis.

PERSONALITY, AUTHORITY, AND ORGANIZATION

Personality and Organization, the title of an influential book by Chris Argyris, expresses succinctly one of the major contemporary interests of public administration specialists. Specifically, what sorts of questions and what sorts of answers may be raised with respect to the problem of the individual who works in or stands before a large-scale organization? One out of seven Americans now works for the government, most of them in organizations of considerable scale. Political scientists, together with students of industrial sociology and psychology, business management, personnel relations, and organization theorists generally, are therefore properly concerned with such questions.
     Chris Argyris (1957) and Robert Presthus (1962), among others, have drawn pessimistic conclusions from their analyses of these problems. To Argyris there is an inevitable clash between personality and organizational structure, between the spontaneous "nonrational" character of individual men and the demands for discipline, coherence, and predictability required by formal organization. If by administrative culture we refer to the psychological orientations of people to organizational elements—goals, means, work conditions— Argyris has shown that even "favorable" orientations will nonetheless frequently mislead the analyst. An agency or bureau may be a "good" place to work only because it is apparently superior to any perceived alternatives. But, Argyris demonstrates, such evidence obscures the genuine tensions that inevitably remain. Friendships,

individual maturation, participatory attitudes tend to be absent in the "best" of organizations.

Robert Presthus, in his stimulating *The Organizational Society*, is similarly pessimistic. Presthus has examined the manner in which personality archetypes, derived largely from Harry Stack Sullivan's theory of personality and from stimulus-response learning theory, emerge from a confrontation with bureaucracy. The three archetypes are derived from the "pattern of accommodations" that individuals make with bureaucratic organization and consists of three sorts: "upwardly mobiles," "indifferents," and "ambivalents." These characterizations and their definitions are among the most insightful in the literature. (Also see Presthus, 1973.)

Of the *upwardly mobiles*, Presthus is concerned with answering a number of questions: what accounts for those individuals who thrive on organizational life, who accept its premises, means, and goals without question? How is their colossal ambition and occasional vanity to be understood? What anxieties prompt the inordinate compensations in which they engage in pursuit of power, income, prestige? What mental aberrations or rational adjustments stir their exhibitions? These are the kinds of questions that Lasswell (1948, 1960) posed with respect to politicians some three decades ago. The variable that receives emphasis from Presthus is formal organization itself, and the manner in which it enchants and mobilizes certain personality types.

The upwardly mobile pursue power, accept direction and control, draw strength from involvement with a powerful institution, are unquestioning in their organizational loyalty, and manipulative toward their subordinates. In subsequent research, Presthus (1965) has found that this theoretical formulation does tend to hold empirically among successful executives.

Indifferents are those who, finding only economic rewards in organizational participation, reject any involvement that extends beyond a fine balance of inducements and satisfactions. Organizational life is viewed as barren, inane, and perverse, a means only of achieving resources to be expended in the world outside the organization. Alienation from work is complete and adjustment is sought in family, neighborhood, community. This particular method of accommodation, Presthus argues, is the one chosen by most bureaucratic employees and constitutes the healthiest possible adjustment to organizational society.

Ambivalents, finally, are torn between seeking the rewards that organizational success can offer and the means that must be used to achieve them—flattery, deference, guile. Unable to resolve this dilemma, which afflicts intellectuals particularly, those who adjust to such a pattern are perhaps the most neurotic.

Such conceptions link naturally with the individual studies of higher bureaucrats and heads of administrative organizations which, although few in number, are intriguing sources of data and hypotheses. Among them we might include Walker's study (1954) of William A. Jump of the Department of Agriculture; Rogow's magnificent study (1963) of Forrestal; Zelig's useful, though incomplete, study (1967) of Alger Hiss; the George and George study (1956) of Woodrow Wilson; as well as the Bullit and Freud study (1967) of the same president. Nowhere, for example, in the Rogow study is it apparent that Forrestal, in spite of an overwhelming sense of guilt, ever questioned the legitimacy of the organizations to which he belonged, the nature of the rewards which he derived from his membership in them, or the policies which he pursued. His psycho-biography fits rather precisely the categories of Presthus's upwardly mobiles. Traditionally, students of bureaucracy have been concerned to understand the structural conditions under which certain personality types could emerge to leadership positions; this kind of question remains central to bureaucratic, indeed to political, analysis. But in an age when the high-ranking state bureaucrat, particularly in the military and foreign policy establishments, can exercise a major influence over the fate of whole societies even through ostensibly marginal decisions, the personality variable assumes an importance in understanding governments that heretofore it may not have. At one point, the aberrations of princes could not always shape history; today the conceptual categories of generals, department ministers, ambassadors often do. It is quite remarkable, and indicative of the work to be done in public administration, that such matters have not been at the forefront of our research agenda. We have tended for the most part to study administration; we have not studied administrators in any depth (Merton, 1940).

The science of administration must deal, then, with the individual personality—its nature, properties, orientations—and the manner in which different personality types engage in and interpenetrate administrative structures. This concern, obviously, involves an interest in theories of personality and the alternative modalities of personality derived from such theories. Political scientists have as yet limited competence in the use of such analytical techniques, but we may hopefully look for some improvement.

The personality-organization relationship extends in another important direction as well, although it is one rarely considered in the literature. Most research into the question of administrative leadership has dealt, in the early literature, with the traits, or "essence," of the "natural" leader and in more recent research, with the situational character of leadership. The general conclusion seems clear that informal leadership in organizations is extended by the group to individuals who fit most closely the nature of group norms and who possess some skills in personal accommodations and conflict resolution (Stodgill and Coons, 1957). Leaders in the Hawthorne studies appeared to be those who met most closely the production norms established by the group; in Blau's study of Federal officials, leaders were those who possessed the greatest work skills. The imperatives of the situation and the values of the group interact to bestow leadership on individuals who, in other contexts, would not emerge as leaders. Formal leadership, as Presthus (1965) has shown, also grows out of one's loyalty to formal norms and to successful task performance as defined by superiors; although, at higher levels particularly, more ascriptive criteria seem to be involved (Dalton, 1959).

But what can one say of the general cultural attitude toward leadership that grants legitimacy to hierarchically structured organizations and acts to undermine the egalitarian values of the culture? The conventional answer to this question is that the socialization of the child into authority relationships at a very early age—in family, school, church, politics—conditions him to grant legitimacy, even prior to organizational membership, to those who hold formal status in the organizations of society. Still, the ambivalence in American society between equality and bureaucratic hierarchy (Lipset, 1963) has never been fully analyzed. What in our culture accounts for the continued fascination in some quarters with "principles" such as the unity of command and the virtue of the single executive? Simon, as we have seen, attacked such principles on a logical and empirical basis, but he did not deal with the reasons for their widespread acceptance. In short, if the *obverse* of a standard cultural proposition makes just as much sense as the proposition itself, how are we to understand the reluctance or inability of people to see the other side of the coin? In this connection, it is interesting to note that *the preponderance of proverbs with which Simon dealt were statements legitimizing centralized authority.*

In a fascinating but unfortunately unpublished study by E. A. Smith (1957), a start has been made in answering such questions. Smith's method is psychoanalytic, and his data are drawn from his experience as a participant observer in a state public welfare agency, and from the administrative science literature. His assessment of Weber's and Follett's writings on bureaucracy, their social impact, as well as his discussion of an actual public administrative system (the welfare agency), derive from an understanding of public bureaucracies as social systems in which the dramas of domestic life have their analogues.

Smith's understanding of Weber takes the following form: Weber's assumption of bureaucratic rationality is twofold: (1) behavior can be rational, and (2) it is in bureaucratic structures, particularly public structures, that rationality *could*, *had*, or *would* replace the personalism and emotionalism of feudal life. Historically, too, the rationalization of family roles proceeded from the development of law, or state power, which limited the arbitrary power of the father. Psychoanalytically, however, the result was "not so much to produce healthy behavior as to sterilize the emotional climate of the family and to freeze behavior into crystallized forms. . . ."; the same processes worked themselves out in the development of bureaucracy, especially its public forms, which was similarly circumscribed by law (Smith, p. 294).

The "functional" character of bureaucracy is not denied by Smith, who contends that the organized hostility that is bureaucracy was the perfect instrument for taking aggressive control of the environment. In operation, then, bureaucracy did not, as Weber suggested, eliminate power factors, nepotism, ascriptive criteria in recruitment and advancement (rationalized "merit" systems, for example, were manipulated to accommodate these practices), but as a *conceptual system* emphasizing neutrality and achievement values, it found its adherents in various elites who saw it as providing support for the status quo. Weber's work must be understood as the cultural product of a culture that emphasized paternalistic supremacy and a hierarchical social structure. As evidence, Smith points out that Weber never seriously considered such factors as multiple formal authorities (a widespread institutional practice in the United States), nor the emotional aspects of organization that are known to every practicing administrator.

Why, then, did Weber's work enjoy such extraordinary acceptance in the United States where cultural variations—a relatively open class system, egalitarian values—differed so greatly from Weber's Germany? Smith's answer is that

> there was present in the American scene a strong emotional need with which the adopting of a foreign conceptual scheme was consistent. Possibly the pace of social change and the continuing political revolution had raised anxieties which were sought to be alleviated by the restoration of a strong-father image and of an authoritarian rule in the work life of the American people.

The ideological components included in Weber's ideal type stem from the "aggressive-submissive pattern between the male parent and the male child" of Weber's Europe, "one easily acted out in homosexual male organizations and easily associated with any activity having a highly aggressive content" (Smith, pp. 299–301).

If true, any culture in which there are all-male (or nearly so) organizations charged with an aggressive limited-objective mission (the armed forces, a Manhattan Project, a corporation) would find in Weber's formulation the ideological content to justify their activities. "Democratically-ordered joint activities," however, would seem to require or demand alternative administrative models and ideologies.

Smith then proceeds to counterpoise an American administrative theorist, Mary Parker Follett, to Weber and his unidimensional "masculine" model of administration (Smith, pp. 300-14). Although Follet did not construct a comprehensive model of administration, as did Weber, several of her ideas have had particular relevance to subsequent theorizing.

First, Follett conceived of organizations as dynamic communications systems in which sensory inputs from any part of an organization could set off an action or response elsewhere in the system. Through such reactions new social systems, i.e., new patterns of interaction, emerge, and with them, new personal and organizational values. Command and control from a Platonic (or Weberian) headquarters were foreign to her system; interdependence was central. Follett referred to this systemic phenomenon as *circular response*, a concept that is analogous to the "feedback" of more recent literature.

Second, Follett was concerned with understanding what she was to call, and what is still called, *functional* authority—a problem dealt with more recently in Victor Thompson's *Modern Organizations* (1961). Authority, she suggested, stemmed not only from formal status but from expertise and specialized knowledge, rather a contrast to Weber's conceptions of strict supervision and rigid discipline.

Finally, the question of organizational *integration* was of interest to Follett, as it has been to subsequent theorists. Integration was seen as a form of conflict resolution quite different from, say, capitulation (where conflict is resolved through power in a zero-sum fashion), or compromise (where there are universal losses to offset universal gains). Instead, integration is a process of conflict-resolution in which there are no losses to offset added increments of satisfactions. In a society which emphasizes aggression and guilt, integration may, as Smith notes, be a utopian solution to organizational conflict. Aggression inhibits integration by clouding perspectives as to the possibility of achieving integration; similarly for guilt which produces a need for self-punishment or loss for any gains received. From a psychoanalytic point of view, Smith argues that organizational integration is difficult in large part because integration at the most basic family level is culturally constrained.

Thus, the normative content of Follett's work, which centered on circular response, functional authority, and integration as positive goods, deemphasized the aggressive components present in Weber's system, and incorporated more passive and feminine elements.

Whether or not Smith (p. 314) is correct in suggesting that the ideology in Follett's work stemmed from a genteel spinsterhood, "an emotional content drawn from her fantasy life, idealized and beneficent to an improbable degree because it was never subjected to the test of being lived out in marriage," is a matter for more competent authority to decide. In any event, Follett's model would seem more applicable than Weber's to organizations with "soft," or people-oriented, outputs, with multiple missions, or to those staffed with professional employees (see Bennis, 1966).

ORGANIZATIONAL EFFECTIVENESS

Public agencies present, as do all organizations, two "faces" to the world: the face that confronts the resource markets from which they must derive their sustenance, whether physical, sociopsychological, or symbolic, and the face presented to that segment of the world that the organization services, regulates, rewards, or punishes. The relationship between these two sets of activities has frequently been taken as the means by which organizations may be evaluated in terms of their effectiveness. There is some virtue in this approach: it tends to remove biases stemming from subjective assessments of organizational policies or goals, and it brings to bear, ostensibly, a truly universal concept useful in the evaluation of all organizations regardless of size, culture, or activity. In market oriented organizations, the gauge has been useful, although it is limited to the extent that extraneous variables, e.g., depressions or shifting consumer preferences, may explain a declining performance, rather than any failure on the part of the firm. In nonmonetary market oriented organizations—that is, most public agencies—the gauge is less reliable, however, simply because the relationship between inputs and outputs is more circumspect and extremely difficult to trace. This fact, however, constitutes an analytical, not a social, problem, and it may yet be possible with more precisely sophisticated models than now exist to establish input/output ratios for most public agencies. Indeed, this is one of the major current requirements of organizational, not to say political, theory (see Kaufman, 1973; Zentner, 1973).

Still another technique of organizational evaluation, provided by what has been called the "goal" model, attempts to determine the extent to which organizations are successful—if at all—in achieving their goals. (Goal specificity, in the Parsonian system, is the defining characteristic of formal organizations.) Since goals are typically perceived future states, however, such an approach typically leads only, as Etzioni has said, to "stereotyped" conclusions: social and cultural systems are always somewhat out of joint, and analysis will indicate that all or most organizations as social systems fail to attain their goals, which are nearly always stated in cultural terms. One virtue of the goal model, however, is that, as in the input/output model, goals are taken as given, thus eliminating one form of observer bias.

Etzioni (1960) has posed as an alternative method of evaluation a "systems" model, which (1) stays at the social and does not concern the cultural level, (2) is concerned with organizations as multifunctional units (not all resources are or can be goal directed), and (3) attempts to state the conditions under which goal-attainment activities are pursued. Seen in these terms, a prison that "fails" in its official goal of rehabilitating inmates cannot be said to have failed if externally derived resources are limited to the point where only adaptive problems (say of custodianship or organizational survival) can be met, or where official goals are inconsistent with what the larger society is willing to tolerate. Superb management, trained and dedicated staff, may not be "successful" under these conditions. The important point is that many public organizations face a forceful environment but can act on that environment only in limited and discrete ways.

A suggestion: the criterion of efficiency, *if* one is concerned with using it in public administration analysis, might well give way to a broader conception; specifically, to the concept of effectiveness and all that it implies in the evaluation of organizations. A most important book providing a set of propositions relating to this question is James L. Price's *Organizational Effectiveness* (1968).

Price has consolidated the findings and implications of some fifty mostly book-length studies of administrative organizations (involving, for example, the Forest Service, mental institutions, colleges, employment agencies, and corporations). His purpose is to isolate the determinants of effectiveness defined as the achievement of operative, as opposed to official, goals (i.e., what an organization *is* actually working towards and not what its officials *say* it is working towards). It is interesting that the bulk of Price's book is given over to an analysis of the internal and external political systems that bear on effectiveness. Also relevant to effectiveness are such factors as the economic system, the organization's control system (the mechanisms which encourage conformity to organizational norms), as well as more general influences such as population and ecology.

The argument is both detailed and complex, and cannot be reproduced here. But two conclusions which relate to the interaction of political systems and administrative success are particularly relevant to public administration. (1) On the basis of Price's analysis, he draws the conclusion (p. 93) that an internal political system will contribute most to effectiveness when it is *"legitimate, rational-legal, highly centralized with respect to tactical decisions* (except where there is a high degree of complexity), and *maximally centralized with respect to strategic decisions."* (2) Of external political systems, he concludes that such systems will contribute most to effectiveness when there is a high degree of *"autonomy;* an ideology which has high degrees of *congruence, priority,* and *conformity; co-optation; major elite-cooptation; a high degree of representation; major elite representation; and a major elite constituency"* (p. 132).

CONCLUSION

The confusion of much work in public administration is clear from an examination of a variety of sources. Waldo (1968, pp. 465- 78) for example, cites three "important developments" in the field that have occurred since 1948; of the three, only one, I suspect, would be deemed important by many specialists. In short, there seem to be profound differences over the direction that the study of public administration should take. The first development that Waldo cites is the "case method" approach, particularly as developed by the Inter-University Case Program (Stein, 1952). One may readily grant that *some* case studies (Selznick, 1949; Wildavsky, 1962) are important to the extent that they blend theory and evidence in a self-conscious explication of particular administrative processes. Using any standard of scientific relevance, however, the Inter-University Case Program studies are certainly outside the mainstream of social science. They are atheoretical—indeed, antitheoretical—in the extreme, and methodologically simplistic. Even as pedagogical devices they are increasingly irrelevant in a period when so many students have been exposed to the standards of serious research, both in their public administration as well as other social science courses.

A second development cited by Waldo, the emergence of Program Planning Budgeting, is (1) not all that new, and (2) not a development in research, theory, or teaching but in administrative practice. Indeed, it is a technique of enhanced managerial control, and harbors a thinly disguised ideology. As such, it is a datum of research, in the same way that a rationalized mass media is a datum for students of political parties, or in the same way that statistics, national income accounting, input-output analysis, operations research, or monetary and fiscal theories, are devices that administrators may or may not utilize in the pursuit of whatever goals move them. That technical-rational factors are of increasing importance in that pursuit is, of course, obvious. But the scientific questions always remain: how are such techniques used, in whose interests and with what consequences? The third post-1948 development in public administration cited by Waldo—an increased emphasis in comparative administrative systems—is indeed important. A caveat might be added that although most comparative research has been usefully cross-cultural, little intranational comparative research has yet been undertaken, although Peter Blau's work (1968) makes important strides in that direction.[1]

Genuinely comparative studies of public bureaucracies are quite rare (most "comparative" studies are in fact single-nation studies). There are few efforts indeed as broadly conceived as Blau's recent and massive cross-organizational studies, i.e., his inquiry into hierarchy in 250 governmental agencies. Blau's conclusions—that organizations requiring highly qualified staff tend toward centralization; that many-leveled hierarchies are associated with size, few major formal divisions, and automation; and that many-leveled organizations are more "self-regulating" and less exposed to direct intervention from top management—are not only conclusions that would be important in any study, but are particularly so because of the increased confidence we may have in them. Such confidence stems not only from the rigor of Blau's research design, which is impressive, but also from the number of factors that can be analyzed in a study of such scale. To replicate and extend such studies will require that scholars have access to a greater share of the social product than is now the case and that they extend their perspectives beyond the traditional one-case focus (see Smith, 1975).

Or consider a recent, and on the whole imaginative, effort by Keith Henderson (1966) to integrate the diverse history and current trends of public administration. Henderson has attempted, through a kind of neo-Hegelian perspective, to collapse the history of public administration into three periods in which the "thesis" was supplied by a "structural emphasis" extending from 1887 to 1945; an "anti-

---

1. Concurrently with the appearance of his "Public Administration" (1968), Dwight Waldo sponsored a conference of young professionals on "The New Public Administration." The movement that has resulted from the Minnow-brook Conference may have profound consequences for public administration because of the normative concerns emphasized by its converts. The proceedings of the conference were edited by Frank Marini, *The New Public Administration: The Minnowbrook Perspective* (1971). Recent surveys of trends in public administration are Nicholas Henry, *Public Administration and Public Affairs* (1975) and Frederick C. Mosher, ed., *American Public Administration: Past, Present, Future* (1975).

thesis" or "behavioral-environmental" emphasis from 1945 to 1958; and a "synthesis" or "organizational" emphasis from 1958 forward. The usefulness of this dialectic is not particularly clear. Pre-1948 writers such as Follett and Barnard were not "structuralist" (although they were perhaps the most important writers of the 1930s and 1940s), nor do the second and third periods appear to be meaningfully characterized by the terms behavioral-environmental and organizational. The *Administrative Science Quarterly* began publishing in 1956, reflecting a prior concern with the sociopsychological analysis of organizations; Presthus's *The Organizational Society* appeared in 1962 and is thoroughly modern, but would appear to fit best Henderson's second category.

Not only is there confusion about the nature and history of public administration, but the instrumental and hidden character of many bureaucratic arenas has left blind spots in our understanding of bureaucracy and national politics as they currently function. Although the situation is changing (Clark and Legere, 1969; Davis, 1972), we still lack good and sufficient inquiries into such substantively important decision-making institutions as the Federal Bureau of Investigation, the Central Intelligence Agency, and the State Department; but even in agencies of a nonsecurity nature, serious studies are embarrassingly rare. We are almost totally ignorant as well of many microbureaucratic but crucial decision-making arenas: the director's review in the Office of Management and Budget, the staff activities of the National Security Council, the deliberations of interagency committees, the conferences of the Joint Chiefs of Staff. Such institutions are vitally important to an understanding of politics and policy making in the United States; indeed, they are every bit as critical to that concern as are congressional committees, the Supreme Court, or the national committees of the political parties. Yet as features on the political landscape, they are virtually uncharted except for journalistic reports which vary considerably in sophistication but which, in any event, remain typically unrelated to systematic political science.

It is probable, of course, that many existing behavioral propositions, say from the small group literature, are applicable to such systems. The arcane manner in which they operate, however, means that (1) we can never really be sure of this, since the fact of secrecy may very well influence behavior in ways not apprehended by such propositions, and (2) that a science excluded from its own phenomena is seriously compromised. Some inroads into the problem of bureaucratic access have been provided by recent legislation, but access to much sensitive organizational materials is still limited (see Simpson, 1976).

Public administration is at once the most advanced and the most retrograde of political science's traditional fields. It is advanced in those instances where organizational analysis, built by a variety of disciplines, has added to our understanding of public organizations. It is perhaps most retrograde with respect to an appreciation of the role of public administration in policy development, i.e., in politics. In spite of some commendable attempts to establish the connection between administration and politics, such efforts have usually been insufficiently systematic and have not been imbued with the theoretical clarity that one might hope for. One has only to contrast studies of public administration with studies of the electoral process for this fact to stand out in sharp relief. Voting studies began with an emphasis on social background and political choice (Lazarsfeld et al., 1948), moved to a concern with intervening (psychopolitical) variables and choice (Campbell et al., 1960), and now tend strongly in the direction of establishing cross-cultural linkages between aggregate choices and public policies (Campbell et al., 1966). In public administration, such systematic progression of effort has not really developed. In fact, efforts by public administration specialists have not even attained the linkages established in the early voting studies which focused upon SES-religion-residence variables *and* behavior. For example, the Warner et al. study, *The American Federal Executive* (1963), and the Brookings Institution studies (Jennings, 1964a, 1964b), constitute two very large and important survey research projects which delineate in great detail many of the sociopsychological characteristics of national bureaucrats. But the political and administrative theorist needs to know much more: what are the decisional consequences of such variables? Under what conditions do such factors modify the formal and informal structures of an organization? But more than that: how do such variables affect public policy?

Public administration has been the forgotten land of political science, although this may well be changing. Political scientists must go where politics occurs (Rehfuss, 1973); and few would deny that, in American society, politics is more closely connected with national bureaucracies than ever before.

6. INTERNATIONAL RELATIONS

Michael Haas

SCOPE

International relations, according to many scholars, is not a subfield within the discipline of political science. Instead, international relations is claimed to be an autonomous discipline of its own. The argument proceeds as follows. First, the study of international relations as a separable body of knowledge began after the rise of political science itself: the earlier journals and professional associations of political scientists date from the last half of the nineteenth century, whereas programs of international studies were initiated largely after World War I. Second, there are separate departments and schools of international affairs at major universities. Third, there is a mood among international relationists that they are regarded as second-class citizens within political science departments, as well as within national and regional professional associations of political scientists in which they hold membership; such a mood is reinforced by the dearth of international articles in political science journals and the underrepresentation of international relations scholars on committees and boards of professional political science organizations. Fourth, students are more attracted to international studies programs than to any of the other traditional subfields of political science, so international relations scholars feel that they are not in an interdependent relationship with their colleagues. Fifth, new journals and professional associations have arisen within the community of international relations, area studies, and cross-national studies. Notable among the journals are *International Organization*, *International Studies Quarterly*, *Journal of Conflict Resolution*, *Journal of Peace*

Special note: Manuscript received in 1969.

183

Research, and *World Politics*. The International Studies Association, the Society for International Development, and organizations among scholars interested in Africa, Asia, Latin America, the Middle East, and the Soviet world have emerged since World War II. Indeed, a major terminological distinction has gained currency in recent years: *international studies* is regarded as the sum of area studies, comparative studies, and international relations, pursued by scholars from all of the conventional academic disciplines. This formulation posits that all of the components of international studies are in symbiotic relationships with one another, thus making a separate treatment of international relations a bit artificial in juxtaposition with the wider academic home in which it plays a central role.

How can a separate chapter on international relations be justified within a volume on aspects of political science? For each of the five arguments presented above there are quite reasonable counterarguments. First of all, the fact remains that more international relationists are inside political science departments and organizations than outside, though this is by no means clear for the larger field of international studies. Second, the formation of separate departments of international relations is on the downswing; schools of international affairs tend to span the breadth of all international studies and may thereby undergo a rebirth and proliferation within universities with political science departments whose focus has become too narrow. In the third place, as international relations journals have increased, fewer articles are submitted to political science journals by these scholars; professionals have turned their attention and interest to the newer organizations, which are far more exciting intellectually than the stultifying atmosphere to be found among political science organizations nowadays. Such trends may, of course, change in time. A major argument against a separable international relations discipline is whether it is worth all the effort to draw careful boundaries around units and levels of analysis. Empirically there would appear to be no difference between behavioral regularities found at the international level and those found at the national or subnational level. Analytically there is no paradigm unique to international relations. What is the utility of isolating scholars on the basis of subject matter when they can achieve unity of interest by dint of their mutual concern with politics? In an era of fragmented knowledge, the counterargument goes, there will be more gain in the quest for unified knowledge on matters affected by or relevant to the political arena. International politics is no more divorced from international economics than national politics is from national economic realities. Moreover, international behavior is linked inextricably with national politics (Rosenau, 1969b).

Further insight can be gained by looking at alternative theoretical approaches within international relations. While students of domestic politics were persuaded that power was the central concept of politics, the study of international relations started as a self-conscious effort to reject power politics. Woodrow Wilson, himself an eminent political scientist, chided statesmen for making war in pursuit of power. The League of Nations was formed and supported by international relationists as an alternative to war, as a means for resolving nations' differences. These self-styled *idealists* were thus unprepared for the machinations of Mussolini, Hitler, and other leaders who testified to the pervasive role of power in world politics. The *realists*, especially Hans Morgenthau (1967), accepted a *power politics paradigm* for international relations,[1] while students of domestic politics in countries emerging from the economic depression of the 1930s were transcending the power paradigm to ascertain how cooperative systems of behavior and democratic principles could operate so benignly as they did in the era of the New Deal.

The overwhelming superiority of the United States after World War II posed a fundamental puzzle for advocates of the power paradigm within international relations. The United States did not choose to use its thermonuclear arsenal for fear of a doomsday situation; the Soviet Union also withheld its nuclear weapons from actual use. Neither major power could control the United Nations or bully those nations in Asia and Africa that were achieving their independence. There was a bipolar confrontation of force in most sections of the globe; with power no longer a decisive factor in the outcome of international disputes, scholars sought out new paradigms to comprehend the ambiguities of the stalemated nuclear age. Behavioral scholars in domestic politics were fascinated by shifts in voter alignments as twenty years of Democratic presidents gave way to a Republican victory by Dwight Eisenhower. Although some international relations research dealt with national votes within the United Nations, the vote was a far more trivial phenomenon within international, as opposed to intranational, politics. Much of behavioral international relations has constituted a search for an appropriate empirical unit of analysis. Hence, trends within political science and international relations diverged once again, and international relations became a rich domain for theoretical inquiry. Six paradigms have been developed since the mid-1950s.

Decision-making theory sorts out interpersonal elements of foreign policy dynamics. As sketched by Snyder, Bruck, and Sapin

---

1. For a more extensive review of international relations theories, see Haas (1970a).

(1962), a decision-making analysis of international relations involves the researcher in assembling data on spheres of competence, information and communication, and motivation. All is reduced to one atomic behavioral act, the decision. Decision-making theory has been developed by Robinson and Snyder (1965), Robinson and Majak (1967), Rosenau (1970), and Haas (1969a), to include cognitive, affective, evaluative, and structural aspects at each of a number of key nodes in a decision process.

Strategy theorists look upon interactions between countries as tranmutable in terms of a process of calculations for maximizing payoffs, and are thus concerned less with the process of deciding than with the content of alternative choices as screened through a matrix of utilities, costs, and benefits. Kahn's *On Thermonuclear War* (1960) has been the seminal work in this field, though Schelling (1960, 1966) has developed more of the social-scientific applications of the game theoretic approach to questions of military and political strategy than has Kahn (see also Coffey, 1971).

Communication theory, as applied to international relations by Karl Deutsch (1963, 1966a), looks for social networks of relations as the underpinnings of orderly international transactions. Nation building, national unification, supranationalism, and the maintenance or erosion of alliance ties are thus supposed to be a function of the frequency, intensity, and valence of interactions between national units.

Field theory generalizes the communication theory position into a view that state behavior is a function of a set of basic national attributes, one of which might be communication factors. Inspired by Quincy Wright (1955), such scholars as Haas (1967) and Rummel (1965) have been attempting to derive a set of basic national attributes that might account for such outputs as levels of foreign conflict.

Equilibrium theory is pursued by thinkers who view the major happenings of international politics as transformations from one type of system to another. Following Kaplan (1957), a main interest has been whether bipolar worlds are more stable than multipolar systems. Classical balance of power theory has preferred multipolarity; its modern advocates are Deutsch and Singer (1964). Bipolarity has been espoused by Waltz (1964, 1967). Rosecrance (1963, 1966) takes a middle position, arguing that each system of power stratification has its own advantages and pitfalls.

Structural-functional theorists, finally, seek to gain an overview of the terrain of international relations before hypothesizing specifically about its subject matter. Alger (1963a), Masters (1964), Modelski (1961), and Deutsch (1968) have been among the most prominent expositors of structural-functionalism in international relations.

Along with the growth in international relations theory, there has been an expansion in focuses for study. Traditionally, international relations was divided into the rubrics of foreign policy, international organization, international law, and international politics. Newer paradigms not only have challenged the utility of such a procrustean division, but also have raised such questions as:

1. What goals do nations seek in world politics, and how do leaders determine which goals and means to pursue? What is regarded as political and nonpolitical within the society of nations?
2. Which countries are most and least likely to align with each other, and for how long?
3. What background characteristics of leaders, attributes of nations, and systemic factors, dispose countries to exhibit different styles of foreign behavior?
4. What are the bases of support for preserving the status quo, or for desiring to change world conditions among international communities, whether bilateral, local, regional, or worldwide in scope? What kinds of citizens are actively interested in international relations?
5. What are the components and limits of national power? How unequal is the distribution of resources among nations of the world? How do weaker countries survive?
6. Under what conditions do new actors emerge and old actors disappear in the world polity? How do international organizations get support for an expansion in their activities?
7. How do leaders of states collect information about the realities of international affairs? How are world events perceived?
8. Is there a collectively sanctioned and authoritative decision-making process in international systems? How do nations reach agreements with each other on substantive matters?
9. When will states behave in accordance with international law and custom rather than anarchically? What is the extent of concern for preserving the independence of other nations, and for the freedom of peoples in other countries?
10. How are collective inter-nation plans for development implemented?
11. Which among various tools of statecraft—coercion, diplomacy, propaganda—are most likely to be chosen to pursue foreign policies?
12. What are the most likely methods for resolving conflicts and disputes between international actors?

Each of these twelve questions explores a different function that may be performed within international systems by such structures as states, international organizations, leaders of states, and the like. Since various actors and eras can be compared by using categories to describe the twelve types of problems, we have the potential for an all-encompassing theory of international structures and functions. Accordingly, following up an earlier effort to develop a structural-functional approach to international relations (Haas, 1965a), each of the questions may be said to pertain to the categories presented in Table 1.[2] The concepts themselves imply no axiomatic theory, but are to be used as convenient organizing labels for surveying empirical research on international relations in this chapter.

Before proceeding, it will be useful to define the key terms of structural-functional analysis. We can define *functions* as generic types of tasks or activities. Politics ordinarily is regarded as involving pressures from various interests to obtain rewards from official sources. Political functions can therefore be placed into three categories: some are concerned with inputs into authoritative centers, some deal with decision deliberations, and others are involved with outputs from such sources. There are four input functions, which are customarily performed outside formal political structures: articulation, aggregation, socialization, and support. Withinputs are gate-keeping, recruitment, supervision, and plan making. Output functions are rule adapting, implementation, enforcement, and direction. Political systems differ according to the manner in which functions are performed. Where functions are performed intermittently, the system is called *primitive;* in *mature* or *developed* political systems, functions are performed with great frequency. *Underdeveloped* political systems fall between these two poles. Mature political systems perform the functions self-consciously, or *manifestly;* function performance in primitive political systems is *latent*, that is, it is usually an unconscious byproduct of a nonpolitical activity, the political implications of which are not entirely perceived. Members of the Congress of the United States are aware that they are engaged in rule making, but political aspects of a weekly gathering of elders in a tribal council may be undecoded by the participants.

Just as controversy exists on whether international politics constitute the equivalent of a primitive political system (Masters, 1964)

2. The twelve questions presented as a basis for organizing this chapter are not unlike those used by Deutsch (1968) to justify his division of the study of international relations into a number of convenient categories. What is unique about the twelve questions herein is that they are generated from a coherent structural-functional framework, which is developed more elaborately in Haas (1974).

TABLE 1. Functions of a Political System[a]

Behavioral Aspect	Temporal Aspect		
	Inputs	*Withinputs*	*Outputs*
Goal Attainment	(2) aggregation	(8) plan making	(10) implementation
Adaptation	(1) articulation	(6) gatekeeping	(9) rule adapting
Pattern Maintenance	(3) socialization	(5) recruitment	(11) enforcement
Coordination	(4) support	(7) supervision	(12) direction

[a]Numbers in parentheses refer to numbered questions listed and discussed in the text.
  Source: Michael Haas and Henry S. Kariel (eds.), *Approaches to the Study of Political Science* (San Francisco: Chandler, 1970), p. 463. Reprinted by permission.

or are instead overpoliticized (Levi, 1964), most of the major research questions remain unanswered. While political science in general experienced a prolific outpouring of empirical and quantitative studies in the 1960s, international relations scholars were still debating and refining theoretical formulations without subjecting them to rigorous scientific analysis. This may seem an unusually harsh judgment, but it is shared by such an eminent political scientist as Heinz Eulau (1968), for the fact is that only about a dozen quantitative, book-length investigations have emerged as a consequence of the behavioral revolution in international relations. Most of the empirical literature is in a shorter form, in professional journals or as chapters in essay collections. Policy makers and students of international affairs thus find that the most sophisticated analyses available to them are researched incompletely and written in a language that appeals more to a technically proficient audience than to laymen. One of the purposes of this chapter is to provide a guide to this scattered yet significant and growing body of knowledge. Under each of the twelve headings there will be a formal definition of the function, a discussion of alternative approaches, a description of relevant sources of data, and a summary of findings thus far derived from research employing a quantitative design.

INPUTS INTO THE INTERNATIONAL POLITICAL ARENA

Within most of the international systems with which we are familiar, the assertion of demands by an actor signals a starting point in a political encounter. The demands may be realistic, idealistic, or unrealistic, and they are directed toward other international actors in order to trigger a decision-making process. The input phase of international politics, in short, consists of verbalizations and anticipations of possible future states of affairs.

1. Articulation

To *articulate* an interest is to state a group demand on political system. In international politics, articulation occurs when leaders of one government, on behalf of their nationals, propose action that affects another government. Since the international arena is composed of geographically distinct actors, most activity in the world polity must filter through segmentally organized governmental structures. Informal mediation of conflict by intermediate private groups occurs much less than in domestic political systems, where individuals may join groups whose overlapping membership may lead to a mitigation in the irreconcilability of articulated group interests. International articulation is performed mainly by such institutional interest groups in the world polity as the nation-state and the empire.

The frequency in performance of the articulation function is related to the relative self-sufficiency and geographic propinquity of units in the international system. States that need resources not produced at home will attempt to engage in commercial intercourse or to conquer foreign lands, provided that logistics do not impose a prohibitive cost factor. Dealings between the segmental empires in the centuries before the Roman Empire were minimal because transportation was crude and hazardous; intraimperial dealings had the properties of international relations (Bozeman, 1960). Developments in technological skill during the Industrial Revolution simultaneously made necessary an integrated supply of natural resources in the developed countries, and made possible the technological capacity for maintaining far-flung empires. It was believed that it was more efficient to have an empire than to conclude trade agreements. With the independence of former colonies in the twentieth century, the day has arrived when nearly all international articulation is formal, or state to state.

A consequence of the politicization of international affairs is that when one unit absorbs another, whether voluntarily or by coercive means, the loss in one unit's sovereignty brings to an end its ability to articulate goals that will be considered an input into the world polity. In the late Middle Ages, German free cities were legitimate articulators within the Hanseatic League, but the League preempted their ability to articulate in the international arena. The degree of hierarchy of the international system determines the degree to which

articulation is specialized or dispersed; effective articulation is concentrated in the most powerful unit of a hierarchical system, and
there is less concentration the more equal the distribution of power
among units in the system.

Most international articulation is particularistic: it is an expression of a country's perceived "national interest." Nations claiming
that they espouse universalistic policies, those that are in the "world
interest," seldom veil the particularistic gains that would accrue from
adoption of their goals.

Empirical analyses concerning articulation are to be found amid a
few dozen case studies, from E. E. Schattschneider's *Politics, Pressures and the Tariff* (1935) to Glenn Paige's monumental *The Korean
Decision* (1968). The process of calculating which goals to express is
the province of foreign policy decision-making theorists, who have
followed the lead of Snyder, Bruck, and Sapin (1962) in examining
structural, cognitive, and motivational elements that play a role in
determining foreign policy choice (Willrich and Rhineland, 1974).

Most students of articulation have preferred to undertake partial,
rather than holistic, applications of Snyder's decision-making approach, and an assortment of studies on the foreign policy-making
process has thus appeared without being knit together theoretically.
The role of the executive has been studied by Hilsman (1967), Pruitt
(1964), Halpern (1974), and Sapin and Snyder (1954). The most
recent treatments on legislatures are by Carroll (1966) on the House
of Representatives, and Robinson (1962a) and Frye (1975) on both
chambers. Interest groups and political parties have fascinated
Almond (1950), Cohen (1957, 1963), Bauer, Pool, and Dexter
(1963), and Rosenau (1963). Rosenau's (1970) ongoing team investigation of comparative foreign policy-making promises to deparochial-
ize the overattention to American processes and thus find out which
kinds of structural arrangements have what effects over a large
sample of countries, thereby following up such single-country studies
as Deutsch and Edinger's (1959) analysis of German foreign policy.

Cognitive and perceptual aspects of foreign policy calculation
have received closer attention in recent years. The role of ideology,
sketched imaginatively by Leites (1951), has been more relevant for
long- than for short-range articulation (cf. Triska and Finley, 1965).
Subjective probabilities and uncertainty are seen as decisional elements by Wohlstetter (1962) and Russett (1967b). Perceptions are
content analyzed by Holsti (1962b), Holsti, North, and Brody
(1968), and Zinnes (1968), revealing that decision makers obsessed
with emotional and affective considerations will so structure their
images of reality as to justify policies that are maladaptive and futile.
Misperceptions are studied through survey research in Christiansen

(1959), and through nonfrequency content analysis by White (1966). Charles Hermann simulates the environment of foreign policy decision makers in *Crises and Foreign Policy* (1969) and tests some twenty-six hypotheses about the effects of threats, surprise, and crisis moods.

2. Aggregation

When two or more states consciously reduce mutual incompatibilities in articulated foreign policy goals with the air of presenting a single, harmonized, and joint demand upon the international system, they have engaged in *aggregation*. Several demands are pooled so that a combination of states can pursue a common set of goals with a greater chance of their attainment. Aggregation results in a simplification of the number of articulated goals in the international arena.

In international systems unaccustomed to peaceful resolution of conflict, manifest aggregation is performed largely within shaky coalitions of states shortly before and during wars. Aggregation may also be latent. The extension of a state's frontiers by conquest, bringing formerly independent units into subjugation, entails latent aggregation on behalf of the new realm. To promote the retention and efficient exploitation of new lands on the periphery, an imperial power has to temper foreign policy demands relevant to the inner core of the empire. So long as colonists consent to rule by a "mother" country, colonial rule is a voluntarily accepted form of international aggregation. By the 1770s many American colonists had changed their opinions about their status and sought to throw off English aggregation of their interests. Similarly, protectorates often are welcomed as aggregative devices by which weak powers agree to let major powers manage their foreign affairs; as the scope of domestic affairs left to the local rulers shrinks, the aggregation is regarded as illegitimate.

The most frequent manifest aggregators appear to be the strongest members of blocs and treaty organizations; superior resources and diversified interests place them in leadership roles. A strong unit has a head start in securing adoption of its articulated goals, so it may seek to add enough adherents to its camp in order to achieve a general consensus on its point of view.

Informal aggregation involves an oral agreement or entente. For aggregation to be formal, an official declaration or treaty must be on paper. When the British and French carved out spheres of influence in the Indochinese peninsula, they were informally agreeing to aggregate on behalf of the native peoples. A geographical distribution group in the United Nations aggregates informally insofar as it lacks regular meetings and has no administrative organization. The Arab caucus, which has had a permanent headquarters and regular times for conferences since the early 1950s, aggregates formally. Aggregative alliances and treaty arrangements vary from being self-executing, thus requiring no formal organization, to those that establish permanent machinery, such as the institutions of the European Economic Community. In intermediate cases, such as a treaty dealing with water resource development of an international river, an ad hoc intergovernmental commission may be established to provide a continuous forum for interest articulation and aggregation. An example is the St. Lawrence Seaway Commission.

One effect of aggregation is the reduction of particularistic goals, although completely universalistic goals do not necessarily emerge. Instead, the national interest is restated as the coalition, bloc, or regional interest. One view is that these aggregated intermediate interests make resolution of conflicts more difficult by inhibiting a spirit of cross-coalition compromise in attempts to negotiate settlements of issues. The contrary view is that the experience of successful aggregation educates states on the advantages of abandoning national selfishness and intractability.

Data relevant to articulation, as discussed in the previous section, include case study analyses of decision making, simulations, content analyses, and roll-call voting in the United Nations. Aggregation analysis, which has come into vogue just recently, has relied extensively on roll-call voting data as well as on compilations of the number of types of alliances and coalitions among countries.

Bloc voting research has enjoyed popularity since Hovet's *Bloc Politics in the United Nations* (1960). The identification of homogeneous clusters of countries has been continued by Alker and Russett (1965), who find that divisions on East-West cold war issues do not carry over into the North-South cleavage about the need for a world redistribution of resources.

Alliances have been categorized into defensive pacts, nonaggression pacts, and ententes, in an enumeration by Singer and Small (1968) that covers the years 1815 to 1945; they have supplemented the list (1969) through 1965. Using these data Singer and Small (1968) found that alliances appeared to deter wars in the nineteenth century but have been precursors to twentieth century wars, whereas Haas (1970b) examines the same data and finds that the presence of many alliances is associated with bipolarity, which in turn is a relatively peaceful way of stratifying power in international systems (see Singer and Small, 1972; Holsti, Hopmann, and Sullivan, 1973). Although mutual advantage is regarded as the cement of alliances,

Russett (1970) discovers that the most powerful partner in an alliance will tend to invest a much larger share of its resources in order to hold the alliance together. Insofar as a state desires to play a leadership role and has noneconomic goals in mind, it will sacrifice or redistribute its resources to its junior partners (Burgess and Robinson, 1969). A nation that avoids alliances entirely is likely to have considerable hostility toward leaders of the alliances, moreover (Choucri, 1969).

Functional and political integration is a more durable form of institutionalized aggregation. The cases reviewed by Deutsch and associates (1957) in the North Atlantic area suggest that unification is more likely to be successful before states have achieved industrialization; pluralistic (functional) security communities are recommended for the advanced countries today. Further research on regional mergers and institutional devices is provided by Etzioni (1965, 1966) Nye (1971), and Blase (1973).

3. Socialization

As social animals, men learn to respond to certain stimuli in a manner that they believe will lead to desired rewards. The behavior of nation-states conducted by their national elites is as structured as that of individuals; they respond to a conditioning of their activities. The process of learning what roles a state can assume, what patterns of behavior it can follow, is referred to as *socialization*. Role conformity and role deviance gauge the degree to which actors in international relations are fully or imperfectly socialized. Socialization gives a state a distinctive national style of performing other functions within international systems.

The latent sources of socialization to international political behavior are ideologies, belief systems, and social norms. Underlying cultural values shared by foreign policy elites establish patterns of behavior of international actors. Belief systems, whether religious, democratic, aristocratic, collectivist, or nationalist, contain general propositions that are accepted as standards of behavior. Christian ethics conditioned medieval international politics, just as Marxism-Leninism guides actions of Communist countries.

Manifest socialization about the nature of the international system is acquired through direct or vicarious experience of the behavior of foreign units interacting in the international arena. Leaders of countries are in a position to see the extent to which expectations of domestic international socialization are unrealistic on specific policy questions in light of the structuring of the international system.

Foreign policy proposals of nonelites may be consistent with domestic ideologies but impracticable. Elites and well-informed persons ordinarily can best predict what consequences follow from certain kinds of behavior of states in the international arena, and according to Ernst Haas (1958), European elites built the European Economic Community in spite of nationalistic pressures because they had been able to develop a sense of mutual trust and camaraderie in their negotiations.

The manifest socialization by a decision maker consists specifically in determining traditional diplomatic orientations of countries, in assessing the proper balance between objectives and commitments (ends and means), and in discovering the rules that need to be observed to maintain international systems. An individual is imperfectly socialized within an international system if he receives his international socialization only as a latent by-product of national socialization. A state's international behavior will be more effective the greater the degree of influence of its internationally socialized elites.

Traditionally, Americans are said to be prone toward legalism and abstract idealism, the British toward power balancing, Germans toward Continental domination. These traditional orientations are consistent with the dominant ideologies of meliorism, pragmatism, and rationalism, respectively. Junior diplomats are promoted if they owe allegiance to these notions of their superiors. National plenipotentiaries at conferences presume that other nations will continue to have the same national style, and reciprocal role expectations will be mutually reinforcing until there is a radical turnover of elites.

Because it is assumed that states will attempt to achieve what is in their own "national interest," there is a bias in international systems toward particularistic socialization. There is some evidence, however, that participation in international organizations involves a certain degree of universalistic socialization. Representatives of states learn to think more in terms of the world interest after they have talked to their opposite numbers in other delegations at the United Nations (Alger, 1963b). Ideological socialization may be performed within blocs by a bloc leader specialized in the socialization function; pragmatic experience in the international environment is obtained diffusely. Powerful states discover that they can lead coalitions, dictate rules to weak states, and either fight or coexist with states of equal power. States increasing or decreasing in power have difficulties in learning appropriate roles. Because of Germany's growing might in the early twentieth century, its leaders were tempted to bid for hegemony in Europe—for which Germany was twice unprepared. The post-1945 decline in French power has tempted its decision makers to play a vetoing role, as in the European Defense Community and the early British application for entry into the Common Market.

One traditional approach to the study of international socialization is to analyze "isms" and foreign policy continuities in diplomatic history. The sociocultural approach traces patterns of national behavior to nonpolitical group life or to child-rearing practices in nations (Leites, 1948). A third approach is the elite study or the biography, in which the social and psychological backgrounds of decision makers are considered (Lasswell, Lerner, Rothwell, 1952; Raser, 1966). A fourth approach is to specify rules known to well-socialized actors in a variety of international systems; system maintenance and system change can be assessed by determining under what conditions actors fail to learn these rules (Kaplan, 1957).

Three types of factors are viewed as possible predisposing elements in the decision making of international actors. In keeping with Singer (1961) and Waltz (1959), these are the psychological, sociological, and systemic levels of analysis. Data sources vary at each level.

The concern with perceptions in articulation overlaps with the broader concern for psychological aspects of decision making, which have been codified by Klineberg (1964), Stagner (1967), and De Rivera (1968). Public opinion data and experimental findings are surveyed extensively in articles in Kelman's *International Behavior* (1965) and Rosenau's *Domestic Sources of Foreign Policy* (1967). Clinical appraisals of individual leaders appear in George and George (1956) and Rogow (1966).

Sociological factors have been assessed rigorously during the last decade. Domestic conflict has been found unrelated to foreign conflict by both Rummel (1963) and Tanter (1966). But the same aggregate statistical data have been reanalyzed by Haas (1965b, 1969b) and Wilkenfeld (1968, 1969), and a positive relationship has been discovered instead. The role of rank disequilibrium has been described by Galtung (1964, 1968) and Lagos (1963). Social correlates of foreign policy opinions have been delineated by Rieselbach (1966a), Bobrow and Cutler (1967), and Bobrow and Wilcox (1966); many other studies are contained in Kriesberg's *Social Processes in International Relations* (1968).

The claim that bipolar power distributions are inherently precarious and unstable has captured the interest of systemic theorists such as Kaplan (1957), Rosecrance (1963, 1966), and Waltz (1964, 1967). Bipolar systems with spiraling arms races have been studied by Richardson (1960a,b) and Boulding (1962). But Haas (1970b) finds that wars are more frequent in multipolar eras, upsetting the predictions of classical balance of power theory.

4. Support

Although allegiance to international systems is ordinarily lower than it is to national polities, Easton's (1965b, p. 390) definition of the *support* function allows for such a possibility: "actions or orientations promoting and resisting a political system, the demands arising in it, and the decisions issuing from it."

Data concerning support would consist of opinions expressed in survey research or content-analyzed statements of decision makers. As Choucri (1969) finds, leaders of nonaligned states have a hostile disposition toward the thermonuclear giants, the U.S.A. and the U.S.S.R. The lack of support for international systems stems from its inchoate structure. While bloc followers may back up bloc leaders in a bipolar or multibloc system, manifestations of support for the system as a whole lack a clear point of reference. One may claim that the acceptance of a current modus vivendi constitutes latent performance of the support function nevertheless. Indeed, transformation of the system to some other model would be fraught with so much uncertainty that states reaffirm existing power stratification arrangements quite frequently insofar as they engage in incremental foreign policies. The designs of a Napoleon or a Hitler for fundamental reconstruction of the international order may be entertained secretly by leaders in starry-eyed moments of megalomania, but such goals are seldom pursued.

Only the Charter of the United Nations and similar documents in regional intergovernmental organizations provide a set of symbols that may approximate a universalistic orientation for the actors within the world polity. Even so, ceremonial events, a flag, and a pledge of allegiance are notably lacking at the international level, although there is a United Nations Day and a UN flag. As Claude (1966) argues forcefully, international organizations generate support insofar as their members consciously seek collective legitimization. Lip service to the goal of world peace and justice for all is fashionable within speeches delivered at the United Nations, but support is far more particularistic when the audience addressed is in a domestic setting. One of the advantages of regional communities is that a state can support the interest of the region while not appearing to desert its domestic constituents. Holsti and Sullivan (1969) report that China was far more deviant in attitudes within the Communist bloc than was France as a heterodox member of the Western bloc, and they attribute this difference to the amount of pluralism tolerated within each bloc in the first place. Similarly, it has been found that Chinese hostility toward the West is highest when Peking and Moscow are not engaged in an altercation or a border incident, whereas intrabloc dissension dampens China's hostility concerning countries in the non-Communist world (Holsti, 1966).

Theories of international communication and integration approach the question of transnational loyalties most directly. Exchanges of trade, diplomatic representatives, common memberships in international organizations, and the formation of new regional communities, are all seen as minimal aspects of mutual support between countries. According to Deutsch and associates (1957) and Etzioni (1965), the most important factors accounting for peaceful communities and mergers between states are similar values, preferences, and a common attachment to symbols. Although an alliance indicates aggregation, such an arrangement is only a potential sign of support between partners should a critical situation arise. Richardson (1960b) finds that former allies seldom go to war with each other, though the memory of former friendships wears off quickly. British-American relations are chronicled in terms of communication theory in a study by Russett (1963), who finds that Britain's share of American attention declined as the United States rose to world prominence and began to consider its relations with many other countries (see also Pentland, 1973).

Another approach in locating inter-nation support and collaboration is to ask elites and various publics whether they are inclined toward nationalistic or internationalistic views. McClosky (1967) finds that rigid personalities espouse nationalism, and his analysis of political leaders show them to favor internationalist options. Ascertaining whether loyalty toward one's country is incompatible with transnational loyalties, Guetzkow (1956), however, has found that group identification is a more generalizable characteristic: those forming a strong attachment to their own country are also likely to be world-minded.

DECISION MAKING WITHIN THE INTERNATIONAL POLITICAL ARENA

Most of the authoritative allocations of values in international systems are made by the major powers, but since such entities enjoy far less of a monopoly on coercive means than do governmental elites within national polities, small powers do have a great deal to say about the systems in which they often serve as a disconsolate proletariat.

5. Recruitment

In all systems there is a division of labor; some units specialize in the performance of tasks to which they are best suited. Leaders, for example, are chosen to direct activities and to supervise maintenance or changes in systems. In some domestic political systems, leaders are recruited formally by means of elections; but in international political systems, leadership accrues to the most influential states.

Lasswell and Kaplan (1950) suggest that *influence* can be measured by eight components—power, respect, rectitude, affection, well-being, wealth, skill, and enlightenment. In general, one would suspect confirmation of their agglutinative hypothesis, namely, that states high on one factor will be high on others. Galtung (1964) hypothesizes that a state failing to achieve such an equilibrium in rankings will attempt to redress the imbalance by force, if necessary. Except for the situation in which leaders are chosen formally in international organizations on the basis of such considerations as respect and rectitude (cf. Singer and Sensenig, 1963), however, power and wealth are the most important components of international influence (Bartlett, 1973; Alpert, 1973; M. R. Singer, 1972; Spiegel, 1972; Calleo and Rowland, 1973).

A concomitant of recruitment is world stratification of influence and of international role differentiation. In *unipolar*, imperial systems there is one dominant power; other units may be linked either democratically or in an authoritarian manner. *Bipolar* systems are *tight* if all members of the system are in the orbit of one of two power centers; *loose* bipolar systems contain two major blocs with some nonaligned states. Similarly, there may be tripolar, quadripolar, polypolar, or multipolar systems. As the degree of influence stratification declines, role differentiation can be correspondingly more dispersed. Historically, the most frequent systems are unipolar; Rome, for example, produced a stable role fusion in a single center through dominance and acquiescence. As influence is more diffusely distributed, states jockey for leadership roles by means of a continuous increase in national components of influence. Unipolar systems have greater stability than dispersed systems, particularly fragile eras of multipolarity (Haas, 1970b).

Recruitment is studied in four ways in international relations research. One approach attempts to derive a "power formula" by some combination of indicators, such as military resources, economic resources, administrative capacity, and motivation for war (Claude, 1962; Jones, 1954; Knorr, 1970; Morgenthau, 1967; Organski and Organski, 1961; Organski, 1968; Brodie, 1973). Two historians, Simonds and Emeny (1935), show specifically how these components are integrated by countries seeking power in the 1930s. In runs of the Inter-Nation Simulation at Northwestern University, Brody (1963) experimentally created a bipolar system and then arranged for nuclear weapons to spread beyond the bloc leader, aiming thereby to study the effects of nuclear proliferation on power structure.

The results of his study show that bipolarity remained but was maintained much more loosely, while most countries turned to economic pursuits; in several cases, however, war was declared and fought to a conclusion. There is need for the experimental approach in studying recruitment because most relevant data on national power for present situations are often top secret and thus cannot be examined within an academic setting.

6. Gatekeeping

The traditional concern about imperialism in world politics (Moon, 1926) focused largely on how industrialized countries intervened to prevent less advanced peoples from attaining sovereign status. To decide which entities shall be members or nonmembers in world politics is to engage in *gatekeeping*, a concept first developed by the novelist Franz Kafka to refer to nondecision-making processes in domestic politics (cf. Bachrach and Baratz, 1962a). Gate-opening involves the creation of new entities, such as Belgium from the United Netherlands in the early nineteenth century; gate-closing occurs when a larger power swallows up buffer states on its periphery. A third way for a new entity to rise as a member of an international system is for a faction in a domestic civil war to attract outside intervention: as long as the Falange's opposition to the Spanish government was defined as a domestic war by the European powers, its status was that of a subnational actor; but when German, Italian, and other troops were dispatched to fight in the quarrel, the Falangists achieved an international significance.

Gatekeeping over issues is performed more covertly than gatekeeping over membership in an international system. An issue such as disarmament is usually not open to discussion within international systems, except between powers that maintain very friendly relations; instead, the limitation and control of certain types of weapons is apt to be discussed. Because there are few resources independent of members of international systems, states with prized resources strictly control any efforts to reallocate their resources on a more universalistic basis, unless, as in the case of Perry's "opening" of Japan, both sides stand ready to gain reciprocally from having a wide number of issues freed for discussion. One of the more unexamined questions in international relations is under what conditions disputes become negotiable, and when international organizations expand the scope of their activities. Klingberg (1966) predicts the termination of war on the basis of casualties suffered by the losing countries; Tanter (1967) and Beattie (1967) consider task expansion of international organizations in their investigations of international political development.

The *grand debate* approach to peace (Claude, 1964) is premised on the view that international organizations can serve to open the range of issues discussable before a forum in which universalistic expressions are more acceptable. In this respect international systems are more likely to have gatekeeping performed by formal, specialized institutions today than national systems, where anomic and non-establishment interest groups are likely to raise new issues for consideration.

Accordingly, it has become fashionable to discard the concept of sovereignty and to refer to degrees of penetration instead. Herz (1959) has surveyed ways in which states can be penetrated formally: by economic sanctions, by propaganda, and by the use of aerial warfare. Scott (1966) and Rosenau (1970) examine informal penetration, a condition in which the real centers of power in a state are held by rulers or agencies located in other states. Communist satellites are penetrated informally via Communist parties; former colonies are still penetrated economically in a manner referred to as neocolonialism within the new states of Africa and Asia. The military penetration of Southeast Asian countries up to the mid-1970s was a source of caustic debate. In search of empirically homogeneous international regions, Russett (1967a) in effect decomposes the world polity into definable subsystems with memberships based upon similarity in United Nations voting and trade interchange. And these subsystems also delimit boundaries to the performance of international supervision, the next function to be discussed.

7. Supervision

Decision making presupposes information concerning the nature of a situation, the means at the disposal of decision makers, and the feasibility of various alternative courses of action. Supervision consists of fact gathering and observation with the aim of piecing together an orderly conception of realities.

Media, especially newspapers, television, and radio, provide the ordinary citizen with information about international affairs (cf. Robinson, 1967). A two-step flow model, with news going to opinion leaders and thence to most members of the public, has been proposed by Katz and Lazarsfeld (1955); this would appear especially appropriate for international news, with which most persons lack direct and meaningful experience. Almond (1960a), and Deutsch and Merritt (1965) trace fluctuations in opinions and attention to foreign news as a function of the importance of the issue. Nevertheless, most news is likely to convey incomplete images. Markham (1961) and Abu-Lughod (1962) find coverage highly skewed toward major powers rather than a balanced treatment in the press (cf. IPI, 1953). Many observers have also noticed that editors will tend to feature news in the framework of earlier attitudes instead of allowing new information to challenge existing stereotypes (Kriesberg, 1946; Oliphant, 1964; Schillinger, 1966). News distortion, however, can be due to the biases of a recipient more than to biases in coverage (Holsti, 1962b; Eckhardt and White, 1967).

For the citizen fortunate enough to undertake foreign travel, it is possible to gain insights that will modify ideologically based views (Isaacs, 1961; Gullahorn and Gullahorn, 1962; Bauer, Pool, Dexter, 1963; Angell, 1969). Information for foreign policy elites is gathered much more systematically. Indeed, Ogburn (1960) has provided a detailed description of various channels through which an item of information can travel in the United States State Department. Xydis (1956) notes that the press in other countries can be scanned to derive a notion of public and official attitudes on foreign policy issues. Cohen (1963) indicates that the press is used as a check against governmental sources of news, the latter derived principally from diplomatic reports. And diplomats frequently travel abroad to obtain firsthand information on new conditions and to participate in international conferences.

The act of supervision consists of overseeing the behavior of actors. If a United Nations representative in South Korea observes an advance of North Korean troops which violates an internationally agreed boundary, his perception of the violation—if communicated—is an instance of supervision.

Procedural supervision is performed by protocol officials of individual foreign ministries and by parliamentarians at international conferences. Substantive supervision is conducted by each country on its own, or by officials of international organizations assigned to observer teams. For example, in 1956 the Soviet Union desired the "free reliberation" of the Hungarian nation but would not admit the United Nations Secretary General to Budapest to oversee events, which took place instead under the watchful eyes of Russian airplane pilots.

In United Nations questions involving small powers, the performance of the supervision function often constitutes what Claude (1964) refers to as preventive diplomacy. When a crisis arises, the formula is to dispatch United Nations personnel as observers to the scene of the dispute. Given orders only to fire if fired upon, the effect of interposing the UNEF in Suez between Egyptian and

British-French-Israeli forces was to implement a cease-fire in a latent manner while the mission manifestly "observed" the military forces.

Data on supervision come from two main sources. Insofar as diplomacy is the most highly institutionalized form of the state observation of conditions in the international arena, we would look for diplomatic exchange data to reveal networks of formal state interaction (Singer and Small, 1966b). There are some 25,000 diplomats assigned abroad in the world today, according to Alger and Brams (1967). The second source of information is through nonofficial media of communication such as mail, the world press, radio, and television, all of which are susceptible to content analysis (cf. Lasswell, Lerner, Pool, 1952; North, Holsti, Zaninovich, Zinnes, 1963) and transaction flow analysis (cf. Brams, 1966; Gleditsch, 1967).

Diplomatic styles and practices have been codified by Nicolson (1963), but this aspect of supervision is largely bilateral in character. Multilateral diplomacy occurs within international organizations, and the main political function of such institutions at the international level has been to give publicity to disputes between nations in a supervisory, rather than decision-terminating, capacity (cf. Claude, 1964). Alger (1963b, 1965), for example, has demonstrated that UN participation can serve as a learning experience that makes for a more world-minded corps of diplomats. It is the informal discussions, rather than the stylized public speeches, which garner maximum information for diplomats (Alger, 1968). The extent of international communication, surveyed in its qualitative richness by Davison (1965), has been found to have a direct relation to the size of the actor communicating. Just as unicellular organisms are functionally diffuse and have many transactions with their environment, small countries tend to have a high proportion of foreign mail and trade. As a country becomes more developed economically and its share of foreign intake declines proportionally, its internal preoccupation increases (Deutsch, 1956a; Deutsch and Eckstein, 1961).

8. Plan Making

When designs to allocate resources within international systems are being decided upon, plan making is occurring. The most frequent setting for *plan making* is a bargaining situation involving negotiations. Although overt negotiations have been subjected to close scrutiny by both traditional and behavioral scholars, the concept of tacit bargaining has arisen more recently in an effort to understand the nature of deterrence. Because plan making might be unilateral on the part of any member of an international system, in the sense that a country directly affected might not be consulted on a move, scholars have come to realize that all states maintain certain postures toward other states in order to deter undesired, unilateral moves.

A plan is made when a standard of behavior is specified by a source in an authoritative manner.[3] To be authoritative, a plan must be clothed in legitimacy, which means that its acceptance ordinarily must be based more on consent and acquiescence than on coercion. The simplest example of a plan is a two-power treaty in which there is a mutual pledge to observe the terms prescribed in the document; this is a type of particularistic plan. Universalistic plans are contained in multilateral conventions. Most resolutions in the United Nations are not plans insofar as they only express pious goals in which implementation is left to individual states, some of which may continue to misbehave with impunity. Plan making differs from aggregation in that the latter occurs when two or more countries pool demands to strengthen the likelihood of their attainment; when plan making is completed, demands of one state upon another have been met in principle and remain only to be put into practice.

A large number of important and authoritative international decisions are made in specialized international organizations, where they are regarded as nonpolitical allocations of values (Sewell, 1966). The UN seldom functions as a true political decision making body. UN decision making on economic and social questions, analyzed by Hadwen and Kaufmann (1960), has several positive effects. However, the mere dispatch of intermediaries and peace observation teams seldom constitutes a step toward the authoritative reallocation of international resources, despite its extremely useful function of cooling off tempers of countries in a crisis (Young, 1967; Wainhouse et al., 1966). In Kriesberg's (1967) analysis of collective decision making in international systems, the lack of normative consensus is singled out as the most insurmountable factor. Nevertheless, contemporary thermonuclear powers agree that disarmament and deescalation are desirable, but they have not yet agreed to a program involving significant arms reduction. It is simpler to reciprocate a posture of deterrence than one of tension reduction (cf. Etzioni, 1967).

Much of deterrence research shades off into the study of more direct bargaining situations, where the operational codes suggested by Iklé (1964) are immediately relevant. Results of such investigations, as surveyed by Sawyer and Guetzkow (1965), and by Gallo

---

3. The term "plan" is almost equivalent to "policy" but has been endowed with a more general meaning in Miller, Galanter, and Pribram (1960).

and McClintock (1965), demonstrate only a sketchy awareness of overall processes. Meeker, Shure, and Moore (1964) find that the threats associated with deterrence lead to payoffs that are far less satisfactory for both sides than more empathic negotiations. There is much consistency in the experimental studies concerning the benign outcomes associated with high levels of communication among participants in a negotiation process (Fouraker and Siegel, 1963; Pilisuk and Rapoport, 1964). Concessions in the experimental games of Bartos (1967) were made by softer bargainers facing tougher negotiators, but concessions in Soviet-American disarmament negotiations have been correlated with positions of relative military weakness on the part of the conceding country (Jensen, 1965).

OUTPUTS INTO THE INTERNATIONAL POLITICAL ARENA

Changes in value allocations throughout international systems assume many forms. Customarily, they have been studied in terms of the principal tools of statecraft such as economic transactions, verbal exchanges, and the application of force and coercive sanctions.

9. Rule Adapting

If a demand placed upon a country is regarded as worthy of immediate adoption, the decision-making process is for the most part shortcircuited; an arduous effort to aggregate and to perform the plan making function is unnecessary. Demands are seen as routine, however, only when they are viewed as conforming to an existing set of rules and procedures. When demands appear to bring existing norms and rules of conduct up to date, such as in the light of changes in technology, *rule adapting* has occurred. In national political systems, rule adapting is performed most conspicuously in legislatures and courts, where law is defined or modified incrementally. International law, however, occupies a less central role in international systems, even though its scope is defined so broadly as to include provisions of treaties and customary forms of state behavior.

For a system to be maintained in an orderly manner, predictability in the exchange of goods, symbols, and services is required. Substantive aims of members of systems are achieved most efficiently where there is agreement on norms and standards of behavior. Social systems have certain norms which specify behavior that conforms to, or deviates from, attainments of man's needs in a particular environmental setting. These norms give rise to rules of conduct that simplify goal attainment.

In world politics there are two generic types of outputs; both are contained in international law and practice. *Procedural rules* relate to the etiquette of international political behavior. *Substantive plans* deal with concrete allocations of rewards accruing to groups that bargain in interest conflicts. One example of a procedural rule in international politics is the specification in the United Nations Charter of conditions for summoning a meeting of the Security Council. An example of a substantive output is the decision by the International Court of Justice that Cambodia had more of a claim to disputed territory than did Thailand; legal principles were weighed to determine a judgment, and the Thais acquiesced.

International law lends itself to case analysis, as in McDougal's inspired *Studies in World Public Order* (1960) and in the more recent *International Law and Political Crisis* (1968) by Scheinman and Wilkinson, both of which demonstrate the specific uses of law in conditions of intense disputes. Although many textbooks on international law are organized as casebooks, the sum of procedural rules of the international system is not synonymous with what is contained in international legal codes. The positivist school of international law regards manifestly written rules—treaties and legal decisions—as the major sources of law. Such rules are adapted in a latent fashion as certain practices or norms of state behavior arise and are accepted gradually by other states. In nonpositivist international law, however, custom, equity, and natural law are more likely to be invoked in nonpolitical disputes between states. It has been the task of Carlston's *Law and Organization in World Society* (1962) and of Coplin's *The Functions of International Law* (1966) to analyze the diverse uses of international law and thereby the scope of the rule adapting function. In contrast with law within countries, nonlegal regularities in international behavior (that is, custom) are more frequent sources of rule adapting in international systems (see Barros and Johnson, 1974).

Procedural rules of diplomatic behavior were developed by Richelieu, codified by Callières (1919), and have been expanded subsequently at international conferences. Treaties dealing with such specific matters as trade, as well as those establishing international organizations, customarily contain procedural rules for the fulfillment of the substantive aims. Ambassadorial negotiations proceed according to diplomatic protocol; plan making in organs of international organizations is guided by procedures concerning time and places of meeting, methods of voting, and other constitutional requirements. For example, the advisory opinion of the International

Court of Justice that the United Nations is an entity with legal standing in international law contained a procedural implication, namely, that the UN may bring suit in a court of law. With the procedural rule decided, it became possible for a substantive suit to be brought in connection with the assassination of the United Nations mediator in Palestine, Count Bernadotte.

An emphasis on law in action rather than law in books has been stimulated considerably by *The Political Foundations of International Law* (1961), by Kaplan and Katzenbach, and has received restatements by such scholars as Irvin White (1969). Sources of behavioral data on international law consist of the number and types of treaties contracted between countries, as well as various aspects of international courts—the nature of their judges, the decisions, and the votes cast.

Oakes and Mowat (1918) provide one of the earliest compilations of treaties, but systematic analysis of Soviet treaties is one of the earliest efforts in behavioral international legal research. Triska (1964) summarizes findings from his classification of Soviet treaties by asserting that there has been a trend away from political-ideological motives and toward economic aims. As the U.S.S.R. withdrew from treaties contracted by the Tsarist regimes, it undertook economic agreements more and more. Today one-third of Soviet treaties are economically oriented, and indicate the extent to which the revolutionary temper of Soviet foreign policy has cooled into a preference for prosperity under an international status quo. A larger project, supervised by Rohn (1968), has assembled and coded treaties documented in the UN Treaty Series for purposes of information retrieval and, ultimately, correlational analysis.

Courts of international law have attracted much attention on the part of quantitative scholars. Rosenne (1955) compares the current International Court of Justice with the former Permanent Court of International Justice, which existed contemporaneously with the League of Nations; he finds that the PCIJ was used more frequently than is the ICJ. Nagel (1966) develops a predictive model to determine the outcome of cases to which the United States is a party. Jarvad (1968) notes that the most powerful states are the principal litigants in the ICJ but that their actions are motivated largely by desires to enhance their prestige as law-abiding members of the family of nations, for the weakest nations have on the average recognized the jurisdiction of the ICJ much longer than the strongest nations. Low-ranking nations are more likely to refer to general norms and future consequences, rather than particularistic rules and present circumstances which undermine the aim to make the scope of international law more pervasive.

In domestic situations, a case that is settled out of court relieves the strain on judicial systems. But this is not true in international systems, where a nonlegal settlement entails a widening of the sphere of politics and a narrowing of the scope of law. We now turn to the remaining output functions, which are politicized to a high degree.

10. Implementation

Once a treaty is ratified or a gentlemen's agreement finalized by a handshake, it may never be put into operation. International plans may be dormant or active. *Dormant* plans may include those that are unenforceable or obsolete. *Active* plans are those which are executed, and for which noncompliance is likely to be punished; in short, two functions—implementation and enforcement—are involved. The initial execution of a plan is *implementation*. If implementation falls short of expectations, one reaction may be to recognize the impracticability of the plan and to abandon it, but another response may be to engage in *enforcement*, that is, to inflict deprivations on noncompliant actors. Noncoercive implementation is frequent in stable social systems; it is costly and disturbing to a system to enforce rules with great frequency. The chronic instability of international systems is due to the larger role of enforcement, wherein strong states seek to impose their will on weaker states. Examples of procedural implementation and substantive enforcement occurred in the Congo in 1960. The authorization of the ONUC force by the United Nations, in accordance with Charter procedures, was implemented quickly, as African troops assembled under the command of General von Horn. The substantive plan, directing ONUC to bring about a unification of the Congo, was enforced by resorting to force only after Katangese forces resisted implementation of the UN order to cease fire.

Whether international implementation is unilateral, bilateral, or multilateral, two main tools of statecraft can be used—words and deeds. Some writers expand this list of tools to include diplomacy, propaganda, and economic or military actions. Such techniques may be employed as inputs, withinputs, and outputs, equally appropriately. We are interested here primarily in how such modes of state behavior are involved in carrying out international plans and, thus, in the way in which such outputs feed back into the input stage, generating demands for new plans or for the continuation of old ones.

Diplomacy in corridors of the United Nations has already been discussed as a socialization factor (Alger, 1963b); the codification of diplomatic rules of protocol is of interest to students of rule adapting; and the collection of information by diplomats constitutes a source for international supervision. What concerns us here is how diplomats engage in international administration, a subject that owes its origin to the pioneering work of Norman Hill (1931). The practice of diplomacy to conduct day-to-day operations has been called *overseasmanship* by Harlan Cleveland and others, who summarize the role of public and private representatives of the United States in *The Overseas Americans* (1960). Yet another analysis of diplomats *qua* administrators is provided by Thayer (1959).

Data on diplomatic exchange have not been collected in abundance, though Brzezinski (1961) assembles a careful summary of delegations exchanged among leaders of states in the Soviet bloc. Brams (1968), in turn, has analyzed these data to derive a measure of levels of prestige hierarchy within the Communist camp.

The study of diplomatic implementation within international organizations, especially at the regional level, has tended to stress progress in nonpolitical realms as a possible catalyst for multinational political cooperation. Ernst Haas's notion of spillover in *The Uniting of Europe* (1958) has been used as an organizing device for studying when agreements reached within one functional sphere make additional agreements in other spheres more feasible and pragmatically desired by the countries involved (cf. E. Haas, 1964). Pointing to the thriving Common Market institutions, where an increasing load of business is transacted, Haas argues that integration is increasing in Europe. Focusing on attitudes (Deutsch, Edinger, Macridis, Merritt, 1967) and trade patterns (Alker and Puchala, 1968), other scholars find decreased integration in Europe and more internal preoccupation with unforeseen problems of disequilibrium created by the new regulations of the Common Market. Similar problems are noted in other regions by Eide (1966) and Reinton (1967).

International administration in the United Nations has been surveyed by Sharp (1961, 1963). The largest share of the UN budget is devoted to social and humanitarian aims, the success of which has been chronicled by Asher and associates (1957). International administration by empires has intrigued both Bozeman (1960) and Jones (1923).

Data on propaganda, another tool of statecraft, consist of verbal symbols and nonverbal images conveyed in visual media. The content analyses of Lasswell (1927) and George (1959a) are most familiar to political scientists as evidence of how wartime propaganda can serve as inputs into strategic planning (cf. Daughtery and Janowitz, 1958). But the most systematic research on propaganda and attitude change has been conducted by social psychologists, who have demonstrated,

for example, that rational appeals are superior to fear-arousing messages (Janis and Feshbach, 1953; Hovland et al., 1957; cf. Klapper,
1960).

Economic tools of statecraft have yet to be researched exhaustively as a means for implementing international plans. Analyses of
the impact of foreign trade, tariffs, and commodity regulations have
been conducted by economists with an international relations specialization (cf. Schelling, 1958; Lagos, 1963; Myrdal, 1956). Political
scientists have been content to uncover the existence of trading blocs
(Russett, 1967a; Brams, 1966). Foreign aid has been examined as a
politically motivated aspect of power politics (O'Leary, 1967; Liska,
1960; Morgenthau, 1962b; Montgomery, 1962) more often than as a
positive assistance to economically developing countries (Pilvin,
1962; Wolf, 1964).

11. Enforcement

When members of a system are perceived to be insubordinate, it
is incumbent upon elites to enforce procedural rules and substantive
agreements if basic patterns of the system are to be maintained.
Since major powers are likely to be at odds, international enforcement would be continually turbulent were leaders of countries to act
in an unrestrained manner. In international organizations, procedural
rules are generally enforced by presiding officers—and successfully—
in the face of opposition by powerful members of the international
system so long as the universalistic character of the rule is clear and
the style of enforcement is regarded as mild and polite.[4]

Enforcement of substantive plans involves the use of threats or of
actual diplomatic, economic, or military sanctions, thus placing the
bulk of the burden of enforcement on states with many resources
available to be committed to gain compliance at whichever cost
accords with a country's priorities in values. Universalistic enforcement comes under the heading of collective security, which has been
tested with some success only in the case of Korea (Claude, 1964;
Goodrich, 1953).

Enforcement is an infrequently performed function in the international system when compared with national systems, since individual lawbreakers in a country can be incarcerated more easily.
Countries starting wars have been decreasingly likely to win in

---

4. Nicholas (1967) describes the case where the Chairman of the General
Assembly threatened to cut off the interpretation system from delegates of the
Soviet Union who, in the opinion of the chair, were out of order. Such a threat
was extremely effective in maintaining a procedural rule.

modern times (Deutsch and Senghaas, 1969), and according to Russett (1965), internal warfare has a higher incidence than external warfare. Moreover, it is well known that most warfare deaths are due to nonbattlefield fatalities (Prinzing, 1916; see also Hiscocks, 1974).

Although economic sanctions (Hoffmann, 1967) and economic warfare (Gordon and Dangerfield, 1947) have received some attention, scholars look to war and its causes as the principal focus for studying international enforcement. At the personality level, doves and hawks have been contrasted in national cross-sections of public opinion as well as in college classrooms (Bobrow and Cutler, 1967; Bobrow and Wilcox, 1966; McClosky, 1967; Galtung, 1967; Carter, 1945), and it has been found that doves are college-educated, middle-aged, Jewish, nonauthoritarian, and politically active. Decision-making case studies reveal that decisions to go to war involve information underload, psychological frustration, cultural ignorance, and issues that are regarded as crucial (Haas, 1969a). War-prone states are major powers, economically and politically stagnant, and engage in arms races (Haas, 1971). The international system breeding the most warfare is multipolar in character (Haas, 1970b).

Warfare *qua* enforcement, of course, has been described in textbooks on military history, such as the one by Fuller (1961). But the costly and inconclusive nature of limited wars in modern times, plus the unthinkability of nuclear warfare, has directed the interest of scholars to methods for deterring potential aggressors.

Deterrence theory initially was based upon the conceptual innovations of game theory (Kahn, 1960; Morgenstern, 1969), but through the leadership of such thinkers as Schelling (1960) it has been taking more real-world factors into account. Data in deterrence research varies from aggregate case analysis to experimental games. Richardson (1960a, 1960b) finds that progressive arms buildups turn into runaway arms races. Russett (1967b) finds that a major power will defend a minor power under threat of attack when there is a high degree of interdependence between the two states, especially when the linkage is economic. Rapoport and Chammah (1965) report on ways in which players of experimental games prefer to be noncooperative or can be induced to achieve mutually satisfactory outcomes. Nevertheless, a leader of a country who perceives his state as invulnerable will resist all efforts at compromise (Raser and Crow, 1966). And, concluding a summary of deterrence research over a twenty-year period, Raser (1969b) brands deterrence strategies a failure: they have actually made the world less secure, for no system of deterrence can simultaneously provide both adequate threat and reassurance against its preemptive use in a surprise attack.

12. Direction

Our final concept has been defined as "the more detailed guidance of the conduct of foreign affairs and the execution of policies which have been formulated" (Padelford and Lincoln, 1962). *Direction* involves the coordination of operational elements of foreign policy toward specific targets, and thus most specifically implies conflict resolution and conflict termination (see Mendlovitz, 1974).

Preconditions to conflict termination have been analyzed in detail across many types of phenomena by Coser (1961). Yet according to Quincy Wright (1955), most international conflicts are resolved by becoming obsolescent. Alternatively, the balance of power is said to operate as an invisible hand which regulates and equilibrates international systems (E. Haas, 1953b; Claude, 1962; Zinnes, 1967). Direction is performed quite infrequently, most states preferring to remain in ambiguous relations with each other—with conflicts expressed in a muted and indirect manner rather than becoming so sharp in intensity that vital interests will be perceived as being involved. The termination of international conflicts once required the signing of treaties of settlement following major wars, but the growing institutionalization of international relations in the twentieth century has meant that much more direction is performed by specialized, formal bodies, from plenary bodies of intergovernmental organizations to tribunals with a worldwide jurisdiction.

When conflicts are terminated inside international institutions, a more universalistic style pervades the settlement. But when wars are concluded, the more frequent possibility is for the weaker side to capitulate to a particularistic set of terms favoring the victor in the struggle. Decisions to surrender have been surveyed by Kecskemeti (1958). Klingberg (1966) informs us that as a state's casualties rise above 4 percent of its total population, it undergoes a period of war weariness; states that hold out beyound the 4 percent level are likely to have fewer perceptual linkages between the ruling elites and the public at large and hence to be undemocratic forms of government.

One of the newest fields of inquiry to emerge has been the investigation of modes of conflict resolution. Hanrieder (1966) has suggested the probability that one method or procedure will be able to operate within a variety of systemic conditions. His suggestions have been used to guide the tabulation of disputes resolved by majority will or balancing in U.N. organs (E. Haas, 1968) and parallel K. J. Holsti's (1966) classification of awards, passive settlements, compromise, submission-withdrawal, conquest, and avoidance.

CONCLUSION

Each of the theories of international relations reviewed in this chapter assigns primacy to one or more of the functions enumerated above. Power theory places the recruitment function at the center of attention, arguing that states with more power will perform the other eleven functions more frequently and more successfully. Decision-making theory focuses on articulation, and thus encompasses the whole of international relations by accepting the tacit postulate that ultimately all of the other functions are consequences of decisions made at the national level. Strategy theory concentrates on enforcement. Field theory is basically a model of international socialization. Communication theory overlaps the aggregation function (where it studies the conditions under which states harmonize their goal demands jointly), the supervison function (which deals with information inputs into decision making), and the concept of spillover as used by investigators of implementation whith intergovernmental organizations. Equilibrium theory hypothesizes a fundamental linkage between enforcement propensities and the power structure of an international system. Through a structural-functional framework it is possible to see that these strands of theory are working in relative isolation from one another, hence suggesting the utility of convergence through a broader treatment.

The structural-functional approach to the study of international relations would appear to qualify as a broad gauge theory of international relations. It classifies the major elements of international systems and enables their interrelationships to be located within a unified framework. It integrates the traditional attention to diplomatic history, international law, and organization with more recent advances in systematic empirical analysis. It encourages the statement of commonly held propositions in a more precise manner. But functional categories are removed by an inferential leap from actual behavior; they supply a conceptual overlay for organizing knowledge and thus guide a survey of the literature even when no propositions unique to functionalism are formulated.

Perhaps the greatest advantage of a functional approach to international relations is that it avoids parochialism; it can apply to non-Western, premodern international systems. The complete testing of propositions generated by functionalism involves a comparative study of historically distinct international systems (Modelski, 1962; Haas, 1970b). Before such cross-historical comparison is possible, however, there is a need for far more systematic knowledge about relationships between variables that apply to the contemporary era.

A quantitative literature based on articles and fugitive and varied sources has begun but has failed to achieve exhaustiveness on any single subject. While world leaders persist in pursuing reckless policies in every corner of the globe, the time has come for scholars in international relations to provide sound advice to policy makers before our time for reflection as well as for continued existence comes to an end.

PART 3

TOOLS AND TECHNIQUES
OF RESEARCH

7. SURVEY RESEARCH

Donald M. Freeman

The use of survey research to study political phenomena is more clearly identified with the "Behavioral Era" than any other technique of data collection (Dahl, 1961b, p. 765). Articles and research reports based on survey data did not begin to appear in the journals of the discipline until after the Second World War, that is, at approximately the beginning of the behavioral era. We should acknowledge that political science owes a great debt to marketing research, sociology, psychology, and social psychology for their early groundbreaking work with survey methods, and all of the social sciences are in debt to those scholars in the field of mathematics who deal with the theory of probability and statistics (see Hennessy, 1970b, pp. 83-92). The importance of the rise of social survey research for the "Behavioral Protest Movement" can not be overestimated: it permitted the political scientist to make inferences about individual political behavior, to make precise statements about large populations, and to study the component parts of complex populations in ways not possible before.

One can chronicle the rising importance of survey research in political science by a simple count of journal articles relying on the technique. We have made such a count for the *American Political Science Review, Journal of Politics,* and *Western Political Quarterly,* considering the years from 1948 to 1968. These data are reported in Table 1. The "Behavioral Credo" reads "whenever possible quantify one's data" (Somit and Tanenhaus, 1967, pp. 176-80). The impetus to quantify is clearly visible in the national and two regional journals, with a gradual increase in quantitatively oriented articles from 1948

Special note: I wish to acknowledge the debt I owe to Jerry L. Rankin, my research assistant at the University of Arizona, for the collection of the data reported in Tables 1 and 2.

T A B L E 1. Proportion of Articles Using Quantitative and Survey Data for Three Political Science Journals by Year of Publication, 1948-1968

Proportion of Articles		1948	1949	1950	1951	1952	1953	1954	1955	1956	1957	1958
		American Political Science Review										
With Quantitative Orientation		4.8	2.3	12.2	8.7	17.8	20.9	31.7	22.5	18.2	14.0	26.8
Based on Survey Data		0.0	0.0	7.3	2.2	4.4	7.0	7.3	7.5	6.1	2.3	9.8
	$N =$	(42)	(44)	(41)	(46)	(45)	(43)	(41)	(40)	(33)	(43)	(41)
		Journal of Politics										
With Quantitative Orientation		9.0	9.4	16.7	0.0	6.9	5.0	0.0	14.3	24.0	19.0	16.7
Based on Survey Data		0.0	0.0	0.0	0.0	3.4	0.0	0.0	0.0	8.0	0.0	4.2
	$N =$	(33)	(32)	(30)	(31)	(29)	(20)	(23)	(21)	(25)	(21)	(24)
		Western Political Quarterly										
With Quantitative Orientation		0.0	2.3	8.6	8.1	10.0	11.4	2.8	9.4	12.7	19.6	20.0
Based on Survey Data		0.0	0.0	0.0	0.0	0.0	0.0	0.0	3.1	0.0	5.4	0.0
	$N =$	(28)	(43)	(35)	(37)	(30)	(36)	(36)	(32)	(55)	(56)	(45)

Proportion of Articles		1959	1960	1961	1962	1963	1964	1965	1966	1967	1968	Total
		American Political Science Review										
With Quantitative Orientation		19.4	16.7	23.1	28.6	31.4	40.0	51.4	68.3	66.7	62.3	28.4
Based on Survey Data		16.1	8.3	6.1	2.4	5.7	5.7	5.4	22.0	15.6	15.1	7.4
	$N =$	(31)	(36)	(39)	(42)	(35)	(35)	(37)	(41)	(45)	(53)	(853)
		Journal of Politics										
With Quantitative Orientation		13.0	26.3	24.1	37.0	24.3	31.6	30.3	29.0	50.0	36.1	20.4
Based on Survey Data		0.0	5.3	13.8	3.7	2.7	10.5	12.1	6.5	10.0	5.6	4.4
	$N =$	(23)	(19)	(29)	(27)	(37)	(38)	(33)	(31)	(30)	(36)	(592)
		Western Political Quarterly										
With Quantitative Orientation		22.6	25.0	22.2	16.3	34.9	45.8	33.3	43.2	38.6	31.1	21.7
Based on Survey Data		1.6	1.8	3.2	7.0	11.1	6.3	7.9	10.8	10.5	8.9	4.2
	$N =$	(62)	(56)	(63)	(43)	(63)	(48)	(63)	(37)	(57)	(45)	(978)

to 1968, until roughly two-thirds of the articles in the national journal and one-third of the articles in the regional journals are based on quantitative data. Likewise, there is a gradual and clear increase in the proportion of articles based on survey data.

In the three journals for 1948 and 1949, no article based on survey data appears. Beginning in 1950, at least one article based on survey data appeared in each volume of the national journal, but survey based articles made no consistent appearance in the regional journals until after 1959. If we divide the journals under consideration into two roughly equal time periods, 1948-1958 and 1959-1968, the trends we want to note are much more boldly stated by the data. See Table 2.

In the decade 1959-68, the national and regional journals in political science published at least three times as many quantitatively oriented articles as they had in the previous decade. In the same comparative time periods they published at least twice as many articles based on survey data. The *American Political Science Review*, the preeminent journal in the discipline, has been more receptive to quantitatively oriented articles and to survey data based articles than the two regional journals. And at least one-fourth of all quantitatively oriented articles appearing in the national and regional journals from 1959 to 1968 were based on survey data, though many other quantitative techniques of data collection were available to political scientists.

T A B L E 2. Proportion of Articles Using Quantitative and Survey Data for Three Political Science Journals by Decade, 1948-1968

Proportion of Articles		1948-1958	1959-1968
		American Political Science Review	
With Quantitative Orientation		16.1	42.6
Based on Survey Data		4.8	10.4
	$N =$	(459)	(394)
		Journal of Politics	
With Quantitative Orientation		10.7	30.7
Based on Survey Data		1.4	7.3
	$N =$	(289)	(303)
		Western Political Quarterly	
With Quantitative Orientation		10.4	30.9
Based on Survey Data		1.1	6.7
	$N =$	(441)	(537)

Until very recently, survey research has largely been a tool for the student of American politics and political institutions. Though our journals attempt to maintain a balance of published articles among the various fields of the discipline, 90.4 percent of the articles in the *American Political Science Review* and 76.9 percent in the *Journal of Politics* (1948–1968) that used survey data were studies in the American field. The extent to which the survey has been the special tool of the researcher in that area is obvious in Herbert McClosky's excellent treatment of "Survey Research in Political Science" (1967). Eighty-nine percent of the citations in his bibliography are for studies in the American field. Students of American politics have a big head start over their colleagues in other fields in the discipline in the use of the sample survey (probably on account of the voting studies), but extensive use of the technique has begun in the other fields, especially in comparative politics (Converse and Dupeux, 1962; Butler and Stokes, 1969; Merritt and Rokkan, 1966; Frey et al., 1969; Holt and Turner, 1970; Rokkan et al., 1970; O'Barr, Spain, and Tessler, 1973).

In these introductory paragraphs we have tried to demonstrate that survey research is a technique of investigation which is of increasing importance to the political scientist. We have avoided the standard introductory questions: "What is it?" "When is it used?" and "When should it not be used?" Survey research is a technique or tool of data collection. The data collected pertain to a universe or population of interest to the researcher. Rather than taking a complete census of the relevant population, the researcher takes a sample, which must be drawn by procedures carefully laid down in advance so that the researcher knows the accuracy of estimates he will make and the confidence he can place in his findings.

Survey research can be used to study almost all political phenomena involving individual behavior, but it is obviously limited by the capacity of the respondent to remember, to distort, or to report objectively events, motivations, or acts. It has been used to study the political behavior of elites, groups, and masses. For example, it has been used to study the following elites: legislators (Wahlke et al., 1962), lobbyists (Milbrath, 1963), party officials (Eldersveld, 1964), congressmen (Miller and Stokes, in Campbell et al., 1966, pp. 351–72), senators (Matthews, 1960), civil servants (Stanley, 1965), and professional soliders (Janowitz, 1960). It has been used to study formal and informal groupings in society: the political behavior of Jews (Fuchs, 1956), the International Typographical Union (Lipset et al., 1956), the impact of religion on behavior (Lenski, 1961), the United Auto Workers (Kornhauser et al., 1956), and the political behavior of Negroes in the South (Matthews and Prothro, 1966). It has been used repeatedly to study American voting behavior, the studies from Michigan's Survey Research Center being the most important examples. (The two major SRC studies were: Campbell et al., 1960 and 1966; see also Rossi, 1959.) It has also been used to study processes and institutions central to Western political systems; for example: who has power (Dahl, 1961a), how are citizens socialized (Hess and Torney, 1967), what are the dimensions of citizen duty to the state (Almond and Verba, 1963), and the functions of public opinion in a democracy (Key, 1961 and 1966; McPhee and Glaser, 1962). These are only a few of the hundreds of significant studies which have relied heavily on survey data (Glock, 1967).

Many of the most important subjects on the research agenda for the political science profession are not likely to be studied through survey research. The evolution of political institutions, for example, cannot be easily explored with the survey. Some subjects can be more efficiently studied using another technique: for example, communications patterns in small groups may be studied effectively using participant-observer methods. Only after the research topic has been chosen and carefully defined into a series of hypotheses should the investigator adopt a particular research technique.

Sometimes the investigator must choose another technique of data collection as an alternative to survey research because of the costs involved. A small survey study, of a limited universe, can consume a surprising amount of money. A large-scale, national study can only be funded with the help of the major foundations and typically costs a quarter of a million dollars (*ISR Newsletter;* Sudman, 1967; Mayer, 1964). Every stage of survey research is costly in human and financial resources: designing the study, drawing the sample, printing the interview schedules, training the interviewers, conducting the fieldwork, coding the interviews, and analyzing the results. Large-scale survey studies may require the employment of up to two or three hundred persons on the staff and in the field. The time consumed between drawing up a research proposal and publishing the findings may be more than five years. *The American Voter* (Campbell et al.) is a study of the 1952 and 1956 presidential elections that was published in 1960. The fieldwork for *Negroes and the New Southern Politics* (Matthews and Prothro) was conducted in 1961 (Southwide cross-section) and 1962 (student); it was published in 1966. The proposals for these two studies were obviously submitted to the foundations a year to two before fieldwork began. (On funding major research projects, see Zallen and Zallen, 1976.)

Most of the large-scale, significant survey research projects for political science have been conducted by one of three research centers, which I will introduce briefly at this point. *The Bureau of Applied Social Research* was established in 1937 at Princeton as the

Office of Radio Research under a Rockefeller grant and under the directorship of Paul F. Lazarsfeld and associates Hadley Cantril and Frank Stanton. It moved to Columbia University in 1940, gradually expanded its research interests, and changed its name from the Office of Radio Research to the Bureau of Applied Social Research in 1944. Two of the earliest voting studies were conducted by the Bureau; its staff was especially active in government contract research during the Second World War; and it continues to be active in the areas of urban problems and methodology (Lazarsfeld, Berelson, and Gaudet, 1944; Berelson, Lazarsfeld, and McPhee, 1954; Bureau of Applied Social Research, 1966). *The National Opinion Research Center* was established in 1941 at the University of Denver under the direction of Harry H. Field and was moved to the University of Chicago in 1947. It is a multipurpose, nonprofit research organization which does a wide range of survey research work for government agencies, universities, and private organizations (Mack, 1961; Allswang and Bova, 1964). *The Survey Research Center* of The University of Michigan is a component of the Institute for Social Research. It was founded in 1946 by Rensis Likert and Angus Campbell. Respectively the first and second directors of the Survey Research Center, they had been associated with the Division of Program Surveys of the United States Department of Agriculture, a governmental research agency which had been doing survey research since 1939. The Survey Research Center carries on a wide variety of independent research funded by foundations, it does contract research for governmental agencies, and it frequently conducts surveys for research projects housed at other universities (Institute for Social Research, 1965a, 1965b, 1968, 1969a, 1971). Surveys also are conducted out of research centers at leading universities all over the country, but the three centers discussed above have been the leaders; they have trained more new practitioners, and they have been responsible for more methodological innovations than all of the other research centers added together.

Like modern medicine, survey methodology has many general practitioners and a few celebrated specialists. The literature has gradually begun to reflect an increasing level of specialization. Some of the most important academic specialists are on the staffs of the three research centers noted above. However, there are many other specialists doing applied work in the fields of marketing research and public opinion polling. The professional association in which academic and applied survey methodologists share their findings, discuss ethical standards, and try to solve mutual problems, is the American Association of Public Opinion Research, founded in 1946 (Hart and Cahalan, 1957). They adopted as their official organ the *Public Opinion Quarterly*, which was first published in 1937. The student of survey research methodology should keep up with the *Public Opinion Quarterly*, but in the sampling and data analysis components of the subject, he will frequently need to turn to the leading journals in statistics.

In the limited space available for this chapter, I can by no means give the student a detailed introduction to survey research and its literature, but will cover briefly the following general subjects: design, sampling, questionnaire construction, interviewing, coding, analysis, polls and pollsters, critics, trends in survey design and analysis, secondary analysis, and data repositories.

RESEARCH DESIGN

The design of survey research is a special case under the general heading of the design of social research. The canons of modern science dictate that good social research proceed by a carefully laid out plan, a plan which keeps the research team goal conscious and on guard against loose habits of mind.

As there is no one path to discovery, there is no one set of steps in research. However, by relying on the research design literature, we can extract some of the components which should be included in a research plan. (1) There must be a thorough explication of the central research question, which will lead the research team into (2) a survey of background and related studies, including those related bodies of data stored in data repositories. (3) The central research question should then be defined into a series of subquestions or hypotheses for investigation. At this stage in the research design, the investigators need (4) to carefully define those concepts and variables involved in the study, an operation which will entail exploring measurement problems related to the study. If a concept is relatively new and unexplored, preliminary methodological studies may be necessary to build scales, indices, or other operational definitions (see chaps. 17 and 12 in this volume). (5) The research team will then need to select the population or universe to be studied. If survey research is to be the tool of data collection, (6) a sampling procedure suited to the research task needs to be selected. The choice of the universe to be studied and the sampling procedure to be used are heavily dependent on the financial resources available; and the sampling procedure is further limited by the sampling frames available and by the precision with which the research team wishes to make estimates. (7) Drawing up the research instrument—the questionnaire—and deciding on how it will be administered are conditioned by the preceding components of the research plan. The instrument should be pretested and suitably revised before going into the field. The research design should include a plan for (8) conducting the field work, (9) designing the coding manual, (10) coding the interviews, and (11) analyzing the results. Finally, (12) there should be a plan for reporting the findings of the study to the academic and related communities.

This brief introduction is oversimplified, of course; however, the reader must realize that each component of research design is related to every other component. A complete plan is a prerequisite to good social research and is even more of a prerequisite for good survey research. Unless the research team has considered carefully the variables to be studied, and included the relevant questions in the study; unless they have formatted the data properly; unless they have drawn a sample which will permit comparisons of relevant subpopulations within the universe; then the analysis cannot be satisfactorily completed. The analysis plan, more than any other component, can expose the inadequacies of other parts of the research design. The research plan is a vehicle with which the research team can control error, minimize bias, and, in general, minimize variance that might be the product of the research process itself.

The last generation of political scientists read a series of works on methodology and research design which are still being used: Selltiz Jahoda, Deutsch, and Cook, *Research Methods in Social Relations* (1959); Festinger and Katz, *Research Methods in the Behavioral Sciences* (1953); Eulau, Eldersveld, and Janowitz, *Political Behavior* (1956); Lazarsfeld and Rosenberg, *The Language of Social Research* (1955), updated by Lazarsfeld, Pasanella, and Rosenberg in 1972; Lerner and Lasswell, *The Policy Sciences* (1951); Lindzey, *Handbook of Social Psychology* (1st ed., 1954); and Ackoff, *The Design of Social Research* (1953). One must be impressed that these works have remained useful and have not been significantly dated by the last decade of methodological innovation.

Five general works on methodology are outstanding, and should become the classics of this generation of political scientists: Kerlinger, *Foundations of Behavioral Research* (1964); Lindzey and Aronson, *Handbook of Social Psychology* (2d ed., 1968); Sjoberg and Nett, *A Methodology for Social Research* (1968); Blalock and Blalock, *Methodology in Social Research* (1968), and Greenstein and Polsby, *Handbook of Political Science* (1975). An excellent general work on the ethics of social research is Sjoberg, *Ethics, Politics and Social Research* (1967).

The serious student of methodology will want to consult an emerging body of literature on the logic and philosophy of research in political science (Wasby, 1970; Isaak, 1969; Greer, 1969; Frohock, 1967; Meehan, 1965, 1968, 1969). There are about a dozen teaching manuals available for introducing the undergraduate to research methods; some of them are very useful and quite sophisticated (for example, Buchanan, 1969, 1974; Benson, 1969). A number of quality introductory methods texts are available, largely from sociology; if the advanced texts assume more in the way of background and preparation than the student has had, then he should begin with one of these texts (Phillips, 1966; Riley, 1963a, 1963b; Chapin, 1955; Thomlinson, 1965; Simon, 1969; Goode and Hatt, 1952; Doby, 1967; Denzin, 1970; Madge, 1965; McCormick and Francis, 1958; Buchler, 1961; Lerner, 1958b; Miller, 1970a; Smith, 1975; Smith et al., 1976; McGaw and Watson, 1976).

Finally, there are a limited number of works on survey design and analysis. The classic older work is Hyman, *Survey Design and Analysis* (1955). A more recent, and highly regarded, work is Rosenberg, *The Logic of Survey Analysis* (1968). A third work, Selvin, *The Logic of Survey Analysis* (1966), is more abstract, more causal-model-oriented, and more directly tied to the third-generation computer. (See also Pelz, Magliveras, and Lew, 1968; Converse, 1969; Beshers, 1965; Evan, 1959; Zeisel, 1957.)

SAMPLING

Sample designs fall into two major generic classifications: probability samples and nonprobability samples. The distinguishing characteristic of a probability sample is the sampler's ability to calculate the chance that some member of a population will fall into the sample. Among the probability sample designs used today, I will discuss: pure random samples (or simple random samples), skip-interval samples (also called systematic samples and equal-interval samples), area random samples (a form of stratified random sampling), and block samples with quotas. Though not often used by social scientists, we shall discuss two types of nonprobability samples: quota samples and purposive samples.

The model on which all sampling is based and on which all sampling theory ultimately rests is the *simple random sample*. Unfortunately, most populations of interest to social scientists are far too large and complex to be sampled in this fashion, since every element in the population must be listed for the sample to be drawn. Those populations for which total lists exist (or for which total lists can be prepared at reasonable cost), and which are relatively homogeneous, can be sampled in this fashion. For example, assume that we would be interested in studying the partisan attitudes of a small liberal arts college of, say, 1,500 students. These 1,500 names could be placed in a drum, thoroughly mixed, and a sample of 150 students drawn. A much simpler and probably more rigorous process is recommended for drawing a pure random sample, using a table of random numbers: each of the 1,500 student names is assigned a number from 0001 to 1500; entry is made into a table of random numbers, typically by stabbing at the page with a pencil; and 150 numbers falling between 0001 and 1500 are drawn (replacing duplicate numbers). The names corresponding to the numbers constitute the sample (see Blalock, 1960, pp. 393-6; Palumbo, 1969, pp. 343-5).

An approximation of a simple random sample can be secured with a *skip-interval sample* (equal-interval or systematic sample). Rather than using a table of random numbers to draw a sample of a 1,500 student liberal arts college, we could number the alphabetical list of students from 0001 to 1500, and take a sample of 150 by the following process: 1500/150 gives us our interval of 10; using a table of random numbers, pick a starting number between 01 and 10, say 7; take student number 07 and every tenth student after 07; that is, 17, 27, 37, and so on (see Kish, 1965, pp. 113-23). The list used to draw a skip-interval sample must be in some nonsense or random order (e.g., alphabetical). If segments of the list are arranged in some particular order (i.e., army rank, position in a firm, office in a party), the interval may repeatedly choose a particular quality or value and substantially bias the sample.

As in the case of a simple random sample, the skip-interval sample can only be used when lists of persons or dwelling units are available, or when such lists can be prepared at reasonable cost. Since the *Census of Housing* lists dwelling units by blocks for all Standard Metropolitan Areas, one can easily draw a skip-interval sample of dwelling units for cities; coupled with random selection of respondents in the designated dwelling units (Kish, 1949), the researcher has an approximation of a random sample with a known probability for the selection of every respondent. The skip-interval, block sample (with clustering of selected dwelling units for cost reduction) is lucidly described in Backstrom and Hursh, *Survey Research* (1963).

To study large, complex (heterogeneous) populations (e.g., the American voting public), social scientists are most likely to use an *area random sample*. By area random sample we mean that the universe (for example, continental United States) is stratified by area and a multistage sampling procedure is followed which produces a random selection of respondents (i.e., the sampler knows the probability of any one area, dwelling unit, and respondent falling into the

FIGURE 1. SRC Sampling Method

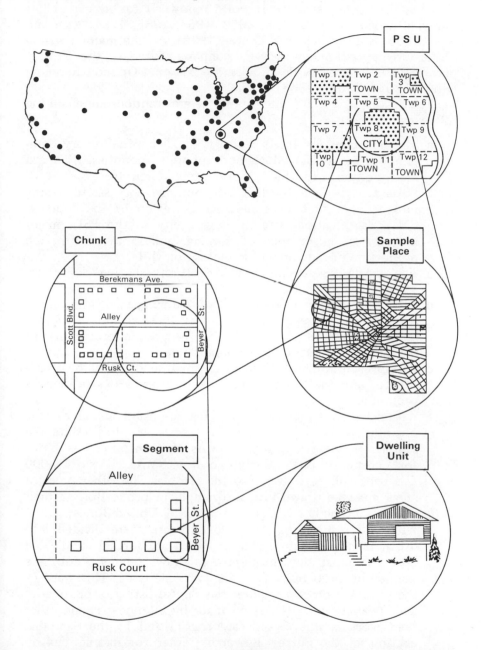

Source: Survey Research Center, Field Office, *Interviewer's Manual* (Ann Arbor: Institute for Social Research, University of Michigan, 1969), p. 8-2. Copyright 1969 by The University of Michigan. Reprinted by permission.

sample). The Survey Research Center of the University of Michigan's Institute for Social Research is world renowned for its use of this sampling procedure (see Kish, 1952, 1953, 1965, 1967; Kish and Hess, 1965; Survey Research Center, 1969). All the major research centers use approximately the same sampling procedure, though they may use other terms to describe it (see National Opinion Research Center, 1964a, 1964b, 1966).

The Survey Research Center draws the area random sample in the following manner (see Figure 1):

a. The continental United States is divided into Primary Sampling Units (PSUs) which correspond to counties, Standard Metropolitan Areas (SMAs), or clusters of counties.
b. PSUs are grouped together into homogeneous strata, taking into account such characteristics as region of the country, SMA classification, size of largest city in the PSU, major industry or major type of farming, and in the South, the proportion of the population that is nonwhite.
c. The twelve largest SMAs (called "self-representing" PSUs) are automatically selected.
d. One PSU is drawn from each of the sixty-two other strata (called "nonself-representing" PSUs); these strata are approximately equal in size. Each PSU is given a probability of selection in proportion to its population.
e. Within each PSU, substrata are formed on the basis of urbanization, and the heavily urban substrata are also stratified by economic level.
f. Within the substrata, secondary areas are listed, and an average of three to six of the secondary areas are drawn into the sample. In the twelve largest SMAs, the central city is drawn for a certainty; in the thirty-two other SMAs, cities of 50,000 and over will be drawn into the sample. The other types of areas must be drawn into the sample in proportion to their presence in the universe (i.e., continental United States).
g. Within the substrata, the secondary areas are divided into urban blocks and rural chunks which are further subdivided into segments; the entire process draws segments into the sample by probability (i.e., random) methods. This stage of the sampling process requires the careful listing of boundaries and dwelling units (DUs) on maps by interviewers and other field workers; the records are transmitted to the Sampling Section at the Survey Research Center for instructions on drawing the DUs in which interviews will be taken.
h. Segments typically contain from four to twelve DUs, and an average of four DUs are drawn from each segment; the Sam-

pling Section gives such careful instructions to the field that all choice of DUs is taken out of the hands of the interviewers: *no substitution of DUs is permitted.*

i. From the first knowledgeable adult the interviewer contacts at each selected DU, a list is secured of all persons eligible to be interviewed, in order, from oldest to youngest male, and oldest to youngest female. A respondent selection table (based on tables of random numbers) attached to the interview cover sheet identifies the respondent; *no substitution for the designated respondent is permitted* (see Kish, 1949).

From such a sample the investigator can make estimates about the United States voting public and the voting public of the nation's major regions. Usually enough interviews are taken in the New York metropolitan region to make estimates for that voting public. However, one can not make estimates by states or congressional districts from this sample. Scholars who use data collected by area random sampling procedures (or any sampling procedure, for that matter) in secondary analysis should secure from the original research team a clear understanding about the types of inference the sample will support.

The National Opinion Research Center has undertaken extensive methodological research on *block samples with quotas* (also called probability samples with quotas). The sampling process is very much like the area random sample down to the selection of urban blocks and rural chunks. At that point respondents are selected by quotas based on the probability of being available for an interview. NORC has developed four strata relevant to availability: men under thirty, men over thirty, employed women, and unemployed women. Because of the social and political significance of race, quotas are typically assigned on this variable as well. Estimates on this sampling procedure have been reasonably close to those based on area random samples. The researcher should, of course, consider the precision with which he wishes to make estimates and the nature of the block sample with quotas before electing to use it. The block sample with quotas has the following advantages: it does not require callbacks; therefore, data can be collected much more quickly, and the costs of data collection are substantially reduced (a callback sample may cost three times as much per case as a quota sample). This is a probability sample *only* if the quotas do actually control for the respondent's availability for being interviewed and if interviewers carry out their assignments with precision (see Sudman, 1967, p. 6 ff.; National Opinion Research Center, 1967a).

Before 1948, a methodological battle raged in the opinion research industry about the comparative merits of *quota sampling* and probability sampling (Hochstein and Smith, 1948). Quota sampling, *a nonprobability form of sampling,* had dominated the industry up to that time, and marketing research had also relied heavily on quota sampling. The failure of public opinion polls to predict Harry S. Truman's victory over Thomas E. Dewey was a product of many factors (see Mosteller et al., 1949; Campbell, 1950), but sampling techniques deservedly received a great deal of attention, and probability samples generally replaced quota samples in the opinion research industry (Mendelsohn and Crespi, 1970, p. 73 ff.).

Quota sampling proceeds much like area random sampling down to the block and rural chunk; however, voting precincts can be used as either a primary or a secondary sampling area. At the block or chunk level, interviewers are assigned quotas of respondents with certain characteristics based on major demographic variables. The demographic characteristics on which quotas are based are proportioned to their presence in the universe population (relying on census data, informed estimates, and other available guidelines). The more relevant a particular variable is to the survey project, the more important a quota criterion it becomes. There are three major criticisms of quota sampling. First, ultimate selection of the respondent is placed in the hands of the interviewer who can significantly bias the selection process; to save time, interviewers may pick respondents in limited geographical areas, resulting in the clustering of respondents. There may be a limited spread within quotas, and interviewers may "force" respondents into quota cells near the end of their assignment when cells more difficult to fill are reached. Bias may be further introduced by the interview setting, which need not be in a dwelling unit (i.e., interviews may be held in public parks, offices, stores); in general, the control of respondent selection is abdicated by the sampling section to the interviewer in the field. Second, even the most carefully defined quota sample is so divergent from probability models as to make it impossible to "place quota sampling on a sound theoretical basis" (Stephan and McCarthy, 1958, p. 190). Formulae for estimating sample variance and errors are based on probability theory, and are not transferable to quota sampling. Last, the investigator using probability sampling can compare survey estimates against check data (i.e., census results, voter registration lists, voter turnout, etc.) as a measure of accuracy. Students of the quota sample find that a sample may yield an accurate estimate on one variable and be significantly in error on another. (On quota sampling see Stephan and McCarthy, 1958; Moser, 1952; Kish, 1965, p. 562 ff.)

The *purposive sample* (also called judgment or expert choice sample) is another form of nonprobability sample, and one which must be seriously considered by the social scientist to handle certain special research tasks. This form of sampling is one in which the researcher selects typical or representative units with which to make estimates relating to a population in which he has an interest. Of course, no social scientist would suggest a general use of purposive sampling, say to make estimates for the American voting public. Rather than selecting areas by probability techniques, *a purposive selection of areas* can be used to draw relevant units into a sample. For example, a study of the politics of the "company town" could be more meaningfully carried out if the sample areas included a mill town, a mining town, and a logging town; the researcher should choose towns which are uncontaminated or pure types. Proper control towns (non-mill towns) would need to be carefully selected to control (match) as many relevant independent variables as possible. Finally, convenience and reduction of costs might dictate the selection of certain towns. To study public opinion in the United States regarding the uses of atomic energy, the Survey Research Center purposely selected matched communities, half of them near atomic energy activities. Purposive selection *can also be used to draw relevant persons* into a sample which might only approximate the universe being studied but would also provide the range of accurate information desired. For example, a study of disaster victims' attitudes toward government services could be more detailed and accurate if collected immediately after the event and without waiting for the development of a sample (see Kish, 1965, p. 19; Stephan and McCarthy, 1958, p. 374 ff.).

The serious student of sampling will want to explore the following works. Perhaps the most distinguished treatment of sampling is Kish, *Survey Sampling* (1965), the authority on the area random sample. Stephan and McCarthy, *Sampling Opinions* (1958), surveys a great deal of the literature and develops a variety of excellent comparisons of sampling procedures and results. Other general works on sampling are Cochran, *Sampling Techniques* (1963); Deming, *Some Theory of Sampling* (1950); Yates, *Sampling Methods for Censuses and Surveys* (1960); Sukhatme, *Sampling Theory of Surveys with Applications* (1954); Hansen, Hurwitz, and Madow, *Sample Survey Methods and Theory* (1953); Conway, *Sampling* (1967). (See also Kish, 1953; Chein, 1964; Sudman and Bradburn, 1974.) Good introductions to sampling are presented in general texts on survey research, which I will introduce next, and in the books on research design treated earlier in this chapter.

The most highly regarded concise treatment of survey research with which the interested student should begin his reading is Moser, *Survey Methods in Social Investigation* (1958). Other general works one should consult are Young and Schmid, *Scientific Social Surveys and Research* (1966); Parten, *Surveys, Polls, and Samples* (1950); Backstrom and Hursh, *Survey Research* (1963); Babbie, *Survey Research Methods* (1974); and Weisberg and Bowen, *Introduction to Survey Research and Data Analysis* (1976).

Most surveys are designed to make estimates for one point in time. Measuring change requires a special sample design. Repeated surveys provide a limited estimate of change in a particular attitude or characteristic in a universe. For example, the Gallup Poll from 1965 to 1968 charted the course of the American public's declining support for the Vietnam War. However, there was no evidence that the group opposing the war in March of 1965 continued to oppose the war in 1968—some of the group might have changed to support the war. *Panel studies* can provide a map of fluctuations of opinion at successive time intervals. By panel studies, we refer to reinterviewing the same sample. Panels present special methodological problems: (a) some respondents will not agree to be reinterviewed; (b) some will be uncooperative enough to deny a satisfactory, completed interview; (c) some will move and be difficult to locate, raising reinterview costs; (d) some will die; and (e) the reinterviewing of respondents can destroy spontaneity or "innocence" of response. For all of these reasons, the researcher must constantly check the panel for representativeness. Perhaps the ideal, but most expensive, check for representativeness one can use is a matched control sample to be interviewed simultaneously with the panel at a relevant stage in the study—sometimes several control samples will be desirable. The two voting studies conducted in 1940 and 1948 by the Bureau of Applied Social Research were early and elaborate panel studies (Lazarsfeld, Berelson, and Gaudet, 1944; Berelson, Lazarsfeld, and McPhee, 1954). The Survey Research Center, in its voting studies, has regularly interviewed its samples before and after elections, and has conducted one panel study of *Stability and Change in Attitudes and Behavior of the American Electorate* covering the elections of 1956, 1958, and 1960. On panel studies, see Kish, 1965, p. 469 ff.; Moser, 1958, p. 112 ff.; Glock, 1955; Newcomb et al., 1967; Lazarsfeld, 1948; Hottois, 1969; Levenson, 1955.

In this brief treatment of sampling we have excluded the mathematics and theory of design. Complete understanding of the subject entails training in probability theory, statistics, and mathematics through elementary calculus. The literature we have cited handles these formal aspects of sampling, but does so in such a fashion that the untrained and uninitiated can often skip passages of symbolic notations and formulae and still build an understanding of essential concepts.

QUESTIONNAIRES

Care and precision are required at every stage of a survey research project. This is especially important to remember in a discussion of drawing up and pretesting the questionnaire (sometimes referred to as the research instrument, interview schedule, or the protocol). A good research design is the best guard against error in drawing up the research instrument, but good design alone will not control the potential for error or bias in (1) the wording of the questions, (2) the selection of the form in which to ask the questions, (3) the order in which the questions will be asked, and (4) the use of scales or indices to measure complex variables. I will discuss each of these topics, and then close this section with a statement on the special problems of mailed questionnaires.

Question Wording

Before wording the questions, it is necessary to reexamine the nature and scope of the study. This requires a complete explication and a thorough listing of the various components of the research subject. What hypotheses are to be tested? What have related studies revealed? What data, on what variables, will be needed for the analysis of the research subject? It would be tragic to discover that needed data have not been collected *after* the field work is completed.

Questions must be worded to collect the information needed for the study; therefore, the language of each item in the schedule must be carefully analyzed to be sure it will accomplish its precise goal. Questions should be as direct and as short as possible to ensure ease of comprehension and retention by the respondent. Simple and clear language is always desirable, regardless of the universe being studied. Technical terms and highly specialized language should be avoided for lay publics, but they can be used and will be quite an asset to a study if fully understood by the population being examined. On attitudinal items especially, only one thought should be incorporated into a question. Words with double meanings, emotional connotations, or with the potential to be misunderstood, should be avoided.

It is much easier to list rules for the wording of questions than it is to follow them. Sometimes the application of one rule entails the violation of another; for example, to write a clearer question may require writing a longer one.

Questions must be worded objectively to avoid biasing responses. The questionnaire must not include value-laden words and themes, except to deliberately test for a reaction; it must not expect or anticipate a response pattern; it must permit the respondent to be unknowledgeable as well as knowledgeable. Experienced professional men (doctors, lawyers, counselors, etc.) who rely heavily on interviews in their work are frequently shocked at hearing one of their own interviews on tape. They are shocked because they hear themselves leading the respondent with careless and biased questions. For this reason, more and more professionals rely on a structured interview schedule which their client fills out prior to the oral interview.

Some years ago specialists in survey research talked about "hard" and "soft" data questions. In general, factual questions were regarded as "hard," and attitudinal questions were regarded as "soft." The "hard" or "soft" distinction is clearly untenable. Such hard data questions as those pertaining to education leval and occupational classification involve prestige, and respondents may report a higher level of education or higher status title for their occupation than is actually the case. Or, to consider another example, in a nation which values "civic duty" the nonvoter must be permitted to report not voting in a particular election without embarrassment or he may falsely report that he did vote as would be expected by the norms of "the system." Or, to consider a final example in the old realm of "soft" questions, respondents must be permitted to tell the interviewer that they know nothing about, or have no opinion about, an issue that is clearly on the public agenda for resolution at the moment.

Replication of questions from other survey studies is a convenient and time conserving practice. It is also incumbent upon those designing questionnaires to maintain as much comparability with other studies as possible. For example, designing a new measure of occupational status, and abandoning the "standard" questions available, could only be justified by the research team's belief that these "standard" questions would not yield the information needed for their particular study.

Pretesting the questionnaire is an absolutely essential check for violation of the principles discussed above on question wording. Along with good research design, it is excellent insurance against every type of error in questionnaire construction. Pretesting should be a genuine trial run; therefore, every attempt must be made to simulate the final fieldwork setting. Most important, the pretest respondents must be similar to the respondents in the universe to be studied. It will not suffice to "try out" the questionnaire on a college class (unless the study pertains to college students). One pretest may not be sufficient to "debug" a questionnaire. If substantial changes are dictated by the initial pretest, the revised questionnaire should be checked out in the field with another pretest.

Questions drawn from other studies, even highly successful ones, should also be pretested. Questions written for a cross-section of the American people may yield reliable and valid but not very *useful* data when directed to an elite or to one distinctive segment of society. Questions may not be reliable (*reliability* refers to a question's ability to obtain the same results over time). And, finally, questions can yield valid estimates in one study and invalid estimates in another study (validity means that the estimates closely approximate the true value in the population). In summary, the pretest can help the research team select useful, reliable, and valid questions.

Question Form

Questions may be classified broadly as "open" or "closed." Open-ended questions permit the respondent to reply in his own words. If the open-ended question seeks a rather simple factual response (for example, "In what year were you born?"), it is little different from a closed question. The open-ended question which seeks a broader response is more intrinsically interesting to the social scientist. It permits the respondent to reply in detail, to volunteer the subtle nuances of his opinions, to report the intensity of his opinion, and to reveal something of the affective content of his opinion. An excellent example of the open-ended question is a sequence used by the Survey Research Center to measure short-term forces in American national elections: "What do you like about the Democratic party? What do you dislike about the Democratic party? What do you like about the Republican party? What do you dislike about the Republican party?"

The great rewards the researcher reaps in richness of detail with the open-ended question are offset by two factors: (1) content analysis of the responses is difficult and time consuming, and (2) special care must be taken by the interviewer not to lead the respondent when probing for a full response. Because of these limitations, the researcher should make every effort to close a question if the pretest indicates that only four or five responses will be secured by the question in its open form.

There are many different types of closed questions, but the two essential types are dichotomous and multiple choice. Dichotomous questions typically seek yes-no or agree-disagree responses. For example, "Do you remember for sure whether you voted in 1968?" The multiple-choice question typically consists of asking a question and reading the possible responses; if the list is especially difficult to comprehend, a card with the alternatives should be handed the respondent. No card would be required for "Are you single, married, divorced, or widowed?" However, a question with seven or eight possible responses, like income of the household, would require a card.

The open and closed classification by no means exhausts the subject of question form. A respondent can be asked to respond to a picture, a story (real or hypothetical), or some other such catalyst. A respondent may be asked to indicate his position on a "ladder," his feeling on a "thermometer," or place himself, his family, or his community on some other scale or continuum. And the respondent can be asked to make pairings between persons (or events, concepts, or matters central to the study) and a variety of adjectives. These examples are largely related to scale and index construction, which will be treated briefly below.

Question Order

The questionnaire must be introduced to the respondent in such a manner as to insure his cooperation. In a letter of introduction, or in an opening statement, the respondent should be told the general nature of the study and should be informed as to its sponsorship and legitimacy. It is customary to tell the respondent in general terms how he has been selected to be interviewed; for example, "your name has been selected purely by chance from a list of registered voters." Most respondents are willing to be interviewed and to give from thirty minutes to one hour of their time, and a good many respondents are flattered that they have been chosen. Nonetheless, the opening statements should be designed to involve the respondents in the study and to maximize the chance that they will cooperate fully.

The initial set of questions should be designed to disarm the potentially reluctant respondent and to lead him gently into the questionnaire. There is no inflexible rule about the form of the opening questions, but most public opinion questionnaires begin with open-ended questions; for example, "What would you say are the major problems facing the country today?" Certainly the research team will want to avoid controversial items in the initial battery of questions, and they should also include questions that the respondent can readily answer.

The questionnaire should be organized into generally homogeneous sections. For example, in a voting behavior questionnaire, you might open with a section on current issues or public problems, proceed into a section on the respondent's political history, move on into a section evaluating the current campaign, get the respondent's reaction to a rather lengthy battery of attitudinal items, and close with a section on the respondent's occupational status and other personal information. By grouping the questions together, you avoid jarring shifts of subject matter and make the experience as orderly for the respondent as possible. Throughout the questionnaire the research team should use "transitional statements" to warn the respondent that the interviewer is changing from one line of questioning to another. In the Negro Study, for example, the following transitional sentence was used: "This finishes the regular part of the interview. Now we need to ask a few more questions about you so that we can compare the answers of people in different age groups, men with women, people in different jobs, and so on" (Matthews and Prothro, 1966, p. 516).

Within a specific content area (i.e., attitudes on civil rights), the open-ended or general question should always precede the closed or more specific question. For example, if the questionnaire included five specific questions on current policy issues (i.e., the Middle East, busing, pollution, crime rates, and unemployment), it would be meaningless to later ask the respondent to volunteer a list of problems facing the nation. For a thorough examination of a specific subject, the research team may use a sequence of questions (called by many a "funnel sequence") beginning with general questions and ending with quite specific ones. George Gallup suggests a "quint-amensional plan of question design" which includes (1) a screening question to find out whether the respondent has thought about the issue or knows anything at all about it; (2) open-ended questions to secure general feelings or knowledge in the respondent's own words; (3) questions on specific components of the subject or the respondent's attitudes about it; (4) questions seeking explanations for the respondent's feelings; and (5) questions on how strong these feelings are (Oppenheim, 1966, p. 40).

There are many other format and organizing conventions, of which I will treat three in closing this section. First, the questionnaire will include many questions that are dependent or contingent upon other questions; that is, if the respondent's answer is "No" or "Don't Know," you can skip the dependent items. Therefore, the questionnaire should be arranged so that those blocks of questions which are closely related are together, and so that dependent questions can be boxed (or otherwise noted) for easy omission, if such is warranted. For example, the interviewer need not proceed to ask a battery of questions designed to record a respondent's voting history if the respondent initially says that he has never voted.

Second, the questionnaire should be printed in clearly arranged patterns to help the interviewer efficiently record answers and skip contingency questions without skipping the wrong sections. Indentation, ruled boxes around sequences of questions, skipped spaces, and any other good visual aides will help to avoid interviewer recording errors in the field. For mailed questionnaires and all other self-administered questionnaires, the format has to be even more carefully designed.

And finally, questionnaires can be precoded to the extent that they are made up of closed questions, or that the research project director can anticipate the exact pattern of information he seeks. Many pollsters precode their questionnaires, going so far as to use graphite-sensitive scoring sheets which can be used to punch data cards, thereby speeding up the data analysis when interviewing is completed, and, theoretically at least, reducing coding and punching errors.

Measurement of Complex Variables

Some of the most interesting variables in the study of political behavior are quite complex and require the development of special measuring devices called scales and indices. For example, consider the complex nature of the following concepts: anomie, conservatism, cynicism, personal competence, class identification, civic duty, religiosity, authoritarianism, and racism.

An index is a summary of items in one dimension of the behavior being studied: the researcher assumes that there is a relationship between the items, and that the summary variable is more meaningful than any single item. In *The People's Choice*, for example, Lazarsfeld, Berelson, and Gaudet found that their Index of Political Predisposition explained voting behavior better than any simple variable. The Index of Political Predisposition included religion, level of socioeconomic status, and residence (Lazarsfeld, Berelson, and Gaudet, 1948, p. 174). Socioeconomic status is also an index and is typically defined as a summary of the occupation of the head of the household, the education of the respondent, and the income of the whole household. Another excellent example of an index is the variable "involvement" used in *The American Voter*. In that study, involvement is defined as a summation of interest in the campaign, concern over the election outcome, sense of political efficacy, and sense of civic duty. Involvement is a very powerful complex variable in explaining turnout (Campbell et al., 1960, pp. 96–110). Though it is much wiser to plan for index construction before going into the field (and thereby being sure to include all of the needed items in the questionnaire), an index can be constructed after fieldwork is completed. The Index of Political Predisposition and the Involvement Index are good examples.

There are a number of different types of scales used in the study of political behavior. McLemore and Bonjean have discussed "Some Principles and Techniques of Scale Construction" elsewhere in this volume, so I will not duplicate their effort. One can scale votes, political participation, and other types of political events and behavior, but we are primarily interested at this point with attitude scaling.

An ideal scale, or measuring device, should have the following properties:

1. *Unidimensionality* or *homogeneity*. That is, it should measure one quality or dimension of behavior as nearly as possible.
2. *Linearity and equal intervals* or *equal-appearing intervals*. It should follow a straight-line model and should entail some sort of scoring system, preferably one based on interchangeable units. Attitude scales assume the straight-line model, but scoring units are difficult to devise and of doubtful interchangeability.
3. *Reliability*. Over time, the scale should produce the same results.
4. *Validity*. The estimates should closely approximate the true value.
5. *Reproducibility*. The respondent's score tells us where he can be placed on a straight-line model and what his attitudes would be on the other items in the scale (Oppenheim, 1966, pp. 121-23).

No ideal scaling technique exists. Each of the best known methods of attitude scaling has strengths and weaknesses; each meets some, but not all, of the criteria listed above.

Guttman scales are the best known of all attitude measuring devices. Items selected into the scale pertain to some component of the complex variable, or at least this is the judgment of the investigator. Guttman specified a series of technical requirements that a scale must meet, the last of which is a .900 coefficient of reproducibility. Actually, an investigator can scale by the Guttman method a series of items that are of little meaning; therefore, one important aspect of a Guttman scale is the good judgment of the analyst. Scalogram analysis is especially concerned with unidimensionality and reproducibility—the items in the scale have the properties of being ordinal and cumulative. (This paragraph and the two which follow are influenced by Oppenheim, 1966, pp. 120-59.)

Two other types of scaling, *multiscaling* and *factorial scales*, rely heavily on the judgment of the investigators as to which items will be used in the questionnaire; and further, they call for the investigator's assessment or judgment of the value of the scales produced by the scaling process. With multiscaling, the investigator uses the computer to search all items and build scales on intercorrelations between items. The minimum correlation score is set in advance as the guide for scale building. Factorial scales are built in much the same fashion; the computer is programmed to search for underlying factors. Both multiscaling and factorial scales focus especially on unidimensionality. With either process, scales can emerge that are difficult to name and appear to have little meaning; however, these are efficient, time-conserving methods of scaling and, if the analyst is willing to discard those scales difficult to name or of little meaning, they are very sound ways to proceed.

Thurstone scales are built on the judgment of a panel of judges (who should be closely matched, if possible, to the population to be studied). A pool of items is prepared relating to the concept to be measured; the judges are asked to ignore their personal feelings and place the items in eleven piles that are ordered from most to least favorable toward the subject under investigation. The researcher then eliminates items on which too large a spread (variance) in judgments has emerged, and the medians for the remaining items are calculated. The items that are then selected into the scale (typically twenty to twenty-two of them) are chosen at relatively equal intervals on the hypothetical continuum of the scale. When administered as a scale, respondents check the items with which they agree, and the mean values for those items become the respondent's scale score. *Likert scales* are built from a pool of items, related to the concept under investigation, which are administered to a pretest sample. Respondents are asked to place themselves on a five point attitude continuum running from "strongly agree" to "strongly disagree," with "uncertain" as the midpoint. The items are then assigned weights from one to five (taking care to reverse the scores for negatively worded items), and the cumulative score of each item is calculated. The best method of determining which items to retain in the scale is to correlate them with some external criterion; but that is rarely available, so correlation scores are calculated between items, and those with the highest correlation scores are retained. When the scale is completed, it is administered just as in the pretest, and the mean score of the item values becomes the scale score of the respondent. Unidimensionality of Thurstone scales must be tested by the internal consistency of the items in an evaluative pretest; unidimensionality is the chief concern of Likert scales. The reproducibility of Thurstone scales is difficult to judge, and with Likert scales it is impossible, because the same scale score can be achieved in many different ways.

We make these brief comments on scaling only to point out that there may be a need for a preliminary investigation (perhaps a lengthy and expensive one) if new measuring instruments must be devised. Fortunately, a great many scales and indices have been developed by other scholars as survey research has grown, and one of those available may serve a project's need. There are now four major collections of scales and indices that should be consulted by designers of sample surveys: Bonjean and McLemore, *Sociological Measurement: An Inventory of Scales and Indices* (1967); Robinson, Athanasiou, and Head, *Measures of Occupational Attitudes and Occupational Characteristics* (1969); Robinson, Rusk, and Head, *Measures of Political Attitudes* (1968); and Robinson and Shaver, *Measures of Social Psychological Attitudes* (1969, 1973). The last three of these have been developed by the staff of the Institute for Social Research at Michigan.

Mailed Questionnaires

A mailed questionnaire is feasible when the universe to be sampled is relatively homogeneous and when the potential to motivate a response is high. Leaders of various types have been studied with mailed questionnaires and the response rates have occasionally been very good (for example, party leaders, voluntary association leaders, national convention delegates, and civil servants have been studied successfully by mailed surveys).

The cover letter for a mailed questionnaire has to involve the respondent enough to convince him to take his time, fill out the questionnaire, and return it; so the purpose of the study, the promise of its findings, the standing of the sponsoring agency, or some other good office, must weigh on the respondent to induce him to cooperate. In experiments with mailed questionnaires, the type of delivery has influenced the response rate; that is, the response rate has gone up with the level of special handling postage (i.e., first class, air mail, special delivery, and registered mail). The format, question order, and directions for a mailed questionnaire must be more carefully designed than similar components of a questionnaire which will be administered face to face. If the questionnaire is very complex, asks the respondent to search his files for information, or burdens him in some other such fashion, the response rate will go down and the number of partially completed questionnaires will go up.

To provide for follow-up mailings to those who have not returned their questionnaires, project directors usually stamp a number on the questionnaire. Respondents may protest this system of numbering as a loss of anonymity, and they may clip off the number or fail to return the questionnaire as a result. Of course, anonymity of responses will be protected, because the project will never publish the responses tied to the respondent's name, but this is not always easy to explain. Either as a primary system, or as a back-up system of identification, the project can code the back of the return envelope with a colored dot corresponding to a spot on a two-way grid (A through J across the top, and one through nine down the side, for example).

To the researcher with limited funds, the mailed questionnaire may be the only feasible way to collect needed data. A mailed questionnaire is inappropriate for many of the most interesting populations, because the response rate would never be sufficient; however, used carefully, and for the right populations, it is a valid instrument for data collection.

On questionnaire design and wording questions, there are two fine works: Oppenheim, *Questionnaire Design and Attitude Measurement* (1966) and Payne, *The Art of Asking Questions* (1951). See also the general works on survey research cited earlier, and Kornhauser and Sheatsley (1964). On scaling and index construction see especially Togerson, *Theory of Methods of Scaling* (1958) and Edwards, *Techniques of Attitude Scale Construction* (1957); see also Summers (1970), Rieselback (1966b), Remmers (1957), Gullikson and Messick (1960), Barnette (1964), Cataldo et al. (1970), Shaw and Wright (1967). On validity studies, see Crossley and Parry (1950), Clausen (1968), Cahalan (1968). On mailed questionnaires, see Glaser (1966), Crotty (1966).

INTERVIEWING

A good questionnaire is one designed to help the interviewer collect the information essential to the successful completion of the research project, but the interviewer's performance can destroy the communication process and result in the collection of meaningless information. In this section we will cover the interviewer's task, qualities of good interviewers, the training of interviewers, and the overall nature of the fieldwork operation.

The Interviewer's Task

Robert L. Kahn and Charles F. Cannell treat the interview as "communication" in their classic work, *The Dynamics of Interviewing* (1957). The chief task of the interviewer is to motivate the respondent to communicate, as fully and accurately as possible, the information needed for the research project. The first component of the interviewer's task is to motivate the person selected in the sample to accept the role of "respondent."

On the cover sheet of the questionnaire, the interviewer should be supplied with information about the study in order to communicate to the potential respondent. The interviewer should tell the potential respondent precisely who he is, what agency or research center he represents, the general nature of the study, how the respondent was chosen to be interviewed (in easily comprehended language), and approximately how much time will be needed for the interview.

If the respondent is reluctant to be interviewed, the interviewer must ascertain the reason for the reluctance and apply the appropriate technique to secure cooperation. If the respondent doubts the legitimacy of the interviewer (for example, seeing him as a salesman, bill collector, or as an undesirable of some sort), the interviewer can use his credentials and letter of introduction. He may ask the respondent to check his legitimacy with the local Chamber of Commerce, local Police Department, or with the home base of the research center or agency. If the respondent pleads a lack of time, the interviewer can offer to arrange the interview to meet the respondent's time schedule, to come back later, or he can describe the time demands of the interview in more precise and detailed terms. If the respondent appears to be threatened by the nature of the interview or of the interview process, the interviewer will need to try to reassure him by mentioning the "confidentiality and anonymity of the responses," by telling him of other people's doubts which disappeared after the beginning of the interview, or by adopting some other supportive and positive strategy to create a spirit of trust and communication.

"Once the respondent has agreed to be interviewed, a specific relationship has been initiated between him and the interviewer, and mutual expectations are in the process of being established" (Kahn and Cannell, 1957, p. 53). The interviewer must sustain his role in a professional manner, and maintain the dynamic, two-way communication process. When this is done well, we say the interviewer has "rapport" with the respondent. As the interview proceeds, the interviewer has to steer the respondent away from distractions (TV, children, callers, and the like), must be alert to disturbances caused by sensitive questions, and, if necessary, reassure the respondent of the relevancy of the study or the purpose for any parts of the questionnaire.

In building rapport, the interviewer should avoid building a personal relationship which would distort his role. His chief job is to ask the questions exactly as they are printed and to secure undised information; therefore, the relationship should be friendly, but professional. If, for example, the respondent views the interview as a contact with a new friend, he may contrive responses designed to reinforce that friendship, rather then giving candid and truthful responses (Richardson et al., 1965, pp. 281-4).

It is essential that the interview be conducted with a minimum of *error*. Authorities on interviewing have classified interviewing error as either *random error* or as *bias*. Because of the chance nature of "random error," one mistake tends to cancel out another; however, "bias" is systematic, or one-directional and cumulative. Bias can seriously distort estimates based on data collected in a study.

As the term implies, there is no patterning to "random error." This term applies to such interview behavior as skipping a question accidentally, or checking the wrong answer box (though the question was asked correctly and both the interviewer and respondent were communicative). Other examples would include accidentally skipping a phrase, line, or sentence in a question; or inadvertently inverting Arabic numerals while recording the respondent's age, income, or length of residence. The most obvious or flagrant random errors may be caught and corrected by the interviewer or coding staff when editing the completed questionnaire; however, internal evidence is rarely sufficient to make corrections, since many people interviewed proffer inconsistent patterns of response.

Bias is a serious problem for the survey analyst. As Kahn and Cannell have written, "Such errors are not random, because each has a characteristic effect and direction" (1957, p. 169). Bias has a cumulative effect, as we noted above. In the examples of random error used in the last paragraph, we used "accidentally skipping a phrase in a question," a chance, perhaps one-time occurrence. Now, we have a different matter entirely if the interviewer's personal distaste for that one phrase in a question leads him to omit it consistently in the fieldwork: this is a matter of bias. Bias, according to Kahn and Cannell, "is the intrusion of any *unplanned* or *unwanted* influence in the interview" (1957, p. 176).

Potential for biasing results can be identified in the background characteristics, in the attitudes, and in the motives of the interviewer and the respondent. The behavior of both in the course of the interview can bias results. Finally, we should recall from the last section of this chapter that the questionnaire itself can be poorly designed, leading, and in general a poor measuring instrument.

Let us consider three examples of differences in background characteristics which have the potential to bias interview results. It is unlikely that a black respondent will give full and frank responses to a white interviewer, especially on matters relating to black attitudes toward the politics of change. An interviewer from a markedly higher social class than the respondent is likely to be told what the respondent thinks he wants to hear, as a matter of deference to his status in life. And, finally, a young female interviewer interviewing an older male respondent may find him patronizing and trying to control the timing and flow of the interview. We can control, to some extent, for differences in background characteristics during the recruitment of interviewers. It is especially important to control for those characteristics related to the chief purpose of the study. Moreover, through training, interviewers learn to be aware of the danger of background differences, and work to minimize their disruptive effects.

The interviewer must not permit his own attitudes and motives to intrude into the interview. His goal is to measure the respondent's attitudes and to collect information undistorted by his own personal views. The interviewer must not react (orally, with facial expressions, mannerisms, or in any other way) to the respondent's answer to a question. The interviewer must not permit his own personal view to appear in a "rewording or clarification" of a question, or in a probe follow-up to an open-ended question. One strategy used to make the interviewer aware of his own attitudes and opinions is to require him to fill out the questionnaire himself before he goes into the field to administer it to others.

Not only must the interviewer not permit his own attitudes and motives to intrude into the interview, but further, he must guard against any distortion of the questions he asks. Questions should be asked precisely as they are printed. If the respondent's answer is incomplete or nonresponsive, the question should initially be repeated. If clarification is necessary, it should be done very carefully, and the interviewer's clarification should be recorded in the margin of the questionnaire.

In using open-ended questions, the interviewer must learn to use objective, nonleading, or nondirective probes. In probing, the interviewer needs to motivate the respondent to communicate more fully without distorting the question, suggesting an answer, or judging what the respondent has already said; and probing must be carried out without damaging the existing rapport. The nature of the probe will vary with its purpose. For example, probes are used to (a) get the respondent to go ahead, to complete his answer, or to give the fullest response; and (b) to get the respondent to substitute an adequate answer for an inadequate one.

In probing to get the fullest response, three strategies have been suggested by Kahn and Cannell (1957, p. 207):

1. The interviewer can indicate that he has received and recorded the first response and is waiting for more ("I see," "yes," "uh huh").

2. The interviewer can pause and look expectantly at the respondent.
3. The interviewer can use one of a dozen objective, neutral phrases, all of which mean "tell me more about it."

When the respondent has given an inadequate response, the interviewer must assess the response, try to detect the cause of the inadequate response, and then move to stimulate a full response with an objective probe. Many times, repeating the question will evoke a full response, but sometimes it will be necessary to emphasize the key phrase(s) in the question, or to clarify the question, or to define a term used in the question. The interviewer must keep in mind the possibility that probing under these circumstances can damage the existing rapport. Irrelevant or inaccurate responses may indicate either misunderstanding on the respondent's part, or an unwillingness to talk about the particular subject; and the interviewer must try to find out which is the case. If the respondent says he does not want to talk about the subject, the interviewer must make an effort to diagnose the problem while working to keep the interview going.

In carrying out his task, the well-trained interviewer keeps the purpose of each question in mind. Probing is essential to getting the information for which the question was asked, but nondirective probing can be learned through effort and experience. In time, as the interviewer gains experience and poise, he is able to pace the interview to the particular respondent and circumstances.

Qualities of Good Interviewers

Not everyone can be a good interviewer; indeed, some essentially able people are surprising failures at the task. For example, as one part of the University of Michigan's Representation Study, members of the United States Congress were to be interviewed. The study directors decided to use Congressional Fellows as interviewers because of their backgrounds and their availability in Washington. Though Congressional Fellows are very bright, highly educated, and quite knowledgeable, they failed to get the interviews. Efforts of the study directors themselves to get the interviews were not successful. Ultimately, the study directors called a group of experienced interviewers, a part of the field staff of the Survey Research Center, to Washington, and they secured the interviews. Undoubtedly, interviewing congressmen is a more demanding task than interviewing a cross-section of the American people, but you should not operate under the assumption that *anyone* can be a good interviewer.

The following quote from Richardson, Dohrenwend, and Klein, in *Interviewing* (1965, p. 274), is a good summary of the skills needed by an interviewer. The quote also serves as a good connection between the discussion of the interviewer's task and this one:

> Certain readily definable skills are demanded of the schedule interviewer, and these skills are required in a rather considerable degree because his behavior is so closely restricted by the requirements of the schedule of questions. Most of these are skills in interpersonal interaction. The schedule interviewer must maintain an appearance of spontaneity and interest with each new respondent, even after having used the schedule in scores of earlier interviews. In every interview, he must maintain painstaking attention to accuracy and detail in asking the questions and recording and coding the responses; he must gain and maintain participation, using as closely as possible a standard statement of purpose; he must tolerate the difficulties of locating respondents and sometimes encountering refusals and rebuffs; finally, he must have sufficient self-confidence to initiate contacts with one stranger after another and not display anxiety and hesitancy lest this be sensed by the respondents and lead to a refusal to participate.

What qualities in persons are related to these skills?

Though the great research centers have been attentive to this subject, and some research has been conducted on it by academic and commercial survey analysts in the United States and abroad, "Little systematic research has been done to isolate the personal variables that contribute to interviewers' effectiveness. . . ." (Richardson et al., 1965, p. 271). Authorities are not in agreement on "desirable qualities," and the lists of attributes available amount to an "ideal" or "model" not easily applied to mortals. The balance of this section will be devoted to listing the qualities which appear on many checklists. The reader will readily note that few people will be able to meet *all* of the criteria.

The basic demographic characteristics of good interviewers appear on every checklist. I will discuss sex, age, level of education, social status, and racial or ethnic background. In an ideal world, the interviewer's characteristics should match the respondent's characteristics. Obviously, this is impossible; therefore, you seek the interviewer who minimizes the differences that count the most.

Studies of interviewer effect have indicated that better results are obtained when the interviewer and respondent are of the same *sex* and age. In addition, these studies show that a more successful interview is secured from a woman interviewing a man than from a man interviewing a woman, though the differences noted are not great. Both men and women are employed by large and small research centers and projects, but the great majority of interviewers are women. The dominant position of women in fieldwork is probably more directly the result of the part-time nature of the job than any theoretical advantage in employing women. Men are likely to need and secure full-time jobs, and they typically have more time limitations on accepting interviewing assignments than do women. In the last decade, with its attendant rise in urban violence, it is a simple fact that a female interviewer is less "threatening" to more potential respondents than is a male interviewer.

The *age* requirement for interviewers is roughly linked with *maturity*, though the two variables are not necessarily related. Interviewers for the great research centers overwhelmingly come from the ages of between thirty and fifty. Younger (and older) persons *can* undoubtedly be good interviewers. Because of a lack of financial backing, many small-scale studies have been conducted using college students as interviewers, and quite a few of these studies have made important contributions to knowledge. It is a fact, nevertheless, that substantial age differences between the interviewer and respondent can bias interview results. The great research centers have secured their best results from early middle-aged female interviewers.

It requires a *bright* interviewer to communicate with respondents, to grasp the purpose of the questionnaire in all of its component parts, and to detect nonresponsive or partially responsive answers. Most research centers hire college graduates or, occasionally, persons with some study in college. *Level of education* (like age = maturity) is no guarantee of alertness, intelligence, and perceptiveness, so recruiters must gain some independent insight on this quality.

Good interviewers must be able to relate to persons from different *social classes*. Perceived status differences can bias a respondent's answers (as noted earlier). Obviously, no one person is perfectly able to converse with people from all status levels, but research centers look for the *adaptable* interviewer who can most minimize bias based on the status differences between himself and respondents. (On interviewing low income respondents, see Weiss, 1966.) In the training period, field supervisors watch for evidence of genuine discomfort on the part of an interviewer faced with a respondent of another class or status. *Personal appearance* is very important in controlling for status differences. Besides being clean and neat, the interviewer should be neither overdressed nor shabbily dressed; should have neither an elegant hair style nor an unsightly one. Basic, widely accepted modes of dress will minimize the class or status differences.

If at all possible, interviewers should be matched to respondents of the same *race* and the same *ethnic group*. It has been fairly well established that black respondents will not speak to a white interviewer with full candor, especially when the subject of the interview is the race question and attendant social issues (Axelrod, Matthews, and Prothro, 1962). Though Puerto Rican and Mexican-American respondents have been successfully interviewed by Anglo interviewers, studies need the acceptance of the subculture community, and a goodly proportion of the interviewing staff must be bilingual (Freeman, 1969; Welch, Comer, and Steinman, 1973). The more central the variables of race or ethnic group are to a study, the more important it is that interviewers be of the same race or nationality.

The demographic characteristics that pertain to interviewers can stand as surrogates for personal characteristics (for example, age for maturity, and education level for intelligence); therefore, the distinction between *demographic* and other *personal* characteristics is not overly clear, but I have used it anyhow, to effect some grouping of the attributes assigned to interviewers. In the discussion of other personal characteristics of interviewers, the following will be treated: interpersonal skills, personal competence, motivation and interest, ethics, experience, health, and ability to work without close supervision.

An interviewer must like people of both sexes, and genuinely enjoy listening to what they have to say. I do not mean to repeat naive old cliches about "rapport," but a successful interviewer is personable and possesses strong *skills in interpersonal communication*. There is, undoubtedly, a variety of tests of gregariousness, interpersonal relations, and communicability, but observation of role playing in interviews and field trials will most likely afford enough evidence to evaluate a potential interviewer in this regard.

Persons who can interact with others and communicate with ease undoubtedly have a high sense of *personal competence*. That is, they feel fully able to handle matters, people, and details in their personal lives. Interviewers have to have confidence in themselves, and some ego strength, to be able to knock on strangers' doors, get into the respondent's home, and hold his attention for a period of time ranging from thirty minutes to an hour or more. In addition, one has to have self-confidence to run the risk of being rejected. Richardson et al., comment in this area about the problem of stress:

> Ability to withstand stress is an important factor in the selection of interviewers. In some situations, stress can affect the interviewer's effectiveness in two ways: not only can it reduce the level of his own skills and activities but, if it visibly reduces his self-confidence, it may make respondents less willing to participate or may reduce the quality of their participation [1965, p. 280].

A genuine *interest* in what other people think will *motivate* an interviewer to withstand the stress of his job. His interest must be broad, and include a genuine curiosity about people, events, attitudes, differences between people, and about life in general. If money is the chief motive for someone applying to be an interviewer, he should be told that there are other, easier ways of making money. Interviewing is an ideal job for a housewife able to shed the responsibility of children, who wants to stay alive to the changing world and has a genuine urge to do something significant.

Research firms and projects seek interviewers with a strong sense of *integrity* and a highly developed sense of personal *ethics*. The interviewer's ethical system should compel him to adopt good *professional practices*. Respondents and field supervisors should always be told the truth, only the respondent's true responses should be reported on the questionnaire, and a respondent's interview should be held in the strictest confidence. The essential ethics of social research require that all respondents be treated with dignity and respect.

The more *experience* an interviewer has, the better his performance. Regardless of other controls used (sex, age, education, etc.) in studies of interviewer success, "experienced" interviewers outperform inexperienced interviewers. Experienced interviewers gain a higher response rate, with fewer callbacks, and they secure a better, more complete interview than an inexperienced interviewer (Durbin and Stuart, 1951). In hiring "experienced" interviewers, however, research centers try to avoid persons who have been trained in drastically different types of fieldwork and persons who continue to serve on another field staff or research project. The former may have learned a set of practices that he must "unlearn." The latter has conflicting loyalties, may be overcommitted, and may let the project down at a critical moment when interviews must be completed.

Interviewing is hard work, demanding commitment and alertness to the details of the task; therefore, an interviewer must be in *good health*, without physical limitations or infirmities. Though interviewers travel by automobile or mass transit to the general location of the fieldwork, lengthy walking, standing, and working under difficult conditions are attendant to the job and are quite taxing physically. For many studies, interviewers serve the sampling section or the project directors by doing block-by-block listings of dwelling units for substantial geographical areas, which is quite exhausting.

And finally, interviewers must be responsible people who *perform their tasks without continuing, immediate supervision*. Interviewers have to accept the responsibility of fulfilling their assignment; this means getting into the field by midmorning and staying out until the middle of the evening, without being told to do so. This self-starting, independent quality is essential to expediting fieldwork when it must be completed within limited, acceptable time frames. Early in an interviewer's training, a supervisor may accompany him in the field and observe some interviews. All quality field operations require random field checks to assure that interviews completed were valid, but most interviewing is, in essence, not supervised.

The Training of Interviewers

The large research centers maintain a nationwide staff of interviewers and field supervisors under the direction of a centralized field section staff, and new interviewers are added gradually to fill any vacancies which occur. These additions to the permanent staff are trained on an individual basis most of the time. The purposes of this chapter can best be met by discussing the recruitment and training of a block of interviewers for a study, rather than focusing on the individualized training given to those joining a permanent field staff. However, the recruitment and training processes are essentially the same whether one is referring to replacements for a permanent staff, or to a block of interviewers employed for a particular research project.

If a study were about ready for fieldwork to begin, those responsible for directing the interviewing would advertise in newspapers the basic job description and a method of applying for employment. Initial applications should be made to a post office box or to the newspaper account number. On the basis of the preliminary applications, the field director then would mail out personnel action forms to be filled out and returned, or call in applicants for a personal interview. Either through the interview or the personnel action forms, information should be collected to permit the field director to screen out applicants who are not likely to be good interviewers. At the end of the recruiting process the list of potential interviewers should be longer than necessary to conduct the fieldwork, because some of the applicants will drop out during or after the training, and the fieldwork director will want to drop some other applicants at the end of the training period. When an applicant is invited to the training session, it is standard practice to pay a stipend (typically $15.00 to $25.00 per day) and expenses (food, lodging, and travel if necessary).

A training session of at least one full day (preferably two days) should be scheduled. A motel with dining facilities and a large conference room is a good site for training sessions, because time is conserved if trainees do not have to go out for meals and if the entire group is housed together. It is essential that the final version of the questionnaire, cover sheet, flash cards, and field specifications be ready in advance of the training session, and all other appurtenances of the interviewer should be available for the training session (that is, clipboards, approved pencils and pens, maps, sampling instructions, credentials, and so forth).

The large research centers publish manuals for interviewers and field supervisors. These vary in content, depending on whether they were written principally for interviewers or for the field supervisors to use in training interviewers, but all of them are very useful for the student of survey research. The Survey Research Center's *Interviewer's Manual* (1969) treats the nature of the center's work, the sample survey, learning to interview, sampling, and the center's administrative procedures. The National Opinion Research Center prints a similar manual (NORC, 1945) and a shorter one on interviewing entitled *A Brush-Up on Interviewing Technique* (NORC, 1962). Principally for its field supervisors, NORC also publishes a *Manual of Procedures for Hiring and Training of Interviewers* (1967c). Other research centers publish similar manuals or circulate detailed memoranda on operating procedures. These materials are available for a nominal fee to students of survey research.

Interview specifications ("spex," or interview goals or purposes) provide the interviewer with a thorough introduction to a project. Included in the spex (as NORC calls them), are the nature of the project, clear sampling instructions, a question-by-question commentary on the goals of the questionnaire, instructions on filing reports, and any other general instructions peculiar to the particular project to which they pertain. The spex are a ready reference tool in the field, and if they are well designed, the interviewer will be able to solve most of his problems with them. When NORC or SRC begin a national study, they mail out the spex for the project with the assignment, and interviewers are urged to read them thoroughly and carry them with them in the field.

The most important phase of the training program is that devoted to various practice sessions: (1) role playing, (2) trial interviews, and (3) observed or taped trial interviews. The trainees can interview either each other or experienced staff members during role playing. The trainee acting as a respondent is learning, not just helping his partner, because he sees the interview process from another point of view. The field director can assume the role of respondent for one trainee, while others observe the process. This permits the field director to "play out" some of the problem respondents every interviewer will ultimately encounter in the field. Recordings of interviews illustrating successes and failures in handling the various parts of questionnaires can be played for a group of trainees (Kahn and Cannell, 1957, pp. 239–40).

The trial interviews submitted by a trainee can be evaluated by the fieldwork director, who will mentally compare them with work submitted by experienced staff interviewers. Some criteria for evaluation are: completeness, mistakes in following contingency item directions, the nature of the probes written in the margins, and the conversational tone which is the hallmark of an accurately recorded interview. An observed interview is a superior way of evaluating an interviewer, and in the training period, the experienced observer can inject himself into the interview when he spots a major error, thus immediately showing the trainee his mistake in context and offering a suggestion for avoiding the mistake again. Recorded interviews permit good evaluation, and the supervisor and trainee can listen to the tape together, going over its strengths and weaknesses.

Training sessions should be conducted in a businesslike manner, but also in a friendly and open one. Applicants are potential new professional interviewers. Their backgrounds qualify them for treatment as novice professionals. The coffee breaks, meals, and question periods offer an opportunity for the staff to relate personally with the trainees and ease beginners' fears and tensions so that a fair role playing experience and set of trial interviews is possible. At the end of the training period, some trainees cannot be retained as interviewers. In all fairness, those not retained deserve the best explanation one can give them, but this particular chore is never easy for the training staff.

Nature of the Fieldwork Operation

Most survey projects seek to measure some attitudes which are sensitive to events in the public sector; therefore, it is essential to complete the fieldwork within a limited time. Typically, it is deemed wise to complete most of the fieldwork within one week, allowing for a day or two beyond the week for clean-up work on difficult respondents. Meeting the time constraints requires good cooperation between the fieldwork director, the field supervisors, and the interviewing staff.

The fieldwork director must be sure that all necessary materials are in the hands of the interviewers and that they receive his full support in their work. In every community where interviews are to be taken, the Police Department and the Chamber of Commerce must be fully informed of the project. Some responsible members of the project staff must be available by phone for "trouble" calls from interviewers and for "legitimacy check" calls from potential respondents. If the project is to be conducted under the sponsorship of one unit of a larger agency (for example, a department or research unit of a university), the public relations arm of the parent agency should be advised that the study is in the field.

Interviewers are expected to fill their assignments as soon as possible, and help with the clean-up phase of the project if possible. Any difficulties should be reported to the immediate field supervisor. As the interviewer finishes each interview, he is required to read it over and "edit" it. Editing, in this sense, has quite a different meaning from the literary definition of the word, for no respondent answer is changed. If the interview was taken in pencil (a no. 2 pencil is always preferred), it should be edited in pen or colored pencil. The interviewer's editing includes being sure that the handwriting is legible; marking errors in asking contingency questions or errors in omitting items (Not Ascertained, N/A); and adding marginal notes to clarify a response. And, finally, the interviewer must fill out time sheets, expense reports, and any other field reports required.

In addition to supplying materials to interviewers and responding to their requests to solve problems, field supervisors conduct field checks. The supervisor randomly calls at dwelling units where interviews have been reported, or he phones reported respondents, or he mails a two-way postcard to ascertain that the interview was actually conducted. In any one of these field checks, the simple question is "Our records show that on March 15th Mary Brown, a member of the Project field staff, called at your home to interview you. I am just calling [writing] to be sure that Miss Brown did a good job with the interview. How did you think the interview went?" Of course, the central purpose of the question is to ascertain whether the interview did take place. As a final phase of the field check operation, the superivisor should carefully read completed interviews looking for any unusual patterning of responses, a possible indication of fraudulent interviews, but more likely an indication of interviewer bias.

There are, potentially, two bases on which interviewers may be paid: by the hour, or by the unit (interview) of work completed. The major research centers pay portal-to-portal hourly wages plus expenses, and this is much the superior practice to follow. If a per unit salary were paid, the temptation would persist to rush the fieldwork, and no pay would be received for callbacks to dwelling units or for waiting for respondents (Hilgard and Payne, 1944). Since the research project is vitally interested in a high response rate and a high quality effort at data collection, the hourly wage is the wise policy. Occasionally, the hourly basis of payment leads to an interviewer "padding" his pay by overreporting his time. If such a problem develops with a permanent member of the interviewing staff, a carefully worded note of caution usually brings future reports into line.

To conclude this section on interviewing, let us review the literature. There are four outstanding general works on interviewing, and I have used them extensively in this section: Herbert H. Hyman et al., *Interviewing in Social Research* (1954); Robert L. Kahn and Charles F. Cannell, *The Dynamics of Interviewing* (1957); Stephen A. Richardson, Barbara Snell Dohrenwend, and David Klein, *Interviewing: Its Forms and Functions* (1965); and Raymond L. Gorden, *Interviewing: Strategy, Techniques, and Tactics* (1969). The Hyman work reflects the rich experience at NORC, and Kahn and Cannell are, respectively, program director and head of the field staff at SRC. Both editions of the *Handbook of Social Psychology* contain excellent articles on interviewing: the entry in the first edition is by Eleanor and Nathan Maccoby (1954), and that in the second is by Kahn and Cannell (1968). Two works are available on interview costs, the first reflecting experience at SRC, the second, at NORC: Charles S. Mayer, *Interviewing Costs in Survey Research* (1964) and Seymour Sudman, *Reducing the Costs of Surveys* (1967). We have been concerned throughout this chapter with the structured, cross-sectional survey; for other approaches see Lewis Anthony Dexter, *Elite and Specialized Interviewing* (1970).

CODING AND ANALYSIS

After all fieldwork has been completed, the coding staff proceeds to develop a code book. This process may require weeks or months. In this section I will try to describe as fully as space will permit: (1) the general features of a code book, (2) the process of designing codes, (3) the coding operation, (4) punching the coded data, and (5) the analysis process.

The Code Book

A code book serves several different functions: it is a record of the research operation, a set of precise directions and codes to direct the coding operation, and a guide to any person undertaking either the primary or a secondary analysis of the data.

As a record of the research operation in the scientific tradition, the project director tells other social scientists about the quality of the research effort. In a *preface* there should be a statement on the type of sample used, the response rate, any weighting operations necessary to perform on the sample to use the data, and any limitations imposed on the analyst by the nature of the sample or data collection operation. If there are problems inherent in the storage or condition of the data, the potential analyst needs to be warned.

Also, as a part of the record function, the code book must contain the precise *questions* and *interview instructions* from the questionnaire. It does not suffice to give a simple heading, "Education of the Respondent," and the appropriate codes. The question used to elicit the data on education must be included, because the form of the question can influence the quality of the data. Analysts need to know what instructions were given to the interviewers on probing for answers to an open-ended question. For example, on an open-ended question on "current public problems," an interviewer instruction might read: "Probe for up to *five* different problems."

The code book also contains the *codes* by which coders convert verbal symbols into numerical symbols and the *coding instructions* which guided the coding operation. Instructions given coders can be as important to the analyst as interviewer instructions.

Code books also include *frequency counts* of responses to virtually all questions. Typically, no frequency count is included for the complex, multiple-response, multiple-column coded questions, or for certain items included primarily for identification purposes. Frequency counts are very helpful in planning the analysis of the data and in verifying analysis output or the accuracy of analysis decks. In planning the analysis, for example, frequency counts on "income" permit the collapsing of categories by the analyst into three relatively equal, synthetic categories of "high, medium, and low income." And after computer runs are done or an analysis deck has been punched, it is always wise to compare the frequency counts from the code book for several variables against the frequency counts for the same variables on the "A Deck" or the output. Frequency counts are usually typed in the left margin of the code book.

Code books are laid out, and data punched, in a pattern which follows the standard *IBM card* as a storage unit. With the advent of the last three generations of computers, data are actually stored and processed on computer tape, but the IBM card has become a conventional, easy to handle, basic record unit, and all code books are a listing of the cards or decks of data (see Bisco, 1965; Janda, 1969).

Designing Codes

To the extent that a questionnaire is made up of closed, multiple-choice, or dichotomous response questions, *precoding* is possible, and the effort needed to construct a code book is minimized. However, large-scale studies in the social sciences typically include a variety of open-ended questions, and the attendant questionnaires require a great effort to build a code book. To the extent that questions have been replicated from other studies, *codes should be replicated*, with such amendments as are absolutely necessary, to insure comparability. As noted previously in this chapter, it is hardly necessary to construct new questions on such items as occupation, income, and religion; codes for these questions are available and should be used.

Before the staff begins to design the code book, it is wise to have a clear plan of how the work will proceed. The order in which the codes will appear needs to be planned, and the number of columns necessary to store the data for each question must be listed. After the basic plan is established, all of the staff should meet for a survey of the plan and assignment of duties.

Open-ended questions pose the great problem for the staff. A careful *content analysis* must be made of the responses. For example, every distinguishable thought, pattern of behavior, or other type of response, should be copied on three-by-five cards; the cards can then be grouped into categories. One of the most difficult facts for the novice to accept is: *you are going to lose some information.* If you have 1,500 respondents, you can, theoretically, have 1,500 different code categories, and this would defeat the purpose of the whole enterprise. In general, the following test is a good one for establishing code categories: no coding category or subcategory should be retained if it will be used for a trivial number of responses. However, if the study has hypothesized that a certain response or pattern of responses will be minimal, the code should permit a careful recording of any such response(s), no matter how few.

When the codes have been drawn up, the *temporary code book* is typed and reproduced in sufficient quantities for use by the staff. All members of the coding staff should then meet with the project director and the coding supervisor for instruction on the use of the code book and any reference works to be used in coding (for example, most occupation codes are based on the U.S. *Census of Occupations*). Members of the coding staff should recognize the coding supervisor as the authority in all questions which will arise (though the supervisor may confer regularly with the project director). After instructions, the coding staff should begin coding a random sample of the questionnaires to test the temporary code book, and the entire group will need to meet frequently to discuss difficulties. It is wise to have several coders code the same questionnaires and compare the results. During this trial phase, coders should *not* confer on coding decisions on an individual basis—coding problems should be brought up at group meetings.

After the testing phase is completed, a group meeting should be held to check every coder's copy of the *corrected preliminary code book*. This can easily be done if the coding supervisor reads aloud all corrections entered in the master copy of the temporary code book while each coder checks his individual copy. Then all of the coding sheets produced during the trial phase are destroyed, and the final coding process begins. Further changes in the code book should be made only when absolutely necessary.

Examples of Codes

A one-column code is fairly easy to conceive. For example, consider the following one (ICPSR, 1971, p. 82):

Question 56. In the elections for President since you have been old enough to vote, would you say that you have voted in all of them, most of them, some of them, or none of them?
1. All of them
2. Most of them
3. Some of them
5. None of them
6. Voted, NA how many
7. None of them because not old enough to vote before or not a citizen before. Resident of Washington, D.C.
8. DK
9. NA

A two-column code is a bit more difficult, but the following one (ICPSR, 1971, pp. 107-8) is illustrative. Note that both columns or both digits of the code should have some significance. The first column should permit a logical, informed, useful collapsing of the data.

R's Education [question omitted]
00. None
11. 1 Grade
12. 2 Grades
13. 3 Grades
14. 4 Grades
15. 5 Grades, or 1st to 8th grade, NA exact level
16. 6 Grades
17. 7 Grades
21. 8 Grades
31. 9 Grades

32. 10 Grades
33. 11 Grades, or 9th–12th grade, NA exact level completed
41. 9 Grades plus non-college training
42. 10 Grades plus non-college training
43. 11 Grades plus non-college training
51. 12 Grades
61. 12 Grades plus non-college training
71. Some college
81. Bachelor's degree (4 years college). BS, BA, AB, AB IN TH, B ARCH, B CH E, BCL, BCS, BD, BE, B ED, BFA, BJ, B LIT, BSA, BSC, BSED, BSFS, BS IN CE, BS IN CHE, BS IN ED, BS IN LS, JCB, LITB, LLB, PHB, SB, STB
82. Master's degree. MS, MSC, MA, MAT, MBA, MDS, MED, MFA, EDM, LLM, MPH, MPA, MS IN LS, MSW, MUSM, SM, STM, MMUS, MFS
83. PHD, LITD, SCD, LHD, DFA, DLIT, DPH, DPHIL, DSC
84. LLD, JD, JSD, SJD
85. MD, DDS, DVM, VS
86. DD, JCD, STD, THD
98. DK
99. NA

Note that this particular two-column code meets an important coding convention: namely, whenever possible and economically feasible, code detailed data to a level you may never need, because the secondary analyst may need it, or may desire to collapse the data in a different pattern from that of the primary analyst.

A three-column code is more complex, but it is designed in the same fashion. Each column has a particular meaning. For example, let us consider one of the most important series of questions in SRC's election studies (ICPSR, 1971, pp. 7, 9):

Question 3. Is there anything in particular that you like about the Democratic party? (What is that?)

Question 4. Is there anything in particular that you don't like about the Democratic party? (What is that?)

Question 5. Is there anything in particular that you like about the Republican party? (What is that?)

Question 6. Is there anything in particular that you don't like about the Republican Party? (What is that?)

The first digit of the code is designed to capture the direction of the response:

1. Pro Democratic
2. Anti Democratic
3. Pro Republican
4. Anti Republican

The second digit captures a gross category of the substantive content:

0. Likes People Within Party
1. Government Management
2. Government Activity, Philosophy
3. Domestic Policies and Conditions: Welfare and Economic
4. Domestic Policies and Conditions: Other
5. Foreign Policy
6. Like Party Because Bad For, Has Kept (Will Keep) in Check [Groups]
7. Like Party Because Good For, Better For, Has Kept (Will Keep) in Check [Groups]
8. Party Responses
9. Other

The last digit codes the specific substantive content of the response. For example, consider the third digit of the pro-Democratic "Leaders" response for the 1964 election study (ICPSR, 1971, pp. 253-68):

101   Johnson
102   Kennedy
104   Roosevelt
106   Humphrey
107   Local and National Democratic Leaders
108   Democrats Have Good Leaders. Like Leaders.
109   Other

The first digit says "Pro Democratic" response; the second, "Likes People Within Party"; and, in the case of the code 101, the third digit says the object of this positive, Democratic response is "Lyndon Johnson."

The codes should provide the categories necessary to adequately describe *missing data*. Five particular categories are conventionally used:

DK: respondent answered "don't know"
RA: respondent "refused to answer"
NA: not ascertained by the interviewer
IA: question is inapplicable for the particular respondent
Other: meaningless response or an unclassifiable response

Preliminary tallies may permit the staff to omit the "refuse to answer" category on all except a few of the most sensitive questions (like age, vote, income, or racial attitudes). Some code books are built with only a limited category or two to capture missing data, making no distinction between "not ascertained," "refused to answer," and "don't know." These are quite different categories of missing data, and code book designers should be very certain that they will not need these discrete categories to support their analysis. Collapsing missing data categories can be a false economy of time.

In designing codes, it is always wise to use logical patterns of numbers and to be consistent in the use of the same codes for identical or similar responses. The code "O" for the categories "none," "inapplicable," and "no follow-up panel study interview" seems quite natural and logical. Furthermore, it is helpful to coders and analysts alike to know that "yes" and "no," or their counterparts in dichotomous questions, will invariably be coded "1" and "5." Likewise, it is good to set the code for each of the categories of missing data and follow those codes throughout the study.

Every card (or deck) must contain certain identification data: (1) the respondent identification number, (2) the study identification number, and (3) the card (or deck) number. The respondent identification number is necessary to tie the respondent's record together in the data file, and it is especially useful in replacing torn IBM cards, replacing an erased section of a tape, or in cleaning errors from the data set. The study number on every card prevents the mixing of data sets. Since most survey studies have more than one card of data per respondent, it is wise to repeat the card number on every card to avoid any possible confusion of one card with another. With tape storage of data, the card number is not as important, so long as one knows the manner in which the card images or card records have been read onto the tape.

The Coding Operation

The training of the coding staff and their attentiveness to their task are important to the overall quality of the research project. Many of the qualities needed to become a good interviewer are also essential to becoming a good coder. A coder needs to be bright, interested in people—and the world in general—and motivated to do a good professional job. Coders are not an appendage to the research operation—they are involved in the whole process. They need to know the general nature of the project and the particular goal or purpose of each question asked if they are to intelligently code responses.

The formal training of coders is as important as the formal training of interviewers. Coders may be added to the staff in two waves: after an initial group has been employed to help with the content analysis, code building, and the debugging of codes, a second group can be added for the final coding process. (Large research centers maintain a coding section with a continuing, trained staff.) Before the final coding process begins, the coding supervisor should formally train the coding staff on the goals and purposes of questions, how to apply the codes, and all of the forms and rules to be followed in the coding operation.

The physical setting needs to be appropriate to the coding operation. Plenty of space needs to be available for each coder—space to spread out the code book, the interview, coding sheets, and any reference materials necessary. The coding supervisor's office should be nearby if not adjacent to the coding room. The physical work setting should maximize the security of the questionnaires and coding sheets. Actually, there is little danger that anyone would want to destroy the anonymity of the responses; the greater danger is that a questionnaire might be lost in the massive flow of paper going out of the coding room. From the beginning, it is wise to store questionnaires in filing cabinets, take them out in blocks for coding, and return them daily to their appropriate storage place.

Beyond the code book, there are some elementary rules needed to guide the coding operation. For example, editing of interviews by coders should be done only in one (designated) pencil color to distinguish notations made in the field from those made in the coding operation.

At first, coding will go slowly, and then the coders will begin to pick up speed. After a few weeks, the coders will have memorized almost the entire code book, and coding will go along rapidly. When coding picks up, it is time for the coding supervisor to remind the staff that accuracy is of paramount importance. Memory can be faulty; carelessness is a potential result of speed. It is important that the coder stay alert and maintain his interest and motivation if he is to do a professional job (Roth, 1966).

As in other phases of survey work, bias and error enter into coding. Early in the coding operation, the supervisor should personally check the work of each member of the staff and be especially alert to potential bias on the coder's part. If the coder has strong personal views which constitute an evaluative context for judgment coding, he may need to be replaced. If, on the other hand, he has misinterpreted the purpose for which a question was asked, a clarification of the purpose permits an immediate adjustment on the coder's part. Every study should (and few studies do) conduct a systematic *intercoder reliability check*. That is, every Nth interview coded should also be coded by another member of the staff, and, unless there is very high agreement between the coders, there is a problem in some phase of the coding operation.

Analysis

When the data have been "cleaned," appropriate validity checks (if any) have been performed on the study, and the sample has been evaluated on the basis of available check data, the final edition of the code book can be prepared, including the frequency counts. In reality, analysis often begins before the data have been fully "cleaned" or the final code book prepared, but this is risky.

Analysis is a formidable subject. If the research design was a good effort, the analysis plan is already prepared. It will certainly be amended, or elaborated upon, but changes will mostly spring from novel or surprising findings. The original storage decks of data will be extended as indices are constructed or items scaled and the summary scores added (these manipulations are often performed and the scores are added items in the final edition of the code book).

During analysis, it may be necessary to call on the computer center for programming assistance. However, in the last decade several significant analysis and statistical computer program packages have been designed and made available across the country. The three best-known packages are: BMD or the Biomedical computer programs (UCLA); SPSS (Stanford); and OSIRIS (Michigan). One or more of these program packages will soon be available in almost every computer center in the country. With limited skills the analyst can perform the analysis of his data in any way he wishes, generating the necessary statistics, using a program or several programs from one of these packages. The analyst need not be a programmer: he addresses the computer in English (not Fortran). And if the subroutine the analyst needs is not available, or if he has special problems, advice and assistance can be secured from one of the large research centers at minimal cost. If the analyst's institution is a member of the Inter-University Consortium for Political and Social Research, or the Roper Center, one service these memberships offer is special programming assistance.

The following works have been especially useful in writing this section, and I recommend them to the reader: "The Quantification of Questionnaire Data," chapter 9 in Oppenheim, *Questionnaire Design and Attitude Measurement* (1966); Janda, *Data Processing Applications to Political Research* (1969); Blackman and Goldstein, *An Introduction to Data Management in the Behavioral and Social Sciences: the Use of Computer Packages* (1971); Harkins, Isenhour, and Jurs, *Introduction to Computer Programming for the Social Sciences* (1973); and Ralph L. Bisco, "Social Science Data Archives: Technical Considerations" (1965). See also Bisco, *Data Bases, Com-*

puters, and the Social Sciences (1970); Nie, Brent, and Hull, *Statistical Package for the Social Sciences* (1970); Tufte, *Data Analysis for Politics and Policy* (1974).

POLLING AND POLLSTERS

If public opinion polls were a central concern of this section, much space would have to be devoted to the history of polling, which I shall only outline here. Public opinion measurement in the United States had its origins in straw polls taken in the early nineteenth century. After World War I, when the country's manufacturing and industry produced a surplus economy, marketing research became a business tool for planning and manipulating the market. In the mid-1930s, several of the nation's leading marketing research specialists turned to public opinion polling. The first great names in the field were George H. Gallup, Archibald Crosley, and Elmo Roper: in 1936, at the same time the *Literary Digest* published its disastrously erroneous straw poll, Gallup, Crosley, and Roper published reasonably accurate public opinion polls predicting a Roosevelt victory. The polling industry survived its own disastrous predictions of a Dewey victory over Truman in 1948 mostly because it publicly confessed its error in continuing to use quota sampling and in failing to take late measures of opinion trends (Gallup's data collected late in the 1948 campaign showed a Truman surge, but Gallup refused to accept his own estimates). Since then, the polling industry has grown dramatically, both in the United States and abroad. In recent years, the polls have had a remarkable record of accuracy, and the polling industry has become very conscious of its responsibility in the conduct and reporting of its polls (Hennessy, 1970b, pp. 67–92; Roll and Cantril, 1972, pp. 5–11).

Thousands of polls are available to political scientists for secondary analysis; most of them are stored at the Roper Center (Williams College) and at the Louis Harris Political Data Center (North Carolina). Of course, polls are designed to serve a basically different function from surveys. Pollsters seek primarily to predict, and secondarily to explain. Polls are likely to be based on short questionnaires, with fewer open-ended questions, and without many of the complex measures found in surveys. However, some polls (especially those taken for campaign planning, or to serve some information purpose) are fully as complex and sophisticated in design as academic surveys.

Since the large pollsters have become syndicated reporters of their data (to newspapers, news magazines, and to universities), they take regular, systematic readings of public opinion. Identical questions are asked periodically about the country's leadership, party affiliations of voters, and major public policy questions in the United States. Repeating an example cited earlier using *Gallup Index* data, an analyst can plot the surge and decline of American support for the war in Vietnam from 1965 to 1972. Of course, these are not panel data, but the comparability of the several estimates over time is quite good.

Though poll data are not always coded, punched, and stored according to conventions accepted in the academic community, the secondary analyst can control for these problems. Only a few researchers have made use of poll data. For example, V. O. Key, Jr., used poll data in writing his last book, *The Responsible Electorate* (1966), in which he explored the "rationality" of "the American voter" by studying "stand patters" and "shifters" in elections from 1936 to 1960. He discovered that a rational decision, in gross terms, is made by the shifter; that is, the shifter's move is congruent with his policy preferences and group identifications (Hyman, 1972, pp. 196-200). Pool, Abelson, and Popkin (1965) did their simulations of the 1960 and 1964 presidential elections using poll data.

There are four studies I should cite on polling and pollsters: Rogers, *The Pollster* (1949); Mendelsohn and Crespi, *Polls, Television and the New Politics* (1970); Bogart, *Silent Politics* (1972); Roll and Cantril, *Polls* (1972). On the 1948 polls see Campbell (1950) and Mosteller et al. (1949). On the AAPOR and the worldwide polling fraternity see Hart and Cahalan (1957), Wallace (1959), Wilson (1957). Also see Roper (1957), Gallup and Rae (1940), Chase (1962), Cantril (1961), Popkin (1966); Rosenbloom (1973).

TRENDS AND CRITICS

The two most pronounced trends in survey research in the last decade are (1) the exporting of survey methodology abroad, with a concomitant development of comparative studies, and (2) the emergence of more complex study designs, resulting in complex data sets.

One indication of the spread of survey methodology abroad is the number of foreign affiliations with the Inter-University Consortium for Political and Social Research: forty-four foreign universities and research institutes were affiliated with the Consortium in 1976, including members from Brazil, Denmark, Japan, Kuwait, Canada, Holland, Australia, Belgium, Norway, Germany, England, Switzerland, Sweden, and Israel. In addition, Gallup International has affiliates in every major country in the free world.

Examples of comparative or joint research projects involving scholars in two or more countries are growing in number annually. Consider the following examples, a few of the many available: Campbell and Valen's study of party identification in Norway and the United States (1961); Converse and Dupeux's study of the political socialization of the electorate in France and the United States (1962); the same authors' study of the appeals of the "Victorious General," Eisenhower and De Gaulle (in Campbell et al., 1966, pp. 292–345); Butler and Stokes's study of the English voter (1969); Almond and Verba's comparative study of *The Civic Culture* in five nations (1963). Election study data are available through the Consortium for many countries, including Australia, France, England, Canada, Norway, Holland, and Japan. (See also Rokkan et al., 1970; Merritt and Rokkan, 1966; Holt and Turner, 1970; Frey et al., 1969; Campbell, 1962).

Five studies undertaken in the last two decades are illustrative of the trend to complex designs and complex data sets: Matthews and Prothro's Negro Study, Stokes and Miller's Representation Study, Converse's (SRC's) United States Elections Panel Study, Jennings's Political Socialization Study, and Prothro and Kovenock's Comparative State Politics Study.

The Negro Study included (1) a Southwide cross-sectional sample of voting age adults, (2) a sample of voting age Negroes in the South, (3) a cross-sectional sample of Negro college students in the South, (4) in-depth studies of four southern communities, chosen to represent a range from most permissive to most repressive toward Negro political activity, (5) a massive collection of aggregate political and social data for the South, and (6) the 1964 SRC Election Study, which included questions necessary to measure change in attitudes and voting behavior in the South between 1960 and 1964 (Matthews and Prothro, 1966).

The Representation Study is an empirical testing of representation theory, exploring the linkage between public attitudes and policy outcomes in the United States House of Representatives. For this study, the following data were collected: (1) a nationwide sample of voting age adults clustered in 116 congressional districts in 1958, (2) interviews with all the incumbent congressmen, (3) interviews with all the opponents (if any) to incumbent congressmen, (4) subsequent roll-call votes of the elected congressmen, and (5) aggregate political and social indicators for the districts studied (Miller and

Stokes in Campbell et al., 1966, pp. 194-211, 351-72). At the same time that the Survey Research Center was conducting the cross-sectional survey for the Representation Study, one segment of SRC's Panel Study was in the field. The Panel Study includes reinterviewing the same sample of voting age adults in 1956, 1958, and 1960. With this first major national panel study, Converse will be able to assess continuity and change in the American electorate with a confidence unparalleled in behavioral research (for an article based on the data see Campbell et al., 1966, pp. 78-95).

The objective of the Political Socialization (or High School Senior) Study was "to ascertain the values and beliefs held by high school seniors about public affairs and politics and to determine the differential impact of various agents in shaping the values and beliefs" (Jennings and Fox, 1968, p. 429). To support this research, the following data were collected: (1) personal interviews with a national probability sample of high school seniors, (2) a self-administered questionnaire to the whole senior class in schools selected into the sample, (3) an interview with one or both parents of every high school senior chosen for a personal interview, (4) an interview with social studies (broadly construed) teachers in each school selected in the sample, (5) an interview of the principal of each selected school, and (6) data on the school characteristics, and the social studies courses offered at each school from 1962 to 1965 (Jennings and Fox, 1968; Langton and Jennings, 1968; Jennings and Niemi, 1974, 1975; Niemi, 1974).

The final example is a long needed study of comparative state politics which was conducted by the Institute for Research in Social Science at North Carolina. The 7,800 interviews taken just after the 1968 presidential election for this study include (1) a national probability sample of voting age adults, drawn in such a manner to permit (2) analysis by seven regions, and (3) probability samples for thirteen states. In the past, national election study samples have been designed to permit inferences by region, but could not support inter-state comparisons (Kovenock and Prothro, 1973; Wright, 1974; Black et al., 1974; Schneider, 1976).

CRITICS OF SURVEY RESEARCH

The survey has more than a few critics. Some of the critics oppose the behavioral movement, quantitative analysis, and the scientific orientation of political science in recent years, so that attacks on the survey are part of a general attack on trends in the discipline

(McCoy and Playford, 1967; Charlesworth, 1962; Berns, 1962). Other critics are less hostile; they have pointed out problems of survey analysis only to improve the technique, and have written critiques of shortcomings in survey analysis without attacking the methodology of survey research (Williams, 1959; Kendall and Lazarsfeld, 1950; Key, 1960b).

Some of the critics question the validity of the entire survey operation. They argue that samples of inanimate objects in science (say, rocks) can never be compared to samples of human beings; that human beings respond from a complex personality and experience; that human beings adjust attitudes or change opinions; and that pulling one attitude out of the context in which it has meaning and classifying it with dozens of other points of view similarly distorted is hardly "scientific." To these critics, users of the survey are pseudoscientists or worse; they contribute to a dehumanizing movement in which the dignity of human values and the human spirit are lost in a process of classifying, counting or manipulating (the popular slogan is "do not fold, bend, spindle or mutilate"). Indeed, these people who deny a science of human behavior go on to say that even were such a science possible, we should not pursue it: if man's behavior can be described, plotted on a graph, and explained, then man can be manipulated and true freedom will be lost.

There are other questions raised about the survey. "Do they [respondents] tell the truth?" Is the reply given by the respondent "the answer"? Should survey analysts treat a reply as the ultimate datum to be gained? Or, "Does behavior follow opinion?" Does not the mind "toy with or play with" ideas on which a person would never act? Do the analyst and respondent distinguish between the *ideal* nature of questions asked and answers given and the *real* nature of the world in which the respondent lives, interacts, and responds? "What is the meaning of the data collected?" Survey responses are converted to numerical values (with a certain loss of meaning) and then they are manipulated by categories noncongruent with the real world, and finally an analysis is performed using statistical operations which may or may not be appropriate for the data under analysis. What meaning does the analyst gather from this process?

Other critics have pointed out that survey analysts study "only the obvious," and reach conclusions "everybody already knew to be correct on the basis of intuition or simple observation." Or, to take up another line of criticism, users of surveys have to focus their studies on the simple taks, those amenable to the survey as a measuring instrument—so the appellation "out-house counters or man-hole counters" is carried over from the earlier accusations against sociology and anthropology. Given this accusation of "simple-mindedness," it is hard to understand the following, oft-used, accusation: "survey analysts put too much confidence in their data; they read too much into it; much of their data should be marked 'use with caution.' " There is, unfortunately, too much truth in the following two interrelated critiques of the survey: (1) too often the survey is poorly grounded in theory, has little to guide it in data collection, and is therefore essentially meaningless or can make but a shallow contribution to knowledge; and (2) survey analysts suffer from a disposition to report their findings in simple descriptive data reports, amounting to rather long research notes—they act like the academic world will be suitably impressed with their data, and genuine analysis, theory-building, and explanation were not required.

V. O. Key, Jr., wrote a perceptive evaluation of "the political relevancy of surveys" in his very favorable review article on *The American Voter* (Key, 1960b). Political survey analysts have profited immensely from Key's critique, but its message should be reasserted frequently. Key wrote that the findings of previous survey studies had "been primarily of sociological or psychological interest." "Ultimately the concern of the student of politics must center on the operation of the state apparatus in one way or another." Further, Key wrote, the very nature of the survey instrument "tended to encourage a focus of attention on microscopic political phenomena more or less in isolation from the total political process." The many survey studies, all at the individual or micro level, must be related to macro-level questions if they are to have true meaning for the political scientist. Moreover, survey studies, even panel studies, are a "snapshot of a ponderous and complex system as it moves through time." And Key concluded his essay with this summary of his central theme:

> Survey technique brings into systematic view the attitudes and outlooks of the mass of the people, but it is extraordinarily difficult to relate those findings to the workings of government, the payoff of the political process. *[The American Voter]* takes steps toward an understanding of the relations of governors and governed by its theory of the place of elections in the governing process. Yet both the practitioner and the theorist of democratic politics assume that elections are not the whole of democracy and that a continuing interplay between elite and mass occurs. Our systematic knowledge of that interrelationship is most limited; no little mystery remains about the bearing of mass attitudes and preferences on the day-to-day workings of democratic regimes [Key, 1960b, pp. 60-61].

Those using the survey need to be very aware of the criticisms summarized in this section, but the two most compelling pieces of advice they should keep in mind are: (1) ground studies in theory, and (2) make the studies relevant for a science of politics.

SECONDARY ANALYSIS AND DATA REPOSITORIES

Though public opinion polling dates back only to 1935 and only a few survey studies of major significance were undertaken before 1950, thousands of polls and surveys have now been taken. In this concluding section, secondary analysis of poll or survey data, and the rise of the data repositories to store and disseminate these studies, will be discussed.

By secondary analysis we mean any research use of a body of data *other* than that conceived and carried out by the original principal investigator(s). In Hyman's definitive work on the subject, he defines the term as "the extraction of knowledge on topics other than those which were the focus of the original surveys" (1972, p. 1). A tremendous investment in human and financial resources has been made in the multitude of polls and surveys stored in data archives; yet, their full potential for analysis has not been realized. In fact, authorities on secondary analysis are astonished at the minimal reuse, or "retreading," of poll and survey data.

The economic benefits of secondary analysis are obvious. It can be conducted for a fraction of the cost of a primary study and, moreover, the secondary analyst helps to bring out the full potential of the data collected by the primary analyst. The fledgling researcher is unlikely to secure the level of foundation funding needed to undertake a major primary study, but he can usually find the resources to undertake a secondary analysis. Graduate students in particular should avoid primary data collection (to conserve time and resources); if his major professor is not engaged in a project to which the doctoral candidate can have access, the candidate should turn to data available in archives. The established scholars and research centers that do command support from the foundations have made their data and their know-how available to the novitiate. In the opinion of Herbert Hyman, this openness of the established scholars and centers avoids oligarchy in survey research, in that it provides upward mobility to the young scholars who can make a break-through in publications by secondary analysis, and then make a claim on the foundations for support of their primary research projects (Hyman, 1972, pp. 9-70).

There are many other assets to be gained from secondary analysis. A prior secondary analysis may strengthen the design of a new primary research effort. There are times when the intrusion of a primary research effort is socially unwise because of public unrest or dislocation, and a secondary analysis will fill the researcher's needs. Certainly the discipline should not support a primary research effort and run the risk of eroding the public's good will toward the survey when a secondary analysis would do as well. Secondary analysis is an important aid in exploring the past, and it will support long-term trend studies. It will support comparative studies between nations and within nations at different time periods. In carrying out secondary analysis, the researcher is forced to improve his analytical tools, to be innovative, and to look for creative ways to manage data or solve data problems. Theory-building, concept formation, and the ability to think broadly and abstractly are improved by the very nature of secondary analysis. In the process of "rummaging around" in other studies at different time periods, the analyst is forced out of the normal (and probably narrow) patterns of thinking and proceeding. (This paragraph is a summary of points made by Hyman, 1972, pp. 1-24.)

Secondary analysis is not without its problems and pitfalls. The first and simplest problem is the availability of studies which will serve or fit the researcher's needs. Even if the analyst finds studies which seem supportive of the design, some variables may be missing; questions, codes, or scales to measure a variable may not be identical in two or more studies he wishes to use. Secondary analysis is beset by a potential for error: error in the design of the secondary analyst as well as error attendant to the primary research effort. The secondary analyst must design his study with caution—he must not unthinkingly and arbitrarily combine data sets, weight samples, or detach subsets of data, though these are strategies available to him; he must consider the full import of his procedures in the given context. Throughout this chapter on survey research I have discussed the potential for error in the survey; the secondary analyst must try to find out what error permeates a particular primary data set he wishes to use, and the further back in time a data set was collected, the more difficult it is to find out the true nature of a study (Hyman, 1972, pp. 25-31 et passim).

The problems of secondary analysis can be controlled. If all the needed variables cannot be found in appropriate studies, the secondary analyst may have to *build a new measure* from whatever indicators are available or decide to accept a weaker *substitute variable*. A sample design inappropriate for the study may be made appropriate by a *weighting* process, or the *awareness* of the nature of the sample may be all the secondary analyst needs to control for possible error.

The secondary analyst can literally redesign and reuse data collected by others. Polls which had no planned relationship with one another can become the basis for a time series study. One attitudinal survey can be linked to an aggregate data set for secondary analysis. If the particular variables to be explored are scarce in a population, and cells tend to become too small to support analysis, several samples taken about the same time can be combined to produce a super sample with an N of thousands. "Retreading" the data in secondary analysis can be as creative and sound as the analytical powers of the analyst permit. (See case studies in Hyman, 1972, passim; Glaser, 1962.)

Hyman's definitive treatment of the *Secondary Analysis of Sample Surveys* (1972) has substantially influenced this section. This book is an appraisal of the potentials of secondary analysis, a guide to its methodology, and includes a number of case studies illustrating the successful application of secondary analysis. Anyone about to undertake secondary analysis should read Hyman.

Data Repositories

The canons of science require the analyst to report his findings to the scholarly community in such a manner as to make replication possible. No rule is really required—the spirit of the survey community is one of cooperation. Requests for questionnaires, code books, and data are invariably honored, with these exceptions:

1. The cost of reproducing the code book and the computer time to store data on the requester's tape *may* be assessed.
2. If the primary analysis of the data set has not been finished and the research report published, the data *may* be withheld.

Actually, code books and data sets are often supplied to potential users (especially to graduate students) at no cost, and many times a data set is released to a secondary analyst before the primary analysis has been published. If a particular study is assigned to an archive, the principal investigator can refer all requests for servicing the data set to the archive. The growing number of requests from secondary analysts for code books and data sets helped to spur on archival developments in the United States in the last decade.

When the Council of Social Science Data Archives decided to advertise the existence of its members and their holdings in 1967, twenty-five data banks were included in the brochure (Council of Social Science Data Archives, 1967). The June 1973 issue of *ssdata: Newsletter of Social Science Archival Acquisitions* listed thirty-four data banks. The American archives on these lists are of several types:

1. Five of them are major, general purpose archives.
2. Some of the remaining ones are well known for a special function they have performed (for example, consider the following: the Latin American Data Bank at Florida; the Social

Science Information Center at Pittsburgh, which is especially known for its comparative political elites data; and the Social Science Data Library at Chapel Hill, which is the repository for Harris Poll data).
3. The remaining archives are a variable group: some of them are virtually state archives; others are built around a few major studies; and a few are primarily a users' center for local faculty and graduate students, with a very small proportion of the data being unique to the archive.

In other words, a few giants have dominated the archival developments in the United States. They are the multiple-purpose, general interest centers which regularly receive the bulk of foundation funding awarded for studies or archival development.

The five major, general purpose archives in the United States are: the Roper Public Opinion Research Center, the Inter-University Consortium for Political and Social Research, the International Data Library and Reference Service (Berkeley), the National Opinion Research Center (Chicago), and the Bureau of Applied Social Research (Columbia). The two archives having the greatest influence on political science at this time are the Roper Center and the Consortium; these two centers illustrate how rapidly secondary analysis has grown (with concomitant growth in archives) in the last decade and we will focus our attention on them. (On Berkeley, see Survey Research Center, Berkeley, 1965; Mitchell, 1964. See Bureau of Applied Social Research, 1966. On NORC, see Allswang and Bova, 1964; Mack, 1961.)

The Roper Center was founded in 1946, and in 1947 Elmo Roper and Associates transferred to Williams College all the materials from their public opinion polling dating back to 1936. In 1957 it became a general purpose archive to serve academic, government and other data users. In 1964 it organized the International Survey Library Association, the arm of the Roper Center which provides for institutional membership. "Originally, the center held the basic data from 177 surveys conducted by Roper Research Associates. By 1971, the data bank contained the original response data from approximately 9,000 surveys ... contributed by 117 survey research organizations in 68 countries. Annually, the center acquires between 400 and 500 additional data sets" (Roper Public Opinion Research Center, 1972). In 1971 there were fifty-one educational institutions affiliated with the Roper Center.

One third of the surveys at the Roper Center were conducted in the United States by national, regional, and state organizations. The remaining two-thirds were carried out by survey research groups in 67 other countries. Over 80% of the studies are omnibus surveys containing questions on a variety of topics. Because of the omnibus nature of most of its surveys, the center uses the individual question as a basic indexing unit. Each question is assigned to one or more of the 70 major and 1400 minor topical categories in the Center's indexing system [Roper Public Opinion Research Center, 1972].

The Roper Center is the world's oldest and largest opinion data archive. Faculty and students at institutions affiliated with the center have (for an annual fee) access to its data, can request data analysis, and can secure advice on research problems. Those from nonmember institutions can ask for the same services and an individual fee will be charged. From 1957 to 1962 approximately 2,500 scholars had made use of Roper Center data; in 1971 accesses to data had grown to nearly 2,000 per year (Hastings, 1963, 1964; Roper Public Opinion Research Center, 1965+).

The Inter-University Consortium for Political and Social Research was organized in the summer of 1962 as a cooperative arrangement between twenty-one universities and the Survey Research Center at Michigan. The goals of the consortium were

(1) the development of data resources; (2) the establishment of a formal training program for graduate students and faculty; (3) the stimulation and facilitation of new research; and (4) the operation of a clearing house for the improved communication of information about ongoing research [Miller, 1963].

Those organizing the consortium expected it to remain a rather small membership group, but they were to be surprised. The five-member council elected in 1962 to make policy for the consortium included some rather distinguished political scientists: James W. Prothro, chairman, David Easton, Robert E. Lane, Austin Ranney, and William H. Riker. At first, the consortium was primarily known for its American politics emphasis, especially in voting behavior. However, their archival resources are drastically changing. They now include American politics, comparative politics, international relations, and historical data. In extending its data collection, cleaning the data, and formatting and preparing them for dissemination, the consortium has been the recipient of foundation support, especially from the National Science Foundation. Summer training programs in quantitative methodology for graduate students and junior faculty began in the summer of 1963 and have continued ever since. The consortium has also sponsored many high-level data conferences designed as catalysts for data production and for the use of new data holdings. It has supported new lines of research, encouraged foundation support for them, and has been an innovator and disseminator of computer software packages. The consortium staff is available for consultation on research and data management problems. The consortium itself is supported from three sources: institutional membership fees, the University of Michigan, and special program grants and contracts. The breakdown for the expenditure of its 1972–73 budget of $891,900 was: 43 percent, technical services to members; 23 percent, archival development; 13 percent, summer training program; and 21 percent, consortium administration. Over 220 universities and research institutes were members of the consortium in 1976.

It would be hard to compare the extent of the usage of consortium data to that of Roper Center data. The consortium encourages all institutions with the computer facilities to do so to acquire complete studies on tape and make them available to users on their campus—code books are shipped automatically to all member institutions for any newly accessed studies. Because it holds such a great mass of data, this strategy is not possible for the Roper Center. The consortium and the Roper Center have quite different data collections: the Roper Center is primarily known for its collection of poll data, and the consortium for its collection of survey and aggregate data from academic sources. In addition, the Roper Center maintains much closer ties with the commercial polling industry and with the AAPOR, while the consortium is in the thicket of academic competition for major foundation support (see Inter-University Consortium for Political Research, 1969a, 1969b, 1973a, 1973b; Miller, 1963; Miller and Converse, 1964; Bisco, 1964; and closely related to the consortium, see Institute for Social Research, 1965a, 1965b, 1969a, and the ISR *Newsletter*).

In the winter of 1962, as an offshoot of the initial organizational meeting of the consortium, a committee of eight was formed to plan for the Council of Social Science Data Archives. The Committee of Eight developed a plan for a loose confederation of social science data archives in the United States. The NCSSDA was a planning, policy-making, and information-disseminating group for coordinating and publicizing the activities of archives. It was a supra-archive cooperative organization. The National Science Foundation funded the organization for at least six years.

The NCSSDA was designed to produce a forum in which the archives could deal with one another, try to build cooperation, and solve problems outside of a spirit of rivalry (which had existed in some cases). They wanted to minimize the self-centered, emerging, independent research centers. Members noted that research designs were not cumulative and that surveys were underanalyzed. They sought to lick the problem of the rapid search for data and its nation-wide transmission; therefore, it sought and secured a grant to support an experiment in telecommunications between divergent computer installations. The council was never to pass negative sanctions and was not to become the agent for fund gathering for archives, but it was to lead in the development of archives. It led in the development of standard formatting of data and of the machine readable code book. It encouraged new archives to accept specialized roles which needed to be developed. In trying to gain access to new bodies of data, NCSSDA encouraged a breakthrough to data collected by the mass media, encouraged the adoption of new computer programs for content analysis to reduce coding costs, and pointed to data collections in countries where no archives existed to store them. It advocated the development of an inventory of all survey and poll studies and an index to studies and variables included in them. To help develop the skills needed in the new age of archive development, the NCSSDA sponsored several annual conferences; for example, the fourth conference held in 1967 was on "Modern Computer Analysis of Complex Social Science Data Bases," and the fifth conference in 1968 was on "The Use of Archives for the Study of Public Policy Issues."

The council was established with an administrative organization at Columbia University in 1965 under the executive directorship of William A. Glaser. It offered real promise of solving some of the problems in the age of the survey. In 1968, the administrative office moved to the University of Pittsburgh under the executive directorship of Ralph Bisco. However, with the advent of the Nixon administration and the attendant limitation of funds for the social sciences, battles for those funds broke out among the archives, and the council was one of the victims of the struggle.

If there is a hope for the programs suggested by the council, that hope probably rests in the consortium. The consortium has taken up many of the projects of the council, but other archives must accept the consortium's leadership. The Laboratory of Political Research at the University of Iowa has taken up one of the roles of the council (with NSF funding); in September 1971 it began to publish *ssdata: Newsletter of Social Science Archival Acquisitions*, a quarterly listing of data acquisitions at all cooperating archives with an annual index of subject headings. For the first two years *ssdata* was distributed free of cost to all interested social scientists. Even with the contributions of the consortium and the emergence of *ssdata*, there is still a need for a supra-archival agency (Sessions, 1974).

(The foregoing discussion of the National Council of Social Science Data Archives has been based on mimeographed materials distributed by the council entitled "Newsletter," "Plans for the Council," "News and Notes," Announcements of Annual Conferences, and "The Constitution of the Council," dating between 1965 and 1968. Of the many articles on data library developments, see the following: Lefcowitz and O'Shea, 1963; Converse, 1964b; Bisco, 1965; Bisco, 1966; Converse, 1966b; Nasatir, 1967; Bisco, 1967; Council of Social Science Data Archives, 1967; Scheuch et al., 1967; Mitchell, 1968. For a warning on potential misuse and abuse of data banks, see Westin and Baker, 1972.)

CONCLUSION

In spite of the high costs in human and financial resources attendant to survey as a research technique, surveys and polls seem to increase each year. All of the major users of survey and poll data are increasing: the academic community finds it a very powerful technique of research; virtually every major candidate for political office has one or more polls taken; government agencies want surveys of their clientele groups and the public in general; and many surveys are taken by pollsters for the communications media to inform their various publics.

Though the survey is vulnerable to bias and error at every stage of the research process, the social scientist has the capacity and understanding to control for these hazards. A significant proportion of the *Public Opinion Quarterly* and other journals is devoted to methodological research, and specialized journals have been initiated to deal with methodology per se; for example, see *Social Science Research* (first published in 1972) and *Political Methodology* (first published in 1974).

And, finally, the survey is certainly going to grow in importance with the increased use of the technique in major comparative studies and with the design of large-scale, complex data sets. The data repositories make survey studies available at a minimal cost to universities, their graduate students, and their faculties, and there is little doubt that secondary analysis of data held in these repositories will be very fruitful for political science and social science in general.

8. CONTENT ANALYSIS

Ole R. Holsti

"Content analysis," wrote Abraham Kaplan in 1943, "is the statistical semantics of political discourse." This rather restrictive definition is no longer widely accepted, but it does serve to remind us of the close historical relationship between the development of content analysis and political inquiry. In this chapter I shall consider several aspects of this relationship.[1] What is content analysis? For what classes of research problems are political scientists likely to find it useful? What are the different types of content analysis research designs? What are some of the political studies which have used this technique? What are the implications of recent developments which make it possible to undertake content analysis by computers?

WHAT IS CONTENT ANALYSIS?

Nearly all social and humanistic research depends in one way or another on careful reading of written materials. What, then, distinguishes content analysis from any careful reading of documents? Although definitions of content analysis have tended to change over time with developments in technique and with its application to new problems and types of materials, there is wide agreement that it must

Special note: Substantial parts of this chapter are drawn from my chapter of the same title in the *Handbook of Social Psychology*, 2d ed. I am indebted to Gardner Lindzey, Elliot Aronson, and Addison-Wesley Publishing Company, editors and publisher of the *Handbook*, for generously permitting me to do so.

1. The present discussion is limited to a summary survey of the "why" and "what" aspects of content analysis. Space does not permit a review of such "how" questions as categories, coding, systems of enumeration, sampling, reliability, content analysis by computers, and the like. These are discussed at length in Holsti (1969).

meet the requirements of *objectivity*, *system*, and *generality. Objectivity* stipulates that the judgmental processes must be carried out on the basis of explicitly formulated rules and procedures which will enable other analysts to replicate the research. The investigator must be explicit about his procedures and criteria for selecting data, for determining what in the data is relevant and what is not, and for interpreting the findings. *Systematic* means that the inclusion and exclusion of content or categories is done according to consistently applied rules. This requirement clearly eliminates analyses in which only materials supporting the investigator's hypotheses are admitted as evidence.[2]

Important and necessary as these two criteria are, they are not sufficient to define content analysis or to distinguish it from related endeavors. An index or bibliography is concerned with the content of certain types of documents. Both can be done objectively and systematically; indeed, usually more objectively and systematically than most content analyses. But neither is undertaken with any theoretical purpose in mind. They are merely listings of terms or titles according to specified rules (e.g., alphabetically), and the list itself is the intended end product. On the other hand, content analysis includes listing of the content of documents according to specified rules, but this represents only an intermediate step toward answering some research question. *Generality*, then, requires that the findings have theoretical relevance. A datum about content takes on meaning only when we compare it with at least one other datum— other attributes of the documents, documents produced by other sources, characteristics of the persons who produced the documents, or the times in which they lived, or the audience for which they were intended. The link between these is represented by some form of theory.

These three requirements, as necessary conditions for all scientific inquiry, indicate that, in general terms, content analysis can be considered as the application of the canons of scientific research to the analysis of communication content.

Along with general consensus that objectivity, system, and generality are defining characteristics of content analysis, two other pro-

2. These requirements can also be illustrated by a negative example. In a book purporting to demonstrate the intellectual inferiority of certain racial groups, the authors culled from both reputable and highly suspect sources all materials supporting the thesis of racial inequality, while virtually disregarding the quantitatively and qualitatively superior evidence in support of the contrary thesis (Weyl and Possony, 1963). Although these findings were presented as a "content analysis" of the literature relating racial origin to intelligence, a "study" of this type clearly fails to satisfy even the loosest definition of objective or systematic research.

posed requirements have generated considerable debate in the recent literature. Must content analysis be *quantitative?* Must it be limited to the *manifest* content, or may it be used also to probe for more latent aspects of communication?

The quantitative requirement has often been cited as central to content analysis, both by those who praise the technique as more scientific than other methods of documentary analysis and by its severest critics. There is, however, considerable disagreement about the meaning of "quantitative" as applied to content analysis. The most restrictive definitions are those which require that content analysis measure the *frequency* with which symbols or other units appear in the text (e.g., Leites and Pool, 1942, pp. 1-2; Janis, 1943, p. 429). This definition assumes that frequency is the only valid index of concern, preoccupation, intensity, and the like. Often this is in fact the case, but there is also ample evidence that measures other than frequency may in some instances prove more useful. This view also places a number of standard content analysis methods on the borderline of acceptability, and it removes some of the most imaginative content analysis studies from our consideration. A pioneering application of content analysis, the RADIR (Revolution and the Development of International Relations) studies, combined frequency and nonfrequency techniques; each editorial in the sample taken from a series of "prestige newspapers" during a sixty-year period was coded according to the appearance or nonappearance of certain key symbols (Lasswell et al., 1952). Thus a strict frequency count, including multiple use of any symbol within an editorial, was not employed.

Some definitions equate content analysis with *numerical* results (Kaplan and Goldsen, 1949, p. 83). Others are still less restrictive and include studies in which findings are reported in such terms as "more," "less," or "increasing" (Berelson, 1952, p. 17). The case for designing content analysis to yield numerical data—although not necessarily in terms of frequency—is a powerful one. Foremost among the arguments is the degree of precision with which one's comparisons and conclusions may be stated. They also permit a more precise answer to a recurring question raised by case studies: with what degree of confidence can one generalize from the results obtained in the sample under study? But the use of statistics is not dependent upon recording frequency counts or any other single system of enumeration.

Finally, there is a group which accepts the distinction between "quantitative" and "qualitative," but which insists that systematic documentary studies of the latter type constitute an important, and perhaps more significant, form of content analysis. According to one viewpoint, a quantitative restriction leads to bias in the selection of problems to be investigated, undue emphasis being placed on precision at the cost of problem significance (Smythe, 1954; Barcus, 1959). Related to this general criticism is the view that one can draw more meaningful inferences by nonquantitative methods (Kracauer, 1952). Qualitative content analysis, which has sometimes been defined as the drawing of inferences on the basis of appearance or nonappearance of attributes in messages, has been defended largely, though not solely, for its superior performance in problems of applied social science. Alexander George (1959b, p. 7) cites instances in which qualitative analysts were able to draw more accurate inferences from studies of Nazi propaganda during World War II than those using quantitative techniques. Proponents of qualitative techniques also question the assumption that, for purposes of inference, frequency of assertion is necessarily related to the importance of the assertion; these critics suggest that the single appearance—or omission—of an attribute in a document may be of more significance than the relative frequency of other characteristics (George, 1959b). But even studies which identify and draw inferences from the unique aspects of each document are not simply qualitative; rather than counting frequencies, the analysts have chosen to formulate nominal categories into which one of two scores are recorded—present or absent.

Although the issues underlying the quality-quantity debate are not trivial ones, the position taken here rejects the rigid dichotomy which is sometimes implied. Measurement theorists are generally in agreement that qualitative and quantitative are not dichotomous attributes, but fall along a continuum. In short, all data are potentially quantifiable. Moreover, whether stated explicitly or not, many of the most rigorous quantitative studies use nonnumerical procedures at various stages in the research. Because content analysts are not generally agreed on standard categories, even for given classes of problems or variables, the investigator must often develop his own for the question at hand. Before constructing categories, he may want to read over a sample of his data to get a "feel" for the types of relevant symbols or themes. Prior to coding, he may also read over the data to identify any idiosyncratic attributes which, if not taken into account, might adversely affect the results. After coding and analysis of data have been completed, he may want to check the "face validity" of the quantitative results by rereading parts or all of his documents. Conversely, quantitative results may highlight qualitative aspects of the text which might otherwise have escaped the analyst's scrutiny. Thus, for purposes of definition there are few compelling reasons for excluding studies which fail to conform to any specified level of measurement. Rather, I take the view that there are various levels and types of measurement possible with verbal data (as there are with other types of data), and that each carries with it certain assumptions (which may or may not be warranted in a specific instance).

A second major source of disagreement among those defining content analysis is whether it must be limited to *manifest* content—that is, the surface meaning of the content—or can content analysis be used to analyze the deeper layers of meaning embedded in the content? The manifest-latent controversy can be considered at two levels. The requirement of objectivity stipulates that at the *coding* stage of research, the stage at which specified words, themes, and the like are located in the text and placed into categories, one is limited to recording only those items which actually appear in the document. "Reading between the lines," so to speak, must be reserved to the interpretation stage, at which time the investigator is free to use all of his powers of imagination and intuition to draw meaningful conclusions from the data.[3]

The second aspect of the manifest-latent issue concerns the *interpretation* of results. This debate is essentially one concerning the dimensions of communication which may properly be analyzed (Morris, 1946). Earlier definitions tended to limit content analysis to questions of *semantics*, the relationship of signs to referents, and to questions of *syntactics*, the relationship of signs to signs (Kaplan, 1943; Janis, 1949; Berelson, 1952). The restriction against analysis of the *pragmatic* dimension of language, the relationship of signs to those that produce or receive them, was usually based on the difficulty of drawing valid inferences about the causes or effects of communication directly from content data.

As has been the case in the quantity-quality debate, the recent trend has been in the direction of a broader definition (Cartwright, 1953, p. 424; Barcus, 1959, p. 19; Stone et al., 1966, p. 5). But the differences between the broader and more restrictive views are not as great as suggested at first glance. Both Kaplan (1943, p. 223) and Janis (1943, p. 437) excluded pragmatic content analysis because inferences as to the causes or effects of content can rarely be validated solely by analysis of the messages themselves. That is, inferences were limited to describing attributes of documents; inferences about characteristics of those who produced messages or ef-

---

3. A vivid example of "reading between the lines" is Shneidman's (1961, p. 26) inference that the patient who announces "I am Switzerland" is, by equating that country with freedom, expressing a desire to be released from hospital confinement.

fects upon those who received them were excluded.[4] On the other hand, proponents of a broader definition are generally aware of the dangers of inferring intentions, values, motives, and other characteristics of communicators without some independent sources of corroborating evidence; hence, they usually assume that content analysis data will be compared, directly or indirectly, with independent (that is, non-content) indices of the attributes or behavior that are inferred from documents.

For present purposes, a broad definition of the method will be adopted: *content analysis is any technique for making inferences by objectively and systematically identifying specified characteristics of messages.*[5] In somewhat more succinct form, this definition incorporates the three criteria discussed earlier: content analysis must be objective and systematic, and, if it is to be distinguished from information retrieval, indexing, or similar enterprises, it must be undertaken for some theoretical reason.

WHEN TO USE CONTENT ANALYSIS

Content analysis is not relevant to all documentary research. It can rarely be used to determine the truth of an assertion, or to evaluate the aesthetic qualities of campaign rhetoric.[6] Moreover, if the analyst uses documents to settle limited issues of fact, such as to determine whether the *New York Times* supported Carter or Ford in 1976, methods other than content analysis could be used more efficiently. But the data the investigator seeks from the content of documents can rarely be reduced to such simple factual questions.

One approach to documentary research is exemplified by a manual which suggests dependence upon "a sort of sixth sense that will alert you to tell-tale signs" (Gray, 1959, quoted in Dibble, 1963, p. 204). The difficulty with such advice is not that it is wrong, but rather that it may be insufficient. Intuition, insight, or a brilliant flash born of experience, thorough knowledge of one's data, imagina-

4. While definitions restricting inferences from content data were widely accepted until the 1950s, many earlier studies did in fact draw conclusions, often implicitly, about the causes or effects of communication.

5. This definition was developed jointly with Philip J. Stone in conjunction with his book on computer content analysis (Stone et al., 1966).

6. It can, of course, be used to determine the truth of an assertion about the content of communication. The statement "Jimmy Carter made more references in his 1976 campaign speeches to the need for federal action to aid the cities than did his opponents" can be shown to be true or false by content analysis of the speeches made by the two candidates.

tion, or luck are perhaps always present in creative research. But the same idiosyncratic qualities of intuition which render it important in some stages of research, especially in formulating the problem and in drawing inferences from the data, make it less useful in others. Intuition is not a substitute for objectivity, for making one's assumptions and operations with data explicit where they are open to critical purview. Nor is it a substitute for evidence. There is, finally, one further limitation of intuition that is particularly relevant for content analysis: language is complex, and even the trained analyst with keen insight may find it difficult to draw all relevant evidence from his data unless he uses systematic methods.

The limitations of relying solely upon ordinary reading of documents may be illustrated by White's study (1947) of Richard Wright's autobiography, *Black Boy*. Although White was a trained psychologist, his preliminary appraisal of the book failed to uncover a number of major themes. Systematic content analysis, however, revealed Wright's emphasis on personal safety, failure to identify with other blacks, and lack of interest in social goals. In general, then, content analysis will be useful whenever the problem requires precise and replicable methods for analyzing those attributes of documents which may escape casual scrutiny. In such cases the analyst will find the objective and systematic methods involved in content analysis advantageous *as a supplement to, not as a substitute for*, the other intellectual tools he brings to bear on his problem.

More specifically, content analysis is likely to prove useful for at least three general classes of research problems which may occur in many types of political inquiry. First, it may prove useful when data accessibility is a problem and the investigator's data are limited to documentary evidence. The analyst who has direct access to his subjects may well find that other research techniques provide better data more directly and at lower cost. When restrictions of time or space do not permit direct access to the subjects of research, they must be studied "at a distance," with the consequence that other research techniques (interview, questionnaire, observation, and the like) are not applicable. If the subject is no longer alive, he can be studied only through the record of his activities, through what his contemporaries set down about him, or through whatever writings he has left. In some instances the third category constitutes the most revealing, and occasionally the only surviving, source. Under these circumstances the options may be reduced to two—use the documentary evidence as skillfully and imaginatively as possible, or don't do the research at all. Content analysis may thus serve as a "last resort" approach to research when more direct techniques of analysis are ruled out by circumstances.

There are also occasions when even the investigator who *has* direct access to his subjects may prefer to collect his data through some form of content analysis. If it is important to get repeated measures of the subjects' values, attitudes, and the like over a period of time, and if one has reason to believe that continued interaction between analyst and subject may affect the nature of responses, then content analysis of the subject's statements may be a useful way to gather the required data. An important feature of content analysis is that it is a "nonreactive" or "unobtrusive" research technique (Webb et al., 1966).

Content analysis of documents may also be useful as a supplementary source of data. In the words of a Chinese proverb, "The palest ink is clearer than the best memory" (quoted in Webb et al., 1966, p. 111). A related application of content analysis, even when direct access to the subject poses no difficulty, is to develop an independent line of validation for data obtained through other methods. The investigator may check the results of questionnaire or interview data by comparing them with content analyses of the subject's statements. For example, a study of public attitudes and concerns used both survey data and content analyses of letters to mass-circulation magazines (Sikorski et al., 1967). The analyst who has used open-ended questionnaires or interviews may also find that he can best utilize such data by content analyzing them. In a cross-national study, *Youth's Outlook on the Future*, the investigators used content analysis on both open-ended questionnaires and the subjects' autobiographies about their futures to the year 2000 (Gillespie and Allport, 1955). Another illustration of content analysis used in conjunction with other techniques appears in a study of community social structure. Names of persons and associations appearing in two local newspapers in "Illini City" were tabulated. As a result of this study, Janes (1958) concluded that the sociologist can use such newspaper data both as a reconnaissance tool and as a supplement to other information on community structure. These examples illustrate the "multiple operation" approach to research (Webb et al., 1966, pp. 3-5). When two or more approaches to the same problem yield similar results, our confidence that the findings reflect the phenomena in which we are interested, rather than the methods we have used, is enhanced.

Second, some form of content analysis is often necessary when, given certain theoretical components of the data themselves, the subject's own language is crucial to the investigation. The social scientist often requires information of a subtlety or complexity which renders casual scrutiny inadequate, even if undertaken by a skilled and sensitive reader. One would have little confidence in rough estimates of the degree of "need achievement" in various literary products regardless of the investigator's skill or training.

Finally, content analysis may be helpful when there are technical advantages because the volume of material to be examined exceeds the investigator's ability to undertake the research by himself. In studies of newspapers, government documents, propaganda materials, and many other forms of communication, the analyst must usually limit his study to a *sample* of the documents. Findings from the sample of documents selected for study can then be used to make inferences about the larger universe from which it was selected. But unless the sample is drawn in such a way as to make it representative and unless relevant characteristics of the sample are described precisely, inferences about the entire set of documents will be dubious at best.

Another approach to the problem may be to employ one or more assistants. Whatever the merits of the investigator's sixth sense, when assistants are used he must be able to translate his methods of analysis into explicit rules to insure an acceptable degree of consistency and uniformity (i.e., reliability) in his results. Failure to do so will raise serious problems and confound the analyst in drawing conclusions from his data. Sampling and employing assistants are not, of course, mutually exclusive solutions to be the problem of data volume: they are often used together.

CONTENT ANALYSIS RESEARCH DESIGNS

All communication is composed of six elements: a *source* or sender; an *encoding process* which results in a *message;* a *channel* of transmission; a *detector* or recipient of the message; and a *decoding process*. Content analysis is always performed on the message, but the results may be used to make inferences about all other elements of the communication process. To the classical formulation of these questions—"who says what, to whom, how, and with what effect" (Lasswell et al., 1952, p. 12)—I shall add one more: "why?"

Each of these questions may be subsumed under research designed for three different purposes. The investigator may analyze messages to make inferences about characteristics of the text, causes, or antecedents of messages, or effects of the communication. These three categories differ, as summarized in Figure 1, with respect to the questions which will be asked of the data, the dimension of communication analyzed, and the types of comparisons.

The most frequent application of content analysis has been for the purpose of *describing the attributes of the message*. The type of

FIGURE 1. Content Analysis Research Designs

Purpose	Branch of Semiotics	Types of Comparison	Question	Research Problem
To describe characteristics of communication	Semantics (sign/referent) Syntactics (sign/sign)	Messages Source A 1. Variable X across time 2. Variable X across situations 3. Variable X across audience 4. Variables X and Y within same universe of document	What?	To describe trends in communication content To relate known characteristics of sources to the messages they produce To audit communication content against standards
		Messages Source Type A/ Messages Source Type B	How?	To analyze techniques of persuasion To analyze style
		Messages/Standard: 1. A priori 2. Content 3. Noncontent	To whom?	To relate known characteristics of the audience to messages produced for them To describe patterns of communication
To make inferences as to the antecedents of communication (the encoding process)	Pragmatics (sender/sign)	Messages/Nonsymbolic Behavioral Data 1. Direct 2. Indirect	Why?	To secure political and military intelligence To analyze psychological traits of individuals To infer aspects of culture and cultural change To provide legal evidence
			Who?	To answer questions of disputed authorship
To make inferences as to the effects of communication (the decoding process)	Pragmatics (sign/receiver)	Sender Messages/Recipient Messages Sender Messages/Recipient Behavioral Data	With what effect?	To measure readability To analyze the flow of information To assess responses to communication

Source: Ole R. Holsti, "Content Analysis," in Gardner Lindzey and Elliot Aronson (eds.), *Handbook of Social Psychology*, 2d ed. (Reading: Addison-Wesley, 1968), vol. 2, p. 604. Reprinted by permission.

research design will depend on the questions which the investigator seeks to answer and on his data. In order to state meaningful conclusions, however, *all* content data must be compared to some other data, in accordance with the dictum "Securing scientific evidence involves making at least one comparison" (Campbell and Stanley, 1963, p. 6). When content analysis is used to describe text, there are three basic types of comparisons that can be made. The analyst may compare documents derived from a *single source* in several ways. One application of this method is the comparison of messages for the purpose of drawing inferences about trends. The investigator may also compare messages from a single source in differing *situations*. This design is applicable for determining the effect of changed circumstances on specified characteristics of communications. The proposition that the character of an audience affects the content and style of communication has been tested in a number of content analysis studies. In this case, the research design calls for comparison of the messages produced by a single source across different *audiences.*

Comparisons of communication content across time, situation, or audience are intermessage analyses. A research design may also be based on the relationship of *two or more variables* within a single document or a set of documents. Hypotheses may also be tested by comparing the messages produced by *two or more different sources*. Usually the purpose is to relate theoretically significant attributes of communicators to differences in the messages they produce.

Finally, content data may be compared to some *standard* of adequacy or performance. Many studies have employed *a priori* standards defined, often implicitly, by the investigator's preferences. Even when a priori standards are made explicit, such deviations as "bias" have rarely been operationalized in a satisfactory manner. An alternative to the deductive approach is to derive standards inductively from *content data.* A representative sample of messages produced by a class of communicators may provide norms against which the products of any single communicator may be compared. A third type of standard against which content data may be compared is one defined by *noncontent indices*, such as aggregate data or expert opinion. A classic study of this type compared the incidence of minority group characters in popular magazine fiction with census data (Berelson and Salter, 1946; see also DeFleur, 1964).

Many research designs use two or more types of comparisons together. For example, hypotheses about the relative potency of role and personal variables in decision making were tested by analyzing the statements of Democratic and Republican senators (comparisons across sources) during the Truman and Eisenhower administrations (comparisons across situations) (Rosenau, 1968; see, however, the reanalysis of the data in Stassen, 1972).

The second major classification of studies is that in which the text is analyzed in order to make *inferences about the causes or antecedents of the message*, and more specifically, about the author. Within the communication paradigm, messages are examined for the purpose of answering the questions "who?" and "why?"

The problem inherent in this use of content analysis is that the relationship between a person's statements and his motives, personality, intentions, and the like, is at best only vaguely understood. Owing to possible differences in encoding habits, inferences about the antecedent causes of messages drawn solely from content data cannot be considered self-validating. Thus, however precise our measures of communication content, it is hazardous indeed to assume, without corroborating evidence from independent sources, that inferences about the author can be drawn directly from content data.

One of the more vigorous debates among content analysts is that between proponents of the "representational" and "instrumental" models of communication. The former take the position that the important aspects of communication are "what is revealed by the lexical items present in it" (Pool, 1959, p. 3; cf. Osgood, 1959). Words are assumed to "represent" accurately the author's inner feelings; thus there are constant, though probabilistic, relationships between the content of the communication and the underlying motives of their authors. The latter argue that it is not the face meaning of a message, but what it conveys in a given situation, that is important (George, 1959b; Mahl, 1959). In this view communication is seen as an instrument of influence; hence the content of messages may be shaped by the communicator's intent to manipulate his audience in certain directions. The position taken here, that inferences as to the intentions or feelings of authors drawn from content data need corroboration through independent evidence, is somewhat closer to that of the instrumental school. It does not deny the existence of regularities between content and its causes; rather it accepts the view that because regularities may be of a limited type (e.g., for certain classes of communicators, in specified situations, and so on) we need evidence beyond that provided by content analysis of the messages.

In order to draw valid inferences about sources from the messages they send, the content data may be compared *directly* with independent behavioral data. Inferences based on an *indirect* relationship between symbolic and other forms of behavior are much more frequent in the content analysis literature. The logic of such inferences can be stated as a syllogism: in a given situation, individuals whose behavior patterns are known to be A, B, and C, produce messages with characteristics X, Y, and Z respectively. If in similar circumstances a source produces messages with attribute X, the inference is that it was related to behavior pattern C. A classic example of this research design is the comparison between Nazi propaganda themes with the books, periodicals, and transoceanic cables of certain domestic organizations suspected of sedition, in which content analysis revealed significant similarities on a number of dimensions (Lasswell, 1949). In this case the likenesses in the messages of *two separate sources* served as the basis for inferences about the similarity of motives—support for the German war effort.

The research design may also focus on the relationship of events to symbols from a *single source*. The propaganda analyst may examine messages for attributes that have in the past provided a clue to certain types of policies. In general, inferences are based on some demonstrated relationship between events and symbols for the same or for comparable communicators. One weakness of many content analysis studies is that such a relationship between symbolic behavior and other forms of behavior has been assumed rather than demonstrated.

The third major classification of content analysis studies is that in which *inferences are made about the effects of messages* (the decoding process) upon the recipient. The question "with what effect" is, in some respects, the most important aspect of the communication paradigm. The effects of propaganda, campaign speeches, and other forms of political appeal are central to many research problems. There is strong evidence that persons interpret and assimilate the content of communication in light of their beliefs about the credibility of the source, situational, personality, and other factors. Thus, the investigator wishing to assess the effects of communication cannot confine his analysis merely to the content of the messages; his research design must also include evidence about the recipient of the communication.

As in the other types of research design, the sender's message serves as the data. Two types of comparison can be used to measure the impact of the message. First, the investigator may determine the effects of A's messages on B by content analyzing B's subsequent messages. An alternative approach to studying the effects of communication is to examine other aspects of the recipient's behavior; for example, his behavior before and after receiving the message.

These, then, are the basic designs which can be employed in content analysis research. We turn now to a survey of some political studies in which they have been used.

USES OF CONTENT ANALYSIS

Content analysis encompasses a widely varying set of techniques which have been employed to analyze many forms of symbolic materials relating to politics. Limitations of space restrict this review to a small sample of the literature. Only a few studies of each type can be described, and then only in summary fashion. Citations keyed to other studies listed in the reference section will be used to supplement the review, but even this bibliography can encompass only a fraction of the entire literature.

Characteristics of Content: What

Content analysis has been used most frequently for research problems in which the question can be answered *directly* from a description of the attributes of content. In such studies the content data serve as a direct answer to the research question, rather than as an indicator from which other characteristics are to be inferred.

To Describe Trends in Communication Content. Interest in measuring trends in attitudes relevant to international politics has stimulated considerable analysis of the printed media. An early study applied scaling techniques developed by Thurstone to Chinese and Japanese materials during the Far Eastern crisis of 1930- 32 (Russell and Wright, 1933). The same techniques were used to examine trends in American attitudes toward Japan and China along a favorable-hostile continuum (Wright and Nelson, 1939).

After the outbreak of World War II, Lasswell (1941) suggested that a "world attention survey" be conducted by ongoing analyses of the world's press. This idea subsequently led to an extensive survey of political symbols as one aspect of research on Revolution and Development of International Relations (RADIR). The studies were designed to test hypotheses relating to a "world revolution" by identifying and mapping trends in the usage of those symbols expressing major goal values of modern politics. One "prestige" newspaper from each of five countries—the United States, Great Britain, France, Germany, and the Soviet Union—was analyzed for the period 1890- 1949. Editorials appearing on the first and fifteenth day of each month were coded for the presence of 416 key symbols, including 206 geographical terms and 210 major ideological and doctrinal symbols. Each time a symbol appeared, it was scored as present; and further, expressed attitudes toward the symbol—approval, disapproval, or neutrality—were recorded. Data from 19,553 editorials were used to trace changing focuses of attention and attitude, as indexed by key symbols, for the sixty-year period (Pool, 1951, 1952a, 1952b).

Other studies have examined trends in Soviet May Day slogans (Yakobson and Lasswell, 1949), symbols used by the Communist International (Leites, 1949), twentieth-century propaganda (Kris and Leites, 1953), acceptance speeches of American presidential candidates (Smith et al., 1966), social optimism and pessimism in American Protestantism (Hamilton, 1942), and racial stereotyping in advertisements (Cox, 1970; Colfax and Sternberg, 1972).

Trend inventories have varied widely in purpose and quality. Such studies can be useful for identifying major changes across long periods of time, and are relatively easy to undertake; on the other hand, surveys depending on gross categories often conceal more information of interest than they reveal. According to one source, "systems of classification may be inadequate and unstandardized; nevertheless, if a system is used consistently over a time period valuable facts may appear" (Albig, 1938, p. 349, quoted in Berelson, 1952, p. 29). This seems a dubious premise upon which to stake very much research effort.

To Relate Known Characteristics of Sources to the Messages They Produce. Important aspects of social research test such hypotheses as "Sources with characteristic A are likely to produce messages with attributes w and x, whereas those with chracteristics B are likely to produce messages of types y and z."

The relationship between political orientation of media and the nature of their news reporting has been an area of considerable research in Europe and the United States. As early as 1910 Max Weber (quoted in Krippendorff, 1966, p. 5) urged that "we will have to start measuring, plainly speaking, in a pedestrian way, with the scissors and the compass, how the contents of the newspapers has quantitatively shifted in the course of the last generation."

Interest in the role of the press in electoral campaigns has been especially strong. Several studies have sought to determine whether editorial support is systematically related to other aspects of campaign coverage, such as the amount of space devoted to stories about each candidate. Evidence from such investigations is mixed, depending largely on the selection of newspapers and elections. Blumberg (1954) examined thirty-five American dailies during the 1952 campaign and found little evidence of bias in news coverage. This finding was supported by Markham and Stempel (1957). Studies of fifteen "prestige" dailies during the 1960 and 1964 campaigns indicated that "as a group they gave the Democratic and Republican campaigns virtually equal amounts of space in their news columns" (Stempel,

1961, p. 157; Stempel, 1965). But analyses of dailies in Florida and California revealed that endorsed political candidates received better news coverage (Kobre, 1953; Batlin, 1954).

A serious limitation of investigations based on space measures is that they tap only a single dimension of bias. Some rough equality of space allocation may be a necessary condition of unbiased coverage, but probably it is not sufficient. During the 1940 campaign the press and radio *focused* on Roosevelt by a margin of 3:2, but *favored* Willkie by better than 2:1 (Lazarsfeld et al., 1944, p. 117). The more subtle, and probably more important, methods of slanting news have received less attention than measures of space. One exception is an analysis of eight major daily newspapers during the 1952 campaign. Newspapers were rated on eighteen indices, including size and tone of headline, placement of stories, number of biased remarks, number of pictures, and total column inches of stories on various pages. These measurements gave strong indication of systematic bias in favor of the endorsed candidate (Klein and Maccoby, 1954).

Differential coverage of "civil rights" stories has also been related to various characteristics of newspapers, including geographical location, ownership (black, white), and political orientation. The findings have generally supported hypotheses of systematic quantitative and qualitative differences in news coverage (Broom and Reece, 1955; Carter, 1957; Breed, 1958).

Content analysis has frequently been used on documents produced by political action groups. Comparative analysis of Communist publications was used to develop a model against which perceptions and experiences of former party members (determined by interviews) could be compared (Almond, 1954). The American business community (Cochran, 1953; Lane, 1951; Bernstein, 1953), right-wing organizations (Wilcox, 1962; Abcarian and Stanage, 1965), and various groups of lobbyists (McPherson, 1964) are among other groups whose publications have been analyzed.

A variety of materials have been used in cross-national studies. Examination of news coverage by CBS and the CBC yielded data on the relative incidence of violence, protest, and war on American and Canadian television (Singer, 1970-71). Speeches by top leaders in eighty-six countries were analyzed for the purpose of identifying and comparing national role conceptions (K. J. Holsti, 1970). Two studies compared the literature and songs of youth groups in Nazi Germany and the United States. The German literature placed significantly greater stress on national loyalty, national identification, and determination, whereas American Boy Scout materials emphasized altruism, religion, and creativity (Lewin, 1947). A parallel study of children's songbooks yielded similar results (Sebald, 1962). German sources stressed national loyalty, obedience, and heroic death, and paid less attention to the beauty of nature, play, and Christianity. Content analysis of such materials can reveal important international differences at a specified point in time, but further inferences, unsupported by independent data, are often open to question. A case in point is Sebald's generalization, based solely on Nazi songbooks issued in 1940, that the modal character of Germans is basically authoritarian.

To Audit Communication Content against Standards. Historically, a major impetus toward development of content analysis was a concern for judging various types of documents. Dovring (1954) cites an interesting example of content analysis in eighteenth-century Sweden. Publication of a collection of ninety hymns, *Songs of Zion*, aroused concern among officials of the Lutheran state church who feared that the hymns were adversely affecting public opinion. Content analyses, based on the frequency with which certain themes related to Christ appeared, led opponents of the hymns to conclude that they threatened the doctrines of the established church. Content analysis was also used by the other side in the controversy to show that many words which were condemned when they appeared in *Songs of Zion* were praised when they appeared in other hymnals.

The more direct antecedents of content analysis may be found in studies by reformers and "muckrakers" of the American press around the turn of this century, some of them stimulated by concern over the spread of yellow journalism (Speed, 1893; Matthews, 1910; Tenney, 1912). Much of this early research has justifiably been criticized for subjective and arbitrary procedures. Interest in standards of the mass media, and especially in their presentation of political subjects, has been sustained, however, and many serious technical problems of the early investigations have been resolved.

A study of three major American news magazines—*Time, Newsweek*, and *U.S. News and World Report*—against the standard of "responsibility in mass communication" indicated that the "neatly reconstructed picture of the world" they present is often biased, distorted, or factually false" (Bagdikian, 1959). While apparently strong evidence of systematic bias was presented, the absence of explicit coding categories or sampling methods raises some questions about the findings. A rigorous study of the same news magazines during the period of the 1960 presidential nominating conventions revealed that each magazine treated the conservative candidates (Richard Nixon and Lyndon Johnson) more favorably than the liberal ones (Nelson Rockefeller and John F. Kennedy) (Westley et al., 1963; see also Ash, 1948, for a study of magazine treatment of the Taft-Hartley Act).

An analysis of six types of bias (attribution bias, adjective bias, adverbial bias, contextual bias, outright opinion, and photographic bias) revealed that *Time* used each technique extensively to describe recent American presidents. *Time*'s presentation of Truman was totally negative, Eisenhower was depicted in an unambiguously favorable light, and only Kennedy was described in somewhat balanced terms (Merrill, 1965). "Repeated distortion and misinformation" were also discovered in public affairs articles in *Reader's Digest* (Christenson, 1964).

The most common weakness of studies using an a priori standard stems from the absence of a clearly defined basis for judgment, rather than from technical problems of applying content analysis to the data. What constitutes "adequacy" in news coverage? Or, how close to "equal time/space" must the media come to be considered "fair"? It is doubtful whether unbiased reporting of every controversial situation calls for equal presentation or evaluation, as is sometimes assumed by indices of bias. Often the investigator's own values serve as the standard of comparison, but failure to define such terms explicitly makes it difficult to interpret findings.

One answer to the difficult problem of defining standards against which to audit sources is to make comparisons against other sources; that is, general norms for classes of communicators are developed inductively. The investigator may then rank sources along one or more dimensions. A more precise method, the technique of "successive approximations," was used to construct a "socialization-sensationalism" index. Six rough indicators were first applied to a large number of newspapers to identify those with highest scores on socialization *(Christian Science Monitor, Wall Street Journal)* and sensationalism *(New York Daily News, New York Daily Mirror)*. Detailed analysis of these newspapers yielded a more precise scoring system which can be used to rate any newspaper (Kingsbury and Hart, 1937).

A different approach was used to assess the *New York Times*'s coverage of the Russian Revolution and its aftermath. As a standard against which to measure the performance of the *Times*, the researchers' assessment included only seven Russian events, the occurrence of which was beyond any dispute: for example, overthrow of the Kerensky provisional government by the Bolsheviks in November 1917. Analysis revealed that coverage of these events was inadequate and misleading: "In the large, the news about Russia is a case of seeing not what was, but what men wished to see. ... The Russian policy of the editors of the *Times* profoundly and crassly influenced their news columns" (Lippmann and Merz, 1920, pp. 3, 42).

Characteristics of Content: How

To Analyze Techniques of Persuasion. For the last four decades, and particularly during World War II, considerable research has focused on propaganda. Often the purpose has been to infer intentions of communicators from propaganda content, a type of analysis to be discussed later. The remaining research has aimed at developing a theory of form, style, and the structure of persuasive communication.

A pioneering study of this type was Lasswell's analysis of propaganda techniques during World War I, in which four major objectives of propaganda and appropriate techniques of appeal for each goal were identified: to mobilize hatred against the enemy; to preserve the friendship of allies; to preserve the friendship and, if possible, to procure the cooperation of neutrals; and to demoralize the enemy (1927, p. 195). More quantitative methods were used to examine the organization, media, techniques, and symbols of Communist propaganda in Chicago during the depression of the 1930s (Lasswell and Blumenstock, 1939).

"Value analysis," a set of categories for studying personality from written materials, was used to compare the propaganda style of Hitler and Roosevelt (White, 1949; for a detailed explanation of value analysis, see White, 1951). The same method and categories were found useful for distinguishing writings by political figures of various ideological persuasions: Khrushchev, Stalin, Hitler, Mussolini, Goldwater, Hoover, Churchill, Kennedy, and Franklin Roosevelt (Eckhardt, 1965). Techniques of other propagandists which have been examined by content analysis include Father Coughlin (Lee and Lee, 1939), and Gerald L. K. Smith (Janowitz, 1944).

Several sets of categories for describing and analyzing various aspects of propaganda have been proposed. One scheme, developed at the Institute of Propaganda Analysis, enumerates content (name calling, testimonial, bandwagon, and the like) and strategic (stalling, scapegoating, and so on) techniques which have been identified in propaganda (Lee, 1952, pp. 42-79, 210-34). Other studies have examined atrocity propaganda (Jacob, 1942), arguments related to Swedish acquisition of nuclear weapons (Ohlström, 1966), German-British (Bruner, 1941), and Soviet-American propaganda (Garver, 1961) efforts against each other.

Research has not been limited to official governmental propaganda. For example, campaign biographies a form of persuasive literature which appears on the American political scene quadrennially, have been analyzed (Brown, 1960). Research has also focused on letters to congressmen (Wyant and Herzog, 1941), to various newspapers in the United States (Foster and Friedrich, 1937; Toch,

Deutsch, and Wilkins, 1960), the Soviet Union (Inkeles and Geiger, 1952, 1953), and Communist China (Wang, 1955), and to a magazine by radical right wingers (McEvoy, Schmuck, and Chesler, 1966).

The most evident weakness of propaganda analysis has been the absence of systematic research to relate categories of appeal, techniques, and dimensions (and combinations of these), to effects. What types of appeals are most effective? Under what circumstances? For which subject matter categories? One exception is a detailed investigation of Kate Smith's war bond drive. Content analysis was used to identify characteristics of her appeals which might be expected to elicit particular responses from the audience. The validity of inferences based on the content data was then checked by interviewing the audience (Merton, 1946). But in the main, questions about how technique and content of appeals are related to effects have remained unanswered.

To Analyze Style. Political rhetoric, especially that of American presidents or presidential candidates, has been a favorite subject for study. One approach is illustrated by a study of Woodrow Wilson's speeches (Runion, 1936). Categories were developed around grammatical aspects of discourse—sentence length, sentence structure, and figures of speech. Following in this tradition is Wolfarth's (1961) comparison of John F. Kennedy's inaugural address with those of all preceding presidents. Much of the analysis is devoted to word and sentence counts, with considerably less attention to policy content or presentational style of the addresses.

Some of the more imaginative studies of rhetorical style have developed categories other than word counts, sentence length, and the like. A study of broadcast addresses by Eisenhower and Stevenson during the 1956 campaign related substantive and stylistic categories (Knepprath, 1962). Shepard (1956) examined various content attributes of Henry J. Taylor's radio talks for General Motors. The issues and symbols which Taylor discussed were identified, and his treatment of them was coded as favorable, neutral, or unfavorable. Assertions were further coded as factual or interpretative, and for the type of evidence presented: statistics, examples and comparisons, analogies and figurative language, testimony, or none.

An interesting analysis of political rhetoric is found in a study of the 1960 presidential campaign designed to test the assertion that in their televised debates John Kennedy and Richard Nixon "made clearer statements of their positions and offered more reasoning and evidence to support their positions, than they did in other campaign situations" (Ellsworth, 1965, p. 794). The data clearly revealed a far higher incidence of analytic, evidential, and declarative content during the televised debates than during the other addresses.

A similar technique of coding was used to test the hypothesis that ideological distance between candidates increases the amount of policy discussion in campaign addresses in 1960 and 1964 (Ellsworth, 1967). Although the presidential candidates in 1964—Lyndon Johnson and Barry Goldwater—were assumed to be further apart ideologically than were Kennedy and Nixon four years earlier, no significant difference in the amount of policy content was found. The data did, however, indicate that the ideological content of political rhetoric—defined as statements regarding "the nature or character of man, society, government, or the relationship between them"—was significantly higher in 1964 than in 1960.

Characteristics of Content: To Whom

To Relate Known Attributes of the Audience to Messages Produced for Them. Studies to relate audience attributes to message content are often undertaken with a view to testing some form of the general proposition that communicators tend to cast their messages in the idiom of the intended audience.

Two studies have demonstrated that John Foster Dulles effectively identified the distinguishing characteristics of his audience and directed his political appeals to those attributes. Both during his efforts on behalf of the Japanese Peace Treaty of 1951 (Cohen, 1957) and during his later tenure as Secretary of State (Holsti, 1962a), the content of Dulles's rhetoric was guided in part by the nature of those to whom his appeals were addressed.

Albrecht (1956) analyzed short stories in large-circulation magazines with lower *(True Story, True Confessions)*, middle *(American, Saturday Evening Post)*, and upper *(Atlantic, New Yorker)* status readers, recording the distribution and evaluation of ten "family values." Stories produced for each status level strongly supported American family norms as a group. The data also indicated, however, that stories produced for the lower class were most conservative in attitude, and those in upper-class magazines were most liberal with respect to family values.

Interpretations of findings relating audience attributes to communication content are generally of three basic types: that authors *write differently* for dissimilar audiences, that the messages *reflect* basic value differences of the audiences, or that such materials *shape* the values and predispositions of the audience. The first interpretation presents the fewest problems of validity and can be made directly from attributes of the content. The second explanation is a variation of the theme, often debated with respect to the mass

media, that producers of communication are only giving audiences
"what they want." Whether or not this is true, such inferences
generally require either direct or indirect confirmation with independent data. The third interpretation is concerned with the effects of
communication and it, too, is tenuous unless supported by data
other than the description of the content.

To Describe Patterns of Communication. How are patterns of
communication affected by situational or systemic changes? Analysis
of documents written by leaders of the Dual Alliance and Triple
Entente nations during the summer of 1914 indicated that as war
approached, there was a significant increase in messages exchanged
within alliances, with a concomitant decrease in inter-coalition communication (Holsti, 1972b). Messages produced in seventeen "Inter-
Nation Simulations" revealed that after all members of an alliance
had obtained nuclear weapons, the modal pattern of communication
changed from a "wheel" configuration to an "all channels" pattern
(Brody, 1963).

The Antecedents of Content: Why

Among the most interesting and challenging research problems
are those about the causes and effects of communication. What
motives, values, beliefs, and attitudes are revealed in a person's
writing or speech? What can we learn about a culture by examining
documentary evidence? What is the relationship between exposure to
information and cognitive or attitudinal changes? These are but a few
of the questions to which content analysis has frequently been
applied.

To Secure Political and Military Intelligence. An important
impetus to the development of content analysis was a large-scale
propaganda research effort during World War II. Social scientists,
many of whom made significant theoretical and methodological
contributions to content analysis, were engaged by the Federal
Communications Commission, Library of Congress, and Justice
Department to study these materials.

The most difficult problem, because of the constraints within
which the propaganda analyst operates, is that of establishing criteria
for inference. The FCC used both *direct* and *indirect* techniques. The
first method operates from a *representational* model of communication, in which the investigator assumes that words in the message are
valid indicators of intentions, irrespective of circumstance. This
method was used to assess the degree of collaboration between
German and Italian propaganda agencies. Because the content of

German and Italian broadcasts were consistently different, analysts concluded that there was no collaboration. This inference was proved correct by evidence which became available after the end of the war (Berelson and De Grazia, 1947).

The single step approach to propaganda analysis has been criticized for two deficiencies: past regularities are often based on a very few cases, and the method is insensitive to changes in propaganda strategy, which may render past correlations invalid.

An instrumental model of communication, in which it is assumed that the important aspect of the message consists in what it conveys, given context and circumstances, underlies the indirect method of inference.[7] The initial step in the indirect method is to establish the propaganda goal or strategy underlying the characteristics of content. A series of interconnected causal imputations are derived from this point (George, 1959a, p. 41).

Despite many difficulties facing the analysts, documentary material on the Nazi conduct of the war indicated that FCC inferences were accurate in an impressive number of cases. For a two-month period (March–April 1943), 101 out of 119 inferences made by the German section were scored as correct. Of methodological interest is the finding that frequency and nonfrequency indicators were about equally successful (George, 1959a, pp. 264–6).

To Analyze Psychological Traits of Individuals. It is a widely held belief among social scientists and humanists that symbolic behavior of the individual can provide important psychological data about personality, values, beliefs, intentions, and other characteristics of the communicator. Personal documents may take many forms, ranging from a diary or intimate letters to autobiographies and speeches addressed to a wide audience. They may also be produced specifically for research purposes. To obtain data for testing five hypotheses about the effects of social catastrophe, Allport, Bruner, and Jandorf (1953) held a prize competition for the best essay on "My Life in Germany before and after January 30, 1933," the date Hitler and the Nazis came to power. The competition drew over 200 responses averaging more than 100 pages in length.

A study of Richard Wright's autobiography, *Black Boy*, was described earlier to illustrate the point that content analysis of documentary materials may reveal information that would have escaped even the skilled analyst using more impressionistic techniques (White, 1947). Quite different kinds of documents, Justice

7. For a further discussion of the representational and instrumental models, see Pool (1959) and Mitchell (1967).

Robert Jackson's legal opinions, were analyzed and related to other aspects of his behavior in an effort to reconstruct continuities and changes in his legal philosophy (Schubert, 1965c). Several hypotheses derived from theories of attitude change were tested by an analysis of John Foster Dulles's statements about the Soviet Union. Analysis of more than 400 documents supported the general hypothesis that Dulles consistently interpreted new information about Soviet policies, intention, and capabilities in a manner consistent with his beliefs about the fundamental nature of the Soviet system (Holsti, 1967).

Political rhetoric has been analyzed to infer personality traits of the speaker from logical and cognitive characteristics of his verbal production (Shneidman, 1963). Theoretical bases of this approach are the premises that all humans engage in thinking or reasoning, that there are many styles of reasoning, and that from the idiosyncratic characteristics of a person's logical processes one can infer other attributes of that individual. To illustrate his method, Shneidman (1961, 1963) examined the logical styles of Kennedy and Nixon on their first two television debates, and that of Khrushchev in speeches delivered after the collapse of the Paris "Summit" Conference and at the United Nations. Shneidman's inference regarding the personalities of Kennedy, Nixon, and Khrushchev appears to have considerable face validity, but pending considerable further research, the psychological correlates of logical styles are only working hypotheses. Nevertheless, as a method of studying style, this technique represents a substantially more sophisticated approach than earlier attempts to analyze political discourse through content analysis (Hayworth, 1930; Runion, 1936; McDiarmid, 1937).

Content analysis has also been used to assess psychological variables in the context of foreign policy decision making. One approach, a continuation of the Lasswellian tradition, has emphasized elite values and ideology. In the absence of direct measures, Soviet and American publications representing political, economic, labor, military, scientific, and cultural elites were examined to identify major values. Although Soviet and American value preferences were found to be symmetrical in some respects and incompatible in others, the data also revealed that elites in both nations displayed a strong tendency to act and speak in such a way as to magnify differences between them (Angell et al., 1964; see also Eckhardt and White, 1967, a test of the "mirror image" hypothesis using documents produced by John Kennedy and Nikita Khrushchev).

A second approach to foreign policy studies has focused on analysis of documents written by officials holding key decision-making roles. The basic assumption is that foreign policy decisions, like all decisions, are in part a product of the policy maker's perceptions; that if men define situations as real, they are real in their consequences. Again, the choice of content analysis is based largely on the inability in most cases to use observational methods to assess the perceptions, attitudes, and values of foreign policy leaders at the time of decision.

An initial study tested two basic hypotheses about the relationship between perceptions of threat and perceptions of capability during the 1914 crisis (Zinnes et al., 1961). After these data were recoded to permit analysis on the basis of intensity as well as frequency, hypotheses relating to perceptions of capability and injury were reexamined. Decision makers of each nation most strongly felt themselves to be victims of persecution and rejection precisely at the time when they were making policy decisions of the most crucial nature (Holsti and North, 1965). Related studies have tested several models of hostility in international communication (Zinnes, 1963; Zinnes et al., 1972), and have compared the 1914 content analysis data with those derived from simulations (Zinnes, 1966; Hermann and Hermann, 1962, 1967).

Other analyses within the framework of a model linking actions and perceptions have consistently shown that the more intense the interaction between parties, the more important it is to incorporate perceptual variables, as indexed by content data, into the analysis (Holsti et al., 1968; Zaninovich, 1964; Choucri, 1967).

Several prominent hypotheses in the decision-making literature were tested using documents from the 1914 crisis. The data revealed that as stress increased, decision makers perceived time as an increasingly salient factor in formulating policy and they became preoccupied with short-term, rather than long-range, implications of their actions. Leaders in various capitals of Europe also perceived the alternatives open to them as decreasing, and those of their adversaries as increasing, as they came under more intense stress. On the other hand, conscious efforts on the part of American and Soviet leaders to extend decision time and keep alternatives open apparently contributed to nonviolent resolution of the Cuban missile crises. It was revealed that during that time, both sides tended to perceive rather accurately the nature of the adversary's actions. Unlike the situation in 1914, efforts by either party to delay or reverse the escalation were generally perceived as such, and responded to in a like manner (Holsti, 1972b).

To Infer Aspects of Culture and Cultural Change. Anthropologists, sociologists and students of political culture have examined societal artifacts to describe constant and changing characteristics of cultures. Content analysis may prove especially useful in such studies because various forms of documents often constitute the major surviving source of evidence about past cultures. Research of this type can be illustrated by a series of studies centering on hypotheses relating *need of achievement* and *inner/other direction* to major stages in cultural development.

A person with high *n* of *achievement* is someone who wants to succeed, who is energetic and nonconforming, and who enjoys tasks which involve elements of risk. The hypothesis that a society with a high percentage of individuals with high *n* of *achievement* will grow in influence and power because it contains a strong entrepreneurial class which will tend to be active and successful—particularly in economic activities—was tested by scoring samples of literature from the periods of growth (900–475 B.C.), climax (475–362 B.C.), and decline (362–100 B.C.) of Greek civilization (McClelland, 1958). The area within which Greece traded in the sixth, fifth, and fourth centuries B.C. was used as a measure of the growth, climax, and decline of Greek power and influence. When compared to trade area, the findings supported the hypothesis that expressions of *n* achievement index stages in the development of a civilization. An independent check on these results was made by analyzing inscriptions on vases produced in various eras of Greek civilization (Aronson, 1958). The results substantiated the other findings; signs of high *n* of *achievement* were significantly more frequent in the period of growth and less frequent in the period of climax. The same system of content analysis has also been used in other cross-cultural studies (McClelland, 1961; McClelland and Friedman, 1952).

According to some students of American culture, there has been a notable trend from the "Protestant ethic" or inner-direction to a "social ethic" or other-direction (Riesman et al., 1950). On the assumption that inner- and other-direction could be measured by achievement motive and affiliation motive (as defined by McClelland, 1958) respectively, children's readers for the period 1800–1950 were analyzed to determine whether these psychological variables index observed cultural change in the United States. The results indicated that achievement motivation in the readers increased steadily throughout the nineteenth century and began to decline only around the turn of the century. Changes in achievement imagery were, however, highly correlated with the number of patents granted, which also reached a peak at the end of the nineteenth century, and have since declined. During the same period "affiliation motives" increased and the incidence of moral teachings declined (De Charms and Moeller, 1962; see also Dornbusch and Hickman, 1959).

These studies illustrate some of the many possible ways in which content analysis of social and historical documents can be used to test hypotheses. At the same time, it should be pointed out that there are many pitfalls, aside from such technical problems as coding reliability, to be avoided. A most important problem, one rarely resolved beyond doubt, is the selection of materials which do in fact represent the culture, or at least some significant segment of it. Do newspapers, drama, or literature of a period, taken collectively, represent merely a manifestation of the authors' personalities, or do they reflect the more general milieu?

A partial solution to the problem is to rely on materials which meet the criterion of popularity, as was done in the study of achievement motivation in Greek literature. A second approach involves examining materials which explicitly perform the function of transmitting and instilling social norms. Socialization materials which have been content analyzed include folk tales (McClelland and Friedman, 1952; Colby, 1966a, 1966b), children's readers (De Charms and Moeller, 1962), youth manuals (Lewin, 1947), songs (Sebald, 1962), textbooks (Walworth, 1938), and government controlled newspapers (Fagen, 1967).

A third method is to use one or more independent indices against which to correlate content data. In their comparative study of German and American drama during the 1927 season, McGranahan and Wayne (1948) used six separate sets of data, both content and noncontent, to support their conclusion that there were real and persistent differences in the psychology of Germans and Americans. Each supplementary test supported findings based on content analysis, thereby increasing confidence in them.

To Provide Legal Evidence. During World War II the United States government asked Harold Lasswell to analyze certain materials and to testify about their content in four cases of suspected criminal sedition. The purpose was to demonstrate that statements by the accused publishers conformed to enemy propaganda themes. Materials ranged from over two hundred books in English and Russian in the *Bookniga* case to eleven issues of the periodical *The Galilean*, published by William Dudley Pelley. Eight tests were developed to analyze the materials, the results of which were accepted in evidence by the court (Lasswell, 1949, pp. 177-8). It has been pointed out that "There is almost no theory of language which predicts the specific words one will emit in the course of expressing the content of his thoughts" (Lasswell et al., 1952, p. 49). In the absence of such a theory, a posture of considerable skepticism is warranted toward use of content analysis data for other than descriptive purposes in legal proceedings.

A form of content analysis intended to yield only descriptive information has been used by the Federal Communications Commission to determine whether radio station owners conform to prescribed standards. The FCC has ruled in unambiguous terms that content analysis is an acceptable evidentiary technique if the data are deemed to be of adequate quality (*Content Analysis*, 1948, p. 914).

On the whole, content analysis has been used sparingly as a source of legal evidence. Literary infringement cases are perhaps the legal area in which it might be used most suitably (Sorensen and Sorensen, 1955). Existing tests suffer from precisely those deficiencies which can be remedied through careful content analysis. The tests developed in the sedition cases, as well as those developed by "literary detectives," might well provide more reliable data than evidence gathered by impressionistic scanning.

The Antecedents of Content: Who

Was James Madison or Alexander Hamilton the author of *The Federalist Papers* nos. 49–58, 62, and 63? This is one of many problems of literary detection which have been investigated by content analysis. The belief that each person's style contains certain unique characteristics is an old one, and methods of inference from statistical description of content attributes go back at least to the nineteenth century (Mendenhall, 1887). But because there are so many possible characteristics of style which might be used to discriminate between authors, the major task is that of selecting proper indicators. For example, sentence length, often thought to be a useful index, proved useless in the case of *The Federalist Papers*—the known writings of Madison and Hamilton averaged 34.59 and 34.55 words per sentence respectively. The frequency of 265 words in their writings, however, strongly supported the claim of Madison's authorship (Mosteller and Wallace, 1964). Politically important but infrequently appearing words turned out to be far less effective discriminators than the high-frequency function words. This finding is consistent with one generalization which has emerged from other studies of the unknown communicator in painting, literature, and music: it is the "minor encoding habits," the apparently trivial details of style, which vary systematically within and between communicators' works (Paisley, 1964).

Other statistical methods for identifying authors from content characteristics have emerged from studies of the "Quintus Curtius Snodgrass Letters" (Brinegar, 1963), and the "Junius Letters," a series of political pamphlets written between 1769 and 1772 (Ellegård, 1962).

The Results of Communication: With What Effect

The basic format of content analysis research designed to study the effects of communication is: if messages have attributes A_x, B_x, and C_x, then the prediction is that the effect on the recipient will be A_y, B_y, and C_y. Content analysis describes the relevant attributes of the independent variables (A_x, B_x, and C_x), but, as indicated earlier, any direct inference as to effects from content is at best tenuous. That effects of communication are related not only to attributes of content but also to predispositions of the audience is well established; the evidence demonstrating this relationship is too voluminous to review here (cf. Berelson, 1942; Klapper, 1960; Hovland et al., 1953; Bauer, 1964). Suffice it to say that owing to the variety of audience predispositions and decoding habits, the effects of communication cannot be inferred directly from the attributes of content (what) or style (how) without independent validation.

This problem was anticipated in an early proposal to measure public opinion by quantitative newspaper analysis. Woodward's (1934) research design incorporated systematic efforts to test the relationship between public attitudes and newspaper content. Often, however, this relationship is simply assumed to exist. For example, frequencies of British and American place names[8] in colonial American newspapers were tabulated to index sentiments of national identity (Merritt, 1966). But the absence of evidence demonstrating that the appearance of these symbols shaped (or reflected) feelings of national identity calls into serious question inferences drawn from the content data. Measures of effects may be derived from analyses of subsequent messages produced by the recipient to determine if they are consistent with predicted effects or from noncontent indices of the recipient's behavior.

To Analyze the Flow of Information. The effect of communication is sometimes analyzed by comparing the source and content of incoming information with that of outgoing information. Foster (1935, 1937) examined the flow of news to the United States from the outbreak of hostilities in Europe in 1914 until the American declaration of war on Germany in April 1917. The data revealed that American readers were almost wholly dependent upon news directly from, or dispatched through, the Entente powers. Thus, events such as the German invasion of Belgium were reported almost exclusively by news received from Germany's enemies. As war approached, the proportion of news from American sources increased sharply, as did news containing some appeal favoring American participation.

---

8. The utility of such categories as indicators of national identity is highly questionable. For a further discussion, see Holsti (1969, chap. 5).

Content analysis was used to determine whether the Associated Press and United Press International, each of which had full-time bureaus in Havana, were responsible for charges of inadequate public information about the Cuban revolution. All stories about Cuba filed during December 1958 were analyzed. Scores were computed for percentage of available AP and UPI information used, and the prominence (headlines, placement) with which it was displayed. On the basis of the comparison between information received by newspapers from AP and UPI and that published by those dailies, the author absolved the news services from charges of inadequate coverage (Lewis, 1960, p. 646).

Studies employing some form of content analysis to chart the flow of news include Carter (1957), Schramm (1959), Hart (1961), and Galtung and Ruge (1965).

To Assess Responses to Communication. One aspect of the effects of a communication is the degree to which its symbols become assimilated by its audience. Prothro (1956) tested the hypothesis that political symbols of the New Deal have become a permanent part of the American tradition, and that not even successful spokesmen for conservatism reject them. The first Acceptance, Inaugural, and State of the Union addresses of Hoover, Roosevelt, Truman, and Eisenhower were coded for relative frequencies of *political appeals* (government aid, government regulation, national power, and the like) and *demand symbols* (for example, peace, freedom, faith, controls, initiative). While demand symbols distinguished Hoover and Eisenhower from Roosevelt and Truman, Eisenhower's political appeals were free from any repudiation of the New Deal, which supports the hypothesis.

Soviet newspapers and domestic and foreign broadcasts were analyzed to assess the effects of Voice of America broadcasts. Thematic analysis was used to code more than 2,500 references to VOA. These data revealed that the Soviets, rather than posing a counterimage of Soviet virtues, responded by counteracting the image they assumed VOA had created of the United States (Inkeles, 1952; see also Massing, 1963).

COMPUTERS IN CONTENT ANALYSIS [9]

Content analysis usually requires a skilled and sensitive coder, the very type of person who soon becomes bored and frustrated by the

9. Space limitations do not permit a description of presently available computer content analysis programs. These are described in Stone et al. (1966), Holsti (1969), and Gerbner et al. (1969).

tedious and repetitive nature of the task. Manual methods of content analysis may also suffer in varying degrees from other limitations. Some methods are expensive and time consuming. Moreover, many techniques lack flexibility and possess only limited ability to deal with complex units. A number of such problems associated with manual coding can be minimized or overcome by use of computers, but computers are not currently able to undertake all of the repetitive and routine chores associated with content analysis.

What, then, can computers do, and what can they not do? The most general answer is that they can do any task for which the analyst can prepare unambiguous instructions. It is a truism that a computer cannot appreciate good poetry, but if the investigator were able to specify all the necessary and sufficient conditions for a good poem, then the computer could be used to judge poetry according to those criteria. More specifically, we can identify certain classes of research problems for which computers are likely to be of significant assistance.

First, computers are likely to be especially useful when the unit of analysis is the word or symbol, and inferences are to be based on the frequency with which it appears. This is a chore that computers do well at almost unbelievable speed, and many versions of word count programs are available.

Second, when the technique of analysis is a complex one, the ability of computers to deal with a large number of variables simultaneously may prove very useful. Because the capacity of even a well-trained human coder for committing extensive instructions to memory is limited, reliability is likely to suffer. Many forms of contingency analysis, in which inferences are based on the occurrence of two or more concepts in a sentence or any other specified unit of text, are also of such complexity that computers can perform the necessary coding tasks with significantly higher reliability than human judges.

Third, when there is strong reason to suspect beforehand that completion of the research will require many different analyses, having the data on IBM cards for machine analysis will probably save many hours—if not months—of labor. In some types of exploratory studies the analyst may be able to state his goals unambiguously, but he may not be certain which of several possible operations on his data will best enable him to achieve his purposes. This type of research should, however, not be confused with "fishing expeditions" in which the goals of inquiry are little more than a hope that some interesting findings will emerge.

Fourth, if the documents are to be reused for a series of investigations, the initial costs of preparing the data, when spread over several studies, may render computer analysis far less costly than any manual technique. This may be a particularly appropriate manner of calculating research costs when the data in question are very basic documents. For example, all American major party platforms since 1844 were initially analyzed by computer to test several hypotheses relating to concerns for economic values (Namenwirth, 1969). They are being reexamined in a broader analysis of other politically relevant values (Namenwirth and Lasswell, 1970). It seems unlikely that even the latter study will exhaust all questions for which political scientists, historians, sociologists, and others might analyze party platforms.[10] When viewed in this light, the initial costs of data preparation for computer analysis seem small indeed.

There are also a great many other research problems for which manual techniques are likely to prove superior to computer analysis. First, for the "one-shot" study in which a single analysis of rather specialized documents will suffice, the overhead costs of computer analysis may be prohibitively expensive. Pending the availability of optical scanners capable of transforming the printed page into machine-readable form directly, the text must be punched on to IBM cards, a cost of no small magnitude if the data are extensive. If the analyst must prepare a "dictionary"[11] for his variables rather than borrowing one already available, research costs are further increased.

Second, computer analysis is usually impractical when the volume of data is large, but only a limited amount of information from each document is required. A case in point is an analysis of French and Chinese documents for themes relating to alliances, such as "Praise (or condemnation) of NATO," and "Praise (or condemnation) of the U.S.S.R." (Holsti et al., 1973). To have keypunched over six hundred documents totaling some three thousand printed pages for the limited purposes at hand clearly would not have been justified.

Third, when the research problem calls for the use of space or time measures, simpler instruments such as the ruler will yield sufficiently precise answers at a far lower cost. However, computers may be very useful in the final stages of research for purely numerical and statistical operations (cross tabulations, correlational analyses, and the like).

10. This does not, of course, imply that computer content analysis represents the only or even the best way to analyze party platforms. For an interesting example of manual techniques applied to platforms, see Benson (1961). But even the investigator who used manual techniques might find it useful to have such documents available at a central archive in card form for supplementary analyses.

11. Dictionaries for computer analysis are discussed in Stone et al. (1966), Holsti (1969), and Stone (1972).

Fourth, the case for or against computer use for thematic analysis is less clear-cut. Thematic analysis usually requires not only specifying the occurrence or co-occurrence of certain words, but also the relationship between them. At present there are two approaches to the problem, both of which involve a combination of manual and computer effort. One solution is to specify relationships between parts of themes by some form of syntax coding prior to keypunching (Stone et al., 1966; Holsti, 1969; Miller, 1967), but the added research costs may be considerable. Alternatively, the analyst may use the computer to retrieve and print out all themes in which certain words occur, and then sort them out manually. Finally, one might employ the following procedures: (1) extract manually the relevant themes from the text; (2) sort them manually into various classifications (e.g., statements evaluating India, statements about India acting, statements about India as the target of others' actions); and (3) use computer analysis on the resulting data (Loomba, 1971, 1972). Whether any of these approaches to thematic analysis is more satisfactory than doing all the coding manually will depend on the nature of the inquiry.

At present, most computer content analysis programs fall into one of two categories. Those of the first type are essentially word count programs, the output consisting of the frequency with which each word in the text appears. The second type of computer system—that of the "General Inquirer" family of programs (Stone et al., 1966)—is characterized by a dictionary system in which text words are looked up in the dictionary and automatically coded with information representing the investigator's frame of reference and assumptions. The coded text can then be manipulated, categorized, tallied, and retrieved according to the analyst's data requirements.

Implications of Computers in Content Analysis

The most apparent characteristic of computers, the ability to analyze text reliably at almost unbelievable speed, requires no further elaboration. Less obvious but perhaps of greater importance are the following points.

First, it is perhaps ironic that the severest limitation of computers—their nontolerance of ambiguity—actually contributes to the quality of inference by forcing greater rigor, discipline, and clarity into the planning of research. The investigator using computers for content analysis is forced to make every step of his research design explicit. The most valuable contribution of computers in content analysis research is often made long before the first data tape is mounted on a computer or the first printout is produced. The need to state one's problem with the clarity required by computers can have far-reaching consequences, even to the point of requiring the analyst to confront the questions "What am I doing, and why?" Thus it is not wholly facetious to suggest that all content analysis should be designed *as if* it were to be done by computer.

Second, when data are punched on IBM cards, they are amenable to reanalysis as often and for as many different purposes as desired. In conventional content analysis research, the analyst almost of necessity instructs coders to prepare the data to yield answers for a limited number of research questions. If a new hypothesis suggests itself after the data have been coded, the investigator often must choose between recoding the data and dropping the new idea because he is "locked in" by his research design. Data on IBM cards, on the other hand, can be rerun to test hypotheses that had not even been considered at the time of data preparation.

Third, the use of computers enables the analyst to undertake very complex data manipulations, such as contingency analyses involving numerous variables, which often cannot be done reliably or economically by hand. When computers are used, the problem of scoring reliability is completely resolved; this does not mean, of course, that the investigator can assume the validity of his results.

The availability of computer assistance will also facilitate (but certainly not make inevitable) research of wide scope—both across time and space—on the problems of critical importance. Content analysts have often been criticized for bypassing research questions of this type (e.g., Stephenson, 1963). Such studies are not, of course, impossible to design and execute by manual techniques. But we should not casually dismiss the lesson of the RADIR research on political symbols in the early 1950s. The enormous labors associated with analyzing documentation running into millions of words proved a deterrent to further studies of a similar scope. Well before the computer era, the authors of the RADIR studies foresaw the need for computer assistance in large-scale content analysis research (Lasswell et al., 1952, p. 63).

Fourth, documents punched on IBM cards can readily be reproduced and exchanged between scholars. There already exist several examples of such exchanges, both within and between disciplines. As a result, serious discussion and planning for central data archives to replace informal data sharing are taking place in various disciplines.

Fifth, computers can free the scholar from many of the most laborious chores associated with content analysis research. The computer, like any tool properly used, can enhance the creativity of the scholar by freeing more of his time for those indispensable ingredients of significant research—the original idea, the creative hunch, the insight that is necessary to make "facts" meaningful.

Despite this optimistic appraisal of the implications of computers, it may be well to conclude on a more cautious note. Just as all research does not lend itself to content analysis, not all content analysis should be done by computer. It is important to remain aware of the dangers in what Kaplan (1964, p. 28) called the "law of the instrument," exemplified by the child who, when given a hammer, suddenly discovers that everything needs pounding. Man and computer each has unique capabilities which are required in different combinations, depending upon the nature of the inquiry. Well-designed research will divide the labor in a way that permits each to do the tasks best suited to those capabilities. For some research, computer assistance is necessary, but it can never be sufficient.

Nor should the limitations of computers be overlooked. Bad data on IBM cards, magnetic tape, or printout, are still bad data. Perhaps the single greatest danger in the use of computers is that a misplaced faith may lull us into accepting the validity of findings without a critical consideration of the steps preceding and following machine processing. Computers cannot save a sloppy research design, nor will they transform a trivial research problem into an important one. There is no guarantee that they will not be used to inundate us with studies of great precision and little importance. The machine output only reflects the skill and insight—or lack thereof—with which the investigator formulated his research design. Thus, the investigator's insight and imagination remain the most important ingredients of significant political analysis.

9. SOME BASIC APPROACHES TO THE MEASUREMENT OF ROLL-CALL VOTING

Aage R. Clausen

The analysis of recorded votes in democratic assemblies can provide the historian, the sociologist, and the political scientist with an extraordinary opportunity to study the factors affecting the policy outputs of a variety of political systems and subsystems. This opportunity is underscored by the historical reach of the voting records. For example, the roll-call record for the entire life of the United States Congress is available and is being prepared for analysis.[1]

There are, of course, limitations on the types of information to be gleaned from the voting record. If the purpose is one of uncovering special advantages to particular interests, e.g., a favorable paragraph in a complex bill, the voting record may be of little use. However, if the purpose is one of explicating the major policy cleavages, of measuring the impact of forces extending across the political system, of describing the life cycle of ideological struggles, of observing the birth and demise of political coalitions, the public record of the legislative assembly assumes a well-deserved preeminence as a source of data.

A brief dispensation is sought for the criticisms that the recorded vote does not represent the legislator's attitudes, that it does not faithfully reflect his position as it is exhibited in other activities on the same legislation, that it is meant for public consumption of an image that the legislator wishes to present. The dispensation is accomplished by observing that the meaning of the recorded vote is to be established by analysis. Studies purporting to explain the

Special note: I am indebted to Herbert F. Weisberg for an exceptionally careful reading and very helpful comments and to Donald Freeman and Hayward R. Alker, Jr., for their well-taken observations.

1. For information on the character and the availability of the roll-call data contact Dr. Jerome Clubb, Executive Director, Inter-University Consortium for Political and Social Research, University of Michigan, Ann Arbor, Michigan.

patterns of voting are then subject to criticism. But this is far removed from the criticism which discounts the voting record because it doesn't reflect what someone thinks it should, a normative judgment of little relevance for the anlysis itself.

The primary concern of this chapter is to consider (1) some of the alternatives one has in performing roll-call analyses, (2) the choices to be made among a variety of statistical representations of the voting behavior, and (3) some of the implications that attend these choices.[2] I have restricted my attention to operations designed to produce general measures of legislative voting behavior out of the voluminous file of discrete individual votes. Thus, I give little attention to the explanation of voting acts beyond that which is implicit in the voting measures. However, in the concluding section of this chapter is a brief discussion of the advantages inherent in a longitudinal analysis as regards the explanation and understanding of roll-call voting behavior.

The first, and major, part of this chapter is organized in terms of the three basic intralegislative relationships that are assessed by the measurement models that I shall discuss. These relationships are (1) between persons, (2) between roll calls (items), and (3) between the individual and the group of which he is a member. A distinction will be made between the statistical measurements that are appropriate for the first two types of relationships—inter-item and inter-person— and those appropriate for the individual-group relationship. The interchangeability of the statistics used in inter-item and inter-person relationship analysis needs brief attention before we move on to a consideration of the inter-person, inter-item, and individual-group relations, in that order.

The similarity of the statistics commonly used to represent inter-person and inter-item relationships is illuminated by observing the fourfold table into which the entries are made for analysis of either relationship. (Throughout the chapter, our attention will be confined to the dichotomous Yea-Nay vote condition, leaving the treatment of absences [abstentions] to the more specialized treatments of the problem associated with particular studies.) The ubiquitous fourfold table follows:

	Yea	Nay
Yea	a	b
Nay	c	d

2. More comprehensive treatments of the variety of statistical models including multidimensional models, which have been used, or which may be

When the analysis is based on the inter-item relationships, the cell entries are the *number of legislators* who respond to two items in each of four possible ways: YY, YN, NY, NN. When the focus is upon inter-person relationships, the cell frequencies show the *number of items* on which two persons agree (YY, NN), and disagree (YN, NY).

A variety of descriptive statistics may be calculated on this fourfold table to summarize the relationships between items or between individuals. The implications that follow from the choices among these statistics will be discussed in the separate sections on inter-item and inter-person relationships. Let us begin by considering some of the purposes and methods of analyzing inter-person relationships.

INTER-PERSON RELATIONSHIPS

Paired-Agreements Analysis

In paired-agreements analysis one observes the frequency with which each possible pairing of legislators agrees on a set of roll calls. In terms of the fourfold table, the number of agreements is the sum of the cases in cells a (YY) and d (NN). A percentage agreement score can be computed by dividing the total number of agreements by the total number of roll calls on which both legislators cast a vote. This has the advantage, relative to a simple count of agreements, of removing the effect of absences on statements of the relative level of agreement across legislator pairings.

A well-known study of legislative behavior using the paired-agreements approach is Truman's study of the Eighty-first Congress. It is concerned with the patterns of intraparty voting and the organization structure implied in the patterns. The intraparty structures are identified in terms of the sets of legislators whose paired agreements scores exceed the minimum established for inclusion in a cluster or bloc, or for location on the fringe of a bloc. Roll-call voting behavior is used for this purpose on the grounds that

> those members of the legislative body who characteristically choose the same side of a series of policy issues are in a sense both choosing each other and at the same time revealing the possibility of some degree of association prior to the announcement of their votes ... That is, a succession of identical or markedly similar divisions within a legislative party or compara-

used, in the analysis of roll-call voting are provided by Alker (1967), Anderson et al. (1966), Weisberg (1968), and MacRae (1970).

ble groupings reveals its gross structural tendencies; moreover to the extent that they are persistent, these divisions lead to the entirely reasonable assumption that their members are not only aware of their similarity of view but also may have been actively associated with one another prior to or in consequence of these choices [Truman, 1959, pp. 43–44].

A characteristic of paired-agreements analysis is its insensitivity to the probability of chance agreement between legislators whose decision premises are different. Thus, for any two legislators a certain proportion of agreements will occur across a set of roll calls even though the two men have arrived at their vote decisions on each roll call independently. Furthermore, the level of chance agreement varies as the distribution of Yea and Nay votes varies for the two legislators. This point is illustrated in Table 1, which shows the relationship of legislator A to legislators B, C, and D. In each case, A agrees with the other legislators at the level expected by chance, given their individual vote distributions; yet the percentage agreement declines from 68 percent agreement with B, to 50 percent with C, and to 32 percent agreement with D.

The chance level of agreement is arrived at by computing the probabilities of each of the four combinations of Yea and Nay votes given the proportion of Yea and Nay votes cast by each legislator. For example, over a set of 100 roll calls both A and B vote Yea .8 of the time. According to probability theory, the probability of Yea agreement between A and B is .8 × .8, or .64. This proportion multiplied by the total number of roll calls yields the expected number of Yea agreements across the 100 roll calls. These computations are repeated for each cell of the table, using the relevant row and column proportions.

A number of statistics have been suggested as alternatives to the paired-agreement frequency, or percentage, scores; whether or not they are inherently superior alternatives is neither presumed nor at issue here. These statistics compare the *observed* level of agreement with the *expected* (chance) level of agreement. To distinguish them from the nonprobabilistic paired agreement scores, they will be referred to as coefficients of agreement. Three such coefficients will be discussed in the next section.

TABLE 1.   "Expected" Levels of Agreement

		Legislator B			Legislator C			Legislator D		
		Yea	Nay		Yea	Nay		Yea	Nay	
Legislator A	Yea	64	16	80	25	25	50	16	64	80
	Nay	16	4	20	25	25	50	4	16	20
		80	20	100	50	50	100	20	80	100

Coefficients of Agreement

The three statistics to be considered are the phi coefficient, which is equivalent to the Pearson product moment r on a 2×2 table (Alker, 1965; pp. 83—4), phi/phi max (for a discussion of the appropriate calculation see Guilford, 1965), and A_{ij} (an index of agreement proposed by MacRae, 1966). Phi will be considered first, particularly as it compares to the percentage agreement score. This comparison lays the groundwork for a comparison of the index of agreement (A_{ij}) with the phi coefficient. Finally, the phi/phi max coefficient will be discussed.

Phi is equal to the difference in the cross-products of the diagonal cells, $ad - bc$, divided by the square root of the product of the four marginals of the fourfold table.[3] Phi is zero when the observed cell entries match those expected by chance, given the marginals of the items. Operationally, the zero coefficient results when the product of the two "agreement" cells equals the product of the two "disagreement" cells.

Viewed from afar, the phi coefficient and the percentage agreement score look very much alike in that both are dependent upon the ratio of agreements to disagreements. However, closer inspection of the behavior of the two statistics reveals a substantial degree of independence, because the value of phi is dependent upon the way in which the agreements and disagreements are distributed about the four cells. Under the condition of a constant percentage agreement score, the following proposition holds: as the two modes of agreement, YY and NN, approach numerical equality, the phi coefficient moves toward a higher positive value. Conversely, as the two modes of disagreement, YN and NY, approach numerical equality, phi moves toward higher negative values. Phi is the product of these two functions. The fact that the phi coefficient may assume the same value for a variety of percentage agreement scores, noted earlier in Table 1, is the other side of the same coin.

The difference observed between the percentage agreement score and the phi coefficient promotes the realization that the phi coefficient of agreement between legislators is affected by the direction or polarity of the motions being voted upon (MacRae, 1966). An example of a shift in polarity is provided by the motion to recommit and the motion for passage. Here, even though the legislator's posi-

---

3. Given the cell entries a, b, c, d,

$$\text{phi} = \frac{(a \times d) - (b \times c)}{\sqrt{(a+b)(c+d)(a+c)(b+d)}}$$

tion remains the same, his vote changes between Yea and Nay. Consequently, the level of agreement between two legislators will be represented by different phi coefficients on the same substantive issues as a function of the variation in the distribution of affirmative and negative responses that is induced by variations in the polarities of the motions presented to them.

This instability of the phi coefficient has led Duncan MacRae (1966) to suggest an alternative statistic, A_{ij}: the index of agreement between legislators i and j. *The significant difference between this index of agreement and the one provided by phi is that the probability of chance agreement between two legislators is based on the Yea and Nay frequencies for each roll call rather than upon the Yea and Nay distributions for the individual legislators.* Consider roll call A, on which 80 percent of the legislators vote Yea and 20 percent vote Nay. If a Yea is scored as a 1 and a Nay as a 0, the mean vote score for the set of legislators will be .8. Two legislators, i and j, voted Yea. Each of their votes is scored 1. The agreement score for them is computed by multiplying (1) the difference between the mean assembly score and the individual score of i by (2) the difference observed for j: (.2) (.2), or .04. If both legislators had voted Nay, their agreement score would have been (0 - .8) (0 - .8), or .64. In either case of disagreement, the disagreement score is - .16. Agreements on individual roll calls will always make positive contributions to the total agreement score, with greater weight given to agreement on roll calls as the probability of chance agreement decreases. Conversely, disagreements make negative contributions to the total agreement score according to the same rule.

It would be incorrect to leave the impression that MacRae's argument against the use of the phi coefficient for this type of analysis has been universally accepted. Both his index of agreement and the percentage agreement score have been criticized by Sidney Ulmer (1967), who continues to favor the phi coefficient, at least under certain conditions.

It is sufficient for our purposes here to underscore the point that *there are at least two ways of estimating the expected, or chance, level of agreement between two individuals.* One estimate, in the case of phi, is based on the distribution of Yea and Nay votes for the individual; the second estimate, in the case of the index of agreement, is based on the distribution of Yea and Nay votes on each roll call on which a pair of legislators has voted.

A third coefficient which has been used in correlating individuals is phi/phi max. This is the ratio of the observed phi to the maximum phi that is possible, either negative or positive, given the Yea-Nay vote distributions of two individuals. Phi has the characteristic that there is only one condition under which it may vary from -1.0 to 1.0: when the Yea-Nay vote distributions for both legislators are 50/50. When both legislators have the same relative proprotions of Yea and Nay votes, phi may reach 1.0 but not -1.0. When the relative proportions of Yea and Nay votes are mirror images (80/20, 20/80), phi may reach -1.0 but not 1.0. If none of these conditions holds, the maximum phi will be somewhere *between* -1.0 and 1.0. The purpose, therefore, of phi/phi max is to provide a statistic which can achieve the maximum value of 1.0 or -1.0 regardless of the marginals of the individual vote distributions. By relating the observed phi to the maximum obtainable, this property is preserved. The question is, do we *want* to preserve it?

It would seem to be undesirable to use a coefficient designed to represent individual similarities which allows as much dissimilarity as permitted by phi/phi max. It is possible, for example, that two legislators may be represented by phi/phi max of 1.0 when one votes Nay 10 percent of the time and the other votes Nay 90 percent of the time:

		A			
		Yea	*Nay*		
	Yea	10	80	90	
B	*Nay*	0	10	10	phi/phi max = 1.0
		10	90	100	phi = .11

The very fact that phi requires the vote distribution to be similar if the individuals are to be judged as similar, ignoring to some extent the manner in which their agreement and disagreements come about, seems to be a valid basis for preferring phi to phi/phi max.[4]

This discussion of the coefficients of agreement, plus the section on percentage agreement scores, is preliminary to a consideration of how these statistics are to be used in developing summary indicators of legislative behavior—at the inter-person level. In the section on percentage agreement scores, Truman's use of paired agreement scores in identifying clusters of legislators was presented in brief. The

4. One exception to this statement of preference for phi over phi/phi max is found in the condition where the items are unidirectional in terms of the underlying dimensions. In this instance, phi/phi max could be more appropriate; however, this implies a knowledge of the data that would not be available, ordinarily, without a prior analysis of inter-item relations.

following section will be devoted to a further consideration of variants on the basic cluster approach to the analysis of individual similarities and dissimilarities.

Cluster Analysis

Cluster analysis is given the status of a basic approach to the comparison of individual voting profiles in this paper as a matter of expository convenience that is suitable to the level and scope of presentation. Its essential "basicness" is not being championed.

The term "cluster" and the term "bloc" are sometimes used as synonyms in the literature of research on inter-person relations, and ambivalence about preferred usage is sometimes resolved by the use of "cluster-bloc." I shall use "cluster" as the more neutral term, with none of the connotations of "bloc" in legislative analysis, and shall eschew the use of "cluster-bloc" as a redundancy.

A cluster of legislators is so designated because the measure of agreement being used indicates a level of similarity among a subset of legislators that these legislators do not share with other members of the legislature. A variety of criteria may be employed (Tryon, 1959). For example, if there are two or more clusters of individuals, the measure of agreement within each cluster should have a higher value than the measure of agreement between the members of the two different clusters. The criterion for cluster membership may be set at a specified level or it may be stated in relative terms; it may be established as an average level of agreement across the members of the clusters or it may be applied to each individual pairing within and between the clusters.

It is quite feasible to identify clusters of legislators from a matrix of agreement scores by visual inspection and paper and pencil rearrangements of the matrix to bring out the clusters—as long as the number of legislators is relatively small and one wishes to identify only the grossest structure of inter-personal relations. However, when the number of legislators approaches that found in the United States Senate, or when the anticipated structure is complex, the pencil and paper and visual scanning techniques become quite difficult, enormously time consuming, and in the end possibly unsatisfactory.

The advent of the computer has made it possible to perform cluster analysis using whatever form of clustering procedures suits the individual researcher. A variety of clustering models have been suggested and used in roll-call voting analysis. The procedure to be discussed, factor analysis, generalized beyond the definition of clusters but it can be used also for the identification of clusters of persons (Fruchter, 1954; Harman, 1967). When factor analysis is performed on the correlations between individuals, it is referred to as a Q factor analysis to distinguish it from R factor analysis, which is applied to the correlations between items.

A description of the factor analytic model in terms of its mathematical detail is beyond the scope of this section. However, a nodding acquaintance with the technique can be established by comparing its output with that of a simple cluster analysis. For purposes of illustration, and in line with usual procedures, let us use phi coefficients. In addition, let us assume that the factor analysis is directed at a "simple structure" solution which is used quite often and is favored because it facilitates the interpretation of the results (for an example see Russett, 1966a). In this solution, the factor structure that is imposed is one that seeks to minimize the factoral complexity of each individual's behavior.

Consider a set of positive correlations between six legislators such that the correlations among legislators A, B, and C are relatively high, as are the correlations among D, E, and F, with relatively low correlations between the members of the two three-man clusters (Table 2). The product of the simple structure factor analysis would tend toward two major Q factors and a few smaller ones. One of the factors would be oriented to the ABC cluster, and the other to the

TABLE 2.   Matrix of Inter-Person Correlations

		Legislators					
		A	B	C	D	E	F
	A	–	84	90	35	40	28
	B		–	79	28	33	15
	C			–	25	23	19
Legislators	D				–	95	92
	E					–	83
	F						–

DEF cluster. This would be indicated in the factor output by relatively high factor loadings of legislators A, B, and C on the first factor and relatively high factor loadings of legislators D, E, and F on the second. The statistical interpretation to be placed on these results is that whatever is producing agreement among A, B, and C, loaded highest on the first factor, is much less important for the agreement among D, E, and F. Similarly, the relatively high loadings of D, E, and F on the second factor indicate that the bases of the similarity in their voting profiles have relatively little to do with the voting behaviors of A, B, and C.

A contrasting condition is one in which two clusters form on a single Q factor. This occurs if all of the correlations between the six legislators in our example are relatively high but the correlations between the two three-member sets are *negative* while the correlations within each set are positive. The factor analysis would show the members of one cluster to have high positive loadings and the members of the second cluster to have high negative loadings on a common Q factor. This indicates that whatever is responsible for agreement within each cluster is also contributing to the high disagreement between clusters.

As may be readily appreciated, the Q factor analytic technique provides a relatively painless way of identifying voting clusters and giving some indication of the variety of factors linked up with the various clusters. Unfortunately—or fortunately, depending upon one's tolerance of indeterminacy—the researcher has a number of different factor solutions to choose from when performing the analysis. For example, he may require statistical independence between factors, or he may choose to allow the factors to be correlated with each other to some predetermined level. Until there is a closer mesh between the theory concerning the behavior in question and the theory implied in the various factor solutions, the choice of a factor solution is likely to be made on the basis of experience. Here the criterion has a pragmatic base: which solution provides results that are most readily interpreted? Somewhat ironically, this criterion may be employed at the same time that the researcher is pointing to the objectivity with which the voting behaviors have been analyzed. However, it is only within the constraints established by the choice of one analytic model over the other that the data analysis can be said to be objective. This is not to argue against experimentation but to show it for what it is, the substitution of one set of assumptions for another.

The necessity of making assumptions in the selection of the appropriate statistical operations is paralleled by the need to make assumptions in the selection of the roll calls to be used in the analysis. Indeed, how does one choose the roll calls most suitable for an analysis of the structure of relationships between legislators, whether these are conceived of as blocs, coalitions, or like-minded legislators who vote together without prior consultation?

Roll-Call Selection

The analyst who approaches his task with a particular structure in mind, with at least some notion of the conditions under which that structure may be expected to emerge (if it exists at all), may be able to designate the roll calls relevant to the anticipated structure of inter-person relations. In other words, he is making certain assumptions about the behavior in question, and on the basis of those assumptions is hypothesizing a voting structure which may or may not emerge.

In an attempt to avoid preconceptions, an approach often virtuously intended, the researcher may eschew purposive subselection and throw all the roll calls into the hopper. (Where the total roll-call set is simply unmanageable, a representative sample may be chosen by random selection.) This approach may also be used when the analyst doesn't have the foggiest notion of what to expect. However, assumptions have *not* been avoided. Instead, the analyst would appear to be assuming that the structure sought is a pervasive one extending over the entire spectrum of legislative issues. Structures that are specific to more limited roll-call domains certainly run the risk of being obscured beyond the point of statistical recognition by being mixed together, as agreements in one area are countered by disagreements in another. Nor does it do to accept the rather facile argument that the inclusion of all the roll calls is a first exploratory device. The exploratory instrument is too blunt; it is the safecracker doing his work with boxing gloves on. The most tenable position is to recognize the assumptions being made, and to label the analysis as one that *is* designed to bring out the pervasive structure.

Interpretation

The final point to be considered with regard to inter-person analysis of legislative voting behavior is interpretation. Where the definition of the clusters is used to promote the observations of similarities and differences in the attributes of individual legislators—party, region, constituency, tenure, age—as these attributes relate to the voting structure, the interpretive problem is not particularly difficult. It *may* be inconclusive. However, most students of roll-call voting behavior are not content unless they can say something about the issues that induce cohesion and conflict. At this point, the utility of the inter-person approach comes into question. Having performed the inter-person analysis, one must now turn about to look at the content of the roll calls that appear to be most productive of the various cluster relations. However, if one is ultimately concerned with the issue content of legislative voting structures, it would seem most reasonable to begin there. This may be accomplished by *first* looking at inter-item relations to identify item clusters and *then* observing the attributes of the legislators associated with the corresponding alignments.

MODELS OF INTER-ITEM RELATIONS

The statistical operations performed in an inter-item analysis are highly comparable to those carried out in the inter-person analysis. Again the presentation will be based on clusters, except that now it is the items that are clustered. The clusters are established on the basis of the inter-item correlations that reflect the degree to which the same legislative alignments appear for two or more items. No particular substantive interpretation of the clusters and the accompanying alignments is presumed; it must be inferred.

A distinction will be made here between two types of coefficient commonly used in roll-call item analysis. The first type is represented in its most general form by the Pearson product-moment *r;* its equivalent for the 2 × 2 table is phi. The second type of coefficient is represented in its most general form by the Goodman and Kruskal gamma (1954); in the 2 × 2 table its equivalent is Yule's (1911) *Q*.[5] Phi/phi max (Wood, 1968) and the tetrachoric *r* (Weisberg, 1968) have also been used as alternatives to gamma *(Q)*. In the remainder of the discussion, we shall use "*r*" and "gamma" to represent the two types of coefficient.

The major difference between *r* and gamma, with which we are concerned, refers to the conditions under which each of these statistics may reach unity (- 1 or 1). Unity is achieved for *r* when all of the cases in a 2 × 2 table fall in one of the pairs of diagonal cells. Gamma

---

5. For the cell entries given previously,

$$Q = \frac{(a \times d) - (b \times c)}{(a \times d) + (b \times c)}$$

imposes much less severe constraints in that its maximum value is reached when any one of the four cells is empty. Examples are given below:

		(2)					(2)		
		Yea	*Nay*				*Yea*	*Nay*	
(1)	*Yea*	40	20	60	(1)	*Yea*	40	0	40
	Nay	0	40	40		*Nay*	0	60	60
		40	60	100			40	60	100
	r = .667		gamma = 1.0			*r* = 1.0		gamma = 1.0	

A similar distinction was made earlier with reference to phi and phi/phi max where it was observed that phi is dependent upon the marginals as well as upon the entries in the cells whereas phi/phi max, subsumed under gamma in this presentation, is dependent entirely upon the arrangement of cases in the four cells. The distinction is reintroduced here in a more general form to set the stage for a discussion of the assumptions inherent in two different approaches to roll-call item analysis. Although there are variants on each of these approaches, we can proceed most expeditiously by considering the best-known example of each: (1) Guttman scale analysis (gamma), and (2) *R* factor analysis (*r*). *R* factor analysis may be performed using a variety of coefficients, including gamma; comments on that will be reserved until later. Let us first consider the Guttman scale model.

Guttman Scale Analysis

The Guttman scale model was introduced by Louis Guttman as a test of the assumption that a given set of items is responded to by a given population in terms of a single dimension (Stouffer et al., 1950). The model assumes that an ordered relation exists among the items, and among the individuals, and that both items and individuals are ordered on a single dimension. To keep from getting too abstract, let us use a liberal-conservative dimension as an example.

In the simplest case of dichotomous items, the Guttman model states that all subjects occupying a higher order position will respond positively to all items in a lower order position (See Table 3, part A). In the example, all legislators who are more liberal than the liberal option provided by a set of roll calls will support the liberal option.

All subjects in lower order relation to a given set of roll calls will respond negatively to them; in the example, all legislators less liberal than the liberal option provided by individual roll calls will respond by taking the conservative option. For a set of three items and four legislators, where both legislators and items can be ordered in this fashion, the pattern of response is as shown in Table 3, part B.

The marginals entered in Table 3, part B, bring out the point that in a Guttman scale, items in the lower order position will attract a higher proportion of positive responses, while subjects in the lower order positions will make fewer positive responses. Furthermore, the ordering of subjects and items is unambiguously defined in that the individual with the higher order position will always respond positively to all items receiving a positive response from individuals in lower order positions, in addition to responding positively to one or more additional items.

In the early applications of Guttman scale analysis, the researcher performed the test of scalability by a rather laborious ordering and reordering of items and subjects aimed at minimizing the discrepancy

T A B L E 3.　Three Perspectives on the Guttman Scale

Part A. Order Relations: Items and Persons

Items:	(1)	(2)	(3)	
Persons:	A (− − −)	B (+ − −)	C (+ + −)	D (+ + +)
Order Relations:	Lower . . . . Higher			
General:	Negative . . . . Positive			
Scale Continuum Specific:	Conservative . . . . Liberal			

Part B. Perfect Scalogram

	Items			
	(1)	(2)	(3)	
A	−	−	−	0
B	+	−	−	1
C	+	+	−	2
D	+	+	+	3
	3	2	1	

Part C. Inter-item Relations

		(2) +	(2) −	(3) +	(3) −
(1)	+	2	1	1	2
	−	0	1	0	1
(2)	+			1	1
	−			0	2

between the observed response pattern and the Guttman model pattern. Having achieved the best possible orderings, the researcher then counted the number of responses not fitting the scale pattern. According to convention, following Guttman's suggestion, the proportion of such "error" responses should not exceed .10. This requirement is expressed in the minimum level set for the coefficient of reproducibility (1.00 - proportion errors): .90. Thus, the coefficient of reproducibility should be .90 in order to infer the condition of unidimensionality. This is, of course, an arbitrary criterion, and any claim of unidimensionality requires further validation.[6]

As a substitute for the ordering and reordering of items and individuals to find the best-fitting pattern, one may test the scalability of a set of items by observing their intercorrelations, a pair at a time. Where a perfect scale exists, the relationship between each pair of items is that expressed by the fourfold table with one empty cell. This is illustrated in Table 3, part C, which shows the relationships among the three items in the scalogram in part B; the table entries are drawn directly from the scalogram. Given the properties of the two types of coefficient discussed earlier, the statistic to be used in representing the scalar relationship should be gamma, which is 1.0 for each item pairing. A rationale for the use of Yule's Q (gamma in the 2×2) has been presented by MacRae (1965). Phi/phi max has been used in the same context, but it has not been discussed fully as an alternative to Q (Wood, 1968).

After the researcher has selected the correlation coefficient that seems most satisfactory to him, he must decide how high the correlations must be before he is satisfied that a particular cluster of items meets the Guttman scale requirements. MacRae has used a minimum Q of .8, although he certainly recognizes that there is nothing magical about that value. Even if the minimum correlation established is justified in terms of the reproducibility of the resultant scales, we are back with the same old problem: how high should the reproducibility be before unidimensionality is established? To repeat, unidimensionality must be validated by other means in subsequent analyses. However, some criterion must be established if the research is to proceed, a problem to be dealt with later in a more general context.

6. The coefficient of reproducibility has been criticized for its insensitivity to the chance variation in reproducibility accompanying the variation in the item marginals, and in the number of items forming a scale. A number of alternatives to the coefficient of reproducibility have been proposed to cope with this problem. However, since the original Guttman scale construction format will not be considered further, a detailed discussion of the coefficient of reproducibility as a criterion of unidimensionality will not be presented.

Scoring

Another decision is faced when it comes time to assign scores to the individual legislators in order to position them along the scale, e.g., from most extreme liberal to most extreme conservative. Clearly, the least burdensome approach is some variant on the simple summation of positive responses across the set of items included in the scale. A score may be assigned that is equivalent to the total number of positive responses made by each individual. Or a mean score may be assigned by dividing the raw score (number of positive responses) by the number of items. Or the scores may be "standardized" by dividing (1) the difference between the *individual score* and the mean score for all individuals by (2) the standard deviation of the raw scores. Absences may be treated in a variety of ways; among these are (1) scoring the responses to each roll call as 0, 1, 2 for conservative, absent, and liberal, respectively, and (2) excluding the absences from the scoring and computing mean or standard scores.

A more burdensome approach to scoring is to adhere to the Guttman scale scoring. This involves a number of steps: (1) an inspection of the response pattern of each individual, (2) the assignment of scores to the perfect model response patterns, which are commonly equivalent to the number of positive responses, and (3) the assignment of the error response patterns to the perfect patterns that they resemble most closely, and giving them the perfect pattern score. Note that if it were not for the error response patterns, the simple summation and Guttman scale scoring of individuals would be the same.

The scoring of the individuals with imperfect response patterns can be ambiguous. For example, what assignment is to be made for the error pattern + + - +? There are two choices, the perfect patterns + + + + and + + - -. In using the Guttman model, one must assume that either the negative response to the third item or the positive response to the fourth item is in "error," i.e., it is not a response that is made in terms of the underlying dimension. If the judgment is made that the third item response should have been positive, the individual's scale score becomes a "4." If the fourth response should have been negative, the scale score becomes a "2." In contrast, the simple summation scoring of positive responses would split the difference at "3."

It seems reasonable to consider the simple summation scoring as a compromise between the reality of human behavior and the ideal of the Guttman model of behavior. This compromise finds support on two counts.

First, there is the pragmatic basis for the simple summation scoring. It consists of the observation that the Guttman scale scoring and the simple summation scoring become more highly correlated as the number of items in the scale increases. This dovetails with the principle of measurement that the reliability of a scale increases with the number of items. It is well recognized that the Guttman model is not put to a strong test when the number of items is small; in the case of dichotomous items Guttman recommended a minimum of ten items. Consequently, where there is the lowest correlation between the two scoring methods there is the least support for choosing the Guttman scoring over the simple summation scoring. And where the Guttman model might provide a basis for choosing between the two methods of scoring, practically speaking it makes little difference.

Second, in support of simple summation scoring as an alternative to Guttman scale scoring, the validity of the Guttman scale model may be challenged. Indeed, how realistic is it to adhere strictly to the requirement that all individuals located at the same position on an underlying continuum should respond positively to *all* items in a lower order position and negatively to *all* items in a higher order position? More precisely, how reasonable is it to require that all items have the same ordering for *all* individuals and to treat every response not meeting that requirement as an error? Let us consider a probability model of voting behavior as an alternative to the deterministic Guttman scale model (Torgerson, 1958).

The probability model states that individuals in a higher order position have a higher *probability* of responding positively to any item in the scale. (Items fitting this model are referred to as monotone.) This model is comparable to the Guttman model in that the relative *order* position of items and individuals determines the probability of a positive response—as opposed to a proximity model[7] in which the *distance* between the item and the individual will determine whether the individual rejects or accepts the items. However, the probability model does not require that the ordering of items be identical for each individual although it does require a fair degree of comparability in the item orderings from one individual to the next. The model also assumes that individuals occupying the same position on a continuum have the same probability of responding positively

7. The proximity model has been neglected in roll call analysis despite its relevance for certain legislative voting situations, as when both conservatives and liberals reject an item of legislation because it is too far removed from the ideals held by both. A notable exception to this general neglect is provided in Weisberg's (1968) discussion of the model's relevance for legislative voting and his application of it to voting on the Compromise of 1850.

to each item. However, this allows some variation in the composition of the subset of items to which the positive responses may be made by persons at the same position. Concretely, individuals with the same score, based on a simple summation of positive responses, will respond positively more frequently to lower order items, where the item order position is an average ordering across all individuals, than to higher order items. However, their individual response patterns will be subject to as much variation as their identical summation score permits. The similarity in the individual response patterns will increase as the correlations (gamma) between the items increase to the point where a perfect Guttman scale is present. The Guttman scale is the best possible even where the probability model assumptions are used, but this does not imply that the deterministic properties of the Guttman scale model need be written into one's measurement model.

What does the probability model say about legislative behavior? It says that two or more legislators who are equally liberal will manifest their liberalism in somewhat different behaviors as other factors intrude upon their decisions. (A comparable position is advanced in a more general form by Peak, 1953.) On a given roll call, one legislator may opt for the conservative position while his like-minded colleagues vote liberal. This could occur as a function of the first legislator's constituency pressures on that measure, the payment of a debt to one of his colleagues, leadership pressures for a needed vote, and even his failure to correctly perceive the intent of the specific motion. Similarly, his fellow occupants of a scale position may be drawn away on other roll calls for some of the same or additional reasons. The probability model allows a certain degree of independence between individual behavior patterns because it states that individuals occupying the same scale position are alike only in their *probabilities* of making positive responses to the several items in a scale.

In more general substantive terms, the probability model says that it makes sense to think of legislators ordered on, say, a liberal-conservative continuum, from extreme liberal to extreme conservative. Furthermore, as one moves from the extreme liberal pole toward the conservative pole, one expects to see fewer liberal votes being cast without necessarily expecting legislators located at the same position to respond with liberal votes on exactly the same items. The link-up of the probability model and the simple summation scoring (Torgerson, 1958, pp. 373, 385) comes in the willingness to score each of these liberal votes as a manifestation of liberalism without discounting some as errors because they do not fit into the perfect Guttman scalar mold, or scoring conservative votes as liberal because the Guttman model says they should be.

The foregoing discussion of scoring methods and the deterministic model versus the probabilistic model brings us again to the criteria for defining item clusters, earlier introduced and set aside for later consideration. Since this is an extremely difficult decision area, prudence dictates that I restrict myself to the presentation of some possible alternatives.

Correlational Criteria: Defining Scale Clusters

One procedure for defining scale item clusters has already been discussed, that of establishing a minimum coefficient of reproducibility to be met, either within the Guttman scaling format or more indirectly through the specification of a gamma correlation that satisfies a coefficient criterion. An alternative method is to require that the correlation of each item with other members of a cluster be higher than its correlation with any item outside the cluster. Along the same lines, but less severe in its constraints, is the requirement of an average correlation of an item with other members of the cluster that is higher than its average correlation with items outside the cluster. A variant on the average within- and without-cluster correlations is the *coefficient of "belongingness,"* the ratio of the *average within-cluster correlations among item pairs to the average correlation between items within and items outside a cluster* (Harman, 1967, pp. 118–21). The procedure here is to find the two or three items with the highest reciprocal correlations and to add items to this original set until the coefficient of belonging drops below a certain level or shows a sharp drop with the addition of an item. The choice of the item to be added is dictated by the average correlation of that item with the cluster that is being built, always selecting the item with the highest average correlation.

The advantage that accrues to the clustering procedure using a criterion of relative within-to-without correlations is the elimination of the necessity to specify an arbitrary minimum correlation, although there will undoubtedly still be some items whose cluster assignment is quite arbitrary. For each of the individual clusters that result from the application of the relative magnitude procedures, the statistically based interpretation is that the roll calls in a given cluster have more in common with each other than they do with items outside the cluster. There is, however, no presumption of unidimensionality. Nor does one presume any particular content regarding the common character or characteristics of the alignments on the roll calls in a cluster. It is possible that a single attitude dimension is reflected in a cluster; on the other hand, the cluster may represent a transitory coalition formation; or both. To understand the clusters is to study them.

Unfortunately, there are certain disadvantages associated with the relative-magnitude cluster methods. Compared to the arbitrary minimum criterion method, the relative-magnitude methods are quite complex in application to large matrices because of the large number of inter-item comparisons and computations that must be made. In addition, there is the risk of producing a large number of small clusters that are quite highly related to each other. The indices constructed on these clusters will also be highly interrelated. This creates problems in the statistical analysis of the variables related to the various voting indices in that high correlations between voting indices place constraints on the possible range of variation in the correlations of different indices with a single variable. Thus if two indices are correlated at the .90 level, their individual correlations with another variable cannot be too different.

A practical rather than a theoretical argument can be made therefore for the specification of a minimum level of inter-item correlation for the inclusion of items into a cluster that is low enough to permit statistical discriminations between clusters. I am disposed to err on the side of setting the minimum too low for three reasons. (1) The statistics used in the subsequent analysis are unlikely to be sensitive to subtle differences in the relationships between explanatory variables and the voting indices, a problem compounded by the relatively weak explanatory power of many of the associated variables. (2) Whatever minimum level of correlation is established, there will be a substantial number of correlations that are much higher. For example, in setting the minimum Q at .6, a correlation of .7 is rare with many correlations in the .8 and .9 ranges. (3) Should the clusters appear heterogeneous in content, and an inspection of the intra-cluster correlations reveals the existence of two or more subclusters, remedial steps can then be taken. Whatever clustering method is used, the resulting clusters should not be treated as sacrosanct. Statistics are an aid to judgment, and they provide a test of our judgment, but their use does not call for a suspension of critical judgment based on a knowledge of the phenomenon under study.

(Incidentally, the need for exercising judgment and making choices in the statistical analysis of voting behavior calls for a parenthetical note regarding the use of a minimum correlation criterion to define roll-call clusters. This procedure may appear to some to be an example of a crude methodology. Yet it is quite comparable to the practice of setting maximum limits on the correlation between the factors to be extracted in an oblique factor analysis and the requirement in an orthogonal factor analysis that the factors be statistically unrelated. There is perhaps a tendency to ignore the existence of such simple arbitrary judgments when the analytic model is mathematically complex.)

A brief summary of the ground covered in this section is in order. We began with the Guttman scale model, which assumes a difficulty ordering of items and a capability ordering of individuals. The gamma (Q) correlation was introduced as a means of clustering items which fit the Guttman model. The deterministic requirements of the Guttman model, represented by the requirement of an identical ordering of items for each individual, were relaxed to fit a probabilistic model of voting behavior. The probabilistic model allows for some variation in the difficulty ordering of items across individuals, and for some variant on the simple summation scoring of individuals. The amount of variation in the difficulty ordering of items across individuals is controlled by the minimum gamma correlation permitted for item inclusion in a cluster; as the correlation increases, the probabilistic model approaches the ideal status of the Guttman model. Finally, it is to be emphasized that the meaning to be attached to the legislator alignment for a given item cluster is not a matter of a priori judgment but a subject for further analysis.

A discussion of factor analysis follows with primary attention given to comparisons between R factor analysis and Guttman scale analysis, where the factor analysis is based on r-type coefficients.

R Factor Analysis

One of the major reasons cited for the use of factor analysis is its capacity to analyze item responses at a multidimensional level. Thus if individual items are responded to in terms of more than one dimension, or subsets of items are located on different dimensions, factor analysis provides a means of explicating the dimensional structure of the responses. The potential for complexity in legislative voting certainly provides grounds for exploring the utility of factor analysis.

Factor analysis applied to the correlations between items is referred to as R factor analysis, to distinguish it from the Q form applicable to inter-person relations. In passing, let it be noted that one may be tempted to assume that the factors extracted in a Q factor analysis may be treated as the equivalent of the factors generated in an R analysis. The discussion in the literature indicates that this assumption should not be made too casually, and possibly not at all, without more empirical evidence of its validity (Ross, 1963).

In the earlier discussion of Q factor analysis, it was suggested that it is possible to arrive at a factoral interpretation of a relatively small matrix of correlations by a visual inspection. This is particularly true where the simple structure solution is applied so as to minimize the factoral complexity of the individual items—a relatively unique identification of items with a single factor. For example, if inspection of the matrix of correlations reveals one or more clusters of items, the factor analysis will tend to show as many factors as there are clusters, with additional factors accounting for the intercluster relations and the variations in the inter-item correlations within the clusters. As the complexity of the inter-correlations increases, and as the number of items increases, visual inspection may prove too difficult.

The choice of the simple structure factor solution is often favored because it facilitates interpretation of the factors in terms of the items with the high loadings on (correlation with) the individual factors. Paradoxically, this choice is away from the multidimensional capabilities of the factor analytic model. There remains the further decision regarding an orthogonal or an oblique factor solution; unrelated or related factors. It has been argued that the oblique solution is preferred for legislative voting on the grounds that it is unreasonable to *assume* that the factors affecting voting behavior are unrelated. We know only too well that a variable such as party is related to variables that characterize constituencies and that both may be related to attitude dimensions. The researcher who is compelled by the logic of letting the data speak for themselves is naturally drawn to the oblique solution that places fewer constraints on the structure of the factoral space, allowing related factors to emerge while not foreclosing on the emergence of unrelated factors.

Without further discussion of the intricacies of factor analysis, I shall report on some of the comparisons that have been made between factor and scale analysis. These comparisons will be restricted to factor analyses based on the r-type coefficient.

Factor and Guttman Scale Comparisons

The comparison of scale and factor analysis begins with a contrived set of data. Six items were scored to form a perfect scale; they were also scored to form three pairs such that the marginals in each pair were relatively similar whereas the marginals differed substantially from one pair to the next. Phi (r) coefficients were then computed between each pair of items: The relevant data are shown in Table 4 (Clausen, 1964).

T A B L E 4.   Matrix of Phi Coefficients: Perfect Scale Items

Items		(1)	(2)	(3)	(4)	(5)	(6)
	% Pos.						
(1)	80	–	.87	.55	.50	.29	.25
(2)	75		–	.63	.58	.33	.29
(3)	55			–	.90	.52	.45
(4)	50				–	.58	.50
(5)	25					–	.87
(6)	20						–

Note that the correlations (boldface) between items at each of the three general difficulty levels are more than .23 higher than the correlations between the items located at the different levels of difficulty. From this observation, it is anticipated that the three item pairs will emerge along three factors.

A factor analysis of the matrix, using both an orthogonal solution (Kaiser's varimax rotation of principle axes) and an oblique one (Carroll's biquartimin rotation) does, in fact, produce the three anticipated factors. The highest correlation between any pair of factors in the oblique solution is .31.

In another contrived test, this one reported by Wilkins (1962), seven perfect scale items were factor analyzed and two factors emerged in contrast to the single dimension of the scale analysis.

It is often the case, however, that the differences spelled out at a theoretical level are much less apparent in practice. Through the courtesy of James C. Lingoes, a set of roll-call data on which both a scale and a factor analysis had been performed was made available (1962). The analysis was based on 112 roll calls taken in the Eighty-third Senate covering seven issue domains: farm policy, taxation, foreign aid, atomic energy, tidelands oil, McCarthy censure votes, and Communist subversion.

Scale analysis produced eight scales containing seven items or more. The seventy-six items included in the eight scales were then factor analyzed utilizing a simple structure rotation of orthogonal factors.

Discussion of the results of this scale-factor comparison will cover two points: (1) the effect of item difficulty upon the factor structure as it relates to the scale structure, and (2) the content specificity/generality of factors and scale dimensions.

An inspection of the factor loadings of the items in the eight scales provides strong evidence that the factor structure is affected by item difficulty. Using the two scales with the most items for illustrative purposes, data are presented which give (1) the positive marginals of the items in percentages, (2) the factor with the highest loading for an item, and (3) the loading of the item on that factor (Table 5) (Clausen, 1964).

It is rather remarkable to observe the neatly arranged strata of principal factor loadings forming down the scale item ordering. The data shown are limited to the two largest scales; however, it can be reported that on only one seven-item scale is the homogeneity of the strata disturbed. As the variation in the difficulty of the items decreases, items in a scale tend to be split over only two factors. In only one scale do all items have their highest loading on a single factor. Significantly, this is a scale with minimal variation in item difficulty: 70 to 55 percent positive.

On the second point of comparison between the scale and factor analysis, the level of specificity/generality in the content of the scales and factors, the evidence is that the scale dimensions tend to be more general in content. Five of the factors may be described as single issue factors with but one of them having a single roll call drawn from a different issue domain. These five factors account for forty-four out of the sixty-eight items classified in the seven issue areas listed previously. In contrast, only three scales are clearly dominated

T A B L E 5.   Item Difficulty Stratification of Factor Loadings

% Pos.	Factor	Loading	% Pos.	Factor	Loading
86	3	.43	83	2	.49
82	3	.87	74	2	.88
77	3	.40	73	7	.47
73	7	.47	65	7	.54
66	7	.67	59	7	.58
56	7	.73	58	7	.62
52	7	.89	52	7	.78
51	7	.83	49	7	.67
49	7	.76	48	7	.55
48	7	.69	48	6	.59
47	7	.72	48	6	.64
44	7	.49	32	6	.54
28	5	.88			
28	5	.88			
27	5	.92			
25	5	.87			
15	5	.57			

by a single issue domain, and these account for only twenty-two of the sixty-eight classified items. The detailed breakdown of the issue classifications is shown elsewhere (Clausen, 1964, pp. 76- 87).

Comparable findings have been reported in a methodological study of interview items used to assess the effects of experiences associated with American Fulbright and Smith-Mundt awards to students and teachers. In two areas of investigation, single Guttman scales divided into two factors. The finding in each case was that separate factors were found at the opposite ends of the Guttman scales, a result that is understandable in terms of variation in item difficulty (Gullahorn, 1967, pp. 52- 3).

Clearly the evidence supports the distinction that should be made between factor and scale analysis as regards the differences that may appear between factors and Guttman scale dimensions. However, this also leaves open the question: which is preferable?

The fact that Guttman scales may be more general in content, due to the lack of constraints imposed by the variation in item difficulty in a factor analysis using an r-type coefficient, is not an unmixed blessing. When a scale analysis is used to identify roll-call clusters in a set of items drawn from several issue domains, it can occur that items whose manifest content is quite heterogeneous will be included in a single scale. This is less probable in a factor analysis as roll calls in particular issue areas will tend toward a similarity in vote decisions and thereby have a better chance of exhibiting relatively high correlations. Accordingly, a factor analysis may be easier to interpret, in part because it loses the information that there is scalar consistency in the legislator's votes across two or more issue areas.

The Guttman scalar approach does protect against the possibility that items which really do belong together are not spread across two or more dimensions (factors), as might be the case for two roll calls with disparate marginals in the same issue area. However, in making the argument for the use of the Guttman scalar model as the best of all possible worlds, one must also be prepared to carefully study the content and alignments associated with given clusters and to make considered judgments on the advisability of partitioning some clusters into subclusters that can provide meaningful and useful indices of legislative voting behavior.

As a final comment on factor and scale analysis, I want to reemphasize the possibility of using factor analysis on statistics such as gamma (MacRae and Schwarz, 1968; Weisberg, 1968). Although such statistics do not conform to the formal mathematical requirements of factor analysis, a computer-programmed factor analysis that is capable of working over a large set of items may be quite useful for the identification of issue clusters.

Let us now turn from inter-item relationships to person-group relationships, as measured by the Rice index of cohesion.

INDIVIDUAL-GROUP RELATIONS

It is quite easy to confuse the measurement of the cohesiveness of a group, as manifested by the voting behaviors of the group members, with a measure of agreement among the individuals comprising a group. The confusion may be lessened by recognizing that in the measurement of group cohesion the relational nexus is between the individual and the group, whereas in a measure of inter-individual agreement the relations that are observed are between individuals (Clausen, 1967a). In the latter case, one individual's vote is compared with another's; in the former instance of group cohesion, each individual's vote is compared with the vote that was expected of him as a member of a group. In these terms, group cohesion is manifested by the degree to which the members of a group vote in conformity with a norm of group behavior.

The Rice index of cohesion is operationally consistent with the definition of group cohesion presented here *if* one accepts the group position to be the one reflected in the position taken by the majority of the members of the group (Rice, 1924a). This can be seen in the calculation of the index of cohesion: the proportion of the group comprising the group majority on a roll call *minus* the proportion comprising the group minority. If the group divides evenly, with no majority position, the index is 50/50, or 0. If all members of the group vote the same way, the index is 100/0, or 100.

Not everyone will be satisfied with the majority group position as the operational definition of the group position or norm. Indeed, it is conceivable that whatever is used to indicate the group position—the leadership position for example—may be supported by less than a majority of the group. However, this does not alter the validity of the proposition that a measure of group cohesion should represent a summary of individual-group relationships rather than a summary of inter-person relations.

Equating measures of inter-person relations with measures of group cohesion is particularly dangerous when a probability-based coefficient such as phi is averaged across individual pairings. As was observed earlier, the correlation between individuals across roll calls is subject to variation as a function of the distribution of cases in the agreement categories and in the disagreement categories. In the present case, the use of an average phi coefficient is suspect, for it will tend to vary according to the distribution of Yea and Nay group majority positions. An illustration of this is provided by calculating the expected phi coefficient when group members move between the group majority and minority positions in a random fashion, as would be the case if no intra-group clusters existed.

Consider the example of a group of 100 members that divides 80/20 on each of a series of 100 roll calls. There are 50 Yea-majority votes and 50 Nay-majority votes. On each of these subsets, the expected frequencies for each of the modes of agreement and disagreement for any member pair is calculated across the 50 roll calls given the probabilities of agreement and disagreement associated with each roll call. Both the probabilities and the frequencies are shown in Table 6 for the Yea-majority subset (Table 6, part A), the Nay-majority subset (Table 6, part B), and the total set of 100 roll calls (Table 6, part C). The expected phi coefficient of inter-person agreement for each pairing is shown to be .36.

Assuming the same level of cohesion but changing the distribution of Yea and Nay majority votes to 70 and 30 respectively, the correlation drops off to .32; a 90/10 distribution of Yea-Nay majority votes produces a correlation of .17. And when all of the majority votes are either Yea or Nay, the correlation drops off to 0.

The variation in the expected correlation among individuals that occurs when the distribution of Yea and Nay majority votes varies, while the level of cohesion as measured by the Rice index remains constant, illustrates the discontinuity that can exist between measures of group behavior and individual behavior. It is interesting to note that the percentage agreement score expected for the member pairs would not change with a change in the distribution of Yea and Nay majority votes.

T A B L E 6. Expected Phi Coefficient of Agreement: Group Member Pairings

	Part A. Yea-Majority Set			Part B. Nay-Majority Set			Part C. Total Roll-Call Set	
	Yea	*Nay*		*Yea*	*Nay*		*Yea*	*Nay*
Yea	(.64)	(.16)		(.04)	(.16)			
	32	8		2	8		34	16
Nay	(.16)	(.04)	+	(.16)	(.64)	=		phi = .36
	8	2		8	32		16	34
N =		50 +			50 =			100

Parentheses indicate probabilities.

Another illustration of the same general point is drawn from a consideration of the impact of bifactionalism within the group upon the average phi coefficient. Suppose that the 80/20 divisions observed on each roll call for the present group were due to two internally cohesive factions in consistent opposition to each other. Regardless of the distribution of Yea and Nay majority votes (excluding the unique condition where the majority votes are either all Nay or all Yea), the average correlation for the parent group will be .354.[8]

The correlation of .354 that will appear when the present group is split into warring camps, regardless of the distribution of Yea and Nay majority votes, is to be compared with the *expected* correlation that is at its maximum of .36 when the distribution of Yea and Nay majority votes is even and drops off to 0 when all of the majority votes are cast either as Yeas *or* as Nays. This means that when the average correlation is used as a measure of cohesion, there will be a general tendency for the *condition of bifactionalism to produce a higher cohesion score* than would be obtained where there are no members who tend to adopt either the group majority or minority positions. The difference in the two measures of cohesion increases as the distribution of Yea and Nay majority positions becomes more uneven.

One point that may be obscured by this discussion, although it is actually implicit in it, is that although inter-individual agreement measures may be suspect as measures of group behavior *once the group has been defined*, it may be quite appropriate to use them as means of identifying groups. This observation is implicit in the foregoing discussion because the bifactionalism observed in the hypothetical example would also have been observed if the group had been defined by inter-person agreement measures. The result would have been the definition of two groups instead of one.

Apart from the comparison of the index of cohesion with inter-individual coefficients, it is not my intent to defend the Rice index of cohesion as an instrument of roll-call analysis. Its statistical deficiencies are too well known. The principal statistical deficiency of the Rice index of cohesion is associated with its use as a measure of group influence. This application is questionable because of the

8. The average correlation is computed knowing that there will be a perfect positive correlation for every pairing within each subset ($80 \times 79/2 - 20 \times 19/2$, or 3,350 within subsets pairings), a perfect negative correlation for each pairing across the two subsets (80×20, or 1,600 trans-subset pairings) with a mean correlation of .354 [(3,350 − 1,600)/4,950]. In the unique condition of uniformity in the direction of the majority votes cast by the group, the correlations within subsets are undefined since all of the entries will be in a single cell while the correlations across subsets will be perfectly negative. If the within subset pairings are scored as perfectly positive, the average correlation will again be .354.

absence of statistical controls on nongroup factors that may be operative to produce the observed level of cohesion. Thus members of a party may vote together for a variety of reasons other than their allegiance to their party. However, this does not preclude the possibility of using the Rice index of cohesion as a measurement of group behavior for which an explanation is sought in subsequent analysis.

Rice (1924a) also suggested an index of group difference (similarity) called the "index of likeness," which has been neglected thus far. The negelect is perhaps well deserved today since the function of this index can be performed by computing a phi coefficient on the association between group membership and vote. One example should suffice. On roll call X, seventy members of Group A vote Yea, and thirty members Nay; in Group B, thirty vote Yea and seventy, Nay. The group difference measure is the difference in the proportion of Group A voting Yea and the proportion of Group B voting Yea (Nays may be used instead). In the present case the calculation would be .70 - .30 or .40. Now let us enter the same values in a table showing the relationship between group affilation and vote:

	Group A	Group B	
Yea	70	30	100
Nay	30	70	100
	100	100	

$$\text{phi} = \frac{(70 \times 70) - (30 \times 30)}{\sqrt{100 \times 100 \times 100 \times 100}} = \frac{4000}{10000} = .40$$

The match of the two statistics in this case is perfect. It is true that the match will not always be perfect, with differences emerging with great disparities in group size and skewed vote distributions. Generally, the group difference measure, unlike the cohesion index, makes no unique contribution to the measurement of legislative voting. Furthermore, it makes sense to use the phi coefficient of association because this fits in with the general class of correlations between voting and other variables.

A Prejudiced Viewpoint

Among the variety of methods of studying roll-call voting behavior that have been reviewed, the inter-item approach appears to have distinct advantages. First of all, there is its immediate concern with the patterns of relationships between roll calls with early information on the content of the roll calls that are grouped together. The scoring of the individuals that follows shows which legislators are similar in their voting behaviors and which are dissimilar, with an indication of the degree of similarity given by their relative score positions. Furthermore, these measures of similarity are made in terms of particular subsets of roll calls, thereby providing the researcher with issue referents. Finally, the inter-item approach is not embarrassed by the statistical problems that appear to intrude upon the inter-person and the individual-group analytic models. There remain, of course, the problems of interpretation. The meaning of a particular dimension or factor is always difficult to establish.

A major contribution to our understanding of roll-call behavior and the forces impinging upon it may well emerge from a greater attention to longitudinal analyses. Such studies are now becoming possible with the aid of the computer in processing the vast array of data provided in the roll-call record. The payoff from the longitudinal study is certainly going to be worth the effort.

LONGITUDINAL STUDIES

The longitudinal analysis of no more than two Congresses provides valuable information about the measures of voting constructed in each. For example, which of the indices of voting are reflecting enduring voting patterns and which are not? Does the content of the roll calls associated with two highly correlated measures from different Congresses indicate the continuity of a policy dimension, or are the alignments in the two Congresses of a coalitional form with considerable variation in the content of the particular roll calls on which the coalition emerged? (A discussion of the "measurement identity" problem in longtitudinal analysis is found in Clausen, 1967b.)

The confidence that one has in the interpretation of a voting measure based on a single point in time can be rudely shattered by either a step forward or a step backward into time. On the other hand, one may obtain interpretational confirmation in the time comparison.

There is also the multiplier effect of longitudinal analysis; studying two Congresses instead of one raises more questions than it answers. For example, the study of two Congresses may reveal a small to moderate change in the correlation of party with a particular dimension. When one Congress is under study, it is all too easy to generalize the observed correlation. However, a change from one

Congress to the next may raise the question "Does the change represent a trend, or is it perhaps due to measurement irregularities or to a short-lived disturbance in the political atmosphere?" The addition of a third Congress is unlikely to resolve the problem. The root of the problem is that our confidence in the validity of the single point-in-time measurement has been shattered, and along with it our confidence in the generalizability of any relationship observed for a span of time. This is part of the excitement, and the frustration, of the longitudinal analysis.

The longitudinal study of congressional voting behavior has been given a tremendous boost by the Inter-University Consortium for Political Research through its conversion of 180 years of legislative history into machine-processable form. For a goodly portion of those 180 years, a record of electoral, economic, and social history is also available for computer analysis (see chap. 20).

One of the central concerns of political studies that may be explored through this vast array of data is that of the role of the political party in our political system. Since the Civil War we have had a two-party system, with at least a superficial continuity. Yet today the most definitive statement, which has earned ceaseless repetition, concerning partisan effects on legislative voting behavior is that party is the best *predictor* of voting in our possession. Unless questioned further, we may let this statement stand in its quivering nakedness in the hope that someone will unwittingly clothe it with the respectability of an *explanation*. The truth of the matter is that we have considerable difficulty in separating the condition in which the party makes the legislative man from that in which the man makes the legislative party. Here the longitudinal study can come to our assistance in providing a basis for observing change and stability.

As an illustration, I present an analytic model of partisan influence in legislative voting. This model is, to say the least, embryonic. However, it may serve as an indication of the kinds of question that may be posed of a longitudinal study and that are impossible to ask of a study limited to one point in time.

The suggested paradigm of partisan influence on legislative voting behavior is presented as a series of conditions. The conditions are stated in ideal terms whereas the judgment of partisan influence must be made in terms of the approximation of the data to the paradigm across the set of conditions.

Condition A: The ordering of legislators on a voting dimension shows no overlap in the scale positions occupied by the members of the two parties.

Condition B: When a personnel turnover occurs for a legislative seat, with respect to measures of a party dimension in two Congresses, the new member adopts a scale position conforming with his partisan affiliation either in *agreement* with his predecessor if partisan *continuity* is maintained or in disagreement with his predecessor if partisan *turnover* occurs.

Conditions A and B are interdependent in that A cannot be met for successive Congresses unless B is met. However, where A is not fully satisfied, partial satisfaction of condition B provides support for the partisan influence proposition.

Condition B is particularly important in the contest between a model of constituency influence and one of partisan influence. If the constituency model holds, partisan turnover should be limited in its effect upon the representation provided a given electoral constituency because members of different parties will be constrained by the constituency pressures impinging upon the representative's voting decisions.

Condition C: The correlation of scale orderings from one Congress to the next reduces toward a limit of zero when party affiliation is held constant.

Condition C-1:   When partisan pressures are resisted by party members in terms of transient conditions with individually idiosyncratic effects upon the members, the correlation of scales at time one and time two will be zero within the party.

Condition C-2:   When the partisan influence is in the form of a partisan ideology, party members may be ordered on this ideological dimension with the effect of lessening the reduction of the inter-scale correlation within the party.

Condition C-3:   When individual party members are ordered on a party loyalty continuum the reduction of the intra-party inter-scale correlation will be constrained.

There is no certainty, but some possibility, that conditions C-2 and C-3 may be distinguished by the content of the scales at times one and two. Under condition C-2, one would expect continuity in the manifest content of the scales given the issue content of an ideology. In contrast, where condition C-3 holds, the manifest content of the scales need not exhibit continuity, since the issue content of partisan objectives may shift from one time to the next. Note that the character of the partisan influence in condition C-1 is subject to the same indeterminancy as characterizes C-2 and C-3 in that the partisan alignment may reflect an ideological partisan dimension on which no reliable ordering was established, possibly because of the cohesiveness of the party members, or it may be the product of partisan pressures without ideological content.

The data manifestations of the variety of party influence conditions suggested here provide a basis for evaluating the character and scope of partisan influence. Included within the scope is the breadth of the partisan influence across issue domains and the continuity of the partisan influence over time. The character of the partisan influence refers to the different ways one may interpret a party-associated dimension with the aid of longitudinal data.

The possibility of identifying the existence and establishing the duration of ideological partisan dimensions is of obvious importance in studying the role of the political party in the political system. Just as one example, if one discovers an ideological partisan dimension that reaches through time, one has a basis for further investigation of the role of the political party as an agent of ideological socialization. Is the partisan ideology the property of a small elite segment of the population, with socialization taking place as the individual enters actively into partisan politics, or is it the property of a broader segment of the electorate?

Alternatively, to the extent that one observes shifting issue focuses in voting alignments attributable to partisan influence, evidence may be adduced in support of the brokerage function of political parties. Here the purpose of the parties is one of maximizing electoral support by identifying and responding to the demands of present and potential supporters.

The parties may be observed serving both types of function, ideological and brokerage, in different issue areas. One of the advantages associated with historical studies relevant to the understanding of current legislative behavior is that these studies make it possible to develop analytic models (such as, but more complete and refined than, the one suggested here) consistent with particular theories in a variety of contexts, with subsequent application to current politics. As indicated with respect to the ideological partisan dimension, it seems inevitable that the probing analysis of legislative behavior will lead to innumerable questions about components and processes of the political system. I know of no more solid, or more extensive, base to proceed from than the voting record of legislative bodies.

10. SIMULATION AND GAMING

John R. Raser

The scene is a large auditorium, bare except for fifteen partitioned cubicles or "offices," each fitted out with a desk and chair. The cubicles are grouped into widely separated sets of three; over each set is a different flag and a placard bearing the name of a make-believe "nation": Algo, Erga, Ingo, Omne, Utro.

From the hall comes the sound of marching feet as fifteen uniformed naval officer-candidates approach the auditorium. Once at the threshold, however, they break ranks and dash into their cubicles, eager to start the afternoon's work as national decision makers.

The chief decision maker of Omne smiles in satisfaction as he scans a mineographed report; his nation's standard of living has risen since morning, his proposed alliance with Ingo has been ratified, and because of a research-and-development breakthrough, his large nuclear force is becoming invulnerable. He rapidly scribbles a message to Utro, warning his rival against further military aid to Algo.

Across the room, Algo's foreign minister is scowling as he reads a mimeographed newspaper, the *World Times*. A secret message to his ally, Erga, has been intercepted by enemy intelligence and is blazoned in the "international" press; his scheme for a joint tariff barrier against Ingo is wrecked. In the adjoining cubicle, Algo's economic minister is drafting a proposal for a trade agreement with Omne.

Meanwhile, messages are piling up on the desk of Utro's chief decision maker. When he comes to Omne's ultimatum, he angrily pushes the rest aside and dashes off a statement for the *World Times*; he will expose Omne's reckless belligerency and declare Utro's decision to guarantee peace by strengthening its own military power. Soon a bell rings. In each "nation" the economic and foreign ministers leave their desks and assemble in the office of their chief decision maker for a cabinet meeting. . . .

Several weeks later, in the "real world," a report goes to the United States Department of Defense. Some of the social-psychological assumptions underlying the proposal to develop an Anti-Ballistic Missile Defense System, the report states, have been cast into serious doubt in an inter-nation "simulation."

A group of general officers wearing the uniforms of the United States Army, Navy, and Air Force are huddled around a large table in a bomb-proof underground room. They are tense; an air of crisis envelops them. One of them addresses the man across the table. "But Chairman Kosygin," he says, "trying to exploit the American mistake is likely to anger the French. It could have serious consequences for our own relations with the Quai d'Orsay."

"Nevertheless, Comrade Telenskii," comes the reply, "I'm convinced it's worth the risk. It will almost certainly weaken the Chinese position in Southeast Asia. I talked to them at lunch and. . . ."

These American military officers go to their beds that night with a new grasp of the complex ramifications of any decision they make, for they have played out a "scenario" set in the Kremlin, in which each played the role of a Russian decision maker. . . .

With worried frowns, special staff assistants to the Council of Economic Advisors pore over a computer printout which charts the U.S. economy for the next six months. They check the inputs again. All the parameters are accurate. They check the assumptions built into the program; yes, they are realistic. No doubt about it—they agree that in six months the economy will be overheated. They begin to draft a report to the president recommending a higher income tax. . . .

All these people have been playing serious adult "games" of "let's pretend," games that involve them in contingency planning, crisis gaming, role playing, scenario construction, economic modeling, or—to use a more comprehensive and common term—"simulation." Much as children take a space trip in ships made of cardboard cartons and chairs, or play house, researchers in universities, government agencies, and private industry are, in all earnestness, creating artificial "worlds" and simulating complex social, economic, or political situations. By playing out these "games" and analyzing both their consequences or outcomes and the intermediate steps that led up to them, scholars are attempting not only to learn more about the social-behavioral world but to cope with crucial human problems, problems as complex as bureaucratic decision making or as deadly as thermonuclear warfare.

Simulation gaming is "in," and the burgeoning interest in this new technique is due, in large part, to recent developments on several fronts in the social sciences: the dramatic advances in machine computational and analogizing capabilities; the increased emphasis on examining complex systems of interaction as a means of understanding social phenomena and consequent concern with interdisciplinary research; and the growing stress on multivariate analysis, on rigorous specification of assumptions and relationships, and on temporally dynamic rather than static theories. Because simulation gaming is now becoming a standard technique, familiarity with the type of thinking on which it is based is a prerequisite for understanding contemporary social and behavioral science research.

Furthermore, the epistemological and methodological considerations which are at the heart of simulation work—the problems of theory building, hypothesis testing, inference, and validity—are also at the heart of all scientific endeavor. By exploring these problems in connection with simulation in this chapter, we shall also be exploring an important area in the philosophy of science.

We shall be concerned then, not so much with *what* simulators are doing, as with *why* they are doing it. (For descriptions of what simulators do, see Guetzkow et al., 1963; Orcutt et al., 1961; Scott et al., 1966; Raser, 1969a; Laponce and Smoker, 1972.) I shall deal chiefly with the scientific concepts that are fundamental to simulation building, the problems confronting the simulator, the distinction between simulations and "games," the role of simulation and gaming in the development of theory and, finally, the validity of this technique.

But first, a caution: the terms "simulation games" and "gaming" should not be confused with "game theory." Game theory constitutes, first, a set of mathematical tools for dealing with explicit types of conflict situations, and second, a method of selecting the best strategies for obtaining the highest payoff under given conflict circumstances (Brams, 1975). A social science simulation or game, on the other hand, is a representation, an operating model, of a social-behavioral system. It is a functional substitute for the "real thing"; by examining the changes in the simulated system as it "runs," the theorist can explore the processes of the system under study more cheaply, safely, or effectively than if he tried to investigate them in nature. Thus simulation gaming is, essentially, an application to the social and behavioral sciences of the chief experimental technique of the physical or "hard" sciences.

BASIC CONCEPTS

Science is based on a set of conceptual tools, the processes of analogizing, theorizing, and model building. Let us begin, then, by discussing these processes and their relationships.

Analogy and Theory

"The vessel ploughed through the water" is a metaphor, i.e., a verbal analogy which points out that certain characteristics of the vessel's motion and its relation to the water resemble those of a plow furrowing the earth. Like all analogies, the statement calls attention to *the resemblances in some particulars between two things otherwise unlike.* By plucking out, or *abstracting,* those resemblances, an analogy enables us to ignore the myriad complexities of a concept, or of reality, in order to focus on a single aspect. Thus analogy is a powerful tool of thought by which the complex is made simple, the abstract is made concrete. As Morris Cohen observes, most basic concepts in science—e.g., "force, energy, cause"—are anthropomorphic analogies, "fictions [which], like maps and charts, are useful precisely because they do not copy the whole, but only the significant relations" (1944, p. 99).

For example, the concept of "containment" which has provided both a rationale for solving specific international problems and a basis for creating and developing political theory, is an analogy that enables us to think about complicated political problems in terms of such concrete everyday objects as cartons, buckets, cages, and the like, and thereby serves as a bridge between the simple, the concrete, the specific, and the complexities with which we wish to grapple. An analogy is a terse and economical way of making a statement about reality—and though like any other statement, it may be true or false, it is a way of narrowing down and focusing our thinking.

Similarly, a *theory* is a terse and economical statement, or set of statements, about some aspect of reality, past, present, or predicted. It is a "way of keeping in mind a vast amount while thinking about very little." A theory attempts to describe the elements or *components of a particular reality* (the "referent"), and to *specify the relationships among them.* Like analogy, theory abstracts from the universe of data those elements and their relationships that are germane for the purpose at hand, and ignores those that are not. Hence, like analogy, theory expresses a particular view of the referent, and usually deals with aspects of it that are not immediately

evident to the senses. Theories (and hypotheses, which are provisional guesses about reality) provide a bridge between the known and the
as yet unknown. They are "guides in the labyrinth of possibility"
(Cohen, 1944, p. 17). In an important sense, all theories are analogies.

Theories, Models, and Simulations

In their most familiar form, theories are expressed as verbal or
mathematical statements about the *structure of the subject matter*.
For example, a fundamental theorem of human behavior states that
"Men will act on the basis of that which they perceive"; it declares,
in other words, that the structure of human behavior is such that
there is an essential relation between two of its components, acting
and perceiving. Because its terms are so nonspecific, it would be
difficult if not impossible to express this theory mathematically.

Many theories, however, can be expressed in both verbal and
mathematical terms. A crucial theorem of Keynesian economics, for
example, may be stated verbally—"National income is equal to the
sum of consumption, investment, and government expenditure—or
mathemetically:

$$Y = C + I + G$$

The equation can be quantified and its terms manipulated. Given the
dollar figures for C, I, and G, projected for the current year, the total
national income for that year can be predicted and verified.

Unlike the verbal theory, the mathematical statement not only
describes the structure of its referent, but *in itself exhibits* that
structure. This form of theory is called a *model*, and most mathematically expressed theories are models. By allowing us to manipulate its
structure, a model enables us to predict, in a very concrete way,
future states of the reality we are investigating. One of the most
elegant and economical examples of a mathematical model is
$E = mc^2$"; when its symbols and the relations among them are
manipulated according to rule, the outcomes tell us something about
the realities represented in the model: energy, matter, velocity, and
their interdependencies.

Not every theory is a model, but every model is a specific form
of theory; hence models are a subclass of theory. To make this more
clear, let us consider the verbal theory, "A molecule is composed of
two or more atoms linked by bonding forces." The theory *implies* a
model but is not itself a model. Now compare that statement with
the Tinker Toy representation of a methane molecule in Figure 1.

The model pictured is in itself a system which can be physically explored. Given knowledge of the rules that govern the system, one may investigate its possibilities by adding and subtracting balls and rods indefinitely; exploring its structure will not only tell us something about the structure of the methane molecule, but something about the larger system of which it is a part.

To the extent that investigations in the model provide the same outcomes as investigations in the referent, the model may be considered "valid." And while the findings derived from exploring the model must always, of course, be tested against reality, if they fail the test, the model may suggest what to look for.

A model, then, is a specific form of theory; it allows us, in a sense, to "play" with the theory, to speculate in a rather physical, concrete way. But it cannot represent the *functional* relationships among the components, or the *processes* characteristic of the system. As James G. Miller points out, the structure

> of a system may remain relatively fixed over a long period or it may change from moment to moment, depending upon the characteristics of the process in the system. . . . Process includes the on-going *function* of a system. . . . [It] also includes history . . . mutations, birth, growth, development, aging, and death. . . . Historical processes alter both the structure and the function of a system [1965, p. 209].

A *simulation* is a dynamic or *operating model* of a system. It represents the *functional* as well as the *structural* relationships

FIGURE 1. A Model of the Methane Molecule

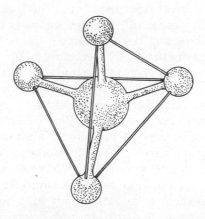

Source: John R. Raser, *Simulation and Society: An Exploration of Scientific Gaming* (Boston: Allyn & Bacon, 1969), p. 7.

among the components, and changes over time in the model correspond to changes over time in the system being modeled. This distinction between the representation of structure only and the representation of both structure and process is crucial to the difference between a model and a simulation (see Brunner and Brewer, 1971).

Simulating Social Systems

Many laboratory experiments in the physical sciences are simulations of one sort or another. Simulations of social systems, however, are necessarily more primitive than simulations of physical systems, for as John Madge says:

> One point on which all social scientists from Comte and Spencer to the present day have been agreed is that human behavior is less predictable than the events with which previous scientists have had to deal. . . . Some people conclude that . . . every individual has some capacity of choice which enables him to vary his conduct in partial independence of forces acting upon him. Others believe that, although human behavior is fully determined by circumstances, these circumstances in all their ramifications are so numerous and unknowable that we can never hope to predict how any individual or group will respond to a given situation [1953, pp. 21-2].

Were these conclusions correct, we could never hope to simulate a social system—unless we wanted to build a random-events generator. Nevertheless, mankind is convinced that there are patterns and regularities in individual and social behavior. Indeed, the very term "social system" conveys the belief that the social-behavioral universe is not random, for "system" implies an entity composed of lawfully interacting, interrelated parts—whence the adjective "systematic," meaning "orderly, methodical, predictable."

And there is a slowly growing body of social science knowledge that does enable us to posit some regularities in human behavior, if only in an often primitive and statistically "probabilistic" way. On the basis of these observed regularities, we can attempt to simulate social systems and subsystems. Such attempts, however, involve certain intricate questions of methodology. At the heart of these considerations is the concept of *pattern*—as a way of viewing the organization of systems, as an epistemological tool, as a guide in designing social science research, and as a justification for using simulations and games to study human behavior. The importance of "pattern" will emerge in the following discussion.

System: "Information" and "Entropy"

We must begin by looking more closely at the term "system," using the twin concepts of *information* and *entropy* as a way of characterizing a system of any kind. "Information" is not used here in the familiar sense of knowledge gained about something (although that, too, is implied); it is used in the more technical sense as denoting the *amount of formal patterning or complexity in a system*, the degree of order or structure, the predictability. In short, the more "information" there is in the system, the more *certainty* it contains. "Entropy" is lack of information, i.e., randomness, unpredictability, uncertainty; the opposite of information, it is sometimes therefore called "neginformation." To better understand information and entropy, consider the three types of system shown in Figure 2.

System I is composed of two units, (A) and (B), which are interdependent, and whose relationship to each other is fully known; knowing the state of (A) therefore tells us the state of (B), and we have a perfect information system. It contains no entropy and hence is completely predictable. It is an "ideal type" in the Weberian sense; that is, no such system could actually exist, because there would always be some uncertainty or "play" in the system—at the atomic or molecular level, if not elsewhere. But there are many "high-information" systems. The simplest analogue of such a system is a balance scale; a less perfect but multi-unit example is an internal combustion

FIGURE 2.   Three "Systems"

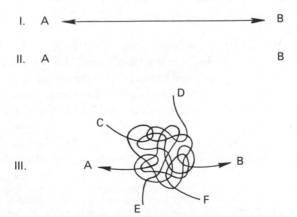

Source: John R. Raser, *Simulation and Society: An Exploration of Scientific Gaming* (Boston: Allyn & Bacon, 1969), p. 21.

engine, for if we know the position of one piston we can state with a high degree of confidence the position of every other part of the engine. Given the state of only one part, we can predict the state of the whole system.

Even in a high information system, the units need not have quite this kind of relationship. The state of one unit does not necessarily disclose the states of all others. But if the *relationships* among the units are known, and if we know the state of all but one of the units, the state of that unit can be predicted. For the purposes of study, for example, we can regard water and environment as a system. If we know the state of the water—how pure it is, how much pressure it is under, how much it is being "jiggled," and so on—we can determine the exact temperature at which it will freeze. Such statements as "If A is x, then B is y" are the stuff of which the "laws" of science are constructed. And as implied by both examples, we need not limit ourselves to A and B. We can also add C, D, E, and so on. Many complex physical entities are formally patterned, high information systems, and simulating them is simply a matter of calculation and finding analogues, which is often exceedingly complicated and difficult, but essentially an engineering problem.

Now consider System II. Since there is no relation between (A) and (B), we should more accurately refer to this as a "nonsystem." Knowing the state of (A) tells us nothing whatever about the state of (B); there is no pattern, no information. This system is characterized by randomness, lack of organization, and unpredictability; it represents complete entropy. The "ideal type" of such a condition would be a totally disordered universe in which each particle is completely unrelated to any other. All events would be random and completely unpredictable.[1]

It is unlikely that such a condition exists in the universe, for we have reason to suspect that everything may be at least partially determined, but we simply don't know in what way. Still, we live in the midst of what *seems* to be an infinitude of nonsystems, characterized from *our* observational viewpoint by a high degree of entropy. There is no apparent relation, for example, between the emergence of pop art in America and the decline of the sardine population in Pacific waters. If we knew more about our social

1. It must be borne in mind that "random" has a somewhat different meaning in statistics where the term describes, not the state of the system, or the data in the sample, but the *process* by which a sample is obtained. Thus randomness is not a property of an individual sample but rather of the sampling process. In statistics, therefore, perfect randomness provides perfect information, because only to the degree that a sample is random can the mathematical laws of probability be applied. The statistician strives to discover the pattern of sampling variability in terms of which the sample must be interpreted.

system, we might be able to discover a connection—as was found between freight car loadings and sunspot activity. But only a clever metaphysician might be able to establish any relation between the number of books on my shelf and the production of yak butter in Tibet. Unless we could demonstrate that the two are related, we simply could not simulate such a nonsystem.

What about System III? In this system we have good reason to believe that there is information, order, and predictability, but the unknowns are multitudinous, and the connections ("linkages") between (A) and (B) are so tangled that we can't predict much about (B) from knowing a good deal about (A).[2] This is a description of most social science phenomena.

Simulating a Social "System"

Nevertheless, despite the extreme complexity of human social behavior, simulators in the social sciences believe that they are dealing with a true system containing information, rather than with a nonsystem or a state of entropy; they are sure, that is, that some of the "particles" of the social-behavioral "universe" are interrelated, that human behavior and societal functioning are *not* random but are characterized by a whole spectrum of states of determination ranging from complete disjointedness to nearly complete determination. The theoretical problems of social science simulators are similar to those of physical scientists, merely more difficult. But their practical problems are enormous.

It is simply impossible to simulate a system unless one has an adequate understanding of how it operates. We can say, for example, that there is quite probably some relation between "culture" and the behavior of national decision makers, but we cannot determine what that relation is, to what degree it influences their behavior, whether the relation is direct or indirect, or whether it is true of every decision maker. We do not have answers to these questions partly

2. An instance of System III involving tangled linkages between two subsystems—one human, one avian—is the puzzling correlation in Denmark, long observed and well authenticated, between an increase in the birth rate (A) and the number of stork nests (B). The most obvious explanation—that storks bring babies—had to be rejected. (A) and (B) turned out to be indirectly linked through their relationships with two additional components in this interesting "system": newly married couples (C) who in pre-apartment house days almost invariably built new houses (D), upon whose chimney storks built nests.

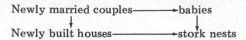

Newly married couples ──────▶ babies

Newly built houses ──────────▶ stork nests

because there are so many intervening factors we can't control in order to test the hypotheses, partly because there are large gaps in the network of social-behavioral theory, partly because we have neither the resources nor the tools to measure, in a meaningful way, either "culture" or "decision-making behavior," and partly because we don't know how much randomness there is in social-behavioral phenomena.

It is clear that such phenomena cannot be fully simulated—i.e., replicated—until social scientists fully observe and describe them. So the inability to replicate is due less to limited simulation engineering skills than to the lack of adequate social science theory and data. But despite very incomplete understanding of the phenomena they are trying to model, and because they are convinced that trying to simulate them is worthwhile for a variety of reasons, scholars "take a stab at it." They turn to "piecemeal" and "skeletal" simulations and to "games."

Partial Simulations

A "piecemeal" simulation is one in which the researcher attempts to simulate only a very small segment of social behavior and to study it intensively. The choice of the segment is usually based on a conviction that the nature of the units which compose this segment, and the relationships among them, are fairly well established; that is, there is an "island of theory" or a "microtheory" which describes this particular segment with a fairly high degree of confidence. For example, a computer simulation has been developed which embodies an island of theory as to the relation between personality and decision-making behavior during an international crisis (Pool and Kessler, 1965). Piecemeal simulations provide a scientifically "sterile" laboratory, since all the factors but the one under study are held constant, and the dependent variable (e.g., personality configuration) can be systematically varied. However, the findings may not be generalizable to the nonsterile and richly complicated real world. Indeed, when human subjects are involved, the laboratory setting may itself bias the results.

The researcher may take the opposite tack by using a "skeletal" simulation. Instead of focusing on a strictly delimited type of social interaction, he tries to simulate a large and complex system such as "international relations." Recognizing that he cannot identify all the units of the system, much less the nature of the relationships, he selects those units and relationships about which he has the most information. Using them as the "bones," he builds a skeleton of international relations. He hopes that by continually gathering more data in the field, by operating the simulation over and over and thus learning what is pertinent and what is not, he will slowly be able to flesh out the bones of his skeleton until—someday—he has a more complete simulation of the system he is studying. In the meantime he must continuously bear in mind that he has abstracted and crudely, even cruelly, abbreviated: that his simulation is to real life what a skeleton is to a living man. And it is precisely here, in the abstraction and abbreviation, that danger lies.

The skeletal simulation is particularly vulnerable to the danger of the "excluded variable." The very core of simulation, as of analogy and theory building, is abstraction. But *what* to abstract from reality for inclusion in the simulation must be determined by an intelligent evaluation of what is crucial to the operation of the system. Under social, financial, and intellectual pressures to "create a product"— that is, to come up with an operable simulation—the scholar's rules for abstraction may become less rigorous. The variables embodied in the simulation are likely to be those about which he knows the most, rather than those which he has determined to be most crucial; availability of information may become the most powerful selection criterion. One of the advantages of using simulations in research, however, is that if important variables have been neglected, the outcomes of the simulation are apt to be absurd. This is why simulation plays so important a role in theory building, as will be discussed more fully later.

Both piecemeal and skeletal simulations present a second danger to the scholar, the danger of forgetting that the outcomes are likely to be inadequate. Since a simulation has "face validity"—that is, since it is *called* a simulation of human conflict, international relations, or whatever—to forget that it may not really simulate any of these things is easy, and the temptation is great to give the results a good deal more weight than they deserve.

In a simulation the rules for translating external variables into simulation variables are highly formal; "tight and tough." All substitutions and analogies must be defended; the relations between variables must be carefully specified; the operation of the simulation must be governed by mathematical rules. Clearly, then, the translation of variables must be based on adequate theory and data.

"Games"

Where data are scanty or theory is weak, still another, and many think more profitable, approach is to drop the idea of "simulating" in the strict sense. Instead, the researcher constructs a skeletal model which serves as the framework for an open-ended "presimulation" or "game." He *tentatively postulates* the entire model; he may leave the empty spaces open or may fill one or more with a substitute which will then itself become an object of study with the goal of eventually filling the space more accurately. In a game, therefore, the rules for translation of real-life variables are less demanding than in a simulation; it is possible to "play around" and "make do," for the model embodies only a set of tentative hypotheses; it is an informal sketch of reality, a first approximation.

The property that usually contributes most to the informality of a game, and perhaps the most important distinction between a simulation and a game, is the use of human players as an essential component of its operation. The players serve both as a substitute or *surrogate* for a missing or inadequate variable, and as a "black box." For though the players are constrained by the "rules of the game" (the postulated relationships among the core variables), their behavior is unprogrammed. The often surprising interactions among the players and between the players and programmed environment turns the game into a complex laboratory, generating new data which can then be used to improve the model (Belch, 1974).

Thus a *game can serve both as a "presimulation"—an admittedly inadequate framework for conducting research leading to improvement of the framework itself—and as a laboratory for studying basic principles of human behavior*. This "gaming" approach to simulation construction is somewhat similar to lifting oneself up by one's bootstraps or, perhaps more accurately, like rebuilding a boat while it is under sail. Though this may seem like an exercise in absurdity, there are sound reasons for advocating it as a research strategy, as we shall now see.

Validity

Whether we turn to games as a laboratory for studying the behavior of human subjects or as a means of elaborating and refining theory which can then be embodied in a simulation devoid of human participants, we confront certain basic epistemological questions. Can we learn anything about the real international system, for instance, by studying a skeleton, simulated international world and its surrogate decision makers? What kind of logic allows us to generalize from a simulated system to a real one? The answer to such questions is based on some assumptions about *how* we know what we know, about the "uniformity of experience," and about the validity of inference as a means of learning something about reality.

How can we be confident that our theories are valid? It is a basic tenet of science that one tests a theory, *not by proving it true*, but by *failing to prove it false* and thus increasing our confidence in it. One way to do this is to state the theory explicitly, hypothesize about the phenomena which should occur were the theory correct, and then see if those phenomena do in fact occur. If, in repeated observations, the predicted phenomena do not occur, we feel justified in assuming that the theory is false. If they do occur, our confidence in the theory is increased. The more tests the theory passes, the more often we fail to prove it false, the greater is our confidence.

Our confidence is further heightened if we can devise "competing" or alternative theories to explain observed phenomena, extract hypotheses from them, test them, and find that they fail. Disproving the alternative theories increases our confidence in the original theory. More and more challenges can be put to a theory; there is no point at which we can say for certain that all possible alternative explanations have been eliminated, but as the challenges become more and more "farfetched," our confidence in the theory grows.

Pattern Matching

I have used the term "farfetched" intentionally, since it is precisely in the decision as to what is "farfetched" and what is "reasonable" that a difficult epistemological question arises. In simple terms, a theory is judged reasonable to the extent that it *fits in with other theories* in which we have confidence. Thus a number of theories have been put forth to explain the path of the planets around the sun. But there is only one theory that is consistent with all the other theories about phenomena that are part of the system—gravity, the age of the solar system, etc. We therefore accept the one theory that fits into the network of theory, and reject the others. Hence the internal logic of the network of theory is itself a kind of "proof" of the validity of any particular section of the web. And conversely, the better *new* bodies of data-supported theory fit into the network, the more confidence we have in the network itself. We look at the whole network, or "pattern," and to the degree that bits of data or theories "match" the pattern, our confidence in the accuracy of data, theory, and pattern is increased.

Moreover, it is only because we have previously identified the complex "whole," or pattern, that we can surely identify any single "particle." Think of the difficulty of identifying a particular star on a clear summer night. No single star is identifiable by itself without the pattern of stars surrounding it as identifying context. Let me repeat: *Insofar as we can be certain of identifying any single particle, it is because we have previously identified the whole.* Research into basic cognitive processes demonstrates that at the most primary level of perception and cognition, no sense impression can be understood without a pre-established frame of reference. This is how learning takes place. Slowly, an interpretive structure is built, a context for evaluating information, which is elaborated and modified with each new perception. This kind of "knowing" which comes from the recognition of patterns and thus of the subunits of those patterns—the perception of a Gestalt—is called *distal* knowledge.

And this "pattern-matching" approach has become a powerful epistemological tool in dealing with discrete, "punctiform" or "proximal" bits of data whose significance is not evident. In an illuminating discussion of pattern matching as a scientific approach, Donald Campbell says that "both psychology and philosophy are emerging from an epoch in which the quest for punctiform certainty seemed the optimal approach to knowledge." The conventional, logical positivist, inductive approach, says Campbell, involves gathering isolated, puntiform bits of data in a specific area of interest, fitting them together into part-theories and, one step at a time, trying to construct more comprehensive, all-embracing theory. But, Campbell continues, we do not recognize and identify the complex whole by identifying its particles and establishing their relationship; rather, it is the complex whole about which we can have the more certain knowledge, and which enables us to know something about the elements or particles of which it is composed (Campbell, 1966, p. 83).

And it is distal knowing, pattern matching, which enables us to confront a collection of fragments—bits of punctiform data, each of which is, by itself, uninterpretable—and suddenly see the entire pattern or context. We describe this experience as "insight," "revelation," "suddenly making sense of the whole thing." All such descriptions express the recognition that when an entire pattern or context is grasped, *each part of the pattern* is also more clearly apprehended.

Measurement Error

Pattern matching is also a powerful epistemological tool for dealing with problems of measurement error. For as we know, the measurement of any single phenomenon is inevitably subject to error, to "meter fallibility." In essence, all knowledge is indirect, filtered through our senses; punctiform certainty is a mirage. But as Campbell points out, when all observation points or "meter readings" are graphed together, they give us a *pattern* by which we can match theory to data. A priori, any of the points could be wrong, but by graphing the points, "the fringe of error" is distributed, and the pattern-matching model of relating theory to data allows us to grant the error of any single meter reading without requiring us to impeach the theory. Furthermore, and even more important, in the absence of an overall framework or pattern we would be hard put to *interpret* the measurements (Campbell, 1966, pp. 100–2).

And now we are back to our starting point, for pattern matching is the process referred to earlier as "messing around," the bootstrap operation of constructing a presimulation or "game." Instead of waiting until the nature of all the elements is determined before building a simulation, we tentatively postulate the entire model, and use human players or other surrogates for missing variables. By watching the behavior of the operating subparts and noting how they "fit" with its other parts, we can check and refine both the subparts and the model as a whole. And in a game—as in putting together a jigsaw puzzle, painting a picture, or writing a poem—the "empty spaces" may themselves suggest what parts are needed. The incomplete pattern suggests its own completion.

Another powerful rationale for constructing a tentative but "complete" game is that it can provide a stimulating laboratory for studying human behavior. By building an operating game which incorporates the central features of that which we wish to study, even if those features are only rough approximations of reality, we can provide a wide range of stimuli for the human subjects, and offer them the opportunity for a wide range of behaviors, for in the game situation, as in the real world, everything is complicated, messy, and tangled. The game, then, serves as a rich and complex laboratory for testing hypotheses and for developing new theory.

Inference

The argument that such an intricate laboratory is superior to a "simple" and well-controlled one is based on Spinoza's dictum that the *pattern of research* should be the same as the pattern of that being studied. Applied to the design of laboratory experiments, this is pattern matchingof a somewhat different sort and in a different context.

One way we gain information about the world is by inference. We measure, under controlled conditions, the behavior of some sample of a population; because we assume a certain uniformity of experience, we then infer that the findings about the sample can be applied to the whole population, subject of course to the limitations imposed by the sampling method. This is the technique used in survey research with highly valid results.

Alternatively, we may measure the behavior of some *entity* (not an actual sample) thought to *resemble* the population in question. We then infer that the behavior of the surrogate tells us something about the behavior of the population. It is generally assumed that the more the surrogate resembles the population of interest, the more confidently may inferences be made. The experimental psychologist interested in learning behavior typically studies rats in cages and mazes; and from the behavior of these surrogates, he draws inferences about the learning process in humans. But he extrapolates more confidently from primate behavior than from rat behavior. The game approach goes a step further; it suggests that the more closely the *laboratory* resembles the situation to which inferences are made, the more valid the inferences, and the more useful in creating or developing theory. The representative sampling of subjects is extended, by the game approach, to the representative sampling of situations. The soundness of this rationale is demonstrated by recent findings that the behavior of rats, mice, and other common experimental animals is distorted by the austerity of the usual laboratory environment. When the setting is enriched, made more complex, more representative of the real world, the animals manifest far richer, more varied, and often quite different behaviors (Kavenau, 1967).

Suppose one is interested, as a social scientist, in learning about the decision-making behavior of chiefs of state as a function of personality. For obvious reasons one cannot study chiefs of state directly and hence must use surrogates. Pattern matching requires that two rules be followed: (1) as much as possible, the surrogates should resemble the chiefs of state; and (2) as much as possible, the situation in which each surrogate is placed should be like that in which the chief of state operates. Both rules, however, are often broken for very good reasons. Because of limited resources, research subjects must usually be chosen on the basis of availability, not suitability. And laboratory environments are usually made as austere as possible, first, because data gathering is easier, and second, because of the belief that research is improved if all variables except the one under study are rigidly controlled.

But this contravenes Spinoza's dictum. The more closely the laboratory setting matches the situation under study, the more confidently may the researcher generalize his findings to the real world. Hence, if we are interested in the interaction between human beings and the system (or situation) of which they are a part, games provide the ideal laboratory environment, for their greater complexity more nearly resembles the real world than does the usual experimental setting of flashing lights, buzzers, and the like.

So "gaming" is based on observing a phenomenon, ascertaining the pattern inherent in it, and using it as a starting point from which to fill in the gaps. Thus, new data and theories are generated, and at the same time a rich laboratory is created which can be used as a vehicle for studying complex human and systematic behavior.

But note that in constructing a game or presimulation, one does *not* pluck the essential elements *out* of the observed world and use them as building materials for the laboratory replication. Rather, one simply observes the phenomena, determines what the crucial elements and relationships are, and finds a way of *representing* them in the replica through the judicious use of analogue materials, or substitutes. What game and simulation builders actually do, then, is to abstract, simplify, and substitute.

SIMULATION BUILDING

In building either a model or a simulation, *abstraction, simplification*, and *substitution* are the "name of the game." They are central to the process, and not merely inconvenient limitations on the goal of perfect replication which could be overcome with more funds, better facilities—or more comprehensive theory. By abstracting, simplifying, and substituting, more clarity is introduced into the model than exists in the referent system, and it is in this that one usefulness of modeling lies.

Abstraction and Simplification

It is important to recognize that for some purposes a very simple model is preferable to a more complicated one, if for no other reason than that it is cheaper and easier to manipulate. The crucial questions facing the simulation builder concern *which* elements, *which* relationships, *which* processes to abstract, and which can be neglected. In other words, he must select those variables that are both *relevant* and *essential*.

The question of relevance can be determined only within the framework of his particular goal. If his purpose is to study the aerodynamic qualities of a new plane design, the wooden-model-and-wind-tunnel simulation will do; a detailed and accurate representation of an aircraft in flight would include much expensive and distracting rubbish. If, on the other hand, his purpose is to test the useability of a new control panel, he might build a life-sized mockup of the panel and omit everything else.

And he might be wrong! For the theories regarding human performance—reaction time, attention span, fatigue, etc.—and their relations to such variables as vibration, noise, space limitation, the presence or absence of other people, are so primitive that the investigator would be hard put to know what to include and what might be excluded in order to obtain useful and generalizable results. If he fails to take relevant variables into account, even though he cannot replicate them, or if he fails to specify the system components and processes, he risks omitting elements that are not only relevant but essential!

Substitution

Nevertheless, he need not build a perfect replication of a plane interior in order to include these essential elements. He may *substitute*. It has been suggested that models entail two basic kinds of substitution, *replica* and *symbolic:*

> Replica models . . . are material or tangible and look like the real thing [such as] toy automobiles or models of an interplanetary rocket. Symbolic models . . . use ideas, concepts, and abstract symbols to represent objects. They don't even resemble the real thing. They use lines and arrows to symbolize information flow, and things like diagrammatic blocks to symbolize the major elements of a system [Chapanis, 1961, pp. 115–16].

Obviously, the model itself is a substitute, a replica or symbolic representation of the referent system. Though highly simplified, the small wooden airframe and wind tunnel is a replica model that abstracts the relevant properties of the referent: the relationship between air currents and the configuration of a plane in flight. A computer program which simulates an economic system is a symbolic model; so is a system of pipes, valves, pumps, and colored liquids used for the same purpose, even though it is tangible. Similarly, the components of the model may be replica or symbolic substitutes or both. The question of what is substituted for what is crucial. The small wooden plane is a substitute for the million-dollar monster, but its configuration must accurately represent that of the referent. And while the researcher may have carefully calculated the relationship between the size of his model and the air current forces in the wind tunnel, he may have forgotten weight or surface texture. Does air flowing over a wooden surface have the same effect as air flowing over polished metal? If theory tells him it doesn't, he must either build his model of polished metal or find a substitute which theory tells him will represent that particular variable.

For the model builder, the problem is that of analogy—finding substitutes that resemble in important particulars the otherwise unlike referent components. For the simulation builder, the problem is that of finding an *analogue*—"something *similar in function* but different in structure and origin." He must be sure that the relevant properties of the model are not only similar to those of the referent, but that they *interact* with each other and with another entity in the same way as do those of the referent. Moreover, a single component may have several properties. "Human performance" is the sum of a variety of interrelated properties which are, in turn, affected by, and hence related to, the environment. If the simulation builder fails to reconstruct the relationships accurately, he falls into the trap of false or incorrect analogy, and may end up with a "model" as absurd as that of the apocryphal orator who cried, "I smell a rat, I see him floating in the air, but mark me, I shall nip him in the bud!"

Not all models, of course, are physical representations; they may be entirely symbolic, and the substitutes may be "iconic" (pictorial representations, such as flow charts or diagrams), verbal (description in words), or mathematical (representation by symbols and formulae of elements and relationships in the model).

In a simulation, all three may be used to assist description, but the substitutions usually involve electronic and/or physical aspects as well. In a computer simulation of an economic system, for example, all the substitutions are symbolic: the mathematical model of the system (e.g., "$Y = C + G + I$") is cycled on the computer with each cycle representing a designated time period; the electronic processes substitute for the economic processes under study. In a "man-machine" simulation such as the inter-nation simulation mentioned at the beginning of this chapter, each "nation" is symbolically represented by human players and by a mathematical model which specifies the essential economic and political variables and the relationships among them. Other components of the inter-nation system are introduced into the model by the verbal descriptions and rules given the human players. Changes in the variables resulting from choices of the human decision makers are calculated according to the mathematical formulae.

Human Players as Substitutes

The players may serve either as surrogates (symbolic representations) for a known variable, or as substitutes (replica representations) for a *missing* variable. To illustrate: suppose we wish to explore the relation between the crisis decision making of real-life chiefs of state and their personality configurations, a question of some relevance to political science theorists. If we wish to clarify theory about certain cognitive functions—information processing under stress, for example—we might construct a purely symbolic model and write a computer program consisting of two simulated decision makers, each programmed with different personality characteristics related to attention span and selective perception. As the simulation "runs," each receives messages, analyzes them in accordance with his programmed personality constructs, and responds. If we wish, we can systematically vary the programmed characteristics to determine the effects of different personality configurations on decision making. Indeed, this is precisely what has been done in an all machine simulation (Pool and Kessler, 1965, pp. 31-8).

But what about the personality variables that are *not* programmed, and what about the situation variables—cultural factors, goal orientations, means of attaining the goal, economic and political constraints, interactions among chiefs of state, degree of personal involvement—all the messy real-life complications in which human decision makers are usually entangled? How do these affect the operation of the entire "system" of which the decision makers are a part? To begin to find out, we can select human players whose salient personality traits are similar to those of known real-life decision makers; in this case the subjects are replica substitutes, or surrogates, for the "decision-maker" variable of the model. Though we now have a game rather than a simulation, its functioning will more nearly represent the referent world, the "setting of application," to which we wish to generalize than did the piecemeal computer simulation described above. The verbal reports of INS players demonstrate that a man-machine game does provide a high degree of realism; they describe the time pressure, the information overload, the burden of responsibility and worry and situations too complicated to sort out; they describe their inability to rely on the accuracy of reports and on the competence of those who carry out directives, and so on. And their reports have a familiar ring, echoing the reports of decision makers in similar real-life situations.

On the other hand, the human players may substitute for a *missing* variable. Suppose a scholar has set himself the goal of accurately simulating a specific social system: international politics. His thinking might go something like this:

"It's foolish even to try, at this point, to simulate the system, for I don't know enough about it, but I'll use the best theory and data at my disposal and see what I come up with. For example, I know that 'culture' (whatever that means) surely has an important effect on the behavior of national decision makers, but I don't know just what. I could leave out the culture variable and see whether the game operates as observations in the real world suggest it ought. Or I could plug in a 'black box,' the closest substitute I can contrive for the missing culture variable, and study it as I operate the game.

"I could use college students of different nationalities. I know they are not really analogues of national decision makers, but they do give me a way of finding out something about the influence of culture on decision-making behavior. And from what I learn about the decision-making behavior of real people with different cultural backgrounds, perhaps I can start to build a *theory* about the culture variable in international decision making. In any case, I can keep on improving the game, testing new hypotheses as they are suggested by the outcomes of the game; in addition, by focusing on the *system* characteristics—changed levels of tension, and the like—I can also learn more about the reaction of human decision makers to different environmental conditions, even though the players are regarded, for research purposes, as 'black boxes' that are simply part of the system.

"I could, on the other hand, focus on the subjects themselves—on how they respond to various stimuli, on how their personal characteristics affect their behavior, and how they interact with their fellows as a function of these variables. In this case, changes in the state of the system will be interesting only to the degree that they reflect the subjects' choices. The system, the 'machine' part of this man-machine game, simply provides an 'environment' for studying a wide range of human behavioral responses, but I can see to it that the machine environment has the same characteristics of overload and uncertainty, of ambiguous, threatening, and probabilistic situations, as does the real international system. Within limits, I will have a laboratory which is an analogue in important respects to the system I wish to study. In either case, the game will allow me to sort out cause and effect as I could never do by observing the real international system."

WHY SIMULATE?

Like more conventional laboratory experiments, simulations have certain advantages over observations in the real world: *economy*, *safety*, *visibility*, and *reproducibility*. While the first two are obvious—for example, one can economically and safely investigate *some* of the consequences of thermonuclear warfare by building a computer simulation—the last two merit discussion.

Visibility

Phenomena under study are frequently more visible in a simulation because they are *physically* more accessible and hence more readily observed, or *conceptually* more accessible and hence more readily grasped. Watching smoke flow past an air foil in a wind tunnel is physically much easier than trying to measure the air flow past the wing of a plane in flight. And some phenomena are virtually inaccessible in nature; for example, strategists cannot study the relationship between the amount of destruction in thermonuclear warfare and weather conditions, weapons yield, weapons reliability, time of warning, or extent of preparation. A computer simulation can be programmed to make accessible a complete range of information.

Phenomena may be conceptually more accessible in a simulation, and hence more visible, because the elimination of all but the salient and relevant elements highlights and clarifies the relationships and processes under study. This is particularly true in social science simulations, for the phenomena in the referent are frequently so confused and chaotic that it is hard to make any sense of them at all. The student who wants to understand world affairs, the researcher who wants to test basic principles of international relations, is face to face with the tangled System III described earlier. Where should he start? What should be observed? What is relevant? What are the relationships? But in a simulation of international relations which incorporates most of the salient elements in simplified and explicit form, both student and researcher can grasp the general outlines, the operating framework of the international system, by working with the simulation. It *simplifies* and *clarifies* a system whose complexity obscures specific phenomena. And upon the initial structure of the game, the researcher can build the details in which he is particularly interested. So simulations aid visibility by making certain kinds of phenomena more accessible to manipulation, observation, and measurement, and by introducing clarity into what is otherwise complex, chaotic, or confused.

Reproducibility

The final advantage of simulations—their reproducibility—is particularly valuable for the social science researcher, for this allows him to study repeatedly events which might occur but once, or not at all, in the real world. There are two good reasons for wanting to do this. The first involves the element of *chance*, the need to gain some understanding of the effects of events whose frequency of occurrence simply can't be predicted. The researcher can build chance into the operation of his model with "Monte Carlo" techniques, or by letting the simulation run often enough to allow all the possible outcomes to occur, and then observing how often in fact they do occur.

Second, because a simulation is reproducible, the researcher is permitted to play the fascinating game of "What might happen if . . .?" For he may, should he wish, simulate a set of circumstances and then introduce the "if. . . ." In the terminology of research, it allows him to observe the effects of different kinds of manipulation of the input variables: he can change assumptions, alter the input parameter values, modify the relationships among elements of the system, and intervene in the ongoing processes—and, because time is compressed in a simulation, he can observe in a day processes which might occur only during months or years in the real world. In everyday language, he can mess around with the model. He might want to find out, for example, "What difference would it make in the international system if the chief of state of a major power is highly paranoid as opposed to self-confident and trusting?" The complexity of the real international system, the ambiguity of the "linkages," virtually defies the identification of cause-effect relationships, even could he observe a paranoid real chief of state. In a simulation he can carry out controlled experiments that yield profitable insights into how the system operates under such a condition.

Unexpected Payoffs

In addition, simulations may serve as an "early warning system," suggesting or demonstrating the *potential* effects of powerful variables, or baring unforeseen contingencies. Moreover, by staging a future event, the simulator, or the players in a game, can live through a variety of contingencies, analyze their causes and results, and be better prepared to cope with them should they occur. Army maneuvers, i.e., military games, are large-scale simulations which serve this purpose.

Finally, simulation and games are "serendipity-prone." Unexpected findings are often generated that suggest new areas for exploration and hypothesis testing. For example, analysis of data from a study with the inter-nation simulation uncovered perceptual distor-

tions arising from one nation's achievement of nuclear invulner-
ability. Such an effect had never been predicted in the literature, but
once it occurred in the game, considerable evidence could be found
for it in the real world. Thus the unexpected outcome called for a
new hypothesis with serious empirical implications: that a seesaw
race in weapons development might result in ever greater perceptual
distortions among nations, with consequences which could be
catastrophic.

As a research method, then, simulation and gaming has important
advantages over naturalistic observation and experiment. In addition,
the attempt to *construct* a simulation contributes in significant ways
to the generation and construction of theory.

Theory Building

First, game or simulation building, more effectively than most
other scholarly activities, disciplines theory and stimulates the "need
to know." Kaplan says:

> Models have this merit; . . . [they] save us from a certain self-deception.
> Forced into the open, our ideas may flutter helplessly; but at least we can
> see what bloodless creatures they are. As inquiry proceeds, theory must be
> brought out into the open sooner or later; the model simply makes it sooner
> [1964, pp. 268–9].

Almost everyone who has tried to build a game or simulation
confesses that his first contact with it generated more intellectual
soul searching than he had ever previously been forced to undergo. It
is one thing to accept a verbal theory. It is quite another to define it
operationally in order to express it in a simulation. Every concept—
every noun, every verb—must be specified in terms of actual behavior. Nor is it enough to state the functional relationships in some
general form. The processes of the system must be specified in terms
of increase and decrease, of degree and direction.

The would-be model builder must ask himself what sort of data
are needed to specify these relationships and processes, and whether
the data exist in terms of the definitions at which he has now arrived.
He is forced to be *explicit*, *logical*, and *accurate*, and so is confronted
with the magnitude of his ignorance, and the fuzziness, inconsistency, and lack of coherence of his concepts. Indeed, game building
has led to the repudiation of a theory when the spotlight of simulation showed the theory to be meretricious.

Second, simulation building expands the scholar's horizons, and
invites him to reconnoiter unexplored terrain. It is impossible, for

example, to build a model of an international system, or even of a single nation, without taking cognizance of economic and psychological factors as well as political and social factors. A serious attempt to simulate any but the most trivial phenomena quickly convinces the scholar of the artificiality of interdisciplinary boundaries. The literature, the methods, the data, the concepts, the analogies from related disciplines suddenly become tormentingly relevant—"tormentingly" because he must acquire at least a rudimentary understanding of the language of other disciplines; he must examine the congruence of his own concepts and methods with those of other disciplines. Simulation building breaches the walls that encapsulate specialized "fields of study," and encourages the integration and communication of knowledge. The problem-oriented approach of the simulation builder is a very effective way of overcoming disciplinary parochialism. It may eventually lead to the development of a single "language," a set of concepts and basic principles, which will unify the various behavioral sciences into a unitary science of behavior.

The need for rigorous explication and for including theory and data from other disciplines, often reveals new possibilities that might otherwise be missed, and that have important implications for theory. In the "bootstrap" process of simulation building, playing around in so rich an environment, exploring interactions so complicated, the scholar is almost guaranteed insights and outcomes that open up whole new areas for exploration, theory construction, and hypothesis testing.

Fun and "Games"

Finally, simulation building has yet another payoff for the scholar. The elaborate, subtle, and satisfying play aspect of creating a "pretend" world, coupled with the tremendous challenge of making that world as realistic a representation as possible, produces deep involvement. Gaming and simulation building are magical activities, the sort of "play" that engages a poet with words, an artist with form and color. The researcher quickly becomes obsessed by a desire to fill in those "blank spots" where theory and data are missing; he is possessed by an intellectual and emotional drive far more powerful than pure curiosity, for now he is goaded not only by his scholarly interest in knowledge for its own sake, but by a lust for knowledge with which to perfect his simulation. Gaming capitalizes on man's desire for situational involvement for its own sake, and on his inherent urge to construct aesthetically and rationally satisfying systems—his need to create order out of chaos (his "negentropic" instinct?).

In sum, then, I have argued that simulation allows the scholar to investigate, safely and economically, phenomena that he might otherwise be unable to investigate at all because they are relatively inaccessible or invisible, or impossible to study in nature; and that simulation reveal unforeseen contingencies and unexpected possibilities. I have further argued that the effort to build a simulation is, in itself, an epistemologically sound and powerful goad to the development of theory. And I have argued the presimulations or games, though they embody incomplete models and tentative postulation, constitute a rich and complex laboratory for studying human behavior—a laboratory that is superior, because of its complexity, to the conventionally sterile setting of most social science experimentation. We must now confront the throny and unresolved problem of *validity*.

ARE SIMULATIONS VALID?

"Are games and simulations valid instruments for research in the social sciences?" The question appears at first glance to be a very simple one. We are really asking "How good are the findings?" or, more explicitly, "Do simulation outcomes accurately reflect what happens in the real world?" This accords with a dictionary definition: "*valid* implies being supported by objective truth or generally accepted authority." But when we deal with validity in the context of research, we can seldom appeal to "truth" or "authority." We are in a vastly different domain, that of the philosophers of science, where there are no hard and fast "laws," only greater or lesser degrees of "probability." Even more vexing, the question of validity differs depending on the type of research. A valid theory describes process and relationships accurately enough to predict new processes or additional relationships with a high degree of probability. A valid psychological test interprets behavior more convincingly than other methods. A valid hypothesis is one that has not been disconfirmed in spite of strenuous efforts to do so. In science, we might say, "Valid is as valid does," and it is clear that we are concerned with *degrees* of validity, rather than with an absolute.

Valid Methods versus Valid Results

But the validity question has two faces: one must distinguish between the validity of a *method* and the validity of the *results*. We presuppose, as an article of faith, that the validity of the results is related to the validity of the method. Shall we simply declare, then, that the proof of the pudding is in the eating, that if the method is valid, the results are sure to be, or that if the results are valid, the method must be? We cannot. Scholars have been known to use impeccably valid methods only to arrive at demonstrably invalid results. For example, standard intelligence tests validly measure certain cognitive functions *within the context of Western middle-class culture.* There is now ample evidence that their results are invalid in other cultural contexts. On the other hand, a method which violates all the canons of scientific procedure may nevertheless produce "true" or accurate results. Yesterday's old wives' nostrums are part of today's pharmacopoeia.

In spite of the slipperiness of the concept, validity is a pragmatic question to the scholar. His efforts are bootless if they do not further the increase of knowledge—and "knowledge" *implies* "validity." How then shall we judge the validity of a method such as simulation?

Isomorphism versus Usefulness

The temptation is great to measure the validity of a model according to how accurately and completely it represents reality; more technically, according to its "isomorphism to the referent." We believe that if the model is faithful to reality, we have a right to infer that the outcomes of manipulating the model will be identical to outcomes in the real world. But testing for isomorphic fidelity in the social-behavioral universe, replete as it is with myth, error, unexplored territory—and randomness—is almost impossibly difficult. What shall we use as a standard for comparison? How shall we judge the validity of the model's structure, if we don't know the structure of the referent? In any case, when we are dealing with symbolic models or with analogues, validity does not, as we saw earlier, presuppose replication. I shall argue, therefore, that as a criterion of validity isomorphism is not only inappropriate but is also *inadequate.* It is both more consistent with modern concepts of scientific theory and more fruitful to judge the validity of a particular simulation—and, indeed, the validity of gaming as a method—in terms of its *usefulness,* its usefulness in solving empirical problems or in increasing knowledge. The criterion of usefulness raises two further questions: "Useful for *what?*" and "Useful *compared* to what?"

Consider a table model of the solar system composed of balls and wires. If isomorphism is the criterion, the model is clearly invalid. But if we ask whether the model is *useful,* the answer is "Yes, indeed." For the purpose of acquainting students with the geometry of the solar system it is probably far more useful than a highly accurate verbal description, set of equations, or two-dimensional drawing. Thus, we can say, "The most valid (that is, most useful) model or method is the one that best contributes to knowledge." But we must then ask, "Knowledge for what *purpose*?" Wayman Crow and Robert Noel (1965) argue that in employing the usefulness criterion, attention should be shifted to the *information* one wishes to gather and the *purpose* for which it is to be used. We may then ask, "How useful for the purpose is the information produced by this method, as compared to some alternative method?"

Again, this implies that a method valid for some purposes may not be valid for others, and hence that the accuracy and precision of a method are not the sole considerations. Indeed, gaming experience demonstrates that for teaching or theory building, a simple, inaccurate, and incomplete game which contains intriguing concepts and obvious challenges is a greater incentive to improving the model than is a highly accurate computer simulation; hence the game is more "valid."

In using games for research, however—for generating data, testing theory, exploring or "messing around"—isomorphism is nearly always salient. Harold Guetzkow (Guetzkow and Jensen, 1966) suggests that the adequacy of a social science game can be assessed by asking, "To what extent does the game generate processes and/or outcomes similar to those observed in the referent?" Here the criterion is "isomorphism" of results. This criterion is implied by Richard Brody (1964), who considers that confidence in a game is increased (1) if it can reproduce an actual historical event, given the actual antecedent situation; (2) if it reliably predicts future events; (3) if the processes observed in the game are those that would be predicted to occur were the game valid; or (4) if hypotheses are confirmed or disconfirmed in the game much as theory predicts they would be if tested in the referent.

Criteria for Validity

The simulation literature contains still other and somewhat different sets of validation criteria, but all, I think, can be distilled into four ideal requirements. Thus a simulation can be considered valid for research purposes to the degree

1. that the environment seems realistic to the subjects, where an all-man or man-machine simulation is used as a "complex environment" laboratory;

2. that the structure of the model (the theory and assumptions upon which it is built) is isomorphic with that of the referent;
3. that the processes observed in the system are isomorphic with those observed in the referent; and
4. that it is able to reproduce historical outcomes or to predict the future.

Only where human players are involved are all four criteria applicable. In all-computer simulations or models of economic systems, the first criterion is irrelevant, and the third criterion cannot be met, since the processes that occur during cycling are so highly aggregated and so invisible as to defy analysis. Nevertheless, economic simulations can quite accurately predict gross economic trends over fairly short time periods, and compared to other methods of economic predicting, simulations are superior because they require far less time and manpower. If usefulness is the overriding criterion, then one must assess the validity of each specific game with respect to its specific purpose, and apply the criteria in accordance with the goal.

For man-machine games, it is the last three criteria which present the greatest difficulties. Nevertheless, the limited evidence available suggests that many game processes may be more isomorphic with those in the referent than would be expected. Each new version of the inter-nation simulation, for example, is evaluated in terms of the existing body of theory and data from international relations, and the model is constantly brought into closer conformity with what is known of the referent system. This game, it is safe to say, will remain for a very long time to come a dynamic research technique rather than a true—i.e., isomorphic—representation of the international system. But therein lies its great usefulness. Furthermore, it may be that process validity is not highly dependent on structural isomorphism. If so, then in studying human behavioral processes, actual isomorphism is less important than that the environment seem realistic to the players, that it conform to *their* idea of reality. In any case, considerable experience with games indicates that as realistic laboratories they rate very well, and certainly better than the available alternatives.

Visualizing the Unknown

But as I have suggested throughout this chapter, it is as a theory-building device that games and simulations are most useful, and hence most "valid." There is, however, a deeper sense in which one can ask the question of validity—a sense which is indirectly rather than directly related to the criterion of usefulness that I have emphasized. Does gaming reflect, or is it based on, an appropriate philosophy of science? It is my underlying thesis here that scientific activity is fundamentally a matter of matching patterns, of creating frameworks for inquiry, of discovering analogies, of fitting systems together, rather than of simply discovering "truth" through the incremental addition of particles of fact. Gaming does reflect and build on this philosophy. If the philosophy is appropriate, gaming is valid.

Against great odds, social science researchers and theorists try to apply in their own fields the methods and epistemology of the physical sciences. They may be heartened, therefore, by reading *The Double Helix*. This book is a delightful and unpretentious account of how James Watson and Francis Crick used what is essentially the gaming and pattern-matching approach to achieve what has been called the greatest breakthrough in the twentieth century, the discovery of the structure of the DNA molecule. On the face of it, their undertaking was foolhardy, if not foolish. "Most likely," writes Watson, "we had to know the correct DNA structure before the right model could be found." They kept asking, "Which atoms like to sit next to each other?"; they spent their time constructing tentative models and "fiddling around" with them to find "the prettiest way for a polynucleotide chain to fold up" (Watson, 1968). Like the social science game builder, they tried to learn about reality by visualizing the unknown.

But as Jacob Bronowski points out:

> This is how the scientific method really works: . . . we *invent* a model and then *test* its consequences. . . . It is the conjunction of imagination and realism that constitute the inductive method. . . . Albert Einstein could not have made a visible model of his space-time; and yet space-time *is* a model, and so is every discovery, and it takes its power from the closeness with which the consequences that flow from it match the real world [1968, pp. 381–82].

Isomorphism is the end result, not the starting condition.

11. "MODELS" IN POLITICS

Gordon Tullock

In the social sciences the word "model" seems to serve much the same role as the word "theory" in the natural sciences. Exactly why we do not refer to "theory" in social sciences when we have a logically rigid structure of some sort, but call it a "model," while the physical sciences refer to the same thing in their area as a theory, is not clear. It probably is a development of the history of the discipline. Whatever the reason, there is considerable difference in the usage of these words in the different disciplines. Further, there is even a difference as to whether their subject matter is within the discipline. In economics, for example, one of the standard subjects is "the history of economic thought." This is, in essence, a history of the development of economics with careful examination of the work of the early economists. Most of the natural sciences do not teach their students the history of the science itself. That is left to a separate discipline called the history of science. In political science, on the other hand, the history of the development of political science is given considerably more emphasis than it is even in economics, and it is called theory.

Granted that the meaning of words is essentially arbitrary, there is no reason why we should complain about the meaning of these words in these different disciplines, but we must keep it in mind. Further, the use of the word "theory" for the history of the development of political thought means that another word is needed to deal with the political science equivalent of the theory in the natural sciences. To fill this gap, the word "models" has been chosen. Thus, in this chapter I shall talk about political models, but this is simply bowing to custom. If I were completely free, I should refer to these matters as political theory and refer to the subject matter now taught in political courses as History of Political Thought.

What, then, is a political model? The answer is perfectly simple in principle but extremely difficult in application. A model is a logically rigid chain of reasoning proceeding from certain assumptions through a structure of reasoning to certain deductions. In order for it to be a model in political science, we add the additional requirement that there be some reason to believe that the political world behaves in a manner such as to "fit" the model. It will be immediately seen that a model is not a particularly new phenomenon either in the natural sciences or in the political sciences. Examples will be found in Aristotle and many other classical thinkers. Indeed, in this as in so many other areas, one could say that Aristotle was an example of the modern scientifically oriented man who happened to live in ancient Greece. In two thousand years we have, generally speaking, managed to make very, very great improvements on his thought, but this is not because we are brighter or more logically coherent than he, but simply because we have been able to build on the earlier work.[1]

The above definition of a "model" is superficially very simple and easy, but it actually raises very difficult issues. These may be taken up in almost any order, but I should like to begin by discussing a special kind of political model which is used by all political thinkers and which is characteristically not thought of as a model. Let us suppose that I predict that the black wards in Chicago will, in the next election, go Democratic. This prediction is clearly the outcome of a very simple political model. I am assuming (and I must say in this case that the assumption is backed by a great deal of empirical evidence) that blacks vote Democratic more often than they do Republican. I then note that the wards to which I am referring are black and deduce from these two facts that they will vote Democratic. This type of extremely simple model is used regularly, continuously, and consistently by all students of political science and indeed by all students of any subject.

Many of my readers may, in fact, regard the above reasoning as not really being a "model" but as some kind of empirical statement. Clearly, the empirical evidence for the assumption is strong, and the statement about the real world, i.e., that the Chicago black wards will vote Democratic, is readily testable, but the fact remains that I have achieved it by a rigidly correct line of reasoning. I may, of course, not give the line of reasoning in detail in writing an actual article in a political journal because I would assume that my readers would be able to follow it without my carrying out every step. If I happen to be producing an elaborate mathematical demonstration of some point, I would also skip those steps that I felt my readers could duplicate without my wasting ink on them.

1. Newton's famous remark "If we have seen so far, it is because we have stood on the shoulders of giants" is relevant here.

But this extremely simple type of model raises very, very few real difficulties in the real world and is not in any sense controversial. The more complex models to which I now turn are frequently criticized. These criticisms are, I believe, largely the result of misunderstandings. The problems of a complex logical model and a simple logical model are basically the same, although there may be more difficulties in the longer model. But the difference is a matter of degree, not of principle. In each model we have some assumptions, a chain of reasoning, and a conclusion. In each model the questions are two: (1) "Is the logical chain of reasoning correct?" and (2) "Does the chain of reasoning describe the real world?" The fact that the chain of reasoning may be long in one model and short in the other is of some interest, but is not really decisive for problems of pure methodology.

Nevertheless, in the remainder of this chapter I propose to talk mainly about the types of political models which involve fairly complex chains of reasoning. The reason I shall do so is mainly that it is very boring to discuss the extremely short chains of reasoning involved in the type of model I have outlined above. Also, some readers may think that there *is* a distinction between short chains of reasoning and long chains; hence a discussion in terms of long chains may be more enlightening for them than a discussion in terms of short chains. Turning, then, to these rather long chains of reasoning, we may loosely refer to them as consisting of three parts: the assumptions, the reasoning, and the conclusions. As a general rule, the reason we have developed these theories is that we are interested in their conclusions. We want a way of manipulating the real world, and for this purpose we seek out theories which will tell us things about the real world we did not know before the theory was invented. Characteristically, these things will be found in the conclusions rather than in the assumptions.

The fact that we are normally more interested in the conclusions than in any other aspect of the theory has been used by positivists as a basic argument to the effect that we should ignore the assumptions if the predictions of the theory turn out to be validated. This seems to me to be something of an oversimplification. Surely, if I were given my choice of a theory the assumptions of which were all true and the conclusions of which were all false, or a theory the assumptions of which were all false and the conclusions were all true, I would choose the latter. It would be a much more useful tool in dealing with the real world. But what we would really like to have is a theory in which both the assumptions and the conclusions are true. Unfortunately, in the imperfect state of knowledge as it exists today we sometimes do have to make choices. When we do have to make these choices, it seems to me that the positivist's choice is the correct one. We should look to the conclusions, not to the accuracy of the assumptions. Nevertheless, we should always realize that this is very decidedly a second-best procedure. What we actually want is a theory which proceeds from truthful assumptions to truthful conclusions by way of a correct line of reasoning.[2]

The relationship of the theory to the real world is also a matter which requires a certain amount of discussion. First, it should be noted that as a characteristic matter it is not possible to directly test the theory *qua* theory with respect to any real world phenomenon. There may occasionally be cases where the theory produces specific deductions with respect to the real world but more commonly it is necessary to deduce from the theory a specific statement about the real world and then test that specific statement. Thus, for example, let us take an assumption that is very commonly found in theories of human behavior; that is, that behavior is to some extent rational. Perhaps in the next thousand years we will learn enough about psychology that we can test this statement by examining people's minds and finding out whether they are, indeed, to some extent rational.

In the present state of knowledge, however, this is impossible and we test the hypothesis by deducing from it certain other propositions. For example, I add an additional assumption: most people would rather not be burned to death. Then with the use of the rational assumption which amounts to saying that people generally speaking take action to achieve their goals and my assumption about goals, i.e., people will avoid being burned to death, I produce the prediction that most people who are in burning buildings will attempt to get out. We now have a general statement about the real world. From it a specific statement about specific people can be deduced. This latter statement is then subject to empirical testing. As a matter of fact, of course, I presume that no one would bother to test my little theory, since the results of the test are, in this case, fairly obvious.

There are, however, a number of special problems. One of them is that no theory in economics, physics, or political science ever completely states the conditions for its validity. This is not an

2. It should be noted that in some famous cases the line of reasoning has been improper. From the time Newton and Leibniz invented the calculus until the nineteenth century, this operation was supported by invalid proofs. Thus we had a rather remarkable situation in which mathematicians, physicists, etc., all over the world were using a mathematical tool which had been demonstrated by Bishop Berkeley to be invalid. With the development of the concept of limits in the nineteenth century, valid proofs of the calculus were developed. The fact remains, however, that for a very long period of time very good scientists were using a line of reasoning which, according to the best knowledge of their day, was invalid.

inherent defect in the theory, but simply a statement of the fact that most theories anticipate that people who might turn to tests in the future will make certain basic assumptions of their own. For example, one will seldom find any statement in physics predicting certain activities in the real world if certain things are done in which the theorist adds on statements that the experiment should not be attempted during earthquakes, or that if the experimental apparatus happened to be struck by lightning during the course of the experiment, the predicted settings on the dials would not occur. Similarly, in the social sciences we rarely find a complete list of all things which could happen and which would invalidate the deduction about the real world because we assume that the person who uses the theory will use common sense. It is also probable that we could not give a complete statement of all the things which might happen that would lead to the results of the experiment being different from the prediction. This is simply limitation on our imagination, not a basic drawback to the theories.

Another aspect of all theoretical work and one that is rather seldom discussed either in the natural sciences or social sciences concerns what I would like to call the differentiation assumption. When we make up a theory, whether we are physicists or political scientists, we do not claim that we know everything about the real world. It is a commonplace that we do not know everything about even the most simple objects. It would take many scientists many lifetimes to describe completely the eraser on my pencil. Further, with our present knowledge we probably would not be able to achieve anything near a full description. In spite of the fact that we do not believe that we know everything about anything, we nevertheless produce theories. The reason that we can do this is because we believe implicitly or explicitly that a theory dealing with only certain aspects of reality may nevertheless be correct.

Thus, consider the theory I discussed earlier in which we assume that people are sometimes rational. We would deduce from this theory and from our assumption that the reality is differentiable; that if we set up the experimental apparatus which I described (burning buildings) we would find a good many of the people in these buildings attempting to get out. In this case, I suppose we would be rather surprised if we found anyone who didn't, but one can think of special circumstances which might lead to someone choosing to remain within. In more complex theories we of course turn to statistical procedures. In recent years, for example, radar has been used to measure the distance from the earth to the moon and from some of the near planets. The radar return signal is a very feeble signal compared to the amount of static which is picked up by the antenna at the same time. Nevertheless, believing that the radar signal is there, we use statistical methods and are able to disentangle this one aspect of the reception, the radar bounced off the planet, from the large amount of background noise.

This view that the real world is differentiable, that we can study one aspect of it and find the effect of this aspect, is perhaps most clearly visible in the work of engineers. They will start with a rather simple equation dealing with one particular aspect of a piece of machinery. They will then produce another equation dealing with another aspect and integrate the two equations into a larger equation. This process will then be continued until an equation which looks so long that no reasonable man would even think of trying to solve it is produced. The engineers then proceed to solve it, and obtain various optima in design. This is a very old technique and proceeds from the assumption that you can take a number of special aspects of reality and integrate them to produce a larger and more comprehensive picture of a number of what we may call major aspects, or a major aspect. We have no proof that the world is that differentiable and that considering it aspect by aspect is a valid procedure; nevertheless, without this implicit assumption, the human mind being finite, we would never have been able to discover anything about the real world and the assumption is the foundation of all of our knowledge.

Our method of dealing with the world, then, is of necessity a statistical one. We produce a theory of some sort which in political science we call a model. This theory cannot in the present state of the world be all-inclusive. It is of necessity a theory of some aspect of the world. Thus the deduction that is produced about the real world is also not the totally descriptive one. It will be a partial description. Characteristically, this means that we must use statistical methods to separate out the "noise" produced by other aspects of reality from the "signal" produced by the effect that our theory deals with. Since the development of statistics is one of the great wonders of the human mind, this is not a disadvantage but it must be kept in mind. We should not anticipate that any theory will show a one-to-one correspondence with the totality of reality. If the theory produces a valid result, this merely means that we will get a tendency towards the results predicted. This tendency may be more or less obscured by noise originating from other factors with which we have not yet been able to deal.

What I have been saying in the past few paragraphs is very rarely mentioned in books on method but is, in fact, a commonplace if one considers what scientists actually do. Most scientific theories, whether they are in physics, biology, or the social sciences, produce statements about the reality which (if we test them) turn out to be not exactly true. In part, the inexactitude of the theories no doubt reflects the imprecision of the measuring instruments, but in part it also reflects the fact that the real world is a complex place and the particular theory that we are testing describes not the whole of that world but simply some significant part of it. Those parts of the world which are not described by the existing theory have their effect on the results and hence the theory produces not a perfect picture of the world but a picture of the effects of part of the world on another part of the world. The outcome is, then, a prediction which is statistically verifiable but which is seldom exactly what happens.

Many of the complaints about the inaccuracy of assumptions of theories turn very largely on the simple fact that these theories do not completely describe the initial state of affairs. It will be said, for example, that the men in my little theory of the burning building are not always rational and not all human beings have equally strong aversions to being burned to death. No doubt this is quite true and no doubt, therefore, if we performed an experiment (let us say, burning down a hotel, having first wired it with closed circuit television so that we could observe the behavior of all the people in it) we would find that different people left the hotel with different degrees of speed and efficiency. This would not invalidate the theory, but it would indicate that the theory is not a complete one. Our objective in the world is to obtain complete theories, but it must be admitted that we are now thousands of years from that goal.

The characteristic theory today, whether it is a physics theory or a model in political science, assumes certain things about the real world which are not a complete description of the real world and in some cases, no doubt, are slightly inaccurate. From this, then, it deduces certain consequences in the real world, and when we test these consequences we find that they are not perfect fits to the real world. Our problem normally is not a choice between a perfect theory and no theory, but between a number of different theories of different degrees of imprecision.

How, then, do we select our theories? Roughly, we can divide statements about the world into two categories: the very simple theories of the sort I gave in an example earlier, in which we predicted the behavior of the black wards in Chicago, or theories with a much higher degree of logical structure. The general rule used in choosing between theories is to choose the "simplest" theory which will explain the phenomenon. In this rule, however, the word "simple" has quite a different meaning than it does in ordinary English. Surely the simplest theory to describe any result is a very short direct theory: for example, the theory that opium causes people to sleep because it has dormative properties. In practice, however, this is not what is meant by "simplicity" in theories. What we actually aim for in "simplicity" is a large number of predictable outcomes from a small number of initial assumptions about the real world. In other words, we look for a logical structure which has many implications instead of a few. Progress is characteristically noted when we find theories which have a high degree of ability to explain much from relatively little input. This frequently means that we choose a complex theory over a simple one, but this choice is not a direct desire for complexity. Indeed, if we have two theories which explain the same phenomenon with the same input, we will choose the simplest (using the word "simple" in its ordinary English sense). The rule is not to choose the simplest theory in the sense in which the word is normally used in English, nor to choose a complex theory, but to choose that collection of theories which explains the most with the least in the way of assumptions as an input.

There seems no reason why political science should be any different from physics in this respect. Many of the arguments that one encounters against the use of "models" in political science are actually arguments against specific models. For example, it may be said that people are not rational and hence those models that involve an assumption of rationality are incorrect. Leaving aside temporarily the question of whether people are or are not rational, this is clearly not an objection to a complex line of reasoning *per se*, but an objection to one particular assumption which is quite frequently used in such complex chains of reasoning. The step from an attack on a particular model to an attack on models in general is clearly logically illegitimate. No doubt, it was true in 400 B.C. that there were no correct theories of physics of any degree of logical structure. One could not deduce from that that no such theories were possible. Similarly, a demonstration that no existing models of political structure were valid would not be a proof that such models are impossible. Needless to say, in my opinion there is no disproof of the current existence of such models, but even if there were, no general conclusion could be drawn from it.

If we examine the social sciences, we immediately observe that there is a striking disparity in the number of fairly elaborate models that are used in different areas. In economics, elaborate, mathematically sophisticated models have been used for over a hundred years. Every new issue of the economics journals produces more elaborations on these models. Further, by now these models can be regarded as very highly confirmed. The development of computers and modern statistical theory led to a period of testing of the economic models in the late 1950s and early 1960s with the result that the theoretical work has been demonstrated to have a reasonably close correspondence to the real world.

A second area in which there are a fair number of reasonably complex models is one particular aspect of foreign affairs, i.e. that part which can be dealt with by game theory. As it happens, here the models are much simpler than those in use in economics—perhaps because they have been recently invented, and we have not had many scholars working on them—and the empirical confirmation is much weaker. In fact, there are many people who would argue that it is nonexistent. When we turn out away from these areas, however, we are confronted with a surprising paucity of elaborate theoretical structures in the social sciences. The recent development in political science, which is very largely an importation of economic techniques and constructs, is I think the largest single collection of theory which will be found outside of economics in any of the social sciences. These theories are as yet rather recent, and clearly could stand a good deal of further work. At least up to now, the degree of empirical confirmation that they have received is not high. The empirical problems raised by these theories is, in general, not that they are in conflict with the empirical evidence but that the empiricists in political science have, in general, not made any serious effort to test them—perhaps because they have difficulty following them. What tests have been run seem (on the whole) to support these newer theories. Nevertheless, it must be admitted that the basic reason for regarding them as correct (at the moment) is simply that they make use of a number of tools which have been very successful in economics, and that the theories have internal coherence and make predictions about the real world which appear to be true from common experience. Clearly, we need much more empirical testing in this area, but it will require the development of new techniques and of a higher degree of sophistication before these tests can be regarded as of any great value.

In a sense, the introduction of these economic methods has so far had more effect on political science by a change in the way in which people look at politics than in terms of the strict models themselves. The view that the voter is choosing among alternatives in terms of his personal preference schedule rather than making an effort to determine what is in the public interest leads to quite a different attitude towards the voting process. It can also be the foundation of very elaborate chains of reasoning, as a number of scholars have demonstrated, but it is probable that the very simple change in attitude has to this day been more important than the complex theories themselves.

A difference in attitude has also come with the introduction of essentially economic models into political science. There has been a movement to what we can call cooperative model building. If we examine the work of William H. Riker (1962), Anthony Downs (1957, 1967), Mancur Olson, Jr. (1965), Kenneth J. Arrow (1963), Duncan Black (1958), James M. Buchanan (1967), and Tullock (1967), we find that there is relatively little dissent among them. In general, they use each others' books as sources and do not engage in very much controversy among themselves. Further, when, as for example in Riker's remarks about Downs (Riker, 1962, p. 33), one of them alleges that another has fallen into error, the person who is accused of the error normally rather quickly accepts the accusation, or the person who has made the accusation agrees that he himself is in error and withdraws it. That this is unusual in political science I take it most of my readers will agree.

The reason, I think, is that the use of a set of rather similar logical models makes it very hard for individuals to defend genuine errors. Undoubtedly all of us do make errors; but the structure of the work which is now called "model building" in political science is such that in general any difference of opinion between two people on some portion of the models can normally be rapidly cleared up. Where there are continuing differences of opinion among these scholars in this field, they are normally recognized by all parties as being differences about matters on which, at the moment, no definite conclusion can be reached. In such cases, the theorists will be in general agreement that eventually the problem will be settled and that it is an important one, and that their present differing opinions are of little authority.

Once again, this change in attitude, although quite sizable from traditional political science, is not in and of itself a revolution. It simply reflects the fact that it is hard to maintain an erroneous model against the criticism of people who understand the model as well as you do. Thus, clear errors are normally rather rapidly eliminated and differences tend to persist only in those areas where the models do not give a definite outcome. Needless to say, these latter areas may be important, but the fact that all of the model-building community is aware of the fact that the conclusions are not very definitive means that there is relatively little heat in discussing these differences. It is to be hoped that this attitude, which differs so sharply from the controversy between the behavioralists, for example, and the followers of Leo Strauss, will become more common in political science as time goes by. Indeed, it must be admitted that most of the behavioralists are moving rapidly in this direction in any event. A reduction in the amount of heat may not lead to more light, but it is, generally speaking, an indispensable first step toward that goal.

Still, this chapter is about models and not about political science in general. I cannot, of course, in the brief compass of the remainder of this discussion give an example of a really elaborate chain of reasoning and then discuss its application. Let me, however, give one of the oldest propositions of the "new political theory," one of the earliest modern models in politics, and discuss very briefly one particular deduction from it together with the empirical information which confirms it. I shall then give a very recent and rather more complex theory which has not yet had much of any empirical testing. The first and simplest theory is normally associated with the name of Paul Samuelson and is entitled "The Theory of Public Goods." I should explain that, like any theory that is now a good many years old, most specialists in the field would regard it as an approximation and that there are more recent theories which fit reality better. These more recent theories, however, are complex, and the very simple and powerful model introduced by Samuelson will do as an illustration. Samuelson pointed out that there are certain activities which benefit a great many people and for which it is substantially impossible to restrict the benefits to a selected group of people. Under these circumstances, nobody may be motivated to provide the activity at all. (See Niemi and Weisberg, 1972.)

Consider, for example, a lighthouse. All ships that pass in the night would, at least before the invention of radar, benefit from its existence. If any private person or company chooses to build a lighthouse, however, it will have no way of preventing others from using it. It would be very hard, moreover, to imagine a way in which it could collect a toll from people who saw the lighthouse from a vast distance and used it for navigation. Under the circumstances, only an individual or company which had a very large number of ships of its own passing along the coast would be motivated to put up a lighthouse. Further, once it had put up the lighthouse, it would find it was impossible to recover the funds invested, since it would not only reduce the number of wrecks suffered by the owner's ships, but it would also reduce the number of wrecks suffered by other ships and they would (in a competitive market) cut their rates to the point where the owner was unable to obtain return on the money he put into the lighthouse.[3]

Samuelson says that under these circumstances it would not be likely that the lighthouse would be built by anyone. He points out, however, that if all shipowners got together and hired someone to coerce them to pay individual assessments for the lighthouse, they

3. In a monopolistic or an oligopolistic market the inability to get the money back is also demonstrable but with considerable complications.

could all be better off. Thus, they would be wise to set up an instrument of coercion for the purpose of coercing themselves. Samuelson then goes on to demonstrate that this intellectual apparatus can be used to justify a very large part of the activities which governments, in fact, carry on. The more complex apparatuses which have been developed in recent years provide an even better fit to the real world.

One of the defects of traditional political and economic theory has been the absence of any real rule for determining what activities should be carried on by the government and what by private persons. The tradition has been either to depend on tradition itself, i.e., the government should continue doing what it is now doing and private market should do what it is doing, or to make ad hoc arguments for any given activity being either government or private. Samuelson's public goods theory, with more recent modifications, appears to provide a necessary, although not a sufficient, condition for activities being conducted by the government rather than by private market. Such traditional governmental activities as the military forces of the country or the maintenance of domestic order are almost perfect examples of Samuelsonian public goods. It is clear they would not be provided in suitable quantity by the market.

If we go through the rest of government activities, we find that a large number of the traditional activities of the government are of this nature. Further, the rule not only justifies many traditional government activities but indicates that a number of new government activities, such as control of air and water pollution or financing of research, are suitable for government activity. It also calls into question certain activities which the governments have traditionally undertaken. At the moment, for example, it would seem that there is no reason why the government should be interested in the operation of the postal service. It is also by no means obvious that the government should be subsidizing higher education.[4] Thus we have a very simple, relatively obvious, theoretical apparatus which turns out to have very great power to produce normative conclusions about the real world.

But is the theory offered by Paul Samuelson correct? To answer this question we need some empirical test in the real world. Clearly, if the test is to take the form of having, let us say, eight countries in which the postal service is government run and eight in which it is privately run, and if we waited fifty years to observe the results, we

----

4. I trust the reader will excuse me for not giving any detailed derivation of these conclusions from the simple model. This has been done in Tullock, *Private Wants, Public Means* (1970).

would be unable to offer any immediate conclusions. Further, the experiment would be so vastly expensive that we might not feel that the additional information obtained was worth it. It is not necessary in testing a theory, however, to test its every implication. We can deduce from the theory simple and modest conclusions, and then look at the real world and see whether the theory is, in fact, confirmed. The theory of public goods has been tested very largely by this method.

I do not intend to run through a long series of such tests, but I will give an example, one which is out of the realm of traditional political science. It is, however, clearly a test of the theory. One of the intriguing features of the new approach to political science is that it tends to eliminate the traditional boundaries of the field. Using the new approach, we frequently find ourselves dealing with problems which have not been dealt with by traditional political scientists. On the other hand, we may quite frequently also find ourselves unable to deal with problems which have been dealt with by traditional political scientists. Whether this is an advantage or a disadvantage I shall leave to the reader to decide. It is, however, a necessary consequence of the use of the model building technique, since it is, on the whole, unlikely that a newly designed model will have exactly the same boundaries of application as some traditionally defined field of study.

Now to apply this model. At Rice the students have organized a faculty rating system. This faculty rating system, which is voluntary and which distributes its information freely, uses a very simple procedure. A random sample of the students in any given class is sent a questionnaire by a student committee. It is hoped that they will fill out these questionnaires and return them to the committee, and the committee then puts the results of this questionnaire together and publishes a report. Clearly, this report is of great value to students choosing their courses for the next semester. In examining the report, I have been particularly impressed by the superiority of its course descriptions compared to those in the university catalogue. The rating of the professors, of course, is also something in which the students (and the administration) are very much interested.

Note, however, that here we have a public good. Any individual student who contributes by filling out the form or by participating on the committee which integrates the various forms into the final report is performing a service for the other students. If, however, he refrains from either of these activities (let us say, he fails to submit his form), the reduction in the quality of the report is very small. Further, for him personally the reduction is zero because he is presumably not thinking of repeating the course he should report on.

If the benefit to other students were the only motive moving the students, we would predict that none of them would bother to fill out their forms. In practice, of course, most students have other reasons for filling out forms. For example, the "grading" of the professor is, I think, something that they enjoy doing. Nevertheless, the theory of public goods seems to indicate that many students will not bother to fill out the forms. In practice, this is what happens. Less than half of the students who are sent the forms bother to fill them out and return them, even though it is a matter of only a few moments. As a result, the report is necessarily much poorer than it would be if all the students were willing to invest a few minutes every year to filling in the report on their professors. If the form did not give them the opportunity to work off their spleen on the professors (a "private" good), I suspect that the returns would be zero.

This is not quite all, however; the committee that puts the forms together and makes the final report is clearly confronted with a rather large amount of work to produce something which will benefit themselves, in part, but mainly other students. They get some gain themselves, since they tend to be students who are active in university politics, but not a great deal. Under the circumstances, one would predict that they, on the whole, would do a casual job of putting the report together. Anyone reading the report and noting the innumerable errors in grammar and punctuation, and the sentences that don't seem to mean anything, very rapidly realizes that the students are (in fact) behaving in accord with this prediction.

Let us contrast this Rice rating system with another very similar institution. The Texas A & M Department of Economics for a number of years has required graduating seniors who are majors in economics and who have a B grade or better to provide a fairly detailed evaluation of the courses and teachers. This evaluation is used exclusively for the administrative convenience of the Department of Economics and of those professors who care to see what the students think of them. Further, as I have noted, it is filled out by graduating students and hence would be of no direct value for the individual student who fills it out. He will be out of school by the time it is compiled.

Note, however, that in this case the element of coercion is present. The individual fills out this form, not to contribute to a public good, but to obtain a private end, i.e. his degree. We can therefore predict that substantially all students will carry out this requirement, and that is what does happen. The Texas A & M student body is of much lower quality than that at Rice and probably somewhat less motivated to benefit "the public" than the student body at Rice. Further, from the standpoint of the students themselves the positive benefit of producing their questionnaire evaluation is lower at Texas A & M. Nevertheless, the theory of the public good indicates that we will get much better performance at Texas A & M than at Rice, and when we look at the real world we find out that this indeed happens.

Thus we have a very simple model which predicts certain things about the behavior of people in the real world and which fits the real world very neatly. The outcome will surely not surprise anyone, but note that the theory of public goods upon which this conclusion has been based does not make use of any of the tools of classical political analysis. It was, in fact, originally published in economic journals and has been an important part of economics courses, those which deal with taxation, for a number of years. The theory in fact simply argues that certain areas require coercion and recommends it in those areas.

Note that I have done nothing in the way of statistical investigation, but if any of my readers are concerned about this matter I am sure they can carry out the investigation themselves. But note also that although the theory seems to fit the real world, it clearly is not a total description. Some students at Rice do fill in their questionnaires. In fact, enough do so that it is possible to produce these faculty ratings even though the ratings are not anywhere as good as they would be if a higher level of participation was achieved. Further, at Texas A & M a few students escaped filling out the questionnaires for one reason or another. Thus we have a theory which predicts correctly a difference in the behavior of the student under these two situations. It also points to an intuitively appealing explanation, but it is clearly not a full description of their behavior.

We could, I imagine, think of additional little theories which could be used to improve the predictive ability of this one. For example, we might expect that if the university faculty had made a concerted effort to prevent the publication of these faculty ratings and had failed, that the students in the year in which the event had occurred would probably fill out more forms than in other years. This would be much more primitive theory than the theory of public goods, but we would (I think) anticipate that statistical testing would show that it also was true. I am sure that my readers could think of many more conditions which would affect the likelihood of filling out the questionnaires. The existence of these additional conditions, however, does not in any way impair the validity of the public goods model. Like any other theory, it refers only to one aspect of reality. Like any other theory, the real world is more complex than the assumptions the theory provides, and hence we do not anticipate a perfect fit of the predictions of the theory and the real world. Perhaps with several thousand years more of investigation we will obtain theories which have a perfect fit in the real world. Unfortunately, at the moment we have not reached this stage.

Let us, however, turn to a more important example of the new political theory.[5] One of the usual complaints about democracy is that the voters are relatively ignorant of the choices which confront them in political voting. Traditionally, political scientists have argued that the voters should become more informed in order to cast a more sensible ballot. Model builders have approached this belief not by preaching its virtue but by inquiring how much information the voter should acquire, assuming that he is in fact attempting to maximize his return. Put differently, they have taken into account the fact that information is not free, and have engaged in cost-benefit analysis to find out how much information the voter should acquire.

In order to see how this is done, consider Equation (1).

(1) $$x = P_D \times V \times A$$

where x = payoff, P_D = party differential, V = vote effect, and A = accuracy of judgment $(-1 < A < +1)$. This equation shows the payoff to the voter as computed by the voter who has not made any particular effort to acquire any information in order to cast an informed vote. The equation is simple, but perhaps a few words are in order as to the meaning of the concepts. The party differential $[P_D]$ is simply the value which the voter anticipates, both directly to himself and by way of his desire to do good to other people, from the party which he chooses winning. Note that it is not the absolute value of government by, let us say, the Democrats, but what he regards as the difference between the benefit of government by the Democrats or government by the Republicans. Generally speaking, one can think of this figure as the amount that the voter would be willing to give in order to determine the outcome, granted that the determination of government were put up to auction as the Praetorian Guards used to put up the Roman Empire. Strictly, in order to make this operational, we should assume that the market for credit is rather better than it actually is, and that the voter can mortgage his future earnings so that he can take into account future as well as present sources of income in making bids. As we shall see, however, the exact size of this figure is not very important.

The second term $[V]$, the effect of the vote, is simply the *ex ante* likelihood that the individual's vote will make some difference

5. The following sections are based largely on the work of Anthony Downs, *An Economic Theory of Democracy* (1957) as elaborated in my own *Toward A Mathematics of Politics* (1967).

in the election. For an American presidential election, this figure would vary from election to election, depending on the number of people that are expected to vote and the anticipated closeness of the election; but if we assume that it is on the order of 1/10,000,000, we shall not be far wrong. Finally, we have the accuracy of judgment. This is a rather unusual term, but it is necessary if we are to talk about improving information. If I think it is desirable to improve my information about any choice which I am thinking of making, what effect does this have? Obviously, the answer to this question must be that it improves the accuracy of my choice in terms of some ideal standard. Thus, I might now feel that the Democratic party's victory in Virginia in the fall of 1976 is to my advantage. I realize, however, that I know relatively little about Virginia politics and that if I knew a great deal more—if I were perfectly informed, to borrow a term from economics—it is conceivable I might choose to vote Republican. Let us say that I assume that the information I now possess is good enough so that I have a 75 percent chance of being right in my evaluation of the Democratic party. I have chosen to make A vary between -1, for a zero probability of being right, and +1, for a certain probability of being right, so that a 3/4 chance of being right would give A a value of .5. This is rather unusual, but not illegitimate, and makes the equation a little simpler.

This estimate of the accuracy of one's own judgment is, as I said, rather unusual in equations or even to talk about, but it is clear that if we are going to consider improving someone's knowledge, this type of argument is necessary. Improving knowledge does improve the accuracy of the output. Note further that it is possible that improving my knowledge might change my estimate of the size of the party differential. I do not attach any variable to the party differential to indicate this, partly for simplicity but partly for theoretical reasons. The equation has to be considered *ex ante*, that is before I undertake any search for information. At that time, I would assume that increasing information might change the size of my party differential; but if I thought that it was likely to increase the party differential, that would mean that I felt that somehow or other I had the wrong party differential and knew the direction of movement necessary to improve it. This is clearly impossible, because it would mean that my party differential was different than it actually is. Hence, the party differential, although it will be changed by raising the value of A, will change in an unpredictable direction and the anticipations of the outcome of this process discount down to the present party differential.

Let us put a few numbers into our equation. Assume that the amount that I would pay to have my choice succeed to the presidency is \$10,000, which I imagine is higher than most people would in fact be willing to pay. Let us use 1/10,000,000 as V and assume that A is equal to .5, which means that I feel that I am apt to be right three times out of four. The outcome is shown in Equation (2).

(2)   Payoff = \$10,000 × .0000001 × .5
                                = \$ .0005

It will be noted that it is, to put the matter mildly, very small, which is the reason that I said that the value of the party differential is of relatively little importance. If the individual party differential were \$10,000,000, a wildly unlikely figure, this number would be only 50¢.

Let us now consider an individual contemplating improving his information about the campaign. Suppose that he proposes to watch two speeches, one by each of the candidates, on television, and that the result of this is that he will be unable to watch two programs that he normally would prefer. Let us assume that the switch from a program which he enjoys to a political speech will give him less entertainment, and that the value of the two speeches is thus -10¢. That is, if he were presented with the choice of hearing the two speeches or the alternative programs, and was not interested in improving his vote, he would be willing to pay 10¢ for the privilege of watching the programs. Let us further assume that he feels that watching these two programs will improve his ability to decide which party he should favor from 3/4 to 4/5, which is an extremely optimistic estimate of the value of the information to be obtained from two political speeches.

The appropriate equation to determine whether there is a positive or negative payoff for this effort to obtain additional information is shown in Equation (3).

(3) $x_i = (P_{Di} \times V \times A_i) - (P_D \times V \times A) - C_I$

where x_i = payoff with additional information, P_{Di} = party differential with additional information, A_i = accuracy of judgment with additional information $(-1 < A < +1)$, and C_I = cost of information. Equation (4) shows the result with the numbers we have been using.

(4) x_i = (\$10,000 × .0000001 × .6) - .0005 - .10
                  = -.0999

It will be noted that the payoff is negative and hence the individual should not bother to get additional political information.

Before turning to a further discussion of this equation and pointing out certain limitations on it, we should begin by noting that the outcome does indicate that the average man, in ignoring the preaching of his betters, has been behaving quite rationally. Further, it indicates fairly clearly that individuals in advising people to become well informed in order to cast an intelligent vote have been giving bad advice. It is possible that the man giving the advice will himself be benefited by the voters following his advice. After all, most of the people who give this advice are in the business of communicating to the public and can say almost anything they wish at no cost. This is particularly so since they normally not only tell the voter he should become well informed, but also proselytize for their own political position. Granted the low or zero cost which they face in this operation, they may be behaving rationally while their listener is behaving equally rationally in ignoring their advice.

Returning to the implications of the equation itself, clearly, individuals do not use this particular method of making up their minds. The algebra I have been using is so simple that most junior high school students would have no difficulty following it; however, most adult Americans have forgotten what they learned in junior high school. Further, they characteristically devote relatively little conscious thought to making up their minds on such matters. Of course, that is what the equation implicitly advises them to do. It can be said that they have been behaving quite rationally, in terms of the equation, in not bothering to work the equation out. The problem here is similar to that raised in the famous debate in the *American Economic Review* between Fritz Machlup (1946, 1947) and Richard A. Lester (1946, 1947) on the rationality of behavior of human beings in purely economic transactions. (The Machlup-Lester debate has been widely reprinted; for example, in Clemence, 1950, Vol. 2, pp. 104- 79.) As Machlup pointed out, the average person, in deciding whether or not to pass another car on a two-lane highway, probably does not engage in the elaborate mathematical calculations which an engineer would use to determine whether there was enough space (Machlup, 1946, pp. 534- 35). On the other hand, his behavior in most cases is very closely approximated by these equations. It seems likely, therefore, that some kind of mental process similar to the engineer's equation is involved, although probably it has been gone through a few times and has become routine. In many cases, the man who is learning to pass another car never makes the calculations himself at all; he simply accepts his instructor's estimate of distances and, over time, learns to use the same estimates himself.

A similar situation exists in the equations given here. It would be ridiculous to assume that individuals engage in this type of direct calculation by consciously using algebra. It is also probable, however, that in a less precise way they *do* make these calculations, and do decide to watch "All in the Family" instead of Jimmy Carter on television.

It should not be deduced from this that the electorate is totally ignorant. In the first place, there are a good many people who get a certain amount of entertainment out of active participation in politics or at least out of following politics. Unfortunately, these people seem to be much like the baseball fan. They back one party, and when they pick up additional information, this is as unlikely to change their vote as is information to switch a Cub fan to backing St. Louis.

There are other people, however, who gain a good deal of knowledge about politics as a sort of by-product of other activities. If you listen to the evening news broadcasts at all (and they completely block the networks at certain times) you will pick up some political information. Further, if you read newspapers solely for the sports section, you will nevertheless see front page headlines when you buy the paper, and you will thus will get some political information. The political managers themselves are, of course, fully aware of the fact that many voters know very little about politics, and do a good deal of advertising which is intended to appeal to what we may call the "impulse voter." Highway signs, doorbell-ringing campaigns, commercial spots on television, etc., are mainly aimed at the relatively ill-informed voter who, it is thought, may be quite readily influenced. It should be pointed out that the empirical evidence does indicate that the better your information in politics, the less likely you are to change from one party to another.[6]

What we would deduce from all of this is simply that we must accept it as a fact that the voter will be relatively badly informed under present circumstances. Can we do anything about this? This question has been answered in the affirmative many times. The idea that the voter must be educated is one of the standard justifications for free education in the United States. Further, it was one of the reasons why the founding fathers arranged to subsidize the transmission of printed matter by mail. Returning to the early part of this

6. There is a limitation on this. Those people who tell investigators that they have received *no* political information at all in the last year or so are apt to stick with the party which they had voted for before. Apparently the optimal target for electoral propaganda is a man who has very little information about politics, is not much interested in it, and who is thus likely to be swayed by some relatively minor bit of propaganda like a television commercial or a billboard. Those who are seriously interested in politics and whose information level is such that only a full-dress speech would significantly affect them, are much less easily swayed by political propaganda. Since this type of propaganda is also much more expensive, the tendency of the campaign managers to put very heavy emphasis on the short spot, the highway billboard, and door-to-door solicitation is understandable.

essay, the argument is a public good argument. It is believed that, although it is not very rational for me to become well informed, I nevertheless may be injured if everyone else is also ill informed; hence, it is desirable from my standpoint to agree with other persons to coerce ourselves to become more informed.

There are two problems with this traditional argument; the first is that it is not obvious that improving voter information would benefit us particularly. There is now a great deal of empirical evidence indicating that majority voting in a democracy tends to lead to an outcome which is close to the preferences of the "dead center" voter. There is no reason to believe that improving voter information would change this. In fact, it should strengthen the tendency to move toward the dead center voter because the voters will know more accurately what the politicians are proposing to do. If, then, the outcome of improving voter information is simply that the voting outcomes are closer to the dead center of the voting mass (in other words, that the random variance is lower), it is not clear that this should be regarded as any great advance. It can be demonstrated that it would reduce the average level of dissatisfaction of the voters, but, granted the fact that the improved information changes the shape of their subjectively perceived preference map, it is not clear that this is a net advantage either.

The argument for improving information, then, must be that it would change in an efficient direction the things that voters wanted. It would not be that the Republicans would not continue to try to get to the dead center of political positions, but that, with improved information on the part of the voters, these dead center opinions would be "better" than thcy are now. Let me use an economic analogy. Suppose that we gave all people in the United States compulsory courses in automobile engineering. This would probably not greatly change their choices among Fords, Chevrolets, Plymouths, etc. It is likely, however, that over time the designers of these cars, selling them to much more expert purchasers, would begin putting into the cars advantages which are not observable to the present ignorant automobile owner, but would be observable to a specially trained man. One could regard this as an improvement in efficiency.

The result of educating voters might have a somewhat similar effect. On the other hand, it might not. It is, in any event, not clear that this is a desirable use of public resources. It should be noted that, in terms of political practicality, only the slightest improvement in information of all the voters is likely to be acceptable to the voters now, and hence is likely to be politically possible. This may be unfortunate, but we must accept it as true. It is arguable that requiring every person who is eligible to vote to take a fairly stiff examination on the political situation in the country,[7] and then fining him $50 if he flunked, would improve the efficiency of our democracy. It is wildly unlikely that the voters would accept this proposal in their present state of ignorance. What they might accept would be the use of some minor government funds to sponsor special political programs on the public television network. They would not be compelled to watch it, and the tax cost of the programs would be very tiny.

I have observed, in talking to people about the improvement of voter information, that almost everyone feels improving information would move the outcome closer to his own preferences. There is, in fact, no reason to believe this is so. You, the reader of this book, might find that you gain by improved voter education, or you might find that with improved voter education you are in a much less desirable position. To take but one example, I think in general most voters are under the impression that a state government actually cannot do very much in the way of "disciplining" a state university. They tend to feel that it is really impossible for a state government to get a university to teach the kind of things that the citizens want, prevent certain types of "undesirable" political activity on campus, etc. This is, of course, untrue. A state legislature has a perfect right to refuse to appropriate any money for a university or to put almost any condition it wishes on these appropriations. Most academics are strongly opposed to the type of voter education which would indicate the actual powers which politicians and the voters have over universities. They prefer that the voters remain in ignorance in this area.

The actual gains from improving voter education would be rather like those from improving the information a man has about automobiles. In both cases, it would lead the designers of either the automobiles or the platform to make available a superior selection of alternatives which they place before the customer-voter because they feel that his information is higher. Efficiency gains are possible in the sense that we may now not be taking advantage of alternatives which we would choose if they were placed before us. These will not be placed before us until our information is greater. It is, however, by no means sure that this is so; it should be kept firmly in mind that the improved efficiency might mean an improvement in the degree of satisfaction of the average man, and a reduction in the degree of satisfaction of the average intellectual. Intellectuals, after all, are a minority and their preferences do not and should not count for very

7. Who would draft the examination is of course a problem.

much in determining whether a given decision is optimal or not. Thus, even if it could be, strictly speaking, demonstrated that improvements in the performance of our government could be obtained by improved information, it is by no means certain that the preference functions of intellectuals would be "maximized" by this change.

But this difficult question, one which I think has been canvassed relatively little in traditional political science, is one which I cannot answer here. Indeed, the point of this essay has not been to answer questions or to solve the great classic problems of political science, but to give a short introduction to a new approach to the problems of political science. This new introduction starts with a radically different set of tools, asks somewhat different questions, and comes up with answers which, in many cases, are again radically different. In a very real sense, it is revolutionary. Revolutions, of course, are not always desirable. It may be that a rational man would be a counterrevolutionary in this particular uprising. Still, one thing that can be said for revolutions is that they are exciting, regardless of which side you are on, and it would seem sensible for political scientists to familiarize themselves with this one. They may want to join the revolutionaries or the forces of suppression, but, in any event, they won't be bored.

12. SOME PRINCIPLES AND TECHNIQUES OF SCALE CONSTRUCTION

S. Dale McLemore and Charles M. Bonjean

MEASUREMENT AND THE SOCIAL SCIENCES

Kant's dictum (Smith, 1958, p. 93) that "thoughts without content are empty; intuitions without concepts are blind" appears to have gained general acceptance both within and across several social science disciplines. Numerous writers, representing both rationalistic and empiricistic emphases, have commented upon the mutual dependence of theory and research, of concepts and operations. Parsons (1961a, p. 32), for example, in a discussion of areas of consensus within sociology states that

> probably the greatest consensus exists regarding the applicability to our discipline of the general canons of the scientific method . . . .
> This agreement clearly includes the role of theory in science . . . . Despite differences of emphasis . . . the old battle of theory *versus* empiricism may be considered to be over.

Some would argue however, as has Merton (1957, p. 85), that "this very unanimity suggests that [such] remarks are platitudinous"; and in fact, this verbal rapprochement does encompass broad differences in scholarly styles. Many students of politics work mainly on problems of a high order of abstraction where measurement is frequently difficult, indirect and intuitive (see, for example, Lipset, 1959, pp. 69-105), while others work "close to the data" where elaborate and precise measurement procedures may be highlighted (see, for example, MacRae, 1958).[1] Nevertheless, the acceptance in principle of the interdependence of conceptual and operational procedures represents

---

1. A useful analysis of some implications of such differences of style is given by H. D. Price (1963, pp. 704-43).

a significant intellectual advance in that one is no longer obligated to defend either side of numerous false dichotomies.[2] One may, for instance, agree with Thorndike's proposition (Guilford, 1936, p. 3) that "whatever exists at all, exists in some amount" (and is therefore measurable), without necessarily subscribing to naive, "raw," or atheoretical empiricsim: "Generalizations can be tempered, if not with mercy, at least with disciplined observation; close, detailed observations need not be rendered trivial by avoidance of their theoretical pertinence and implications" (Merton, 1957, p. 85).

On the basis of such reasoning, it is assumed for the purposes of this discussion that the rules of scientific method are applicable to an understanding of human social behavior and that "the development of a theoretical science . . . would seem to be virtually impossible unless its variables can be measured adequately" (Torgerson, 1958, p. 2). This view implies at a minimum that at least *some* of the concepts which enter into the propositions of theories must *at some point*— either directly or indirectly—be related to reality through rules of correspondence or operational definitions (Gibbs, 1967, p. 75; Torgerson, 1958, pp. 4–5). It should be noted that this statement recognizes the existence, and the importance for theory, of some concepts which may be intrinsically immeasurable. Also for the purposes of this discussion, measurement is taken to be "the use not only of a metric, but also of ordinal position and even of mere enumeration" (Stouffer et al., 1953, p. 591).

The issues involved in measurement and hence the decisions an investigator must make are many.[3] In spite of the increasingly empirical nature of the social sciences and the growing body of literature on research methods, "we will find the measurement process as anything but an easy task, because none of our tools have the precision or the fool-proof character we want" (Stouffer et al., 1953, p. 594). Our goal in this chapter, given the limitation of space, is simply to indicate something of the range of problems and choices which social scientists have addressed in relation to the topic of this chapter. We acknowledge in advance that our presentation treats some of these crucial issues only superficially and, in some respects, skirts or entirely ignores others. The reader is advised here as he will be later in our presentation to make extensive use of the references cited in the bibliography at the end of this volume.

2. For a vigorous rationalistic critique of empiricism in political research, see Storing (1962).

3. Particularly relevant discussions of several of these issues are in Alker, 1965, pp. 13–28 and Torgerson, 1958, pp. 13–40.

SCALE CONSTRUCTION IN POLITICAL RESEARCH

Scaling methods are appropriate when a researcher wishes to order certain units—individuals, states, nations, countries, or any other relevant unit—in terms of some characteristic(s) or variable(s) either as an end in itself or as a step toward further analysis. The different types of scales commonly used in political research appear to vary according to the types of research problems, the types of data gathered, and the units selected for analysis. As an illustration, consider some pertinent problems which may be encountered in the effort to construct a device to be used in a sample survey to measure the political conservatism or liberalism of individuals who participate in a series of interviews. Assume that the many important problems concerning the aim of the study, the selection of the sample, the training of the interviewers, the design of the interview schedule, and so forth, have been solved satisfactorily, or for some other reason are not of immediate concern.

Under these circumstances, how are responses which are related to political liberalism or conservatism to be elicited from the interviewee? Should he simply be asked how liberal or conservative he considers himself to be? Or should the matter be approached less directly or in greater detail? That the question format may influence the response distributions has long been known in the social sciences (see, for example, Centers, 1949). The respondent's answer might be structured somewhat by presenting him with a card on which appear several labeled categories ranging from "very liberal" to "very conservative" and asking him to place himself within one of these categories. He might be asked instead a series of questions concerning his voting behavior or his preference for certain candidates or policies and then, on the basis of his answers, be assigned to one of the same categories which could have appeared on a card. Any number of possibilities may occur to the investigator; but these are all likely to be representative of one of two broad kinds of scales: *rating scales* and *attitude scales.*[4] When the rating scale is utilized, "someone makes a judgment about some characteristic of an individual and places him directly on a scale defined in terms of that characteristic" (Selltiz et al., 1959, p. 344). The "someone" making the judgment may be the respondent, the interviewer, or a third party; and the rating scale may be described in words or it may be graphic. When, instead, an attitude scale is utilized, the instrument is "constructed in such a way that the score of the individual's responses places him on

4. Some alternative modes of classification in this field are discussed in Schmid (1966, pp. 349–50) and in Torgerson (1958, pp. 41–60). Our classification and discussion are indebted heavily to Selltiz et al. (1959, pp. 344–84).

the scale" (Selltiz et al., 1959, p. 344). The questions may be constructed and the scores may be calculated in a number of ways. The items comprising the instrument may be written by the researcher for his own specific purposes, or they may be taken from the existing literature, or both.[5]

The most prominent types of attitude scales are Thurstone, Likert, and Guttman. Other well-known techniques associated with scaling are factor analysis, the Q-sort, the semantic differential, and latent structure analysis.[6] Most of these techniques are responses to certain methodological problems which have arisen from researchers' experiences with rating scales; thus, rating scales provide a convenient point of departure for an understanding of some aspects of the problems of validity, reliability, and levels or precision of measurement.

RATING SCALES

Rating scales of different types are frequently utilized in public opinion polling and other forms of survey research. They provide the researcher with a rapid and easily interpretable method for gathering information on a relatively large number of variables. Generally the researcher constructs a rating scale with reference to at least the following considerations: (1) Is the scale to be graphic or verbal? (2) Is the respondent to rate himself or is he to be rated by the interviewer? (3) Is the rating to be made in comparison to a specific group, or is the basis of comparison to be "global" or unspecified? The graphic technique has been very popular and has been well analyzed (see Guilford, 1936, pp. 263-84). Typically, the graphic scale consists of an unbroken line which contains several numbered, equidistant segments and some brief descriptions. The line indicates the variable in question, and the descriptions along the line are intended to denote the degree and/or intensity of individual differences with respect to that variable. The number of distinct scale points and the number of descriptions which are placed along the scale will vary with the research problem, the preferences of the investigator and the degree to which raters can reliably distinguish

5. Some efforts to systematize the existing literature are Bonjean, Hill, and McLemore (1967); Miller (1964, 1970a); Robinson, Rusk, and Head (1968); and Shaw and Wright (1967). See also Maranell (1974).

6. The logic of some types of scale analysis may be generalized to variables other than attitudes and therefore these techniques are frequently used by political scientists for the development of nonattitude scales.

the various scale positions. If, on the basis of an interview, one wished to determine the degree of a respondent's interest in foreign aid, for example, the interviewer might be instructed to ask several questions concerning certain aspects of foreign aid and then to mark a position on the graphic rating scale shown as Figure 1. The simplicity and flexibility of such a device is fairly apparent. But in this example, the interviewer was the rater and no basis for comparison was specified. Instead, the respondent could be asked to rate the degree of his interest in foreign aid and some specific group could be designated as the basis for comparison. A major advantage of the graphic rating scale is that it leads directly to the assignment for each respondent of an "interest in foreign aid" (or some other) score which may reflect with some precision the continuous character of the underlying variable.

The verbal rating scale is an alternative technique for defining a continuum and locating the scale points. To pursue the foreign aid example a bit further, suppose that the respondent has been asked to say whether a particular appropriation should be voted by Congress, and that the interviewer has been asked to rate the respondent's answer in terms of a five-point scale. The points on the scale may be labeled as "expresses complete and unqualified agreement" through "expresses complete and unqualified disagreement." Additionally, each scale-point label may be accompanied by a brief or detailed description of the kinds of expressions of opinion which would identify the appropriate point along the continuum for a given respondent. One advantage of this technique is that it is suitable for the rating of the answers given to open-ended questions. In this case, several judges who have been trained specifically for the purpose may determine independently the appropriate scale score for the respondent.

With this brief discussion of rating scales as a foundation, let us turn now to a cursory review of some of the most important and persistent issues to be found in the field of the measurement of attitudes and behavior.

F I G U R E 1. Rating Scale of Interest in Foreign Aid

INTEREST IN FOREIGN AID
(Put a check mark at the point on the line which best describes
the degree of the respondent's interest in foreign aid)

SOME METHODOLOGICAL ISSUES

Validity

The basic issue facing any researcher is that of *validity*—whether an instrument measures what it purports to measure. The major difficulty in assessing validity is created, of course, by the necessity of having an external or independent criterion against which to evaluate a given instrument. For example, if individual A has been rated on the scale presented above as being "extremely interested" in the matter of foreign aid, how can one be sure that this designation is correct? On the assumption that the respondent's show of interest was indeed extreme, it is nonetheless possible that the variable being measured was not just an interest in foreign aid but was rather a general interest in foreign affairs, or an interest in all political matters, or a general interest in financial transactions. When an investigator attempts to establish the validity of a scale by referring to an external standard of evaluation, then the status of *that* standard may be questioned; and if one possessed an unimpeachable external standard he would, in most instances, utilize it in preference to some derivative.

In spite of this problem, there are several reasonable, if less than perfect, approaches to the validation of measures of attitudes and behavior. Although there is considerable variation in the names which different authors assign to these approaches, as well as in the number of subtypes distinguished, the principal types are (1) face validity, (2) predictive validity, and (3) construct validity.

The effort to demonstrate that a measuring device is "on the face of it" or "manifestly" valid is related to the effort to establish that certain truths are "self-evident" or that a mathematical or logical relation holds "by inspection." As suggested above, there is little about the "interest in foreign aid" illustration which logically compels one to accept its validity. A strong case for face validity usually is easier to construct when behavioral rather than attitudinal variables are under examination. For instance, if political participation were to be measured by noting the frequency with which an individual votes, attends precinct meetings, campaigns for a candidate, or runs for public office, the "manifest" relevance of the measures to the variable in question might seem defensible. It could be argued, however, that apparent differences among individuals with respect to political participation are due to some other difference which happens to be correlated with the behavioral measures selected. As Goode and Hatt (1952, p. 237) have noted, "it is not wise to rely on logical and common-sense validations alone. Such claims for validity can at best be merely plausible and never definitive."

Predictive validity, sometimes termed pragmatic validity, involves the prediction of a specified behavior or set of behaviors from a knowledge of an individual's scale position. One might, for example, expect that an individual who was rated as "extremely interested" in foreign aid would read many newspaper and magazine articles on that subject, frequently discuss the matter with friends, write his congressman letters, and engage in similar behavior. None of these criteria is infallible, to be sure, and problems arise if the scale is more effective as a predictor of one criterion than of others. Still, the successful prediction of several ostensibly relevant performances may increase the researcher's confidence that his scaling device reflects the intended variable and is therefore valid to some degree.

Construct validity is less direct and more difficult to describe succinctly than the two preceding types. Many of the variables of interest to political scientists (for example, liberalism-conservatism, self vs. collective orientation, faith in public officials, political efficacy and many other variables) are not simple ideational reflections of observable phenomena; they are complex mental constructs based upon, but abstracted from, reality. These abstractions, moreover, are generally made in relation to some underlying theory or set of theoretical propositions and they may be defined either partially or completely in terms of other constructs in the theory, rather than in terms of directly observed phenomena. Hence, many of the most interesting and theoretically powerful constructs (those which are presumed to "explain" or "account for" empirical relationships) may not have a manifest connection with a particular scaling device or may not be invalidated by a weak relationship to a single event or behavior. When a construct is utilized in a set of interrelated hypotheses, a number of predictions arise; and some of the predictions may be confirmed by weak or moderate relationships as well as by strong ones. Under these conditions, the internal consistency of the outcomes of a variety of expectations lends support *both* to the validity of the measurements of the construct in question and to the set of hypotheses within which the construct is embedded. The failure of any one of the predictions, in like manner, calls into question both the validity of the measurement and the hypothesis upon which the prediction is based. Such a failure requires that the analyst give further attention to theory construction as well as to measurement procedure. Through this process of testing and refinement, support may gradually accumulate in favor of both the technical and theoretical validity of a construct. A more detailed explication of construct validity (as well as other types) may be found in Cronbach and Meehl

(1955, pp. 281-312) and a publication of the American Psychological Association (1954, pp. 13-28).

No matter how much care is exercised in the development of a valid instrument for the measurement of human behavior or attitudes, it is likely that the scores gathered through its application will still be affected to some extent by factors other than the one the investigator intends to study. For example, if it is noted that two respondents are "quite interested" in foreign aid, the identity of their scale positions could reflect a genuine agreement between them on this subject; however, this identity also may arise because one of the respondents truly is "quite interested" while the other believes that appearing to be "quite interested" is likely to win him the approval of the rater (see, for example, Edwards, 1953). Had "interest in foreign aid" been measured instead by asking respondents to agree or disagree with a series of statements, some of the agreement among them might be due to differential tendencies to show agreement or disagreement in general, rather than to their true interest in the topic of immediate concern (see, for example, Couch and Keniston, 1960). Difficulties of this sort give rise to systematic errors in measurement—errors which if undetected or uncontrolled, reduce the degree of validity of the measurement instrument.

Reliability

In addition to the possibility that systematic errors may be present in the assignment of individuals to scale positions, there are several well-known sources of variable error. An individual's scale position may appear to have changed from one point in time to another even when it actually has not and when the ratings were not appreciably affected by systematic errors in the measuring instrument. Variations in the respondents' vigor, health, mood, motivation, and so on may affect their scale scores. The extent to which an instrument produces consistent measurements because it is unaffected by sources of variable error is described as its reliability. It should be clear that if a scale were satisfactorily established as being valid, then it also would be sufficiently reliable; however, perfect predictive validity and/or the complete satisfaction of the requirements of construct validity are seldom achieved in practice. Therefore, in addition to the variations due to true differences among the objects under study and to systematic errors, variations in measurements due to the unreliability of the instrument usually are present. Since the total amount of variation is due to all of these factors, it follows that the investigator must interest himself in the reliability of a scale as a necessary condition to the assessment of its validity.[7]

A scale for determining a respondent's "interest in foreign aid" which showed him to be "extremely interested" one day and, as a result of temporary fatigue, to be "not at all interested" one week later, would be of little use to the political researcher. The various methods which have been developed for the estimation of reliability are too numerous and detailed to be described here; however, whether the method is based upon comparisons of scores gathered with a given instrument at different points in time (test-retest) or on comparisons of scores gathered on presumably equivalent instruments at a particular point in time (alternate forms or split-halves), the analyst's underlying strategy is to make plausible inferences concerning the probable sources of variations in the scale scores he observes. This rationale and the operations associated with it are discussed in a number of standard sources including Guilford (1956, pp. 435- 60) and Gulliksen (1950, pp. 193- 229).

Levels of Measurement

Before returning to a discussion of specific scaling techniques, some consideration of one final methodological issue is essential. This involves the meaning of scale scores once they have been assigned. The meaning of a scale score is defined in part by the extent to which the researcher may infer from it the respondent's position in relation to all aspects of the variable being measured. A scale score's meaning also is dependent upon the level of measurement involved.

The process of distinguishing qualitatively among certain individuals, objects, or events, and noting the frequencies in the resulting categories, is considered by most methodologists to yield the lowest level of measurement.[8] Some scholars (for example, McGregor, 1935) would insist that the process of naming or labeling (for example, categorizing individuals as Democrats, Republicans, Independents, or Other) is qualitative in nature and does not constitute measurement. Most, however, would consider the set of categories and frequencies as a nominal scale.[9] Such scales involve merely the

7. An interesting exception to this rule may occur if the "scale" approximates a battery of single-item scales. For a discussion of this point, see Selltiz et al. (1959, pp. 178–79).

8. The following discussion has been influenced strongly by Selltiz et al. (1959) and Torgerson (1958).

9. The term "scale" is used in the literature to stand for both the levels of measurement (as in this portion of the discussion) as well as for various *types* of measuring instruments. A definition of "scale" in the second sense will be offered below.

determination of *"equivalence* or *nonequivalence,* with respect to the attribute in question, between the given object and other objects placed in a given category" (Selltiz et al., 1959, p. 190); and while numbers may be assigned to represent the categories thus derived, no mathematical relations exist between them. One may count the number of objects placed in each category, or compute the mode, or establish the existence or strength of an association between the types of one characteristic (for example, party affiliation) and the types of another characteristic (for example, religious affiliation), but the basic operations of arithmetic do not apply. Because it is frequently desirable to make distinctions of degree rather than of kind, the nominal scale is of limited usefulness. Higher orders of measurement are necessary for the assessment of questions relating to "more" or "less."

The ordinal level of measurement, as the term suggests, is achieved when the researcher can rank the individuals, objects, or events under investigation in terms of a particular variable. Such ranking procedures are quite common, are very useful, and involve very few assumptions. If the researcher has established, with due regard to questions of validity and reliability, that individual A is politically more conservative than individual B who, in turn, is more conservative than individual C, and so forth, then he has devised at least an ordinal-level measurement procedure. This level of measurement involves no assumption that the magnitude of the difference in political conservatism which exists between individuals can be specified; thus, a scale score of 30 is larger than, but not necessarily twice as large as, a score of 15. For this reason it is sometimes said that measurement at the ordinal level provides the investigator with a "rubber yardstick." Nevertheless, the utility of devices which permit the ordering of data is well established in all branches of science.

The interval level of measurement, by contrast, *does* involve the assumption that the units of measurement represent equal distances along a continuum; however, no assumption is made concerning a zero point. Because interval scales in the social sciences are rare, this level of measurement will be illustrated with the Fahrenheit thermometer. The unit of measurement, the degree, represents a fixed distance through which the column of mercury contained in the thermometer moves; but the zero point is arbitrary. Consequently, one may state that a *change* of ten degrees is twice as great as a *change* of five degrees, but one may *not* state that a temperature of forty degrees is twice that of twenty degrees.

The ratio scale, an interval scale containing an absolute, rather than an arbitrary, zero point, provides the highest level of measurement. Examples of ratio scales in the social sciences presently are restricted to variables such as age, income, units of production,

number of votes, days absent from work, and other such nonattitu-
dinal phenomena.[10]

Each level of measurement "involves a possible gain and a possible loss" to the researcher (Phillips, 1966, p. 168). When the lower
order (nominal and ordinal) levels of measurement are used, precision is lacking; however, as the higher orders of measurement are
utilized, the investigators' assumptions increase in number and strin-
gency. Hence the "price" one must pay for increased precision is an
increase in the number of assumptions which must be made and
justified; conversely, if one operates only on the basis of assumptions
which are easily met, the most powerful tools of statistical analysis
may be inapplicable.

One of the most important controversies in the measurement
literature concerns the behavioral scientist's ability to operate at the
interval level. Few would argue that the ratio level is usually achieved
with existing techniques or, conversely, that we are restricted to the
nominal level; rather, the debate centers on whether social scientists
are restricted to those methods which are pertinent to ordered
data—the so-called nonparametric methods—or whether one is justified in assuming that he has established equal intervals along a
continuum and may therefore apply the more powerful parametric
methods.

That the simple rating scale discussed earlier is especially vulnerable in regard to problems of validity and reliability and that it
provides only a low level of measurement should be obvious to the
reader. The approaches to scaling discussed below may be viewed as
efforts to solve these problems. (See also Blalock, 1974.)

THURSTONE SCALING

Basic Considerations

Thurstone's methods of scaling have been developed with particular reference to the measurement of social attitudes.[11] The basic
intention has been to create valid and precise tools for the measure-

10. A possible exception involves the recent application of magnitude
estimation to social science phenomena. This technique, originally used by
psychophysicists in the 1930s, measures the perceived magnitudes of "real"
variables in a manner that "seemingly" produces genuine ratio-level data. The
method is described by Stevens (1966), Hamblin et al. (1974), and Shinn
(1970). Its application in the development of a measure of political dissatisfaction can be found in Welch (1971).

11. The following discussion is heavily indebted to Edwards (1957).

ment of attitudes through the application of psychophysical scaling methods (Thurstone and Chave, 1929, pp. 1- 21). Instead of permitting the interviewer, respondent, or some other person(s) to determine a subject's score on a rating scale, the researcher's effort is directed toward the construction of a series of standardized items or statements which differentiate as exactly as possible the degree of an individual's favorable or unfavorable feelings toward an attitude object.[12] In this manner, the task of creating valid and precise rating scales discussed above is in effect subdivided into more manageable, if more tedious, elements.

Thurstone has developed three principal methods of selecting, arranging, and scoring attitude scale items: (1) the method of paired comparisons (see Edwards, 1957, pp. 19- 82; Thurstone, 1927a, 1927b, 1959, pp. 39- 49, 67- 81); (2) the method of equal-appearing intervals (discussed below), and (3) the method of successive intervals (see Edwards, 1957, pp. 120- 48). Each of these methods involves the use of a group of "judges," and in each case the judges are asked to determine the degree to which various statements are favorable or unfavorable toward an attitude object; but the techniques for eliciting the judgments vary as do some of the problems which the researcher must face.

No matter which technique is used, it is assumed that items pertaining to a given attitude object (e.g., war, Congress, a legislative bill) can be secured, and can be judged as denoting various degrees of favor or disfavor (or perhaps neutrality) toward the specified object. Other items, however, will be ambiguous and will attract a wide range of judgments, being labeled by some as favorable, and unfavorable by others. Still other items will not seem to the judges to be pertinent to the attitude object and thus will be discarded as irrelevant. In this manner, an original sample of items is reduced to an ordered subset of valent, unambiguous, and relevant items which are taken to represent various locations along a continuum of attitudes toward a given object. It should be emphasized that the judges are not instructed to report whether *they* are favorable or unfavorable toward the object in question; rather, they are asked to determine the extent to which various statements denote such differences in attitude. Thus, the focus is upon the degree of sentiment associated with each item, *not* upon the attitudes of the judges. No matter which Thurstone technique is utilized, the selected subset of items is then assumed to represent the range of sentiments which one might express in relation to the attitude object. Once the attitude scale has been constructed, the researcher is able to locate a given respondent

12. Two discussions of the status of the concept of attitude are DeFleur and Westie (1963) and Scott (1968).

in relation to the several points along the scale by asking him whether he agrees or disagrees with the scale items. Presumably, the respondent is most likely to endorse those items which correspond in direction and degree to his own attitudes toward the object under study.

The Method of Equal-appearing Intervals

The basic feature of this method of Thurstone scaling involves presenting judges with a relatively large number of statements, each typed on a separate card, and asking them to sort the cards along an eleven-interval continuum representing equal steps throughout the range of affect toward a given attitude object. Judges frequently are able to assess hundreds of items in this manner in a relatively short period of time.

This method has been used by Droba (1931, pp. 96–111) in the construction of a militarism-pacifism scale. Droba began by collecting 237 statements expressing varying degrees of militarism-pacifism from the literature on war and peace and from written opinions of 120 students. ne hundred and seven of the statements were discarded by inspection as being too long, too ambiguous, or irrelevant. The remaining 130 statements were evaluated by 300 judges, all of whom were students at the University of Chicago.

Each student judge was given an envelope containing, in part, the instructions, the statements typed on separate cards, and eleven index slips numbered in roman numerals from I to XI. Each judge was asked

> to put on slip I those statements which he believed express the most extremely militaristic opinions. On slip XI he was requested to put those statements which he believed express the most extremely pacifistic opinions, and on slip VI to put those which he thought express neutral opinions. On the rest of the slips he was instructed to arrange the statements in accordance with the degree of militarism and pacifism expressed in them [Droba, 1931, p. 98].

After the judgment had been completed, a count was made of the frequency with which each statement had been placed in each of the eleven intervals. This is shown in Table 1 for the two statements which became items 11 and 28 in the final form of the scale. It can be seen that item 28 appeared to most judges to express a very militaristic point of view. No judge thought the statement expressed any degree of pacifism, and only one judge thought it could be regarded as neutral. There is less agreement in regard to item 11,

TABLE 1. Judges' Ratings of Two Militarism-Pacifism Items: Frequencies (f) and Cumulative Percentages (cp)

Item No.	Item		I	II	III	IV	V	Interval VI	VII	VIII	IX	X	XI
28.	There is no progress without war.	f	194	67	21	13	4	1	0	0	0	0	0
		cp	65	87	94	98	99	100	100	100	100	100	100
11.	The evils of war are slightly greater than its benefits.	f	2	3	7	13	28	20	180	33	9	5	0
		cp	1	2	4	8	17	24	84	95	98	100	100

Source: Data drawn from D.D. Droba, "A Scale of Militarism-Pacifism," *Journal of Educational Psychology* 22 (February 1931): 96–111.

which was placed most frequently within interval VII, adjacent to the neutral interval (VI) and on the pacifist side of the continuum. Only one interval, XI, was not utilized by any judge; and two of the judges felt that this item was very militaristic. It should be clear that both aspects of the distribution—its central tendency and dispersion—are pertinent to an evaluation of a statement's utility as a research instrument. Some measure of central tendency, usually the median, is taken as the *scale value* (S) for each statement; and some measure of dispersion, usually the interquartile range (Q) is taken as an estimate of *ambiguity*. The less agreement there is about a statement, the more ambiguous it is presumed to be and the larger will be the interquartile range (which contains the central 50 percent of the judgments). These values may be determined graphically or they may be calculated.[13] The graphic method was selected by

F I G U R E 2. Judges' Evaluations of Item 11

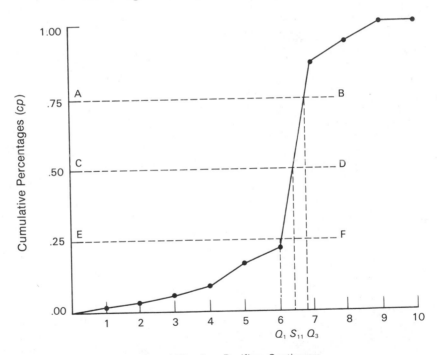

Source: Data drawn from D. D. Droba, "A Scale of Militarism-Pacifism," *Journal of Educational Psychology* 22 (February 1931), 96–111.

13. The necessary computational procedures are described in several well-known texts. See, for example, Blalock (1960, pp. 55–57).

Droba (1931) and is illustrated for item 11 in Figure 2. The median may be found on the graph by dropping a perpendicular from the intersection of the curve and a horizontal drawn at cp = .50 (line CD). The value of the point S_{11} at which the perpendicular touches the baseline is the scale value for the statement. The Q value, which is the distance between cp = .25 and cp = .75, is obtained in a smiliar manner. Horizontal lines are drawn at cp = .75 (line AB), and at cp = .25 (line EF). Perpendiculars are dropped from the two points of intersection with the curve, and the Q value is read directly on the baseline as the difference between Q_1 and Q_3. In the present examples, S = 6.4 and Q = 6.0 - 6.8 = 0.8.[14] With these procedures, the researcher may select a number of items, preferably twenty or more, having scale values which are spread fairly evenly throughout the full range of the attitude continuum under study; and he can select among those items which have similar scale values the least ambiguous ones as revealed by the Q values. Droba, for example, discovered forty-four items from which he constructed two "matched" or roughly equivalent forms of the militarism-pacifism scale.[15] Some of the matched items, representing several points along the continuum, are presented in Table 2 in order of decreasing militarism. An inspection of the table reveals that items 9 and 28 have very similar scale values which lie near the theoretical extreme militarism value of .00, while items 8 and 35 have identical scale values and lie near the theoretical extreme for pacifism.

Once the scale items have been selected, they may be presented— in a random order and without their assigned values—to the respondents in a study. These respondents are asked to place check marks or plus signs by those statements with which they agree. Sometimes respondents are asked additionally to place minus signs by the statements with which they disagree and thus to "vote" for each statement. An individual's score is calculated as the mean or the median of the scale values of the items with which he agrees. For example, if an individual agrees with items 12, 13, 6, and 14 of Form 1 of Droba's (1931) scale, the researcher may calculate the mean of their respective scale values of 3.6, 4.2, 5.2, and 6.0 and assign a score of 4.75 to that individual.[16]

14. For a discussion of some rapid and accurate graphic scoring procedures see Edwards (1957, pp. 91-2).

15. The measure of ambiguity used by Droba (1931, p. 103) was the semi-interquartile range.

16. Droba (1931) devised an "equivalent numbers" technique for scoring the militarism-pacifism scale. He arrayed the items in each form of the scale from most to least militarism (0 signified the most militaristic item in each form). The attitude score was calculated as the sum of the equivalent scores of the items which received plus marks.

TABLE 2.   Selected Matched Items from Droba's Scale of Militarism-Pacifism

	Form 1			Form 2	
Item No.	Scale Value	Item	Item No.	Scale Value	Item
9	0.5	Might is right.	28	0.6	There is no progress without war.
1	3.0	Multitudes are benefited by learning the lesson of wartime discipline.	31	2.9	We cannot hope to do away with war, because it is part of the unending struggle for survival in a crowded world.
10	5.6	The most that we can hope to accomplish is the partial elimination of war.	34	5.6	The most frequent cause of war is the rivalry of nations for possession of territory, markets, concessions, and spheres of influence.
21	8.4	Under the scourge of war a nation has no opportunity for cultural development.	29	8.4	Militarism should be abolished from the curriculum of state schools.
8	10.7	It is the moral duty of the individual to refuse to participate in any way in any war, no matter what the cause.	35	10.7	There is no conceivable justification for war.

Source: Data drawn from D.D. Droba, "A Scale of Militarism-Pacifism," *Journal of Educational Psychology* 22 (February 1931): 96–111.

Several important issues have arisen in relation to the use of Thurstone's equal-appearing intervals scales, only three of which will be mentioned here.[17] First, since the intervals between the adjacent positions on the scale have been judged to be equidistant, the attitude scores may be regarded as representing the interval level of measurement; hence, the investigator may calculate means, standard ' deviations, and other statistics which are based on assumptions appropriate to the interval level. Second, if the scale scores of the items represent genuine locations along the attitude continuum, one would expect that the attentive respondent will endorse only contiguous items which are located at or around his true position with respect to the variable being measured; however, respondents frequently endorse noncontiguous items, which brings into question the meaning of means or medians as representative of the true attitude score. Finally, it is assumed that the opinions of those who act as judges during the item-construction and item-selection phases of scale development do not significantly affect the final form of the scale. Yet to the extent that such opinions do intrude, the meaning of the scale scores and the distances between the intervals becomes unclear. Each of these issues has been the subject of a fairly large and growing literature, and several alternatives to the method of equal-appearing intervals have been developed.[18] Although serious doubts exist concerning the ability of the equal-appearing intervals technique to reveal true interval measurement scores, it has not been established that any of the alternative approaches yield that level of measurement nor that the the alternatives are necessarily superior at the ordinal level. Thus, it seems that Thurstone's method of equal-appearing intervals, even though controversial, is still of great potential value to political scientists.

LIKERT SCALES

Basic Considerations

Among the objections which have been raised against the Thurstone methods, perhaps the role of the judges (including the difficulty in persuading some individuals to undertake the tedious sorting job and the degree to which their opinions may affect item selection) has attracted the most attention. The most influential attempt to circum-

17. These and other issues are discussed in more detail in Edwards (1957, pp. 101–19) and Selltiz et al., (1959, pp. 362–5).
18. See Edwards (1957, pp. 201–19); Webb (1951).

vent the technical problems associated with the utilization of judges
has been presented by Likert (1932), and Murphy and Likert (1938).
The scales which are developed through these alternative procedures
are referred to variously as Likert-type scales, summated scales, or
internal consistency scales.

Murphy and Likert (1938) acknowledge the importance of
Thurstone's approach to attitude scaling. They praise his effort to
equalize the step-intervals in the attitude scale by the application of
psychophysical methods, and they believe that a scale so constructed
yields satisfactory reliability and validity. Nonetheless, they (1938,
p. 26) see their approach as "a radical departure from the concepts
which Thurstone has published as, for example, the use of judges."
Instead of relying upon a group of judges to reveal which items
should constitute a given scale, Murphy and Likert recommend that
the investigator analyze the items for internal consistency.

Techniques of Scale Construction

This approach to scale construction may be illustrated by reference to Likert's (1932) Internationalism Scale and to Lutzker's
(1960; Robinson, Rusk, and Head, 1968, pp. 321- 5) more recent
scale of the same name which is based, in part, upon the earlier
effort.

The first step in the Likert procedure is to assemble a large group
of value or opinion statements concerning the attitude object or its
presumed correlates. For example, to construct his Internationalism
Scale, Likert (1932) conducted a survey of previously used questionnaires on this topic, examined more than 200 newspapers, magazines,
books, and pamphlets and, additionally, "made up" some new items.

The next step in the Likert procedure is to administer these items
to a group of respondents who are asked to express the *degree* to
which they agree (approve) or disagree (disapprove) with *each* statement (Murphy and Likert, 1938, pp. 281- 91). The response format
may consist of as few as three degrees of affect—"agree," "undecided," and "disagree," although the Likert-type format typically consists of five alternatives—"strongly agree," "agree," "undecided,"
"disagree," and "strongly disagree." The use of a number of response
categories, rather than simple endorsement-nonendorsement as is
characteristic in Thurstone scaling, is often cited as one of the
advantages of the Likert technique. Three or more response categories increase the precision of the response, provide a category for
those wishing to state "no opinion" or "undecided," and remove one
source of respondent frustration. For a discussion of these points see

Riley, Riley, and Toby (1954, pp. 283-4). Each response alternative is assigned a value ranging in order from one to three (or five or six as the case may be) so that a response of "strongly agree" will receive the highest score if approval of the item reflects a favorable attitude. This procedure, in effect, presents the respondent with a battery of self-rating scales; however, instead of scoring each item as a separate scale, the values corresponding to the respondent's choices are added (hence, a summated scale) to yield a total score. Finally each item is analyzed in one of two ways (described below) and its value as a scale element is appraised.

The Likert-type approach is illustrated in Figure 3, which presents partial instructions and selected items from Lutzker's (1960)

FIGURE 3. Partial Instructions and Selected Items from Lutzker's Internationalism Scale

You are being asked to participate in a survey of opinions on political topics. Below, you will find a list of statements. Each statement is followed by six "reactions." ... You are to read each statement and then *encircle* the words which best describe your reaction to it.

1. The United States should take more of its problems to the U.N. than it has been doing.

Disagree Strongly	Disagree Moderately	Disagree Mildly	Agree Mildly	Agree Moderately	Agree Strongly
(1)	(2)	(3)	(4)	(5)	(6)

8. All military training should be abolished.

Disagree Strongly	Disagree Moderately	Disagree Mildly	Agree Mildly	Agree Moderately	Agree Strongly
(1)	(2)	(3)	(4)	(5)	(6)

13. The United States should recognize the Chinese Communist government.

Disagree Strongly	Disagree Moderately	Disagree Mildly	Agree Mildly	Agree Moderately	Agree Strongly
(1)	(2)	(3)	(4)	(5)	(6)

26. Any form of international government is impossible.

Disagree Strongly	Disagree Moderately	Disagree Mildly	Agree Mildly	Agree Moderately	Agree Strongly
(6)	(5)	(4)	(3)	(2)	(1)

30. Patriotism and loyalty are the first and most important requirements of a good citizen.

Disagree Strongly	Disagree Moderately	Disagree Mildly	Agree Mildly	Agree Moderately	Agree Strongly
(6)	(5)	(4)	(3)	(2)	(1)

Source: Daniel R. Lutzker, "Internationalism as a Predictor of Cooperative Behavior," *Journal of Conflict Resolution* 4 (December 1960): 426-42. Reprinted by permission of the publisher, Sage Publications, Inc.

Internationalism Scale. A consideration of Figure 3 in relation to our previous discussion of Thurstone scaling makes clear some of the basic differences between the Thurstone and Likert approaches to scale construction. First, the items of the Likert-type scale do not have specific scale values which indicate their position along an underlying continuum. Although it is plausible to assume that item 1 is "internationalist" in direction and that item 26 is "isolationist," it is not clear whether item 1 is *more or less* "internationalist" than item 13; and, *a fortiori*, the magnitude of the distance between these items is unknown. Second, an individual's scale score consists of the *sum* of the values of the responses to *every* scale item, rather than the mean or median of the scale values of the items an individual endorses. Third, each respondent in the initial sample is asked to give *his* reaction to each item. Fourth, even though Lutzker's (1960) scale is intended as a measure of "internationalism," many of the items contain no direct reference to this phenomenon. Such items might well be discarded in the Thurstone process as irrelevant. Finally, the values assigned to the response alternatives, which of course do not appear on the actual questionnaires, are determined arbitrarily.[19]

Before proceeding further, we must return to the question of item selection. Murphy and Likert (1938) experimented with two methods of item selection, each of which is based upon the idea of internal consistency. The first method, referred to as item analysis, is a correlation procedure. The mean of an individual's responses to all of the items is correlated with his score on each item taken separately. In this manner, the investigator is able to determine the extent to which a given item reflects, corresponds to, or clusters with, the rest of the items. Specific items which correlate poorly with the total group of items may be discarded. The remaining items then comprise the attitude scale. The principal problem with this selection procedure is the laborious calculation of the necessary correlation coefficients (Murphy and Likert, 1938, p. 287). The second method of item selection, which utilizes a different criterion of internal consistency, attempts to determine the ability of an item to distinguish those who are located near one end of an attitude continuum from those who are located near the opposite end. An item's ability to distinguish—its *discriminatory power* (*DP*)—is calculated as follows: the investigator determines, on the basis of the total scores to the original items, which individuals comprise the highest and lowest quarters (or tenths) of the distribution. The *weighted* frequency distributions of these two "extreme" groups are compared *for each item* in the original scale. An example of the calculations needed for

19. Lutzker (1960) assigned values of 1-3 and 5-7 to the response alternatives. High scores indicate internationalism.

this comparison, taken from Likert's (Murphy and Likert, 1938, p. 289) Internationalism Scale, is shown as Table 3. The *DP* of the item described in the table is considered to be very high. In general, if the *DP* of an item exceeds .50, it is thought to be usable. In practice, one should not use many items having *DP*s below 1.00. A rapid judgment concerning the probable utility of an item may be formed by an inspection of the frequency distribution column of Table 3. In this case, it is seen that *all* of the individuals in the high-scoring group endorsed the "strongly approve" alternative (5), while *none* of the low-scoring group endorsed it. The probability is low that one would observe such a division if the item really were *not* discriminating effectively between the members of the two groups; therefore this item appears to be a good prospect for inclusion, and the *DP* should be calculated. After the *DP*s have been calculated, the items may be ordered by their ability to discriminate those who are high from those who are low on the attitude under study, and the best fifteen or twenty items may be selected to constitute the final scale.

The principal advantages of the Likert method over the Thurstone methods are alleged to be (1) the avoidance of the use of judges, (2) the simplicity of scale construction, (3) the inclusion of items which are covert measures of an attitude, (4) the avoidance of interval-level measurement assumptions, and (5) the inclusion of a response format which permits the individual to register various degrees of agreement or disagreement. These and other issues have given rise to a critical literature concerning the relative merits of these approaches, and the controversies are still under way (see Tittle and Hill, 1966; Edwards, 1957, pp. 162–71). One particularly important criticism has been directed against both the Likert and the Thurstone methods: that the resulting scales are not *undimensional.*

T A B L E 3. Calculation of the Discriminatory Power (*DP*) of Item 18 from Likert's Internationalism Scale*

Group	N	Frequency Distribution for Item 18					Weighted Sum (WS)	High WS minus Low WS = (D)	D/N = DP
		1	2	3	4	5			
High	9	0	0	0	0	9	45		
								23	23/9 = 2.6
Low	9	1	5	1	2	0	22		

*Item 18: "In the interest of permanent peace, we should be willing to arbitrate absolutely all differences with other nations which we cannot readily settle by diplomacy" (Murphy and Likert, 1938, p. 35).

Source: Gardner Murphy and Rensis Likert, *Public Opinion and the Individual* (New York: Harper & Row, 1938), p. 35. Reprinted by permission.

GUTTMAN SCALES

Basic Considerations

In addition to the criteria discussed up to this point, some students of measurement would add the condition that there be "an unambiguous meaning to the order of scale scores" (Guttman, 1944, p. 50). An important criterion of nonambiguity is that the items comprising a scale be cumulative in nature so that an individual's scale score indicates the response that he gave to each scale item. The development of scales meeting this criterion have been based primarily upon the theory and techniques originally presented by Guttman (1941, pp. 319–48).

In this type of scaling, as in any other, one starts with the notion that for a given attitude object there exists a universe of content or universe of attributes; however, a major purpose of the Guttman approach is the determination of whether scale items come from the same universe of content, i.e., whether the universe as defined by the investigator is *unidimensional*. A scale or universe of content is unidimensional when its component items represent different degrees of favorable or unfavorable sentiment toward a *single* attitude object, or, in the case of behavior, when different forms of behavior have but a *single* content ordering. If items in a scale are from different universes of content, of if the universe itself is multidimensional, then (according to the proponents of the Guttman approach) ordering individuals by scale scores would be an exercise unlikely to contribute to theory and methodology and possibly an exercise devoid of meaning since "it would make little sense to attempt to order people in terms of it . . . if the 'it' is really a 'they'" (Jahoda, Deutsch, and Cook, 1951, p. 199). For example, those items making up the Internationalism Scale presented in Figure 3 may come from a single internationalism-isolationism universe of content, or they may be from several more specific universes including attitudes toward international organizations, attitudes toward military training, and so on.[20] Guttman techniques would offer the investigator the data upon which he could make inferences concerning the answer to this question.

If those items comprising a scale do in fact describe a single dimension, then responses to the items should display a unique

20. This of course suggests that if the universe of content is multidimensional, there may be research situations where it would be *desirable* to construct a multidimensional scale to attempt to measure it. See Goode and Hatt (1952, pp. 285–86), who stress the fact that the criterion of unidimensionality may, on occasion, be inappropriate.

order. For example, assume that 100 respondents have been instructed to agree or disagree with those items listed in Table 4—a sample of items from the universe of attributes labeled as classical conservatism by McClosky (1958, pp. 27-45). Hypothetical percentages representing "agree" responses also are shown in Table 4.

Respondents may agree with anywhere from none to all nine of the items A-I, and may thus be assigned one of ten scores which can be used to order the respondents by the degree to which they subscribe to the classical conservative outlook. This idea is illustrated in Table 5, which indicates that all of the individuals who agreed with item I also agreed with all the others; those who agreed with item H did not agree with item I but did agree with items A-G, and so on. Under these conditions an individual's score reveals his response pattern, i.e. the pattern is *reproducible* from the score. Should the analysis of 100 scale scores yield a pattern as clear and internally meaningful as this one, it is likely (but is not a certainty) that the scale and universe in question are unidimensional. Tables 4 and 5 indicate that an ordered, meaningful relationship is apparent among both items and respondents. On the other hand, if a universe of content is multidimensional, if items are from more than one universe, or if respondents' perceptions of the items vary, then we

T A B L E 4.   Student Responses to Classical Conservatism Items

Item No.	Item	Percent Agreeing
A.	All groups can live in harmony in this country without changing the system in any way.	10
B.	We must respect the work of our forefathers and not think that we know better than they did.	20
C.	If something grows up over a long time, there will always be much wisdom in it.	30
D.	If you start trying to change things very much, you usually make them worse.	40
E.	I'd want to know that something would really work before I'd be willing to take a chance on it.	50
F.	A man doesn't really get to have much wisdom unless he's well along in years.	60
G.	It's better to stick by what you have than to be trying new things you really don't know about.	70
H.	No matter how we like to talk about it, political authority really comes not from us, but from some higher party.	80
I.	I prefer the practical man any time to the man of ideas.	90

Source: Herbert McClosky, "Conservatism and Personality," *American Political Science Review* 52 (March 1958): 31. Reprinted by permission.

would expect *errors* in the response types. There might be instances
where individuals agree with item B, but not with the others, or they
may agree with items C and D but with no others. When responses
deviate from the types shown in Table 5, this represents a lack of
agreement among the respondents in regard to the degree of conservatism manifested by the item content and, in practice, there usually
is some lack of agreement.[21] Even if a perfect pattern were found,
the investigator should not assume that this scale and universe are
unidimensional. Scale analysis itself gives no judgment on content
and, at best, may be used as an auxiliary basis for inference concerning unidimensionality (Guttman, 1950, p. 85). One item may happen
to scale with others; yet it may not reflect the same content because
of chance or similarity in question format. Still another caution is
that Guttman scales are specific to time and the sampled population.
For a given group of people, a universe may be scalable at one point
in time but not another. At that same point in time, a universe may
not be scalable for a different group of people; therefore, the
techniques of scaling outlined below should be applied each time a
cumulative scale is administered.

Techniques of Scale Construction

Items are selected initially in Guttman scaling either as they are
in Thurstone or Likert scaling or, preferably, by a combination of
those techniques. Other factors being equal, "the more items included in a scale, the greater is the assurance that the entire universe

T A B L E 5. Response Types Associated with "Perfect" Scales

Scale Score	Response to Item(s)									Percent in This Category
	A	B	C	D	E	F	G	H	I	
0	−	−	−	−	−	−	−	−	−	10
1	+	−	−	−	−	−	−	−	−	10
2	+	+	−	−	−	−	−	−	−	10
3	+	+	+	−	−	−	−	−	−	10
4	+	+	+	+	−	−	−	−	−	10
5	+	+	+	+	+	−	−	−	−	10
6	+	+	+	+	+	+	−	−	−	10
7	+	+	+	+	+	+	+	−	−	10
8	+	+	+	+	+	+	+	+	−	10
9	+	+	+	+	+	+	+	+	+	10

+ = Agree; − = Disagree.

21. In addition to the factors listed above, chance factors also operate. In a
nine-item scale there are 512 possible response types, only 10 of which represent
perfect scales.

of which these items are a sample is scalable" (Guttman, 1950, p. 79). It has been suggested that at least ten items be used at the outset unless agreement with the items ranges between 30 and 70 percent. If the preliminary sample of items is not large enough to include diverse questions, there is the possibility that four or five items will hold together accidentally (Toby, 1954, pp. 373-4). It also should be kept in mind that the final scale probably will consist of fewer items than the number included in the preliminary sample since most of the steps outlined below involve discarding items which do not meet certain criteria.

Most procedures for the determination of scalability require, at some point, the dichotomization of the responses to each item; however, if a dichotomous response format is employed at the outset, information may be lost and there may be less assurance that a universe is scalable (see the related discussion above under Likert Scales). As a rule, if a dichotomous item has more than 80 percent of the responses in one category or, when more than two response categories are used, if it is impossible to combine categories so that one category will contain at least 20 percent of the responses, then the item should be discarded. Items having divisions more extreme than this may not discriminate effectively among the respondents. Such items also may inflate the reproducibility of the scale and spuriously support the inference of undimensionality; thus, in our example in Table 4, items A and I would be dropped from the scale for these reasons.

As an illustration of the rule that response categories should be combined in such a manner that the division leaves at least 20 percent of the responses in one of the resulting categories, assume that the percentages in Table 4 are for "agree strongly" only and that the responses to item A are (in percent) "agree strongly"—10; "agree"—15; "undecided"—60; "disagree"—10; and "disagree strongly"—5. While one might be inclined to discard the item because of the proportion of ambiguous ("undecided") responses, if it were to be retained, the only acceptable point of division would lie between "agree" and "undecided." Any other dichotomy would yield a percent outside of the acceptable 20-80 range. A second consideration is that if the concern is with "agree" responses, it would be unwise to combine the "undecided" responses with these since such a combination would cloud the meaning of the constructed category. Still a third guide in dichotomizing is the desirability of "spacing out" question responses to help "spread" the respondents into approximately equal groups along the continuum. Suppose that the responses to item B in Table 4 were (in percent) "agree strongly"—20; "agree"—20; "undecided"—10; "disagree"—20; and disagree strongly"—30. Given the other percentages in Table 4, the investigator probably would decide to use the 20/80 division because this places the item between A and C on the scale. Any other breaking point places B at a point on the scale which is occupied already by another item. It has been suggested that "scale questions should be spaced out by more than five percent . . . so that subsequent samples will not show reversals in the scale order of the questions, and . . . to help spread respondents out" (Ford, 1950, p. 516). Taken literally, this rule—in combination with the 20/80 rule—limits to thirteen the number of items one can use in constructing a Guttman-type scale. In practice, it may be difficult to find thirteen items spaced in the manner specified.[22]

Once the extreme items have been discarded, the remaining items are subjected to "scale analysis." A number of alternative techniques may be used to assess the degree to which scale scores permit the response patterns to be reproduced, including (1) the scalogram board technique (Stouffer et al., 1950, pp. 91-121), (2) the Cornell technique (Guttman, 1947, pp. 247-80), (3) the tabulation technique (Goodenough, 1944, pp. 179-190; Ford, 1950, p. 514), (4) the least squares method (Guttman, 1941, pp. 319-48), and (5) pairwise comparison, which is discussed below.

Scale analysis begins with the ordering of items by the percentages of agreement as has been done in Table 4. Suppose that instead of discarding item A, as suggested earlier, the "agree" and "agree strongly" responses are combined. The resulting 25/75 dichotomy permits item A to be placed between B and C. In the case of item I, of course, there is no alternative but to discard because all 90 percent of the responses are "agree strongly." After these decisions, the scale consists of eight items reordered in the suggested manner.

Pairwise comparison involves comparing the response distribution to one item with those of every other item, or at least to the five closest items. This involves constructing fourfold tables showing the relationship of the responses to one item with those of another. Table 6 indicates what the relationship could have been in a hypothetical comparison of items B and A. Since in the previous example, item A has been placed between items B and C, no cases would be expected in cell (b) of Table 6—the "nonscale" cell—*if* the scale were perfectly cumulative and the responses were reproducible from the respondents' scores. This is the case in Table 6; however, perfect

---

22. To make possible the utilization of more items, Stouffer et al. (1952, pp. 273-91) have introduced a procedure through which more than one item may be placed at a single scale point. This procedure—the H technique—is more precise than that discussed here.

T A B L E 6. Hypothetical Responses to Items B and A (in Percent)

		Item A		
		Agree and *Agree Strongly*	*Other* *Responses*	
Item B	*Agree* *Strongly*	*(a)* 20	*(b)* 0	20
	Other *Responses*	*(c)* 5	*(d)* 75	80
		25	75	100

T A B L E 7. Hypothetical Responses to Items B and C (in Percent)

		Item C		
		Agree Strongly	*Other Responses*	
Item B	*Agree* *Strongly*	*(a)* 8	*(b)* 12	20
	Other *Responses*	*(c)* 22	*(d)* 58	80
		30	70	100

scalability is rare and the presence of a few cases in cell (b) may not lead us to conclude that the two items are from different universes. While the level of error tolerated may be established in a number of different ways (see Anderson, Watts, and Wilcox, 1966, pp. 101-3), the simplest criterion is the designation of an absolute percentage ceiling of error for all items in a scale. This level is designated arbitrarily and depends upon the type of risk the researcher wishes to take, but it has been suggested that the number of cases in the nonscale cell should not exceed 10 percent of the total and that the cases in cells (a) and (d) should each be at least twice as numerous as the cases in cell (b) (Toby and Toby, 1954, p. 343). Both criteria are met by the example shown in Table 6 but not by the example in Table 7. There the number of cases in cell (b) exceeds 10 percent and the number of cases in (a) is not twice as numerous as in (b). This means that item B or C or both should be discarded. Further analysis of this type will indicate which is the case. If all responses are cross-tabulated with all others, the results may be summarized simply in a matrix. If check marks are employed to indicate which pairs of items meet the criteria suggested above, the matrix might appear as in Table 8. One may observe the blank in the C row and B column

T A B L E 8.   Item Pairs Meeting Criteria of Scalability

	B	A	C	D	E	F	G	H
B		✓		✓	✓	✓	✓	✓
A				✓	✓	✓	✓	✓
C				✓		✓		✓
D					✓	✓	✓	✓
E						✓	✓	✓
F							✓	✓
G								✓

(which represents the pairwise comparison presented as Table 7), and one may observe further that the criteria also were not met when the responses to C were compared with those to A, E, and G. To be included in a scale, an item must "scale" with all others. When C is removed, the scale criteria are met by all of the other items.[23]

A seven-item scale meeting the relatively rigorous criteria associated with Guttman theory now remains. Because the items have a logical and empirically based order, the respondents may be ordered according to their scale scores in the manner shown in Table 9. It will be noticed that, because of "errors," not all of the response patterns conform to perfect scale types but are assigned scores on the basis of that type they most closely approximate (see again Table 5). For example, respondent (student) 2 agreed with item E but no others. If he were assigned a score of zero, only one error would result—the positive response to E. If he were assigned a score of one, then two errors would result—the negative response to B and the positive response to E; hence, respondent 2 more closely approximates scale type 0 than scale type 1. The decision is even more obvious in the case of respondent 4, who displays only one error when classified as a 2 but who would display more than one if he were placed in any other category. The decision is not so simple in regard to respondent 7, who could be classified either as a 2 or as a 4 with only one error. In this case, two different rules have been suggested: first, assignment to the mean scale score between the two (Anderson, Watts, and Wilcox, 1966, pp. 109-10)—in this case 3; or, second, assignment to that scale type closest to the middle of all categories (Ford, 1950, p.

23. It is possible (but unlikely in this example) that a reanalysis of the relationships between the items, utilizing different combinations of response categories for some of all of the items, would have led to a decision to retain C. It has been suggested by Toby and Toby (1954, pp. 341-2) that all possible 2 × 2 tables representing different response combinations be examined and that the cell frequency criteria mentioned above also be employed in the dichotomization process.

TABLE 9.   Ranking of Respondents by Scale Score

Student	B	A	D	E	F	G	H	Scale Score
1	−	−	−	−	−	−	−	0
2	−	−	−	+	−	−	−	0
3	+	−	−	−	−	−	−	1
4	−	+	−	−	−	−	−	2
5	+	+	−	−	−	−	−	2
6	+	+	+	−	−	−	−	3
7	+	+	−	+	−	−	−	4
8	+	+	+	+	−	−	−	4
9	+	+	+	+	−	−	+	4
10	+	+	+	+	+	−	−	5
11	−	−	+	+	+	−	−	5
etc.								

522)—in this case 4. The alternative selected may well depend upon the nature of the research problem. If the concern is primarily with the distribution of individuals as opposed to items (e.g., the concern with specific legislators' behavior in a roll-call analysis), then it may be preferable to use the first alternative; if the concern is primarily with item content (e.g., the ranking of an issue among a set of issues), then the second alternative may be preferable. This, of course, emphasizes the fact that the distribution of responses shown as Table 9 can be used to rank either the items in the scale or the respondents.

Once the total number of errors has been determined, the adequacy of a scale may be assessed by computing its *coefficient of reproducibility*. This coefficient is simply

$$1 - \frac{\text{total number of errors}}{\text{number of questions} \times \text{number of respondents}}$$

Stated another way, it is the ratio of correct responses to total responses. If Table 9 could have been extended to show all 100 respondents' scale patterns, and if 60 of their responses were errors, then the coefficient of reproducibility in this case would be

$$1 - \frac{60}{7 \times 100} = 1 - .085 = .915$$

A coefficient of .90 has been set forth (Guttman, 1950, p. 77) as acceptable. In addition to this criterion, Guttman (1950, pp. 78-9) has indicated that the pattern of errors should be random. If specific nonscale types occur with some frequency, it is likely that some variable other than that the investigator intends to measure also is reflected in the responses. It has been suggested (Toby and Toby, 1954, p. 316) that there should be no more than 5 percent of the sample in any nonscale type. In fact, if the pairwise-comparisons technique described above is used, it will be unlikely that the coefficient of reproducibility will fall below .90 and that more than 5 percent of the sample will be characterized by the same nonscale pattern.

It has been noted that the coefficient of reproducibility is affected by the number of errors which occur when response patterns are reproduced; it also is affected by the extremeness of the percentage range of items (which is controlled within limits by the item selection criteria) and by the extremeness of the individuals' responses. For these reasons Menzel (1953, pp. 268–80) has suggested a *coefficient of scalability* to supplement the coefficient of reproducibility. This coefficient is

$$1 - \frac{\text{total number of errors}}{\text{maximum number of errors possible}}$$

The maximum number of errors is the sum of the nonmodal responses to each item. For example, given the hypothetical dichotomization of item B, the modal category contains 80 responses and the nonmodal category contains the remaining 20; thus the maximum number of errors for item B is 20. The sum of the nonmodal responses to all items would be 20 (B) + 25 (A) + 40 (D) + 50 (E) + 40 (F) + 30 (G) + 20 (H) = 225 (see Table 4). But the maximum errors also may be calculated by examining the nonmodal responses for each individual. An examination of Table 9 indicates that respondent 1's maximum error possible (or nonmodal response) is 0; student 2's is 1, and so on to student 10, who has a maximum of 2, and student 11, who has 3. Because examination of the first type of nonmodal responses assesses the extremeness of the items while the second type assesses the extremeness of the individuals, both maximum error values are determined. Then the smaller of the two is used in the computation of the coefficient of scalability. If, in our example, the 225 possible errors which are a function of the extremeness of items is the smaller, then the coefficient of scalability is 1 - (60/225) = 1 - .266 = .734. A coefficient of scalability of .65 or higher has been accepted arbitrarily as adequate.

In summary, the criteria for scalability in the Guttman sense include reproducibility (assessed by the coefficient of reproducibility), an acceptable range of marginal percentages (assessed by the coefficient of scalability), a random distribution of errors (assessed by the 5 percent criterion), the number of items (the larger the number, the greater the assurance that the entire universe is scalable), and the number of response categories (the greater the number, the greater the assurance of scalability). The first criterion alone is not a sufficient test for unidimensionality; yet many social scientists report only the coefficient of reproducibility in evaluating their scales and very few report data in regard to all five criteria.

FACTOR ANALYSIS

Factor analysis has not been used extensively to date in the construction of scales, but it has been used successfully and extensively in the related area of index construction (see, for example, Hagood and Price, 1952, pp. 526–30). Because the technique can be used in relation to two of the scaling problems discussed above—the assessment of unidimensionality and the weighting of scale items—a brief description will be offered here. For a more complete discussion of the nature and uses of factor analysis, the reader is referred to Rummel (1967, pp. 444–80). For a discussion of basic principles and computational procedures, there are several adequate sources, including Fruchter (1954) and Harman (1967).

"Factor analysis" is the general term given to a number of techniques which have as their purpose "to determine from the interrelationships of a large number of variables the smallest number of factors (or underlying dimensions) whose associations with the original variables will account for all of the observed interrelationships" (Price, 1942, p. 449). Thus, as one might expect, it has been suggested that the technique may be applied to validate the unidimensionality of Guttman-type scales. Kuroda (1968), for example, administered 71 Likert-type scale items (many from Guttman-type scales) to a sample of 287 registered voters and 19 reputational leaders in a Japanese community. The responses of each sample were subjected to factor analyses to determine the underlying dimensions in the attitudes of the public and its leaders in this community. This involved correlating scores on every item with scores on every other item yielding, in this instance, a 71 × 71 correlation matrix for each sample.[24] Clusters of highly interrelated items are assumed to be indicators of underlying dimensions—an idea related to our earlier discussions of the universe of content and sample of attributes. The

24. Because Kuroda (1968) eliminated one item in one of his analyses, one of his matrices was 70 × 70. For another illustration of the use of factor analysis in scale construction, see Jacob (1971).

dimensions (factors) themselves are then "rotated" to the point where the greatest amount of total variation is explained. This yields a rotated factor matrix with the items presented as the stubs (describing the rows) in the matrix and the factors presented as the captions (describing the columns). Space does not permit a reproduction of the complete matrix from Kuroda's (1968) paper, but part of it is reproduced as Table 10. The figures in the cells are factor loadings, which are coefficients representing the correlation between the item in the stub and the factor in the caption. The proportion of the variation in the 71 items which is explained by a given factor is calculated by summing the squares of the factor loadings for each *column* and dividing the total by the number of variables. The proportion of variation in a given item which is explained by all of the factors combined—the communality coefficient (h^2)—is calculated by summing the squares for each *row*.

The data presented by Kuroda illustrate several points in regard to the use of factor analysis in the assessment of scale unidimensionality. First, Table 10 indicates that among members of this sample at the time the items were administered, one of the four F-scale items (item 4) was more closely related to factor (or dimension) 11 than to that dimension (factor 1) about which the other three F-scale items (1, 2, and 3) were clustered. Another of the items (1) is almost as closely related to two other dimensions (8 and 9) as it is to factor 1. Finally, the factor loadings for the other two items (2 and 3) are relatively low and explain only a small fraction of the variation. In short, the four-item F scale used by Kuroda (1968) does not seem to be unidimensional. The content of the sixteen items comprising the scale suggested to Kuroda (1968) that "collectivity orientation" was an appropriate name for the factor. In addition to the three F-scale items, items from a self-society orientation scale and from a liberal-conservative scale also had high loadings. That one could conceptualize all sixteen variables as "collectivity orientation," but at the same time place them in three related substantive subcategories, reinforces the comments made earlier about the possible utility of using multidimensional scales in some instances (see note 20).

Table 10 also shows that six of the seven items making up a political cynicism scale have high loadings on factor 2, but on no other factors. The seventh item (37) has a higher loading on factor 5, but Kuroda (1968) has indicated that "this is one which, in the eyes of the Japanese, may not be a relevant factor in determining the extent to which one holds politics and politicians in disrepute." In short, this factor analysis suggests that at least five and probably six of the original seven items in the political cynicism scale are

TABLE 10. Portion of a Rotated Factor Matrix for 71 Attitude-Scale Items Administered to 287 Registered Japanese Voters

Item	Factor											h^2
	1	2	3	4	5	6	7	8	9	10	11	
1. What youth needs most is strict discipline, rugged determination, and the will to work and fight for family and country. (F)	.379							.358	-.307			.383
2. Most of our social problems could be solved if we could somehow get rid of the immoral, feebleminded, and crooked people. (F)	.441											.317
3. People ought to pay more attention to new ideas even if they seem to go against the Japanese way of life. (F)	.447										.307	.320
4. The findings of science may someday show that many of our most cherished beliefs are wrong. (F)	.329										.536	.441
35. I don't believe that public officials care about what people like me think. (PC)		.425										.287
37. In order to get nominated, most candidates for political office have to make basic compromises and undesirable commitments. (PC)		.136			.416							.297
39. Politicians spend most of their time getting reelected or reappointed. (PC)		.670										.511
41. Money is the most important factor influencing public policies. (PC)		.689										.538
43. A large number of city and county politicians are party hacks. (PC)		.551										.439
45. People are often manipulated by politicians. (PC)		.668										.519
49. Most politicians in the community are probably more interested in getting known than in serving the needs of their constituents. (PC)		.709										.575

F = F Scale; PC = Political Cynicism Scale

Source: Yasumasa Kuroda, "Attitude Structure of the Public and Its Leaders in Reed Town, Japan," paper presented at the annual meeting of the American Political Science Association, Washington, 1968, pp. 11–12. Printed by permission.

unidimensional for this population at this time. In fact, Kuroda (1968) noted that "this finding suggests the validity of the political cynicism scale constructed through the use of the Cornell technique in earlier works."

Still, not all of the items are equally closely associated with the political cynicism factor; therefore, the factor loadings *could* be used to refine the scales even further by assigning differential weights to the items. The factor loading itself or the square of the factor loading may be used to rescore item responses and thus alter an individual's total scale score. Since item 49 of Table 10 is more closely associated with the political cynicism dimension than item 35, it would be logical to assume that it should contribute more to the total scale score than item 33. This effect can be produced by multiplying each respondent's numerically coded response alternative by the factor loading or its square. These products may then be summed to yield each individual's score. Probably because of the increasingly general availability of electronic computers, the use of factor analysis in political science seems to be on the upswing. For the same reason, it is likely that this technique will be used with greater frequency in constructing scales in the future.

CONCLUSION

The many issues which have been introduced or implied in this brief review of scaling principles and techniques suggest three additional observations which seem especially pertinent at this point. First, it seems clear that students of politics share with investigators in sociology and psychology a steadily increasing interest in problems of measurement; and, as has been true in sociology and psychology, the development of quantitative approaches has raised many difficult questions concerning the relationship of "traditional" and "behavioral" conceptions of man. Problems of the validity, reliability, and precision of observations—taken in a broad sense—are central to some of the most engaging controversies to be found in the disciplines named.

Second, the techniques described above—Thurstone scaling, Likert scaling, Guttman scaling, and factor analysis—have grown principally out of the psychometric tradition; but they are today the common property of several social science disciplines, each of which may encounter distinctive opportunities to refine these techniques, or, let us hope, to devise superior ones. It seems probable, on one hand, that the comparatively frequent utilization by political scientists of

Guttman scaling may lead to developments along these lines which will influence researchers in related fields. On the other hand, political scientists' comparatively infrequent utilization of Thurstone scaling suggests the possibility that further explorations along this line may be fruitful.

Finally, while there has been cross-disciplinary continuity in regard to the principles and general techniques of scale construction, continuity in the development and utilization of specific instruments has been unimpressive. Within sociology, for instance, an analysis of twelve volumes of four of the leading sociological journals revealed that only 50 measures among 2,080, many of which are indices, were used or cited more than six times (Bonjean, Hill, and McLemore, 1967, pp. 13-14). Furthermore, even among the scales which have been utilized most frequently, much remains to be done to establish their validity and reliability. Important efforts to promote continuity in attitude measurement, directed principally toward psychologists, have been completed by Shaw and Wright (1967) and by Robinson and Shaver (1969). A similar undertaking, directed principally toward students of politics, has been conducted by Robinson, Rusk, and Head (1968). Three other valuable compendia have been completed by Robinson, Athanasiou, and Head (1969); Lake, Miles, and Earle (1973); and Maranell (1974). These efforts are evidence of a widespread recognition of the need for a genuine accumulation of trustworthy research tools. Progress in this direction should benefit scholars in all of the social science disciplines.[25]

25. Still, the uncritical application of a scale constructed from responses of one set of respondents and applied to different types of respondents is not likely to meet the criteria of validity and reliability set forth above. This problem is discussed at some length and illustrated by Jacob (1971).

13. PARTICIPANT-OBSERVER ANALYSIS

R. J. Snow

"Participant observation" may be more appropriately called a "style" of social science research than a "method."[1] In sister disciplines to political science, especially in sociology and anthropology where participant-observer research is common,[2] the term means "going into the field" to take on a social role from which to gain perspective and collect data about what social actors do, and how and why they do it. The particular field behavior of the researcher may vary from one extreme of presence without personal involvement in the environment under study, in which *observation* tasks are primary, through observers-as-participants and participants-as-observers, to another extreme of active *participation* in tasks identical to those performed by other participants, in which observation is secondary.[3]

Research designs for participant-observer studies are usually directed toward investigation of a specific problem or social environment, and they normally call for the use of more than a single data collection procedure. Data produced by more or less systematic observation techniques in the particular combination of participant or observer roles adopted by the researcher are usually supplemented by documentary analysis and various kinds of interviewing. The entire flexible role and multiple method procedure may thus be called participant observation.

This chapter surveys some uses of the participant-observer research style in political science, assesses the nature of the approach to social

1. This is the suggestion of McCall and Simmons (1969).

2. A number of participant-observer studies in sociology and anthropology have clear relevance for political science. As the most notable examples, see Warner et al. (1949, 1963), Whyte (1955), Cyert, Simon, and Trow (1956), Wylie (1957, 1966), Vidich and Bensman (1958), Gans (1962), Mair (1962), Blau (1963a), Cohen (1965), and Vidich, Bensman, and Stein (1964).

3. On the field role of the participant observer, see Gold (1958), Junker (1960, pp. 35-9), Janes (1961), and Duverger (1964, pp. 209-22).

science research it represents, and discusses practical questions related to research design, implementation, and analysis.

Political scientists have not been very explicit about their use of participant observation, although many have participated in political events and environments which they later described, especially in the case study literature, in studies of political personalities, and in studies of legislative and bureaucratic institutions and processes. Only a few of these studies show evidence of full use of the privileged access and unique opportunities for systematic observation which their authors' participant roles allowed. Even fewer authors have been explicit in describing for other researchers the particular data collection procedures which direct participation allowed them to employ. A literature on the application of participant-observer analysis in political science has only recently begun to emerge.[4]

In spite of a relative lack of explicitness about method, however, the significant contribution of observation studies to political science may be measured in the detail found in published policy case studies, in the awareness displayed by experienced political scientists of rules and norms of government and political institutions, in the written evidence of close acquaintances with styles, traits, and habits of political personalities, and in innumerable anecdotes sprinkled throughout the political science literature. This enrichment of the discipline results from experience which political scientists have gained as interns, fellows, consultants, advisors, staff members, or as officeholders themselves.

Some of the most insightful and widely read literature on Congress is based on observers' experience. The work of Stephen Bailey (1950), Bertram Gross (1953), Ralph Huitt (1954, 1961), Donald Matthews (1960), and Charles Clapp (1963) depended upon detailed knowledge produced by direct experience. Alan Fiellin (1963) produced his study of informal groups in Congress following experience as a congressional fellow of the American Political Science Association. In-depth studies of congressional decision processes such as those by Robinson (1962a) on foreign policy, Bauer, Pool, and Dexter (1963) on international trade policy, and Eidenberg and Morey (1969) on the passage of the 1965 Elementary and Secondary Education Act, are closely analytical as well as descriptive, and in their methodology they approximate participant observation studies done in sociology and anthropology. Like Fiellin, Charles Clapp, James Robinson, Eugene Eidenberg, and Roy Morey were APSA congressional fellows. Ronald Hedlund (1971) provides a bibliography of writings produced by other congressional fellows, many of which are based on their experiences.

4. See Robinson (1969) and Hennessy (1970a), Hedlund (1971, 1973a, 1973b), and Hirschfield and Adler (1973).

Neustadt's analysis of the presidency (1960) is substantially based on his staff experience in the White House. Less analytical in terms of political science, nonetheless revealing studies of the Kennedy administration have been produced by Sorensen (1963, 1965) and Schlesinger (1965), who were primarily participants and secondarily observers. An analytical study based in part on experience as a presidential counselor during the Johnson administration has been written by George Reedy (1970). The events of Watergate in the early 1970s produced an extended series of explanations and analyses of the cover-up engineered by the Nixon administration, a number of which were written to substantiate claims that their authors were only innocent observers, and not willful participants.

Studies of internal party and campaign processes such as those by Robinson (1962b), Cotter and Hennessy (1964), and Jones (1964) are based in substantial part on participant-observation experience. Robinson served with the Illinois delegation to the 1960 Democratic National Convention, Hennessey with the Democratic National Committee, and Jones with the House Republican Policy Committee. Duane Lockard's writings (1959, 1963) on state government and politics draw on his experience as a member of the Connecticut State Senate.

The study by Ralph and Estelle James (1965) of Hoffa and the teamsters' union is a well-conducted example of the application of participant-observer methods in the study of a politically relevant personality. Fortuitously and unexpectedly invited by Hoffa to travel with and observe him, the Jameses spent six months in close interaction with the teamsters' leader. Lengthy interviews ensued, files were opened, and "total access" to teamsters' records and personnel was arranged. According to the authors, "No assurances were ever given about the conclusions we would reach." This highly unusual study provides an opportunity for a potential participant observer to examine how unique opportunities for interpersonal involvement and access to data, and unforeseen problems of research design and execution such as expense, hostility, and distrust from some participants, come into play in a single study.

Among the most ambitious but little-known participant-observer efforts described in the literature of political science is the study underwritten by the National Center for Education in Politics and carried out by a team of graduate interns assigned for several months to governors' offices in fourteen states. Common data collection categories were devised, similar interviews were conducted, and regular observer reports were collected by each intern. The project was designed and administered by Alan J. Wyner, who also analyzed and synthesized the study materials (1967).

Studies of bureaucratic behavior have used data collection techniques which range from unstructured note taking by participants to highly structured "communications audit" procedures where individual interactions between persons were counted and carefully analyzed. Harold Lasswell and Gabriel Almond (1948) report research in the 1930s in which they successfully employed clerks in a Chicago relief agency as participant observers in a study of the effects of personality type on administrative decisions. The studies by Hyneman (1950) and Blau (1963a, 1967) were produced after Hyneman had served as a bureau administrator and Blau had served as a participant observer. Cohen (1965) used participant observation in a partial replication of Blau's study.

The research by Benjamin Walter (1963, 1966) of internal control relations in municipal administrative institutions used a sophisticated "communications audit" procedure to determine and measure interpersonal transmission of influence. Walter used a team of trained observers randomly assigned to different time periods with various administrative officers in two cities. His study is one of very few in political science which reports hypothesis tests based on data collected through observation.

The communications audit procedure was modified by David Kovenock (1964, 1967) for a study of the impact of personal influence in a congressional subcommittee. The "audit" procedure depends upon both systematic observation and interviewing. Using a coding sheet, Walter and Kovenock recorded instances of direct interaction, both oral and written, between actors under study. Follow-up interviews solicited information about the degree of influence each interaction produced and the extent to which opinion change took place in the communication recipient.

While the Walter-Kovenock procedure qualifies as observation research, such studies may be performed in open settings where access is not limited to "participants." Thus, these studies might be categorized apart from participant-observer research. They are part of a relatively small body of research in political science which depends on data produced through systematic observation where the special kinds of access accorded a participating staff member or intern are not necessarily required. The earliest of these studies was carried out by Garland Routt (1938), who recorded interactions among twelve leaders in a state legislature during the opening fifteen-minute period of eighty-six separate legislative days. His observation data supplemented documentary data and interviews.

The observation procedure used by Chadwick Alger (1968) to record interaction among international diplomats from a visitors' gallery overlooking a committee of the United Nations is an excellent example of the effective use of an ordinary research opportunity and a researcher's fertile imagination in the production of social science data of high quality.

At the level of local government, Minar (1966) and Snow (1966) combined efforts to devise a procedure for systematically recording observed interactions among participants in school board and city council meetings. The procedure was pretested, revised, and employed over a period of several months in city council and school board meetings in five suburban Illinois communities. The observation data produced were of adequate quality for hypothesis testing.

Systematic observation of real political actors in a quasi-experimental situation was carried out by James D. Barber (1966), who obtained the cooperation of members of local government finance committees in twelve New England communities for a research project conducted in the Yale Small Groups Laboratory. Structured policy problems were assigned to each committee, and Barber and his staff intensively observed and recorded their interactions for later analysis.

Like the Walter, Kovenock, Routt, Alger, Minar, and Snow studies, the Barber study is not necessarily dependent on observation by participants. It is appropriate to include mention of these studies because the methods they employ are especially amenable to use by participants, and because they are observation methods specifically devised for application to political science research.

Finally, extensive use of participant observation can be discovered in case studies in political science literature, including studies published by the Inter-University Case Program, as well as in those published by the Eagleton Institute of Politics.

The literature cited here provides firm evidence of the utility of participant-observer methods in political science research. At the same time it suggests that participant observation promises further enrichment of the discipline if it is employed even more systematically than it has been, and if better use can be made of increasing observation opportunities.

The remainder of this chapter deals with considerations relevant to applying participant observation to research problems in political science. Advantages and problems of the general approach to research it presents are first discussed.

APPROACH

One of the features of the developing science of politics has been a tendency for political scientists to borrow proven research methods from sister disciplines. There now seem to be valid reasons for increased attention to the application in political science of partic-

ipant-observation techniques which largely have been developed
elsewhere.[5] The first reason is the apparently increasing availability
of internship opportunities for political scientists and their students.
Hennessy (1970a, pp. 13-18, 123) has enumerated several broad-scale
internship programs currently in operation, and many thousands of
internships which have been granted to faculty and students since
1953. Of these, many were faculty and graduate awards, including
161 which were APSA congressional fellowships. Only a few of these
awards have resulted in published studies (see Hedlund, 1971, app.
B). Robinson (1969) has suggested a number of ideas for making
internships more profitable in hypothesis-testing research. With the
inception in the late 1960s of the APSA Graduate Internships in
State and Local Government, and with innumerable new internship
programs developing between universities and state and local governments throughout the country, increased use of participant-observer
methods may enhance the possibility that such experiences, in addition to their substantial value in providing background for teaching
and career preparation, may be used in ways to benefit research
development in political science (see Hedlund, 1973a, 1973b; Hirschfield and Adler, 1973). Additional information on internship programs can be obtained from the National Center for Public Service
Internship Programs, 1140 Connecticut Avenue, NW, Suite 201,
Washington, D.C. 20036.

Another major reason for attention by political scientists to
participant observation is that certain distinctive advantages may
accrue to a researcher who elects to utilize its techniques with care
and advance planning. The most obvious advantage is the provision
of another data source with which the researcher may supplement
and cross-validate what might be considered "harder" data produced

5. For the limited number of published studies specifically relying on
participant observation there is a surprisingly broad literature on the problems
and opportunities of participant observation and research. The basic guides are
those Weick (1968) produced in social psychology, McCall and Simmons (1969)
in sociology, and Adams and Preiss (1960) in anthropology. Bruyn (1966)
presents a detailed theoretical defense of participant-observation suggestions in
Webb et al. (1966). Good general summaries of observation techniques and the
problems they pose can be found in the numerous guides to social science
methods. A partial list includes Goode and Hatt (1952), Festinger and Katz
(1953), Selltiz et al. (1959), Junker (1960), Riley et al. (1963a), and Duverger
(1964). See also Scott (1965), Whyte (1951), and Whyte's methodological
appendix to *Street Corner Society*, rev. ed. (1955). The leading journal in
participant observation is *Human Organization*, published by the Society for
Applied Anthropology. See also Caporaso and Roos, 1973; Herbst, 1970.

Of related methodological interest is the study of "proxemics," defined as
the study of social distance and spatial relationships, and of "kinesics," the
study of nonverbal communication through movement. Cf. Galton (1885),
Allport and Vernon (1933), Goffman (1959), Hall (1959), and Fast (1970).

by interviews, surveys, or aggregate data analysis.[6] For example, data produced through careful observation may supplement interview data to provide an index of the accuracy of a respondent's picture of himself as an actor in a social environment. A second advantage is that observation research may place a social scientist somewhat closer to the empirical reality he seeks than do some other research procedures. Hebert Gans (1962, p. 350) has written:

> *Participant observation is the only method I know that enables the research-er to get close to the realities of social life. Its deficiencies in producing quantitative data are more than made up for by its ability to minimize the distance between the researcher and his subject of study.

Surveys, interviews, aggregate data analysis, content analysis, simulation, and gaming are all important data collection techniques which are used widely because they offer certain rather predictable possibilities for controlling error in research. Each of these techniques, however, is essentially indirect and dependent upon a document, a respondent, a reporter, a simulate, or a "player" to provide basic study data about human behavior. In such studies a number of points exist at which distortion may enter between discovery of a datum and its ultimate placement in the theory under construction. For example, in survey research a number of steps occur between which data distortion may enter interstitially. Error may enter

1. in translating a research concept into a survey question
2. in the transmission of the question from interviewer to respondent
3. in the respondent's interpretation of the question
4. in his search for a response in his own consciousness
5. in the interviewer's interpretation of the response
6. in the interviewer's recording of the response
7. in the interviewer's report of what he has written when he interprets it at a later time
8. at the time data are analyzed.

In observation research there is potential for distortion, but the points where it may enter are reduced and the number of "screens" through which a datum must pass is decreased. In addition, the "immersion" of the participant observer in the environment under study, if his personal biases and blind spots can be controlled, may provide a rich context or "frame of reference" within which fragmentary or unclear data may be interpreted. (Bruyn, 1966, and Hennessy, 1970a, call this frame of reference "Verstehen" or "under-

6. See Campbell and Fiske (1959) on the increased strength of validation produced by multimethod research designs.

standing." Hedlund, 1971, calls it "feel.") Vidich and Shapiro (1955, in McCall and Simmons, 1969, pp. 301-2), in their comparison of survey and observation methods, write:

> What the survey method gains in representative coverage of a population is probably of no greater methodological significance than the increased *depth* of understanding and interpretation possible with participant-observation techniques. This is evident when we contrast the position of a survey analyst and a participant observer when both face the problem of interpreting the *meaning* of a question.... The observer ... can call upon the wealth of his experience with the linguistic habits, the attitudes, values and beliefs of the group and provide a much richer and probably sounder interpretation.

Becker and Geer (1957, in McCall and Simmons, 1969, p. 322) go still further in their advocacy of participant observation over other data collection techniques.

> The most complete form of the sociological datum, after all, is the form in which the participant observer gathers it: An observation of some social event, the events which precede and follow it, and explanations of its meaning by participants and spectators, before, during, and after its occurrence. Such a datum gives us more information about the event under study than data gathered by any other sociological method. Participant observation can thus provide us with a yardstick against which to measure the completeness of data gathered in other ways, a model which can serve to let us know what orders of information escape us when we use other methods.[7]

Third among distinctive advantages of observation research is the relative flexibility it offers for field stage alteration of research design. As new data are gathered the researcher may discover a need to shift focus temporarily or permanently to a new research goal. Such a shift by a participant observer may be relatively less costly than if a similar shift were required in a survey or interview design where extensive efforts may have already been expended in instrument design and pretesting. Depending upon a researcher's skills, a relatively unstructured situation allows the use of initiative and imagination in data collection, and of following closely a current situation as it develops.[8]

Observation thus offers the researcher the unique opportunity to use his own person and skills in the process of measurement. Quite obviously, this is an involved and intricate task, one which critics of the movement toward a science of politics believe to be more threatening than useful to reliable research. Utilizing one's human

7. See Martin Trow in McCall and Simmons (1969, pp. 332-38) for a comment critical of this enthusiastic endorsement of participant observation.

8. On flexibility and its benefits see Festinger, Riecken, and Schacter (1956, pp. 237-50).

role in social research, however, may allow access to data otherwise unavailable. When the researcher earns confidences and is accepted in his research environment he may probe for access to guarded data sources, tune in on "scuttlebutt" and gossip, and ask questions which he could not ask as an interviewer on a brief visit. As Radke-Yarrow and Rausch have written (1962, p. 1):

> There are specifically human values to human observers—in what they can observe and how they can shift focus as well as in the mistakes they make. There are virtues in the observers being, in some respects, like the observed. Hence, what might be regarded as weaknesses and obstacles can also be potential values of human observers.

Further, and within limits imposed by ethical considerations and the researcher's skills, a participant-observer role may allow a researcher to manipulate a social situation to provide variation on dimensions of the environment which are of particular research interest.

Having pointed out some advantages of participant-observation research, we must consider certain research problems which are unique to situations where an observer is an actor in the arena to be observed. For example, overuse of flexibility by an observer in the field can be a serious threat to the success of a study, and the option to redesign or modify a study plan must be exercised with great care. A lack of structure in research design, or "looseness" inherent in many participant-observer situations, is looked upon by critics as one major problem of the approach.

Riley (1963a, p. 71) suggests that participant-observer studies are subject to two basic types of error. The first is "control error" caused by the reactivity of the researcher, or his personal impact for change in the environment under study. The second is "biased viewpoint error" caused by the selective exposure and selective perception of the researcher, and specifically by the shift of his interest and perception over time. Thus "looseness" and lack of reliability in measurement are perceived to be threats to the accuracy of participant-observation studies. Other potentially serious problems with the approach should be considered as well.

It is an illusion to think that because of "looseness," or flexibility, participant-observer studies are easily implemented. They can be stressful, frustrating, and physically exhausting.[9] A participant observer must be cautious, objective, and must continually assess and evaluate his research procedures, including those aspects of observation which seem to him to be the most routine and uninteresting. He

9. One ardent testimony to the difficulties of participant-observer research is the methodological discussion in Festinger, Riecken, and Schacter (1956, p. 237). See also Whyte (1955).

must record observations regularly and in detail. This especially is important in early stages of the study when, coincidentally, it may also be the most difficult. At early stages, however, the researcher is likely still uncertain about the amount and type of data he may need to complete his study.

In a microcosmic sense, true participant-observation studies exemplify very lucidly what scientific research is all about. In such studies the researcher must deal with reality and with theory at the same time. He moves back and forth in a process of data collection and classification in the real world, and concept formation and theoretical articulation in the hypothetical world.

At the outset, the participant observer must approach a relatively unknown social situation with nothing more than preliminary notions about potentially appropriate research questions. He must move cautiously so as to influence the environment as little as possible while adjusting himself into a plausible participant role and sorting out in his perspective the major parameters and focuses of his research context, such as the actors, their physical locations, observation boundaries, system processes, and research strategies. Almost simultaneously he must attempt to impose rational conceptual order on what he is observing. He thus begins an inductive process of theory building guided by his research interests and his notions about research focuses.

Once the most gross and broad components of the theory are identified and tentatively ordered, the researcher seeks additional evidence for the purpose of articulating and validating the inductive product he has evolved. He thus begins the development of a framework which, as it proceeds, will allow initiation of a phase of deducing hypothetical consequences. If initial formulations are sound, certain kinds of predictable consequences can be deduced. Even as hypothesized consequences emerge, the researcher discovers a need to further refine categories and to collect new data for the purpose of applying tests to predicted relationships. Thus, ideally, the participant observer engages almost simultaneously in data collection, concept formation, hypothesis generation, and hypothesis testing.[10]

In practice, of course, few observation studies in any social science field actually involve all the above stages. Most produce detailed descriptions of their objects, which are normally individuals,

10. In descriptions of their own observation research Blau (1967) and Dalton (1967) show how in practice the various theory building processes are congruent. On the basic theory-building processes of participant observation, see McCall and Simmons (1969, pp. 142–228). See also Kuhn (1962), Glaser and Strauss (1967), and Dubin (1969).

groups, or organizations, leading toward some analytical conjecture in a conclusion. Only rarely are descriptive studies followed up with additional effort, and as stated above, very few hypothesis-testing studies are based on observation data.

It is clear that while one chief value of observation techniques is that they may provide rich qualitative data, these are basically descriptive in most cases, and social scientists may have neither the interest, the funds, nor the time to use such expensive and relatively inefficient methods as observation procedures if their research goals go beyond basic description. The requirements of parsimony, scientific rigor, and economy may force reliance on more stringent and tight research procedures for data collection, the costs and efficiency of which can be more easily predicted, in respect to perceived research gain.

In addition to these constraints, participant-observation research raises important ethical issues. Specifically, how much should other participants know about the objectives of the research project? How should matters of personal confidence be treated? What kinds of interpersonal confidences are acceptable? Which among all events and behaviors will be observed? What will ultimately be revealed in print? Conflicts arise in finding acceptable answers to such questions as these because a researcher must at once maintain the integrity of his project and seek to preserve his own credibility as a participant. He has ethical responsibilities to "science" in terms of the thoroughness and accuracy of his research product, to the preservation of the opportunity for future scientific work in the same environment by another researcher, and, not least, to the subjects of his research.[11]

Sociologist Howard Becker (McCall and Simmons, 1969, pp. 260–75), on the basis of extensive experience using observation techniques, suggests that the implications of a study should be explained as carefully and fully as possible in advance in order that "a proper bargain" between subjects and researchers can be struck prior to the beginning of a study. Then, he suggests, both sides should be expected to honor the bargain, with social scientists realizing that they may be in an advantageous bargaining position because of intimate familiarity with past studies. If researchers agree to censorship prior to publication they should uphold their obligation. If subjects agree to a study they should be expected to allow it. Subjects should be fully informed as to study results wherever possible, perhaps through a series of meetings in which the context

11. On the ethical responsibilities of social scientists, see Beals (1969), Rainwater and Pittman (1967), Sjoberg (1967), and Committee on Professional Standards and Responsibilities (1968).

of the study as it is revealed may cushion the potential controversy surrounding the report.

Researchers should carefully consider how much they can reveal to their subjects about the research focus. Revealing too much may cause reactivity and change in behavior. Not revealing enough may inhibit acceptance of the researcher because of mistrust. Before entering the field situation the researcher should have clearly in mind how he will respond when asked, "What is your paper topic?" or "What is it you are doing here?" In general, it can be suggested that he reveal as much of his research intent as possible, short of those aspects of the study which might arouse opposition, suspicion, or which might occasion change in normal behavior patterns.

Ethical problems arise regarding what is watched and what behaviors are recorded. A researcher must be selective in what he records because of his limited access, the constraints on his time, problems of regular record keeping, and out of regard for the rights of others. Information potentially harmful to other participants in personal matters should be treated with great care. Overzealous interest in interpersonal disputes, romances, financial or emotional problems, or the like may potentially destroy acceptance of an observer, as well as the personal life of the subject if such information were ever revealed.[12]

Further ethical issues revolve around the content of the final research report. Becker suggests that neither facts nor conclusions should be published which are not necessary to the support of the study thesis. Neither should they be published, he says, if they might cause suffering out of proportion to the scientific gain of making them public. The publication of *Small Town in Mass Society* (Vidich and Bensman, 1958) is frequently cited as an instance where members of the small New York community studied were allegedly recognizable in the book, and where the self-image of the community was thought to be substantially affected. Ralph and Estelle James relate in their volume (1965) the deflating impact of one of their chapters on Jimmy Hoffa, its principal subject. Laurence Wylie (1957) discusses village reaction to the publication of his French community study. I recall a meeting of graduate students with Charles Adrian, author of *Four Cities*, during which he expressed

12. In regard to the ethics of what behavior is observed and recorded one may note the controversy in sociological literature regarding observation studies of casual sexual encounters between both heterosexual (Roebuck and Spray, 1967) and homosexual persons (Humphreys, 1970). The appropriateness of such studies is discussed by Von Hoffman, Horowitz, and Rainwater (1970). One might also consider the experimental research of Masters and Johnson (1966) based on observation of sexual relations involving over time more than 700 persons.

reluctance when asked to reveal the names of the cities he studied. Chris Argyris (in Adams and Preiss, 1960, pp. 122–23) amplifies Becker's suggestion about discretion in publishing study results. He suggests that it is psychologically unhealthy for a researcher not to feel responsibility for the proper use of his product if his research results may in any way be used against or toward other human beings. Argyris says, "Only children and mentally ill persons are freed of this responsibility, the former only temporarily." Thus, distinctive advantages accrue and unique problems emerge in applying participant-observation research in political science. Discussion of research design may suggest means for resolving some problems discussed and for enhancing some advantages.

DESIGN

Every scientist observes. Watching and recording stasis and change in phenomena is the most basic activity of scientific research. In much of science, however, "watching" is a highly sophisticated process involving intricate measurement apparatus. Although the levels of methodological development clearly differ, the search for accurate and nonreactive measurement devices is no less a feature of social science development than it has been of development in the so-called hard sciences. The utility of observation techniques in measurement depends in large part upon research design.

Based on a combination of methodological procedures, participant observation offers extensive flexibility in research design. One feature of the procedure, as suggested above, is that it may be employed in situations in which, because of lack of information about major variables in observation contexts, it would appear that *no* advance research design is possible. Beginning research with decisions unmade as to major variables and data collection techniques, and with potential informants and respondents yet unidentified, can be a stimulating and productive experience. In such instances, a researcher must be able to accept initial ambiguities, and in view of the uncertain potential gain of his research, to justify the expense and time a lack of structure requires. Practical political internships with research goals are good examples in political science of instances where unstructured research designs are often imposed by lack of adequate advance acquaintance with the observation context. Intentionally unstructured designs offer the possibilities that discovery can be maximized and that the native intelligence and insights of the researcher can be extensively utilized in the research process (see Lohman, 1937, and Kluckhohn, 1940).

The extent to which research designs are developed preceding observation field work depends primarily upon the number and scope of central research questions and the level at which the researcher intends to seek answers. To isolate a central question or series of questions for observation research on the basis of limited advance information is a difficult task, but the initial work required to order alternative research questions before field work begins will be abundantly rewarded. There are a number of common means for discovering feasible central research questions, the most obvious of which is a review of literature relating to the major actors, processes, and institutions relevant to the observation context. Literature searches for studies in need of replication or validation, for basic untested propositions or hypotheses, or for other unresolved issues of potential interest to the observer, will be of proportionately greater value to the study the earlier they are applied in research planning.

If the researcher seeks answers to central research questions at the level of basic description, extensive advance planning may not be required. Such studies may succeed with the establishment of basic data categories, and the collection of observation records during the field period. If observation research is undertaken as a source of validational data supplementary to data produced primarily from another source, enough advance planning will be required to assure that data needs are clear, and that data collection categories are established prior to field work.

If the researcher needs observational data of a quality sufficient for hypothesis testing, he will need extensive advance planning to become as familiar as circumstances allow with the major actors and variables involved in the observation environment prior to working out a final design. Finally, if the researcher plans to manipulate certain aspects of an observation environment for purposes of experimentation, he imposes upon himself the need to understand thoroughly the parameters and characteristics of the environment so that his manipulations are effective and adequately protective of other participants involved. Thus, the extent to which research is structured and designed in advance in observation studies depends directly upon the goal of the research.

Progress in determining central research questions and the levels at which they might be answered will allow initial assessment of data needs which will underlie the basic research design. Data needs might be determined in conjunction with a pre-field examination of the broad range of available data sources which the observation context

offers. In addition to general data sources such as libraries, newspapers, political speeches, fugitive campaign materials, press releases,
propaganda from local political organizations, office files, and access
to the mail, observation designs normally employ interviewing, informants, and direct observation.

Selection of informants in whom the researcher may confide and
from whom he may elicit highly useful and semiguarded information
is a common occurrence in observation studies. The informant's
word is taken as validly as is the researcher's own personal record,
and by confiding in him and asking him for information the participant observer extends himself both spatially, in the sense that the
informant may occupy a different physical location than the
observer, and historically, in the sense that the informant will likely
have had more extensive experience in the relevant environment than
the observer.[13]

Another common practice in participant observation is the selection of certain key participants to serve as occasional respondents in
more or less formal interview situations for the purpose of reporting
on specific events or providing in-depth information. Some features
of the research environment are closed to access or understanding by
the observer and are only available through the willingness of other
participants to provide information.

Several types of direct-observation and data-recording procedures
are common to field situations and should be built into research
designs. Most important in this regard is the chronological record of
events which should be written or dictated regularly, preferably
daily. It may contain descriptions of individuals, events, actions,
explanations, interpretations, assignments, records of conversations,
and miscellaneous comments. Use of checklists in keeping the daily
record complete is suggested by Selltiz et al. (1959, pp. 209-10) and
by Richardson in Adams and Preiss (1960, pp. 124-39).

Another basic type of observation data concerns the rules and
norms in a given environment which may be learned both through
participation and through observing the interaction of others. Easy
adjustment into a participant-observer role is greatly facilitated if
early attention is paid to the norms of personal interaction and the
common rules governing the environment. As much as possible, the
researcher at the design stage should become familiar with the physical locations from which he will be observing. He should attempt
also to determine the character of organizational arrangements, both

13. Kahn and Mann (1952) discuss the development of "partnerships" in
research. Campbell discusses the use of the informant in interviewing. Whyte
used "Doc" as an informant in *Street Corner Society* (1943). Dalton discusses
his relationships with "intimates" (1967, pp. 76-81).

formal and informal, so that his initial role orientation to the field might be made with attention to establishing confidences and keeping open channels of communication with key staff members. Hennessy (1970a, pp. 103–22) suggests, on the basis of his analysis of internship experiences, ways in which awareness of qualities of the research environment and qualities of interns may relate to each other in the presentation of the kinds of conditions appropriate for meaningful research

A third type of observation data, specific enumerations of events or behaviors, may be required in a research design. Robinson (1962b) relates having counted and categorized speeches at the Democratic National Convention according to themes. He also counted rounds of applause by members of the Illinois delegation during speeches and noted the varying degrees of interest expressed by delegates. Enumerations may be relatively easy to obtain in many observation contexts. For example, a participant observer on the staff of a U.S. senator may wish to know how his senator's time is allocated among constituents, lobbyists, staff conferences, committee work, and personal activities. Several sources of data are available to him. First, depending on his location, he may watch and record traffic into and out of the office. Second, he may utilize the register which guests normally sign when they visit a Senate office. Third, he can look at the records of the office receptionist regarding traffic into and out of the reception area. Fourth, the senator's personal secretary has records of his schedule; and fifth, the senator's administrative assistant, along with the personal secretary, might be enlisted as an informant. Enumeration of visitors and reliance on informants for time data should allow reconstruction of a senator's day, and then the analysis of whatever subset of the collected data the researcher wishes to isolate.

Decisions about data needs for a specific research design should thus be based on a review of the array of potential data sources from which an observer may draw, ranging from traditional documentary records through interviews and use of informants, to several types of observation and enumeration.

In addition to considerations of research intent and data availability, a number of other basic issues relevant to scope and accessible resources determine the research design. These issues include the number of observers that can be used, the number of observation sites to be studied, the time allocated, and the availability of additional supporting resources such as mechanical and clerical assistance.

First, how many observers will there be? Most participant-observer studies involve a single researcher, but availability of additional personnel may allow (1) broader research focus if observers are located in the same or similar environments; (2) comparison, if observers utilize similar data collection procedures and categories in different but similar environments; (3) inter-coder reliability checks, if enumeration and observation schemes are sufficiently developed to warrant them; and (4) teamwork, wherein two researchers can join efforts, with the first as interviewer and the second as observer in an interview situation (Gorden, 1969). Wyner's (1967) extensive team of observers using common data collection procedures in fourteen governors' offices produced an extremely rich body of data. The use of three observers in the Minar (1966) and Snow (1966) studies allowed inter-coder reliability checks on observation coding procedures, which added credibility to the study. Two participant observers in the Festinger, Riecken, and Schacter (1956) study communicated with each other important information about basic data needs and important events among the cultist group they infiltrated.

Second, how many observation sites are to be utilized? Advantages of more than a single observation site are the same as or closely parallel to those provided by more than a single observer. For example, the value of a study of campaign processes might be greatly increased if trained participant observers using similar research plans could be placed with both or all of the major competing candidates during a period of several weeks prior to an election. Even a single observer, however, might enhance the value of his study if he can develop access to more than one observation site. In urban areas, for example, where many separate units of local government are located close to each other—each with similar legal authority standardized by state laws—a single observer might divide his participant-observer time among several sites in search of comparative data in which he has an interest.

Third, how much time is available? Generally speaking, the longer the time available, the better will be the study. Acceptance of an observer into an environment by others requires some time, as does the observer's own socialization into his role. Time requirements should be analyzed during research design, and the time allocated, the scope, and the intent of research should be arranged in direct correlation with each other.

Finally, what resources in addition to observers, sites, and time are available? Through adequate funding or borrowing such resources as mechanical and clerical assistance, the possibilities of data collection through observation may be greatly enhanced. When, for example, photography (Collier, 1967), photoelectric counters, and audio or video tape recorders can be utilized in nonreactive ways (see Webb et al., 1966, pp. 142–70), semipermanent records of special events, interviews, routine interactions, traffic flows, or other aspects of the observation environment, can be made for close subsequent and repeated analysis. Using small group methods, or behavioral coding schemes, such records can produce high-quality quantitative data.

Good clerical assistance, including the use of a dictaphone, is of special importance in observation research as needs begin to build for keeping daily records, coding communications, and for filing extensive bodies of data.

The presence of mechanical and clerical assistance also enhances the researcher's ability to utilize more than a single method in collecting data relating to the same phenomenon, and thus to engage in "multiple operationism" with a view toward increasing reliability in the study (see Webb et al., 1966, pp. 1-5).

In sum, considerations of scope and intent of research, data needs and availability, and the accessibility of supporting resources are fundamental to research design in participant observation.

IMPLEMENTATION

How does the participant observer proceed in the field? In a word, the answer should be "cautiously." During the initial field period, the observer will be the observed, and his early mistakes will linger. Until he has earned trust and some supportive personal acquaintances, and until he becomes aware of the norms of interpersonal relations, his data collection efforts should be withheld; or if begun, they should be tentative, and humbly employed (see Dean, Eichhorn, and Dean in McCall and Simmons, 1969, pp. 68-70).

Three basic considerations emerge as most important for implementation of observation research. They relate first to role and task selection and observer skills; second to strategic locations and procedures for observation, including where, when, and how to record and store data; and third to maintaining accuracy and objectivity in data recording.

First impressions formed of the researcher and of his role as he begins participant observation will be of great importance to the ultimate success of the study. Ideally, those persons well established in the research environment will perceive the newcomer as affable, as a peer, as one willing to work hard, and as one who poses little threat to their roles. The degree of threat posed depends in part upon the participant-observer role selected (Olesen and Whittaker, 1967). To the extent that the observation context involves interaction with other people, Argyris (Adams and Preiss, 1960, p. 122) suggests that a role as a passive researcher observer is more likely to arouse anxiety than is a role as an active participant who seeks identification as "one of the team." Davis (1964, p. 355) and Junker (1960, p. 38) have suggested that extremes in role selection, those of pure observation on one end and pure participation and self-analysis on the other, tend to gather less information than intermediate stances on observers participating or participants observing.[14] Davis writes, "The complete *participant* adopts a cover that restricts his perceptions and often interferes with the maintenance of detachment, while the complete *observer* lacks rapport and, if known, frequently proves an upsetting irritant to the group" (emphasis added). Junker adds that the complete observer "is strictly an imaginary role," inasmuch as the mere presence of an observer will have some impact upon the environment which renders him something of a participant. Argyris (Adams and Preiss, 1960, p. 122) reinforces the suggestion that the complete observer role may be nonproductive of results: "If he [the observer] expects people to express their thoughts and feelings freely to him, he cannot conceal his own thoughts and feelings completely from them."

Ideally, a nonessential but potentially contributing position in the research environment may be available such as (in a political science context) a special projects research assistant, a writer, or a temporary assistant to a central organizational figure. Such a position is preferable first because it may appear relatively marginal and thus less threatening to permanent staff members. Second, it will be more "comprehensive" in the sense that it may provide periodic opportunities for changing physical locations within the observation environment. Third, it allows an observer to demonstrate his willingness early in the field period to work hard. If his position is marginal, but one in which he can prove his productivity, doing so will help him to develop others' confidence and trust in him. Such a position will allow the researcher to become more broadly acquainted with other participants through discreet requests for advice and task direction. Finally, its marginality and flexibility will allow some autonomy useful for occasional unobtrusive note taking.

Personality factors and the human relations skills of a researcher will have a direct bearing upon success in observation, as will his social position, age, sex, and national origin. While there may be few means to control the impact of such variables, their potential effects should be continually considered in data evaluation. Some of the particular characteristics of an observer may prove beneficial in a research situation. South African anthropologist David Brokensha

14. The appropriateness of role and its relation to the quantity and quality of data produced is a point debated in the literature. For a statement on the utility of total personal immersion into a social situation, see Garfinkel (1967). See also Bruyn (1966, pp. 12, 178–81) and Hennessy (1970a, pp. 103–4) on the concept of *Verstehen*.

informed me that his native British accent made him a "neutral" in a Mexican-American farm-worker community in central California. It also established him as a "stranger" from whom either the most basic or the most probing questions, innocently asked, were acceptable.

An enterprising observer may look for unique opportunities to enhance the quality of the data he can obtain through interaction and observation. Social events offer good occasions, since normal organizational roles are altered to a nonwork context which may allow special insight into informal group organization. In the interaction context, he may also develop "reciprocities" whereby a small, discreet, and ethical service or favor may be rendered another participant in such a way as to enhance friendship and trust in his favor. Knowledge of the researcher's study and desire to preserve one's favorable place therein may in itself provide a potential reward which will induce cooperation from permanent participants.[15]

The participant observer may discover that the strategic physical location of his desk or working space in the research environment will have direct implications for the quality of data he is able to collect. Selection of a locus in an environment will involve trade-offs, since access to certain sites will limit access to others in most field situations. Depending upon research interests, a researcher should locate himself strategically to maximize observation opportunities if he can do so without offense to others. In a government or political office an observer may seek proximity to a primary communications center. These may include the desk or office of an organizational official or central staff member, or they may be file rooms, mail rooms, reception desks, or switchboards.

Whatever the physical location of the observer in the environment, a number of possibilities afford themselves for systematic data recording. To the extent possible, regular field notes and enumerations should be recorded at the time and on the spot where notable events occur. The observer should avoid long lapses of time between the occurrence of significant events and his recording of them. Use of a dictaphone or small tape recorder will help immensely. He will maximize the amount and quality of his data and reduce distortion if he can make immediate notations of significant occurrences.[16] Festinger, Riecken, and Schacter (1956) report that their observers found it useful—in the intense environment which they studied for

15. On the notion of "reciprocities," see Gusfield (1955), Wax (1957), or Adams and Preiss (1960, pp. 90–123), which contains them both. See also McCall and Simmons (1969, pp. 2, 68–70).

16. A report by the Behavioral and Social Sciences Survey Committee of the Social Science Research Council (1969, p. 49) states that man, according to research, "can retain in short term memory about seven 'chunks' of information, a chunk being any unit that is thoroughly familiar to him such as a number, a

When Prophecy Fails—to retire periodically to the bathroom to make observation notes. William Whyte (1955) was elected secretary of the street corner gang in which he participated, thus enabling him to make extensive notes in a way which did not arouse suspicion.

In addition to recording field notes, a number of systematic observer protocols are potentially applicable to political science research. Included are those alluded to above which have been applied by Walter (1963, 1966), Kovenock (1964, 1967), Alger (1965), Minar (1966), Snow (1966), and Barber (1966). Borgatta and Crowther include potentially useful protocols and practical direction in their workbook (1965). Verba (1961) discusses research methods for small groups, as do Heyns and Zander (1953), and Heyns and Lippitt (1954). Suggestions for research design and specific measurement amenable to participant observation are made by Delbert C. Miller (1964, 1970). Madron (1969) explains in detail some political science applications of Bales's (1950, 1952) interaction process analysis, as well as some other observer rating scales.

There are occasions in participant observation, however, when it is not convenient to make written field notes or complete protocols because of the possibility that suspicion might be aroused. In such cases researchers have utilized other techniques to make enumerations and records. James Robinson bent paper matches in a matchbook each time a particular event occurred during a brief period of intense interaction in which he was a participant observer. I have made records with thumbnail marks in styrofoam cups, paper napkins, and wooden pencils. Pencil marks on napkins, menus, envelopes, small note pads, and the like can be used for enumerations in situations where detailed field notes or compilation of observer protocols are impossible.

In preparing written records such as field notes and protocols it is useful to make more than a single copy so that at the analysis stage some might be available for clipping and classification into category files. One copy should be retained as a chronological record.

Efforts toward maintaining objectivity and accuracy in recording data will increase the acceptability of research results by other social scientists. There are quite normal tendencies among observers to be highly selective in what data are recorded and thus to omit much detail, to be uneven and inaccurate in recording, as well as to misunderstand individual behaviors and to make improper and unjustified associations between them. These are the kinds of weaknesses in the human being as a measuring device which invite skepticism about the utility of

---

familiar word or the name of a friend." Researchers find this phenomenon to be "surprisingly consistent for many different kinds of tasks, and quite consistent among persons." Thus, the necessity for regular and frequent recording of events is underscored.

participant-observation research (Schwartz and Schwartz, 1955). Among the most effective correcting devices open to an observer in the field is to confide principal conclusions to an informant in order to check their validity. Informants may also be helpful in assessing the degree to which the researcher himself has been productive of change in the environment he is seeking to understand.

In addition to these types of error, there are strong pressures in field situations to abandon personal detachments, to take sides (Colfax, 1966), and thus to conclude a report of participant observation as an apologist or a partisan, defending a position rather than providing an analysis. Such pressures may be especially strong in political science contexts where advanced undergraduates, graduate students, and faculty members have had direct involvement with political campaigns, staff service, or even holding political office. They may be intensely aware of and sympathetic to the vulnerability of some political actors, as well as of the very personal and sensitive nature of much interaction in politically relevant environments. Such close exposure to the persons and arenas which are the objects of much political science research may produce a number of possible effects upon a participant observer. It may produce "blind spots," making him unable to see certain aspects of the environment he is studying. It may dull his sensitivity to certain "routine" processes and patterns of interaction which may be central to research interests but taken for granted by the observer because they are taken for granted by the observed. In anthropological research this kind of desensitizing overexposure is referred to as "going native." It may lead the researcher to lose perspective, to abandon regularity of effort, and to conclude that nothing significant is happening for his research because everything appears to be so "normal" (see S. M. Miller, 1952).

Although difficult and demanding of personal discipline, an effective check against going native is regular and systematic recording of observation data, especially including the daily record. Category checklists, maintaining a regular schedule of respondent interviews, conversations with informants, and the routine drudgery of compiling and storing study data, probably more than any other influence, will keep uppermost in the mind of a researcher the central goals and focus of his research.

ANALYSIS

The title of this chapter, "Participant-Observer Analysis," implies correctly that analytical activity is a *constant* part of the process of participant observation. Analytical thinking begins with the general approach to observation field work when initial concepts and definitions of the research environment are being sought. It continues through the stages of research design and study implementation, and is summarized and extended during post-field consideration of the collected body of research data. The implications of the constant process of analysis are that data must be maintained in good order, with regularity, and with care as to quality and accessibility.

Constant analysis implies that basic research categories and data collection procedures are being continually examined and evaluated during the period of research. Glaser (1965) argues in this vein that the most effective use of participant observation in building theoretical constructs is the procedure of "constant comparison," which calls for ongoing assessment of the basic goals, categories, concepts, and directions of research through continuous reflection of the meaning and place of new data as they are collected.

It is thus necessary at the outset of research activity to develop a scheme for imposing order and accessibility on the data as they are collected. McCall and Simmons (1969, pp. 75–76) suggest two different data-indexing schemes for rendering accessible the extensive details recorded in daily records and field notes. One scheme, developed by Whyte (1960), is based on a continuous categorization and indexing of data as they are collected, using three columns on a page. The first column is used for basic reference material including date of collection, document or page numbers, and data location. The second column is used for identification of persons present, involved, interviewed, or informing, and the third column is used to identify the relevant topical categories on which data exist. This hand-indexing system appears cumbersome, but it allows exhaustive categorization of field notes, and renders them more available. Index guides by individual topic can be created, so that every reference to a particular topic in field notes is quickly available.

A more efficient and less demanding scheme is suggested by McCall. It is more efficient in that it facilitates addition of new categories, and less demanding in that it eliminates the need for extensive hand indexing. McCall has experimented with typing field notes directly on a duplicator stencil so that several copies can be run off corresponding with a number somewhat larger than the number of predetermined data categories he has established. Each page is dated and numbered, and one chronological field-record file is maintained. Data pertaining to the study categories are circled in red, and the dated pages on which they appear are placed in appropriate topical folders. If new categories are established, extra copies of past field notes can be quickly scanned for relevance. Periodically, during the field work, materials in each topical folder are summarized into a "position paper," which requires a summation of existent data, and which may point to new insights and a need for additional data categories.

Such indexing schemes, especially the latter, provide opportunities for imaginative analysts to "mine" the field data for potential *quantitative* information. For example, *post hoc* analysis of field notes and enumeration of visits by legislators to the office of a governor during a legislative session might be fruitful if the enumeration were compared with a record of major legislative events of the session. It might show, for example, that visits from opposition party legislators to the governor decrease immediately after the latter engages in publicized partisan political activity. Opposition party visits might increase, on the other hand, suggesting the occurrence of bargaining, following the occurrence of a show of legislative independence of the governor by his own party legislators. Further analysis might show a slowdown of legislative-gubernatorial interaction within the same party to have immediately preceded the show of legislative independence. Daily records, documents, interview reports, and informant notes may all be examined with the specific idea of discovering useful quantifiable data. Thus, indexing schemes and "data mining" are means of continuously analyzing data and rendering them more accessible and comprehensible.

The researcher has a number of options open by which to assess the *quality* of the data he has gathered. It should be understood that certain limitations on quality are inherent in the participant-observation approach. They have been discussed above, and will only be summarized here. Participant observers will tend to collect data which are biased nonrandomly because of limited access to interactions and events, because of biases in observer perception and modification of the observer's frame of reference over time, and because the observer himself has impact on the environment which is difficult to assess. Other more subtle data biases may enter as well. As a part of continuing analysis researchers should be as fully aware as possible of the potential bias of data. In the research report the biases should be fully explained, as should any evidence that some of the biases have been predicted and controlled by the research design.

Control on data bias or "error variance" may be exerted, as suggested above, by "multiple operationism," or by seeking more than a single measure of important phenomena. Webb et al. (1966, pp. 1-5) suggest that strength in analysis results from converging weaknesses of measurement. If the data base contains interview materials, informant reports, and observation data, all of which converge to shed light on a single explanation, the case for the validity of the explanation will be much stronger, as will the case for reliability of each individual measurement. Bruyn (1966, pp. 180–85) relies on George Homans in making specific suggestions relative to criteria for assessing the quality of observation data. In summary, his criteria include (1) adequate time spent in observation, (2) physical closeness of the observer to the observed group, (3) a variety of social circumstances and status opportunities within which the observer has been able to relate to his subjects, (4) familiarity of the observer with the language of the subjects, and (5) intimacy without overinvolvement achieved by the observer with the subjects. Bruyn states, "Our confidence in the observer's report increases as his ability to answer well to all of these requirements increases."

After the data quality has been ascertained, the analyst's task is the integration of data into patterns of relationship in accordance with preliminary theory. The question is "How does it all fit together?" or "How can I tell what it means?" In a certain sense, making it all fit together is an act of special insight and skill because of the mass of the data and its primarily qualitative character. Barton and Lazarsfeld (McCall and Simmons, 1969, p. 163) state the problem thus: "What can a researcher do when confronted by a body of qualitative data—detailed, concrete, non-metric descriptions of people and events, drawn from direct observation, interviews, case studies, historical writings, the writings of participants?"

Following a review of some 100 studies based on qualitative data, Barton and Lazarsfeld made generalizations about the use of qualitative observations in theory building. They discovered (1) that some single qualitative observations are analyzed alone because they raise particular problems and demand single explanations, either because they are unexpected and anomalous, or because they indicate evidence of some broader-scale social phenomenon not readily observable other than by qualitative assessment; (2) that some qualitative observations appear to fit together or are, on the basis of an adopted rule, grouped in descriptive categories; (3) that certain groups of observations or categories of description appeared to be related to each other in causal ways; and (4) that in some instances, observations or descriptive categories fit together in "matrix formulations" which have the character of basic theoretical formulations. Barton and Lazarsfeld define a "matrix formulation" as "a descriptive concept on a higher level which manages to embrace and sum up a great wealth of observations in a single formula" (McCall and Simmons, 1969, p. 192). Their review of literature thus reveals that through inductive analysis qualitative observations can, at various levels and to varying degrees, be fitted together in the construction of theory.

At the point where theoretical formulations are emerging, the analytical emphasis shifts to their articulation and, as Becker and

Geer (1960, p. 288) state it, to the search for "negative cases." If and when they are found, the search for data and theory begins anew.

Webb et al. (1966, p. 1) wrote *Unobtrusive Measures* to suggest that the narrow range of research methods utilized in social science should be broadened to include new and unique measurement possibilities. They wrote:

> Today, some 90 percent of social science research is based upon interviews and questionnaires. We lament this overdependence upon a single fallible method. Interviews and questionnaires intrude as a foreign element into the social setting they would describe, they create as well as measure attitudes, they elicit atypical roles and responses . . . *But the principal objection is that they are used alone* [their emphasis].

This essay suggests that there is utility in efforts to directly measure human behavior, that it is useful in political science research to watch and record, more or less simply, human and organizational behavior in politically relevant settings, and that participant-observer analysis can usefully supplement interviews, questionnaires, and other research methods as a data source in political science.

14. THE ANALYSIS OF AGGREGATE DATA

Carl Beck and Douglas K. Stewart

A theory of social science data presumes social science theory. It is pointless to discuss problems of data as though they had no relationship to conceptual or theoretical problems. Today, an unfortunate propensity exists on the part of many to dichotomize knowledge into two independent realms of discourse: to view data-related problems as technical problems and to view theoretical problems as unrelated to data. A chasm in contemporary social research is perpetuated when the empirically oriented social scientist categorizes the theoretician as being abstract and idealized and when the theoretically oriented social scientist views the empiricist as a statistician or, even worse, as a stand-alone computer. This chasm results in the bifurcation of political science and adds credence to the argument that it is less than relevant to contemporary life. It is only in the mesh of theory construction and data analysis that fruitful research and knowledge can be generated (Andrain and Apter, 1968; LaPalombara, 1968; Deutsch, 1966b).

There is some disagreement in political science as to what is meant by theory. We agree with Raymond Aron that

> a theory is a hypothetical, deductive system consisting of a group of hypotheses whose terms are strictly defined and whose relationships between terms (or variables) are most often given a mathematical form. The elaboration of this system starts with a conceptualization of perceived or observed reality; axioms or highly abstract relationships govern the system and allow the scientist to rediscover by deduction either appearances that are thereby fully explained, or facts that are perceptible through devices, if not through the senses, and that temporarily either confirm the theory or invalidate it [Aron, 1967, p. 186].

In this research orientation, data become relevant as they explicate the conceptualization of perceived or observed reality, either supporting (not confirming) that conceptualization or causing it to be amended.

Too often, both empirical and theoretical problems are treated as existing in disjoint domains. In this chapter we are concerned with the use of aggregate data. We shall discuss the structure of data and the ways in which they can be manipulated. Our major posture is that operations undertaken on data, whether individual or aggregate, must be mappable into symbolic operations within a theory. For example, calculating the arithmetic mean involves summing over all observations and dividing by the number of observations. The social scientist should be sure that the two operations (summation and division) can be represented by the social science theory in use. If we agree on this orientation, empirical problems can be taken to represent theoretical problems. We have set an exacting task for social research. For example, if we find in a particular re-search project that the use of means on the one hand or medi-ans on the other produce different results, we must conclude that this paradox exists simply because the theory that shaped the research is insufficiently explicit as to which measure of cen-tral tendency is appropriate. In this context, then, there are no pure empirical problems.

It is sometimes argued that if a theory generates predictions with respect to unavailable data, the research problem is an empirical one. We should turn the statement around, however, and suggest that it is a weakness of the theory that it does not predict anything with respect to observable information. It is a nonfalsifiable theory in practice, if not in principle. A recurrent theme of this chapter is that various so-called empirical problems can be traced either to a lack of theoretical rigor, or to a failure to match operations on data to operations of theory (Coombs, 1964; Churchman and Ratoosch, 1959).

There are numerous uninterpreted theories such as the theory of point sets, the theory of mathematical statistics, and the theory of probability. Empirical social science involves developing rules of correspondence between observable data and the elements, relations, and operations of an uninterpreted theory. With the development of such rules of correspondence the theory becomes interpreted or empirical.

The behavioral revolution in the study of politics has led to two major research styles: the use of information based upon the observa-tion of individuals, and the use of information based upon the observation of collectivities, usually nation-states or regions within states (Scheuch, 1966). In the United States, the dominant research style has been the study of individual behavior and the analysis of data based upon sophisticated interviewing of the electorate

(Campbell et al., 1960). The high degree of confidence in the information, the extent of conceptual clarity of those persons observing and explaining voting behavior, and the theoretical sophistication of the researchers, have buttressed this orientation. In Europe, however, there has been a "long and honorable tradition" of working with aggregate data, particularly census data (Scheuch, 1966, p. 131). These intellectual traditions have tended to perpetuate themselves. However, with the increased cross-fertilization of research styles, one of the contemporary motifs in social research in the United States is the use of information descriptive of nation-states for the purpose of making broad comparisons between national states (Banks and Textor, 1963; Russett, 1964).

With increasing regularity, aggregate data are utilized in contemporary social research. Of particular promise in this regard is the formation of complex data sets from such diverse sources as census tract data, precinct voting data, and survey data. The mixing of information from several sources often introduces serious problems when the reporting units are not identical (e.g., census tract data and precinct data). In general, statistical geographers are particularly sophisticated with respect to such problems. Two sources of worth are Neft (1966) and Berry and Marble (1968).

PROBLEMS IN THE USE OF AGGREGATE DATA

We define "aggregate data" as "data descriptive of collectivities such as areal, cultural, or political units." Aggregate data are relevant to a rich variety of theoretical units of analysis. Any variable used to describe a collectivity is an aggregate variable. Such variables are defined in terms of the operations undertaken on a specified set of elements. To draw out the relationship between the data and the theory, we must be able to specify the measurement function that associates one value with each element in a set of observations. We should allocate more of our resources to the specification of the measurement function, but, in every piece of research, purely administrative problems intrude upon our ability to do this (Hammond, 1964).

Erwin K. Scheuch (1966) has noted that there is both enthusiasm and suspicion in the use of aggregate data. The enthusiasm for aggregate data stems from the present capability of individuals to undertake research that a generation ago only the most massive research institutes could undertake. Suspicion arises from the nature of the data now available for secondary analysis and the analytical problems that face the user of aggregate data. We have already emphasized that most problems associated with the use of aggregate data can be viewed as problems in theory. This, however, makes them no less troublesome. Some purely administrative problems exist as well.

Accessibility

Until the last decade, only a few academic centers and government agencies possessed machine-readable data and were willing and organized to make their data available to other scholars. Fortunately, an increasing number of research projects, academic institutions, and government agencies are now becoming archives for social science data (Bisco, 1968). Since 1960, at least fifty social science data archives have been formed in academic centers alone, and a number of networks have been developed for sharing data bases. Among these are the Council of Social Science Data Archives (Bisco, 1968) and the Inter-University Consortium for Political and Social Research (Miller, 1965).[1] Despite these efforts, a number of problems confront the potential user as he attempts to find out whether information relevant to his research interest has been collected and is available to him. The majority of users do not know the most likely sources of needed machine-processable information; the potential user is confronted with a diversity of manual, semiautomated, and low level automated retrieval systems (Bisco, 1968). The nexus of these two conditions can result in extreme frustration. Therapeutic steps are being taken, but at this time, support for such remedies is far from adequate for bringing about a cure.

Accuracy

Aggregate data tend to come from diverse sources, as from a particular research project or from data bases established for administrative or political purposes. They also tend to take different forms. In the case of the *Cross-Polity Survey*, for example, a group of experts was used to rank polities in terms of an array of variables as a complement to quantitative indices. Quantitative indices alone were not employed, because they were unavailable, unreliable, or incapable of being validated. "Statistics for many variables, especially where the newer nations are concerned, are notoriously suspect"

1. Since this writing the council has been disbanded.

(Banks and Textor, 1963, p. 14). "In general, there is a clear tendency for the quality and availability of data to rise with the level of economic development in a country" (Russett, 1966, p. 97). Most social scientists are acquainted with cases in which data have been deliberately distorted for political reasons, even in advanced industrialized societies.

Relevance

"How do we define a party member? The reply varies according to the party: each holds to a concept of membership which is peculiar to it" (Duverger, 1955, p. 37). The meaning of party membership may not be a significant problem when a researcher is studying the structure of political parties in a manageable number of states. It becomes a very significant problem when someone else, remote from the conceptual problem, uses membership data as one factor in an array of factors in order to describe a particular unit or to compare that unit with another one. What party membership actually means in differing historical periods, or in differing countries, is a key question, but that question becomes lost when party membership is used in conjunction with, for example, another set of 100 additional variables.

Another class of problem that confronts the user of data collected for other purposes concerns what social scientists call censored data. Here we have in mind coding categories that are too broad for the purposes of the secondary analyst. If "nonwhite" is a reporting category in a study, how can one extract characteristics of American Indians? The variable is not the one required by the investigator.

To no small extent the nature of the findings of relationships between various attributes—whether aggregate or individual—depends upon how the data are categorized. Kenneth Janda points out that at least three carefully constructed studies have explored the relationship of urbanization to inter-party competition. In the research process, the three studies categorized the variables in different and arbitrary fashions. Conflicting interpretations of such findings can result in neither staunch support for nor rejection of the relationships postulated by the theory (Janda, 1965, 1969).

One basic strategy seems crucial to this problem: to code the information required as empirically (as exactly) as possible. Instead of categorizing income into five or ten categories, record income: instead of using arbitrary designations for class, record all of the relevant information available that can be used to describe class. This simple strategy makes it possible to aggregate or disaggregate data while minimizing the degree by which the unexplicated conceptual biases of a coder—or of a researcher—intrude upon the data. It also enables a person to replicate research. Every decision about how to treat certain sets of information is recallable through a search of the computer program used to form indices.

Censored data constitute a general problem for any empirical analysis. If the desired variable is unavailable, should one desist from empirical inquiry or should one "patch up" the research design in order to use what is available, though not ideal? In general, we believe it is better to use less than ideal variables than to terminate research. We emphasize the theoretical aspect of the issue. In support of our position, a "strong" theory is more likely to enable us to estimate the desired parameter from the observed value than is a weak theory. In the limiting case, a very strong theory would enable us to determine the "dishonesty bias" of a closed society. On occasion, however, the available indicators are so far removed from the desired indicators that any analytical outcome is irrelevant. This is an important consideration that the researcher ought to confront before undertaking a lengthy project.

The Measurement Function

An important problem relative to the use of aggregate data is the measurement function. This is especially bothersome in the case of historical and cross-cultural data. We may superficially define a measurement function as a rule that associates one and only one value with each element in a set of observations. In the case of historical or cross-national data, measurement functions often vary. For example, the rules used to categorize responses to a question on employment may vary drastically over time and reporting agencies. Another, perhaps less significant, example is the difference in referents for "billion" in the United States versus the United Kingdom (a thousand million versus a million million or 10^9 versus 10^{12}). In addition to formally stated rules, we must be aware of the complex bureaucracies that generate most aggregate data. Such bureaucracies are relatively imperfect data collection instruments and may introduce additional variability. A particularly serious form of this problem occurs when the measurement function is itself related to one or more of the variables of theoretical interest. An obvious instance of this problem is the case of government compiled data and the nature of the political regime If some descriptor of governmental form is a variable of interest and the variable supplied by that government is also of interest, the relation between the two may be confounded if the measurement function is itself a function of governmental form.

The Ecological Fallacy

William S. Robinson (1950) reminded the behavioral science community of the impropriety of attributing "ecological" (i.e., areal) correlations to individuals. Consider the possibility of two independent effects, a within-group and a between-group effect (alternatively, individual level and group level effects, respectively). Figure 1 shows a simple example. We have two attributes, A and B, and we are able to identify some aggregate (as the city) in terms of the proportion A and proportion B, P(A) and P(B). We have drawn two lines, one for individuals who have attribute A and one for those who do not (A and ~A, respectively). A brief inspection should make clear the two statements: (1) the between-city effect of A on B is positive, and (2) the within-city effect of A on B is negative. In short, if B is a desideratum, the optimal combination is to be a non-A among A types, and the worst combination is to be an A type among non-A types. We may decompose a "total" effect into two factors: a within-group effect and a between-group effect (see Davis, Spaeth, and Husson, 1961). We may generalize Robinson's point in the following way: *employ data appropriate to the nouns and the predicates of the theory.* This is an important but often overlooked statement. In the following section we explore other cases in which this principle is ignored (see also Dogan and Rokkan, 1969).

FIGURE 1.

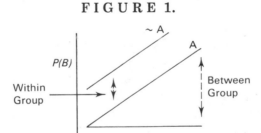

THE UTILITY OF AGGREGATE DATA

If it is inappropriate to test individual-level assertions with aggregate data, it is similarly inappropriate to test macroscopic propositions with individual-level data. Thus, the utility of aggregate data relates to the area of propositions regarding aggregates. Consider a developmental hypothesis to the effect that industrial development creates both an industrial working class and an industrial upper class.

Clearly, we are not hypothesizing that the more working-class an individual is, the more upper-class he is; that is, the appropriate unit of analysis is not the individual but some economic unit such as geographic region or nation-state. Thus, the appropriate unit of analysis should be indicated by the theory. A theory that is unclear as to the appropriate level of aggregation is an unclear theory.

We adopt the position that the *level of analysis* is defined in terms of the unit and the context of analysis. In the following examples, contexts rather than units are changed.

Under the assumption of a fixed national product, the income of capital and labor can be expected to be negatively related (i.e., what one gains, the other will lose). Across time we expect the incomes of the two classes to be positively related as a function of general economic activity. Moreover, if we were to compute the correlation between the level of air pollution experienced by families and the income of families of the world, we would expect a positive association due to industrialization (i.e., both increased income and increased pollution are "fruits" of industrialization). Were we to compute the same measure of association within a given metropolitan area, we might well find a negative association (i.e., those with the economic wherewithal will live in relatively less polluted areas). In these cases, the unit of analysis has remained constant; we choose to call what has been varied the context of analysis.

Many social science theories are inadequately explicit in defining the context of their propositions.

Unit and Context

Thus far, unit and context have been only intuitively defined. Let $\bar{X}_N$ be the mean air pollution for a nation, let $\bar{X}_R$ be the mean air pollution for a region, and X_i the air pollution for the residence of an individual. For much statistical work, the deviation of an observation from a mean is of central importance (in the present case, when we speak of high or low pollution, we mean relative to average pollution). Thus, we can present the individual relative to the nation as $X_i - \bar{X}_N$, the region relative to the nation as $\bar{X}_R - \bar{X}_N$, and the individual relative to the region as $X_i - \bar{X}_R$. The equality of $X_i - \bar{X}_N = (\bar{X}_R - \bar{X}_N) + (X_i - \bar{X}_R)$, then, holds. Ecological data are of the form $(\bar{X}_R - \bar{X}_N)$. Therefore, the ecological analyst should tread cautiously in making inferences regarding $(X_i - \bar{X}_N)$. The individual level analyst deals with $(X_i - \bar{X}_N)$, but too often ignores the presence of $(\bar{X}_R - \bar{X}_N)$ in his observation. That is, if the analyst purports to test a proposition that relates two individual variables by means of presumed personality dynamics, he should not ignore the group contamination of individual variables. An interesting datum for the sociology of science is that whereas the ecological fallacy is well known among political scientists and sociologists, the opposite problem of "correlated means effect" (or, more simply, the group contamination of individual variables) is not widely recognized among these investigators.

The following definition formalizes this discussion:

$$X_i = \frac{\sum\limits_{j=1}^{N_i} X_{ij}}{N_i}$$

where X_{ij} is the value of X for the jth element of the ith collection and N_i is the number of observations in the ith collection; i denotes the context and j denotes the unit of analysis. Thus, in forming deviation scores of the form $(X_{ij} - \bar{X}_i)$, X_{ij} represent the units of analysis and $\bar{X}_i$ represent the contexts.

Hayward Alker (1966) has discussed the utility of contrasting the association between variables while varying the context (but not the contextual level). For example, is the association between propensity to vote and educational attainment the same in developing nations as it is within developed nations? In this case, we are considering the homogeneity of regression in alternative contexts. But we can also consider differences obtaining for different unit and context levels. In the pollution-income example, we consider three different (unit-context) combinations (although, of course, one was derivative, given the other two). The observed relation where the individual is the unit and the world is the context is the result of two mechanisms: where the economic region is the unit and the world is the context, the mechanism invoked to explain a positive association is industrialization. Where the individual is the unit and the economic region is the context, we invoke the ability to pay for a clean environment to explain the negative association. The consideration of phenomena at different levels of analysis (unit-context) serves to point up varying systemic properties.

Robert Crain (1968) has provided a set of findings that show what occurs when the level of analysis is changed:

1. The higher the individual level of educational attainment, the more likely is the individual to favor school integration (individual-nation).

2.   The higher the percentage of high school graduates among adult, white members of a community, the less likely are its schools to be integrated (community-nation).

This example raises an additional point not previously discussed: policy outputs are not the same as attitudes. The investigator operating at more than one level of analysis must be careful to note that variables appropriate to one unit of analysis are often inappropriate to another—variables with similar names are indeed different.

STATISTICAL PROCEDURES

In the vocabulary of the data analyst, the units of analysis are conventionally termed observations. An observation is represented by one or more values for a set of variables. The set of values may be presented in vector form in the following manner:

$$O = \{ x_i, x_2, \ldots, x_j, \ldots, x_m \}$$

Thus, the observation O is defined as a set of values over m variables. If we are dealing with n observations, we are confronted with n vectors of length m, which may be "stacked" to form an n-by-m matrix (i.e., a matrix of n rows and m columns) in which a row represents an observation and a column represents a variable. Even a small matrix represents more information than can be conveniently considered simultaneously. It is for this reason that we have recourse to summary or descriptive statistics. The purpose of a summary index is to extract some facet of the information contained in a data matrix. As such, summary procedures are concerned with the task of data reduction.

If we expect one scalar to somehow represent n-by-m scalars, it is clear that we are sacrificing some detail for the sake of parsimony (parsimony, it should be noted, is an aesthetic principle much admired by finite intellects). In addition to the descriptive or data reduction functions of statistics, there are inferential or decision-making applications for statistical theory. These applications are possible because various summary statistics (t, F ratios, r, etc.) have known sampling distributions. Such techniques deal with questions having to do with sampling variability and hence are inappropriate if one is not dealing with a sample. This point is too often overlooked in the behavioral sciences. One often encounters the application of sampling statistics to nonsample data. This prompts us to surmise that chance is as basic to Western thought as cause, and equally as unexplicated. We shall not belabor the point, other than to note that most descriptive statistics have known sampling distributions which may be utilized by the analyst working with sample data.

Univariate Statistics

Summary indices dealing with a single variable include measures of central tendency (mean, median, mode, proportion), dispersion (variance, range, uncertainty), and the shape of a distribution (kurtosis, modality). These measures are of interest when they may be contrasted with either theoretically generated expectations or two domains (e.g., the dispersion in nation A with the dispersion in nation B). Careful consideration of one's purpose will normally provide evidence that at least one of these contrasts is of interest. For example, the median family income in the United States is not of interest in and of itself. Moreover, a cross-national contrast of median family income is not, in and of itself, of particular interest. Such a contrast is usually associated with some simultaneous contrast (e.g., political stability). In this regard, we are in agreement with Zetterberg: "I will not dignify one-variate statements by calling them propositions" (1963, p. 12).

Bivariate Techniques

Conditional probabilities is probably the most intuitively acceptable bivariate technique. The conventional notation for probabilities is as follows:

$P(A)$	the probability of A
$1-P(A) = P(\sim A)$	the probability of non-A
$P(A \cap B)$ or $P(A, B)$	the probability of the joint occurrence of A and B
$P(A:B)$ or $P(A/B)$	the probability of A given B (This is a conditional probability and B is said to be the "conditioning event.")

(Note that, in general, $P(A:B) \neq P(B:A)$ and that they are quite different conceptually.)

Two events, A and B, are said to be statistically independent if $P(A \cap B) = P(A) \times P(B)$. If this condition holds, it can be shown that $P(A) = P(A:B) = P(A:\sim B)$. It is the equality of the two conditional probabilities, $P(A:B) = P(A:\sim B)$, that is probably most intuitively satisfying, for it tells us that under conditions of statistical independence, knowledge of one event (in this case, $\sim B$ versus B) does not affect out expectation with respect to another event, $P(A)$.

The most frequently used bivariate index of association is the Pearson product-moment correlation, r. Numerous other indices exist, and are preferred in specific cases. However, we restrict our discussion to this index. We have already noted the definition of statistical independence with respect to probabilities, i.e., $P(A,B) = P(A) \times P(B)$. The definition of statistical independence of real variables is formally similar: $E(X \times Y) = E(X) \times E(Y)$. The correlation coefficient, a simple transformation of the left-hand term, may be interpreted in various ways. At the most superficial level it can be taken as a measure of the degree to which two variables "go together." One step beyond this interpretation is that of predictability—the higher the absolute value of r, the more predictable one variable is from another. In addition, there are geometric interpretations—r is the cosine of the included angle of two vectors.

An interpretation that is relevant to a discussion of aggregate data views r as a measure of goodness of fit of observations in a two-dimensional space to a linear function in the space. That is, the greater the absolute value of r, the better is the fit of a bivariate distribution to a straight line in the plane. If r is a measure of goodness of fit to the optimal linear function, there are no assumptions, let alone any assertions, regarding level of measurement. It should be noted that this approach is quite independent of questions regarding the statistical significance of any value of r.

In some exploratory work undertaken with William Love (Stewart and Love, 1968), one of the authors conducted some analyses of the data base reported in *The Civic Culture* (Almond and Verba, 1963). These analyses will be used as illustrative examples of the various techniques reported here.

Ten variables (reflective of perceived political efficacy, interpersonal ideology, perceived impact of national government on day-to-day affairs of respondent, and similar topics) were correlated with nationality. Nationality, which would normally be considered a nominal variable, was transformed into a vector of "dummy variables." Given that a variable is a set of elements, mutually exclusive and exhaustive over a specified domain of observables (alternatively, one may say that a variable is the range or co-domain of a measurement function), one may construct a set of variables, each comprised of one of the original elements and its complement. In the present case, the original variable was "nation" and its range included "United States," "United Kingdom," "Italy," and "West Germany." From this original single variable of four possible values, we construct four new variables of two possible values each:

United States	United Kingdom	Italy	West Germany
1. Yes 0. No	1. Yes 0. No	1. Yes 0. No	1. Yes 0. No

It should be clear that for any individual included in the study, his score vector will include a single 1 and three 0's. Because of this, if we know the individual's score on any of three of the four dichotomies, we can perfectly predict the score for the remaining variable. This condition is known technically as a linear dependency. The presence of a dependency in a data matrix creates analytic problems (the rank is less than the order, therefore the determinant goes to zero). Two approaches are available: (1) where a nominal variable contains K categories, create only $K-1$ dummy variables; or (2) include a few contrived score vectors in the data matrix. The latter approach was used in the analyses reported here. Because of constraints for space, we are unable to explicate fully the procedures used in creating the following examples. They should therefore be interpreted solely as illustrative of the techniques presented. Finally, for some reassurance on the issue: "Perhaps part of the trouble lies in the use of the term 'dummy' variable. There is nothing artificial about such variables; indeed in a fundamental sense they are more properly scaled than conventionally measured variables" (Suits, 1957). It should be clear that variables so formed are not normally distributed, and, therefore, tests of the statistical significance of r are inappropriate. The correlations between attitudinal items and nations are shown in Table 1.

In general, we note very low correlations between nations and attitudes. This indicates poor fit of the bivariate distributions to the optimal linear function. Whenever one imposes "strong" models on "weak" data, one should not expect very good fit between the two. A positive correlation indicates that as one variable increases, the other variable increases in magnitude. The converse is the case when a negative correlation obtains. The absolute magnitude of the correlation indicates the strength of this association.

Earlier, we emphasized the importance of the mean from which observations are deviated. For many analytic purposes it is inappro-

T A B L E 1.   Matrix of Correlations between Ten Attitudes and
Four Nations

Attitudinal Variables	Nations			
	United States 14	*United Kingdom* 11	*Italy* 13	*West Germany* 12
1.	−.246	−.071	.170	.247
2.	−.112	.088	.178	−.097
3.	−.098	−.030	.177	.020
4.	.062	.101	−.082	−.122
5.	−.067	−.021	.005	.103
6.	.026	.052	.038	−.114
7.	−.027	.091	.062	−.114
8.	−.107	−.052	.164	.068
9.	.011	−.062	−.021	.074
10.	−.130	.060	.152	−.026

*Item descriptors are as follows:
1. Can people be trusted?
2. Do you follow political affairs?
3. Frequency of discussing political affairs.
4. Range of people with whom you are willing to discuss politics.
5. Are politics and government too complicated for the average man to understand?
6. How well do you think you understand national and international issues?
7. How well do you think you understand local issues?
8. Are most people inclined to help others or look out for themselves?
9. Willingness to become politically active.
10. How much effect has the national government on your day-to-day life?

priate to deviate individual observations from the grand mean. Instead, it is worthwhile to deviate observations from the mean for a defined context. We may then aggregate the within-group covariances to form a pooled within-group measure of association. On the other hand, we may wish to conduct a true aggregate analysis, in which case we assign collectivities their mean scores, sometimes extracted from the variables observed for individuals. There is a common propensity to weight the large collectivities more heavily than the small collectivities when undertaking this type of analysis. For many purposes, however, the collectivity is the unit of analysis; there is, then, no justification for weighting them differentially on the basis of population or any other such characteristic. Similarly, in this case we would be likely to deviate observations from the mean of means rather than the grand mean (i.e., from the mean of unweighted means rather than from the mean of weighted means).

Figure 2 demonstrates an instance in which mean scores are used. Here, we explore the association between careers in the government bureaucracy and careers in party ideology of persons who composed the politburos of five countries during four time periods. In each case the number of persons in the politburos varies. The politburo has become the unit of analysis and all politburos are then treated as equal despite the difference in size. The plotting of these relationships (Figure 2) reveals a strong negative association between the two variables in Romania, Bulgaria, and Czechoslovakia. In the cases of Hungary and Poland we see a mixed pattern. Moving outside these

F I G U R E 2.   Politburo Officials in Five Eastern European Countries

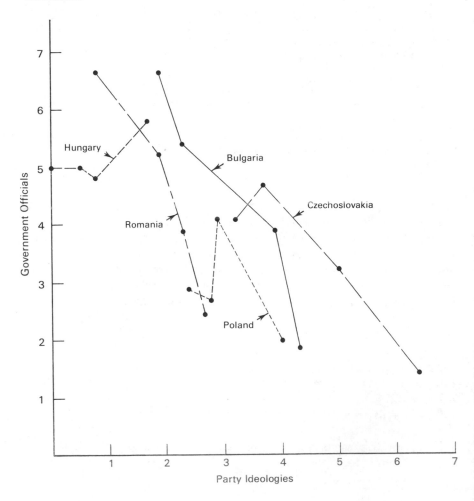

data, Poland and Hungary, of course, were most affected by "New Course" politics. Note that the observed overall effect is negligible because of different within-nation and between-nation effects.

Multivariate Techniques

Descriptive statistics are useful for data reduction or simplification. Imagine, then, that the data matrix n by m is now represented by an m-by-m matrix of correlations among the m variables. Although the amount of information has been greatly reduced (we assume $m < n$), it may be desirable to further reduce the data. Techniques that operate on correlation matrices are often termed "multivariate," and this convention will be adopted here.

The multivariate technique most often encountered in the social sciences is factor analysis. One reason for its apparent ubiquity is that the term is generic and refers to a class of techniques. The most basic technique currently used is principal components analysis. Consider the case of m observations, each one of which has been assigned values on two variables (X and Y). We may represent the m observations as m points in a two-dimensional space. The two axes (X and Y) represent a basis for the space. The alternative bases may be pictured as constituting rotations of the X and Y axes in the plane, which (a) maintain X and Y at right angles and (b) leave the points on the plane undisturbed. A unique rotation exists that has useful properties. An axis onto which the points may be projected that maximizes the dispersion of points is termed the first principal component. If X and Y are viewed as alternative indicators for the concept so that we desired to form a scale of the two items, we might wish to accept the first principal component as the scale. We are then willing to accept a score on the first component as the best single scalar representing the information contained in the pair of scores on X and Y. The reader who is familiar with linear regression will detect a similarity between the first principal component and the least squares line of regression. It should be noted, however, that the least squares line of Y on X is not coincident with the least squares line of X on Y, except in the instance of perfect correlation (i.e., r is equal to the cosine of the included angle of the two regression functions). Thus, the first principal component is best viewed as a line midway between the two regression functions.

In the case of more than two variables, the definition of principal components remains as stated: the first principal component is that linear combination of the variables that represents maximum variance; the second principal component is that linear combination of the variables that represents maximum variance with the constraint that it is at right angles to the first principal component (instead of "right angles," we normally say "orthogonal" or "uncorrelated"), and so on, for as many components as there are variables (given m variables, there may not in fact be m principal components, but this is ignored for the current treatment). Each component is a linear combination of the m variables. A set of m coefficients or "weights" is therefore associated with each component (i.e., for each variable there is a coefficient that is used to multiply the scores on that variable). The set of coefficients is termed a "characteristic vector" or "eigenvector." The most useful way to interpret the principal components is to inspect the correlations between the observed variables and the components. These correlations are commonly termed "factor loadings."

If we denote the correlation between the ith variable and the jth component as L_{ij}, the proportion of variance of the ith variable associated with the jth component is the square of the correlation, or L_{ij}^2. The sum of the squared loadings of the m variables with the jth component can be interpreted as the amount of variance associated with that component. This is known as the "characteristic root" or "eigenvalue." An eigenvalue of less than unity informs us that a component has less variance associated with it than a variable has (unit length variables are assumed throughout). Given that factor analyses are often undertaken to obtain a simplified representation of the information in hand, attending to m constructs rather than m variables is a loss rather than a gain in simplicity.

Returning to the *Civic Culture* data (Almond and Verba, 1963), we inspect the correlations (loadings) of ten attitudinal variables with

TABLE 2.   First Component Loading Pattern

Attitudinal Variables	Nations			
	United States	United Kingdom	Italy	West Germany
1.	.289	.259	.045	.119
2.	.690	.713	.745	.769
3.	.674	.682	.711	.686
4.	−.357	−.282	−.632	−.562
5.	−.468	−.465	−.454	−.511
6.	.785	.746	.831	.842
7.	.647	.607	.753	.615
8.	.216	.221	.187	.182
9.	.609	.404	.341	.495
10.	.517	.517	.528	.200

the first principal component for each of four nations (see Table 2). Variable 6 has the highest correlation with the first component of each of the four countries. (The question asked of the respondent was how well he feels he understands national affairs.) On the other hand, variables 1 and 8 are consistently the lowest (absolute) correlations. The interesting point of this finding is that these two variables deal with interpersonal ideology (e.g., "Can people be trusted?") and they were the only items of this type among the ten (all of the remaining eight deal with political interest, understanding and relevant behavior). Given a superficial similarity across the four nations in this regard, we note one interesting difference. Variable 10 is correlated with the first component in excess of .50 in the solutions for the United States, the United Kingdom, and Italy. Its loading in the West German solution is only .200. This variable has to do with perception of the impact of the national government upon the respondent's day-to-day life. Thus, in West Germany this variable is only slightly related to a general political interest and participation dimension—the opposite is true for the other three nations. A superficial inspection of the second components (Table 3) indicates that this dimension is largely defined by the two interpersonal ideology variables (numbers 1 and 8).

The analyst, therefore, selects the first K $(K < M)$ components for further inspection and analysis. In so doing, the researcher has accepted a model of reduced rank. In short, the analyst is willing to ignore lesser constructs (often tacitly defining them as "error") and to concentrate on those constructs that are associated with greater amounts of observed variance. Often, the eigenvector or vector of factor loadings associated with a given principal component is not

T A B L E   3.   Second Component Loading Pattern

Attitudinal Variables	Nations			
	United States	*United Kingdom*	*Italy*	*West Germany*
1.	−.675	.594	.774	−.727
2.	:071	.005	.186	.034
3.	.131	−.145	.205	−.230
4.	−.117	.202	.115	.255
5.	−.127	.208	−.028	−.259
6.	.155	−.134	−.131	.193
7.	.102	−.057	−.176	.318
8.	−.766	.711	.652	−.522
9.	−.108	−.193	−.235	.021
10.	.001	.291	−.113	−.220

clearly interpretable (i.e., the component does not possess face validity for any of one's theoretical constructs). In this case, it is common to rotate some of the components. If one accepts a model of rank k, the first k components will be rotated. The goal of rotation is a more interpretable pattern of factor loadings.

One approach to an understanding of canonical correlation is to view it as the most general form of linear regression analysis. Given two standardized variables, X and Y, we predict Y from X with the following equation:

$$Y_i = bX_i + e_i$$

where Y_i is the value of Y for the ith observation, X_i is the value of X for the ith observation, e_i if the value of a random variate for the ith observation, and b is the regression coefficient or slope (which in this case is equal to r, the correlation coefficient). Of course, when estimating the value of Y_i from X_i we do not know e_i and therefore speak of the estimated value of Y_i as $\widehat{Y}_i$ (read "Y hat"). The equation of concern is simplified to

$$\widehat{Y}_i = bX_i$$

It is then obvious that $\widehat{Y}$ is a linear function of X and is therefore perfectly correlated with X. We may interpret the correlation between x and y as the correlation between Y and $\widehat{Y}$. This interpretation is worthwhile when we turn to the question of multiple correlation, in which we predict Y from several variables. In this instance, $\widehat{Y}$ is a linear combination of the several independent variables. Hence, multiple correlation is properly interpreted as the correlation between the optimal linear composite $\widehat{Y}$ and Y. (For this reason, it is not correct to speak of multiple correlation as the correlation between one variable and several variables.)

Just as a zero-order correlation can be interpreted as a special case of multiple correlation, multiple correlation can be interpreted as a special case of canonical correlation. If we are concerned with only the first canonical root (as was Hotelling, 1935), we may consider two vector variables X and Y and form a linear composite of each so that the two linear composites are maximally correlated. The linear composites are termed "canonical variates" (or "factors") and the correlation between the two canonical variates is called the "canonical correlation." Subsequent canonical variates can be viewed as those formed with all preceding canonical variates partialed.

Earlier, correlations were computed between nationality and various attitudinal items. The technique used involved transforming a single nominal variable into several dichotomous variables. Therefore, this was actually a canonical analysis, undertaken by using the ten

T A B L E   4.   First Canonical Function

	Canonical Correlations			
	United States	*United Kingdom*	*Italy*	*West Germany*
Nationality	.69	.22	.61	.62

Loadings of Attitudinal Variables			
1.	−.800	6.	.099
2.	−.218	7.	.035
3.	−.390	8.	−.454
4.	.321	9.	−.088
5.	−.227	10.	−.286

Canonical r = .43

attitudinal variables as one set and the four dichotomous nationality variables as the other set. Table 4 shows a strong association between attitudinal variables 1 and 8 and the first canonical function. These are the same interpersonal ideology items that were essentially un-correlated with the first components in each of the four countries. In short, of these ten variables, these two are most important for explaining between-nation differences, but they are at least important with regard to within-nation differences. This intriguing finding is indicative of the potential of cross-level analysis. The ability to decompose gross effects into their component effects can lead to increasingly sophisticated theoretical formulations.

SUMMARY

In the preceding pages we have argued for the hegemony of theory in the conduct of research. Operations undertaken on data, whether individual or aggregate, must be mappable into symbolic operations within a theory. Empirical problems should be taken to represent theoretical problems. If a theory does not predict anything with respect to observable information, it is a weak theory. In other words, various so-called empirical problems can be traced either to a lack of theoretical rigor or to a failure to match operations on data to operations of theory.

With increasing regularity, aggregate data are utilized in con-temporary social research. Problems arising in the use of aggregate data concern their accessibility for secondary analysis, the accuracy of their sources, and their relevance to various specific research projects. Difficulties may also emerge in specifying the measurement function, for the strength of aggregate data is directly related to the adequacy of the theoretical explication of the measurement functions (through which data are related to theoretical entities and operations). The utility of aggregate data rests on the accurate specification of the unit and context of analysis. The appropriate unit of analysis should be indicated by the theory; a theory that is unclear as to the appropriate level of aggregation is an unclear theory.

Aggregate data are essential to the testing of macroscopic theory. They are relevant to a rich variety of theoretical units of analysis. The availability of aggregate data and the power of univariate, bivariate, and multivariate statistical techniques allow contemporary political scientists to explore dimensions of politics heretofore only intuited. The potential of that exploration rests, we believe, in how well we allow theory rather than data to shape our analyses.

15. COMMUNITY POWER: CONCEPTS, METHODS, AND INTERVENTION

Bert E. Swanson

The analysis of and reports on the American community have shifted considerably with each generation of scholars and the changing concepts and techniques of social scientists. Each generation has made its own contributions, to be used or ignored by the next, in the search for knowledge. The community has become the testing place for social and political theory and is the observatory of perhaps the most dynamic, yet the most disquieting and disintegrating, aspect of American life. Each intellectual discipline, with the possible exception of economics, has taken the community as its focus for empirical investigations. Each study—virtually all are individual case studies—has not only entertained generations of readers with narrative and descriptive history but produced fragments of insights about the American city as well.

There are a few scholars in the present generation who have gone beyond the single case study of a community as a necessary step in building viable theories about communities and their power dynamics. Some have begun to emerge in comparative community studies with a small number of cities. (For a comparison of four communities, see Agger, Goldrich, and Swanson, 1964; Williams and Adrian, 1963; Alford, 1969.) Some have begun to study a few variables for a larger number of cities and explain policy outputs (see Hawley, 1963, pp. 422-31; Clark, 1968, pp. 576-93; Eulau and Prewitt, 1973). A handful of scholars have from time to time conferred and explored the possibilities of a large-scale comparative community study project. For example, the participants in one conference were concerned with

intra-community political power or influence relations; relationships between and among various portions of the community power structures, e.g., various aspects of leader and follower relationships in community power structures and economic and social structures; relationships between political and administrative decision-making; and relationships between community politics and regional and national politics [Swanson, 1962, p. 1].

The participants of this conference agreed that the community should be conceived as a general behavioral system rather than a loosely integrated geopolitical unit. The participants sought system-level concepts and variables to explain the community as a viable entity. They agreed on the urgent need to substitute the comparative study of many communities for the past series of single case studies. They would replace a single point-in-time analysis with a dynamic analysis using the community as an experimental laboratory. They viewed the community as undergoing rapid change in the direction of industrialization, urbanization, and bureaucratization; and last, they viewed the community as linked to regional, national, and possibly international sets of events.

While some scholars have compiled lengthy inventories of studies in an attempt to synthesize the vast array of findings, others have engaged in a series of dialogues, debates, and heated arguments over the discrepancies in their findings (see the following inventories: Milbrath, 1965; Berelson and Steiner, 1964; Bell et al., 1961; Clark, 1967b, pp. 291-316; Walton, 1966, pp. 430-8; Press, 1962; Gore and Hodapp, 1967; Aiken, 1970; Gilbert, 1972; and Lane, 1959). Although some have raised a number of important questions and problems in their efforts to explain the dynamic processes of community decision making, others have tried to formulate their findings into meaningful concepts, propositions, and typologies on urban policies—"who gets what, when, and how."

Ironically, the greatest dispute has developed between sociologists and political scientists over the methods to be used in studying power relations in American communities (Gilbert, 1966). The methodological disagreements are important, as Linton Freeman and his associates have pointed out, since the methods employed determine in large measure the outcome of the research (Freeman et al., 1960). What needs careful scrutiny is the relationships between the definition and measurement of variables, the methodological strategies and tactics, as well as the general and specific nature of the findings of the investigations.

Those ready to engage in future research could choose either to review and evaluate these past studies in order to formulate new theoretical perspectives or to start afresh without benefit of past efforts. I have chosen, instead, to draw selectively upon the past and to classify the growing number of empirical community studies into four major patterns. The first is the group of *stratification* studies that assumed or did not provide a sufficiently elaborated conception of social stratification as it relates to community power and decision making. The second is the set of studies that discovered a *power elite* or inner cliques of economic dominants who control community affairs. The third is the number of studies that identified *pluralistic* leadership patterns showing power to be more broadly shared and sufficient mechanisms to allow for democratic decision making. The fourth is the group of studies that reveal *multifaceted* systems and that go beyond the determination of few or many key leaders to include a concern for the linkages or lack thereof of the masses to leaders, prevailing ideologies, "rules of the game," and stages in the decision-making processes.

Several distinctive research methods and techniques have been used in the study of community power. The first, *positional*, is a

T A B L E 1. Positional, Reputational, and Issue-Decisional Definitions of Power and the Accompanying Research Techniques

Type of Power	Conception of Power	How It Is Described	Techniques Employed	Principal Products of Research
Positional Power *(Structural)*	Power that can be mobilized if available resources are used. Ordinarily employed in private decisions.	Identification of the institutions, organizations, and offices in the community that have potential power.	Documents. Informants.	List of persons in the most influential offices. Resources of persons and organizations. Records of results achieved.
Reputational Power *(Sociometric)*	Power that is imputed to persons and organizations and institutions. Employed variously in both private and public decision-making.	1. Identification by judges of the most influential leaders, organizations, and institutions. 2. Description of roles played by influential leaders.	Interviews with panel of judges, informants, and with influential leaders.	List of leaders considered most important, and their participation patterns.
Issue-Decisional Power *(Issue-Relevant)*	Power that can be assigned to persons, organizations, and institutions through the debate of public issues or promotion of public projects. Employed mainly in decisions on public matters.	1. Identification of recent issues that are considered most important in the life of the community. 2. Identification of the persons and the roles they played in resolving issues or projects.	Interviews with persons associated with issues or projects during decision-making. Attendance and recording of decision-making meetings.	List of most influential leaders in recent issues. Analyses of roles played.

Source: Delbert C. Miller, *International Community Power Structures* (Bloomington: Indiana University Press, 1970), p. 8. Copyright © 1970 by Indiana University Press. Reprinted by permission.

structural approach that associates power with the position one holds in the institutional life of the community. The second, *reputational*, relies on the sociometric choices of knowledgeable, influential, and active participants. The third, *decisional*, attempts to trace those who participate in and influence a particular set of decisions on community issues. Each method has been generally associated with one of the above patterns of community power. For example, the reputational approach has tended to identify power elite patterns while the decisional approach appears to discover pluralistic leadership patterns. In fact, Miller associates these three methods with the types of power system (see Table 1).

The intellectual watershed in community studies occurred in the post-World War II period of the 1950s and 1960s. From each approach a number of research considerations are reviewed here. They include the questions raised or the stated problem; the concepts, or the stated propositions and hypotheses; the general approach or method used; the model of the systems formulated or typologies constructed; and the general findings or theory developed.

COMMUNITY STRATIFICATION THEORY

In their classic case study of Middletown, the Lynds used a cultural anthropologist's approach not to prove any thesis, but "to record observed phenomena, thereby raising questions and suggesting possible fresh points of departure in the study of group behavior" (Lynd and Lynd, 1929, p. 3; see also their second report, 1937). They participated in local life, collected and examined documentary materials, as well as interviewed, formally and informally, a wide range of local citizens and leaders. They replicated their study of the same small community a decade later and used the economic depression of the 1930s as a natural experiment to examine the intertwined processes of industrialization and urbanization. Their findings were confirmed in a series of other community studies that established the pattern that those who govern either dominate or reflect the social structure. (Among the more widely used are Warner and Lunt, 1941; Hollingshead, 1949; and Baltzell, 1958.) Dahl describes the holding of political resources in a patrician oligarchy as "cumulative inequality: when one individual was much better off than another in one resource, such as wealth, he was usually better off in almost every other resource—social standing, legitimacy, control over religious and educational institutions, knowledge, office" (Dahl, 1961a, p. 85).

By the second study it was quite clear to the Lynds that the X family governed Middletown in almost every aspect of its community life. As one local citizen expressed it:

> If I'm out of work I go to the X plant; if I need money I go to the X bank, and if they don't like me I don't get it; my children go to the X college; when I get sick I go to the X hospital; I buy a building lot or house in an X subdivision; my wife goes downtown to buy clothes at the X department store; if my dog strays away he is put in the X pound; I buy X milk; I drink X beer, vote for X political parties, and get help from X charities; my boy goes to the X Y.M.C.A. and my girl to their Y.W.C.A.; I listen to the word of God in X-subsidized churches; if I'm a Mason I go to the X Masonic Temple; I read the news from the X morning newspaper; and, if I am rich enough, I travel via the X airport [Lynd and Lynd, 1937, p. 74].

The X family was not only "a reigning royal family" but an intimate part of a stratified class system that included the business class that governed Middletown. In their first study the Lynds formulated a two-class system: (1) the business class, constituting 29 percent of the population and concentrating their activities on *people*; (2) the working class, constituting 71 percent of the population and focusing their activities on *things*. This was later refined into a six-level class system.

The economic depression heightened the role of the X family and the socioeconomic stratification process and "tightened" the control net of the leadership over the community. The Lynds describe process control of the X family and the business class as follows:

> That the control is at very many points unconscious and where conscious, well-meaning and "public spirited," as businessmen interpret that concept.

> That the control system operates at many points to identify public welfare with business-class welfare.

> That there is little deliberate effort from above to organize local bankers, businessmen, and leaders of opinion into a self-conscious "we" pressure group; but that this sharply centripetal tendency of Middletown's businessmen is normal behavior in capitalist, credit-controlled culture where there is a potential control-center in the form of vast personal resources of demonstrated willingness to lend a friendly hand.

> That, so long as the owners of such vast personal resources exhibit a public-spirited willingness to help with local problems leadership and control tend to be forced upon them by circumstances, and their patterns tend to become the official guiding patterns.

> That, viewed at any given time as a going concern, this centrally-hubbed control agency both may and does operate in many subtle and even

ordinarily unintended ways to "welcome little fishes in with gently smiling jaws," with an accompanying loss to the latter of independent leadership. Those who try to be independent tend to be regarded, as the local phrase puts it, as "gumming the works" [Lynd and Lynd, 1937, p. 99].

Given high levels of alternating exasperation and cynical apathy regarding the local civic administration, the X family and the business class used group sanctions and taboos that were solidified into laws. In monopolizing all the stages of decision making, they depend for their maintenance not upon the support of public opinion but upon official enforcement. The key instrumentality to this end is the office of the mayor, who operates behind the scenes, with only minor protest in the open.

The Lynds' study received wide acclaim. But there were those, such as Polsby, who placed the research findings of the stratification theorists, especially the Lynds, into serious question. Polsby not only disagreed with the generalizations and propositions underlying their work but attacked them on methodological grounds. The propositions of the stratificationists under attack are, simply stated, that the political and civic leaders are subordinate to the economic upper class that rules. Within the upper class a power elite governs in its own interest, which is the basis of social conflict between the upper and lower classes. Polsby believes that these generalizations no longer hold and, more important, suggests that they may never have been true at all, given the methodological inadequacies:

> (1) Data are given which tend to discredit or disprove a proposition, but the refutation of the proposition is never explicitly formulated; (2) the methods of a study either do not test hypotheses or permit premature confirmation by avoiding or by-passing direct tests; (3) refutations are recognized by authors as occurring in their data, but extraneous, *ad hoc* explanations are constructed or extenuating circumstances claimed, so as to evade the necessity of giving up the propositions [Polsby, 1963, p. 14].

ELITISTS VERSUS PLURALISTS

Polsby's attack was only a small part of a larger and more vigorous debate between those who believe and/or have found that American communities are governed by either power elites or pluralistic groupings. A number of considerations may account for the different theories and findings. Of course, one explanation may be the very real differences in characteristics and power structures of the communities under study. More relevant for this exploration are important methodological concerns. Thus, one explanation for the differences in community power findings may be the intellectual discipline of the investigator, as Anton suggests (1963, p. 430) and Gilbert documents (1965, p. 31). "As expected," Gilbert writes, "sociologists are more likely to describe a pyramidal structure, and the others are more likely to describe one that is multi-pyramidal." Another related explanation is the ideological position of those conducting community studies. As Connolly points out about "elitist" and "pluralist" theories, the investigator "comes to political inquiry predisposed to describe and explain the environment in certain ways; he is equipped with an incipient interpretation which appears plausible to him and which tends to receive the support of those reference groups to which he is linked by ties of origin, conceptual organization, beliefs, and values" (Connolly, 1967, p. 48). There are those, of course, who believe community power is not very relevant anyway. Wolfinger states, "Power is not a very useful or interesting general empirical concept in any event, and trying to analyze local politics in terms of a 'power structure' imposes a number of sterile rigidities without substantial accompanying theoretical strength" (Wolfinger, 1974).

The most plausible explanation links these factors of intellectual discipline and ideologies to the methods and units of measurement used by the investigators. That is, sociologists using the "reputational technique" generally find elite or pyramidal power structures; political scientists using decision-making models and event analysis generally find more dispersed or pluralistic power structures. For example, Walton's secondary analysis of thirty-three power structure studies of some fifty-five communities revealed that "the reputational method tends to identify pyramidal power structures, while the decision-making approach discovers factional and coalitional power structures" (Walton, 1966 pp. 430–38).

This paradoxical situation is sharply pointed up in the two classical studies by Hunter and Dahl in their seemingly different pictures of community power and decision making (Hunter, 1953; Dahl, 1961a); The discussion presented here is somewhat representative of the one that has stirred the social sciences and that has also encouraged the development of new concepts, insights and methodological approaches. The following discussion simultaneously compares Hunter's power elite of Atlanta, Georgia, with Dahl's pluralistic democratic system of New Haven, Connecticut.

While both authors appear to begin with essentially the same research problem of trying to determine who, if anyone, rules (Dahl, 1961a, p. 1; Hunter, 1953, p. 1), they differ considerably on their conceptions and research methods and techniques. (For a systematic review of the conceptual differences and problems found in the study of community power, see Clark, 1967a, pp. 271–86. He focuses on fifteen aspects, including anticipated reaction, direct and indirect influence, patterns of value distribution, scope, visibility, power bases, efficiency of power application, the zero-sum problem, the allocation of resources, and the stratification of power.)

Hunter's reputational technique included compiling lists of leaders occupying positions of prominence in civic organizations, business establishments, education, office holders in village politics, and persons prominent socially and economically. Fourteen "judges," persons who had lived in the community for some years and who had a knowledge of community affairs, were asked to select from each one, in rank order of importance, ten persons of influence, meaning that they have an ability to lead others. The judges were also asked to choose from a list of fifty organizations the ten most influential. The nominated leaders were then interviewed; their responses became the basis of the analysis (Hunter, 1953, pp. 255- 63).

Dahl's decisional approach, on the other hand, was sixfold: (1) to study changes in the socioeconomic characteristics of incumbents in city offices to determine whether any rather large historical changes may have occurred in the sources of leadership; (2) to isolate a particular socioeconomic category and then determine the nature and extent of participation in local affairs by persons in this category; (3) to examine a set of "decisions" in different "issue-areas" to determine what kinds of person were the most influential according to one operational measure of relative influence, and to determine patterns of influence; (4) to survey random samples of participants in different issue-areas to determine their characteristics; (5) to survey random samples of registered voters to determine the characteristics of those who participate in varying degrees and in varying ways in local affairs; and (6) to study changes in patterns of voting among different strata in the community (Dahl, 1961a, pp. 330- 40).

A power elite is a political system where power is concentrated in the hands of a few, with rather fixed socioeconomic barriers between the leaders and the nonleaders, with private citizens rather than government officials comprising the largest proportion of the top leadership, and with a high level of political manipulation. In a power elite not only is power monopolized by a few, but there is little prospect that it will ever be widely shared. The power elite community generally is associated with a monolithic power structure. An example is the small company town that has not experienced a population influx from diverse ethnic or racial backgrounds. The system is characterized by a small number of social and civic organizations and generally has only one political party. Hunter found Atlanta to be under the control of "economic dominants." Leaders of finance and industry prevailed on all the big issues and most of the small ones. They made up a more or less homogeneous group, united in their operations. They recognized cliques among themselves. They tended to form as subgroups of an integrated whole, rather than as competing factions, each seeking to dominate the others.

A pluralistic democracy, on the other hand, is a political system where power is actually or potentially widely shared, where the power strata are relatively permeable, where the government officials constitute a large proportion of the top leadership, and where the level of manipulation is comparatively low. The democratic community generally is characterized by a pluralistic economic system that is more industrialized, a bureaucracy that is more differentiated, and a social structure that is more heterogeneous than in the power elite. Even more important, power is divided among competing political parties and social and civic organizations. In New Haven, Dahl found a New England oligarchy that had been transformed into a polity where leaders of a number of countervailing sectors of society, from the old Yankees to the newly arrived ethnic society, all had a voice in the city's functions. New Haven leaders were bargaining for the groups they represented with the leaders of other groups. This behavior takes place in a system where nearly everyone is committed to the rules of the game—democracy with a loyal opposition.

Dahl characterizes the American belief in democracy and equality much as does Lipset, who asserts that the paradoxical relationship between achievement and equality finds an association between equality of power among the people and equality of social conditions. As Dahl puts it, the latter is not "a necessary prerequisite" of the former,

> but if, even in America, with its universal creed of democracy and equality, there are great inequalities in the conditions of different citizens, must there not also be great inequalities in the capacities of different citizens to influence the decisions of their various governments? And if, because they are unequal in other conditions, citizens of a democracy are unequal in power to control their government, then who in fact does govern? How does a "democratic" system work amid inequality of resources? [Dahl, 1961a, p. 3].

Dahl lists four answers. One is political party competition that organizes the unorganized, provides power to the powerless, and presents policy alternatives. Second, he says, there is the struggle between the interest groups. Third, there is "beneath the facade of democratic politics a social and economic elite" (Dahl, 1961a, p. 6). The fourth alternative is the theory of mass society, that is, an older, stratified, class-based social structure is destroyed by a mass of individuals—rootless, aimless, and without strong social ties—who are ready to bind themselves over to some political entrepreneur who will cater to their tastes and desires. These exploitative leaders who command the masses have the capacity to destroy, but they do not provide any stable alternatives.

In the contemporary American community Dahl maintains that the socioeconomic notables certainly are not the "ruling elite" composed of the patricians of an earlier day. They do, however, exercise their influence on specific decisions, particularly those involving economic prosperity or business interests. He maintains that the smart politician avoids a direct confrontation over the values sought by socioeconomic notables.

Dahl makes a significant contribution to our understanding of urban politics when he explores five patterns of leadership that provide integration of the political system. However, he fails to include some patterns that appear to encourage disintegration. Apparently the assumption here is that leadership and politics constitute essentially an integrative process. The first pattern is "covert integration by economic notables" (Dahl, 1961a, pp. 184-220), a pattern similar to that found in studies of the Lynds and Hunter. In this pattern, the leaders consist of the unified group of private citizens who make decisions about community policies through private negotiations and discussions and not in a public place. They secure their influence from their wealth, social standing, and economic dominance.

The second pattern is an "executive-centered 'grand coalition of coalitions.'" In this coalition of public officials and private individuals, the former coordinate the policies and draw upon the special skills and resources of the latter. Dahl associates this pattern with vigorous chief executives, such as President Franklin D. Roosevelt and Mayor Richard Lee of New Haven. The executive-centered coalition tends to be more ephemeral, fluctuating in strength, even dissolving when the leaders no longer can reconcile their strategies and goals.

Note the contrast: covert domination by economic notables places the public official in a supportive relation to those with wealth, social standing, and corporate position, while the executive-centered coalition treats the prerogatives of public office, legality, and legitimacy as independent sources of influence that carry their own weight. The covert elite may create pessimism or a sense that public officials are simply puppets, because the upper class reduces the strategy of peaceful reform via politics and thus suggests that change must

> come about either through the gradual action of outside factors, like changes in industrial organization or technique, or else through a revolution-

ary seizure and transformation of the state by leaders of social segments who for some reasons cannot win election and obtain public office. The hypothesis of integration by an executive-centered coalition, by contrast, allows for the possibility that reformists or radical coalitions (as well as conservative ones) may, by peacefully winning elections, obtain control of the powers of government and introduce durable changes in the distribution of access to influence, wealth, education, and social standing [Dahl, 1961a, p. 186].

The third pattern of leadership is a "coalition of chieftains," where integration takes place mainly by negotiation among the chieftains, as opposed to the executive-centered coalition, where integration is achieved mainly by means of skills and resources of an elected leader, such as the chief executive or mayor. The fourth pattern is that of "independent sovereignties with spheres of influence." In New York City, for example, Sayre and Kaufman (1960) found a system of petty sovereignties, each centered around an issue area controlled by a different set of top leaders whose goals and strategies are adapted to the particular segments of the communities that happen to be interested in that specific area. As long as there is no conflict between the participants or between the areas, there is no need for much communication or negotiation. However, the petty sovereigns begin to fight it out when conflicts arise over scarce resources or when someone believes coordination or cooperation is necessary between the agencies or participants in two areas, such as youth-serving activities or the comprehensive approach of Mobilization for Youth in the ghetto. This is Dahl's fifth pattern of leadership: "rival sovereignties fighting it out."

> Possibility of conflict is minimized by mutually accepted spheres of influence, combined with a strong presumption that the *status quo* must be adhered to; it is also understood that if disagreements arise they are to be resolved by implicit, or occasionally explicit, bargaining among the petty sovereigns without an appeal to the populace or other external authorities [Dahl, 1961a, pp. 188–89].

Both Hunter and Dahl unfortunately report on a different community, which precludes the comparative value of their findings. Each, however, specifies some of the conditions of holding power, whether it be institutional in nature or concerning the more informal relationships between the leaders who hold power and the strata below them. When examining a plan of urban development, Hunter contends that the major economic leader handled the problem of securing a policy decision while the mayor brought the issue to the attention of the public. Thus, Hunter rates and delineates the power personnel of Atlanta into four categories:

FIRST RATE: Industrial, commercial, financial owners, and top executives of large enterprises.

SECOND RATE: Operations officials, bank vice-presidents, public relations men, small businessmen (owners), top-ranking public officials, corporation attorneys, contractors.

THIRD RATE: Civic organization personnel, civic agency board personnel, newspaper columnists, radio commentators, petty public officials, selected organization executives.

FOURTH RATE: Professionals such as ministers, teachers, social workers, personnel directors, and such persons as small business managers, higher paid accountants, and the like [Hunter, 1953, pp. 107-8].

Hunter used a schematic diagram (see Figure 1) to present a generalized pattern of policy formation. The diagram shows the patterns discerned as common to both institutional structures of economics and government and professional and civic associational structures. The recruitment, circulation, and accountability of elites is a central concern for elite theorists (see Prewitt and Stone, 1973).

Dahl's exploration of the cohesiveness among the power elite was measured by the degree of overlap between those holding social, economic, and political power. He then examined the

F I G U R E 1. Generalized Pattern of Policy Committee Formation Utilizing Institutional and Associational Structures

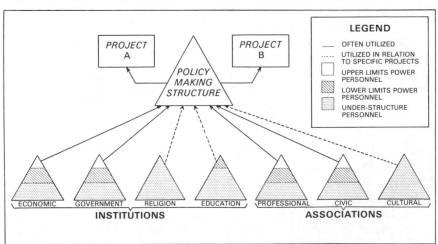

Source: Floyd Hunter, *Community Power Structure* (Chapel Hill: University of North Carolina Press, 1953), p. 91. Reprinted by permission.

same set of participants to see if they were active and influential in the three decisional arenas of political party nominations, urban redevelopment, and public education. He found little overlap (approximately 6 percent) of institutional membership or social interaction between public officials (who hold elective office as well as party offices), people considered social notables (those invited to the annual assemblies, cotillions), and people considered economic notables or economic dominants (those with position and influence over corporations, banks, utilities, business firms and those with property valued at a quarter of a million dollars or more). While Dahl found these notables were scarcely a ruling elite, he did find them influential in specific decisions involving them directly.

> Moreover, politicians are wary of their potential influence and avoid policies that might unite the notables in bitter opposition. Fortunately for the politician, it is easy to avoid the implacable hostility of the notables, for living conditions and the belief system of the community have not—at least so far—generated demands for local policies markedly antagonistic to the goals of businessmen and notables. What would happen if such demands ever developed is not easy to predict. But judging from the fate of the patricians, competitive politics would lead in the end to the triumph of numbers over notability [Dahl, 1961a, p. 84].

From this perspective Dahl formulates the important distinction between direct and indirect influence. As for the former, many constituents have no direct influence, most have very little, subleaders have more, and only a tiny group exerts great influence. As for the latter, most citizens possess a moderate degree of indirect influence, subleaders have more, and top leaders exert considerable indirect influence on one another, "for each is guided to some extent by what he believes is acceptable to some or all of the other leaders" (Dahl, 1961a, p. 164).

For Hunter, an elite system exists and persists when three elements—fear, pessimism, and silence—prevail in the following pattern: there are "expressions of fear in community life among the top leaders. Pessimism is manifested among the professionals and silence is found in the mass of the citizenry in Regional City" (Hunter, 1953, p. 223). The fear of the leaders is not personal cringing from the raw facts of life but part of a "cautious approach to any new issue which may arise and is apparently rooted in the feeling that any change in the existing relations of power and decision in the community would be disastrous for the leaders who now hold power (Hunter, 1953, p. 223).

Not only did the leaders in Regional City fear reform and the posing of political questions, but they used coercive and violent means to put down dissident factions. The pessimism of the professionals is based on the conflict between serving in a subordinate role to the power elite from whom they are isolated and fulfilling their professional obligations to improve the living conditions of the disadvantaged. They find their efforts part of a "ritualistic panorama" often failing to reach the point of effective action. "Action results when a plan fits the relatively narrow interests of the policy-makers, but on many issues there is community paralysis and inaction" (Hunter, 1953, p. 234). The bulk of the citizenry, silent and apathetic, have no voice in policy determination. Hunter notes that "the method of handling the relatively powerless is through . . . warnings, intimidations, threats, and in extreme cases, violence" (Hunter, 1953, p. 241).

Dahl's interest in the political process led him to examine and explain transformation of the changing leadership patterns. He noted that a number of old American cities pass through a transformation from a system in which their resources of influence were highly concentrated to one where they are dispersed. Thus, New Haven has changed from a "system of *cumulative inequalities* in political resources to a system of noncumulative or *dispersed inequalities* in political resources" (Dahl, 1961a, p. 228). He found the following six characteristics of dispersed inequality to be:

1. Many different kinds of resources for influencing officials are available to different citizens.
2. With few exceptions, these resources are unequally distributed.
3. Individuals best off in their access to one kind of resource are often badly off with respect to many other resources.
4. No one influence resource dominates all the others in all or even in most key decisions.
5. With some exceptions, an influence resource is effective in some issue-areas or in some specific decisions but not in all.
6. Virtually no one, and certainly no group of more than a few individuals, is entirely lacking in some influence resources [Dahl, 1961a, p. 228].

Part of the transition is reflected in the changing leadership patterns in New Haven. Dahl studied the mayors to test who governs this community and found that over a period of two centuries New Haven gradually changed from an oligarchy to a pluralistic system.

In the first period (1784–1842), public office was almost the exclusive prerogative of the patrician families. In the second period (1842–1900), the new self-made men of business, the entrepreneurs, took over. Since then, the "ex-plebes" rising out of working-class or lower middle-class families of immigrant origins have predominated. These transformations reflected profound alterations in the community, in the course of which important resources for obtaining influence were fragmented and dispersed. Wealth was separated from social position by the rise of industry, and public office went to the wealthy. Later, popularity was divorced from both wealth and social position by the influx of immigrants, and public office went to the ex-plebes, who lacked wealth and social position but had the advantage of numbers [Dahl, 1961a, p. 11].

As for the future, Dahl speculates that "the new men in local politics may very well prove to be the bureaucrats and experts—and politicians who know how to use them" (Dahl, 1961a, p. 62).

To decide upon and carry out a particular community project, the power elite of Hunter's Regional City proceeded with a highly *informal* process in appointing a policy committee, holding a series of meetings involving a relatively closed and inclusive group of men of power. As the project is formulated the group membership is enlarged, bringing in top-ranking organizational and institutional leaders who play specific roles in securing community acceptance. "The newspapers will finally carry stories of the proposals, the ministers will preach sermons, and the associational members will hear speeches regarding plans" (Hunter, 1953, p. 92).

Dahl's discussion of strategies concentrated on the role of the mayor in the executive-centered coalition. Mayor Lee of New Haven systematically began to seek control over key decisions. He centralized his influence through his appointive powers to dominate the many boards and commissions. The mayor's men then took charge *within* their agencies, knowing that they could call upon the mayor to back them up. When decision involved negotiations *outside* the agency, the mayor took charge.

> Yet it would be grossly misleading to see the executive-centered order as a neatly hierarchical system with the mayor at the top operating through subordinates in a chain of command. The mayor was not at a peak of a pyramid but rather at the center of intersecting circles. He rarely commanded. He negotiated, cajoled, exhorted, beguiled, charmed, pressed, appealed, reasoned, promised, insisted, demanded, even threatened, but he most needed support and acquiescence from other leaders who simply could not be commanded. Because the mayor could not command, he had to bargain [Dahl, 1961a, p. 204].

These two studies received considerable attention and became cause for debate. Atlanta, for example, has been studied by two political scientists. The first was Banfield's simplistic "guesswork" approach, which provides a political roadmap of factual information (Banfield, 1965). Banfield found no power elite in Atlanta. Instead he found a political system ruled by politicians with the help of the press and two voting blocs, the first consisting of the businessmen and the white middle class, the second of the black community. While Atlanta has a weak-mayor form of government—he nominates heads of departments but the city council elects them—the mayor's real influence comes through the nominations of strong department heads, his own persuasive ability with the city council, and his capacity to marshal community support. As for the interest groups, the business community has considerable importance, but its members disagree among themselves. The press is influential, especially in the field of race relations. Labor, while politically aggressive in screening candidates, is not considered particularly influential. The black community, however, is viewed as having an unusual degree of influence.

The second study is a systematic reexamination of the Hunter thesis on Atlanta by Jennings, who states that

> the central decision-makers are not uniformly drawn from the ranks of those with the highest economic status. In fact, the "pure" economic dominants were almost uniformly lowly politicized and only slightly involved in significant issues in the community. This evidence should effectively dispel the notion that economic position is invariably correlated with political power in Atlanta. At the same time, some economic notables are quite influential. To put it another way, ranking economic position is only one of a number of factors related to political power and, by itself, is unlikely to be the decisive factor . . . Although a homogeneous elite does not rule Atlanta, a coalition of actors, organizations, and institutions does tend to prevail in most important community issues. The main components of this coalition are the business-civic, the governmental-political, and the older Negro leadership [Jennings, 1964, pp. 122–200].

Jennings tries to account for the discrepancy by suggesting that there may have been a change in the political and social structures over time. There may also have been a shift in orientation and conceptualization of power in the decision-making process as Jennings questions the validity of Hunter's sociometric techniques. Certainly, during the decade between the two studies, the advent of federal programs such as urban renewal, highway construction, housing, and airport development, all financed from outside the system, may have had considerable effect on decision-making processes. The fact that these are all public programs could have the effect of rearranging power relations, especially of emphasizing the role of governmental officials. Furthermore, race relations in Atlanta have altered substantially with the advent of school desegregation, the civil rights movement, and urban riots. Jennings takes a middle ground and concludes by saying, "In essence, then, the structure is neither so monolithic as Hunter claims in his earlier work on Atlanta nor so fragmented as other metropolises appear to be" (Jennings, 1964, p. 201).

While there have been no follow-up studies, Dahl's interpretation on New Haven has provoked many comments. Hunter, for example, in reviewing the study, states:

Finding that between one-fourth and one-half of 1 percent of the population of New Haven have anything at all to do with the development and execution of community policies comes as no particular surprise to anyone familiar with community affairs, nor does it surprise Professor Dahl—although it obviously troubles him as it does many students of communities elsewhere. He readily records that democracy in New Haven is related to social ritualism, ceremonialism, high-order delegation, social referents, and business-politician bossism. He is not at all ready to designate such an array of leaders as an "elite" group, nor as a "power structure." He protests that the persons he talked to and talks about have historically evolved from an aristocratic set of patricians, ex-plebes and entrepreneurs into a "pluralistic political system" cued by an "executive centered order."

I have no trouble in understanding that "democratic pluralism" is at work in the upper reaches of the one-half of 1 percent of the policy-making array of New Haven. The fact that Dahl finds no connection between this narrow band of civic democrats and the large body politic does not, as suggested, surprise anyone. Yet in such a vacuous state of affairs where there seem to be no connections between anyone in relation to community policies, the question of "who governs" remains haunting [Hunter, 1962, pp. 517-19].

Other investigators have attempted to test many of Dahl's findings. Presthus, in a study of two communities, disagreed with Dahl. For example, he found leaders had a "virtual monopoly of typical 'influential resources' compared to the community rank and file" (Presthus, 1964, p. 420). He also found considerable overlap of leaders from one institutional area to another.

MULTIFACETED SYSTEMS

A much broader and more eclectic approach is needed, one that at times is intuitive and impressionistic. Bachrach and Baratz suggest that further research should begin

not, as does the sociologist who asks, "who rules?" nor as does the pluralist who asks, "does anyone have power?"—but by investigating the particular "mobilization of bias" in the institution under scrutiny. Then, having analyzed the dominant values, the myths and the established political procedures and rules of the game, he would make a careful inquiry into which persons or groups, if any, gain from the existing bias and which, if any, are handicapped by it [Bachrach and Baratz, 1962b, p. 952; see also 1970].

They borrow from Schattschneider's sense of the mobilization of bias in that "all forms of political organization have a bias in favor of exploitation of some kinds of conflict and the suppression of others because *organization is the mobilization of bias.* Some issues are organized into politics while others are organized out" (Schattschneider, 1960, p. 71).

In a multifaceted, comparative study of four communities, I participated in a comprehensive effort to formulate systematic concepts and to measure the distribution of power and influence as well as the leadership and ideological patterns that determine decisional preferences and outcomes. As political sociologists we were able to go beyond the methodological dispute between the reputational and decisional approach. We used a multiphase research strategy including random samples of citizen attitudes and behavior and reputational leadership analysis, as well as case studies of specific decision-making processes and events. In addition, a historical perspective was introduced with measurements over time and the predictive ability of the analysts was tested in "natural experiments." (For a detailed discussion on the methods used, see the Operational Definitions in Agger, Goldrich, and Swanson, 1964, pp. 688–759.)

Sensitive to the quarrel among elitists and pluralists, leaders were classified not only as being nominated by other leaders but by their activity of having taken part in political decision making and being satisfied. Then, using sociometric techniques, the leaders were found to cluster into viable ideological "inner cliques." The leadership pattern varied not only by the number of cliques but also by the political ideologies they held on policy perspectives and decisional preferences. These ideologies and preferences were gleaned from open-ended interviews, published statements, and correspondence. The operational ideologies discovered in this study include orthodox, progressive, and Jeffersonian conservatives, community conservationists, liberals, and radical rightists and leftists, as well as black and white supremacists (Agger et al., 1964, pp. 14–32).

In the smallest community (2,500), Farmdale, a single Jeffersonian conservative clique dominated the community affairs. They believed in hard work, shunned the problem of city life as the place of lazy, impatient persons looking for immediate rewards, and they abhorred political controversy and community conflict. (The leadership structure of Farmdale is described in Figure 2.)

In the largest community (110,000), Metroville, a white progressive conservative clique prevailed as autocratic guardians who pos-

FIGURE 2.   Farmdale: Manifest Leadership Group Structure

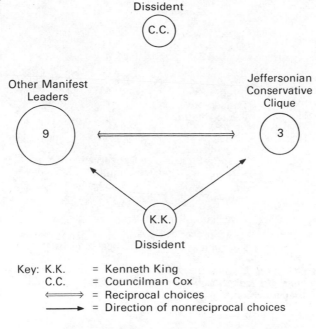

Key: K.K.   = Kenneth King
     C.C.   = Councilman Cox
     ⟸⟹   = Reciprocal choices
     ⟶   = Direction of nonreciprocal choices

Source: Robert E. Agger, Daniel Goldrich, and Bert E. Swanson, *The Rulers and the Ruled*, rev. ed. (Belmont: Duxbury, 1972), p. 141. Reprinted by permission.

sessed wisdom as to what is the community's interest. This clique had the economic, social, and political power to defeat any competitors, such as proprietors, factory workers, or blacks. They viewed civic troubles and demands for substantial change as originating with outsiders. The manifest leaders of the black subcommunity were also a progressive conservative clique, "accommodating" to the influence of their white benefactors. (Metroville's leadership structure is described in Figure 3.)

In Oretown, a small community (15,000), there were two competing inner cliques—orthodox conservatives versus community conservationists. There was also a liberal clique of latent leaders. The conservatives perceived the community as having sets of competing interests with their primary loyalties given to the businessmen. They believed in the principles of nonpartisanship, efficiency, low taxes, and the absence of spoils politics. They operated on a model of economic scarcity. The community conservationists, on the other

F I G U R E 3. Metroville: Manifest   Leadership   Group
Structure

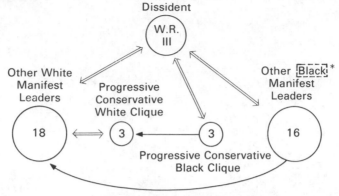

Key: W.R. III = Williston Russell, III
      ⟺   = Reciprocal choices
      ⟶   = Direction of nonreciprocal choices

Source: Robert E. Agger, Daniel Goldrich, and Bert E. Swanson,
The Rulers and the Ruled, rev. ed. (Belmont: Duxbury, 1972), p. 141.
Reprinted by permission.

hand, see the community as a collectivity of mutually interdependent parts to be governed by constitutional representatives. They
operated on a model of abundance supporting public programs that
preserved community harmony. (See Figure 4 for a representation of
the Oretown leadership structure.)

In Petropolis (100,000) there were three competing cliques. The
pattern is similar to that of Oretown, with the exception that the
liberals are active and there is a liberal black clique. The Petropolis
conservatives were bitterly anti-union, sharply racist, and believed
strongly in a surplus of cheap labor providing the necessary conditions for strengthening the moral fiber, while poverty was a punishment for past and present sins. They feared any black-white-labor
political machine that would increase taxes and mismanage and
corrupt the local government. The orthodox conservatives not only
preferred white industrial-financial rule but had a high sense of
cultural class.[1] The community conservationists supported immediate major moves to expand the scope of local government to halt
or slow down further deterioration in community spirit. While they

1. The sense of cultural class refers to political values, beliefs, opinions,
judgments, and ideas about the polity as well as to matters of manners, morals,
money, and music (Agger et al., 1964, p. 24).

F I G U R E 4. Oretown: Manifest Leadership Group Structure

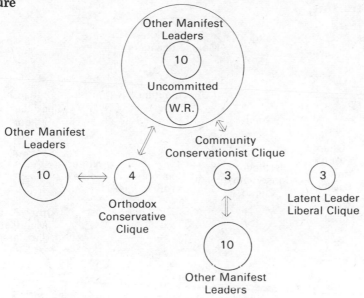

Key: W.R. = Wilbur Rake
⟺ = Reciprocal choices
⟶ = Direction of nonreciprocal choices

Source: Robert E. Agger, Daniel Goldrich, and Bert E. Swanson, *The Rulers and the Ruled*, rev. ed. (Belmont: Duxbury, 1972), p. 144. Reprinted by permission.

had no master plan, they had advocated a set of civic improvement policies, including those on race relations, new industry, redevelopment of the central business district, urban planning and governmental reorganization—particularly annexation of industrial areas and consolidation of city and county. (Figure 5 represents the manifest leadership structure of Petropolis.)

The analysis revealed that the political-leader inner cliques were extremely articulate, had relatively well-developed political ideologies, and did three things more consistently than other political leaders:

First, they propounded general doctrines of their political ideologies; second, they applied those doctrines to decisional questions and announced the "proper" decisional preferences and outcomes to others; third, they acted as the chief of staff, the planners of the broad strategies to be followed by members of their groups, in the making of the political decisions that would affect the scope of government in their communities [Agger et al., 1964, p. 427].

F I G U R E 5. Petropolis: Manifest Leadership Group
Structure

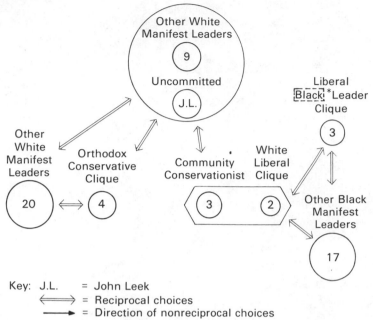

Key: J.L.   = John Leek
      ⟺   = Reciprocal choices
      ⟶   = Direction of nonreciprocal choices

Source: Robert E. Agger, Daniel Goldrich, and Bert E. Swanson,
The Rulers and the Ruled, rev. ed. (Belmont: Duxbury, 1972), p. 142.
Reprinted by permission.

We formulated a typology to classify local community political
systems. This included the indicators of power structures and regimes. The power structure is based on two dimensions: the extent
to which political power is distributed broadly or narrowly throughout the citizenry, and the extent to which the ideology of the
political leadership, in regard to the scope of government, is convergent or compatible on the one hand or divergent and conflicting on
the other. It is obvious that if there were only one political leadership group sharing a single ideology, the type of power structure
would be consensual (see Figure 6).

The second measure in our typology is regimes. The writings of
democratic philosophers have identified two variables that define the
extent to which a regime, regardless of its type of power structure, is
democratic or undemocratic. The first variable is the extent to which
the citizenry feels able to use elections, if necessary, to attempt to shift
the scope of government and the probability that legitimate efforts to
affect the scope of government (whether to shift or to maintain it)
would be blocked by the use of illegitimate, negative sanctions. Thus,
by "regime" we mean the "rules of the game" of political decision

making as leaders and citizens interpret, conform, or attempt to change them. The sense of electoral potency refers to the citizens' conviction that they can use elections to put men into office who will respond to their decisional preferences. It does not mean that they must feel sanguine about their prospects of electoral victory in the short or even in the long run. If they are not optimistic about their long-run chances, however, it may be that their sense of being able to use elections will atrophy into apathy and alienation. It should be noted, however, that participation may be low rather than high, and the distribution of power may be narrow rather than broad, even in situations of relatively optimistic electoral potency (see Figure 7).

F I G U R E 6. Types of Power Structure

Distribution of Political Power among Citizens

		Broad	Narrow
Political Leadership's Ideology	Convergent	Consensual Mass	Consensual Elite
	Divergent	Competitive Mass	Competitive Elite

Source: Robert E. Agger, Daniel Goldrich, and Bert E. Swanson, *The Rulers and the Ruled*, rev. ed. (Belmont: Duxbury, 1972), p. 38. Reprinted by permission.

F I G U R E 7. Types of Regime

Probability of Illegitimate Sanctions Blocking Efforts to Shift the Scope of Government

		Low	High
Sense of Electoral Potency	High	Developed Democracy	Guided Democracy
	Low	Underdeveloped Democracy	Oligarchy

Source: Robert E. Agger, Daniel Goldrich, and Bert E. Swanson, *The Rulers and the Ruled*, rev. ed. (Belmont: Duxbury, 1972), p. 44. Reprinted by permission.

A decision-making model was developed to analyze community policy formulation. It used six stages: (1) policy formulation, (2) policy deliberation, (3) organization of political support, (4) authoritative consideration (event: decisional outcome), (5) promulgation of the decisional outcome, and (6) policy effectuation (Agger et al., 1964, pp. 40–51). The critical stage in establishing public policy is the fourth stage—authoritative consideration—which is the stage at which the political participants seek to have their greatest influence. They therefore are most active in the first three stages. Because the political systems of Oretown and Petropolis included competitive mass power structures and developed democracy regimes, the authoritative-consideration stage took place more frequently in an open, public setting and the decisions were of a public issue character, whereas in Farmdale, with its consensual elite power structure and guided democracy regime, and in Metroville, a consensual elite with an underdeveloped democracy regime, a closed private setting with restricted decisional consideration was more characteristic. This does not mean government officials were never the political leaders in Farmdale and Metroville but were frequently so in Oretown and Petropolis. Nor does it mean that there was a smaller proportion of elected government officials in the political leadership of the consensual elite than in the competitive mass. But it does mean that in the former there was a greater tendency for outcomes to have been decided by the time the formal authorities publicly engaged in authoritative consideration in their official forums.

The strategic concerns of political leadership are not only to respond to and support sets of demands for a shift in the scope of government but to balance these demands against the more complex processes of building support for themselves, as well as nurturing and building a sense of political community. Demands can and do emanate from all sectors of the political stratum. Those demands that are not repressed from fear of illegitimate sanctions or feelings of political inefficacy, however, reach at some point the political leaders who are in an influential position to control, respond, modify, or reject the demands. In the competitive mass, for example, it is more likely that there will be greater citizen participation that will encourage the development of subsidiary political organizations. These organizations provide the mechanisms and potentially increased articulation of demands and mobilization of support for competing leaders of differing ideological groups. In the consensual elite, the climate is highly unlikely to encourage citizen participation, while demands will remain low and support will most likely be generated through control by the elite.

The leadership roles in relationship to the decision-making processes differed considerably in the differing political systems. In Petropolis and Oretown they spent more of their time and energies in the deliberative and organization-of-political-support stages, trying to build the mass support necessary to influence officials. The flow of demands generally came from a few citizens to an aspiring or actual leadership group which in turn transmitted them, often modified, to a larger proportion of citizens who could embrace these demands as their own. By contrast, the political leaders of Farmdale and Metroville seldom activated political messages back to any substantial proportion of citizens. In fact, there were distinct major impediments to the development and articulation of demands in these two communities. In the guided democracy of Farmdale, potential demands either remained prepolitical and private, taking the form of diffused political discontent, or became specific administrative demands; thus, few demands became public issues. In the underdeveloped democracy of Metroville, the fear of illegitimate sanctions repressed the development and articulation of demands as well as the

TABLE 2.   Public Policy Outputs on Four Communities

Political Decision-Making Process	Farmdale	Metroville	Oretown	Petropolis
I. Economic Reorganization				
A. Economic Base	4 rejections	2 successes 3 rejections	4 rejections	2 successes 1 rejection
B. Stimulation of Business	1 success 2 rejections	2 successes 2 rejections	1 success	3 successes
II. Civic Improvement				
A. Housekeeping Services	1 success 4 rejections	3 successes	1 success	no attempts
B. Community Planning and Guided Development	1 success 1 rejection	1 success 5 rejections	1 rejection	2 successes 2 rejections
C. Recreation	2 rejections	2 rejections	no attempt	no attempt
D. Health	no attempt	1 success 1 rejection	1 rejection	1 rejection
III. Social Organization	no attempt	2 successes	no attempt	3 successes 4 rejections
IV. Government Reorganization	1 rejection	2 rejections	1 success 2 rejections	1 success 2 rejections
TOTAL	3 successes 14 rejections	11 successes 15 rejections	3 successes 8 rejections	11 successes 10 rejections
Percent Successes	17.7	42.3	27.3	52.4

Source: Adapted from Robert E. Agger, Daniel Goldrich, and Bert E. Swanson, *The Rulers and the Ruled*, rev. ed. (Belmont: Duxbury, 1972), pp. 195–260.

formation of independent, competitive political-leadership groups.

An analysis of the public policy outputs on shifting the scope of government suggests that no single factor such as power structure determines the degree of success (see Table 2). Any explanation should include the interrelationships between the types of power structure, regime, and political ideology as well as social, economic, and political goals, conditions, trends, projections, and alternatives (Swanson and Swanson, 1970).

SUMMARY

The following paradigm (Table 3) summarizes the general state of knowledge about community power. It uses the four approaches—

T A B L E 3.   Paradigm of Four Approaches on Understanding Community Power

	Stratification	Elite	Pluralist	Multifaceted
Who governs? (leadership)	Upper socioeconomic class	Top economic dominants	Competitive interest groups and political leaders	Leaders of social and cultural groups/classes
Where? (kind of community)	General	General, variation depends on type of economic base	General, variation depends on competitive skills in using resources	Variable, depends on type of power structure and political regime
When? (under what conditions)	Integration social and economic forces	Economic forces prevail, inducing pessimism, fear, and silence	Degree of socioeconomic diversity determines degree of competition	Depends on effort and strategy in participation in various stages of decision-making process
How? (strategy)	Class control of all aspects of communal life	Inner clique excludes others from forumulation of policy	Bargaining on policy and influence implementation through appointments and regulations	Multistrategic based on relative influence
To what end? (cost benefits on outcomes)	To control (power to maintain power and wealth)	To dominate (wealth to maintain wealth and power)	To bargain to minimize losses and maximize interest	Depends on prevailing ideologies serving social and cultural class interests

stratification, elite, pluralistic, and multifaceted—and attempts to answer five key questions: "Who governs?" (leadership), "Where?" (kind of community), "When?" (under what conditions), "How?" (strategy), and "To what end?" (cost benefits).

There is one common finding in all the studies of American communities: that there are few who are reputed to be influential or are actually playing a significant role in determining public policy. The approaches differ primarily on the degree of competition they believe to exist among the few and the reason for that competition. The stratificationist and the elitist stress socioeconomic class status, the pluralist stresses competing interest groups, while the multifaceted approach emphasizes ideologically based groups. There is, as I observed before, a similarity in the findings of stratification and elite theorists with the exception that economic determinism and control of the decision-making stages are somewhat more pervasive for the former. There are sharp differences between the elitists and the pluralists on "who gets what, when, and how." The elite theorists proceed with an analysis of *control* mechanisms in contrast to the pluralists' more *regulative* system, which stresses political competition, strategic skills, and bargaining. The pluralists use individuals and interest groups as the basic unit for analysis and a mini-max cost-benefit analysis on what influentials seek and receive from their energy and political resources. Similarly, the pluralists discern a bargaining strategy on policy formulation and the reliance on appointed authorities to supplement policy, rather than the monopolistic control of policy formulation and implementation of the stratificationists, and the discriminatory-exclusionary process of forming policy and determining who implements it of the elitists.

The multifaceted approach presents a far more conditional portrait of the exercise of power and influence in a variety of American communities. The answers to the questions depend on the variables of the constructed typologies of power structures and political regimes. The influentials in local communities were found to be leaders of ideological and class interests and their risks and rewards are largely determined by the values of the prevailing group or groups. The comparative-typological approach allowed for the classification of communities not previously developed by the other three schools of though. It also delineates not only the distribution of power but also the effect of such essential variables as ideological competition, sense of political efficacy, and the use of illegitimate sanctions. It establishes useful insights for the development of strategic and tactical concerns for discovering community dynamics and change.

A PLEA FOR PLANNED INTERVENTION

Obviously, much research remains to be done on American communities, especially as they face the urban crises arising from rapid social and racial change, economic decline and fiscal insolvency, and political conflict and problems of the legitimacy of authority. Some students of community power structures will and should continue the search for power considering Simpson's questions: (1) "What does the government do, who benefits from it, and who does not?" (2) "Who decides what the government will do?" (3) "Through what processes do the decision makers decide?" (4) "What are the causes of variation in numbers 1, 2, and 3?" (For comments on Clark, 1967a, see Simpson and Olson, 1967, pp. 287-96.) More effort should be given to comparative community studies across national or cultural boundaries (see Miller, 1970b, pp. 259-79). However, other students of urban politics should begin to apply the pool of relevant social science knowledge we have developed over the years (see Report of the Special Commission on the Social Sciences of the National Science Board, 1969).

The multifaceted incursion into the narrow elite-pluralist debate allows those interested in the science of politics to develop a deeper understanding of community power. This requires going beyond making simple observations of the political process and engaging in theory building through action-research, which involves engaging in clinical diagnostic probes and sensitive intervention techniques for change. Planned intervention not only provides the opportunity to test the validity of our social science theories and insights but can aid in community problem solving. (How intervention strategies fit into the role of social scientists and change agents in local communities is discussed in Swanson et al., in press.) Without action-research it is difficult to translate theoretical concepts into operational research terms or into specific practical application for citizens, administrators, and politicians. (This discussion is based on a five-year project, "Mobilizing Leadership for Effective Community Action," funded by Title I of the Higher Education Act of 1965, and the Marshall Field Foundation.) The observer faces the enormous problem of gaining access to the policy makers and overcoming the insulation of the decision-making process. Political prototyping, a form of action-research I have used, eases the breakthrough of some of these barriers, as the social scientists develop working relations and events require translation of theoretical concepts into securing effective community action (Dobyns, Doughty, and Lasswell, 1971).

To overcome these problems and make our theoretical work more relevant, while at the same time testing the validity of some of our insights, we at the Institute of Community Studies explored the use of political prototyping as our major effort to mobilize leadership for effective community action. Specifically, the prototype experience involved some eighteen change-agent inputs concerning such community problems as racial segregation and urban redevelopment. We were especially interested in finding ways to develop community leaders who could more effectively respond to citizen demands and introduce them to the nature of their changing community, in part through self-study and in part through consultant studies and discussion. They learned to assemble, analyze, and report on complex local problems as well as to evolve feasible proposals for community action. Then, of course, they engaged in the process of gaining approval from other leaders and citizens as well as making direct contact with city and other officials who were in authority and could take the necessary action.

Here community leaders were going through the process of learning while doing and trying out what seems feasible. Our work was directed toward the following seven specific objectives:

1. opening up and maintaining channels of communications between leadership groups;
2. developing a sense of reality about social change, exploring the myths and assumptions that lie behind public policy;
3. examining the public-private mix of community programs, services, and activities as well as learning how to effectively accept and use external assistance;
4. learning the workings of the system and the interrelationships of the various community institutions and groups, probing to see what factors are critical in securing community action;
5. following closely the progress of community agencies and programs such as urban renewal, public school desegregation, and the antipoverty program;
6. defining and stating the key community problems, formulating programs with a sense of priorities for action;
7. evolving workable leadership patterns and coalitions which were realistic in face of the changing community.

Prototyping is suggested as an addition to basic data survey, which should provide answers to the following questions:

Who are the significant *participants* (official or unofficial)? What are the participants' *perspectives* of the outcomes (values) they seek, their prospects of success, and the groups with whose fate they identify themselves? What *arenas* are specialized in the task? What assets (*base values*) are at the disposal of participants seeking to influence results? What *strategies* do they employ in managing these base values to affect outcomes? With what immediate and long-range results (outcomes and effects)? [Lasswell, 1963, p. 47].

Lasswell acknowledges that "trend data," usually collected by historians and political scientists, in many ways are insufficient to meet the criteria of science and policy. He therefore suggests that we consider the possibility of linking experimentation, prototyping, and intervention as a comprehensive strategy of policy innovation. This linkage becomes important in an effort to extend the findings of more highly controlled experimental settings to field situations where there is an ongoing decision-making process. Prototyping for Lasswell is "the effective pursuit of enlightenment," where "innovation, typically small scale, is made in political practice, primarily for scientific purposes" (Lasswell, 1963, p. 99).

Our experience in political prototyping has reaffirmed some of the general findings on community power and impotence and their changing nature that were reported in *The Rulers and the Ruled* (Agger et al., 1964). While there we became aware of the ideological undercurrents of public policy; here the dialogue really revealed the operational interrelatedness of economic and social, as well as political, values. If one value was predominant, it certainly would have been economic, ranging from a concern for the economic viability of the community to the specifics of policy, from tax abatement for urban renewal to proposals for industrial development as a means to bolster or diversify the tax base of the community. There was growing concern, however, for the accompanying social consequences of urban renewal in the relocation of business and residential tenants, especially among the blacks, who have fewer alternatives and choices available to them.

It seems as though most urban systems in America have grown too rapidly and have been unable to retain the essence of democracy. Their social and economic structures have so factionalized the systems that there is a low sense of political efficacy among the people and a low rate of participation in community affairs as well as a fear of and wish to avoid community contention, controversy, and conflict. The scope of government has expanded slowly and often too late to meet the real needs of the citizens. The administrative officials are removed and insulated from the people whom their programs are to serve.

I believe that if a leader desires to prepare his community to meet the political change that lies ahead of most American towns, he should provide his people with an *accurate* and increasingly high sense of political efficacy; encourage mass participation by and for *all*; risk political controversy; shift to increase the scope of government to meet the needs of the people; and professionalize the bureaucracy to serve the public but not to completely govern the system. (For a more detailed discussion of the interrelation of these six factors, see my "Political Change in the Small American Community," in Gore and Hodapp, 1967, pp. 124-54.) To do otherwise is to countenance the growing deterioration of democratic ideals in the world of oligarchic reality.

We also explored beyond a surface interest the role of the political party in ethnic politics as it is played out in the urban scene. Instead of looking for "ticket balancing" and "gentlemen's agreements" on Protestant, Catholic, and Jewish representation on the local school boards, we began to describe and understand the complex set of relationships that forms the basis for the major factions—black, Jewish, and Italian—in their struggle for power over the scarce and highly prized urban space.

There was, among the participants, in our experience, at least an implicit recognition that the prototype was effective in the redistribution of economic, social, and political values, as certain decisions were made. The redistribution, however, favored those least concerned with social justice. Thus, in terms of power, one became well aware who were the most powerful, who were less so, and who were impotent. Interestingly, there seemed to be a tendency for those already powerful to gain more strength, in part at the expense of their opposition.

Finally, political prototyping, while highly intricate and time-consuming, is a necessary and sufficient experience to discover the relationship between community power and change. The procedure not only makes it possible to test the general propositions in the social sciences but also to formulate alternative explanations of the community decision-making process. I have found prototyping to provide a greater opportunity than any of my other experiences, such as assistant to a United States senator or serving in a fellowship capacity to the mayor of a big city or as special assistant to the commissioner of a public housing agency.

In prototyping, I began to perceive the larger, system-level implications of political influence and their impact as they relate to meeting human needs. We have only begun our prototyping experience and need to do much more, both theoretically and practically, in this area. We need to test out the value of various processes for transforming urban political systems: professionalization, management, reform, politicization, mediation, and creative tension (Swanson, 1969, pp. 288-92). Certainly one must be committed to spending a considerable number of years in an attempt to fully understand, perhaps to modify and/or reverse, the general direction of community decisions, attitudes, and ideologies that have been generations in the forming.

It is hoped that action-research and planned intervention will enrich our knowledge about community power. However, it should be viewed as a complementary approach, along with present methods and innovative strategies, that will focus on several relatively neglected areas central to understanding the American community of tomorrow. First is the effect of caste and class, especially on the black struggle for equality—black power and ghetto riots—as well as white resistance and "backlash" (see Harris and Swanson, 1970). Second is managerial power in the rise of the "administrative state" and the protest and demand for "community control." (See Sayre and Kaufman, 1965; Lowi, 1964a; Altshuler, 1970; and Yates, 1973.) Third is the growing importance of knowledge and information and the struggle for its control. Fourth is the confluence of coercive forces, including those of the invisible government of organiized crime, authoritarianism on the right and left, and the use of the repressive tactics of illegitimate sanctions by public authorities.

PART 4

FOUNDATIONS, APPROACHES, AND METHODS

16. PHILOSOPHY AND SOCIAL SCIENCE: A PHENOMENOLOGICAL APPROACH

Maurice Natanson

This chapter is concerned with a philosphical description and analysis of some fundamental problems in social science; it is not intended as an inquiry into political philosophy, although I believe that the themes to be examined and the methodological considerations to be probed are indeed relevant to political theory. On the whole, I shall be interested in issues which form a part of what might be termed an epistemology of the social world. By that I mean a study of the conditions of our knowledge and experience of social reality. Given the social world, what are the essential, constitutive elements of knowing which make that world possible? And even within the large methodological perspective, I shall not turn to a survey of major types of approach and position in the philosophy of social science. Rather, I shall limit the focus to the formulation and elucidation of a phenomenological standpoint, contrasting that position with a more nearly naturalistic-behavioristic approach. In these terms, a number of issues will *not* be discussed here: the logic of explanation, the meaning and role of hypothesis and law in the social sciences, the structure of models. To the extent that I shall touch on such problems, it will be because they are relevant to the phenomenological position I shall develop. In brief, then, it is with distinctively philosophical questions that I am concerned, and I am going to turn to them from the standpoint of philosophical methodology rather than the history of political theory or its concrete problems. There are, of course, some disadvantages to such a procedure. Those who believe (and with some justification) that methodological issues are best examined in the context of substantive work in a discipline may be rather wary of my plans, but I would urge them to keep an open mind and to think of what follows as a fresh conception of the province of methodology. To turn to an epistemology of the social world will mean to take as ultimately relevant to political theory the problems of intersubjectivity, mundane existence, and sociality itself. If such themes have an unfamiliar ring, it may be that the unfamiliar may indeed lead us to hidden possibilities and that students of political science may, if only in a heuristic sense, find new sources and ideas in the epistemological vantage point from which this essay derives. At the end I hope to make clearer the excitement as well as utility of a phenomenological approach to social science in general and political theory in particular.

THE NATURE OF PHILOSOPHY

It may be possible to clarify the meaning of an epistemology of the social world by first locating the meaning of epistemology in philosophy. I am not interested in tracing a history of the term in classical thought. Let us rather turn to its placement in the practice of philosophy, understood and taken in a certain way, one which will become more evident as we go along. Earlier, I raised (and left hanging) the question "Given the social world, what are the essential, constitutive elements of knowing which make that world possible?" The central terms of the question deserve some analysis. "Given the social world"—for, to begin with, we are as ordinary human beings, men in the world, involved in an ongoing reality of work, love, strife, and reflection. We are *in* the world without asking about it or wondering why it is. If we ask philosophical questions about "being in" the world, we are no longer in the initial placement of mundane existence. "Given," then, in this perhaps peculiar way of speaking, refers to what is unquestioningly and naively accepted as real. The given is not a gift but an orientation, not a mathematical posit but an attitude. It points back to some prior state of tacit knowing in which men locate their guidelines for both action and reflection. "Given the social world," then, means naively accepting language, history, fellow men, and their interaction.

Starting with the social world as given, philosophy reflects on that givenness, asks about it, turns to it questioningly. What are the essential, constitutive elements of knowing? Suppose one were to take a language—English, for example—as "given" and then ask about its essential, constitutive elements. What would they be? We may at least suggest that in addition to vocabulary, syntax, and other formal aspects of language, there are certain structural features which demand notice: predication (the fundamental subject-object relationship), the continuity or sequential connectedness of English sentences as they build into larger units of paragraph, chapter, and totality, and the "sedimentation" of meaning, to use a phenomenological term, i.e., the genesis and buildup of meaning borne by the words and concepts of our language. To turn to the constitutive elements of English, then, would be to ask how our language is possible and to determine the grounds from which meaning arises. In our daily, run-of-the-mill use of English at home, in the office, at the playground, such formative powers of language are taken for granted in the sense of being assumed, presupposed, in discourse. To turn to language questioningly in the epistemological sense is to attempt to make manifest the latent reality of the mundane. In considering the social world as our theme, we must proceed in a way similar to our questioning of language. What are the formative powers which underlie and constitute the social domain? Later on, I shall try to present some answers to this question. For the present, let us say that an epistemology of the social world is the built-in response to the need for basic clarity about the assumptions of men in daily life (and, as we shall also see, the common-sense starting point of naturalistically oriented social science) and the taken-for-grantedness with which they organize their spheres of action.

Philosophy, as has been at least immanently revealed thus far, is a critical enterprise. Recognizing and delineating what is given, it then proceeds quickly to challenge the conditions of givenness. The challenge here is a purely critical, not a skeptical one, as far as I am concerned. The fundamental issue is not whether what is given is "real" but rather what taking it as real signifies and presupposes. Thus, man in the world, man thrust into the sociality of mundane events, does as a matter of psychological fact act in such a way as to indicate his acceptance of the "real." More fundamental, apart from his behavior, there is an egological dimension to his grasp of the real; he accepts it in a profoundly sure sense of immediate actuality as real, i.e., as real for him. We meet here a theme of the "naive" or "taken for granted" way in which common-sense men, men in everyday life, involve themselves in mundane experience and interpret its component elements or at least the events which are built out of those elements. Philosophical analysis is intrinsically set over and against the taken for granted, for the "obvious" truth of the world about us and ourselves in that world cannot be examined or even entertained as a theme for discussion as long as we begin analysis by presupposing that "of course" the familiar world about us is, in its basic aspects, as it appears to be. The first and essential step in philosophy is the recognition that the "obvious" demands the most cautious and sensitive analysis.

The notion of philosophy I am proposing here—philosophy as the critique of common-sense experience—stands in an odd relationship to the large pragmatic motive of some philosophical work and the purely theoretic character of some aspects of logic. That is, the critical inquiry into the nature of what is taken for granted in mundane experience is not primarily validated by the "utility" of such analysis, nor is it an exercise in pure thought. Rather, philosophy is the illumination of the world in which we live, the bringing into clarity of its constitutive history—the story of its meaning-structure. Our orientation is toward the placement of men in daily life who interpret the world and each other as evident and unchallengeable ultimates, ineluctable "data" of all human reality, but the central problem that arises when we extend our philosophical glance toward that theme is that what most needs analysis is the sense of "ultimacy" which attends daily life. What ordinary men will never believe, William James once said, is that their experience of the world is a fraud. Taking the "role" of a common-sense individual, I may put the case this way: "Everyday life is like a machine which is always in operation, whose inside mechanism I've never inspected, whose physical principles of operation I'm ignorant of, and which has never broken down. Since it works so smoothly and efficiently, I've never concerned myself about it, hardly given it a thought. *Were* it to become defective, however, I don't know who I'd call in or consult about repairs. I'd be caught in an unusual situation." Indeed I would! If we take the machine analogy seriously, part of what would have broken down when everyday life is impaired is the very meaning of "consultation," for being able to turn for help to neighbors, telling them what's wrong, asking them to come in and take a look, and trusting them to advise and assist us, is precisely part of and integrally bound to the meaning of "everyday experience." The failure of that precious machine means the disintegration of any coherent scheme for diagnosis of what is wrong or action to correct what is faulty. Mundane experience is built on the assumption that whatever else may go wrong, it—everyday life itself—is invincibly permanent and efficacious.

A paradox seems to have been generated: if philosophy is to be the critique of everyday experience, how can the philosopher (any more than anybody else in daily life) find a place outside of mundane existence from which to examine it? On what fulcrum can the philosopher who seeks to "move" the world conceptually place his lever? The language of "in" (or "within") and "out" (or "outside") is deceptive and misleading. Mundane experience is encompassing in the sense of being the conceptual and interpretive ground in which human reality is rooted. We are "in" the world in the way in which the Kennedys are "in" politics, not in the way in which the cigars are in the humidor. "In" is more nearly a temporal than a spatial term, or at least we might say that the spatiality of "*in*-volvement" in politics or life is situational rather than cartographical. When we ask for a way "out" of the impasse of any effort to inspect daily life from "within," the answer must be responsive to the temporal and situational horizon of the question. In these terms, the way "out" is through radical reflection. To the extent that I can make common-sense experience an explicit object for examination, I am able to escape the apparent circle of mundane involvement. But *radical* inspection must mean that in rendering the taken for granted explicit, I must include in my methodological purview the subjectivity of the *taking* (in the taken for granted). My own basic orientation in accepting the world as real must be no less examined than the individual things or events accepted as real. In radical reflection, the philosopher turns back upon his own experience-of-the-world and subjects it to rigorous scrutiny. Remaining in the world as a common-sense man, the philosopher nevertheless transcends it by reflecting upon it in the remarkable and uncompromising way which, as I have suggested, alone merits the name of radicality.

THE RELATIONSHIP BETWEEN PHILOSOPHY AND SCIENCE

Isaiah Berlin once pointed out that if you want an answer to a formal question, you go to a logician, and if you want a factual question answered, you go to a scientist; but if your question concerns neither fact nor formal considerations, then it is philosophical. If we understand by "science" natural science, then for our immediate purposes we may say that matters of fact are first of all distinguished from matters of value. Other distinctions will follow soon, but for the moment let us concentrate on the fact-value duality. The natural scientist need take no stand on the question either of the worth of his activity or of the value-quality of what he investigates. To the extent that he makes value judgments about helping to make atomic bombs or elements of bacteriological warfare, he is operating as a man, as an ethical creature, as a philosophically concerned individual. Matters of fact, however complex, are in this view intrinsically neutral in ethical terms. The philosopher, to look at the other side of the matter, is professionally immersed in value questions. They fall into his bailiwick with a decisive thud and refuse to be ignored or sidetracked. Nevertheless it would be both naive and misleading to assume that by rather simple decision we can brand the scientist value-free and the philosopher value-bound. Both scientist and philosopher are highly complex beings, who do not suddenly spring into life when their professional work is being done and then are transmogrified instantaneously when they leave the laboratory or the study. Nevertheless the distinction between fact and value holds. To see it in its full force it is necessary to move from the scientist and philosopher as agents, to science and philosophy as disciplines. Whether or not a particular scientist is able to set definitive limits to his interest in questions of value, his discipline is responsible for so doing. Margenau (1950, p. 465) writes that

> natural science contains no *normative* principles dealing with ultimate goals; physical reality is the quintessence of cognitive experience and not of values. Its significance is in terms to stable *relations* between phases of experience, and since it draws its power from relations, reality cannot create an *unconditional* 'thou shalt.' To know physical reality is to know where to look when something is wanted or needed to be seen; it is to be able to cure when a cure is desired, to kill when killing is intended. But natural science will never tell whether it is good or bad to look, to cure, or to kill. It simply lacks the premise of an "ought."

But there are other major considerations which separate the nature and career of science and philosophy. In particular, I would point to the "additive" versus the "renewing" functions of the two domains. By the "additive" aspects of science I mean the historical-systematic continuity of such disciplines as mathematics and physics. A student of physics today is able to learn what has been done in a special branch of that science by consulting the appropriate treatises, journals, etc. Each time someone enters upon the study of physics, it is not necessary for him either to work alone or to reconstruct on his own the entire corpus of the science. To the contrary, it is assumed that he will start where his scientific predecessors have left off. One can then "add" to solid and reliable work already done. I am suggesting that the additive aspect of science is essential to its character and that the matter stands differently in philosophy, where what I have termed a "renewing" function exists. By renewal I mean the turning to one's own concrete existence, one's own distinctive experience, one's own history, and trying to build a philosophical edifice from its elements. Having to make one's own way, having to start from where and what one is—these are endemic to the demands of renewal. When a tiger is born, Ortega somewhere says, it is the same thing all over again, but when a human being is born, that is unique. More than anything else, the need for renewal in philosophy is rooted in the intimate connection between the philosopher and philosophy. The great theorems proved by Euclid, Pythagoras, or Fermat can be understood perfectly without knowing anything of the personality of their discoverers. It is not so simple to divorce Plato, Aristotle, and Descartes from their philosophical discoveries. A closer look at "renewal" is necessary.

Edmund Husserl (1960, p. 2) says in his *Cartesian Meditations* that

> anyone who seriously intends to become a philosopher must "once in his life" withdraw into himself and attempt, within himself, to overthrow and build anew all the sciences that, up to then, he has been accepting. Philosophy—wisdom (*sagesse*)—is the philosophizer's quite personal affair. It must arise as *his* wisdom, as his self-acquired knowledge tending toward universality, a knowledge for which he can answer from the beginning, and at each step, by virtue of his own absolute insights.

The philosopher is related to his professional work through the large current of his experience, and that includes his immediate perceptual activity as well as his cognitive, memorial, imaginative, emotive, and conative life. His search for knowledge must begin with a fundamental and intransigent fact: the general or even universal features of his experience are embedded in a concrete, historical, and individuated career—his actual life. Furthermore, his point of access to the transindividual pattern of his experience must necessarily by by way of his specific situation, his age, his translation of the socio-cultural world in which he lives. It might appear as if the "subjective" point of access I am emphasizing means that knowledge is, if not impossible, at least relative to the individual, that a form of first-person skepticism would be inescapable. Actually, I am arguing in the opposite direction, toward a docttine of essence, but a full account of the matter must wait for a later discussion of phenomenology. For the present, let me say simply that the search for knowledge must pass the considerable and rigorous test of individual experience and that the way to wisdom is through subjectivity.

In addition to the discussion of the question of value and the additive-renewal issue, there is one other problem we must turn to in this brief assessment of the relationship between philosophy and science. What about understanding in contrast to power? It was Comte, of course, who gave us the formula: "*Savoir, pour prévoir, pour pouvoir.*" In this sequence, power is the indwelling goal of knowledge and prediction is the mediating instrument between the two. Knowledge, then, carries an implicit arrow within it—it points toward its fulfillment and validation in practice. The Comtian genius is still with us, and at *this* point there is little difference between the nineteenth- and twentieth-century versions of positivism. If there is a distance between knowledge (understanding) and power, there is also an internal nexus between them which deserves comment. We are the inheritors still of the metaphysical legacy of Descartes: the split between mind and body, between consciousness and the "external" world, between what Descartes termed *res cogitans* and *res extensa*. Once severed, self and world become insulated in such a way that what goes on in the former demands an observable corollary in the latter. Thought, then, needs the agency of efficacious translation in the "real" world, the practical world. Those whose ideas seem to be above or remain apart from consequential practical results are tolerated as ineffectual: the poets and the philosophers find themselves thrown together as surprised allies after their Platonic battles. The nineteenth century reaches the height of the complaint: interpretation is not enough; the world must be changed! But if we are the heirs to Cartesian metaphysics, we may renounce the inheritance or at least give up that aspect of his view which keeps us from reassessing the place of mind in nature. Marx's philosophy was an interpretation of the world which helped to change it because, apart from the dramatic historical and political relevance of his ideas, significant interpretation is a mode of action. This may be less apparent in philosophies which are not directed to social and political matters, but it is all the more important to recognize that conceptual analysis is continuous with practice. Indeed, the latter is lame as well as blind without it. There are, of course, variant levels or strata of both idea and act. For a discipline to seek to clarify its basic terms and to develop its theoretical base is inevitably to affect its results and application to reality. "Knowledge is power," then, in a prepragmatic sense: the means as well as the seeds of change are to be sought in the conceptual matrix of science. The initial act of reflection and the search for clarity are the primary moments of the realization of power. Nowhere is there greater justification for this view than in the philosophy of the social sciences.

PHILOSOPHY OF THE SOCIAL SCIENCES

Common-sense men and social scientists very often share a philosophical outlook which has been characterized as "naive realism," i.e., the view that the world is as it appears to us and that in perceiving it we have legitimate access to its nature. For normal men in ordinary life, then, what they perceive is veridical, the trust they place in daily life warranted, and the hypotheses they construct on the ground of their experience are valid. The coinage "naive realism" should not be thought of as having a perjorative quality. In fact, "naive" realism is a rather sophisticated position (when it is advanced and defended by philosophers acutely aware of what they are proposing); the difficulty with it in its unself-reflective form is that it makes fundamental philosophical judgments without either being aware that it does or appreciating the implications of those judg-

ments for both common sense and social science. The central implication of naive realism as far as the philosophy of social science is
concerned is that philosophy may reflect upon a genuine social
reality, composed of real people in actual situations whose action
impinges on the ongoing scene: like figures in a Brueghel dance, the
movement is energetic; but unlike pictorial reality, the consequences are real. The difficulty with all of this from a philosophical
standpoint is that in addition to being unclear, the assumption of the
veridical character of the "social" bends or predisposes subsequent
analysis toward a root prejudice: mundane life needs no critique; it is
lucidly veridical. Rigor demands that we settle for nothing less than
clarity, and so we must inspect the haunts of naive realism and
attempt to arrive at a more nearly independent judgment about the
nature and station of mundane existence as a theme of social-scientific inquiry.

From Plato's Allegory of the Cave on in the history of philosophy, it has been said that the proper business of the philosopher is
to transcend the transitory, fragmented, illusory, error-ridden domain of everyday life (the World of Becoming) in order to arrive at
knowledge, i.e., what is permanent, unified, real, and true (the World
of Ideas). In these terms, it has been suggested that Plato turned
away from the problems of mundane existence and so denied a
central aspect of philosophical inquiry. By giving precedence to the
World of Ideas he discounted the source of our human reality. John
Wild (1959, p. 63) writes:

> We may doubt whether the objective universe is in any sense prior to the
> human life-world and independent of it. This idea fails to fit the facts of
> social and individual history. Man existed in the concrete world for many
> millennia before the appearance of rational reflection and science. Further-
> more, the human thinker must grow up in the everyday world before he
> becomes a philosopher or scientist. Lost in his investigations of what he calls
> other regions, and even other worlds, he may forget when and where he is.
> But actually his theories belong to human history, and he remains in the
> same moving world as the rest of us. Science begins in the *Lebenswelt*,
> proceeds in a special region within it, and ends by being purposefully used
> to transform it. If we were to give a picture of *these* facts in terms of Plato's
> famous myth, we would have to invert the image.

The initial description of the situation of the prisoners in the Cave,
the very setting of the myth, is outside the shadow-world Plato
describes. To note that the prisoners are chained is not to be a
prisoner. Indeed, to speak of "prisoners" is to make an implicit claim
to a standpoint outside the Cave. Whatever else we may say about
Plato's myth, it is at least true that the description he offers of life in
the Cave is not itself ephemeral and contingent. Untruth, then, has

its own structure: there is a veridical aspect to be disclosed in illusion. This view has important implications for philosophy of the social sciences.

The world of everyday life, the "taken for granted" world, as Alfred Schutz (1972a) called it, is the prime locus of man's existence and action as a social being. Prior to any act of formal scientific observation, the individual intends and interprets the meaning of his and his fellow men's action. The locus of everyday existence as immediately lived and naively interpreted by ordinary men and women and children—the denizens of mundanity—is, to use Husserl's term, the life-world (*Lebenswelt*). Following Schutz, we might list some of the basic features of the everyday world and try to indicate the outline of a general inventory of the structural elements comprising the life-world. To begin with, to put the matter in first-person terms, I find myself always as part of the world, involved in its ongoing life. However, it is from a particular vantage point that I perceive both the physical and the human world: I find my fundamental location in terms of my body. Starting from where I am (where I am, that is, as a physical no less than a psychic being), I see objects and events (and fellow men as well) as "there" in terms of my "here." You are nearby or distant depending on my "here." Now it is essential to note that the relationship between the "here" and the "there" is an experiential one, not a purely conceptual or deductive phenomenon. That is to say, it is in my naive perception of the Other as "over there" that the significance of my being "here" is disclosed. I do not deduce the presence of the Other as distant from me because I "know" in terms of a yardstick measure that he is twenty feet away. Twenty feet from is "near" or relatively "distant" according to my interest in and relationship to the Other. Furthermore, there is a "reciprocity of perspectives" (Schutz, 1962a, p. 11 ff.) between us: I take it for granted that if I were to move to where the Other now is, I would see things in essentially the same way he does. Still more, I assume that what holds true for me also holds true for him: that if he were to change places with me, he would view things as I do. Of course, we are speaking of the more limited aspects of perception at this point. If the door is to my right as I face the wall, then I assume that it will also be seen in the same perspective by anyone else standing where I am and facing in the same direction. There are larger implications regarding the "reciprocity of perspectives," but I shall not consider them here. It should be evident, though, that social and cultural horizons are also involved in taking for granted the exchange of places—that if I were an unemployed, impoverished black man in a deteriorating urban ghetto, I would see the world in a way distinctively appropriate to that perspective.

In addition to the "reciprocity of perspectives," there is a second fundamental feature of the life-world: it is taken as intersubjectively valid for all normal individuals. Not only can I exchange places with you, but I take it for granted that what I find when I do so can be successfully communicated to other people. The world is, then, "ours" from the outset: we are, by virture of being men, capable of sharing not only language but a universe of meaning. I do not achieve an intersubjective ground *when* I take the place of the Other, nor is there an inductive recognition of the mutuality of experience; rather, it is because *we* share the social world to begin with that perspectival exchange is possible. With this notion of intersubjectivity, we come to a root phenomenological problem which the social sciences must face in the most radical way. I shall return to it later on. For the moment, I shall say that most empirical social science commences analysis by presupposing the thematic problem of intersubjectivity. Third, the experience which I have of the social world is, in a certain crucial regard, universal. I do not take my experience of objects, events, or of persons to be, strictly speaking, individual. My impressions, attitudes, judgments, etc. may, of course, be said to be idiosyncratic in the sense that they are mine and not yours, but they possess a generalizable feature: they can be expressed as ideas through propositions which are comprehensible to anyone. The severe limits of moment to moment perception in individual psychological acts of the experiential world are not reflected in a fragmentation in their significance for other people. My knowledge of the world is in its very nature formulated in terms of universals and remains saturated with the claim to generality. Once again, the vital impulse to universality is a shared phenomenon: I take it for granted, and assume that my alter ego does as well, that what we think, believe, judge, say, and even wish and hope for involves a common universe of meaning. Failures in that communality are, ultimately, comprehensible only in terms of the very generality which has proved faulty in some regard. (Cf. Straus, 1958, p. 146 ff.).

This quick sketch of a few features of the life-world permits us to glimpse the outlines of the task which faces the philosopher of the social sciences. My point is this: rather than starting with men in action, collectivities, political power, and the large systems of social relationship, the clue to such high level phenomena is to be found in the domain of daily life I have pointed to. Whatever interpretations we may make of the world, we must come to terms with their grounding in everyday life, for it is within the life-world that each of us, as a mundane being, gives credence to or denies the interpretive constructions we find in the world, whether they derive from social scientists, fellow men, or the historical and cultural framework of our lives. As a common-sense man I define and translate social reality. Whether I do so brilliantly and imaginatively or stupidly and ignorantly, I help to constitute the social order by my perception of it and my action in it. The peril of starting with the terms, definitions, and theories of the social scientist is that they bear within them the hidden attitudes and assumptions not only of philosophy but of common sense itself. By turning to the bedrock of mundane life, we are attempting to establish a philosophical foundation on which social reality can be reconstructed. The task is twofold: we are interested in the general philosophical problems underlying social reality, but we are also concerned with exploring a particular avenue of philosophical analysis, the distinctively phenomenological approach to the taken for granted world. The next step in the argument will be an attempt to contrast the methods involved in such an approach with those employed by philosophers and social scientists who take a different view of matters than we have. Between the polarities of a phenomenological and a behavioral view of daily life, we shall find some further methodological clarification of the roots of social science.

POSITIVISTS AND INTUITIONISTS

In speaking of "positivists" and "intuitionists," I am following the distinction proposed by W. G. Runciman (1963, p. 8), who writes:

> The positivists are those who in general regard the social sciences (under which they may well include history) as methodologically equivalent to the natural sciences; that is to say, they regard the differences between the two as being of a purely technical kind. The intuitionists strongly reject this claim, but they do so on one or both of two main grounds which need to be carefully distinguished. The first is that every historical event is unique in a way that the experiments or replications of natural science are not: an experiment can always be repeated, but never a segment of history. The second ground (which is, however, not entirely unrelated to the first) is that human behavior has meaning to the agents performing it.

Although the choice of contrasting terms—positivists and intuitionists—may be different, the contrast is hardly new. The classical neo-Kantian distinction between the natural and the cultural sciences is, of course, precisely what is involved. More recently, "objectivists" have been paired with "subjectivists" (Natanson, 1963). Whatever the terminology, the opposition is clear: on the one hand, there are those who accept the methodological tenet that human action is completely available to the observer of human behavior, i.e., in overt action, speech, gesture, etc. On the other hand, there are others who are convinced that the meaning of human action is defined primarily by the actor himself and, moreover, that what presents itself behaviorally to the observer is a fragment (albeit an important one) of man's social being. A closer inspection of each position is needed.

The Positivists

Though the term must be used with some caution, I think it fair to say that a "behavioristic" thesis underlies the positivist's view of human action (cf. Charlesworth, 1962; Wann, 1964). Whatever the epistemological status of mind or consciousness, the behaviorist holds that its character and "content" are fully displayed in the overt action or behavior of the individual. Of course, "behavior" is taken in wide sense, so that it includes everything from dreams (as reported by the dreamer), emotions (as evidenced in psychophysiological changes in the organism), conceptual systems (presented in the writings or speech of theoreticians), and the large perceptual stream of each person's life (as revealed in the complex totality of man's performance in the world). In terms of this view, for something to be a possible datum for scientific description and analysis, it must necessarily show itself in some form which can be either directly perceived by an appropriately trained observer or inferred on the basis of what is overtly given. The basic vantage point and the methodologically inescapable axis of interpretation is the duality of observer and observed. Behavior, then, is behavior *for* fellow men. Moreover, the entire conception of what is considered to be appropriate scientific method for the observer's work derives from the model of the natural sciences. Ideally, formalized language is the most revealing means for understanding social phenomena. The turn to informal description may be necessary because of the immaturity or incompleteness of the discipline involved. The natural science ideal is of paramount importance to the behavioristic conception of human action (cf. Beck, 1968).

It should be emphasized that the positivist's conception of social science, though it is based on the natural science ideal, does not ignore or deny the differences between some of the disciplines involved. Thus, the methodological problems facing economists are quite different from those facing a psychologist. Nor is it absolutely certain who is permitted to answer to the roll call of the social sciences. History, linguistics, and jurisprudence are either borderline relations or partial members. It is argued, however, that despite the distinct differences between them, the guiding methodology proper to social science may be extended to them with the assurance that as social science advances, the principle of application will be vindicated. Taken together in their methodological continuity, the differing social sciences are also recognized by the positivists as having noteworthy differences from the natural sciences. But again, an undergirding continuity of inquiry is stressed. On this score, the views of social scientists have not changed significantly in the past generation. A recent pronouncement by Homans is not essentially at variance with views expressed by Lundberg (1939) over thirty years ago. Homans (1967, p. 28) writes:

> There are scholars who argue that, if social science is a science at all, it is a radically different kind of science from the others, and that it makes a mistake pretending to be the same sort of thing. I do not believe this in the least. The content of the propositions and explanations is naturally different in social science, because the subject matter is different, from what it is in the others, but the requirements for a proposition and an explanation are the same for both. And so long as the compulsion to be scientists does not rob us of our native wit and prevent our seeing what is there in nature to be seen, I believe that the social sciences should become more like the others rather than less.

The unstated premise of the argument for the natural science ideal in the social sciences is that the paradigm of knowledge is indeed evinced in mathematical physics. Part of the latent content of the positivistic position is the assumption that prediction and, ultimately, control are, as we have seen earlier, the riches of the kingdom of science.

The Intuitionists

If the behavioristic doctrine underlies the outlook of the positivists, what may be called an "intentionalistic" thesis is fundamental to the intuitionists. "Intentionalism" may be defined as the view that human action is a function of the meaning which the actor ascribes to his act. There is, then, an intentional relationship between the actor and his act. The intuitionist holds that that relationship can be probed from two standpoints: that of the observer and that of the agent. Primacy is given the agent because it is he who has knowledge of what he means by his act, it is he who knows the time structure of his act (when it begins and when it ends), and it is he who is the source of the interpretive reality valid for each man's life. Without turning to the situation of the concrete individual and trying to appreciate its scope, structure, and texture, it is impossible to understand a given act in its richness and variegation. If the observer is limited to the overt behavior of the individual he studies, then he is faced with a double difficulty: first, he has merely the surface of the act, not its core, and so he is forced to extrapolate beyond the given to the meaning of the act; second, he finds it difficult if not impossible to comprehend meaningful decisions the actor makes which do not appear in overt form, e.g., decisions not to act, not to run for office, not to vote. The domain of "negative" acts, as they have been called (Schutz, 1962a)—we might also term them "covert acts"—surely constitutes a vital aspect of social reality, of tremendous importance to such disciplines as political science and economics no less than to psychology and anthropology. The problem of intention goes even deeper, for the relationship of observer and observed is not as simple or at least as methodologically unproblematical as it may seem.

The privileged position of the scientific observer cannot go unquestioned, especially in the social sciences. The activity of the observer presents a rather odd problem to the positivist, for if we are to follow the behavioristic thesis, only another observer can explain the behavior of the observer. As George H. Mead (1934, p. 106) put it in criticizing the rather reductionistic position of the founder of behaviorism: "You can explain the child's fear of the white rat by conditioning its reflexes, but you cannot explain the conduct of Mr. Watson in conditioning that stated reflex by means of a set of conditioned reflexes, unless you set up a super-Watson to condition his reflexes." The difficulty is aptly caught by the old story about the behaviorist who meets another behaviorist and says, "You are fine! How am I?" It would seem, then, that the scientific activity of the observer is transcendent to the rules of his method. But more is involved than a special instance of a limiting case. The observer is also an actor on the social scene. Even if we were to grant him procedural independence from the run of common men, we must still try to understand his mode of behavior. We can do this, on positivistic grounds, only if *we* are not in question, i.e., if our role as observers is deemed beyond methodological inspection. Since the one who is doing the observing is free of behavioristic strictures, and since there is a plurality of such observers, it would seem that at least one significant segment of the social world—the operative domain of the social scientist—cannot be understood in positivistic terms, at least not without a basic inconsistency.

The freedom which positivism seems to give to the scientific observer finds certain epistemological limits in the very act of observation. In its extreme form (which I present here for provocative and contrastive purposes and not because I am advancing any arguments along these lines), there is what might be called the "observo-centric predicament" (to match the "egocentric predicament" Ralph Barton Perry, 1960, described in a famous article): how can the observer ever get beyond his own observational skin? Is he not really restricted to describing himself when he observes the behavior of others? As an epistemological (not a social-scientific) problem, Bertrand Russell gave a remarkable if perplexing account of the physiologist who looks at another man's brain. "What he sees," Russell (1946, p. 705) writes, "is in his own brain and not in the other man's." We need not say that to indicate the analogous if more limited problem in social-scientific observation. The observer there is a center for perceptual activity: he sees and hears and sniffs and touches his fellow men. Just as vital to the perceptual unity of his role, he has knowledge about them from historical and cultural sources. As a valuing creature, he is a storehouse of past judgments about men as well as a value-insti-gating source. But in all of this, the observer's microcosm of perception and knowledge, memory and imaginative consciousness, is alive with *his* intellectual and attitudinal activity. It is ultimately *his* impressions, sensations, ideas, and images which form the matrix of his judgment and decision. It is not necessary to argue for a philo-sophical idealism to be able to assert that the privileges the observer gives to himself are hardly extended to his fellow men. Man as a mundane being, as an actor on the social scene, is put into a methodological corner; he is the victim of an act of epistemic discourtesy. If the observed individual's behavior must be described, analyzed, and explained by the scientific observer, then who is responsible for describing, analyzing, and explaining the observer's behavior? And what positivistic sense can be made of the individual who reflects upon his own behavior? What about the psychoanalyst analyzing his own dream? The observo-centric predicament haunts the positivist's methodology. His troubles do not end there, however, for even if we leave aside the question of methodological consis-tency, we are still faced with the more profound difficulty of how an observer-centered theory can account for the full intentional range of human action. We must return to the idea of "negative" action.

In ordinary discourse we distinguish between intentional and accidental behavior. Slamming a door in someone's face is a highly insulting act if the situation clearly shows that the door slammer knew precisely what he was doing. However, having a door close on you when the one releasing it was unaware that someone was behind him cannot be put in the same class of purposive action. The external physical event itself (the movement of the door) cannot reveal the meaning of what took place. In a sense, the meaning is left open or ambiguous until we find out what is ordinarily termed the "motivation" and intent of the actor. It is clear that social reality teems with events and situations which are highly subtle witnesses to or evidences of attitudes and plans. Without knowing whether it was intended, we cannot evaluate a social act, and without understanding the situational placement of the actor, we are unable to appreciate the significance of his silences, his refraining from expressing an opinion, his refusal or reluctance to choose sides. We come, then, to recognize that the overt aspect of any act is merely a fragment of the much larger intentional domain the actor occupies. To understand our fellow men it is necessary to reconstruct the negative no less than the positive features of their performances in the social world. Only in this way is it possible to allow for and to honor the full range of man's social commitments, involvements, flights, and denials. The intuitionist has no need to isolate covert from overt acts, for he turns to the total domain of man's action as a continuous expression of attitude, choice, and understanding. The most obvious physical act— striking another person with one's fists—has a different meaning depending on whether the individual is trying to injure the other, ward off the other in a purely self-protective way, give one's boxing companion at the gym or club a friendly jab, or outpoint one's opponent in an Olympic match. Beyond this, however, what the individual intentionally refrains from doing in his striking the other is just as central to the meaning of the blows dealt. What manifests itself in behavior, then, is incomprehensible in its status *as action* without some additional interpretation by those on the social scene. In truth, such interpretation is a fact of daily life. If that is so, then the next major problem we must face is the exploration of a methodology suited to the clarification of social reality in its intentional as well as behavioral aspects. Phenomenology has the strongest claim to being the philosophy *par excellence* of social action.

PHENOMENOLOGY

I am speaking of the phenomenology of Edmund Husserl and his followers. Boldly stated, phenomenology is a discipline concerned with the description and analysis of immediate experience. The "phenomena" which phenomenology seeks to elucidate include any thing which may be or become an object of consciousness. The means by which the phenomenologist carries on his work involves a rich methodlogy whose procedures I shall try to outline as I go along. At the outset, however, a number of terminological difficulties must be recognized which often prevent a fair as well as a full appreciation of Husserl's thought. Let me turn to the brief definition I just gave and consider its language. "Immediate experience" should be understood as including everything the individual perceives, taken in its straightforward and unmediated givenness. Of course, thinking, imagining, remembering, and willing are included in the generic concept of perception. Perhaps the most helpful point to recognize about immediate experience is that for all its immense availability, men in ordinary daily life rarely turn to the given without deeply rooted preconceptions and preinterpretations. The attitude of man in daily life is not neutral but slanted in a nonself-conscious manner. Such an attitude—Husserl terms it the "natural attitude"—makes precise and unprejudiced description quite difficult, if not impossible. To describe directly and thoroughly is to attempt to seize the given—the phenomena—in their "originary" character, that is, to confront experience without distorting it. And to do analysis in phenomenological terms is to explore the constitution of the meaningful world, a task I shall examine more closely. Altogether, then, to define phenomenology as concerned with the description and analysis of immediate experience is to turn to a way of seeing and understanding. The elucidation of that way must begin with the naive order of daily life.

The Natural Attitude

Within the round of our everyday affairs, each of us rarely raises philosophical doubts about the world or our experience of it. Rather, we simply take for granted its metaphysical and epistemological nature. We assume unreflectingly that the world is real, that it is pretty much as it appears to us, that my experience of it is much like yours, that *we* share the same sights, sounds, and wonders, and that whatever problems present themselves may be considered and responded to within the ordinary framework of our lives. The belief of common-sense men in the veridical character of their lives is, for Husserl, the most deeply rooted feature of man's existence. Were it not for the fact that another discipline has appropriated the term "unconscious," making it hazardous for us to use the word without tedious distinctions, we might well call the belief of man in the natural attitude an "unconscious" affirmation of the real. Husserl speaks rather of a "doxic" positing and means by it an orienting but unreflective commitment to the truth of experience. Earlier, I spoke of naive realism and its philosophical involvement. Now it is appropriate to say that within the natural attitude, common-sense men build their lives on the assumption that naive realism is indeed the final or at least the unchallengeable truth. The categorial content of the attitude in question (Husserl, 1931, speaks of the "General Thesis" of the natural attitude) deserves some further explanation.

In speaking of "our" world each of us within the natural attitude assumes that the world of everyday life is historically grounded, linguistically shared or at least sharable, pragmatically utilizable and controllable, mutually accessible, and transmittable to our children and their children in essentially the same form. In philosophical terms, the natural attitude includes the thesis of intersubjectivity, the fundamental assumption that communication with fellow men is possible. Furthermore, it is assumed by common sense that a causal relationship pertains between the elements of mundane experience, so that our acts in the world are essentially efficacious. Daily life, then, is a realm of action as well as appreciation, and to be involved in the affairs of men in such a way is to turn almost automatically to the genesis of an event—to what caused it—in order to understand it. The habit of mind which looks to the origin of an event as the basis for comprehending it is a feature of scientific no less than mundane interpretation. Though it has its root in the natural attitude, the causal approach to experience is essentially grounded in a conception of consciousness which holds the latter to be a facet of nature. The phenomenological critique of that naturalistic thesis involves a refutation of "psychologism."

Psychologism

We may define psychologism simply as the view which holds that the structure and content of consciousness are bound to and determined by its neurophysiological conditions. If we understood the brain perfectly we would understand consciousness perfectly. Before considering the large aspects of the problem of psychologism, let us ask a small question concerning the brain-consciousness thesis. Would a better understanding of neurophysiology help to clarify further the mathematical proposition that two plus five equals seven? Would the truth of that proposition be more thoroughly demonstrated or revealed if the neuroanatomy of the cortex were known in a more detailed way? What connection is there between what happens in the brain and the truths of arithmetic? Let us transpose the question. Obviously, there are individual differences in the way in which minds work, but is "Two plus five equals seven" any more or any less certain if the arithmetician is nimble or languid in his figuring? Along with the late nineteenth- and early twentieth-century symbolic logicians, Husserl repudiated a psychological grounding to logic. The truth of mathematics is formal and not individual. Two plus five equals seven because of the rules of the language of arithmetic and not because of anything that happens in the nervous system. Clearly, in order for mathematics to be done there must be mathematicians who think, but *what* they think as mathematicians is independent of the concrete, physical processes which constitute the neurophysiological conditions of the brain's operation. To confuse the *what* of thought with the physical *how* of the brain is to be guilty of psychologism. The problem of structure and origin goes still further, however, for what is at issue in psychologism is, more than the foundations of logic, the status of consciousness in nature. In addition to denying the psychologizing of logic, Husserl also refuses to naturalize consciousness. To be sure, consciousness has a physical dimension, but it also has a universe of structural elements and relationships which are independent of what happens in the nervous system. The goal of phenomenology is to redeem consciousness by understanding it in its purely significative structure, liberated from its psychological trappings and its causal nexus with nature. In these terms, consciousness has a privileged position in the study of both man and nature, for all descriptions and analyses are ultimately brought before the court of consciousness for interpretive adjudication. Whether or not the individual judge was a happy or a miserable child, whether he loved or detested being a law student, whether his wife cherishes or is indifferent to him, whether his colleagues respect or patronize him, he is, *as a judge*, confronted with concrete cases involving concrete issues. He may judge wisely or not, but his decision must necessarily turn to the juridical content of the case and must take into account the system of law within whose province the judge must locate himself professionally. So with consciousness, we may say that whatever its distinctive psychological characteristics, it has a field of operation whose meaningful elements and whose formal nature may be examined in noncausal, distinctively phenomenological terms.

Phenomenological Method

To move from the natural attitude and a psychologistically oriented approach to experience to a more nearly neutral and philosophically independent position is one of the immediate goals of phenomenology. There are other interests, of course, but it is first necessary to see how phenomenologists proceed to realize their first goal. What methods do they employ? The essential procedure, called *epoché* (suspension), is a setting aside of the fundamental belief in the natural attitude, i.e., a placing in abeyance of one's ordinary believing in the world. Since the natural attitude itself is not self-consciously entertained or reflectively grasped by men in daily life, it is necessary to render that "believing-in" explicit ("thematic," a phenomenologist would say) so that it can be examined and understood in its implications for the nature of mundane experience. *Epoché* in its most simple form means deciding to refrain from accepting as real the events and objects of our experience. Instead of naively "taking them as real," the phenomenologist abstains from that root judgment. Instead, he views the content of experience in its direct presentation to him and withholds any predication of "real" or "unreal," "existent" or "not existent" with regard to the phenomena. Along with the methodological decision to abstain from taking the world as real, there is the additional and correlative setting aside of the causal, valuational, and historical aspects of the phenomena at issue. The point, then, is to turn to what presents itself in experience *as* and *insofar* as it does without consideration of why the phenomena appear as they do, whether it is desirable or not that they take the form they do, or what shape they have taken in the past and may have evolved from. The most subtle feature of *epoché* is the pervasive and far-reaching character of the believing it seeks to thematize. The natural attitude underlies man's involvement in all particular projects in mundane life. It is not belief in this or that portion of experience which is at issue but a basal and most immanent believing which extends to all aspects and contents of the real. The world as naively given to us is affected profoundly by our attitudes and commitments to it. What occurs in phenomenological *epoché* does not change or alter the physical universe—nature is not thrown into methodological turmoil—but merely makes it possible to turn to man's world in a fresh and direct manner. One of the first recognitions which is secured by *epoché* is that the believing in the world which it seeks to comprehend is *ours*; *we* take experience as real. In a way, my very point of access to experience is saturated with an intersubjective intention. Before it is possible to succeed in a phenomenological scrutiny of experience, the constitution of the social dimension of believing in the world must be understood. *Epoché* is a preliminary step to the uncovering of a deeper field for analysis, that of the nature of conscious life, of the building up of a shared realm of experience, and of the expression of man's sociality in the world of everyday life. What phenomenological method leads to is a distinctive conception of the nature of consciousness, and that in turn involves a further step in method.

Intentionality

In turning to the experiential world in its unmediated givenness and in looking for the grounding of the "we" aspect of believing in the world, the phenomenologist is trying to specify the *phenomena*, in the strict sense, of which his discipline purports to be the *logos*. The clue to grasping the phenomena directly is in the doctrine of the intentionality of consciousness. If all acts of consciousness are essentially directional in character, if they intend some object (in the sense of something "meant"), then it may be possible to explore their formative features without making reality claims and without invoking a causal-genetic procedure for the translation of phenomena to their psychological or historical beginnings. That exploration is indeed the phenomenologist's line of advance. He utilizes what Husserl termed "phenomenological reduction," placing in brackets the world and "our" believing in it as a part of the natural order and coming instead to pure consciousness, understood at last as an epistemically privileged realm. As Aron Gurwitsch (1966, pp. 94–5; cf. Schutz, 1966) writes:

> By the phenomenological reduction, the integration of consciousness into the real world is severed. Consciousness is no longer regarded as a particular mundane domain among other domains, nor are acts of consciousness considered as mundane events which occur in the real world and, therefore, depend causally or functionally upon other mundane events. Under the phenomenological reduction, acts of consciousness are considered solely as experience of objects, as experiences (this term understood in the broadest possible sense) in and through which objects appear, present themselves, and are apprehended as those which they are and as which they count. By the phenomenological reduction, *consciousness* is fully disclosed as a *unique realm of absolute priority*, because it reveals itself as the medium of access to whatever exists and is valid. The phenomenological reduction permits us not only to make but also to exploit this disclosure, i.e., to render it fruitful for concrete analyses and investigations.

Through reduction, the phenomenologist is able to turn his gaze directly to the intentional flow of consciousness as revealed by its acts and the objects intended by those acts. The "object-pole" of intentionality is the full range of all that which is "meant" by thinking, willing, desiring, judging, and all the rest. The "subject-pole" of the intentional structure involves the act-character of such intendings. The relatedness of the two poles to the real world and to real people may, in turn, be examined from the vantage point of intentional consciousness. Thus, we may speak of the "real world" as meant-as-real or the real-life individual as intended-as-concrete. What is opened up through phenomenological reduction is the fundamental domain of consciousness, freed of its complicty with nature and made available for display to a categorially unencumbered mind. At the same time, the reduction returns us to the living specificity of mundane reality.

The Life-world

Each of us lives in two worlds, one the large reality of history and the arena of "public" affairs, the other the microcosm of our individual daily lives. Although the former precedes the latter in historical terms (we are born in a certain century, in some place, with parents who speak a particular language), the point of epistemological access each man has to history is the microcosm of his own life. It is through my clear or vague conception of how international politics works that I interpret current questions of diplomacy and national interest. And the grounds for my political insight or confusion are to be found in the structure of that world of daily life which phenomenology strives to illuminate. The life-world is the primal region from which and in which are developed the assumptions which constitute the ground of mutual understanding between man and fellow man, which constitute what is "common" in common sense. For example: Within the life of any community there is a certain familiarity which pervades the intimate region of home, the office or factory, and the contours of one's neighborhood. Familiarity, however, is rarely examined or discussed in either a philosophical or even a psychological way. Presumably, a psychological approach to the notion would turn upon some elements of genetic development: conditioning, repetition, the biology of memory. About the phenomenon of familiarity itself, however, it is doubtful that there would be much said, for the phenomenon is so evident, so close to us, that we are blind to it. For the phenomenologist, familiarity is a structure of the life-world which can be elucidated in terms of such elements as temporality, spatiality, and embodiment, that is, the experience of the flow of inner time, the grasp of one's placement in the world from some "here," and the individual sense of one's own body as a being present to the world. In these terms, familiarity has a history, a genesis which can be explored by attending to its constitutive elements in their givenness rather than in their causal setting. Husserl spoke of a "sedimentation of meaning" involved in the constitution of experience. For our purposes, we may take that phrase to signify the building up of meaning in all spheres (including the special domains of art and science) from formative elements apprehended in the life of childhood and steadily expanded in the growth of the individual in the social world. Taken in this way, the life-world is a vast preserve which contains the roots of all possible experience, an infinite reservoir of the language and imagery of all mankind. Still, the life-world should not be understood to be making a kind of anthropological claim for universal features of the contents of all societal orders. The specific features of a given life-world may and do indeed vary from culture to culture as well as from age to age within the same culture. What remains invariant is the sense of coherence presupposed in any world we recognize as a human domain—that, for example, in any possible society, there must be a structure of daily life, a taken for granted routine of mundane life, a constitutive realm of the familiar. A phenomenology of the social world must turn to such grounds if a comprehensive and searching philosophy of the social sciences is to be achieved.

PHENOMENOLOGY AND SOCIAL SCIENCE

Alfred Schutz, more than anyone else, has shown the relevance of phenomenology for social science. I shall follow his lead in presenting a quick survey of some of the implications and applications of this position for social-scientific knowledge.

The Biographical Situation

"Man finds himself," Schutz (1962a, p. 9) writes,

at any moment of his daily life in a biographically determined situation, that is, in a physical and sociocultural environment as defined by him, within which he has his position, not merely his position in terms of physical space and outer time or of his status and role within the social system but also his moral and ideological position. To say that this definition of the situation is biographically determined is to say that it has its history; it is the sedimentation of all man's previous experiences, organized in the habitual possessions of his stock of knowledge at hand, and as such his unique possession, given to him and to him alone.

In this sense, each person has a series of relationships and involvements which, though they may be generalizable in terms of categories and types, are unique to him: his parents, his home, his teachers, his friends, his work. Obviously every man has parents, but what defines *my* biographical situation is *this* mother and *this* father, *this* home they have created, *this* world they have generated. Thus, I share with my fellow men the outlines of a biographical situation, but the concrete instantiation of my life makes possible the determinate qualities of facing and living in the world as I actually do. There is a voluntative aspect of my biographical situation, for I may *choose* to give emphasis to certain aspects of my home and work or tend to ignore their importance. The biographical situation is not a mechanism made up of fixed pieces which grind out a necessary product, but rather we must understand it as a mobile reality in which the individual is free to select, emphasize, or slight the features we have outlined. The central fact is that the biographical situation is inescapable not only for the ego but is also essential in any effort to interpret the acts of one's alter ego. Man and fellow man are irretrievably caught in their biographical situation.

Typification

All interpretation of the world of daily life, for Schutz (1962a, p. 7),

> is based on a stock of previous experiences of it, our own or those handed down to us by parents or teachers; these experiences in the form of "knowledge at hand" function as a scheme of reference. To this stock of knowledge at hand belongs our knowledge that the world we live in is a world of more or less well circumscribed objects with more or less definite qualities, objects among which we move, which resist us and upon which we may act. Yet none of these objects is perceived as insulated. From the outset it is an object within a horizon of familiarity and preacquaintance-ship which is, as such, just taken for granted until further notice as the unquestioned, though at any time questionable stock of knowledge at hand. The unquestioned pre-experiences are, however, also from the outset, at hand as *typical*, that is, as carrying open horizons of anticipated similar experiences.

To typify is, most basically, to abstract from the concrete richness or variability of empirical reality to its type-aspect, its class, kind, or generic characteristics. In phenomenological terms, typification is the primal activity of consciousness rather than a later sophistication of mind. From the outset, then, we see objects, men, animals, and events in their typified aspects, experiencing them as boxes, fellow men, elephants, and celebrations rather than agglutinations of sensory attributes or conceptual predicates. As we mature in our understanding of everyday life, we extend rather than deepen our knowledge of the way in which the social order works. In a few domains we may have expert or at least thorough knowledge, but in the great majority of areas of our involvement in and with the world we have only a "general" notion of how things work. It is enough, for practical purposes, if I know how to write a draft on my bank account, take it to the teller, and receive cash in the transaction. I need know nothing of the work of clearing houses to function adequately as a check writer. All I need for that purpose is a typification of "banks" and "banking procedures." The genius of social man is his capacity to typify.

Interpretive Understanding

In being grasped by common-sense men in typified and typifying terms, the social world is in its very nature a meaningful unity. My knowledge of my fellow men, taken as a complex of typifications, arises in a world in which others no less than ourselves define their intersubjective existence as bearing a meaning for the actors who populate the social world. Understanding, or what Max Weber termed *Verstehen* (interpretive understanding), is, for Schutz, the clue to sociality. "From the beginning," he says (1964, p. 9)

> this orientation through understanding occurs in cooperation with other human beings; this world has meaning not only for me but also for you and you and everyone. My experience of the world justifies and corrects itself by the experience of the others with whom I am interrelated by common knowledge, common work, and common suffering. The world, interpreted as the possible field of action for us all: that is the first and most primitive principle or organization of my knowledge of the exterior world in general.

In the literature of the history of social science, *Verstehen* is conceived of as an important tool for social scientific work as well as a framework, for methodological purposes, which the social scientist can utilize in his professional labors. In Schutz's phenomenological translation of the concept, interpretive understanding is the way in which mundane men comprehend each other. Rather than being thought of as an instrument which the methodologist employs, interpretive understanding is characterized as an inevitable part of social reality. Clearly, such a reading of *Verstehen* is not intended to deny in any way the valid and important function of the theory at the level of the social scientists's operations. Instead, the relationship between social scientist and common-sense man is seen in its true complexity: the task of the social scientist utilizing the theory of *Verstehen* is to apply it to the *already* preinterpreted and structured world of daily life in which men have performed interpretive acts in the very process of living their ordinary lives. The constructs which the social scientists self-consciously utilize must then catch the meaning constituted by the constructs naively created and applied by common-sense men trying to come to terms with each other.

The Social Scientist

The scientific observer, as I noted earlier, is in a special position with respect to the social world he inspects, for he is and yet is not part of that world. The "attitude of the social scientist," Schutz (1962a, p. 36) writes, is that of a mere disinterested observer of the social world. He is not involved in the observed situation, which is to him not of practical but merely of cognitive interest. It is not the theater of his activities but merely the object of his contemplation. He does not act within it, vitally interested in the outcome of his actions, hoping or fearing what their consequences might be but he looks at it with the same detached equanimity with which the natural scientist looks at the occurrences in his laboratory.

The social scientist has exchanged his biographical situation as a citizen of daily life for that of the scientific situation of the observer. To be sure, he may return to, regain his common-sense placement by performing an *epoché* suited to that transformation. As long as he remains a formal observer, however, he relinquishes his position in the temporal and spatial reality of mundane existence and gives up his personal history. What he attains in turn is a responsibility to the state of his discipline and a place in its historical development. If we accept this view of the proper role of the social scientist, we are still faced with the question of how he comes into relationship with the everyday world he transcends. The answer is that the social scientist appropriates the typifications of actors in mundane life in their purely formal nature; that is, he builds models which make clear the relationship of certain kinds of acts for certain kinds of actors. In daily life the typifications lead back to a concrete person; in scientific analysis they point to another model. If a point of contact between science and life has been established, it is still metaphysically uncertain whether and how the social scientist finds an integral placement in the real world which both makes his function possible and yet excludes his personal presence.

Social Science and Philosophy

Whatever the status of the social scientist may be, we must look to his performance, to the work he accomplishes. The question to which we are led is "What philosophical sense can we make of social science?" Perhaps philosophy mediates in some way between science and life, between the "sanitary" mode of existence of the biography-free observer and the biography-infested condition of the ordinary man. Mediation may be understood in several senses here. Philosophy provides a vantage point from which both the pure constructs of science and the applied constructs of daily life can be viewed. Furthermore, both the scientist and the citizen are free, despite all the obvious handicaps and immense difficulties, to reflect on their modes of operation. Philosophy is possible for mundane life. Philosophy is also necessary to science to the extent that the investi-

gator is concerned with illuminating the presuppositions and implications of his own discipline. But there is still another aspect of
mediation. Philosophy brings the results of social scientific work
together with an original, indeed a radical, mode of interpretation.
There is in philosophy a hermeneutical disposition which leads the
inquirer to reflect on the design and signification of scientific results.
What is at issue here is not a matter of a synthetic viewing of limited
or disjointed materials. Rather, I am speaking of a shift in perspective
which makes it possible (and even necessary, in an odd way) for the
viewer to penetrate the object (to move into the work which has
been done) and search out its formation and internal possibilities.
The art of interpretation involved constitutes a form of mediation
between research and reflection. The upshot of this notion of hermeneutics as mediation is that "results" have two faces: they are
most evidently bound to the observer's design and refer back to his
investigations; at the same time, however, they are linked to or are at
least open to the reconstruction of the analyst who brings to them
his own schemas of interpretation. Janus-faced, then, the materials of
social science look both to their scientific originators for validation
and to an unintended philosophical audience for another and no less
significant evaluation.

My discussion of social science and philosophy has led me
beyond the views expressed by Schutz, but there are analogues and
sources in phenomenology for the position advanced. It was Husserl
who maintained that there is an isomorphism between the realms of
empirical analysis and transcendental analysis. In a sense, the "same"
phenomena may be examined from within the natural standpoint or
viewed from within the transcendentally reduced sphere. It is a
matter of attitude and also a question of what we are looking for.
Although it is not possible to move from the sphere of daily life (the
natural attitude) to the transcendental realm without performing the
phenomenological reduction, it is possible to bring descriptions made
from within the former orientation into transcendental view. We do
not have two distinct and separate worlds; the empirical and the
transcendental are corollaries which can both be illuminated by the
necessary phenomenological steps. Thus, the phenomenologist does
not purport to do empirical work, but nevertheless he is in a position
to reflect on the products of that work from a radically different
standpoint. The reverse does not hold: one cannot legitimately
locate, let alone criticize, the results of transcendental description
and analysis outside of the transcendentally reduced sphere. Of
course, *talk* about both empirical and phenomenological work
can be entertained in ordinary discourse and can be brought into
the street or carried on in offices or studies, but the content of

the work performed is fugitive in principle to such sectors of science and life. We have a parallelism without an invasion; an isomorphism without a cross-penetration. In these terms, phenomenology and social science may be seen to enrich each other as philosophy is the mediating agent in their encounter. Still more, to agree actively or passively to the splitting off of philosophy from science, science from philosophy, is to deny the meaning of both endeavors and to weaken their foundations. But it is not "science" in the utterly nonphenomenological sense which we can somehow contain and try to isolate (or, conversely, which can attempt to cloister itself). Science—*knowledge*—is already phenomenologically sedimented; it needs only to fulfill its own ultimate interest in arriving at philosophical lucidity. And from the other side, philosophy chokes its own sensibility if it pretends to be science-free. Its relation to both the empirical and the mundane is integral to its own career. Philosophy and science cannot be compartmentalized, as Merleau-Ponty (1964b, pp. 101-2) points out in a passage which admirably concludes the argument:

> The segregation we are fighting against is no less harmful to philosophy than to the development of scientific knowledge. How could any philosopher aware of the philosophical tradition seriously propose to forbid philosophy to have anything to do with science? For after all the philosopher always thinks *about something*: about the square traced in the sand, about the ass, the horse, and the mule, about the cubic foot of size, about cinnabar, the, Roman State, and the hand burying itself in the iron filings. The philosopher thinks about his experience and his world. Except by decree, how could he be given the right to forget what science says about this same experience and world? Under the collective noun "science" there is nothing other than a systematic handling and a methodical use—narrower and broader, more and less discerning—of this same experience which begins with our first perception. Science is a set of means of perceiving, imagining, and, in short, living which are oriented toward the same truth that our first experiences establish an urgent inner need for. Science may indeed purchase its exactness at the price of schematization. But the remedy in this case is to confront it with an integral experience, not to oppose it to philosophical knowledge come from who knows where.

PHENOMENOLOGY AND POLITICAL THEORY

The general problem of the applicability of phenomenological philosophy to political theory cannot be resolved either by making a priori claims or by attempting to press specific phenomenological procedures into service so that empirical issues can be examined.

Indeed, the question of applicability is itself complex and its meaning far from clear. The consideration of a few criticisms of phenomenology which have come from social scientists may help to explain my reluctance to rush to quick conclusions in a domain which is still in the process of being established. In his discussion of the "limited usefulness" of Husserl's phenomenology for political theory, Arnold Brecht (1959, p. 382) writes that

> we cannot hope to find elements of absolute certainty in political questions, especially in questions of justice, law, and government, through Husserl's phenomenological method alone. He once observed, quite consistently, that law and government are factors in the external, transcendent world, which must be "bracketed," i.e., excluded from direct attention, in phenomenological research ... And indeed, how could he ever have arrived at statements on objective requirements of justice, or even only on universal postulates in these fields, through his investigations of the "subjectivity of the ego"? His original intentions had never been to ascertain even the reality of Is; how could he have claimed ability to reveal the validity of Ought? What he wanted to do, and succeeded in doing, was merely to lay bare the ultimate, original experiences which lie at the bottom of human consciousness, regardless of what certainty these inner experiences may give us as to the external world.

Before commenting on this objection I must note that it is not a repudiation of the relevance of phenomenology for political theory but only a warning about its limitations. Still, the points made are serious and do have important implications for the potential applicability of phenomenological method to substantive issues in political theory. A response is surely warranted.

Without trying to go into a detailed analysis of Brecht's interpretation of phenomenology, I shall say first that the *distinction* Husserl makes between essence and fact is not a *separation* of the two. Whatever presents itself in actual experience may be interpreted in phenomenological terms. The Is and the Ought of political experience may both be taken "as meant," that is, in their intentional character. As a purely descriptive and analytic enterprise, phenomenology does not assume the task of recommending normative concepts, but that does not mean that it cannot turn to them as they have been historically given and as they may be hypothesized. Bracketing does not mean excluding but only differentiating for methodological purposes. And subjectivity is, above all, vitally in touch with the phenomena of reality and so, for Husserl, with the ways in which men experience the real. Second, even if it were true that phenomenological *method* cannot get at political reality, it is still open as to whether that holds as well for phenomenological *philosophy*. The latter is more than the techniques it employs; it is a constructive effort to comprehend the totality of man's being. If that philosophy was left by Husserl still in its infancy, we should not conclude that it is incapable of maturing. If for no other reason, we must recognize that Husserl's writings on the "crisis" of Western man and science go beyond the apparent neutrality of method and offer, in the best sense, an evaluation of the Is and the Ought embedded in our history and embattled in our present. The possibilities of phenomenological method are only now becoming clear; the future of phenomenological philosophy is on the far side of twentieth-century knowledge.

Another and quite widespread criticism of phenomenology as an organon of social-scientific theory in general (and a fortiori of political theory in particular) may be summed up this way: At best, the results of phenomenological work, the specific propositions it articulates, are either valid because they are so abstract as to be empirically contentless or acceptable because in their validity they apply to a highly limited stratum, one which has but a marginal connection with the major issues in social science. The specific judgments which phenomenology makes regarding the social world are, in this view, seen to be either limited to a few truisms or else disguised and only contingent empirical statements. If one looks to phenomenology for necessary truths which have empirical reference (judgments which are both a priori and synthetic), the result is highly disappointing. Arguing along this line, Hans Neisser (1959, p. 209) writes:

> What are the invariants of the acts in which we understand and participate in the social world? First, the ego lives. It would have to organize its life as a human being in some fashion even if it were a solitary Robinson. The world around it has also the function of serving its needs—this is an eidetic insight, but the "how" is empirical and changing. Secondly, the ego lives in a "social world," i.e., in communication with other entities regarded as similar in basic traits to the ego. Is this an eidetic necessity? Certainly not: the ego could consider these entities as particles in a kind of molecular Brownian movement, which displays certain regularities; and the descriptive content of the ego's subjective experience as well as the conceptual organization of this subjective experience will differ according to which of the two approaches the ego considers as appropriate. But, it may be argued, we are born into a social world by which we orient our acts and actions—they do not fit the Brownian movement approach. Let us take the fact of the social world of other human beings as the only suitable starting point of social science, as an invariant feature of a certain class of acts; can we obtain further eidetic propositions which would form the basis of social science? *I have not been able to find any.* The few remarks in Husserl's writings are nothing but a restatement of the definition of the social world, except for slips into the empirical.

Again, in fairness to the author it must be emphasized that Neisser is not condemning Husserl's work; rather, his "objections are directed against his desperate attempt to claim for phenomenology a function which his own analytical work has not performed and, in our opinion, cannot perform." (1959, p. 212) And once more, I must restrict myself to a few comments. The central role of the doctrine of essence in Husserl's thought leads to some imbalance in the understanding of phenomenology if we regard the latter chiefly as a means of grinding out synthetic, a priori propositions which may then be used to legislate universal and necessary laws in social science, as their Kantian equivalents did for the epistemology of the natural sciences. Not propositions but the conceptual reconstruction of the social world is what we must look for. Of course, that reconstruction is presented to us in books and articles which are composed of sentences. What is central to the phenomenologist's reports, however, is the theoretical map he gives us of the structure of social reality. Essences are nothing else but the meaningful structure of the world which the social scientist takes as the object of his inquiry. In practice, then, the phenomenologist gives us a description and analysis of the social. Thus, Alfred Schutz's study, *The Phenomenology of the Social World* (1967), is a systematic effort to present a reconstruction of the taken for granted world of everyday life by showing its essential components, strata, and such fundamental elements as the time-structure of social action. Yet Neisser (1959, p. 210) argues that Schutz's book is "based much less on phenomenology than even the author assumed, and much more on empirical knowledge (excepting of course the purely methodological parts). Naturally, we have a considerable body of knowledge drawn from *common experience* and scarcely open to doubt—this does not make it eidetic." Granted that Schutz is, self-consciously, attempting a phenomenology of the natural attitude which does not utilize the standpoint of transcendental phenomenology, I can still point out that the "common experience" which Neisser emphasizes is precisely the theme of Schutz's analysis. Within the natural attitude we take it as beyond doubt that our familiar world is true and our knowledge of it quite reliable, but the thematic belief which establishes that certitude of "common experience" is opaque to those who base their lives on it. Recounting some of the components of "common experience" is hardly equivalent to accounting for its givenness and even for its very possibility as a foundation for mundane life. In attempting to provide an inventory of the constitutive elements of everyday life and establishing the guidelines of its anatomy and function, Schutz not only transcends empirical knowledge but indeed provides a basis from which the empirical can be grasped as a possible mode of human expression. The phenomenology which emerges is itself a theory of social reality if not yet a full-fledged philosophy of the social. In any event, these considerations have prepared the way for a glance at some examples of phenomenology applied to basic issues in political theory. We shall consider the concepts of situation, representation, power, and nihilism.

Situation

Recalling my discussion of the "biographical situation" and of the "here" and "there" of our placement in the world, we may say that to be "situated" is to find oneself confronted by the weight of a certain past, the pressure of present possibilities, and to choose one's way toward the future. As Sartre (1948, p. 60) put it, "what men have in common is not a 'nature' but a condition." The choice that they make of themselves is also a choice of their situation, a way of defining their world. If men interpret a political crisis as resolvable, then a central dimension of the political reality is that confidence in a successful outcome. "Confidence" is analyzable, then, in other than purely psychological terms. Whether or not confidence is warranted, whether it be well grounded or foolhardy, it is a structural feature of the situation to be understood. It should be pointed out that here we meet a concept fundamental to sociological theory. The phenomenological approach to "situation" converges with W. I. Thomas's (1928, p. 572) thesis that "if men define situations as real, they are real in their consequences." Also, we come to a meeting of themes with Max Weber's postulate of the subjective interpretation of meaning. In all of these theories, what is real is what is *meant* as real, and the understanding of the alter ego, of an institution, a political party, or a government *in fact* includes what we think they think, how we gauge their attitude to us, and how we reconstruct the situation they live within. In short, the question is "How do we define their definition of the situation?" (see Hamburg, 1955). As long as the subjective is given a purely genetic explanation, as long as we turn to subjectivity as a product of causal processes, so long do we avoid the direct apprehension of political reality. The phenomenological approach to that reality is an effort to display its component elements and to trace their operation in the constitution of social structure.

Representation

Whatever the type of political organization of a society, it is a fact inwoven in the texture of sociality that a "standing-for" relationship between the individual and his "representative" is possible. Individual existence is self-transcending, for the concrete person is, in his very individuality, both typified and typifying in certain regards. He is "a" small businessman, "a" householder, "a" participant in the political process. Between his specificity as *this* individual with his unique biographical situation and his type-character as "one" among many, there is generated a double tension: from the vantage point of individuality, concrete existence is enhanced immeasurably by its capacity to find a place in symbolic action; from the standpoint of the general or universal categories of the social order, the person is able to carry out and instantiate the life of the society and of history in the presence of actual situations. In these terms, the representative character of society is not a chance product of history; history is the product of an essential capacity of the concrete to generate the universal. Human society, as Eric Voegelin (1952, p. 27) points out,

> is illuminated through an elaborate symbolism, in various degrees of compactness and differentiation—from rite, through myth, to theory—and this symbolism illuminates it with meaning in so far as the symbols make the internal structure of such a cosmion, the relations between its members and groups of members, as well as its existence as a whole, transparent for the mystery of human existence.

Within social order, then, the "representative" arises as the symbolic possibility of the concrete individual, as the possibility of his extension beyond his "here" and "now" to the totality of history, or at least to the compass of his society's unified organization and coherence. My "representative" stands for me within a larger order of society which also "represents" me. The "mystery of human existence" may then be understood as a phenomenon for philosophical reconstruction. Its essence is man's self-interpretation, through which the symbolic character of his concrete life is identified and illuminated.

Power

The distinction between the "public" world of politics and history and the life-world of individual interpretation and action makes it possible to reapproach the concept of power as a feature of intramundane existence. Within the natural attitude, common-sense men *intend* the life-world as a controllable and efficacious domain, i.e., as a field in which power is both exertable and exerted. We must leave open the question "What is the source of power?" Instead, we may say with Radbruch (1950, p. 115) that "all power rests on the recognition, willing or unwilling, of those subject to it." In life-world terms, I find myself in a reality which feels the effects of the "outside" scene of national and international politics. That "outside" world has forces which can at any moment enter into and disrupt the microcosm I inhabit. At the same time, I realize that the capacity of the macrocosm to affect the cosmion of my daily life rests upon fellow men who serve as its agents and who "represent" the power of the state because in their roles they perform the *epoché* essential to the military, to the police, to the militia, or to the secret service. My world can be disrupted not only because the forces of the state fulfill their roles, follow their orders, but also because I accept and make way for their operation: I *recognize* their action and so, in a secondary but no less vital way, empower them. A fundamental intention, then, underlies social order and involves the assumption, powerfully maintained, that social roles will be performed in typical ways, that agents of the state will act in such a way that the intimacy and familiarity of the life-world of the individual will be punished by abstract behavior. By that I mean to contrast the warmth and fondness of mundane attachments each of us has within the life-world with the anonymity and abstractness of "official" deeds and activities. Of course, it would be a gross falseness and an unwarranted sentimentalization of the life-world to suggest that within it there are no roles played or abstract action undertaken (cf. Natanson, 1970). Rather, there is a horizon of familiarity in terms of which the individual locates himself in anonymous roles (purchaser of stamps from a machine, telephone caller asking for information, passenger in the subway train) which are still insulated from the macrocosm. Power both establishes and threatens that insulation.

Nihilism

The intention which supports and guides the meaning of power also points in another and no less crucial direction: toward a continuity of experience which lends itself to rational comprehension. Beyond suggesting that the dimensions of time are bound to each other in some integral fashion, I am saying that there is an immanent commitment in coherent experience which demands and expects that each act of interpretation and consciousness is relatable to subsequent acts, that human experience is not a random collection of bits or hunks of history but that there is a sequence and a consequentiality to all human reality. The impulse to continuity and coherence is not self-justifying, nor is it pragmatically validated. Since it is antecedent to any possible set of verifying circumstances and to any determination of value, the intention of continuity is a priori to any particular empirical organization of mundane life and to any form of political activity. Commitment to the intention is an originary act of consciousness, a primordial involvement of man's spirit. Its denial or internal disruption may be defined as the meaning of nihilism. Clearly I am not concerned with programs or theses of political action in the narrower sense. Rather, I am really wondering about phenomena which thus far have been only dimly perceived: the demoniac aspect of Nazism, for example. There it is not specific acts which can be totaled up and condemned; it is the brooding incoherence underlying acts of terror and bestiality which demands recognition and comprehension. Perhaps the power involved in constituting the macrocosm and microcosm is internally threatened by an attraction to sever and splinter the intention of coherence: the urge to destruction which haunts the builder. It is not necessary to overstate the case and say that the fulfillment of nihilism would mean the annihilation of value. It is possible to envision a more modest but no less appalling result: the decline of civilization and the relinquishment of reason to, in Max Weber's language, "specialists without spirit or vision and voluptuaries without heart" (see Strauss, 1953, p. 42). Phenomenological philosophy is a countervailing force whose mission is the vindication of reason and the repudiation of madness. I shall turn to that theme in a postscript.

It might seem as if a phenomenological approach to political theory demanded an abandonment of empirical research in favor of an examination of the nature of intentional consciousness as it constitutes such structures as situation, representation, power, and as it is canceled and defiled in nihilism. I think it idle to ask students of political theory somehow to set aside their work and become phenomenologists. And I think it profitless to urge that phenomenological procedures be used in place of the developed methodologies which political scientists in fact employ. The phenomenological moral is quite different: Look to your philosophical grounds! If that advice were followed with rigor and ultimate seriousness, the phenomena which Husserl asked us to return to would be close at hand. And if philosophy were taken radically, the phenomena would be given a unified expression in the form of a *logos* which would testify to the capacity of reason to sustain itself against external destruction and interior dissolution (see Natanson, 1973).

17. ON THE ROLE AND FORMATION OF CONCEPTS IN POLITICAL SCIENCE

Paul F. Kress

> *"Don't let us quarrel," the White Queen said in an anxious tone. "What is the cause of lightning?"*
>
> *"The cause of lightning," Alice said very decidedly, for she felt quite certain about this, "is the thunder—no, no!" she hastily corrected herself. "I mean the other way."*
>
> *"It's too late to correct it," said the Red Queen: "when you've once said a thing, that fixes it, and you must take the consequences."*
>
> —LEWIS CARROLL

The scholar who undertakes to describe characteristic and proper research practices for his discipline commits at least the sin of hubris, even if he somehow escapes that of folly. This is especially the case in those sciences of man which, rightly or wrongly, have not developed a set of generally accepted procedures for dealing with recognized problems, or, in the language of Thomas Kuhn, the practicing of "normal science" (1962). As Phillip Hammond's instructive collection of research biographies illustrates, personal style and constraints of the field situation may produce a bewildering variety of legitimate strategies (1964). It is not only that differing techniques are employed, and in varying mixes and sequences, but there often seems rather little agreement about the nature of the phenomena under investigation, even when they are designated by the same word. When researchers are able to agree upon the elements which constitute a state of affairs (for example, a sense of political efficacy or alienation), they frequently cannot agree whether these elements are present at any given moment, let alone over time. Some teachers of methodology, despairing that helpful recommendations can be distilled from such disciplinary anarchy, advise their students to adopt a multiple strategies approach to all research problems, apparently in the hope that what escapes or remains ambiguous in one light will be illuminated and clarified by another.

This advice is attractive to most undogmatic minds for its apparent endorsement of openness and tolerance; should not, after all, each strategy and tool have its day in court, and full opportunity to demonstrate the merits of its case? The difficulty, of course, is revealed by the metaphor. Courts render decisions on the basis of evidence which, though factual in character, is carefully circumscribed by the rules of admissability, proper inference, cross or adverse examination, and so on. A great many of these rules are deemed basic and necessary to a wide variety of civil and criminal proceedings, but *are* there comparable rules of "due process" which can be said to underlie the judicial system of science? On what grounds or in what arena may our multiple strategies be asked to prove themselves? (Kress, 1974a). The question is perplexing because the apparently compelling response, that a research strategy is vindicated by its results, contains a disquieting circularity (Kaplan, 1964). Every such strategy is in some respect self-validating in terms of its definition of problems, rules of inference, and sense of significance (Friedrichs, 1970).

Thus the categories of the subconscious and the techniques of free association and symbolic analysis employed by psychoanalytically oriented scientists presuppose that certain ways of knowing are possible and that other kinds of knowledge are reliable. Alternative strategies such as game theory, sample survey, content analysis, participant observation, and controlled experimentation contain their own presuppositions, which may be shared, or contradictory, or simply have no relationship to one another at all (Charlesworth, 1967). These presuppositions are usually left implicit in the writings of research scientists, but when made explicit and systematically articulated, they constitute the epistemological foundation of the strategy, or, to recall my earlier analogue, the due process rules of a particular scientific judicial system. The circularity involved in evaluating a strategy by its results consists, then, in this: that *in some measure* we must accept the epistemological foundation as legitimate in order to employ the strategy in the first place. To suggest a homely analogy: if a man believes he should be judged by the enemies he makes, it will do us little good to test the success of his strategy by studying his friends (though we may certainly object a priori to his standard itself).

If this were the end of the matter we might well despair of scientific method entirely, for the fruits of inquiry would then be viewed as so many self-fulfilling prophecies. As we shall see later, this need not be the case since certain self-correcting mechanisms (e.g., a means for falsifying results) can be made a part of the strategy. It remains, however, that such safeguards become themselves a part of the due process rules themselves or "domain assumptions" (Gouldner, 1970).

THE THREE LEVELS OF METHOD

There are two primary lessons I wish to emphasize at this point. The first is an injunction to the researcher to be aware of the epistemological rules which underlie the strategies he employs—further, that his awareness be both sympathetic (to fully exploit the sensitivity of his instruments) and critical (to guard himself against systematic oversights). The second lesson is more complex, but essential to the discussion which follows. I want to suggest that what have thus far been called research strategies or "approaches" (I would reserve the word "theory" for a more specialized use) may profitably be thought of as subsisting on three levels of analysis or abstraction. The most fundamental, or to reverse the image, the "highest" most general, level is the epistemological, sometimes called the "philosophical." Justus Buchler points to something of this kind:

> There is another sense in which the expression "a methodology" designates the rationale of a method. The rationale is assumed to be a kind of structure inherent in the method rather than a set of policies or strategies relating to its conduct. Hence it needs exposure. In this sense, a methodology is the "theory" or "philosophy" of a method, the attempt to chart it or interpret it not merely in terms of its putative goal, or the interests of its practitioners, but in terms of its relation to other methods and to other human considerations. It is to philosophers, therefore, rather than to practitioners, that the exposure or formulation is assumed to belong [1961, p. 125; Sellars, 1963].

In these terms, the philosophy of method deals with the *justification* of certain procedures, and here the matter of values arises within both the framework and the substance of the strategy (Edel, 1964; Habermas, 1971). Following Abraham Kaplan, I would accept as examples of epistemological questions those at the level of the following: what is the nature of causality; is the universe ruled by determinism or chance; how is a belief in induction justified? This is a realm of very general, basic, and abstract concerns, and is easily contrasted to the third level, which I shall here call that of "research technique." Included here are such operations as scale construction, the drawing of sample populations, and administration of projective tests. These are the tools, the instrumentation with which we reach into the subject under scrutiny. While it is relatively easy to illustrate the issues which belong to realms one and three, the intervening level is much more difficult to describe, in part because of the diversity of issues encountered there, and in part because those issues *are not often resolved there*. We are instead tempted to seek resolution by pressing "back" to the epistemological level for justification through reason, or "down" toward vindication through instrument application (Radnitzky, 1968; Kisiel, 1973).

I shall argue that this middle level is the proper focus of the "methodologist"; that he must seek such boundaries to his activities that will relieve him of obligation to become either philosopher of science or technician. But at the same time he must view those boundaries as highly permeable; that is, the methodologist should be able to point to the paths along which his concerns lead back to epistemology and down to technique. This middle level is the jugular vein of the scientific enterprise, and no element in the realm is more crucial than *the concept*. In the remaining pages of this essay I shall attempt to describe the difficulties and processes through which concepts are formed and function in this methodological realm, though it will now and then be necessary to imbed that discussion in epistemological bases and technical issues (Horkheimer, 1974). Before beginning that effort, however, it may be helpful to offer a few illustrations to make my idea of a methodological realm somewhat less of a residual category (Bakan, 1969).

Political scientists have long been bemused by the concept of power. From Plato to Dahl, the idea that politics somehow intimately involves the ability to direct the behavior of others against their wills has held strong appeal, and some theorists have hoped that the monopoly of the means of coercion (ultimately the ability to take life) could serve as the distinguishing mark of political authority (Weber, 1947a). To let inquiry rest here, however, is to mistake the beginning for the end of analysis. We need now to ask: how are we to understand the phenomenon of power as it operates among men, or, perhaps even more basically, how are we to recognize the appearance of power in diverse contexts (Bendix, 1963; Przeworski and Teune, 1970)? Recent disciplinary controversies illustrate the importance of these questions. While some researchers conceive of power as a "substance," capable of being possessed and denied, others view it as a "relationship," requiring definition in terms of acquiescence as well as command (Key, 1960a).

These differing conceptions of power may appear to be purely verbal and not worthy of serious concern, but in fact they lead their respective adherents to quite distinct research orientations and value positions. To conceive of power as a substance is to urge upon the researcher a primary concern with its *locus;* whether defined in terms of geography, institutions, class, or personality the question becomes, who now holds power? There is the further implication that those outside this locus are effectively without power, and the suggestion that power is a scarce item, incapable or unlikely to be increased or shared. Power is something exercised upon the ruled. A formulation of this kind leads us to consider the power relationship as one of domination rather than authority; that is, it appears as a one way street. If, conversely, we opt for the relational concept of power, we expect to find the possessors circumscribed by the degree to which the ruled will tolerate commands. Such a view not only endows the subjects with a kind of veto power and thus encourages us to think in terms of authority and legitimacy, but it opens the possibility of increasing the sum total of power available to the entire society. Power, in other words, is no longer conceived as a zero sum game (see chap. 15).

Further analysis is possible. The dispute between power elite and pluralist interpretations of community political structures illustrates both normative and procedural differences. There is surely an affinity between the substantive sense of power, the idea of an elite of power holders, the reputational or ascriptive method of researching the issue, and a critical political ideology (Mills, 1956; Hunter, 1963; Agger et al., 1964). On the other side, one may encounter a sense of power as relational, the idea of policy as the outcome of pluralist conflict, the decisional research strategy, and a more sanguine view of American democracy (Dahl, 1958, 1961a, 1966). This is not to argue that there is some inherent or logically necessary relationship among these elements, or that to begin with one concept of power is to be committed to a single strategy or set of values (Charles Taylor, 1967). It is, however, to say that these positions seem to cohere and to constitute alternative cognitive maps of the political universe which make sense to scholars of contemporary American politics (Bachrach, 1967; Bachrach and Baratz, 1962b; Polsby, 1963; Walton, 1966). This is by no means a new problem for social science as Blau's analysis of Max Weber's use of the term *Herrschaft* nicely demonstrates (1963b).

My second example of methodological analysis of a concept, borrowed from psychology but basic to many fields, is the idea of repression. An epistemologist would certainly press his analysis back to the category of the unconscious, and ask in what sense things can be "in" the mind without our consciousness of them. He would want to understand the nature and status of such theoretical entities as id, ego, and superego, and what they mean for our beliefs about memory and mind (Skinner, 1965; Scriven, 1965). If we move in the other direction from the concept of repression, we encounter therapeutic techniques such as free association and hypnosis, such diagnoses as Oedipus and Electra complexes. Again, as in the case of power, concepts are not fully determined by epistemology, nor technique by concepts, but the fact remains that concepts draw our efforts and attentions in certain directions, that illumination of one area is achieved by contrast to a surrounding darkness (Parsons, 1949, pp. 27–41). To put the matter in terms which I shall elaborate below, it is not that a particular conceptual language forbids expression of certain ideas (though this may occasionally be the case); it is rather that some expressions are *favored* by the rules of a particular language system. Some ideas are easier to express than others, and this is true in large part because substantive images interpenetrate and underlie methodological principles (Kress, 1966; Landau, 1961; Schneider and Bonjean, 1973).

CONCEPTS AND PERCEPTION

With these brief illustrations in mind let us pass on to confront the central questions of this essay:

What are concepts?
What is their function in inquiry?
How are concepts formed?

A provisional, though by itself unsatisfactory beginning, is to ask how, in fact, we use the word "concept," that is, which are possible permissible usages and which are inadmissible (Foucault, 1971)? What are synonomous, analogous, and contrasting terms? A standard compilation of synonyms gives "idea," "conception," "notion," "thought," and "impression," and lists as contrasting terms "percept," "image," and "sensation" (Webster, 1942). Turning to "conception" and "idea" we find a similar listing of synonyms, and an even wider array of analogous terms: "opinion," "view," "belief," "conviction," "persuasion," "sentiment," and "hypothesis." Examination of synonyms for "hypothesis" seems at length to move us toward greater rigor, or perhaps simply suggests the clank of science to our ears: "conjecture," "surmise," "guess," "deduction," "inference," and "conclusion."

The circle may have been somewhat tightened by this exercise, for we like to think that words such as "deduction" and "conclusion" have rather firm meanings. It remains, however, that deduction and conclusion are technically considered quite different, and if we must also accept conjecture, surmise, and even guess, we may surely not feel content to rest our search. The full difficulty of this approach to understanding is encountered if we try the experiment of imagining various usages: Jones's concept of power; Jones's idea of power; his view, or notion, of power; his convictions or hypotheses, or sentiments, about power. Some of these uses may jar us, and some we might think improper, but all are permissible, and a great many, I venture to add, strike our ears as indistinguishable. If we further consider that this exercise has made use only of nouns, not of their innumerable adverbial and adjectival forms, and that we have not put these examples in paragraph context, the difficulties of obtaining a consensus by this method seem overwhelming.

Must we then conclude that inquiry into usage is futile? The answer probably turns on our expectations, but it would be premature to conclude that we are in no respect advanced. We have at least explored some of the obstacles to understanding, and gained an appreciation of the possibilities as well as the constraints of language rules. Abraham Kaplan's emphasis should not be forgotten: terms are purposive utterances which acquire a bundle of permissible uses called the usage of that term (1964; Dufrenne, 1963). Insofar as they are purposive, concepts are our tools, but because usages shape our very ability to think, and because our need for communication imposes stable conventions, they are also our masters (Freire, 1972). The examination of usage can be a means of liberation, as I shall try to show by recalling that the contrasting terms to "concept" include "percept," "image," and "sensation." Within these contrasts lies an entire history of epistemological thinking whose exploration leads to some central issues of concept formation. (See Graber, 1976.)

I have earlier called concepts the jugular vein of the scientific enterprise, but reflection on the range of associated meanings examined above might well suggest that this is too modest a claim—that in fact, concepts are the stuff of thought itself, whether artistic, mythic, religious, or commonsensical (Piaget, 1971; Lévi-Strauss, 1966, 1969). The way is now open to ask whether there can be nonconceptual thought, and what such a phrase might mean. Since the days of Locke, especially his *Essay Concerning Human Understanding*, a powerful philosophical school has argued that the senses constitute blank slates, or, in more contemporary terms, receptor mechanisms, which are written upon by external stimuli. These stimuli, signals from whatever is "out there," were held by Locke to constitute the sole source of human knowledge about the world. (This widely accepted interpretation may also do less than justice to the subtlety of Locke's position [Nyman, 1973].) They are, presumably, received as "raw" experience, sensation, sense data, or perception. It is this unformed material which constitutes the stuff of *conceptions*, or the products of the active mind. In this view we might say the perception is a kind of sensory/mental activity that is free of the mediation of concepts.

Several observations should be made about this legacy. It had considerable difficulty in distinguishing the elements of the process, i.e., in demarcating the object source of stimulation, the sensation itself, the nature of perception, and its translation into mental state or idea. Ogden and Richards once lamented:

> The use of the term "concept" is particularly misleading in linguistic analysis. There is a group of words, such as "conception," "perception," "excitation," which have been a perpetual source of controversy since the distinction between happenings inside and happenings outside the skin was first explicitly recognized. Processes of perceiving caused in an interpreter by the action on him of external objects have been commonly called "perceptions," and so, too . . . have those objects themselves. Other processes, more abstract or less obviously caused references, have similarly been called "conceptions." [1952, pp. 99–100; Dewey and Bentley, chap. 1].

Of greater interest to the methodologically concerned is the manner in which this Lockean tradition has valued perception and suspected conception. While the latter suffered from a tinge of fictitiousness, and seemed to lead to recalcitrant problems of whether "that" is or is not a chair, the former appeared certain if inchoate. This preference suggests a mistrust of nature shared by Descartes, most notably in his skeptical hypothesis of a malign spirit systematically deceiving him. It did, however, seem safe, even to the mind of the doubting Hume, that while we might well question the presence of a table, an impression of "brown rectangular patch" could be accepted. This desire to make knowledge rest upon direct reportage of perception has persisted in our century in the efforts of Carnap and others to develop a purely phenomenal language happily free of conceptual elements (1936, 1937).

But conceptual thinking has proved highly resistant to banishment. In the post-Humean philosophy of Immanuel Kant, concepts were restored to the center of scientific thinking. Summaries of thought as complex as Kant's are inevitably and properly suspect, but David Hawkins's words lie within permissible limits of simplification.

> The main problem in Kant's analysis of knowledge was the existence, as he believed, of a body of general knowledge that was inextricably involved with the description of our experience but did not, in any obvious way, owe its validity to the findings of experience. In his own terminology such knowledge was *a priori*—that is, known to be true independent of empirical fact—yet synthetic, making assertions beyond the bare elucidation of the

meanings of our concepts. Our experience of the physical world, in particular, involves, in our perceptions, an orderliness and a reproducibility without which such experience could not be distinguished from fantasy or hallucination. The concepts of space and time were related to the ways in which we order our perceptions of the physical world; they were required by, rather than learned from, such perceptions [1967, p. 56].

Speaking of the category of time, John Gunnell notes that for Kant,

time was not merely a property of a relation between things or an idea formed by successive sensations as maintained by Locke, Hume, and Condillac. Time was subjective, but a priori—it was a form of intuition by which experience was ordered; knowledge was grounded in experience, but time was not derived from experience. In this way Kant avoided the relativism of the empiricists and made time meaningful for science while preserving its internal base. But the internalization of time inevitably put its "reality" in jeopardy and made it a problem for psychology [1968a, p. 21].

While Kant sought to guarantee the sense of time, more skeptical minds would be led to ask how we could be confident that our perceptions were "correct," and further, that they were similar among men. This is indeed a psychological problem but, as Hawkins relates, it is much more.

Once the principle was established that the forms of perceptions—and by extension the forms of belief—were mind-dependent and not determined by the intrinsic character of things perceived, it was only necessary to add that these forms were themselves functions of psycho- and sociodynamic development, and one went from Kantianism to all varieties of subjectivism, relativism, and cultural determinism that have at once plagued and enriched modern philosophical thought [1967, p. 58; Piaget, 1951, 1963].

It is important to stress that this line of thought does not rest upon the possibility of individual idiosyncrasy or aberrance alone. A number of powerful theories converge here to present a formidable array of arguments and evidence against any easy acceptance of "objective" concepts. Space prohibits detailed examination of these currents, but their shape and general thrust can be indicated.

We know from psychodynamics and learning theory that early in socialization a child's ability to experience the world may be decisively conditioned; theories of cognitive dissonance and selective perception have shown how much we need to believe that the world is as we or our peers would like it to be (Lazarsfeld et al., 1948; Róheim, 1968). But socialization has dimensions beyond psychology, as the sociology of knowledge, a discipline stemming directly from Kantian categories, suggests. Karl Mannheim has argued that not only does our position within the social structure foster an "interest" or "partial ideology" which shapes our vision, but the entire *Weltan-*

schauung, or "total idealogy" of a class or epoch, imposes limitations upon our most basic ideas (1936; Lukács, 1971; Geertz, 1964). Another direct descendent of Kant, the philosophy of symbolic form, which seeks to explore the basis of such symbolic modes as religion, art, and myth, seems to support a relativism if only because it treats "science" as one among many cognitive and expressive styles (though an "advanced" one) (Cassirer, 1953, 1955, 1957; Langer, 1963).

Symbolism suggests language, and at least two distinct intellectual currents are important here. The first, stemming from analytic philosophy, is Ludwig Wittgenstein's attempt to locate and solve problems within the rules and resources of language. Wittgenstein's legacy is extremely complex, but in brief it may be said that he directed attention to language conceived as different "families of meanings" as the solution to philosophical dilemmas, or, in his telling metaphor, to show the fly the way out of the fly bottle. For Wittgenstein, a recent commentator observed that

> the solution of a philosophical problem is reached through a deeper insight into the real function of the sentences under scrutiny, through an understanding of the language game which is actually being used; hence the task of philosophy becomes purely descriptive in the sense that it states (or ascertains) how various sentences function [Hartnack, 1965, pp. 80-81; Pitkin, 1972].

Just as there is no "game of all games," there can be no language of all languages; each variant is legitimate. The "later" Wittgenstein's position described above is clearly at odds with that of philosophers who seek to develop a "pure" or meta-language to undergird science. It is of tangential but real interest to note the contrast between the imagery of Descartes and Wittgenstein; to the former, philosophy must contend against demonic forces; for the latter, the philosopher functions as physician treating an illness.

Peter Winch, in a recent and controversial volume, has sought to apply Wittgenstein's insights directly to social science, and to cast his arguments in terms of an anthropology (1958; Levison, 1966; Louch, 1966). In giving the argument this flavor, Winch suggests the second strain of the language focus which stems from American anthropology, and is referred to notationally as the Whorf-Sapir thesis. Its central idea "is that language functions, not simply as a device for reporting experience, but also, and more significantly, as a way of defining experience for its speakers" (Hoijer, 1958, p. 93; Chomsky, 1965; Dreitzel, 1970). In this view language appears as perhaps the most crucial cultural element in shaping categories of cognition and awareness, but in permitting some kinds of awareness, it closes off others, and while a scientific-technical language can alter the structure of natural languages, it too has limitations. What, for example, happens to meaning when the Western idea of "cause" is translated for the East Indian as "Karna" or "karma" (Burtt, 1962, pp. 260-1)? Even should we feel that we can liberate ourselves from the strictures of language, there may be subtler constraints imposed by the entire life style of a culture. F. S. C. Northrop's philosophical anthropology insists upon the existence of a fundamental epistemological difference between the Western stress on science, abstraction, and technology, and the Eastern sense of the aesthetic component of immediate experience (1946). R. G. H. Siu suggests that a similar dichotomy can be found in the respective styles of science and the Tao (1957). The extent to which the scientist can transcend these barriers, and the proper way to go about such an effort, are matters of considerable dispute and cannot be considered here (Garfinkel, 1967; Sartori, 1970). It is, however, time to make some assessment of these diverse threats to conceptual integrity.

All, in one respect or another, remind us that science is an activity conducted within the complex matrix of human existence, and that it cannot entirely escape the tyrannies of time, place, person, and culture. To this it may be replied: but even if we could conceive of an alternative, some Jovian perspective beyond space, time, and self, would we not be casting ourselves in the role of creator rather than investigator? (Malinowski, 1967). If it be true that we are largely ignorant yet want to know, is it not the case that science is the means some of us think best able to assist our frail abilities? To wish ourselves more or other than human is perhaps also to wish for power or perspective which would make science unnecessary (Devereux, 1967; Kress, 1971). In this respect should these problems of understanding be seen as deficiencies of science, they may also be considered protests against constraints of the human condition (Foucault, 1972).

But if we vindicate the enterprise of science itself, it remains that the practice of science can be more or less successful. Given that we also do not abandon the activity, how are we to deal with the human and cultural frailties of its practitioners? My discussion thus far has raised two basic questions: (1) "How are we to know the state of affairs?" and (2) "Since science has a public dimension, how are we to communicate that knowledge?" While these questions appear—and in some analytic contexts may be—distinguishable, I shall here discuss them simultaneously, for when we discuss concept formation at the methodological level it seems artificial to ignore the social nature of our thinking (Ziman, 1968). I shall not press the question of relative priorities between symbol and perception any further, but simply accept Bill Harrell's judgment:

The issue is not between the choice of a frame of reference which assumes that symbol systems determine the way in which we perceive reality or that perceived reality is the causal force behind the employment of symbols— both of these assumptions seem to be partially true. The question is when and under what conditions do percepts structure concepts and concepts structure percepts [1967, p. 127].

THE FUNCTION OF CONCEPTS IN INQUIRY

But how, then, are we to advance, given the uncertain object of our quest and the bewildering interpenetration of person, problem, and culture? It is, I think, necessary to begin with what Abraham Kaplan calls "logic in use," with the scientist emersed in his inquiry. What, then, is an "inquiry"? Northrop puts the matter well:

Notwithstanding its importance and the difficulty of handling it effectively, the initiation of inquiry has received very little attention . . . . All the methods for the later stages of inquiry are well known. Countless books about them have been written. But what to do at the very beginning in order to determine which of the possible methods is to be used for the inquiry in question and in order to find among the infinite number of facts in experience the particular ones to which the particular methods chosen are to be applied—with respect to these initial difficulties the textbooks on methodology are ominously silent, or if they say anything their authors unequivocally disagree [1959, p. 2].

Where, continues Northrop, are we to locate the genesis of investigation?

Several incommensurable answers have been offered. For Francis Bacon one begins with fact and proceeds by inductive compilation; this method is today called, usually disparagingly, "brute empiricism." Bacon's aphorisms set out in *Novum Organum* merit the attention of all serious students of social science. Political scientists will recognize Bryce's plea for the compilation of fact as Baconian. While probably in general use in the discipline, most political scientists would hesitate to defend so unsophisticated a view of their practice (Easton, 1953; Jackson, 1972). A second recommendation was offered by René Descartes and has already been partially discussed. Impressed by the apparent certainty and rigor of geometrical demonstrations, Descartes proceeded through doubt to a deductive elaboration of true propositions. This style of inquiry is familiar to political scientists in Hobbes's *Leviathan* and, in this century, George Catlin's *The Science and Method of Politics*; as the discipline turned toward empiricism this approach was discarded as overly rationalistic, though it should be noted that the deductive style is enjoying a renaissance in Robert Dahl's *Preface to Democratic Theory*, and in the articulation of formal models in game and decision theory (Buchanan and Tullock, 1962; Rapoport, 1960; Riker, 1962). In our contemporaries Morris Cohen and Ernest Nagel, Northrop finds a third view of the initiation of inquiry. Rejecting both Bacon and Descartes, they see a felt difficulty as its true genesis; this difficulty or uncertainty stimulates thoughts about its solution which, when formulated as propositions, become our hypotheses (Cohen and Nagel, 1934; Cohen, 1931; Dewey and Bentley, 1949; Nagel, 1956). This method would probably command the allegiance of the majority of contemporary political scientists; most methodology texts recommend the procedure of definition of the problem, formulation of hypotheses, operationalization, moving to the data, and so on. Whether such a scheme represents the actual course of inquiry or not, it is faithfully recited as a preface to most dissertations and research reports (Hammond, 1964; Shils, 1957; Kress, 1974b).

It should be noted that in contrast to Bacon and Descartes, Cohen and Nagel locate the genesis of inquiry at an anterior level— that is, in the problem felt by the investigator—and thus their second or hypothesis stage is comparable to Bacon's and Descartes's first stages. This difference should not be overemphasized for Bacon, and Descartes might well have simply assumed a disposition to inquire; it should, however, be noted that while they would probably have called this disposition "curiosity," the twentieth century prefers "difficulty."

The final formulation to be considered is very much contemporary in this respect. For John Dewey an "indeterminent situation," doubtful in itself, is immediately antecedent to inquiry. It *becomes* a problematic situation in the process of undergoing inquiry. This stage passes into the "determination of a problem solution," reached by analysis of the "constituents" of the problem. There follow other steps involving reasoning and operations (Northrop, 1959, pp. 12-14; Dewey, 1938; Popper, 1968). It is clear that Dewey places considerably more emphasis on the preformulation stages, and his orientation is more "psychological" in this respect than the previous versions of inquiry. It is also clear that he sees inquiry as a process rather than a series of rather clearly demarcated steps. A great deal of our effort, and perhaps the most important segment, is expended *before* we arrive at "facts," "hypotheses," or "operations." Further, Dewey invites us to retrace our steps to alter an unsatisfactory formulation; his entire vision enjoins us to be "open" in every respect: toward the environment, the problem, alternative solutions, and possible reformulations. The values are openness, adaptability, and possibility; to be avoided are structure, rigidity, and finality.

Dewey's account of the nature of inquiry is attractive and powerful, but it purchases flexibility at the cost of introducing a certain looseness. Are there not, we want to ask, some rules which can guide our formulation of problems and solutions, and direct our movement among stages? *Where, for example, do laws and concepts appear within the process?* It should certainly be apparent that the simple account, which sees "concepts" as arising from undifferentiated perceptions, is inadequate (Bruner et al., 1956). As Popper notes, "The belief that we can start with pure observations alone, without anything in the nature of a theory, is absurd" (1968, p. 46). Inquiry may indeed begin from the facts, but these facts are already impregnated by concepts—that is, the frame, emphasis, or focus of observation is a given. To borrow the expressive terms of W. T. Jones, concepts bring certain data to the "foreground" of awareness, permitting other data to remain in the relative obscurity of the "background" (1965). Michael Polanyi has something similar in mind when he speaks of "tacit" knowledge, the cognitive map comprised by our beliefs, values, and expectations (1964). Whether we follow Popper in holding that science begins with a conjecture, or N. R. Hanson in his insistence that physicists start from data, these maps are determinative.

The content of these cognitive structures may vary considerably. We may be led to hold certain expectations as derivations of a sophisticated and articulated theory, or a much more tenuous association may be controlling. "Just as research cannot be initiated without some sense of the significant, so sociological theorizing cannot be developed without a strong sense of what is 'real' in society" (Bendix and Berger, 1959, p. 93). The researcher's "images" are not necessarily revealed by formal propositions, but these often unarticulated intuitions define the "data" of the science and, by implication, set the boundaries of the discipline. As Bendix and Berger note, reflection on the nature of "social fact" in the writings of the classical sociologists goes far to illustrate their differing researches: for Simmel it was "interaction"; for Durkheim, the coercion exercised by society; and for Max Weber, the meaning of action.

It is a facile but seductive response to suggest that such influences upon the formation and use of concepts is an unfortunate testimonial to the immaturity of the social sciences—that considerations of this kind are, for the natural or developed sciences, artifacts of their dark ages. N. R. Hanson and other historians of science have forcefully demonstrated the importance of images in the conduct of physical inquiry. Their role finds vivid illustration in the way inquiry is framed, i.e., the manner in which questions are asked. In discussing Galileo's persistent attempts to account for the behavior of objects in free fall, Hanson notes his early rejection of the concept of impetus.

> The successive actions of impetus occur primarily in time; they are in space in only an inessential way. Ignore the causal aspect of free fall, however, and our ideas veer away from the temporal frame in which these causes successively act. Thinking becomes fixed to the spacial frame in which the "resultant" motion is manifested. Galileo wished to geometrize motion, so he ignored this feature of the impetus theory, and hence the impetus theory as a whole [1958, pp. 40–41].

Thus, though he was later able to recognize the temporal dimension, Galileo's "thinking became orientated in a spatial framework not in a causal, time-dependent one. Why does motion cease? That was Galileo's problem." The matter is not that to opt for certain puzzles precludes, in an absolute or logical sense, the asking of other questions; it is rather that when we frame a problem in particular terms we are *encouraged* to pursue inquiry in some modes rather than others. This observation returns our attention to the intimate connection between symbols and perception, and the function of concepts in communication.

> The argument is simply that the formation of a concept x in any language not rich enough to express x (or in a language which explicitly rules out the expression of x), is always difficult. The conception of x without a notation in which x is expressible need not constitute a logical impossibility [Hanson, 1958, p. 36].

If problems of the notational system are bothersome to physicists, they are especially troublesome to political scientists. How are they to translate certain responses to their interview schedules into such concepts as "powerlessness" or "alienation"? How many civil wars, riots, or shifts of government suffice to brand a regime "unstable"? If "democracy" be defined as electoral participation, what becomes of such other measures as the presence of effective opposition, civil liberties, and social justice? This is not, as some would have it, simply an arbitrary choice of conceptual indicators with clarity the only imperative. Marion Levy is surely correct when he urges that concepts are means of intersubjective communication, usually by words, and that these words need necessarily have intersubjective meanings (1952, p. 227; Jung, 1972). The point, of course, is that language is an already established system.

> The terms of physics thus resemble "pawn," "rook," "trump," and "offside"—words which are meaningless except against a background of the

games of chess, bridge and football. To one ignorant of what happens as a rule in bridge, "finesse" will explain nothing. Even though nothing escapes his view while the finesse is made, he will not *see* the finesse being made [Hanson, 1958, p. 57].

The problem of "intersubjectivity" is, for the social scientist, double-edged. He must be concerned that his concepts "share" a meaning with *both* his subjects or respondents, and his colleagues (Sibley, 1967). In some fashion, through shared or translatable symbols, a community of meaning must come into being (see chap. 16). The fact that the subject matter of behavioral science is itself a complex symbol system has led many researchers to insist that concept formation must have its genesis in the "lived" world or *Lebenswelt* (Schutz, 1962b; Nagel, 1963). Exactly what this procedure requires is an immensely complicated issue in the philosophy of social science which can only be mentioned here, for it involves basic questions about the nature of validation and explanation (Gunnell, 1968b). Some social scientists have embraced phenomenological epistemology while others have sought a grounding in existential psychology, though these labels tend to obscure very diverse formulations (Kariel, 1967; Natanson, 1962; Neisser, 1959; Merleau-Ponty, 1964a; Sartre, 1964; Levi, 1962). Whatever their respective epistemological bases, these approaches usually employ some variation of the methodology of *Verstehen* (Abel, 1948-49; Wax, 1967; Natanson, 1963). "All forms of social life, not merely science, are paradigmatic, and the configuration of intersubjective symbols that comprise a paradigm and that are expressed in actions, institutions, and social relationships constitute social reality and provide 'the directly observable data of sociation' " (Gunnell, 1968b, pp. 184-85). Merleau-Ponty, in describing Husserl's phenomenology, makes the point this way: "Instead of a logical organization of the facts coming from a form that is superimposed upon them, the very content of these facts is supposed to order itself spontaneously in a way that is thinkable" (1964a, p. 52). We have, then, two symbolic systems: that of the *Lebenswelt* and that of science. But while the conceptual system of the latter must be rooted in the former, it is an error to hold that scientific language must "reproduce" its subject meanings, or that it be in all respects "reducible" to them (Waismann, 1955). Gunnell describes the relationship this way:

> While the language and view of reality of both the social and natural sciences supersede that of everyday life in describing and explaining the universe, the symbolic world of everyday life is an object of social scientific inquiry, and the illumination of this world is logically tied to the explanation of social action. While the natural and social scientist alike are concerned with the intersubjective concepts constituting their science, the

social scientist must also be concerned with the intersubjective order of everyday life and language [1968b, pp. 179-80].

An ambitious but still early step toward a theoretical formulation of this position is Berger and Luckman's *The Social Construction of Reality* (1966), though political scientists may find Murray Edelman's *The Symbolic Uses of Politics* (1964) more empirically satisfying.

The interdependency of these two languages is illustrated by this rather typical treatment of concepts by a popular method text: "Aggression is a concept, an abstraction that expresses a number of particular actions having the similar characteristic of hurting people or objects. A *conceptual scheme* is a set of concepts interrelated by hypothetical and theoretical propositions" (Kerlinger, 1964, p. 4). There is no particular problem with this formulation, but neither is it remarkably helpful. Bearing the earlier discussion in mind, we must wonder how we can recognize circumstances of "hurting people" without entering the emotive and cognitive universe of our respondents; in a similar vein, it must appear somewhat artificial to suggest that so rich a concept as "aggression" can be understood in itself. Does it not require a "conceptual scheme" which would include "disinterestedness" or "altruism" or "pacifism" to make the "concept" aggression meaningful? When Kerlinger continues to further distinguish a "construct" as "a concept with the additional meaning of having been created or appropriated for special scientific purposes," we may be excused for wondering whether the ingenuity of distinction has not outstripped its utility.

That text, however, is certainly correct in suggesting that concepts often serve the purpose of aggregating disparate happenings or entities under the rubric of an inclusive symbol. In this respect, "aggression," "democracy," "cooperation," and "matrilineal" are more or less abstract categories which facilitate contrast, comparison, and generalized thought. The most basic function performed by these concepts is that of description: this or that behavior, we are told, is an instance of aggression, democracy, etc. This elementary descriptive function becomes more sophisticated through creation of additional concepts, as when we establish the polar categories of open and closed societies. We may later hope to move toward subtler analysis by locating regimes on some point in a continuum between open and closed. At the moment, however, political scientists seem largely concerned with the elaboration of concepts for essentially taxonomic purposes (Almond and Coleman, 1960; Almond and Verba, 1963; Morton Kaplan, 1957; Macridis, 1955; Mitchell, 1962). A major reason for this preoccupation is the continued popularity of functional and system theories which, despite their avowed intention of treating social dynamics, have concentrated their efforts on taxonomy (Parsons, 1951; Easton, 1965b; Mitchell, 1967a; Buckley, 1967; Young, 1968; Jarvie, 1969).

In addition to their functions in identification, description and comparison, concepts are sometimes said to express causal or explanatory relationships. To perform these more sophisticated tasks, concepts must be imbedded in laws and theories. If concepts are but labels, the process of "attaching" them is one of naming, whether their referents be entities ("America"), events ("Paris Commune"), or operational indicators ("F Scale"). This process of naming may be stipulative or arbitrary, in which case we simply establish a linguistic convention—in Carl Hempel's example, "Let the word 'tigion' be short for (i.e., synonymous with) the phrase 'offspring of a male tiger and a female lion'" (1952, p. 2). This conventional naming or *nominal definition* is usually contrasted to so-called *real definition*, which presupposes a settled usage (Bierstedt, 1959). In attaching real definitions we pass beyond stipulation to the making of claims to the truth of our assertions, and assume the burden of validating them. We may, for example, define the United States Congress as "that body which exercises the national legislative power," but this assertion might be tested in one of two ways. It might be interpreted as a claim that *as words are used* in their accepted meanings, the *definiendum* is indeed synonomous with the *definiens* (Hempel, 1952, pp. 6-14). Hempel would call this procedure a "meaning analysis." Alternatively, the definition of Congress could be read as a claim to an empirical relationship, that *in fact* the Congress and uniquely the Congress performs the national legislative function. The differences between these means of validating the two interpretations of real definitions are not only formal (meaning versus empirical analysis), but they may lead to differing conclusions. In the congressional illustration a meaning analysis might result in a vindication of the definition, while an empirical test which would record the diffusion of national legislative power among many agencies could reject it.

Hempel gives the following account of concept formation: "The explanatory and predictive principles of a scientific discipline are stated in its hypothetical generalizations and its theories; they characterize general patterns or regularities to which the individual phenomena conform and by virtue of which this occurrence can be systematically anticipated" (Hempel, 1952, p. 1). "Explanation," in this view, consists in subsuming particular phenomena under general or covering laws. Explanation and prediction thus have the same logical form: "explanation is always deductive no matter how covertly" (Brodbeck, 1968, p. 9). If we know that whites desert apartment buildings when black occupancy reaches 40 percent, we explain a particular exodus while we predict it. Brodbeck cautions, however, that there are no "explanatory concepts"; only sentences which assert matters of fact, and thus express laws, have such power.

Though we cannot explore the issue here, there is considerable dissent from this "hypothetico-deductive" account. Kaplan (1964) speaks of "semantic" explanation or the substitution of a familiar for a strange word, and P. W. Bridgman once spoke of explanation as the point at which curiosity rests (1927; Rapoport, 1953). Other criticism of the "H-D" account has come from Stephen Toulmin's argument that explanation and prediction are distinct operations, Hanson's reconstruction of the process of scientific discovery, and Gunnell's case for philosophical explanation in social science (Toulmin, 1961; Hanson, 1958; Gunnell, 1968b; Charles Taylor, 1964; Richard Taylor, 1966).

THE EVALUATION OF CONCEPTS

But whether we are viewing concepts as descriptive, taxonomic, predictive, or explanatory, the important question is "Are they significant?" We are accustomed to hearing concepts described as "rich," "barren," or "mistaken," but what do we understand by such words? Insofar as concepts are simply names they cannot be said to be true or false (except in the circumstances that settled usage is violated in speech), nor are precision of definition and explicitness of operations alone reliable indices of significance. It is sometimes suggested that the more abstract is a system of notation the more powerful are its concepts, and the example of mathematics is urged in demonstration; but Kaplan's cautionary voice should be heeded here. Unless, he remarks, abstract notation can provide a function, it is of little value; the power of mathematics lies in its ability to sustain such relationships as ordinality, cardinality, and transitivity, but political notation falls far short of this standard.

Harold Lasswell's much discussed hypothesis concerning political motivation is a case in point:

> The most general formula which expresses the developmental facts about the fully developed political man reads thus:
> $$p\}d\}r = P,$$
> where p equals private motives; d equals displacement onto a public object; r equals rationalization in terms of public interest; P equals the political man; and $\}$ equals transformed into [1960, pp. 75–76].

Strictly speaking, Lasswell should not have used the term "equals," for no measure of magnitude was intended. He should have said "stands for," but even granting that a measure of notational economy is achieved, it is purchased at the cost of a certain pretentiousness. Professor Lasswell is himself far too sophisticated to make this error, but his choice of nonverbal symbolization does suggest that an "advance" rather than a substitution has been affected.

May Brodbeck brings us closer to an adequate idea of significance: "The more laws into which a concept enters, the more significant it is, because the more we know about how it is connected with other things" (1968, p. 8). Later she assures us that "to look for a good concept is to look for a law." The stress upon laws is, of course, a consequence of her devotion to the hypothetico-deductive mode of explanation, but we need not read her remarks so narrowly. It is the *connections* the concept establishes or suggests among laws, or facts, or other concepts which mark its significance. This is part of what is meant by richness, and its importance is indicated by the frequency with which we hear the injunction to imbed concepts in theory. What is sought is a pattern, a coherence, a cognitive map which can structure and illuminate experience, and those concepts which express more of this needed coherence are generally of greater significance (Zilsel, 1941; Zaffron, 1971).

It is necessary to distinguish this kind of richness from the level and range of concepts. Terms such as "input" and "output" are highly abstract and general categories, as is "boundary maintenance," but they are formal rather than rich. By contrast, the concept of "alienation" even when applied to an individual is rooted in a comprehensive social theory, and is closely linked to such other ideas as "powerlessness," "hostility," and "isolation" (Feuer, 1963b; Meszaros, 1970; Ollman, 1971; Horkheimer and Adorno, 1973). A similar observation might be made of the contemporary stress on uniformity and law in the structure of theory. Both the case study method, and the ideal typical analysis of Max Weber, have developed and employed some of the most significant concepts in all social science literature. Political science abounds in landmark case studies which have given direction to a major part of the field at one time or another. One immediately recalls Beard's still vital view of the Constitutional struggle (1965), Odegard's pioneering study of an American interest group (1928), the work of Key and Mackenzie on American and British parties (1949, 1955), Selznick's examination of Bolshevism (1952), Snyder and Paige's reconstruction of the decision to defend South Korea (1958), Mason's biographies of Stone and Brandeis (1946, 1956), and Neustadt's perspectives on the contemporary presidency (1960).

Weber's uses of the ideal type are varied and imaginative; they include types employed as bases for taxonomies, means of imaginary experiment (or historical reconstruction), end points of continua, and sources of general hypotheses (Rhoads, 1967; Martindale, 1959). Types are "constructed" from empirical materials, but the aim is less to draw a blueprint of reality than to exaggerate its dominant features. The complex of attitudes, values, and social relations which constitute Weber's analysis of the Protestant ethic and the rise of capitalism deliberately accented such beliefs as predestination and postponed consumption to illustrate their mutual affinity. A construct of this kind may be used for any of the purposes noted above; the point is that concepts developed from study of unique historical or cultural configurations, even those which do not claim to reflect matters as they happened or are, may have versatility and significance at least equal to concepts embedded in general laws (Zaffron, 1971). As Rhoads observes, ideal typical analysis does not necessarily conform to the logic of classes, but beyond this it may even tolerate contradictory or "illogical" elements (1967; Parsons, 1949).

A further means of assessing the significance of concepts is suggested by Arthur Koestler's study of creativity in the arts and sciences. The essence of the creative act he describes as the "bisociation of matrices," or the process of bringing two previously distinct frames of reference together in a new way. Employing examples ranging from the pun to Gestalt psychology Koestler argues that discovery involves seeing the familiar in a new, even incongruous, fashion (Havelka, 1968). While it may well be a risky enterprise to identify creative moments in political science, I suspect that the master metaphor of the *Republic*, Plato's exploration of the state as man writ large, would satisfy many readers. A more contemporary and perhaps more controversial illustration might be the famous chapter in *Voting* in which the author's intent seems to be to effect a drastic revision of classical democratic theory: to argue that citizen apathy, ignorance, and partisanship contribute to the good political life (Berelson et al., 1954). Boguslaw's attempt to view the systems engineers of the Rand Corporation as heirs of the Western utopian tradition may seem sensible, even obvious to some, but must be startling, perhaps disquieting, to many of those involved (1965). Freud's great therapeutic insight that the control mechanisms of a culture are themselves a source of destructive aims and energies is yet another example of what Kenneth Burke has called "perspective by incongruity."

Koestler's argument is relevant here less for its success in illuminating the mysteries of creativity than for its reinforcement of the claim that significance is best viewed as conceptual richness: "A concept may be regarded as a relatively stable aggregate or 'cluster' of receiving-transmitting circuits, with a kind of nuclear core: the verbal label" (1964, p. 645; 1949). Without devaluing either clarity or rigor, Koestler points to the importance of "connotative matrices" in all conceptual thought, and asks us to consider our "circuitry systems" capable of extensive "rewiring."

To review, we judge the significance of concepts on many dimensions. *Ceteris paribus*, clarity and precision of definition should be valued, as should the expression of laws and connections to theory. More abstract concepts may have greater generality and thus more power, though this dimension must be modified by that of richness. Whether the suggestion that concepts which subsume others be called "meta-concepts," and we then progress to third and fourth order subsumptions, has merit, must probably depend upon the degree of deductive rigor we judge that a particular effort requires (Haas, 1974). Concepts may derive their significance from an ability to join aspects of previously unrelated theories or matrices. We usually experience these with a shock of recognition, a sudden, surprised appreciation that ideas can be so ordered (Wolin, 1969). There is a final dimension to concept significance which I shall try to illustrate by referring once more to Kuhn's analysis of scientific revolutions. These, he tells us, are recognizable by noting the appearance of a "paradigm work." By this term he means "to suggest that some accepted examples of actual scientific practice—examples which include law, theory, application, and instrumentation together—provide models from which spring particular coherent traditions of scientific research" (Kuhn, 1962, p. 10). Paradigm works share two essential characteristics. "Their achievement was sufficiently unprecedented to attract an enduring group of adherents away from competing modes of scientific activity. Simultaneously, it was sufficiently open-ended to leave all sorts of problems for the redefined group of practicioners to resolve" (Kuhn, 1962, p. 10; Lakatos and Musgrave, 1970).

There are a number of other characteristics of paradigms as defined by Kuhn, and it is by no means clear that political science has attained the status of a paradigm science despite the imprimatur lent that claim by recent and prestigious commentators (Almond, 1966; Truman, 1965). Leaving that issue aside, I propose that Kuhn's two defining characteristics can be adapted to the evaluation of concept significance. Concepts, as Brodbeck observes, slice our experience into meaningful patterns, and another way to put this is to say that they teach us which questions to ask and how to ask them. Significant concepts suggest questions, but in such a way that they leave a variety of problems yet to be investigated. Examples are not difficult to cite. The conviction that societies might be seen as organisms subject to Darwin's hypotheses of species evolution proved remarkably fertile for American historians and social scientists of the early twentieth century (Hofstadter, 1955). Ferdinand Tönnies's use of the *Gemeinschaft-Gesellschaft* distinction has, in a variety of formulations, dominated sociological thinking for nearly a century (Etzioni, 1968). In more contemporary terms we would have to mention the idea that polities have "nervous systems" (Deutsch, 1963); Erikson's focus on "identity crises" in early socialization (1950, 1958); the development of Michels's elite-mass polarity by Mills, Kornhauser, and Lipset (1959); Lipset et al. (1956, 1962); Easton's employment of the language of systems theory (1965b); Mannheim's analysis of ideology and rationality (1936); and Arendt's suggestive concepts of "public" and "action" (1958).

Many other equally deserving examples could be cited, but these should serve to illustrate this final dimension of significance. Each has captured the imagination of the field by sharing an exciting way of ordering experience: through investigating a new variable, as did McClelland's study of children's fairy tales (1961); asking an old question in a new way, as did McLuhan (1962); linking previously distinct matrices, as did Lasswell (1960); or setting forth a full-bodied "grand theory," as did Parsons and Shils (1951). None of these achievements, despite their grandeur, exhausted or "closed" the inquiry it initiated; rather, the impetus of their insights extended beyond the scope of the works themselves.

The lesson for political scientists concerned with concept formation seems clear—to develop concepts is to look for problems. But how is a sense of the problematic itself to be learned? The question is formidable, for if any contemporary scientists or educators know how to teach creativity they have kept the secret very well indeed. Still, if the argument presented here has merit, a few suggestions might be made.

1. Researchers should be aware of the "theory," or more broadly, the tradition from which their concepts stem. More specifically, they should be alive to major perspectives, strengths, and problems of that tradition as well as its areas of deemphasis or neglect.
2. While continuing to seek clarity and precision of statement, political scientists should imbed their concepts in the broadest possible context of theory.
3. Because few researchers find one tradition or theory fully adequate to their purposes they must cultivate an appreciation of various sources of inspiration and imagination.

4. They should cultivate the flexibility of mind which permits the interlacing of investigative matrices through innovative conceptual formation.

Basic to all these recommendations is a thorough grasp of the discipline of political science, and the broadest possible appreciation of relevant trends in cognate fields. Some colleagues will caution against the dangers of dilettantism and eclecticism inherent in these recommendations (Scheffler, 1967; Landau, 1972); they would be right to issue that warning, provided that it is accompanied by an admonition against premature closure and an unhistorical satisfaction with the contemporary (Kariel, 1969). The story of scientific advance has been one of the tensions between discipline and innovation, and the future of a science of politics is unlikely to prove the unique exception.

18. SYSTEMS THEORY AND STRUCTURAL-FUNCTIONAL ANALYSIS

Fred M. Frohock

ORIGINS

Systems analysis, like many ideas, has an unclear past. The popular mind marks its entry into political science with a pair of articles in the mid-1950s, Gabriel Almond's "Comparative Political Systems" (1956) and David Easton's "An Approach to the Analysis of Political Systems" (1957). Easton's critique of the history of theory in an earlier volume, *The Political System* (1953), suggests that the political theorist need look no further for origins. But the persistent explorer can find versions of the structural-functional approach of systems theory in many earlier works. Aristotle, for one, developed a theory of social action replete with functional categories. How Almond and Easton differ from Aristotle yields more than a fair share of stories, but in their views of function can be found the appropriate starting point for this essay.

Aristotle's functional categories are action oriented. Like most behavioralists today in the social sciences, he was primarily interested in what a thing *does*. Unlike most behavioralists today, he recognized essential functions, those which "define" agents. In classical philosophy, the virtue of any agent is that activity which cannot occur in the absence of the agent. Virtue is, roughly, a characteristic function. For example, the virtue, or characteristic function, of the eye is to see; for in a world without eyes, seeing is impossible. The eye which sees well, fully, is, accordingly, a good or virtuous eye. This same exercise was applied by Aristotle to human beings. The virtue of man is intelligence, *nous;* for without man, thinking is impossible. Thus the virtuous man is one who fully exercises his intelligence. So, for Aristotle, some functions, as virtues, are essentially related to what a modern theorist would call "structures": without the structure, the function does not occur; and the function sets out that which is essential about the structure.

Two other features of Aristotle's functionalism are important here. First, action is always seen in context. For Aristotle, an event is to be taken not only in terms of its particular features, but also in terms of its place in a larger whole. Second, events for Aristotle are directed *toward* some end. Aristotle held four kinds of causality: formal (what is it), material (out of what is it made), efficient (by what agent), and final (for what end). The most important cause for Aristotle is the end toward which a thing is directed. The extended context of action thus includes not only the location of an event in a larger social or biological whole, but also its end-state, or that which it is to become. It is worth remarking that for Aristotle all life, and not just human life, is purposive. But ends can be consciously known only by man, thus leaving the events of nature with purposes but without what we would call "intentions."

One obviously hesitates to speak of virtue as occupying a central role in modern functional analysis. But some of Aristotle's other concerns do not fit badly. It is a source of satisfaction among structural-functional theorists that they view social life in terms of process. This can be traced in sociology at least back to Talcott Parsons's action schema (Parsons and Shils, 1951), but in political science one need look no further than Easton's recommendations in *The Political System* (1953) to focus less on institutions (like constitutions and legal systems) and more on behavior (like congressional committees and White House aides). It is obvious that institutions are also patterns of behavior. But an emphasis on process will have two consequences for political inquiry. First, it will call attention to behavior which is not institutional in the legal or constitutional sense, like the committee system in the House of Representatives. Second, institutions themselves will be viewed not as static structures but as fluid matters of behavior, processes with outcomes, a view in keeping with Aristotle's dictum that institutions must be seen in terms of what they *do*.

Functional analysts also view action as purposive, as did Aristotle. But here the important differences between Aristotle's functionalism and the functionalism of modern social analysis become evident. The purpose or end of an event was, for Aristotle, its final cause. The end exists in the event in a state of potentiality. It is normally accepted today that human behavior is goal oriented. But goals in modern functional theory are not taken as a state of potentiality (as Aristotle saw them). They are taken as present facts. To say that there are ends for action is, for social scientists today, to say that some actor is in a certain state of mind in the present. So, while for Aristotle the future state of an event can direct its present behavior, for the contemporary functionalist ends are thoughts of the future existing in the present. Modern structural-functional theory is thus like Aristotle's functionalism in relying on ends to define action and unlike it in reducing final causality to efficient causality.

The idea of function itself has changed from Aristotle to the present time. The term "function" does not today normally include any notion of characteristic activity. If a parallel can be drawn between the classical meaning of an agent and either of the currently more fashionable words "structure" and "institution," then no structure or institution is said today to have a characteristic activity which could not occur without the structure or institution in question. In fact, the opposite is true. Alternate structures or institutions are said to be able to satisfy any given function. The converse is also held (as, again, it was not by Aristotle), which is that structures or institutions may have several functions, none of which may be definitive. The function of food distribution, for example, may be carried out by any of a number of structures, including the political machine or the political party; and either of these two structures may carry out a variety of functions. Essential relationships, in the sense of necessity between factual arrangements and functions, have been jettisoned in modern social science. The eye not only does many things besides see, but also seeing can be done by things other than the eye. Or, to avoid the absurdity, there are no parallels between the eye and the parts of the social order in modern functional theory.

Finally, it is clear that the normative concerns of Aristotle, his attempts to describe and justify the good polity, are not prominent in contemporary structural-functional theory. Values are taken today primarily as expressions of feeling, as what an actor desires or judges ought to be the case. Thus values enter social inquiry as facts, as statements describing the attitudes, feelings, or judgments of actors. Aristotle maintained, on the other hand, that value statements do make truth claims, and so may enter our intellectual concerns as true-false statements on the ideal polity. In short, the classical inquiry into the just or moral polity is excluded from modern structural-functional theory precisely on the basis of a theory of value which, unlike the classical thesis, denies value statements any truth-function.

SOME BASIC IDEAS

Having considered (briefly) how contemporary functional theory is unlike its classical origins, we may now appropriately examine current affairs in structural-functional analysis. One helpful way to begin is by outlining some primary ideas and terms.

1. Social events are conceptualized in terms of their consequences for the social system in which they occur. Events which have positive consequences for the social system are said to be functional; those with negative consequences are dysfunctional; and in some theories (but not all) those with neutral consequences are said to be eufunctional. If we allow that events may have features other than those associated with system consequences, then structural-functional analysis does not focus on those dimensions of social action which are unrelated to the coordinates of a system. Events are structured and ordered in accordance with the definition of a system guiding the analysis.

2. *Structure* and *function* can be distinguished in terms of form versus content. *How* something is done is a structure. *What* is done is a function.[1] Example: the distribution of goods and services to meet minimal human needs of survival is a necessary function of any social system. How these goods and services are in fact distributed is a question of social structures. Any of a number of social forms can perform the function in question, including political machines, the federal government, and others (Merton, 1956). And any of these structures may have alternative functions. So, again, no necessary relationship exists between structures and functions. What we have is a factual relationship. Certain things are done (functions) in societies by certain social forms (structures). The precise relationship between particular functions and structures is a variable of the particular society under scrutiny.

A rough analogy to the structure-function distinction can be found in the distinction we often draw between rules and content in scientific theories. Structures can be seen as similar to rules of inference and evidence which are common to a variety of theories. Sometimes procedural rules are the only common feature of theories which differ radically in what they contain in the way of substance. We say that procedural rules are constant while content varies, suggesting, in terms of the analogy to social structure and function, that certain procedures (read "structures") are compatible with a wide (although not infinite) variety of content (read "functions").

Where the analogy with scientific theories revealingly breaks down is on the other side of the coin: theoretical content may not so

---

1. There are obvious variations on this schematic description. Fred Riggs, for example, defines structure as a basic pattern of activity which is repeated, and function as the result of any such pattern. But this is, I believe, a definition consistent with the account here: basic patterns can express *how* something is done, while outcomes may be described as *what* is done. (See Riggs, 1962, 1964.)

easily be expressed by a variety of procedural rules as functions by structures. Procedures in theories are adopted, in part, to disallow certain content, that which is generally seen as specious. We cannot shop around for different rules to state that regarded as unfounded by established rules. Scientific theories rest on some rough idea of *correct* rules of inference and evidence. No comparable sense of correctness can be found in structural-functional theory. It would, in fact, be considered quite parochial—even, to use a word in fashion not so long ago, ethnocentric—to specify one set of social structures as "valid" for the realization of any and all functions. Variance occurs rather, from the perspective of function as well as structure: functional patterns may legitimately take on any of a number of structural forms.

A sense of "incompatibility" replaces the harder "validity" of scientific theories. If we operate with a less than infinite range of functions for any particular structure, and functions as not expressible in terms of all possible structures, it is but a small step to the incompatibility of some structures with some functions. Such incompatibility is conceptually enlarged with the identification of some functions as necessary for the maintenance of any society. For example, a religion that holds animals as sacred in a society requiring the slaughter of animals for minimal food requirements may be said to be a structure incompatible with basic (maintaining) functions. This quasi-normative requirement of universal functions is normally set at a low level of maintenance, often embracing only the bare minimum for physical survival. But it is the reference point which allows generalizing judgments that specific structures are functional, dysfunctional, or—on occasion—eufunctional.

3. A *system* can be formally defined as a set of interacting elements in a state of mutual dependence. This definition is large enough to take in the behavior of almost any aggregate. In part, this is what systems analysts intend. The claim is normally made that a wide range of behavior, perhaps all behavior, possesses certain shared characteristics; and, further, that these common features are the most important features of behavior. All systems, for example, are said to have boundaries, possess requirements which must be fulfilled in order for them to maintain an existence, and are composed of elements which are mutually dependent in the sense that a change in one part of the system unavoidably changes some other part of the system. Most systems are also dynamic, meaning that the rates and quality of the exchanges between system elements alter over time, even though boundaries may remain constant. Finally, goals are postulated for most systems, if not all, and certainly human behavior is taken as goal oriented.

Structural-functional theory also includes the idea of subsystems within the social system concept. A subsystem is distinguished analytically from the concept of a social system on the basis of non-general features ascribed to social events. Some social events are taken as economic elements, some as political elements, and so on. Elements in a subsystem are still considered elements in a social system, but the subsystem is only a partial factor in the social system. The political system, which occupies the interest of the current discussion, is generally defined as the directive subsystem in society. In its most widely known definition, it is specified as those social events which are involved in the authoritative allocation of values (see Easton, 1953, 1965b). This feature, "authoritative allocation," sets off the political system as a subsystem, distinct from other subsystems (such as economics).

All political systems are said to perform certain functions. Precisely what these are is a point of difference among structural-functional theorists. Almond, in the article mentioned earlier, distinguishes *input* and *output* functions. Input functions are the consequences of structures for the political system and output functions are consequences of the political system for other social structures. A certain amount of difficulty obtains for this distinction. If input functions occur *outside* the political system then it is not clear what the character of these functions is. They appear political, are necessary conditions of the political system (it is said, in fact, that all political systems "perform" these functions), and yet they are said to be outside the boundaries of the political system. One can reasonably ask, "What is *inside* the political system?" Such circumlocutions have led other theorists to add another category of functions, "with-inputs," to designate inputs which occur within the political system (Easton, 1965b). And, of course, the same extra designation must be made for outputs.

Almond's input functions are interest identification, interest aggregation, political socialization and recruitment, and political communication. These functions have been pared down over the years by various theorists to leadership selection and interest identification. Generally, input functions have been taken as *demands*, *supports*, and *apathy* (a later addition to the earlier input functions). Output functions for Almond are rule making, rule application, and rule adjudication. Another version of these functions is rule making, settlement of disputes, and rule application. The more general way of stating the output functions is that they consist of *rewards* and *deprivations*. On this account, input functions reflect the attitude of nonpolitical elements toward political elements and output functions reflect the attitude of political elements toward nonpolitical elements. It is helpful to recall here that political elements are frequently viewed as types of directive behavior.

These input and output functions are necessary and sufficient conditions for a political system. No political system can exist without them, and whenever they exist a political system exists. Politics, in this way, is conceputalized universally. This, at any rate, is the claim.

SOME CRITICISMS

Structural-functional analysis has been subject to four major criticisms in recent years. Three have been widely discussed for a considerable time, while the fourth is of more recent vintage. This is an interesting reflection in itself on the state of functional analysis in political science, for the fourth criticism is by a considerable margin the most important. The first three will, for these reasons, be treated at once, and more briefly, than the fourth criticism.

1. Is functionalism a distinctive way of accounting for experience? Or can it be reduced to other forms of explanation? (Davis, 1959). One form of explanation which has had considerable influence on political science is the "covering law" explanation. Those who support this version of explanation (Hempel, 1966) maintain that an event has been explained when it can be subsumed under an empirical law. Normally this also requires an assumption of causality, in the sense that from a description of antecedent conditions and the covering law the event which is explained can be deduced.

A second form of explanation rests on certain claimed deficiencies for the covering law thesis. First, it is often maintained that the variety and complexity of social phenomena make covering law explanations only idle models with little relevance to social reality (Popper, 1969). In such a view, a deductive-nomological account will still be a possible way to see social experience, but the lawlike relationships it states are vacuous in that they almost never occur in social experience. Second, it can be maintained against the covering law thesis that there may be causal connections between events which are not covered by a law (Scriven, 1969). We may, for example, explain in retrospect a random event by citing its antecedent conditions, but the event still may not be deducible from a description of the antecedent conditions and a covering law. The evolution of almost any physical attribute is an example of this point, where a satisfactory account of the attribute may be given after the fact but without satisfying the deductive requirements of the covering law explanation. Third, it can be argued that certainty is possible prior to, and even independent of, explanation, in the form, say, of prescientific knowledge (Polanyi, 1964). Thus a covering law explanation is not the establishment of certainty in conditions of uncertainty, but the reflection of prescientific knowledge. This being so, it follows that the proper concern of social inquirers is with the particular conditions of such knowledge, not a causal explanation of it (for causal explanations presuppose, and do not investigate, such knowledge).

The form of explanation which, its supporters maintain, avoids these criticisms is a "context" version of explanation (Toulmin, 1960, 1964; Scriven, 1969). This form of explanation relies on criteria of adequacy locatable within particular social contexts, and what makes an explanation a good explanation in one context will not necessarily make it a good explanation in another. So, the argument goes, what is needed in social inquiry is less a stipulation of abstract standards and more of an empirical investigation into the actual standards and rules by which explanations are made and accepted as adequate. A legal explanation, for example, will be of a different form with different adequacy requirements than, say, an explanation in biology. Supporters of the context view of explanation assert that such differences must be revealed and used as the source for adequate explanations. Reconstructing adequacy criteria and form, as the covering law adherents do, merely obscures and distorts these differences. The perjorative claim of the contextual argument is that no scientist, not even the physical scientist, follows the deductive model in the pursuit of science; and, of course, no one ever claimed that ordinary people explain in deductive fashion. This, if true, leaves the deductive model as the curious possession only of philosophers of science like Nagel and Hempel, and, of course, strengthens the support for a consideration of contextual factors (Gunnell, 1968b).

Still a third way we may explain social events is by revealing reasons for action (Winch, 1958). For example, if someone walks across the room and closes the window, a reasonable way to account for the action is to ask the person why he closed the window. If he responds with a statement to the effect that it is cold in the room, then we have an explanation for his actions. A reason need not be something always accessible to the actor, something he can put forward as a way of explaining his actions, for we may say that there *is* a reason for a given action even if no one *has* that reason in the sense of being able to forward it when asked. But a reason must be a statement which makes the action intelligible. Reasons for action are obviously not causal antecedents. We may have all of the reasons for an action yet not be able to deduce what the actor is going to do. A "reason-supported" explanation makes sense of an action without providing general laws of explanation or prediction.

It is clear that a functional account of social phenomena does not take the form of any of the three versions of explanation briefly described above. It is not, first, a version of the deductive-nomological form, for no necessary connection is maintained between structures, or between structures and functions. From a given function one cannot deduce any facts; from facts one cannot deduce functions; and from facts one cannot deduce other facts with the help of functional statements. Second, as we have seen, functional explanations are not limited to any particular contexts, but rather contain propositions about maintenance requirements for any society. Third, functions cannot be reduced to what people intend or offer as reasons for their actions, for intentions and reasons can be functional, dysfunctional, or eufunctional (Merton, 1956). Nor do functions merely make social events intelligible. They also state how any event contributes positively or negatively to the maintenance or realization of some state of affairs. It follows that a functional account is a distinctive way of accounting for phenomena, not equivalent to any of the three standard forms of explanation, though whether explanation can occur in the fullest sense using only functional categories is another question.

2. Does structural-functional theory in fact explain? The answer to this question is, by most accounts of explanation, no. Strictly speaking, structural-functional theory is really not an empirical theory at all.

All versions of what constitutes an adequate explanation share certain requirements. The primary feature of all empirical theories, whatever the explanatory form adopted, is that they be capable of falsification. This does not mean that every proposition in a theory must itself be capable of factual verification. Many theoretical propositions are constructs which are taken as given for other propositions which *can* be confirmed or disconfirmed. That the universe is finite may be presumed for a variety of theories without serious thought that it can be adequately confirmed. On a more modest plane, certain causal relationships are often assumed as the basis for other factual statements. One also can scarcely imagine how to confirm or disconfirm the various statements about rational behavior scattered throughout the social sciences. Theoretical statements of this sort do not, in themselves, explain anything. They are, however, connected to statements which do offer explanations, and they are dismissible (if not falsifiable) in that experience is decisive in their retention.[2]

The primary propositions of structural-functional analysis are like many of the theoretical constructs indicated above in the sense that they are not falsifiable, but they are unlike these theoretical constructs in that one cannot envisage how they might be dismissed with experience. Consider the range of functional propositions which outline the input and output functions of a political system (see above). No amount of data can bring about the rejection of these statements, for they are simply not empirical propositions. They are, taken charitably, methodological rules. The primary function of such propositions is to define the categories in which data will be gathered, which is an a priori task. This task is, however, more than metaphorical. Functional propositions connect to factual statements in distinct ways. Data on voting, for example, may be clearly conceptualized as an input function. Other conceptualizations are possible, of course, but this does not affect the functional view of voting. Most discussion on the explanatory power of functional theory fails to keep separate the dimensions of structure and function. Factual statements are statements about structures, and explain relationships between states of affairs. Functional statements are definitional propositions which provide for the conceptualization of social events in one way instead of another. Functional propositions hence do not *explain* any events. They tell us how to view events. They are of the order of, say, theoretical categories in psychology (for example, the ego-id-superego trio of Freudian theory). One does not ask whether they constitute good explanations. The proper question is "What other view of events will replace them?"

3. The third criticism of structural-functional analysis grows out of, and on occasion precedes, the first two. It is the assertion that the concepts in functional theory are at such a high level of abstraction that they cannot be operationalized in any satisfactory manner. At first glance this certainly seems true. One need not look far to find examples. Parsons's pattern maintenance, Easton's gatekeeper function, and Almond's interest aggregation all seem sufficiently loose and abstract to make the point. Yet the point can be made another way upon closer inspection. It is not that these concepts cannot be stated in ways which allow for measurement. It is that they can be measured in so *many* ways.

2. See Karl R. Popper for the most famous presentation of the falsification thesis, primarily *The Logic of Scientific Discovery* (1959) and *Conjectures and Refutations* (1963).

It is helpful to view social concepts as falling on a continuum marked by levels of abstraction. The lowest level contains words which have a fairly specific factual content. At this level might be found terms such as "stamp," "vote," "phone," etc., in Western social systems. (The qualifying clause locating these terms in one part of the world is necessary simply because whether factual content is specified or not turns on social convention. One can easily imagine social contexts where not a single one of the examples has any indisputable factual meaning.) The second level contains terms which are not factually specified, but need only indices for the specification. An example of such a term is "unemployment." This term can be measured in numerous ways, depending upon the purpose of the measurement. Yet the measurement can be carried out with precision once the purpose is established. The third level of abstraction is characterized by terms which need both dimensions and indices before measurement can be effected. Often, but not always, these terms carry a great deal of emotive content. An example of such a word is "freedom." It is interesting to note that this word does not need factual specification to function importantly in the discourse of politics.

In formal logic a set of transformation rules would be available to derive a secondary meaning from a primary term. But the connections between third-level political terms like "freedom" and possible instances of the term are tenuous in the extreme. Part of the problem is the general ambiguity of such words in the context of political behavior. The apparent disjunction between how people define "freedom" in the abstract and in terms of factual content has been documented in the literature (e.g., Stouffer, 1955; Campbell et al., 1960). But the spectacle of cognitive dissonance does not exhaust the problems of measurement. It is, as indicated earlier, a two-step process. While a less general term like "employment" can be elaborated with indices like relevant populations, distinctions between those who do and do not seek work, and the like, a term like "freedom" must be translated into less general terminology before indices can be established. In this case, one would identify dimensions of the word, such as self-satisfaction, autonomy in securing goals, and so on. Then these dimensions would be given indices for purposes of measurement.

The point to these brief remarks on operationalizing language is that the vocabulary of structural-functional analysis, like any more-or-less descriptive language, can be measured if we are prepared to go through the necessary steps. The abstract quality of functional concepts may result in conflicting interpretations of relevant dimensions and—even—indices. But dissensus in measurement is not equivalent to no measurement at all. We can measure, though what it is we mean to measure is open to the fourth criticism.

4. The fourth criticism is directed at the type of status of the conceptualization of "politics" which provides that subsystem we call "the political system." It focuses on an issue vital because of its centrality to structural-functional theory in political inquiry: the entirety of what we mean by "politics" as a reasonably distinct species of action. Two prominent conceptualizations of "politics" have surfaced in recent years, one concentrating on "function," the other on "structure." We shall see more clearly the limitations and possibilities of structural-functional theory if we critically focus on each conceptualization in turn.

POLITICS AS "THE AUTHORITATIVE ALLOCATION OF VALUES"

When David Easton published *The Political System* in 1953, political science was viewed as a discipline in search of a definition. One problem with the field of inquiry which now seems outstanding was the tendency of many political analysts to pick out some institution and claim for it the proper locus for political inquiry. It is easy now to see how such an approach is deficient; for whatever institution is chosen as the point of a study, a case can always be made, on slightly different facts, for a rival institution. For example, if Congress (or its committees) are selected, someone can always lay claim for the presidency as the controlling factor in political life; if the presidency, then someone can argue that a "power elite" is the *eminence gris* behind the office of the chief executive. The simplest way to resolve disputes over institutions is to ask a different question: "What is it that institutions *do* that makes them candidates for political study?" With such a question, we are not asking the older, institutional question, "What is the *structure* for the expression of politics?" but, rather, "What is the expressing *function* of politics?"

The specification of politics as "the authoritative allocation of values" is an attempt to identify the defining function of political life (Easton, 1953, 1957). It defines that which all political systems do whatever the arrangements might be that carry out the defining function. All forms of government, dictatorships as well as democracies, seem to allocate values authoritatively. Perhaps of even more importance, it is no longer necessary to argue which institution defines political life. We will now be able to look for the function of politics, "the authoritative allocation of values," and study politics in whatever institution performs this function. If the function is performed by the presidency, good. If, however, it is performed by General Motors, fine also. In such a case we will simply take General Motors as the effective political unit in the society. Not only does this functional emphasis avoid criticisms that the wrong social unit has been chosen, but it also provides for a conceptualization of politics as a system of actions:

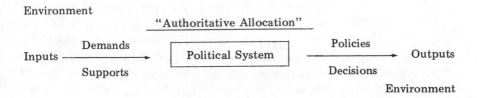

It is important to see that shifting one's focus from institutions to functions also means adjusting the lens of one's viewing equipment: politics is now not a static unit, but rather a flow of a certain *type* of action which may occur in any of a variety of social structures. Demands and supports are transformed into policies and decisions by means of actions which authoritatively allocate values, a function which many institutions can carry out. If we set aside for the moment the issue of whether there is *any* single defining function, or characteristic, of political life, then the question we want to be sure of answering correctly is "Does the 'authoritative allocation of values' adequately define politics?" One helpful way of answering this question is to look carefully at each word in Easton's definition and try to determine if it covers all, or a substantial slice, of political life.

1. **Authoritative.** Easton allows as how a policy is authoritative when "people feel they must or ought to obey it." One difficulty which can be pointed out immediately with this specification is that *feelings* may have little to do with some political events. In the strongest traditions of political life, social customs may govern behavior more effectively than any overt directive from political leaders. Preindustrial societies, indeed the politics of many small rural towns in America, can be seen as directed by the authority of "Things have always been done this way." In such cases, policies may be carried out from habit, not from any feeling about what must or ought to be done. We must also allow for the unintended consequences of action. It is commonly acknowledged today that many of

the Head Start programs ambitiously developed for education in the 1960s had unforeseen and unplanned effects. If we view policy as the outcome of a decision process, then practices can authoritatively govern behavior in a way having little to do with how people perceive (feel about) these policies in the shortrun.

A second difficulty in "authoritative" is with the idea of *obedience*. Certainly many policies do elicit "obey-type" responses. The use of federal troops, for example, disposes the average citizen to comply by heeding the explicit or implicit imperative a policy supported by force represents. But other policies are not imperative in form and do not require obedience for compliance. Look at the language of the Civil Rights Act of 1964. Two main provisions of the act prohibit (1) unequal standards in voter registration procedures, and (2) discrimination or segregation in public accomodations on the grounds of race, color, religion, or national origin. Further, the attorney general is required to act on behalf of any person denied equal access to public accomodations. Fines and imprisonment are cited as modes of enforcement.

Certainly this act contains strong rules which registrars, owners of public accomodations, members of school boards, and employers (among others) have to obey, but the act does not require minority groups not in those categories to do anything. The law is more accurately seen, from the perspective of *these* groups, as providing access and opportunity, not as issuing commands which they must obey. Similarly, the extension of the franchise to women in 1920 did not require women to vote anymore than the legalization of abortion today requires women to have abortions. Such actions can be called rule-establishing, or rule-permissive, policies. They either (a) change the framework of politics by establishing new rules and/or new players, or (b) provide the conditions for doing certain things. In neither case are the appropriate responses of *all* citizens accurately described by the word "obey."

2. **Allocation.** Is politics always a form of allocation? When we allocate items, we distribute them among recipients. Distribution is a common enough theme in contemporary politics. It is even easy to see the political system as primarily concerned with distribution as it extracts resources (through taxes, primarily) and spends monies. Such policies as social security, welfare payments, poverty programs, aid to education, urban reform, and many others, are "strong" allocationist programs: they take resources from some segments of society and distribute them to others. But other policies do not square so easily with allocationist formulas. Regulatory policies like civil rights laws, law enforcement, electoral reform—these are not allocationist except in a marginal way. They seem, more precisely, to

be directed at ensuring conformity with certain rules rather than with allocating resources. Other political actions do not seem to fit the idea of allocation at all: establishing roles and offices at all levels of government, organizing groups to maintain social practices (like political parties, congressional committees), reinforcing symbolic values.

Two types of public issue are not even logical candidates for allocation: (1) public goods, and (2) ethical issues which must be resolved within a public policy framework. A "pure" public good is generally defined as any good which is (a) nonexcludable, meaning that it is consumable by everybody if available at all, and (b) supply-irreducible, meaning that consumption does not diminish supply (Samuelson, 1954–55). Pure public goods may be a rare commodity, but many goods either approximate the "pure" standard, or are characterized with one of the two defining attributes of pure public goods. Clean air, for example, is a close·instance of a pure public good. All in a geographical region can consume it whenever it is available and the supply, while not technically inexhaustible, is only marginally diminished by consumption. National security policies often represent nonexcludability, for ensuring the defenses of an entire society will profit all within the society no matter who finances or arranges the defenses. Now, whatever we want to say about the distributive efforts required to make public goods available (with some expending more time and resources than others), such goods are not strongly allocatable in the normal sense of making things available to some while denying them to others. Certainly public goods are unlike, say, welfare payments, which *do* distribute society's resources. A public good, unlike a distributive good, is available to all once it has been made available at all.

The second kind of issue not adequately described by "allocation" is that taken as ethical. Frequently, ethical issues are not within the public domain. Whether one is obligated to attend church services every Sunday may be a proper topic for moral and/or religious regulation, but it is in many societies a matter of indifference to public authorities. Some moral issues, however, intertwine with legal rules. Killing is typically enjoined by both moral and legal rules, though it may be prohibited for different reasons in each case (against God's law in the first instance, say, and contrary to social stability in the second). On occasion moral issues require public resolution in order to secure sanction for certain practices. Abortion is a moral issue currently supported and condemned by those of opposed moral convictions, but involving as it does the joint actions of doctors and hospital staffs as well as patients, the law must stipulate what is permitted on the issue. Now again, whatever the distributive effects for a society of a pro or con abortion policy, disputes over the legalization of abortion are not primarily concerned with distribution, but rather with the issue of whether abortion is desirable as a public practice. Resolving these disputes is not a question of allocating values, or even of choosing one allocative arrangement of values over another, but of settling on what *ought* to be valued by the society on this issue.

It is also helpful to maintain a distinction between maximization (or production) and allocation. Economists are ever prone to use pie slicing as an analogy for allocationist policies. If one group gets a larger slice of the pie, then the others must get less. In politics, such activities are often called zero-sum, for gains to some require commensurate losses to others. But, while the idea of pie slicing is excellent for understanding family dinners and even many forms of politics, the *size* of the social pie can also be a issue for political action. Government incentives to businesses to increase production, for example, may unavoidably favor some groups at the expense of others, but the primary intention of such policies may be only to increase the resources of a society, something not even indirectly intended by primarily allocationist policies like welfare programs. Increasing the productive capacity of a society may even affect purely distributive policies, for if the pie gets larger as it is being cut, then losses to another group may be compensated by gains measured from a previous point in time. Given that political societies can maximize goods as well as distribute them, then "allocationist politics" seems to capture only one dimension of political activity.

3. Values. One of the more difficult words to interpret in any language is "value," and these difficulties are no less pronounced in political discourse about values. Political policy can allocate values in two prominent ways: (a) by rearranging the attitudes of citizens which express values, or (b) by distributing the things which are valued by citizens. In (a), policy will be aimed at changing or maintaining the value sets of a population, as might be the case if a government wants to "educate" its citizens about a policy regarded as necessary on grounds other than simple consensus. On (b), policy can distribute the goods and services which are the favored objects of attitudes. Distributing "things" are among the more visible actions of a political system. That family of policies roughly grouped under "urban affairs" is an example of "thing" allocation. On the assumption that houses, public and private, are items of value, the variety of programs sponsored by the Federal Housing Administration and the Urban Renewal Administration are attempts to allocate valued items.

Still a third sense of "values," however, is not covered by either (a) or (b). This is the sense in which values refer to disputes over what *ought* to be valued. An allocationist formula is most comfortably fitted to what is valued, either the expression of values in attitudes or the range of items held in favor. Authentic disputes over what ought to be held as valuable will not be equivalent to efforts at attitude change or maintenance, or to distributions of valued things. They will be actions aimed at clarification, at settling on primary standards and rules, and at reaching basic conclusions about the "good life." Public debates over euthanasia, for example, are evaluative activities of singular importance for medical policies, but unlike the more familiar types of allocationist politics in not being action aimed at distributing anything.

So: politics as "the authoritative allocation of values" is effective in relocating the concept of politics in the area of *function* rather than particular *institutions*. But the relocation carries several liabilities, primarily (a) an interpretation of "authoritative" that concentrates on what people feel they must or ought to obey, which excludes such events as traditional behavior and unintended consequences, extreme coercion, rule-establishing or rule-permissive actions, bargaining; (b) a fix on "allocation" at the expense of regulatory actions, criteria-establishing actions, an accomodation of public goods, and maximization policies; and (c) an insensitivity to "values" as what *ought* to be valued in society.

POLITICS AS "AUTHORITY PATTERNS"

A second prominent conceptualization of "politics" has been developed around the notion of authority patterns as the *structure* of politics. Harry Eckstein has suggested that political relations are profitably viewed as a subset of asymmetric relations (Eckstein, 1973). An asymmetric relation, for Eckstein, is roughly comparable to one where "someone affects more than he is affected, controls more than he is controlled, and/or gets more of what is allocated" (1973, p. 1146). In short, asymmetry favors one party to the transaction more than the other party. It is obvious that not all asymmetries can count as political relations. When a father orders his infant son to bed in the evening no political act has been consummated. Naturally some might maintain that *all* asymmetries are potentially political, perhaps even overtly political. A thoroughgoing Marxist, for example, might well maintain that family relations have explosive implications for political systems. But for those like Eckstein who want to calibrate the concept of politics more finely, such an extension casts the net too widely: the differences between events covered by the class of all asymmetries is so heterogeneous as to be useless for effective research. If, for example, we say that the actions of a president in vetoing a bill and the actions of a father in sending his son to bed are both political, and we have no other device in our concept of politics to reflect any differences between the two actions, then the conceptualization is spread too thin to accommodate the rich variation of social, and political, life.

In order to respect social variation, Eckstein suggests that only some types of asymmetrical relation properly count as political, specifically those which are (1) in social units, (2) in hierarchically ordered segments, and (3) concerned with the direction of these social units. Other types of asymmetries, those *not* characterized in these three ways, are not political. Those asymmetries which *do* have these characteristics are political, and are designated by Eckstein with the appellation "authority patterns."

1. A social unit for Eckstein has several features. First, it is a collective individual, meaning that it is not constituted by a single individual but by "corporate" people—collections of people organized in accordance with some principle, as for example General Motors, the Democratic Party, Syracuse University, and so on. Second, the activity characteristic of a social unit is recurrent and patterned. It is the transaction that occurs, in Eckstein's turn of phrase, not between a customer buying an item from a clerk, but between employers and employees. Third, the members of the social unit tend to self-identify in terms of the unit, much as a congressional representative will perceive himself as a member of the corporate body we call the U.S. Congress. Fourth, social units can have goals distinct from the goals of the individuals comprising the unit. For example, if the U.S. Senate votes 60-40 in favor of increasing the minimum wage, then the Senate's goal (increase the wage) is at variance with the goal of the forty-member minority (do not increase the wage).

Social units can even have goals to which, in a technical sense, *none* of the members of the unit subscribes (though Eckstein does not develop this). This is the case with the compromise candidate. Consider a three-member group with preferences for candidates A, B, C, and D. The ranking according to vote and weight for each of three voters is as follows:

	Voter 1	Voter 2	Voter 3
(4)	A	C	D
(3)	B	B	B
(2)	C	D	A
(1)	D	A	C

An electorate arranged in terms of these preferences will give candidate B nine votes, candidates A, C, and D seven votes apiece. Candidate B is the "choice" of the group, even though no member of the group has chosen him. In such cases, it is possible to say that the social unit (the electorate) has a goal (the selection of candidate B to represent it) which is shared by no individual member of the unit (voter 1, 2, or 3). Whether social units can really "choose" or advance goals is a complicated topic which needn't be pursued here. It is enough to understand that the outcomes of social processes need not coincide with the intentions of the individuals comprising the social process.

Finally, social units for Eckstein involve the "differentiated allocation of roles or division of labor attuned to the unit's goals, together with definition of tasks, duties, responsibilities, and rights appropriate to the roles" (1973, p. 1150). Put in another language, social units are not uniform patterns of action but are rather constituted by a variety of actions related in some way to the outcomes of social activity. A bank, for example, will typically be a distributive arrangement of social efforts, people doing a variety of things, oriented toward the goals of profit and, possibly, service.

2. Hierarchically ordered segments of a social unit are those in which some segments are, on a variety of grounds, regarded as "higher" than others. Social units with hierarchically ordered segments are stratified, arranged in terms of ascending, or descending, parts. An organization chart describes stratification in many businesses. But less formal relations can also be stratified, those within traditional patriarchal families, for example, where the father is considered head of the household. Families with recent views on lateral, more nearly equalitarian, relationships may not be stratified. In Eckstein's view, only hierarchically ordered segments of a social unit are fertile conceptual ground for political relationships.

3. The direction of social units is a type of social action with four variations: (1) the general management of the unit, an activity which includes defining the social unit's goals and the means to attain these goals, regulating conduct, assigning roles, coordination of member performance; (2) the recognition of role incumbents with special rights and responsibilities; (3) the issuance of directives, which are prescriptions backed by sanctions, negative and positive; and (4) the activation of perceptions of legitimacy, those special moral qualities that justify rights, privileges, and primitive behavior otherwise deemed immoral or amoral.

The study of politics is, on the view described here, properly aimed at authority patterns, defined as asymmetric relations among hierarchically ordered members of a social unit that involves the direction of the units. Does this specification of "politics" provide a stronger conceptualization than "the authoritative allocation of values"?

Advantages

1. Concentrating on "authority patterns" has the initial advantage of restricting the scope of politics without yet encountering the older problems which institutional studies occasioned. It is not, for example, the "state" which is identified with "authority patterns," or any particular institution, but a type of structure. This type of structure can be seen as the equivalent of state organizations even where such organizations do not exist, but is not a particular institution of politics. Thus the type of error risked in the identification of, say, a presidency or a congress as the locus of politics, where the wrong institution may have been selected and even a cultural bias introduced into the analysis, is avoided with the reliance on "authority patterns." On the other hand, the scope of politics has been narrowed from the purely functional emphasis of "authoritative allocation." "Authority patterns" denotes not just a type of action, as does "authoritative allocation," but a type of action with special characteristics (in social units, in hierarchically ordered segments, concerned with unit direction). So while a functional specification covers an extremely broad field in its concern only with action-types, the accumulation of structural features that "authority patterns" represents more accurately focuses on the "political" dimensions of action.

2. A second advantage in using "authority patterns" is that it introduces the important concept of public, or corporate, persons in the specification of politics. "Collective" individuals are unlike single, or private, individuals in important ways. Social wholes, for example, are not "born," and do not die, like individuals. The pathology of the state is not an appropriate topic for physicians of human physiology (or psychology). More important, however, is that a range of actions is attributable to the social whole which cannot be attributed to individuals. Men and women as individuals may kill, for example, but only societies can go to war. Or again: societies may kill as retributive punishment, but individuals may not. To see "politics" as an expression of functional relationships obscures this important collective or corporate sense of political action. A conceptualization which, like "authority patterns," introduces social units into the sphere of politics will have the power to recognize the fact that political transactions are often between public rather than private figures.

3. Still a third advantage is that the kinds of activity described by "authority patterns" are broader in scope than the more narrow imperative model assumed in "authoritative allocation." Statements that cover general management activities, the recognition of rights

and responsibilities, activation of perceptions of legitimacy, as well as more explicit guides to action, are more realistic descriptions of the scope of political life than the simpler account of authoritative policies as those which people must or ought to obey. A more complete sense of the variety of politics is set out with the interpretation of "directives" for social units, including the rule-establishing and rule-permissive actions (franchise extension, creation of offices, roles) not adequately handled by the idea of obedience to commands.

Disadvantages

1. The most pressing disadvantage of the "authority patterns" view of politics is its inability to accommodate symmetrical transactions. A symmetrical transaction, reversing the terms of asymmetries found in "authority patterns," is roughly comparable to any transaction where all parties are equally affected, no one controls more than he is controlled, and goods are evenly distributed. Bargaining transactions qualify. One reason that New York City officials have bargaining sessions with city employees is that city officials cannot successfully control them. A settlement of grievances is required which all parties can accept voluntarily, not through dominance by one party over the other. Symmetrical transactions are those typically studied under the rubric of political economy, where exchange rather than simple control characterizes the events. Such transactions are obviously vital in politics, and that the "authority patterns" version of politics cannot cover them presents a glum liability for this conceptualization of political action.

It is also important to avoid thinking that even the rough characteristics of both asymmetries and symmetries, those dealing with (a) affect, (b) controls, and (c) distribution, must all be present in the same way and with the same magnitude each and every time there is one or another of the two types of transaction. Bargaining, for example, is clearly a case of equal control, or even the absence of control, but the outcome of a bargain may favor some parties more than others (some getting more goods than others). Again depending on the outcome, some parties in a bargain may be more affected by the transaction than others, especially if they feel more intensely about the issues at stake, or if their interests are more vitally involved. Similarly, even an extreme asymmetrical transaction, say a máster-slave relationship, may be one of complete control without realizing the other two rough characteristics in the same way. Though perhaps unusual, one can imagine the authoritarian actor, in some situations, as being more affected by the fact of control than the subordinate who is controlled. If absolute power corrupts absolutely, then the corrosive effects of controlling another may be more intense and, as a result, more decisive for the power holder as his control is greater. What makes such a situation intelligible is the possibility of effects resulting *from* control, as distinct from the effects *of* control. A slave is affected as he is controlled. But power may also have an effect on the slaveholder, a corrupting one if Lord Acton is to be believed. Less difficult to imagine, and perhaps more common, is the reversal of benefits in asymmetries. Obviously a ruler may rule in the interests of those he controls, either through beneficence, miscalculation, or some perverse combination of these.

2. The moral to be drawn from the possibility of overlapping characteristics is that we have a second disadvantage for the "authority patterns" conceptualization: in addition to the inability of the specification to handle the large areas of political life set out as "symmetries," it also only imperfectly reflects some finer distinctions in politics. Instead of using (a) affect, (b) controls, and (c) distribution as a single group of features representing (1) "authority patterns" if they are asymmetrically arranged, or (2) symmetrical transactions otherwise, it seems better to concentrate on one, *control*, as the decisive distinction between asymmetries and symmetries. This concentration on "control" then allows that the *type* of transaction, asymmetrical (control by one, some, over others) versus symmetrical (parity of control, or no control), is distinct from the *outcome* of transactions (affect, distribution of goods).

3. A third disadvantage of the "authority patterns" view is the minimal attention paid to implicit rules as a directive force in political affairs. Implicit rules can be of various types. The strongest type in the literature of political theory is "tradition," where the norms or customs of a society actually direct behavior, though no one in the society may be aware of such rules. The anthropologist Claude Lévi-Strauss has identified "kinship rules," which effectively govern behavior though no member of a society may be able to state these rules. Among these rules is the incest taboo, which is both natural and cultural (Korn, 1973). It generates formal rules like "Each member of the society is assigned a marriage type" (Kemeny, Snell, and Thompson, 1957). Such rules can be effectively seen as causal antecedents for behavior, but they can easily remain unconscious directives for the society's members. If we are serious about conceptualizing the full scope of political life, we must allow unconscious rules, or traditions, a strong status in directive theories of society.

4. A fourth disadvantage of "authority patterns" is the indifference of the phrase to conditions of no-authority. While we may want

to view the terms "authority" and "authoritative" as necessary for governing activities, the various senses of "politics" can easily extend to nongoverning actions. When candidates vie for convention votes in state primaries, they are engaged in nongoverning political actions. Such activities seem analogous to types of game, those consisting of opponents making a series of tactical, or even strategic, moves in response to each other's actions, and with a payoff attached to the outcome of the game. Unlike such symmetrical transactions as bargaining, no one is getting anyone to do anything, except in the marginal sense as such action is instrumental to winning. The goal of such games is securing the payoff, not in any primary sense controlling or directing the behavior of other players. When politics is like a competitive game, with autonomous players intent on winning, the phrase "authority patterns" seems particularly inappropriate as a description; for one of the conditions of competitive games is that ability and chance determine outcomes, not authority.

5. A final disadvantage of "authority patterns" is the inability of the concept to handle singular events. In one sense it may be unfair to indict a conceptualization for ignoring a type of action while praising the concept's capacity for covering the opposite type of action; for singular actions may be seen as the other side of the coin representing the collective and patterned dimensions of social units. But while corporate and patterned actions may figure heavily in politics, a calculation strongly supported by the fact that social action *is* typically recurrent and patterned, singular events can be important politically as well. Consider for the moment the spectacle of assassinations. If we accept the conclusions of the Warren Commission, then Lee Harvey Oswald was the lone assassin of President John F. Kennedy. No corporate or collective body was author of the assassination. No recurrent or patterned activity was involved, indeed its very singularity (at that time in American history) gave it its stunning quality. Yet the assassination was surely a political act. Even the word "assassination" has come to have a political connotation, ascribing political dimensions to the word "murder."

What we have in singular events are possibilities for politics not exhausted by the idea of a social unit. Assassinations are social events. They *may* also be part of a social pattern. If insurance companies, for example, can calculate in actuarial tables the losses which violent crimes bring to clients, then there is no reason to think that the violent crime of assassination could not also form a recurrent activity (as the later events of the 1960s in America seemed to suggest). Murdering the leader of a country may even take the form of institutionalized political change, substituting for more prosaic methods like elections. But, on the other hand, assassinations are still political events even if they are *not* social patterns. If, as hypothesis, the human race had learned of assassination from Aristotle's discussion of tyrannicide in the *Politics*, and if no assassination had as a matter of mundane fact ever taken place in human history before the events of November 22, 1963, in Dallas, Texas, the murder of President Kennedy would still have been an obvious political act.

Again, as with the earlier inspections of politics, the rich complexity of political life imposes additional distinctions on our conceptualization. Assassins are public figures, institutional in the sense that the political quality of the event is indifferent to who occupies the role, or even the motives and intentions of the person who is the assassin. If Marina Oswald, Oswald's wife, had killed Kennedy, the political dimensions of the action would have been, all things considered, roughly comparable. If a jealous husband had shot John Kennedy because Kennedy was the lover of his wife, the action still would have been an assassination (since it would have been impossible to shoot John Kennedy, lover, and not—at that time—also shoot John Kennedy, president). But institutions, marking off public events, need not be recurrent in fact or represent corporate bodies in fact. The fact of an assassination can be a singular event, done by one person and never repeated, and therefore as unlike the recurrent patterns of employer relationships to customers as any two events can be. Yet singular events can be political in all senses in which patterned events can be: each can direct behavior, affect numerous people, change or maintain institutional arrangements, allocate goods, and so on. What political events seem to require in our conceptualizations is the reflection of *both* singular events *and* events in a social unit (where they are collective and recurrent).

We have, then, in the use of "authority patterns" a mix of advantages and disadvantages. The primary advantages are (1) that the specification is more precise than *functional* definitions in focusing on a type of *structure*; (2) that public, or corporate, actors are introduced; and (3) that the scope of the specification extends beyond the imperative model of politics. The primary disadvantages are (1) that the specification cannot accommodate symmetrical relationships, thus excluding such obvious candidates for political action as bargaining transactions; (2) that some ambiguity occurs in the failure to single out *control* from *affect* and *distribution* in distinguishing symmetries from asymmetries; (3) that minimal attention is paid to implicit rules; (4) that the defining terms are indifferent to conditions of no-authority (conditions vital to "game" accounts of politics); (5) and that singular events are ignored.

POLITICS: THE POSSIBILITY OF A GENERAL THEORY

One important implication of these critiques of two prominent conceptualizations of politics, the one functional and the other structural, is that "politics" may be a term so heterogenous that no set of necessary and sufficient conditions can be identified for the application of the term to experience. In effect, a taxonomic "definition" of politics, consisting in the identification of a single property shared by all events we are warranted in calling "political," may be contrary to ordinary political events. We may have instead a natural variety of political life so rich in internal differences that several senses of the "political" may be required. Such a cluster of items may have to be organized on several basic dimensions, not on only one. The most likely chart, on the basis of the discussion here, would be along the lines of (1) species of behavior, (2) conditions of behavior, (3) kinds of good, and (4) kinds of actor. Then an outline can be drawn up to map the fuller scope of political life suggested up to now.

I.   Species of Behavior
    A. Generic Forms
        1. Prescriptive direction (including power, in the traditional sense), defined as A getting B to do X by means of a command or recommendation. *Example:* President Dwight Eisenhower forcing compliance of school integration in Arkansas in 1956 by the use of federal troops.
        2. Bargaining transactions, defined as A and B getting each other to do X by means of a binding agreement to which each party assents. *Example:* The wage settlement between Mayor John Lindsay and New York City sanitation workers in 1968.
        3. Game tactics, defined as a series of actions by which two or more opponents, A and B, under conditions of uncertainty and risk with a payoff to one or more players defining the outcome of the actions. *Example:* Any presidential primary election.
        4. Noncognitive direction, defined as any direction or constraint of A and B by habits, customs, tradition in the general sense, or the congenital endowments of political actors. *Example:* Lévi-Strauss's kinship patterns.
    B. Locus Forms
        1. Criteria-establishing, defined as A and/or B establishing or maintaining any basic rules constituting political life. *Examples:* Constitutional amendments, Supreme Court

interpretations, franchise extension, or, specifically, the U.S. Civil Rights Act of 1964.
2. Contextual-establishing, defined as A and/or B changing or maintaining the internal conditions of political life. *Examples:* Assignment of offices and duties, providing options, organizing groups, or, specifically, rule-permissive actions like the New York State abortion law.
C. Resource Forms
1. Maximizing, defined as any effort to increase goods and resources in society. *Example:* Tax rebates to heavy industry.
2. Allocationist, defined as any effort to distribute goods and resources in society. *Example:* Welfare policies.

These three types of political behavior, A, B, and C, are presented neither as exhaustive accounts of politics nor as mutually exclusive categories. Variations on any of them can yield new classifications. For example, representative forms, say a fiduciary relationship, may transform game tactics dramatically. And certainly many of the categories can be combined in interesting ways. Bargaining, for example, can aim at either maximization or allocation. (Others do not combine happily with each other; for example, noncognitive direction is inconsistent with game tactics.) The outline simply expresses some broad distinctions in political life which the single-phrase, or taxonomic, approach to defining politics cannot recognize.

II. Conditions of Behavior
A. Authority versus no-authority, defined as (respectively) the presence versus absence of control by one party(s) over another.
B. Scarcity versus abundance, defined as (respectively) the absence versus availability of goods with respect to demand.
C. Certainty versus uncertainty, defined as (respectively) the necessary versus contingent relationship of outcomes to the actions which lead to outcomes.
D. Risk versus no-risk, defined as (respectively) the possibility of loss versus the absence of loss possibilities.

One important point to notice about these conditions is that different types of action are sometimes (a) defined by conditions, and (b) rational or irrational in various conditions. On (a), for example, conditions of (A) no-authority, (B) uncertain outcomes, and (D) risk define that species of behavior we call game tactics. On (b), for example, the resource action of maximizing will be more rational in conditions of scarcity, that of allocating will be more rational in conditions of abundance. These conditions, then, can be viewed as identifying some basic settings in which political behavior occurs.

III. Kinds of Goods
  A. Public, defined as any good which is (1) nonexcludable, meaning that it is consumable by everyone if available at all, and (2) supply-irreducible, meaning that consumption does not reduce supply. *Example:* National security.
  B. Competitive, defined as any good which is (1) excludable, meaning that it can be consumed by some at the expense of others when available, and (2) supply-reducible, meaning that consumption does reduce supply. *Example:* Automobiles, houses.
  C. Ethical, meaning any good which represents an issue of what *ought* to be the practices of a society.

It is an easy matter to see that this typology of goods provides overlaps between A-B and C: either public or competitive goods can be, or lead to, ethical issues. On the other hand, some ethical issues, like that of abortion, are not easily categorized as either a public or competitive good (and in fact can be considered as a "good" only by considering social practices as "goods"). The most helpful way to see this typology is not as a set of mutually exclusive categories, but as an outline of the (sometimes overlapping) forms social goods can assume.

IV. Kinds of Actor
  A. Egoist versus altruist, defined as (respectively) self-interested versus other-interested actors.
  B. Perfect versus imperfect knowledge, defined as (respectively) situationally complete or transcendent knowledge versus situationally incomplete knowledge.
  C. Rational versus nonrational, defined as (respectively) having the capacity to deliberate on relevant considerations and act in accord with rules versus not having the capacity to deliberate on relevant considerations and act in accord with rules.
  D. Representative versus nonrepresentative, defined as (respectively) acting for another versus acting for oneself.
  E. Corporate versus individual, defined as (respectively) a collective (group, organization) versus a single-unit actor.

These characteristics set out what kinds of actor play the political game. The characteristics mesh with, and reflect on, other components in the cluster of items. For example, imperfect knowledge is a state of mind paralleling the conditions of uncertainty required for gaming situations. The actor characteristics also reflect the diversity of politics, where either side of any of the paired characteristics may be found among political figures. And, as with the other items in the cluster, the characteristics are not mutually exclusive, for, as we all know, representative actors can be both rational and nonrational.

Generally, this outline of some dimensions of political life reflects a diversity any student of politics can observe. Political behavior can cover a variety of items, including regulation, bargaining, assigning roles and offices, extraction of resources, maximizing, allocating, changing the rules or conditions of the game, and other actions which both overlap with each other and extend to forms probably impossible to catalog exhaustively, and certainly impossible to describe with a single-phrase taxonomic "definition" of politics. This variety of political life also provides for a variety of theoretical approaches to politics. Perhaps the most important distinction in approaches is between a power-oriented approach (control, authority) and an exchange-oriented approach (bargaining). Though supporters of each approach often (though not always—witness Eckstein's concession that symmetrical relations are beyond the pale of his "authority patterns") try to reduce the opposition to their own terms, it seems more reasonable to adopt a nonreductive approach and investigate political events in terms of their apparent diversity rather than by means of some imposed uniformity.

A recognition of variety should not, however, be taken as an assumption that distinctions always emerge in terms of separate events. Even a family of units can converge on a single political experience. Look, for example, at the number of items represented in a criminal trial. The defense lawyer (a) represents his client, (b) is an egoist in earning his fee and maintaining his reputation, but (c) is operating to ensure the interests of his client, (d) opposes the prosecuting attorney in game conditions (uncertain outcome, risk, imperfect knowledge, payoffs), (e) yet is constrained in his actions by regulations on procedures and evidence, (f) can bargain with the opposition (plea bargaining), (g) but is subject to the imperatives issued by the judge (backed by coercion, e.g., contempt citations), and so on. A law court is not a microcosm of the political arena. But the example of a convergence of political dimensions suggests that any political experience may be a mixed and complicated combination of family items.

The effects of such variety in "politics" on structural-functional theory is, in two senses, decisive.

1. If no single-phase, or taxonomic, conceptualization of "politics" is possible, then we do not have a species of political action which will allow a single subsystem of politics. We have several subsystems (if we maintain in any way the idea of a "system"), perhaps operating at different logical levels. Each of the four main categories of political items—behavior, conditions, goods, actors—can provide a type of political system, and even the distinctions within these categories can yield system types. For example, an imperative system of politics is unlike a system conceptualized on the notion of gaming tactics. The attempt in both functional and structural approaches to "define" politics in taxonomic terms seems doomed in the face of the natural heterogeneity of politics; and, if doomed, then the idea of politics as a subsystem of action conceptualized along such a definition also must fail. There is, in short, not *a* political system, but at least *several* political systems, if any "system" of politics can be said to occur at all.

2. The idea of a "system" of political action is itself jeopardized. A system, let us recall, is a set of interacting elements in a state of mutual dependence. The idea of a "set" in systems theory complements the taxonomic approach to defining. A set, defined formally, is a number of items associated for any reason. But to form a system the elements in a set must be related to one another in some dependent way, so that what affects some elements in the set will affect others. Suppose, however, that we replace the taxonomic conceptualization of politics with a cluster-concept. Then political events will not share some common property, like members of a logical class, but will be grouped in what has been called a "family resemblance" way (Wittgenstein, 1953): like members of a family, several distinctive features may be distributed among the family members, so that high cheekbones, full mouths, great height, etc. may be family traits, but the distribution of the traits is not uniform. They rather crisscross in various, and even (ultimately) unconnected ways, like patterns on a quilt, so that every member of the family has one or another of the identifying features, but no one "defining" feature is shared by every member of the family. If politics is a cluster concept, and the critical discussion of the two taxonomic conceptualizations, functional *and* structural, suggests that it is, then the events covered by the term "politics" may be sufficiently heterogeneous to deny the dependent quality of a system. Like many real families, "politics" may cover a set of elements so unlike one another in important respects that what affects some members has no relationship to what affects others. We then have a "family" of political items, but not a "system."

The historical significance of this turn of affairs should not be missed. The empiricist dismissal of essential definitions, the main pillar of support for functional concepts in classical political philosophy, has finally led to the gloomy possibility that a general theory of politics on structural-functional terms is not feasible. The irony of this state of affairs will be richly appreciated by those who maintain the classical approach in contemporary political thought.

19. TOWARD A MACROSOCIOLOGY: ELEMENTS OF A THEORY OF SOCIETAL AND POLITICAL PROCESSES

Amitai Etzoni

A macrosociology is needed both on theoretical and on pragmatic grounds. Theoretically I suggest that societies and polities have *emergent* properties, which it is fruitful to treat as the subject of a distinct subtheory, macrosociology. Such a theory is not to replace general theory, which deals with the *universal* properties of all social units, from the dyad to the world community (e.g., level of integration). But both macro- and microsociology are additional tiers on the top of this shared base, one dealing with the particular properties of macrounits (e.g., nations, classes), and the other with properties of microunits (for example, family, work teams, and friendship groups). While sociological theory holds for general, micro- and macro-subtheories, history is a macroscopic process.[1] It is on this level that sociological and historical perspectives can be authentically and systematically joined.

From a pragmatic viewpoint, a disciplined study of the substantive problems of society—such as modernization, democratization, change of status relations among major collectivities, societal reallocation of wealth, and political integration of previous autonomous

Special note: This article was written during my fellowship at the Center for Advanced Study in the Behavioral Sciences. I am indebted to Sarajane Heidt, Fred DuBow, Miriam Gallaher, and Astrida Ilga Butners for comments on earlier drafts. A prior version of this article was published in *The Academy of Management Proceedings*, 27th Annual Meeting, Washington, D.C. (December 27-29, 1967), pp. 12-33. During the period in which this article was written, I benefited from a grant from the National Science Foundation (GS-1475).

1. We usually do not refer to the history of microunits; there is a distinct term for the genetic study of persons or families—"genealogies." Sometimes this is referred to as "life history" or "family history," but when the term "history" is used without additional characterization, it evokes a macrodynamic perspective. Universal elements of theory are not predicated on any specific unit. They can have a history, as part of the history of ideas of sociology, but not as part of the history of society.

units—cannot be much advanced without a systematic analysis of macroscopic factors.

The most basic distinction here, for reasons that will become evident below, is between guided and "ongoing" change, between change which is consciously directed and change which happens as a matter of course. The higher the ratio of guided change over ongoing change, the greater the danger of rebellion of instrumentality against the primacy of societal goals, and that collectivities whose vested interests rest in the realm of instruments might divert societal guidance to serve their goals. Hence, as has often been pointed out but never made the cornerstone of a sociological theory, the key problem of guided change is the development of more effective methods of societal guidance that will ensure the primacy of societal goals.

A MACROSOCIOLOGICAL PERSPECTIVE

Macrosociology Defined

I suggest that macroscopic (social) units have emergent properties above and beyond those of microscopic (social) units and beyond universal social properties. One can support this suggestion on tentative *pragmatic grounds*: let us try it out and see if it will enable us to gain some insight into substantive societal problems. One can further support the suggestion on *empirical logical grounds*: that macroscopic emergent properties account for a significant part of the variance of sociological data; i.e., explanation of those data cannot be reduced, without a significant residue (i.e., unaccounted for variance), to propositions drawing only on microscopic or universal properties. Finally, it can be supported on *logical grounds*: a three-level referent structure—of subunits, units, and supraunits—can be applied at any level of analysis, e.g., roles, families, and neighborhoods. There is in principle no reason that one cannot apply the same structure to subsocieties, societies, and suprasocieties. Thus, this differentiation is a private case of a universe of formal, hierarchical relations.

Whatever track one follows, the units of analysis need to be substantively designated. In doing so we adhere to a *functional approach* in that acts are defined as macroscopic if their consequences are macroscopic—i.e., affect the properties of macroscopic units. An act, let us say a peasant uprising, is in itself neither micro- nor macroscopic; its consequences might be both microscopic (a few families were destroyed) and macroscopic (a change of political institutions and stratification was forced). The same act might thus be studied from both viewpoints. However, because of the hierarchical nature of the concepts, while acts that have macroscopic consequences always also have microscopic ones, those with microscopic consequences may or may not have macroscopic ones. Some cutoff point in time is always to be specified because in the long run there might be consequences to the consequences that would move them from the microscopic to the macroscopic level. Macroscopic theory deals with the acts that have macroscopic consequences and with the relations of these consequences to each other, not exploiting their microscopic effects as long as they, in turn, do not have macro-consequences within the period specified.

We characterize social units according to where the majority of their consequences lie. Macroscopic units are those whose primary acts effect changes in properties of subsocieties, societies, or suprasocieties. General Motors is macroscopic for American society; the Chinese restaurant next door probably is not. Families are usually not macroscopic, but those of absolute rulers are. Units that are part of the referent framework—subsocietal, societal, and suprasocietal units—are macroscopic by definition. Small groups—such as families, teams, friendship groups—are the units of microsociology.

Two Kinds of Reductionism

Two kinds of reductionism are prevalent in the social sciences. One reduces social or political analysis to the level of a universal theory of action or to psychology. This reductionism in effect denies both sociology and political science as distinct theoretical disciplines. It is widely embraced by philosophers, anthropologists, and psychologists. Sociologists and political scientists tend naturally to profess to realize that their disciplines require a distinct theory, but their actual analyses are often—and, it seems, increasingly—psychological or draw entirely on universal variables. This is particularly common in studies that use survey data about attitudes of individuals, e.g., studies of political sociology that deal only with aggregate data about various categories of voters, explaining their voting behavior by attitudes they hold (e.g., on a conservatism-liberalism scale) or by personality variables they possess (e.g., degree of authoritarianism). The explanatory processes are clearly intrapersonal. For instance, an individual who holds one attitude will tend to hold others that are consonant because dissonant attitudes cause a psychic cost or pain; or, aggressive attitudes toward foreigners fulfill a superego need. While various procedures for transition from such data to social analysis and suggestions for combination of such data with "global" data about the social units themselves have been advanced (Lazarsfeld and Menzel, 1961, pp. 214-17), most studies do not carry out such analysis.

The second kind of reductionism is to microsociology, on the ground that micro- and macrosociological theories are isometric and hence studying small groups will provide all the theoretical statements needed to understand relations among macroscopic variables (e.g., studies of cohesion of small groups are used to explain class solidarity), or else the existence of macroscopic emergent properties is a priori denied. Another example of this reductionism in political science can be seen in veto-group analysis of national politics, which attempts to explain the macrobehavior of legislative output and executive policies in terms of the relations among political groups, their qualities and dynamics. Relatively little independent explanatory power is granted to national institutions themselves, to national leadership, or to ruling classes. A major outcome ascribed to the aggregate of the actions of the veto groups is blockage, stalemating the polity. Whatever national action does occur cannot, within the limits of this approach, be credited to (or blamed on) any one group or coalition of groups, because all groups affect the national action, like vectors feeding into a vector diagram (Riesman, Denney, and Glazer, 1950; Dahrendorf, 1961, pp. 175-206; Kornhauser, 1961, pp. 252-67).

This reductionistic approach is further exemplified in the attempts to determine on the basis of transactional analysis the nature and dynamics of bonds that tie units into communities—whether these be nations, suburbs, or tribes. The transactions studied include telephone calls, letters, telegrams, trade, and tourism. Macroproperties (e.g., the integration level of the communities) are perceived as the product of transactions among the units, not as the result of supraunit actions. In general, the more transactions that occur, the more the units are viewed as related, and the more the supraunit, the community, is seen as integrated (Deutsch and Savage, 1960, pp. 551-72; Deutsch, 1956a, pp. 143-60; Deutsch, 1964, pp. 75-97; Gross, 1967, pp. 315-31). The reductionism from macrosociology to microsociology, which has already been forcefully called to our attention (Mills, 1959; Moore, 1958, pp. 111-59; Wolin, 1960, pp. 429-34), is much less widely acknowledged by the majority of sociologists and political scientists who work with empirical data than is psychological reductionism. Here, it is not just a matter of a threshold that is disregarded in actual research, but one whose very claim is questioned (Mack and Snyder, 1957, pp. 107-8; M. Deutsch, 1965).

Substantive Assumptions

Those engaged in macrotheory building tend to follow one or two major approaches as to what substantive assumptions are to be made about the nature of the macroscopic units, their properties, and their dynamics. I suggest a combination of the two approaches and add a third ingredient. Before we turn to explore these approaches, I shall briefly note the criteria used for differentiation among them.

I am interested in developing a general theory for macroscopic (social) change, which is a formal concept for sociopolitical (or societal) history. Societal change, obviously, is affected both by factors which the participants control and by those beyond their control, a mix of guided and ongoing change. *The approaches under discussion differ in the assumptions they make about the ratio of one kind of change as against the other.* The collectivistic theories see chiefly ongoing changes; voluntaristic ones focus on guided change. The *collectivistic view* of society—as an actor oriented toward itself—is rather passive; the *voluntaristic view* is hyperactive. A third or *synthetic approach*, which I favor, balances these two approaches.

I am dealing here with analytic languages (or metatheories), each one of which is used to formulate several theories. As I am concerned only with laying bare their most basic assumptions, no attempt is made to do justice to any specific theory or to assumptions concerning other dimensions than the one explored: their *explanations of* societal change.

Sociologists are most familiar with collectivistic theories. Social system theories, functionalist models, anthropological-cultural theories of configuration as well as phenomenological ones are collectivistic and basically passive. They do not recognize systematically a seat of action on the macroscopic, societal level. Scanning major theoretical writings of these traditions shows that concepts such as goals, knowledge, decision making, and strategies—all typical concepts needed to characterize an actor who guides a change process— are absent or appear only infrequently and mainly in relation to microunits and not macroscopic ones. The typical society under study is treated as if it had no government, and political processes are described only as ongoing. The balance-of-power theory of international relations provides a good example of this approach (E. Haas, 1953a, pp. 370-98; Seabury, 1965; Hinsley, 1963). The state of international affairs is viewed as determined by the actions of the various units (nation-states). War, should it occur, is the result of an "upset" in the balance, which in turn is explained by the emergence of a new coalition between the units, by changes in the power of some units, or by the appearance of new units in the particular historical situation. However, no collectivistic supraunit is assumed to have the capacity to correct the balance. Even when a balancer is introduced, it is seen as merely one more unit whose self-interest dictates weighing one side of the scale to safeguard the balance, rather than as a supraunit force. It is somewhat like a rook moving to prevent a checkmate, with all the figures knowing and observing the rules of the game but with no player to guide them.

Differentiation is representative of many other theories that could be utilized as an example of this approach. Over the past few years, the concept has increasingly been used by Parsons, Smelser, Eisenstadt, and others[2] to relate societal change to functional-structural analysis (Parsons, 1961c, pp. 219- 34; Parsons and Bales, 1953; Smelser, 1959; Zelditch, 1955, pp. 305- 51). The core image, which is typical of the collectivistic approach, is taken from biology, where we find "simple" units that split into two or more, each one more "specialized" than the previous. All the functions carried out by the simple unit are also carried out by the differentiated ones, except that now each of the functions has a substructure of its own, a "differentiated" unit. Most biological studies do not ask what propels the transition, or to what degree the transition may be guided by a unit other than units which are being differentiated. Those who did raise these questions in biology dealt with the function of codes in guiding the transition from a simple to a differentiated unit. The code, which is found in the undifferentiated unit, holds in an "abstracted" form (as an information pattern or model) a fully differentiated design of the future unit toward which the simple unit is to evolve. Research focuses on what the code specifically contains and how its "messages" are transmitted to the evolving unit[3] (Grodins, 1963, pp. 16- 26; Pohley, 1961, pp. 443- 58). In sociology so far, by and large, the question which the conception of a code answers for biology (i.e., what guides differentiation) and its *consequences* are studied, but not its guidance mechanism (Etzioni, 1959, pp. 476- 87; 1963, pp. 407- 21). In other words, the process is viewed as ongoing and the unit merely subject to it, i.e., as passive.

The voluntaristic approach is almost unknown in contemporary sociology. Voluntarism was quite influential in political science until recently, especially in the study of international relations between

2. Studies of favorable environmental conditions are not to be confused with those of guidance mechanisms. These are inputs and not system qualities by which the reaction of the system is to be explained and which cannot be assumed. Most of these are ad hoc anyhow—dealing with the contact of non-whites with the white civilization.

3. For results of experiments with animals in which the brain was disassociated from the embryo and the effects of such disassociation on the embryo's development, see Heinz-Joachim Pohley (1961, pp. 443- 58).

the two world wars and in studies of administration or formal organizations[4] (Goodrich, 1959; Stein, 1959, pp. 233- 54; Scott, 1939; Jackson, 1952). Essentially, there are two major voluntaristic approaches: one views the societal actor as if he were a nonrational being, and the other views him as if he were rational. The nonrational voluntaristic approach perceives societal units as acting like macropersons—responding to drives, emotions, and beliefs (Pye, 1961, pp. 205- 21; Leites, 1948, pp. 102- 19). Since these are beyond the actor's control, this version has a passive element. Its voluntarism lies in its explanation of societal behavior as the response to one actor's drives and urges. Many psychoanalytical interpretations of national conduct, some psychological writings on societal action, and earlier anthropological and sociological views of national character are representative of this approach (Klineberg, 1964; Riessman and Miller, 1964, pp. 29- 38; Waltz, 1959; Nett, 1958, pp. 297- 303).

Rationalistic voluntarism is more activist: it assumes that the macroactor is not only free to compel his "body" to express his will, emotions, and urges but is also able to modify his will in accord with information gained and by sequential reasoning (Cook, 1949, pp. 553- 64). Man, it is conceded, does not always act rationally, but this is due to limitations on his knowledge, on his capacity to analyze, and on his decision-making model. Provided with better information, computers, and models, man would not only think but would also act more rationally. Value and power conflicts, it is held, can be solved through arbitration, mediation, negotiation, or by "splitting the difference" (Scott, 1939; Jackson, 1952). In short, no permanent or major limitations on the active orientation are recognized; the world is seen not as an atom-filled container or a quasi-organic tissue but as the product of an omnipotent agent.

Varying degrees of rationalistic voluntarism can be found in administrative science and branches of political science. In studies of administration, it is most evident in the scientific management approach (Gulick and Urwick, 1937; Pfiffner and Sherwood, 1960) and in some schools of decision making (Shubik, 1964; Marschak and Hurwicz, 1946; Buchanan and Tullock, 1962; Tullock, 1965; Black, 1958). Although never so popular in political science as it was in economics, rationalistic voluntarism was quite important before World War II, particularly in the field of international law and

4. Among the contemporary writers along this line, see those who believe that changes in the United Nations charter, especially weighted voting, would significantly enhance world government, and that direct election to a European parliament would lead to the United States of Europe. See, in particular, L. Goodrich (1959), Eric Stein (1959, pp. 233- 54), J. B. Scott (1939), and E. Jackson (1952). Most writings in the "conflict resolution" and "problem solving" traditions are voluntaristic, often to a high degree.

organization (Downs, 1957; Baumol, 1952; Wright, 1965; Wheare, 1964; Carr, 1956; Hyneman, 1959).

Hans Morgenthau, who has contributed significantly to the reduction of voluntarism in political science, depicts its rationalistic version as follows:

> One school believes that a rational and moral political order, derived from universally valid abstract principles, can be achieved here and now. It assumes the essential goodness and infinite malleability of human nature, and blames the failure of the social order to measure up to the rational standards on lack of knowledge and understanding, obsolescent social institutions, or the depravity of certain isolated individuals and groups. It trusts in education, reform, and the sporadic use of force to remedy these defects [1954, p. 3].

The influence of rationalistic voluntarism has waned during the last three decades, although it often survives in diluted form in which more extensive ad hoc limitations on rationality and the freedom to act are recognized. Recently, however, the rationalistic model has seen a measure of revival (Simon, 1957a; Olson, 1965; Downs, 1957; Rosenau, 1974). In part, this is associated with attempts to use computers to explain macrobehavior (although the association is historical rather than necessary), to apply game theory and other rationalistic models to military strategy and foreign policy (Schelling, 1960) and to study macrosocial behavior with some of the less structural cybernetic models (Miller, 1956, pp. 29- 65; Dechert, 1965, pp. 15- 20; Mehl, 1957, pp. 410- 19).

Another well-known voluntaristic-rationalistic model is the legal-constitutional approach to societal change. Its adherents hold that new societal systems, e.g., unions of states, can be generated by forming a constitution or revising it, and that societal structure, e.g., the steepness of the stratification, can be drastically altered by legislation. The 1789 meeting in Independence Hall in Philadelphia is viewed as having created an American polity out of a confederation, and enactment of inheritance and progressive tax laws is expected to level economic differences, just as civil rights acts are believed to be a major instrument for desegregation. Without asking here if and under what conditions these assumptions are valid, the model of societal change used should be noted. It is that of a group of sensible leaders—founding fathers, Congress—who, having examined a problem and found a solution, bring it into being by their action. A limited degree of "unanticipated consequences" is anticipated, but distortion of processes due to latent dysfunctions, replacement of goals, and above all, failure to proceed significantly due to resistance of the body of society, are not part of this view. It had direct parallels in the scientific management school and "formal organizational" theory, where managements draw up blueprints and charts and implement them (Gore and Dyson, 1964; Gulick and Urwick, 1937; Buchanan and Tullock, 1962).[5]

For our purposes, one rationalistic-voluntaristic model is of particular interest for reasons that will become evident below, namely, the cybernetic model. The source of the model, it is important to realize, is the mechanical guidance of machines, that is, the development of machines that take over control functions the way "lower order" machines, the supervised ones, took over earlier performance ("work") functions. The cybernetics model most frequently applied entails a decision-making center, and a communication network that carries the messages from the center to the units under supervision and feedback messages from the units to the center. The underlying assumption of the model, similar to that of the functionalistic full-integration model, is that in principle the center can guide the system. "Disturbances" are recognized, e.g., overloading of the decision-making center; various solutions are worked out assessing priorities to messages. Similarly, gaps in the communication networks might appear, let us say, due to poor relay, and correction is provided (e.g., by including redundant lines).

When this model is applied to societal analysis, the government is viewed as the cybernatorial overlayer of society which provides it with a decision-making center, a communication network to member units, and feedback mechanisms. One of the most distinguished and influential political scientists of this generation, Karl W. Deutsch, has developed this application of the cybernatorial model (Deutsch, 1963).

The irrational-voluntaristic model is held mainly by psychoanalysts who write about societies, some psychologists, and a few anthropologists (Leites, 1948, pp. 102-19; Waltz, 1959; Buchanan, 1949, pp. 496-505). The tendency is to view society as man writ large, each society interacting with other societies basically the way one individual interacts with others. For instance, the United States and the Soviet Union misunderstand each other, which leads to frustration, which generates aggression, etc. Improved communication between the sides is expected to increase their reality testing and cooperation. Charles E. Osgood, a former president of the American Psychological Association, is one of the best-known representatives

5. An important segment of decision-making studies view the actors as being able to make rational decisions, while lack of complete information and computation capacities limit his capacity to guide the unit for which he decides. These are viewed as ad hoc limitations. In principle, the more information he collects and the better his computers, the more effective decisions he is expected to make. For a study of "group" behavior explained in terms of individualistic goals, see Mancur Olson, Jr. (1965).

of this approach (Osgood, 1962). While it is diametrically opposed to the rationalistic approach in terms of the substantive assumptions about the mechanisms at work, which here are subconscious and emotional, the parallelism is complete, as this voluntarism too views society as basically acting as a monolithic unit, being able to change, for instance, from a hostile to a cooperative mood as if it had one will (Osgood, 1962).[6]

There is an interesting difficulty posed by the use of a voluntaristic viewpoint in studying political action. Those adopting a voluntaristic point of view tend not to take into account sufficiently the degree of integration of the group under study. This is particularly true for studies of interest groups. Actually, these groups are sometimes highly integrated and sometimes aggregates, and their political action differs considerably according to their degree of integration, a fact that is not duly recognized in many interest-group studies (Bentley, 1949; Freeman, 1965; Easton, 1953; Zeigler, 1964; Ehrmann, 1958). This leads to an underestimation of the latitude of an interest group's leadership when the group's membership is poorly integrated, and an overestimation of this factor when it is highly integrated. The same limitation is found in the studies of the relations between public opinion and decision-making elites which view the public as several aggregates, such as more and less educated or more or less committed citizens, disregarding the fact that public opinion is, to a considerable degree, generated in societal units in which an educated and committed minority may lead the rest of the members (Stouffer, 1955). In using a purely voluntaristic viewpoint, these difficulties must be avoided.

In summary, all the voluntaristic approaches see one main seat of action, and in principle recognize no limitations to "man's," i.e., society's, capacity to change. In that sense they are all hyperactive, because these theories do not include as an integral part variables that can account for the forces that resist change, that block or distort implementation of the will.

Toward a Synthetic Approach

I suggest that a synthesis of the collectivistic approach, which in effect focuses upon *ongoing* processes and change, and a voluntaristic-cybernatorial approach, largely concerned with *guided* processes

6. Voluntarists, who face the question of the nature of the actor of the differing units of analysis, maintain their monolithic assumption by assuming a close relationship among the units, for instance, between the president (or power elite) and public opinion. See, for instance, Osgood (1962).

and change, would provide for a more balanced theory of societal change, especially of modern societies in which both kinds of changes are prevalent. It also balances the nonrational focus of the collectivistic approach, which tends to stress the study of societal ties of sentiments and values, with the rationalistic perspective cybernetics often exhibits. A third major element that both approaches tend to neglect is added, that of a conception and theory of power.[7] By power I mean a relational attribute which indicates the capacity of one unit to overcome the resistance of the other(s).[8]

The central position of power for my theory is manifest in my seeing in each society (and in each societal unit) an internal struggle between the guidance mechanisms and the passive elements, and not just an external, interunit struggle. The outcome of this struggle significantly determines the capacity of a societal unit to act upon itself (to effect its own change) as well as to act externally and hence also to influence the patterns of the supraunit of which it is a unit. Supraunits are composed of units that have at least some cybernatorial capacities and power, as well as having, in principle, some such capacities and power of their own, on the supraunit level.

The collectivistic approach sees the members of the collectivity, configuration, or system as closely tied to each other. While some leeway or "play" is recognized, basically units cannot be moved around or changed unless other units change more or less simultaneously. If they do not, various pathologies are expected, described in such concepts as social lag and imbalance (Rosenstein-Rodan, 1943; Nurkse, 1953). And, as no guidance center is assumed—a center whose assumption would entail also assuming moveable and changeable, less "tied" units—the question of the source of the capacity to transform the units or the ties does not arise. Power has at best a marginal, external role and a theoretical status. As a matter of fact, most collectivistic theories do not include the concept of power at all, while in others it is tacked on, post hoc.

The voluntaristic cybernatorial model stresses the importance of communication and information, the manipulation of symbols, and largely excludes power other than that involved in manipulation of symbols. No resistance of the units is in principle expected. It focuses on the problems of generating well-calculated messages, of relaying the messages from the center of the units, and of providing

7. Voluntarism neglects mainly the relationship between the guiding mechanism and the "body" of the actor, and less so in the relationship among actors.

8. Much has been written about the difficulties of defining power. To go into all the objections here would require more space than this entire article. My reasons for holding that the above definition is operational are stated in *The Active Society* (1968).

reliable feedbacks, but once the messages reach the performing units, no power is assumed necessary to overcome their resistance to the message. If the feedback indicates that the message did not trigger the expected action, the assumption is that the message was inappropriate (and the effective center is expected to revise it) or was distorted on its way because of communication difficulties, not that the message was appropriate and was "read" loudly and clearly, but was not backed up by enough power. Symbols, changes in patterns of information or meaning, are transmitted, not power;[9] it is a matter of the nerves, not the muscles of government (Deutsch, 1963).

Rather than characterizing my approach as one of collectivistic-voluntaristic power analysis, I shall refer to it as a theory of societal guidance. My theory of societal guidance draws on both the collectivistic and the voluntaristic approaches. It differs significantly on one major dimension from both—it does not assume that the societal unit it deals with is a monolithic or highly integrated unit. Authors of both traditions have argued that this assumption is just a heuristic device, a standard against which reality can be measured, and not an assumption about the nature of reality itself (Schelling, 1962, pp. 421-32; Schelling, 1960). However, even for those who remember that they are dealing only with a heuristic device, these models introduce the mistaken perspective that deviations from the standard are pathological, limited, and correctable; and they provide no model for the study of low integration or low compliance situations, which are abundant. We assume no particular relationship between the societal actors under study. The actors might relate to each other completely externally without any shared bonds, a situation approximated by nations in a state of all-out war. Or the actors might be related by complementary or shared interests which bind them with ties that are limited to the transactions themselves and which are inherently unstable, because changes in the environment or in the actors that will change the interests concerned will lead to an abandonment of the relationship. Further, the actors might be bound by shared values and institutionalized norms, which bind in a more "generalized" and stable way because commitments are nonrational and may have a moral force.

Relations might be classified accordingly as coercive, utilitarian, or normative (Etzioni, 1968). While there are symbolic elements in all three kinds of relationships, the core of the utilitarian and the coercive is nonsymbolic. Normative relations have the symbolic as the primary link; however, even in the coercive, a symbolic element

9. Symbols are cognitive, not expressive, and hence have no motivational power.

exists, e.g., threats to use force play an important role in coercion. Utilitarian relationships draw heavily on interests and material objects, and besides the symbolic relation to the object (as has been stressed in the institutions of property), the nature and the distribution of the objects themselves are of much importance. The same holds for means of violence as the basis of coercive relations; too much has been made by contemporary sociologists of the symbolic element of legitimation in the concept of authority and too little of the other component, the actual capacity to use force.

I have argued elsewhere that these three kinds of relationships are analytically exhaustive, i.e., that every concrete relationship can be analytically classified in terms of various combinations of these three basic ones (Etzioni, 1961). The threefold conception of bases of societal order seems to answer the criticism raised by Dahrendorf and others on the symbolistic and nonconflict nature of prevailing sociological theory (Dahrendorf, 1958, pp. 115- 27; Coser, 1964, pp. 20- 6). It should be noted that each of these relationships can be either horizontal or hierarchical—i.e., a relationship either of actors having similar values, interests, or force, or of actors that are subject to an actor who has power of one kind or another over them. All the members of a cohesive group are committed to each other, but the commitments of leaders and followers are asymmetric. Exchange between roughly equal units, and between those which are not, is basically different. This difference between hierarchical and horizontal interactions, neglected in many traditional as well as more recent writings, is central to the present approach.

Societal and Political Processes

Before discussing the relationship between system, structure and transformability, the relationship between societal and political processes needs to be investigated. Political processes have two societal functions: to combine subunits into a societal unit, to make out of parts a whole, and to guide societal action toward the realization of societal values as expressed via the political processes. Thus, the concept of political process provides an answer to the question of how, empirically, a societal "will" is expressed. If these processes are distorted, the expression of the members' needs will also be distorted. The service of both functions assumes some awareness of the societal whole and its parts, a measure of responsiveness to the members' needs, and some command of power and its purposive exercise. In short, for a societal entity to exist, political processes are required. Political processes are the main control mechanism of societal action. (They may be inadequate or distorting but their effect remains the central one.) Hence, the study of the interplay between guidance processes and ongoing ones, between activation and passivity, is an indispensable component of any theory that can hope to account for societal action.

Because the prevailing sociological tradition is collectivistic and several major schools of political science are relatively voluntaristic, the language of societal action must draw on both these disciplines and bridge this interdisciplinary border. More specifically, the societal action approach draws on the sociological perspective in making societal units rather than individuals or political units the core units of analysis, and in viewing both their internal make-up and their relations as having the qualities of a system. But neither the societal units nor the relations among them are assumed to be given or to change only as the result of ongoing processes. (While some societal units do have a highly "fixed" structure and accommodate to ongoing processes with little self-control, a full sociopolitical theory—which has to encompass modern society as well as primitive and historical ones and has to deal with religious and social movements, political parties, complex organizations, and states as well as with ethnic groupings and classes, and with the interaction between more active and more passive subunits—must include, on the most basic level, the concept of a unit capable of a measure of self-guidance, an active societal unit.) Some societal units may have very little self-control, others a great deal, and still others an intermediate amount. While there can be a societal unit without a controlling overlayer, a theory of societal processes without one is markedly incomplete (Horowitz, 1972).

The language of societal action draws on political science for its greater concern with the malleable and active aspects of societal units than is common in prevailing sociological theories. Political science deals to a large extent with states rather than societies, with administration rather than informal organization, with parties rather than ethnic groupings or classes, and with voting rather than interaction (Dahl, 1961b; Truman, 1951b, pp. 37-9). In recent years, however, political scientists have become increasingly concerned with the limitations social bonds impose on macro action (Halpern, 1964), and some sociologists have become more interested in guidance mechanisms. Thus, a line of analysis has been evolving that bridges the traditional gap between these two disciplines (Lipset, 1960; Deutsch, 1963; Porter, 1965; Schurmann, 1960). With these developments in mind, it is now time to turn to a consideration of the interrelationships between system, structure, and transformability.

System, Structure, and Transformability

Over the last decades the term system has been applied increasingly loosely, to a degree that it has lost an essential quality of a concept, the ability to differentiate one referent from another. There is no relationship which has not been at one point or another directly or by implication characterized as a social system, including the relationships between the drivers of cars on a freeway. The essence of the concept as used in sociology, it seems, is collectivistic; no relationship makes a system unless there are nontrivial feedback effects among the members. If half of the American housewives were to have a cup of change-of-pace tea instead of another cup of coffee, the Brazilian economy would be damaged. This does not make these distinguished ladies and the Brazilian coffee plantations one system, however, because what happens to the Brazilian economy will not have significant feedback effects on the American housewives.

I see three kinds of relation: *situations* in which there are interunit relations but no feedback loops; *systems* which assume nontrival interdependence among the member units; and *communities* which assume an integrative supraunit capacity. Each of these three concepts covers a sector of a "closeness"-of-interaction continuum, and hence within each sector one might refer to more or less "tight" relationships (e.g., more vs. less integrated units).

A system might be a relatively concrete concept referring to relations among units of action—tribes, nations, organized classes—or a relatively abstract one, referring to relations among variables. Systems of either kind have boundaries which should not be confused with their structures. Boundaries determine which unit or variable is a member and which is not; structures characterize the specific pattern of relationship among the members. Boundaries change much less frequently than structures; the same system may, over time, have many structures.

Societal units whose structure includes an overlayer can partially guide the change of their *nonsocietal* situation, their relations to other actors, and their own internal structure. Relatively passive actors are those who react to environmental changes more than they introduce changes in their environment; they adapt by changing their internal makeup, but the nature of their adaptation is itself often affected by external factors, including more active societal units. More active units are more able to initiate change both in themselves and in their environments, in accordance with their preferences.

Second, relatively passive units tend to be *ultrastable*, in the sense that when challenged they tend to introduce variants of the existing structure, attempting to maintain the same basic institutional solution. More active units have a *self-transforming capacity*, i.e., they can create on the cybernatorial level a map of a not-yet-existing future-system, and guide their self-change toward the realization of a new structure, which is not a variation of the existing one but a basically new pattern. This capacity allows them to (a) adapt successfully to a much larger variety of environmental changes, (b) participate much more actively in changing the environment, and (c) actualize more of their own values. The study of the conditions under which the capacity for self-transformation increases and of the elements involved is an integral part of a theory of societal guidance; it ties systematically the study of encompassing societal changes, planned and unplanned, to structural-functional analysis.

The tension between ongoing processes and guided ones is central to the theory of societal guidance. To realize his values, an actor seeks to guide processes; but in doing so he faces the constraining effects of other actors in the situation, his system or community ties to others, and the institutionalized consequences of both his and their earlier actions.[10]

The degree to which an actor is active depends on his cybernatorial capacities, his power, and his consensus-formation capacity. Each one of these factors has both an internal and an external dimension: how much he knows about himself and about others, how much he can mobilize power over members *and* over nonmembers, to what degree he can gain the support of subunits and of external units. Since it is useful to refer to both cybernatorial and power capacities together, I shall refer to them jointly as his ability to *control*. When his skill in mobilizing consensus is also taken into account, I refer to his ability to *guide*. As I grant to the subunits and other units in principle the same capacities as to the actor under study, his capacity to be active is obviously not optimized by maximizing his control capacities but by optimizing the combination of control and consensus formation—that is, by maximizing the capacity of his guidance mechanisms.

We turn now to explore these factors in some detail. Our approach is at first analytic, in that each factor is explored as if all the others were held constant; in the following section I shall take a more synthesizing and historical view of actors that are becoming more active generally, on all major dimensions. In the analytic section I compare briefly both societies and subsocieties. (Suprasocieties are not discussed here.) The societies I focus on are political—that is, encapsulated in a state which serves as their organizational tool for both control and consensus formation. Similarly, the

10. He faces other factors, too, such as conditions of the nonsocial environment, but those are not the focus of the present study.

subsocietal actors are collectivities that have organizational "arms," such as working classes which have labor parties and unions. Collectivities which have not been organized are treated mainly for comparative purposes.

The purpose of the following discussion is strictly to illustrate the kind of factors my theory focuses on and not to provide here a set of propositions (not to mention data) in support of the theory. The statements, however, have the basic structure of propositions; each proposes that if all other conditions were equal, a change of the specific variable discussed would correlate in the way specified with the active capacity of the unit under study.

The State of Macroanalysis in the Various Social Sciences

Most social sciences do not distinguish between micro- and macroscopic units and subtheories. Some so clearly focus on one kind of unit that the distinction seems unnecessary or not relevant. The subject matter of psychology is personality, which is neither a micro- nor a macrosocial unit; political science's subject matter is macroscopic, though the tendency toward psychological reductionism and micropolitics seems to be on the rise (Wolin, 1960). To the degree that anthropology is concerned with preliterate societies, the difference between micro- and macrounits seems to present itself less than it would in the study of modern societies, and it is rarely observed. Interest in the transition from man to Man, which disregards both the micro-macro and the psychosocial thresholds, is still more common in this discipline than in most others (Kaplan, 1957, pp. 87-121), and is probably most often found in psychoanalytic writing about societal behavior. In sociology, the micro-macro threshold was much ignored during the last generation, especially in America, and since World War II has been largely ignored in Europe. This neglect, however, has been pointed out forcefully over the last decade, and there has been some gain both in macrosociology and in recognition of the threshold (Moore, 1966, pp. 475-82).

The micro-macro distinction is established in economics, with studies of business firms usually being treated as microeconomics and those of the national economy as macroeconomics (Heilbroner, 1965). It would appear, however, that the concept of emergent properties has not been fully recognized. Boulding, for example, views macroeconomics as the *study of aggregates*, while microeconomics is seen as dealing with member items (individual industries, particular commodities). This amounts to interunit analysis without introducing emergent properties. It is small wonder, therefore, that he finds it "difficult" to explain why "many propositions which are true of individuals or of small groups turn out to be untrue when we are considering the system as a whole" (Boulding, 1955).

The terms "macro" and "micro" are, as a rule, defined by denotation (Merton and Barber, 1963; Rokkan and Valen, 1960; Milbrath, 1965; Rokkan and Campbell, 1960). The distinction between universals and micro- and macroemergent properties is not drawn; universals and microvariables are often collapsed into one category, which leads to the inference that since some of these "microvariables" apply also to the macro level, the distinction between macro- and microanalysis is not valid. Often, even when the difference between *behavior* on the two levels is clearly recognized, as with regard to individual versus national debt, the theoretical distinction is less widely utilized (Friedman, 1953; Knight, 1936).

The distinctions I advance here seem to be of value for all social sciences. For psychology, their employment would more clearly focus the question of whether a society can be studied as isometric with personality. In political science, they would clarify the difference between aggregate studies of voters, their personality and friendship patterns, on the one hand, and those of national political processes on the other. Above all, they would better prepare sociology (though other changes are needed as well) for historical analysis and for the presentation of an action theory of society.

CONTROL FACTORS

Cybernatorial Capacities

Societal units differ in their capacity to collect, process, and use information. This holds not only for corporations that compete over a market, but also for political parties (Kennedy is believed to have used social sciences more effectively than Nixon in the 1960 campaign), federal agencies (the air force is thought to be superior in this respect to the navy and the army), and civic organizations (the NAACP's capacity to use information increased between 1955 and 1970).

The input of knowledge into a societal unit follows, I suggest, the same basic patterns other inputs do; that is, it might be blocked (and hence partially or completely lost for action purposes) at each stage of the process. Societal units have varying facilities for collecting information ("raw material" input). This capacity seems to be associated with economic affluence but not in a one-to-one relationship. If we were to order countries (or other societal units) by their average income per capita and then score their capacity to collect information, let us say, in terms of expenditure on research, we expect that the most affluent units would have a much higher capacity than the next affluent ones, while the remaining units would have few such capacities at all. Four powerful federal agencies in the United States, the Department of Defense, the National Aeronautics and Space Administration, the Atomic Energy Commission, and the Department of Health, Education, and Welfare, spent more of the federal research and development (R & D) funds than the thirty-odd other agencies combined, or 91 percent of the available funds: Defense, 47 percent; NASA, 28 percent; AEC, 8 percent; HEW, 8 percent. Three affluent states out of fifty gained more than 50 percent of these R & D funds: California, 35.1 percent; New York, 10.7 percent; Massachusetts, 5.6 percent.[11] Societal units' spending on information has much accelerated in the last generations as compared to earlier ones.[12] In short, patterns of interunit distribution of information seem significantly more inegalitarian than are those of the distribution of economic assets.

The ratio of investment in *collecting* over *processing* information is an indicator of the sophistication of the cybernetic overlayer and the knowledge strategy to which the particular unit subscribes. The United States and Great Britain, it seems, tend to invest relatively highly in collection; France, at least until recently, has stressed processing.[13]

A societal unit that emphasizes disproportionally the collection of information will, I expect, have a fragmented view of itself and its environment; it will have many bits but no picture, like a survey study before tabulation. Such processing, I suggest, will tend to be associated with drifting (or passivity), as information that is not

11. Data on states' receipt of federal funds for R & D are from the *Statistical Abstracts of the United States: 1968*, table 780, p. 528; and refer to "Federal Prime Contracts and Grants Awarded for R & D States: 1965." Data on agency expenditures of R & D funds are from the National Science Foundation, *Federal Funds for Research, Development and Other Scientific Activities, Fiscal Years 1967, 1968, and 1969*; vol. 17, NSF 68-27, p. 32.

12. Thus, for instance, the United States' total federal expenditure on R & D in 1969 is estimated to have reached $17.6 billion; in 1959, $5.8 billion; in 1949, $1.1 billion. Data refer to fiscal years. They include R & D plans. See National Science Foundation, *Federal Funds for Research, Development and Other Scientific Activities, Fiscal Years 1967, 1968, and 1969*; vol. 17, NSF 68-27, p. 3.

13. This is one meaning that is implied when the Anglo-Saxon tradition is characterized as "pragmatic" and the French as rationalistic. For some evidence, related to differences in economic planning, see Andrew Shonfield, *Modern Capitalism: The Changing Balance of Public and Private Power* (New York: Oxford University Press, 1965), pp. 151-75.

sufficiently processed is in effect not available for active societal guidance.

On the other hand, a unit that overemphasizes *processing* is expected to have an "unempirical" view of itself and its environment, because it will tend to draw more conclusions from the available information than are warranted; it is similar to acting on the basis of a poorly validated theory. Thus, overprocessing is expected to be associated with hyperactivity, as the actor assumes he knows more than he does. Master plans used to guide economic development are typically hyperactive in their assumptions. Finally, societal units whose collection and processing are relatively balanced (not in absolute amounts but in terms of intrinsic needs of the guidance mechanisms) are expected to have comparatively more effective controlling overlayers, all other things being equal, and to be active without being hyperactive.

Information that has been processed might still be wasted as far as the societal unit is concerned if it is not *systematically introduced into the unit's decision-making and implementation overlayer* (Homans, 1950, pp. 369–414), where the main societal "consumption" of information takes place. Two major variables seem useful for characterizing the different arrangements societal units have for interaction between the knowledge-producing and the decision-making units; one concerns the relative degree of autonomy of production, the other, the effectiveness of communications of the "product." It is widely believed that structural differentiation between the producers and consumers of information is necessary; fusion of the two kinds of unit—for instance, in the management of a corporation—is viewed as dysfunctional both for production of knowledge and for decision making. For societal units whose knowledge and decision-making units are differentiated, various modes and forms of articulation and communication exist whose relative effectiveness remains to be explored. Here I can touch on only one aspect of this intricate subject.

The controlling overlayer itself has layers upon layers; processing is superimposed on the collecting of information, both in the logical sense that the one presupposes the other, and in the structural sense that those engaged in processing have higher ranks and more power to mold the societal input of knowledge than those who collect information (Hilsman, 1956). Differences in the internal *structure* of the control overlayer affect the total action capacity of societal units. The division between those who work within a given knowledge framework and those who seek to transform it, and the structural relations between them, seem to be of much cybernatorial importance. Consumption and, to a degree, processing, of knowledge are inevitably in part political processes. That is, which part of the available knowledge is used and what conclusions are reached on the basis of the knowledge are in part determined by political factors. These include considerations of the knowledge producers in terms of the internal politics of the organizations in which knowledge is processed, their affiliations with political groupings in the society at large, and the differential absorption by various political actors of the knowledge produced, according to its political rather than intrinsic value. The core of the politicization of knowledge lies not in deliberate or subconscious slanting of facts but in the interpretive and judgmental elements most items of knowledge include. It is not, as some students of administration would have it, that knowledge units simply produce information and the political decision-making elites add the judgment. The producers of knowledge play an active role in formulating the judgments.

Within this context, one issue is of special significance for the theory of societal guidance: the effect of the relative investments in two sections of the cybernatorial overlayer—*viz.*, "transforming" versus "stable" knowledge production. Transforming knowledge rechecks and potentially challenges the basic assumptions of a system. "Stable" knowledge elaborates and respecifies, even revises, secondary assumptions within the framework of a basic set which is taken for granted. Most decision-making elites most of the time seem to prefer "stable" over "transforming" knowledge production, to seek closure on basic knowledge assumptions precisely because they cannot be selected and reviewed on wholly empirical grounds. Hence, once consensus has been reached on the basic assumptions of a world view, a self-view, a view of others, or of a strategic doctrine, etc., it is expensive politically, economically, and psychologically for the elites to transform these assumptions. They hence tend to become *tabooed* assumptions, and knowledge production comes to be limited to specifics within the limits of the assumptions. At the same time, the ability to transform basic perspectives is sharply reduced and with it the capacity for *societal* self-transformation. The societal units survive as long as the range of tolerance of their knowledge and societal pattern allows for sufficient adaptation to environmental changes, but such adaptation tends to become increasingly costly.

More active units have supralayers that can be activated to review and transform tabooed assumptions. A comparison of corporations that have shifted to a new line of products, restructured their internal organization, and found new markets when their old markets were gradually lost, with those whose sales and profits declined or "died" because of lack of innovations, suggests that transforming corporations maintained R & D units which were not only exempt from the tabooed assumptions but were also, among other things, expected sporadically to review these assumptions. That is, part of their institutionalized role was to engage in "search" behavior precisely where the decision-making elites would otherwise settle for "satisfying" solutions (Simon, 1955b).

The societal parallel of this cybernatorial arrangement is not difficult to see. The intellectual community acts as one major societal R & D unit, as a critical examiner of tabooed assumptions. Under what economic, political, and sociological conditions it can fulfill this function and what, if any, functional alternatives exist are questions social scientists have much feeling about—but there is surprisingly little systematic research (Coser, 1965).

These questions can be studied for any society and any societal units. As the input of knowledge becomes a major *guided* societal activity (more than 75 percent of expenditure of the R & D funds is federal), as the ratio of this input as compared to other societal inputs is increasing, both in relative expenditure and in sociopolitical importance, the macrosociology of knowledge becomes an unavoidable part of studies of societal change. Typically, earlier studies of a society stressed the size of its population, territory, and GNP; the present approach adds the number of Ph.D.'s a society "turns out," the size of its professional manpower, and its investment in research and develpment as indicators of a major societal variable. Sociology of knowledge traditionally focused on the social conditions under which true states are made (Merton, 1957); macrosociology of knowledge focuses on the societal conditions under which knowledge for societal purposes is produced and consumed, opening a whole new field of inquiry for study of societies (Hogg, 1963; Price, 1965; Wiesner, 1965).

Societal Decision Making

The head of the societal control overlayer is a decision-making elite—the sociopolitical equivalent of the electronic center. The elites choose between alternative policies, issue signals to the performing units (guide the underlayer), and respond to feedback information. (The body of the overlayer is made up of communication networks which tie elites to other member units and a power hierarchy.) Sociologists have studied elites by asking how "closed" versus "open" they are to members of various societal units, how dispersed control is among them, and how they relate to each other. But these are not cybernatorial considerations. They belong under the heading of consensus formation (e.g., closed and completely open elites are believed less effective for consensus formation than relatively open ones) and the study of power relations (e.g., hierarchy plus decentralization is believed more effective than monopolization of control by one elite or its fragmentation among several). Cybernatorial aspects of elites have been studied largely by nonsociologists and have not been systematically related to analysis (Deutsch, 1963; Kuhn, 1963). The cybernatorial study of elites concerns the procedures used by the decision-making elites, the strategies employed, and the communication networks that lead from the elites to the performing units and back.

When elites engage in decision making they draw on an implicit or explicit societal theory as to what the relations among the units under control are like, and as to how much and by what means these can be guided by the elites (Zinnes, 1966, pp. 474-502; Kelman, 1965, pp. 43-334). The validity of these theories varies from elite to elite; the greater the validity the more effective one would expect the decision making to be, which in turn is positively associated with the degree to which a social unit is active. This proposition is not earthshaking, nor are many other ones concerning the conditions under which decision making is effective. However, the inclusion or omission from a societal theory of a set of propositions about effective decision making is of much importance. It is indicative of a central position regarding the nature of society and of societal change.

In seeking to explain the action or change of a societal unit, most sociologists are more inclined to explore "background" conditions, from the level of economic resources the unit commands to the educational opportunities of elite members, than to study the decision-making procedures the elites follow. There is a widely held assumption that such "background" factors constitute the basic substructure which both sets the main limits of variability of societal action and change (e.g., poor countries lack the capital needed to develop) and specifies the main factors which determine what divisions will be made among whatever options are left open (e.g., because of the revolution of rising expectations democratic elites cannot defer increase in consumption). Differences in decision-making procedures are considered either "dependent" variables or trivial. In comparison, sociobernetics views the societal actors as having more autonomy. "Background" factors are viewed as setting a broad frame; which course is followed within its limits is affected by cybernatorial factors, among which decision-making procedures are significant elements. An effective elite might defer consumption increase in a poor country, and thereby lead toward a stable development.

Actually, many of the underdeveloped nations are not poor in resources or overpopulated, but are poor in cybernatorial capacities, that is, the quality of their elites is low in terms of ability to guide change. For instance, in 1930 the economic indicators of Canada and Argentina were similar. [14] Canada since then has continued to develop, while Argentina remains underdeveloped. A typical "background conditions" approach would stress the presence of the Protestant element in the one country and its absence in the other, as well as the differences in the Catholic stock in the two countries (in Argentina it is more that of southern Spain and Italy, in Canada that of the French). These differences are expected, á la Weber, to correlate with attitudes favorable to capitalism.

An elite study would add the difference between the responsive, democratic government of Canada and the authoritarian leadership of Argentina. True, this difference in leadership is in part due to differences in societal structure; e.g., Canada would not "tolerate" a Perón. But unless one assumes a one-to-one relationship between background factors and elite conduct and assumes that elite conduct has no significant independent effect on background factors, the analysis of the nature of the elites has to be included as an integral part of a theory of societal processes. It suffices to contrast the development of each country under different governments following different decision-making procedures, e.g., Perón and Illia in Argentina, to highlight the importance of systematically including the study of elites.

One typical decision societal elites in charge of guided change often have to make, at what are relatively critical turning points, is between acceleration and deceleration of the processes of change they guide. When a societal change is initiated—whether it be collectivization of farms, federation, or desegregation—resistance tends to accumulate because existing patterns are backed up by vested interests which are often threatened by the changes. As a change advances there is often at least one critical turning point at which resistance rises to a point where it endangers the control of the elites. The president thinks he might not be reelected, the government believes it might be overthrown, or a part of the country might secede. The decision the elites then face is between acceleration, in hope of "overpowering" the opposition and reaching a stage at which the support of those that will benefit from the new pattern will rise, or slowing down to give more time for the opposition to be worked out, circumvented, educated, or otherwise dealt with.

Obviously the question is not which one procedure or strategy is in the abstract the more effective; the question is under what societal

14. *El Desarrollo Económico de la Argentina*, E-CN. 12-429, add. 4 (1958), pp. 3–5.

conditions one is more effective than the other *and* under what conditions an elite chooses the suitable as against the unsuitable strategy. In a comparative study of four cases we found two elites that accelerated and two that decelerated in face of a "premature" situation, i.e., a situation where opposition was high and forces in support of the change weak. The accelerating elites lost control (in the U.A.R., Syria rebelled and seceded; the West Indian Federation was disbanded). The decelerating elites are still in control, though in one of the two cases (the Scandinavian system) the elite had to decelerate so much that the process of change (unification) came to a standstill, while only in the fourth case (the European Economic Community) was continuation of the process assured by deceleration (Etzioni, 1965).

Other societal decisions, often debated ideologically but rarely studied analytically and systematically, concern the conditions of militancy versus moderation, or confrontation versus coalition politics, and the wholistic versus the gradualist approach. These and similar strategic decisions draw on explicit·or implicit theories about the nature of societal linkages and control factors, such as how far a government can be relied upon as an agent of transformation, what will be the result of mass activation of apathetic publics, or how much will "spillover" in one societal sector generate change in others. Here lies the main link between the study of societal decision making and of societal input of knowledge.

The quality of decision making gains in importance the more active a societal unit is by other criteria. Obviously the more activated a unit is and the more assets it has, the more advantages it can gain by effective use of them, and the more it can waste them if it uses them ineffectively. For passive units, which barely guide their own processes, "background" factors are of much importance; for units that react more creatively to their environmental as well as to internal challenges, it is the quality of decision making that is of much importance. Under what structural conditions elites make more effective decisions, all other conditions being equal, is a question that has been barely explored sociologically.

Cybernatorial factors other than processing of information and decision making include various attributes of societal goals, such as the clarity of their formulation, and the degree of compatability of the various goals a unit pursues. Also important is the quality of the communication networks that lead from the decision-making elites to the performance units and back, including number and intensity of gaps, "noise" on the line, etc. As my purpose here is not to list all these factors, but to illustrate the main categories, let us turn now from cybernatorial factors to the second element of control, power.

Control: Power, Its Sources, and Its Mobilization

Societal Assets and Power. Societal structures are not just patterns of interaction of actors, patterns of expectations and symbols, but also patterns of allocation of societal assets, the possessions of a societal unit. These can be classified analytically as coercive, utilitarian, and normative, concerning respectively the distribution of means of violence, material objects and services, and symbols. A measure of the assets a societal unit or subunit possesses is *not* in itself an indication of its actual power, but only of its *potential*. Assets might be used to generate more assets, be consumed or stored, *or* might be used to overcome the resistance of other actors, which is what by definition societal power means. (This does not mean necessarily to force other actors; their resistance might be overcome, for instance, by offering a payoff.) In exploring the relations between assets and power, it is essential not to shift the frame of reference in mid-analysis. Conversion of assets into power at time t^1 might lead to more assets at time t^2; in time t^1, however, the generation of power entails a "loss" of assets.

A central predisposition of sociobernetics is that the relationship between assets and power is a "loose" one—that is, the amount of assets allocated to a societal unit in a given structure is a poor predictor of how much societal power the unit will have. The amount of power generated depends significantly on the *intra*unit allocation of the assets among alternative usages. A unit poor in assets can in principle command more power than a much more affluent one, if the poor unit assigns more of its assets to power "production." (With half the GNP, the U.S.S.R. maintains a defense budget similar to that of the U.S.)

The societal context affects the fraction of the assets a unit possesses that can be converted into power; this potential for conversion is not freely set by the societal actor (e.g., that black Americans are less politically active than Jewish Americans is in part due to differences in educational opportunities). However, I suggest, the degree of intraunit assignment of assets to power is a relatively more malleable attribute than the amount of assets the unit possesses (at any given point in time). It is here that an important element of voluntarism enters the societal structure. A comparison of colonial societies in the years immediately preceding the "takeoff" of national independence movements with those immediately after they won their independence seems to show that the "takeoff" involved more change in the relative *use* of assets for power than in the assets base itself. For example, the American civil rights movement, which between 1953 and 1965 transformed important segments of the black American population from a passive to an active grouping, entailed much more of a change in mobilization of power than in amount of assets (Wilson, 1965, pp. 3–7).

Mobilization. Each societal unit has at any given point in time a *level of activation* which we define as the ratio of its total assets that are available for collective action. The percent of the GNP spent by the government, the percent of the labor force employed by it, and the percent of knowledge producers that work for it are crude indicators of national activation level. "Mobilization" refers to an upward change in the level of activation, to an increase in the fraction of the total assets possessed by a unit that are made available for collective action by that unit. ("Demobilization" refers to a reduction in that level.)

The level of activation of most societal units most of the time is very low; if all their assets are taken into account, usually less than 10 percent are available for unit action. Hence relatively small percentage changes in the level of mobilization may largely increase the action capacity of a unit. For example, an increase of 10 percent in the assets of a unit that are mobilized might more than double its action capacity. Major societal transformation, such as revolutions and the gaining of national independence, usually involve relatively high mobilization. The secret of the power of social movements lies in part in the relatively high mobilization which their asceticism and the intense commitment of their members allows for.

Aside from the asset base a collectivity possesses and the amount of power it is mobilizing, the *kind* of power mobilized also affects the action capacity of the unit. To employ power is, by definition, to overcome resistance, but in society as in nature each application of power generates a counterpower, a resistance of its own (the result of the alienation of those who were made to suspend their preferences in favor of those of the power wielders). While all power applications have this effect, some generate more alienation than others.

In estimating the effect of the use of a particular kind of power on the relationships between the power wielder and the subjects, it is essential to take into account that this is as a rule a "generalized" relationship. That is, while a particular instance of exercise of power may generate little alienation, repeated use may generate much. Even when no alienation is manifest, it might accumulate covertly and express itself indirectly.

When the power relationship is explored (and not just described), if the power used is coercive (if it involves the use of force or imposes severe deprivations on the subject), all other things being equal, resistance will tend to be high. If utilitarian power is applied, power which rests on rewarding the subject with material goods and objects, resistance to the power wielder's demands will be lower. If normative power is applied, power which has its basis in the individual's involvement in the particular matter, then the resistance will be lowest of all. (Actually even some net gains in future capacity to act may be achieved when normative power is applied, as it may reduce resistance to future acts.) Most power wielders may prefer to use the less alienating kinds, but there are limitations on their capacity to mobilize these kinds as well as on their understanding of the dynamics involved, with the consequence that they may opt to use the more alienating kinds of power (Etzioni, 1961), even where this is not otherwise necessary.

A study of control thus adds to the exploration of the asset base of a unit, the degree to which it is mobilized for collective action and which kinds of power are mobilized. These added factors in turn determine to a considerable degree how alienating control will be, and whether relations between the elites and the other units will be those of open conflict, encapsulated conflict, or cooperation.

CONSENSUS FORMATION

Consensus Defined

So far, guidance of change has been explored from a "downward" view, from the controlling overlayer to the controlled underlayer; even the discussion of communication feedback and subject resistance has been from the viewpoint of a controlling center. The main difference, though, between societal and electronic cybernetics is that in the societal we take into account systematically that the controlled units have some of the controlling capacities themselves: they input knowledge, make decisions, pursue goals, and exercise power. Hence the capacity of any one unit to act is determined only in part by its ability to control the others; it is similarly affected by the degree to which the goals it has chosen to pursue and the means it employs are compatible or in conflict with those preferred by other units, i.e., degree of consensus.

Consensus, the congruence of preferences of the units concerned, is viewed by typical collectivistic theories as largely given (or changing under the impact of ongoing processes); voluntaristic theories tend to view it as open to manipulation by charismatic leadership and/or mass media. From a sociobernetic viewpoint, consensus is the result of a process in which given preferences *and* guided efforts affect the outcome, which is a changing consensus. Many studies have applied such a perspective; in sociobernetics it finds a theoretical home. How much consensus is actually achieved changes with a variety of sociopolitical factors and cannot be explored here.

Control and Consensus

There is a trade-off curve between control and consensus; that is, for any given level of activation, the more consensus, the less need for control; and the less consensus gained, the more need for control. Which "mix" is used is of course not without consequences; it affects the level of alienation and of resistance, and hence the future capacity to act. It is important to realize that when both consensus *and* control are higher, more change can be guided than when both are lower, without an increase in alienation. (The additional consensus absorbs the additional alienation which the additional control would generate.)

Consensus Formation Structures

To illustrate a sociobernetical study of consensus formation, let me briefly compare "built-in" and "segregated" consensus formation structures. In a built-in structure, consensus formation is by and large the output of ongoing interactions among the societal units. Consensus formation in smaller and less complex preliterate tribes seems to rely largely on ongoing interaction between the member families. Consensus is to a degree produced in Soviet society in the process of interaction between factory managements, union leaders, and party officials, though the prime function of these interactions is not consensus formation but is economic and administrative in nature—in the downward guidance sense of the term (Berliner, 1957; Huntington, 1965, pp. 129-90). In a segregated structure, political units (such as parties and legislatures) exist as distinct from societal ones, and societal differences are translated into political ones before consensus concerning collectivization is worked out. Segregated structures seem more effective for consensus formation than built-in ones, though they can produce only enough to back up comparatively low levels of activation. They are like a sophisticated machine that cannot be used for heavy duty.

In the search for a structure that would allow for more guided change and higher consensus, a search that is far from completed, "voluntary planning" as developed in France in the postwar years and by the European Economic Community has gained much attention. There is less separation of political and societal units than in the segregated structure (typical of totalitarian regimes). Above all, the knowledge input units are not related only to the decision-making units but are also tied into the consensus-forming process, thus informing the controlled and not just the controlling units, and remodeling the judgments that information units produce—on the basis of interaction with *both* groupings.

Comparative studies of consensus formation ought to supplement and in part to replace the comparative study of constitutions and formal studies of governments. To supplement, because we need studies of both the political institutions and consensus formation which will relate these institutions to societal groups and relations among them. To replace in part, because the studies of political shells have proved too rigid and simplistic for many purposes. The study of democracy might illustrate this point.

As "democracy" was traditionally defined—"the rule of the majority"—the concept was unable even to distinguish between totalitarian and democratic regimes. The more subtle implication of the definition (provision for the institutionalized change of the party in office) still disregarded less formal democratic mechanisms, such as changes in the coalition partners and the factions represented inside the ruling party in response to changes in societal power. Moreover, by exclusion, it defined the government of such countries as West Germany and Israel as nondemocratic. Neither the Christian Democratic Union nor the Mapai has been voted out of office since the establishment of the two states, and whether or not these parties can be voted out is an open question. Also, the formal study focuses on parliaments and parties as the consensus-forming agents, but these are rapidly losing their effectiveness as the power of the executive rises. Thus, a policy that meets all the criteria of a formal democracy might still not generate enough consensus for the prevailing level of activation, not to mention increased levels which are both needed and occurring, thus leaving the society with substandard consensus leading either to accumulative alienation or to curtailment of activity.

Similarly, the important differences among the consensus formation processes of various totalitarian and authoritarian societies as well as the changes that occur in these processes over time can scarcely be studied in formal terms; the very characterization of regimes as totalitarian or authoritarian attempts to analyze these in terms of their formal characteristics. These processes of consensus formation are further obscured by the tendency to classify regimes as one-, two-, or multiparty states. In comparison, a sociobernetic study of consensus formation provides a less institutional and more "societal" approach.

A SYNTHESIZING VIEW: THE ACTIVE SOCIETY

I turn now to illustrate the synthesizing perspective on societal change that can be attained once our understanding of the various components of sociobernetics is more advanced, since at the present stage little more than a brief illustration can be provided. Using control (cybernatorial capacities and power) and consensus formation as two dimensions of a property space, I characterize, in an ideal-typical manner, a society which is high on both as comparatively active; low on both as passive; high on control but low on consensus as overmanaged; and low on control but high on consensus as drifting.

The *passive society* is approximated by highly primitive societies. Their low level of societal self-control is obvious. Their consensus is collectivistic and static, but it is largely not mobilized around societal goals, and there is little machinery to *form* consensus when additional consensus is needed. Hence, while "background" consensus might be high, the consensus *formation* capacity is low. One indicator of this low capacity is that when primitive societies do act, coercion often plays a rather central role in overcoming resistance (Morris, 1965).

The *active society* maintains a level of activation that is not lower and is possibly even higher than that of overmanaged societies, and it forms at least as much consensus as drifting societies. This is possible because the active society commands more effective control and consensus-forming mechanisms; it can rely more on the less alienating kinds of power, especially on the normative. Also, high consensus requires a high level of activation and realization of some of the variety of goals the various subsocieties and the society as a unit are committed to. Effective control, in turn, requires support of those subject to the control; hence raising the level of control without at the same time raising alienation requires a high capacity to form consensus. Thus, high control and high consensus, high activation and low alienation are mutually reinforcing. Finally, the active society has the highest capacity of the four ideal types for self-transformation, which is the ultimate safeguard against widespread alienation as it makes possible that the rise of radically different goals and subsocieties may still be accommodated within the same system.

The active society is largely a utopia which does not exist, though it is not a utopia in the sense that no society might become one, for its functional requirements do not appear to violate any sociological law. Social-movement societies, such as Israel in 1948, approximate such an active society. A main difference between a social-movement society and the active one is that the latter stabilizes some social-movement features such as high consensus formation and intense commitment, rather than merely passing through such a phase. (The mechanisms for stabilization cannot be discussed in the present limits of space; for a further discussion, see *The Active Society*.)

The *overmanaged*, high-control, low-consensus type is approximated by the totalitarian societies. Typically, they have inadequate consensus formation structures, and those they have are mainly of the built-in type. Societal action is oriented to hyperactive goals, which later are scaled down, as consensus mechanisms here do not allow discovery beforehand of where and how much resistance will be encountered in the various subsocieties as various societal changes are introduced. Typically, too, use of alienating kinds of power is high.

Whether overmanaged societies are transformable and what kind of society they will become if they are, are two widely debated questions. The argument is between those who see democratization as taking place and those who argue that the totalitarian societies are ultrastable (Mosely, 1962; Almond, 1960a). This dichotomy seems not to exhaust the possibilities. Democratization seems unlikely because democracies are themselves no longer well adapted, as their present control and consensus mechanisms are insufficient for the higher level of activation needed, and because there is no legitimation of democracy or democratic experience in the history of most contemporary totalitarian societies. On the other hand, it seems hard to maintain that totalitarian societies are not transformable in view of the far-reaching changes of the U.S.S.R. since 1917.

The direction of any such change might be toward an active society whose level of control is relatively closer to that of totalitarian societies than of the democratic ones, whose less-segregated consensus-formation structure is closer to the totalitarian built-in one than the democratic segregated one, and whose social-movement character can draw on legitimation of the most charismatic period of totalitarian societies. The sharpest transition needed would be from reliance on force and propaganda as central means of compliance to a focus on education and normative power; such a transformation, as drastic as it is, may be easier than a shift to a utilitarian focus characteristic of capitalistic democracies. In fact, this is the direction of change already evidenced by the U.S.S.R.

Drifting societies are approximated by capitalist democracies. Their most important relevant feature is that they act as societies to introduce significant structural changes only when the need to act is "overdue" (Etzioni, 1965, pp. 81-82), is a "crisis," when broad consensus can be mobilized before action is taken. Second, the action taken often does not remove the lag as the changes introduced are the fruit of compromise between the more conservative and the more change-oriented subsocieties. The second major reason that capitalist democracies are drifting societies is that the more powerful subsocieties draw societal assets for their own consumptions and power, either by neutralizing the societal controls or by slanting them to serve their subsocietal interests. In either case, as far as the society at large is concerned, it is not guiding its processes and change.

CONSENSUS, EQUALITY, AND ACTIVATION

Here a conceptual addition must be introduced to tie the concept of consensus formation to those of asset analysis and alienation, an addition found in the concept of equality. Equality is higher the closer the distribution curve of assets approximates a straight line, i.e., groupings of the population that are equal in size possess equal amounts of assets. No society is completely egalitarian, but there are obviously significant differences in the degree of inequality. These in turn are associated, though of course not on a one-to-one basis, with differences in power. Now, when consensus is formed it reflects the power relations among the members; the policy agreed upon tends to be closer to that preferred by the more powerful subsocieties. It is as if the weaker members say to themselves that they had better go along with a suggested policy in which their concurrence is traded for some concessions, for fear that otherwise the powerful would impose a policy even more removed from their preferences. The amount of alienation that remains in the weaker units, however, is clearly related to the measure of inequality. Consensus which leaves little or no alienation can be formed only under conditions of comparatively high equality.

While this cannot be demonstrated here, I suggest that there is a secular historical trend toward a reduction in inequality among the subsocieties making up the capitalistic democracies, although so far this reduction has been limited. (The trend is fairly obvious as far as political rights and status symbols are concerned; it is less clear with regard to economic well-being.) Continuation and acceleration of such a trend, if it were to take place, would move democratic societies in an active direction by allowing the formation of more consensus with less alienating undertones, and more facing of societal problems before they are overdue, i.e., toward a high level of activation. A major force which propels the transition from a drifting to an active society is the mobilization of the weaker collectivities; this is triggered by the spread of education, by changes in employment opportunities, and by other factors that generate imbalanced status sets, as well as by the priming effect of elites, especially intellectual ones. As this statement is rather central to my conception of societal change as far as the transition of Western societies into the postmodern (see below for definition) period is concerned, the assumptions implied should be briefly outlined.

As I see it, transformation of capitalist democracies is not propelled by *conflict* among *classes*, but by *interaction* among *organized collectivities*. Thus, the societal units may be an ethnic group, a race, a national community, and not just a class; the relationship might be of coalition, limited adversary, etc. rather than all-out conflict; and, above all, the unit of action is not the collectivity per se, but that part of it which has been mobilized into organizational structures. Thus, history is not affected by the working class as such, which is a passive unit, but by labor unions, labor parties, social protest movements that mobilize a segment of the working class. (The same could be said about the civil rights movement and black Americans, national independence movements and colonial people, etc.)

Collectivities are bases of *potential* power, but generally only a small fraction of these potentialities are actualized for purposes of societal action and change. The capacity of any societal actor to influence the pattern of societal change, i.e., his actual societal power, depends as much on his capacity to mobilize—i.e., *on the outcome of the internal struggle between mobilizers and the apathetics*— as on the actor's potential power base.

It might be said that the capacity to mobilize is itself determined by the distribution of assets *among* the collectivities; that the more powerful units hold down the capacity to mobilize of the weaker societal units. While this is a valid observation, it is also true that the mobilization of any collectivity reduces the capacity of other collectivities to hold it down. For each point in time, hence, it is necessary to study not only the power potential of a societal actor but also his mobilization capacity, which affects his actual power at this point in time. The dynamic analysis then proceeds by comparing changes in potential and actual power over time and the effects of changes in the power of some actors over that of the others. A study of societal change which focuses largely on the stratificational relations among collectivities (as Marx did and in which he was corrected to a degree by Lenin), not to mention one which excludes power analysis altogether, provides at best a fragmental theory of societal change (Wolin, 1960).

What does all this imply for the change of capitalistic democracies? In these societies, too, most members of most collectivities have a formal right to participate in the political process, i.e., an egalitarian political institutional status unmatched in their societal positions. An increasing number are also gaining an education, which has a mobilizing effect (Milbrath, 1965). For historical reasons which need not be explored here, campus groups, professionals, clergy, middle-class members of ethnic minorities, all of which command political skills, are allowed to act as mobilizers, though under various constraints. And, I suggest, with weaker collectivities becoming increasingly mobilizable, and with an increase in the number of mobilizers, the total effect is increased societal power of the heretofore weaker and underprivileged collectivities. The effect of the mobilization of weaker collectivities, which is only in part neutralized by countermobilization of more powerful collectivities, is to transform the society in the direction of a relatively more egalitarian and active one. Whether such transformation will sooner or later lead to a showdown between the powerful and the mobilizing collectivities, or the mobilization will run out of steam on its own, or the scales will be tipped for an active society—that is, whether a structural transformation will take place—are questions the study of sociobernetics points to but cannot at present answer.

Both the overmanaged and the drifting society seem to be tending toward becoming an active society (rather than either of the less active types becoming the prevalent type). The new means of communications and of knowledge technology may be working in this direction in both kinds of society; continued mobilization of the weaker collectivities in capitalist societies and increased pluralism in totalitarian societies may also be supportive of such a transformation. Under what conditions an active society will be advanced is a major subject of macrosociology. The new cybernatorial capacities that have become increasingly available since 1945 offer a new range of societal options and hence mark a period that might be referred to as the postmodern one. Nineteen forty-five marks also the opening of the atomic age and hence suggests that a major issue for macrosociology, not touched upon here, is that of changing not the systems' structures but their boundaries. The question of which conditions favor and which block the rise of active societies and the transformation of an anarchic world into a communal one, I suggest, is regained for systematic sociological study by such approaches as that of sociobernetics.

20. THE HISTORICAL-ANALYTICAL APPROACH

Jerome M. Clubb

During the past few decades the study of politics has been increasingly marked by an effort to apply scientific modes of investigation and explanation. This effort has led to the development of powerful methodological and conceptual tools which in turn have been productive of findings and generalizations of at least limited predictive and explanatory power. These successes have worked to inspire confidence in the possibility and value of the scientific study of politics both among students engaged in the general enterprise and among many politicians, statesmen, and others concerned with practical political situations and problems. The behavioral approach to the study of politics, which will be taken for present purposes as generally synonymous with a scientific orientation in political studies, is, however, primarily a development of the years since World War II. In the main, practitioners of this general approach have been concerned with contemporary phenomena. As a consequence, many of the most important and impressive findings and generalizations about politics are based primarily upon investigation of the events and phenomena of a limited time period, essentially the years since 1945. Until very recently, historical political phenomena have been largely neglected.

The politics of even the distant past have, of course, been intensively studied by professional and amateur historians and, to a much lesser degree, by other social scientists. While the value of this work is undeniable, it is also clear that these efforts have serious limitations as contributions to scientific knowledge of the political life of the past or of politics more generally. To many social scientists, both the methods employed and the evidence which historians have relied upon most heavily seem largely impressionistic and not subject to the procedures of verification and replication demanded, at least as a goal, by contemporary social science. More important, perhaps, is that historical studies have tended to be primarily descriptive and concerned with the unique and episodic. Indeed, many historians have argued, virtually as a professional canon, that the development and use of generalizations and theories is neither possible nor desirable in the study of human affairs (Potter, 1963). Thus their work has tended to lack the theoretical orientation usually considered a vital goal in the scientific study of human affairs, and their work does not fully compensate for the failure of other social scientists to concern themselves with the phenomena of the past.

The growth of interest in recent years among political scientists and other students of politics, including historians, in systematic investigation of historical political phenomena communicates well-justified dissatisfaction with this general state of affairs. The necessity of studying political phenomena in a variety of situational contexts has long been recognized, and students have devoted attention to comparative studies across nations, cultures, regions, and subnational groupings. The logic underlying such studies suggests the value of historical investigations. When confronted with conclusions based upon a limited period of time, it is justifiable to ask whether these conclusions have relevance beyond that time period, just as it is justifiable to ask whether findings based upon a single area or nation have general relevance. The tendency to neglect history has the effect of unnecessarily reducing the range and variety of political phenomena available for study and of restricting the number of cases or examples of particular phenomena to be investigated. Historical evidence affords the opportunity to examine a wider variety of political phenomena in a wider variety of contexts than would be possible if investigations were limited to the investigator's immediate present. Historical investigations, in short, can facilitate findings of greater generality and increase the researcher's confidence in the validity and relevance of his work. Without a well-developed historical or time dimension, moreover, the study of politics can hardly hope to cope with developmental processes or with the problem of change more generally, and the risk of an excessively static view of political life is inevitably increased.

No lengthy effort to explain the absence of a well-developed historical dimension in the emerging science of politics is required at this point. Several general issues may be noted briefly, however, in order to eliminate certain possible objections to the use of historical evidence, and to provide a basis for more detailed discussions to follow.

It seems clear that social scientists have tended to focus their attention primarily upon contemporary phenomena, in part out of an understandable concern for relevance. At first glance the investigation of the events of the remote past can hardly seem as important or rewarding as investigation of more recent ones. For the student who feels that social science should aid man in orienting himself in the world and contribute to the development of solutions to human problems, investigation of the past may seem an essentially unproductive luxury. However understandable, these views may well be based upon an unscientific attitude. The goal of science is, after all, the development of working hypotheses, theories, and laws of the greatest possible generality. To develop such generalizations, investigation of a wide and varied range of relevant phenomena is necessary. Study of the political life of different nations, cultures, and subnational groupings can contribute to the development of theoretical formulations which help to predict and explain the characteristics of a single limited area. Similarly, the study of political phenomena in a variety of historical contexts can, in principle, contribute to the development of generalizations and theories which serve to explain the characteristics of the investigator's own or other historical contexts. In short, it is the theories and generalizations developed through the study of politics that contribute to the solution of human problems. To the degree that historical evidence can be useful in the development of such generalizations, that evidence is fully as relevant as the evidence provided by the more contemporary world.

More significant arguments against the use of historical evidence in the social sciences have to do with the nature of historical evidence and knowledge. To state the matter in oversimplified and somewhat distorted terms, it has been contended that the study of the past does not allow scientific procedures of direct observation and verification and that, hence, knowledge of the past cannot be admitted as scientific knowledge. Only a little thought may suggest the strict epistemological accuracy and the irrelevance of this criticism of historical investigations. It is obvious that the past no longer exists and that only the residue of past events, not the events themselves, can be studied. On the other hand, it is also clear that events are studied after they occur. The political scientist normally does not base his analysis of the electoral process solely upon his direct observation of a single election, but upon extensive additional evidence of which only a small part can be in any sense considered the product of direct and immediate observation. Normally his evidence includes essential elements of earlier elections, and he describes processes at work during the particular election and campaign which he could not observe directly and can only infer from the results of the election. In these terms, then, "historical" and "contemporary" investigations differ in the relative distance in time between the investigator and the phenomena investigated; but strictly speaking, all political scientists must study the past.

Examination of events of the relatively remote past inevitably differ from more contemporary ones in terms of the quantity and nature of available evidence and, to a lesser extent, in terms of the methods of data collection which may be used. The investigator interested in the causes, nature, and consequences of revolutionary upheavals, for example, might well decide to examine the great revolutions of modern history, including the French and Russian revolutions, as well as more recent revolutions. In carrying out his investigations of the revolutions of the more remote past he would not, of course, be able to conduct public opinion surveys or interview leading participants. But even in the case of more contemporary upheavals, and particularly those that involve "closed" societies, his opportunity to use techniques of data collection that involve direct observation would be severely limited. Rather, the data available for the study of revolutions, however remote or proximate in time, tend to be "natural" data, including the writings of participants and observers, the documents produced by officials and public and private agencies, and the "public record" data recorded by social bookkeeping systems. As will be seen, the use of such evidence, whether bearing upon events of the remote past or upon more contemporary events, poses special problems of evaluation, involves heavy reliance upon inference, and places a premium upon particular research procedures.

HISTORY AND THE SCIENCE OF POLITICS

Perhaps the most commanding reason for the use of historical evidence is lack of confidence in findings, generalizations, and theories based upon investigation of the phenomena of a single point in time or a limited chronological period. This general problem can be illustrated by brief consideration of the nature of the contemporary era as compared with earlier time periods. While the years since 1945 may appear to have been marked by rapid and even chaotic change to those fated to live through them, a little consideration will serve to demonstrate that these years have also been characterized by major elements of continuity and homogeneity. The international environment during these years has been more or less consistently marked by bipolar tensions and is in this respect unlike the multipower system of, for example, the nineteenth or eighteenth century. Similarly, a relatively high level of affluence, advanced technology, and well-developed communications facilities have also been relatively consistent characteristics of these years. To be sure, change along these dimensions of life has occurred, and not all nations, cultural areas, and social groups share equally in these attributes of contemporary life. Even so, modern-day affluence, technology, and communications could hardly have been dreamed of in even well-developed Western nations a short century ago. Thus the conditions of life and with them the conditions and determinants of politics inevitably differed in more remote time periods from those of more recent years. Moreover, while it is undeniable that affluence, advanced technology, and communications are by no means evenly distributed in the contemporary world, it also seems clear that even impoverished social groups and relatively underdeveloped nations feel the impact of these characteristics of modern life if only in terms of goals to be achieved and as sources of a sense of deprivation.

Findings based upon investigation of the evidence provided by such a limited chronological period, however intensive the investigation, may well be time bound and limited in generality and relevance to the particular era considered. Continuity and discontinuity within such a period may be observed and precisely measured, but it is impossible to know whether these mark significant changes or merely limited fluctuations in a longer trend or pattern. Generalizations based upon observation and measurement of such fluctuations may provide little guidance in understanding earlier phenomena and, more important, provide only inadequate guidance for the future. The search for causal relations may be frustrated if investigations are limited to a single period in time. The number of particular cases of general phenomena may be few within a single chronological period, and the range and variety of political phenomena available for investigation within any given time period are similarly limited. Because contextual conditions such as level of affluence, technology, and communications are often relatively constant within a single era, the effort to identify and isolate the impact and causal significance of such conditions is made more difficult if only a single era is considered. Changes in the effectiveness of party organizations in legislative bodies, as measured through interviews and analysis of voting behavior within a particular time period, may be seen as the product of new ideological currents or of changes in patterns of constituency interests. Seen in a longer time perspective these changes may appear as special cases of a longer trend or pattern produced by changes in contextual characteristics. The development of communications and transportation facilities may have worked to increase both the visibility of legislative activities to constituents, as well as the visibility of constituency interests to legislators, or these developments may have served to introduce new mechanisms which allow the legislator to appeal more directly to constituents with less reliance upon the party organization.

In these terms, then, the past can be seen as a kind of laboratory for the study of politics which can be used to formulate hypotheses and test those based upon investigation of more contemporary phenomena, to examine developmental processes and trace trends and changes across time, and to investigate the genesis of particular phenomena and processes. Such a formulation may justifiably provoke objections. The use of the past as a laboratory may be seen as contrary to the effort to reconstruct the past for its own interest and value, which has often been expressed as the goal of historical research. Suffice it to say at this point that I am not concerned with the goals of historians here, although the concluding section of this essay may be considered relevant to some of the preoccupations and assumptions of professional historians.

For present purposes a more important objection to the above formulation will center upon the connotation of experimentation which the word laboratory involves. The limitations of historical evidence, the fact that the investigator concerned with past phenomena cannot create additional evidence that better suits his purposes, and the obvious impossibility of controlling past events, all seem to suggest the impossibility of experimentation where the past is concerned. The general accuracy of these objections can be admitted, however, without undermining the utility of historical evidence. In the first place, experimental conditions, in the sense used in the physical sciences, can rarely be achieved in the investigation of political phenomena whatever their locus in time in relation to the investigator. The student of even the most contemporary phenomena can rarely control all the circumstances of his investigation. Except in severely limited ways, he cannot summon up at will additional cases of a particular phenomenon in order to test and refine his hypotheses and increase his confidence in their generality. Nor can he, again except in very limited ways, secure the precise repetition of an event while adjusting and controlling a single variable to determine its impact as a genuine experiment would require. Thus it seems clear that, in political studies in general, investigations at best can only rarely resemble a genuine experimental situation.

Despite the limitations of historical data and the necessary lack of conformity between research concerned with past events and a model experimental situation, it seems clear that historical investigations do have advantages. By examining specific instances of a general phenomenon or class of phenomena in a variety of historical contexts it may be possible to better identify the significance of particular contextual characteristics present only in some of the instances studied. Thus, through the use of historical evidence, otherwise uncontrollable elements of political situations can, in effect, be controlled and varied to better estimate their causal significance. Within the limits of available evidence, historical events and individuals are open for study to a degree that more contemporary events and individuals often are not. Problems of confidentiality and sensitivity to possibly damaging revelations are less serious where historical investigations are concerned. Historical events and processes are closed and their outcomes are known. The past is insensitive to the process of inquiry, and the investigator can have no impact upon the attitudes and behavior of historical individuals as he could in the present. In short, while the conditions of a model experimental situation cannot be achieved in historical investigations, some elements of such a situation can be approximated sometimes more effectively than if one were studying more contemporary events.

Perhaps the most important goal of scientifically oriented investigations of historical phenomena is that of formulating and testing hypotheses which look toward the development of empirically based general theories of human behavior. This goal can, of course, be appropriately seen as underlying and constituting a basic requirement of all scientifically oriented studies utilizing historical evidence, or for that matter more contemporary evidence, including studies that are essentially descriptive or exploratory in nature.

One category of such studies is composed of investigations of varying numbers of specific examples of general classes of events. In one sense, at least, Arnold Toynbee's monumental *Study of History* (1935–61) admirably illustrates this particular utilization of historical evidence on a grand scale. Through examination and comparison of all historical civilizations from the ancient world to the present, Toynbee attempted to plot the life cycle of civilizations and to identify basic characteristics and processes common to the birth, life, and death of these historical phenomena. Since civilizations have existed in a variety of historical contexts and in numerous patterns of relations with each other, Toynbee attempted through comparisons to distinguish between the characteristics common to all civilizations and the specific characteristics of particular civilizations produced perhaps by peculiar historical contexts. Brinton's early study of revolutions (1952) is a less monumental but still grand-scale example of this type of investigation. By studying and comparing the particular events, characteristics, and conditions of four great historical revolutions Brinton attempted to identify the elements and characteristics common to revolutions in general. A further illustration of this general category of historical investigation is provided by

Eisenstadt's study of the political systems of bureaucratic empires (1963). This study is a particularly important illustration in view of Eisenstadt's effort to apply the methods and conceptual tools of the social sciences to the study of history, and for his explicit attempt to find "patterns or laws in the structure and development" of the political systems studied.

These are, of course, the works of master scholars which have proven productive and fertile both in terms of the generalizations about human affairs which they present and more important, perhaps, in terms of the stimulus to the use of comparative methods in the study of historical phenomena which they have provided. They provide useful illustrations of the investigation of a number of specific examples of a general class of human experiences in order to discover general attributes, characteristics, and processes common to the entire class. In the longer term such investigations look toward the development of theories and laws of human behavior similar to those of the natural sciences, although to attribute these latter goals to Toynbee and Brinton may well be inaccurate and tend to falsify the philosophical orientation of their work.

Despite their importance and value, consideration of the limitations of such works is also instructive (Black, 1966). In the first place, the research and erudition required to carry out studies of this scope, even when the number of cases is limited, are beyond the capacities of most investigators. Moreover, the scale of the phenomena considered is such that the number of cases of each one available for investigation is necessarily limited even when the entire sweep of human history is considered. Phenomena of such large scale also inevitably present serious definitional problems. As Black points out, scholars disagree as to conceptual boundaries and definitional characteristics of such events as civilizations and revolutions and, as a consequence, comparisons on such a grand scale are rarely concrete and specific enough to allow precise generalization. For these reasons, generalizations and theories based upon such large-scale studies, while provocative, often inspire only limited confidence.

Examination of more limited and specific phenomena provides, at least at this stage in the development of the study of politics, a more satisfactory means to formulate and test hypotheses relevant to political affairs. Ripley's studies of leadership patterns in the American Congress (1967, 1968) provide examples of such studies involving the use of historical evidence. By examining and comparing patterns of congressional leadership in varying circumstances of partisan control over the central government and in varying historical contexts, Ripley attempted to elucidate the role of party leaders, to identify changes in leadership functions in Congress, and to assess leadership patterns and other factors conducive to legislative success. In these studies Ripley had the advantage of a comparatively brief time span and a well-defined institution characterized by structural continuity. Thus problems of definition and boundary conditions were less severe.

Investigations of historical occurrences are probably most useful when designed to test limited and well-defined hypotheses which relate to broader conceptual frameworks or theories. In these terms, the studies by Singer and his associates of the relations in history between the development of international alliance systems and the incidence of war are useful illustrations. One of these investigations was intended to test two basic hypotheses: "The greater the number of alliance commitments in the [international] system, the more war the system will experience," and "the closer to pure bi-polarity the system is, the more war it will experience" (Singer and Small, 1968). These hypotheses were, of course, related to broader propositions bearing upon the international system. Through systematic collection, codification, and analysis of basic historical data relevant to the world international system from 1815 to 1945, an attempt was made to test these propositions (see also Deutsch and Singer, 1964; Singer and Small, 1966a, 1966b).

In these works Singer and his associates were concerned with international phenomena, and their work dictated collection of data bearing upon a relatively long time period and relevant to the entire international system. In his study of the relation between information flow and partisan attitudes, Converse (1966a) suggests a somewhat more limited use of historical evidence. On the basis of data provided by public opinion surveys conducted in the 1950s and early 1960s Converse advanced several propositions bearing upon the relation between varying levels of information about politics held by the American electorate and the stability of partisan attitudes within the electorate. However, the high level of information generally available to the electorate due to the advanced communications systems of the 1950s and 1960s presented an obstacle to full investigation and pursuit of the phenomena with which he was concerned. Thus Converse suggested that examination of popular voting trends in the nineteenth century, when the communication system was less well developed and the volume of information available to the electorate was much lower, would provide a test of these propositions.

Perhaps the most obvious use of historical evidence in the study of politics involves examination of processes that occur across long periods of time. Political institutions and systems obviously change with the passage of time. It is debatable whether such changes can be appropriately described in terms of such organic analogies as growth and decay, and explained in terms of processes internal to the particular system, as has often been attempted. On the other hand, it is clear that long-term processes of change do occur. These processes can be studied by examining nations and cultures passing through different stages of a long-term process at the same chronological point. But despite the utility of this approach, it does not facilitate analysis of the general development process as a whole and may not allow identification and analysis of variables which are part of the world historical context. To accomplish these goals, the investigation of such processes in historical depth is necessary. In these terms, studies of political modernization and development, and investigations of changes in the function and structure of political institutions, are obvious examples of the use of historical evidence to develop knowledge of political phenomena (see, for example, Lipset, 1963).

Historical evidence has also been employed in what may be termed genetic studies. Frequently, contemporary processes and other phenomena cannot be fully understood without consideration of their origins, and, as a consequence, investigation of historical evidence is necessary. One example of this use of history is provided by Campbell, Converse, Miller, and Stokes (1960, pp. 149–67). In their work these authors employed sample surveys conducted in the 1950s to systematically discover patterns of political attitudes in the American electorate and to relate these patterns to electoral behavior. It was recognized, however, that attitude patterns in many cases antedated the 1950s. To investigate the formation and nature of particular attitudes, respondents in public opinion surveys were asked to recall their voting behavior during earlier years and their reactions to particular events in the past. In this way it was possible to estimate the relevance of the events of the 1930s to the formation of partisan identifications and political attitudes still present and of importance in the 1950s. This procedure, moreover, provided further evidence of the durability over time of American political attitudes. This illustration exemplifies the use of a limited but interesting form of historical evidence, the recollections of participants in the present-day political process. However, other investigators (for example, Key, 1956; MacRae and Meldrum, 1960; Silva, 1962; Pomper, 1968; Clubb and Allen, 1969, 1971; Burnham, 1965, 1970; Ladd, 1970) have examined historical voting returns to gauge the impact of particular events and social forces upon the development of patterns of partisan affiliation within the electorate.

The preceding discussion does not, of course, provide a comprehensive review of studies of political phenomena which draw upon historical evidence. Rather, a few investigations have been touched upon to suggest that investigation of historical events can serve to formulate and test hypotheses, to examine developmental and other long-term processes, and to discover the genesis of particular political institutions and phenomena. This general categorization has, of course, been used for purposes of illustration, and it should be clear that actual investigations usually fall into more than one of these general categories. Deliberate stress has been placed upon the use of historical evidence to test and refine well-defined and carefully formulated hypotheses. As will be seen, this emphasis is dictated not only by considerations of economy and convenience in research, but also by the nature of historical data and knowledge.

THE NATURE AND USE OF HISTORICAL EVIDENCE

From what has been said to this point it should be apparent that the use of historical evidence in political studies neither involves a particular conceptual approach analogous, for example, to the functional or institutional approaches, nor requires a special body of methodological tools. Rather, the conceptual and methodological tools that have been found fruitful in the investigation of contemporary politics are, with few exceptions, applicable to the study of the political life of the past. Certainly, the canons of scientific investigation are fully applicable to studies that involve a historical dimension.

On the other hand, the nature of historical evidence presents certain problems and imposes limitations that are confronted less severely or not at all by researchers concerned with contemporary political life. Discussions of the nature and value of historical investigations for the social sciences have often called attention to the limitations of historical evidence. Historical materials have been described as fragmentary, incomplete, and impressionistic, with the implication that the study of the life of the past cannot approach in rigor, precision, and accuracy studies of more contemporary life. Still other commentators have noted the great mass and volume and the diffuse nature of historical evidence, particularly that bearing upon the modern era, and have suggested that these characteristics prevent their effective use. As it happens, both of these commentaries contain substantial elements of truth, although neither constitutes an insurmountable obstacle to the use of historical evidence in the systematic study of politics.

Historical evidence can best be seen as the residue of normal processes of human life. The researcher concerned with past events cannot, in most cases, employ methods of direct observation and inquiry to create information that specifically suits the purposes of his investigation. He can sometimes collect information by questioning surviving participants in past events, as in an example described above (Campbell et al., 1960, pp. 149-67), but this source of historical information is subject to the frailties of human memory and strictly limited by the human life span. By far the greatest volume and the most important historical evidence, moreover, was not originally created with the needs and interests of social scientists in mind. Rather, these materials were, in the main, created by ongoing processes of society including governmental and administrative activities and simple communication between individuals. It is true that data collected by social scientists of the past are available in considerable abundance, particularly for relatively recent years. All too frequently, however, the interests of social scientists of the past do not coincide with those of contemporary researchers.

The processes through which historical materials have been preserved impose further limitations upon the investigator. Societies, groups, and individuals have usually shown interest in preserving the records of their own past. On the other hand, not all records have been systematically saved; some have been destroyed accidentally and still others deliberately to avoid damaging revelations or to reduce the encumbrances presented by growing masses of records. Well-intentioned efforts have been made to select records for preservation in terms of their historical value. Unfortunately, interests and criteria of value have changed over time, and often the criteria of the past are not the same as those of later social scientists.

Historical Source Materials

As will quickly become apparent, no brief discussion can fully describe the range and variety of historical evidence or provide a comprehensive indication of the many guides to historical source materials. In this section the major types of historical source will be briefly discussed, and in a subsequent section references will be given to major guides and bibliographies. For purposes of convenience and brevity, attention will be focused primarily upon the United States with occasional references to other nations. It should be clearly recognized, however, that this provincialism is primarily a matter of convenience. Many of the major categories of historical evidence mentioned are also available for most other nations.

Voting records constitute the most obvious and perhaps the most valuable form of evidence relevant to historical political phenomena.

In the case of the United States, election returns for a large number of local, state, and national offices can be found for the nineteenth and twentieth centuries and, in less abundance, for earlier years as well. In American history popular voting has not been limited to the election of candidates to particular offices. A very large number of policy questions, including questions relevant to the form, structure, and functions of government, have also been decided by popular vote on referenda, initiatives, and amendments to state constitutions. Obviously, voting data are at least potentially available for all nations characterized by popular participation in government. While suffrage requirements have varied from nation to nation and from one time period and office to the next, these materials provide a continuing record of the candidate preferences of the electorate and a useful means of assessing popular reactions to the issues of the day, public interest and involvement in political life, and of tracing trends in public opinion across time.

The *records of legislative bodies* constitute a further array of voting data bearing directly upon political processes. Legislative voting records are by no means limited, of course, to central legislatures such as the American Congress or other national parliaments. In the United States, for example, voting is an intrinsic element in the conduct of legislative business not only in Congress but in state legislatures, city councils, county boards of supervisors, and a variety of other governmental organizations. For the Congress of the United States, a comprehensive series of roll-call votes is available in relatively convenient published sources for all the years since 1789. Similar series are also available for most states stretching back in time to territorial days and, indeed, for several of the original states, such materials are to be found for even the seventeenth and eighteenth centuries. For many cities, similarly lengthy series are available for common councils and other legislative agencies. These materials provide a record of countless collective decisions on matters of public policy and of the positions taken on these matters by large numbers of individuals. As such they provide, as Clausen suggests in chapter 9, a vital source not only for the investigation of the functions and nature of these agencies themselves, but also for investigation of changing policy interests, of shifting political attitudes and ideologies, and of the response of governmental figures to societal problems. Nor are voting records of this sort limited to those of formal governmental legislative agencies. Collegial judicial agencies frequently deliver decisions on the basis of a kind of voting procedure, and these records thus constitute a fruitful source of information for the investigation of judicial and governmental processes. A host of private organizations ranging from private clubs to labor unions and political parties employ voting procedures either in general assembly or in their governing councils to transact business of organizational and sometimes public concern.

The value of voting records to the study of past politics requires little elaboration. However, governmental and private agencies have also collected and preserved large quantitites of *information which describe the characteristics of individuals, groups, and populations of geographic areas.* These sources allow assessment of the conditions of life and the determinants of politics in the past and afford a means to gauge the consequences of political actions. Since 1790, systematic censuses have been taken by the government of the United States. In the beginning they were little more than enumerations of the population of the nation for purposes of apportioning representation in Congress. But even in the earliest national censuses, population was enumerated by sex and age, and as slave or free, and the results were tabulated at the county level as well as for certain subcounty units. In the latter half of the nineteenth century the census enumeration was expanded to collect data bearing upon income, the ethnic composition of the population, internal migration, religious affiliation, economic production, and employment, as well as other characteristics of the population and the nation. Since the late nineteenth century the periodic national census has steadily expanded both in scope and quality. Thus the federal census reports (Dubester, 1950), the published tabulations resultant from these enumerations, provide a rich source of systematic statistical information describing the characteristics of the population and of geographic areas for more than 170 years of American history. Most Western nations have also regularly conducted national censuses of a quality and magnitude at least comparable to those of the United States (Willcox, 1940). The various national censuses, moreover, can frequently be supplemented by the local and state ones conducted occasionally in many nations. (For American state censuses, see Dubester, 1948.) For the most part, national censuses are a phenomenon of modern history, although occasional censuses were also taken during the Middle Ages and even in the ancient world (Willcox, 1940; Price and Lorwin, 1970).

In most cases, the results of these censuses are most conveniently available in aggregated form. The bulk of the census materials for the United States, for example, is aggregated data describing particular population groups or geographical areas. In terms of geographical areas, by far the largest volume of published census data is recorded at the county level, although substantial bodies of material are also recorded for smaller units, including towns, cities and other subcounty units. A search of national archives, however, will frequently

reveal the original manuscripts recording the actual individual enumerations from which published tabulations were compiled. For the
United States, the original enumerations for the federal censuses of
1790 through 1900 can be obtained from the National Archives, and
the original returns from subsequent censuses will become available
in later years. The original enumerations provide, in effect, a limited
but useful social survey of the entire population of the nation. Thus,
national censuses can provide not only a rich source of aggregated
descriptive data but of data bearing directly upon individuals as well.

National and local censuses do not, of course, constitute the only
source of statistical materials pertinent to the study of patterns of
life and the conditions and determinants of political affairs of the
past. Most governmental agencies, both local and national, collect
and systematically preserve substantial arrays of numeric information
in the course of carrying out administrative and governmental activities. *Budgetary accounts, appropriations records*, and *tax receipts*
constitute a systematic record of governmental activities across pro-
longed periods of time. These materials provide a record of the level
of activities of government, the functions performed by it, and the
allocation of societal resources through it (Deutsch, 1956b). Again
for the United States, specific governmental agencies, including the
Bureau of the Budget, the Office of Education, and the Bureau of
Labor Statistics, are particularly noteworthy for the compilation and
preservation of statistical information. In nations such as the United
States, moreover, many public agencies below the national level
perform a variety of functions and regularly compile data as a
by-product of these activities. Budgetary records and other governmental accounts are, of course, maintained by most, if not all,
nations. As a consequence, these records are a source of relatively
comparable data for most nations of the world.

Various other categories of basic statistical data are also compiled
as a part of ongoing societal life. Among these are *vital statistics*
recording births, deaths, marriages, and other information bearing
upon the life histories of individuals, and frequently these sources
record information beyond the simple facts of birth and death. The
crime statistics compiled by most governmental agencies—often, unfortunately, quite indifferently—provide information relevant to the
quality and nature of life in countless individual communities as do
such sources as *wills*, *tax records* and *building permits*. Nor is the
collection and preservation of basic statistical materials limited to
governmental and public agencies. A variety of private agencies also
generate voluminous records of use to students of historical political
life. For many nations, including the United States, churches systematically accumulate records bearing upon the lives of parishioners,

and businesses, hospitals, fraternal organizations, and trade unions are similarly often a source of useful information.

Quantitative and readily quantifiable historical materials of the sort discussed thus far, however, constitute only a fraction of the total body of evidence relevant to the political life of the past. Abundant textual materials are also available to the political researcher concerned with historical events and processes. Several general categories of textual source materials will readily come to mind. *Governmental and other official documents* exist in considerable quantity, frequently in published form, and have long served as a basic source of information for the study of historical political and governmental processes. These materials include constitutions and charters relevant to the formal structure and functions of government; statutes and other legal documents; the official papers of governmental officers; diplomatic correspondence; and reports and proceedings of a variety of governmental agencies, to mention but a few examples of this general category of historical sources.

The *private papers* and other writings of individuals constitute still another category of textual source materials. The *diaries, letters, memoirs, autobiographies*, and other writings of a very large number of prominent and not so prominent figures of the past have been diligently collected and preserved, and often provide a source of private, more or less candid, and "inside" information bearing upon events of the past. The *mass media* are also highly useful historical sources. The files of a large number of newspapers and magazines are to be found in many libraries and other repositories, and include accounts and editorial commentaries upon numerous historical events as well as individuals who were considered newsworthy. For later years, *recordings* and *films* have been preserved and are useful sources of historical information. *Biographical records* are a further source of information for the study of the past. City directories provide limited but useful information about countless individuals and may sometimes be used to discover the characteristics of particular areas and population groups and to trace changes in residential patterns and social and economic conditions over time. Bluebooks, legislative directories, obituary columns, and other similar sources contain basic biographical information bearing upon large numbers of individuals and afford a means to systematically trace career patterns and to identify the characteristics of particular groups.

Sources such as official documents, personal records, and news media are often termed subjective or qualitative in nature and are more or less sharply differentiated from more quantitative materials such as voting records, statistical compilations, and the like. Often this distinction involves the implicit or explicit view that data in the former category are less useful and reliable than those in the latter. It is ture, of course, that textual sources such as those discussed in the preceding paragraph record the personal views, opinions, and experiences of individuals, and include their subjective interpretations and evaluations. On the other hand, even statistical compilations are sometimes based upon subjective observation and classification systems. Moreover, while textual sources are often colored by qualitative judgments and frequently record subjective personal impressions, it does not follow that they cannot be systematically investigated and subjected to quantitative analysis. As suggested above, through systematic categorization and coding, the information contained in biographical sketches and directories can be converted to quantitative form, subjected to statistical analysis, and made the basis for systematic statistical comparisons of the characteristics and backgrounds of particular groups (see, for example, Schlesinger, 1957, 1966). Through devices such as content analysis (discussed in chapter 8), the personality traits of individuals and the impact of events and changing circumstances upon them may be systematically investigated, and attitudes and patterns of opinion examined and subjected to quantitiative analysis and measurement (see, for example, Cochran, 1953; Merritt, 1966; and Holsti et al., 1968).

The present discussion does not, of course, provide an exhaustive description of historical source materials. Several major categories of such material have been briefly described, but a little imagination will quickly suggest numerous other sources of historical information. Novels and other fictional writings can sometimes be of particular value for the interpretation both of past events and other source materials. Social scientists have called attention to the value of "physical traces" in contemporary social research (Webb et al., 1966). This form of evidence can obviously also be of value in historical studies. The size and physical characteristics of historic buildings, for example, can sometimes provide important clues as to the nature of the political life and institutions of the past. Cemetery and death records, including tombstone inscriptions, have been employed to assess the social structure and other characteristics of present and past societies. It should be clear, then, that society and government themselves have produced and preserved vast and varied bodies of evidence of both direct and indirect value to the investigator concerned with past political phenomena.

Evaluation and Use of Historical Evidence

These various categories of historical data have clear and obvious value for the study of politics, but, unfortunately, historical materials are also marked by serious limitations. As noted earlier, the volume and bulk of extant historical source materials and their diverse nature constitute severe obstacles to effective use by political researchers. Indeed, the mere task of surveying historical sources to identify and locate potentially useful data can constitute an undertaking of considerable magnitude. No comprehensive guide to historical source materials is available, and specialized guides are too numerous to be listed. However, the *Historian's Handbook* (Gray et al., 1964) provides a brief but useful starting point in the search for relevant data, and the American Historical Association's Guide to Historical Literature (Howe et al., 1961) provides a more substantial beginning.

These guides are, however, primarily useful as guides to textual materials. A considerable volume of historical material of this sort is available in relatively accessible published form. Through photoduplication processes many libraries have substantial holdings of historical newspapers and other periodicals. Considerable effort has also been devoted to the collection, organization, and preservation of unpublished source materials such as letter collections and other personal accounts, and major collections of these materials are to be found in libraries and other obvious repositories (Hamer, 1961). Although these materials are by no means centralized, textual sources are characterized by at least a semblance of organization and accessibility.

Statistical materials for the study of the past present a somewhat different problem. Obvious collections, such as census tabulations for the United States and other nations, and legislative voting records, are available in published form. But on the whole, less effort has been devoted to the collection and organization of statistical source materials for the study of politics than to textual sources. Many of the quantitative source materials discussed above, including election returns, tax records, and so on exist only in fragmentary form in widely scattered sources ranging from state and local archives to a host of obscure publications, and no comprehensive guide to these materials has been prepared (see, however, Schmeckebier and Eastin, 1961; Press and Williams, 1962; and Price and Lorwin, 1970).

For the investigator to effectively pursue his research goals, moreover, analysis and manipulation of very large amounts of quantitative data is necessary, and statistical tools are required which are often cumbersome and time consuming indeed when employed manually. Although electronic data processing equipment opens the way for the performance of truly prodigious tasks of data manipulation and analysis, these devices do not in themselves facilitate large-scale and fully effective utilization of the several categories of quantitative historical evidence mentioned above. The researcher still faces the laborious task of locating and collecting materials relevant to his research goals, and the work of coding, organizing, and converting data to a form susceptible to machine manipulation must be carried out.

Fortunately, these related problems have prompted noteworthy cooperative efforts. Investigators now regularly make materials that they have collected, organized, and converted to computer-readable form for their own research purposes, available to other investigators. Indeed, to hoard such resources is increasingly seen as a serious breach of scholarly ethics. This cooperative spirit has also given rise to noteworthy institutional innovation. A number of automated data repositories have appeared in recent years in the United States and in other nations (Bisco, 1967). These new organizations collect and maintain bodies of research materials in a form readily susceptible to machine analysis and make these materials conveniently available to the research community.

For those interested in the systematic investigation of past political phenomena, the Inter-University Consortium for Political and Social Research, located at Ann Arbor, Michigan, is the best example of these new scholarly resources. The consortium has assembled large-scale collections of historical political materials which are available in computer-readable form for scholarly use. These include county-level returns for elections to the offices of president, governor, senator, and representative for the United States from 1789 to the present; basic county-level descriptive material taken primarily from the United States Census Reports, 1790 to the present; and complete roll-call records for the United States Congress from the First through the present. Additional bodies of historical source materials are also being collected, and work is now underway at the consortium and in other countries that are looking toward the creation of similar collections of automated data relevant to other nations.

Problems related to the mass and volume of statistical data for the study of past political phenomena will not, however, be completely eliminated by such cooperative efforts. The quantity of these data is such that it is impossible to anticipate a time at which all relevant quantitative historical data will reside in computer-readable form in an easily accessible automated data repository. Rather, political researchers will frequently face the necessity of collecting and organizing specific bodies of data peculiar to their own research interests. In any event, the problems of collection and organization of historical data resources are by no means the only obstacles in the way of effective utilization of these materials.

As noted elsewhere, historical source materials tend to be fragmentary and discontinuous. These characteristics result both from the manner in which these data were originally created and the winnowing processes of time which have worked to preserve some materials and to destroy others. As a consequence, the student investigating the voting patterns of earlier years, for example, will often find that the returns for crucial elections in particular areas were either never collected or lost in the course of time, and in either event cannot be found. If his investigation leads him from major to lesser local offices, he will usually find relevant voting data steadily more fragmentary and difficult to locate. As he attempts to shift his investigation to smaller geographical units in order to refine his focus and test hypotheses more precisely, increasing difficulty will be encountered in locating relevant data.

For the United States, the study of historical election patterns is seriously complicated by the absence of a centralized agency for collecting and preserving these materials. But problems of discontinuity are also encountered even in the case of historical data that have been systematically collected and centrally compiled and preserved. In many nations periodic censuses have been taken with admirable regularity and have produced large bodies of basic information of value to the study of politics. In early years, however, national censuses were limited, both in terms of the quantity of information collected and the methods employed, and they have steadily expanded in size and quality with the passage of time. As a consequence, the information provided by such censuses varies greatly over time and is particularly limited for early years. The American census, like censuses of other nations, has been marked by changes of interest and focus and by varying budgetary circumstances. Collection procedures have been modified, definitions and tabulation categories changed, and particular categories of information omitted and new categories added. As a result, the data provided by census sources varies considerably from one census to the next and is frequently lacking in consistency.

Historical textual materials tend to be fragmentary in still other senses of the word. Little thought is required to recognize that letters, diaries, memoirs, and other personal documents tend to reflect the views, attitudes, and experiences of a very limited segment of society. Historically, ordinary men and women did not write letters and record their experiences and views with the same frequency as did members of elite groups. In earlier time periods particularly, when the illiteracy rates were high, ordinary men and women lacked the educational resources and motivation to record their experiences. Even when they did, their families and society more generally did not make the same effort to preserve their writings as was made in the case of more prominent and notable individuals. Thus personal documents must be seen as primarily the product of the upper echelons of society, and the researcher who uses such materials to infer mass attitudes, motivations, and behavior is on uncertain grounds indeed. Contemporary research (for example, Converse, 1964a) has clearly suggested that the attitudes of elite groups show relatively little similarity to mass attitudes. Nor can it be assumed that personal documents necessarily constitute a valid reflection even of elite attitudes, opinions, and experiences. Some individuals relied primarily upon fact to face communication rather than written forms of expression and did not concern themselves with leaving records for posterity.

Much the same limitations are characteristic of other forms of textual historical evidence. The biographical sketches referred to above, although they exist in great number, cannot be taken as providing a valid sample of the total population of the area and time period to which they are relevant. Rather, these materials are usually concerned with individuals who were considered both by themselves and their contemporaries as in some respects notable. Lesser men and women were only infrequently the subjects of biographical treatments. Similarly, the accounts and commentaries upon historical phenomena provided by the mass media cannot be taken uncritically as a reflection of mass attitudes and behavior patterns. Few would be willing to assert that the editorial page of the *New York Times* today provides a valid reflection of public opinion or that the accounts of events contained in that newspaper necessarily present completely valid and accurate observations. Much the same reservations must be exercised where accounts provided by the mass media of the past are concerned.

Historical source materials also often present difficulties for the investigator in terms of interpretation and assessment of accuracy, value, and significance. In many cases the procedures by which statistical materials were originally collected and tabulated are by no means clear. Similarly, the definitions and classification systems employed are sometimes not fully explained. As a result, problems of evaluating the accuracy of data are compounded, and the researcher encounters difficulty in determining the precise meaning of otherwise significant data. Frequently the process or phenomenon to which the data are relevant is only partially understood and the data therefore are subject to varying interpretations. The voting records of legislative bodies are a case in point. In the American Congress, for example, major policy questions are decided by means other than recorded votes; all issues do not reach a record vote, however crucial they may be; individual congressmen do not vote on all issues; and the votes they cast are a reflection of a variety of factors ranging from organizational characteristics of Congress to constituency influences as well as the individual congressman's personal views. Roll-call votes are, in short, by no means simple data, their interpretation is difficult, and conclusions cannot be drawn in a simple straightforward fashion.

Perhaps the most frequently noted shortcoming of historical sources has to do with matters of accuracy, reliability, and bias. Common sense will serve to suggest many of the sources of error in historical materials of interest to the student of politics. Even in contemporary elections, the vote count is sometimes demonstrated through recounts to be inaccurate, and it is obvious that in earlier years before the invention of such aids to accuracy as voting and adding machines, the count was probably less accurate than it is today. It is likely that when counting was entirely manual, the count in one-sided races was particularly subject to error as enumerators and poll watchers suspended their work when the victor became obvious. It may be surmised that in the past, minor party candidates suffered particularly from the failure of poll workers to fully count their votes. Fraud and corruption are further sources of inaccuracy in historical election data, although their incidence has probably been exaggerated. Systematic enumerations and compilations are also subject to error. The accuracy of the census enumeration in outlying and frontier areas in earlier years may well be doubted, just as the enumeration of lower income groups in major urban areas was perhaps often incomplete (as was the case in the 1960 census of the United States). Statistics relevant to crime, delinquency, and other social disorders are of great potential value to the student as indications of the performance and quality of the political system. But as has often been pointed out, the lack of a centralized recording agency, differences in law enforcement procedures, and the absence of uniform definitions, both from one locale and from one time period to the next, severely limit the utility of this important category of historical information.

The reliability of textual sources is also obviously open to question. As suggested above, textual sources frequently have the advantage of providing accounts of past events and phenomena based upon actual experience and direct observation. It must be recognized, however, that information of this sort cannot be accepted uncritically as fully accurate and free of bias. Personal accounts, perhaps inevitably, suffer from bias and frequently involve large elements of self-justification. Even the most honest and fair-minded person tends to account for events in which he was a participant in terms of his own point of view and often presents a more favorable account of his own action than was justified. Explanations of personal motivations are perhaps particularly suspect in this respect. Personal experience will doubtlessly suggest the difficulty of accurately assessing and explaining after the fact one's own reasons for adopting a particular action. Obviously, official governmental reports and documents are also sometimes characterized by biases and inaccuracies of this sort. Those responsible for the preparation of such documents were rarely in a position to know all relevant information from direct experience and were probably often inclined to present information biased in their own favor whether inadvertently or in order to deliberately mislead.

In part, at least, these may be seen as problems of interpretation. The letters or other personal writings of historical political figures may not provide an accurate account of past events or an unbiased explanation for the adoption of particular courses of action. Similarly, governmental reports may provide only inaccurate explanations of the bases for particular decisions and only biased accounts of historical situations and problems. On the other hand, systematic analysis of such materials may serve to identify the psychological traits, attitude patterns, and orientations of historical groups and individuals. Clues as to states of mind provoked by historical events and to decision-making processes may be implicit in such materials. Obviously, to extract this information the researcher must be prepared to employ sophisticated analytic techniques and to apply the findings of psychology and the other social sciences in order to penetrate beneath the level of explicit exposition.

Fortunately, historians and other social scientists have developed rather elaborate and relatively effective guides and procedures for the use and evaluation of source materials (see, for example, Gottschalk, 1950; Gottschalk et al., 1951; and especially Naroll, 1962). These rules and procedures obviously merit careful consideration.

It should go without saying that the investigator concerned with past events and phenomena should give preference in his work to primary as opposed to secondary sources. Unfortunately, precise differentiation between these two categories of historical information is difficult to make. For present purposes, however, primary sources may be crudely defined as sources which provide information based upon direct observation of the event or phenomenon considered or which are the direct products of the phenomena or processes studied. Election returns and census reports based upon direct counts and enumerations are in this category, as are constitutions or charters for the investigation of the formal structure of government, and congressional speeches for the study of congressional behavior. Secondary sources are derivative materials which are not based upon direct observation, although they may be based on primary sources. Scholarly reports obviously fall into this latter category. These distinctions are by no means precise, and it should be clear that whether a source is considered primary or secondary may depend upon the purposes for which it is used. In these terms, editorial commentaries in newspapers might be a primary source for the study of historical elite opinion, but a secondary source for the study of governmental processes. (For a more elaborate classification of source materials, see Naroll, 1962, pp. 30–32.)

The authenticity of historical sources, and for that matter more contemporary sources as well, is sometimes open to question. Forgeries and fraudulent documents and tabulations are not unknown, and the bases for reports and tabulations are sometimes unclear. Historians have developed careful procedures for coping with problems of authenticity. Consultation of basic treatises on historical method will suffice to introduce the interested reader to these techniques (for example, Gottschalk, 1950).

Perhaps the most critical problem encountered in the use of historical sources concerns evaluation and assessment of their accuracy, credibility, and reliability. Historical and even contemporary source materials are frequently marked by inaccuracy. It is useful, however, to distinguish between two types of error that may be characteristic of source materials: error which is random in nature, and error which is the product of systematic bias (Narroll, 1962). Random error results from such factors as careless or incomplete observation, or unsystematic inaccuracies in enumeration, tabulation, or computation. Bias can be the result of the prejudices or prior assumptions of observers, or of enumeration, recording, or calculating procedures which introduce systematic inaccuracies. In the case of data marked by random error, recorded values are equally likely to be either greater or lesser than the true values, while in biased data recorded values tend to consistently diverge in one direction or the other from true values.

These two types of error have significantly different consequences for the investigator. Error of the first type, because unpredictable, is the most difficult to compensate for and correct and is more likely to work to obscure true relations than to produce erroneous findings. If the direction of bias is known, on the other hand, correction and compensation procedures can be employed more easily, but this type of error is most likely to lead to the discovery of erroneous relations and to produce invalid findings. In other words, simple mistakes in counting the vote in elections are unlikely to result in systematically assigning a higher vote to specific candidates, but they may work to obscure associations between the strength of specific candidates and particular geographic areas or economic and social groups. On the other hand, if poll workers systematically undercounted the vote for minor party candidates, a possibility suggested above, the researcher might conclude that voter turnout was low and that popular satisfaction with the political alternatives provided by major parties was greater than was actually the case.

In his useful discussion of data quality control, Naroll (1962) has suggested a variety of systematic procedures for assessing and evaluating the accuracy and credibility of source materials. Some of his suggestions may be usefully adapted to the purposes of the present discussion, although the brief and rather liberal adaptation presented here should not be taken as a substitute for consulting his work.

When possible the researcher should draw upon alternative sources. By comparing sources, errors and discrepancies can sometimes be identified and reconciled. All information relevant to collecting and recording procedures should, of course, be carefully considered. The explicitness and the detail characteristic of source materials can provide an indication of their reliability. The investigator may feel greater confidence in the accuracy of explicit and precise sources, and explicit and precisely phrased sources require less inference and interpretation by the researcher and afford less opportunity for intrusion of his own biases. By the same token, when procedures by which data were originally collected are stated clearly and in detail, the investigator is in a better position to judge the reliability of the data and may feel greater confidence in the quality of the original work. The internal consistency of source materials should also be considered. Textual reports are often marked by explicit or implicit internal contradictions which may suggest that the report is unreliable. In the case of statistical sources, internal comparisons and tests for consistency can facilitate identification of possible errors or anomalies. Thus comparison of election returns for a given area from one election to the next may reveal sharp changes in voting patterns. These may indicate changes in voter sentiments, but may also be an indication of erroneous or fraudulent returns. By comparing voting returns with population figures, the nature of such fluctuations can sometimes be ascertained.

The characteristics of the authors of reports or of recording agencies can also provide clues to the reliability of sources. The qualifications of the author or recording agency may suggest greater or lesser reliability. The researcher may feel greater confidence in data recorded by a group or agency, such as the U.S. Bureau of the Census, which is professionally and continuously involved in the collecting and recording of information, than in material collected by amateur or special interest groups. Along these lines, the education and training of the reporter may be an indication of his ability to observe and report events correctly. The degree of involvement by the reporter in the event or process reported may provide an indication both of the likelihood that the report is complete and of possible biases on the part of the reporter. Agreement or disagreement between reporters with differing points of view can also facilitate evaluation of the reliability of source materials and allow the development of composite and more reliable descriptions of particular events or processes which draw upon several sources. The time lapse between an event and the actual preparation of the account of that event should also be considered. Obviously, human memory is frail, and the longer the time between the event and the preparation of the account, the greater the opportunity to forget elements of the event and for the author's own preconceptions and prejudices to intrude. The opportunity of the reporter to actually observe the particular event or process should be considered. Accounts and reports usually contain elements of hearsay and inference, and these elements can frequently be identified if the position of the reporter is considered.

Of course, neither these nor any other set of general rules can suffice, in themselves, as completely adequate checks and safeguards against the inaccuracies, biases, and other limitations that are often characteristic of historical source materials. Students who utilize these materials in their research are well advised to consult the manuals and handbooks concerned with source and evidence evaluation prepared by historians and other social scientists. These works convey the results of experience in dealing with concrete historical materials in research situations. But there is no substitute for caution, sensitivity to human frailties, and simple common sense where these materials are concerned. By exercising much the same caution and critical sensitivity in dealing with historical materials as one exercises in dealing with contemporary news reports and other information sources, many of the limitations and pitfalls of historical data will be avoided.

Problems of Research and Analysis

It has been suggested, then, that a wide variety of historical evidence is available to the researcher in considerable abundance. Historical sources, however, tend to be fragmentary and incomplete and are frequently marked by error and bias. The researcher concerned with past phenomena, moreover, cannot control either the original collection or the preservation of data, and he is compelled to rely primarily upon materials which were originally created to serve purposes other than social science research. Although these general problems do not constitute arguments against the use of historical evidence in political research, they do have consequences and implications for the investigation of past phenomena which merit careful consideration.

One of the immediate implications of this general situation is that the researcher usually does not have information bearing directly upon the historical phenomena with which he is concerned. Nor can he supplement available data through direct observation. This obviously dictates that the investigator be familiar with available information resources and be prepared to make imaginitive use of extant sources. Among other things, he should be able to capitalize upon evidence of events that did not occur as well as on evidence of those that did. As suggested elsewhere, in legislative bodies not all issues reach a record vote, and, indeed, not all possible issues receive consideration in any form. Frequently, the categories of issues which were not voted upon or which were not considered can provide useful indications of attitudes among legislators or of the relation between their behavior and constituency interests. By the same token, the relative amount of time devoted to various types of issues can provide useful but not obvious information. The fact that political parties do not contest all races may provide an indication of the assessment by party leaders of the strength of their party among particular social and economic groups.

These propositions suggest more general imperatives for the investigation of past events. If the researcher is to capitalize upon available data he must be prepared to employ inferential procedures. The investigator might, for example, wish to pursue propositions relevant to the relation in the nineteenth century between income levels and electoral participation, or electoral identifications with particular parties. For such an investigation, voting returns would necessarily be a principal source. But these data provide evidence of only one form of electoral participation and do not provide a direct and uncomplicated indication of partisan identifications. Many other factors, aside from partisan identification, work to shape the voter's decision at the polling place. In this example, moreover, the researcher would probably find that valid income data were not collected for at least some of the years and geographical units with which he was concerned. He might be willing to conclude, however, that educational levels, for which data are available, constitute a valid indication of income levels, and proceed to test his hypothesis by comparing the vote for the party in question with educational data. It would be necessary to recognize, of course, that education and income, while doubtlessly related, are by no means the same thing.

In order to refine his test, the investigator might find it desirable to explore the statistical relation between income and education during other time periods for which data for both variables are available. In so doing, his goal would be to gain more precise knowledge of the relation between these two phenomena in order to improve the basis for his use of education as an indicator of wealth and to increase his confidence in his capacity to adequately test his hypothesis. Clearly, such a research strategy could result in erroneous conclusions. While it is possible that a close relation between income and education exists and has been relatively consistent regardless of time or place, this assumption is not demonstrated, and to transfer relations observed at one time period to another involves a possible erroneous inference. Even so, if the tentative nature of investigation is recognized, an inferential leap of this sort may be justified. In carrying out such an operation, the researcher can be seen as doing no more than constructing additional tests of his hypothesis, although at the risk of either reinforcing invalid conclusions or undermining valid ones.

This simple illustration serves once again to call attention to more general propositions relevant to historical investigation. The researcher must be prepared, in the absence of directly relevant data, to employ indicators which indirectly and imperfectly measure the particular process or characteristics with which he is concerned. In order to capitalize upon available historical data he must be flexible in formulating hypotheses and research problems. Often, hypotheses and research problems which are not testable or cannot be investigated directly in their original form because relevant data do not exist can be modified, or implications deduced which are susceptible to testing and investigation in terms of available information. In so doing, hypotheses should be carefully and explicitly formulated, and all assumptions and inferential steps should be considered and made explicit in order to identify possible sources of invalid findings.

It may well be accurate to say, in fact, that historical investigations require more careful attention to the formulation of hypotheses and research problems and to the design of research than do investigations of more contemporary phenomena. The researcher concerned with present-day problems has greater opportunity to collect data that bear directly upon his work. Since the researcher concerned with the past must make do with extant data, he must make heavier use of assumptions and inferences and draw upon generalizations and theories developed by the other social sciences. Thus, care and imagination in the use of data and in the formulation of research procedures is required if maximum use is to be made of existing resources; and assumptions, inferences, and generalizations employed must be made explicit and their implications recognized if the limitations of findings are to be understood.

These generalizations also suggest possible hazards in the conduct of historical investigations. It should be clear, of course, that historical investigations require familiarity with the characteristics of the historical period considered. Particularly in comparative historical studies and in historical studies designed to test hypotheses based upon more contemporary phenomena, it is often assumed, either implicitly or explicitly, that two or more eras are similar except in terms of the specific processes or characteristics under consideration. Indeed, these assumptions of similarity are central to historical comparisons and, more generally, to investigations designed to identify the impact and causal significance of particular processes or characteristics. It is obvious, of course, that no two historical eras (or for that matter no two physical events) are ever precisely alike. The scientific investigator is, however, often willing to assume on the basis of his best investigations that historical eras are sufficiently alike to allow him to design tests of the significance and influence of particular characteristics.

Unfortunately, despite a researcher's best efforts it may happen that unanticipated dissimilarities are present in such an investigation. Once again, the point can be illustrated by an obvious example. Various researchers have called attention to the high level of voter participation and to the remarkable stability of voting patterns in the late nineteenth-century United States as compared to the middle decades of the twentieth century. Various factors have been suggested to account for these observed changes, including developments in communication facilities and the growth of dissatisfaction with the responsiveness of the political system to popular needs and interests. These same researchers have also raised the possibility that the observed changes in voting patterns may be in some measure the product of less spectacular and neglected developments such as changes in registration procedures and voting regulations, which made it more difficult to vote, and changes in ballot form, which made it easier for voters to switch from one party to the other in elections and which worked to reduce the consistency of the party vote (see, for example, Burnham, 1965, 1970; Converse, 1966a, 1972; and Rusk, 1967, 1970).

This is, of course, an obvious and limited illustration, but it may serve to demonstrate the ease with which dissimilarities between historical eras could be overlooked and erroneous conclusions drawn. In this particular case, it would have been easy to assume that such basic structural characteristics as registration procedures and ballot form have remained constant, or that changes in these characteristics had little significance. To do so, however, might have resulted in overstated or erroneous findings. In general, social scientists who turn to historical investigations are sometimes prone to assume that the relations and structural attributes observed in the contemporary era were also characteristic of other historical time periods. Needless to say, such similarities are matters for investigation and cannot merely be assumed.

Historical Accounts

Social scientists whose work involves investigation of the past are almost inevitably compelled to consult and rely upon accounts written by historians. Even though original sources are used in conducting research, it is usually necessary to rely upon historical works for accounts of the course of events and for descriptions of the institutions, processes, and personalities of historical eras. All too frequently, however, the "standard" and so-called definitive works of master historians, particularly, are accepted without the healthy skepticism with which all scholarly works should be greeted. It is appropriate, therefore, to briefly explore the nature of historical accounts and to suggest in general terms some of the procedures involved in their preparation.

It should not be necessary to point out that historical accounts should be subjected to careful and critical evaluation before the information that they provide is accepted. Students of the past, like all investigators, are capable of poor and mistaken work, and it should be recognized that the study of the past is dynamic, as are all scholarly disciplines. New evidence often comes to light, and findings are often refuted or refined by later investigations. This does not mean, of course, that only the latest work is valuable, but it does call attention to the need for cognizance of recent investigations.

Several obvious guides for the evaluation of historical accounts can be cited. The use of sources should be considered: is the work based upon primary sources? Does it make use of relevant sources, and is their use careful and critical? Does the account take into consideration the work of other historians and social scientists? The author's goals and purposes in writing should also be examined. Particular works may well be designed to serve purposes that are not in keeping with the investigator's interests. A textbook, for example, written for use in beginning courses is usually not adequate for the needs of the more advanced investigator except, perhaps, in terms of the broad and general outline of past events that it provides.

These general evaluative propositions suggest more fundamental considerations. Perhaps the most frequently announced goal of historians, at least in the past, has been to reconstruct the past "as it actually happened." A premium has been placed upon empiricism, and historians have insisted that investigations of past events should not be affected by preconceived theories and notions and that historical sources should be allowed to "speak for themselves." It should be clear that these goals, stated here in somewhat exaggerated form, cannot be taken literally. In the first place, a description of a past event or process is inevitably an abstraction from reality. The sources available to the historian are incomplete, and he cannot hope to know or describe all aspects of a past event "as it actually happened." Moreover, even within the limits imposed by his incomplete sources, the historian cannot describe all aspects of a past event that can be known. A description of all elements of even a trivial event would result in a volume of literally immense proportions. Clearly, the historian includes in his account only those aspects of past situations which he considers relevant and important.

Historical accounts are then shaped by those criteria, as well as by empirical historical evidence. Unfortunately, these criteria are frequently unexpressed. They include, however, such factors as the historian's own interests and purposes in writing, and considerations of a dramatic appeal and interest value. More important, these criteria also include the historian's assumptions about causal relations in human affairs, and generalizations about human motives, behavior, and institutions derived from such sources as personal experience and the findings of the social sciences as well as historical evidence. It is, of course, these assumptions and generalizations that allow the historian to identify relevant and important elements of past situations and to link those elements to each other in terms of determining and causal relations (see, in this general connection, Pressly, 1954; Potter, 1963; Berkhofer, 1969; Fischer, 1970).

These procedures are necessary in some degree and are not in themselves subject to categorical criticism. In many if not most historical accounts, however, such assumptions and generalizations are implicit rather than explicit and are often, indeed, apparently unrecognized. Thus they are rarely critically evaluated, and when made explicit and subjected to critical assessment, they often appear biased, outmoded, and untenable in the light of contemporary social science, and sometimes, in fact, in the light of common sense. Needless to say, the social scientist who draws upon historical accounts in his work must recognize such implicit assumptions and generalizations and subject them to searching evaluation. The consequence may be to undermine the credibility of otherwise useful historical accounts.

CONCLUSION

In this discussion, attention has been called to the value of historical evidence and investigation in the study of politics, but perhaps greater stress has been placed upon the limitations of histor- ical evidence and the difficulties and hazards of historical investiga- tion. As has been observed, historical investigations do have some advantages over those concerned with more contemporary phenom- ena, and it would be possible to overemphasize the differences between the two categories of research. The findings of contempo- rary investigations are also tentative, and the quantity and quality of evidence available for such investigations is also limited.

Even so, historical studies have limitations and present difficul- ties that are in some ways more severe than those characteristic of more contemporary studies. The critical argument for the use of historical evidence in the study of politics does not, however, turn primarily on questions of relative difficulty and uncertainty of re- sults. To limit the study of politics to contemporary research with a premium placed upon methods of direct observation could only work to slow the development of the science of politics. Hypotheses, theories, and generalizations could not be tested until appropriate situations occurred; long-term trends and processes could not be satisfactorily investigated. If one believes that a science of politics can serve humanly valuable ends, then investigation of past politics is clearly indicated whatever the difficulties and uncertainties involved.

21. IMPROVING THE USEFULNESSES OF THE CASE STUDY

Edwin A. Bock

This chapter, written mostly in the early 1970s, considers past and possible future uses of the case study in political science. Underlying it are the following beliefs and politics requires a variety of methodologies; (2) that the relative popularity of these methodologies will alter as new items appear on research agendas and scholarly enthusiasms change; and (3) that political scientists will, and should, continue to seek significant truths in somewhat independent ways, with imperatives arising from their individual abilities, opportunities, and particular senses of scientific vocation (Pye, 1968, pp. 241-42; Polanyi, 1958).

It is also assumed here that what Waldo has said about the case study in public administration is likely to be true in political science:

> The evidence strongly suggests that the case method will become a permanent feature of the study and teaching of Public Administration. At the same time the evidence clearly indicates that the case method will not come to dominate study and teaching in a way comparable to the dominance of case method in the study and teaching of law during recent generations [Waldo, 1968, p. 469].

The aim in this chapter is not to argue that the case study should become relatively more prominent at the expense of some other research style. Rather, it is to consider the range of serviceabilities that the case study seems to offer political scientists as of the early 1970s and to suggest how some key limitations might be overcome, thereby increasing these usefulnesses.

GENEALOGICAL INFLUENCES

By the 1960s political science case studies existed in such profusion and in such a variety of forms and qualities that it will

674

shortly be necessary for me to define what sort of case studies I am and am not discussing. Yet thirty years earlier, one could count on one hand the number of political science studies that would fit under a generously broad definition of the term. How the genre arose in political science and what attitudes and purposes pushed its development are matters that help one to understand its peculiarities and potentialities.

Before 1930 the case study had been established in other American academic disciplines. The method had, of course, a considerable history in medical research writing and clinical teaching. The case method had been introduced in law at Harvard around 1870 and had become internationally prestigious in that field by the turn of the century, except, of course, in countries following the Roman-Napoleanic law tradition. By the mid 1920s, under a dean who had graduated from the Harvard Law School, the practice of teaching primarily by exposing would-be executives to real case problems or situations had become the proud, well-financed, and much imitated method of instruction at the Harvard Business School (Copeland, 1954).

Approaching political science from another direction, case studies in the sense of descriptive process reports of findings of empirical field research existed in social anthropology (Malinowski, 1922), social psychology, and sociology (Small and Vincent, 1894; Thrasher, 1927). Studies in this tradition had penetrated American political science by the end of World War II, having moved on a course through such points as *Middletown* (Lynd and Lynd, 1929, 1937), *Suye Mura* (Embree, 1939) and, finally and irresistibly, the Japanese-American Relocation Center in Arizona described in Leighton's *The Governing of Men* (1945). In a separate but sometimes intertwined tradition, American political scientists, like historians and sociologists, were, by the 1930s, familiar with descriptive historical studies and biographical studies that depended in part on use of diaries, life histories, or accounts of participant observers (Clarendon, 1704; Ostrogorski, 1902; Thomas and Znaniecki, 1927; Gosnell, 1924; Wooddy, 1926; Dollard 1935).

One can detect case study beginnings in at least three different sectors of twentieth-century American political science after the urban and antitrust muckraking period. Beard's *An Economic Interpretation of the Constitution of the United States* (1913, 1935) was partly in the descriptive, action-sequence style one would expect from a historian-political scientist. A less debatable nomination for the first modern political science case study is Odegard's (1928) methodologically unselfconscious action study of the Anti-Saloon League. Odegard credited the idea for his study to Arthur Macmahon, his Columbia professor, who had been a student of Beard's.

Another landmark in this sector is Schattschneider's *Politics, Pressures and the Tariff* (1935). Like Odegard's book, it was the product of field research for a doctoral dissertation at Columbia. So was Zeller's *Pressure Politics in New York* (1937).

The Odegard and Schattschneider books had in common something that turned out to be of lasting importance for the evolution of the case form. They dealt with *policy making*. They preceeded a flow of realistic studies of New Deal policy making that blended process with substance in such matters as social security (Douglas, 1936), sugar pricing (Dalton, 1937), shipping and merchant marine (Zeis, 1938), and the coal industry (Parker, 1940). These works alerted some in the rising generation of political scientists to the usefulness of the case study style, although the name itself was seldom used. One can see with hindsight that they initiated a connection between policy making research and the case form that has continued down to contemporary investigations of policy making and metapolicy making (Dror, 1968, 1970; Lowi, 1964c, 1971; G. D. Greenberg et al., 1973).

Possibly the first methodologically explicit application of the case study in modern American political science occurred in another sector. It stemmed at least partly from its author's experience with psychiatry, medicine, and social anthropology. He was Harold Lasswell, and the work was an ingenious, rigorous field study that still repays careful reading: *The Participant Observer: A Study of Administrative Rules in Action* (1935a). Lasswell acknowledged the aid of a graduate student then in his twenties, Gabriel Almond. The senior author had earlier demonstrated the usefulness of case histories and medical case records to political science in the now famous book published in *his* twenties, *Psychopathology and Politics* (1930).

Another sector in which political science case studies appeared in the 1930s was the then relatively rambunctious one of public administration, which was stimulated by foundation support through the Public Administration Committee set up by the Social Science Research Council (SSRC) in 1934 in the New Deal atmosphere of expanding federal agency activity (Gaus and Anderson, 1945; Friedrich, 1947). One of the early acts of this mixed body of public administration experts, practicing administrators, and political science association mavericks was to support "capture and record" field studies of aspects of the work of the Roosevelt administration. One such study was led by Macmahon. He and Millett used personal histories in *Federal Administrators* (1939). They interviewed, examined files, and observed officials in action. Some of their research data appeared years later in *The Administration of Work Relief* (Macmahon, Millet, and Ogden, 1941).

In 1938 the SSRC's Public Administration Committee consti-
tuted a subcommittee on "Research Material on the Administrative
Process." The extensive minutes of the two-day meeting (Charles S.
Ascher was secretary) show that it was devoted entirely to the
question of how to develop "cases." Members included Luther
Gulick, Leonard White, John Corson, Donald Stone, Henry Reining,
Jr., a youngish Princeton assistant professor named George Graham,
and William E. Mosher, dean of the new Maxwell School at Syracuse.
All apparently accepted White's definition of a case study as

> including the statement of relevant facts involved in an administrative
> problem, a decision taken with reference thereto, and the results arising
> therefrom, gathered for the purpose of (a) testing a hypothesis, (b) illus-
> trating a significant administrative situation or (c) providing material for
> critical consideration by students [see Social Science Research Council,
> 1940, pp. 21–23].

After this beginning, the members wrestled for a day and a half
with many of the methodological difficulties of case studies that are
predictable fare in today's scope and methods courses when their
proprietors deliver the customary review and critique of the case
study: Could cases validate theories? Could cases serve both research
and teaching purposes at the same time? Should the SSRC seek cases
of "pathological" or "normal" situations? Finally, how could cases
be prepared so that their data would be comparable or additive?
"Several hours' " discussion was devoted to attempting to formulate
"hypotheses or questions" to be investigated with cases. White proposed one sizzler: *"The efficiency of a public office varies inversely
with the number of veterans employed."* Dean Mosher—who earlier
had declared that "as a group of social scientists, the committee was
interested in the testing or verification of hypotheses, in the hope
that by observation of many comparable episodes general principles
or laws would emerge"—proposed on the second day a hypothesis
that exuded a hearty tang of familiarity with real-world government
and a characteristic confidence that scholarly field work in a clinical
style would yield answers of concurrent scientific and civic value. It
read: *"A properly staffed budget bureau is the proper agency
through which the legislature should make contact with the departments; it should not depend upon the senatorial presence* [i.e.,
winning manner] *of the bureau chief."*

The product that finally resulted from this heady planning session was a three-volume, loose-leaf set of short "case reports" published by Public Administration Service, Chicago, after editing by
Joseph McLean and Mrs. V.O. (Luella Gettys) Key. In them, public
officials reported with edited brevity and muffled pride how they
had dealt with stated categories of middle managerial problems.

The next important steps in the public administration–public policy sector were taken by, or at the instigation of, E. Pendleton Herring, who in 1944 was seeking to develop suitable materials for a new course instituted by the faculty of the Harvard Graduate School of Public Administration. Herring had done considerable Washington field work for his *Group Representation before Congress* (1929), which had resulted from his doctoral dissertation at Johns Hopkins. He had been a member of the SSRC Public Administration Committee in the thirties and had participated in planning some administrative histories of federal war agencies in the early forties. (The preparation of these histories, incidentally, involved such political scientists as James Fesler, V. O. Key, and Harvey C. Mansfield.) Herring and his colleagues at Littauer were mindful of the great successes credited (especially by Harvard president James Conant) to the use of the case method at the Harvard Business School in the training of effective wartime government administrators. With the potent aid of Oliver Garceau, then a political science instructor and a recent M.B.A. who had prepared teaching materials at the business school, Herring used graduate students to prepare case studies about current federal administration problems.

In 1948, the Carnegie Corporation (Herring then served as its staff associate) began to support an effort by an inter-university consortium (a committee of five professors of political science and economics) to design and secure the preparation of public administration–policy formation case studies. This work culminated in 1952 with Harold Stein's influential casebook, *Public Administration and Policy Development*, and with the creation of the Inter-University Case Program as an enlargement of the original group of sponsoring institutions. (The loose inter-university arrangement was deliberately chosen by Herring in preference to the single-school, "Harvard Vatican" approach that had characterized the initial development of the case method in law and business administration.) Stein, it is important to observe, had had considerable Washington experience at higher administrative levels. He was a forceful man of taste, literary skill, commitment, irony, and horse sense. These strengths were fortified (in the eyes of his sponsors) by the sterling credential that he had never read a textbook on public administration. He was counseled in the selection and editing of his cases by a sponsoring committee and a staff that included Paul Appleby, Merle Fainsod, Oliver Garceau, George Graham, Arthur Macmahon, Harvey Mansfield, Edward Mason, Don Price, and the late and rare Wallace Sayre. His case writers included Paul Ylvisaker, William Riker, Arthur Maass, Jack Peltason, Norton Long, and Louis Koenig.

The quality of the Stein casebook, supplemented by a summer conference at French Lick, Indiana, at which Fainsod and others demonstrated the art of teaching in case study discussions, won a beachhead of acceptance for what might be termed the ICP-public administration type of case study among American political scientists. This beachhead widened as the number of high-quality cases increased, partly by continued production under the aegis of the ICP and partly by able efforts of individual scholars in public administration and in other sectors of political science. Many of the political scientists who worked at preparing these cases, and many political scientists who were the first to respond positively to the appearance of the Stein casebook, had had some government experience in the New Deal or in emergency wartime agencies. Waldo has described the early spirit of this case movement in public administration:

> The case movement ... arose out of a dissatisfaction with the Public Administration of the Twenties and Thirties ... It represented a search for "reality", a desire to view the administrative world afresh, in its wholeness and without false theory and oversimplifying assumptions. In this aspect its motives were scientific. (That is, careful observation and the collection of data are usually thought to be first steps toward an empirical science.) ... There was an obvious ... intent to portray the intricate interrelation of administrative processes with political processes ... there was also a new emphasis upon policy.... In my own view the emergence of the case method in the late Forties is related to the response of Public Administration to behavioralism. To the then young, now middle-aged generation of Public Administrationists this *was* behavioralism ... the beginning of a genuinely scientific inquiry; and it represented a more appealing version than the alternatives, as represented especially in [Herbert Simon's] *Administrative Behavior* [Waldo, 1968, pp. 468-69].

THE RANGE OF POLITICAL SCIENCE CASES

Activities of scholars *outside* the public administration case study movement had much to do with the achievement of a viable swarm of high-quality case studies in the larger universe of political science. It was undoubtedly the impressive quality, range, and value of their cases as well as Stein's that explained the full acceptance of the style by the mid-1960s. The fifties had opened with the appearance of two book-length case studies resulting from doctoral dissertations at Harvard and Columbia, respectively, Bailey's *Congress Makes a Law* (1950) and Riggs's *Pressures on Congress* (1950). Lane produced a book of case materials on parties and interest groups for the introductory political science course in 1952. Meyerson and Banfield's *Politics, Planning and the Public Interest* appeared in 1955. So did Palamountain's sophisticated (doctoral) study of the Robinson-

Patman Act, *The Politics of Distribution* (prepared under Fainsod), as well as casebooks in civil rights and security investigations (Yarmolinsky, 1955), and one in technical assistance administration and politics (Teaf and Franck, 1955). Important book-length cases (Cohen, 1957; Davison, 1958) and cases in journals (Paige and Snyder, 1958) began to appear in the field of international relations and foreign affairs. In 1957 the Eagleton Institute started issuing cases in practical politics under the editorship of Paul Tillett.

By the mid 1960s, the case study had become an accepted form of scholarly research and writing in American political science. Special foundation support to establish the style no longer seemed justifiable, at least in America. When such support was turned off, production of case materials did not stop. On the contrary, during the rest of the 1960s it continued to expand. One reason was that the pipelines of such organized efforts in the case field as the ICP and the Eagleton program, continued to yield new cases for the purpose of illuminating or exploring important political, governmental, or policy areas (Bock, 1963, 1965; Tillett, 1965; Mosher and Harr, 1970). But the growth in political science case study writing had evidently spread and taken hold far beyond the boundaries of such enterprises.

During the 1960s, as before, political science cases were produced for teaching, research, or operational purposes, or sometimes a combination of the three (Bock, 1962, pp. 93–104). (The operational category included studies prepared, sometimes with government agency sponsorship, to serve as aids in actual policy making or other operations.) A considerable part of the expansion in case writing in the 1960s occurred in thesis and dissertation writing (Finkle, 1960; Wildavsky, 1962) and on the teaching materials side. The demand for case materials for teaching undergraduate and more specialized courses enlarged considerably, and commercial publishers encouraged political scientists to prepare case collections to meet the demand (Westin, 1962). Some of the casebooks produced with these aims were based on original research and were of sufficiently high quality to be useful for analytical purposes and for the function of advancing the understanding of faculty as well as students (Silverman, 1959; Carper, 1962; Christoph and Brown, 1969). Others were hurriedly fashioned out of the *New York Times* or other secondary sources.

The growing number of case-style studies prepared primarily for research purposes fall, from a methodological standpoint, into two categories. In the first are the studies produced because the directors of large research investigations wanted to use them as one element in their total armament of research and reporting methods. Sometimes this was because the case style could serve a useful purpose as an instrument of reconnaissance or for getting at a certain type of reality. Sometimes it was because it counterbalanced or complemented or checked the other research styles used in the project. Conspicuous examples appeared in *Union Democracy* (Lipset, Trow, and Coleman, 1956), Dahl's *Who Governs?* (1961a), and *American Business and Public Policy* (Bauer, Pool, and Dexter, 1963).

A second source of research-oriented cases came from political scientists who found the case style the most suitable one for exploring and explaining their subjects. One of the best-known examples of this use of the case study is Neustadt's *Presidential Power* (1960, 1976). His later *Alliance Politics* (1970) was based partly on an operational case study made for President Kennedy and his secretary of defense. An outstanding later example was Derthick's *Uncontrollable Spending for Social Services Grants* (1975). Methodologically important examples under this heading are Paige's *The Korean Decision* (1968), which concluded with forty-nine general propositions, and Mosher's *Governmental Reorganizations* (1967). The latter work was the result of a laborious five-year experimental effort at using one dozen case studies to explore the participation hypothesis in organizational theory.

Other research-oriented case-style studies of high quality have illuminated a variety of political science areas. A few examples:

DEFENSE: Hammond's *Super Carriers and B-36 Bombers* (1963), Stein's casebook *American Civil Military Decisions* (1963), Wohlstetter's important *Pearl Harbor: Warning and Decision* (1962), and other studies (Schilling, 1962; Art, 1968; P.M. Smith, 1969).

FOREIGN AFFAIRS: *Essence of Decision* (Allison, 1971), *Diplomats, Scientists and Politicians* (Jacobson and Stein, 1966), *Programming Systems and Foreign Affairs Leadership* (Mosher and Harr, 1970).

NATIONAL PLANNING AND ECONOMIC DEVELOPMENT: Devons's *Planning in Practice* (1950), Hansen's *The Process of Planning* (1966), Hirschman's *Development Projects Observed* (1967), and Allen and MacLennan's *Regional Problems and Policies in Italy and France* (1970).

STATE AND URBAN POLITICS: Martin, Munger, and Associates' *Decisions in Syracuse* (1961), Mowitz and Wright's *Profile of a Metropolis*, Altshuler's *The City Planning Process* (1965), and others (Kramer, 1969; Still, 1950).

NATIONAL POLICY POLITICS: Sundquist's *Politics and Policy* (1968), Moynihan's *Maximum Feasible Misunderstanding*

(1969), Cleaveland's *Congress and Urban Problems* (1968), and Pierce's *Politics of Fiscal Policy Formation* (1971).
SCIENCE AND GOVERNMENT: Gilpin's *American Scientists and Nuclear Weapons Policy* (1963) and others (B. Smith, 1966; Lambright, 1969; Henry 1968).

There has also been an increasing flow of case materials about foreign governments. Two outstanding studies were originally prepared for operational purposes and were then made available to scholars (Rush, 1958; Leites, 1959). Others were produced by American scholars for research and/or teaching purposes (Ylvisaker, 1958; Eckstein, 1958a, 1960; H. H. Wilson, 1961; Wengert and DeLéon, 1957; Cohen, 1969; Braunthal, 1972). Possibly more significant for comparative studies in the long run are the increasing efforts of foreign scholars and institutes (Bock, 1962; Beck, 1967); for example, in England (Willson, 1961; Rhodes, 1965; Gregory, 1967; R. A. Chapman, 1969; B. C. Smith, 1969), the Philippines (De Guzman, 1963), Nigeria (Murray, 1969), and India (Narula, 1963; Butani, 1969; Indian Institute of Public Administration, 1972).

DEFINITION AND DISTINCTIVE QUALITIES

The preceding review of the expanding range of uses and the growing output of political science case studies, whether for teaching or research purposes or both, should establish that this particular genre is not the private property of any one school of scholars, nor are its features petrified in a form suitable only to one sector of the discipline. The variety of case-style materials now utilized in political science and other social sciences exceeds the available terminologies (e.g., "case," "case report," "case study," "case history," etc.). This condition, and the fact that the case study style is evolving in response to new applications, makes precise definition necessary here, because these terms can mean different things to different scholars, even within political science and public administration.

The worst possibility of misunderstanding can be eliminated by emphasizing at the start that the term "case study" is used here to mean considerably more than just any examination, in the political science universe, of any one particular as compared with a generality to which it seems to be related. It is common practice ("Colonialism—The Case of Upper Gonkaland") to use the term "case" to refer, for example, to the detailed, static analysis of one country's electoral system or social welfare legislation in comparison to those existing

elsewhere throughout the universe, or to some general model. That is
not the kind of case study that is the subject of this essay.

The key elements of the style of political science case study dealt
with here are the following:

1. It is a focused study and description of the forces, conditions,
and sequences of human actions that led to, or affected, a particular
outcome that is of interest to political science. The outcome is often
a specific one such as the nomination of a candidate, the making of a
policy decision, or the depiction of the consequences of a particular
urban renewal program. Sometimes the outcome/subject is more
diffuse: the changing nature of a party headquarters organization
over a set time period, the evolving relationships of a mayor and a
police chief, or a week in the life of a president. Although most
political science cases up to 1970 focused on the process that led up
to the making of decisions, after that date an increasing number of
cases described the outcomes of policies. Of these, many were
produced (sometimes with funding from federal agencies) to aid in
evaluation of new programs.

2. The case study deals with action, with dynamic sequences and
relationships, not with static analysis.

3. The element of time is always prominent. Compared to much
historical writing, a case study deals with a relatively compact sequence of activity and a more tightly focused set of forces. (Thus,
happily, the superb 700-page AEC history of the development and
use of the atomic bomb by Hewlett and Anderson, 1962, fits under
the definition, as does V. P. N. Menon's *The Transfer of Power in
India*, 1957. Ashton's classic 100-page history, *The Industrial Revolution*, 1966, does not.) Also, the case study usually describes processes in which the element of time is significant. It is because they
are static rather than real-time descriptions of action sequences that
what Crozier (1964) terms "cases" in his valuable study of French
bureaucratic behavior would probably not fit under this definition.
Nor would the descriptive material in Blau's *Dynamics of Bureaucracy* (1963) that has been dissected away from a living time
context.

4. Typically a case writer will seek to convey to his readers with
literary skill and precision how the principal characters in the real-life
situation perceived events at the time they were occurring. The
intentions, strategies, interpretations, and perspectives (not just the
actions) of these central characters, or their organizations, often
form a valuable part of the case. If the author incorporates data
uncovered later but not known to the actors at the time, he distinguishes them in his narrative from what was contemporary knowledge. The case writer often seeks to enable the reader to understand

sympathetically the actions of the central actors. He does not try to score off them on the basis of hindsight, at least not in the narrative portions of his study.

5. Case studies are based usually on participant observation, interviews, and examination of primary documents (files, letters, internal memoranda, etc.). A few high-quality, effective teaching cases have been prepared from secondary sources. So have many worthless ones.

6. A notable quality of the authors of cases that are highly admired by aficionados of the genre is intense curiosity about, and interest in, the real world of government and politics. One quickly senses in these authors the clinician's high respect for reality. To them, like Lasswell's (1970) systems-minded "emerging policy scientist," anything that affects the outcome that is the subject of their research is worthy of study, whether or not it fits existing theory, existing scientific fashions, or existing disciplinary boundaries. The case study style fits their needs because it permits the inclusion of the multiple, interrelated factors that affect most significant outcomes in public affairs, and because it permits the inclusion of accidental factors, about which the same may be said. This is one reason that many esteemed practitioners of the case study style feel an obligation and a utilitarian necessity to "see without preconception and report without prejudice" (Waldo, 1962, p. 42). Yet this tendency is not usually the product of an undiluted positivism that believes that facts speak for themselves. Outstanding case writers are intensely aware that, like other conscientious scientists, they are necessarily subject to cross-pressures that require fine professional judgments. On the one hand, they must have strong scientific sensibilities if they are to detect and wrest significant order from the complex hurly-burly of real life. On the other hand, they feel the obligation to follow the courses of actual reality and the obligation not to adjust the evidence (which they alone may possess) even in minor literary ways to fit their theoretical or scientific eagernesses.

7. The case study also differs from history because it has acquired special rules of fair dealing between author and reader. These are similar in some respects to the ground rules that prevail in the reporting of medical cases or of experiments in natural sciences. They derive also from the pedagogical use of cases in business administration. The distinctive characteristic is that the author feels obliged to present the reader with all the relevant data before thrusting on the reader his conclusions or opinions. He also calls attention to data that could not be obtained. The aim is to put the reader on a plane of equal factual knowledge with the author by the

time the latter offers his analyses or interpretations. Thus, a case writer would not tell the reader at the start that something happened because, for example, there was not enough citizen participation. First he would describe what actually did happen and what the conditions of citizen participation and other relevant conditions actually were. This special characteristic of the style exists partly because case studies have been in the past, and to some degree still are today, prepared to be used in "case method teaching" discussions. Here the aim is partly to strengthen the student's ability to think for himself, to improve his judgment, and to develop his courage to make decisions on the basis of incomplete evidence. To achieve this teaching purpose, which exists more in public administration than in political science, the student needs to feel that, having read the case, he knows as much about the particular reality situation being discussed as anyone else in the classroom, including the instructor.

The cardinal features of the political science case study style, and the main elements of conscientiousness that motivate and discipline some of its more admired exemplars, are thus drawn from a variety of lineages. Yet the genre does not fall entirely within any one of the separate traditions that conveyed it into political science.

The elements and definitions, whose presentation is now concluded, are what characterize the type of political science case style that is being discussed here. It will have occurred to the reader, perhaps, that some works consciously prepared and marketed as case studies will not fit these standards, while other works will, even though their authors may never have heard of the term "case study." In fact, some studies squarely in this style and of immense significance to political science were not prepared by or for an audience of political scientists (Devons, 1950; Titmuss, 1950; Hersey, 1951; Martin, 1948; Talese, 1969; Oberdorfer, 1971; Newhouse, 1973; Quinlan, 1974).

Any taxonomy creates borderline disputes, and it may be observed that the political science case style would be infinitely poorer if it could not include, at least as honorary examples, such valuable studies as Wylie's *Village in the Vaucluse* (1964), Bedford's *The Faces of Justice* (1961), and Swanberg's moving account of the confrontation behavior of the unfortunate commander of Fort Sumter in *First Blood* (1957). There remains the question of biographical material. The criteria laid out above would, on the ground of diffuseness, exclude Freeman's biography of Lee (1935) but not Rogow's psychiatric-political biography, *James Forrestal* (1963), or Frankel's valuable *High on Foggy Bottom* (1969).

THE MAIN USEFULNESSES OF THE CASE STUDY

After thirty years of growing experience with the case style in political science, what can be said about its demonstrated and potential usefulnesses? The more important matters may be summed up under three heads, the first two of which will then be discussed in detail.

First, it has been shown that the case study is especially useful for exploring, discovering, and communicating significant aspects of public policy making and implementation in the real-world context of politics, organization, and personalities, aspects that probably could not or would not be delivered by any other scholarly style of research. These capabilities have not been so well deployed or so well utilized on behalf of the discipline as they might, for reasons discussed in the concluding section below.

Second, it has been shown that the case study can be synchronized beneficially with other forms of research and with systematic theory in political science, and that it is necessarily neither a methodological loner nor an urban guerilla out to interrupt scientific inquiry. Here also improvements could bring greater benefits to the discipline.

Third, it has been widely concluded that the case study style has high teaching values (Banfield, 1960; Long, 1965; Somers, 1956), and although this is not a matter for further discussion in a book on methodology, it is significant that the egalitarian atmosphere of case teaching—in the sense that the student and the instructor have equal access to the case's basic facts and to its author's analyses about a problematic complex of current reality—is congenial to the modern style of student-faculty relationships. Perhaps it is also irrelevant to dwell on the fact that those who have prepared major cases, whether senior professors or dissertation writers, have usually reported gratification with an extraordinarily valuable learning experience. At the same time, it is now certain that the preparation of a substantial case study calls for considerable abilities and, in the case of graduate students, special exertions on the part of dissertation supervisors. Experience to date has provided no evidence that the case style can convert second-class scholarship into a first-rate piece of political science writing.

Exploration, Discovery, New Hypotheses—The Problem of the Remarkable Case

The case study has been exceptionally useful as one of the few political science instruments for reconnaissance, exploration, and

discovery that can be applied to the study of momentous, consequential matters of public affairs and to the effective communication
of such data in ways that carry precision and understanding (Neustadt, 1970; Mosher and Harr, 1970; Head, 1970; Lambright, 1968,
1973; Henry, 1968; Chapman, 1968; B. C. Smith, 1969; Juergensmeyer, 1964; Palamountain, 1955, 1965; D'Souza, 1969; Anderson,
1964; Wohlstetter, 1962; McConnell, 1960; Leites, 1959; Stein,
1949). It is a style that gives the researcher freedom (Crain, 1968,
p. 5) to follow his "white whale." It is exceptional in its ability to
deal with the involved sequences of interaction of large public affairs,
with the "bounded uncertainty" (Shackle, 1969, p. 271) of government decision making, and with the tortuous dynamics of power,
personality, urgency, and substantive interest that often go into
major policy making (Pye, 1968, p. 246). At the same time it can
show the involvement of less dynamic contextual influences such as
substantive or technical limitations, organizational, cultural, and economic settings, and legal limitations (Wengert, 1961; Whelan, 1969).
These features make the case style also a potent source of new
hypotheses if it is properly used.

Has an eager welcome been extended by political scientists in
recent years to the suggestive case-style data brought back for them
from the otherwise inaccessible lands of consequential political affairs and the uncharted islands of potentially momentous new policy
areas and new forces of social change? Not always. Some methodological grandees disdain or ignore these Columbian accounts
of new realities. The explorers tell of new phenomena, but they
have brought back no gold ducats that—to indulge in an infla-
tionary anachronism—will fit the hometown parking meters. The
complaints are that these are merely long anecdotal accounts,
that their gross, uncouth data will not fit the slots of existing
refined analytical instruments, and that these data deal with nonrepresentative situations and are therefore of little use for scientific inquiry.

These complaints are not kindly received by the political scientists who have exerted themselves to use the case style for exploration of new phenomena about which there is neither much
knowledge nor much thoretical appreciation (as distinguished from
those who prepare cases for more systematic use within relatively
well-known and theoretically mapped areas). From their perspective,
the first complaint boils down to saying, in effect, that existing
disciplinary paradigms and analytical awarenesses will not accommodate the unfamiliarities and complexities of momentous new realities. Mindful, for example, of the growing body of reports that
much broader—and even wider interdisciplinary—perceptions are
needed if scientists in general and policy scientists in particular are to

understand new patterns of movement and the vital current problems of contemporary society (Dror, 1968, 1970; Lasswell, 1970), the explorer type of political science case researcher is apt to see the above-mentioned complaints as the equivalent of a plea to keep the door of the Platonic cave closed so that a fuller, more direct view of the actual world will not destroy our satisfaction with the meager shadows of inadequate theory. Case-style materials that describe such contexts more fully and sensitively than most other varieties of political science writing thus are fated to become bearers of unwelcome news to some systematic theorists, and to ask that such upsetting news be recognized as a discovery is rubbing it in. Yet several recent surveys of the state of what political science or policy sciences have to contribute to our current understanding of public policy making have again emphasized the inadequacy of systematic contemporary policy studies that cut themselves off from contextual forces. The most recent is a 1976 foundation paper prepared by Douglas Yates, Jr., of Yale's new School of Organization and Management.

A complaint that deserves consideration is that remarkable cases (especially discovery and exploration cases and those dealing with momentous affairs) yield data of little political science value because they describe nonrepresentative situations. Representativeness is related to frequency, to ordinariness, to regularity. On the other hand some actions of government and politics—starting a war, for example—have great and irreversible effects on the viability of a nation and the state of human society. Such actions are, both in life and by definition, unusual (not to say unique). To suggest that a case study of dissident-employee pressure forcing a secretary of HEW to resign is of little value unless there is already in existence a class of similar incidents that can make it ordinary, or unless some clerical snippet of established systematic theory can be attached to accord it an entrance permit to our serious scientific consideration, seems like methodological Gongorism.

Even if one eliminates from consideration the value of momentousness and great impact on human society, the disciplinary implications of unqualified application of the representativeness criterion are forbiddingly severe. The regularities in any one small entity are often imperfect, and, as Wilfred Beckerman noted in his devastating review of the second Club of Rome report, they often decrease in the most primitive relationship with another entity. As that relationship is subjected to a variety of different conditions, the regularities often become still fewer (Mansfield, 1951). And when great chains of interaction relationships and conditions are formed, as in the handling of almost any piece of public business with its inherent uncertainties (Shackle, 1969), the elements of regularity and of ordinariness decrease severely in relation to the elements of uniqueness and unpredictability. One can say of most public affairs what has been said of battles: namely, that achieving a true understanding of their outcomes makes it necessary to study them in the full context of intertwined conditions, intentions, and accidents (Macintyre, 1969; Tolstoi, n.d.). Thus, unless the nonrepresentativeness criticism is considerably qualified, it seems to imply—since, unlike Schrödinger's (1945) particles, individual political actions do not necessarily become more regular in the mass, especially in free societies—that many important matters of public affairs are at present beneath our methodological dignity.

Finally, what becomes of representativeness in social science in a time of increasing change? In a world of increasing newnesses, in which fanatic as well as humane elements search for uniqueness and disorder while others under the stress of chaos exaggerate orderliness to be able "to live with our death" (Vizinczey, 1969, pp. 21-22), scientific inquiry must—without becoming entirely disorderly itself—find improved means of understanding profoundly the unique, the unusual, and the complex. One possibility is suggested by the enduring walls of the prehistoric fortress of Sachuaman near Cuzco. They derive their strength not from a binding matrix of concrete, which would in any event have been incapable of supporting their massive blocks, but from the irregularities in these enormous stones and the ingenious and understanding way they have been fit together.

The discovery-exploration-hypothesis-generation type of productivity of the case style is not confined to its application to new or bizarre areas. Many of its contributions of new knowledge have been new qualitative observations about aspects of familiar institutions and patterns of activity. It is the literary form of the case, which permits the communication of such qualitative data, as it does data about time and change, that makes it worthwhile for researchers to take note of significant subtleties: the vital elements that Polanyi (1958, p. 373) has called "the tacit coefficient of knowing." These include a range of elements from personal feelings to the distinct atmosphere of a police headquarters. There are subtle but ineluctable dynamic patterns, tricks of the trade, or rules of the game that are evident, for example, in *The Double Helix* (1968), in journalists when one is being interviewed, or in dock workers when one tries to take delivery of a shipment (Oram, 1970). About such influences, cases can bring scholarly recognition and tacit understandings that may have discovery effects within the realm of the familiar. One thinks, for example, of the perception of the balance of power and of the stoic irony of the 1961 presidency conveyed by reading of President Kennedy's remark that he was going down to Oklahoma to open that damned bridge and to kiss Bob Kerr's ass. Or the statement of the wizened Brooklyn police official about how to tell what department policy was: "You go up to headquarters and listen to what they are talking about in the hall" (Logue and Bock, 1953).

No inventory of the usefulnesses of the case style should ignore its capability, and thereby its encouragements to the researcher, to report material of this kind (P. M. Smith, 1969; Melnik and Leites, 1958; Leites, 1959) and bring it to the attention of political science as a matter worthy of a fuller, and perhaps more systematic investigation and consideration (Leites, 1969).

Other Research Contributions

For purposes of exposition, the preceding section has overstated the case study's separateness from all other forms of scientific inquiry in political science. There are important examples of cases being used for discovery and exploration not alone but in combination with other styles, as in Bauer, Pool, and Dexter's *American Business and Public Policy* (1963). Combining case-style material with quantitative data is now such a frequent practice that it is barely worth mentioning. Nor, despite the opposing thrusts described above and the strains that result from what Norton Long has called the case study's necessary role in "editing" theory, is there a fundamental antagonism between the case style and systematic theory.

As a contributor to the development of theory in roles other than exploration and discovery, the case style has special strengths and limitations. At the start, cases contribute data about current realities to the common stock of empirical knowledge that political scientists draw on in considering what is worth teaching and what is worth inquiring into (Long, 1965, p. 119). Then, as Fesler (1962, p. 78) has noted in a characteristically thoughtful discussion of the relation of cases to theory, cases help sort out plausible from implausible hypotheses. Evidence to support a proposition from at least one life case in the stock of the discipline's empirical knowledge is often considered a minimum credential for its serious consideration. The role of the case in validation and invalidation of propositions is part of a larger discussion of empirical testing that is doubtless given fuller attention elsewhere in this volume. I shall note here that negative cases can certainly invalidate propositions, as demonstrated in the comparison of actual crisis behavior in the Cuban missile affair with conclusions drawn from Europe in 1914 (Wohlstetter and Wohlstetter, 1965). And they certainly can cut down the pretentiousness of propositions, as shown in Mosher's (1967, p. 534) use of cases in investigating the participation hypothesis.

The single case by definition is not comparative, and the impossibility of using a single case to prove a hypothesis is widely accepted. To prepare five or ten rigorously comparative cases, when it is possible at all, is a demanding, time-consuming effort: one too extravagant (for both tester and reader) to be used for the validation of small-gauge propositions. On the other hand, theories about large affairs may require case-style data as part of a total testing effort. The writings of some respected thinkers, and our increasing awareness of the extent of forces of accident and irregularity in momentous public affairs, make it reasonable to raise the question whether a broad but specific theory about the dynamics of such affairs, whose complex assumptions are supported by three large case studies, is not so well and truly certified as a narrower and shallower proposition would be by 100 verifications (Glaser and Strauss, 1965; Polanyi, 1958, p. 135; Berlin, 1969, p. xxvi).

Another usefulness offered by the case in this connection is its employment to corroborate hypotheses raised by data of another style in the same research project. "Diversity in research strategy may do more to increase confidence in our conclusions than merely replicating the same research design in a large number of situations" (Ostrom, 1957).

Finally, there is the often misunderstood matter of the usefulness of case data by other scientists and for purposes other than the one for which it was gathered—especially for purposes of generalization. One expression for this is "transferability of case data." "Are the data in cases 'additive'?" is another way of putting the question, and the answer in scope and methods courses is quickly in the negative before moving on to other matters. In fact, experience in the last ten years shows much evidence that *case data can be additive and transferable.* Sundquist (1968) used data from Cleaveland's (1968) casebook. Dahl used Muir's *Metal Houses* data in *Who Governs?* (1961). Neustadt used several ICP cases as a basis for analysis in *Presidential Power* (1960, 1976). Mosher (1967) made effective systematic use of five cases prepared before his research design was even envisioned in his comparative analysis of reorganization cases. Bauer used Chapman (1968) as the basis of an analysis of organizational strains affecting research and development enterprises. Building on his well-known *World Politics* essay, "American Business, Public Policy, Case Studies and Political Theory" (1964), Lowi used seventeen major cases in his *Four Systems of Policy, Politics, and Choice* (1971).

A most ambitious and original blending and analysis of data from a great variety of cases prepared by others was described in the book by Davis and Weinbaum (1969). The authors analyzed the occurrences of interactions in thirty-two metropolitan case studies written by over twenty different authors. More recently, Greenberg, Miller, Mohr, and Vladeck (1973) have attempted more ambitious systematic methods of comparing data from twenty-four public policy cases on behalf of developing further public policy theory.

ACHIEVING LARGER USEFULNESS

The case style, as noted, has some inherent limitations. But the major impediments to achieving fullest benefit from the style are those that are self-inflicted by its practitioners. It is the purpose of this concluding section to suggest how some could be overcome.

A key symptom of underachievement in the use of cases in political science is the high rate of unemployment of large quantities of dearly won case data. Evidently, the profession has not paid careful attention to all of the significant case materials that have been produced in the last twenty years. To what should one attribute this condition? Apart from general factors such as differences in taste, preoccupation with one's own ideas and scientific styles, and the like, there are the case-avoidance needs described above in discussing the inhospitableness of some political scientists to discovery data. But these are explanations about the avoiders. The fact is that there are defects on the side of the case producers that furnish a justification to those predisposed to ignore important data in case studies. The defects fall under two headings. First, there are simply too many insignificant cases to make it easy, under present conditions, for someone to identify the significant ones. A contributing factor to this difficulty in locating cases relevant to one's interests is that only a small portion of case style materials is reviewed (probably under 10 percent) and there is as yet no central agency that indexes case materials with the thoroughness applied by the Harvard Business School, for example, to business administration cases (Intercollegiate Case Clearing House, 1968). Second, more cases need to reach the high standards of reliability and precision that the best ones have shown to be possible. This must be done if case data are to be more fully transferable, more usable—in pieces or as wholes—by others for their own generalizing or analytical purposes. A grading and labeling procedure for cases and some other innovations are proposed in the discussion of this second topic, to which I now turn.

Scholars sometimes are understandably uncertain about how much to rely on data in cases (a) because there is uncertainty about their degree of accuracy and dependability and (b) because the data themselves may be presented so as to fall tantalizingly short of just that degree of precision required for the reader's analytical purposes. As Pye (1968, p. 247) notes, the writer of descriptive studies may cite several contributing factors as having led to an outcome but may fail to indicate precisely how they combined to bring it about and which factor was most influential.

For dependability and precision, there are no inherent limitations that make case-style data less true to life than any other style. On the contrary, its literary form in the hands of a skilled writer may be used to communicate nuances and complexities of action far more accurately than any other. The difficulty is that one does not always know if a man is choosing his words carefully or, alternatively, engaging in assembly-line thought and using prefabricated phrases. (In a different manner, a somewhat similar difficulty sometimes arises in making additive use of survey data gathered by different teams in different parts of the country about the same questions, but two wrongs are not additive into one right.)

The problem of uncertain dependability of case data starts with differences from one case writer to another in the effort made to achieve accuracy. The author preparing cases mainly for teaching is subject to certain forces for inaccuracy. The author of research cases is subject to others (Bock, 1962, pp. 99-104). Marginally conscientious scientists in each group may succumb. So may men whose powerful intellects bully their reality data in their masters' urgency to lead fellow scientists to important new theories, as Jones (1955, p. 430) says was true of Freud and as Lambright (1973) implies was true of Langmuir, to cite instances tactfully distant from contemporary political science. Such forces for bias affect every political science style. But much can be done to protect the reliability and hence the transferability of case data.

The first act is to make explicit the criteria used in the selection of the case subject and in the collection of the case data. The reader must know if the absence of a particular element is due to the author's not having looked for it or to his having failed to find it.

Next comes the matter of sources. Transferability of data requires that the reader have a true picture of the sources of case data and of the records and persons that were inaccessible. In doubtful instances, a statement by the writer assessing the depth and correctness of key data is almost essential.

Soon after one raises the matter of identifying and grading the sources of case data one is led into the complicated subject of *research ethics*, confidentiality of sources, the Freedom of Information Act, the scientist's need to know, the government's need to encourage subordinates to speak up(ward) frankly, the government's need for informed and knowledgeable criticism from the outside, and the individual's right of privacy (Delany, 1960; Shils, 1959; Webb et al., 1966; *Science* 1967, p. 535). And one is led, as in Dickinson's agonizing case, *German and Jew* (1967), to the human relationship between the research scientist and the observed human being:

> The author identifies with the human beings who people these pages: there but for the vagaries of chance go I. . . . It would pervert this identification and destroy this texture if the people who have made this book possible and to whom the writer owes an inviolable gratitude were exposed to the effects of the stereotypes that suffering and ignorance have attached to many of the matters dealt with [1967, p. x].

It is no coincidence that it is usually in the case style that such matters arise more frequently than in other styles. The case study, in fact and in the fears of those observed and depicted, can cause political turbulence and real career damage. At the same time, its quality is utterly dependent on the fullest cooperation of at least a minority of insiders (to get interview data and to get access to records that can confirm or disprove self-serving recollections).

The nub of the problem for transferability of case data is illustrated by two important case-style works, Neustadt's *Alliance Politics* (1970) and Sundquist's *Politics and Policy* (1968). Both are men of high reputations for probity and for access to many pipelines to inside Washington knowledge. Sundquist gives his reader a careful statement of sources and of gaps in his data, but then comes the remark: "These [more than 100] interviews were usually conducted on a 'not for attribution' basis. Throughout this book, where sources are not indicated for information not available in published form, the confidential interview can be assumed to be the source" (1968, p. 8). Neustadt, rather more sorrowfully, conveys a similar message.

Anyone with experience in the preparation and editing of descriptive materials knows how easy it is to paint over gaps in data with a skillful use of words. Or how easy it is to stretch the data, sometimes against the grain of reality, to fit one's stirring new hypothesis. How much more easy it is to succumb to such practices if one is able to dispense with naming sources, and if one knows that no one else can ever replicate one's study! The two writers cited are above succumbing to such temptations, but how can the reader, the potential data user, know one scientist's conscience from another?

There are, to be sure, some effective means for increasing the dependability of case data under these circumstances. One is the selection of authors of high standards, with sophisticated knowledge of theory and life, and with no inhibitions against writing frankly. A second is incessant, unyielding insistence—as a dissertation supervisor or the director of a research enterprise—on accuracy and precision in the presentation of case data. Here one can take advantage of a built-in force for correctness in the case style: the author must, after all, present data that satisfactorily explain the outcome. But experience shows that all of these aids alone cannot guarantee completeness, accuracy, and precision. In fact, experience in using *accepted* Ph.D. dissertations as starting points for case studies in the Inter-University Case Program from 1957 to 1973 shows a devastatingly high (over 70 percent) number with substantial inaccuracies, omissions, and biasing of critically important data. Like the commercial publisher, but with more regret, the dissertation supervisor has little means of knowing whether the factual data in a dissertation are correct, complete, or biased.

What would greatly improve the usefulness of case data is *the introduction of a system of grading the accuracy and dependability of case-style studies,* a system similar to those that protect consumers of meat and tires. A beginning would be the working out of standards under the aegis of a body like the American Political Science Association. For top grading, a case-style study would have been written for a scientific purpose, its author would have had full access to persons and papers, and the draft would have been reviewed and commented on at least once by the main characters, along the lines followed in preparing ICP cases. Provision might also be made for a scholarly ombudsman (a) to render a grading on studies in which sources have had to be protected and (b) to render advisory judgment when the officials who review drafts say they are inaccurate and the authors speak with tightened throats about academic freedom. Resolution of differences in the latter situations could take the form sometimes already used of permitting the portrayed officials to make their critical rejoinders in footnotes. In the operation of the grading system, a special (possibly voluntarily self-graded) category might be created for those abominable teaching-only cases that cause professional journals to decide to review almost no cases at all: the ones written entirely from secondary sources (or from other authors' research cases) and rushed directly into print in time to exact due tribute from the captive book buyers in this year's introductory courses. If a grading service existed, it might also be put to use improving the reliability of case-style dissertations by circulating for review by the portrayed officials a sampling from each major university's recently accepted dissertations. One might then know what value to place on data in each such dissertation, and, incidentally, something about the standards of supervision in the different political science departments.

A final innovation for improvement on this score is an extension of the practice recently instituted for West European research materials at Yale: making available to serious researchers the tapes of oral interviews or the written notes on which a writer based his case.

MORE SIGNIFICANT CASES

The other major impediment to full employment of significant case data by political science is that there are so many insignificant ones that they make it difficult—in the absence of journal reviewing or of indexing—to locate the ones that are important. The number of highly significant cases has steadily increased, but so has the number of cases of small worth for analysis. The fact that cases are given little critical review does not encourage case writers to see each of their data as of potential significance to some fellow political scientist, yet such a perspective would doubtless be a force for greater accuracy and precision. If there were a higher proportion of significant and reliability-graded cases, more political scientists would use them, and if more political scientists used cases and raised questions about the value and meaning of their data, more producers of cases would feel a greater incentive to achieve the highest standards and usefulnesses of the method.

Initiating such a beneficial cycle of uplifting interactions requires, plainly and simply, a higher output of significant cases. So does the much more important mission of keeping political science mindful of important new realities and the apparently sudden emergence of new public policy issues and of severely different urgencies thrust on the public sector. To me, both purposes will be well served by greater deployment of case-writing effort in the sector of the style's most demonstrated strength: its utilization for discovery and exploration of new realities, new conditions, new urgencies, new areas of public policy. Lambright's remarkable (1973) study of the manner by which weather modification capability matured into certain particular kinds of contemporary national policy questions rather than other kinds is an example of how the style can serve to bring an appreciation of a momentous change in reality into the disciplinary awareness of political science. One hopes there can be many similar discovery and reconnaissance usefulnesses for cases. If this and other exploratory and discovery values of the case style could be expanded, and if such cases could succeed in alerting the main body of political scientists to important new forces and issues *before* rather than after they have led to decisions, everyone in the discipline would benefit, not least our students (who would have a fighting chance of catching up to the march of events) and our systematic theorists.

As part of an overall disciplinary effort to increase the relevance and potency of political science, the case-study writer serving in an exploring and discovering role is not confined to what is germane to existing theoretical systems. Especially in times of sharp changes, it seems indisputable that the case study can yield important scientific values by discovering and exploring knowledge that is as yet unappreciated, undifferentiated, unaccounted for, or unknown by existing theory and its more closely attached methodologies.

PART 5

TOWARD A SCIENCE OF POLITICS

22. AN ASSESSMENT OF FUTURE TRENDS

Donald M. Freeman

This final chapter has three general purposes: (1) to offer an overview of the contents of the book, (2) to review past trends in the discipline, and (3) to determine some potential trends in the future of political science. In writing this chapter I am reminded of the oft-quoted critic who said that meterologists' forecasts would be more accurate if they predicted tomorrow's weather on the basis of the actual weather of today. Deprived of measuring instruments comparable to those available to the meteorologist, we *must* forecast on the basis of the past.

This book has been designed and written largely as a mainstream-discipline-affirming work. Our point of view is certainly not shared by all political scientists, but we believe it reflects the view of a good majority of the fraternity and also of the leadership of its associations. In affirming the direction of the discipline in the last two decades, we are mindful of the potential for a dramatic or massive reorientation of political science, like that which took place after 1946 in the behavioral revolution, but no such reorientation seems likely in the coming decade. Gradual change, in more flexible professional associational frameworks, in a discipline now grown tolerant of a plurality of values, interests, points of view of colleagues, and of a plurality of means of pursuing the multiple interests of the profession, seems to me to be the path of the future (McCoy and Playford, 1967; Melanson, 1975; Blondel, 1976).

THE PAST AS FUTURE

Political science is a very young discipline or profession in the United States.[1] The relevant dates of our beginnings as a discipline

701

are three: 1880, the first graduate school of political science at Columbia; 1903, the founding meeting of the American Political Science Association (APSA) at Tulane University; and 1906, the publication of the first number of the *American Political Science Review (APSR)*. The growth of political science as a profession was slow. For example, (1) few Ph.D.'s were granted in the discipline until well into the twentieth century;[2] (2) the founding meeting of the APSA drew an attendance of only twenty-five; and (3) for some years, the APSR was dwarfed in reputation by such journals as *The Annals* and the *Political Science Quarterly*. Initially, political science was typically housed in a joint department with one or more of the other social sciences, and this was a common practice until after World War II, except in the larger universities and colleges.

From the very beginning there was disagreement in the ranks of the discipline over many important matters. Somit and Tanenhaus (1967) have sorted out the discipline's history and chronicled the principal movements and schisms in its ranks—their book is required reading for serious students of political science. Some of the key fights, which have recurred every generation, have been over the following questions: (1) the possibility of a science of politics, (2) the civic education function of the profession, (3) the relationship of the political scientist to the government and society within which he functions, (4) the direction and performance of the *APSR* and what might be done to correct its "faults," and (5) the legitimate scope of interests within the purview of the discipline. As if especially cursed by the gods, political science seems doomed to reconsider these same disputes for all ages to come.

Protest Movement I: Behavioralism

The behavioral movement is typically dated from 1946, forty-three years after the birth of the APSA; however, the roots of the movement were planted in the 1920s and 1930s at the University of Chicago. The causes of the movement have been ably analyzed by Dahl (1961b) and Somit and Tanenhaus (1967, pp. 173 *ff.*), and yet there is still one more possible construction which can be placed on these events. Was this not the *identity crisis* of an adolescent profes-

1. In chapter 1 Evron Kirkpatrick has ably documented the ancestry, birth, and rise of American political science; therefore, this commentary will only reassert points I wish to use as a springboard to look into the future.
2. Somit and Tanehaus (1967, p. 58) *estimated* the annual Ph.D. output as "from 1885 to 1900, three or four; from 1900 to 1910, six to ten; from 1911 to 1915, ten to fifteen; and from then to 1921 about eighteen to twenty."

sion? At Chicago in the 1920s and 1930s Charles E. Merriam trained a new generation of leaders for the profession who questioned the limited goals of the profession and its methods of inquiry. How did political science differ from other social sciences, especially history? What was political science's special province of interests? If political scientists were limited to historical-institutional-legal analysis (often based only on library research), how did it differ from history? When Merriam's students took over the leadership of the discipline (as they did after World War II), they were joined by many other inquiring young Ph.D.'s, the search for a distinctive identity for political science in the social sciences was pressed forward, and then solved (for their generation at least). So successful was the behavioral movement that its principal tenets have been substantially internalized in the profession, and most commentators agree that political science is in a "postbehavioral era." On the other hand, and contrary to the views of the vocal antibehavioralists of a decade ago, the internalization of behavioralism by no means blotted out the previous heritage of the profession—in the behavioral movement only another dimension was added to the complex and rich experience of political science in the United States.

The importance of Merriam to behavioralism suggests some comment at this point on leadership. John W. Burgess and Charles E. Merriam each exemplifies the ability of one person to make a lasting impact on a profession. Burgess is the father of American political science through his founding influence on the graduate school at Columbia. Burgess pressed the Columbia administration into committing the resources for the school, went to Europe to recruit the initial faculty, and in general modeled Columbia's school of political science after the German universities of the day (these Germanic beginnings are still influential in graduate study today). Merriam is the father of modern political science through his leadership at Chicago in the 1920s and 1930s and through his students who became the leaders of the behavioral movement. If there is a new "Moses" (or Burgess or Merriam) in the profession, he (or she) has not been clearly recognized as such. The survey of the literature of political science found in part 3 of this work reveals, among other things, that the number of truly distinguished scholars in the discipline is quite large, and no particular man stands out as *the* leader. In the 1950s and 1960s V. O. Key, Jr., was certainly the most revered and widely recognized political scientist—now, no such preeminence is accorded any one scholar. Consider this *partial* list of senior scholars: Harold D. Lasswell, David B. Truman, David Easton, Herbert A. Simon, Karl W. Deutsch, Hans J. Morgenthau, Robert A. Dahl, Angus Campbell, C. Herman Pritchett, Gabriel A. Almond, Austin Ranney, and Heinz Eulau. Skipping down to the next generation of professionals, there is an equally impressive list of men who have already made a mark on the profession, but they promise much more creative writing in the future. A *partial* list of such men includes: Nelson Polsby, Aaron Wildavsky, Richard L. Merritt, Larry Wade, Ira Sharkansky, Harmon Zeigler, Jorgen Rasmussen, Charles O. Jones, Frank Sorauf, Anthony Downs, J. David Singer, Raymond Tanter, Kenneth Janda, Donald R. Matthews, and Philip E. Converse. With the ranks of professional leadership substantially enlarged over that of any previous generation of political scientists, perhaps no one scholar can command the attention of a majority of the profession, and perhaps no one scholar will ever find the discipline in such a state of readiness for leadership as Merriam found it in the twenties and thirties.

Protest Movement II: The Caucus

Until the mid-1960s, the business of the APSA was handled rather quietly by the governing council of the APSA, the editor of the *APSR*, the executive director of the APSA, and a very few members who were willing to show up at the dull annual business meetings. In the mid-1960s the peaceful, almost private, conduct of association affairs ended—as one shocked member of the council put it after the business session in 1967, "My God, we had a motion from the floor," an unprecedented event. By the end of the decade, the services of the American Arbitration Association had been secured to aid in the conduct of business meetings and to handle elections and referenda by mailed ballot.

Before 1967 there were plenty of grievances, real or imagined, in the APSA, but they were usually not formally filed or dealt with; after 1967, every grievance, real or imagined, got a hearing, and the Caucus for a New Political Science became the principal agent for aggregating dissenting points of view. The catalysts which produced the caucus were (a) the war in Viet Nam, (b) the social revolution and unrest in the cities, and (c) the extensive organized dissent in the United States in the 1960s. One of the founding statements of the caucus is a letter from H. Mark Roelofs, caucus chairman, to Evron M. Kirkpatrick, executive director of the APSA, dated October 3, 1967; the letter contained five resolutions for transmittal to the officers of the APSA. The first of these resolutions was the organizing statement of the caucus:

> Whereas the American Political Science Association, at its conventions and in its journal, has consistently failed to study, in a radically critical spirit, either the great crises of the day or the inherent weaknesses of the American

political system, be it resolved that this caucus promote a new concern in the Association for our great social crises and a new and broader opportunity for us all to fulfill, as scholars, our obligations to society and to science.

The second resolution called for a plenary session and full day of panels on the Viet Nam War; the third urged the APSA to resist all government efforts to get the names of student and faculty groups on campuses; the fourth urged the APSA to poll its members on the war. The fifth and last resolution committed the caucus to studying areas of political science which had been ignored, and it was this last resolution which became the basis of the caucus-conducted panels at the professional meetings from 1968.

The caucus immediately became a force in professional associational politics: it altered completely the character of business meetings, ran rival slates of candidates for associational offices, set up its own panels at professional meetings, and became virtually a rival "political party" within the profession opposing the "establishment."

Associational elections in the 1970s have been hard-fought, interesting battles. In addition to the "caucus slate" and the "nominating committee slate" (supported by the Ad Hoc Committee and the Committee for a Fair Election headed by Donald Herzberg and Warren Miller), endorsements of candidates have been coming from the Black Caucus, the Women's Caucus, and the Chicano Caucus. There is clear evidence of slate building from both "parties"; there is impressive bloc voting in the elections; and the two major "parties" engage in coalition formation with the various minority caucuses by nominating their leaders or endorsing some member of their slate. The Caucus for a New Political Science has won some victories at the APSA ballot boxes, but the APSA is still predominately a "modified one-party system" and is likely to remain so.

The caucus has been a "lightning rod" to draw together those with grievances in the association, and much like Eugene McCarthy's candidacy in the 1968 New Hampshire presidential preferential primary, the caucus following is a heterogeneous one (see Graham and Carey, 1972). The heterogeneity of the caucus following increases the potential voting power of the group, but it presents substantial problems in maintaining unity in the group. *Some* of the grievances articulated through the caucus are: the APSA is run by a closed, small, elite group; the reviewing practices of the *APSR* and other journals are questioned, along with the articles actually selected for publication; the programs of the annual meetings are run by the establishment, staffed by their friends, and include irrelevant panel topics and panel papers; not enough attention has been focused on good teaching in the APSA; women and other minorities, they argue, have been systematically disadvantaged within the discipline; and, finally, the APSA leadership is charged with manipulating the foundations and the publishing industry. A great number of committed antibehavioralists have been involved in caucus efforts, but the caucus is not primarily an antibehavioral "party."[3]

The Caucus for a New Political Science has clearly made an impact on the APSA and has, in my opinion, the following accomplishments to its credit: the committee structure and attendant programs of the association were expanded and invigorated (to some degree on pressure from the caucus); the new opinion and newsletter journal of the APSA, *P. S.*, which began publishing in 1968, has been enlivened by caucus participation; either because of or in spite of the caucus, the panels of professional meetings are well publicized a year in advance and participants are more openly recruited than ever before (it is still not perfect, but it is better); the conduct of associational business by the council is more fully reported than ever before and more members of the association know about its affairs; slate-building and association politics have produced representation for minorities on the council; some small share of the credit for the more open recruiting policies for new appointments should be accorded the caucus, and this would include the equal employment movement as well; and finally, with the hard-fought APSA elections, more attention than ever before has been directed on the selection of officers (especially the president)—a decade ago, few seemed to care who got elected.

The caucus has had virtually no impact on the *APSR*, and if any trend is discernible in the regional journals, it is that they are more selective of articles, contain fewer "relevant" pieces, and are more professionally managed than ever before. There has been no redirection of the profession in line with the interests of the caucus (for example, the caucus could get "baby-sitting service" for the women members of the APSA at the annual meeting, but it never got a resolution passed condemning the war in Viet Nam). For a time, caucus demands for more programs, and the attendant activities of association committees, cost more than APSA's annual income would support. And, finally, it must be said that caucus resolutions and political maneuverings have been a distraction to the profession and have caused needless and undue friction.

3. I am making no effort at this point to analyze these charges or grievances. I do urge the reader to reflect on them and do some investigation. There is more truth in some of the charges than in others. There was discrimination against minorities, and perhaps the APSA as a group should have spoken out more clearly on the subject, but surely all discrimination can't be charged against the association. Likewise, all associations, and most groups, in my experience, are run by a small group of leaders, but the APSA council is not a closed group.

The national associations of the other social sciences had insurgent movements in their ranks in the 1960s and 1970s, and they were quite similar to the Caucus for a New Political Science. So, factionalism came to all the associations; the insurgents were especially outspoken about the war and the social unrest of the 1960s; and the movements drew especially strong support from young professionals. The increased size of the associations, the plurality of interests and functions encompassed in any association, and a lack of consensus on professional goals, suggest the rise of factionalism. Perhaps the caucus in the 1960s was a wave of the future.

Trends in Personnel, Funding, and Publishing

Gone are the halcyon days of the 1950s and 1960s when, for over a decade, newly minted Ph.D.'s could pick an appointment from several job offers. Mobility was always possible and salaries were clearly affected by the seller's market setting. All of higher education was expanding rapidly, but political science was a special case. All over the country joint departments were divided, and independent political science departments were established; they immediately experienced rising enrollments of majors, and therefore expanded teaching staffs. The growth of political science permitted rapid promotions (with the attendant perquisites) for young professionals, because the higher ranks were largely uncluttered. Departments were well financed; travel was supported generously; and teaching loads were being gradually adjusted downward. The scarcity of senior staff permitted a maximum impact for the new behaviorally oriented young Ph.D.'s. The expansion of political science took place during a period of widespread regard for education, and legislatures, trustees, and foundations were generally supportive of higher education.

In the late 1960s the war in Viet Nam produced substantial campus unrest, and public support for education eroded. The permissive climate on campuses gradually disappeared; enrollments began to stabilize; and funding for universities was limited. In the early 1970s the supply of Ph.D.'s caught up with the demand. The APSA established a personnel service, which had an immediate clientele, this time in a buyer's market. By 1972 major departments that advertised a new position could expect to receive hundreds of applications, literally more than they could afford to process and fully investigate. Actually, political science did not have a crisis situation: 70 percent of those seeking appointments in 1972 had found one by June 1, and many appointments always open up in the summer after legislative budgets have made their way through the mysteries of boards of regents' processing.

For the future, we can expect continued growth in the profession. More schools are offering the M.A. and the Ph.D., and, with some modest cyclical ups and downs, the Ph.D. output will continue to rise. However, there will be a much more stable profession with closer review of performance and slower awarding of tenure and promotion. Political science will establish a more normal cycle of replacement through gradual educational expansion and the retirement and death of senior men. A larger share of Ph.D.'s will come from nonprestige departments (a trend which has been clear for some time, Somit and Tanenhaus, 1967, p. 159), and the Ph.D.'s from these departments have, at least in recent times, been able to secure appointments about as well as their comrades from prestige departments.

In 1970, as a direct result of the new market situation, the APSA began two efforts which will certainly grow in the coming decades: (1) annual manpower studies of professional political scientists and positions available for them, with projections for the future, and (2) the establishment of a departmental services program under the direction of a standing APSA Committee of Department Chairpersons. For the first time the APSA will produce, for member departments who pay an annual fee, a set of essential professional services which will include the *Biographical Directory* (continuing an old service), annually updated lists of department chairmen and changes of address for members of the APSA, a set of pamphlets on careers in political science (for undergraduates), a *Guide to Graduate Study in Political Science*, revised annually, and an information service which will cover salaries, positions, ranks, growth in enrollments, and other pertinent data for the nation's political science departments. These programs project an image of a more active association, offering more and more services to the profession.

In the late 1960s and early 1970s, as noted earlier, funding for departments tightened up, and the available research funds from private foundations and from the government were limited. With more limited travel funds, for example, attendance at the annual meeting of the APSA declined and fluctuated sharply, depending on the location of the convention city. Research funding simply did not keep pace with the expanding political science fraternity, and the federal government has been shifting priorities, moving funds to new programs, canceling some and tapering off other old programs (gone in 1975 was the Institutional Grants Program; added in 1972 and 1973 was a new set of grant programs called RANN, Research Applied to National Needs). In 1972 and 1973 a new difficulty arose: a department could secure a favorable review for a proposal and then find that the federal government had decided not to spend the money Congress had appropriated. With funds limited, and the competition for them much sharper, the established departments or prestige departments are going to get the lion's share of what is available (they have always done well, Somit and Tanenhaus, 1967, p. 167 *ff*.), and major funding for less prestigous departments and research centers will be even more difficult to obtain than usual.

In the 1950s and the early 1960s the publishing industry expanded simultaneously with the rapid growth of political science. The older presses were busy signing contracts (with tempting advances) and considering spin-offs (the establishment of splinter publishing houses off the parent unit) for tax advantages. In the late 1960s and early 1970s, the publishing industry's economic fortunes changed. First, campus unrest cut into the sale of books; second, the cost of editing, production, and publishing rose drastically; and third, the used-book companies organized so effectively that they could make handsome profits off the sale of used books (which students bought at slightly lower prices than they would pay for a new copy). Though the publication explosion which began in the 1950s continues on into the 1970s, book companies must be more cautious than ever before in signing commitments, and large advances on the signing of a contract have virtually disappeared.

Costs of production have also made times difficult for the *APSR* and the regional political science journals (most of which are subsidized). As noted earlier, the quality of the journals has definitely improved, and they are all more professionally managed than they have ever been before. The *APSR* has in the late sixties and early seventies fallen further and further behind in its publishing schedule, developing a backlog of accepted, but not yet published, manuscripts. In the same time period, there has been a dramatic proliferation of new, specialized journals that have appeared in comparative politics, international politics, teaching, research methods, and data repositories, to mention just a few. This growth should take some of the pressure off all journals except the *APSR*. Because of its preeminence, every scholar prefers the *APSR* as the vehicle of publication. For several years, proposals have been discussed calling for more numbers of the *APSR* per year, the establishment of another journal under APSA sponsorship, or some other form of expansion, but this move calls for greater investments of money from the APSA and time from the editorial staff, neither of which is readily available.

NEW DIRECTIONS IN SCIENCE

The philosophical underpinnings of modern political science have been borrowed from the physical sciences. The noteworthy successes of physical science in this century attracted the attention of the social sciences, and imitation followed. As Harold Lasswell has so ably stated in *The Future of Political Science* (1963, p. 161):

> We can predict with confidence that, if the institution of study itself continues, it will be applied to power and government. The scientific approach to any phase of the natural or social order is so deeply embedded in our civilization that, if any one group of scholars fails to apply it to a field for which they are presumably responsible, the field will be taken away from them and cultivated by more strongly motivated and capable colleagues under other labels.

With Lasswell, I believe there is no turning back from the scientific movement in political science—the whole body of theory which has been developed and the whole research tradition now institutionalized are permeated with the conventions and canons of science.

The last two generations of political scientists were trained in traditional philosophy of science as stated by the works of men like Bertrand Russell, Karl R. Popper, Hans Reichenbach, Alfred North Whitehead, Richard B. Braithwaite, Ernest Nagel, A. J. Ayer, and Carl G. Hempel. Undoubtedly the works of these men will continue to be influential for some years to come. However, younger philosophy of science specialists have been turning their attention to a phenomenological approach to the philosophy of science, and this appears to be the new, corrective wave of the future.

Maurice Natanson has argued in a compelling fashion for a phenomenological approach to the philosophy of science in Chapter 16 of this book. The obligations of a phenomenological approach on the researcher and on research design are more demanding than those of traditional philosophy of science. In the past, empirically oriented political scientists have collected and analyzed data on attitudes, actions, and events with but rare concern for the context of the behavior, the meaning of the behavior for the individual actor, or anything like a full awareness on the part of an actor of how his behavior fits into a dynamic, ongoing system. Phenomenology puts on the social scientist the new burden of sorting out the full meaning of attitudes, actions, and events. This challenging new way of looking at science asks the scientist to go beyond behavior to the meaning of behavior.

THE DOMAIN OF POLITICAL SCIENCE

Twenty years ago doctoral candidates typically elected three or four fields of study: a major field, minor fields in political science, and a field of related study. At preliminary written and oral examinations, students were responsible for the entire literature of each field. Mercifully, examining committees were tolerant of some spots of ignorance, and most of the time committees sought to find out what candidates did know more often than what they did not know. The outer limits of the discipline's domain have been stretched to the point that today the major fields have been broken down into subfields, and doctoral candidates typically are responsible for groups of subfields within the major fields. Where entire department faculties used to attend oral examinations, today committees of three or five are appointed for each student, and examinations are tailored far more precisely to the student's specialization. Changes in the structure of graduate programs and the content of examinations reflect the growth of the discipline's interest, the increased specialization within its ranks, and the radical expansion of the literature of political science.

Part 2 of this book is a survey of the literature of political science. I chose to classify the literature into the five "traditional fields" of the discipline knowing that "these are old wineskins holding new wine." Specialists in public law and constitutional politics no doubt would be happier with a sixth field surveying their literature and special interests (rather than forcing this range of interests into the American institutions and political behavior section). The burgeoning literature in the subfields points up the artificiality of our "five-field classification of the literature." Whole sections could be devoted to such subfields as area studies, political change, political socialization, voting behavior, empirical theory, normative theory, organizational theory, small group theory, international law, national security policy, and deterrence theory.

The far-flung boundaries of our discipline and the plurality of interests it contains sometimes seem to foreshadow a formal organizational subdividing of interests. As Michael Haas has pointed out in chapter 6, many international relations specialists think of themselves as an independent branch of knowledge, not a field of political science, and there are a number of independent departments of international relations. In the last decade the schism between the theorists and other members of the political science department at Berkeley led to an unsuccessful secession movement. At Michigan there have been occasional conflicts between the Department of Political Science and the Political Behavior Program, and the latter goes along on a relatively independent course. And, finally, public administration is frequently established in a separate school and has controlling interests in institutes or centers of government and public affairs (sometimes virtually in isolation from the institution's department of political science).

However, the boundaries (or scope) of political science's interests are sure to be pushed out further. The experts writing our surveys of the literature in part 2 all call attention to the changing parameters of the fields. On comparative politics Kaufman and Rosenau write, "The field of comparative politics is presently in a state of ferment. Its boundaries are expanding. Its focuses are proliferating. Its research strategies are multiplying. Its storehouse of conceptual equipment is overflowing." And Chandler writes, "The field of political theory is undergoing redefinition." The cross-fertilization of public administration with the new thrust in policy studies has been a tremendously invigorating move, though Wade says that "public administration is at once the most advanced and the most retrograde of political science's traditional fields. . . . It is most retrograde with respect to an appreciation of the role of public administration in cross-national policy development, i.e., in politics."

In the past, political science has given up far too many of its legitimate spheres of interest to other disciplines. As Buchanan has noted, we have studied the policy-making processes without giving much attention to the impact of those policies enacted (for example, we have let education specialists study the impact of state budgeting on the quality and nature of public education systems). Early in the development of an environmental awareness in this country, we abdicated the entire subject area to biologists and cultural geographers, and for an inordinately long time we abdicated the study of the transition of societies (including the institutions of government) from the primitive to the modern stages to anthropologists. Political science must give more attention to rapid technological, social, and environmental changes and their attendant political consequences; for example, we have a legitimate interest in the developing law of outer space, in the political consequences of the international monetary system, in the consequences of the information systems revolution, in the political consequences of zero population growth, and in the whole process of the allocation of resources, as the world appears to be moving into a new age of scarcity in which the "have" and "have not" nations are drastically changed. We can be assured that at every point along the boundaries of political science's legitimate domain another discipline waits to stake its own new claim.

TOOLS OF THE TRADE

At no time in political science's history have its research scholars been armed with more tools and techniques of data collection than the present. In every case, political science owes a great debt to other social sciences for developing the tools we have now adopted as our own. For example: much of what we know about participant-observation analysis comes from anthropology and sociology; power attribution techniques were invented by Floyd Hunter, a sociologist; the advancement of the science of index and scale construction was most notably aided by psychology; today's political science specialists in the analysis of aggregate data are much aided by work in economics, especially in econometrics; thanks to an early pioneering work by Harold Lasswell, political science had a hand in developing content analysis, but the technique has greatly benefited from work done by communications scientists and sociologists.

Part 3 of this book includes chapters on nine different tools or techniques of data collection and analysis available to political scientists. I asked the authors of these chapters to write about how the researcher employs the tool, about the tool's strengths and weaknesses, and to give examples of its use in political and social science.[4] Beyond these three essentials, each author made his own decision about what to include in his chapter.

A tool or technique of data collection is not an end in itself (except, perhaps, for a methods specialist); it is a means of answering questions. The novice political scientist sometimes misses this point and picks research topics amenable to a particular tool or technique which has caught his fancy. It is true that many professionals develop special strengths in one or two techniques and continue to use these limited types of data for a professional lifetime. The experience of some of our most distinguished researchers strongly suggests that the young professional seek out those research questions which intrigue him and then select the appropriate data (and tool of data collection) to permit him to answer the questions.

Consider, for example, the research career of V. O. Key, Jr. His *Southern Politics* (1949) and *American State Politics* (1956) rest on the analysis of aggregate data, in-depth interviews with political leaders, and a historical-analytical analysis of much of his data. However, the tools he used and the data he collected were not the strengths of his work—these works are classics because of Key's insights and analytical powers. The careful reader of Key's works is impressed with the array of posits tested in each volume. Key's last two works, *Public Opinion and American Democracy* (1961) and *The Responsible Electorate* (1966), rest on survey data and poll data. In the first book he systematically explored the linkage function of

4. No rigid format was imposed on any author. For this reason, some authors give greater attention to method and others give greater attention to applications.

public opinion between the voter and his government, and in the last book he set out to correct what he believed to be overstatements in voting study findings of issue unawareness and issueless voting on the part of the electorate. In other words, Key's powers as a researcher depended on his theorizing and his analytical skills, not on the data or the tools he used to collect them.

There are very few published accounts of research projects, and one fears that if there were more they might be self-serving rather than wholly accurate accounts. Three notable volumes contain researchers' descriptions of their projects and the joys and sorrows of pursuing answers to their questions, and they are highly recommended to our readers: Walter, *Political Scientists at Work* (1971); Everson and Paine, *An Introduction to Systematic Politics* (1973); and Hammond, *Sociologists at Work* (1964).

When a research question has been "discovered," or "formulated," there may be several ways of pursuing it, and no one of the available research strategies may appear to be more meritorious than the other(s). Of course, the costs in time and other resources may simplify the choice (be mindful that costs are always an important factor in research decisions). For example, one could study grassroots political leadership using the survey or participant observation. Key primarily used aggregate data in his *Southern Politics* (1949), while Matthews and Prothro relied primarily on the survey in their *Negroes and the New Southern Politics* (1966). Berelson et al. studied democratic theory and the vote in one of the pioneering survey studies, *Voting* (1954), and Downs studied the same topic with an economic model in his *Economic Theory of American Democracy* (1957). One could study the legislative process in the United Nations with roll-call analysis or gaming; and content analysis or in-depth interviews could be used in a study of the political views of newspaper editors. Of course, sometimes several different types of data are necessary and mutually supportive in a research strategy (see my commentary on complex data sets in chapter 7).

A study need not be grand in size or scope to make a contribution to research in the discipline. To consider V. O. Key's work again, I can point to his article "A Theory of Critical Elections" (1955), which became the "realigning elections" in the famous typology of elections found in *The American Voter* (Campbell et al., 1960). Key studied the variance between the behavior of traditional, "Yankee" towns and towns with substantial hyphenated-American populations, and discerned a clear realignment of these New England towns tied to the 1928 candidacy of Alfred E. Smith. Dahl's classic *Who Governs?* (1961) is a study of one city, New Haven, and Lipset et al. (1956) tested Michels's "Iron Law of Oligarchy" thesis in one labor union in a work which made a profound contribution to the literature of social science.

Research should be soundly grounded in theory. In other words, the *substance* of the research question is important, but the *form* of the question is also important (one test of form is "Is it amenable to empirical examination?"). Further, it is important *how the research question relates* to other questions being asked in the discipline and to bodies of questions which have been answered (more or less satisfactorily), and which constitute a body of theory. So, I have said that the substance, the form (syntax), and the relationship of the research question to other bodies of theory are important, but I should further state that the words we use in the research questions are also important. The most important words are called "concepts," and concept formation is but a component of the general subject of theory building. In general, we judge concepts on their clarity, precision, and meaningfulness, but the subject is much more complex than this simple sentence and has been given a sound interpretation by Paul Kress in chapter 17.

SOME WAYS OF VIEWING AND USING DATA

John W. Burgess and his colleagues at Columbia in the 1880s had all studied at German universities. They imported into political science in this country a method of inquiry we can awkwardly describe as a comparative-historical-legal-institutional approach. For several generations this was the dominant research approach or research methodology in political science. Since that time, every new method of inquiry or approach to subject matter has come upon the discipline like a breath of fresh air.

In 1908 Arthur Bentley published *The Process of Government*, containing the group theory of politics, and this approach has been revived and reinvigorated in every generation since. In 1951 David B. Truman restated the group theory in *The Governmental Process*. The essence of the group theory is that politics is a process of interaction of groups and that the outcome of the process is policy. Group theory is one of political science's most celebrated approaches to study political phenomena, in spite of the many critiques which have been directed at its basic assumptions. Even its critics use the concepts of group theory, and virtually every basic text bears some trace of the influence of the theory.

These approaches are two from a rather extensive inventory available to political science. In part 4 of this book we have chapters treating five approaches or methods of study widely used by political scientists: structural-functional analysis, systems theory, macroanalysis, the historical-analytical approach, and the case study approach. The interchangeable use of the terms "approach" and "method" in this literature will no doubt trouble the reader, and indeed it has troubled the whole discipline. "Approach" is a way of viewing data, and "method" is a way of using data; the latter is the more rigorous term. The two terms could be used interchangeably, I think, for the case study and for the historical-analytical method. Systems theory and structural-functional analysis, and macroanalysis are, I think, clearly approaches to the study of politics, not methods of analysis.

Eastonian systems theory, as first presented in *The Political System* (1953), is fully as celebrated an approach as the group theory—its special terminology permeates the literature, and basic texts always include some reference to systems analysis. The structural-functional approach of systems theory has especially been influential in the comparative study of politics in the last decade. In addition to the usefulness of group theory, systems theory, and structural-functional analysis to guide and suggest research, all three approaches are outstanding teaching devices and help students to order and interpret information.

The three authors of the other selections in part 4 are distinguished advocates of the approaches they discuss. Etzioni has called to the attention of social scientists (not economists) the uncritical way in which we fail to distinguish between micro- and macro-level phenomena; in looking to the individual unit of analysis, we may miss the larger movements and developments in longer time frames. Clubb is a historian and the executive director of the Inter-University Consortium for Political Research; he examines in chapter 20 the potential use of historical evidence and discusses its limitations. Bock is president of the Inter-University Case Program, and surveys the extensive use of case studies over the years in political and social science, especially in public administration. A large proportion of the dissertations and theses written in political science have been case studies, and Bock's chapter 21 is the best treatment of the subject to date.

We have only begun to touch on the approaches amd methods available to political scientists. The most fundamental methods of analysis are taken for granted and were learned in elementary science courses in the first years of collegiate study (i.e., the comparative method, methods of classification, and the building of ideal typologies). Other approaches of note include the policy sciences approach (Lerner and Laswell, 1951); power approaches (Lasswell and Kaplan, 1950); role theory (Wahlke et al., 1962); decision-making theory (Braybrooke and Lindbloom, 1963); a game analogy (Lockard, 1963); and Schattschneider, in his *Semisovereign People* (1960) viewed politics as "conflict." On approaches in general, see Young (1958), Polsby, Dentler, and Smith (1963), Eulau, Eldersveld, and Janowitz, (1956), Haas and Kariel (1970), Wasby (1970), and Golembiewski, Welsh, and Crotty (1969).

BEYOND TEXTBOOKS: LEARNING THROUGH RESEARCH

The student of political science methodology benefits substantially from reading the texts on research design and research methods; and chronicles of major research projects, when available, are also instructive. However, first-hand involvement in a research project is by far the best learning process available. An artificial, antiseptic, purist view of research undertakings can be gained from reading texts in isolation from a first-hand encounter with the problems of research. Texts are replete with warnings about the unreal nature of their "how to do it" introductions to research. One of the most colorful caveats comes from Arthur J. Bachrach (1965, p. ix):

> *People don't usually do research the way people who write books about research say that people do research.* That's my First Law,* a good informal law which may need a bit of elaboration. I mean simply that books on research are, as a rule, statements of general formalized principles and reflect only in an idealized way the actual day by day practice of research. They present the detached view of science and little if any of the fun and frustration. In short, books about research (to mix a metaphor) are white tie and tails; research itself is a pair of blue jeans.

> *My Second Law relates to the problems of planning in research—it states simply that: *Things take more time than they do.*

It is incumbent on professors, in my opinion, to involve as many students as possible in their research projects. In addition to the research experience, the students gain professional socialization through interacting with the project director(s). The highly formal classroom or seminar relationship between professor and student disappears in the field, in the coding room, and in the experimental laboratory.

At the University of North Carolina in the 1950s and 1960s the formal barriers between faculty and students were reduced dramatically by the involvement of students in major research projects. Robert Agger, Fred Cleaveland, Alexander Heard, Don Matthews, and Jim Prothro involved students in the projects which produced

The Rulers and the Ruled, The Costs of Democracy, and *Negroes and the New Southern Politics*. I believe that North Carolina's rapid rise in status in the profession was to a great extent the result of the openness and intellectual excitement generated by these men and their generous invitations to students to become a part of the research process. The output of students at Carolina during this era tends to support this assertion: Lester W. Milbrath, Daniel Goldrich, M. Kent Jennings, William J. Crotty, Lewis Bowman, Bob Boynton, Charles F. Cnudde, and others.

In conclusion, the future of political science as a discipline promises to be exciting. It is a young discipline, constantly reevaluating its boundaries. It has profited handsomely from advances made by the other social sciences. Its growth has made it possible to develop large ranks of young professionals, and each new generation appears to be better trained than the last. In my opinion, our survey of the history, scope, and method of the profession leaves us looking to the future with optimism.

BIBLIOGRAPHY

Abcarian, G. E., and S. M. Stanage
    1965   "Alienation and the radical right." Journal of Politics 27
                (November): 776-96.
Abel, Theodore Fred
    1948   "The operation called 'Verstehen.'" American Journal of Sociol-
                ogy 54 (November): 211-18.
Abramson, Paul R.
    1975   Generational Change in American Politics. Lexington: Heath.
Abruzzi, Adam
    1956   Work, Workers, and Work Measurement. New York: Columbia
                University Press.
Abug-Lughod, Ibrahim
    1962   "International news in the Arabic press: A comparative content
                analysis." Public Opinion Quarterly 26 (Winter): 600-12.
Ackoff, Russell L.
    1953   The Design of Social Research. Chicago: University of Chicago
                Press.
Adams, Richard N., and Jack J. Preiss (eds.)
    1960   Human Organization Research. Homewood: Dorsey.
Adorno, Theodor W., Else Frenkel-Brunswik, Daniel J. Levinson, and
    R.N. Sanford
    1950   The Authoritarian Personality, New York: Harper.
Adrian, Charles R., and Oliver P. Williams
    1963   Four Cities: A Study of Comparative Policy Making. Philadel-
                phia: University of Pennsylvania Press.
Agger, Robert E., Daniel Goldrich, and Bert Swanson
    1964   The Rulers and the Ruled: Political Power and Impotence in
                American Communities. New York: Wiley.
Agger, Robert E., Marshall Goldstein, and Stanley A. Pearl
    1961   "Political cynicism: Measurement and meaning." Journal of Poli-
                tics 23 (August): 477-505.

Aiken, George David
1976   Aiken: Senate Diary, January 1972–January 1975. Battleboro:
            Stephen Greene.

Aiken, Michael
1970   "The distribution of community power." Pp. 487–525 in
            Michael Aiken and Paul C. Mott (eds.), The Structure of Commu-
            nity Power. New York: Random House.

Ake, Claude
1967   A Theory of Political Integration. Homewood: Dorsey.

Albig, W.
1938   "The content of radio programs, 1925–1935." Social Forces 16
            (March): 338–49.

Albrecht, Milton C.
1956   "Does literature reflect common values?" American Sociological
            Review 21 (December): 272–79.

Alexander, Herbert
1976   Financing Politics: Money, Elections and Political Reform. Wash-
            ington: Congressional Quarterly Press.

Alexia, Marcus, and Charles Z. Wilson
1967   Organizational Decision-Making. Englewood Cliffs: Prentice-Hall.

Alford, Robert R.
1963   Party and Society. Chicago: Rand McNally.
1969   Bureaucracy and Participation. Chicago: Rand McNally.

Alger, Chadwick F.
1963a   "Comparison of intranational and international politics." Amer-
            ican Political Science Review 57 (June): 406–19.
1963b   "Participation in the United Nations as a learning experience."
            Public Opinion Quarterly 27 (Fall): 412–26.
1965   "Personal contact in intergovernmental organizations." Pp.
            521–47 in Herbert C. Kelman (ed.), International Behavior. New
            York: Holt, Rinehart & Winston.
1968   "Interaction in a committee of the United Nations General
            Assembly." Pp. 51–84 in J. David Singer (ed.), Quantitative
            International Politics. New York: Free Press.

Alger, Chadwick F., and Steven J. Brams
1967   "Patterns of representation in national capitals and intergovern-
            mental organizations." World Politics 19 (July): 646–53.

Alker, Hayward R., Jr.
1965   Mathematics and Politics. New York: Macmillan.
1967   "Statistics and Politics: The Need for Causal Data Analysis."
            Paper prepared for the annual meeting of the American Political
            Science Association, Chicago (September).

Alker, Hayward R., Jr., Karl W. Deutsch, and Antoine H. Stoetzel
1973   Mathematical Approaches to Politics. San Francisco: Jossey-Bass.

Alker, Hayward R., Jr., and Donald Puchala
1968   "Trends in economic partnership: The North Atlantic area,

1928–1963." Pp. 287–316 in J. David Singer (ed.), Quantitative International Politics. New York: Free Press.

Alker, Hayward R., Jr., and Bruce M. Russett
1965   World Politics in the General Assembly. New Haven: Yale University Press.

Allen, Kevin, and M. C. MacLennan
1970   Regional Problems and Policies in Italy and France. London: George Allen & Unwin.

Allensworth, Donald Trudeau
1975   The Political Realities of Urban Planning. New York: Praeger.

Allison, Graham T.
1971   Essence of Decision. Boston: Little, Brown.

Allport, Gordon W., J. S. Bruner, and E. M. Jandorf
1953   "Personality under social catastrophe: Ninety life histories of the Nazi revolution." Pp. 436–55 in C. Kluckhohn and H. A. Murray (eds.), Personality in Nature, Society and Culture, 2d ed. London: Jonathan Cape.

Allport, Gordon W., and Philip E. Vernon
1933   Studies in Expressive Movement. New York: Macmillan.

Allswang, John M., and Patrick Bova
1964   NORC Social Research, 1941–1964: An Inventory of Studies and Publications in Social Research. Chicago: National Opinion Research Center, University of Chicago.

Almond, Gabriel A.
1946   "Politics, science, and ethics." American Political Science Review 40 (April): 283–93.
1950   The American People and Foreign Policy. New York: Harcourt, Brace.
1954   The Appeals of Communism. Princeton: Princeton University Press.
1956   "Comparative political systems." Journal of Politics 18 (August): 391–409.
1960a   The American People and Foreign Policy. New York: Praeger.
1960b   "Introduction: A functional approach to comparative politics." Pp. 3–64 in Gabriel A. Almond and James S. Coleman (eds.), The Politics of Developing Areas. Princeton: Princeton University Press.
1966   "Political theory and political science." American Political Science Review 60 (December): 869–79.

Almond, Gabriel A., Taylor Cole, and Roy C. Macridis
1955   "A suggested research strategy in Western European government and politics." American Political Science Review 40 (December): 1042–49.

Almond, Gabriel A., and James S. Coleman (eds.)
1960   The Politics of Developing Areas. Princeton: Princeton University Press.

Almond, Gabriel A., and G. Bingham Powell, Jr.
1966   Comparative Politics: A Developmental Approach. Boston:
            Little, Brown.

Almond, Gabriel A., and Sidney Verba
1963   The Civic Culture: Political Attitudes and Democracy in Five
            Nations. Princeton: Princeton University Press.

Alpert, Paul
1973   Partnership or Confrontation: Poor Lands and Rich. New York:
            Free Press.

Altshuler, Alan A.
1965   The City Planning Process. Ithaca: Cornell University Press.
1968   "The study of American public administration." Pp. 55–72 in
            Alan A. Altshuler (ed.), The Politics of the Federal Bureaucracy.
            New York: Dodd, Mead.
1970   Community Control. New York: Pegasus.

American Psychological Association
1954   "Technical recommendations for psychological tests and diagnos-
            tic techniques." Psychological Bulletin Supplement 51 (March).

Anderson, J. W.
1964   "Eisenhower, Brownell, and the Congress." Mimeographed.
            Syracuse: Inter-University Case Program.

Anderson, Lee F., Meredith W. Watts, Jr., and Allen R. Wilcox
1966   Legislative Roll-Call Analysis. Evanston: Northwestern University
            Press.

Anderson, William
1955   The Nation and the States: Rivals or Partners. Minneapolis:
            University of Minnesota Press.
1964   Man's Quest for Political Knowledge: The Study and Teaching of
            Politics in Ancient Times. Minneapolis: University of Minnesota
            Press.

Anderson, William, and John Gaus
1945   Research in Public Administration. Chicago: Public Administra-
            tion Service.

Andrain, Charles, and David E. Apter
1968   "Comparative government: Developing new nations." Journal of
            Politics 30 (May): 372–416.

Angell, Robert C.
1969   Peace on the March. Princeton: Van Nostrand.

Angell, Robert C., Vera S. Dunham, and J. D. Singer
1964   "Social values and foreign policy attitudes of Soviet and Amer-
            ican elites." Journal of Conflict Resolution 8 (3):330–491.

Anton, Thomas J.
1963   "Power, pluralism, and local politics." Administrative Science
            Quarterly 7 (March): 430.

Appleby, Paul H.
1949   Policy and Administration. University: University of Alabama
            Press.

Apter, David E.
1961   Political Kingdom in Uganda: A Study in Bureaucratic National-
        ism. Princeton: Princeton University Press.
1963   Ghana in Transition. New York: Atheneum.
1965   The Politics of Modernization. Chicago: University of Chicago
        Press.
1968   Some Conceptual Approaches to the Study of Modernization.
        Englewood Cliffs: Prentice-Hall.
1971   Choice and the Politics of Allocation: A Developmental Theory.
        New Haven: Yale University Press.
1973   Political Change: Collected Essays. London: Frank Cass.

Apter, David E., and Charles Andrain
1968   "Comparative government: Developing new nations." Pp.
        82–126 in Marian D. Irish (ed.), Political Science: Advance of the
        Discipline. Englewood Cliffs: Prentice-Hall.

Arendt, Hannah
1958   The Human Condition. Chicago: University of Chicago Press.
1963   On Revolution. New York: Viking.

Argyris, Chris
1957   Personality and Organization. New York: Harper.
1964   Integrating the Individual and Organization. New York: Wiley.

Aristotle
1962   Nicomachean Ethics. Translated with introduction and notes by
        Martin Ostwald. Indianapolis: Bobbs-Merrill.

Armstrong, John A.
1973   The European Administrative Elite. Princeton: Princeton Univer-
        sity Press.

Aron, Raymond
1965   Essai sur les libertés. Paris: Calmann-Levy.
1966   Peace and War: A Theory of International Relations. Translated
        by R. Howard and A. B. Fox. Garden City: Doubleday.
1967   "What is a theory of international relations?" Journal of Interna-
        tional Affairs 21 (Winter): 185–206.

Aronson, E.
1958   "The need for achievement as measured by graphic expression."
        Pp. 249–65 in J. W. Atkinson (ed.), Motives in Fantasy, Action
        and Society. Princeton: Van Nostrand.

Arrow, Kenneth J.
1963   Social Choice and Individual Values. 2d ed. New York: Wiley.

Art, R. J.
1968   The TFX Decision. Boston: Little, Brown.

Ash, P.
1948   "The periodical press and the Taft-Hartley Act." Public Opinion
        Quarterly 12 (Summer): 266–71.

Ashby, W. Ross
1956   An Introduction to Cybernetics. New York: Wiley.
1960   Design for a Brain. 2d ed. New York: Wiley.

Asher, Robert E., Walter M. Kotschnig, William Adams Brown, Jr., and
  Associates
  1957   The United Nations and Economic and Social Co-operation.
                Washington: Brookings.

Ashton, Thomas S.
  1966   The Industrial Revolution, 1760–1830. London: Oxford Univer-
                sity Press.

Axelrod, Morris, Donald R. Matthews, and James W. Prothro
  1962   "Recruitment for survey research on race problems in the
                south." Public Opinion Quarterly 26 (Summer): 254–62.

Aydelotte, William O.
  1963   "Voting patterns in the British House of Commons in the
                1840's." Comparative Studies in Society and History 5 (Jan-
                uary): 134–63.

Ayer, A. J.
  1936   Language, Truth and Logic. London: Gollancz.

Babbie, Earl R.
  1974   Survey Research Methods. Belmont: Wadsworth.

Backrach, Arthur J.
  1965   Psychological Research: An Introduction. 2d ed. New York:
                Random House.

Bachrach, Peter
  1967   The Theory of Democratic Elitism. Boston: Little, Brown.
  1973   Political Elites in a Democracy. New York: Lieber-Atherton.

Bachrach, Peter, and Morton S. Baratz
  1962a   "Decisions and nondecisions: An analytical framework." Amer-
                ican Political Science Review 57 (September): 632–42.
  1962b   "Two faces of power." American Political Science Review 58
                (December): 947–52.
  1970   Power and Poverty. New York: Oxford University Press.

Backstrom, Charles H., and Gerald D. Hursh
  1963   Survey Research. Evanston: Northwestern University Press.

Bagdikian, B. H.
  1959   "The newsmagazines." New Republic 16 (February 2): 11–16;
                (February 16): 9–14; (February 23): 9–15.

Baier, Kurt
  1965   The Moral Point of View. New York: Random House.

Bailey, Stephen K.
  1950   Congress Makes a Law. New York: Columbia University Press.
  1955   Research Frontiers in Politics and Government. Washington:
                Brookings.
  1964   "Our national political parties." Pp. 1–20 in Robert A. Goldwin
                (ed.), Political Parties, U.S.A. Chicago: Rand McNally.
  1966   The New Congress. New York: St. Martin's.

Bailey, Stephen K., and Associates
  1955   Research Frontiers in Politics and Government. Washington:
                Brookings.

Bakan, David
    1969   On Method. San Francisco: Jossey-Bass.
Bales, Robert F.
    1950   Interaction Process Analysis. Reading: Addison-Wesley.
    1952   "Some uniformities of behavior in small social systems." Pp.
                146–59 in Guy B. Swanson, Theodore M. Newcomb, and Eugene
                L. Hartley (eds.), Readings in Social Psychology. New York:
                Holt.
Baltzell, E. Digby
    1958   Philadelphia Gentlemen. New York: Free Press.
Banfield, Edward C.
    1958   The Moral Basis of Backward Society. New York: Free Press.
    1960   "The Training of the Executive." Pp. 16–43 in Public Policy.
                Cambridge: Harvard Graduate School of Public Administration.
    1965   Big City Politics. New York: Random House.
    1974   The Unheavenly City Revisited. Boston: Little, Brown.
Banks, Arthur S., and Robert B. Textor
    1963   A Cross-Polity Survey. Cambridge: MIT Press.
Banks, Arthur S., and the Staff of the Center for Comparative Political
Research, State University of New York at Binghamton
    1971   Cross-Polity Time-Series Data. Cambridge: MIT Press.
Barber, James David
    1965   The Lawmakers: Recruitment and Adaptation to Legislative Life.
                New Haven: Yale University Press.
    1966   Power in Committees: An Experiment in the Governmental
                Process. Chicago: Rand McNally.
    1968   "Adult identity and presidential style: The rhetorical emphasis."
                Daedalus 97 (Summer):938–68.
    1969   "Analyzing presidents: From passive-positive Taft to active-
                negative Nixon." Washington Monthly 1 (October):33–54.
    1972   The Presidential Character: Predicting Performance in the White
                House. Englewood Cliffs: Prentice-Hall.
Barcus, F. E.
    1959   "Communications content: Analysis of the research,
                1900–1958." Doctoral dissertation, University of Illinois.
Barfield, Owen
    n.d.   Saving the Appearances. New York: Harcourt Brace Jovanovich.
Barghoorn, Frederick C.
    1966   Politics in the USSR. Boston: Little, Brown.
    1972   Politics in the USSR. 2d ed. Boston: Little, Brown.
Barnard, Chester
    1938   The Functions of the Executive. Cambridge: Harvard University
                Press.
    1948   Organization and Management: Selected Papers. Cambridge:
                Harvard University Press.
Barnette, W. Leslie, Jr.
    1964   Readings in Psychological Tests and Measurements. Homewood:
                Dorsey.

Barros, James, and Douglas M. Johnson
1974   The International Law of Pollution. New York: Free Press.
Bartlett, Randall
1973   Economic Foundations of Political Power. New York: Free Press.
Barton, Richard F.
1970   A Primer on Simulation and Gaming. Englewood Cliffs: Prentice-Hall.
Bartos, Otomar J.
1967   "How predictable are negotiations?" Journal of Conflict Resolution 11 (December):481–96.
Batlin, R.
1954   "San Francisco newspapers' campaign coverage, 1896, 1952." Journalism Quarterly 31 (Summer):297–303.
Bauer, R. A.
1964   "The obstinate audience: The influence process from the point of view of social communication." American Psychologist 19 (May):319–28.
Bauer, Raymond, Ithiel de Sola Pool, and Lewis Anthony Dexter
1963   American Business and Public Policy. Chicago: Atherton.
Baumol, William J.
1952   Welfare Economics and the Theory of the State. London: Longmans, Green.
Bay, Christian
1958   The Structure of Freedom. Stanford: Stanford University Press.
1965   "Politics and pseudopolitics: A critical evaluation of some behavioral literature." American Political Science Review 59 (March):39–51.
1970   "Behavioral research and the theory of democracy." Pp. 327–51 in Henry S. Kariel (ed.), Frontiers of Democratic Theory. New York: Random House.
Beals, Ralph L.
1969   Politics of Social Research: An Inquiry into the Ethics and Responsibility of Social Scientists. Chicago: Aldine.
Beard, Charles A.
1913   An Economic Interpretation of the Constitution of the United States. New York: Macmillan.
1934   The Open Door at Home: A Trial Philosophy of the National Interest. New York: Macmillan.
1935   An Economic Interpretation of the Constitution of the United States. With a new introduction. New York: Macmillan.
1965   An Economic Interpretation of the Constitution of the United States. Paperbound, reprint of 1935 ed. New York: Free Press.
Beattie, Robert R., Jr.
1967   "Toward a theory of international political development." Master's thesis, Northwestern University.
Beck, Carl, and Associates (comps.)
1975   Political Science Thesaurus. Washington: American Political Science Association.

Beck, Lewis White
1968   "The 'natural science ideal' in the social sciences." Pp. 80–89 in
            Robert A. Manners and David Kaplan (eds.), Theory in Anthro-
            pology. Chicago: Aldine.

Beck, Raimund
1967   "Fall-Studien in der Verwaltungswissenschaft." Offenliche
            Verwaltung 14:67. Stuttgart: Kohlhammer.

Becker, Howard S.
1958   "Problems of inference and proof in participant observation."
            American Sociological Review 23 (December):652–60.
1964   "Problems in the publication of field studies." Pp. 267–84 in
            Arthur J. Vidich, Joseph Bensman, and Maurice R. Stein (eds.),
            Reflections on Community Studies. New York: Wiley.

Becker, Howard S., and Associates
1961   Boys in White. Chicago: University of Chicago Press.

Becker, Howard S., and Blanche Geer
1957   "Participant observation and interviewing: A comparison."
            Human Organization 16 (3):28–32.
1960   "Participant observation: The analysis of qualitative field data."
            Pp. 267–89 in Richard N. Adams and Jack J. Preiss (eds.),
            Human Organization Research. Homewood: Dorsey.

Becker, Theodore L.
1964   Political Behavioralism and Modern Jurisprudence. Chicago:
            Rand McNally.
1970   Comparative Judicial Politics. Chicago: Rand McNally.

Bedford, Sybille
1961   The Faces of Justice. New York. Simon & Schuster.

Beer, Samuel H.
1966   British Politics in the Collectivist Age. New York: Knopf.
1967   "Political science and history." Paper prepared for the annual
            meeting of the American Political Science Association, Chicago
            (September). Available from University Micro Films.

Beer, Samuel H., and Adam B. Ulam
1958   Patterns of Government. The Major Political Systems of Europe.
            New York: Random House.

Behavioral and Social Sciences Survey Committee
1969   "Basic research in the sciences of behavior." ITEMS of the Social
            Science Research Council 23 (December):49–54.

Belch, Jean (ed.)
1974   Contemporary Games: A Directory and Bibliography Covering
            Games and Play Situations or Simulations Used for Instruction
            and Training by Schools, Colleges and Universities, Government,
            Business and Management. 2 vols. Detroit: Gale.

Bell, Daniel
1960   The End of Ideology. New York: Free Press.
1973   The Coming of Post-Industrial Society. New York: Basic Books.

Bell, David V. J.
1975   Power, Influence, and Authority: An Essay in Political Linguis-
            tics. New York: Oxford University Press.
Bell, Wendell, Richard J. Hill, and Charles R. Wright
1961   Public Leadership. San Francisco: Chandler.
Bendix, Reinhard
1949   Higher Civil Servants in American Society. Boulder: University of
            Colorado Press.
1956   Work and Authority in Industry. New York: Wiley.
1963   "Concepts and generalizations in comparative sociological stud-
            ies." American Sociological Review 28 (August):532–39.
1964a   Nation Building and Citizenship. New York: Wiley.
1964b   "The age of ideology: Persistent and changing." Pp. 294–327 in
            David Apter (ed.), Ideology and Discontent. New York: Free
            Press.
1968   "Concepts in comparative historical analysis." Pp. 67–81 in Stein
            Rokkan (ed.), Comparative Research across Cultures and Na-
            tions. Paris: Mouton.
Bendix, Reinhard, and Bennett Berger
1959   "Images of society and problems of concept formation in sociol-
            ogy." Pp. 92–118 in Llewellyn Gross (ed.), Symposium on Socio-
            logical Theory. Evanston: Row, Peterson.
Bennis, Warren
1966   Changing Organizations. New York: McGraw-Hill.
Bensman, Joseph
1967   Dollars and Sense: Ideology, Ethics and the Meaning of Work in
            Profit and Nonprofit Organizations. New York: Macmillan.
Benson, Lee
1957   "Research problems in American political historiography." Pp.
            113–83 in Mirra Komarovsky (ed.), Common Frontiers in the
            Social Sciences. New York: Free Press.
1961   The Concept of Jacksonian Democracy. Princeton: Princeton
            University Press.
1967   "An approach to the scientific study of past public opinion."
            Public Opinion Quarterly 31 (Winter):522–67.
Benson, Oliver
1969   Political Science Laboratory. Columbus: Merrill.
Bentham, Jeremy
1948   An Introduction to the Principles of Morals and Legislation. With
            an introduction by Laurence J. Lafleur. New York: Hafner.
Bentley, Arthur F.
1949   The Process of Government. 1908. Bloomington: Principia.
1954   Inquiry into Inquiries. Boston: Beacon.
Berelson, Bernard
1942   "The effects of print upon public opinion." Pp. 41–65 in D.
            Waples (ed.), Print, Radio, and Film in a Democracy. Chicago:
            University of Chicago Press.

1952   Content Analysis in Communication Research. New York: Free Press.

Berelson, Bernard, and Sebastian De Grazia
1947   "Detecting collaboration in propaganda." Public Opinion Quarterly 11 (Summer):244-53.

Berelson, Bernard R., Paul F. Lazarsfeld, and William N. McPhee
1954   Voting: A Study of Opinion Formation in a Presidential Campaign. Chicago: University of Chicago Press.

Berelson, Bernard R., and Patricia J. Salter
1946   "Majority and minority Americans: An analysis of magazine fiction." Public Opinion Quarterly 10 (Summer):168-90.

Berelson, Bernard R., and Gary S. Steiner
1964   Human Behavior: An Inventory of Scientific Findings. New York: Harcourt Brace Jovanovich.

Berger, Morroe
1957   Bureaucracy and Society in Modern Egypt. Princeton: Princeton University Press.

Berger, Peter, and Thomas Luckman
1966   The Social Construction of Reality. Garden City: Doubleday.

Bergmann, Gustav
1957   Philosophy of Science. Madison: University of Wisconsin Press.

Berkhofer, Robert F., Jr.
1969   A Behavioral Approach to Historical Analysis. New York: Free Press.

Berkley, George E.
1975   The Craft of Public Administration. Boston: Allyn & Bacon.

Berleant, Arnold
1967   "The experience and judgment of values." The Journal of Value Inquiry 1 (Spring):24-37.

Berlin, Isaiah
1969   Four Essays on Liberty. New York: Oxford University Press.

Berliner, Joseph
1957   Factory and Manager in the U.S.S.R. Cambridge: Harvard University Press.

Berman, Ronald
1968   America in the Sixties: An Intellectual History. New York: Free Press.

Berns, Walter
1962   "Voting studies." Pp. 1-62 in Herbert J. Storing (ed.), Essays on the Scientific Study of Politics. New York: Holt, Rinehart & Winston.

Bernstein, Marver H.
1953   "Political ideas of selected American business journals." Public Opinion Quarterly 17 (Summer):258-67.
1955   Regulating Business by Independent Commission. Princeton: Princeton University Press.

Berry, Brian J. L., and Duane F. Marble
1968   Spatial Analysis: A Reader in Statistical Geography. Englewood
            Cliffs: Prentice-Hall.

Beshers, James M. (ed.)
1965   Computer Methods in the Analysis of Large-Scale Social Systems.
            Cambridge: Joint Center for Urban Studies of the Massachusetts
            Institute of Technology and Harvard University.

Bierstedt, Robert
1959   "Nominal and real definitions in sociological theory." Pp.
            121–44 in Llewellyn Gross (ed.), Symposium on Sociological
            Theory. Evanston: Row and Peterson.

Bill, James A., and Robert L. Hargrove, Jr.
1973   Comparative Politics: The Quest for Theory. Columbus: Merrill.

Bisco, Ralph L.
1964   "Information retrieval from data archives: The ICPR system."
            American Behavioral Scientist 7 (June):45–48.
1965   "Social science data archives technical considerations." Social
            Science Information 4 (September):129–50.
1966   "Social science data archives: A review of developments." Amer-
            ican Political Science Review 60 (March):93–109.
1967   "Social science data archives: Progress and prospects." Social
            Science Information 6 (February):39–74.
1968   "Continuation and development of the Council of Social Science
            Data Archives." Proposal to the National Science Foundation,
            Washington.
1970   Data Bases, Computers, and the Social Sciences. New York:
            Wiley.

Black, Cyril E.
1966   The Dynamics of Modernization: A Study in Comparative His-
            tory. New York: Harper & Row.

Black, Duncan
1958   The Theory of Committees and Elections. Cambridge: At the
            University Press.

Black, Max
1952   Critical Thinking. Englewood Cliffs: Prentice Hall.
1961   The Social Theories of Talcott Parsons. Englewood Cliffs: Pren-
            tice-Hall.

Black, Merle, David M. Kovenock, and William C. Reynolds
1974   Political Attitudes in the Nation and the States. Chapel Hill:
            Institute for Research in Social Science, University of North
            Carolina.

Blackman, Sheldon, and Kenneth M. Goldstein
1971   An Introduction to Data Management in the Behavioral and
            Social Sciences: The Use of Computer Packages. New York:
            Wiley.

Blalock, Hubert M., Jr.
1960   Social Statistics. New York: McGraw-Hill.

1967   Toward a Theory of Minority Group Relations. New York: Wiley.

Blalock, Hubert M., Jr. (ed.)
1974   Measurement in the Social Sciences: Theories and Strategies. Chicago: Aldine.

Blalock, Hubert M., Jr., and Ann B. Blalock (eds.)
1968   Methodology in Social Research. New York: McGraw-Hill.

Blase, Melvin G.
1973   Institution Building: A Source Book. Beverly Hills: Sage.

Blau, Peter M.
1955   The Dynamics of Bureaucracy. Chicago: University of Chicago Press.
1956   Bureaucracy in Modern Society. New York: Random House.
1963a   The Dynamics of Bureaucracy. Chicago: University of Chicago Press.
1963b   "Critical remarks on Weber's theory of authority." American Political Science Review 57 (June): 305-16.
1967   "The research process in the study of the dynamics of bureaucracy." Pp. 18-57 in Phillip E. Hammond, Sociologists at Work. Garden City: Doubleday.
1968   "The hierarchy of authority in organizations." American Journal of Sociology 73 (January):453-67.

Blau, Peter M., and W. Richard Scott
1962   Formal Organization. San Francisco: Chandler.

Blitzer, Charles
1960   An Immortal Commonwealth: The Political Thought of James Harrington, New Haven: Yale University Press.

Blondel, Jean
1976   Thinking Politically. Boulder: Westview.

Bluhm, William T.
1965   Theories of the Political System: Classics of Political Thought and Modern Political Analysis. Englewood Cliffs: Prentice-Hall.

Blumberg, N. B.
1954   One Party Press? Coverage of the 1952 Presidential Campaign in 35 Daily Newspapers. Lincoln: University of Nebraska Press.

Blume, Stuart S.
1974   Toward a Political Sociology of Science. New York: Free Press.

Bobrow, Davis B., and Neal E. Cutler
1967   "Time-oriented explanations of national security beliefs: cohort, life-state and situation." Peace Research Society Papers 8:31-58.

Bobrow, Davis R., and Allen R. Wilcox
1966   "Dimensions of defense opinions: The American public." Peace Research Society Papers 6:101-42.

Bock, Edwin A.
1962   "Case studies about government: Achieving realism and significance." Pp. v-viii, 89-119 in Edwin A. Bock (ed.), Essays on the Case Method. Brussels: International Institute of Administrative

Sciences. Also, mimeographed, Syracuse: Inter-University Case Program.
1963   State and Local Government: A Casebook. Tuscaloosa: University of Alabama Press.
1965   Government Regulation of Business: A Casebook. Englewood Cliffs: Prentice-Hall.

Bogart, Leo
1972   Silent Politics: Polls and the Awareness of Public Opinion. New York: Wiley-Interscience.

Bogue, Allen G.
1967   "Bloc and party in the United States Senate, 1861–1863." Civil War History 13 (September):221–41.

Boguslaw, Robert
1965   The New Utopians: A Study of System Design and Social Change. Englewood Cliffs: Prentice-Hall.

Bonacich, Edna, and Robert F. Goodman
1972   Deadlock in School Desegregation: A Case Study of Inglewood, California. New York: Praeger.

Bonjean, Charles M., Richard J. Hill, and S. Dale McLemore
1967   Sociological Measurement. San Francisco: Chandler.

Bordua, David J. (ed.)
1967   The Police: Six Sociological Essays. New York: Wiley.

Borgatta, E. F., and Betty Crowther
1965   A Workbook for the Study of Social Interaction Processes: Direct Observation Procedures in the Study of Individual and Group. Chicago: Rand McNally.

Borko, Harold
1962   Computer Applications in the Behavioral Sciences. Englewood Cliffs: Prentice-Hall.

Boskoff, Alvin, and Harmon Zeigler
1964   Voting Patterns in a Local Election. Philadelphia: Lippincott.

Boulding, Kenneth E.
1953   The Organizational Revolution. New York: Harper.
1955   Economic Analysis. New York: Harper.
1962   Conflict and Defense: A General Theory. New York: Harper.

Bower, Robert T.
1973   Television and the Public. New York: Holt, Rinehart & Winston.

Boyd, Richard W.
1972   "Popular control of public policy: A normal vote analysis of the 1968 election." American Political Science Review 66 (June): 429–, and "Rejoinder":468–70.

Bozeman, Adda B.
1960   Politics and Culture in International History. Princeton: Princeton University Press.

Braithwaite, R. B.
1956   Scientific Explanation. Cambridge: At the University & Press.

Brams, Steven J.
1966   "Transaction flows in the international system." American Politi-
            cal Science Review 60 (December):880–98.
1968   "Measuring the concentration of power in political systems."
            American Political Science Review 62 (June):461–75.
1975   Game Theory and Politics. New York: Free Press.

Braunthal, Gerard
1972   The West German Legislative Process. Ithaca: Cornell University
            Press.

Braybrooke, David
1965   Philosophical Problems of the Social Sciences. New York:
            Macmillan.

Braybrooke, David, and Charles E. Lindbloom
1963   A Strategy of Decision: Policy Evaluation as a Social Process.
            New York: Free Press.

Brecht, Arnold
1959   Political Theory: The Foundations of Twentieth Century Polit-
            ical Thought. Princeton: Princeton University Press.
1968   "Political theory: Approaches." Pp. 307–18 in David L. Sills
            (ed.), International Encyclopedia of the Social Sciences, vol. 12.
            New York: Macmillan and Free Press.

Breed, W.
1958   "Comparative newspaper handling of the Emmett Till case."
            Journalism Quarterly 35 (Summer):291–98.

Brezina, Dennis W., and Allen Overmyer
1974   Congress in Action: The Environmental Education Act. New
            York: Free Press.

Bridgman, P. W.
1927   The Logic of Modern Physics. New York: Macmillan.

Brinegar, C.
1963   "Mark Twain and the Quintus Curtius Snodgrass letters: A statis-
            tical test of authorship." Journal of the American Statistical
            Association 58 (March):85–96.

Brinton, Clarence Crane
1952   The Anatomy of Revolution. Rev. ed. Englewood Cliffs: Pren-
            tice-Hall.

Brodbeck, May
1959   "Models, meanings and theories." Pp. 373–403 in Llewellyn
            Gross (ed.), Symposium on Sociological Theory. Evanston: Row,
            Peterson.

Brodbeck, May (ed.)
1968   Readings in Philosophy of the Social Sciences. New York:
            Macmillan. See the excellent bibliography, pp. 737–68.

Brodie, Bernard
1973   War and Politics. New York: Macmillan.

Brody, Richard A.
  1963   "Some systemic effects of the spread of nuclear weapons tech-
              nology: A study through simulation of a multi-nuclear future."
              Journal of Conflict Resolution 7 (December):663–753.
  1964   "Meaning of findings from the Inter-Nation Simulation." Mimeo-
              graphed. Memorandum to Behavioral Sciences Group, China
              Lake, California, U.S.N.O.T.S.
Brody, Richard A., and Benjamin I. Page
  1972   "Comment: 'The Assessment of Policy Voting.'" American
              Political Science Review 66 (June):450–58.
Brogan, Hugh
  1973   Tocqueville. London: Collins.
Bronowski, Jacob
  1968   "Honest Jim and the Tinker Toy model." Nation 206 (March
              18):381–82.
Brooks, Philip C.
  1969   Research in Archives: The Use of Unpublished Primary Sources.
              Chicago: University of Chicago Press.
Brooks, Robert C. (ed.)
  1939   Bryce's American Commonwealth: Fiftieth Anniversary. New
              York: Macmillan.
Broom, Leonard, and Shirley Reece
  1955   "Political and racial interest: A study in content analysis." Public
              Opinion Quarterly 19 (Spring):5–19.
Brown, Ray E.
  1966   Judgment in Administration. New York: McGraw-Hill.
Brown, Steven, and Richard Taylor
  1970   "Objectivity and subjectivity in concept formation: A note on
              the problem of partition and frames of reference." Paper pre-
              pared for the annual meeting of the American Political Science
              Association, Los Angeles (September).
Brown, W. B.
  1960   The People's Choice. Baton Rouge: Louisiana State University
              Press.
Bruner, Jerome Seymour
  1941   "The dimensions of propaganda: German shortwave broadcasts
              to America." Journal of Abnormal and Social Psychology 36
              (July):311–37.
Bruner, Jerome Seymour, Jacqueline J. Goodnow, and George A. Austin
  1956   A Study of Thinking. New York: Wiley.
Brunner, Ronald D., and Garry D. Brewer
  1971   Organized Complexity: Empirical Theories of Political Devel-
              opment. New York: Free Press.
Bruyn, Severyn T.
  1966   The Human Perspective to Sociology: The Methodology of Par-
              ticipant Observation. Englewood Cliffs: Prentice-Hall.

Bryce, James (Viscount Bryce)
1888   The American Commonwealth. 2 vols. New York: Macmillan.
1921   Modern Democracies. New York: Macmillan.
1926   The American Commonwealth. New York: Macmillan.

Brzezinski, Zbigniew K.
1961   The Soviet Bloc. Rev. ed. New York: Praeger.

Brzezinski, Zbigniew K., and Samuel P. Huntington
1964   Political Power: USA/USSR. New York: Viking.

Buchanan, James M.
1949   "The pure theory of government finance: A suggested ap-
            proach." Journal of Political Economy 57 (December):496–505.
1967   Public Finance in Democratic Process. Chapel Hill: University of
            North Carolina Press.

Buchanan, James M., and Gordon Tullock
1962   The Calculus of Consent: Logical Foundations of Constitutional
            Democracy. Ann Arbor: University of Michigan Press.

Buchanan, William
1969   Understanding Political Variables. New York: Scribner's.
1974   Understanding Political Variables. 2d ed. New York: Scribner's.

Buchler, Justus
1961   The Concept of Method. New York: Columbia University Press.

Buckley, Walter F.
1967   Sociology and Modern Systems Theory. Englewood Cliffs: Pren-
            tice-Hall.

Buher, Burton A. (ed.)
1964   Public Administration, a Key to Development. Washington: U.S.
            Department of Agriculture.

Bullit, William C., and Sigmund Freud
1967   Woodrow Wilson. Boston: Houghton Mifflin.

Burdick, Eugene
1959   "Political theory and the voting studies." Pp. 136–49 in Eugene
            Burdick and Arthur Brodbeck (eds.), American Voting Behavior.
            New York: Free Press.

Burdick, Eugene, and Arthur J. Brodbeck (eds.)
1959   American Voting Behavior. New York: Free Press.

Bureau of Applied Social Research
1966   A Report of the Years 1962–65: Including a Bibliography of
            Recent Publications and Reports. New York: Bureau of Applied
            Social Research, Columbia University.

Burgess, J. W.
1891   Political Science and Comparative Constitutional Law. 2 vols.
            Boston: Ginn.

Burgess, Philip M., and James A. Robinson
1969   "Alliances and the theory of collective action: A simulation of
            coalition processes." Midwest Journal of Political Science 13
            (May):194–218.

Burnham, Walter Dean
    1965   "The changing shape of the American political universe." American Political Science Review 59 (March):7-28.
    1970   Critical Elections and the Mainsprings of American Politics. New York: Norton.
Burns, James MacGregor
    1963   The Deadlock of Democracy. Englewood Cliffs: Prentice-Hall.
Burtt, E. A.
    n.d.   The Metaphysical Foundations of Modern Science. Garden City: Doubleday.
    1962   "The value of presuppositions of science." Pp. 258-79 in Paul C. Obler and Henry Estrin (eds.), The New Scientist: Essays on the Methods and Values of Modern Science. Garden City: Doubleday.

Butani, K.
    1969   "Rubber in the Andamans and the rate of return." Cyclostyled for government circulation. New Delhi: Indian Institute of Public Administration.

Butler, D. E.
    1959   The Study of Political Behaviour. London: Hutchinson.
Butler, David, and Donald Stokes
    1969   Political Change in Britain: Forces Shaping Electoral Choice. New York: St. Martin's.

Butow, Robert J. C.
    1954   Japan's Decision to Surrender. Stanford: Stanford University Press.
Cahalan, Don
    1968   "Correlates of respondent accuracy in the Denver validity survey." Public Opinion Quarterly 32 (Winter):607-21.
Caldwell, Lynton K., Lynton R. Hayes, and Isabel M. MacWhirter
    1976   Citizens and the Environment: Case Studies in Popular Action. Bloomington: Indiana University Press.
Calleo, David P., and Benjamin M. Rowland
    1973   America and the World Political Economy. Bloomington: Indiana University Press.

Callières, Francois de
    1919   The Practice of Diplomacy. London: Constable.
Campbell, Angus
    1950   "The pre-election polls of 1948." International Journal of Opinion and Attitude Research 4 (Spring):27-36.
    1962   "Recent developments in survey studies of political behavior." Pp. 31-46 in Austin Ranney (ed.), Essays on the Behavioral Study of Politics. Urbana: University of Illinois Press.
Campbell, Angus, Philip E. Converse, Warren E. Miller, and Donald E. Stokes
    1960   The American Voter. New York: Wiley.
    1966   Elections and the Political Order. New York: Wiley.

Campbell, Angus, Gerald Gurin, and Warren E. Miller
1954   The Voter Decides. Evanston: Row, Peterson.

Campbell, Angus, and George Katona
1953   "The sample survey: A technique for social-science research." Pp.
            15-51 in Leon Festinger and Daniel Katz (eds.), Research
            Methods in the Behavioral Sciences. New York: Holt, Rinehart &
            Winston.

Campbell, Angus, and Henry Valen
1961   "Party identification in Norway and the United States." Public
            Opinion Quarterly 25 (Winter):505-27.

Campbell, Donald T.
1955   "The informant in quantitative research." American Journal of
            Sociology 60 (January):339-42.
1966   "Pattern matching as an essential in distal knowing." Pp. 81-106
            in K. R. Hammond (ed.), The Psychology of Egon Brunswick.
            New York: Holt, Rinehart & Winston.

Campbell, Donald T., and D. W. Fiske
1959   "Convergent and discriminant validation by the multitrait-multi-
            method matrix." Psychological Bulletin 56 (March):81-105.

Campbell, Donald T., and Julian C. Stanley
1963   Experimental and Quasi-experimental Designs for Research.
            Chicago: Rand McNally.

Campbell, Norman
1920   What Is Science? London: Methuen.
1952   What Is Science? New York: Dover.

Cantril, Hadley
1944   Gauging Public Opinion. Princeton: Princeton University Press.
1945   "Do different polls get the same results?" Public Opinion Quar-
            terly 9 (Spring):61-69.
1961   Gauging Public Opinion. Princeton: Princeton University Press.
1965   The Pattern of Human Concerns. New Brunswick: Rutgers
            University Press.

Cantwell, Frank V.
1946   "Public opinion and the legislative process." American Political
            Science Review 40 (October):924-35.

Caporaso, James A., and Leslie L. Roos (eds.)
1973   Quasi-Experimental Approaches: Testing Theory and Evaluating
            Policy. Evanston: Northwestern University Press.

Cardozo, Benjamin N.
1921   The Nature of the Judicial Process. New Haven: Yale University
            Press.

Carey, Alex
1967   "The Hawthorne studies: A radical criticism." American Socio-
            logical Review 32 (June): 403-16.

Carlston, Kenneth S.
1962   Law and Organization in World Society. Urbana: University of
            Illinois Press.

Carnap, Rudolph
    1936–37   "Testability and meaning." Philosophy of Science 3 (October):
               419–71; 4 (January):1–40.
Carney, Thomas F.
    1972   Content Analysis: A Technique for Systematic Inference from
            Communications. Winnipeg: University of Manitoba Press.
Carper, Edith T.
    1962   "Lobbying and the natural gas bill" and "The defense appropria-
            tions rider." Pp. 47–81 and 175–222 in Edwin A. Bock and Alan
            K. Campbell (eds.), Case Studies in American Government.
            Englewood Cliffs: Prentice-Hall.
Carr, E. H.
    1956   The Twenty Years' Crisis. 2d ed. New York: St. Martin's.
Carritt, E. F.
    1947   Ethical and Political Thinking. London: Oxford University Press.
Carroll, Holbert N.
    1966   The House of Representatives and Foreign Affairs. Rev. ed.
            Boston: Little, Brown.
Carter, Hugh
    1945   "Recent American studies in attitudes toward war: A summary
            and evaluation." American Sociological Review 10 (June):
            343–53.
Carter, R. E., Jr.
    1957   "Segregation and the news: A regional content study." Journal-
            ism Quarterly 34 (Winter):3–18.
Cartwright, Dorwin P.
    1953   "Analysis of qualitative material." Pp. 421–70 in L. Festinger
            and D. Katz (eds.), Research Methods in the Behavioral Sciences.
            New York: Holt, Rinehart & Winston.
Cartwright, Dorwin P., and Alvin Zander
    1953   Group Dynamics. New York: Harper.
Carzo, Rocco, Jr., and John W. Yanouzas
    1967   Formal Organizations: A Systems Approach. Homewood: Irwin
            and Dorsey.
Cassinelli, C. W.
    1961   The Politics of Freedom: An Analysis of the Modern Democratic
            State. Seattle: University of Washington Press.
Cassirer, Ernst
    1944   An Essay on Man: An Introduction to a Philosophy of Human
            Culture. New Haven: Yale University Press.
    1953–57   The Philosophy of Symbolic Forms. 3 vols. New Haven: Yale
               University Press.
Cataldo, Everett F., Richard M. Johnson, Lyman A. Kellstedt, and Lester
    Milbrath
    1970   "Card sorting as a technique for survey interviewing." Public
            Opinion Quarterly 34 (Summer):202–15.

Catlin, George E. G.
1927   The Science and Method of Politics. New York: Knopf.
1930   A Study of the Principles of Politics. New York: Macmillan.
1962   Systematic Politics: Elementa Politica et Sociologica. Toronto:
            University of Toronto Press. See also the review by Charles S.
            Hyneman, American Political Science Review 57 (December
            1963):956–57.

Centers, Richard
1949   The Psychology of Social Classes. Princeton: Princeton Univer-
            sity Press.

Chambers, William Nisbet, and Walter Dean Burnham (eds.)
1967   The American Party Systems: Stages of Political Development.
            New York: Oxford University Press.

Chapanis, Alphonse
1961   "Men, machines, and models." American Psychologist 16
            (March):115–16.

Chapin, F. Stuart
1955   Experimental Designs in Sociological Research. New York:
            Harper.

Chapman, Brian
1959   The Profession of Government. London: George Allen & Unwin.

Chapman, R.
1968   "Tiros-Nimbus." Mimeographed. Syracuse: Inter-University Case
            Program.

Chapman, R. A.
1969   Decision Making. London: Routledge & Kegan Paul.

Charlesworth, James C. (ed.)
1962   The Limits of Behavioralism in Political Science. Philadelphia:
            American Academy of Political and Social Science.
1967   Comtemporary Political Analysis. New York: Free Press.

Chase, Harold W.
1972   Federal Judges: The Appointing Process. Minneapolis: University
            of Minnesota Press.

Chase, Harold W., and Craig R. Ducat (eds.)
1974   Edward S. Corwin's 'The Constitution' and What It Means
            Today. Princeton: Princeton University Press.

Chase, Stuart
1962   American Credos. New York: Harper.

Chein, Isidor
1964   "An introduction to sampling." Pp. 509–45 in Claire Selltiz,
            Marie Jahoda, Morton Deutsch, and Stuart W. Cook (eds.),
            Research Methods in Social Relations. New York: Holt, Rinehart
            & Winston.

Cherry, Colin
1957   On Human Communication: A Review, a Survey, and a Criticism.
            Cambridge and New York: MIT Press and Wiley.

Childs, Harwood L.
1930   Labor and Capital in National Politics. Columbus: Ohio State
              University Press.

Chomsky, Noam
1957   Syntactic Structures. The Hague: Mouton.
1965   "Structural linguistics and the philosophy of science." Diogenes
              15 (Fall):111–27.

Choucri, Nazli
1967   "Nonalignment in international politics: An analysis of attitudes
              and behavior." Doctoral dissertation, Stanford University.
1969   "The perceptual base of nonalignment." Journal of Conflict
              Resolution 13 (March):57–74.

Christiansen, Bjørn
1959   Attitudes towards Foreign Affairs as a Function of Personality.
              Oslo: Oslo University Press.

Christenson, R. M.
1964   "Report on the Reader's Digest." Columbia Journalism Review 3
              (Fall):30–36.

Christoph, J. B., and B. Brown
1969   Cases in Comparative Politics. 2d ed. Boston: Little, Brown.

Churchman, C. West, and Philburn Ratoosch
1959   Measurement. New York: Wiley.

Cicourel, Aaron Victor
1964   Method and Measurement in Sociology. New York: Free Press.

Clapp, Charles L.
1963   The Congressman: His Work as He Sees It. Washington: Brook-
              ings.

Clark, Keith C., and Laurence J. Legere
1969   The President and the Management of National Security. New
              York: Praeger.

Clark, Terry N.
1967a   "The concept of power: Some overemphasized and underrecog-
              nized dimensions." Southwestern Social Science Quarterly 48
              (December):271–86.
1967b   "Power and community structure: Who governs, where and
              when?" Sociological Quarterly 8 (Summer):291–316.
1968   "Community structures; decision-making, budget expenditures
              and urban renewal in 51 American communities." American
              Sociological Review 33 (August):576–93.

Clarendon, E.
1704   The History of the Rebellion and Civil Wars in England. London:
              Oxford University Press.

Claude, Inis L.
1962   Power and International Relations. New York: Random House.
1964   Swords into Plowshares. 3d ed. New York: Random House.
1966   "Collective legitimization as a function of the UN." International
              Organization 18 (Summer):367–79.

Clausen, Aage R.
1964   "Policy dimensions in congressional roll calls." Doctoral disserta-
          tion. University of Michigan.
1967a   "The measurement of legislative group behavior." Midwest
          Journal of Political Science 11 (May):212-24.
1967b   "Measurement identity in the longitudinal analysis of legislative
          voting." American Political Science Review 61 (Decem-
          ber):1020-35.
1968   "Response validity in surveys. Response validity: vote report."
          Public Opinion Quarterly 32 (Winter):588-606.

Cleaveland, Frederic N. (ed.)
1968   Congress and Urban Problems. Washington: Brookings.

Clemence, Richard V. (ed.)
1950   Readings in Economic Analysis. Reading: Addison-Wesley.

Cleveland, Harlan, Gerard J. Mangone, and John Clarke Adams
1960   The Overseas Americans. New York: McGraw-Hill.

Clotfelter, James
1973   The Military in American Politics. New York: Harper & Row.

Clubb, Jerome M., and Howard W. Allen
1969   "The cities and the election of 1928: Partisan realignment?"
          American Historical Review 74 (April):1205-20.

Clubb, Jerome M., and Howard W. Allen (eds.)
1971   Electoral Change and Stability in American Political History.
          New York: Free Press.

Cnudde, Charles F., and Donald J. McCrone
1966   "The linkage between constituency attitudes and congressional
          voting behaviors: A causal model." American Political Science
          Review 60 (March):66-72.

Cobban, Alfred
1953   "The decline of political theory." Political Science Quarterly 68
          (September):321-37.

Cochran, Charles L.
1974   Civil-Military Relations: Changing Concepts in the Seventies.
          New York: Free Press.

Cochran, Thomas C.
1953   Railroad Leaders, 1845-1890: The Business of Mind in Action.
          Cambridge: Harvard University Press.

Cochran, William G.
1963   Sampling Techniques. 2d ed. New York: Wiley.

Coffey, Joseph I.
1971   Strategic Power and National Security. Pittsburgh: University of
          Pittsburgh Press.

Cohen, Bernard C.
1957   The Political Process and Foreign Policy: The Making of the
          Japanese Peace Settlement. Princeton: Princeton University
          Press.

1963   The Press and Foreign Policy. Princeton: Princeton University
            Press.

Cohen, Harry
1965   The Demonics of Bureaucracy. Ames: Iowa State University
            Press.

Cohen, Morris R.
1931   Reason and Nature: An Essay on the Meaning of the Scientific
            Method. New York: Harcourt, Brace.
1944   A Preface to Logic. New York: Holt.

Cohen, Morris R., and Ernest Nagel
1934   An Introduction to Logic and the Scientific Method. New York:
            Harcourt, Brace.

Cohen, Stephen S.
1969   Modern Capitalist Planning: The French Model. Cambridge:
            Harvard University Press.

Colby, B. N.
1966a   "The analysis of culture content and the patterning of narrative
            concern in texts." American Anthropologist 68 (April):374–88.
1966b   "Cultural patterns in narrative." Science 151 (February):793–98.

Coleman, James S.
1958   Nigeria: Background to Nationalism. Berkeley and Los Angeles:
            University of California Press.

Coleman, James S. (ed.)
1965   Education and Political Development. Princeton: Princeton
            University Press.

Coleman, James S., and Carl G. Rosberg, Jr. (eds.)
1964   Political Parties and National Integration in Tropical Africa.
            Berkeley and Los Angeles: University of California Press.

Colfax, J. David
1966   "Pressure toward distortion and involvement in studying a civil
            rights organization." Human Organization 25 (Summer):140–49.

Colfax, J. David, and Susan F. Sternberg
1972   "The perpetuation of racial stereotypes: Blacks and mass circu-
            lating magazine advertisements." Public Opinion Quarterly 36
            (Spring):8–18.

Collier, John, Jr.
1967   Visual Anthropology: Photography as a Research Method. New
            York: Holt, Rinehart & Winston.

Collingwood, R. G.
1942   The New Leviathan. London: Oxford University Press, Clarendon
            Press.
1946   The Idea of History. London: Oxford University Press, Clar-
            endon Press.

Committee on Political Parties, American Political Science Association
1950　　　　Toward a More Responsible Two-Party System. New York: Rinehart.

Committee on Problems and Policy, Social Science Research Council
1949　　　　The Behavioral and Social Sciences: Outlook and Needs. Englewood Cliffs: Prentice-Hall.

Committee on Professional Standards and Responsibilities
1968　　　　"Ethical problems of academic political scientists." P.S.: Newsletter of the American Political Science Association 1 (Summer):3–28.

Comparative State Election Project
1972　　　　Explaining the Vote: Presidential Choices in the Nation and the States, 1968. Chapel Hill: University of North Carolina Press.

Conant, James B.
1953　　　　Science and Common Sense. New York: Macmillan.

Connolly, William E.
1967　　　　Political Science and Ideology. Chicago: Atherton.
1974　　　　The Terms of Political Discourse. Lexington: Heath.

"Content analysis: A new evidentiary technique." 1948. University of Chicago Law Review 15 (Summer):910–25.

Converse, Philip E.
1964a　　　"The nature of belief systems in mass publics." Pp. 206–81 in David E. Apter (ed.), Ideology and Discontent. New York: Free Press.
1964b　　　"A network of data archives for the behavioral sciences." Public Opinion Quarterly 28 (Summer):273–386.
1966a　　　"Information flow and the stability of partisan attitudes." Pp. 136–57 in Angus Campbell, Warren E. Miller, Philip E. Converse, and Donald E. Stokes, Elections and the Political Order. New York: Wiley.
1966b　　　"The availability and quality of sample survey data in archives within the United States." Pp. 419–40 in Richard L. Merritt and Stein Rokkan (eds.), Comparing Nations: The Use of Quantitative Data in Cross-National Research. New Haven: Yale University Press.
1969　　　　"Survey research and the decoding of patterns in ecological data." Pp. 459–85 in Mattei Dogan and Stein Rokkan (eds.) Quantitative Ecological Analysis in the Social Sciences. Cambridge: MIT Press.
1972　　　　"Change in the American electorate." Pp. 263–390 in Angus Campbell and Philip E. Converse (eds.), The Human Meaning of Social Change. New York: Russell Sage.

Converse, Philip E., and Georges Dupeux
1962　　　　"Politicization of the electorate in France and the United States." Public Opinion Quarterly 26 (Spring):1–23.

Conway, Freda
  1967   Sampling: An Introduction for Social Scientists. London: George
                Allen & Unwin.
Cook, Thomas I.
  1949   "Democratic psychology and democratic world order." World
                Politics 1 (July):553-64.
Coombs, Clyde H.
  1964   A Theory of Data. New York: Wiley.
Copeland, Melvin T.
  1954   "The genesis of the case method in business instruction." Pp.
                25-34 in M. McNair (ed.), The Case Method at the Harvard
                Business School. New York: McGraw Hill.
Coplin, William D.
  1966   The Functions of International Law. Chicago: Rand McNally.
Coplin, William D. (ed.)
  1968   Simulation in the Study of Politics. Chicago: Markham.
Coplin, William D., Patrick J. McGowan, and Michael K. O'Leary.
  1974   American Foreign Policy: An Introduction to Analysis and
                Evaluation. Belmont: Duxbury.
Cornelius, Wayne A., Jr.
  1969   "Urbanization as an agent in Latin American political instability:
                The case of Mexico." American Political Science Review 63
                (September):833-58.
Corson, John, and Joseph P. Harris
  1963   Public Administration in Modern Society. New York: McGraw-
                Hill.
Corwin, Edward
  1940   The President: Office and Powers. 4th ed., 1957. New York:
                New York University Press.
Coser, Lewis A.
  1961   "The termination of conflict." Journal of Conflict Resolution 5
                (December):347-53.
  1964   The Functions of Social Conflict. New York: Free Press.
  1965   Men of Ideas. New York: Free Press.
Cotter, Cornelius P., and Bernard Hennessy
  1964   Politics without Power: The National Party Committees.
                Chicago: Atherton.
Couch, Arthur, and Kenneth Keniston
  1960   "Yeasayers and naysayers: Agreeing response set as a personality
                variable." Journal of Abnormal and Social Psychology 60
                (March):151-74.
Council of Social Science Data Archives
  1967   Social Science Data Archives in the United States. New York:
                Council of Social Science Data Archives.
Cox, Keith K.
  1970   "Changes in stereotyping of negroes and whites in magazine
                advertisements." Public Opinion Quarterly 33 (Winter):603-6.

Crain, Robert L.
1968   The Politics of School Desegregation. Chicago: Aldine.

Crick, Bernard
1959   The American Science of Politics. Berkeley and Los Angeles: University of California Press.

Croly, Herbert
1909   The Promise of American Life. New York: Macmillan.

Cronbach, Lee J., and Paul E. Meehl
1955   "Construct validity in psychological tests." Psychological Bulletin 52 (July):281–302.

Cronin, Thomas E.
1975   The State of the Presidency. Boston: Little, Brown.

Crossley, Helen M., and Hugh J. Parry
1950   "Validity of responses to survey questions." Public Opinion Quarterly 14 (Spring):61–80.

Crotty, William J.
1966   "The utility of mail questionnaires and the problem of a representative return rate." Western Political Science Quarterly 19 (March):44–53.

Crow, Wayman J., and Robert C. Noel
1965   "The valid use of simulation results." La Jolla: Western Behavioral Sciences Institute.

Crozier, Michel
1964   The Bureaucratic Phenomenon. Chicago: University of Chicago Press.

Cummings, Milton C.
1966a   Congressmen and the Electorate: Elections for the United States House and President, 1920–1964. New York: Free Press.
1966b   The National Election of 1964. Washington: Brookings.

Curry, R. L., Jr., and L. L. Wade
1968   A Theory of Political Exchange. Englewood Cliffs: Prentice-Hall.

Cushman, Robert E.
1925   Leading Constitutional Decisions. 13th ed., 1966. New York: Appleton-Century-Crofts.

Cyert, Richard M., and James G. March
1963   A Behavioral Theory of the Firm. Englewood Cliffs: Prentice-Hall.

Cyert, Richard, Herbert Simon, and Martin Trow
1956   "Observation of a business decision." Journal of Business 29 (July):237–48.

Dahl, Robert A.
1956   A Preface to Democratic Theory. Chicago: University of Chicago Press.
1958   "A critique of the power elite model." American Political Science Review 52 (June):463–69.
1961a   Who Governs? Democracy and Power in an American City. New Haven: Yale University Press.

1961b   "The behavioral approach in political science: Epitaph for a monument to a successful protest." American Political Science Review 55 (December):763-72.

1963   Modern Political Analysis. Englewood Cliffs: Prentice-Hall.

1967   Pluralist Democracy in the United States: Conflict and Consent. Chicago: Rand McNally.

1976   Democracy in the United States: Promise and Performance. 3d ed. Chicago: Rand McNally.

Dahl, Robert A. (ed.)

1966   Political Oppositions in Western Democracies. New Haven: Yale University Press.

1973   Regimes and Oppositions. New Haven: Yale University Press.

Dahl, Robert A., and Charles E. Lindblom

1953   Politics, Economics, and Welfare. New York: Harper.

Dahl, Robert A., and Edward R. Tufte

1973   Size and Democracy. Stanford: Stanford University Press.

Dahrendorf, Ralf

1958   "Out of Utopia." American Journal of Sociology 64 (September):115-27.

1961   "Democracy without liberty." Pp. 175-206 in Seymour Martin Lipset and Leo Lowenthal (eds.), Culture and Social Character. New York: Free Press.

Dalton, John E.

1937   Sugar: A Case Study of Government Control. New York: Macmillan.

Dalton, Melville

1959   Men Who Manage. New York: Wiley.

1967   "Preconceptions and methods in men who manage." Pp. 58-110 in Phillip E. Hammond (ed.), Sociologists at Work. Garden City: Doubleday.

Daughtery, William E., and Morris Janowitz

1958   A Psychological Warfare Casebook. Baltimore: Johns Hopkins Press.

Davies, James C.

1963   Human Nature in Politics: The Dynamics of Political Behavior. New York: Wiley.

Davis, David H.

1972   How the Bureaucracy Makes Foreign Policy: An Exchange Analysis. Lexington: Lexington Books.

1974   Energy Politics. New York: St. Martin's.

Davis, Horace B.

1967   Nationalism and Socialism: Marxist and Labor Theories of Nationalism to 1917. New York: Monthly Review Press.

Davis, James, Joe L. Spaeth, and Carolyn Husson

1961   "A technique for analyzing the effects of group composition." American Sociological Review 26 (2):215-26.

Davis, Kingsley
    1959   "The myth of functional analysis." American Sociological
                Review 24 (December):757-72.

Davis, Morris
    1964   "Participant observers in platonic cities." Midwest Journal of
                Political Science 8 (August):353-71.

Davis, Morris, and Marvin G. Weinbaum
    1969   Metropolitan Decision Processes. Chicago: Rand McNally.

Davis, Otto A., M. A. H. Dempster, and A. Wildavsky
    1966   "A theory of the budgetary process." American Political Science
                Review 60 (September):529-47.

Davis, Vincent
    1967   The Admirals' Lobby. Chapel Hill: University of North Carolina
                Press.

Davison, Walter Phillips
    1958   The Berlin Blockade: A Study of Cold War Politics. Princeton:
                Princeton University Press.
    1965   International Political Communication. New York: Praeger.

Dawson, Richard E.
    1966   "Political socialization." Pp. 1-84 in James A. Robinson (ed.),
                Political Science Annual. Indianapolis: Bobbs-Merrill.

Dawson, Richard E., and Kenneth Prewitt
    1969   Political Socialization. Boston: Little, Brown.

Dawson, Richard E., and James A. Robinson
    1963   "Inter-party competition, economic variables, and welfare
                policies in the American states." Journal of Politics 25
                (May):265-89.

Dean, John P.
    1954   "Participant observation and interview." Pp. 225-52 in John T.
                Doby (ed.), An Introduction to Social Research. Harrisburg:
                Stackpole.

Dean, John P., Robert L. Eichhorn, and Lois R. Dean
    1967   "Observations and interviewing." Pp. 274-304 in John T. Doby
                (ed.), An Introduction to Social Research, 2d ed. New York:
                Appleton-Century-Crofts.

Dean, John P., and William F. Whyte
    1958   "How do you know if the informant is telling the truth?" Human
                Organization 17 (2):34-38.

Debnam, Geoffrey
    1975   "Nondecisions and power: The two faces of Backrach and
                Baratz." American Political Science Review 69 (September):889-99.

De Charms, Richard, and Gerald H. Moeller
    1962   "Values expressed in American children's readers: 1900-1950."
                Journal of Abnormal and Social Psychology 64 (February):136-42.

Dechert, Charles R.
1965   "The development of cybernetics." American Behavioral Sci-
            entist 8 (June):15–20.

Dechert, Charles R. (ed.)
1966   The Social Impact of Cybernetics. Notre Dame: University of
            Notre Dame Press.

De Fleur, Melvin L.
1964   "Occupational roles as portrayed on television." Public Opinion
            Quarterly 28 (Spring):57–74.

De Fleur, Melvin L., and Frank R. Westie
1963   "Attitude as a scientific concept." Social Forces 42 (Octo-
            ber):17–31.

De Grazia, Alfred
1949   Human Relations in Public Administration. Chicago: Public
            Administration Service.

De Guzman, Raul P. (ed.)
1963   Patterns in Decision-Making. Manila: Graduate School of Public
            Administration, University of the Philippines.

Deising, Paul
1971   Patterns of Discovery in the Social Sciences. Chicago: Aldine.

Delany, William
1960   "Some field notes on the problem of access in organizational
            research." Administrative Science Quarterly 5 (Decem-
            ber):448–57.

Deming, W. Edwards
1950   Some Theory of Sampling. New York: Wiley.

Dennis, Jack
1968   "Major problems of political socialization research." Midwest
            Journal of Political Science 12 (February):85–114.

Dennis, Jack, and Donald J. McCrone
1970   "Preadult development of political party identification in West-
            ern democracies." Comparative Political Studies 3 (Ju-
            ly):243–63.

Denzin, Norman K. (ed.)
1970   Sociological Methods: A Sourcebook. Chicago: Aldine.

De Rivera, Joseph H.
1968   The Psychological Dimension of Foreign Policy. Columbus:
            Merrill.

Derthick, Martha
1975   Uncontrollable Spending for Social Services Grants. Washington:
            Brookings.

Desarrollo Económico de la Argentina. 1958. E-CN. 12-429. Add. 4, pp. 3–5.

Deutsch, Karl W.
1953   Nationalism and Social Communication. Cambridge and New
            York: MIT Press and Wiley.

1956a   "Shifts in the balance of communication flows: A problem of
             measurement in international relations." Public Opinion Quar-
             terly 20 (Spring):143-60.

1956b   "Joseph Schumpeter as an analyst of sociology and economic
             history." Journal of Economic History 16 (March):41-56.

1961   "Social mobilization and political development." American Pol-
             itical Science Review 55 (September):493-514.

1963   The Nerves of Government: Models of Political Communication
             and Control. New York: Free Press.

1964   "Transactional flows as indicators of political cohesion." Pp.
             75-97 in Philip E. Jacob and James V. Toscano (eds.), The
             Integration of Political Communities. Philadelphia: Lippincott.

1966a   Nationalism and Social Communication. 2d ed. Cambridge: MIT
             Press.

1966b   "The theoretical basis of data programs." Pp. 27-55 in Richard
             L. Merritt and Stein Rokkan (eds.), Comparing Nations. New
             Haven: Yale University Press.

1968   The Analysis of International Relations. Englewood Cliffs:
             Prentice-Hall.

1969   "Social mobilization and political development." American Pol-
             itical Science Review 55 (September):493-514.

1970   Politics and Government. How People Decide Their Fate. Bos-
             ton: Houghton Mifflin.

1974   Politics and Government. 2d ed. Boston: Houghton Mifflin.

Deutsch, Karl W. and Associates
1957   Political Community and the North Atlantic Area: International
             Organization in the Light of Historical Experience. Princeton:
             Princeton University Press.

Deutsch, Karl W., and Alexander Eckstein
1961   "National Industrialization and the declining share of the inter-
             national economic sector, 1890-1959." World Politics 13 (Jan-
             uary):287-99.

Deutsch, Karl W., and Lewis J. Edinger
1959   Germany Rejoins the Powers. Stanford: Stanford University
             Press.

Deutsch, Karl W., Lewis J. Edinger, Roy C. Macridis, and Richard L. Merritt
1967   France, Germany, and the Western Alliance: A Study of Elite
             Attitudes on European Integration and World Politics. New
             York: Scribner's.

Deutsch, Karl W., and William J. Foltz (eds.)
1963   Nation-Building. Chicago: Atherton.

Deutsch, Karl W., Harold Lasswell, Richard L. Merritt, and Bruce M. Russett
1966   "The Yale political data program." Pp. 81-94 in Richard L.
             Merritt and Stein Rokkan (eds.), Comparing Nations. New
             Haven: Yale University Press.

Deutsch, Karl W., and Richard L. Merritt
1955   Nationalism and National Development: An Interdisciplinary

Bibliography. Cambridge: MIT Press.

Deutsch, Karl W., and Leroy N. Rieselbach
1970   "Empirical theory." Pp. 74–109 in Michael Haas and Henry S.
            Kariel (eds.), Approaches to the Study of Political Science. San
            Francisco: Chandler.

Deutsch, Karl W., and I. Richard Savage
1960   "A statistical model of the gross analysis of transactional flows."
            Econometrica 28 (July):551–72.

Deutsch, Karl W., and Dieter Senghaas
1969   "Towards a theory of war and peace: Propositions, simulations,
            and reality." Paper prepared for the annual meeting of the
            American Political Science Association, New York (September).

Deutsch, Karl W., and J. David Singer
1964   "Multipolar power systems and international stability." World
            Politics 16 (April):390–406.

Deutsch, Morton
1965   "The social psychology of interpersonal bargaining." Paper
            prepared for the annual meeting of the American Psychological
            Association, Washington.

Devereux, George
1967   From Anxiety to Method in the Behavioral Sciences. The Hague:
            Mouton.

Devons, Ely
1950   Planning in Practice. Cambridge: At the University Press.

Dewey, John
1927   The Public and Its Problems. New York: Holt.
1938   Logic: The Theory of Inquiry. New York: Holt.

Dewey, John, and Arthur Bentley
1949   Knowing and the Known. Boston: Beacon.

Dexter, Lewis Anthony
1970   Elite and Specialized Interviewing. Evanston: Northwestern
            University Press.

Dibble, Vernon Kent
1963   "Four types of inference from documents to events." History
            and Theory 3 (2):203–21

Dickinson, John K.
1967   German and Jew. New York: Quadrangle.

Dimock, Marshall E.
1958   A Philosophy of Administration toward a Creative Growth. New
            York: Harper.

DiRenzo, Gordon J. (ed.)
1967   Concepts, Theory and Explanation in the Behavioral Sciences.
            New York: Random House.

Doby, John T. (ed.)
1967   An Introduction to Social Research. 2d ed. New York: Appleton-
            Century-Crofts.

Dobyns, Henry F., Paul L. Doughty and Harold Lasswell
1971   Power and Applied Social Change. Beverly Hills: Sage.

Dogan, Mattei, and Stein Rokkan, (eds.)
1969   Quantitative Ecological Analysis in the Social Sciences. Cambridge: MIT Press.

Dolbeare, Kenneth M.
1969   Directions in American Political Thought. New York: Wiley.

Dollard, John
1935   Criteria for the Life History. New Haven: Yale University Press.

Domhoff, G. William and Hoyt B. Ballard
1968   C. Wright Mills and the Power Elite. Boston: Beacon.

Dommel, Paul R.
1974   The Politics of Revenue Sharing. Bloomington: Indiana University Press.

Dornbusch, Sanford M., and Lauren C. Hickman
1959   "Other-directedness in consumer-goods advertising: A test of Riesman's historical theory." Social Forces 38 (December):99-102.

Douglas, Paul H.
1936   Social Security in the United States. New York: McGraw-Hill.

Douglass, R. Bruce
1976   "The Gospel and political order: Eric Voegelin on the political role of Christianity." Journal of Politics 38 (February):25-45.

Dovring, Karin
1954   "Quantitative semantics in 18th-century Sweden." Public Opinion Quarterly 18 (Winter):389-94.

Downs, Anthony
1957   An Economic Theory of Democracy. New York: Harper.
1967   Inside Bureaucracy. Boston: Little, Brown.

Dowse, Robert E.
1966   "A functionalist's logic." World Politics 28 (July):607-23.

Dreitzel, Hans P. (ed.)
1970   Recent Sociology No. 2: Patterns of Communicative Behavior. New York: Macmillan.

Droba, D. D.
1931   "A scale of militarism." Journal of Educational Psychology 22 (February):96-111.

Dror, Yehezkel
1968   Public Policymaking Reexamined. San Francisco: Chandler.
1970   "Teaching of policy science." Social Science Information 9 (April):101-22.

D'Souza, J. B.
1969   "The bus fare rise." Cyclostyled for government use. New Delhi: Indian Institute of Public Administration.

Dubester, Henry J. (ed.)
1948   State Censuses: An Annotated Bibliography of Censuses of

Population Taken after the Year 1790 by States and Territories of the United States. Washington: GPO.
1950   Catalog of United States Census Publications, 1790–1945. Washington: GPO.

Dubin, Robert
1969   Theory Building. New York: Free Press.

Duffield, Marcus
1931   King Legion. London: Cape & Smith.

Dufrenne, Mikel
1963   Language and Philosophy. Bloomington: Indiana University Press.

Duncan, Hugh D.
1962   Communication and the Social Order. Totowa: Bedminster.

Dunning, William A.
1902–20   A History of Political Theories. 3 vols. New York: Macmillan.

Dunsire, Andrew
1973   Administration: The Word and the Science. New York: Wiley.

Durbin, J., and A. Stuart
1951   "Differences in response rates of experienced and inexperienced interviewers." Journal of the Royal Statistical Society 114 (part 2):163–84.

Duverger, Maurice
1954   Political Parties: Their Organization and Activity in the Modern State. 1951. Translated by Barbara North and Robert North. London: Methuen.
1964   An Introduction to the Social Sciences with Special Reference to Their Methods. Translated by Malcolm Anderson. New York: Praeger.

Dvorin, Eugene D., and Robert H. Simmons
1972   From Amoral to Humane Bureaucracy. San Francisco: Canfield.

Dye, Thomas R.
1966   Politics, Economics and the Public: Policy Outcomes in the American States. Chicago: Rand McNally.
1976   Who's Running America? Institutional Leadership in the United States. Englewood Cliffs: Prentice-Hall.

Dye, Thomas R., and L. Harmon Zeigler
1970   The Irony of Democracy: An Uncommon Introduction to American Politics. Belmont: Wadsworth.
1972   The Irony of Democracy. 2d ed. Belmont: Wadsworth.
1977   The Irony of Democracy. 3d ed. Scituate: Duxbury.

Dyer, Frederick C., and John M. Dyer
1965   Bureaucracy vs. Creativity. Coral Gables: University of Miami Press.

Easton, David
1953   The Political System. New York: Knopf.
1957   "An approach to the analysis of political systems." World Politics 9 (April):383–400.

1964	The Political System. An Inquiry into the State of Political Science. New York: Knopf.
1965a	A Framework for Political Analysis. Englewood Cliffs: Prentice-Hall.
1965b	A Systems Analysis of Political Life. New York: Wiley.
1969	"The new revolution in political science." American Political Science Review 63 (December):1051-61.
1971	The Political System. 2d ed. New York: Knopf.

Easton, David (ed.)
1966	Varieties of Political Theory. Englewood Cliffs: Prentice-Hall.

Easton, David, and Jack Dennis
1967	"The child's acquisition of regime norms: Political efficacy." American Political Science Review 61 (March):25-38.

Easton, David, and Robert D. Hess
1962	"The child's political world." Midwest Journal of Political Science 6 (August): 229-46.

Ebenstein, William
1970	Today's Isms. 6th ed. Englewood Cliffs: Prentice-Hall.

Eckhardt, William
1965	"War propaganda, welfare values and political ideologies: A test of the mirror-image hypothesis." Journal of Conflict Resolution 9 (3):345-58.

Eckhardt, William, and Ralph K. White
1967	"A test of the mirror-image hypothesis: Kennedy and Khrushchev." Journal of Conflict Resolution 11 (September):325-32.

Eckhoff, Torstein E., and Knut D. Jacobsen
1960	Rationality and Responsibility in Administrative and Judicial Decision Making. New York: Humanities.

Eckstein, Harry
1958a	The English Health Service. Cambridge: Harvard University Press.
1958b	"The British political system." Pp. 52-209 in Samuel H. Beer and Adam B. Ulam (eds.), Patterns of Government: The Major Political Systems of Europe. New York: Random House.
1960	Pressure Group Politics. Stanford: Stanford University Press.
1961	A Theory of Stable Democracy. Princeton: Center for International Studies.
1963	"A perspective on comparative politics past and present." Pp. 3-32 in Harry Eckstein and David E. Apter (eds.), Comparative Politics: A Reader. New York: Free Press.
1966	Division and Cohesion in Democracy: A Study of Norway. Princeton: Princeton University Press.
1969	"Authority relations and government performance: A theoretical framework." Comparative Political Studies 2 (October):269-326.
1973	"Authority patterns: A structural basis for political inquiry." American Political Science Review 67 (December):1142-61.

Eckstein, Harry, and Ted Robert Gurr
      1975   Patterns of Authority: A Structural Basis for Political Inquiry.
                    New York: Wiley-Interscience.
Edel, Abraham
      1965   "Social science and value: A study of interrelations." Pp. 218–38
                    in Irving L. Horowitz (ed.), The New Sociology: Essays in Honor
                    of C. Wright Mills. New York: Oxford University Press.
Edelman, Murray
      1964   The Symbolic Uses of Politics. Urbana: University of Illinois
                    Press.
      1971   Politics as Symbolic Action: Mass Arousal and Quiescence.
                    Chicago: Markham.
Edinger, Lewis J.
      1965   Kurt Schumacher: A Study in Personality and Political Behavior.
                    Stanford: Stanford University Press.
      1967   Political Leadership in Industrialized Societies: Studies in
                    Comparative Analysis. New York: Wiley.
      1968   Politics in Germany. Boston: Little, Brown.
Edwards, Allen L.
      1953   "The relationship between the judged desirability of a trait and
                    the probability that the trait will be endorsed." Journal of
                    Applied Psychology 37 (April):90–93.
      1957   Techniques of Attitude Scale Construction. New York: Apple-
                    ton-Century-Crofts.
Ehrmann, Henry W.
      1968   Politics of France. Boston: Little, Brown.
      1971   Politics of France. 2d ed. Boston: Little, Brown.
Ehrmann, Henry W. (ed.)
      1958   Interest Groups on Four Continents. Pittsburgh: University of
                    Pittsburgh Press.
Ehrmann, Jacques (ed.)
      1970   Structuralism. Garden City: Doubleday.
Eide, Asbjørn
      1966   "Peace-keeping and enforcement by regional organizations."
                    Journal of Peace Research 3 (2):125–45.
Eidenberg, Eugene, and Roy D. Morey
      1969   An Act of Congress. New York: Norton.
Eisenstadt, Shmuel N.
      1963   Political Systems of Empires. New York: Free Press.
Elazar, Daniel J.
      1966   American Federalism: A View from the States. New York:
                    Crowell.
Eldersveld, Samuel J.
      1964   Political Parties: A Behavioral Analysis. Chicago: Rand McNally.
Ellegård, A.
      1962   A Statistical Method for Determining Authorship. Goteborg:
                    Acta Universitatis Cotheburgensis.

Ellsworth, John W.
1965   "Rationality and campaigning: A content analysis of the 1960 presidential campaign debates." Western Political Quarterly 18 (December):794-802.
1967   "Policy and ideology in the campaigns of 1960 and 1964: A content analysis." Mimeographed. Carbondale: Southern Illinois University.

Embree, John
1939   Suye Mura: A Japanese Village. London: Routledge & Kegan Paul.

Emmerich, Herbert
1961   A Handbook of Public Administration. New York: Department of Economics and Social Affairs, United Nations.

Erickson, Erik
1950   Childhood and Society. New York: Norton.
1958   Young Man Luther: A Study in Psychoanalysis and History. New York: Norton.
1964   Childhood and Society. 2d ed. New York: Norton.
1968a   Identity: Youth and Crisis. New York: Norton.
1968b   "On the nature of psycho-historical evidence: In search of Gandhi." Daedalus 97 (Summer):695-730.

Erikson, Robert S., and Norman R. Luttbeg
1973   American Public Opinion: Its Origins, Content and Impact. New York: Wiley.

Etzioni, Amitai
1959   "The functional differentiation of elites in the Kibbutz." American Journal of Sociology 64 (March):476-87.
1960   "Two approaches to organizational analysis: A critique and a suggestion." Administrative Science Quarterly 5 (September):257-78.
1961   A Comparative Analysis of Complex Organizations. New York: Free Press.
1963   "The epigenesis of political communities at the international level." American Journal of Sociology 68 (January):407-21.
1965   Political Unification. New York: Holt, Rinehart & Winston.
1967   "The Kennedy experiment." Western Political Quarterly 20 (June):361-80.
1968   The Active Society. New York: Free Press.

Etzioni, Amitai (ed.)
1966   International Political Communities. Garden City: Doubleday.

Eulau, Heinz
1961   "Recent developments in the behavioral study of politics." Paper prepared for the annual meeting of the Northern California Political Science Association.
1962   Class and Party in the Eisenhower Years: Class Roles and Perspectives in the 1952 and 1956 Presidential Elections. New York: Free Press.

1963   The Behavioral Persuasion in Politics. New York: Random House.
1967   "Segments of political science most susceptible to behavioristic treatment." Pp. 32–50 in James C. Charlesworth (ed.), Contemporary Political Analysis. New York: Free Press.
1968   "Preface." Pp. vii–viii in J. David Singer (ed.), Quantitative International Politics. New York: Free Press.
1969a   Micro-Macro Political Analysis: Accents of Inquiry, Chicago: Aldine.
1969b   "Quo Vadimus." P.S.: Newsletter of the American Political Science Association 2 (Winter):12–13.

Eulau, Heinz (ed.)
1966   Political Behavior in America: New Directions. New York: Random House.
1969c   Behavioralism in Political Science. Chicago: Atherton.

Eulau, Heinz, Samuel J. Eldersveld, and Morris Janowitz (eds.)
1956   Political Behavior: A Reader in Theory and Research. New York: Free Press.

Eulau, Heinz, and Robert Eyestone
1968   "Policy maps of city councils and policy outcomes: A developmental analysis." American Political Science Review 62 (March):124–43.

Eulau, Heinz, and Kenneth Prewitt
1973   Labyrinths of Democracy. Indianapolis: Bobbs-Merrill.

Eulau, Heinz, and James G. March (eds.)
1969   Political Science. Englewood Cliffs: Prentice-Hall. Prepared for the Behavioral and Social Science Survey Committee appointed by the National Academy of Sciences and the Social Science Research Council.

Evan, William M.
1959   "Cohort analysis of survey data: A procedure for studying long-term opinion change." Public Opinion Quarterly 23 (Spring):63–72.

Everson, David H., and Joann Poparad Paine
1973   An Introduction to Systematic Political Science. Homewood: Dorsey.

Fagen, Richard R.
1967   "The Cuban revolution: Enemies and friends." Pp. 184–231 in D. J. Finlay, O. R. Holsti, and R. R. Fagen, Enemies in Politics. Chicago: Rand McNally.

Fainsod, Merle
1967   How Russia is Ruled. Cambridge: Harvard University Press.

Fanon, Franz
1965   The Wretched of the Earth. New York: Grove.
1967   A Dying Colonialism. New York: Grove.

Farris, Charles D.
1960   "Selected attitudes on foreign affairs as correlates of authoritar-

ianism and political anomie." Journal of Politics 22 (February):50–67.

Fast, Julius
1970   Body Language. New York: Evans.

Fayol, Henri
1949   General and Industrial Management. London: Pitman.

Feierabend, Ivo K., and Rosalind L. Feierabend
1966   "Aggressive behavior within polities, 1948–62: A cross-national study." Journal of Conflict Resolution 10 (September):249–71.

Feigert, Frank B., and M. Margaret Conway
1976   Parties and Politics in America. Boston: Allyn & Bacon.

Feigl, Herbert, and May Brodbeck (eds.)
1953   Readings in the Philosophy of Science. New York: Appleton-Century-Crofts.

Feigl, Herbert, and Grover Maxwell (eds.)
1962   Minnesota Studies in the Philosophy of Science. Vol. 3. Minneapolis: University of Minnesota Press.

Feigl, Herbert, and Michael Scriven (eds.)
1956   Minnesota Studies in the Philosophy of Science. Vol. 1. Minneapolis: University of Minnesota Press.

Feigl, Herbert, Michael Scriven, and Grover Maxwell (eds.)
1958   Minnesota Studies in the Philosophy of Science. Vol. 2. Minneapolis: University of Minnesota Press.

Feldman, Julian, and Edward Feigenbaum (eds.)
1963   Computers and Thought. New York: McGraw-Hill.

Fenno, Richard, Jr.
1959   The President's Cabinet. Cambridge: Harvard University Press.
1966   The Power of the Purse: Appropriations Politics in Congress. Boston: Little, Brown.
1973   Congressmen in Committees. Boston: Little, Brown.

Fenton, John H.
1957   Politics in the Border States. New Orleans: Hauser.
1966   Midwest Politics. New York: Holt, Rinehart & Winston.

Fesler, James W.
1949   Area and Administration. University: University of Alabama Press.
1962   "The case method in political science." Pp. 65–88 in Edwin A. Bock (ed.), Essays on the Case Method in Public Administration. Brussels: International Institute of Administrative Sciences. Also, mimeographed, Syracuse: Inter-University Case Program.

Festinger, Leon, Henry Riecken, and Stanley Schacter
1956   When Prophecy Fails. Minneapolis: University of Minnesota Press.

Festinger, Leon, and Daniel Katz (eds.)
1953   Research Methods in the Behavioral Sciences. New York: Holt, Rinehart & Winston.

Feuer, Lewis S.
   1963a   The Scientific Intellectual. New York: Basic Books.
   1963b   "What is alienation? The career of a concept." Pp. 127–47 in
               Maurice Stein and Arthur Vidich (eds.), Sociology on Trial.
               Englewood Cliffs: Prentice-Hall.

Field, Guy Cromwell
   n.d.   Moral Theory: An Introduction to Ethics. New York: Dutton.

Fiellin, Alan
   1963   "The functions of informal groups in legislative institutions." Pp.
               59–78 in R. Peabody and N. Polsby (eds.), New Perspectives on
               the House of Representatives. Chicago: Rand McNally.

Finer, Herman
   1941   "Administrative responsibility in a democratic government."
               Public Administration Review 1 (4):335–50.
   1974   The Presidency: Crisis and Regeneration. Chicago: University of
               Chicago Press.

Finkle, Jason
   1960   The President Makes a Decision: A Study of Dixon-Yates. Ann
               Arbor: Institute of Public Administration, University of Mich-
               igan.

Fischer, David Hackett
   1970   Historians' Fallacies: Toward a Logic of Historical Thought. New
               York: Harper & Row.

Fish, Peter Graham
   1973   The Politics of Federal Judicial Administration. Princeton:
               Princeton University Press.

Fisher, Louis
   1975   Presidential Spending Power. Princeton: Princeton University
               Press.

Fisher, Roger D.
   1964   International Conflict and Behavioral Science: The Craigville
               Papers. New York: Basic Books.

Flanigan, William H.
   1968   Political Behavior of the American Electorate. Boston: Allyn &
               Bacon.

Flanigan, William H., and Edwin Fogelman
   1970   "Patterns of political violence in comparative historical perspec-
               tive." Comparative Politics 3 (October):1–21.

Flanigan, William H., and David Repass
   1969   Electoral Behavior. Boston: Little, Brown.

Flanigan, William H., and Nancy H. Zingale
   1975   Political Behavior of the American Electorate. 3d ed. Boston:
               Allyn & Bacon.

Flew, Antony Garrard Newton (ed.)
   1951   Essays on Logic and Language. New York: Philosophical Library.
   1953   Logic and Language. 2d ser. New York: Philosophical Library.

Ford, Robert N.
1950   "A rapid scoring procedure for scaling attitude questions." Public
            Opinion Quarterly 14 (Fall):508-32.

Foss, Martin
1964   Symbol and Metaphor in Human Experience. Lincoln: University
            of Nebraska Press.

Foster, H. Schuyler
1935   "How America became belligerent: A quantitative study of war
            news." American Journal of Sociology 40 (January):464-75.
1937   "Charting America's news of the world war." Foreign Affairs 15
            (January):311-19.

Foster, H. Schuyler, and Carl J. Friedrich
1937   "Letters to the editor as a means of measuring the effectiveness
            of propaganda." American Political Science Review 31 (Febru-
            ary):71-79.

Foucault, Michel
1971   The Order of Things: An Archaeology of the Human Sciences.
            New York: Pantheon.
1972   The Archaeology of Knowledge. New York: Pantheon.

Fouraker, Lawrence E., and Sidney Siegel
1963   Bargaining and Group Decision Making. New York: McGraw-Hill.

Francis, Roy G., and Robert C. Stone
1956   Service and Procedure in Bureaucracy. Minneapolis: University of
            Minnesota Press.

Frankel, Charles
1969   High on Foggy Bottom. New York: Harper & Row.

Frankfort, Henri, H. A. Frankfort, John A. Wilson, and Thorkild Jacobsen
1949   Before Philosophy: The Intellectual Adventure of Ancient Man.
            Baltimore: Penguin.

Freeman, Donald M.
1969   "Interviewing Mexican-Americans." Social Science Quarterly 49
            (March):909-18.

Freeman, Douglas Southall
1935   Robert E. Lee. 4 vols. New York: Scribner's.

Freeman, J. Leiper
1955   The Political Process; Executive Bureau-Legislative Committee
            Relations. New York: Doubleday.
1965   The Political Process. Rev. ed. Garden City: Doubleday.

Freeman, Linton C., Warner J. Bloomberg, Jr., Stephen P. Koff,
    Morris H. Sunshine, and Thomas J. Fararo
1960   "Local community leadership." Paper no. 15. Syracuse: Univer-
            sity College.

Freire, Paulo
1972   The Pedagogy of the Oppressed. New York: Herder & Herder.

Freud, Sigmund, and William C. Bullitt
1967   Thomas Woodrow Wilson, Twenty-eighth President of the United

States: A Psychological Study. Boston: Houghton Mifflin. See also the reviews by Erik H. Erikson and Richard Hofstadter in the New York Review of Books 8 (2, February 9).

Frey, Frederick W., with Peter Stephenson and Katherine Archer Smith
1969   Survey Research on Comparative Social Change: A Bibliography. Cambridge: MIT Press.

Friedman, Milton
1953   Essays on Positive Economics. Chicago: University of Chicago Press.

Friedrich, Carl Joachim
1932   Responsible Bureaucracy. Cambridge: Harvard University Press.
1937   Constitutional Government and Politics. New York: Harper.
1947   "Political science in the United States in wartime." American Political Science Review 41 (October):978-89.
1950   Constitutional Government and Democracy. New York: Harper. A revised edition of Constitutional Government and Politics (1937).
1963   Man and His Government: An Empirical Theory of Politics. New York: McGraw-Hill.
1967   An Introduction to Political Theory: Twelve Lectures at Harvard. New York: Harper & Row.

Friedrichs, Robert
1970   A Sociology of Sociology. New York: Free Press.

Frohock, Fred M.
1967   The Nature of Political Inquiry. Homewood: Dorsey.
1974   "Notes on the concept of politics: Weber, Easton, Strauss." Journal of Politics 36 (May):379-408.

Froman, Lewis A., Jr.
1963   Congressmen and Their Constituencies. Chicago: Rand McNally.

Fruchter, Benjamin
1954   Introduction to Factor Analysis. Princeton: Van Nostrand.

Frye, Alton
1975   A Responsible Congress: The Politics of National Security. New York: McGraw-Hill.

Fuchs, Lawrence H.
1956   The Political Behavior of American Jews. New York: Free Press.

Fuller, J. F. C.
1961   The Conduct of War, 1789-1961. New Brunswick: Rutgers University Press.

Gallo, Philip S., Jr., and Charles G. McLintock
1965   "Cooperative and competitive behavior in mixed-motive games." Journal of Conflict Resolution 9 (March):68-78.

Galloway, George B.
1953   The Legislative Process in Congress. New York: Crowell.
1961   History of the House of Representatives. New York: Crowell.

Gallup, George, and Saul Forbes Rae
1940   The Pulse of Democracy: The Public-Opinion Poll and How It

Works. Reprint. Westport: Greenwood.

Galton, Francis
1885   "The measure of Fidget." Nature 32:174–175.

Galtung, Johan
1964   "A structural theory of aggression." Journal of Peace Research 1
           (2):95–119.
1967   International Repertory of Institutions Specializing in Research
           on Peace and Disarmament. New York: UNESCO.
1968   "A structural theory of integration." Journal of Peace Research 5
           (4):375–95.

Galtung, Johan, and Mari Holmboe Ruge
1965   "The structure of foreign news: The presentation of the Congo,
           Cuba and Cyprus crises in four Norwegian newspapers." Journal
           of Peace Research 1 (1):64–91.

Gamson, William A.
1966   "Game theory and administrative decision-making." Pp. 158–59
           in Charles Press and Alan Arian (eds.), Empathy and Ideology.•
           Chicago: Rand McNally.

Gans, Herbert
1962   The Urban Villagers. New York: Free Press.

Garceau, Oliver
1941   The Political Life of the American Medical Association. Cam-
           bridge: Harvard University Press.

Garfinkel, Harold
1967   Studies in Ethnomethodology. Englewood Cliffs: Prentice-Hall.

Garrison, Lloyd W. (ed.)
1968   American Politics and Elections: Select Abstracts of Periodical
           Literature, 1964–1968. Santa Barbara: American Bibliographical
           Center–Clio Press.

Garver, Richard A.
1961   "Polite propaganda: 'USSR and 'American Illustrated.'" Jour-
           nalism Quarterly 38 (Autumn):480–84.

Gaus, John M.
1947   Reflections on Public Administration. University: University of
           Alabama Press.

Gaus, John M., and W. Anderson
1945   Research in Public Administration. New York: Committee on
           Public Administration, Social Science Research Council.

Gaus, John M., Leonard D. White, and Marshall E. Dimock
1936   Frontiers of Public Administration. Chicago: University of
           Chicago Press.

Geer, Blanche
1967   "First days in the field." Pp. 372–98 in Phillip E. Hammond
           (ed.), Sociologists at Work. Garden City: Doubleday.

Geertz, Clifford
1964   "Ideology as a cultural system." Pp. 47–76 in David Apter (ed.),
           Ideology and Discontent. New York: Free Press.

Gelb, Joyce and Marian Lief Palley
    1975   Tradition and Change in American Party Politics. New York:
                Crowell.

Gellner, Ernest
    1964   Thought and Change. Chicago: University of Chicago Press.

George, Alexander L.
    1959a   Propaganda Analysis. Evanston: Row, Peterson.
    1959b   "Quantitative and qualitative approaches to content analysis."
                Pp. 7–32 in Ithiel de Sola Pool (ed.), Trends in Content Analysis.
                Urbana: University of Illinois Press.

George, Alexander L., and Juliette L. George
    1956   Woodrow Wilson and Colonel House: A Personality Study. New
                York: Day.

Gerbner, George, Ole Holsti, Klause Krippendorff, William J. Paisley, and
    Philip J. Stone (eds.)
    1969   Proceedings of the National Conference on Content Analysis.
                New York: Wiley.

Gerth, Hans H., and C. Wright Mills
    1946   From Max Weber: Essays in Sociology. New York: Oxford
                University Press.

Gibbs, Jack P.
    1967   "Identification of statements in theory construction." Sociology
                and Social Research 52 (October):72–87.

Gilbert, Claire W.
    1965   "Community power studies: Why the differences in findings?"
                Master's thesis, Northwestern University.
    1966   "Community power structure: A study in the sociology of
                knowledge." Doctoral dissertation, Northwestern University.
    1972   Community Power Structure: Propositional Inventory, Tests, and
                Theory. University of Florida Monographs, Social Science, no.
                45. Gainesville.

Gillespie, J. M., and G. W. Allport
    1955   Youth's Outlook on the Future. Garden City: Doubleday.

Gillespie, John V., and Betty Nesvold (eds.)
    1970   Cross-National Research. Beverly Hills: Sage.

Gillispie, Charles C.
    1960   The Edge of Objectivity. Princeton: Princeton University Press.

Gilpin, Robert
    1962   American Scientists and Nuclear Weapons Policy. Princeton:
                Princeton University Press.

Glaser, Barney G.
    1962   "Secondary analysis: A strategy for the use of knowledge for
                research elsewhere." Social Problems 10 (Summer):70–74.
    1963   "Retreading research materials: The use of secondary analysis by
                the independent researcher." American Behavioral Scientist 6
                (June):11–14.

1965   "The constant comparative method of qualitative analysis."
            Social Problems 12 (Spring):436-45.

Glaser, Barney G., and Anselm L. Strauss
1965   "Discovery of substantive theory: A basic strategy underlying
            qualitative research." American Behavioral Scientist 8 (Febru-
            ary):6.
1967   The Discovery of Grounded Theory. Chicago: Aldine.

Glaser, William A.
1966   "International mail surveys of informants." Human Organization
            25 (Spring):78-86.

Gleditsch, Nils Petter
1967   "Trends in world airline patterns." Journal of Peace Research 5
            (4):366-407.

Glock, Charles Y.
1955   "Some applications of the panel method to the study of change."
            Pp. 242-49 in Paul F. Lazarsfeld and Morris Rosenberg (eds.),
            The Language of Social Research. New York: Free Press.

Glock, Charles Y. (ed.)
1967   Survey Research in the Social Sciences. New York: Russell Sage.

Goffman, Erving
1959   The Presentation of Self in Everyday Life. Garden City: Double-
            day.

Gold, Raymond L.
1958   "Roles in sociological field operations." Social Forces 36
            (March):217-23.

Goldrich, Daniel
1966   Sons of the Establishment: Elite Youth in Panama and Costa
            Rica. Chicago: Rand McNally.

Golembiewski, Robert T.
1962   The Small Group: An Analysis of Research Concepts and Opera-
            tions. Chicago: University of Chicago Press.
1967   Organizing Men and Power. Chicago: Rand McNally.

Golembiewski, Robert T., William A. Welsh, and William J. Crotty
1969   A Methodological Primer for Political Scientists. Chicago: Rand
            McNally.

Gomberg, William
1955   A Trade Union Analysis of Time Study. Englewood Cliffs:
            Prentice-Hall.

Goode, William J., and Paul K. Hatt
1952   Methods in Social Research. New York: McGraw-Hill.

Goodenough, Ward H.
1944   "A technique for scale analysis." Educational and Psychological
            Measurement 4 (Fall):179-90.

Goodman, Leo
1959   "Some alternatives to ecological correlation." American Journal
            of Sociology 64 (May):610-25.

Goodman, Leo, and William H. Kruskal
  1954   "Measures of association for cross classifications." Journal of the
              American Statistical Association 26 (December):732-64.

Goodnow, Frank J.
  1900   Politics and Administration. New York: Macmillan.

Goodrich, Leland M.
  1953   "Korea: Collective measures against aggression." International
              Conciliation 494 (October):131-92.
  1959   United Nations. New York: Crowell.

Gorden, Raymond L.
  1969   Interviewing Strategy, Techniques, and Tactics. Homewood:
              Dorsey.

Gordon, David L. and Royden Dangerfield
  1947   The Hidden Weapon. New York: Harper.

Gore, William J., and James Dyson (eds.)
  1964   The Making of Decisions. New York: Free Press.

Gore, William J., and Leroy C. Hodapp
  1967   Change in the Small Community. New York: Friendship.

Gosnell, Harold F.
  1924   Boss Platt and His New York Machine. Chicago: University of
              Chicago Press.
  1927   Getting Out the Vote. Chicago: University of Chicago Press.
  1937   Machine Politics: Chicago Model. Chicago: University of Chicago
              Press.

Gottschalk, Louis R.
  1950   Understanding History: A Primer of Historical Method. New
              York: Knopf.

Gottschalk, Louis, Clyde Kluckhohn, and Robert Angell
  1945   The Use of Personal Documents in History, Anthropology, and
  1951   Sociology. New York: Social Science Research Council.

Gould, James A., and Vincent V. Thursby
  1969   Contemporary Political Thought. Issues in Scope, Value, and
              Direction. New York: Holt, Rinehart & Winston.

Gouldner, Alvin
  1950   Studies in Leadership. New York: Harper.
  1955   "Metaphysical pathos and the theory of bureaucracy." American
              Political Science Review 49 (June):496-507.
  1970   The Coming Crisis of Western Sociology. New York: Basic
              Books.

Graber, Doris A.
  1976   Verbal Behavior and Politics. Urbana: University of Illinois Press.

Graham, George J., and George W. Carey (eds.)
  1972   The Post-Behavioral Era: Perspectives on,Political Science. New
              York: McKay.

Graham, Hugh Davis, and Ted Robert Gurr
  1969   The History of Violence in America. New York: Bantam.

Graves, W. Brooke
1950   Public Administration in a Democratic Society. Lexington: Heath.
1964   American Intergovernmental Relations: Their Origins, Historical Development and Current Status. New York: Scribner's.

Gray, Wood, and Associates
1959   Historian's Handbook: A Key to the Study and Writing of History. Boston: Houghton Mifflin.
1964   Historian's Handbook. 2d ed. Boston: Houghton Mifflin.

Green, Bert F.
1954   "Attitude measurement." Pp. 335–69 in Gardner Lindzey (ed.), Handbook of Social Psychology. Reading: Addison-Wesley.

Green, H. P., and Alan Rosenthal
1963   Government of the Atom. Chicago: Atherton.

Green, Phillip
1966   Deadly Logic. Columbus: Ohio State University Press.

Green, Philip, and Sanford Levinson (eds.)
1969   Power and Community: Dissenting Essays in Political Science. New York: Pantheon.

Greenberg, G. D., J. Miller, L. B. Mohr, and B. C. Vladeck
1973   Case Study Aggregation and Policy Theory. Ann Arbor: Institute of Policy Studies, University of Michigan.

Greenstein, Fred I.
1965   Children and Politics. New Haven: Yale University Press.
1969   Personality and Politics. Chicago: Markham.

Greenstein, Fred I., and Michael Lerner, eds.
1971   A Source Book for the Study of Personality and Politics. Chicago: Markham.

Greenstein, Fred I., and Nelson W. Polsby, eds.
1975   Handbook of Political Science. 8 vols. Reading: Addison-Wesley.

Greer, Scott
1969   The Logic of Social Inquiry. Chicago: Aldine.

Gregor, A. James
1971   An Introduction to Meta Politics. New York: Free Press.

Gregory, Roy
1967   "The minister's line, part II." Public Administration 45 (Autumn):269–86.

Grinker, Roy (ed.)
1966   Toward a Unified Theory of Human Behavior. 2d ed. New York: Basic Books.

Grodins, Fred S.
1963   Control Theory and Biological Systems. New York: Columbia University Press.

Grodzins, Morton
1956   The Loyal and the Disloyal. Chicago: University of Chicago Press.

1966   The American System. Editied by Daniel J. Elazar. Chicago: Rand McNally.

Gross, Bertram M.
1953   The Legislative Struggle: A Study in Social Combat. New York: McGraw-Hill.
1964   The Managing of Organizations. New York: Free Press.

Gross, Llewellyn
1967   "A transactional interpretation of social problems." Pp. 315-31 in Llewellyn Gross (ed.), Sociological Theory: Inquiries and Paradigms. New York: Harper & Row.

Guetzkow, Harold
1956   Multiple Loyalties. Princeton: Center for Research on World Political Institutions.

Guetzkow, Harold-(ed.)
1962   Simulation in Social Science: Readings. Englewood Cliffs: Prentice-Hall.

Guetzkow, Harold, Chadwick Alger, Richard Brody, Robert Noel, and Richard Snyder
1963   Simulations in International Relations: Developments for Research and Teaching. Englewood Cliffs: Prentice-Hall.

Guetzkow, Harold, and Lloyd Jensen
1966   "Research activities on simulated international processes." Background 9 (4):261-74.

Guilford, Joy Paul
1936   Psychometric Methods. New York: McGraw-Hill.
1956   Fundamental Statistics in Psychology and Education. New York: McGraw-Hill.
1965   "The minimal phi coefficient and the maximal phi." Educational and Psychological Measurement 25 (Spring):3-8.

Gulick, Luther H.
1948   Administrative Reflections from World War II. University: University of Alabama Press.

Gulick, Luther H., and L. Urwick (eds.)
1937   Papers on the Science of Administration. New York: Institute of Public Administration, Columbia University.

Gullahorn, Jeanne E.
1967   Multivariate Approaches in Survey Data Processing: Comparisons of Factor, Cluster, and Guttman Analyses and of Multiple Regression and Canonical Correlation Methods. Multivariate Behavioral Research Monograph no. 67-1. Boulder: Society of Multivariate Experimental Psychology.

Gullahorn, John T., and Jeanne E. Gullahorn
1962   "Visiting Fulbright professors as agents of cross-cultural communication." Sociology and Sociological Research 46 (April):282-93.

Gulliksen, Harold
1950   Theory of Mental Tests. New York: Wiley.

Gulliksen, Harold, and Samuel Messick
1960 Psychological Scaling: Theory and Application. New York: Wiley.

Gunnell, John
1968a Political Philosophy and Time. Middletown: Wesleyan University Press.
1968b "Social science and political reality: The problem of explanation." Social Research 34 (Spring):159-201.
1968c "The idea of the conceptual framework: A philosophical critique." Paper prepared for the annual meeting of the American Political Science Association, Washington (September).

Gurwitsch, Aron
1966 Studies in Phenomenology and Psychology. Evanston: Northwestern University Press.

Gusfield, Joseph G.
1955 "Field work reciprocities in studying a social movement." Human Organization 14 (3):29-34.

Guttman, Louis
1941 "The quantification of a class of attributes: A theory and method of scale construction." Pp. 318-48 in Paul Horst, Paul Wallin, and Louis Guttman, The Prediction of Personal Adjustment. New York: Social Science Research Council.
1944 "A basis for scaling qualitative data." American Sociological Review 9 (February):139-50.
1947 "The Cornell technique for scale and intensity analysis." Educational and Psychological Measurement 7 (Summer):247-80.
1950 "The basis for scalogram analysis." Pp. 60-90 in Samuel A. Lazarsfeld, Shirley A. Star, and John A. Clausen (eds.), Measurement and Prediction. Princeton: Princeton University Press.

Haas, Ernst B.
1953a "The balance of power as a guide to policy making." Journal of Politics 15 (August):370-98.
1953b "The balance of power: Prescription, concept, or propaganda." World Politics 5 (July):442-77.
1958 The Uniting of Europe. Stanford: Stanford University Press.
1964 Beyond the Nation-State. Stanford: Stanford University Press.
1968 Collective Security and the Future International System. Denver: Social Science Foundation, University of Denver.

Haas, Michael
1965a "A functional approach to international organization." Journal of Politics 27 (August):498-517.
1965b "Societal approaches to the study of war." Journal of Peace Research 2 (4):307-23.
1967 "Types of asymmetry in social and political systems." General Systems Yearbook 12:69-79.
1968 "Social change and national aggressiveness, 1900-1960." Pp. 215-44 in J. David Singer (ed.), Quantitative International Politics: Insights and Evidence. New York: Free Press.

1969a   "Communication factors in decision making." Peace Research
             Society Papers 12:65–86.
1969b   "Toward the study of biopolitics: A cross-sectional analysis of
             mortality rates." Behavioral Science 14 (July):257–80.
1970a   "International relations theory." Pp. 444–76 in Michael Haas and
             Henry S. Kariel (eds.), Approaches to the Study of Political
             Science. San Francisco: Chandler.
1970b   "International subsystems: Stability and polarity." American
             Political Science Review 69 (March):98–123.
1973   International Systems: A Behavioral Approach. San Francisco:
             Chandler.
1974   International Conflict, Indianapolis: Bobbs–Merrill.

Haas, Michael, and Henry S. Kariel (eds.)
1970   Approaches to the Study of Political Science. San Francisco:
             Chandler.

Habermas, Jürgen
1971   Knowledge and Human Interests. Boston: Beacon.

Hacker, Andrew
1961   Political Theory: Philosophy, Ideology, Science. New York:
             Macmillan.

Haddow, Anna
1939   Political Science in American Colleges and Universities,
             1636–1900. New York: Appleton Century.

Hadwen, John G., and Johan Kaufmann
1960   How United Nations Decisions Are Made. Leiden: Sythoff.

Hagood, Margaret Jarman, and Daniel O. Price
1952   Statistics for Sociologists. New York: Holt.

Haider, Donald H.
1974   When Governments Come to Washington: Governors, Mayors,
             and Intergovernmental Lobbying. New York: Free Press.

Haire, Mason (ed.)
1959   Modern Organization Theory. New York: Wiley.

Hall, Edward T.
1959   The Silent Language. Garden City: Doubleday.

Hallowell, John H.
1954   The Moral Foundation of Democracy. Chicago: University of
             Chicago Press.

Halperin, Morton H., et al.
1974   Bureaucratic Politics and Foreign Policy. Washington: Brookings.

Halpern, Manfred
1964   "Toward further modernization of the study of new nations."
             World Politics 17 (October):157–81.

Hamblin, Robert L., and Associates
1974   A Mathematical Theory of Social Change. New York: Wiley.

Hamburg, Carl C.
1955   "Logic and foreign policy." Philosophy and Phenomenological
             Research 15 (June):493–99.

Hamburger, Joseph
1963   James Mill and the Art of Revolution. New Haven: Yale University Press.

Hamer, Philip M. (ed.)
1961   Guide to Archives and Manuscripts in the United States. New Haven: Yale University Press.

Hamilton, T.
1942   "Social optimism and pessimism in American Protestantism." Public Opinion Quarterly 6 (Summer):280-83.

Hammond, Paul
1963   "Super carriers and B-36 bombers." Pp. 465-567 in Harold Stein (ed.), American Civil-Military Decisions. Tuscaloosa: University of Alabama Press.

Hammond, Phillip E. (ed.)
1964   Sociologists at Work. New York: Basic Books.

Haner, Charles F., and Norman C. Meier
1951   "The adaptability of area probability sampling to public opinion measurement." Public Opinion Quarterly 15 (Summer):335-52.

Hanrieder, Wolfram F.
1966   "International organizations and international systems." Journal of Conflict Resolution 10 (September):297-313.

Hansen, A. H.
1966   The Process of Planning. New York: Oxford University Press.

Hansen, Morris H., and William N. Hurwitz
1951   "Modern methods in the sampling of human populations." American Journal of Public Health 41 (June):662-68.

Hansen, Morris H., William N. Hurwitz, and William G. Madow
1953   Sample Survey Methods and Theory. New York: Wiley.

Hanson, Norwood R.
1958   Patterns of Discovery. An Inquiry into the Conceptual Foundations of Science. Cambridge: At the University Press.
1961   Patterns of Discovery. Cambridge: At the University Press.
1963   The Concept of the Positron. Cambridge: At the University Press.

Hare, Richard Mervyn
1952   The Language of Morals. London: Oxford University Press, Clarendon Press.

Hargrove, Erwin C.
1966   Presidential Leadership: Personality and Political Style. New York: Macmillan.

Harkins, Peter B., Thomas L. Isenhour, and Peter C. Jurs
1973   Introduction to Computer Programming for the Social Sciences. Boston: Allyn & Bacon.

Harman, Harry H.
1967   Modern Factor Analysis. Chicago: University of Chicago Press.

Harrell, Bill
1967   "Symbols, perception, and meaning." Pp. 104-27 in Llewellyn

Gross (ed.), Sociological Theory: Inquiries and Paradigms. New York: Harper & Row.

Harrington, James
1972 The Commonwealth of Oceana. Reprint of 1656 ed. Washington: McGrath.

Harris, Louis, and Bert E. Swanson
1970 Black-Jewish Relations in New York City. New York: Praeger.

Hart, Clyde W., and Don Cahalan
1957 "The development of AAPOR." Public Opinion Quarterly 21 (Spring):165–73.

Hart, Herbert L. A.
1961 The Concept of Law. London: Oxford University Press, Clarendon Press.

Hart, Jim A.
1961 "The flow of international news into Ohio." Journalism Quarterly 38 (Autumn):541–43.

Hartnack, Justus
1965 Wittgenstein and Modern Philosophy. Garden City: Doubleday.

Hartz, Louis
1955 The Liberal Tradition in America. New York: Harcourt, Brace.

Hartz, Louis (ed.)
1964 The Founding of New Societies: Studies in the History of the United States, Latin America, South Africa, Canada, and Australia. New York: Harcourt Brace Jovanovich.

Harvard University Library
1969 Government. Widener Library Shelflist no. 22. Cambridge: Harvard University Press.

Hastings, Philip K.
1963 "The Roper Public Opinion Research Center: An international archive of social science survey data." American Behavioral Scientist 3 (November):9–11.
1964 "The Roper Public Opinion Research Center: An international archive of social science data." International Social Science Journal 16 (February):90–97.

Havard, William C. (ed.)
1972 The Changing Politics of the South. Baton Rouge: Louisiana State University Press.

Havelka, Jaroslav
1968 The Nature of the Creative Process in Art. The Hague: Martinus Nijhoff.

Hawkins, David
1967 The Language of Nature. Garden City: Doubleday.

Hawley, Amos
1963 "Community power and urban renewal success." American Journal of Sociology 68 (January):422–31.

Hawley, Willis D., and Frederick M. Wirt (eds.)
1968   The Search for Community Power. Englewood Cliffs: Prentice-
            Hall.
1974   The Search for Community Power. Rev. ed. Englewood Cliffs:
            Prentice-Hall.

Hayes, Louis D., and Ronald D. Hedlund (eds.)
1970   The Conduct of Political Inquiry: Behavioral Political Analysis.
            Englewood Cliffs: Prentice-Hall.

Hayward, Jack, and Michael Watson (eds.)
1975   Planning, Politics and Public Policy: The British, French and
            Italian Experience. New York: Cambridge University Press.

Hayworth, D.
1930   "An analysis of speeches in the presidential campaigns from
            1884-1920." Quarterly Journal of Speech 16 (February):35-42.

Head, Richard
1970   "The A-7 program." Doctoral dissertation, Syracuse University.

Heady, Ferrel
1966   Public Administration: A Comparative Perspective. Englewood
            Cliffs: Prentice-Hall.

Heady, Ferrel, and Sybil L. Stokes (eds.)
1960   Comparative Public Administration: A Selective Annotated Bibli-
            ography. 2d ed. Ann Arbor: Institute of Public Administration,
            University of Michigan.
1962   Papers in Comparative Public Administration. Ann Arbor: Insti-
            tute of Public Administration, University of Michigan.

Hedlund, Ronald D.
1971   "Participant observation in studying Congress: The Congressional
            Fellowship Program." Mimeographed. Washington: American
            Political Science Association.
1973a   "The Congressional Fellowship Program: Maximizing participant
            observation in studying politics." Pp. 179-200 in Thomas P.
            Murphy, Government Management Internships and Executive
            Development. Lexington: Heath.
1973b   "Reflections on political internships." P.S.: Newsletter of the
            American Political Science Association 6 (Winter):19-25.

Heilbroner, Robert
1965   Understanding the Macro-economics. Englewood Cliffs: Prentice-
            Hall.

Helmer, John
1974   Bringing the War Home: The American Soldier in Vietnam and
            After. New York: Free Press.

Hempel, Carl
1952   Fundamentals of Concept Formation in Empirical Science.
            Chicago: University of Chicago Press.
1965   Aspects of Scientific Explanation. New York: Free Press.
1966   The Philosophy of Science. Englewood Cliffs: Prentice-Hall.

Henderson, A. M., and Talcott Parsons (eds.)
    1947   The Theory of Economic and Social Organization. New York: Oxford University Press.

Henderson, Gordon G.
    1976   An Introduction to Political Parties. New York: Harper & Row.

Henderson, Keith M.
    1966   Emerging Synthesis in American Public Administration. New York: Asia Publishing House.

Hennessy, Bernard C.
    1970a   Political Internships: Theory, Practice, Evaluation. University Park: Pennsylvania State University Press.
    1970b   Public Opinion. 2d ed. Belmont: Wadsworth.
    1975   Public Opinion. 3d. ed. North Scituate: Duxbury.

Henry, Laurin L.
    1968   "The NASA-university memorandum of understanding." Mimeographed. Syracuse: Inter-University Case Program.

Henry, Nicholas
    1975   Public Administration and Public Affairs. Englewood Cliffs: Prentice-Hall.

Herbst, P. G.
    1970   Behavioural Worlds: The Study of Single Cases. London: Tavistock.

Hermann, Charles F.
    1969   Crises in Foreign Policy. Indianapolis: Bobbs–Merrill.

Hermann, Charles F. (ed.)
    1972   International Crises. New York: Free Press.

Hermann, Charles F., and Margaret G. Hermann
    1962   The Potential Uses of Historical Data for Validation Studies of the Inter-Nation Simulation: The Outbreak of World War I as an Illustration. China Lake: U.S. Naval Ordance Test Station.
    1967   "An attempt to simulate the outbreak of World War I." American Political Science Review 61 (June):400–15.

Herndon, James F., and Joseph Z. Bernd (eds.)
    1974   Mathematical Applications in Political Science 7. Charlottesville: University Press of Virginia.

Herring, E. Pendleton
    1929   Group Representation Before Congress. Baltimore: Johns Hopkins Press.
    1936   Public Administration and the Public Interest. New York: McGraw-Hill.
    1940   Presidential Leadership. New York: Farrar & Rinehart.

Hersey, John
    1951   "Profiles: Harry S. Truman: Mr. President." New Yorker, April 7, pp. 42–56; April 14, pp. 38–42.

Herz, John H.
    1959   International Politics in the Atomic Age. New York: Columbia University Press.

Hess, Robert D., and David Easton
1960   "The child's changing image of the president." Public Opinion Quarterly 24 (Winter):632-44.

Hess, Robert D., and Judith V. Torney
1967   The Development of Political Attitudes in Children. Chicago: Aldine.

Hewlett, Richard G., and Oscar E. Anderson, Jr.
1962   The New World, 1939/1946. University Park: Pennsylvania State University Press.

Heyns, Roger W., and Ronald Lippitt
1954   "Systematic observational techniques." Pp. 370-404 in Gardner Lindzey (ed.), Handbook of Social Psychology, vol. 1. Reading: Addison-Wesley.

Heyns, Roger W., and Alvin F. Zander
1953   "Observation of group behavior." Pp. 381-417 in Leon Festinger and Daniel Katz (eds.), Research Methods in the Behavioral Sciences. New York: Dryden.

Hilgard, Ernest R., and Stanley L. Payne
1944   "Those not at home: Riddle for pollsters." Public Opinion Quarterly 8 (Summer):254-61.

Hill, Norman L.
1931   International Administration. New York: McGraw-Hill.

Hill, Walter A., and Douglas Egan
1967   Readings in Organization Theory. Boston: Allyn & Bacon.

Hilsman, Roger
1956   Strategic Intelligence and National Decisions. New York: Free Press.
1967   To Move a Nation. Garden City: Doubleday.

Hinsley, Francis H.
1963   Power and the Pursuit of Peace: Theory and Practice in the History of Relations between States. Cambridge: At the University Press.

Hirschfield, Robert S., and Norman M. Adler
1973   "Internships in politics: The CUNY experience." P.S.: Newsletter of the American Political Science Association 6 (Winter):13-18.

Hirschman, Albert O.
1967   Development Projects Observed. Washington: Brookings.

Hiscocks, Richard
1974   The Security Council: A Study in Adolescence. New York: Free Press.

Hobbes, Thomas
1957   Leviathan. Oxford: Basil Blackwell.

Hochstein, Joseph R., and Dilman M. K. Smith
1948   "Area sampling or quota control? Three sampling experiments." Public Opinion Quarterly 12 (Spring):71-80.

Hofferbert, Richard I.
  1966   "The relation between public and policy and some structural and
              environmental variables in the American states." American Polit-
              ical Science Review 60 (March):73-82.
  1968   "Socioeconomic dimensions of the American states, 1890-1960."
              Midwest Journal of Political Science 12 (August):401-18.
  1974   The Study of Public Policy. Indianapolis: Bobbs-Merrill.
Hofferbert, Richard, and Ira Sharkansky
  1971   State and Urban Politics. Boston: Little, Brown.
Hoffmann, Fredrik
  1967   "The functions of economic sanctions." Journal of Peace Re-
              search 4 (2): 140-60.

Hoffmann, Stanley (ed.)
  1960   Contemporary Theory in International Relations. Englewood
              Cliffs: Prentice-Hall.
  1965   The State of War: Essays in the Theory and Practice of Interna-
              tional Politics. New York: Praeger.
Hofstadter, Richard
  1955   Social Darwinism in American Thought. Boston: Beacon.
Hogg, Quinton (Viscount Hailsham, Q.C.)
  1963   Science and Politics. London: Faber & Faber.
Hoijer, Harry
  1958   "The Sapir-Whorf Hypothesis." Pp. 92-105 in Harry Hoijer (ed.),
              Language in Culture. Chicago: University of Chicago Press.
Hollingshead, August B.
  1949   Elmtown's Youth. New York: Wiley.
Holsti, Kalevi J.
  1966   "Resolving international conflicts: A taxonomy of behavior and
              some figures on procedures." Journal of Conflict Resolution 10
              (September): 272-96.
  1970   "National role conceptions in the study of foreign policy."
              International Studies Quarterly 14 (September): 233-309.

Holsti, Ole R.
  1962a   "The belief system and national images: John Foster Dulles and
              the Soviet Union." Doctoral dissertation, Stanford University.
  1962b   "The belief system and national images: A case study." Journal
              of Conflict Resolution 6 (September): 244-52.
  1965   "The 1914 case." American Political Science Review 59 (June):
              365-78.
  1967   "Cognitive dynamics and images of the enemy." Pp. 25-96 in D.
              J. Finlay, O. R. Holsti, and R. R. Fagen, Enemies in Politics.
              Chicago: Rand McNally.
  1969   Content Analysis for the Social Sciences and the Humanities.
              Reading: Addison-Wesley.
  1972a   Crisis, Escalation, War. Montreal: McGill-Queen's University
              Press.

1972b   "Time, alternatives and communications: The 1914 and Cuban
             missile crises." Pp. 56-80 in Charles F. Hermann (ed.), Interna-
             tional Crises: Insights from Behavioral Research. New York: Free
             Press.

Holsti, Ole R., Richard A. Brody, and Robert C. North
1965   "Measuring affect and action in international reaction models:
             Empirical materials from the 1962 Cuban crisis." Peace Research
             Society Papers 2:170-90.

Holsti, Ole R., P. Terrence Hopmann, and John D. Sullivan.
1973   Unity and Disintegration in International Alliances: Comparative
             Studies. New York: Wiley.

Holsti, Ole R., and Robert C. North
1965   "History of human conflict." Pp. 155-71 in E. B. McNeil (ed.),
             Social Science and Human Conflict. Englewood Cliffs: Prentice-
             Hall.

Holsti, Ole R., Robert C. North, and Richard A. Brody
1968   "Perception and action in the 1914 crisis." Pp. 123-58 in J.
             David Singer (ed.), Quantitative International Politics. New
             York: Free Press.

Holsti, Ole R., and John D. Sullivan
1969   "National-international linkages: France and China as noncon-
             forming alliance members." Pp. 147-95 in James N. Rosenau
             (ed.), Linkage Politics. New York: Free Press.

Holt, Robert T.
1967   "A proposed structural-functional framework." Pp. 86-108 in
             James C. Charlesworth (ed.), Contemporary Political Analysis.
             New York: Free Press.

Holt, Robert T., and John E. Turner
1966   The Political Basis of Economic Development: An Exploration in
             Comparative Political Analysis. Princeton: Van Nostrand.

Holt, Robert T., and John E. Turner (eds.)
1970   The Methodology of Comparative Research. New York: Free
             Press.

Holton, Gerald
1967   "The thematic imagination in science." Pp. 88-108 in Gerald
             Holton (ed.), Science and Culture. Boston: Beacon.

Homans, George C.
1950   The Human Group. New York: Harcourt Brace Jovanovich.
1967   The Nature of Social Science. New York: Harcourt Brace Jovan-
             ovich.

Horkheimer, Max
1974   The Eclipse of Reason. New York: Seabury.

Horkheimer, Max, and Theodor W. Adorno (eds.)
1973   Aspects of Sociology. Boston: Beacon.

Horowitz, Irving Louis
1972   Foundations of Political Sociology. New York: Harper & Row.

Hotelling, Harold
1935   "Analysis of a complex of statistical variables into principal
            components." Journal of Educational Psychology 24 (Septem-
            ber): 417–41; (October): 498–520.
Hottois, James W.
1969   "Panel research in the study of social change." Paper prepared
            for the annual meeting of the American Political Science Associa-
            tion, New York (September).
Hovet, Thomas, Jr.
1960   Bloc Politics in the United Nations. Cambridge: Harvard Univer-
            sity Press.
Hovland, Carl I., and Associates
1957   The Order of Presentation in Persuasion. New Haven: Yale
            University Press.
Hovland, Carl I., I. L. Janis, and H. H. Kelley
1953   Communication and Persuasion. New Haven: Yale University
            Press.
Howe, George Frederick, and Associates (eds.)
1961   Guide to Historical Literature. New York: Macmillan.
Huckshorn, Robert J.
1976   Party Leadership in the States. Amherst: University of Massachu-
            setts Press.
Huitt, Ralph K.
1954   "The congressional committee: A case study." American Political
            Science Review 48 (June):340–65.
1961   "Democratic party leadership in the Senate." American Political
            Science Review 55 (June):333–44.
Huitt, Ralph K., and Robert L. Peabody
1969   Congress: Two Decades of Analysis. New York: Harper & Row.
Huizinga, Johan
1955   Homo Ludens. Boston: Beacon.
Humphreys, Laud
1970   "Tearoom trade: Impersonal sex in public places." Trans-Action
            7 (January):10–25.

Hunter, Floyd
1953   Community Power Structure. Chapel Hill: University of North
            Carolina Press.
1962   "Review of 'Who Governs? Democracy and Power in an Amer-
            ican City' by Robert A. Dahl." Administrative Science Quarterly
            6 (March): 517–19.
1963   Community Power Structure. Garden City: Doubleday.
Huntington, Samuel P.
1965   "Political development and political decay." World Politics 17
            (April):386–430.
1966   "Political modernization: America vs. Europe." World Politics 18
            (April):378–414.

1968 Political Order in Changing Societies. New Haven: Yale University Press.

1970 One-Party Systems. New York: Basic Books.

1971 "The change to change: Modernization, development, and politics." Comparative Politics 3 (April):283–323.

Huntington, Samuel P., and Clement H. Moore
1970 Authoritarian Politics in Modern Society: The Dynamics of Established One-Party Systems. New York: Basic Books.

Huntington, Samuel P., and Joan M. Nelson
1976 No Easy Choice: Political Participation in Developing Countries. Cambridge: Harvard University Press.

Husserl, Edmund
1931 Ideas. Translated by W. R. B. Gibson. New York: Macmillan.

1960 Cartesian Meditations. Translated by D. Cairns. The Hague: Martinus Nijhoff.

Huzar, Elias
1950 The Purse and the Sword. Ithaca: Cornell University Press.

Hyman, Herbert H.
1955 Survey Design and Analysis: Principles, Cases and Procedures. New York: Free Press.

1959 Political Socialization. New York: Free Press.

1962 "Samuel A. Stouffer and social research." Public Opinion Quarterly 26 (Fall):323–28.

1963 "Reflections on the relation between theory and research." Centennial Review 7 (Fall):431–53.

1972 Secondary Analysis of Sample Surveys: Principles, Procedures, and Potentialities. New York: Wiley.

Hyman, Herbert H., William J. Cobb, Jacob J. Feldman, Clyde W. Hart, and Charles Herbert Stember
1954 Interviewing in Social Research. Chicago: University of Chicago Press.

Hyman, Sidney
1972 Youth in Politics: Expectations and Realities. New York: Basic Books.

Hyneman, Charles S.
1938 "Tenure and turnover of legislative personnel." Annals of the American Academy of Political and Social Science 195 (January):21–31.

1940 "Who makes our laws?" Political Science Quarterly 55 (December):556–61.

1950 Bureaucracy in a Democracy. New York: Harper.

1959 The Study of Politics: The Present State of American Political Science. Urbana: University of Illinois Press.

1963 "Review of 'Systematic Politics: Elementa Politica et Sociologica' by George E. G. Catlin." American Political Science Review 57 (December):956–57.

Hyneman, Charles S., and Charles E. Gilbert
1968   Popular Government in American Foundations and Principles.
            Chicago: Atherton.

Iklé, Fred Charles
1964   How Nations Negotiate. New York: Harper.

Indian Institute of Public Administration
1972   Case Studies in Panchayati Raj. New Delhi.

Inkeles, Alex
1952   "Soviet reactions to the Voice of America." Public Opinion
            Quarterly 16 (Winter):612–17.
1969   "Participant citizenship in six developing countries." American
            Political Science Review 63 (December):1100–42.

Inkeles, Alex, and H. Geiger
1952   "Critical letters to the editors of the Soviet press: I, Areas and
            modes of complaint." American Sociological Review 17 (Decem-
            ber):694–703.
1953   "Critical letters to the editors of the Soviet press: II, Social
            characteristics and interrelations of critics and the criticized."
            American Sociological Review 18 (February):12–22.

Inkeles, Alex, and David Horton Smith
1974   Becoming Modern: Individual Change in Six Developing Coun-
            tries. Cambridge: Harvard University Press.

Institute for Social Research
n.d.   Newsletter. Ann Arbor: University of Michigan.
1965a   "List of publications, 1946–1960." Compiled by William Good-
            rich Jones. Ann Arbor: University of Michigan.
1965b   "List of publications, 1961–1965." Compiled by William Good-
            rich Jones. Ann Arbor: University of Michigan.
1968   A Report on Recent Activities. Ann Arbor: University of Mich-
            igan.
1969a   "List of publications, 1966–1968." Compiled by William Good-
            rich Jones. Ann Arbor: University of Michigan.
1969b   Interviewer's Manual. Ann Arbor: University of Michigan.
1971   A Quarter Century of Social Research. Ann Arbor: University of
            Michigan.

Intercollegiate Case Clearing House
1968   "Bibliography: Case and other materials for the teaching of
            business administration in developing countries, South and
            Southeast Asia." Boston.

International Press Institute
1953   The Flow of the News. Zurich.

Inter-University Consortium for Political and Social Research
1969a   "Annual report, 1968–69." Ann Arbor.
1969b   "Biennial report: 1966–1968." Ann Arbor.
1971   The 1964 Election Study. Ann Arbor.
1973a   "Annual report, 1971–1972" Ann Arbor.

1973b   A Guide to Resources and Services of the Inter-University Con-
             sortium for Political Research, 1972-1973. Ann Arbor.

Ippolito, Dennis, and Associates
1976   Public Opinion and Responsible Democracy. Englewood Cliffs:
             Prentice-Hall.

Irish, Marian D. (ed.)
1968   Political Science: Advance of the Discipline. Englewood Cliffs:
             Prentice-Hall.

Isaacs, Harold R.
1961   Emergent Americans. New York: Day.

Isaak, Alan C.
1969   Scope and Methods of Political Science: An Introduction to the
             Methodology of Political Inquiry. Homewood: Dorsey.

Jackson, Elmore
1952   Meeting of Minds. New York: McGraw-Hill.

Jackson, John E.
1974   Constituencies and Leaders in Congress: Their Effects on Senate
             Voting Behavior. Cambridge: Harvard University Press.

Jackson, M. W.
1972   "The application of method in the construction of political
             science theory." Canadian Journal of Political Science 5
             (3):402-17.

Jacob, Herbert
1965   Justice in America: Courts, Lawyers, and the Judicial Process.
             Boston: Little, Brown.
1971   "Problems of scale equivalency in measuring attitudes in Amer-
             ican subcultures." Social Science Quarterly 52 (June):61-75.

Jacob, Herbert, and Michael Lipsky
1968   "Outputs, structure and power: An assessment of changes in the
             study of state and local politics." Journal of Politics 30 (May):
             510-38.

Jacob, Herbert, and Kenneth N. Vines
1965   Politics in the American States: A Comparative Analysis. Boston:
             Little, Brown.
1971   Politics in the American States. 2d ed. Boston: Little, Brown.
1976   Politics in the American States. 3d ed. Boston: Little, Brown.

Jacob, Herbert, and Robert Weissberg
1970   Elementary Political Analysis. New York: McGraw-Hill.

Jacob, Philip E.
1942   "Atrocity propaganda." Pp. 211-59 in H. L. Childs and J. B.
             Whiton (eds.), Propaganda by Short Wave. Princeton: Princeton
             University Press.

Jacob, Philip E., and Associates
1971   Values and the Active Community: A Cross-National Study of
             the Influence of Local Leadership. New York: Free Press.

Jacobson, H. K., and E. Stein
  1966   Diplomats, Scientists, and Politicians. Ann Arbor: University of
              Michigan Press.

Jahoda, Marie, Morton Deutsch, and Stuart W. Cook
  1951   Research Methods in Social Relations. New York: Dryden.

James, Ralph C., and Estelle Dinerstein James
  1965   Hoffa and the Teamsters: A Study of Union Power. Princeton:
              Van Nostrand.

Jammer, Max
  1954   Concepts of Space. Cambridge: Harvard University Press.
  1957   Concepts of Force. Cambridge: Harvard University Press.

Janda, Kenneth
  1965   Data Processing: Applications to Political Research. Evanston:
              Northwestern University Press.
  1968   Information Retrieval: Applications to Political Science. India-
              napolis: Bobbs-Merrill.
  1969   Data Processing. 2d ed. Evanston: Northwestern University Press.

Janes, Robert William
  1958   "A technique for describing community structure through news-
              paper analysis." Social Forces 37 (December):102-9.
  1961   "A note on phases of the community role of the participant-
              observer." American Sociological Review 26 (June):446-50.

Janis, Irving L.
  1943   "Meaning and the study of symbolic behavior." Psychiatry 6
              (November):425-39.
  1949   "The problem of validating content analysis." Pp. 55-82 in H. D.
              Lasswell, N. Leites, and Associates, The Language of Politics:
              Studies in Quantitative Sematics. London: George Stewart.

Janis, Irving L., and Seymour Feshbach
  1953   "Effects of fear-arousing communications." Journal of Abnormal
              and Social Psychology 48 (January):78-92.

Janowitz, Morris
  1944   "The technique of propaganda for reaction: Gerald L. Smith's
              radio speeches." Public Opinion Quarterly 8 (Spring):84-93.
  1960   The Professional Soldier: A Social and Political Portrait. New
              York: Free Press.
  1964   The Military in the Political Development of New Nations.
              Chicago: University of Chicago Press.

Janowitz, Morris, Deil Wright, and William Delany
  1958   Public Administration and the Public: Perspectives toward Gov-
              ernment in a Metropolitan Community. Governmental Studies
              no. 36. Ann Arbor: Institute of Public Administration, Univer-
              sity of Michigan.

Jaquette, Jane S. (ed.)
  1974   Women in Politics. New York: Wiley.

Jaros, Dean, and Lawrence V. Grant
  1974   Political Behavior: Choices and Perspectives. New York: St.
              Martin's.

Jarvad, Ib Martin
1968   "Power versus equality." Pp. 297-314 in Proceedings of the
            International Peace Research Association Second Conference.
            Assen: Van Gorcum.

Jarvie, Ian C.
1969   The Revolution in Anthropology. Chicago: Regnery.

Jenkins, Peter
1970   The Battle of Downing Street. London: Charles Knight.

Jennings, M. Kent
1964   Community Influentials: The Elites of Atlanta. New York: Free
            Press.

Jennings, M. Kent, and Lawrence E. Fox
1968   "The conduct of socio-political research in schools: Strategies
            and problems of access." School Review 76 (December):428-44.

Jennings, M. Kent, and Richard G. Niemi
1974   The Political Character of Adolescence. Princeton: Princeton
            University Press.

Jensen, Lloyd
1965   "Military capabilities and bargaining behavior." Journal of Con-
            flict Resolution 9 (June):155-63.

Jewell, Malcolm E., and Samuel Patterson
1966   The Legislative Process in the United States. (2d ed., 1972.) New
            York: Random House.

Johnson, Chalmers
1964   An Instance of Treason: Ozaki Hotsumi and the Sorge Spy Ring.
            Stanford: Stanford University Press.
1966   Revolutionary Change. Boston: Little, Brown.

Johnson, John J.
1962   The Military in the Underdeveloped Areas. Princeton: Princeton
            University Press.

Jonas, Frank H. (ed.)
1961   Western Politics. Salt Lake City: University of Utah Press.

Jones, Charles O.
1964   Party and Policy Making: The House Republican Policy Commit-
            tee. New Brunswick: Rutgers University Press.

Jones, Ernest
1955   The Life and Work of Sigmund Freud. Vol. 2. New York: Basic
            Books.

Jones, H. Stuart
1923   "Administration." Pp. 112-39 in Cyril Bailey (ed.), The Legacy
            of Rome. London: Oxford University Press, Clarendon Press.

Jones, Stephen B.
1954   "The power inventory and national strategy." World Politics 6
            (July):421-52.

Jones, William T.
1965   The Sciences and the Humanities. Berkeley and Los Angeles:
            University of California Press.

Jouvenel, Bertrand de
1957   Sovereignty: An Inquiry into the Political Good. Cambridge: At
               the University Press.
1963   The Pure Theory of Politics. New Haven: Yale University Press.

Juergensmeyer, J.
1964   "The president, the foundations, and the people-to-people pro-
               gram." Mimeographed. Syracuse: Inter-University Case Program.

Jung, Hwa Yol (ed.)
1972   Existential Phenomenology and Political Theory. Chicago:
               Regnery.

Junker, Buford H.
1960   Field Work: An Introduction to the Social Sciences. Chicago:
               University of Chicago Press.

Kahn, Herman
1960   On Thermonuclear War. Princeton: Princeton University Press.

Kahn, Robert L., and Charles F. Cannell
1957   The Dynamics of Interviewing: Theory, Technique, and Cases.
               New York: Wiley.
1968   "Interviewing." Pp. 526-95 in Gardner Lindzey and Elliott
               Aronson (eds.), The Handbook of Social Psychology, vol. 2,
               Research Methods, 2d ed. Reading: Addison-Wesley.

Kahn, Robert L., and Floyd Mann
1952   "Developing research partnerships." Journal of Social Issues 8
               (3):4-10.

Kalleberg, Arthur
1969   "Concept formation in normative and empirical studies: Toward
               reconciliation in political theory." American Political Science
               Review 63 (March):26-39.

Kaplan, Abraham
1943   "Content analysis and the theory of signs." Philosophy of Sci-
               ence 10 (October):230-47.
1961   New World of Philosophy. New York: Random House.
1964   The Conduct of Inquiry: Methodology for Behavioral Science.
               San Francisco: Chandler.

Kaplan, Abraham, and J. M. Goldsen
1949   "The reliability of content analysis categories." Pp. 83-112 in
               H. D. Lasswell, N. Leites, and Associates, The Language of Poli-
               tics: Studies in Quantitative Sematics. London: George Stewart.

Kaplan, David
1957   "Personality and social structure." Pp. 87-121 in Joseph B.
               Gittler (ed.), Review of Sociology. New York: Wiley.

Kaplan, Morton A.
1957   System and Process in International Politics. New York: Wiley.
1967   "Systems theory." Pp. 150-63 in James C. Charlesworth (ed.),
               Contemporary Political Analysis. New York: Free Press.

Kaplan, Morton A., and Nicholas de B. Katzenbach
1961   The Political Foundations of International Law. New York:
               Wiley.

Kardiner, Abram, and Ralph Linton
1939   The Individual and His Society. New York: Columbia University
            Press.

Kariel, Henry S.
1961   The Decline of American Pluralism. Stanford: Stanford Univer-
            sity Press.
1967   "The political relevance of behavioral and existential psychol-
            ogy." American Political Science Review 61 (June):334-42.
1969   Open Systems. Itasca: Peacock.

Kariel, Henry S. (ed.)
1970   Frontiers of Democratic Theory. New York: Random House.

Karl, Barry
1974   Charles E. Merriam and the Study of Politics. Chicago: University
            of Chicago Press.

Katz, Elihu, and Paul F. Lazarsfeld
1955   Personal Influence. New York: Free Press.

Kaufman, Herbert
1960   The Forest Ranger. Baltimore: Johns Hopkins Press.
1964   "Organization theory and political theory." American Political
            Science Review 58 (March):5-14.

Kaufman, Herbert, with the collaboration of Michael Couzens
1973   Administrative Feedback: Monitoring Subordinates' Behavior.
            Washington: Brookings.

Kaufmann, Felix
1958   Methodology of the Social Sciences. New York: Humanities.

Kavenau, J. L.
1967   "Behavior of captive white-footed mice." Science 155 (March
            31):1623-39.

Kecskemeti, Paul
1958   Strategic Surrender: The Politics of Victory and Defeat. Stan-
            ford: Stanford University Press.

Kearns, Doris
1975   "The benevolent leader revisited: Children's images of political
            leaders in three democracies." American Political Science Review
            69 (December):1371-98.
1976   "Lyndon Johnson's political personality." Political Science Quar-
            terly 91 (Fall):385-409.

Keech, William R., and Donald R. Matthews
1976   The Party's Choice. Washington: Brookings.

Keech, William, and James W. Prothro
1968   "American government." Journal of Politics 30 (May):417-42.

Keefe, William J., and Morris S. Ogul
1964   The American Legislative Process: Congress and the States. 2d
            ed, 1968. Englewood Cliffs: Prentice-Hall.

Kelley, Stanley, Jr., Richard E. Ayers, and William G. Bowen
1967   "Registration and voting: Putting first things first." American
            Political Science Review 61 (June):359-79.

Kelman, Herbert C. (ed.)
  1965   International Behavior: A Social-Psychological Analysis. New
              York: Holt, Rinehart & Winston.

Kemeny, John G.
  1959   A Philosopher Looks at Science. Princeton: Van Nostrand.

Kemeny, John G., J. L. Snell, and G. L. Thompson
  1957   Introduction to Finite Mathematics. Englewood Cliffs: Prentice-
              Hall.

Kendall, Patricia L., and Paul F. Lazarsfeld
  1950   "Problems of survey analysis." Pp. 133-96 in Robert K. Merton
              and Paul F. Lazarsfeld (eds.), Continuities in Social Research:
              Studies in the Scope and Method of "The American Soldier."
              New York: Free Press.

Kerlinger, Frederick N.
  1964   Foundations of Behavioral Research: Educational and Psycholog-
              ical Inquiry. New York: Holt, Rinehart & Winston.

Kessel, John H.
  1968   The Goldwater Coalition: Republican Strategies in 1964. India-
              napolis: Bobbs-Merrill.
  1972   "Comment: The issues in issue voting." American Political
              Science Review 66 (June):459-65.
  1975   The Domestic Presidency: Decision-Making in the White House.
              North Scituate: Duxbury.

Key, V. O., Jr.
  1936   The Techniques of Political Graft in the United States. Chicago:
              University of Chicago Libraries.
  1942   Politics, Parties, and Pressure Groups. New York: Crowell.
  1943   "The veterans and the House of Representatives: A study of a
              pressure group and election mortality." Journal of Politics 5
              (February):27-40.
  1949   Southern Politics in the State and Nation. New York: Knopf.
  1955   "A theory of critical elections." Journal of Politics 17 (Febru-
              ary):3-18.
  1956   American State Politics: An Introduction. New York: Knopf.
  1959   "Secular realignment and the party system." Journal of Politics
              21 (May):198-210.
  1960a   Politics, Parties and Pressure Groups. 4th ed. New York: Crowell.
  1960b   "The politically relevant in surveys." Public Opinion Quarterly
              24 (Spring):54-61.
  1961   Public Opinion and American Democracy. New York: Knopf.
  1964   Politics, Parties and Pressure Groups. 5th ed. New York. Crowell.
  1966   The Responsible Electorate: Rationality in Presidential Voting.
              Cambridge: Harvard University Press.

Kilpatrick, Franklin P., Milton C. Cummings, Jr., and M. Kent Jennings
  1964a   The Image of the Federal Service. Washington: Brookings.
  1964b   Occupational Values and the Image of the Federal Service: A
              Source Book. Washington: Brookings.

Kingsbury, Susan M., Hornell Hart, and Associates
1937   Newspapers and the News. New York: Putnam.

Kirchheimer, Otto
1966   "The transformation of the western European party system." Pp.
            177–220 in Joseph LaPalombara and Myron Weiner (eds.), Polit-
            ical Parties and Political Development. Princeton: Princeton
            University Press.

Kirkpatrick, Samuel A.
1974   Quantitative Analysis of Political Data. Columbus: Merrill.

Kish, Leslie
1949   "A procedure for objective respondent selection within the
            household." Journal of the American Statistical Association 44
            (September):380–87.
1952   "A two-stage sample of a city." American Sociological Review 17
            (December):761–69.
1953   "Selection of the sample." Pp. 175–239 in Leon Festinger and
            Daniel Katz (eds.), Research Methods in the Behavioral Sciences.
            New York: Holt, Rinehart & Winston.
1957   "Confidence intervals for clustered samples." American Sociolog-
            ical Review 22 (April):154–65.
1965   Survey Sampling. New York: Wiley.
1967   "Sampling training for survey research." Mimeographed. Ann
            Arbor: Survey Research Center, University of Michigan.

Kish, Leslie, and Irene Hess
1965   "The Survey Research Center's national sample of dwellings."
            Mimeographed. Ann Arbor: Institute for Social Research.

Kisiel, Theodore
1973   "New philosophies of science in the U.S.A." Zeitschrift für
            allgemeine Wissenschaftstheorie 4(2).

Klapper, Joseph T.
1960   The Effects of Mass Communication. New York: Free Press.

Klaus, Georg
1964   Kybernetik und Gesellschaft. Berlin: VEB Deutscher.
1966   Kybernetik and Erkenntnis. Berlin: VEB Deutscher.

Klein, M. W., and N. Maccoby
1954   "Newspaper objectivity in the 1952 campaign." Journalism Quar-
            terly 31 (Summer):285–96.

Kleinberg, Benjamin W.
1973   American Society in the Postindustrial Age: Technocracy, Power,
            and the End of Ideology. Columbus: Merrill.

Klineberg, Otto
1950   Tensions Affecting International Understanding: A Survey of
            Research. New York: Social Science Research Council.
1964   The Human Dimension in International Relations. New York:
            Holt, Rinehart & Winston.

Klingberg, Frank L.
1966   "Predicting the termination of war: Battle casualties and popula-
              tion losses." Journal of Conflict Resolution 10 (June):129-71.

Kluckhohn, Florence
1940   "The participant-observer technique in small communities."
              American Journal of Sociology 46 (November):331-43.

Kluckhohn, Florence, and Fred L. Stodtbeck
1961   Variations in Value Orientation. New York: Harper & Row.

Knepprath, H. E.
1962   "The elements of persuasion in the nationally broadcast speeches
              of Eisenhower and Stevenson during the 1956 presidential cam-
              paign." Doctoral dissertation, University of Wisconsin.

Knight, Francis H.
1936   Ethics of Competition. New York: Harper.

Knorr, Klaus
1970   Military Power and Potential. Lexington: Heath.

Knorr, Klaus E., and Sidney Verba (eds.)
1958   The International System: Theoretical Essays. Princeton: Prince-
              ton University Press.

Kobre, Sidney
1953   "How Florida dailies handled the 1952 presidential campaign."
              Journalism Quarterly 30 (Spring):163-69.

Koestler, Arthur
1949   Insight and Outlook. New York: Macmillan.
1959   The Sleepwalkers. New York: Macmillan.
1964   The Act of Creation. New York: Macmillan.

Komarovsky, Mirra (ed.)
1957   Common Frontiers of the Social Sciences. New York: Free Press.

Korn, Francis
1973   Elementary Structures Reconsidered. Berkeley and Los Angeles:
              University of California Press.

Kornberg, Allan (ed.)
1973   Legislatures in Comparative Perspective. New York: McKay.

Kornhauser, Arthur, and Paul B. Sheatsley
1964   "Questionnaire construction and interview procedure." Pp.
              546-87 in Claire Selltiz, Marie Jahoda, Morton Deutsch, and
              Stuart W. Cook (eds.), Research Methods in Social Relations.
              New York: Holt, Rinehart & Winston.

Kornhauser, Arthur, Harold L. Sheppard, and Albert J. Mayer
1956   When Labor Votes: A Study of Auto Workers. New York:
              University Books.

Kornhauser, William
1959   The Politics of Mass Society. New York: Free Press.
1961   " 'Power elite' or 'veto groups'?" Pp. 252-67 in Seymour Martin
              Lipset and Leo Lowenthal (eds.), Culture and Social Character.
              New York: Free Press.

Kovenock, David M.
1964   "Communications and influence in congressional decision-
            making: Employing the communications audit technique in a
            U.S. House of Representatives subcommittee." Paper prepared
            for the annual meeting of the American Political Science Associa-
            tion, Chicago (September).
1967   "Communications and influence in the House of Representatives:
            Some preliminary statistical snapshots." Paper prepared for the
            annual meeting of the American Political Science Association,
            Chicago (September).

Kovenock, David M., and James W. Prothro
1973   Explaining the Vote: Presidential Choices in the Nation and the
            States. 3 parts. Chapel Hill: Institute for Research in Social
            Science, University of North Carolina.

Kracauer, Siegfried
1952   "The challenge of qualitative content analysis." Public Opinion
            Quarterly 16 (Winter):631-42.

Kramer, R. M.
1969   Participation of the Poor. Englewood Cliffs: Prentice-Hall.

Kress, Paul F.
1966   "Self, system and significance: Reflections on Professor Easton's
            political science." Ethics 77 (October):1-13.
1970   "On locating partitions: A note on George Devereux's contribu-
            tion to behavioral science." Paper prepared for the annual meet-
            ing of the American Political Science Association, Los Angeles
            (September).
1971   Social Science and the Idea of Process. Urbana: University of
            Illinois Press.
1974a   "On validating simulation: With special attention to simulation
            of international politics." International Interactions 1:40-50.
1974b   "On method in science: A reply to Jackson." Canadian Journal
            of Political Science 7 (March):143-48.

Kriesberg, Louis
1967   "Collective decision-making modes and international conflict."
            Paper prepared for the annual meeting of the American Sociolog-
            ical Association, San Francisco.
1968   Social Processes in International Relations. New York: Wiley.

Kriesberg, Martin
1946   "Soviet news in the 'New York Times'." Public Opinion Quar-
            terly 10 (Winter):540-64.

Krippendorff, Klaus
1966   "Content analysis: History and critical issues." Doctoral disserta-
            tion, University of Pennsylvania.

Kris, E., and N. Leites
1953   "Trends in twentieth-century propaganda." Pp. 278-88 in B.
            Berelson and M. Janowitz (eds.), Public Opinion and Communi-
            cation. New York: Free Press.

Kuhn, Alfred
 1963   The Study of Society: A Unified Approach. Homewood: Irwin
               and Dorsey.
Kuhn, Thomas
 1962   The Structure of Scientific Revolutions. Chicago: University of
               Chicago Press.
 1970   The Structure of Scientific Revolutions. 2d ed. Chicago: Univer-
               sity of Chicago Press.
Kuroda, Yasumasa
 1968   "Attitude structure of the public and its leaders in Reed Town,
               Japan." Paper prepared for the annual meeting of the American
               Political Science Association, Washington (September).
Ladd, Everett Carll, Jr.
 1970   American Political Parties: Social Change and Political Response.
               New York: Norton.
Ladd, Everett Carll, Jr., with Charles D. Hadley
 1975   Transformations of the American Party System. New York:
               Norton.
Lagos Matus, Gustavo
 1963   International Stratification and Underdeveloped Countries.
               Chapel Hill: University of North Carolina Press.
Lakatos, Emre, and Alan Musgrave (eds.)
 1970   Criticism and the Growth of Knowledge. Cambridge: At the
               University Press.
Lake, Dale G., Matthew B. Miles, and Ralph B. Early, Jr. (eds.)
 1973   Measuring Human Behavior. New York: Teachers College Press.
Lamb, Robert, Robert Gilmour, and Charles Gallo
 1974   Political Alienation. New York: St. Martin's.
 1973   "Weather modification: The politics of an emergent technology."
               Mimeographed. Syracuse: Inter-University Case Program.
Lambright, W. Henry
 1968   "Launching NASA's sustaining university program." Mimeo-
               graphed. Syracuse: Inter-University Case Program.
 1973   "Weather modification: The politics of an emergent technology."
               Mimeographed. Syracuse. Inter-University Case Program.
Landau, Martin
 1961   "On the use of metaphor in political science." Social Research 28
               (Autumn):331-53.
 1965   "Due process of inquiry." American Behavioral Scientist 9
               (October): 4-10.
 1972   Political Science and Political Theory. New York: Macmillan.
Lane, Robert E.
 1951   "Government regulation and the business mind." American
               Sociological Review 16 (April): 163-73.
 1952   Problems in American Government: An Introduction to Political
               Analysis. Englewood Cliffs: Prentice-Hall.

1959   Political Life: Why People Get Involved in Politics. New York: Free Press.

1962   Political Ideology: Why the American Common Man Believes What He Does. New York: Free Press.

1969   Political Thinking and Political Consciousness: The Private Life of the Political Mind. Chicago: Markham.

Langer, Susanne

1963   Philosophy in a New Key. Cambridge: Harvard University Press.

Langton, Kenneth P., and M. Kent Jennings

1968   "Political socialization and the high school civics curriculum in the United States." American Political Science Review 62 (September): 852–67.

LaPalombara, Joseph

1966   "Decline of ideology: A dissent and an interpretation." American Political Science Review 60 (March):5–16.

1968   "Macrotheories and microapplications in comparative politics: A widening chasm." Comparative Politics 1 (October):52–78.

1974   Politics within Nations. Englewood Cliffs: Prentice-Hall.

LaPalombara, Joseph (ed.)

1963   Bureaucracy and Political Development. Princeton: Princeton University Press.

LaPalombara, Joseph, and M. Weiner (eds.)

1966   Political Parties and Political Development. Princeton: Princeton University Press.

Laponce, J. A., and Paul Smoker (eds.)

1972   Experimentation and Simulation in Political Science. Toronto: University of Toronto Press.

Larson, Calvin J., and Philo C. Wasburn (eds.)

1969   Power, Participation and Ideology: Readings in the Sociology of American Political Life. New York: McKay.

Laslett, Peter

1956   Philosophy, Politics and Society. Oxford: Basil Blackwell.

Lasswell, Harold D.

1927   Propaganda Technique in the World War. New York: Knopf.

1930   Psychopathology and Politics. Chicago: University of Chicago Press.

1935a   "The participant observer: A study of administrative rules in action." Pp. 261–303 in Harold D. Lasswell, The Analysis of Political Behavior, 1966. Hamden: Shoe String, Archon. This article was published in the April 1935 issue of the Personnel Journal.

1935b   World Politics and Personal Insecurity. New York: McGraw-Hill.

1936   Politics: Who Gets What, When, How. New York: McGraw-Hill.

1941   "The world attention survey." Public Opinion Quarterly 5 (Fall):456–62.

1948   Power and Personality. New York: Norton.

1949   "Detection: Propaganda detection and the courts." Pp. 173-232 in H. D. Lasswell, N. Leites, and Associates (eds.), The Language of Politics: Studies in Quantitative Semantics. London: George Stewart.

1950   World Politics and Personal Insecurity. New York: Free Press.

1958   Politics: Who Gets What, When, How. Reprint. Cleveland: World.

1959   "Political constitution and character." Psychoanalysis and the Psychoanalytic Review 46 (Winter):3-18.

1960   Psychopathology and Politics. Rev. ed. New York: Viking.

1963   The Future of Political Science. Chicago: Atherton.

1969   "Must science serve public power?" Address to the American Psychological Association, Washington (August 31).

1970   "The emerging conception of the policy sciences." Policy Sciences 1 (Spring):3-14.

1971   A Pre-View of Policy Sciences. New York: American Elsevier.

Lasswell, Harold D., and Gabriel Almond
1948   "The participant observer: A study of administrative rules in action." Pp. 261-78 in Harold D. Lasswell (ed.), The Analysis of Political Behavior. New York: Oxford University Press.

Lasswell, Harold D., and Dorothy Blumenstock
1939   World Revolutionary Propaganda: A Chicago Study. New York: Knopf.

Lasswell, Harold D., and Abraham Kaplan
1950   Power and Society. New Haven: Yale University Press.

Lasswell, Harold D., Daniel Lerner, and Ithiel de Sola Pool
1952   The Comparative Study of Symbols. Stanford: Stanford University Press.

Lasswell, Harold D., Daniel Lerner, and C. Easton Rothwell
1952   The Comparative Study of Elites. Stanford. Stanford University Press.

Lasswell, Harold D., and Robert Rubenstein
1966   The Shaping and Sharing of Power in a Psychiatric Hospital. New Haven: Yale University Press.

Latham, Earl
1952   "The group basis of politics: Notes for a theory." American Political Science Review 46 (June):376-97.

Lawrence, Samuel A.
1962   "The battery additive controversy." Pp. 325-68 in Edwin A. Bock and Angus Campbell (eds.), Case Studies in American Government. Englewood Cliffs: Prentice-Hall.

Lazarsfeld, Paul F.
1948   "The use of panels in social research." Proceedings of the American Philosophical Society 92 (November):405-10.

Lazarsfeld, Paul F., Bernard Berelson, and Hazel Gaudet
1944   The People's Choice: How the Voter Makes Up His Mind in a Presidential Campaign. New York: Duell, Sloan & Pearce.

1948   The People's Choice. 2d ed. New York: Columbia University Press.

1968   The People's Choice. 3d ed. New York: Columbia University Press.

Lazarsfeld, Paul F., and Herbert Menzel
1961   "On the relation between individual and collective properties." Pp. 214-47 in Amitai Etzioni (ed.), Complex Organizations: A Sociological Reader. New York: Holt, Rinehart & Winston.

Lazarsfeld, Paul F., Ann K. Pasanella, and Morris Rosenberg (eds.)
1972   Continuities in the Language of Social Research. New York: Free Press.

Lazarsfeld, Paul F., and Morris Rosenberg (eds.)
1955   The Language of Social Research. A Reader in the Methodology of Social Research. New York: Free Press.

Lee, A. M.
1952   How to Understand Propaganda. New York: Rinehart.

Lee, A. M., and Elizabeth B. Lee (eds.)
1939   The Fine Art of Propaganda. New York: Harcourt, Brace.

Leege, David C., and Wayne L. Francis
1974   Political Research: Design, Measurement and Analysis. New York: Basic Books.

Lefcowitz, Myron J., and Robert M. O'Shea
1963   "A proposal to establish a national archives for social science survey data." American Behavioral Scientist 6 (March):27-31.

Leibenstein, Harvey
1960   Economic Theory and Organizational Analysis. New York: Harper.

Leighton, Alexander H.
1945   The Governing of Men. Princeton: Princeton University Press.

Leites, Nathan C.
1948   "Psycho-cultural hypotheses about political acts." World Politics 1 (October):102-19.

1949   "Interaction: The Third International on its change of policy." Pp. 298-333 in H. D. Lasswell, N. Leites, and Associates (eds.), Language of Politics: Studies in Quantitative Semantics. London: George Stewart.

1951   The Operational Code of the Politburo. New York: McGraw-Hill.

1959   On the Game of Politics in France. Stanford: Stanford University Press.

1969   The Rules of the Game in Paris. Chicago: University of Chicago Press.

Leites, Nathan C., and Ithiel de Sola Pool
1942   On Content Analysis. Library of Congress, Experimental Division for Study of War-Time Communications, Document 26. Washington.

1949   "Interaction: The response of communist propaganda to frustration." Pp. 334-81 in H. D. Lasswell, N. Leites, and Associates (eds.), The Language of Politics: Studies in Quantitative Semantics. London: George Stewart.

Lenski, Gerhard
1961   The Religious Factor: A Sociological Study of Religion's Impact on Politics, Economics, and Family Life. Garden City: Doubleday.

Lerner, Daniel
1958a   The Passing of Traditional Society. New York: Free Press.

Lerner, Daniel (ed.)
1958b   Evidence and Inference. New York: Free Press.

Lerner, Daniel, and Harold D. Lasswell (eds.)
1951   The Policy Sciences: Recent Developments in Scope and Methods. Stanford: Standford University Press.

Lester, Richard A.
1946   "Shortcomings of marginal analysis for wage-employment problems." American Economic Review 36 (March):63-82.
1947   "Marginalism, minimum wages, and labor markets." American Economic Review 37 (March):135-48.

Levenson, Bernard
1955   Panel Analysis Workbook. New York: Bureau of Applied Social Research, Columbia University.

Levi, Werner
1964   "On the causes of peace." Journal of Conflict Resolution 8 (March):23-25.

Levi, William
1962   Literature, Philosophy and the Imagination. Bloomington: University of Indiana Press.

Levinson, Ronald Bartlett
1953   In Defense of Plato. Cambridge: Harvard University Press.

Levison, Arnold
1966   "Knowledge and society." Inquiry 9(2):132-46.

Lévi-Strauss, Claude
1966   The Savage Mind. Chicago: University of Chicago Press.
1969   The Raw and the Cooked. New York: Harper & Row.

Levy, Marion J., Jr.
1952   The Structure of Society. Princeton: Princeton University Press.
1969   " 'Does it matter if he's naked?' bawled the child." Pp. 87-109 in Klaus Knorr and James N. Rosenau (eds.), Contending Approaches to International Politics. Princeton: Princeton University Press.

Lewin, H. S.
1947   "Hitler youth and the Boy Scouts of America: A comparison of aims." Human Relations 1 (2):206-27.

Lewin, Kurt
1951   Field Theory in Social Science: Selected Theoretical Papers. Edited by Dorwin Cartwright. New York: Harper.

Lewis, H. L.
1960   "The Cuban revolt story: AP, UPI and three papers." Journalism
            Quarterly 37 (Autumn):573-78, 646.
Lifton, Robert Jay
1961   Thought Reform and the Psychology of Totalism: A Study of
            Brainwashing in China. New York: Norton.
1968   Death in Life. New York: Random House.
Likert, Rensis
1932   "A technique for the measurement of attitudes." Archives of
            Psychology 22 (140, June).
1967   The Human Organization. New York: McGraw-Hill.
Lindblom, Charles
1965   The Intelligence of Democracy. New York: Free Press.
1968   The Policy-Making Process. Englewood Cliffs: Prentice-Hall.
Lindzey, Gardner (ed.)
1954   Handbook of Social Psychology. Vol. 1. Theory and Methods. Vol.
            2. Special Fields and Applications. Reading: Addison-Wesley.
Lindzey, Gardner, and Elliot Aronson (eds.)
1968   The Handbook of Social Psychology. 2d ed. 4 vols. Reading:
            Addison-Wesley.
Lingoes, James C.
1962   "A multiple scalogram analysis of selected issues of the 83rd U.S.
            Senate." American Psychologist 17 (June):295-422.
Lippman, Walter
1922   Public Opinion. New York: Macmillan.
1925   The Phantom Public. New York: Harcourt, Brace.
Lippman, Walter, and C. Merz
1920   "A test of the news." Special supp. New Republic 23 (August):
            1-42.
Lipset, Seymour Martin
1959   "Some social requisites of democracy: Economic development
            and political legitimacy." American Political Science Review 52
            (March):69-105.
1960   Political Man: The Social Bases of Politics. Garden City: Double-
            day.
1963   The First New Nation: The United States in Historical and
            Comparative Perspective. New York: Basic Books.
1966   "Some further comments on 'The End of Ideology.'" American
            Political Science Review 60 (March):17-18.
1968   "Ostrogorskii, Moisei Ia." Pp. 347-51 in David L. Sills (ed.),
            International Encyclopedia of the Social Sciences, vol. 11. New
            York: Macmillan and Free Press.
Lipset, Seymour Martin (ed.)
1969   Politics and the Social Sciences. New York: Oxford University
            Press.
Lipset, Seymour Martin, and Leo Lowenthal (eds.)
1961   Culture and Social Character: The Work of David Riesman Re-
            viewed. New York: Free Press.

Lipset, Seymour Martin, and Stein Rokkan (eds.)
1967   Party Systems and Voter Alignments: Cross-National Perspec-
              tives. New York: Free Press.

Lipset, Seymour Martin, Martin A. Trow, and James S. Coleman
1956   Union Democracy: The Internal Politics of the International
              Typographical Union. New York: Free Press.
1962   Union Democracy. Paperbound. Garden City: Doubleday.

Lipson, Leslie
1964   The Democratic Civilization. Oxford: Oxford University Press.

Liska, George
1960   The New Statecraft. Chicago: University of Chicago Press.
1962   Nations in Alliance: The Limits of Interdependence. Baltimore:
              Johns Hopkins Press.

Lockard, Duane
1959   New England State Politics. Princeton: Princeton University
              Press.
1963   Politics of State and Local Government. New York: Macmillan.
1972   Politics of State and Local Government. 2d ed. New York:
              Macmillan.

Logue, J., and E. A. Bock
1963   "The demotion of Deputy Chief Inspector Goldberg." Mimeo-
              graphed. Syracuse: Inter-University Case Program.

Lohman, Joseph D.
1937   "The participant observer in community studies." American
              Sociological Review 2 (December):890-97.

Long, Norton
1965   "Politicians for hire." Public Administration Review 25 (June):
              115-20.

Loomba, J. F.
1971   "Content analysis of India's image among US foreign policy
              decision-makers." Economic and Political Weekly 6 (December):
              2239-49.
1972   "The relationship of images and political affiliations to orienta-
              tions toward foreign aid for India." International Studies Quar-
              terly 16 (September):351-71.

Lorwin, Val R.
1968   "Historians and other social scientists: The comparative analysis
              of national-building in Western socieites." Pp. 102-17 in Stein
              Rokkan (ed.), Comparative Research across Cultures and Na-
              tions. Paris: Mouton.

Louch, A. R.
1966   Explanation and Human Action. Berkeley and Los Angeles:
              University of California Press.

Lowell, A. Lawrence
1896   Government and Parties in Continental Europe. 2 vols. Boston:
              Houghton Mifflin.
1908   The Government of England. 2 vols. New York. Macmillan.

Lowi, Theodore J.
1963   "Toward functionalism in political science: The case of innova-
           tion in party systems." American Political Science Review 57
           (September):570–83.
1964a   At the Pleasure of the Mayor. New York: Free Press.
1964b   "American government, 1933–1963: Fission and confusion in
           theory and research." American Political Science Review 58
           (September):589–99.
1964c   "American business, policy politics, case studies, and political
           theory." World Politics 16(July):677–93.
1969   The End of Liberalism: Ideology, Policy and the Crisis of Public
           Authority. New York: Norton.
1971   "Four systems of policy, politics, and choice." Mimeographed.
           Syracuse: Inter-University Case Program.

Lukács, Georg
1971   History and Class Consciousness. Cambridge: MIT Press.

Lundberg, George
1939   Foundations of Sociology. New York: Macmillan.

Lutzker, Daniel R.
1960   "Internationalism as a predictor of cooperative behavior." Jour-
           nal of Conflict Resolution 4 (December):426–30.

Lynd, Robert, and Helen Lynd
1929   Middletown: A Study in Contemporary Culture. New York:
           Harcourt, Brace.
1937   Middletown in Transition. New York: Harcourt, Brace.

Maccoby, Eleanor E., and Nathan Maccoby
1954   "The interview: A tool of social science." Pp. 449–87 in Gardner
           Lindzey (ed.). Handbook of Social Psychology, vol. 1. Reading:
           Addison-Wesley.

Machlup, Fritz
1946   "Marginal analysis and empirical research." American Economic
           Review 36 (September):519–54.
1947   "Rejoinder to an antimarginalist." American Economic Review
           37 (March):148–54.

MacIntyre, Alasdair
1969   "From Zutphen to Armageddon." New Statesman (January),
           p. 18.

Mack, Charles S. (comp.)
1961   "Bibliography of publications, 1941–1960." Chicago: The
           National Opinion Research Center, University of Chicago. This
           bibliography is frequently updated by NORC through supple-
           ments available from the NORC Library.

Mack, Mary Peter (ed.)
1969   A Bentham Reader. New York: Pegasus.

Mack, Raymond W., and Richard C. Snyder
1957   "Approaches to the study of conflict: Introduction by the
           editors." Journal of Conflict Resolution 1 (June):107–8.

Mackay, D. M.
1963   "Machines and societies." Pp. 153-67 in Gordon Wolstenholme
            (ed.), Man and His Future. Boston: Little, Brown. See also pp.
            168-87.

Mackie, Thomas T., and Richard Rose
1974   The International Almanac of Electoral History. New York: Free
            Press.

Mackenzie, R. T.
1955   British Political Parties. London: Heinemann.

Macmahon, Arthur W. (ed.)
1955   Federalism Mature and Emergent. New York: Columbia Univer-
            sity Press.

Macmahon, Arthur W., and John D. Millett
1939   Federal Administrators: A Biographical Approach to the Problem
            of Departmental Management. New York: Columbia University
            Press.

Macmahon, Arthur W., John D. Millet, and H. Ogden
1941   The Administration of Federal Work Relief. Chicago: Public
            Administration Service.

MacRae, Duncan, Jr.
1958   Dimensions of Congressional Voting: A Statistical Study of the
            House of Representatives in the Eighty-first Congress. Berkeley
            and Los Angeles: University of California Press.
1965   "A method for identifying issues and factions from legislative
            votes." American Political Science Review 59 (December):
            909-26.
1966   "Indices of pairwise agreement between justices or legislators."
            Midwest Journal of Political Science 10 (February):138-41.
1967   Parliament Parties and Society in France, 1946-1958. New
            York: St. Martin's.
1970   Issues and Parties in Legislative Voting: Methods of Statistical
            Analysis. New York: Harper & Row.

MacRae, Duncan, Jr., and James A. Meldrum
1960   "Critical elections in Illinois." American Political Science Review
            54 (September):669-83.

MacRae, Duncan, Jr., and Susan Borker Schwarz
1968   "Identifying congressional issues by multidemensional models."
            Midwest Journal of Political Science 12 (May):181-201.

Macridis, Roy C.
1955   The Study of Comparative Government. Garden City: Double-
            day.
1968   "Comparative politics and the study of government: The search
            for focus." Comparative Politics 1 (October):79-91.

Macridis, Roy C., and Robert E. Ward
1963   Modern Political Systems: Europe. Englewood Cliffs: Prentice-
            -Hall.

Macy, Jesse
    1904   Party Organization and Machinery. New York: Century.

Madge, John
    1953   The Tools of Social Science. London: Longmans, Green.
    1965   The Tools of Social Science. Paperbound. Garden City: Double-
                day.

Madron, Thomas W.
    1969   Small Group Methods and the Study of Politics. Evanston:
                Northwestern University Press.

Mahl, G. F.
    1959   "Exploring emotional states by content analysis." Pp. 89-130 in
                Ithiel de Sola Pool (ed.), Trends in Content Analysis. Urbana:
                University of Illinois Press.

Mair, Lucy
    1962   Primitive Government. Baltimore: Penguin.

Malinowski, Bronislaw
    1922   Argonauts of the Western Pacific. London: Routledge.
    1967   A Diary in the Strict Sense of the Term. New York: Harcourt
                Brace Jovanovich.

Mann, Dean E.
    1964   Federal Political Executives. Washington: Brookings.

Mann, Floyd C.
    1951   "Human relations skills in social research." Human Relations 4
                (November):341-54.

Mannheim, Karl
    1936   Ideology and Utopia. New York: Harcourt, Brace.

Mansfield, Harvey C.
    1951   "The uses of history." Public Administration Review 11 (Win-
                ter):51-57.

Maranell, Gary M. (ed.)
    1974   Scaling: A Sourcebook for Behavioral Scientists. Chicago:
                Aldine.

March, James G.
    1962   "Some recent substantive and methodological developments in
                the theory of organizational decision-making." Pp. 191-208 in
                Austin Ranney (ed.), Essays on the Behavioral Study of Politics.
                Urbana: University of Illinois Press.

March, James G., and Herbert Simon
    1958   Organizations. New York: Wiley.

Marcuse, Herbert
    1969   An Essay on Liberation. Boston: Beacon.

Margenau, Henry
    1950   The Nature of Physical Reality. New York: McGraw-Hill.

Margolis, Joseph
    1958   "Critical note: Difficulties in T. D. Weldon's 'Political Philos-
                ophy.'" American Political Science Review 52 (December):
                1113-17.

Margolis, Joseph (ed.)
1968   An Introduction to Philosophical Inquiry: Contemporary and Classical Sources. New York: Knopf.

Marini, Frank (ed.)
1971   Toward a New Administration: The Minnowbrook Perspective. San Francisco: Chandler.

Markham, James W.
1961   "Foreign news in the United States and South American Press." Public Opinion Quarterly 25 (Summer):249-62.

Markham, James W., and G. H. Stempel III
1957   "Analysis of techniques in measuring press performance." Journalism Quarterly 34 (Spring):187-90.

Markowitz, Norman
1973   The Rise and Fall of the People's Century: Henry Agard Wallace and American Liberalism, 1941-1948. New York: Free Press.

Marschak, Jacob, and Leonid Hurwicz
1946   Games and Economic Behavior. Chicago: Cowles Commission for Research in Economics.

Martin, John Bartlow
1948   "The blast in Centralia no. 5." Harper's 196 (March):193-220.

Martin, Roscoe C., Frank Munger, and Associates
1961   Decisions in Syracuse. Bloomington: Indiana University Press.

Martindale, Don
1959   "Sociological theory and the ideal type." Pp. 57-91 in Llewellyn Gross (ed.), Symposium on Sociological Theory. Evanston: Row, Peterson.

Martindale, Don (ed.)
1965   Functionalism in the Social Sciences. Philadelphia: American Academy of Political and Social Science.

Maruyama, Masao
1965   "Patterns of individuation and the case of Japan: A conceptual scheme." Pp. 489-531 in Marius B. Jansen (ed.), Changing Japanese Attitudes toward Modernization. Princeton: Princeton University Press.

Marvick, Dwaine
1954   Career Perspectives in a Bureaucratic Setting. Ann Arbor: Institute of Public Administration, University of Michigan.

Marx, Fritz Morstein (ed.)
1940   Public Management in the New Democracy. New York: Harper.

Maslow, Abraham H.
1943   "A theory of human motivation." Psychological Review 50 (July):370-96.
1954   Motivation and Personality. New York: Harper.
1959   New Knowledge in Human Values. New York: Harper.
1970   Motivation and Personality. 2d ed. New York: Harper.

Maslow, Abraham H. (ed.)
1962   Toward a Psychology of Being. Princeton: Van Nostrand.

1968   Toward a Psychology of Being. 2d ed. Princeton: Van Nostrand.
Mason, Alpheus T.
1946   Brandeis: A Free Man's LIfe. New York: Viking.
1956   Harlan Fiske Stone: Pillar of the Law. New York: Viking.
Massing, Paul W.
1963   "The image of the Voice of America as drawn in Soviet media."
            Pp. 308-14 in Matilda W. Riley (ed.), Sociological Research: A
            Case Approach. New York: Harcourt Brace Jovanovich.

Masters, Roger D.
1964   "World politics as a primitive political system." World Politics 16
            (July):595-615.
Masters, William, and Virginia Johnson
1966   Human Sexual Response. Boston: Little, Brown.
Mathiason, John R., and John D. Powell
1972   "Participation and efficacy: Aspects of peasant involvement in
            political mobilization." Comparative Politics 4 (April):303-31.

Matson, Floyd
1964   The Broken Image. New York: Braziller.

Matthews, B. C.
1910   "A study of a New York daily." Independent 68 (January
            13):82-86.
Matthews, Donald R.
1960   U.S. Senators and Their World. Chapel Hill: University of North
            Carolina Press.
Matthews, Donald R. (ed.)
1973   Perspectives on Presidential Selection. Washington: Brookings.
Matthews, Donald R., and James W. Prothro
1966   Negroes and the New Southern Politics. New York: Harcourt
            Brace Jovanovich.
Matthews, Donald R., and James A. Stimson
1975   Yeas and Nays: Normal Decision-Making in the U.S. House of
            Representatives. New York: Wiley.

Mayer, Charles S.
1964   Interviewing Costs in Survey Research. Ann Arbor: University of
            Michigan Press.

Mayhew, David R.
1974   Congress: The Electoral Connection. New Haven: Yale University
            Press.

Mayo, Elton
1945   The Social Problems of an Industrial Civilization. Boston: Grad-
            uate School of Business Administration, Harvard University.

Mazlish, Bruce (ed.)
1963   Psychoanalysis and History. Englewood Cliffs: Prentice-Hall.
Mazmanian, Daniel A.
1974   Third Parties in Presidential Elections. Washington: Brookings.

McCall, George J., and J. L. Simmons
    1969   Participant Observation: A Text and Reader. Reading: Addison-
                Wesley.

McCarthy, Philip J.
    1951   "Sampling: Elementary principles." New York State School of
                Industrial and Labor Relations, Cornell University, Bulletin no.
                15. Ithaca.

McClelland, David C.
    1958   "The use of measures of human motivation in the study of
                society." Pp. 518–52 in J. W. Atkinson (ed.), Motives in Fantasy,
                Action and Society. Princeton: Van Nostrand.
    1961   The Achieving Society. Princeton: Van Nostrand.

McClelland, David C., and G. A. Friedman
    1952   "A cross-cultural study of the relationship between childrearing
                practices and achievement motivation appearing in folk tales."
                Pp. 243–49 in G. E. Swanson, T. M. Newcomb, and E. L. Hartley
                (eds.), Readings in Social Psychology, 2d ed. New York: Holt.

McCloskey, Robert G.
    1964   American Conservatism in the Age of Enterprise, 1865–1910.
                New York: Harper & Row.
    1968   "Bryce, James." Pp. 159–61 in David L. Sills (ed.), International
                Encyclopedia of the Social Sciences, vol. 2. New York: Macmil-
                lan and Free Press.

McClosky, Herbert
    1958   "Conservatism and personality." American Political Science
                Review 52 (March):27–45.
    1964   "Consensus and ideology in American politics." American Polit-
                ical Science Review 57 (June):361–82.
    1967   "Personality and attitude correlates of foreign policy orienta-
                tion." Pp. 51–109 in James N. Rosenau (ed.), Domestic Sources
                of Foreign Policy. New York: Free Press.

McConnell, Grant
    1960   The Steel Seizure of 1952. Indianapolis: Bobbs-Merrill.

McCormick, Thomas C., and Roy G. Francis
    1958   Methods of Research in the Behavioral Sciences. New York:
                Harper.

McCoy, Charles A., and John Playford (eds.),
    1967   Apolitical Politics: A Critique of Behavioralism. New York:
                Crowell.

McCulloch, Warren S.
    1965   Embodiments of Mind. Cambridge: MIT Press.

McDiarmid, John
    1937   "Presidential inaugural addresses: A Study of verbal symbols."
                Public Opinion Quarterly 1 (July):79–82.

McDonald, Neil A., and James N. Rosenau
    1968   "Political theory as academic field and intellectual activity."
                Journal of Politics 30 (May):311–44.

McDougal, Myres S., and Associates
1960   Studies in World Public Order. New Haven: Yale University Press.

McEvoy, J., R. Schmuck, and M. Chesler
1966   "Letters from the right: Content-analysis of a letter-writing
            campaign." Mimeographed. Ann Arbor: Institute for Social
            Research, University of Michigan.

McGaw, Dickinson, and George Watson
1976   Political and Social Inquiry. New York: Wiley.

McGranahan, D. V., and I. Wayne
1948   "German and American traits reflected in popular drama."
            Human Relations 1 (November):429–55.

McGregor, Douglas
1935   "Scientific measurement and psychology." Psychological Review
            42 (May):246–66.

McIlwain, Charles H.
1932   The Growth of Political Thought in the West. New York: Mac-
            millan.

McKean, Dayton D.
1938   Pressures on the Legislature of New Jersey. New York: Columbia
            University Press.

McKeon, Richard (ed.)
1941   The Basic Works of Aristotle. New York: Oxford University
            Press.

McLuhan, Marshall
1962   The Gutenberg Galaxy. Toronto: University of Toronto Press.

McMillan, Claude, and R. F. Gonzales
1965   Systems Analysis: A Computer Approach to Decision Models.
            Homewood: Irwin.

McPhee, William N., and William A. Glaser
1962   Public Opinion and Congressional Elections. New York: Free
            Press.

McPherson, W.
1964   "Lobbying and communication processes." Paper prepared for
            the annual meeting of the American Political Science Associa-
            tion, Chicago (September).

Mead, George H.
1934   Mind, Self, and Society. Edited by Charles W. Morris. Chicago:
            University of Chicago Press.

Mead, Margaret
1964   Continuities in Cultural Evolution. New Haven: Yale University
            Press.

Meadows, Paul
1957   "Models, systems, and science." American Sociological Review
            22 (February):3–9.
1967   "The metaphors of order: Toward a taxonomy of organization
            theory." Pp. 77–103 in Llewellyn Gross (ed.), Sociological
            Theory: Inquiries and Paradigms. New York: Harper & Row.

Meehan, Eugene
　　1965　　　The Theory and Method of Political Analysis. Homewood:
　　　　　　　Dorsey.
　　1967　　　Contemporary Political Thought. Homewood: Dorsey.
　　1968　　　Explanation in Social Science. A System Paradigm. Homewood:
　　　　　　　Dorsey.
　　1969　　　Value Judgment and Social Science. Homewood: Dorsey.

Meeker, Robert J., Gerald H. Shure, and Williams H. Moore, Jr.
　　1964　　　"Real-time computer studies of bargaining behavior: The effects
　　　　　　　of threat upon bargaining." American Federation of Information
　　　　　　　Processing Societies Conference Proceedings 25:115-23.

Mehl, Lucien
　　1957　　　"La cybernétique et l'administration." Revue Administrative
　　　　　　　58:410-19.

Meisel, James H.
　　1958　　　The Myth of the Ruling Class: Gaetano Mosca and the Elite. Ann
　　　　　　　Arbor: University of Michigan Press.
　　1966　　　Counter-Revolution: How Revolutions Die. Chicago: Atherton.

Melanson, Phillip H.
　　1975　　　Political Science and Political Knowledge. Washington: Public
　　　　　　　Affairs.

Melnik, Constantin, and N. Leites
　　1958　　　The House without Windows. Evanston: Row, Peterson.

Mendelsohn, Harold, and Irving Crespi
　　1970　　　Polls, Television and the New Politics. San Francisco: Chandler.

Mendenhall, T. C.
　　1887　　　"The characteristic curves of composition." Science 9 (March
　　　　　　　11):237-46.

Mendlovitz, Saul H. (ed.)
　　1974　　　On the Creation of a Just World Order: Preferred Worlds for the
　　　　　　　1990s. New York: Free Press.

Menon, V. P. N.
　　1957　　　The Transfer of Power in India. Princeton: Princeton University
　　　　　　　Press.

Menzel, Herbert
　　1953　　　"A new coefficient for scalogram analysis." Public Opinion Quar-
　　　　　　　terly 17 (Summer):268-80.

Merleau-Ponty, Maurice
　　1964a　　The Primacy of Perception. Evanston: Northwestern University
　　　　　　　Press.
　　1964b　　Signs. Translated by R. C. McLeary. Evanston: Northwestern
　　　　　　　University Press.

Merriam, Charles E.
　　1920　　　American Political Ideas. New York: Macmillan.
　　1921　　　"The present state of the study of politics." American Political
　　　　　　　Science Review 15 (May):173-85.
　　1925　　　New Aspects of Politics. Chicago: University of Chicago Press.

Merriam, Charles E., and Harold F. Gosnell
1924   Non-voting: Causes and Methods of Control. Chicago: University
            of Chicago Press.
1949   The American Party System. 4th ed. New York: Macmillan. The
            first edition (1922) was by Merriam alone.

Merrill, J. C.
1962   "The image of the United States in ten Mexican dailies." Journal-
            ism Quarterly 39 (Spring):203-9.
1965   "How 'Time' stereotyped three U.S. Presidents." Journalism
            Quarterly 42 (Autumn):563-70.

Merritt, Richard L.
1966   Symbols of American Community, 1735-1775. New Haven:
            Yale University Press.
1967   "European public opinion and American policy: The USIA sur-
            veys." Social Science Information 4 (August):143-60.

Merritt, Richard L., and Donald J. Puchala (eds.)
1968   Western European Perspectives on International Affairs. New
            York: Praeger.

Merritt, Richard L., and Gloria J. Pyszka
1969   The Student Political Scientist's Handbook. Cambridge: Schenk-
            man.

Merritt, Richard L., and Stein Rokkan (eds.)
1966   Comparing Nations: The Use of Quantitative Data in Cross-
            National Research. New Haven: Yale University Press.

Merton, Robert King
1940   "Bureaucratic structure and personality." Social Forces 18
            (May):561-68.
1946   Mass Persuasion: The Social Psychology of a War Bond Drive.
            New York: Harper.
1957   Social Theory and Social Structure. 2d ed. New York: Free Press.

Merton, Robert King, and Bernard Barber
1963   "Sorokin's formulations in the sociology of science." Pp. 332-68
            in Philip J. Allen (ed.), Pitrim A. Sorokin in Review. Durham:
            Duke University Press.

Merton, Robert K., Ailsa Gray, Barbara Hockey, and H. H. Selvin (eds.)
1952   Reader in Bureaucracy. New York: Free Press.

Meszaros, Istvan
1970   Marx's Concept of Alienation. London: Merlin.

Metcalf, Henry C., and Lyndall Urwick (eds.)
1942   Dynamic Administration: The Collected Papers of Mary Parker
            Follett. New York: Harper.

Meyer, Paul
1957   Administrative Organization: A Comparative Study of the Organ-
            ization of Public Administration. London: Stevens.

Meyerson, Martin, and Edward C. Banfield
1955   Politics, Planning, and the Public Interest. New York: Free Press.

Michels, Robert
1962   Political Parties: A Sociological Study of the Oligarchical Ten-
            dencies of Modern Democracy. 1915. Translated by Eden and
            Cedar Paul, with an introduction by Seymour Martin Lipset. New
            York: Crowell-Collier.

Mickiewicz, Ellen
1973   Handbook of Soviet Social Science Data. New York: Free Press.

Milbrath, Lester W.
1963   The Washington Lobbyists. Chicago: Rand McNally.
1965   Political Participation: How and Why Do People Get Involved in
            Politics? Chicago: Rand McNally.

Mill, John Stuart
1950   Utilitarianism, Liberty, and Representative Government. With an
            introduction by A. D. Lindsay. New York: Dutton.

Miller, Arthur H., and Warren E. Miller
1976   "Ideology in the 1972 election: Myth or reality—A rejoinder."
            American Political Science Review 70 (September):832-49.

Miller, Arthur H., Warren E. Miller, Alden S. Raine, and Thad A. Brown
1976   "A majority party in disarray: Policy polarization in the 1972
            election." American Political Science Review 70 (September):
            753-78.

Miller, Delbert C. (ed.)
1964   Handbook of Research Design and Social Measurement. New
            York: McKay.
1970a   Handbook of Research Design and Social Measurement. 2d ed.
            New York: McKay.
1970b   International Community Power Structures. Bloomington:
            Indiana University Press.

Miller, Eugene
1972   "Positivism, historicism, and political inquiry." American Polit-
            ical Science Review 66 (September):786-87. See also pp.
            818-73.

Miller, George A.
1951   Language and Communication. New York: McGraw-Hill.

Miller, George A., Eugene Galanter, and Karl H. Pribram
1960   Plans and the Structure of Behavior. New York: Holt.

Miller, James G.
1956   "Toward a general theory for the behavioral sciences." Pp. 29-65
            in Leonard D. White (ed.), The State of the Social Sciences.
            Chicago: University of Chicago Press.
1965   "Living systems: Basic concepts." Behavorial Science 10 (July):
            193-237.

Miller, R. W.
1967   "An analysis of changes in Chinese descriptions of the Soviet
            Union using the general inquirer content analysis system."
            Mimeographed. St. Louis: Washington University.

Miller. S. M.
1952   "The participant observer and 'over-rapport.'" American Socio-
            logical Review 17 (February):97–99.

Miller, Warren E.
1963   "The Inter-University Consortium for Political Research." Amer-
            ican Behavioral Scientist 7 (November):11–12.
1965   "Inter-University Consortium for Political Research: Current
            holdings." Social Science Information 4 (September):77–84.

Miller, Warren E., and Philip E. Converse
1964   "The Inter-University Consortium for Political Research." Inter-
            national Social Science Journal 16 (1):70–76.

Miller, Warren E., and Teresa E. Levitin
1976   Leadership and Change: The New Politics and the American
            Electorate. Cambridge: Winthrop.

Millett, John D.
1959   Government and Public Service. New York: McGraw-Hill.

Mills, C. Wright
1956   The Power Elite. New York: Oxford University Press.
1959   The Sociological Imagination. New York: Grove.

Mills, Theodore M.
1967   The Sociology of Small Groups. Englewood Cliffs: Prentice-Hall.

Minar, David W.
1966   Educational Decision-Making in Suburban Communities. U.S.
            Office of Education Cooperative Research Project no. 2240.
            Evanston: Northwestern University Press.

Mitchell, Joyce M., and William C. Mitchell
1969   Political Analysis and Public Policy. Chicago: Rand McNally.

Mitchell, Robert E.
1964   "The Survey Research Center, University of California, Berke-
            ley." International Social Science Journal 16 (1):86–89.
1967   "The use of content analysis for exploratory studies." Public
            Opinion Quarterly 31 (Summer):230–41.
1968   "Information services in information storage and retrieval." Pp.
            304–14 in David L. Sills (ed.), International Encyclopedia of the
            Social Sciences, vol. 7. New York: Macmillan and Free Press.

Mitchell, William C.
1961   "Politics as the allocation of values: A critique." Ethics 71
            (January):79–89.
1962   The American Polity. New York: Free Press.
1967a   Sociological Analysis and Politics. Englewood Cliffs: Prentice-
            Hall.
1967b   "The shape of political theory to come: From political sociology
            to political economy." American Behavioral Scientist 11
            (November-December):8–37.

Modelski, George
1961   "Agraria and industria: Two models of the international system."
            World Politics 14 (October):118–43.

1962   "Comparative international systems." World Politics 14 (June): 662–74.

Monroe, John, and A. L. Finkner
1959   Handbook of Area Sampling. Philadelphia: Chilton.

Montgomery, John D.
1962   Foreign Aid in International Politics. Englewood Cliffs: Prentice-Hall.

Montgomery, John D., and William J. Siffin (eds.)
1966   Approaches to Development: Politics, Administration and Change. New York: McGraw-Hill.

Moon, Parker Thomas
1926   Imperialism and World Politics. New York: Macmillan.

Moore, Barrington, Jr.
1958   Political Power and Social Theory. Cambridge: Harvard University Press.
1966   Social Origins of Dictatorship and Democracy. Boston: Beacon.

Moore, Wilbert E.
1966   "Global sociology: The world as a singular system." American Journal of Sociology 71 (March):475–82.

Morgenstern, Joseph
1969   "The uses of power." Current (110, September), p. 3.

Morgenthau, Hans J.
1946   Scientific Man vs. Power Politics. Chicago: University of Chicago Press.
1954   Politics among Nations. New York: Knopf.
1958   "Power as a political concept." Pp. 66–77 in Roland Young (ed.), Approaches to the Study of Politics. Evanston: Northwestern University Press.
1962a   Politics in the Twentieth Century. 3 vols. Chicago: University of Chicago Press.
1962b   "A political theory of foreign aid." American Political Science Review 56 (June):301–9.
1965   Scientific Man vs. Power Politics. Chicago: University of Chicago Press, Phoenix Books.
1967   Politics among Nations. 4th ed. New York: Knopf.

Morris, Charles W.
1946   Signs, Language, and Behavior. New York: Prentice-Hall.

Morris, Donald R.
1965   The Washing of the Spears. New York: Simon & Schuster.

Morse, Chandler
1961   "The functional imperatives." Pp. 100–52 in Max Black (ed.), The Social Theories of Talcott Parsons. Englewood Cliffs: Prentice-Hall.

Morse, Philip M. (ed.)
1967   Operations Research for Public Systems. Cambridge: MIT Press.

Morton, Henry W., and Rudolf L. Tokes (eds.)
1974   Soviet Politics and Society in the 1970s. New York: Free Press.

Mosely, Philip E.
1962   "Soviet foreign policy since the 22nd party congress." Modern
            Age 41 (Fall):343–52.
Moser, Claus A.
1952   "Quota sampling." Journal of the Royal Statistical Association
            115 (pt. 3):411–23.
1958   Survey Methods in Social Investigation. London: Heinemann.
Mosher, Frederick C.
1967   Governmental Reorganizations. Indianapolis: Bobbs-Merrill.
Mosher, Frederick C. (ed.)
1975   American Public Administration: Past, Present, Future. Univer-
            sity: University of Alabama Press.
Mosher, Frederick C., and John Harr
1970   Programming Systems and Foreign Policy Leadership. New York:
            Oxford University Press.

Mosteller, Frederick, Herbert Hyman, Phillip J. McCarthy, Eli S. Marks, and
    David B. Truman
1949   The Pre-Election Polls of 1948. New York: Social Science Re-
            search Council.
Mosteller, Frederick, and D. L. Wallace
1964   Inference and Disputed Authorship: The Federalist. Reading:
            Addison-Wesley.
Mowitz, Robert J., and Deil S. Wright
1962   Profile of a Metropolis. Detroit: Wayne State University Press.

Moynihan, Daniel P.
1969   Maximum Feasible Misunderstanding. New York: Free Press.
Mueller, John E.
1973   War, Presidents, and Public Opinion. New York: Wiley.
Muir, William K., Jr.
1955   Defending "The Hill" against Metal Houses. University: Univer-
            sity of Alabama Press.
Mumford, Lewis
1967   The Myth of the Machine. New York: Harcourt Brace Jovan-
            ovich.
Murphy, Gardner, and Rensis Likert
1938   Public Opinion and the Individual. New York: Harper.

Murphy, Joseph
1968   Political Theory: A Conceptual Analysis. Homewood: Dorsey.
Murphy, Robert E.
1970   The Style and Study of Political Science. Glenview: Scott, Fores-
            man.
Murphy, Thomas P.
1974   The New Politics Congress. New York: Heath.
Murray, A. R. M.
1953   An Introduction to Political Philosophy. London: Cohen & West.

Murray, D. J.
1969   The Work of Administration in Nigeria: Case Studies. London:
            Hutchinson, for the Institute of Administration, University of
            Ife.
Myrdal, Gunnar
1956   An International Economy. New York: Harper.
Nagel, Ernest
1956   Logic without Metaphysics. New York: Free Press.
1961   The Structure of Science. New York: Harcourt Brace Jovanovich.
1963   "Problems of concept and theory formation in the social sci-
            ences." Pp. 191–209 in Maurice Natanson (ed.), The Philosophy
            of the Social Sciences. New York: Random House.
Nagel, Jack H.
1975   The Descriptive Analysis of Power. New Haven: Yale University
            Press.
Nagel, Ernest, and James R. Newman
1960   Gödel's Proof. New York: New York University Press.
Nagel, Stuart
1966   "Judicial prediction and analysis from empirical probability
            tables." Indiana Law Journal 41 (Spring):403.
Nagi, Saad Z., and Ronald G. Corwin (eds.)
1972   The Social Contexts of Research. New York: Wiley-Interscience.
Namenwirth, J. Z.
1969   "Some long- and short-term trends in one American political
            value: A computer analysis of concern with wealth in 62 party
            platforms." Pp. 223–41 in George Gerbner, Ole R. Holsti, K.
            Krippendorff, W. J. Paisley, and P. J. Stone (eds.), Proceedings of
            the National Conference on Content Analysis. New York: Wiley.
Namenwirth, J. Z., and H. D. Lasswell
1970   The Changing Language of American Values: A Computer Study
            of Selected Party Platforms. Sage Professional Papers in Compar-
            ative Politics. Beverly Hills: Sage.
Naroll, Raoul
1962   Data Quality Control: A New Research Technique. New York:
            Free Press.
Narula, B. N. (ed.)
1963   Cases in Indian Administration. New Delhi: Indian Institute of
            Public Administration.
Nasatir, David
1967   "Social science data libraries." American Sociologist 2 (Novem-
            ber):207–12.
Natanson, Maurice
1958   "A study in philosophy and the social sciences." Social Research
            25 (Summer):158–72.
1962   Literature, Philosophy and the Social Sciences. The Hague:
            Martinus Nijhoff.

| 1970 | The Journeying Self: A Study in Philosophy and Social Role. Reading: Addison-Wesley. |
| 1973 | Phenomenology and the Social Sciences. 2 vols. Evanston: Northwestern University Press. |

Natanson, Maurice (ed.)
| 1963 | Philosophy of the Social Sciences: A Reader. New York: Random House. |

National Opinion Research Center
1945	Interviewing for NORC. Denver: University of Denver Press.
1962	A Brush-Up on Interviewing Technique. Chicago: University of Chicago.
1964a	How to List for an Area Sample. Chicago: University of Chicago.
1964b	Steps in a Survey: Reprinted from the Sampler, December, 1962 through May-July, 1964. Chicago: University of Chicago.
1966	Sampling Instructions for Area Probability Samples. Chicago: University of Chicago.
1967a	Block Sampling Instructions. Chicago: University of Chicago.
1967b	Instructions for the Field Count. Chicago: University of Chicago.
1967c	Manual of Procedures for Hiring and Training Interviewers. Chicago: University of Chicago.

National Science Board, Special Commission on the Social Sciences
| 1969 | Knowledge into Action: Improving the Nation's Use of the Social Sciences. Washington: National Science Foundation. |

National Science Foundation
| 1968 | Federal Funds for Research, Development and Other Scientific Activities, Fiscal Years 1967, 1968, and 1969. Washington: GPO. |

Neft, David S.
| 1966 | Statistical Analysis for Area Distributions. Philadelphia: Regional Science Research Institute. |

Neisser, Hans P.
| 1959 | "The phenomenological approach in social science." Philosophy and Phenomenological Research 20 (December): 198-212. |

Nelkin, Dorothy
| 1972 | The University and Military Research. Ithaca: Cornell University Press. |

Nelson, Joan
| 1969 | "Migrants, urban poverty, and instability in developing nations." Center for International Affairs, Harvard University, Occasional Paper no. 22. Cambridge. |

Nett, Emily M.
| 1958 | "An evaluation of the national character concept in sociological theory." Social Forces 36 (May):297-303. |

Neumann, Sigmund
| 1956 | Modern Political Parties: Approaches to Comparative Politics. Chicago: University of Chicago Press. |

Neustadt, Richard E.
| 1960 | Presidential Power. New York: Wiley. |

1970   Alliance Politics. New York: Columbia University Press.
1976   Presidential Power: The Politics of Leadership with Reflections
            on Johnson and Nixon. 3d. ed. New York: Wiley.

Newcomb, Theodore M., Kathryn E. Coenig, Richard Flacks, and Donald P.
    Warwick
1967   Persistence and Change: Bennington College and its Students
            after Twenty-five Years. New York: Wiley.

Newhouse, John
1973   Cold Dawn. New York: Holt, Rinehart & Winston.

Newman, Robert P., and Dale R. Newman
1969   Evidence. Boston: Houghton Mifflin.

Nicholas, Herbert G.
1967   The United Nations as a Political Institution. 3d ed. New York:
            Oxford University Press.

Nicolson, Harold
1963   Diplomacy. 3d ed. New York: Oxford University Press.

Nie, Norman H., Dale H. Brent, and C. Hadlai Hull
1970   Statistical Package for the Social Sciences. New York: McGraw-
            Hill.

Nie, Norman H., G. Bingham Powell, Jr., and Kenneth Prewitt
1969   "Social structure and political participation." Amercian Political
            Science Review 63 (June):361-78; (September):808-32.

Nie, Norman H., Sidney Verba, and John R. Petrocik
1976   The Changing American Voter. Cambridge: Harvard University
            Press.

Niemi, Richard G.
1974   How Family Members Perceive Each Other: Political and Social
            Attitudes in Two Generations. New Haven: Yale University Press.

Niemi, Richard G., and Herbert F. Weisberg
1972   Probability Models of Collective Decision Making. Columbus:
            Merriam.

Niemi, Richard G., and Herbert F. Weisberg (eds.)
1976   Controversies in American Voting Behavior. San Francisco:
            Freeman.

Nisbet, Robert
1970   "Subjective Si! Objective No!" New York Times Book Review,
            April 5, p. 1.

Niskanen, William A.
1971   Bureaucracy and Representative Government. Chicago: Aldine-
            Atherton.

North, Robert C.
1967   "The analytical prospects of communications theory." Pp.
            300-16 in James C. Charlesworth (ed.), Contemporary Political
            Analysis. New York: Free Press.

North, Robert C., Ole R. Holsti, George Zaninovich, and Dina A. Zinnes
1963   Content Analysis: A Handbook with Applications for the Study
            of International Crises. Evanston: Northwestern University Press.

Northrop, F. S. C.
1946 The Meeting of East and West. New York: Macmillan.
1959 The Logic of the Sciences and Humanities. New York: Meridian.

Nurkse, Ragnar
1953 Problems of Capital Formation in Underdeveloped Countries. New York: Oxford University Press.

Nye, Joseph S., Jr.
1968 International Regionalism. Boston: Little, Brown.
1971 Peace in Parts. Boston: Little, Brown.

Nyman, James
1973 "Making things and the theory of making: Lockean politics in epistemological perspective." Paper prepared for the annual meeting of the Southwestern Political Science Association, Dallas.

Oakes, Augustus, and R. B. Mowat (eds.)
1918 The Great European Treaties of the Nineteenth Century. London: Oxford University Press, Clarendon Press.

Oakeshott, Michael
1962 Rationalism and Politics. New York: Basic Books.

O'Barr, William M., David H. Spain, and Mark A. Tessler (eds.)
1973 Survey Research in Africa: Its Applications and Limits. Evanston: Northwestern University Press.

Oberdorfer, Don
1971 TET! Garden City: Doubleday.

Odegard, Peter
1928 Pressure Politics: The Story of the Anti-Saloon League. New York: Columbia University Press.

Ogburn, Charlton, Jr.
1960 "The flow of policy making in the Department of State." Pp. 172-77 in Field Haviland, Jr., and Associates (eds.), The Formulation and Administration of United States Foreign Policy. Washington: Brookings.

Ogden, C. K., and I. A. Richards
1952 The Meaning of Meaning. London: Routledge & Kegan Paul.

Ohlström, B.
1966 "Information and propanganda." Journal of Peace Research 1 (1):75-88.

O'Leary, Michael K.
1967 The Politics of American Foreign Aid. Chicago: Atherton.

Olesen, Virginia L., and Elvi W. Whittaker
1967 "Role-making in participant observation: Processes in the researcher-actor relationship." Human Organization 26 (Winter):273-81.

Oliphant, C. A.
1964 "The image of the United States projected by 'Peking Review'." Journalism Quarterly 41 (Summer):416-20.

Ollman, Bertell
    1971   Alienation. Cambridge: At the University Press.

Olson, Mancur, Jr.
    1965   The Logic of Collective Action: Public Goods and the Theory of Groups. Cambridge: Harvard University Press.

Oppenheim, A. N.
    1966   Questionnaire Design and Attitude Measurement. New York: Basic Books.

Oram, R. B.
    1970   The Dockers' Tragedy. London: Hutchinson.

Orcutt, Guy H., Martin Greenberger, John Korbel, and Alice Rivlin
    1961   Microanalysis of Socioeconomic Systems: A Simulation Study. New York: Harper & Row.

Organski, A. F. K.
    1968   World Politics. 2d ed. New York: Knopf.

Organski, Katherin Fox, and A. F. K. Organski
    1961   Population and World Power. New York: Knopf.

Ortega y Gassett, José
    1958   Man and Crisis. New York: Norton.

Osgood, Charles E.
    1959   "The representational model and relevant research methods." Pp. 33-38 in Ithiel de Sola Pool (ed.), Trends in Content Analysis. Urbana: University of Illinois Press.
    1962   An Alternative to War or Surrender. Urbana: University of Illinois Press.

Ostrogorski, Moisei
    1902   Democracy and the Organization of Political Parties. 2 vols. London: Macmillan. Abr. ed., with an introduction by Seymour Martin Lipset, New York: Quadrangle, 1964.

Ostrom, Vincent
    1957   "Reflections on the use of case studies in teaching and research." Mimeographed. Syracuse: Inter-University Case Program.
    1973   The Intellectual Crisis in American Public Administration. University: University of Alabama Press.

Packenham, Robert A.
    1970   "The study of political development." Pp. 169-93 in Michael Haas and Henry S. Kariel (eds.), Approaches to the Study of Political Science. San Francisco: Chandler.

Padelford, Norman J., and George A. Lincoln
    1962   The Dynamics of International Politics. New York: Macmillan.

Paige, Glenn D.
    1968   The Korean Decision. New York: Free Press.

Paige, Glenn D., and Richard C. Snyder
    1958   "The United States decision to resist aggression in Korea." Administrative Science Quarterly 3 (June):341-78.

Paisley, W. J.
1964   "Identifying the unknown communicator in painting, literature and music: The significance of minor encoding habits." Journal of Communication 14 (September):219-37.

Palamountain, Joseph C., Jr.
1955   The Politics of Distribution. Cambridge: Harvard University Press.
1965   "The Federal Trade Commission and the Indiana Standard case." Pp. 156-284 in E. A. Bock (ed.), Government Regulation of Business. Englewood Cliffs: Prentice-Hall.

Palmer, Norman D.
1975   Elections and Political Development: The South Asian Experience. Durham: Duke University Press.

Palumbo, Dennis J.
1969   Statistics in Political and Behavioral Science. New York: Appleton-Century-Crofts.

Panel on Privacy and Behavioral Research
1967   "Privacy and behavioral research." Science 155 (February 3):535-38.

Pap, Arthur
1962   An Introduction to the Philosophy of Science. New York: Free Press.

Parenti, Michael
1974   Democracy for the Few. New York: St. Martin's.

Parker, Glen L.
1940   The Coal Industry: A Study in Social Control. Washington: American Council on Public Affairs.

Parsons, Talcott
1937   The Structure of Social Action: A Study in Social Theory with Special Reference to a Group of Recent European Writers. New York: Free Press.
1949   The Structure of Social Action. New York: Free Press.
1951   The Social System. New York: Free Press.
1956   "Suggestions for a sociological approach to the theory of organizations." Administrative Science Quarterly 1 (June):63-85.
1961a   "An outline of the social system." Pp. 30-79 in Talcott Parsons, Edward Shils, Kaspar D. Naegele, and Jesse R. Pitts (eds.), Theories of Society. New York: Free Press.
1961b   "The point of view of the author." Pp. 311-63 in Max Black (ed.), The Social Theories of Talcott Parsons. Englewood Cliffs: Prentice-Hall.
1961c   "Some considerations on the theory of social change." Rural Sociology 26 (September): 219-34.
1966   "The political aspect of social-structure and process." Pp. 71-112 in David Easton (ed.), Varieties of Political Theory. Englewood Cliffs: Prentice-Hall.
1967   Sociological Theory and Modern Society. New York: Free Press.
1969   Politics and Social Structure. New York: Free Press.

Parsons, Talcott, and Robert F. Bales
1953   Family, Socialization, and Interaction Process. New York: Free Press.
Parsons, Talcott, Robert F. Bales, and Edward Shils
1953   Working Papers in the Theory of Action. New York: Free Press.
Parsons, Talcott, and Edward Shils (eds.)
1951   Toward a General Theory of Action. Cambridge: Harvard University Press.
Parsons, Talcott, and Neil J. Smelser
1956   Economy and Society: A Study in the Integration of Economic and Social Theory. New York: Free Press.
Parten, Mildred
1950   Surveys, Polls, and Samples. New York: Harper & Row.
1966   Surveys, Polls, and Samples. Reprint. New York: Cooper Square.
Payne, Stanley L.
1951   The Art of Asking Questions. Princeton: Princeton University Press.
Peabody, Robert L.
1964   Organizational Authority. Chicago: Atherton.
Peabody, Robert L., and Francis E. Rourke
1965   "Public bureaucracies." Pp. 802-37 in James March (ed.), Handbook of Organizations. Chicago: Rand McNally.
Peak, Helen
1953   "Problems of objective observation." Pp. 243-99 in Leon Festinger and Daniel Katz (eds.), Research Methods in the Behavioral Sciences. New York: Holt, Reinhart & Winston.
Peltason, Jack W.
1961   Fifty-eight Lonely Men. New York: Harcourt, Brace.
Pelz, Donald C., Spyros Magliveras, and Robert A. Lew
1968   "Correlational properties of simulated panel data with causal connections between two variables." Causal Analysis Project Interim Report no. 1. Ann Arbor: Survey Research Center, University of Michigan.
Pennock, J. Roland
1951   "Political science and political philosophy." American Political Science Review 45 (December): 1081-85.
Pentland, Charles
1973   International Theory and European Integration. New York: Free Press.
Perry, Ralph Barton
1960   "The ego-centric predicament." Pp. 331-37 in Walter G. Muelder, Laurence Sears, and Anne V. Schlabach (eds.), The Development of American Philosophy. Boston: Houghton Mifflin.
Pfiffner, John M., and Frank P. Sherwood
1960   Administrative Organization. Englewood Cliffs: Prentice-Hall.

Phillips, Bernard S.
  1966   Social Research: Strategy and Tactics. New York: Macmillan.
Piaget, Jean
  1951   Play, Dreams and Imitation in Childhood. New York: Norton.
  1963   The Origins of Intelligence in Children. New York: Norton.
  1971   Structuralism. New York: Harper & Row.
Pierce, John R.
  1961   Symbols, Signals and Noise: The Nature and Process of Communication. New York: Harper.
Pierce, Lawrence C.
  1971   The Politics of Fiscal Policy Formation. Pacific Palisades: Goodyear.
Pilisuk, Marc, and Anatol Rapoport
  1964   "Stepwise disarmament and sudden destruction in a two-person game: A research tool." Journal of Conflict Rsolution 8 (March):36–49.
Pilvin, Harold
  1962   "The distribution of long-term funds to underdeveloped countries, 1952–58." Economic Development and Cultural Change 11 (October):41–54.
Pitcher, George
  1964   The Philosophy of Wittgenstein. Englewood Cliffs: Prentice-Hall.
Pitkin, Hanna Fenichel
  1964   "Hobbes's concept of representation." American Political Science Review 58 (June):328–40 (December):902–18.
  1965   "Obligation and consent, I." American Political Science Review 59 (December):990–1000.
  1966   "Obligation and consent, II." American Political Science Review 60 (March):39–52.
  1967   The Concept of Representation. Berkeley and Los Angeles: University of California Press.
  1972   Wittgenstein and Justice: On the Significance of Ludwig Wittgenstein for Social and Political Thought. Berkeley and Los Angeles: University of California Press.
Plamenatz, John
  1963   Man and Society. Vol. 1, Political and Social Theory: Machiavelli through Rousseau. Vol. 2, Political Theory: Bentham through Marx. New York: McGraw-Hill.
Plant, Raymond
  1973   Hegel. Bloomington: Indiana University Press.
Plato
  1935   The Republic. London: Dent.
Pocock, J. G. A.
  1968   "Time, institutions and action: An essay on traditions and their understanding." Pp. 209–37 in Preston King and B. C. Parekh (eds.), Politics and Experience. Cambridge: At the University Press.

Pohley, Heinz-Joachim
1961   "Interactions between the endocrine system and the developing
            tissue in 'Ephestia Kuhniella'." Archiv für Entwicklungsmechanik
            der Organismen 153:443–58.

Polanyi, Michael
1958   Personal Knowledge. Chicago: University of Chicago Press.
1964   Personal Knowledge. New York: Harper & Row, Torchbooks.

Polsby, Nelson
1963   Community Power and Political Theory. New Haven: Yale Uni-
            versity Press.

Polsby Nelson W., Robert A. Dentler, and Paul A. Smith (eds.)
1963   Politics and Social Life: An Introduction to Political Behavior.
            Boston: Houghton Mifflin.

Polsby, Nelson W. and Aaron Wildavsky
1976   Presidential Elections. 4th ed. New York: Scribner's.

Pomper, Gerald M.
1968   Elections in America: Control and Influence in Democratic Pol-
            itics. New York: Dodd, Mead.
1972   "From confusion to clarity: Issues and American voters,
            1956–1968." American Political Science Review 66
            (June):415–28. See also pp. 466–67.
1975   Voters' Choice: Varieties of American Electoral Behavior. New
            York: Dodd, Mead.

Pool, Ithiel de Sola
1951   Symbols of Internationalism. Stanford: Stanford University
            Press.
1952a   The 'Prestige Papers': A Survey of Their Editorials. Stanford:
            Stanford University Press.
1952b   Symbols of Democracy. Stanford: Stanford University Press.
1967   Contemporary Political Science: Toward Empirical Theory. New
            York: McGraw-Hill.

Pool, Ithiel de Sola (ed.)
1959   Trends in Content Analysis. Urbana: University of Illinois Press.

Pool, Ithiel de Sola, Robert P. Abelson, and Samuel L. Popkin
1965   Candidates, Issues and Strategies: A Computer Simulation of the
            1960 and 1964 Presidential Elections. Rev. ed. Cambridge: MIT
            Press.

Pool, Ithiel de Sola, and Allan Kessler
1965   "The kaiser, the tsar, and the computer." American Behavioral
            Scientist 8 (May):31–38.

Popkin, Samuel
1966   "Political uses of survey banks." Paper prepared for the annual
            meeting of the American Political Science Association, New York
            (September).

Popkin, Samuel, John W. Gorman, Charles Phillips, and Jeffrey A. Smith
1976   "Comment: What have you done for me lately? Toward an
            investment theory of voting." American Political Science Review
            70 (September): 779–831.

Popper, Karl
1950   The Open Society and Its Enemies. Princeton: Princeton University Press.
1959   The Logic of Scientific Discovery. London: Hutchinson.
1961   The Logic of Scientific Discovery. New York: Wiley, Science Editions.
1962   Conjectures and Refutations: The Growth of Scientific Knowledge. New York: Basic Books.
1963a   Conjectures and Refutations. London: Routledge & Kegan Paul.
1963b   The Open Society and Its Enemies. New York: Harper, Torchbooks.
1964   The Poverty of Historicism. New York: Harper, Torchbooks.
1968   Conjectures and Refutations: The Growth of Scientific Knowledge. New York: Harper & Row.
1969   The Poverty of Historicism New York: Harper & Row Torchbooks.

Porter, John A.
1965   The Vertical Mosaic: An Analysis of Social Class and Power in Canada. Toronto: Toronto University Press.

Potter, David M.
1963   "Explicit data and implicit assumption in historical study." Pp. 178-94 in Louis Gottschalk (ed.), Generalization in the Writing of History: A Report of the Committee on Historical Analysis of the Social Science Research Council. Chicago: University of Chicago Press.
1966   People of Plenty: Economic Abundance and the American Character. Chicago: University of Chicago Press, Phoenix Books.

Powell, John D.
1970   "Peasant society and clientelist politics." American Political Science Review 64 (June):411-25.

Press, Charles
1962   Main Street Politics: Policy-Making at the Local Level. East Lansing: Michigan State University Press.

Press, Charles, and Oliver Williams
1962   State Manuals, Blue Books and Election Results. Berkeley: Institute of Governmental Studies, University of California.

Pressly, Thomas J.
1954   Americans Interpret Their Civil War. Princeton: Princeton University Press.

Presthus, Robert
1962   The Organizational Society. New York: Knopf.
1964   Men at the Top. New York: Oxford University Press.
1965   Behavioral Approaches to Public Administration. University: University of Alabama Press.
1973   Elites in the Policy Process. New York: Cambridge University Press.

Prewitt, Kenneth, and Alan Stone
1973   The Ruling Elite. New York: Harper & Row.

Price, Daniel O.
1942   "Factor analysis in the study of metropolitan centers." Social
            Forces 20 (May):449-55.

Price, Don K.
1965   The Scientific Estate. Cambridge: Harvard University Press,
            Belknap Press.

Price, H. Douglas
1963   "Are southern Democrats different?" Pp. 740-56 in Nelson W.
            Polsby, Robert A. Dentler, and Paul A. Smith (eds.), Politics and
            Social Life. Boston: Houghton Mifflin.

Price, Jacob M., and Val R. Lorwin
1970   Quantification and History. New Haven: Yale University Press.

Price, James L.
1968   Organizational Effectiveness. Homewood: Irwin.

Prinzing, Friedrich
1916   Epidemics Resulting from Wars. London: Oxford University
            Press, Clarendon Press.

Pritchett, C. Herman
1941   "Paradox of the government corporation." Public Administration
            Review 1 (4):381-89.
1948   The Roosevelt Court: A Study in Judicial Politics and Values:
            1937-1947. New York: Macmillan.
1968   The American Constitution. 2d ed. New York: McGraw-Hill.

Prothro, James W.
1956   "Verbal shifts in the American presidency: A content analysis."
            American Political Science Review 50 (September):726-39.

Prothro, James W., and Charles M. Grigg
1960   "Fundamental principles of democracy: Bases of agreement and
            disagreement." Journal of Politics 22 (May):276-94.

Pruitt, Dean G.
1964   Problem Solving in the Department of State. Denver: Social
            Science Foundation, University of Denver.

Przeworski, Adam, and Henry Teune
1970   The Logic of Comparative Social Inquiry. New York: Wiley.

Putnam, Robert D.
1967   "Toward explaining military intervention in Latin American pol-
            itics." World Politics 20 (October):83-111.

Pye, Lucian W.
1956   Guerrilla Communism in Malaya. Princeton: Princeton University
            Press.
1961   "Personal identity and political ideology." Behavioral Science 6
            (July):205-21.
1962   Politics, Personality, and Nation Building. New Haven: Yale
            University Press.
1966   Aspects of Political Development. Boston: Little, Brown.
1968   "Description, analysis, and sensitivity to change." Pp. 239-61 in
            Austin Ranney (ed.), Political Science and Public Policy.
            Chicago: Markham.

1976   "Mao Tse-tung's leadership style." Political Science Quarterly 91
            (Summer):219-35.

Pye, Lucien W. (ed.)
1963   Communications and Political Development. Princeton: Prince-
            ton University Press.

Pye, Lucian W., and Sidney Verba (eds.)
1965   Political Culture and Political Development. Princeton: Princeton
            University Press.

Quinlan, Sterling
1974   The Hundred Million Dollar Lunch. Chicago: O'Hara.

Radbruch, Gustav
1950   "Legal philosophy." Translated by K. Wilk. Pp. 47-224 in Edwin
            W. Patterson (ed.), The Legal Philosophies of Lask, Radbruch,
            and Dabin. Cambridge: Harvard University Press.

Radcliffe-Brown, Alfred
1957   A Natural Science of Society. New York: Free Press.

Radke-Yarrow, Marian, and Harold L. Rausch
1962   Observation Methods in Research on Socialization Processes: A
            Report of a Conference. New York: Committee on Socialization
            and Social Structure of the Social Science Research Council.

Radnitzky, Gerhard
1968   Contemporary Schools of Metascience. Göteborg: Akademifor-
            laget.

Rainwater, Lee, and David J. Pittman
1967   "Ethical problems in studying a politically sensitive and deviant
            community." Social Problems 14 (Spring):357-66.

Randall, John Herman
1962   The Career of Philosophy: From the Middle Ages to the Enlight-
            enment. New York: Columbia University Press.

Ranney, Austin
1975   Curing the Mischiefs of Faction: Party Reform in America.
            Berkeley and Los Angeles: University of California Press.

Ranney, Austin (ed.)
1962   Essays on the Behavioral Study of Politics. Urbana: University of
            Illinois Press.
1968   Political Science and Public Policy. Chicago: Markham.

Ranney, Austin, and Willmoore Kendall
1956   Democracy and the American Party System. New York: Har-
            court, Brace.

Ransone, Coleman B.
1956   The Office of Governor in the United States. Tuscaloosa: Univer-
            sity of Alabama Press.

Raphaeli, Nimrod (ed.)
1967   Readings in Comparative Public Administration. Boston: Allyn &
            Bacon.

Rapoport, Anatol
  1953   Operational Philosophy. New York: Harper.
  1958   "Various meanings of 'theory.'" American Political Science
               Review 52 (December): 972–88.
  1960   Fights, Games and Debates. Ann Arbor: University of Michigan
               Press.
  1964   Strategy and Conscience. New York: Harper.
  1966a   Two-Person Game Theory: The Essential Ideas. Ann Arbor:
               University of Michigan Press.
  1966b   "The use of theory in the study of politics." Pp. 3–36 in Edward
               H. Buehrig (ed.), Essays in Political Science. Bloomington:
               Indiana University Press.
Rapoport, Anatol, and Albert M. Chammah
  1965   Prisoner's Dilemma: A Study in Conflict and Co-operation. Ann
               Arbor: University of Michigan Press.
Raser, John R.
  1966   "Personal characteristics of political decision-makers: A literature
               review." Peace Research Society Papers 5:161–82.
  1969a   Simulation and Society: An Exploration of Scientific Gaming.
               Boston: Allyn & Bacon.
  1969b   "Threat, crisis, and war." Paper prepared for the annual meeting
               of the Western Political Science Association, Honolulu.
Raser, John R., and Wayman J. Crow
  1966   "A simulation study of deterrence theories." Pp. 146–65 in
               Proceedings of the International Peace Research Association
               Inaugural Conference. Assen: Van Gorcum
Rawls, John
  1955   "Two concepts of rules." Philosophical Review 64 (Jan-
               uary):3–32.
Reedy, George E.
  1970   The Twilight of the Presidency. New York: World.
Rehfuss, John
  1973   Public Administration as Political Process. New York: Scribner's.

Reinton, Per Olav
  1967   "International structure and international integration: The case
               of Latin America." Journal of Peace Research 4 (4):334–65.
Remmers, Hermann H.
  1954   Introduction to Opinion and Attitude Measurement. New York:
               Harper.
Renshon, Stanley Allen
  1974   Psychological Needs and Political Behavior: A Theory of Person-
               ality and Political Efficacy. New York: Free Press.
Reynolds, H. T.
  1974   Politics and the Common Man: An Introduction to Political
               Behavior. Homewood: Dorsey.

Rhoads, John
    1967   "The type as logical form." Sociology and Social Research 51
                (April): 349-60.

Rhodes, Gerald
    1965   Administrators in Action. London: George Allen & Unwin, for
                the Royal Institute of Public Administration.

Rice, Stuart A.
    1924a   "Farmers and workers in American politics." Doctoral disser-
                tation, Columbia University.
    1924b   Farmers and Workers in American Politics. New York: Columbia
                University Press.
    1928   Quantitative Methods in Politics. New York: Knopf.

Richardson, Lewis F.
    1960a   Arms and Insecurity. New York: Quadrangle.
    1960b   Statistics of Deadly Quarrels. New York: Quadrangle.

Richardson, Stephen A.
    1960   "A framework for reporting field relations experiences." Pp.
                124-239 in Richard N. Adams and Jack J. Preiss (eds.), Human
                Organization Research. Homewood: Dorsey.

Richardson, Stephen A., Barbara Snell Dohrenwend, and David Klein
    1965   Interviewing: Its Forms and Functions. New York: Basic Books.

Richter, Melvin (ed.)
    1970   Essays in Theory and History: An Approach to the Social Sci-
                ences. Cambridge: Harvard University Press.

Ridley, Clarence E.
    1958   The Role of the City Manager in Policy Formation. Chicago:
                International City Managers' Association.

Riecken, Henry W.
    1956   "The unidentified interviewer." American Journal of Sociology
                62 (September):210-12.

Rieff, Philip
    1965   Triumph of the Therapeutic: Uses of Faith after Freud. New
                York: Harper.

Riemer, Neal
    1965   "Review of 'Theories of the Political System: Classics of Political
                Thought and Modern Political Analysis' by William T. Bluhm."
                American Political Science Review 59 (Septermber):696-97.

Rieselbach, Leroy N.
    1966a   The Roots of Isolationism. Indianapolis: Bobbs-Merrill.
    1966b   "Personality and political attitudes: A bibliography of available
                questionnaire measures." Mimeographed. Ann Arbor: Mental
                Health Research Institute, University of Michigan.

Riesman, David, Reuel Denney, and Nathan Glazer
    1950   The Lonely Crowd. New Haven: Yale University Press.
    1961   The Lonely Crowd. Abr. ed., with a new foreword. New Haven:
                Yale University Press.

Riessman, Frank, and S. M. Miller
1964   "Social change versus the 'Psychiatric World View.'" American
            Journal of Orthopsychiatry 34 (January):29–38.

Riggs, Fred W.
1950   Pressures on Congress. New York: King's Crown.
1962   The Ecology of Public Administration. New York: Asia Pub-
            lishing House.
1964   Administration in Developing Countries: The Theory of Pris-
            matic Society. Boston: Houghton Mifflin.
1967   Thailand: The Modernization of a Bureaucratic Polity. Honolulu:
            East-West Center Press.

Riker, William H.
1962   The Theory of Political Coalitions. New Haven: Yale University
            Press.
1964   Federalism: Origin, Operation, Significance. Boston: Little,
            Brown.

Riker, William H., and Peter C. Ordeshook
1973   An Introduction to Positive Political Theory. Englewood Cliffs:
            Prentice-Hall.

Riley, Matilda White, and Associates
1963a   Sociological Research. Vol. 1, A Case Approach. New York:
            Harcourt Brace Jovanovich.
1963b   Sociological Research. Vol. 2, Exercises and Manual. New York:
            Harcourt, Brace Jovanovich.

Riley, Matilda White, John W. Riley, Jr., and Jackson Toby
1954   Sociological Studies in Scale Analysis. New Brunswick: Rutgers
            University Press.

Ripley, Randall B.
1967   Party Leaders in the House of Representatives. Washington:
            Brookings.
1969   Majority Party Leadership in Congress. Boston: Little, Brown.
1975   Congress: Process and Policy. New York: Norton

Roazen, Paul
1968   Freud: Political and Social Thought. New York: Knopf.

Robinson, James A.
1962a   Congress and Foreign Policy Making: A Study in Legislative
            Influence and Initiative. Homewood: Dorsey.
1962b   "Rationality and decision-making: The Illinois Democratic deleg-
            ation." Pp. 240–51 in Paul Tillett (ed.), Inside Politics. New
            York: Oceana.
1969   "Participant observation, political internships, and research." Pp.
            71–110 in James A. Robinson (ed.), Political Science Annual,
            vol. 2, 1969–1970: An International Review. Indianapolis:
            Bobbs-Merrill.

Robinson, James A., and R. Roger Majak
1967   "The theory of decision-making." Pp. 175–88 in James C.
            Charlesworth (ed.), Contemporary Political Analysis. New York:
            Free Press.

Robinson, James A., and Richard C. Snyder
1965   "Decision-making in international politics." Pp. 433–63 in
            Herbert C. Kelman (ed.), International Behavior. New York:
            Holt, Rinehart & Winston.
Robinson, John P.
1967   Public Information about World Affairs. Ann Arbor: Institute for
            Social Research, University of Michigan.
Robinson, John P., Robert Athanasiou, and Kendra B. Head
1969   Measures of Occupational Attitudes and Occupational Character-
            istics. Ann Arbor: Institute for Social Research, University of
            Michigan.
Robinson, John P., Jerrold G. Rusk, and Kendra B. Head
1968   Measures of Political Attitudes. Ann Arbor: Institute for Social
            Research, University of Michigan.

Robinson, John P., and Phillip R. Shaver
1969   Measures of Social Psychological Attitudes. Ann Arbor: Institute
            for Social Research, University of Michigan.
1973   Measures of Social Psychological Attitudes. Rev. ed. Ann Arbor:
            Institute for Social Research, University of Michigan.
Robinson, William S.
1950   "Ecological correlations and the behavior of individuals."
            American Sociological Review 15 (April):351–57.
1959   "The logical structure of analytic induction." American Sociolog-
            ical Review 16 (December):812–18.

Roebuck, Julian, and S. Lee Spray
1967   "The cocktail lounge: A study of heterosexual relations in a
            public organization." American Journal of Sociology 72 (Jan-
            uary):388–95.
Roethlisberger, Fritz Jules, and William J. Dickson
1939   Management and the Worker: An Account of a Research Program
            Conducted by the Western Electric Company, Hawthorne Works.
            Cambridge: Harvard University Press.
Rogers, Lindsay
1949   The Pollsters. New York: Knopf.

Rogow, Arnold A.
1963   James Forrestal: A Study of Personality, Politics, and Policy.
            New York: Macmillan.
1966   Victim of Duty: A Study of James Forrestal. London: Hart-
            Davis.
1969   Politics, Personality and Twentieth Century Political Science:
            Essays in Honor of Harold D. Lasswell. Chicago: University of
            Chicago Press.
1970   The Psychiatrists. New York: Putnam.
Rogow, Arnold A., and Harold D. Lasswell
1963   Power, Corruption, and Rectitude. Englewood Cliffs: Prentice-
            Hall.

Róheim, Géza
  1968   Psychoanalysis and Anthropology. New York: International
                  Universities Press.
Rohn, Peter H.
  1968   "The United Nations Treaty Series Project." International
                  Studies Quarterly 12 (June):174-95.
Rokeach, Milton
  1973   The Nature of Human Values. New York: Free Press.
Rokkan, Stein, and Associates
  1964   "Data in comparative research." International Social Science
                  Journal 16 (1):7-97.
Rokkan, Stein, and Angus Campbell
  1960   "Citizens participation in political life: Norway and the United
                  States of America." International Social Science Journal 12 (1,
                  pt. 1): 69-99.
Rokkan, Stein, Angus Campbell, Per Torsvik, and Henry Valen
  1970   Citizens, Elections, Parties: Approaches to the Comparative
                  Study of the Processes of Development. New York: McKay.
Rokkan, Stein, and Henry Valen
  1960   "Parties, elections, and political behavior in the northern coun-
                  tries: A review of recent research." Pp. 103-36 in Otto Stammer
                  (ed.), Politische Forschung. Cologne: Westdeutscher Verlag.
Roll, Charles W., Jr., and Albert H. Cantril
  1972   Polls: Their Use and Misuse in Politics. New York: Basic Books.
Roper, Elmo
  1957   You and Your Leaders: Their Actions and Your Reactions. New
                  York: Morrow.
Roper Public Opinion Research Center
  1965   The Roper Public Opinion Research Center Newsletter. Williams-
                  town: Roper Center, Williams College. Additions to the Roper
                  Center holdings and developments at the archive are noted in this
                  publication.
  1972   Roper Public Opinion Research Center: Celebrating Twenty-five
                  Years of Research on Human Behavior. Williamstown: Roper
                  Center, Williams College.
Rose, Arnold M.
  1967   The Power Structure: Political Process in America. New York:
                  Oxford University Press.
Rose, Richard
  1964   Politics in England. Boston: Little, Brown.
Rose, Richard (ed.)
  1973   Electoral Behavior: A Comparative Handbook. New York: Free
                  Press.
Rosecrance, Richard N.
  1963   Action and Reaction in World Politics. Boston: Little, Brown.
  1966   "Bipolarity, multipolarity, and the future." Journal of Conflict
                  Resolution 10 (September):314-27.

Rosenau, James N.
1963   National Leadership and Foreign Policy. Princeton: Princeton
            University Press.
1966   "Pre-theories and theories of foreign policy." Pp. 27–92 in R.
            Barry Farrell (ed.), Approaches to Comparative and International
            Politics. Evanston: Northwestern University Press.
1967a   "The premises and promises of decision-making analysis." Pp.
            189–211 in James C. Charlesworth (ed.), Contemporary Political
            Analysis. New York: Free Press.
1968   "Private preferences and public responsibility: The relative
            potency of individual and role variables in the behavior of U.S.
            Senators." Pp. 17–50 in J. D. Singer (ed.), Quantitative Inter-
            national Politics: Insights and Evidence. New York: Free Press.
1969a   "The adaptation of national societies: A theory of political
            behavior and transformation." Mimeographed. New Brunswick:
            Rutgers University.
1970   The Scientific Study of Foreign Policy. New York: Free Press.
1974   Citizenship between Elections: An Inquiry into the Mobilizable
            American. New York: Free Press.

Rosenau, James N. (ed.)
1967b   Domestic Sources of Foreign Policy. New York: Free Press.
1969b   Linkage Politics. New York: Free Press.

Rosenbaum, Walter A.
1973   The Politics of Environmental Concerns. New York: Praeger.

Rosenberg, Morris
1956   "Misanthropy and political ideology." American Sociological
            Review 21 (December):690–95.
1968   The Logic of Survey Analysis. New York: Basic Books.

Rosenbloom, David Lee
1973   The Election Men: Professional Campaign Managers and Amer-
            ican Democracy. New York: Quadrangle.

Rosenne, Shabtai
1955   "The International Court and the United Nations: Reflections on
            the period 1946–1954." International Organization 12 (Sum-
            mer):174–87.

Rosenstein-Rodan, P. N.
1943   "Problems of industrialization of Eastern and South-Eastern
            Europe." Economic Journal 53 (June-September):202–11.

Rosenthal, Alan
1974   Legislative Performance in the States. New York: Free Press.

Ross, E. A.
1908   Social Psychology: An Outline and Source Book. New York:
            Macmillan.

Ross, John
1963   "The relation between test and person factors." Psychological
            Review 70 (September):432–43.

Rossi, Peter H.
1959   "Four landmarks in voting research." Pp. 5–54 in Eugene
            Burdick and Arthur J. Brodbeck (eds.), American Voting Behav-
            ior. New York: Free Press.

Roth, Julius A.
1966   "Hired hand research." American Sociologist 1 (August):190–96.

Routt, Garland C.
1938   "Interpersonal relationships and the legislative process." Annals
            of the American Academy of Political and Social Science 195
            (January):129–36.

Rowse, Alfred L.
1963   The Use of History. New York: Collier.

Rubenstein, Albert H., and Chadwick J. Haberstroh (eds.)
1960   Some Theories of Organization. Homewood: Dorsey and Irwin.

Rudner, Richard
1966   Philosophy of Social Science. Englewood Cliffs: Prentice-Hall.

Rummel, Rudolph J.
1963   "Dimensions of conflict behavior within and between nations."
            General Systems Yearbook 8:1–53.
1965   "A field theory of social action with application to conflict
            within nations." General Systems Yearbook 10:193–211.
1966   "The dimensionality of nations project." Pp. 109–30 in Richard
            L. Merritt and Stein Rokkan (eds.), Comparing Nations: The Use
            of Quantitative Data in Cross-National Research. New Haven:
            Yale University Press.
1967   "Understanding factor analysis." Journal of Conflict Resolution
            11 (December):444–80.
1970   Applied Factor Analysis. Evanston: Northwestern University
            Press.
1972   The Dimensions of Nations. Beverly Hills: Sage.

Runciman, Walter G.
1963   Social Science and Political Theory. New York: Cambridge
            University Press.

Runion, H. L.
1936   "An objective study of the speech style of Woodrow Wilson."
            Speech Monographs 3 (September):75–94.

Rush, Myron
1958   The Rise of Khrushchev. Washington: Public Affairs.

Rusk, Jerrold
1967   "The effect of the Australian ballot on split-ticket voting,
            1876–1908." Doctoral dissertation, University of Michigan.s,
1970   "The effect of the Australian ballot reform on split-ticket
            voting." American Political Science Review 64 (Decem-
            ber):1220–38.

Russell, Bertrand
1931   The Scientific Outlook. New York: Norton.

1946   "Reply to criticisms." Pp. 681–741 in Paul Arthur Schilpp (ed.), The Philosophy of Bertrand Russell. Evanston: Library of Living Philosophers.

1955   Human Society in Ethics and Politics. London: George Allen & Unwin.

Russell, J. T., and Q. Wright
1933   "National attitudes on the Far Eastern controversy." American Political Science Review 27 (August):555–76.

Russett, Bruce M.
1963   Community and Contention. New Haven: Yale University Press.

1964   "Inequality and instability: The relation of land tenure to politics." World Politics 16 (April):442–54.

1965   Trends in World Politics. New York: Macmillan.

1966a   "Discovering voting groups in the United Nations." American Political Science Review 60 (June):327–39.

1966b   "The Yale Political Data Program: Experience and prospects." Pp. 95–107 in Richard L. Merritt and Stein Rokkan (eds.), Comparing Nations. New Haven: Yale University Press.

1967a   International Regions and the International System. Chicago: Rand McNally.

1967b   "Pearl Harbor: Deterrence theory and decision theory." Journal of Peace Research 4 (2):89–106.

1969   "The young science of international politics." World Politics 22 (October):87–95.

1970   The Offenses of Defense. New Haven: Yale University Press.

Russett, Bruce M., Hayward R. Alker, Jr., Karl Deutsch, and Harold D. Lasswell
1964   World Handbook of Political and Social Indicators. New Haven: Yale University Press.

Rustow, Dankwart A.
1967   A World of Nations: Problems of Political Modernization. Washington: Brookings.

Rustow, Dankwart A. (ed.)
1968   Philosophers and Kings: Studies in Leadership. Daedalus 97 (Summer), entire issue. See pp. 683–94 for the editor's introduction.

Ryle, Gilbert
1949   The Concept of Mind. New York: Barnes & Noble.

Sabine, George H.
1937   A History of Political Theory. New York: Holt.

1939a   "What is a political theory?" Journal of Politics 1 (February):1–16.

1939b   "Logic and social studies." Philosophical Review 48 (November):168–79.

1961   A History of Political Theory. 3d ed. New York: Holt.

1973   History of Political Theory. 4th ed. New York: Holt, Rinehart & Winston.

Salisbury, Robert
1968   "The analysis of public policy: A search for theories and roles."
            In Austin Ranney (ed.), Political Science and Public Policy.
            Chicago: Markham.

Salvemini, Gaetano
1939   Historians and Scientists. Cambridge: Harvard University Press.

Samuelson, Paul A.
1954   "The pure theory of public expenditure." Review of Economics
            and Statistics 36 (November):387-89.
1955   "A diagrammatic exposition of a theory of public expenditure."
            Review of Economics and Statistics 37 (November):350-56.
1958   "Aspects of public expenditure theories." Review of Economics
            and Statistics 40 (November):332-38.

Sapin, Burton, and Richard C. Snyder
1954   The Role of the Military in American Foreign Policy. Garden
            City: Doubleday.

Sartori, Giovanni
1962   Democratic Theory. Detroit: Wayne State University Press.
1970   "Concept misformation in comparative politics." American Polit-
            ical Science Review 64 (December):1033-53.

Sartre, Jean-Paul
1948   Anti-Semite and Jew. Translated by G. L. Becker. New York:
            Shocken.
1964   Search for a Method. New York: Knopf.

Sawyer, Jack, and Harold Guetzkow
1965   "Bargaining and negotiation in international relations." Pp.
            466-520 in Herbert C. Kelman (ed.), International Behavior.
            New York: Holt, Rinehart & Winston.

Sayre, Wallace S. (ed.)
1954   The Federal Government Service: Its Character, Prestige and
            Problems. New York: Columbia University, American Assembly.

Sayre, Wallace S., and Herbert Kaufman
1959   Agenda for Research in Public Personnel Administration. Wash-
            ington: National Planning Association.
1960   Governing New York City. New York: Russell Sage.
1965   Governing New York City. Paperbound. New York: Norton.

Scarrow, Howard A.
1967   "The function of political parties: A critique of the literature and
            the approach." Journal of Politics 29 (November):770-90.

Schaar, John H.
1961   Escape from Authority: The Perspectives of Erich Fromm. New
            York: Basic Books.

Schaar, John H., and Sheldon S. Wolin
1963   "Essays on the scientific study of politics: A critique." American
            Political Science Review 57 (March):125-50.

Schafer, Charles Lorus
1969 "What to do about convention protesters." Association Management 21 (October):30–37. There were a number of newspaper reports on meetings of learned societies in 1969; see the "New York Times" for September 1969.

Schattschneider, E. E.
1935 Politics, Pressures, and the Tariff. Englewood Cliffs: Prentice-Hall.
1942a Party Government. New York: Farrar & Rinehart.
1942b "Partisan politics and administrative agencies." Annals of the American Academy of Political and Social Sciences 221 (September):29–32.
1960 The Semi-Sovereign People. New York: Holt, Rinehart & Winston.
1969 Two Hundred Million Americans in Search of Government. New York: Holt, Rinehart & Winston.

Scheffler, Israel
1967 Science and Subjectivity. Indianapolis: Bobbs-Merrill.

Scheinman, Lawrence, and David Wilkinson (eds.)
1968 International Law and Political Crisis. Boston: Little, Brown.

Schelling, Thomas C.
1958 International Economics. Boston: Allyn & Bacon.
1960 The Strategy of Conflict. Cambridge: Harvard University Press.
1962 "Nuclear strategy in Europe." World Politics 14 (April):421–32.
1966 Arms and Influence. New Haven: Yale University Press.

Scheuch, Erwin K.
1966 "Cross-national comparisons using aggregate data: Some substantive and methodological problems." Pp. 131–67 in Richard L. Merritt and Stein Rokkan (eds.), Comparing Nations. New Haven: Yale University Press.

Scheuch, Erwin K., Philip J. Stone, Robert C. Alymer, Jr., and Ann Friend
1967 "Experiments in retrieval from survey research questionnaires by man and machine." Social Science Information 6 (April-June):137–67.

Schilling, Warner R.
1962 "The politics of national defense: Fiscal 1950." Pp. 1–267 in Warner Schilling, P. Hammond, and G. Snyder, Strategy, Politics, and Defense Budgets. New York: Columbia University Press.

Schillinger, Elisabeth Hupp
1966 "British and U.S. newspaper coverage of the Bolshevik Revolution." Journalism Quarterly 42 (Spring):10–17.

Schlesinger, Arthur M., Jr.
1965 A Thousand Days: John F. Kennedy in the White House. Boston: Houghton Mifflin.

Schlesinger, Arthur M., Jr. (ed.)
1973 History of U.S. Political Parties. 4 vols. New York: Bowker.

Schlesinger, Joseph A.
1957   How They Became Governor: A Study of Comparative State
            Politics, 1870–1950. East Lansing: Michigan State University
            Press.
1966   Ambition and Politics: Political Careers in the United States.
            Chicago: Rand McNally.
Schmeckebier, Laurence F., and Roy B. Eastin
1961   Government Publications and Their Use. Washington: Brookings.
Schmid, Calvin F.
1966   "Scaling techniques in sociological research." Pp. 348–86 in
            Pauline V. Young (ed.), Scientific Social Surveys and Research.
            Englewood Cliffs: Prentice-Hall.
Schneider, Louis, and Charles Bonjean (eds.)
1973   The Idea of Culture in the Social Sciences. New York: Cambridge
            University Press.
Schneider, Mark
1976   Ethnicity and Politics: A Comparative State Analysis. Chapel
            Hill: Institute for Research in Social Science, University of North
            Carolina.
Schrag, Clarence
1967   "Elements of theoretical analysis." Pp. 220–53 in Llewellyn
            Gross (ed.), Sociological Theory: Inquiries and Paradigms. New
            York: Harper & Row
Schram, Stuart
1966   Mao Tse-tung. New York: Simon & Schuster.
Schramm, Wilbur (ed.)
1959   One Day in the World's Press. Stanford: Stanford University
            Press.
Schrödinger, Erwin
1945   What is Life? Cambridge: Cambridge University Press.
Schubert, Glendon
1960a   Quantitative Analysis of Judicial Behavior. New York: Free
            Press.
1960b   Constitutional Politics. New York: Holt.
1965a   Judicial Policy-Making: The Political Role of the Courts. Glen-
            view: Scott, Foresman.
1965b   The Judicial Mind: The Attitudes and Ideologies of Supreme
            Court Justices, 1946–1963. Evanston: Northwestern University
            Press.
1965c   "Jackson's judicial philosophy: An exploration in value anal-
            ysis." American Political Science Review 59 (Septem-
            ber):940–63.
1974   The Judicial Mind Revisited: Psychometric Analysis of Supreme
            Court Ideology. New York: Oxford University Press.
Schubert, Glendon (ed.)
1963   Judicial Decision-Making. New York: Free Press.
1964   Judicial Behavior: A Reader in Theory and Research. Chicago:
            Rand McNally.

Schumacher, Bill G.
1967   Computer Dynamics in Public Administration. Washington:
              Spartan.
Schurmann, Franz
1960   Ideology and Organization in Communist China. Berkeley and
              Los Angeles: University of California Press.
1968   Ideology and Organization in Communist China. 2d ed. Berkeley
              and Los Angeles: University of California Press.

Schutz, Alfred
1962a   Collected Papers. Vol. 1, The Problem of Social Reality. Edited
              by Maurice Natanson. The Hague: Martinus Nijhoff.
1962b   "Concept and theory formation." Pp. 48–66 in Alfred Schutz,
              Collected Papers, vol. 1, The Problem of Social Reality. The
              Hague: Martinus Nijhoff.
1964   Collected Papers. Vol. 2, Studies in Social Theory. Edited by
              Arvid Brodersen. The Hague: Martinus Nijhoff.
1966   Collected Papers. Vol. 3, Studies in Phenomenological Phil-
              osophy. Edited by I. Schutz. The Hague: Martinus Nijhoff.
1967   The Phenomenology of the Social World. Translated by G. Walsh
              and F. Lehnert. Evanston: Northwestern University Press.
Schwartz, Morris S., and Charlotte G. Schwartz
1955   "Problems in participant observation." American Journal of
              Sociology 60 (January):343–54.

Scott, Andrew M.
1966   The Revolution in Statecraft. New York: Random House.
Scott, Andrew M., William A. Lucas, and Trudi Lucas
1966   Simulation and National Development. New York: Wiley.
Scott, J. B.
1939   Law, the State, and the International Community. New York:
              Columbia University Press.
Scott, James C.
1969   "Corruption, machine politics, and political change." American
              Political Science Review 63 (December):1142–59.

Scott, W. Richard
1965   "Field methods in the study of organizations." Pp. 261–304 in
              James March (ed.), Handbook of Organizations. Chicago: Rand
              McNally.
Scott, Robert E. (ed.)
1973   Latin American Modernization Problems. Urbana: University of
              Illinois Press.
Scott, William A.
1968   "Attitude measurement." Pp. 204–73 in Gardner Lindzey and
              Elliot Aronson (eds.), Handbook of Social Psychology. Reading:
              Addison-Wesley.
Scott, William G.
1967   Organization Theory. Homewood: Irwin.

Scriven, Michael
  1961   "Notes on the discussion between E. Frenkel-Brunswik and B. F. Skinner." Pp. 129–32 in Philipp Frank (ed.), The Validation of Scientific Theories. New York: Collier.
  1962   "Explanations, predictions and laws." Pp. 170–230 in Herbert Feigel and Grover Maxwell (eds.), Minnesota Studies in the Philosophy of Science, vol. 3, Scientific Explanation, Space, and Time. Minneapolis: University of Minnesota Press.
  1965   "Views of human nature." Pp. 163–90 in T. W. Wann (ed.), Behaviorism and Phenomenology: Contrasting Bases for Modern Psychology. Chicago: University of Chicago Press.
  1969   "The covering law position: A critique and alternative analysis." Pp. 94–116 in Leonard Krimerman (ed.), The Nature and Scope of Social Science. New York: Appleton-Century-Crofts.

Seabury, Paul (ed.)
  1965   Balance of Power. San Francisco: Chandler.

Sebald, Hans
  1962   "Studying national character through comparative content analysis." Social Forces 40 (May):318–22.

Sellars, Wilfred
  1963   Science, Perception, and Reality. New York: Humanities.

Sellers, Charles G., Jr.
  1965   "The equilibrium cycle in two-party politics." Public Opinion Quarterly 29 (Spring):16–38.

Selltiz, Claire, Marie Jahoda, Morton Deutsch, and Stuart W. Cook (eds.)
  1959   Research Methods in Social Relations. Rev. ed. New York: Holt, Rinehart & Winston.

Selltiz, Claire, Lawrence S. Wrightsman, and Stuart W. Cook (eds.)
  1976   Research Methods in Social Relations. 3d ed. New York: Holt, Rinehart & Winston.

Selvin, Hanan C.
  1966   The Logic of Survey Analysis. Berkeley: Survey Research Center, University of California.

Selznick, Philip
  1949   TVA and the Grass Roots. Berkeley and Los Angeles: University of California Press.
  1952   The Organizational Weapon: A Study of Bolshevik Strategy and Tactics. New York: McGraw-Hill.
  1957   Leadership in Administration. Evanston: Row, Peterson.

Sessions, Vivian S. (ed.)
  1974   Directory of Data Bases in the Social and Behavioral Sciences. New York: Science Associates–International.

Sewell, James P.
  1966   Functionalism and World Politics. Princeton: Princeton University Press.

Shackle, G. L. S.
  1969   Decision, Order and Time in Human Affairs. 2d ed. Cambridge: At the University Press.

Shannon, Claude, and Warren Weaver
1949   The Mathematical Theory of Communication. Urbana: Univer-
                sity of Illinois Press.

Sharkansky, Ira
1970   Regionalism in American Politics. Indianapolis: Bobbs-Merrill.

Sharp, Walter R.
1961   Field Administration in the United Nations System. New York:
                Praeger.
1963   "International bureaucracies and political development." Pp.
                441–74 in Joseph LaPalombara (ed.), Bureaucracy and Political
                Development. Princeton: Princeton University Press.

Shaw, Marvin E., and Jack M. Wright
1967   Scales for the Measurement of Attitudes. New York: McGraw-
                Hill.

Shepard, D. W.
1956   "Henry J. Taylor's radio talks: A content analysis." Journalism
                Quarterly 33 (Winter):15–22.

Sherif, Muzafer, and Carolyn Sherif
1964   Reference Groups: An Exploration into Conformity and Devia-
                tion of Adolescents. New York: Harper.

Shils, Edward A.
1957   "Primordial, personal, sacred and civil ties." British Journal of
                Sociology 8 (June):130–45.
1959   "Social inquiry and the autonomy of the individual." Pp. 114–57
                in Daniel Lerner (ed.), The Human Meaning of the Social Sci-
                ences. New York: Meridian.
1960   "Political development in the new states." Comparative Studies
                in Society and History 2 (July):382–406.

Shinn, Allen M.
1970   The Application of Psychophysical Scaling Techniques to
                Measurement of Political Variables. Chapel Hill: Institute for
                Research in Social Science, University of North Carolina.

Shively, W. Phillips
1974   The Craft of Political Research: A Primer. Englewood Cliffs:
                Prentice-Hall.

Shklar, Judith N.
1964   Legalism. Cambridge: Harvard University Press.

Shklar, Judith N. (ed.)
1966   Political Theory and Ideology. New York: Macmillan.

Shneidman, E. S.
1961   "A psycho-logical analysis of political thinking: The Kennedy-
                Nixon 'great debates' and the Kennedy-Khrushchev 'grim de-
                bates.' " Mimeographed. Cambridge: Harvard University.
1963   "Plan II: The logic of politics." Pp. 177–99 in L. Arons and M.
                A. Mays (eds.), Television and Human Behavior. New York:
                Appleton-Century-Crofts.

Shonfield, Andrew
  1965   Modern Capitalism: The Changing Balance of Public and Private
              Power. New York: Oxford University Press.
Shubik, Martin (ed.)
  1964   Game Theory and Related Approaches to Social Behavior. New
              York: Wiley.
Sibley, Mulford Q.
  1967   "The limitations of behavioralism." Pp. 57–71 in James C.
              Charlesworth (ed.), Contemporary Political Analysis. New York:
              Free Press.

Siffin, William J. (ed.)
  1957   Toward the Comparative Study of Public Administration. Bloom-
              ington: Indiana University Press.
  1966   The Thai Bureaucracy. Honolulu: East-West Center Press.
Sigel, Roberta S.
  1966   "Political socialization: Some reactions on current approaches
              and conceptualizations." Paper prepared for the annual meeting
              of the American Political Science Association, New York (Sep-
              tember).
  1968   "Image of a president: Some insights into the political views of
              school children." American Political Science Review 62 (March):
              216–26.

Sikorski, Linda A., D. F. Roberts, and W. J. Paisley
  1967   "Analyzing letters in mass magazines as 'outcroppings' of public
              opinion." Mimeographed. Stanford: Institute for Communi-
              cation Research, Stanford University.
Sills, David L. (ed.)
  1968   International Encyclopedia of the Social Sciences. 17 vols. New
              York: Macmillan and Free Press.
Silva, Ruth C.
  1962   Rum, Religion and Votes: 1928 Re-examined. University Park:
              Pennsylvania State University Press.
Silverman, Corinne
  1959   "The president's economic advisers." Mimeographed. Syracuse:
              Inter-University Case Program
Simon, Herbert A.
  1947   Administrative Behavior. New York: Macmillan.
  1952a   "Formal theory of interaction in social groups." American
              Sociological Review 17 (April):202–11.
  1952b   "On the definition of the causal relation." Journal of Philosophy
              49 (July):517–28.
  1952–53   "Comparison of organization theories." Review of Economic
              Studies 20 (1):40–48.
  1955a   "Recent advances in organizational theory." Pp. 23–44 in
              Stephen K. Bailey (ed.), Research Frontiers in Politics and Gov-
              ernment. Washington: Brookings.

1955b   "A behavioral model of rational choice." Quarterly Journal of Economics 69 (February):99-118.

1957a   Models of Man. New York: Wiley.

1957b   Administrative Behavior. 2d ed. New York: Macmillan.

1960   The New Science of Management Decision. New York: Harper.

1964   "On the concept of organizational goal." Administrative Science Quarterly 9 (June):1-22.

1967   "The changing theory and changing practice of public administration." Pp. 87-120 in Ithiel de Sola Pool (ed.), Contemporary Political Science. New York: McGraw-Hill.

1976   Administrative Behavior: A Study of Decision-Making Processes in Administrative Organization. 3d ed. New York: Free Press.

Simon, Herbert A., and Allen Newell
1964   "Information processing in computer and man." American Scientist 52 (September):281-300.

Simon, Herbert, Donald Smithburg, and Victor A. Thompson
1950   Public Administration. New York: Knopf.

Simon, Julian L.
1969   Basic Research Methods in Social Science: The Art of Empirical Investigation. New York: Random House.

Simonds, Frank H., and Brooks Emeny
1935   The Great Powers in World Politics. New York: American Book.

Simpson, Antony E.
1976   Guide to Library Research in Public Administration. New York: Center for Productive Public Management, John Jay College of Criminal Justice.

Simpson, Lewis P.
1976   "The symbolism of literary alienation in the revoluntionary age." Journal of Politics 38 (August):79-100.

Simpson, Richard L., and David M. Olson
1967   "Community politics." Southwestern Social Science Quarterly 48 (December):287-96.

Singer, Benjamin D.
1970-71   "Violence, protest, and war in television news: The U.S. and Canada compared." Public Opinion Quarterly 34 (Winter):611-16.

Singer, J. David
1961   "The level-of-analysis problem in international relations." World Politics 14 (October):77-92.

Singer, J. David (ed.)
1965   Human Behavior and International Politics: Contributions from the Social-Psychological Sciences. Chicago: Rand McNally.

Singer, J. David, and Melvin Small
1966   "Composition and status ordering of the international system:1815-1940." World Politics 18 (January):236-82.

1966a   "National alliance commitments and war involvement, 1815-1945." Peace Research Society Papers 5:109-40.

1966b   "Formal alliances, 1815-1939: A quantitative description."
           Journal of Peace Research 3:1-32.
1968   "Alliance aggregation and the onset of war, 1815-1945." Pp.
           247-86 in J. David Singer (ed.), Quantitative International
           Politics: Insights and Evidence. New York: Free Press.
1972   The Wages of War, 1816-1965: A Statistical Handbook. New
           York: Wiley.

Singer, Marshall R.
1972   Weak States in a World of Powers: The Dynamics of Inter-
           national Relationships. New York: Free Press.

Singer, Marshall R., and Barton Sensenig III
1963   "Elections within the United Nations: An experimental study
           utilizing statistical analysis." International Organization 18 (Au-
           tumn): 901-25.

Siu, R. G. H.
1957   The Tao of Science. Boston: MIT Press.

Sjoberg, Gideon (ed.)
1967   Ethics, Politics, and Social Research. Cambridge: Schenkman.

Sjoberg, Gideon, and Roger Nett
1968   A Methodology for Social Research. New York: Harper & Row.

Skinner, B. F.
1953   Science and Human Behavior. New York: Macmillan.
1965   "Behaviorism at fifty." Pp. 79-108 in T. W. Wann (ed.), Behav-
           iorism and Phenomenology: Contrasting Bases for Modern
           Psychology. Chicago: University of Chicago Press.

Slusser, Robert M.
1973   The Berlin Crisis of 1961. Baltimore: Johns Hopkins Press.

Small, Albion W., and G. E. Vincent
1894   Introduction to the Study of Society. New York: American
           Book.

Small, Melvin
1966   "Reexamining the classic cold war." Journal of Conflict Resolu-
           tion 10 (December):516-23.

Small, Melvin, and J. David Singer
1969   "Formal alliances, 1816-1965: An extension of the basic data."
           Journal of Peace Research 6 (3):257-81.

Smelser, Neil
1959   Social Change in the Industrial Revolution. Chicago: University
           of Chicago Press.

Smith, Barbara Leigh, Karl F. Johnson, David Warren Paulsen, and Frances
    Shocket
1976   Political Research: Methods, Foundations, and Techniques.
           Boston: Houghton Mifflin.

Smith, Brian C.
1969   Advising Ministers: A Case-Study of the South West Economic
           Planning Council. London: Routledge & Kegan Paul.

Smith, Bruce L. R.
    1966   The Rand Corporation. Cambridge: Harvard University Press.

Smith, David G.
    1957   "Political science and political theory." American Political Science Review 51 (September):734-46.

Smith, Edmund A.
    1957   "Public administration and bureaucracy." Doctoral dissertation, Harvard University.

Smith, H. W.
    1975   Strategies of Social Research. Englewood Cliffs: Prentice-Hall.

Smith, M. Brewster, Jerome S. Bruner, and Robert W. White
    1956   Opinions and Personality. New York: Wiley.

Smith, M. S., P. J. Stone, and E. N. Glenn
    1966   "A content analysis of twenty presidential nominating speeches." Pp. 359-400 in P. J. Stone, D. C. Dunphy, M. S. Smith, and D. M. Ogilvie, The General Inquirer: A Computer Approach to Content Analysis in the Behavioral Sciences. Cambridge: MIT Press.

Smith, Norman Kemp (trans.)
    1958   Immanuel Kant, Critique of Pure Reason. London: Macmillan.

Smith, Perry M.
    1969   The Air Force Plans for Peace. Baltimore: Johns Hopkins Press.

Smith, T. Alexander
    1975   The Comparative Policy Process. Santa Barbara: American Bibliographical Center-Clio Press.

Smythe, D. W.
    1954   "Some observations of communications theory." Audio-Visual Communication Review 2 (Winter):24-27.

Snow, Reubin J.
    1966   "Local experts: Their roles as conflict managers in municipal and educational government." Doctoral dissertation, Northwestern University.

Snyder, Richard C.
    1962   "Some recent trends in international relations theory and research." Pp. 103-72 in Austin Ranney (ed.), Essays on the Behavioral Study of Politics. Urbana: University of Illinois Press.

Snyder, Richard C., H. W. Bruck, and B. Sapin (eds.)
    1962   Foreign Policy Decision-Making. New York: Free Press.

Snyder, Richard C., and Glenn Paige
    1958   "The United States decision to resist aggression in Korea: The application of an analytic scheme." Administrative Science Quarterly 3 (December):342-78.

Social Science Research Council
    1940   "Annual report, 1938-39." New York.

Somers, Herman Miles
    1956   "The case study program: Where do we go from here?" Public Administration Review 16 (Spring):77-165.

Somit, Albert
1974   Political Science and the Study of the Future. Hinsdale: Dryden.

Somit, Albert, and Joseph Tanenhaus
1964   American Political Science: A Profile of a Discipline. New York: Atherton.
1967   The Development of American Political Science: From Burgess to Behavioralism. Boston: Allyn & Bacon.

Sorauf, Frank J.
1964   Political Parties in the American System Boston: Little, Brown.
1966   Perspectives on Political Science. Columbus: Merrill.
1968   Party Politics in America. Boston: Little, Brown.
1972   Party Politics in America. 2d ed. Boston: Little, Brown.
1976   Party Politics in America. 3d ed. Boston: Little, Brown.

Sorensen, Robert C., and Theodore C. Sorensen
1955   "Proposal for the use of content analysis in literary infringement cases." Social Forces 33 (March):262-67.

Sorensen, Theodore C.
1963   Decision Making in the White House: The Olive Branch or the Arrows. New York: Columbia University Press.
1965   Kennedy. New York: Harper.

Sorzano, J. S.
1975   "David Easton and the invisible hand." American Political Science Review 69 (March):91-106
1977   "Values in political science: The concept of allocation." Journal of Politics 39 (February):24-40.

Speed, J. G.
1893   "Do newspapers now give the news?" Forum 15 (August):705-11.

Spiegel, Steven L.
1972   Dominance and Diversity in the International Hierarchy. Boston: Little, Brown.

Spiro, Herbert J.
1967   "An evaluation of systems theory." Pp. 164-74 in James C. Charlesworth (ed.), Contemporary Political Analysis. New York: Free Press.

Spitz, Allen A., and Edward W. Weidner
1963   Development Administration: An Annotated Bibliography. Honolulu: East-West Center Press.

Spitz, David
1958   Democracy and the Challenge of Power. New York: Columbia University Press.
1963   The Liberal Idea of Freedom. Tucson: University of Arizona Press.

Stagner, Ross
1967   Psychological Aspects of International Conflict. Monterey: Brooks/Cole.

Stanley, David T.
1965   The Higher Civil Service: An Evaluation of Federal Personnel
            Practice. Washington: Brookings.

Stassen, Glen H.
1972   "Individual preference versus role constraint in policy-making:
            Senatorial response to Secretaries Acheson and Dulles." World
            Politics 25 (October):96–119.

Stein, Eric
1959   "The European Parliamentary Assembly." International Organi-
            zation 13 (Spring):233–54.

Stein, Harold
1949   The Foreign Service Act of 1946. Indianapolis: Bobbs-Merrill.

Stein, Harold (ed.)
1952   Public Administration and Policy Development. New York:
            Harcourt Brace Jovanovich.
1963   American Civil-Military Decisions. Tuscaloosa: University of
            Alabama Press.

Stempel, G. H., III
1961   "The prestige press covers the 1960 presidential campaign."
            Journalism Quarterly 38 (Spring):157–63.
1965   "The prestige press in two presidential elections." Journalism
            Quarterly 42 (Winter):15–21.

Stephan, Frederick F., and Philip P. McCarthy
1958   Sampling Opinions: An Analysis of Survey Procedure. New
            York: Wiley, Science Editions.

Stephenson, W.
1963   "Critique of content analysis." Psychological Record 13
            (April):155–62.

Sternberger, Dolf
1961   Der Begriff des Politischen. Frankfurt: Insel Verlag.
1962   Grund und Abgrund der Macht: Kritik der Rechtmässigkeit
            heutiger Regierungen. Frankfurt: Insel Verlag.

Stevens, S. S.
1966   "A metric for the social consensus." Science 151 (February
            4):530–41.

Stewart, Douglas K., and William Love
1968   "A general canonical correlation index." Psychological Bulletin
            70 (3):160–63.

Still, Raye F.
1950   The Gilmer-Aikin Bills. Boston: Steck.

Stogdill, Ralph M.
1974   Handbook of Leadership: A Survey of Theory and Research.
            New York: Free Press.

Stogdill, Ralph M., and Alvin E. Coons (eds.)
1957   Leader Behavior. Research Monograph no. 88. Columbus: Bureau
            of Business Research, Ohio State University.

Stokes, Donald E.
  1966   "Some dynamic elements of contests for the presidency."
            American Political Science Review 60 (March):19–28.
  1968   "Voting." Pp. 387–95 in David L. Sills (ed.), International
            Encyclopedia of the Social Sciences, vol. 16. New York:
            Macmillan and Free Press.

Stone, P. J.
  1972   "The general inquirer: status report." Mimeographed. Cam-
            brdige: Department of Social Relations, Harvard University.

Stone, P. J., D. C. Dunphy, M. S. Smith, and D. M. Ogilvie
  1966   The General Inquirer: A Computer Approach to Content Anal-
            ysis in the Behavioral Sciences. Cambridge: MIT Press.

Stone, William F.
  1974   The Psychology of Politics. New York: Free Press.

Storing, Herbert J. (ed.)
  1962   Essays on the Scientific Study of Politaics. New York: Holt.

Stouffer, Samuel A.
  1955   Communism, Conformity, and Civil Liberties. Garden City:
            Doubleday.

Stouffer, Samuel A., and Associates
  1949   The American Soldier. Vols. 1 and 2 of Studies in Social Psychol-
            ogy in World War II, 4 vols. Princeton: Princeton University
            Press.

Stouffer, Samuel A., Edgar F. Borgatta, David G. Hays, and Andrew F. Henry
  1952   "A technique for improving cumulative scales." Public Opinion
            Quarterly 16 (Summer):273–91.
  1953   "Measurement in sociology." American Sociological Review 18
            (December):591–97.

Stouffer, Samuel A., Louis Guttman, Edward A. Suchman, Paul F. Lazarsfeld,
  Shirley A. Star, and John A. Clausen
  1950   Measurement and Prediction. Vol. 4 of Studies in Social Psychol-
            ogy in World War II, 4 vols. Princeton: Princeton University
            Press.

Straus, Erwin W.
  1958   "Aesthesiology and hallucinations." Pp. 139–69 in Rollo May,
            Ernest Angel, and Henri F. Ellenberger (eds.), Existence. New
            York: Basic Books.

Strauss, Leo
  1953   Natural Right and History. Chicago: University of Chicago Press.
  1957   "What is political philosophy?" Journal of Politics 19
            (August):343–68.
  1959   What is Political Philosophy? and Other Studies. New York: Free
            Press.
  1963   On Tyranny: An Interpretation of Xenophon's Hero. Rev. ed.
            New York: Free Press.

Strauss, Leo, and Joseph Cropsey (eds.)
1963   History of Political Philosophy. Chicago: Rand McNally.

Strawson, P. F.
1963   Individuals. Garden City: Doubleday.

Stretton, Hugh
1969   The Political Sciences: General Principles of Selection in Social
            Science and History. New York: Basic Books.

Strum, Philippa, and Michael Schmidman
1969   On Studying Political Science. Pacific Palisades: Goodyear.

Sudman, Seymour
1967   Reducing the Cost of Surveys. Chicago: Aldine.

Sudman, Seymour,and Norman M. Bradburn
1974   Response Effects in Surveys: A Review and Synthesis. Chicago:
            Aldine.

Suits, Daniel B.
1957   "Use of dummy variables in regression." Journal of the American
            Statistical Association 52 (280):548-51.

Sukhatme, Pandurang V.
1954   Sampling Theory of Surveys with Applications. Ames: Iowa
            State University Press.

Sullivan, Denis G., Benjamin I. Page, Jeffrey L. Pressman, and John J. Lyons
1974   The Politics of Representation: The Democratic Convention,
            1972. New York: St. Martin's.

Sullivan, Denis G., Jeffrey L. Pressman, and F. Christopher Arterton
1976   Explorations in Convention Decision Making. San Francisco:
            Freeman.

Summers, Gene F. (ed.)
1970   Attitude Measurement. Chicago: Rand McNally.

Sundquist, James L.
1968   Politics and Policy. Washington: Brookings.
1973   Dynamics of the Party System: Alignment and Realignment of
            Washington: Brookings.

Surkin, Marvin
1969   "Sense and nonsense in politics." P.S.: Newsletter of the
            American Political Science Association 2 (Fall):573-81

Survey Research Center
1965   "Annual report, 1964-1965." Berkeley: University of California.

Survey Research Center, Field Office
1969   Interviewer's Manual. Ann Arbor: Institute for Social Research,
            University of Michigan.

Swanberg, W. A.
1957   First Blood. New York: Scribner's.

Swanson, Bert E. (ed.)
1962   Current Trends in Comparative Community Studies. Kansas City:
            Community Studies.

1967   "Political change in the small American community." Pp.
            124-54 in William J. Gore and Leroy C. Hodapp (eds.), Change
            in the Small Community. New York: Friendship.
1969   Decision-Making in the School Desegregation-Decentralization
            Controversies. Bronxville: Institute for Community Studies.

Swanson, Bert E., and Edith Swanson
1970   Community Analysis: Social, Economic, and Political Profiles.
            Ithaca: Consortium on Community Crisis, Cornell University.

Swanson, Bert E., Edith Swanson, and Christopher Lindley
In press   The College and the Community: Evaluation and Design for
            Planned Change.

Swendlow, Irving (ed.)
1963   Development Administration. Syracuse: Syracuse University
            Press.

Sykes, A. J.
1965   "Economic interest and the Hawthorne researches: A comment."
            Human Relations 18 (August):253-63.

Talese, Gay
1969   The Kingdom and the Power. New York: World.

Tanter, Raymond
1966   "Dimensions of conflict behavior within and between nations,
            1958-60." Journal of Conflict Resolution 10 (March):41-64.
1967   "A systems analysis guide for testing theories of international
            development." Paper prepared for the annual meeting of the
            American Political Science Association, Chicago.

Tanter, Raymond, and Richard H. Ullman (eds.)
1972   Theory and Policy in International Relations. Princeton:
            Princeton University Press.

Taylor, Charles
1964   The Explanation of Behavior. London: Routledge & Kegan Paul.
1967   "Neutrality in political science." Pp. 25-57 in Peter Laslett and
            W. G. Runciman (eds.), Philosophy, Politics and Society. 3d ser.
            New York: Barnes & Noble.

Taylor, Frederick W.
1929   Principles of Scientific Management. New York: Harper.

Taylor, Richard
1966   Action and Purpose. Englewood Cliffs: Prentice-Hall.

Teaf, H., and P. Franck
1955   Hands across Frontiers. Ithaca: Cornell University Press.

Tenney, A. A.
1912   "The scientific analysis of the press." Independent 73 (Octo-
            ber):895-98.

Thayer, Charles W.
1959   Diplomat. New York: Harper.

Thomas, Norman C.
1975   The Presidency: Its Contemporary Context. New York: Dodd,
            Mead.

Thomas, William I., and Dorothy S. Thomas
1928   The Child in America. New York: Knopf.

Thomas, William I., and Florian Znaniecki
1927   The Polish Peasant in Europe and America. 1918. New York: Knopf.

Thomlinson, Ralph
1965   Sociological Concepts and Research. New York: Random House.

Thompson, James D.
1967   Organization in Action. New York: McGraw-Hill.

Thompson, Kenneth W.
1960   Political Realism and the Crisis of World Politics: An American Approach to World Politics. Princeton: Princeton University Press.

Thompson, Victor A.
1961   Modern Organizations. New York: Knopf.

Thorson, Thomas Landon
1961   "Political values and analytic philosophy." Journal of Politaics 23 (November):711-24.
1962   The Logic of Democracy. New York: Holt, Rinehart & Winston.

Thrasher, Frederic M.
1927   The Gang. Chicago: University of Chicago Press.

Thurstone, Louis Leon
1927a   "The method of paired comparisons for social values." Journal of Abnormal and Social Psychology 21 (January-March):384-400.
1927b   "A law of comparative judgment." Psychological Review 34 (July):273-86.
1929   "Fechner's law and the method of equal-appearing intervals." Journal of Experimental Psychology 12 (June):214-24.
1959   The Measurement of Values. Chicago: University of Chicago Press.

Thurstone, Louis Leon, and E. J. Chave
1929   The Measurement of Attitude. Chicago: University of Chicago Press.

Tillett, Paul
1965   Cases in Practical Politics: A Manual. New York: McGraw-Hill.

Tingsten, Herbert
1937   Political Behavior: Studies in Election Statistics. London: King.

Titmuss, Richard M.
1950   Problems of Social Policy. London: Longmans, Green.

Tittle, Charles R., and Richard J. Hill
1966   "Attitude measurement and prediction of behavior: An evaluation of conditions and measurement techniques." Sociometry 30 (June):199-213.

Toby, Jackson
1954   "A proposal for handling multiple category items." Pp. 356-71

in Matilda White Riley, John W. Riley, Jr., and Jackson Toby (eds.), Sociological Studies in Scale Analysis. New Brunswick: Rutgers University Press.

Toby, Jackson, and Marcia L. Toby
1954 "A method of selecting dichotomous items by cross-tabulation." Pp. 339-55 in Matilda White Riley, John W. Riley, Jr., and Jackson Toby (eds.), Sociological Studies in Scale Analysis. New Brunswick: Rutgers University Press.

Toch, H. H., S. E. Deutsch, and D. M. Wilkins
1960 "The wrath of the bigot: An analysis of protest mail." Journalism Quarterly 37 (Spring):173-185, 266.

Tocqueville, Alexis de
1945 Democracy in America. 1832. 2 vols. Translated by Phillips Bradley. New York: Knopf.

Tolstoi, L. N.
n.d. The Physiology of War. Translated by H. Smith. London: Walter Scott.

Torgerson, Warren S.
1958 Theory and Methods of Scaling. New York: Wiley.

Toulmin, Stephen Edelston
1953 An Examination of the Place of Reason in Ethics. New York: Cambridge University Press.
1960 The Philosophy of Science. New York: Harper.
1961 Foresight and Understanding. New York: Harper.
1964 The Uses of Argument. Cambridge: At the University Press.
1972 Human Understanding. Vol. 1, General Introduction. Oxford: Oxford University Press.

Toulmin, Stephen, and June Goodfield
1961 The Fabric of the Heavens. New York: Harper.
1962 The Architecture of Matter. New York: Harper.
1965 The Discovery of Time. New York: Harper.

Toynbee, Arnold J.
1935-61 A Study of History. 12 vols.; vols. 1-3, 2d ed. New York: Oxford University Press.

Trilling, Richard J.
1976 Party Image and Electoral Behavior. New York: Wiley.

Triska, Jan F.
1964 "Soviet treaty law: A quantitative analysis." Law and Contemporary Problems 29 (Autumn):896-909.

Triska, Jan F., and David D. Finley
1965 "Soviet-American relations: A multiple symmetry model." Journal of Conflict Resolution 9 (March):37-53.

Truman, David B.
1951a The Governmental Process. New York: Knopf.

1951b   "The implication of political behavior research." Items (SSRC) 5
             (December):37–39
1959   The Congressional Party. New York: Wiley.
1965   "Disillusion and regeneration: The question for a discipline."
             American Political Science Review 59 (December):865–73.

Tryon, R. C.
1959   "Domain sampling formulation of cluster and factor analysis."
             Psychometrika 24 (June):115–35.

Tufte, Edward R.
1974   Data Analysis for Politics and Policy. Englewood Cliffs: Prentice-
             Hall.

Tugwell, Rexford G.
1972   In Search of Roosevelt. Cambridge: Harvard University Press.

Tugwell, Rexford G., and Thomas E. Cronin (eds.)
1974   The Presidency Reappraised. New York: Praeger.

Tullis, F. LaMond
1973   Politics and Social Change in Third World Countries. New York:
             Wiley.

Tullock, Gordon
1965   The Politics of Bureaucracy. Washington: Public Affairs.
1967   Toward a Mathematics of Politics. Ann Arbor: University of
             Michigan Press.
1970   Private Wants, Public Means. New York: Basic Books.

Turk, Herman, and Joel Smith
1968   "Random sampling from an unenumerated population." Sociol-
             ogy and Social Research 53 (October):78–87.

Turner, Julius
1951   Party and Constituency: Pressures on Congress. Baltimore: Johns
             Hopkins Press.

Turner, Ralph H.
1953   "The quest for universals in social research." American Sociol-
             ogical Review 18 (December):604–11.

Ubbink, J. G.
1961   "Model, description and knowledge." Pp. 178–94 in Hans
             Freudenthal (ed.), The Concept and the Role of the Model in
             Mathematics and Natural and Social Sciences. Dordrecht: D.
             Reidel.

Ulmer, S. Sidney
1967   "Pairwise association of judges and legislators: Further reflec-
             tions." Midwest Journal of Political Science 11 (Feb-
             ruary):106–15.

Unger, Roberto M.
1975   Knowledge and Politics. New York: Free Press.

U.S. Department of Commerce, Bureau of the Census
1968   Statistical Abstracts of the United States, 1968. Washington:
             GPO.

U.S. National Center for Health Statistics
1963   Origin, Program and Operation of the U.S. National Health
             Survey. Washington: Public Health Service. A description of the
             developments leading to enactment of the National Health
             Survey Act, and a summary of the policies, initial program and
             operation of the survey.
1964   Health Survey Procedure. Washington: Public Health Service.
             Concepts, questionnaire development, and definitions of the
             Health Interview Survey. Concepts of morbidity, disability, and
             utilization of medical services and facilities; questionnaire devel-
             opment, fiscal years, 1958–1964; and definitions of terms used
             in statistical reports.

Urwick, Lyndall
1944   The Elements of Administration. New York: Harper.

Van Dyke, Vernon
1960   Political Science: A Philosophical Analysis. Stanford: Stanford
             University Press.

Van Riper, Paul P.
1958   History of the United States Civil Service. Evanston: Row,
             Peterson.

Verba, Sidney
1961   Small Groups and Political Behavior. Princeton: Princeton Uni-
             versity Press.
1965   "Comparative political culture." Pp. 512–60 in Lucian Pye and
             Sidney Verba (eds.), Political Culture and Political Development.
             Princeton: Princeton University Press.

Verba, Sidney, and Norman H. Nie
1974   Participation in America: Political Democracy and Social
             Equality. New York: Harper & Row.

Vidich, Arthur J.
1955   "Participant observation and the collection and interpretation of
             data." American Journal of Sociology 60 (January):354–60.

Vidich, Arthur J., and Joseph Bensman
1954   "The validity of field data." Human Organization 13 (1):20–27.
1958   Small Town in Mass Society. Garden City: Doubleday.

Vidich, Arthur J., Joseph Bensman, and Maurice R. Stein
1964   Reflections on Community Studies. New York: Wiley.

Vidich, Arthur J., and Gilbert Shapiro
1955   "A comparison of participant observation and survey data."
             American Sociological Review 20 (February):28–33.

Vizinczey, Stephen
1969   The Rules of Chaos. New York: Saturday Review Press.

Voegelin, Eric
1952   The New Science of Politics. Chicago: University of Chicago
             Press.

Von Hoffman, Nicholas, Irving Louis Horowitz, and Lee Rainwater

1970   "Sociological snoopers and journalistic moralizers: An exchange." Trans-Action 7 (May):4–8.

Von Neumann, John
1958   The Computer and the Brain. New Haven: Yale University Press.

Von Neumann, John, and Oskar Morgenstern
1953   Theory of Games and Economic Behavior. Rev. ed. Princeton: Princeton University Press.

Vose, Clement E.
1959   Caucasians Only: The Supreme Court, the NAACP and the Restrictive Covenant Cases. Berkeley and Los Angeles: University of California Press.

Wahlke, John C., Heinz Eulau, William Buchanan, and Leroy C. Ferguson
1962   The Legislative System: Explorations in Legislative Behavior. New York: Wiley.

Wainhouse, David W., and Associates
1966   International Peace Observation. Baltimore: Johns Hopkins Press.

Waismann, Friedrich
1955   "Language strata." Pp. 11–31 in A. G. N. Flew (ed.), Logic and Language, 2d ser. Oxford: Basil Blackwell.

Waldo, Dwight
1948   The Administrative State. New York: Ronald.
1952   "Development of theory of democratic administration." American Political Science Review 46 (September):81–103. See also pp. 494–503.
1962   "Five perspectives on the cases of the Inter-University Case Program." Pp. 39–63 in E. A. Bock (ed.), Essays on the Case Method in Public Administrative Sciences. Brussels: International Institute of Administrative Sciences. Also, mimeographed, Syracuse: Inter-University Case Program.
1968   "Public administration." Journal of Politics 30 (May):442–79.
1971   Public Administration in a Time of Turbulence. San Francisco: Chandler.

Walker, Robert A.
1954   "William A. Jump: The staff officer as a personality." Public Administration Review 14 (4):233–46.

Wallace, David
1959   "A tribute to the second sigma." Public Opinion Quarterly 23 (Fall):311–25.

Wallas, Graham
1908   Human Nature in Politics. London: Constable.
1915   Human Nature in Politics. 2d ed. Boston: Houghton Mifflin.
1962   Human Nature in Politics. Paperbound. Lincoln: University of Nebraska Press.

Walter, Benjamin
1963   Bureaucratic Communications: A Statistical Analysis of Influence. Chapel Hill: Institute for Research in Social Science, University of North Carolina.

1966   "Internal control relations in administrative hierarchies."
            Administrative Science Quarterly 11 (September):179-206.

Walter, Oliver (ed.)
1971   Political Scientists at Work. Belmont: Duxbury.

Walton, Hanes, Jr.
1972   Black Political Parties: An Historical and Political Analysis. New
            York: Free Press.

Walton, John
1966   "Substance and artifact: The current status on research on
            community power structure." American Journal of Sociology 71
            (January): 430-38.

Waltz, Kenneth N.
1959   Man, the State, and War. New York: Columbia University Press.
1964   "Stability of the bipolar world." Daedelus 93 (Sum-
            mer):881-909.
1967   "International structure, national force, and the balance of
            power." Journal of International Affairs 21 (2):215-31.

Walworth, A.
1938   School Histories at War: A Study of the Treatment of Our Wars
            in the Secondary School History Books of the United States and
            in Those of Its Former Enemies. Cambridge: Harvard University
            Press.

Walzer, Michael L.
1967   "The obligation to disobey." Pp. 185-202 in David Spitz (ed.),
            Political Theory and Social Change. Chicago: Atherton.

Wamsley, Gary L., and Mayer N. Zald
1973   The Political Economy of Public Organizations: A Critique and
            Approach to the Study of Public Administration. Lexington:
            Heath.

Wang, C. K. A.
1955   Reactions in Communist China: An Analysis of Letters to News-
            paper Editors. USAF Personnel Training Research Center, Tech-
            nical Report 33 (January). HHRI Project; Chinese Documents
            Project.

Wann, T. W. (ed.)
1964   Behaviorism and Phenomenology. Chicago: University of Chicago
            Press.

Ward, Robert E., and Dankwart A. Rustow (eds.)
1964   Political Modernization in Japan and Turkey. Princeton:
            Princeton University Press.

Warner, William Lloyd
1963   Yankee City. New Haven: Yale University Press.

Warner, William Lloyd and Associates
1949   Democracy in Jonesville. New York: Harper.

Warner, William Lloyd, and Paul S. Lunt
1941   The Social Life of a Modern Community. New Haven: Yale
            University Press.

Warner, William Lloyd, Paul P. Van Riper, N. H. Marlin, and O. F. Collins
 1963   The American Federal Executive. New Haven: Yale University Press.
Wartofsky, Marx
 1968   Conceptual Foundations of Scientific Thought. New York:
             Macmillan.
Wasby, Stephen L.
 1970   Political Science: The Discipline and Its Dimensions. New York:
             Scribner's.
Watkins, Frederick M.
 1964   The Age of Ideology: Political Thought, 1750 to the Present.
             Englewood Cliffs: Prentice-Hall.
Watson, James D.
 1968   The Double Helix. New York: Atheneum.
Wax, Murry L.
 1967   "On misunderstanding 'Verstehen': A reply to Abel." Sociology
             and Social Research 51 (April):323-33.
Wax, Rosalie Hankey
 1957   "Reciprocity as a field technique." Human Organization 11
             (3):34-37.
Weaver, Richard M.
 1953   The Ethics of Rhetoric. Chicago: Regnery.
Webb, Eugene J., Donald T. Campbell, Richard D. Schwartz, and Lee Sechrest
 1966   Unobtrusive Measures: Nonreactive Research in the Social Sci-
             ences. Chicago: Rand McNally.
Webb, Sam C.
 1951   "A generalized scale for measuring interest in science subjects."
             Educational and Psychological Measurement 11 (Autumn):456-
             69.
Weber, Max
 1947a   The Theory of Social and Economic Organization. New York:
             Oxford University Press.
 1947b   "Politics as a vocation." Pp. 77-128 in H. Gerth and C. Wright
             Mills, From Max Weber. London: Kegan Paul.
 1948   The Protestant Ethic and the Spirit of Capitalism. New York:
             Scribner's.
 1949   The Methodology of the Social Sciences. New York: Free Press.
 1968   Economy and Society. Totowa: Bedminster.
Webster's Dictionary of Synonyms. 1942. Springfield: Merriam.
Weick, Karl E.
 1968   "Systematic observational methods." Pp. 357-451 in Gardner
             Lindzey and Elliot Aronson (eds.), Handbook of Social Psychol-
             ogy, vol. 2. Reading: Addison-Wesley.
Weilenmann, Hermann
 1951   Pax Helvetica: Die Demokratie der kleinen Gruppen. Zurich:
             Rentsch.
 1963   "The interlocking of nation and personality." Pp. 33-55 in Karl
             W. Deutsch and William J. Foltz (eds.), Nation-Building. Chicago:
             Atherton.

Weingrod, Alex
  1968   "Patrons, patronage, and political parties." Comparative Studies
              in Society and History 10 (July): 376–400.
Weisberg, Herbert F.
  1968   "Dimensional analysis of legislative roll calls." Doctoral disserta-
              tion, University of Michigan.
Weisberg, Herbert F., and Bruce D. Bowen
  1976   Introduction to Survey Research and Data Analysis. San Fran-
              cisco: Freeman.
Weiss, Carol H.
  1966   "Interviewing low income respondents: A preliminary view."
              Paper prepared for the American Association of Public Opinion
              Research Meeting, Swampscott, Massachusetts (May 7).
Weissberg, Robert
  1974   Political Learning, Political Choice, and Democratic Citizenship.
              Englewood Cliffs: Prentice-Hall.
  1976   Public Opinion and Popular Government. Englewood Cliffs:
              Prentice-Hall.
Welch, Robert E.
  1971   "The use of magnitude estimation in attitude scaling: Construc-
              ting a measure of political dissatisfaction." Social Science Quar-
              terly 52 (June):76–87.
Welch, Susan, John Comer, and Michael Steinman
  1973   "Interviewing in a Mexican-American community: An investiga-
              tion of some potential sources of response bias." Public Opinion
              Quarterly 37 (Spring):115–26.
Weldon, T. D.
  1953   The Vocabulary of Politics. London: Penguin.
Welsh, William A.
  1973   Studying Politics: Basic Concepts in Political Science. New York:
              Praeger.
Wengert, E. S.
  1961   "Some thoughts on the uses of cases: Advancing the study of
              public administration." Mimeographed. Syracuse: Inter-Univer-
              sity Case Program.
Wengert, E. S., and Primitivo de Léon
  1957   "A case study of decision-making in city government." Philippine
              Journal of Public Administration 1 (2):108–26.
Westin, Alan
  1961   "The miracle case: The Supreme Court and the movies."
              Mimeographed. Syracuse: Inter-University Case Program.
  1962   The Uses of Power. New York: Harcourt Brace Jovanovich.
Westin, Alan F., and Michael A. Baker
  1972   Databanks in a Free Society: Computers, Record-Keeping and
              Privacy. New York: Quadrangle.

Westley, B. H., C. E. Higbie, T. Burke, D. J. Lippert, L. Mauer, and V. A. Stone
    1963   "The news magazines and the 1960 conventions." Journalism
                Quarterly 40 (Autumn):525-31, 647.

Weyl, Nathaniel, and Stefan T. Possony
    1963   The Geography of Intellect. Chicago: Regnery.

Wheare, Kenneth C.
    1964   Federal Government. 4th ed. New York: Oxford University
                Press.

Wheelwright, Philip
    1954   The Burning Fountain: A Study in the Language of Symbolism.
                Bloomington: Indiana University Press.

Whelan, John W.
    1969   "Review of Mosher's 'Governmental Reorganizations.' "
                Duquesne Law Review 7 (Spring):494.

White, Irvin L.
    1969   "A framework for analyzing international law-in-action: A pre-
                liminary proposal." International Studies Quarterly 13
                (Spring):46-69.

White, Leonard D.
    1929   The Prestige Value of Public Employment. Chicago: University
                of Chicago Press.
    1948   The Federalists. New York: Macmillan.
    1951   The Jeffersonians. New York: Macmillan.
    1954   The Jacksonians. New York: Macmillan.
    1958   The Republican Era. New York: Macmillan.

White, Morton
    1959   Religion, Politics and the Higher Learning: A Collection of
                Essays. Cambridge: Harvard University Press.

White, Ralph Kirby
    1947   " 'Black Boy': A value-analysis." Journal of Abnormal and Social
                Psychology 42 (October):440-61.
    1949   "Hitler, Roosevelt and the nature of war propaganda." Journal of
                Abnormal and Social Psychology 44 (April):157-74.
    1951   Value-analysis: The Nature and Use of the Method. Glen
                Gardiner: Libertarian.
    1966   "Misperception and the Vietnam war." Journal of Social Issues
                22 (July):1-164.

Whiting, Allen S.
    1960   China Crosses the Yalu: The Decision to Enter the Korean War.
                New York: Macmillan.

Whorf, Benjamin Lee
    1956   Language, Thought and Reality. New York: Wiley.

Whyte, William F.
    1951   "Observational field methods." Pp. 493-513 in Marie Jahoda,
                Morton Deutsch, and Stuart W. Cook (eds.), Research Methods in
                Social Relations, vol. 2. New York: Holt.

1955   Street Corner Society: The Social Structure of an Italian Slum.
            Rev. ed. Chicago: University of Chicago Press.
1960   "Interviewing in field research." Pp. 352–74 in Richard N.
            Adams and Jack J. Preiss (eds.), Human Organization Research.
            Homewood: Dorsey.

Wiener, Norbert
1954   The Human Use of Human Beings: Cybernetics and Society. 2d
            ed. Garden City: Doubleday.
1961   Cybernetics. 2d ed. New York: Wiley.
1964   God and Golem, Inc. Cambridge: MIT Press.

Wiesner, Jerome B.
1965   Where Science and Politics Meet. New York: McGraw-Hill.

Wilcox, Allen R.
1974   Public Opinion and Political Attitudes. New York: Wiley.

Wilcox, W.
1962   "The press of the radical right: An exploratory analysis." Jour-
            nalism Quarterly 39 (Spring):152–60.

Wild, John
1959   Human Freedom and Social Order. Durham: Duke University
            Press.

Wild, John Daniel
1953a   Plato's Modern Enemies and the Theory of Natural Law. Chi-
            cago: University of Chicago Press.
1953b   The Return to Reason: Essays in Realistic Philosophy. Chicago:
            Regnery.

Wildavsky, Aaron
1959   "A methodological critique of Duverger's 'Political Parties.' "
            Journal of Politics 21 (May):303–18.
1962   Dixon-Yates: A Study in Power Politics. New Haven: Yale Uni-
            versity Press.
1964   The Politics of the Budgetary Process. Boston: Little, Brown.
1974   The Politics of the Budgetary Process. 2d ed. Boston: Little,
            Brown.

Wilkenfeld, Jonathan
1968   "Domestic and foreign conflict behavior of nations." Journal of
            Peace Research 5 (1):56–69.
1969   "Some further findings regarding the domestic and foreign
            conflict behavior of nations." Journal of Peace Research 6
            (2):147–56.

Wilensky, Harold L.
1967   Organizational Intelligence. New York: Basic Books.

Wilkins, D. M.
1962   "Factor analysis and multiple scalogram analysis: A logical and
            empirical comparison." Doctoral dissertation, Michigan State
            University.

Willcox, Walter F.
1940   Studies in American Demography. Ithaca: Cornell University
            Press.

Willer, David, and Murray J. Webster
1970   "Theoretical concepts and observables." American Sociological
            Review 35 (August):748–57.

Williams, Oliver P., and Charles R. Adrian
1963   Four Cities: Study in Comparative Policy-Making. Philadelphia:
            University of Pennsylvania Press.

Williams, Robert
1950   "Probability sampling in the field: A case history." Public
            Opinion Quarterly 14 (Summer):316–30.

Williams, Thomas Rhys
1959   "A critique of some assumptions of social survey research."
            Public Opinion Quarterly 23 (Spring):55–62.

Willrich, Mason, and John B. Rhineland (eds.)
1974   SALT: The Moscow Agreements and Beyond. New York: Free
            Press.

Willson, F. M. G.
1961   Administrators in Action. London: George Allen & Unwin.

Wilson, Elmo C.
1957   "World-wide development of opinion research." Public Opinion
            Quarterly 21 (Spring):174–78.

Wilson, H. Hubert
1961   Pressure Group. New Brunswick: Rutgers University Press.

Wilson, James Q.
1965   Negro Politics: The Search for Leadership. New York: Free Press.

Wilson, James Q. (ed.)
1968   City Politics and Public Policy. New York: Wiley.

Wilson, Woodrow
1885   Congressional Government: A Study in American Politics.
            Boston: Houghton Mifflin.
1887   "The study of administration." Political Science Quarterly 2
            (June):197–222.
1893   An Old Master and Other Political Essays. New York: Scribner's.

Winch, Peter
1958   The Idea of a Social Science. New York: Humanities.

Wirt, Frederick M., Roy D. Morey, and Louis F. Brakeman
1970   Introductory Problems in Political Research. Englewood Cliffs:
            Prentice-Hall.

Wiseman, H. Victor
1966   Political Systems: Some Sociological Approaches. New York:
            Praeger.
1969   Politics: The Master Science. New York: Pegasus.

Wittgenstein, Ludwig
1922   Tractatus Logico-Philosophicus. Translated by D. F. Pears and B.
            F. McGuiness. London: Routledge & Kegan Paul.
1953   Philosophical Investigations. Translated by G. E. M. Anscombe.
            New York: Macmillan.

1973   Philosophical Investigations. 3d ed. Edited by Kenneth Scott. New York: Macmillan.

Wohlstetter, Albert, and Roberta Wohlstetter
1965   Controlling the Risks in Cuba. Adelphi Papers no. 17. London: Institute for Strategic Studies

Wohlstetter, Roberta
1962   Pearl Harbor: Warning and Decision. Stanford: Stanford University Press.

Wolf, Charles, Jr.
1964   The Political Effects of Economic Programs: Some Indicators from Latin America. Santa Monica: Rand Corporation.

Wolfarth, D. L.
1961   "John F. Kennedy in the tradition of inaugural speeches." Quarterly Journal of Speech 47 (April):124-32.

Wolfe, Alan
1969   "The myth of the free scholar." University Review 2 (Autumn):2-7.

Wolfe, Alan, and Marvin Surkin (eds.)
1970   An End to Political Science: The Caucus Papers. New York: Basic Books.

Wolfenstein, E. Victor
1967   The Revolutionary Personality: Lenin, Trotsky, Gandhi. Princeton: Princeton University Press.
1969   Personality and Politics. Belmont: Dickenson.

Wolfinger, Raymond E.
1974   The Politics of Progress. Englewood Cliffs: Prentice-Hall.

Wolin, Sheldon
1960   Politics and Vision. Continuity and Innovation in Western Political Thought. Boston: Little, Brown.
1968   "Paradigms and political theories." Pp. 125-52 in Preston King and B. C. Parekh (eds.), Politics and Experience. Cambridge: At the University Press.
1969   "Political theory as a vocation." American Political Science Review 63 (December):1062-82.

Woll, Peter
1974   Public Policy. Cambridge: Winthrop.

Wood, David M.
1968   "Majority vs. opposition in the French National Assembly, 1956-1965: A Guttman scale analysis." American Political Science Review 62 (March): 88-109.

Wooddy, C. H.
1926   The Chicago Primary of 1926. Chicago: University of Chicago Press.

Woodward, J. L.
1934   "Quantitative newspaper analysis as a technique of opinion research." Social Forces 12 (May):526-37.

Wright, Benjamin F.
    1973   Five Public Philosophies of Walter Lippmann. Austin: University
                of Texas Press.
Wright, Gerald C., Jr.
    1974   Electoral Choice in America. Chapel Hill: Institute for Research
                in Social Science, University of North Carolina.
Wright, Quincy
    1955   The Study of International Relations. New York: Appleton-
                Century-Crofts.
    1965   A Study of War. Chicago: University of Chicago Press.
Wright, Quincy, and C. J. Nelson
    1939   "American attitudes toward Japan and China." Public Opinion
                Quarterly 3 (January):46–62.

Wyant, Rowena, and Herta Herzog
    1941   "Voting via the Senate mailbag." Public Opinion Quarterly 5
                (Fall):359–82, 590–624.

Wylie, Laurence
    1957   Village in the Vaucluse. Cambridge: Harvard University Press.
    1964   Village in the Vaucluse. Rev. ed. New York: Harper.
    1966   Chanzeaux: A Village in Anjou. Cambridge: Harvard University
                Press.

Wyner, Alan J.
    1967   "American state governors and their offices." Doctoral disserta-
                tion, Ohio State University.

Xydis, Stephen G.
    1956   "The press in world politics and in the conduct of foreign
                policy." Journal of International Affairs 10 (2): 201–11.

Yakobson, Sergius, and H. D. Lasswell
    1949   "Trend: May Day slogans in Soviet Russia." Pp. 232–97 in H. D.
                Lasswell, N. Leites, and Associates (eds.), The Language of
                Politics: Studies in Quantitative Semantics. London: George
                Stewart.

Yarmolinsky, Adam
    1955   Case Studies in Personnel Security. Washington: Bureau of
                National Affairs.

Yates, Douglas
    1973   Neighborhood Democracy. Lexington: Heath.

Yates, Frank
    1960   Sampling Methods for Censuses and Surveys. Glasgow: Charles
                Griffin.

Ylvisaker, Paul
    1958   "Modernization of the Foreign Office." Mimeographed. Syr-
                acuse: Inter-University Case Program.

Young, Hugo, Brian Silcock, and Peter Dunn
    1970   Journey to Tranquility. Garden City: Doubleday.

Young, Oran R.
1964   "A survey of general systems theory" and "The impact of general
            systems theory on political science." General Systems 9 (1964):
            61-80 and 239-53.
1967   The Intermediaries. Princeton: Princeton University Press.
1968   Systems of Political Science. Englewood Cliffs: Prentice-Hall.
1969   "Professor Russett: Industrious tailor to a naked emperor."
            World Politics 21 (April):486-511.

Young, Pauline V., and Calvin F. Schmid
1966   Scientific Social Surveys and Research. 4th ed. Englewood Cliffs:
            Prentice-Hall.

Young, Roland (ed.)
1958   Approaches to the Study of Politics. Evanston: Northwestern
            University Press.

Younger, Kenneth
1960   The Public Service in New States. London: Oxford University
            Press.

Yule, G. U.
1911   Introduction to the Theory of Statistics. London: Griffin.

Zaffron, Richard
1971   "Identity, subsumption, and scientific explanation." The Journal
            of Philosophy 28 (December):849-60.

Zallen, Harold, and Eugenia M. Zallen
1976   Ideas Plus Dollars: Research Methodology and Funding. Norman:
            Academic World.

Zaninovich, M. George
1964   "An empirical theory of state response: The Sino-Soviet case."
            Doctoral dissertation, Stanford University.

Zeigler, Harmon
1964   Interest Groups in American Society. Englewood Cliffs: Prentice-
            Hall.

Zeis, Paul M.
1938   American Shipping Policy. Princeton: Princeton University Press.

Zeisel, Hans
1957   Say It with Figures. 4th ed., rev. New York: Harper.

Zeitlin, Maurice
1967   Revolutionary Politics and the Cuban Working Class. Princeton:
            Princeton University Press.

Zelditch, Morris, Jr.
1955   "Role differentiation in the nuclear family: A comparative
            study." Pp. 307-51 in Talcott Parsons and Robert F. Bales
            (eds.), Family, Socialization, and Interaction Process. New York:
            Free Press.
1962   "Some methodological problems of field studies." American
            Journal of Sociology 67 (March):566-76.

Zelig, Meyer A.
1967   Friendship and Fratricide. New York: Viking.

Zeller, Belle
1937   Pressure Politics in New York. New York: McGraw-Hill.

Zeller, Belle (ed.)
1954   American State Legislatures. New York: Crowell.

Zentner, Henry
1973   Prelude to Administrative Theory: Essays in Social Structure and
                Social Process. Calgary: Strayer.

Zetterberg, Hans
1963   On Theory and Verification in Sociology. New York: Tressler.

Zilsel, Edgar
1941   "Physics and the problem of historico-sociological laws."
                Philosophy of Science 8 (October):567-79.

Ziman, John
1968   Public Knowledge: The Social Dimension of Science. Cambridge:
                At the University Press.

Zinnes, Dina A.
1963   "Expression and perception of hostility in international rela-
                tions." Doctoral dissertation, Stanford University.
1966   "A comparison of hostile behavior of decision-makers in
                simulated and historical data." World Politics 18 (April):474
                -502.
1967   "An analytical study of the balance of power theories." Journal
                of Peace Research 4 (3):270-88.
1968   "The expression and perception of hostility in prewar crisis:
                1914." Pp. 85-119 in J. David Singer (ed.), Quantitative Inter-
                national Politics: Insights and Evidence. New York: Free Press.

Zinnes, Dina A., R. C. North, and H. E. Koch, Jr.
1961   "Capability, threat and the outbreak of war." Pp. 469-82 in J.
                N. Rosenau (ed.), International Politics and Foreign Policy. New
                York: Free Press.

Zinnes, Dina A., J. L. Zinnes, and R. D. McClure
1972   "Hostility in diplomatic communication: A study of the 1914
                crisis." In C. F. Hermann (ed.). Contemporary Research in Inter-
                national Crisis. New York: Free Press.

Znaniecki, Florian
1919   Cultural Reality. Chicago: University of Chicago Press.

INDEXES

NAME INDEX

SUBJECT INDEX

Additive-renewal issue in science, 522–23
Ad Hoc Committee for a Representative
 Slate, 705
Administrative Science Quarterly, 181
Aggregate data analysis, 76–79, 462–82:
 accessibility, 465; accuracy, 465; bivariate
 statistics, 472–77; in comparative politics,
 76–79; defined, 464–65; level of analysis,
 468–71; measurement, 467–68;
 multivariate techniques, 477–81;
 relevance, 466–67; statistical procedures,
 471–81; univariate statistics, 472
American Association of Public Opinion
 Research, 222
American Commonwealth, 90–93
American Political Science Association
 (APSA), 117, 695, 702, 704–6, 708
APSA *Biographical Directory*, 708
APSA Committee of Departmental
 Chairpersons, 708
APSA Graduate Internships in State and
 Local Government, 441
APSA *Guide to Graduate Study in Political
 Science*, 708
American Political Science Review, 5, 22,
 45, 51–52, 217–20, 702, 704–6, 709
American politics and political institutions,
 84–122: categories of literature in, 87–90;
 present concerns in, 120–22; trends in,
 119–20
Annals of the American Academy of
 Political and Social Science, 702
Attitude measurement, 147

Behavioralism, 702–4; *see also* Behavioral
 revolution
Behavioral revolution, 22–34:
 characteristics of, 23–24; criticisms of,
 34–41 (from non-behavioralists, 37–41;
 self-criticism, 35–37); father of, 26;
 impact of, 29; reasons for rapid spread of,
 33–34
Bias, in historical analysis, 665–67

Black Caucus (APSA), 705
Bureaucratic model, 170–71, 175
Bureau of Applied Social Research, 221–22,
 273

Canonical correlation, 480
Case approach; *see* Case study
Case study, 674–97: achieving a larger
 usefulness for, 692–96; definition and
 distinctive qualities, 682–86; genealogy of,
 674–79; range of political science cases,
 679–82; uses of the case approach,
 686–92
Categories of political inquiry, 15–21:
 analytic, 17; descriptive-taxonomic,
 17–18; historical, 16–17; prescriptive,
 20–21; scientific, 18–20
Caucus for a New Political Science, 38–41,
 704–7
Censored data, 466
Center for Advanced Study in the
 Behavioral Sciences, 28
Center for Political Studies, University of
 Michigan, 94
Chicano Caucus (APSA), 705
Coefficient of scalability, 430
Columbia University and the birth of
 graduate education in political science,
 703
Committee for a Fair Election, 705
Communication theory, 186
Communications audit procedure, 439
Community power, 483–514: debate
 between political scientists and
 sociologists, 484; multifaceted systems,
 485, 499; planned intervention, 510–14;
 pluralistic models, 485, 488–89; political
 prototyping, 511–13; power elite studies,
 484, 488–89; research methods or
 techniques, 485–86, 506–8 (decisional,
 486, 506–8; positional, 485; reputational,
 486); stratification studies, 484, 486–88
Comparative community studies, 483–84